PROGRESS IN GROUP AND
FAMILY THERAPY

Progress in Group and Family Therapy

Edited by

CLIFFORD J. SAGER, M.D.

Associate Director, Department of Psychiatry (Family and
Group Therapies) Beth Israel Medical Center
Chief of Applied Behavioral Sciences Service, Gouverneur Hospital
Clinical Professor of Psychiatry, Mt. Sinai School of
Medicine of the City University of New York

and

HELEN SINGER KAPLAN, M.D., Ph.D.

Clinical Associate Professor of Psychiatry and
Coordinator of Student Teaching of Psychiatry
Cornell University College of Medicine
Head, Sexual Disorder Program, Payne Whitney Clinic
of the New York Hospital

BRUNNER/MAZEL *Publishers* • New York

Fourth Printing

TO:

BARBARA, PHILLIP K., PHILIP S.,
REBECCA, ANTHONY, PETER,
and last but not least,
JENNIFER

PREFACE

The rapid expansion of group and family therapy is a major phenomenon in modern psychiatry. The promising group and family field has generated an ambience of ferment and openness to new ideas and many gifted clinicians are currently engaged in the quest for better theoretical formulations and more effective therapeutic strategies. At its present stage of development, the pluralism of the group and family modalities is reflected in a bewildering array of methods, applications and theories. Their methods range from marathons to marital therapy; they have been used to treat a wide spectrum of psychiatric disorders from severely ill hospitalized patients to persons suffering from mild interpersonal difficulties; and, most recently, the application of group principles has been extended to enhance the psychological functioning of normal individuals. Finally, group and family therapy employs the theoretical constructs of group process, general systems theory, psychoanalysis, learning theory, and other theoretical models, all of which have evolved distinctive treatment strategies and tactics. However, although they may appear to be disparate at first glance, the variegated contemporary group and family approaches spring from common conceptual foundations, and gain clarity when viewed from a broader theoretical perspective.

The current emergence of a veritable flood of new publications has made it increasingly difficult for professionals to keep pace with developments in the field, let alone to remain alert to the interrelationships between the different group modalities and to the implications of the new data for the understanding and treatment of mental illness.

The decision to publish this series was dictated by these considerations. As such, our purpose is twofold: to periodically select the most significant recent developments in the group and family field and to attempt to present these, as far as is possible, in a meaningful conceptual framework.

AUTHORSHIP

The fifty-two articles included in this volume were selected to provide a comprehensive overview of recent significant theoretical and clinical innovations in group and family therapy. They represent a sampling of the current views and efforts of many of the outstanding creative thinkers in the field. Twenty-eight of these articles are reprints which originally appeared in the professional literature within the past few years. Indeed, initially we had expected this volume would consist primarily of reprints. However, it soon became apparent that this would not ensure comprehensive coverage of the significant areas of progress in this field. Accordingly, when appropriate material on an important topic could not be found in the existing literature, we invited an outstanding expert in that area to contribute to this publication. A total of twenty-four original articles were specifically prepared for this volume. Thus, for example, it was especially difficult to find suitable published material on the interesting newer approaches in group therapy where clinical work has generally taken precedence over writing. Original manuscripts by Robert Goulding on new directions in Transactional Analysis, by Ruth Cohn describing task-centered workshops, James Simkin's contribution on Gestalt therapy, Herbert Fensterheim's discussion of new techniques of behavior therapy in groups, and Spotnitz's innovative approach to the treatment of adolescents, were included for this reason. In addition Anthony's report on his fascinating study of schizophrenic families, Wolf's analysis of the distinctions between psychoanalysis in groups and other forms of group therapy, Masters and Johnson's paper on the rapid treatment of sexual dysfunction, Rabkin's analysis of the My Lai atrocity, Laquer's paper on multiple family therapy and Nathan Ackerman's last thoughts on the current status and future directions of family therapy, among many others, enabled us to implement our primary publishing goal—to keep the reader informed of current clinical and theoretical developments in the field.

FORMAT

The book has been organized into five areas: *Group Therapy, Family Therapy, The Treatment of Marital and Sexual Problems, Special Patient Populations* and *Applications and Extensions*. Two of these areas, *Group Therapy* and *Special Patient Populations,* have been further subdivided into separate sections for greater clarity. In addition, we made an effort to juxtapose material that reflects contrasting positions in order to underscore the richness and diversity of the field.

We have attempted to create an appropriate vehicle for the presentation of the polymorphous collection of material in this volume by writing brief introductions to each Area and Section which are intended to suggest unifying conceptual frameworks for the papers contained therein. In addition, we sought to foster cohesion and continuity of content by including as part of these editorial commentaries suggested cross-references directing the reader's attention to related articles contained in this volume, as well as to those papers that present alternative or contrasting viewpoints.

THE PREPARATION OF THE BOOK

This book is the product of the cooperation of many talented and dedicated friends. The project was initiated and encouraged by that most far-sighted of publishers, Bernard Mazel. Miss Phyllis Joachim, a graduate student in psychology, conducted the background research. We were fortunate in having the dedicated and efficient assistance of Mrs. Barbara Rose, who organized the secretarial and production aspects of the book. We are also indebted to Doctor Stella Chess and Mrs. Doris Bartlett for their valuable suggestions, and to Doctors Saul Scheidlinger and Donald Bloch, editors of the *International Journal of Group Psychotherapy* and *Family Process* respectively, in which many of the articles contained in this volume were originally published. Finally, we wish to express our special thanks to Elaine Cohen, who edited the editorial comments and original manuscripts, and who, by virtue of her insights and talents, made an invaluable contribution to this book.

We found the experience of preparing this book rewarding and exhilarating. It was, in a sense, like assembling a great dinner for discriminating guests: We planned an exciting meal, selected superb ingredients at the best markets; we tried to prepare each course carefully and to serve it well. We hope you enjoy the feast.

THE EDITORS

CONTENTS

xi

INTRODUCTION

Group and family treatment modalities are, first and foremost, clinical techniques, and should be considered in relation to modern theories of the causes and treatment of psychiatric disorders if they are to be fully understood. It would seem appropriate, therefore, to preface the articles in this volume by a brief review of relevant current concepts of psychopathology and treatment methods, and attempt to clarify their relationship to the various group and family approaches described herein.

THE MULTICAUSALITY OF MENTAL ILLNESS

In the last decade impressive advances have been made in the understanding and treatment of psychiatric disorders. Emerging from, and at the same time central to, the theoretical formulations which underlie this progress is the concept that human behavior is multidetermined. Although, in many respects still a mystery, it has become apparent that the many forms and dimensions of human behavior are the product of the complex interplay of multiple biological, psychological, and environmental factors. Mental health depends on the integrity of these underlying determinants.

According to the multicausal model, these biological, psychological, and environmental factors have critical effects on behavior and psychopathology results from various aberrations of these behavioral determinants. Thus, the chemical effects of LSD, an unresolved oedipal conflict, genetically determined central nervous system characteristics which render a patient particularly vulnerable to stress, self-defeating responses to others learned as a result of early experiences, or coping with pathological family interactions can all contribute to the patient's emotional disturbance, and so must be taken into consideration by the therapist.

TREATMENT

The basic strategy of treatment is to identify the factors which have caused the patient's distress and to alter these if possible. A wide variety of pathogenic determinants can be modified by modern treatment methods. Thus, for example, a patient can acquire more effective modes of relating to others in group therapy; paralyzing fears can be extinguished with the tools of behavior therapy; unconscious conflicts that impede functioning can be uncovered, interpreted, and solved in psychotherapy; the family therapist can relieve the noxious familial influences that tax the patient's adaptive capacities; and a simple electrolyte can modify the chemical roots of mania.

However, our efforts to alter the impact of other important behavioral variables have been less successful; and treatment for many prevalent forms of mental illness is still unsatisfactory.

Beyond this broad concept of multicausality, final answers regarding the etiology of psychiatric disorders continue to elude us, and no single comprehensive theory of human behavior, psychopathology and treatment is universally accepted. Indeed, the multicausal view of psychopathology renders orthodoxy or commitment to any one treatment approach untenable.

INDIVIDUAL VS. ECOLOGICAL APPROACHES IN GROUP AND FAMILY THERAPY

Consequently, as is true of psychiatry in general, contemporary divergent developments in the group and family field reflect the current feeling that human behavior has multiple roots, and that change can be brought about by various forms of intervention. For schematic purposes, however, the treatment strategies currently in use may be separated into those which focus on changing the individual patient and those that seek to treat the individual by intervening to change his environment.

Changing the Individual

Psychiatric treatment has traditionally proceeded by attempting to alter various biological or psychological characteristics of the individual patient. Psychological treatment methods, which subsume the group modalities, employ two basic forms of intervention to this end: the "insight" methods utilized by the various schools of psychotherapy, and the newly developed techniques for the modification of behavior by means of behavior therapy. There is a fundamental difference in these two approaches. Proponents of the insight methods seek to foster the patient's recognition of the unconscious conflicts which underlie his problems; in contrast, proponents of the newer behavioral approaches contend that the effectiveness of the learning tactics they employ to modify behavior is not contingent upon the patient's understanding of the origins of his difficulties.

In essence, the insight methods are based on the assumption that permanent changes in psychological functioning can best be effected by bringing various unconscious psychic elements into the patient's conscious awareness, which, presumably, will enable him to exercise greater control over the impulses and attitudes which shape his maladaptive behavior. However, the various schools of psychotherapy differ widely in the tactics they employ to foster such awareness, and also in the unconscious material that is deemed significant. Thus, the psychoanalytic approaches use the familiar tactic of uncovering and interpreting the unconscious conflicts which are believed to underlie neurotic phenomena. In contrast, interpersonally oriented therapists attempt to foster the patient's insight into the dynamics of his maladaptive relationships, and rely on clarification of specifically structured interpersonal transactions for their therapeutic results. Finally, the major tactic of still another group of therapists, who subscribe to the Gestalt, or experiential, approach, is to create situations specifically designed to foster awareness of bodily and emotional experiences which had not been perceived previously by the patient.

Group and family modalities provide the therapist with an opportunity to employ strategies which have proven highly effective in promoting insight, regardless of the particular psychic parameter he chooses to focus on, and they are being used widely to implement this approach. Thus two of the sections in this volume contain papers describing insight-promoting group approaches that contrast sharply, both in the material brought to awareness and also in their tactics employed to this end.

In contrast to the insight methods, some of the newer treatment modalities that are based on learning theory make no attempt to foster the patient's understanding of the roots of his problem. Rather, they create specific reinforcement contingencies which are designed to re-shape pathological facets of the patient's behavior. Once again, group and family modalities, with their multiple interactions and opportunity for trial and error, and potent sources of reinforcement, provide a rich matrix for this behavioral approach as well. The fact that five papers in this volume deal with the application of learning principles reflects the increasing popularity of these strategies in group and family therapy.

Changing the Environment

The concept of multicausality has extended our perspective beyond the individual patient and focused our attention on the broader social context from which psychopathology derives. Recent recognition of the powerful impact of environmental variables, i.e., family dynamics, interpersonal transactions and social forces, has resulted in a shift of therapeutic emphasis: the therapist's exclusive concern with changing the patient's psychic functioning has been extended to changing the pathogenic environment as well. The development of group and family techniques that can effectively modify such ecological determinants offers great hope for improving the treatment of mental illness, and papers reflecting this approach are heavily represented in this volume.

OVERVIEW

Recent advances in group and family therapy epitomize both circular and linear progress. Circular progress refers to the refinement and elaboration of an existing concept, as exemplified by the evolution of ego psychology within the framework of classical psychoanalytic theory. In contrast, linear progress refers to the creation of a radically different solution to a problem, as exemplified by family treatment of schizophrenia.

With specific reference to developments in the group and family field, the evolution of General Systems Theory may well represent true *linear* progress. The systems approach, which conceives of the individual as a dynamic system in constant interaction with his ever-changing environment, has already inspired the development of a number of innovative therapeutic strategies. Although its final significance remains to be evaluated, this approach may ultimately have a powerful impact on our understanding of human behavior and yield truly novel solutions to the problems of mental illness. Group and family methods based on or influenced by general systems concepts are described throughout this book.

While its impact is not as dramatic, circular progress, the improvement and refinement of existing concepts, is no less important, and, as might be expected, actually characterizes the bulk of human inventiveness. This volume also contains many articles which are innovative without rejecting the past, i.e., which describe promising refinements and extensions of existing techniques and theories.

After reviewing the current literature on group and family therapy, one is left with the impression that there is widespread optimism regarding the effectiveness of family and group modalities. It is equally apparent, however, that no final answers or ultimate techniques have emerged as yet. On the whole, treatment methods are still empirical and are not yet solidly founded on a clear understanding of the causes of the disorders being treated. At this critical stage in the evolution of group and family therapy, one is struck, in particular, by the relative paucity of systematic, controlled studies designed to evaluate the therapeutic efficacy of the attractive new techniques currently in use.

Yet, despite these deficiencies, one has the final impression that group and family techniques hold promise, not only for improving the treatment of the mentally ill, but for enhancing the lives of non-patients. People are turning to group experiences in the hope that these will help them to combat the deadening alienation of their lives by augmenting their positive human potential for joy, creativity, growth and love.

H.S.K.
C.J.S.

PROGRESS IN GROUP AND
FAMILY THERAPY

Area I
GROUP THERAPY

Current conceptual orientations in Group Therapy can be divided into two major categories: those which place relatively greater emphasis on group process and those which focus primarily on the individual patient within the group setting. Further, the "individualistic" schools of therapy can be subdivided into approaches which are based on the psychoanalytic theory of behavior, and methods which derive from various alternate models of personality and psychopathology.

Actually, the distinction between the group process and individualistic approaches is an artificial one in that it reflects a difference in emphasis rather than categorical differences. The creative, individual-oriented group therapist does not fail to take the effects of group processes and the ecological determinants of behavior into consideration. He uses the dynamics of group interactions to further the analysis of his patients. Similarly, the therapist whose work is rooted in systems theory and who employs group process extensively, does so not to the exclusion, but rather in the service of fostering the greater sensitivity, competence, and autonomy of each patient in the group.

To some extent, all forms of group therapy, explicitly or implicitly, employ an amalgam of three change-producing agents: group process, intrapsychic dynamics and learning. Nevertheless, the techniques employed in the various forms of group therapy differ substantially. These disparities derive, in part, from differences in the underlying models of personality and psychopathology, from divergent concepts of the crucial dimensions of the group process, and also from contrasting views of the role of reinforcement and conditioning in modifying behavior. Techniques are also shaped by differences in the relative emphasis that is placed on each of the three change-producing agents.

In organizing the material on group therapy we were guided by these considerations. Thus, Area I includes four sections. Group Process Oriented Group Approaches is the topic of the first Section, 1-A. In contrast, the papers included in the next two sections describe group approaches which emphasize treatment of the individual patient. The articles contained in Section I-B explore innovative developments of group techniques which reflect a psychoanalytic frame of reference. On the other

2

hand, the new group approaches described in Section I-C are based on different orientations: Gestalt psychology, Transactional Analysis and learning theory. The fourth and final section in this area on Group Therapy contains papers on the prolific small group movements, including encounter and marathon groups, and concludes appropriately with a report of the first findings yielded by an excellent and important evaluative study of the encounter groups.

H.S.K.
C.J.S.

Area I—Section A

GROUP PROCESS

GENERAL SYSTEMS THEORY

Briefly defined, General Systems Theory conceives of the individual as a process or system; as such, he can best be understood as an integral functioning part of a larger dynamic system, the social matrix. From the moment of birth, man's nervous system is adapted, both structurally and functionally, to operate on the interface of, and within, the substrate of a social system. Moreover, his personality is shaped and modified by his social interactions, by the input and feedback, and by the very organization of the social substrate in which it exists.

General Systems Theory provides the conceptual framework for the ecological approach which has received growing recognition in psychiatry. The far-reaching implications of the systems approach are reflected in such recent developments as the community psychiatry movement, with its emphasis on changing the pathogenic impact of the patient's environment, the development of partial hospitalization programs and therapeutic communities which seek to create an environment designed to foster recovery from mental illness, and family therapy which treats the symptomatic patient by intervening to change his family system.

RELEVANCE OF THE SYSTEMS MODEL FOR GROUP THERAPY

Emphasis on the clinical importance of group dynamics reflects the influence of General Systems Theory. The "group process" approach in group therapy rests on the assumption that powerful group currents exert various profound influences on its individual members, which, for the most part, go unrecognized. Accordingly, "group process" oriented therapists have attempted to identify the nature of the group themes which evoke significant reactions, and the specific effects of these on patients. Therapeutic techniques which derive from this model attempt

5

to modify group-generated determinants of disturbed behavior. To this end, the therapist seeks to clarify the ongoing group process, and the responses it has evoked in the patients who comprise the group. It is assumed that the insight and concomitant mastery the patient achieves in the therapy group will enable him to negotiate more effectively with his family, work and community groups.

There is general agreement among group therapists that transactional factors are important determinants of emotional disturbance, and that group processes exert significant influence on patients' behavior and should therefore be taken into account in treatment. However, the exclusive therapeutic focus on ongoing group processes recommended by "group process" therapists is a source of controversy. Controversy also derives from the fact that proponents of this approach have advanced several divergent group process models which are usually described in terms that do not permit experimental validation. In fact, the greater clinical effectiveness of group process methods as compared to other group approaches has not yet been demonstrated. It is not surprising, under the circumstances, that although some group process models are conceptually attractive and have gained thoughtful adherents, no one system has been universally accepted to date.

THE PAPERS

The first paper in this section, prepared specifically for inclusion in this volume, and based on a recent presentation by Dr. Helen Durkin, provides a concise description of General Systems Theory, and its relevance for group therapy. In addition, this paper clarifies the relationship and theoretical compatibility of systems theory and current psychoanalytic concepts.

Dr. Durkin's article sets the stage for the two following papers which describe group process approaches of current interest. It should be noted, that the methods described in these papers were developed in England. Our purpose in limiting this section to British contributions to this approach was to provide an overview of the current status of group process in England, where it has gained considerable acceptance.

The papers describe two forms of group process oriented therapy that were developed at the Tavistock Clinic. Rioch discusses the work of Bion who proceeds on the assumption that constructive as well as pathological group forces exist, that both exert powerful effects on the individual patient, and that usually he is not consciously aware of these forces or their impact. Bion further contends that participation in a healthy group process fosters constructive behavior. Conversely, participation in a group which is motivated by irrational assumptions typically evokes destructive behavior, although individuals differ inherently in their vulnerability to various pathological group forces. In any event, it is the dual goal of the therapist to clarify irrational group assumptions on the one hand, and to foster the emergence of the healthy "work group," on the other. In the last paper in this section, Heath and Bacal describe still another model, developed by Ezriel at the Tavistock Clinic, in which the crucial dimensions of the group process are considered to be specific kinds of relationships which exist within the group. Both Bion and Ezriel believe that therapeutic intervention should be limited to interpretations of on-going behavior which, supposedly, is motivated by the predominant group process, of which the patients are not consciously aware.

SUGGESTED CROSS REFERENCES

In her paper in Section C of this area, Ruth Cohn provides clinical examples in support of Durkin's thesis that systems theory is not contradictory to psychoanalysis, that the levels at which observed phenomena are described are different, but complemental.

Although not explicitly stated, a systems view underlies all of family and marital therapy, to some extent, and, as such, the articles contained in Areas II and III, on family and marital therapy, respectively, are pertinent to this section. More specifically, in Area II, Laquer's paper on multiple family therapy, Auerwald's article on the interdisciplinary versus the ecological approach to family therapy, and the article by Speck and Attneave, who advocate manipulation of environmental variables, e.g., relatives, neighbors, schools, etc., demonstrate extensions of this approach.

In Area III, the systems approach is explicitly reflected in Sager et al's paper on the marriage contract, in which they discuss marital therapy from a transactional viewpoint, and also in Masters and Johnson's description of their rapid treatment of sexual problems, wherein they view sexual difficulties as symptoms of faulty interactions between marital partners.

In addition, Christmas and Sager, in their articles in Area V, one on the rehabilitation of the impoverished patient, and the second on the development of a partial hospitalization service for impoverished patients, explicitly base their polymorphous therapeutic techniques on an ecological approach that takes into account the multiple and potent effects of the "system" on psychological functioning.

Finally, the National Training Laboratory in this country employs the group process approach extensively in its work with non-patient populations. A description of the Laboratory Training Model may be found in Area V of this volume, on Applications and Extensions.

H.S.K.
C.J.S.

1

ANALYTIC GROUP THERAPY AND GENERAL SYSTEMS THEORY

Helen E. Durkin, Ph.D.

Training Analyst, Postgraduate Center for Mental Health
(New York City)

The recent proliferation of group methods has brought theoretical confusion among us to the point that the scientific credibility of group therapy is threatened; concomitantly, the implementation of broad-scope group programs in large community projects has become increasingly difficult. It is time to work toward greater conceptual clarity and order (13).

General systems theory seems well qualified to resolve this dilemma by providing certain unifying trends for our thinking. In fact, in time, it may come to serve as a more comprehensive structural framework for the group therapies. But one cannot embark on either course until systems theory and its relevance for group therapy have been reassessed. Actually, concepts and techniques derived from systems theory have been filtering into group therapy from group dynamics and family therapy for some time, but these need to be construed more concisely.

An attempt will be made in this article to provide a basis for the careful theoretical reassessment which must precede change. To this end, the fundamental principles of those branches of systems theory which are germane to group therapy, i.e., group dynamics (8) and cybernetics (17), will be presented as precisely as possible. Consideration will then be given to the question of the compatibility of the concepts of systems theory and the concepts of group therapy, with particular reference to analytic group therapy, because this approach offers the greatest challenge to the establishment of a working relationship between group therapy and systems theory.

The Conceptual Framework. Fortunately for our project, systems science is still young and in a fluid state: It is not as yet fully structured (14). Both inductive and deductive methods have been employed in systems research, as have a diversity of models, concepts, and techniques. Quantification is a goal, and a variety of mathematical formulations have been employed to attain it, but in many areas it has not yet been achieved.

In addition to group dynamics and cybernetics, which, as noted above, have particular relevance for group therapy, there are a number of branches of systems theory, e.g., information theory (12), automata theory (10), game theory (15), and decision theory (11). Some of these are organismic in orientation; others are mechanistic. But, regardless of their orientation, the concepts, models, and techniques unique to each are freely combined to conform with the particular subject matter and specific goals of the researcher. Furthermore, no limitation is imposed on the researcher with respect to the system he may choose to study (or, more specifically, with respect to its locus in the hierarchy of systems), as long as he takes cognizance of the relationship between the system he has selected for investigation and its sub- and super-systems. Clearly, then, we are given wide latitude within this framework to explore the conceptual relationship between systems theory and the group therapies.

The Evolution of General Systems Theory

General systems theory is best understood from a historical perspective. It was preceded by the Cartesian era, during which science was dominated by physics, and all scientists, whatever their special area of interest, attempted to systematize their knowledge by the method of reductive analysis. Although it was a fruitful period on the whole, unfortunately for the behavioral sciences, teleology had been ruled out as a remnant of an unscientific age. Thus, if they wanted to be accepted into the scientific fraternity, scientists had to sacrifice investigation of the most vitally human behavior because it was purposive, and were forced to concentrate instead on less complex phenomena.

Eventually, of course, the method of reductive analysis reached a dead end, even in the physical sciences, when the smallest and the largest elements proved intractable to further analysis. Necessity gave birth to quantum mechanics and relativity theory, which led, in turn, to a radical change in the prevailing scientific outlook—and paved the way for systems thinking. Specifically, the old monadic concept of objects gave way to a new focus on their function and relationship. At the same time, the concept of linear causation yielded to that of the circularity of cause and effect. In short, the social sciences came to life. Scientists soon discovered that goal-directed behavior, growth, and creativity could be accounted for scientifically by the dynamic interaction among the component parts of any living system. At last, the relationship between personality as a whole, its function in society, and society itself could be studied in good scientific conscience.

This change in perspective brought about a whole new order of knowledge which soon began to bridge the gaps among the various branches of science: Although the research which now began to pour in from many different countries covered widely different subject matter, it converged on one crucial phenomenon—the organization of complex phenomena. It was noted that similarities appeared regularly, regardless of the nature of the phenomena investigated. And, invariably, these turned out to be similarities in the relationship of their components. This remarkable consonance suggested that the laws of organization could be generalized: The method of isomorphies was found to be productive in crossing scientific boundaries. The next task, then, was to formulate these laws and elaborate on them. Systems theory was on its way. By 1954 an organization was formed, and arrangements had been made to publish a yearbook to facilitate the exchange of ideas among systems scientists (14). Over the years, a great deal of highly sophisticated research, both theoretical and applied, has been reported in these volumes, but for our purposes we need only concentrate on those findings that are pertinent to group therapy.

The Basic Principles of Systems Theory

The crucial discovery that highly diverse, complex phenomena are similarly organized insofar as the relationship of their components is deceptively simple. In fact, the implications of this discovery have changed the entire face of science. More specifically, systems theory postulates that organized complexities or "systems," as they came to be called, are the product of the dynamic interaction among their parts, rather than the sum of their absolute characteristics. In other words, neither the resultant whole nor its new characteristics can be explained by the nature of the parts themselves; they can only be understood as a function of the continuous interchange of matter, energy, and information among these parts. Within this conceptual framework, Hall and Fagan (5) have defined a system as a "set of objects together with the relationships between the objects and between their attributes. The objects are the component parts of the system, the attributes are the properties of objects, and the relationships tie the system together." The world is thus conceived of phenomenologically as a hierarchy of interrelated systems; within this hierarchy, each system faces downward, as it were, toward its sub-systems, and upward toward its super-systems (9).

The Compatibility of Systems Theory and Psychoanalytic Theory

Although they are not always fully understood, today most analytically oriented group therapists consider the basic principles of systems theory, as delineated above, to be compatible with their theoretical orientation. This is a comparatively recent development, however, and the issue of compatibility is still debated vehemently.

Von Bertalanffy (14) and Watzlawick and his co-workers (16) are representative of those systems scientists who consider psychoanalytic theory incompatible with their own views. Thus Von Bertalanffy maintains that psychoanalysis contradicts the basic tenets of modern scientific theory because it subscribes to the concept of linear causation. And Watzlawick et al. consider psychoanalysis at variance with systems theory because it employs the concept of energy, rather than information, as a unit of exchange.

In fact, however, there is a good deal of evidence which points toward conceptual harmony. As is well known, Freud was among the activators of the protest against nineteenth-century scientism, and the first psychologist to break through the taboo against investigating man's essential purposiveness. Moreover, of particular relevance in this context is the fact that he conceived of man as a "bio-psychosocial being," and defined the group in terms of "the reciprocal influence among its members" (3). Clearly, the potential for theoretical harmony was present from the start.

More recently, the theory of personality advanced by ego psychologists attests to the affinity of current psychoanalytic theory with the views of systems scientists. Specifically, within the framework of ego psychology, personality is described in terms of its structure, the unique character of which is determined by the continuous interaction among its sub-structures, i.e., the ego, the id, and the superego. Thus behavior is seen as an attribute of the total personality organization. Each component substructure within this system is similarly organized. For instance, the ego is composed of several nuclei, each of which has a special function and interacts with other nuclei under the aegis of its integrating function. Nor are the environmental systems ignored by the proponents of ego psychology: Hartman formulated his definition of mental health in terms of the "equilibrium which exists among the structures of the personality on the one hand and those of the environment on the other" (7). Within this conceptual framework, the analytic therapy group can be viewed as a psychosocial system which follows the same laws of organization as the individual personality.

In a sense, analytic group psychotherapy also contributed to the modernization of psychoanalytic theory, in that the psychoanalytic constructs it retained as a result of its purely pragmatic task of applying psychoanalytic therapeutic techniques to the group situation were in accordance with the tenets of ego psychology: Both focus on function, relationship, and dynamic interaction. In light of these developments, arguments such as those advanced by von Bertalanffy, become irrelevant because they pertain only to individual psychoanalysis of pre-1921 vintage.

Specific Considerations: The Compatibility of Systems Theory and Analytic Group Psychotherapy

Analytic group psychotherapy, which was introduced at a time when little was known about systems theory, evolved from the desire of its proponents to implement a particular therapeutic technique, rather than the explicit assumptions they held concerning the nature of groups. Nevertheless, from the beginning, it has been based on the implicit assumption, noted above, and attributed to Freud, that a "reciprocal influence [is operative] among the members" of a group. Thus, one might speculate that it was inevitable that the group and its individual components would ultimately be regarded as interrelated systems in a hierarchy of psychosocial systems.

And, in fact, despite the initial preoccupation of analytically oriented therapists with problems of technique, systems views gradually began to filter into analytic group therapy, by a kind of osmosis, from group dynamics and later from family therapy. Concurrently, analytic group therapists became increasingly aware of the fact that the absence of a single member of the group changed the character of the total group constellation, and that changes in the total group mood or emotional preoccupation influenced the behavior of its individual members. It is safe to assume, for example, that if one member expresses tender feelings at a time when the group is engaged in battle, he is likely to receive short shrift. And so today, although they might use the vocabulary of psychoanalysis, rather than that of systems science, most analytic group therapists would agree that the therapy group is an organized complexity (or system) which is the product of the reflexive dynamic interaction among its components. What needs to be emphasized, of course, is that it is the basic structural similarity, not the language, which is decisive. The general laws of organization hold, regardless of the nature of the components of the system, their attributes, or the forces which tie the group together.

Dissenting opinions. Once again, however, there are sharp differences of opinion concerning the compatibility of analytic group therapy and systems theory, which focus on the analytic view of the nature of the relationship of the components of the group. Systems scientists have argued that analytically oriented group therapists consistently view the components of the group in terms of their developmental history. In contrast, group dynamics and communications therapists prefer to deal exclusively with the here and now. Concomitantly, they prefer to rely on observable behavior, rather than on less exact inferences regarding unconscious infantile motivation. And it is because they consider it more reliable that they prefer the concept of information to that of energy. Finally, analytic group therapists, like group dynamics and communications therapists, deal with events at the interface between systems. They differ, however, in that analytic group therapists stress the source of the input for the component individuals, while the group dynamics and communications therapists concentrate on the effect of the total system upon its components.

Other discrepancies have been noted as well: Watzlawick et al. (16) make the particular point that in other group therapies the attributes are "persons-in-communication," in contrast to the "intrapsychic attributes" of psychoanalysis. But these authors miss the point that the members of the analytic therapy group regularly translate their intrapsychic conflicts into the communicated behavior. It is a mistake to regard the interaction of intrapsychic components as a closed system.

In fact, a delineation of the cardinal features of the transference will serve to refute all of the arguments, delineated above, which have been advanced by those who contend that analytic group therapy is essentially incompatible with systems theory:

1. The transference is translated into clinically observable behavior, and is manifested by obvious distortions of perception and behavior in the group situation.

2. In essence, therefore, it is a here and now phenomenon—a point often missed by systems scientists.

3. The inference that such behavior is derived from unfinished childhood drives can be verified empirically by the patient's associative communications.

4. The fact that translating it into its original terms does effect changes in the form and content of the communicating of group members testifies to the validity of the transference both as a theoretical concept and as a change agent.*

In the group situation, the individual transferences interact as the members simultaneously seek to establish relationships which will gratify (or ward off) their infantile needs (Ezriel, 1950). Their interaction produces a new whole, a transference network (Foulkes, 1957, 1964), which may be viewed as the group equivalent of the transference neurosis. It should be noted, however, that close inspection of the nature of this interaction reveals individual trends that cannot be attributed solely to unconscious infantile motivations; rather, it is multidetermined: The individual's input is also derived from physiological and complex current psychological needs.

At first glance, the concept of the transference may seem irreconcilable with communication theory. Yet an objective inspection of this phenomenon, in the light of ongoing systems research (16) suggests a more fertile outlook. The phenomenon may be perceived, for example, as a behavioral attribute of personality organization which constitutes a reactivation of the caretakers of childhood. It originates during the process of individuation, and serves the special function of avoiding repeated pain. Over a period of time, the transference emulates other specialized functions in that it tends to become mechanized to varying degrees. Concurrently, there is a loss of spontaneity in the affected areas. In cases of severe conflict, it may dominate the individual's behavior, in which event it regularly interferes with valid communication. Thus the whole thrust of the interpretation of transference phenomena is aimed at breaking through this mechanization and restoring spontaneity.

It is this author's contention that this capacity for transposition into systems terms has a structural base. If so, it is strong evidence in support of the conceptual compatibility of systems theory and analytic group therapy. Obviously, this compatibility must be confirmed—or disproved —by appropriate research. The evidence suggests, however, that even

---

* H. T. Glatzer (4) has provided some excellent clinical evidence in support of these statements.

in areas where there are clear-cut differences of opinion, complementarity (rather than contradiction) is a distinct possibility. If such a possibility does exist, the present controversy may, when the need for defensiveness has died down, give way to a productive technical reciprocity.

Analytic Group Psychotherapy as a Method of Effecting Systems Change

Systems research has demonstrated that the method for changing systems must be appropriate to "the components, their attributes, and the forces that tie the system together." Moreover, the techniques must be appropriate to the goals of the therapist. New techniques derived from systems research may be devised in the future. Or established techniques which have proven effective may be employed, provided they are not contradictory to modern scientific principles. Inasmuch as it fulfills these criteria, the technique of interpreting transference resistance in group psychotherapy would be considered a suitable method for effecting systems change.

In order to maintain the stability achieved by their transferences, both individuals and groups, like the members of a family, characteristically expend a good deal of energy in their efforts to ward off anything which threatens their precarious balance. Analytically oriented therapists call this phenomenon transference resistance, and make systematic interventions (metacommunications) in order to break through the patient's mechanized transference behavior (transactions) and restore spontaneity. As soon as he becomes aware of the extent to which past experiences are distorting his present group relationships, the patient has the option of choosing alternative behavior. Analytic interventions provide him with this information, and serve thereby to release the energy bound in his distorted communications.

To the best of this author's knowledge, systems theory has not yet produced a more effective technique. However, the "therapeutic paradox" described by Haley (1963) and Watzlawick (16) seems to come closest to this goal. Briefly, this technique consists of employing paradoxes which are calculated to put the patient into a double bind, and force him to change in order to avoid yielding to what he perceives as the therapist's demands. Thus it would seem that the "therapeutic paradox" involves engaging in the kind of power struggle with the patient (albeit "for his own good") which we are trying to help him give up. The attitude of concerned neutrality seems more in line with the goal of therapy. However, as mentioned earlier, the field is still young; future collaborative research efforts will undoubtedly produce many modifications and innovations.

Summary and Conclusions

It was suggested in this article that general systems theory may provide the much needed unifying trends for the expanding and conceptually fragmented field of group therapy. As a first step toward this end, an attempt was made to provide a reasonable basis for the theoretical evaluation which must precede such a reorientation. Those basic tenets of systems theory which are germane to group therapy were reviewed, and its conceptual compatibility with psychoanalytic theory, and analytic group therapy, in particular, was considered. Thus the concept of the transference, which epitomizes the sharpest differences of opinion on this score, was reviewed in the light of systems concepts.

On the basis of the available evidence, the author concluded that the two conceptual systems are harmonious in principle, and that their differences will eventually prove to be complementary rather than contradictory. Plans are currently underway to employ suitable research techniques to test a series of hypotheses which reflect this point of view.

REFERENCES

1. BATESON, G. & RUESCH, J. (1965) *Therapeutic Communication*, Norton, New York.
2. DURKIN, H. (1964) *The Group in Depth*, Intl. Univ. Press, New York.
3. FREUD, S. (1921) *Group Psychology and Analysis of the Ego*, Hogarth, London.
4. GLATZER, H. (1969) *Working Through in Group Psychotherapy*, Intl. J. Group Psychother.
5. HALL, A. & FAGEN, B. (1956) *Definition of System*, Genl. Systems Yearbook I, p. 18.
6. HALL, C. & LINDZEY, G. (1954) *Handbook of Social Psychology*, Addison/Wesley, Cambridge, Mass.
7. HARTMAN, H. (1964) *Essays on Ego Psychology*, Intl. Univ. Press, New York.
8. LEWIN, K. (1951) *Field Theory and Social Science*, Harper & Row, New York.
9. MILLER, J. (1955) *Toward a General Theory of Systems*, Am. Psychol. Jnl., Vol. X, p. 513.
10. MINSKY, M. (1967) *Computation, Finite and Infinite Machines*, Prentice-Hall, Englewood Cliffs, New Jersey.
11. RAPAPORT, A. (1959) *Critique of Game Theory*, Behavioral Science I, pp. 303-315.
12. SHANNON, C. & WEAVER, W. (1949) *The Mathematical Theory of Communication*, Univ. of Illinois Press, Urbana, Ill.
13. SCHEIDLINGER, S. (1968) *Therapeutic Approaches in Community Mental Health*, Social Work XIII, p. 3.
14. VON BERTALANFFY, L. (1968) *General System Theory*, Human Relations, Braziller, New York.
15. VON NEUMAN, J. & MORGENSTERN, O. (1946) *Theory of Games and Economic Behavior*, Princeton Univ. Press, Princeton, New Jersey.
16. WATZLAWICK, P., BEAVIN, J., & JACKSON, D. (1967) *Pragmatics of Human Communication*, Norton, New York.
17. WIENER, N. (1948) *Cybernetics*, John Wiley & Sons, New York.

2

THE WORK OF WILFRED BION ON GROUPS

Margaret J. Rioch, Ph.D.

Professor of Psychology, The American University (Washington, D.C.)
Chairman of Group Relations Conference Committee,
The Washington School of Psychiatry

The shift in perspective from the individual to the group is difficult to make in actual practice although it is often given lip service. It is like a shift to a higher order of magnitude, which is not easy when the lower order is in itself very complex and by no means thoroughly understood. But the shift is necessary in order to grasp social phenomena. From this perspective it is often possible to see the problems of the individual or the pair in a new light. This is well known to family therapists, who find an individual child or a marital relationship more comprehensible when seen in the framework of the entire family.

The Washington School of Psychiatry-Tavistock Conferences provide opportunities for members to study behavior in large groups of 50-60, in small groups of 10-12, and in intergroup situations. No particular theoretical framework is prescribed, and staff members come with various theoretical points of view and from various professional orientations, including sociology, psychology, psychoanalysis, and business administration. But Bion's concepts have been especially useful to the staff since they formulate group psychological processes in integrative terms. A. K. Rice, who has directed most of the British and American conferences since 1962, was strongly influenced by his membership in a training group conducted by Bion in 1947-48, as well as by Bion's theories.

Reprinted by permission from PSYCHIATRY, 1970, Vol. 33, No. 1, pp. 56-66.

Much of the material on which Bion based his theories and many of the examples which he gives come from the small groups which he conducted at the Tavistock Clinic. He does not deal exclusively with these, however, but also discusses large social institutions such as the army and the church. His interest in group processes was stimulated when, as an officer in the British Army during World War II, he was engaged in the selection of men for leadership roles and in charge of a rehabilitation unit of psychiatric patients. He began at that time to think of treatment of the whole society of the hospital not as a makeshift to save psychiatric manpower, but as the best way to get at the malady as he perceived it, namely the inability on the part of the patients to function adequately as members of society or, in other words, as group members. He saw this inability with reference both to the hospital community and to society at large.

Because Bion's name is so much associated with groups and because he emphasized the phenomena of total fields rather than of individuals he is sometimes thought of as having reified the idea of the group or as having talked about the group as a mythical entity instead of talking about human behavior. This is not the case. He defines a group as a function or set of functions of an aggregate of individuals. It is not a function of any one part separately, nor is it an aggregate without a function.

For example, if a dozen strangers are lying by chance in the sun on the same beach they do not constitute a group according to this definition. But if someone in the water cries for help and the twelve individuals respond by trying to save the swimmer from drowning in some kind of concerted action, however rudimentary the concertedness may be, they have become a group in that they now have a function. This may last for only a few minutes or it may turn into an organization of life savers which goes on for years.

Although Bion thinks and speaks of instincts, he does not postulate a herd instinct or a group mind. He thinks that ideas of this kind are often developed by people in groups, but that when they occur they are symptomatic of regression. In his opinion groups bring into prominence phenomena which can best be understood if one has some experience of psychotic phenomena as well as of normal and neurotic behavior. The belief that a group or group mind exists, as something other than a function of a number of individuals, appears to Bion to be a distorted figment of the imagination which emerges when people are threatened with a loss of their individual distinctiveness.

He emphasizes that people do not have to come together in the same room to form a group. In his view a hermit in a desert is inevitably a member of a group and cannot be understood unless one knows what the group is from which he has separated himself geographically. People have to come together in a room in order that group phenomena may be demonstrated and elucidated but not in order that they should exist. This is similar to the situation in psychoanalysis in which the patient has to enter into a therapeutic relationship with the analyst in order that the analyst may demonstrate and analyze the transference, but not in order that transference phenomena should exist.

Bion's central thought is that in every group two groups are present: the "work group" and the "basic assumption group." This may all sound less mysterious if one says that in every group there are two aspects, or that there are two different ways of behaving. Bion's terminology is a short cut which may lead to the belief that he thinks of each group of ten people as consisting of twenty invisible people sitting in two separate circles and talking, now in normal rational voices and now in another voice as in O'Neill's *Strange Interlude*. And in fact he does think in this kind of metaphor. At the same time he is quite clearly aware that it is a metaphor, which some of his less poetic readers tend to forget. He does not mean that there are two groups of people in the room, but that the group behaves as if that were the case, and he considers that this is the unconscious fantasy of the people in the group.

His concept of the work group will be described first and then that of the basic assumption group. The work group is that aspect of group functioning which has to do with the real task of the group. This exists in a committee which has come together to plan a program, or a staff of an organization which proposes to review the activities of the past year, or a small group met to study its own behavior. The work group takes cognizance of its purpose and can define its task. The structure of the group is there to further the attainment of the task. For example, if a group needed to collect dues it would appoint a treasurer. But it would not appoint a finance committee unless there were real matters of policy to be taken care of by such a committee. The number of vice presidents would be limited by the functions which vice presidents had to perform. The number of meetings would be dictated by the amount of business which had to be conducted. The leader of the work group is not the only one who has skills, and he leads only so long as his leadership serves the task of the group. The members of the work group cooperate as separate and discrete individuals. Each member of the group belongs to it because it is his will and his choice to see that the purpose of the group is fulfilled. He is therefore at one with the task of the group and his own interest is identified with its interest. The work group constantly tests its conclusions in a scientific spirit. It seeks for knowledge, learns from experience, and constantly questions how it may best achieve its goal. It is clearly conscious of the passage of time and of the processes of learning and development. It has a parallel in the individual with the ego, in Freud's sense, in the rational and mature person.

Groups which act consistently like the one just described are very rare and perhaps even non-existent in pure culture. A large part of Bion's theory has to do with why groups do not behave in the sensible way just described as characteristic of the work group. Man seems to be a herd animal who is often in trouble with his herd. Ineffective and self-contradictory behavior seems at times to be very common in groups —even though highly effective functioning is common at other times. The work group is only one aspect of the functioning of the group. The other aspect is the one which Bion calls the basic assumption group.

Bion is probably best known popularly for the names which he coined for the three kinds of basic assumption groups—namely, the dependency, the fight-flight, and the pairing groups. It should be emphasized that he himself used the word "adumbrated"—that is, vaguely outlined— to characterize his classification of these groups, and it may well be that the classification should be made differently or that other categories should be added. This is not the main point.

It is important to understand what the term *basic assumption* means, for otherwise one may get lost in the description of the three kinds which Bion adumbrated and forget the more important point, which is the commonality of all three. Basic assumption means exactly what it says— namely, the assumption which is basic to the behavior. It is an "as if" term. One behaves as if such and such were the case. In pre-Columbian days seafaring men operated on the basic assumption that the world was flat and that they might fall off its edge. Therefore they did not venture very far from the coast. So on many different levels, by observing the behavior of individuals and of groups, one can tease out the basic assumptions on which they operate. Bion uses the term to refer to the *tacit* assumptions that are prevalent in groups, not to those which are overtly expressed. The basic assumptions of the basic assumption groups are usually outside of awareness. Nevertheless, they are the basis for behavior. They are deducible from the emotional state of the group. The statement of the basic assumption gives meaning to and elucidates the behavior of the group to the extent that it is not operating as a work group.

According to Bion there are three distinct emotional states of groups from which one can deduce three basic assumptions. The first of these is the dependency basic assumption.

The essential aim of the basic assumption dependency group is to attain security through and have its members protected by one individual. It assumes that this is why the group has met. The members act as if they know nothing, as if they are inadequate and immature creatures. Their behavior implies that the leader, by contrast, is omnipotent and omniscient. A group of sick, miserable psychiatric patients, for example, and a powerful, wise, loving, giving therapist easily fit this picture. The power, wisdom, and lovingness of the therapist are, of course, not tested. The patients are often united in the belief that if they sit long enough, the wise leader will come forth with the magic cure. They do not even need to give him adequate information about their difficulties for he knows everything and plans everything for the good of the members. In this emotional state the group insists that all explanations be extremely simple; no one can understand any complexity; no one can do anything that is difficult; but the leader can solve all difficulties, if he only will. He is idealized and made into a kind of god who will take care of his children. The leader is often tempted to fall into this role and to go along with the basic assumption of the group.

But since no one really can fill this role and since anyone who is doing his job will refuse to fill it, he can never succeed in meeting the group's erpectations. In failing to be the omniscient and omnipotent leader of these people who are presenting themselves as inadequate weaklings, he inevitably arouses their disappointment and hostility. The members will try for a long time to blind themselves to this and will try not to hear what he says in interpreting their dependency to them. They often try quite desperate maneuvers to wring his heart and to force him to take proper care of them. One of the most frequent maneuvers is to put forth one member as especially sick and requiring the special care of the leader. Such a member may actually be pushed by the others into a degree of distress which he had not really felt at all, but the group needs someone who will wring the leader's heart or else show him up to be an unfeeling demon. The interesting thing is that whereas the group seems to be concerned about this poor person and his trouble, it is actually more concerned about the group aim to get the leader to take care of it and to relieve its feelings of inadequacy and insecurity. A person who falls into this role can very easily be carried away by it until he oversteps the bounds, and then he may find himself abandoned by the group.

When the leader of such a group fails to meet expectations, as he is bound to do, the group searches for alternative leaders. These are often eager to accept the role, and to prove that they can do what the original leader could not do. This is a temptation which the group offers to its more ambitious members. When they fall for it, they are usually in for the same fate as the original leader.

One of the frequent concerns in the dependency group has to do with greed. This is understandable enough since in manifesting the kind of childlike dependency characteristic of this basic assumption, the group members are perpetuating a state appropriate to an earlier stage of development and each one is demanding more than his share of parental care. There is often conflict in this group between the dependent tendencies and the needs of the individuals as adults. Resentment at being in a dependent state is present as well as a desire to persist in it. Although anger and jealousy are expressed, they do not usually arouse a tremendous amount of fear because of the basic assumption that a super-being exists in the form of the leader, who will see to it that the irresponsibilities of the members will not go too far and will not have dire consequences. There is often conflict between the desire to express feelings irresponsibly and the desire to be mature and consider consequences. The basic assumption dependency group in pure culture does not exist any more than the work group in pure culture. But the more it tends to be dominant over the work group, the more the relationship of the members to the leader takes on the characteristics of a religious cult. The work function will often then be felt as a challenge to a religion. Some of the same phenomena will occur which have occurred in the world in the conflict between science and religion, as if the claims of science were challenging the claims of religion. The words or writings of the leader become a kind of Bible and the group engages in exegesis of his works. This tends to happen particularly if the leader has already demonstrated his human inability to satisfy the demands of the group for a deity. His written words or remembered words may then be taken in place of his person.

The outside world often looks cold and unfriendly to the basic assumption dependency group. Sometimes when the members feel deserted by their leader, they forget their internal squabbles, close ranks, and snuggle up to each other like little birds in a nest. A warm groupiness develops which gives a temporary sense of comfort and security. To challenge this is heresy and is persecuted as such.

The second basic assumption group is that of fight-flight. Bion joins these together as two sides of the same coin. The assumption is that the group has met to preserve itself and that this can be done only by fighting someone or something or by running away from someone or something. Action is essential whether for fight or for flight. The individual is of secondary importance to the preservation of the group. Both in battle and in flight the individual may be abandoned for the sake of the survival of the group. Whereas in the basic assumption dependency group the sick person may be valued for his ability to engage the leader as a person who will take care of others, in the fight-flight group there is no tolerance for sickness. Casualties are to be expected.

A leader is even more important than in other basic assumption groups because the call for action requires a leader. The leader who is felt to be appropriate to this kind of group is one who can mobilize the group for attack or lead it in flight. He is expected to recognize danger and enemies. He should represent and spur on to courage and self-sacrifice. He should have a bit of a paranoid element in his makeup if he wishes to be successful, for this will ensure that if no enemy is obvious, the leader will surely find one. He is expected to feel hate toward the enemy and to be concerned not for the individual in the group but for the preservation of the group itself. An accepted leader of a fight-flight group who goes along with the basic assumption is one who affords opportunity in the group for flight or aggression. If he does not do this, he is ignored.

This basic assumption group is anti-intellectual and inimical to the idea of self-study; self-knowledge may be called introspective nonsense. In a group whose avowed purpose or work task is self-study, the leader will find when the group is operating in basic assumption fight-flight that his attempts will be obstructed either by expressions of hatred against all things psychological and introspective, or by various other methods of avoidance. The group may chitchat, tell stories, come late, be absent, or engage in innumerable activities to circumvent the task.

In groups engaged in more overt action, it is possible to observe the close connection of panic and the fight-flight, and uncontrolled attack are really all the same. He says that panic does not arise in any situation unless it is one that might as easily have given rise to rage. When the rage or fear are offered no readily available outlet, frustration arises which in a basic assumption group cannot be tolerated. Flight offers an immediately available opportunity for expression of the emotion in the fight-flight group and meets the demands that all basic assumption groups have for instantaneous satisfaction. Attack offers a similarly immediate outlet. Bion thinks that if the leader of such a group conforms to the requirements of the fight-flight leader he will have no difficulty in turning a group from headlong flight to attack or from headlong attack to panic.

The third basic assumption group is that of pairing. Here the assumption is that the group has met for purposes of reproduction, to bring forth the Messiah, the Savior. Two people get together on behalf of the group to carry out the task of pairing and creation. The sex of the two people is immaterial. They are by no means necessarily a man and a woman. But whoever they are, the basic assumption is that when two people get together it is for sexual purposes. When this basic assumption is operative, the other group members are not bored. They listen eagerly and attentively to what is being said. An atmosphere of hopefulness pervades the group. No actual leader is or needs to be present, but the group, through the pair, is living in the hope of the creation of a new leader, or a new thought, or something which will bring about a new life, will solve the old problems and bring Utopia or heaven, or something of the sort. As in the history of the world if a new leader or Messiah is actually produced, he will of course shortly be rejected. In order to maintain hope, he must be unborn. Bion emphasizes the air of hopeful expectation which pervades the group. He says it is often expressed in clichés—such as, "Things will be better when spring comes" —or in simple-minded statements that some cure-all like marriage or group therapy would solve all neurotic problems. Although the group thus focuses on the future, Bion calls attention to the present, namely the feeling of hope itself, which he thinks is evidence that the pairing group is in existence even when other evidence is not clear. The group enjoys its optimism, justifying it by an appeal to an outcome which is morally unexceptionable. The feelings associated with this group are soft and agreeable. The unborn leader of this group, according to the basic assumption, will save it from feelings of hatred, destructiveness, and despair—both its own feelings and those of others. If a person or an idea should be produced by such a group hope will again be weakened, for there will be nothing to hope for. The destructiveness and hatred have not really been reduced and will again be felt.

These then are the three basic assumption groups which Bion describes. It is clear enough how different they all are from the work group. Although each one has its own characteristics, the basic assumption groups also have some characteristics in common. Basic assumption life is not oriented outward toward reality, but inward toward fantasy, which is then impulsively and uncritically acted out. There is little pausing to consider or to test consequences, little patience with an inquiring attitude, and great insistence upon feeling. Basic assumption members often are confused, have poor memories, are disoriented about time. They do not really learn and adapt through experience but actually resist change, although they may shift very readily from one basic assumption to another. Often there are reminiscences about the good old days. The language of such groups is full of clichés, or repetitive phrases, and of vague and loose generalizations. Another important aspect of the basic assumptions is that they are anonymous. They are not formulated by any one member in the group and cannot be attributed to any one member. No one wants to own them. There is a kind of conspiracy of anonymity, which is facilitated by the fact that identities and names get mixed up; statements are attributed falsely or vaguely. The basic assumptions seem to be the disowned part of the individuals, and individuals seem to fear the basic assumptions as if they might take over and leave nothing of the mature, rational persons in the group. Since the basic assumptions are anonymous, they can function quite ruthlessly, which is another reason why they are feared. There is much vicarious living in a basic assumption group, particularly through roles, so that often a person becomes fixed in a role which the group needs for its own purposes and then cannot get out of it. Basic assumption groups also constantly attempt to seduce their leaders away from their work function.

Neither the work group nor the basic assumption group exists in pure culture for very long. What one sees in reality is a work group which is suffused by, intruded into, and supported by the basic assumption groups. One can make an analogy to the functions of the conscious ego, which are suffused by, invaded by, and supported by the irrational and unconscious aspects of the personality. So it seems that the basic assumptions represent an interference with the work task, just as naughty, primitive impulses may interfere with the sensible work of a mature person. And this is one important side of the picture. There is another, more positive side to the basic assumptions, however, which Bion emphasizes just as much as the negative aspects, and that is the sophisticated use of the proper basic assumption by the work group. For example, a work group such as a hospital can and should mobilize the basic assumption dependency in the service of its task of taking care of sick patients. Bion identifies the church as that major institution in society which mobilizes and uses in a sophisticated way the basic assumption dependency; the army as that one which mobilizes basic assumption fight-flight; and the aristocracy as that one which is most interested in breeding and therefore mobilizes pairing. Whether or not the aristocracy can still be considered to exist, even in England, as an important institution is an open question, along with what takes its place if it does not. Bion himself does not think that the aristocracy can be considered to be a real work group which uses its basic assumption in a sophisticated way, for if the work group characteristics were dominant in the aristocracy then the interest in breeding would be manifest in some such way as a subsidy of scientific genetics research. But this is obviously not the case. If we consider the army, for example, it is clear that the relevant basic assumptions badly interefere with its function if they get out of hand. Fight-flight when engaged in simply as irrational basic assumptions lead to panic or ill-conceived attack. However, when mobilized in a sophisticated way, fight-flight represents the motive force for battle and for organized withdrawal. As indicated earlier, both the work group and the basic assumption group are abstractions; they are concepts which are useful in thinking about ways of functioning which occur in groups. Bion's idea is that both are occurring simultaneously, but to varying degrees, in all groups.

It is necessary now to introduce another one of Bion's concepts, namely that of valency. This is a term which is used to refer to the individual's readiness to enter into combination with the group in making and acting on the basic assumptions. A person may have a high or low valency depending on his capacity for this kind of combination, but in Bion's view it is impossible to be a human being without having some degree of valency. The thing that Bion is trying to do with all his concepts and constructions is to produce useful ways of thinking about man in his function as a social animal. In his concept of valency he is saying that everyone has the tendency to enter into group life, in particular into the irrational and unconscious aspects of group life, and that people vary in the amount of tendency they have in this direction. Bion thinks of this tendency as something which is manifested on a psychological plane to be sure, but which is so basic to the human organism that it should not be thought of as purely psychological. He thinks of it as biological and speaks of it as analogous to tropism in plants rather than as analogous to more purposive behavior. By borrowing a word from physics rather than from psychology or sociology he emphasizes the instantaneous and involuntary aspects of the kind of behavior he is talking about, which he calls instinctive. Valency in the basic assumption group corresponds to cooperation in the work group. But whereas cooperation requires thought, training, maturity, and some degree of organization in a group, valency requires none of these. It simply occurs spontaneously as a function of the gregarious quality in man.

Individuals vary not only in the degree of valency which they manifest but in the kind to which they have the strongest tendency. With some it is toward basic assumption dependency; some toward fight-flight; some toward pairing. Every human being has the capacity for all three, but usually one or another valency predominates. This has nothing to do with whether a person has been psychoanalyzed or not. It is not possible to analyze valency out of a human being as one is supposed to be able to analyze neurosis. For effective functioning in groups, however, and especially for leadership functioning, it is desirable to know oneself well enough to know to which valency one tends. An effective society uses the valencies of its members to serve its various purposes. For example, the educator can find a good outlet for his valency toward basic assumption dependency. The combat commander can use appropriately his valency toward basic assumption fight-flight. The valency toward basic assumption pairing finds a useful expression in individual interviewing and, of course, in family life. There are various types of chairmen and directors of organizations. One type will be solicitous for the welfare of his members and will take a special interest in the weaker ones or in anyone who is sick or disabled. Another will see his main function as fighting for the interests of his organization against any outside or inside attack. Another will find that he does his job best by going around after hours to each one of his members separately, convincing each one of what he wants done. When the meeting takes place everyone is already in agreement and the decisions have all been made. Any and all of these ways can be effective, though each one may be more appropriate at one time than at another.

In the naive or unconscious fantasy, the leader of the dependency group has to be omnipotent; the fight leader has to be unbeatable and the flight leader uncatchable; the leader of the pairing group must be marvelous but still unborn. But in the mature work group, which is making a sophisticated use of the appropriate basic assumptions, the leader of the dependency group is dependable; the leader of the fight-flight group is courageous; and the leader of the pairing group is creative.[1]

For effective functioning the basic assumptions must be subservient to and used in the service of the work task. They make good servants and poor masters. The various tales about fantastic machines, demons, genii, and so forth, who perform miraculous tasks for their masters until one

---

[1] For these formulations the author is indebted to a personal communication from A. K. Rice, who wrote approximately these words in *Learning for Leadership*, p. 72.

fine day they take over and go on a binge of destruction, are mythical representations of the capacity of human beings for harnessing tremendous energy effectively and at the same time of the danger of such energy when it is not harnessed. *The Lord of the Flies* provides another illustration of what happens when the work group is weak and the irresponsible basic assumption group takes over.

The work task is like a serious parent who has his eye on intelligent planning. The basic assumptions are like the fun-loving or frightened children who want immediate satisfaction of their desires. What Bion emphasizes is that both exist and that both are necessary. The basic assumption group, however, exists without effort. The work group requires all the concentration, skill, and organization of creative forces that can be mustered to bring it into full flower. The writers who derogate groups as tending to reduce the intellectual abilities of the individuals in the group are, according to Bion, talking about the basic assumption functions, not work group functions. Bion holds to a very consistent middle way between the glorification and the derogation of the group. The latter is to be found in Jung's statement, "When a hundred clever heads join in a group, one big nincompoop is the result, because every individual is trammelled by the otherness of the others."[2] Bion holds that a group, like an individual, may be stupid and cruel or intelligent and concerned. He does not hold that great achievements are always those of the individual working in solitude. He says that in the study groups he has been in he has made interpretations of behavior just because he believes that the group can hear them and use them, and experience has borne him out. In his own words, he attributes "great force and influence to the work group, which through its concern with reality is compelled to employ the methods of science in no matter how rudimentary a form" (p. 135).

Individuals seem to fear being overwhelmed by their valency for group life; or one might put it that they fear being overwhelmed by the basic assumptions. It is not uncommon in self-study or therapy groups to hear phrases like "the fear of being sucked in by quicksands," or "the fear of being homogenized," which express the fear of being immersed in the group and thus losing one's individuality. Bion thinks that there is not actually so much danger as people think there is of being overwhelmed by the basic assumptions. He has a healthy respect for people's capacities to function on a work level. He thinks that in groups met to study their own behavior, consistent interpretation of the basic assumption

---

[2] Quoted from a letter from C. G. Jung (Illing, p. 80).

tendencies will gradually bring them into consciousness and cause them to lose their threatening quality. The parallel here to the psychoanalysis of unconscious impulses is clear. Presumably, the more the basic assumption life of the group becomes conscious, the more the work task can emerge into effective functioning.

But the individual in a group is not always convinced of this. Bion thinks that the task of the adult in establishing adequate contact with the life of the group or groups in which he lives is truly a formidable one. His first, second, and often third attempts are likely to be failures and to result in regression. When individuals in a group feel that they have lost or are about to lose their individual distinctiveness, they are threatened by panic. This does not mean at all that the group disintegrates, for it may continue as a fight-flight group; but it does mean that the individual feels threatened and very likely has regressed.

Bion says clearly that he thinks of the value of a group experience as the conscious experiencing of the possibilities of the work group. This must be differentiated from the coziness and so-called closeness of feeling in the basic assumption group. The work group which Bion is talking about does not depend upon great amounts of love or warm feelings or an oceanic oneness of the group members. It does depend upon the increasing and developing ability of each individual to use his skills responsibly in the service of the common task. It is not anything like the "togetherness" which is a function of the fear of being alone or on one's own. In the work group, each individual is very much on his own and may have to accomplish his own part of the task in a very lonely way, as for example someone who is sent upon a secret mission or someone who has to make the ultimate policy decision where the buck stops. The reluctance to take the final responsibility for decisions and actions can be seen as a basic assumption dependency phenomenon and is not a characteristic of the work group member, especially not of the work group leader.

The anxiety which one tends to feel in groups and the difficulties with which group membership faces one stem from the double danger of either being isolated like a sore thumb of the total body which may be amputated, or being swallowed up by the total body and losing oneself. When the basic assumption group is strong, the individual tends to feel either in danger of being victimized and extruded, or swallowed up in the anonymous unanimity of group feeling. The usual case, even when work elements are present, is that the individual is wavering somewhere in between the two dangers, with an uneasy sense that he is in a dilemma out of which no right way can be found.

When anxiety becomes severe the group may, as Bion says, resemble the mysterious, frightening, and destructive Sphinx. The Sphinx was made up of disparate members. She had the seductive face of a woman and a body composed of parts of powerful and dangerous animals—the lion, the eagle, and the serpent. To those who wished to pass by her she posed the riddle: "What walks on four legs in the morning, two at noon, and three in the evening?" Those who could not answer she flung to their deaths over the cliff, and that included everyone until Oedipus came by and told her that it was man.

Oedipus had been to Delphi to try to find out who really were his parents; and later too, to his sorrow, he searched for the murderer of the king. He sought after knowledge even when it meant his own undoing. Not by chance was it this man who, as the legend has it, grasped immediately the concepts of time, change, and development implicit in the riddle of the Sphinx. So long as we think in static terms that there *is* an entity which walks on four legs or which *is* the personality or which *is* the group, we can never grasp the complex and apparently disparate phenomena of the world, in time, in which we live. When Oedipus grasped the complexity in an intuitive vision of the whole, the fearful Sphinx threw herself off the rock. But unfortunately she constantly climbs back up again and waits with a new riddle for a new Oedipus to come by.

When the Sphinx lies in wait with her dreadful question, representing the frightening complexity and uncertain behavior of the world, especially the world of groups, one feels terrified at what John Fowles calls "the eternal source of all fear, all horror, all real evil, man himself" (p. 448).

But the same man or the same group which has filled the world with horror at its capacity for evil can also amaze by its capacity for good. If the Sphinx were to ask, "What is it that on Monday is wrangling, cruel, and greedy; on Tuesday is indifferent and lazy; on Wednesday is effectively and intelligently collaborative?", one could easily answer, "That is man and it is also ten men in a group." If she asked, "What made the difference?", a few partial answers could be given. One of them is that on Wednesday the group had a clear goal to which all of its members wanted to devote themselves. Another is that the roles of the members were clearly defined and accepted. Still another has to do with the boundaries between this and other groups. But if the Sphinx were to go on and press about what to do in order that the Wednesday behavior should become more constant and the Monday and Tuesday behavior less frequent, we *might* find ourselves with no satisfactory answer hurtling over the cliff.

REFERENCES

BION, W. R. *Experiences in Groups,* Basic Books, 1959.
FOWLES, JOHN. *The Magus,* Dell, 1967.
ILLING, HANS A. "C. G. Jung on the Present Trends in Group Psychotherapy," *Human Relations* (1957) 10:77-83.
RICE, A. K. *Learning for Leadership,* London, Tavistock Publications, 1965.

3

A METHOD OF GROUP PSYCHO-THERAPY AT THE TAVISTOCK CLINIC

E. S. Heath, M.D.

Director, Rosehill Institute of Human Relations (Toronto)

and

H. A. Bacal, M.D.

*Hon. Psychiatrist, Tavistock Clinic and Tavistock Institute
of Human Relations (London, England)*

With rare exceptions (Berne, 1963; Whitaker and Lieberman, 1964) there have been few references in recent textbooks or journals to methods of group psychotherapy developed at the Tavistock Clinic in London.[1] The purpose of this paper is to describe and discuss one of these, a relatively distinct technique of group psychotherapy which involves the use of here-and-now interpretations of the unconscious group theme, followed by interpretations of each individual's way of contributing to it. This method of group psychotherapy is not more widely known not only be-

Reprinted from the INTERNATIONAL JOURNAL OF GROUP PSYCHOTHERAPY, Vol. 19, 1969, pp. 21-30.

The authors are grateful to Drs. J. D. Sutherland and Henry Ezriel of the Tavistock Clinic, London, for their reading and criticism of the manuscript.

[1] The other main approach to group therapy practiced and taught at the Tavistock Clinic is that developed by W. R. Bion, about which the above notes are to be taken only as an introduction. For further details, see *Experiences in Groups*, W. R. Bion, Tavistock Publications, 1961.

cause of the small number of articles in the American literature pertaining to it, but also because the theoretical basis for the method has been developed mainly in Great Britain, with a slower dissemination of the theory to North America.

HISTORY

The early emigration of Melanie Klein from Berlin to London meant that the development of her ideas about unconscious object-relations had its greatest impact on the work of members of the British Psycho-Analytical Society. These ideas were enlarged upon by Melanie Klein (1932, 1948, 1952), Fairbairn (1941, 1944, 1952, 1963—summarized by Sutherland, 1963) and others. At the same time, there has developed an increasing reliance on the role of transference interpretations by the analysts of the "English School" (e.g., Strachey, 1934) which is by no means confined to the students of Melanie Klein.

Bion (1961), in attempting to apply psychoanalytic understanding to experimental groups at the Tavistock Clinic, found that he could characterize the emotional pattern or culture of the total group in several ways. Thus, at a particular time, groups were either in what Bion termed "W" (Work group) or "BA" (Basic Assumption) activity, which was, so to speak, anti-work. The latter types comprised BA Dependency, BA Pairing, or BA Fight-Flight. Bion's experience was such that a pattern might last for a few moments or even for several sessions. One pattern would give way to another because of interpretations or because of guilt or anxiety about the common movement. In his groups, Bion adhered to transference interpretations referring to the "here-and-now."

Group theory and method were elaborated further by Ezriel (1950, 1952, 1956, 1957), also at the Tavistock Clinic. Ezriel tried to look behind the phenomenologic patterns of group action and to gauge the group interaction in terms of the unconscious common group tension, or the unconscious psychodynamic pattern, that the group was trying to deal with at a particular moment. Further, Ezriel added that the group action can be described in terms of three relationships, all of which are necessary to interpret. This is the method which will be described more fully in this paper. We would emphasize that the following is colored by the authors' understanding and usage of Ezriel's method.

THEORY

Disconnected thoughts, affects, and actions of an individual at any particular time during a psychotherapy session belong together dynamically, i.e., they are meaningfully related and arise from a common unconscious source. Ezriel has extended this hypothesis to groups (Ezriel, 1957, p. 112). Haphazard remarks of the group members are related to each other and may become the expression of a common group tension. If a remark made by a member "clicks," i.e., some aspect of it is relevant to, and can fit into, the ongoing dominant unconscious fantasies of the rest, then it is taken up by others and becomes the unconsciously determined topic of the group—the "common denominator" of the dominant unconscious fantasies of all the members. Each group member deals with this "common group tension" in his own particular way, i.e., in terms of his own defenses. The group then becomes structured so that the object-relations in it correspond in some way to what is required of the various unconscious object-relations of each individual member in relation to the common group tension. This involves the individual's unconscious attempts to manipulate other members, including the therapist, into appropriate roles.

The limiting of interpretations to the here-and-now is based upon the assumption that everything the patient says or does in any one session is a way of expressing an unconscious need to establish a particular relationship with others at that moment. Strachey (1934) emphasized that it is the analysis of the transference in the here-and-now relationship which represents a "mutative interpretation" and can permanently change the patient's unconscious needs. These principles are felt to be meaningfully applicable to group psychotherapy. Ezriel argues that the historical content can be abandoned in the interpretation because dynamic needs behind the material produced in a session do not arise from real events but from unconscious structures which are based on a combination of actual events, distorted memories of actual events, and the conscious and unconscious fantasies clustering about them. The linking-up with the patient's individual past is not done by the therapist; the patient will usefully do this part of the work himself if the interpretation is accurate and pertinent.

A further principle is to restrict all therapeutic intervention to interpretations. Noninterpretative remarks are not made because it is felt that these interfere with the maximum use of the group therapist as a projection screen (Ezriel, 1957, p. 110).

Although, in practice, interpersonal transactions between the group members are interpreted—as usual, in terms of the common group tension and structure—the therapist's role in all of them is felt to be crucial. The group, consciously or unconsciously, attempts to establish a certain pattern of behavior in relation to the therapist and to each other. This is the "required relationship." The group attempts to establish this relationship in order not to get involved in another relationship which is desired but more strongly feared. This is the "avoided relationship," avoided because the group believes it would lead to a third, the "calamitous relationship" (Ezriel, 1956, p. 111). Since group members do not have a common past or a common life outside the group, interpretations centered on the common group tension must adhere only to the here-and-now (Ezriel, 1956, p. 115). An interpretation of this sort to the group as a whole (i.e., delineating the three relationships) is followed by showing each group member his individual way of dealing with the common group tension.

Ezriel claims that dealing with the unconscious fantasies in the here-and-now enables the patients to deal by themselves with their real problems outside.

METHOD

At the Tavistock Clinic, all varieties of neurotic and character disorders are included in groups. The ideal composition has not been worked out, but the value of heterogeneity in diagnosis is implicitly agreed upon. Both men and women are included in each group to provide situations in which fantasies about heterosexual, triangular object-relations can easily be attached to appropriate group members. A group may contain a borderline psychotic patient; some therapists feel that inclusion of such a patient may be helpful due to his ability to detect and verbalize his or others' unconscious needs. A group with members of widely different I.Q.'s or social status is avoided to prevent isolation of individuals. In effect, the bulk of Tavistock patients are from the higher I.Q. brackets. Seven to nine members is considered to be optimal, and meetings are usually once per week. A group usually goes on for about three to five years. The fall-out rate has been fairly consistent over recent years. In the average group of eight, losses of two or three members occur within the first year, and it is common practice to introduce two new members together during this period in the history of the group. The longer a group goes on, the more difficult it is for psychotherapeutically "unsophisticated" patients to fit in with the work of the group. Phillipson (1958) has shown that it is usually in the third year of treatment that people in such groups begin to get the most benefit. The sessions of one to one and one-half hours are often tape-recorded with the microphones in sight, and any paranoid anxieties about these are regarded as group material. Some of the groups agree beforehand to meet behind a one-way screen as part of the teaching program of the Clinic.

The above historical and theoretical remarks can be supplemented by examples of the technique. First, a few comments about the initial session. The patients are usually seen individually by the group leader prior to the first session. In the first session the members arrive at the room and are met by the therapist who remains silent. Confronted with such a situation, frequently the dependency needs of the members are aroused, along with anger and anxiety that these needs may not be met, and a common (usually unconscious) group attempt may then develop to deal with these feelings. All sorts of things may begin to happen: nervous queries about what they are expected to do, attempts by some to become substitute therapists, even some conscious feelings of helplessness or anger, etc. Then a three-tiered interpretation is made: i.e., what they are talking about (e.g., how does a group work?, attempts to engage the leader in conversation, etc.—the required relationship) is to enable them to avoid expression of something else (e.g., angry, dependent, and helpless feelings—the avoided relationship) for fear of what might happen to them if they did (e.g., rejection by the therapist, embarrassment, more helplessness, etc.—the calamitous relationship). Then the therapist goes around the group pointing out the particular contribution of each member to the common group tension and structure, i.e., the three relationships characteristic for each individual.

The following is an example of the first session of a new group of two men and four women:

After preliminary remarks about the procedure for calling the group from the waiting room and the holiday period and times, the therapist fell silent. The group was silent for about two minutes with most of the members looking at the therapist. One woman began to interrogate the other members as to their occupations. The anxiety in the room then seemed to go down. Several members volunteered that they would prefer another job to the one they had, and they joked with apparent anxiety. This, in turn, decreased when they switched onto how they spent their spare time relieving their boredom, e.g., dancing, television. One married woman talked of what she and her husband did, e.g., going to his club. A man who had separated from his wife talked of how he couldn't get people to be interested in him. The young woman who was "running" the group said she couldn't get people interested in her either. The therapist interpreted that they were talking about how to relieve feelings at home and at work and that they were letting someone be a substitute leader (the required relationship) in order to avoid talking about their feelings in the treatment room, i.e., those needs to be cared for by himself (the avoided relationship) and that they did all this because they wished to avoid the anxiety should these needs not be fulfilled by the therapist (the calamitous relationship). The therapist then went around and pointed out how the woman had to handle her dependency needs by herself assuming leadership, how the married woman dealt with hers by describing how her husband cared for her, and the lonely man expressed his by complaining that no one was interested in him. He interpreted that all of these, as well as their talk about preferring other jobs and their attempts to relieve boredom by entertainment, were defenses against the anxieties associated with the expression of their dependency needs toward the therapist.

The result of this interpretation was that the young woman who "ran" the group said angrily that anyone would do what she had done. Another woman member talked of her lack of trust in people. The man who was separated from his wife turned to the group leader and asked for permission to smoke. The young woman went on to talk in an angry manner about how one needed to sound out people first before one could trust them.

While observers may feel that other dynamic patterns exist in this material, most would probably agree that the interpretation covers the common unconscious pattern of the group. What is unique about this method is the nonutilization of outside events, outside relationships, or past events in the interpretation.

A further example will be given from a group which had been meeting weekly for a year and a half:

There were four patients present. Miss A. was telling the group about her date over the previous weekend and commented that if she thought of marrying this man, who was not Jewish, her mother would do everything to stop it. She went on to talk about the many ways in which her mother clung to her and showed disapproval of her behavior. The whole group took up the theme. Mr. V. said that his mother would have been horrified if he had married someone who was not Catholic. Miss R. described how her mother actually spoke in a disparaging way about her fiancé because he was non-Catholic, implying he was an outsider who would understand nothing. Mr. L. told the group that he had in fact married a non-Jewish girl, and his family had taken a long time before they came around to accepting her. The therapist made the following interpretation: whereas the group was talking about the unfavorable reaction of parents, particularly mothers, to their forming a permanent sexual liaison with someone of another faith (the required relationship), what they did not see was that here in the group there were two Jews and two Catholics—by each faith both sexes represented—and he wondered whether they were really discussing these outside situations to avoid feelings and thoughts about each other (the avoided relationship) because this "parent"—the therapist—might react unfavorably (calamitous relationship). The therapist then went around and pointed out the three relationships for each member, e.g., whereas Miss A. talked about an inhibited relationship with a non-Jewish man (the required relationship) to which her mother would react in the particular way she described, she couldn't talk about her wish for this sort of relationship with the other male group members because the therapist-parent might smother her with restrictive disapproval. The response was electric: Miss A. and Mr. V. began to confront each other (Mr. V. with considerable anxiety) about their sexual thoughts and wishes about each other. Mr. V. remarked that he had thought of going to bed with her and had talked jokingly about this outside the group after the last session. Miss A. wondered, nervously, whether he was circumcised.

It has not been found that such direct interpretation of this sort in the here-and-now leads to sexual acting out. In fact, in this instance, the air was cleared for further exploration of these patients' individual sexual problems.

Silent patients pose a difficulty in any group. It is felt that their participation is frequently one of identification with the unconscious common group problem, and it is interpreted as such. Dreams are regarded as part and parcel of the run of material.

DISCUSSION

In a descriptive paper it is not necessary to go too deeply into theoretical issues. The transference situation can, of course, be seen as something not peculiar to treatment, but which happens when (and even before, in fantasy) one individual meets another, and thus all behavior in a group may contain attempts to solve relationships with unconscious fantasy objects which are residues of unresolved infantile conflicts. It is possible, however, that the amount of this will vary from moment to moment, even in the same patient. When a patient relates a traumatic event that happened to him on the way to the Clinic, one can interpret it as, in some way, expressing feelings about the group in the here-and-now rather than the there-and-then which he is telling about. However, sometimes patients are preoccupied with reality matters outside, and the transference links are weak indeed. To the authors, it also seems possible that the silent patient may be off on another trend and is not "clicking" with the rest of the group in his silence. Also, the term "transference" is perhaps used somewhat loosely. Although transference is said to begin when (or before) individuals meet, this has to be distinguished from the "transference neurosis" in which the distortions are not temporary and cannot be corrected without a great deal of working-through.

More orthodox therapists would not make deep interpretations early in treatment. However, Ezriel feels that harmful results like severe anxiety reactions or missed sessions occur if they are not made (Ezriel, 1950, p. 71). In practice, there seems to be a hierarchy of interpretations that respects some sort of timing. Early on, interpretations pertaining to relationships between group members tend to be given more often than interpretations about relationships with the therapist. For example, early on, an oedipal interpretation about competitiveness among the men for the women would be phrased in terms of their anxiety about competing with each other, and probably only later on would it be consistently interpreted primarily in terms of their anxiety about competition with the therapist. Also, in early sessions there seems to be a greater stress on interpretation and less use of the avoided relationship and the calamitous relationship (or the connection made between the avoided and calamitous relationships, sometimes termed the "because clause").

Even if current fantasy object-relations are structures not necessarily related to the real past, this does not rule out the possibility of altering these by interpretation of how they seem to be linked to the real or fantasied past. In practice, it is assumed that the patient can link up the transference interpretation with the past "although the interpretation may have contained no reference to his current life outside the analytic situation or his past" (Ezriel, 1957, p. 112). This presupposes capacities that possibly not all patients possess.

There may be differences of opinion as to what exactly is "the avoided relationship." In addition, we ourselves question the validity of one of the premises in this therapy, i.e., that whatever we observe is always primarily defensive in character. Some of the observations may be samples of the kinds of relationships that people are consciously or unconsciously striving for.

Ezriel's evaluation of the effect of the interpretation by topologically measurable changes in the material which follows the interpretation is to be welcomed as a useful method of attempting to check the validity of interpretations by prediction. At the same time, however valuable this might be from moment to moment as a check upon one's interpretative activity, the evaluation of results and of improvement cannot be made only on how patients progress topologically but must also include how they handle present conflicts in the there-and-then as compared with earlier conflictual situations.

Finally, the method seems to offer a useful solution to the ever-present dilemma of whether to deal with "the group" or with the individuals comprising it.

SUMMARY

A method of group psychotherapy developed and taught at the Tavistock Clinic, London, has been described and evaluated. The method involves the recognition of unconscious common group themes which develop in psychotherapy groups. These are interpreted in terms of on-going "here-and-now" relationships between the group members, but particularly between them and the group leader. The method involves the use of a particular type of three-tiered interpretation: the on-going group material is interpreted as being a required relationship, which may or may not be unconscious, which operates as a defense against an unconscious theme (the avoided relationship) which is avoided because of the fear that it would lead to a calamity. Following the group interpretation, the leader then goes around and interprets the particular way in which each member deals with the common group tension. The unique contribution of this method is the focus upon the on-going unconscious dynamic processes and tensions in the group.

REFERENCES

BERNE, E. (1963) *The Structure and Dynamics of Organizations and Groups.* New York: Lippincott.

BION, W. R. (1961) *Experiences in Groups.* London: Tavistock Publications.

EZRIEL, H. (1950) A Psychoanalytic Approach to Group Treatment, *Brit. J. Med. Psychol.*, 23:59-74.

———— (1952) Notes on Psychoanalytic Therapy: Section II, Interpretation and Research, *Psychiatry,* 15:119-126.

———— (1956) Experimentation within the Psycho-Analytical Session. *Brit. J. Phil. Sci.,* 7:29-48.

———— (1957) The Role of Transference in Psycho-Analytical and Other Approaches to Group Treatment. *Acta Psychother.* 7 (Suppl.):101-116.

FAIRBAIRN, W. R. (1941) A Revised Psychopathology. *Internat. J. Psychoanal.*, 22:250-279.

———— (1944) Endopsychic Structure Considered in Terms of Object-Relationships. *Internat. J. Psychoanal.,* 25:70-93.

———— (1952) *Psycho-Analytical Studies of the Personality.* London: Tavistock Publications.

———— (1963) Synopsis of an Object-Relations Theory of Personality. *Internat. J. Psychoanal.,* 44:224-225.

KLEIN, M. (1932) *The Psycho-Analysis of Children.* London: Hogarth Press.

———— (1948), *Contributions to Psycho-Analysis*. London: Hogarth Press.

———— (1952) *Notes on Some Schizoid Mechanisms (1946) in Developments in Psycho-Analysis*. London: Hogarth Press.

PHILLIPSON, H. (1958) The Assessment of Progress after at least Two Years of Group Therapy. *Brit. J. Med. Psychol.*, 31:32-41.

STRACHEY, J. (1934) The Nature of the Therapeutic Action of Psycho-Analysis. *Internat. J. Psychoanal.*, 15:127-159.

SUTHERLAND, J. D. (1963) Object-Relations Theory and the Conceptual Model of Psycho-Analysis. *Brit. J. Med. Psychol.*, 36:109-124.

WHITAKER, D. S., & LIEBERMAN, M. A. (1964) *Psychotherapy Through the Group Process*. New York: Atherton.

Area I—Section B

PSYCHOANALYTIC APPROACHES

In contrast to the group-process oriented approaches discussed in the preceding section, psychoanalytically-oriented group treatment techniques are among those that focus on the individual.

The distinctive features of the psychoanalytic approach to group treatment derive from its unique underlying theoretical constructs. The highly complex psychoanalytic model of personality and psychopathology makes specific genetic, topographical, and structural assumptions concerning the human psyche, and the genesis and dynamics of various forms of psychopathology. Psychoanalytic treatment, whether it is provided in an individual or group setting, reflects this theoretical position. To illustrate, psychoanalytic theory postulates that conflicts which derive from specific experiences at specific stages of development result in specific forms of neurotic behavior in later life. The crucial therapeutic implications of this central thesis lie in the fact that the patient is unaware of these conflicts, and actively resists their emergence into conscious awareness. The young child erects primitive defenses to protect himself against emotional disasters; the adult patient is afraid, unconsciously, to relinquish his analogous resistances and defenses which preclude conscious recognition of the forbidden impulses, feelings, etc., which underlie his conflicts. Accordingly, it is the task of the psychoanalyst to penetrate these defenses in order to foster awareness and concomitant resolution of the patient's pathogenic unconscious conflicts, and the classical psychoanalytic treatment techniques, which involve a specifically structured interaction between analyst and analysand, were developed to implement these goals.

However, group therapists who are committed to the psychoanalytic model of the human psyche maintain that psychoanalytic theory is not irrevocably wedded to the classic dyadic analytic techniques. Indeed, in

43

some respects, group methods may be more effective than the techniques utilized within the dyadic relationship' in implementing the essential goals of psychoanalytic treatment. The greater advantages of group analysis are considered to lie in the fact that the individual members of the therapy group evoke a wide spectrum of transferences, help each other to overcome certain tenacious resistances, foster the "working through" of intellectual insights and facilitate the translation of cognitive understanding into effective interpersonal behavior. Thus while the analysis of the individual patient clearly represents the focus of their efforts, psychoanalytically-oriented group therapists are not oblivious of the therapeutic implications of group dynamics. Rather they use their knowledge of group process, often exquisitely and creatively, in the service of analyzing their patients.

THE PAPERS

Above all, the psychoanalytically-oriented group therapist formulates his patients' problems in analytic terms, and guides his treatment accordingly. In her article in this section, Glatzer assumes that the symptoms typically manifested by the oral character neurotic—anger, depression, immaturity, unproductiveness, and disturbances in relating to others—had their genesis in distortions in the patient's earliest perceptions of his mother, prior to the age of one and one-half, i.e., during the "oral" phase of development when dependency, intense rage, and omnipotence are crucial psychological issues. Dr. Glatzer points up the advantages of group therapy for patients in this diagnostic category. Thus she discusses the utilization of group process in engaging difficult "oral" patients in therapy, in overcoming their tenacious resistances and archaic defenses, in "working through" their insights, and also in helping the therapist to deal with countertransferential reactions which might impede treatment if it were conducted on an individual basis.

Glatzer's article is followed by a paper by Edrita Fried, which provides another example of the use of group process within a basically psychoanalytic frame of reference, one that derives, however, from the epigenetic concepts of ego-psychology. Fried is deeply impressed with the issues of individuation and activity versus dependency and passivity, which she feels to be central to a wide spectrum of highly prevalent neurotic problems. Pathological passivity in adult life is seen as related to failure to achieve an independent identity and adult relationships with parental figures. Thus Fried's clinical efforts focus on helping patients to achieve such individuation, and in her article she describes the advantages of group therapy in facilitating the implementation of this goal. Specifically, Fried takes therapeutic advantage of the opportunities provided by those inevitable phases of group therapy in which the transactions of the group are dominated by the hostile and rebellious feelings of its individual members. She uses the patient's response to such group trends to foster resolution of pathological conflicts which center on the patient's dependency needs, and to facilitate the acquisition of independent, mature behavior.

The first article in this section delineates of the differences between group psychoanalysis and other forms of group therapy, which currently constitute a source of confusion. Wolf and his colleagues, who have been deeply involved both in psychoanalysis and in group therapy, contrast psychoanalytic group treatment with other group therapy approaches, and summarize their significant points of variance in theory, technique and treatment goals.

SUGGESTED CROSS-REFERENCES

Group therapy techniques, which like the psychoanalytic approaches described herein, focus on the individual patient, but are based on different models of personality and psychopathology, may be found in Section I-C of this area. Approaches based on an alternate conceptual orientation, which places a relatively greater emphasis on group processes than on the individual, are contained in the preceding section in this area.

The techniques used by Markowitz and Kadis in their treatment of marital problems, as described in Area III, are based on psychoanalytic theory, and, to some extent, the influence of psychoanalytic concepts can also be discerned in Lidz's fascinating paper on "The Influence of Family Studies on the Treatment of Schizophrenia" in Section IV, on the Application of Group and Family Approaches to Special Patient Populations.

Finally, Dr. Fried's view that the attainment of individuation and independence is an important treatment goal for a wide spectrum of patients is shared, explicitly and implicitly, by many contributors to this volume. However, there is great diversity in the methods used to achieve this. Thus, for example, Spotnitz, in his article on the treatment of adolescents, in Section IV-B, describes the use of a family therapy technique to implement this goal. Fensterheim discusses the use of role-playing and reinforcement for this purpose in Section I-C; Simkin's article, also in Section I-C, elucidates the use of the Gestalt approach of inducing the patient to experience excluded aspects of himself; and, in contrast, in his article in Section IV-A, Lidz advocates the use of dynamic interpretations to foster the patient's independence and maturity.

H.S.K.

C.J.S.

4

PSYCHOANALYSIS IN GROUPS: CONTRASTS WITH OTHER GROUP THERAPIES

Alexander Wolf, M.D., Emanuel K. Schwartz, Ph.D.,

D.S.Sc., Gerald J. McCarty, Ph.D., and

Irving A. Goldberg, Ph.D.

We will try here to explain in a new way the assumptions and constructs implicit in the kind of group therapy that has become identified as psychoanalysis in groups and to provide a theoretical and practical basis for distinguishing it from the other group therapies.

The exact origins of psychoanalysis in groups need not be determined. It is sufficiently clear that the traditional psychoanalytic approach led to a rejection of the group as a treatment milieu (2). Psychoanalysis demanded non-interactivity on the part of the therapist, passivity on the part of the patient, privacy, regression, inturning, a focusing on the intrapsychic rather than on the interpersonal, a pursuit of history, anonymity on the part of the participants, and emphasis largely upon one person, the patient. The traditionalists tended to deny that the values, the personality, the commitments of the therapist had an influence upon the results. They emphasized the mirror quality of the therapist's functioning.

It is no small wonder therefore that the early forms of group therapy

Adapted from Chapter 1 of *Beyond the Couch* by Alexander Wolf, M.D., Emanuel K. Schwartz, Ph.D., D.S.Sc., Gerald J. McCarty, Ph.D., Irving A. Goldberg, Ph.D., New York: Science House, 1970, pp. 1-26.

were largely nonanalytic, experiential, educational. It was not until Trigant Burrow that an attempt was made to understand the nature of individual neurosis on the basis of social role and social behavior; he was the first to apply psychoanalytic psychology to a group of persons who sought the resolution of deeper internal conflicts. It is this kind of therapy, psychoanalysis in groups, that we are discussing.

We have a strong commitment to psychoanalytic psychology and an equally strong conviction that psychoanalytic methods can be successfully applied to treatment in a group setting. Our focus is on an understanding of unconscious processes and motivation, the significance of resistance, transference, and dreams, the importance of historical determination in current behavior, the necessity for working out and working through of psychodynamic and psychopathological mechanisms. These are the concerns of the psychoanalyst whether he works in the individual situation or the group. The additional dimensions and modifications necessary to treat ten or a dozen patients simultaneously in a group constitute what follows. We shall try to analyze the essential characteristics of group therapy and those special elements required if the therapist wishes to do psychoanalytic work with patients in a group setting.

Most group therapy is characterized today by two essential elements: first, the presence of authority and peer vectors, and second, multiple reactivities, both of which require the presence of not less than two patients in addition to the therapist. Such therapy centers on the phenomenology and the sociology of the group, the manifest behavior and verbalized communications of the members. The therapist leads in exploring the nature of behavior as it appears, as it is spoken, and as it is observed by the members within the context of the group.

To these characteristics of group therapy, psychoanalytic group therapy adds another. It is this third dimension that differentiates psychoanalytic group therapy or, as we call it, psychoanalysis in groups, from all other forms of group therapy. This fundamental ingredient of psychoanalytic group therapy may be identified as working with *unconscious material,* or the exploration of intrapsychic processes. Group therapy with this additional dimension works not only with the phenomenological, the manifest, but it searches for an understanding of what is latent in patient interaction and function. Here the therapist leads the exploration of unconscious processes by using free association and the analysis of dreams, resistance, and transference. Seeking for unconscious processes and motivations and exploring projected behavior lead necessarily into history, away from the emphasis upon the here and now. Only when the third element is added, namely the investigation of latent, unconscious, intrapsychic material, do we convert group therapy into analytic group therapy.

This kind of therapy sponsors individuation and heterogeneity. When the group and the therapist explore each patient in depth, they discover how each person differs from the next in his history, development, and current psychodynamics. A working out takes place, making the group members more interesting to one another, exposing not only their differences in pathology but their differences in healthy resources as well. There is a complementation in difference, a novelty that stimulates all the participants to try to understand and accept their differences. At the same time, this searching in depth may show members certain areas of commonality as well.

Nonanalytic group therapy promotes similarities with less concern for differences; in psychoanalytic group therapy, increased emphasis is placed upon the differences, the uniquenesses of the members. This is in part a consequence of the necessity to explore individual history and pursue psychodynamic formulations. Both kinds of group therapy permit the presence and recognition of similarities and differences among the patients; it is a matter of where the emphasis is placed as a result of the kinds of operations. The greater the exploration of the manifest, the greater the likelihood of emphasizing similarities, homogeneity. The greater the exploration of the latent content, the past, history, psychic determinants, the greater the likelihood of emphasizing individual differences, heterogeneity and diversity.

It is relevant here to discuss for a moment the question of inhibition in the development of neuroses. Perhaps it is useful to regard in some degree the problem of neurosis as one not so much of inhibition as of compulsive conformity. The patient in childhood has been subjected to a series of verbal and nonverbal directives that have shaped his character. He has then conformed to the demands of the mother, father, and siblings, to certain ways of adapting himself for emotional survival. In nonanalytic group therapy, he is encouraged to continue to act out this kind of conformity. Through the exploration of intrapsychic processes, he begins to see in more detail the nature of his conformity. He tries to find his way out and to recover his repressed ego. Analytic group therapy then sponsors nonconformity, individuation, recovery of the lost self.

Since heterogeneity and individuation seem to be characteristic of psychoanalytic group therapy, the question may be asked whether the constitution of the patient membership needs initially to be heterogeneous as well. It is our experience that manifest and latent heterogeneity exists in all groups. The therapist may consciously organize his groups, however, along specific lines, selecting patients for certain similarties. But even in that event, unless homogeneity is demanded by the leader, the chances are that the group will become more and more diversified with the passage of time.

There is also the question whether psychoanalytic group therapy can be done at all with a group of patients who are constituted along homogeneous lines—for example, patients in a psychiatric hospital, or inmates of a prison, or a group constituted entirely of homosexuals, or a group made up exclusively of males or of females. As we have indicated, such a group, unless it is forced to maintain this original identity, will tend to become more and more diverse. But once it is conceived along homogeneous lines, limitations will be placed on the extent to which analytic exploration can be done. If a therapist who had a group made up only of men did analytic therapy, a time would come in treatment when the men would demand that women be introduced into the group. In our experience, group members request that the other, the diverse, be brought into the group. This could be one indication that the therapist was doing analytic therapy.

A new kind of activity is added in analytic group psychotherapy. Not only is there interaction between the therapist and patients and among the patients, but now the therapist introduces to the group his role as interpreter of the nature of unconscious processes. Members of the group soon learn to add this to their repertory of activities. The therapist interprets fantasies, dreams, free association, slips of the tongue, identification, transference, resistance, defensiveness, displacement, and neurotic alliance. The patients soon became aware of these phenomena in themselves and in others and interpret such manifestations to one another, sometimes correctly, sometimes incorrectly. This is a new kind of work that takes place only in psychoanalytic group therapy. This is not only a period of working out but a period of working through, of insight that enables the patient to understand his disorder so that he can struggle to resolve his problems with the affirmation and support of the therapist and group members (3).

The following is a comparison of the differences in *emphasis* in the two categories of group treatment:

Nonanalytic Group Therapies	*Analytic Group Therapies*
1. the group as a whole	1. the individual
2. the here and now	2. the there and then
3. bipersonal psychology	3. multipersonal psychology
4. manifest behavior	4. latent content

Nonanalytic Group Therapies	*Analytic Group Therapies*
5. group dynamics	5. unconscious motivation
6. homogeneity	6. heterogeneity
7. similarity	7. difference
8. conformism	8. individual uniqueness
9. adjustment	9. insight and freedom
10. interaction	10. self-examination
11. interpersonal processes	11. intrapsychic processes
12. less anxiety	12. more anxiety

Although many of the characteristics of analytic group therapy may be taken over by the nonanalytic group therapist, unless the emphasis is placed upon the exploration of the latent, it is not analytic group therapy. This does not mean that the analytic group therapist emphasizes only the unconscious manifestations and processes. In fact, we would consider a person who emphasized only unconscious processes to the neglect of manifest behavior to be a therapist doing individual psychoanalysis in front of the group. In order to do psychoanalysis in groups, we must heed these three ingredients: horizontal and peer relations, multiple reactivities, and working with unconscious material, but with an emphasis upon the exploration of intrapsychic processes. However, this does not mean that group dynamics, individual similarities, and manifest behavior, for example, are neglected or denied. Additionally, the analytic therapist strives to be aware of the necessity of limits for the patients as well as for himself.

The analytic therapist leads the group from the level of multiple interaction to the level of investigating unconscious motivation. In this way the genetic determinants of the experiential data of behavior become available for exploration. On the other hand, multiple reactivities may support resistive and defensive behavior, whether in the course of interpersonal or intrapsychic exploration. Interpretations by patients are not systematically timed. A therapist will consider when to introduce an interpretation to a patient, but a group member will generally not do so.

A Point of View

After many years of working analytically with patients in individual and group settings, we have come to the conclusion that therapy is more than a series of hypotheses concerning the development and functioning of personality, the nature and origination of psychopathology, the cause of anxiety and the defense mechanisms used to deal with it, and the ways in which the patient relates to illusion and reality. We have come to the conviction that in addition to these theoretical and technical constructs, which are applicable to doing psychoanalytic treatment with a patient, the therapist as a human being enters into the treatment situation as an important factor. The development of psychoanalysis in which emphasis has shifted from focus upon the patient to focus upon the relationship, and more currently to focus upon the person of the therapist, is in part what we are talking about here (1). It is more than theoretical persuasion and the technical know-how of the psychoanalyst that effect changes in the persons who come for treatment (4). There is more communicated in an analysis than the historical origin of a patient's intercurrent behavior or a consciousness of unconscious processes within the self.

These additional facets have sometimes been called the educational aspects of psychoanalysis, but we feel that this is a derogatory label. We are, rather, committed to the idea that the psychoanalyst as a person enters into the analytic relationship. This does not mean that he gives up his objectivity, his neutrality, his commitment to listening and exploring the patient or making the patient's needs central to the therapeutic experience. What it does mean is that the personality of the psychoanalyst enters globally into the relationship and that there are transtherapeutic experiences that the patient has in the interaction with the person of the analyst, his philosophy of life, his system of values.

Although we are committed not only to working with the individual patient but to helping him find his way with other human beings, to a socialization, to a gregariousness, to his commitment to working and living within a group, we are nevertheless aware of the importance of his personal growth and development and his ability to think and stand on his own two feet. In spite of the fact that this is a statement about psychoanalysis in groups, we wish not to ignore the truth that for each patient his own personal development is central. In the pursuit of these two objectives we have proposed the alternative session, the meeting of the members of a group without the physical presence of the therapist, which has become the hallmark of psychoanalysis in groups.

We cannot conclude with any better expression of our own position than the words of Joseph Wood Krutch in his "Epitaph for an Age": "The more we teach adjustment, group activity, getting along with a group, and so forth, the less any individual is prepared for the time, so likely to come in any man's life, when he cannot or will not call upon group support. Ultimately security for him depends upon the ability to stand alone or even just to be alone. Belonging is fine. But to belong to anything except oneself is again to give a hostage to fortune."*

---

* *The New York Times Magazine,* July 30, 1967, p. 10.

REFERENCES

1. SCHWARTZ, E. K. "Non-Freudian Analytic Methods," in *Handbook of Clinical Psychology,* edited by B. B. Wolman. New York, McGraw-Hill, 1965.
2. ———— "Psychoanalysis in Groups: Resistances to Its Use," *American Journal of Psychotherapy,* 17:457-464, 1963.
3. WOLF, A. "Psychoanalytic Group Therapy," in *Current Psychiatric Therapies,* Vol. IV, edited by J. Masserman. New York: Grune and Stratton, 1964.
4. WOLF, A. & SCHWARTZ, E. K. *Psychoanalysis in Groups.* New York: Grune and Stratton, 1962.

5

TREATMENT OF ORAL CHARACTER NEUROSIS IN GROUP PSYCHOTHERAPY

Henriette T. Glatzer, Ph.D.

Supervisor, Postgraduate Center for Mental Health
Assistant Clinical Professor, Department of Psychiatry,
Albert Einstein College of Medicine

Within the past several decades, there has been a fundamental change in the clinical picture of the neuroses. The patients seen in current clinical practice frequently present character problems, rather than classic neuroses. The character neurotic may, of course, manifest ego patterns which correspond in general to those found in the classic neurotic; however, he differs significantly from the classic neurotic in that he does not experience his symptoms as ego-alien. Indeed, in neurotic character disorders, of the "modern neuroses," to use Fenichel's term (8), the personality is so enmeshed in the illness that there is no borderline between personality and symptoms, between health and illness.

More specifically, character neurotics typically manifest a general rigidity and inflexibility, which limits their range of adjustment and growth and/or involves them in various types of antisocial, asocial, or dysocial acting-out behavior. Nevertheless, the patient sees the pathological behavior devices which make up his character as "natural"; he experiences them as syntonic. Moreover, since character neuroses do not include symptoms, they are not experienced as a source of suffering by the patient, except to the degree that he is dissatisfied with his performance or its consequences. Thus, as compared with the classic neuroses, neurotic character disorders represent relatively more successful modes of adjustment for the individual, at least in terms of his comfort. In light of these considerations, the fact that the treatment of character disorders poses formidable problems comes as no surprise.

The primary aim of this article is to demonstrate the greater efficacy of group, as opposed to individual therapy in the treatment of a particular form of neurotic character disorder, i.e., oral character neurosis. As a preamble to this discussion, an attempt has been made to describe the treatment problems intrinsic to neurotic character disorders in general, and their greater amenability to solution in a group setting. Once these background data have been provided, the genesis and psychodynamics of oral character neurosis, the resistances typically manifested by this patient category, and the concomitant use of group treatment techniques to deal with these resistances, can be discussed in detail and with greater clarity.

The Therapeutic Tasks in Neurotic Character Disorders

In neurotic character disorders, the pathological attitudes habitually adopted enable the ego to deal with instinctual forces, assure satisfaction, reconcile conflicts, and achieve some degree of adjustment within a particular interpersonal and social environment. It follows, then, that the powerful defending forces of the ego are employed against treatment, and are used to maintain the illness: The pathological behavior devices employed by the patient serve to ward off the breakthrough of dangerous instinctual impulses. Analysis of the layer of anxiety and guilt which, to paraphrase Fenichel (8), have interposed between the original impulse and the ultimate pathological behavior pattern will bring the instinctual impulses to the surface. Frequently, however, the therapist must mobilize these affects before they can be traced to their original sources. The reasonably conflict-free ego, so essential to the success of treatment, seems in these cases to be entangled in character resistances. The initial therapeutic task, therefore, is to separate the reasonable observing ego from its compulsively defended part. More precisely, the therapist has the difficult dual task of making these patients understand that their habitual ways of reacting are pathological, and that their neurotic behavior patterns derive from repressed intrapsychic conflicts. In group psychotherapy, the members of the group support the therapist's efforts toward this end. The therapist can use the reasonable ego of the other group members, which enables them to recognize their own pathological behavior, to strengthen and confront the reasonable part of the ego of the patient, who is more apt to see in others what is ego syntonic in himself.

Analyzing the overt manifestations of character attitudes, such as behavior which has been taken over by the musculature, is a good first step toward thawing out the frozen energies of chronic defenses. The group facilitates this process. When the group analyst calls attention to outward signs of the patient's character defenses, e.g., his tense expression, nervous laugh, restless finger-drumming, the odd tone of his voice, these observations are often confirmed by other members of the group who can see what the patient is unable or unwilling to see. Thus the therapist gets help from the group in his efforts to break through the patient's characterological armor, so that the repressed anxiety which stems from controversial feelings and thoughts may rise to the surface.

In fact, such observations are frequently made by group members on their own, i.e., without prompting from the therapist. Group members learn quickly from the therapist how to recognize surface forms of character traits. Moreover, once they have learned to spot such behavior, they begin to look for the meaning behind it: Having become aware of the fact that these behavioral characteristics disguise anxiety which stems from unresolved intrapsychic conflicts, they initiate independent efforts to extract the underlying connotations which may be more effective than the therapist's interventions. And, of course, this process is facilitated by the fact that, within the permissive group setting, members are encouraged to express their frank opinions about each other freely. While ordinarily the patient will resent this apparent eagerness on the part of his peers to "pick on" his attitudes, intonations, or whatever, his resentment is tempered by the realization that their criticism is motivated by a genuine desire to help him. Another important therapeutic consideration relates to the fact that, in contrast to the therapist, the patient's peers are less likely to be perceived unconsciously in the projected image of the bad parent; consequently, he finds it easier to accept their criticism.*

As noted above, character defenses may be directed not only against forbidden impulses. And, at times, defensive attitudes are not directed against the situation in which the anxiety may arise, but only against the anxiety itself (23). Because powerful quantities of countercathexis are invested in the defense against anxiety, the patient in individual character analysis must frequently experience general feelings of dis-

---

. * Obviously, this would not apply only to those patients in the group who present character disorders.

comfort, with long periods of hostility and resentment toward the therapist, before he can actually experience the anxiety evoked by repressed feelings and memories. Once again, the group process may provide a short-cut to this essential therapeutic goal. When the patient's mannerisms or other behavioral patterns are particularly obvious and/or irritating, several members may focus on a specific character defense, and their concentrated effort may, in itself, give rise to a good deal of anxiety in the patient. Obviously, if the attack is sadistic, or the ego of the patient appears to be too threatened, the therapist must intervene, not only to clarify the factors which precipitated the assault, but also, when necessary, to interpret the attackers' need to crush the patient. More often than not, however, this concerted approach is just dynamic enough to have a strong effect on the patient so that he releases the anxiety which leads, in turn, to the emergence of the repressed feelings and memories. When a patient who has thus been "assaulted" opens up, the other group members usually react with sympathy and understanding which serves to reassure the patient and helps to alleviate his anxiety, so that eventually that particular pathological character defense becomes less rigid.

Another major difficulty in individual character analysis relates to the fact that the patient frequently uses the therapist as a target in acting out his pathological, ego-syntonic defenses, coupled with the fact that the therapist has no clear way of getting the patient to understand the implications of his behavior. It is easier to resolve this problem in the group setting. The group member who manifests a suspicious or derogatory attitude toward the therapist, for example, is often brought up short by the contrasting attitudes of the other group members; or they may feel sufficiently outraged by the patient's "fantastic" charges against the therapist to provide him with tangible evidence to the contrary. At other times, the patient's hopelessness and despair about the value of therapy, or his feeling that the therapist is incompetent, or unwilling to help him, are often countered by incontrovertible evidence of the progress made by other patients in the group. Conversely, the group is also helpful in combatting the patient's eroticized transference, or, more specifically, the intense pseudo-positive transference resistance, in which the patient fantasizes himself as the favored patient of the god-like therapist. In the group setting, he is confronted with evidence to the contrary; moreover, the down-to-earth critical opinions of his behavior expressed by the therapist and by other group members serve to further counteract such transference phenomena.

Finally, the fact that the therapist's interpretations of the patient's behavior are reinforced by the group enhances their impact. The patient finds it difficult to discount the therapist's observations when others share his opinions and/or make similar observations on their own initiative.

THE TREATMENT OF ORAL CHARACTER NEUROSIS

This author has studied the character resistances of orally regressed patients for many years, and described the therapeutic problems posed by the pregenital phenomena manifested by oral character neurotics, and their greater amenability to solution in a group treatment setting, in several recent publications, (16-19). As noted earlier, the techniques used to deal with resistances of these patients can best be understood in terms of their genetic-dynamic determinants.

The Psychogenesis of Oral Character Neurosis

The therapeutic techniques developed by the author are based on the theoretical assumption that the oral character neurotic experienced greater difficulty in giving up the magical fantasy of omnipotence. In the normal course of development, the need to adapt to reality forces every child to modify his original autocratic belief that nothing exists outside of himself. The separation of the ego from the external world is a gradual process, however, and a longing for the original objectless state persists. Thus the child attempts to reverse the separation of ego from nonego by projecting unpleasant sensations onto the external world. During that stage of development which Freud described as the purified pleasure ego (11), everything good is considered self-endowed, i.e., ego, and everything bad is seen as coming from the outside, i.e., nonego.

Inasmuch as she represents the first external frustrator of infantile delusions of grandeur, the mother becomes the principal target of the child's rage and aggression. The hostility which the affront to his narcissism evokes in the child is projected onto the mother in the form of the pre-oedipal "witch fantasy" which is incorporated into the superego (bad maternal superego), and then changed into guilt which is turned against the ego. But in those children who later develop a marked narcissistic neurosis, the pre-oedipal "witch fantasy" is repressed, and undergoes little modification by reality. Their narcissism, wounded by reality restrictions, makes them insist on maintaining the earliest illusions of grandiosity. In their rage, they seek "reimbursement" from their external frustrators. The depth of their original narcissism makes it difficult for them to divert and sublimate this aggression by identifying with the parents; nor is pleasing their parents by behaving in an approved manner a source of gratification. In these narcissistic and angry children, the long maturational period renders a satisfactory expression of aggression impossible; consequently the accumulation is discharged into the superego, which accounts for its severity: The aggression which is taken over by the superego is transformed into guilt and depression. The aggression which remains in the ego serves a defensive function, and is used to provoke rejection and punishment. It is the weak ego's way of attempting to preserve the infantile delusion of omnipotence: "*I force parent (environment) to punish me.*" In other words, this masochistic solution by the infantile ego is an attempt to out-maneuver the environment's efforts to impose the reality principle; concomitantly, it constitutes an attempt to outwit the punishing superego by unconsciously enjoying punishment and libidinizing the overwhelming guilt. In short, the bruised ego seeks to maintain its illusion of omnipotence by reducing punitive authority to absurdity.

Psychodynamics

When such individuals become patients, they repeat this infantile power struggle in treatment. The masochistic victories they achieve over the therapist, by keeping therapy at a standstill, are an unconscious source of narcissistic gratification. Nevertheless, these patients often seem to be overwhelmed by feelings of self-deprecation, of hopelessness and helplessness; although they seem to want to love and be loved, their efforts are always spurned. The therapist must be alert to the fact that this despondency is actually a façade to cover up their omnipotent power fantasies. Interpreting only the dependent longings and oral greed of these patients who feel deprived and rejected, without a deeper analysis of the more regressed masochistic bond to the "bad" pre-oedipal image, is of minimal value in mitigating their self-pity, their endless need to prove to the world that they are still unloved, unwanted, and unworthy.

These patients unconsciously seek to reinforce the masochistic bond to the bad pre-oedipal image by repeating their experience with the rejecting mother. Consequently, they look for affection and respect in impossible situations and deliberately choose objects who are incapable, for one reason or another, of supplying the love for which they purportedly yearn.

Frequently, the dejection of the oral character neurotic represents a form of revenge. As a rule, he seeks to demonstrate to the world that the "bad" mother made him so sick that no authority is powerful enough to help him. Moreover, these patients may act out their fundamental angry reproach to the pre-oedipal mother through the use of positive as well as negative magic gestures (18) : In the positive magic gesture, the patient indicates by his actions that he wished to be treated lovingly and kindly in his childhood, and denies the fact that he deliberately provoked rejection or punishment. He behaves as though he were drinking up all the good milk that the "good" therapist is giving him. But his pseudo-cooperative behavior and the pseudo-insights he achieves, which leave him relatively unimproved, testify to the irony of his actions. The fact is that such a patient gets an unconscious kick out of ridiculing the therapist who, to all intents and purposes, has come to symbolize the parent. His unconscious intent is to show how senseless this parent actually is. In the negative magic gesture, the patient dramatizes the commands of his stern parents to demonstrate their cruelty. He may, in addition, attempt to evoke his mother's coldness and rejection once again, by mimicking her unapproachable, intolerant, and unresponsive manner, as he perceives it.

In the oral character neurotic, provocative aggression often serves as a defense against the patient's anxiety about his nuclear passivity. Feeling passive is equated with the possible loss of the infantile fantasy of omnipotence, which is equated, in turn, with a complete loss of ego. Insofar as his unconscious provocative aggression makes the patient feel that he is actively in control of his environment, he feels safe. Conversely, as long as he remains passive, he is at the mercy of the hostile world. Provoking the environment to reject him gives the patient the illusion of power. Moreover, the rejection itself serves a dual purpose: For one, it enables the patient to consciously rationalize his attack on authority (mother) without feeling guilty, and/or it provides justification for his self-pity as the innocent victim of a malicious world.

The Efficacy of Group Treatment

Interpretation of the patient's provocative aggression is an essential step in achieving therapeutic movement. This author has learned, in the course of her extensive experience, that to treat such aggression as a basic wish instead of a defense against the fear of passivity is to foster oral resistance and leave the deepest conflict untouched. In short, the patient must be helped to understand and accept the fact that his provocative behavior is a defense against his fear of passivity and/or masochism. Deeply resistive oral characters do not readily acquire this insight in individual psychotherapy. As a ready-made parental imago, the therapist evokes a basic negative transference. Consequently, these patients not only resist, but often react in a wounded or self-pitying way to his attempts to point out this ego-syntonic defense. This therapeutic task is facilitated in a group treatment setting, however.

In such a setting, this provocative defense may take a variety of predictable forms: The pseudo-aggressive oral character often intellectualizes in an invasive manner, by monopolizing the group session with repetitious complaints, by inundating the group with dream material, and, finally, by laughing at and ridiculing all interpretations of his behavior as resistance. But it becomes increasingly difficult for the patient to laugh at such interpretations by the therapist or a particular member of the group, when they are supported by other group members, who will typically go to great pains to demonstrate to the patient that his behavior in the present group situation confirms the validity of these observations.

Intellectual verbosity, which may present a serious obstacle to progress in individual treatment, is frequently halted abruptly—and effectively—by other members of the group who have pressing problems of their own, and therefore do not hesitate to interrupt this obstinate defense cycle. Moreover, when interpretations of this defense come from the patient's peers, they are less threatening to his sense of omnipotence. Consequently, he is more receptive to the repeated efforts of his fellow group members to confront him with evidence which clearly demonstrates that his angry, provocative, or despairing attitudes do not stem primarily from realistic factors, but are manifestations of the general rigidity of his behavior.

Similarly, the oral neurotic's subtle use of magic gestures to elicit rejection and anger can be handled more effectively in the group. Inevitably, this self-defeating pattern is repeated with specific members of the group, thus enabling the therapist and/or the other members to observe and interpret it in the dynamic here-and-now. And, as he plays out the same theme in assorted keys with different members of the group, the patient is given ample opportunity to recognize the validity of these interpretations, and, ultimately, to experience his unconscious provocative behavior as ego-alien. The various ways in which he masochistically induces the others, including the therapist, to conform to his internal image of the rejecting mother stand out in bold relief as a chronic behavior pattern. And, once this has emerged, the group situation helps in still another way. The usual narcissistic blow suffered by the patient when his masochism is exposed for analysis is tempered by his awareness of the frequency with which other group members manifest masochistic behavior.

Passive-dependent oral characters, in whom the ego functions of reality testing and critical judgment are impaired, often present latent resistances in the form of a "deceptive" positive transference wherein they treat the therapist as a real parent, not "as if" he were a parent. Patients with such severe ego disturbances have difficulty in maintaining the psychic equilibrium necessary for a transference neurosis. Consequently, the therapist's failure to fully reciprocate their "love" causes them great suffering. Analysis of the pseudo-positive transference as it arises is very important because it may help to elucidate the meaning of their love for and dependence on the therapist, and thus shorten the period of unrequited love which is an agonizing experience for the impoverished ego. The affront to the patient's narcissism is often lessened by virtue of the fact that these interpretations serve to undermine his masochistic fantasies of being the "rejected" one.

Analysis of the superficial positive transference is especially difficult to accomplish with strongly inhibited patients: Their primitive distrust of the pre-oedipal mother creates too much anxiety to permit them to give up the "deceptive" positive transference which serves as a defense against their negative transference to the therapist. As a result, they often remain fixed in their passive masochistic dependency state, despite persistent interpretations by the therapist. Such interpretations, to the effect that the patient is making a game of the analysis, that despite his "armored" smile of agreement, it is clear that he harbors strong negative feelings toward the therapist, rarely elicit a response in individual therapy. In contrast, the group milieu can be helpful in easing this transference deadlock: Other patients by-pass the patient's positive façade and react to the patient's underlying hostility. These reactions frequently force the patient to respond spontaneously and explosively, which paves the way for an expression of hostility toward the therapist.

Indications of therapeutic progress typically evoke negative reactions in oral dependent characters. They are reluctant to acknowledge any improvement in their behavior. It is almost as if the narcissistic infant in these patients has to be pressured into perceiving the therapist as the good mother, giving them nourishing milk. Even in the middle and final stages of treatment, when improvement is hard to deny, they continue to repudiate any tangible gains or refuse to credit the therapeutic process with any positive change in their behavior, and, in fact, try in subtle ways to off-set such change. The group's realistic appraisal of the patient's improvement, as they contrast his current functioning with his former behavior, often forces him to recognize the gains he has made in treatment. Moreover, in emphasizing the reality of the changes which have occurred in the patient, the group plays an active role in helping him to give up his persistent masochistic tie to the pre-oedipal "witch," and to begin identifying instead with the "giving mother" and the "given child."

The Role of the Group Therapist

It has long been the opinion of this author that it is unproductive to assume a neutral passive position with strongly resistive character problems, and in recent years a growing number of therapists have come to the same conclusion. The passive approach over-frustrates these basically passive patients and intensifies their masochism so that the transference resistance is strengthened. Analytic silence merely reinforces these patients' fantasy of the "bad, non-feeding" mother. Moreover, the passive, permissive attitude of the therapist may also increase the patients' anxiety. For, in concealing his real opinion of their acting out, the therapist conveys the impression that he is an insincere, frightened, and impotent parent.

Amelioration of the countertransference. The stubborn resistances and noxious quality of the defenses employed by the oral character frequently evoke a strong countertransference in the therapist. The group situation tends to ameliorate this impasse in several ways. For one, the group therapist, by virtue of his unique role as participant-observer, is able, and indeed required, to give up the passivity which is expected of him in the dyadic relationship. The mere fact that he can be more active, franker, and spontaneous in his relationship with these patients helps to alleviate his countertransference feelings. Secondly, in those rare instances when the therapist's countertransference to these adversely affects his clinical competence, the group provides him with the adjunct help he requires to stand up to their insatiable oral demands, and to dynamically interpret their resistances instead of gratifying their neurotic needs. Since, as noted above, the demands of those patients are actually masochistic defenses, they can never be gratified; rather, their function as defenses requires constant interpretation. The danger lies in the possibility, however remote, that the therapist's own unresolved masochism may make him submit to his patients' oral insistences, by letting them run on endlessly and fruitlessly, in which event the masochism of the therapist serves to reinforce the masochism of his patients. Once again, the members of the group, once they have been alerted to the subtle manifestations of these masochistic defenses, can make up for the therapist's blind spots. In fact, the group may become the corrective, firm parent who discourages acting-out, exaggerations, and caricaturing of treatment. It may, in addition, become the active, feeding parent to the "starving" silent patient when the therapist has been immobilized by his countertransference.

SUMMARY

In summary, orally regressed neurotic characters are generally regarded as extremely resistive and discouraging patients because of their excessive narcissism, weak, unadaptable ego, clinging passive dependency, intense infantile rage, strong psychic masochism, and their intense need to provoke aggression. This author has found, however, that patients in this category are more likely to respond to treatment when it is provided in a group setting.

This hard core of oral character neurotics who frequently resemble borderline psychotics because of their tenacious masochistic defenses often find it easier to recognize the rigid and inappropriate defenses they habitually employ after they have seen similar defenses enacted by their group peers. Watching others play out their various senseless and stubborn delaying tactics stimulates such patients to question their own inflexible behavior when it is challenged or interpreted. Moreover, in the group setting, they are made aware of the fact that the acknowledgment of anxiety by their peers does not demean them; nor do they become passive and vulnerable objects for annihilation as a result. They find instead that the uncovering of conflicts evokes sympathy, and produces tangible help by all the members of the group, including the unconsciously-feared therapist who is perceived as the "bad mother."

REFERENCES

1. ALEXANDER, F. (1933), "Relation of Structural and Instinctual Conflicts," *Psychoanal. Quart.*, 2:185-6, 206.
2. —— & SAUL, L. S. (1937), "Three Criminal Types as Seen by the Psychoanalyst," *Psychoanal. Rev.*, Vol. XXIV, No. 2.
3. BENDER, L. & SCHILDER, P. (1936), "Aggressiveness in Children," *Genetic Psychol. Monog.*, Vol. XVIII, Nos. 5 and 6, 410-524.
4. BERGLER, E. (1949), *Basic Neurosis.* New York: Grune & Stratton.
5. BRUNSWICK, R. M. (1940), "Preoedipal Phase of the Libido Development," *Psychoanal. Quart.*, 9:293-319.
6. DURKIN, H. (1951), "Analysis of Character Traits in Group Therapy," *Int. J. Group Psychother.*, 1:133-143.
7. FERENZI S., "Stages in the Development of the Sense of Reality," *Sex in Psychoanalysis.* New York: Basic Books, 213-239.

8. FENICHEL, O. (1945), *Psychoanalytic Theory of Neurosis*. New York: W. W. Norton.
9. FREUD, A. (1954), "Psychoanalysis and Education," *Psychoanalytic Study of the Child*, IX: 9-15.
10. FREUD, S. (1914), "On Narcissism," *Collected Papers*, 4:30-50. London: Hogarth Press, 1946.
11. —— (1915), "Instincts and Their Vicissitudes," *Collected Papers*, 4:60-83. London: Hogarth Press, 1946.
12. —— (1925), "Negation," *Collected Papers*, 5:181-185. London: Hogarth Press, 1950.
13. —— (1931), "Female Sexuality," *Collected Papers*, 5:252-272. London: Hogarth Press, 1950.
14. —— (1937), "Analysis Terminable and Interminable," *Collected Papers*, 5:316-357. London: Hogarth Press, 1950.
15. —— (1930), *Civilization and Its Discontents*. London: Hogarth Press, 1946.
16. GLATZER, H. T. (1959), "Analysis of Masochism in Group Psychotherapy," *Int. J. Gr. Psychother.*, 9:158-166.
17. —— (1959), "Notes on the Preoedipal Phantasy," *Am. J. Orthopsychiat.*, 29: 383-390.
18. —— (1962), "Narcissistic Problems in Group Psychotherapy," *Int. J. Group Psychother.*, 12:448-455.
19. —— (1965), "Aspects of Transference in Group Psychotherapy," *Int. J. Group Psychother.*, 15:167-176.
20. JACKSON, J. & GROTJAHN, M. (1958), "Treatment of Oral Defenses by Combined Individual and Group Psychotherapy," *Int. J. Group Psychother.*, 8:373-382.
21. LAMPL-DE GROOT, J. (1946), "The Preoedipal Phase in the Development of the Male Child," *Psychoanalytic Study of the Child*, 2:75-83.
22. RAPPAPORT, E. A. (1956), "Management of an Eroticized Transference," *Psychoanal. Quart.*, 25:515-529.
23. ZILBOORG, G. (1933), "Anxiety Without Affect," *Psychoanal. Quart.*, II.

6

INDIVIDUATION THROUGH GROUP PSYCHOTHERAPY

Edrita Fried, Ph.D.

Associate Clinical Professor of Psychiatry
New York Medical College
Training Psychoanalyst, Postgraduate Center for Mental Health
(New York City)

One of the accepted and declared goals of all psychotherapy is to enable patients to achieve identity, independence, and a rootedness that rests within the self. In the literature outlining the developmental phases of childhood from the point of view of psychoanalytic ego psychology, self-rootedness has been termed "identity" (Erikson, 1968), "individuation" (Mahler, 1968), and "self-differentiation" (Eisenbud, 1967), and has received a great deal of attention. In the context of group therapy with adult patients, on the other hand, the phenomena associated with the emergence of individuation have received scant consideration. There has been much systematic and important discussion about identification with the group leader (Scheidlinger, 1955) and with group members and the whole group (Scheidlinger, 1964), about focal conflicts and conflict solutions, and about group coherence, but little attention has been paid to the need of group members, as they grow emotionally, to achieve distance from the therapist so as to fight off primitive desires for identification and fusion and to emerge as individuals in their own right. Yet, only if the group members gradually gain the conviction that each member has the right to his own rhythm, to

Reprinted from INTERNATIONAL JOURNAL OF GROUP PSYCHOTHERAPY, Vol. XX, Oct. 1970, No. 4, pp. 450-459.

the individualized mold of his existence and his ideals, can the goal of therapy be achieved: the ability to love, not through identification, submission and fusion, but as a reasonable, autonomous, separate human being.

The therapy group as a whole, although initially focused on the leader and held together in part by primitive identifications with him, gradually becomes ever more autonomous if it is conducted appropriately. It administers itself ever more efficiently. In the final stages, most, if not all, of the members achieve a peer feeling with one another and with the leader. After considerable anxieties have been understood and shed, and after conflicts between submission and angry protest have been settled, a good feeling arises; the group members become cooperative with one another and feel fond of the leader, though they have become familiar with his shortcomings.

In the child, individuation, in terms of physiological, psychological, and social maturation, is assumed to start at the end of the second year of life. As the encompassing dependence on the mother that is the core of the symbiotic phase wanes, as the child begins to acquire the rudiments of body autonomy, as new ego skills are acquired, the now semi-liberated child wants more often to do than to be done for. The famous, "No, me do it," signifies that the small human being wants to make his first tries at approaching the world on his own two feet. He is reaching out for individuation.

In higher measure than we usually acknowledge, the striving for individuation—for forming convictions that are truly self-made and for relying on inner strength to cope with perils and pleasures—continues throughout any vital life. Never is there an end to the process of achieving self-determination and self-expression. It may be a source of anxiety and tension, but it is also a source of pride. The neurotic achieves a sense of self in circular, seemingly self-defeating, and highly negativistic ways. The healthier person does so through active self-shaping.

When people have been hampered in the normal development of individuation, usually through parental interference of one kind or another, they develop symptoms and character traits that are partly egosyntonic but eventually lead to ego-alien experience. Depression, passivity that is punctuated by hostility and restlessness, and very low self-esteem that gives rise to feelings of helplessness are a few of the rather ego-alien experiences. In increasing numbers, such individuation-deprived persons turn to group psychotherapy for help, although they are not necessarily aware that one of the things wrong is a flawed sense of identity and self-determination.

Several schemata that describe the normal sequence of phases to be expected in groups have been worked out by observers and interpreters of group dynamics. Such schemata, whose usefulness can be great, outline with broad strokes the successive stages through which any group goes or should go to complete a full and fruitful group life cycle. The behavior displayed in each phase and the ways in which the group deals with it are communicated in the "interaction language" and the "acting in" (Ormont, 1969) as well as "acting out" conduct which groups use to express themselves or to cover up what they fear to express. The well-known and widely-used schemata developed by Schutz (1958) describes three essential phases of group development. Schutz calls the first group phase that of "inclusion" and states that during this period the members are primarily concerned with acceptance and nonacceptance. Do the others like me? Does the leader give me equal time? Will I be able to keep up with this group? These are the typical, often unverbalized questions with which group members are preoccupied in the inclusion phase.

A predecessor to the "inclusion phase" may be noted in groups with several borderline or schizophrenic members. This is a "narcissistic phase" in which the members behave like hermits and do not relate. Communications can best be described as a "collective monologue," and any attention of which the members are capable is focused solely on the leader.

As greater coherence is achieved and the members become used to the idea that they are fairly safely installed in their group (a feeling resembling that of a satisfactory mother-child symbiosis), the prime concerns change. Individual members, subgroups, or the entire group now start to focus on the degree of autonomy that the group and the leader will permit. Members begin to express open resentment if they feel they are not being understood. They find satisfaction in challenging each other, especially the strong group members but, above all, the therapist. Whereas in previous sessions the members may have noted how similar they were to one another, and the phrase, "I feel just like you," was clearly heard in a chorus of largely submissive expressions or actions, now the members want to say, or show through their behavior, how they are different. The struggle for individuation has begun. It is always accompanied by hostility and aggression, which serve as reinforcement for the emerging self that is now to take on a separation struggle from the leader and the others. Schutz calls this phase the "power phase," but it could also be termed the strength phase. The prime concerns at this stage are: Who among us are the strong ones? Now I am going to challenge the therapist and some members. I am glad I am different from X. Why did I ever think I was the same? The third and final group stage in Schutz's scheme is called the "intimacy phase." It is characterized by cooperation and peer feeling among members and is achieved only if a lot of challenge has been expressed in the power or strength phase.

Group development schemata that describe the main stations along the continuum of group progression seem to imply, at times, that a group as a whole moves as a rather cohesive entity through the various phases. Concerning the phase that interests us in this context, that of individuation and of self-originated strength and power, it is rare for all members to cope with the central experiences of individuation at the same time. In actual practice, as group therapists know, group members do not tend to sing in chorus. Indeed, unanimous concern with individuation and a concerted challenge of other group members, the therapist, and the value of group therapy are not desirable. If all, or nearly all, members of a group are simultaneously in the power phase, the variety within the group that is the essence of good group composition is reduced to a danger point. If every member challenges the theraipst at the same time, the tension level can become too high.

The reason a schemata of group dynamic movement is useful is not as an aid in developing methods of equalizing the developmental pace of each patient but to help the therapist to make diagnostic distinctions; for example, between hostility that derives from the frustration of passivity and hostility mobilized to fortify the patient's ego during the power struggle. An illustration of this occurred in a therapy group in which only one individual was preoccupied with her rights, with the need to express opposition and to question the helpfulness and abilities of the therapist. All other members, caught in the passivity of the inclusion phase, failed to encourage this group member's legitimate and desirable development. Filled with guilt over being the only protester in the group and despairing of obtaining support from the other members, the rebellious patient wanted to leave the group. Soon after the therapist began to help other patients to express certain doubts and challenges, the situation became rectified and the group moved ahead, though not as a total unit in which everyone expressed opposition and protest at the same time and with equal strength. The young woman who had felt guilty and separated from the others because of her quarrelsome quest for identity, individuation, and strength welcomed the forward movement of the others and stayed on in the group.

WHAT GOES ON DURING THE INDIVIDUATION-STRENGTH-POWER PHASE

When group members become preoccupied with the question of how to achieve the sense of a separate and functioning self, disagreements with the therapist increase. Anger, rage, and humor appear more frequently, and giggles are not uncommon. Patients feel a greater need to form pairs or subgroups of three and four, especially when the leader's interpretations or the group's behavior toward the leader create anxiety. On such occasions, pairing can represent forward development, particularly for patients with borderline personalities or schizophrenic symptomatology whose guilt and anxiety over presenting opposition to the leader may be great. The only condition that should be imposed on this kind of "acting out" is that the group and the therapist be kept up to date about outside meetings and exchanges.

During the struggle for individuation, patients tend to request that the therapist substantiate every comment made. Interpretations, accepted at first, may be turned down on later inspection, or interpretations rejected immediately may later be digested and accepted. Group members who earlier focused their eyes primarily on the leader and addressed him rather than their peers may begin to shift away from this prime focus. Talk and interchange become ever more "crosswise" and interdependent as members realize that the other participants have valuable contributions to make. Group members who struggle for individuation and condemn the group method or the therapist during this process will be contradicted by others who also struggle for individuation, by participants who are still in the inclusion phase, or by patients who already have a feel of their own strength and individuality and are in the third phase of "affection," "intimacy," and "cooperation." Those who doubt the validity of an oppositional member's (individuation-seeking individual's) disregard for the group process or the therapist should be encouraged to be specific, for specificity is the life blood of good group therapy or any valid therapy. It is useful if counterclaims that the group is worthwhile are borne out by specific illustrations and memories of exchanges that promoted growth.

It is sometimes assumed that group cohesion and group work suffer if members *openly and directly* criticize the leader and make him the prime target of attack, and it is suggested that group members instead do better if they attack a scapegoat and displace their anger (Kaplan, 1967), but I cannot share this assumption. Most groups, most of the time, can tolerate severe criticisms of the leader, and group survival does not require that external targets be used and the leader spared. Functioning groups are usually divided, with the members having individual, divergent opinions on specific issues. In a group in which there is total union, or total dis-union, chances are high that something is wrong, either with the com-position of the group or the group dynamics.

As a rule, if one, two, or several people in the individuation-power-strength phase attack the therapist, their remarks are modified or coun-tered by others who have a good word for the leader. The following exchange illustrates this:

> *Dubin* (struggling for autonomy and individuation) : Everything in this group is shitty. She [the therapist] is just full of bull if she says I attack as I feel weak. The truth is I am a bastard. It's as simple as that. No schmanzy-fancy explanation necessary.
> *Strong* (already has gained some sense of individuation and strength) : Sure, sometimes she [the therapist] is wrong. She says things so simply I think she is naïve. But I can give examples when she helped a lot right here. Brilliant. I sort things out. Stops me from generalizing, having tantrums, and feeling like God.
> *Warmly* (has certain sense of strength and individuation) : If I disagree with her I ask questions, or I ask you other people ques-tions. Dubin, you should try it. You are mad at her because you are still too much of a kid with her.

The criterion which dictates whether individual patients, and eventu-ally the entire group, will move into the individuation-strength-power phase and later out of it and into the intimacy stage depends on the countertransference of the therapist. Therapists resemble maternal fig-ures. Mothers can only tolerate growing separation from their children if they like independence and do not need a creature to be dependent on them to feel worthwhile. So it is, too, with the therapist. To help group patients through the struggle for individuation, the therapist has to be able to accept attack without becoming vengeful. The therapist must find gratification in the expanding independence of patients and find the patients' growing ability to challenge and to stand on their own feet more rewarding than continued overestimation of and submission to the leader. What we see when patients reach the individuation-strength-power phase are concomitant, small-scale revolutions. Skillful therapists, those who understand the desirable sequences in individual and group development and have overcome countertransferences to the challenges and attacks that often accompany individuation, comprehend that palace revolutions are not an attempt to boycott treatment. Indeed, they con-stitute important forward thrusts that introduce and promise develop-menal progress. Revolutions in group therapy, unless they are motivated merely by blind hatred and destructiveness, are necessary stages of human growth. In the course of a small revolution the individual prepares and partly sets up his autonomy, his emancipation from the hangover of parental coercion, and his eventual individuation. At some period during the life of a group every patient-follower has to become a rebel.

THE IMPORTANT DIFFERENTIATION BETWEEN TWO KINDS OF ANGER

The many states of anger and rage that are displayed in therapy groups have vastly divergent genetic origins and functions. To focus on just two important kinds, the first type can be called "tantrum anger." Anger designed to get attention, it is experienced by patients who are rooted in a narcissistic transference. If they are borderline or schizophrenic, they want exclusive attention and are often ready to destroy anyone who blocks their road to the focal therapist-maternal figure. Generally these patients are stuck for a long time in the narcissistic phase and then later in the inclusion phase. The tantrum anger is also felt fairly regularly by so-called neurotic patients during the inclusion phase. They, too, wish to get special attention, as a rule primarily from the therapist, and they still hold on to a belief in their own omnipotence and become insulted when they are frustrated. In terms of Berglerian ideas about masochism (Bergler, 1959), these patients get angry when the therapist thwarts them or seems to thwart them, and then either turn their rage against themselves or else have an investment in provoking the therapist so that his or her supposed monstrous indifference and callousness become apparent. At times, groups may help such tantrum-harboring individuals to shield their rage behind apparent benevolence toward the leader (Glatzer, 1965).

The second type of anger with which we are concerned in the context of individuation may be called the "opposition anger." It is genetically anchored in the childhood resentment against parents who tampered with the little boy's or girl's attempts to try out autonomous moves, to start the separation from the parent, to lay the groundwork for individuation. In group therapy such angers tend to be expressed rather than suppressed. They differ from the tantrum angers because they do not blow over quickly but are tenacious and protractedly expressed over a period of time. The attacks and criticisms made by group members in the "power" or "strength" phase are often quite rationally substantiated. The patient who wants to "set himself up in an emotional business of his own," as indeed he should, usually manages to gripe about flows in treatment and deficits of the therapist that can be observed by other members and have a quality of realness. If the tantrum rages connected with the narcissistic transference and the inclusion phase have a masochistic flavor, then the opposition rages have a paranoid cast to them.

Group therapists owe it to their work to make differential distinctions between the tantrum, "I-want-everything" rage and the opposition, "My anger helps me to fight authority better," rage. Though most patients frequently shift from one form of anger to another, making discriminations sometimes difficult, the diagnostic task is essential, for each anger calls for different understanding, for different interpretation, and different corrective experiences. In the long run, the tantrum rage-besieged patient will have to learn to accept frustration as a part of life. When this patient moves toward individuation and uses anger in order to fortify him in the struggle with authority, his anger has to be interpreted as an ego device designed to assist the tension-creating struggle for autonomy. The anger has to be respected and at times even encouraged.

As an example, a group of eight patients became more belligerent in the second year of treatment. In particular, five of the members, three men and two women, after criticizing lovers or mates, engaged in angry outbursts against the therapist. The three other group members were protective of the therapist, to whose benevolence they still clung. Occasionally, two or three of the belligerent members became submissive and tried to fall back on methods of ingratiation with the therapist. Most of the therapeutic interpretations were very brief, merely emphasizing the rebellious group members' motivation for the attack, namely, to get distance and independence from the leader with whom they had previously been much involved.

Responding to doubts, criticisms, attacks, and distortions launched for the purpose of supporting the individual's and the group's struggle for autonomy, individuation, and growing independence from the leader is of little or no therapeutic value to the patients if the external realities of the situation are stressed. To a patient who attacks because that is his admission ticket to personal independence, it matters little whether he has hit accurately on the actual or visible defects of the therapist. What counts above all is that this patient wants to get out of the nest, to rid himself of the danger of fusion, and he is using hostility and criticism as a means to become independent. Group members who seek individuation need not be asked to weigh the *content* of their complaints but the *process*. The process is to become separated, individuated, to acquire strength, to try out one's own wings. What is at first accomplished through frequently unwarranted though fairly reasoned attack is later achieved through genuine strength.

CONCLUSIONS

In conclusion, patients who have severe paranoid leanings and are borderline cases or schizophrenics with paranoid ideas of persecution make therapeutic work in the "power-strength" phase, where individuation is the chief concern, often difficult. If such patients are included in groups—I myself do accept one or two such personalities in groups of neurotics with character disorders—one has to expect that their attacks will become contagious when others strike out for individuation and use hostility for the sake of personal support against authority. When other, not strikingly paranoid, group members fight because of the fortification they experience from their more outrightly paranoid colleagues, it has to be pointed out that the newcomers to the individuation struggle are not sailing under their own flags. At times, if borderline and schizophrenic group members become too abusive of one another, of the therapist, or of the group method, it is necessary to ask them to leave the group unless rage can be modified and controlled to a degree commensurate with the group's tension tolerance. On the three occasions in the past twenty years when I asked a patient who, aware of slips made by the therapist or group member, abused the privilege of criticizing rather than using it, to leave the group, the results were good. The group consolidated. I was told later by two of the three patients that the insistence that they leave helped them to use other treatment situations constructively.

REFERENCES

BERGLER, E. (1959) The Basic Neurosis. New York: Grune & Stratton.
EISENBUD, R. J. (1967) Masochism Revisited. Psychoanal. Rev., 53:520-532.
ERIKSON, E. H. (1968) Identity, Youth and Crisis. New York: Norton.
GLATZER, H. (1965) Aspects of Transference in Group Psychotherapy. This Journal, 15:167-187.
KAPLAN, S. R. (1967) Therapy Groups and Training Groups. This Journal, 17:473-503.
MAHLER, M. S. (1968) On Human Symbiosis and the Vicissitudes of Individuation. New York: International Universities Press.
ORMONT, L. R. (1969) Acting in and the Therapeutic Contract in Group Psychoanalysis. This Journal, 19:420-432.
SCHEIDLINGER, S. (1955) The Concept of Identification in Group Psychotherapy. Amer. J. Psychother., 9:661-672.
———— (1964) Identification, the Sense of Belonging and of Identity in Small Groups. This Journal, 14:291-306.
SCHUTZ, W. C. (1958) Firo. New York: Rinehart.

Area I—Section C
NEW APPROACHES

In the past five years, three new approaches to group therapy—Gestalt therapy, Transactional Analysis, and therapeutic techniques derived from learning theory—have generated a great deal of enthusiasm among therapists and patients alike. However, the grounds for this enthusiasm appear to be primarily experiential, rather than based on scientific evidence. For although they are conceptually attractive, these new approaches do not represent startling theoretical innovations; rather, they are extensions and adaptations of traditional theoretical models. Nor can this enthusiasm be attributed to the greater efficacy of these approaches, for evaluative studies of their clinical effects, with the exception of behavior therapy, are still forthcoming.

It may be speculated, however, that the great interest engendered by these approaches stems from the fact that they often provide immediate rewards for the patient, as well as for the therapist who employs these techniques. Compared with traditional group treatment methods, the new modalities require greater activity on the part of therapist and patient, and their participation in dramatic and satisfying emotional experiences. In general, therapists are pleased with the conceptual foundations of these modalities, comfortable in their new roles, and, of course, their enthusiasm is due, in no small measure, to the favorable responses they have evoked from their patients.

This section includes original contributions on Gestalt or experiential therapy, on TA, and on the use of behavior therapy in groups. These papers describe recent innovations in each of these respective models, and assume some familiarity with these basic premises. Accordingly, for the edification of those readers who have a limited knowledge of these newer systems, brief synopses of the salient concepts of personality and psychopathology and the therapeutic principles of each of these approaches are presented below. In addition, contrasts and similarities are also discussed.

GESTALT THERAPY

Concept of Personality

Gestalt therapy, in contrast to psychoanalysis, is not based on a highly complex structural concept of personality. Psychic functioning is conceived of as dynamic process which consists of the continuous formation and destruction of "gestalten." A "gestalt," or configuration, is a theoretical construct which postulates that awareness of a need or wish leads to the formation of a perceptual and cognitive field which contains the elements necessary for gratification of the need. Once a particular need (or wish) has been fulfilled, its gestalt is destroyed and another gestalt is permitted to emerge. To illustrate, obtaining a drink of water destroys the drinker's thirst gestalt, with its memories and images of the kitchen, water tap, the shelf where glasses are kept, etc., and a new gestalt, subserving the wish to socialize, for example, or to finish work, achieves prominence. Gestalt formation is considered to be an inherent property of the CNS which mediates the organism's growth and development and its interactions with the environment.

Concept of Psychopathology

In essence, psychopathology is viewed as a disturbance of this dynamic process. More specifically, the concept of phobic avoidance is central to the Gestalt model of pathogenesis. Thus the major precipitating factor in mental illness is the compulsion to "avoid" crucial aspects of the self—wishes, feelings, thoughts—or to actively exclude these from conscious perception because they are sources of pain and/or fear. The fact that such disconnected psychic elements are not available for gestalt formation (and gratification) means that some areas of experience have never been integrated into the personality and mastered. Consequent unresolved conflicts and resentments exert powerful and deleterious effects on the individual and constrict his functioning. Accordingly, the psychic elements the individual has sought to avoid, which underlie his conflicts, are termed "unfinished business," which constitutes a core concept in Gestalt therapy.

Therapeutic Techniques

It is the aim of Gestalt therapy to enable the patient to consciously experience previously avoided thoughts, feelings, and sensations, i.e., to finish his "unfinished business," and thereby promote impulse control, autonomy, integration, and growth. Gestalt therapists contend that the mere conscious experiencing of these excluded aspects of the personality will, in itself, result in conflict resolution and the attainment of psychic "freedom." Thus therapeutic emphasis is on the "here and now," i.e., on fostering the patient's conscious perception of on-going sensations and body states, fantasies, and emotions. Patients are encouraged to "stay with" these emerging perceptions, i.e., to permit themselves to perceive and experience unpleasant sensations, confusion, and the pull of conflicting urges. Further, they are urged to identify with and take responsibility for these aspects of themselves. The paper prepared by Simkin for inclusion in this section illustrates one aspect of this approach, specifically, the Gestalt use of dreams to implement its essential treatment goals. Briefly, the therapist asks the patient to "be" all the elements of his dream, as a means of fostering his awareness of previously unperceived aspects of his self.

The Gestalt techniques are considered by many to be highly effective in facilitating conflict resolution and in dealing with defenses and resistances, and many individual as well as group therapists have incorporated various Gestalt methods into their therapeutic armamentaria.

Comparison with Other Approaches

For the most part, the methods used by the psychoanalyst are manifestly different from those employed by the Gestalt therapist, who does not encourage his patient to recall early childhood experiences or to verbalize his associations. Rather, the Gestalt therapist seeks to foster perception of current experiences, and his techniques to this end may include such dramatic tactics as encouraging the patient to talk to different aspects of his self, or sharing his fantasies with the patient.

At the same time, however, the psychoanalytic and Gestalt approaches are also similar in certain important respects. Most importantly, the concept that unconscious psychic elements are pathogenic is central to both systems, and it is the central aim of both to make the patient conscious of these unconscious elements. On the other hand, they contrast sharply in their concepts of the nature of the material which has been repressed or "avoided," and also in the methods used to make such material accessible to consciousness. Ruth Cohn, who has had extensive experience in the use of both analytic and experiential methods, compares these approaches and delineates their essential differences and similarities in her paper in this section.

There are interesting similarities between Gestalt and the learning approaches as well. From the standpoint of the behaviorist, the non-perception of unpleasant experiences which Gestalt therapists believe to be the source of conflict—and mental illness—has been reinforced by the avoidance of pain. Hence, depending on the particular techniques he uses, it is the task of the therapist to expose the patient to such phobic material in the non-threatening "here and now," or have him experience these previously frightening (and avoided) situations in fantasy in order to "desensitize" him.

Thus, Gestalt therapy is similar to other systems in many respects, but a final feature that distinguishes it from other approaches and makes it attractive to many workers in the field is its positive direction and goals. Gestalt therapists do not focus exclusively on the treatment of psychopathology; they also work to develop the positive elements of the patient's personality—his sensory awareness, and his capacity for growth and joy.

Group Applications

The focus in Gestalt therapy is clearly on the individual. However, the method is used almost exclusively in groups. As originally conceptualized by Perls, the group acts spontaneously to choose a specific patient for the therapist to work with at a particular time, and seems to heighten the intensity of the individual's experience. Further, as the therapist works with one patient, other members of the group usually find that certain aspects of the transaction mirror their own life experiences and problems, and they also "learn" in this fashion.*

However, some workers have attempted to make more deliberate use of group process to implement experiential therapeutic goals. In this section, Alger describes his innovative use of video tape to heighten the impact of the therapeutic experience and make it more vivid, and to stimulate group interaction and social feedback which help the patient to work through his new experiences.

In the search for techniques to augment the central goal of treatment, i.e., enhanced self-awareness, experiential therapists are also experimenting with such procedures as nudity, revelations of a personal nature by the therapist, sexual activity, etc., which have given rise to considerable controversy. In her paper in this section, Mintz discusses the theoretical issues involved in one such method which advocates physical contact among group members.

---

* For further information about the Gestalt method the reader is referred to "Gestalt Therapy Verbatim" by F. Perls. Real People Press, Lafayette, Cal., 1969.

According to Eric Berne, its originator, TA encompasses a systematic theory of personality and psychopathology, and an active treatment method derived from these theoretical constructs.

Concept of Personality

The TA model of personality is similar to that postulated by psychoanalytic theory in that it makes comparable topographic and structural assumptions concerning the human psyche. There is a greater emphasis, however, on the patient's characteristic interpersonal transactions, and the theoretical constructs that describe personality seem more immediately related to the patient's experiences and perceptions.

According to TA, the psyche is comprised of three phenomenologically distinct "ego" states which gain ascendency in different situations and which find expression in characteristic behavior patterns. These ego states have been labeled the emotionally immature child (C), the judgmental parent (P), and the rational adult (A).

Concept of Psychopathology and Therapeutic Techniques

Pathological behavior is said to result from various aberrations of the three ego states, which cause their inappropriate emergence, and result in behavior that is destructive to the patient. The characteristic expressions of the patient's ego states can be deduced from the nature of his interactions with the therapist and with members of the group, and the clarification and conscious control of these expressions constitutes the "structural analysis" phase of treatment. The goal of this initial phase of treatment is to put the patient's "rational adult" in charge, so to speak, and so motivate him to participate in the transactional phase of treatment during which his pathological transactions and life strategies are analyzed.

Central to the TA theory of psychopathology is the concept of unconscious compliance with early parental wishes or "injunctions" ("witch messages"). In essence, transactional analysts contend that the patient structures his life so that it will follow a "script" which is consistent with the early parental injunctions, and repeatedly engages in various transactional strategies, such as the familiar "games people play," to support —and maintain—this "script." The second phase of TA is designed to foster the patient's conscious awareness of these transactions, and also of his life script, and thereby bring these under the control of his Adult.

Comparison with Other Approaches

TA shares with psychoanalysis, and also with Gestalt therapy, the central thesis that aspects of the self that are unconscious are pathogenic; therefore, it is the task of therapy to bring these unconscious psychic elements to consciousness. As is true of psychoanalysis, TA relies on insight and understanding to facilitate changes in behavior. In contrast to psychoanalysis, however, TA places relatively greater emphasis on the analysis of current transactional patterns and compliance with the parents' unconscious injunctions, of which the parents as well as the patient are unaware.

In addition, the TA concept of the "strokes" and "stamps" that reward pathological behavior patterns, and so serve to maintain them, is analogous to the behaviorist concept of "reinforcement." Like behavior therapy, TA attempts to structure the therapeutic situation so that no "reward" for immature behavior is forthcoming. On the other hand, unlike the behavior therapist, the transactional analyst also relies on the patient's intellectual recognition of the reinforcement contingencies for behavioral change.

Group Applications

TA was initially developed as a group technique; analysis of the patient's behavior within that setting facilitates identification of his underlying ego state, the nature of the games he plays, and his life script. The group is also used experientially to foster the patient's vivid experience of his ego states and "strokes," and, finally, the TA group is structured as a learning opportunity where new transactional patterns are tried and reinforced.

Robert Goulding—a student of Berne's—has extended and refined TA theory. His paper in this section deals with the important question of the mechanism by which a parental wish is translated—in *some instances*—into a life-long pattern of compliant behavior which is often highly destructive to the individual. Goulding believes that the crucial variable is an active decision, made early in life, to comply with the parental injunction. Accordingly, he helps the patient to "write" a new life script by helping him to make a re-decision, motivated by his healthy desire to foster his own best interests, rather than his fear of parental disapproval, etc.*

---

* Berne's book, *Transactional Analysis in Psychotherapy*, contains a comprehensive description of TA methods. Grove Press, New York, 1961.

BEHAVIOR THERAPY

Behavior therapy differs sharply from psychoanalysis, TA, and Gestalt therapy in that it makes no assumptions about personality structure. In addition it does not rely for its therapeutic results on bringing unconscious material into awareness.

Concept of Psychopathology

The various techniques for the modification of human behavior subsumed under this approach are based on the theoretically attractive and logical assumption that many types of pathological behavior are learned, and can therefore be learned, or modified. Neurotic symptoms, including phobias, sexual dysfunction, compulsive behavior, obsessions, inhibitions, etc., as well as pathological modes of relating to others, e.g., excessive timidity and submissiveness, or competitiveness and aggression, can be attributed to the individual's failure to acquire appropriate responses or to his having learned maladaptive reactions. Furthermore, although it is a source of pain and discomfort, pathological behavior persists, because it is reinforced, overtly or covertly, or, in the case of phobias, because avoidance of the phobic object or situation prevents the possible extinction of the phobia.

Therapeutic Techniques

The behavior therapist assesses each unit of behavior that needs to be modified in terms of its reinforcement or extinction contingencies and formulates his treatment plan accordingly. Specific therapeutic strategies are designed to implement various goals. More precisely, the therapist may seek to eliminate maladaptive responses, such as fear, which mediate neurotic behavior; remove the rewards from and, in certain instances, "punish" undesirable instrumental behavior; or he may attempt to establish and reinforce alternate more adaptive forms of behavior. Many ingenious and effective techniques for the modification of behavior, based on such learning principles, have been devised. Thus, for example, the fact that learning can take place in fantasy has been exploited in the desensitization techniques which employ imagery; in the treatment of psychophysiological disorders, sensory feedback devices are being developed to teach patients to control visceral responses, such as heart beat and blood pressure; and aversive contingencies are being used to treat alcoholism and sexual problems.

Group Applications

The learning potentials inherent in group and family settings are currently being explored. Potentially useful variables for behavior modification in these settings include the strongly reinforcing effects of social approval, on the one hand, and the adverse effects of rejection and criticism, on the other. Group settings also make available models for appropriate behavior and provides the opportunity for "in-vivo" desensitization or extinction of fears of assertion, of sexual impulses, authority, etc.

Fensterheim has prepared a paper for inclusion in this section on his use of groups in "assertive training," a technique which has not been described hitherto in the literature. To state his thesis briefly, Fensterheim contends that excessive timidity and failure to assert oneself have wide deleterious psychic ramifications in terms of constricting the patient's self-concept, productivity, and interpersonal relationships. His technique entails the use of certain group processes to foster rapid acquisition of appropriate assertive behavior patterns.*

SUGGESTED CROSS-REFERENCES

Additional data on the current increasing use of learning theory and behavior therapy in group and family modalities may be found in Ferber and Ranz's paper on setting reachable goals and assigning workable tasks in family therapy, contained in Area II, which also contains a paper on behavioral approaches in family and marital therapy by Lieberman, as well as in Stuart's description of the use of operant conditioning techniques in the treatment of marital discord in Area III. Area III on Marriage and Sex also includes a paper by Masters and Johnson describing the rapid treatment of sexual dysfunction. Although not explicitly formulated in behavioral terms, the technique used by these workers is consistent with behavioral principles inasmuch as it fosters mutual reinforcement of desirable sexual responses and the opportunity to extinguish inhibiting sexual attitudes. The paper by Birk *et al.* in Area IV describes a method of treating homosexual men which combines group and behavior therapy.

Finally, experiential techniques designed to foster self-awareness are extensively employed in sensitivity, encounter and marathon groups. These small group phenomena are described below, in Section I-D.

H.S.K.

C.J.S.

---

* A truly comprehensive volume on the behavior therapies has not yet been published. However, further information on this subject may be found in J. Wolpe's *The Practice of Behavior Therapy* (Pergamon Press, Elmsford, N. Y., 1969), and A. T. Yates' *Principles and Practice of Behavior Therapy* (Wiley, New York, 1970).

7

PSYCHOANALYTIC OR EXPERIENTIAL GROUP PSYCHOTHERAPY: A FALSE DICHOTOMY

Ruth C. Cohn

Director, Workshop-Institute for Learning-Living (New York City)

Often a young group therapist will speak to me of a personal dilemma engendered by having more than one supervisor. For example, one supervisor may say to him: "If you hide, how do you expect your patients to dare to become and be themselves? You have a right to your feelings as a human being; and these feelings will help patients learn to be authentic individuals, unashamed of their thoughts and emotions." The second supervisor might say the opposite: "You can't expect to help your patients with their problems while you are burdening them with your own; they have a right to your full attention. Check your own feelings silently and discover whether they are induced by the patient's pathology or by your own unresolved problems, and speak only when reasonably certain this is purely in the patient's interest."

I would like to share with you my own viewpoint with regard to this controversy within our profession. This is my hypothesis: All correct therapeutic interventions initiate curative processes which affect the patient's total personality. This occurs when the intervening stimulus facilitates the patient's recognition of any significant part of important personal reality that he was previously unaware of or detached from. Such curative processes occur when the patient receives messages that help him to: 1) repair distortions in his perceptual and cognitive world,

Reprinted from THE PSYCHOANALYTIC REVIEW, Vol. 56, No. 3, 1969, pp. 333-345.

2) add emotional content to previously deprived or depleted personality areas, 3) free physical mobility from prior rigidity.

While therapists offer differing stimuli with greater or lesser emphasis on each of these three levels according to their various orientations and personalities, the patient's innate tendency toward health will expand the curative process so as to affect his total organism. Such processes may be likened to giving injections to a physically ill patient; almost regardless of where the drugs enter the body, the total organism will be affected through the therapeutic intervention.

I believe that the psychotherapeutic process can be initiated by a variety of interventions, such as the use of interpretation to promote insight or a realistic encounter geared toward a curative experience. It may, for instance, be promoted by a therapeutically oriented total here-and-now experience, by an analytic weaving of threads between the past and present, or by emphasis on values, future goals, or working directly with body defenses.

Individual preferences do not relieve us from searching for and refining optimally effective methods and professional skills. We have to investigate, explore and increase our knowledge as to what techniques may be most helpful to a given patient at a specific time. Consideration must be given to the patient, the therapist, and to the methods in all their intricate specificities and variant conditions. Each patient has permanent as well as temporary *patterns of receptivity to therapeutic interventions,* which are determined by his constitution, by his character, his immediate energy level, acute motivations, tensions, etc. Correspondingly, each therapist has typical patterns of activity and response, specific trained skills and variant convictions in different periods of his life, as well as moods of the hour. Analysts may conceptualize patterns within the framework of libidinal cathexis, transference matrix and resistance, while experientialists may define the same phenomena as relating to growth potential, inauthenticity of encounter, and avoidance patterns. *The therapist's task is to strive towards establishing procedures which aim at meeting up with the patient's optimal receptivity and to recognize how he can best function in the patient's interest.*

My hypothesis is that the patient's innate growth potential responds positively to the recognition of any important factor of his personal reality. Therefore the therapist's acceptance of the patient's reality initiates a fluid curative process. If the therapist misconceives an important facet of the patient's reality, an obstacle to the curative process occurs. Even such error, however, is not fatal to the therapeutic process if the patient has achieved an autonomy level which allows him to react positively to a negative stimulus.

"Match or Miss" interventions connote the therapist's skill at recognizing the patient's receptivity and reality. The matching intervention presupposes the therapists' ability to recognize health as well as pathology, and to accurately gauge the patient's optimal receptivity and energy level at any given moment. The point in time when such recognition occurs may be accompanied by an "aha" experience, a glow of heightened awareness, or just a fleeting surprise that a disagreeable head or neck tension has disappeared. The "miss" intervention is generally (although not always) countertherapeutic. It may occur through faulty communication processes, which miss the patient's reality on any one level or through failure to recognize the patient's limitations on psychological or somatic levels.

I then perceive the curative process in therapy as a fluid intrapsychosomatic event which is derived from an interactional here-and-now experience and involves the totality of the there-and-then of past and future. It proceeds towards a new here-and-now which has integrated the therapeutic stimulus and process of the recent therapeutic event. Such stimulus is derived from an interactional process between the patient, therapist(s) and/or a group.

CASE EXAMPLE: THE SAME CASE IN TWO GROUP THERAPY SETTINGS

I would like you to follow me on an imaginary trip with a patient, Dina, into the group therapy sessions of Dr. Allen Ashley (analytically-oriented group therapy) and Dr. Eric Emory (experiential group therapy). Let us follow Dina (a real person) as she interacts with these two therapists and their groups (who are also real). However, for the sake of essential rather than factual truth, let us take poetic license and create two episodes which occur simultaneously.

Dina is the patient on whom I would like you to focus your attention. She is 35 years old, married and has one two-year-old child. She speaks in a barely audible voice without intonation whenever she talks about herself at any length. But she is capable of sounding vigorous and vivacious when speaking about others. Her facial expression, accordingly, is either masklike and dead or quite animated.

(In this episode, all italicized material relates to the *thoughts* of therapist and patient.)

PSYCHOANALYTIC GROUP THERAPY

Dina: (*I must force myself to talk . . . I feel so terrible . . . it's difficult . . . but I have to push myself . . .*) Bob . . . my husband . . . last night again he came home late . . . I was up . . . the baby had just gotten up for a glass of water and when the door opened I tried to smile and act casual . . . not as if I was hurt. (*They also know why he was out . . . he must have another woman . . .*) He was furious with me and walked out of the kitchen (*Maybe he's jealous of the baby . . . but I can't help that—I won't neglect him.*) Afterwards, in bed . . . he turned to the wall . . . and I cried all night. (*I need his body next to mine . . . I need to cuddle up . . . I don't want to tell this to the group.*) I just can't help being so depressed when he comes home late.

Sharon: Oh, why don't you break it off . . . get rid of him. You have no idea how much better off I am since I separated from my husband. He used to run around with women like that . . .

Dina: (*Sharon doesn't understand . . . I can't be without Bob . . . I love him . . . being next to him . . . and I need him for Freddy . . . maybe I'm not bright enough for him, or sexy enough and he found someone better.*)

Craig: You know, I don't blame him a bit. If I had to put up with Dina's whining and nagging, I wouldn't bother to come home either. Blah blah blah . . . all the time . . . nothing the poor guy ever does is right . . . and that crying voice . . . just like my mother . . . she just keeps going on and on . . .

Dina: (*I feel tight . . . my stomach . . . throat . . . choking . . . don't move, it hurts too much . . . Craig hurts . . . what did he say? I don't know what he said.*)

Jane: Craig, how can you be so cruel? Don't you hear how upset Dina is . . . she can hardly talk.

Craig: Ah! You're another one to talk . . . another ball breaker . . . you, Dina, Sharon . . . you're all experts in the art.

Dina: (*Why doesn't Dr. Ashley say something . . . help . . . he is silent . . . he must feel the same way as Craig about me . . . what did Craig say?*)

Morty: I can't see this at all, Craig . . . I'd be upset too if my wife came home late every night . . . but . . . there's something about Dina's voice . . . that low voice . . . you have to strain. I want to listen and I can't.

Dina: (*Morty is nice . . . Now I remember what Craig said . . . he accused me of nagging Bob.*)

Jane: Whenever Dina speaks, I feel like I shouldn't take up time with my stupid problems . . . her's are so much worse . . .

Dina: (*Oh, Jane . . . I'm sorry . . . she needs Dr. Ashley more than I do and I take up all the time . . . Damn, I need him so—right now and he just sits there.*)

Dr. Ashley: (*Dina's crying. She looks confused . . . bewildered . . . it's better than that whining . . . I can't stand that voice . . . it gets on my nerves . . . sickening masochism . . . guilt as a defense. If only she fought people openly . . . I'll be cautious.*) You seem to be close to tears. Dina, I wonder what is going through your mind.

Dina: I feel awful . . . just awful . . . I think Bob feels . . . you know . . . like Craig said. And it's my fault. If I were more cheerful . . . if I could smile like Jane . . . my little sister is that way, always smiling even when it hurts . . . and I can't and I know Bob hates it.

Dr. Ashley: (*Her conscious guilt acts as a defense against showing any aggression.*) You think it's all your fault?

Dina: I know it is and I don't really feel like talking here because (*because they'll jump on me*) . . . because I get on everyone's nerves.

Dr. Ashley: (*Maybe she does . . . she often gets on mine.*) Craig was the only one who said you get on his nerves. You seem to have a radar system for negative judgments . . . you always hear only the negative.

Dina: (*What is he saying? . . . can't think . . . speak somebody! . . . please . . . I can't talk.*)

Dr. Ashley: (*I guess she went blank . . . heard me negatively, too . . . maybe I can help her see where this defense comes from . . .*) I wonder why you go blank now . . . what of your childhood comes to your mind with regard to "negative judgments"?

Dina: (*Nothing . . . nothing . . . they're going to bed next door . . . Mummy, Daddy . . . radar station for the negative . . .*) No . . . nothing . . . They . . . my parents . . . they just didn't pay any attention to me . . . I had to be quiet when Daddy came home . . . except for when I had good report cards. I had to be quiet . . . always . . . when my parents went to sleep I had to whisper to my dolls so they wouldn't hear me . . . and I couldn't wake Sis up . . .

Dr. Ashley: Perhaps if your dolls could speak, they would tell us how angry you were at your parents for having to be quiet, for having to give so much to your sister and to them. And how you lost your voice.

Jane: Dina, your voice was loud just before . . . I wonder why.

Dina: (*Damn it . . . why does she interrupt? . . . blank . . .*) I didn't notice my voice.

Sharon: Dina is being a good girl . . . answering all of Dr. Ashley's questions.

Craig: I'm glad he's giving it to her . . . she needs to be told plenty . . .

Dr. Ashley: (*I gave her an important interpretation . . . a connection from the hostility she knew about and told to her dolls to her withholding aggression now . . . to Craig, Jane, Bob . . . I guess me, too . . . her choked voice . . . I let it rest at that and go to Craig; he's so blind to his hatred and is setting me up as his male ideal, not mine . . .*) Craig, you really have it in for Dina . . . for Sharon and Jane, too . . . they must do something to your system . . .

Craig: You bet they do!

(Later that evening at home)

Dina: (*Dr. Ashley doesn't like me as much as Jane or Craig . . . he only gave me such a short time and he stayed with Craig all evening. I know he doesn't really like me but he never says so. He must really, really hate me . . . and Bob, he can't stand me either . . . I don't care. No, I do care. Why doesn't Dr. Ashley stay with me? I hate him . . . . I hate him . . . I feel like smashing my fist on his bald head . . . How can that be? I'm not that way . . . Freddy loves me . . . my dolls come to my head . . . they used to love me, too . . . that's funny . . . now I talk to myself as I did to Irmie and Edith, my dolls . . . and they liked me . . . even when I thought of letting the faucet run over and drown everybody, the whole house except me and Irmie and Edith . . . I'm really funny . . . if I listened to myself like my dolls did . . . I'd like me. Funny . . . I like that thought: "I'd like me. I'd like myself." Go ahead, Dr. Ashley . . . just ignore me . . . hate me . . . see how much I care! I hate you all . . . that's a good one . . . "my dolls like me and I like me and I hate you" My head feels good now.*) Bob, did I ever tell you that I used to sing? That was before I got these lousy headaches . . . when I was still in school . . . I was the best singer . . .

Bob: No, I didn't know that . . . but I know you've got a great voice . . . I like your voice when you sing.

In this brief episode, Dr. Ashley intended to lead Dina toward the recognition of her repressed hostility which manifested itself in her masochistic way of torturing Bob by her as-if-crying reproaches, and torturing the group and analyst by her manner of speech. The method used here is: 1) professional attitude—the therapist speaks to and about the patient without revealing his own experiences; 2) leading questions which go along with Dina's resistance of guilt feelings defending against hostility

("You think it is all your fault?") ; 3) leading questions oriented toward important memories; 4) interpretation of Dina's repressed anger.

Although the analyst had promoted a process of insight into the dynamics of repressed hostility, Dina was emotionally preoccupied with the feeling that Dr. Ashley did not like her. This feeling represented a mixture of transference illusion and a perception of Dr. Ashley's unexpressed annoyance which she interpreted into the transference connection of his disliking her. This kept her awake and worried. Her awareness of her own hatred for Dr. Ashley's "disliking" her and preferring 'other children" fused with the memory of her revealing her rage about her parents to her dolls and their successor, the husband, and the baby, Freddy. This heightened awareness deepened into the experience of a recognition, here manifested with an awakening sense of humor and an ability to communicate with Bob on a nonmasochistic level.

EXPERIENTIAL GROUP THERAPY

Dina: (*I must force myself to talk . . . I feel so terrible . . . it's difficult but I have to push myself.*) Bob . . . my husband . . . last night again he came home late . . . I was up . . . the baby had just gotten up for a glass of water and when the door opened I tried to smile and act casual . . .

Dr. Eric Emory: Please speak louder! Do you smile when you are angry?

Dina: (*Push . . . voice choked . . . I can't . . . I can't talk louder.*) I don't want to upset Freddy with our problems.

Morty: You know that can't be done . . . not upset our children . . .

Dina: (*I'm not going to let Freddy suffer like I did, Morty doesn't understand . . . he hasn't got any children.*)

Craig: What a phony! She is the phoniest.

Dina: (*What did he say? I can't understand . . . he's angry . . .*)

Sharon: Craig's at it again . . . ignore him, Dina. So what happened between you and Bob?

Dina: He was . . . just furious . . . when he got into bed, he turned to the wall . . . (*I can't tell them this. I can't stand sleeping alone.*)

Eric: (*I feel irritated, annoyed.*) Dina, I really can't hear you without straining a lot . . . I feel irritated now.

Jane: It's difficult to hear her . . . but I understand . . . she's choked up . . . it's painful to talk about it.

Sharon: So maybe it wouldn't kill you to strain a little, Eric . . . After all, you're not having her troubles.

Eric: I don't want to strain. Dina can talk louder.

Dina: (*I want Eric to listen . . . to help . . . and Eric looks so pleased with himself . . . he doesn't care about me . . . why should he?*)

Jane: You should stay with Dina, Eric . . . really you should.

Eric: (*Jane plays Dina's voice.*) What troubles you, Jane?

Jane: I think Dina needs you now and you should stay with her.

Eric: I don't want your "shoulds." I don't need them. I want to stay with you now. Speak for yourself, Jane!

Jane: My problems are not big like Dina's. They don't involve a husband and child.

Sharon: Right! My problems were cut in half the day I left Mike. I keep telling Dina she should get rid of Bob . . .

Dina: (*Eric doesn't care about me, he doesn't like me. What's wrong with me? He's so nice to everyone else.*) Sharon, I can't leave Bob. Everything that's happened is my fault. If I were cheerful and agreeable like Jane, Bob might come home on time.

Morty: You don't know what you really feel, Dina. You whisper when you talk, and you want to smile when you're hurt or angry.

Dina: (*Morty confuses me . . . I feel like crying . . . I don't want them to know.*)

Eric: What is it, Dina?

Dina: Nothing . . . go on to someone else.

Eric: You look as if you're crying.

Dina: (*I won't.*) No.

Jane: The group isn't Freddy. He is little. But we can take it.

Dina: I don't want to cry here . . . I cry all the time when I'm alone . . . last night . . . all night.

Eric: An image flashed through my mind just now . . . the huge ocean . . . with just one little boat . . . way out . . .

Dina: (crying) (*I'm in that boat . . . all alone.*) Nobody listens . . . they never listen . . . when you need someone . . . nobody is ever there . . . you, Eric, you don't care either, with your pleased self-adoring smile on your face . . . you never, never care . . . all you care about is the money you take home to your wife.

Eric: Yes, Dina, I do care about my wife and my money. But I care about you too. And your rage hit me right now. It hurts. But now you speak for real and I can hear you.

Dina: No, you don't. You never do.

Eric: You can say this now. I feel relieved.

Craig: She thinks you are as phony as she is.

Eric: For heaven's sake, Craig, can't you see when someone is real?

Craig: You must know that she is phony.

Eric: I wonder if there isn't more to you, Craig, than this one-way track.

Dina: (*There he is again . . . he takes on Craig . . . I shouldn't feel so jealous . . . but he always does it . . . he always drops me . . .*)

(*Later that evening at home*)

Dina: (*I just don't get Eric . . . I got so furious . . . he always listens to everyone but me. I guess I do talk in a low voice . . . but Jane always manages to hear me. He did look sad though . . . and he helped me cry . . . the boat . . . I am in a boat . . . far away, Mummy and Daddy in their bedroom, that's when I used to talk to my dolls. I was so lonesome I told them how I felt about Sis getting everything . . . she was just like Jane, so concerned and cheerful and sweet . . . no, but maybe they didn't really care about her either, she says so, they were too egotistical, money, money, money, that's all they ever talked about and screamed at each other for. Mummy complained she couldn't buy clothes for us . . . I didn't want any clothes . . . All I wanted was for them to stop screaming . . . Egotistic? I never thought of that . . . like Eric, money, money . . . he doesn't want to "strain" himself for me, just wants money, who cares . . . I don't want to talk to him. No, that's not true. I say he doesn't want to listen but I really don't want him to know how I feel. When I screamed at him, I felt better though . . . and he said he did . . . Maybe I should have told my parents, they might have listened and understood, about my not wanting them to scream, not wanting clothes . . .*) Bob, I wonder . . . no . . . I'd like to know how you felt when you came home last night.

Bob: Fine, until I got a look at that expression on your face. I was really sorry to be late again, but you looked as if you didn't give a damn about the reason . . . so I just didn't feel like explaining.

Dina: I feel so unsure . . . about your loving me.

Bob: This is the one thing I can't stand about you—it hurts me when you don't trust me.

Eric (therapist) openly stated his needs. He stressed what was comfortable for him together with his thoughts, imagery and feelings directed toward Dina (and the other group members). This openness was used by Eric as a major tool for stimulating the curative process. He offered Dina, by his frank expressions, the opportunity to give vent to her own impotent rage. Dina, whose life history indicated that she was most creative in solitude, reconstructed the group process later on in her mind and made meaningful connections from the therapeutic session to her childhood. She pondered about Eric's seeming callousness, which appeared inconsistent with his relatedness to her and his empathic imagery. From there, Dina was able to consider her parents' "egocentricity" in the light of their marital problems and relatedness to their children. She was now on the way toward the recognition of her own "egoistic" magic formula: "Parents and therapists must live for their children and patients, and must understand them without spoken words." Having dimly recognized this feeling, she spontaneously communicated in a direct verbal way with Bob.

In both therapy sessions, Dina experiences a process of recognition, which was initiated by the therapist's interactions. Dr. Allen Ashley maintained a primarily objective attitude and led Dina directly toward insight of dynamic connections between the repression of hostility in the past and her present defensively masochistic behavior. Dr. Eric Emory presented himself as a man with personal feelings and subjective needs and he facilitated Dina's awareness of her own feelings by this authentic encounter.

In both instances, the fluid curative process involved the patient's total personality. Dr. Ashley's patient worked from induced insight towards emotional and physical release; Eric's patient used her encounter for gaining insight.

People are psychobiological entities whose past experiences and future anticipations meet at the pinpoint of the here-and-now. This little space-place, however limited, is the only moment of freedom and action which is ours in living. This crosspoint of past and future is therefore also the only meeting ground in which therapist and patient can interact. All psychotherapy therefore occurs in the here-and-now of intervention and receptivity—a two-way road with a one-way emphasis. However, since the here-and-now, as defined by the fluid process of the there-and-then, is past and future, the therapeutic process involves all previous experiences and the anticipated future of both the therapist and the patient.

Although I hypothesize the therapeutic effectiveness of all therapy as based upon the fluidity of curative process, I do not wish to understate differences and effectiveness of the two methods. I would like to propose that experientialism, if based upon psychodynamic concepts, is not a departure from, but a continuation of, Freud's search.

Freud, in his practice and theoretical framework, came steadily closer to the application of the here-and-now principle of modern experientialism. His discovery of the phenomenon and concept of transference established the present as the forum of therapeutic intervention. His concept of resistance served to pinpoint, within the here-and-now of psychoanalysis, the power of defenses as operant in the analytic process. Correspondingly, the emphasis in the doctor-patient relationship, which had initially been seen as representative of the medical model, also underwent changes. The analyst's personality was seen as contributing, for better or for worse, to the therapeutic process. Concepts of "the therapeutic personality" and the "educational experience of psychoanalysis" rely heavily on the "corrective experience" of an interpersonal event. However, the psychoanalyst's tools are still primarily seen as his using questions, comments, dynamic interpretations and a professional accepting attitude.

The experiential viewpoint has taken the personal involvement of the therapist in the corrective experience one step further. Intensification of personal communication and exploration of the immediate encounter are continuations of Freud's conceptualization of transference and resistance as active agents of the past in the present. The experiential psychotherapist's primary tools are his perceptivity of the patient's feelings, his acuity in understanding verbal and nonverbal statements and his revealing his personal experience of the patient to him. Such revelation fuses subjective and objective perspectives of the patient's personality and behavior. *The effect of authentic, open communication replaces one-sided patient-related interpretations. The therapeutic means is seen as interpersonal rather than intrapsychic truthfulness. If, however, experientialists neglect the meaning of the past as operant in therapeutic processes, unrealistic denial takes place which is countertherapeutic.* (This holds equally true for today's frequent denial of the significance of intellectual insight in the therapeutic process. As Freud states: the voice of the intellect is low, but penetrating.)

While, in psychoanalysis, interpretations foreshadow future insight and integration, experientialism uses interpretations as cementing forces for the just-experienced therapeutic intervention. This is a natural outgrowth of Freud's maxim of "staying with the surface" (the immediacy of the here-and-now) and interpreting "just a step ahead" of the patient (but not more).

Both analytic and experiential schools use participant group members as assistant therapists. Analysts speak of multiple transference; experientialists of group encounter. While patients are inclined to gear their behavior toward therapists' theoretical and practical expectations, the history of group therapies parallels the general historical trend toward experiential emphasis within the psychoanalytic process. Group therapy as a method has been highly instrumental in helping the classical psychoanalyst to accept the efficacy of greater experiential openness. The powerful force of transference distortions becomes most obvious in groups when patients continue to see their peers with their subjective-colored glasses, regardless of the fact that they know each person's history and characteristics. This is equally true for the continuation of transference projections onto group analysts, whose behavior is more exposed to their groups than to individual patients.*

SUMMARY

The seeming juxtaposition of psychoanalytic versus experiential group psychotherapy is seen as a false dichotomy. The author hypothesizes that all curative processes are fluid. All therapeutic interventions are effective if they lead to the integration of personally significant aspects of reality previously unavailable to the patient. The intrapsychosomatic curative process guides constructive processes from one personality level to all others. Thus, psychoanalytic insight leads to release of emotional and physical tension, and experiential encounter promotes psychoanalytic insight. Differences—but not a dichotomy—exist and relate to the role of the therapist and the emphasis on the here-and-now versus the there-and-then within the therapy session. The author sees a historical trend beginning with Freud's conceptualization of transference and resistance and evolving toward more experiential attitudes in psychodynamically oriented individual and group psychotherapy.

---

* In a group analytic cotherapist setting with my colleague, Dr. Max Markowitz, we discovered that our patients, for long periods of time, continued to see us as dominant or submissive according to their transferential matrix; some patients assigned the role of the domineering partner to my male colleague, some to myself.

8

THE USE OF DREAMS IN GESTALT THERAPY

James S. Simkin, Ph.D.

During the past half dozen years increased emphasis has been placed on the use of dreams in gestalt therapy. This important therapeutic advance can be attributed in large measure, to the work of Perls, who first made reference to the use of dreams in gestalt therapy as early as 1966, in his paper on "Gestalt Therapy and Human Potentials" (1), and three years later, devoted the major portion of one of the last books written before his death to transcripts of his dream work seminars at the Esalen Institute (2). We are indebted to Perls for his concept of the dream as an existential message, the meaning of which can become obvious if the dreamer is willing to work on his dream by a process of owning (identifying with) the various parts of his dream. An attempt has been made in this article to contribute to the further clarification of this concept.

The Therapeutic Function of the Dream

In accordance with the principles of gestalt theory, the gestalt therapist assumes that a dream is a script, written by the dreamer, in which all of the parts of the dream, both animate and inanimate, are representations of the whole, i.e., of the person doing the dreaming. Thus dreams might be expected to provide a useful vehicle for illustrating some of the basic goals of gestalt therapy. As Yontef has pointed out, "In Gestalt therapy dreams are used to integrate and they are not interpreted" (3). More specifically, the over-all goal is to foster awareness, to guide the patient to unite his thoughts with his feelings. He is also encouraged to take appropriate risks in the process, and these, in turn, serve to enhance his self-reliance.

The Dream Enactment Procedure

With respect to the imposing task of unravelling "meanings," that is, the complex problem of exploring the significance of dream symbols, gestalt therapy offers an approach rich in possibilities. One of the most effective means of exploration consists of a dramatic enactment of the dream by the dreamer. In the process, the unique qualities of the dreamer's inner world are revealed. And, almost invariably, the elaborate material produced permits the dreamer to get in touch with aspects of himself which he has been avoiding.

The enactment procedure can be summarized as follows: Usually, the therapist begins by asking the patient to recount his dream in the first person, using the present tense. He is then asked to assume the identity of one of the animate or inanimate elements in his dream, then to take on the identity of a second element, then a third, etc. Some gestalt therapists prefer to start with those aspects of the dream which are easily identified, and then ask the patient to shift to the more ego-alien material. In contrast, other therapists prefer to have the patient start with the aspect of his dream which is least identifiable.

Regardless of where one starts with the dream material, the basic rule of gestalt therapy, staying with what is in the foreground, is observed. Thus, if the dreamer is focusing on—in touch with—an animate aspect of his dream, he will be asked to continue to assume that identity until he has explored all its implications. If the therapist observes the use of body language on the part of the patient as he recounts his dream, the dreamer is asked to focus his awareness on what became foreground for the therapist at that moment, and work with that material.

Apart from its value for the individual, in a small-group setting, the dream work of one patient often triggers the recollection of dreams in other group members. Concomitantly, being present during the working through of dream material encourages others to risk working of their own dreams. Finally, not infrequently, dream enactment engenders feelings of closeness and intimacy between the dreamer and other group members.

Clinical Example

The transcript of the enactment of a dream which follows will serve to illustrate the principles and techniques described above—and their efficacy. The patient recounted his dream in the setting of a group workshop, in which approximately fifteen persons participated. He had worked with several members of this particular group before, and was very close to a few. When the patient completed his dream work, he was asked to address all the people in the workshop.

Transcript

P: I want to work on a dream, a very recent dream. I had this yesterday; in fact, last night. In the dream, my youngest daughter, who is about eight years old, gets chopped up with a hatchet. Specific part of her body, her leg is chopped off. And the hatchet is wielded by a boy in the neighborhood that I know, and I'm watching. She is sitting on the floor by a table, and he come under the table and hacks up her foot, her leg. And I intend to stop him and I struggle with him but I can't prevent him from doing this. Finally I wrest the hatchet away from him, and it is too late. She is in great pain and dies on the spot. And then he attacks me, barehanded. And I hit him, not with the sharp edge of the hatchet, I hit him with the back of the hatchet on his leg, just enough to stun his leg so that he can't run after me. But not to do him any real damage. And then I stand off, where I'm safe from him, and tell somebody—a woman that I don't recognize— who is standing there that I was powerless to stop him and that I can't understand it. I woke from this dream in a great fright and trembling. The most vivid dream I've had in a long time.

　　Dr. Simkin: O.K. Now start by being *(your daughter)*. In the first person, present tense.

P: I am *(name)*, sitting under the table and this guy comes—crawls under the table and he's coming at me with the hatchet. I don't know what he's going to do. But he starts chopping up my foot, and it hurts a lot. And I can't understand it. It doesn't make any sense. And daddy is there, and he can't do anything about it, and I can't figure it out. Somebody do something!

S: Please go on as she.

P: I particularly can't figure out why anyone would want to hurt me. I am the most healthy, the most natural of any one around. This was an association I had to her. That's all for her.

S: Oh no. You are changing your dream.

P: I didn't do the part where it hurts.

S: Please continue.

P: O.K. (*Sigh*) I'm embarrassed.

S: What's embarrassing?

P: I'm embarrassed to holler out that my leg is hurting.

S: Please continue.

P: Ow, you chopped into my leg; ow, my foot is hurting; ow, it's going up my leg. Somebody do something; something is happening to my leg. They're chopping it all up, it hurts . . . I must be blocking something out.

S: You did not go through the dying.

P: O.K. I'll resume: chopping up my leg, and it's bleeding, and daddy isn't stopping him, and it hurts and I'll die. I'm dying. I don't know how to portray dying, violent death of this type.

S: I don't believe you. (*Long Pause*) What are you doing?

P: I'm touching my lip and thinking.

S: Trying to figure it out, perhaps.

P: Yes. How to portray dying and make it convincing to you.

S: See if you can make it convincing for your daddy.

P: (*Pause*) I can't do that.

S: What can you do?

P: I can sit and wish that my daddy would do something.

S: O.K. Now would you be the boy who is crawling under the table? The hatchet-wielder.

P: (*Pause*) There is (*name*) sitting on the floor. I'll chop her up right now. Get under this table where nobody can get me. By the time they get to me, I'll have chopped the leg good. I'm really good with this hatchet, too. King-pin with the hatchet; just watch my smoke. It's a gas, a ball. And I climb under the table and, before any one knows what's happening, I'm chopping up her leg. Every stroke cuts right through the bone; it's great. And blood all over the floor, it's a gory mess. I've never done anything so exciting in my life! Here comes that idiot father, trying to stop me, and he'll never make it. Because I got this table in between. Finally I got her chopped up enough that she's going to die from it, and I can't do any more. That bastard! He got the hatchet away from me. I'll go and get him! Ow, he hit me in the leg; I can't run. What does he think he's doing? I can use the hatchet and I can chop good; he hits me in the leg with the back of it. What an idiot! (*Pause*)

S: What do you experience?

P: A perplexity: this is a side of me I am not acquainted with. If this is part of me, then I certainly—

S: *If* this is part of you?

P: O.K. It's part of me that I don't recognize and don't admit consciously. A hatchet-wielder? That's not my image.

S: A sneaky hatchet-wielder.

P: O.K.: under the table.

S: Yes. Does that become a bit more recognizable?

P: Slightly: I've had a history of sneakiness. But that . . . (*voice trails off*)

S: What's just happened?

P: I just became aware of the color of your suit. Yellow and red! For quite some time, I've been working out into the open the sneaky things I do. And I was under the impression that I'd pretty much changed that. I am very surprised to discover this aspect of being sneaky. Not so surprised, since this is an aspect that I don't recognize as sneaky.

S: Now be the hatchet.

P: Hatchet? I'm about the sharpest, keenest hatchet that ever existed. An edge that will go through bone, can kill in one clean sweep. Just aim me right and one blow does it. Real fine, sharp hatchet: the best.

S: Be the other side.

P: The dull side? (*Pause*) As the dull side of the hatchet, I am not very effective. I can strike a temporary blow, I can hold things off. I can't make a clean strike. I can't be used effectively. I can only blunt, I can numb for a time. But I can't cut.

S: Now be the table.

P: I'm protection for the boy who climbs under the table, I'm protection for the hatchet. I am no protection for (the girl).

S: You are protection for two out of the four people or objects.

P: No protection for (myself).

S: I don't believe that. I believe that you are protection for (the dreamer).

P: I don't see what the table protects him from. In the dream, I'm in his way. Prevent him from going to (his daughter's) rescue.

S: Yes.

P: Are you suggesting that this does something for him?

S: Yes. (*Pause*) What just happened?

P: I put my hands in my pocket. Thinking again. Trying to figure out what it does for (own name).

S: What does putting your hands in your pockets do?

P: Gives my hand a definite place to be. A safe place for my hands.

S: Now be the vague woman.

P: I'm a complete bystander. I'm not involved with any of the people in the drama, with (any of them). I am the fringe of the scene, totally useless. I can barely see what's going on. I can't understand much of what (he) is saying to me, I can hardly hear his words. The whole thing is a vague, foggy event to me; I'm out of it.

S: And now be (you).

P: Goddam, look what's happening. I didn't see that boy go under the table with the hatchet. He's on (my daughter). My God, he's chopping her leg. I have to stop him.

S: What's happened to your hands?

P: I took them out of my pockets.

S: Please go on.

P: I have to stop him. I'll run, I'll grab him. I'm grabbing him. I'm holding on to him, fighting with him and he is still chopping away. I can't understand that; I'm fighting with him, I'm strong, but I'm not preventing him from continuing to chop. I don't seem to be able to stop him. And it's going to be too late and (my daughter) is screaming, and there is blood, and I'm powerless—not that I'm not trying. I'm trying, but apparently, I'm not trying in the right way. I'm not preventing the damage.

S: Yes.

P: And I blame myself for not doing this.

S: How do you blame yourself?

P: I'm a grown man. I should be able to keep a small boy from chopping her with a hatchet, by taking the hatchet away from him.

S: You can't do this.

P: I can't do it.

S: So you are going to have to figure out some other method.

P: To prevent the damage. This I don't see: here is the kid, under the table, chopping with the hatchet, and I'm standing back from it. All I can do is run to the scene and try to take the hatchet away. And this I am doing.

S: With?

P: —all my energy, all speed.

S: And?

P: I'm ineffective.

S: Right.

P: And I'm in a panic, in a sweat, because I can't be effective. That's exactly how I woke up from the dream: in a sweat, trembling, and in panic. Powerless.

S: I am curious about (the you) in the dream: how do you finally wrest the hatchet away from the boy?

P: I don't know. It seems as if he gives it up when he's through.

S: Yes. There is the key. (*Pause*)

P: I make a connection to going through with something that's finished.

S: Right. This boy is not going to stop until he is through: he's getting the kicks. And he has a very effective instrument.

P: But it's *inconceivable* to me that I just stand by and wait until he's done.

S: What's your choice?

P: I must try to top him.

S: How?

P: (*Pause*) By holding his arm back, or taking the hatchet away.

S: That doesn't work. He's not going to stop until he's through.

P: My attitude is: if (daughter) is getting chopped, I've got to do something.

S: What's your choice?

P: Either to try directly to stop him, or to let him finish. That does not make any sense: I don't know what my choice is! I don't see any choice.

S: Good, I'm going to be helpful.

P: Who's laughing?

S: I think the boy is going to chop until he's finished. I think your only choice is to be a hero.

P: That's to let him chop me instead.

S: Of course.

P: This never occurred to me in the dream!

S: Of course not! In the dream you are panic-stricken and terrified. But here you have the opportunity to be a hero. And I am suggesting this is your choice.

P: (*Pause*) I'm lost. To save my daughter, that sounds good; but how can I do that?

S: I am just trying to be helpful.

P: And I appreciate it. (*Rustling in the crowd*)

S: If you remember, in Gestalt Therapy, we assume that every part of the dream is a part of you. The hatchet is you, both the sharp side and the blunt side. (Your daughter) is you, (you) is you, the table is you, the murderous kid is you, etc., etc. All of these are parts of yourself. The part of you that is (your daughter) is the innocent part, the "healthy" part. That's the part that gets killed by the savage little monster. And you are not offering (you) as the victim (instead of your daughter) . . . What are you doing?

P: Thinking. This makes a lot of sense. If thereby I could save the (daughter)-part, it would be a most worthwhile sacrifice. I was just thinking: when this comes up in situations, I don't see such a choice. It never occurs to me to make the (Me) part of the dream the victim.

S: This (you) in the dream is quite ineffectual: He's a good actor, and he can get panic-stricken, and he can blame himself, and he can play mea culpa, and he can talk to vague women who can't even hear him.

P: Who needs it?

S: You do! (*Small laughter in group*) You are bright enough not to damage the murdering little kid in you, and just to stun him and hold him off a while. Bright enough to see how adequately you can cut to the bone. You can kill.

P: But apparently not bright enough to recognize this choice when it comes up.

S: Yes. You need the terrified and bumbling (you) much more.

P: Let's say, I am more accustomed to being that. It seems to me I need help to recognize the possibility of sacrificing this ineffective bumbling.

S: All right: I have a suggestion.

P: Shoot!

S: Go through your dream once more and change it any way you like. First Person, Present tense . . . What are you doing?

P: Thinking.

S: What did I ask you to do?

P: You asked me to go through the dream and change it any way I like.

S: And what are you doing?

P: Planning how I am going to change it.

S: Too bad. (*Laughter*) Already you are giving (you) his usual role!

P: Fantastic!

S: Not so fantastic!

P: This is what happens!

S: Yes, of course! What are you doing now?

P: I am choking back laughter. (*Pause*) Now I'm really confused.

S: Stay with your confusion.

P: (*Deep breath*) That was quick.

S: What happened?

P: No desire to laugh any more!

S: All right: What would you like to do at this moment?

P: I'd like to go through the dream. (Daughter) is sitting on the floor—

S: What just happened?

P: I stopped in confusion about what tense to use, and who I am telling the dream: (She) is sitting on the floor, (etc.).

S: Now I am confused. (She) is not sitting on the floor!

P: No: she always was! Near the table.

S: She was not sitting with the table protecting her.

P: Next to the table on the floor, so that it was difficult to get to her and the table is in the way. The person who was most under the table was the boy with the hatchet. So this boy climbs under the table, aiming for (her). And what I do now is I go for the table, and I kick the table over. With the table kicked over, the boy stops going for (her) and turns on the table with his hatchet.

S: Are you willing to sacrifice the table?

P: Oh yes! Gladly!

S: Are you sure?

P: No. I don't know what the hell the table is.

S: Yes, you do! The table is the key to everything.

P: If I could hack up that table, I would give that kid a hand. That would be a real pleasure.

S: And everything will be out in the open.

P: Right: that's where I want it, anyway!

S: O.K. What I'd like you to do now is to make the statement to everybody in the room, one at a time. "I want things out in the open. I don't want things under the table, etc." One sentence quickly to each person.

P: I want things out in the open. I don't want things under the table. (*Repeats with slight variations in inflection*)

S: What do you experience?

P: Pounding of my heart, excitement. A certain amount of embarrassment. I feel unbalanced.

S: Which side?

P: Left side forward, the right side back. As I was going around the room, I had the impression I was talking mostly from my guts, and very little understanding of what this means. Once or twice a recognition.

S: There is a Yiddish expression which is most appropriate now: Mazel-tov!

P: O.K. Thank you.

REFERENCES

1. PERLS, F. S. Gestalt Therapy and Human Potentials. In Otto, H. A. (ed.), *Explorations in Human Potentialities.* Springfield, Ill.: C. C. Thomas, 1966, Chap. 35.
2. PERLS, F. S. *Gestalt Therapy Verbatim.* Lafayette, Calif.: Real People Press, 1969, pp. 73-216.
3. YONTEF, G. M. *A Review of the Practice of Gestalt Therapy.* Trident Shop, California State College, Los Angeles, 1969, p. 28.

9

NEW DIRECTIONS IN TRANSACTIONAL ANALYSIS: CREATING AN ENVIRONMENT FOR REDECISION AND CHANGE

Robert Goulding, M.D.

Director, The Western Institute for Group and Family Therapy

INTRODUCTION

In the past decade, group therapy techniques have undergone a marked change at The Western Institute for Group and Family Therapy. Our current approach to treatment evolved gradually over this ten-year period. However, the seeds for change in our theoretical and therapeutic orientation were planted when we began to learn about Transactional Analysis from the late Eric Berne:* Under Berne's tutelage, we became aware of the fact that each of our patients was actually three people, and that their behavior and feelings changed with remarkable rapidity, depending on which ego state was in control: One moment we were watching a frightened child, the next moment we were

---

The pronoun "we" is not used in an editorial sense in this article. Although she did not participate in the actual preparation of this material for publication, Mary Goulding, M.S.W. collaborated with the author in the implementation of the therapeutic innovations described herein. Moreover, she was responsible for many of the new theoretical concepts, discussed in detail below, which underlie these innovations, e.g., the classification of Injunctions, rejection of the term "Witch Message," and recognition of the fact that the patient's ability to "forgive" his parents is crucial to the success of treatment.

* We have operated on the assumption that the professional audience for whom this volume was designed would have a general knowledge of the principles of Transactional Analysis. Consequently, only those concepts which are central to our thesis have been discussed at length in the text.

listening to a stern parent, and then, only seconds later, we were listening to a rational, realistic, problem-solving adult; and we began to realize that our patients characteristically assumed one of these three identities, i.e., Parent, Child, or Adult, at various points in their transactions with others. Once we had acquired these insights, we became aware of the frequency with which our patients demonstrated the same kinds of feelings after a series of similar transactions; we learned to recognize the games they were playing. In addition at this point, we began to realize that our patients' transactions and games were part of a larger plan, of a life script they had "written" as children, and which they were determined to follow to its inevitable tragic end. Thus it seemed to us that they almost deliberately behaved in ways which reinforced and served to perpetuate their feelings of worthlessness, rage, alienation, etc., so that in time they began to feel that they had no choice but to kill themselves, or kill someone else, or run away, or escape by going crazy or withdrawing.

Once we had become familiar with the basic concepts of Transactional Analysis, we began the process of analyzing ego states, the transactions between ego states, the games, the scripts, on the assumption, held by Berne and his followers, that if our patients were made aware of their feeling and behavior patterns, they would be able to change them. It soon became apparent, however, that this approach was not effective in a sufficient number of cases, and we began to change our therapeutic methods in the group: Obviously, it was not enough to sit around, waiting for our patients to develop this awareness, waiting for them to change as they "worked through" whatever it was they were supposed to be working through. Instead, we began to work quickly and carefully to "tease out" the patient's feeling and behavior patterns, to confront him with an exact model of his games, rackets, etc., which could be drawn, illustrated, felt. At the same time, our basic therapeutic orientation underwent some modification: Specifically, we began to recognize the importance of the Injunction and Decision which underlay these patterns. We came to understand that the patient's script, his games, rackets, etc., served to support a particular Injunction he had been given in childhood and the particular Decision he had made surrounding that Injunction. And, finally, we began to realize that although we could make the patient acutely aware of his feeling and behavior patterns, he would not be able to change those patterns until he was able to make a new Decision and so free himself from the Injunction. Thus, in recent years, our efforts have focused on creating a therapeutic environment which is truly conducive to change, or more precisely, to the process of

Redecision—on an emotional, as well as a cognitive level—which must precede change.

The Injunction

We learned from Berne that certain kinds of behavior, certain kinds of feelings, are often preceded by certain kinds of parental messages. Berne called these parental messages "Witch Messages"; we refer to them as "Injunctions," and consider the term "Witch Message" to be anti-therapeutic. By definition, the Injunction is a message given to the child by the parent's internal Child, usually (but not always) without the awareness of the parent's Adult. In essence, the message tells the child how he can achieve recognition, i.e., under what circumstances he can expect to receive strokes from Mother or Father.

There is some difference of opinion among transactional analysts as to the extent to which these messages may vary in content. Berne, Steiner, Karpman, and others who attended the San Francisco Seminars, felt there were many possibilities, depending on the exact words used. We believe that there are only a few Injunctions, and that often they are never actually spoken; rather, they are inferred by the child from his parents' actions. The first five Injunctions we picked up were *"Don't Be," "Don't Be You," "Don't Be a Child," "Don't Be Grown Up,"* and *"Don't Be Close."* Subsequently we identified two more—just plain *"Don't,"* and *"Don't Make It";* and then we picked up still another— *"Don't Be Sane"* (or well).* Finally, although we are not yet certain of the frequency with which it occurs, recently we became aware of the Injunction *"Don't Be Important."*† Another just added is *"Don't Belong."*

As noted above, as we acquired additional clinical experience, we began to recognize that these Injunctions, which had been given to our patients when they were children by an irrational part of their parents, were, in fact, the real force behind the scripts they were in, and the games they played to support those scripts.

---

* Presumably, we would have picked up this Injunction much sooner if we had been seeing more psychotic patients. In recent years we have been working primarily with therapists who are candidates for training in Transactional Analysis. Consequently, we have lost touch with this segment of the patient population. Apparently, however, there are enough therapists around with serious problems, so that in time we were able to pick up the "Don't Be Sane" Injunction.

† This Injunction was brought to our attention by Edward Frost, one of our trainees from the ministry.

A depressed, suicidal woman of forty-four, who had done things to drive people away all her life, could relate her depression to the Injunction not to be, which had been given to her as a child by her mother. The patient had been told over and over again that she alone was the cause of her mother's unhappiness; that if she hadn't been born, hadn't been conceived, mother could have gone to college, or would never have gotten married, or could have had a career in opera, or would not have developed hemorrhoids, etc. And what all this, together with all the non-verbal messages the mother sent out, added up to was "Don't Be." Even after forty years, the patient continued to obey that Injunction, continued to behave in ways which would heighten her feelings ·of worthlessness, her sense of alienation—and add credence to the Injunction. Thus she showed us how she added up the evidence of all the bad things that happened to her so that she would have enough bad feelings to support her depression. And when she couldn't find the evidence, she made bad things happen to her so that she could feel depressed. Or if she did not feel sufficiently depressed at a given moment, she would fantasize something in the past or the future to be depressed about; or, when all else failed, she would think about the war, the political situation, etc., and become pathologically depressed.

Because the Injunction is often implanted by strokes given by the parent at the time he transmits his "message," the child comes to perceive his failure to obey the Injunction as posing a threat to his psychological survival. These strokes, or units of recognition, may be positive or negative. Obviously, in the *"Don't Be"* Injunction, they are usually negative. But if no positive strokes are delivered, then negative strokes become very important: The child would rather be treated badly than completely ignored. Strokes may also be categorized as unconditional or conditional: Parents may love their child unconditionally, just for being; or they may love him just for doing things they approve of; or he may be loved for both being and doing. Similarly, parents may dislike a child just for being; or he may receive negative strokes only when he does something bad, and be ignored the rest of the time; or he may receive both unconditional and conditional negative strokes. The child who is given a *"Don't Be"* Injunction is often slapped and scolded by his parent just because he exists. As a general rule, however, the *"Don't Be"* Injunction is implanted by conditional as well as unconditional negative strokes: The child will be slapped and scolded if he tries to break the bars of his crib, bangs his head, throws his bottles around, spills his milk, throws his toys on the floor, etc. If, on the other hand, he is quiet, can be left alone in his room for long periods, doesn't get in anyone's way, doesn't "bug" anyone, he will be ignored. Thus the child learns that his parents will give him strokes (i.e., recognition) for being bad and forget that he exists if he is good. And now he is in a quandary: If he is recognized, he hurts; but if he does nothing to deserve a spanking or scolding, and that's the only way he can attract his parents' attention, he is lonely—and loneliness is infinitely more painful. There is still another possibility: If the child is given an Injunction to stay out of the way, and gets positive strokes for staying out of the way, he will begin to realize that he will be loved for not being there, and scolded if he is. And this type of situation, in which the parent actually gives the child warm, loving strokes, when he obeys an Injunction, however irrational, may have an even more noxious effect, in terms of the child's future development.

As a child, while his father was away in the war, the patient received a "Don't Be You" (i.e., Don't Be a Boy) Injunction from his mother who dressed her little boy in girl's clothes, and then loved him for being a "girl." Furthermore, the mother really hated men, so that even the Counter-Injunction, which came from the mother's Parent, was Don't Be a Boy. Thus, the patient saw no alternative but to decide to go along with the Injunction. As long as he remained a boy, he wouldn't get strokes because mother didn't want "him," she wanted "her." Having made a decision to comply, he became depressed and proceeded to gather evidence to knock himself off.

Given these data, one can predict the kind of life script the patient developed for himself with a fair degree of accuracy: When he was first seen, the patient was a homosexual whose behavior might best be described as frenzied; in addition, he was depressed, suicidal, alcoholic, and blind. Over a two-year period, several therapists worked with the patient to extricate him from the *Don't Be a Boy* Injunction and the early Decision he had made surrounding that Injunction, and to help him to make a Redecision about his maleness. At the end of those two years, the patient was no longer suicidal, but he was certainly not well, and he was still blind. At this point, the patient decided to undergo surgery to change his sex, discussed his problem with the staff of a University-affiliated hospital, and, after considerable effort, persuaded both the surgical team and the psychiatric team that such an operation was justified. Shortly after he started a course of hormonal treatments prior to surgery, the patient began to dress in women's clothes and work as a housekeeper. In addition, while he was receiving hormonal treatment, his blindness, which was central, with a vision of 20/800 peripherally, disappeared, and he/she no longer felt depressed. Subsequently, both stages of surgery were completed, and for over two years the patient has been doing well, living and loving as a woman. She is now married and has two step-children.

This case illustrates the power of the Injunction, but it also serves to highlight an aspect of the Injunction which has not received enough attention in the literature, namely, the trap the therapist may fall into if he allows the patient's contract to be influenced by his own convictions. Thus if, despite his stated goals, the patient persists in his determination to stick with the early Injunction he was given, after considerable work has been done, the therapist would do well to re-examine and, possibly, revise his own commitment to implement that contract.*

The Decision and Its Sequelae

Once we recognized the influence of the Injunction, and were able to specify the various forms it might take, we became aware of another element, one that we think Berne and his close followers missed: If Mother said, from her irrational Child Ego State, *"Don't Be,"* the child had to agree, i.e., to make a *Decision* not to be, if that Injunction was to hold any power.

Many children get a *"Don't Be"* Injunction from a parent who doesn't want them, but only certain children decide not to be. Others respond differently; they decide to ignore their parent's message, regardless of the consequences. We are not sure why some children do not feel impelled to obey an Injunction, but there are several possible explanations: Obviously, the other parent often plays a crucial role in such cases. To illustrate, if mother says, from her crazy irrational Child, *"Don't Be,"* but father says *"Don't listen to her, she's nuts; she's mad at life, not at you,"* then, in all probability, the child will be able to get through his early years without deciding to kill himself someday. Similarly, if a father says *"Don't Grow Up"* to his sexy nine-year-old daughter, she may well decide to obey his Injunction, to remain a little girl so that father will love her, unless her mother says *"Don't listen to him. It's OK for you to grow up; give him time and he'll love you anyway. And even if he doesn't, it really won't be that important after you've grown up and left home."*

There is a second possible explanation: the child may remain uncommitted to a parent's Injunction, even when it is not countermanded by the other parent, if he is mature enough emotionally to recognize that his psychological survival does not really depend upon his parents, that he can get the recognition and support he needs from parent surrogates.

The point is that the child doesn't have to buy the Injunction. And if he does buy it, he doesn't have to stay with it forever. Accordingly,

---

* Obviously, this would not apply to the suicidal patient.

we provide our patients with an opportunity to change their early Decisions. At times, they may even make the same Decision they did as children (except for the Decision not to be), for although it may have had an adverse effect on his early development, that Decision would now be considered relatively "safe." For example, the child who decides to obey the Injunction *"Don't Be a Child"* often works hard from the time he is six years old to accomplish things, and is amply rewarded for his efforts, but isn't really enjoying life. In fact, this Injunction frequently underlies the life script of the professional who undertakes further training in his spare time; who continues to strive for recognition as a grown up, and does not permit himself to enjoy child-like pleasures. Even when he is relaxing, he may be pushed by his internal Parent to get off his rear end and get something done. He has two choices—to decide to have fun, be a child at times, and then be alert to the deprivation he feels, recognize its source and look for strokes from people around who are also interested in having fun. Or, second choice, he can decide to stay with the original decision of not being a child, and stop hassling himself about his inability to have fun, instead of doing things which preclude having fun, such as going into debt so that he can't, or fighting with his wife when its time to have sex.

What needs to be emphasized is the fact that the great majority of children do make an initial decision to go along with the Injunctions which are given to them, although the effects of this decision may vary considerably, depending, of course, on the content of the Injunction. For obvious reasons, the *"Don't Be"* Injunction would be expected to have the most serious implications. Thus if the child feels impelled to obey the *"Don't Be"* Injunction, then at some point in his young life, he may make one of the following Decisions surrounding that Injunction:

1. If things get too bad I'll kill myself; or
2. I'll get you even if it kills me; or
3. I'll get you to kill me; or
4. I'll show you even if it kills me.

There are other decisions that can be made, of course. These are listed by way of illustration. The point is that, whatever form it may take, once the child has made such a Decision, he has forfeited his autonomy. There is a good chance that he will remain stuck in the Injunction and in a script which must support it.

Thus we began to see a picture unfold, which was repeated over and over again: An Injunction from the Child ego state of the parent (or

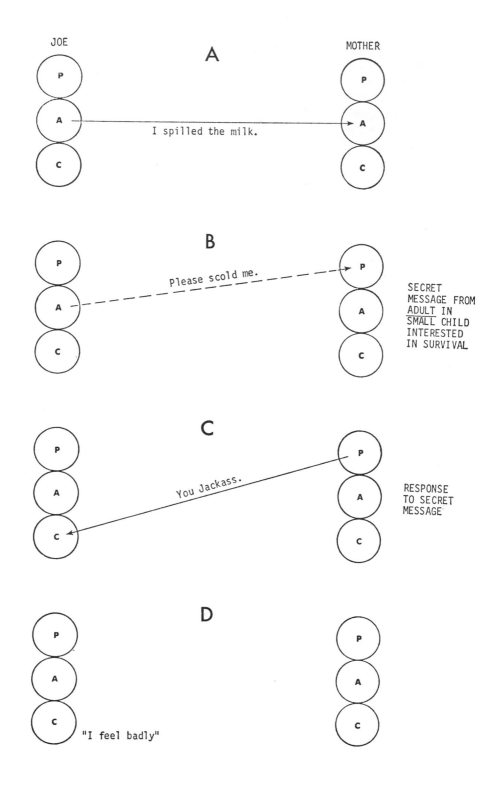

parent surrogate) had been followed by a Decision made by the patient to go along with that Injunction, after which the patient developed a set of bad feelings that were consistent with that Decision; began to play games to maintain or support those bad feelings (the feelings which we call rackets); began to collect those bad feelings and the bad things that happened, so that he could cash them in later for the suicide, or depression, or the anger or anxiety which the script calls for.

The Games. The ways in which the games the patient plays serve to support the Injunction and the script he is in, emerge clearly in the following clinical illustration:

> Joe, who was the oldest of several children, had been born before his mother was married, and had been given a "Don't Be" Injunction: If it weren't for him, the other kids would have enough to eat; and if it weren't for him she wouldn't have had to get married, and wouldn't have all those kids in the first place. As might be expected, the Injunction not to be had been implanted by negative strokes. And so Joe learned very early in life that the way to get recognition was to do something bad, and the way to feel was depressed and sad, and decided that if things got too bad he could always knock himself off.
>
> At first, he got recognition in all kinds of ways, e.g., by getting his mother to scold him for spilling the milk, etc. And he began to equate being scolded with being loved. Thus he was motivated to start playing the game, as the patient often is, by his need to ensure his psychological survival.
>
> To trace the evolution of this process, first, he spilled the milk; second, he sent his mother the secret message, *"Please scold me";* third, she complied with his request; fourth, his mother's negative strokes evoked bad feelings which he collected and cashed in for his first suicide attempt when he was only six. Fifth, while Joe was probably conscious of this whole procedure when he was a small child, as a data-processing Adult he was not aware of what his Child was doing. Consequently, as Joe grew up he continued to play the Game, *Kick Me,* and, from his Child position, asked to be kicked (and loved) over and over again.

Thus, the definition and description of a game (Kupfer-Goulding) is:

1. Ostensible (usually) adult stimulus
2. Secret Message
3. Response to secret message
4. Pay off of bad feelings
5. Entire series of transactions are not within awareness of adult (unconscious if you wish, although I hate to use unc.)

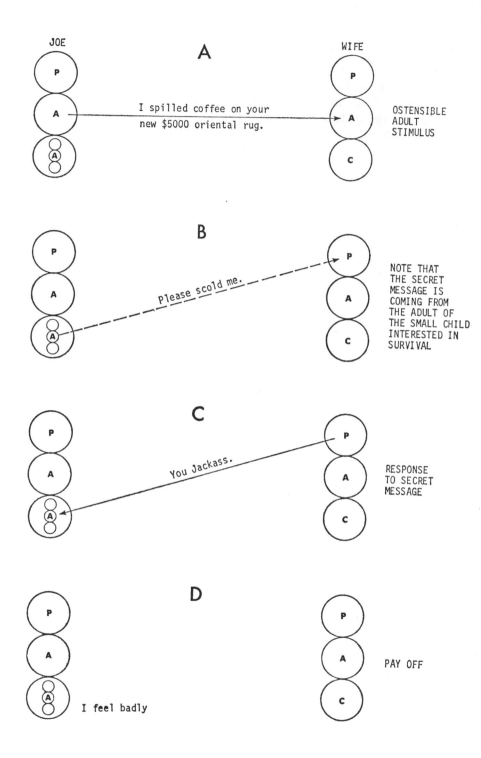

The First Act Experience. To review, then, the individual gets an Injunction from his parent, which is implanted by strokes (which may be positive or negative, conditional or unconditional), makes a Decision around that Injunction, and then develops a script to support the Injunction. Sometimes, however, the child has some kind of first act experience, in the course of which he develops some bad feelings from the strokes he gets and the things that happen to him, but also gets some satisfaction from the strokes, and often, when young, some kind of reward for his bad feelings. As demonstrated below, when it occurs, it is this first act experience which sets the pattern for the feelings and modes of behavior that the child retains until (and if) he decides to change.

A patient came to the Institute, depressed and suicidal, shortly after I had decided to give up my private practice to devote my time to teaching, training, and conducting workshops. Actually, she had been depressed on and off all her life, but in the last several years her depression had become acute; for some time now, she had been suicidal, and had made two abortive attempts to kill herself. The patient attributed her depression to the fact that her husband had divorced her two years earlier and had since remarried. What she was really saying now, from her Child position, was *"Please come back so that I can stop being depressed,"* although what she said out loud was *"How can I help being depressed when I don't have the man I love anymore."*

Because the patient had been a friend of the family, she wanted me to treat her. I explained why that would not be possible, and suggested that she see one of my associates. She agreed, but even after she had been in treatment for several months, she continued to feel acutely depressed. She had a new rationalization, however. When she came into the office and ran into me, she said *"How can I help being depressed when I don't have you as my therapist?"*

And then one day when we met by chance in the reception room, I was struck by the fact that her behavior simulated a first act experience that she might have developed for herself as a child. As soon as she saw me, she said *"If you don't see me today, I'm going to kill myself."* I warned her not to try to blackmail me: *"If you feel suicidal, I'll arrange to have you admitted to the hospital, but I won't see you."* At this point, she began to cry like a child, and I asked her if she remembered the first time she didn't get her way, and cried until she did. She recalled that when she was five or six years old she had wanted a particular doll for Christmas. When she got the wrong doll she had cried and cried until her father finally went out, the day after Christmas, and got her the right one. Clearly, then, she had actually had a first act experience in which being depressed and crying got her the goody she was looking for, at which point being depressed and crying acquired some magical power.* Apparently, she had done the same thing over and over again with her husband, until he finally refused to play his part in the act. But even after he had divorced her and married someone else, she continued to believe that her depression had the power to bring him back. Indeed, it was only after she got in touch with the shame of carrying on this way, that she was able to give up the first act, and to knock off her depression instead of herself.

The Rackets. The bad feelings, or rackets, that we hold on to, then, are those feelings, often copied from our parents, which we experienced and got rewards (strokes) for when we were little children, which we subsequently came to believe had some magic power, and which fit into the script or the first act in that they serve to support the particular Injunction we were given. A little child's bad feelings frequently serve an important function, of course: The young child, who is totally dependent on others, must use every possible means of attracting attention if his basic psychological and physiological needs are to be gratified. But the bad feelings that we hold on to, or play games to get, or use as an excuse to withdraw, which don't motivate us to take Adult action, are rackets.

One need only drive down any freeway with different people and watch their behavior to be convinced of the ubiquity of rackets. A few drivers can turn on their radios and listen to music while they go where they have to go, without permitting the behavior of other drivers no matter how provoking, to feed their bad feelings. But they are the exceptions. For the rest, some are in a state of fury throughout the trip; they get angry when other drivers tailgate, or cut in, or even when they come onto the freeway from a side street; some are so confused by the traffic and by the signs that they begin to feel disoriented; some are depressed by the traffic; some are frightened by all the Kamikaze pilots, etc. The patterns are the same: They say, *"The traffic is making me anxious today,"* but they are also anxious lying in bed thinking about the next day's traffic. Or they say, *"Who wouldn't be depressed when they have to drive in this traffic every day,"* but they never look for a house or apartment closer to their job, or try to find a job closer to home. Or they try to excuse their irrational anger on the grounds that, *"Everyone in my family gets angry easily, it comes from having red hair"* (gene theory); or *"What's going on in the world makes me angry"* (cosmopolitan theory); or *"I have a lot of unconscious hostility"* (Pseudo-Freudian theory). The point is that they are all refusing, in different

---

* We realize, of course, that this episode was probably a screen memory, but it would still be considered to constitute a first act experience.

ways, to assume responsibility for themselves, to exercise their autonomy. Instead they stay in the rackets their parents taught them, stay in their script or their first act; play games, or, if it becomes necessary, use fantasy to support the rackets and script.

A participant in one of our workshops can be actively involved in

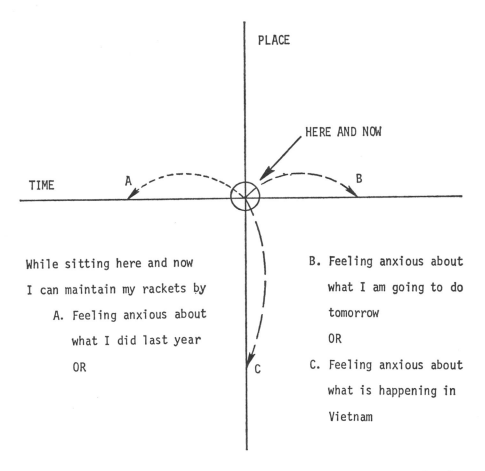

PLACE

HERE AND NOW

TIME   A   B

While sitting here and now
I can maintain my rackets by
   A. Feeling anxious about
      what I did last year
     OR

C

B. Feeling anxious about
   what I am going to do
   tomorrow
   OR
C. Feeling anxious about
   what is happening in
   Vietnam

what he is doing then and there; or he can be anxious about what he will do when the workshop meets again; or he can be anxious about what the other people in the group thought of him at the last workshop; or he can even be anxious about what is happening in Viet Nam, and the possibility that China might enter the war. Although he is probably not aware of it, his anxiety is a racket: He is using a bad feeling, which comes from his irrational Child, as an excuse to withdraw.

We see, then, everyone is in the same bag to some extent. In fact, we rarely train a professional, even one who has had years of psychoanalysis, or Gestalt therapy, or TA, or whatever, who doesn't still have some Injunction, some script that he's still following. Thus, for example, the therapist who feels frustrated because his patients don't get well faster is probably doing something that prevents them from changing, or is setting goals for himself in the therapist-patient relationship that he won't live up to (won't, not can't), or he is actually letting the patient exercise some measure of control over his feelings by using techniques which he knows will backfire, e.g., by telling the patient what to do and then being frustrated when (of course) he doesn't do it. Chances are that when this therapist was four, Daddy told him, in some way, to cure Mommy, and he is still trying to cure patients from his four-year-old position.

THERAPEUTIC INNOVATIONS: REDECISION

Precipitating Factors

As we developed our skills at putting these pieces together, we began to realize that, frequently, just when the group was ready to deal with some important point, the time would be up, and we would have to send everyone home so that we could get to the next group. And so we determined to increase the time traditionally allotted to a single group treatment session. At first, we experimented with the three-hour group, then the six-hour group, the twelve-hour group, and finally we tried the weekend marathon—which proved the most effective approach of all. It seemed to us, and it also seemed to them, that when our patients worked together continuously for three days, they often accomplished as much as they had in six months of regularly scheduled therapy sessions. We then began to hold weekend marathons, not only for intact groups, but also for groups of patients selected from the larger population, who had reached an impasse in their therapy. We were impressed by how much more they were able to learn about themselves, about the Injunction, their early Decision and its consequences; impressed by the fact that once they became aware of the origins of their feelings and behavior, they frequently began to stop playing their serious games. On the other hand, we had to face the fact that although our patients might be able to stop playing their serious games, and were no longer determined to pursue a life plan which would end in suicide or homicide, they were not really prepared to give up their entire script, or all their rackets and games. They often found new ways to maintain their rackets; they often continued to play some other less serious game (e.g., the alcoholic might stop drinking only to start playing the Debtor game).

Apparently, no matter how favorable their initial response to the weekend marathon, our patients were unable to progress beyond a certain point in therapy. As we became increasingly aware of what Gestalt therapists call "the impasse," we began to realize that it related to the danger of giving up the Injunction and the Decision: Usually, a patient reached an impasse in his treatment because he was listening to the early Injunction given to him by his parent, and facing the fantasized threat of the parent's rage if he changed his original Decision to go along with that Injunction. In other words, he equated giving up his early Decision with the loss of the love and nurturing he was getting, or expected to get if he was a good boy and did what mother or father wanted. Thus we were presented with clinical evidence in support of our observation, noted earlier, that the power of the Injunction lies in the fact that it carries with it the threat that love (and/or recognition) will be withdrawn, or never offered unless the patient goes along with it. Even when his parents had been dead for many years, the patient continued to behave as if they would come back and love him, or love him in the afterlife, provided he stayed with the Injunction and the Decision. It was this fantasied threat of psychological retaliation, then, that seemed to account for the impasse our patients reached, and which precluded their further progress in treatment.

As noted above, we recognized almost from the outset that the treatment methods developed by Berne and his followers, although beautifully clear and crisp insofar as they made the patient aware of his life patterns, were not really getting the patient out of his bag. At about this time, we were exposed to the Gestalt methods used by Fritz Perls and James Simkin, and to Virginia Satir's family methods, and over a ten-year period we experimented with these and other treatment techniques. And we found that no single traditional approach to treatment—traditional Berne, traditional Perls, or whatever—really created an environment for change, i.e., an environment which would foster the resolution of the impasse as a prerequisite for change. On the other hand, however, we recognized the potential effectiveness of an eclectic approach, composed of various elements drawn from each of these sources. Thus we began to develop a distinctive style of therapy which combined the traditional techniques which had grown out of our early indoctrination in psychoanalysis and the psychodynamics of behavior, with Berne's TA and my own variations on TA (including stroking for change and not stroking for non-change), with Perls' and Simkin's Gestalt methods,

Satir's family techniques, and occasionally some psychodrama. In short, we sought to combine traditional techniques which foster cognitive awareness with techniques which foster emotional awareness: Over weekends of intensive therapy, we taught the patient the TA approach and worked with him concurrently in the Gestalt approach so that he could get through his impasse by making a Redecision. Only then did he really begin to change, to stop playing games, to stop maintaining his rackets, to stop following his life script—and to become autonomous.

Treatment Techniques

We use several methods to help the patient reach a Redecision. Often, Redecision is reached when the nuclear family is recreated, as Satir does with her sculpting, or when the patient engages in a fantasied dialogue with his parent:

> A twenty-year-old girl who was hung on a *"Don't Grow Up"* In- junction was able to fantasize a dialogue with her father, in the course of which she told him *"I'm not going to stay a baby for you."* Then, in the manner of patients who are in Gestalt therapy, she told each member of her group in turn, *"I'm not going to stay a baby."* And now there was a dramatic change in her appearance: She took her hands away from the front of her crotch, she straight- ened her shoulders, her voice dropped almost an octave, she pushed her breasts out, sucked her abdomen in, started moving her hips seductively. In short, she looked like a twenty-year-old woman in- stead of a nine-year-old girl—and felt the change deep down in her guts.

Often Redecision can also be reached by Melges' method of allowing the patient to fantasize about his future, to predict where he will be ten years from now if he continues in his present life script, and where he will be ten years from now if he changes. He may then make a Redeci- sion based on the projection of his future.

Thus, at this stage in our professional development, we work quickly and intensively to get to the early Injunction and Decision, and create an environment for change, an environment in which the patient will learn to stop playing games to support his rackets which, in turn, pro- vide him with the evidence he needs to stay in his life script. In essence, of course, all TA therapists share these goals. Our approach differs from the traditional techniques used to date in that we don't expect the pa- tient to give up his games just because he has become aware of the fact that he's been playing games, or because he's been told they're neurotic; and we realize that he won't expect to give them up because they make him feel bad. Rather, we create a therapeutic climate in which the patient can make a new decision regarding the Injunction which underlies his life script. Once he has made this Redecision, his games and rackets become obsolete. There's no need for him to play *Kick Me,* if he isn't going to add up the kicks and try to cash them in for a free suicide—if, in short, he's made a new decision surrounding the *"Don't Be"* Injunction he was given as a child. There's no reason to get into an uproar with his wife in order not to be close, if he's made a new Decision not to go along with his parent's *"Don't Be Close"* Injunction. And if, on the other hand, he's decided to stick with that Injunction, if his Adult has made an uncontaminated decision not to be close, he doesn't need to provoke an argument to avoid closeness.

Redecision versus the counter-injunction. Some of the more orthodox TA therapists take the position that the patient can only give up the Injunction, which comes from the parent's Child, if he goes into the Counter-Injunction, which comes from the parent's Parent. Thus if the patient received a *"Don't Be"* from his parent's Child, but his parent's Parent said *"Work Hard, Succeed,"* the patient would be "cured" if he decided to switch to the Counter-Injunction. In addition, a number of TA therapists, Schiff and Steiner, in particular, often treat from their Parent, or, more precisely, assume the role of the patient's "good" parent. Thus Jaqui Schiff encourages her schizophrenic patients to deny their real parents completely, and reparents them in a belated attempt to provide them with the consistent, rationale parents they never had.

Apparently, Schiff's method has been successful. However, we question its therapeutic value over the long term. If the patient recognizes that he made the wrong decision at some point in his early life because it seemed to be the only decision he could make at the time, then he can change that decision. Instead of trying to change the content of the Injunction, which, in a sense, has become part of the patient's neurophysiology, he can redecide not to listen, to act on his own. Obviously, he cannot achieve autonomy if he stops listening to the Injunction of one parent only to begin listening to the Injunction of another parent, who happens to be the therapist. Steiner believes that if a suicidal patient gets a *"Don't Jump"* Injunction from his therapist often enough, when he gets to the edge of the San Francisco Bridge he'll hear the therapist saying *"Don't Jump,"* and won't. I would suggest that if the patient makes a new Decision regarding the *"Don't Be"* Injunction he was given, if he redecides, on his own, not to kill himself, he won't get to the edge of the bridge in the first place.

The Injunction versus the "witch message." Not surprisingly, those

TA therapists who think of the patient as a victim of his parents, who believe that the best way to get the patient to give up the Injunction is to encourage him to deny his parents, typically conceive of, and refer to the Injunction as the witch message. In fact, one TA therapist used to have his patients dance around a circle singing "Ding Dong the Witch Is Dead," at the conclusion of each marathon.

This technique sounds very exciting and like fun. The trouble is that it doesn't allow the patient to really say goodbye to the past. It helps him to hold on to his image of his mother and father as witches, and to maintain his negative feelings toward his parents. The patient cannot give up his Injunction until he lets his parents go; he cannot function autonomously until he stops shifting the responsibility for his behavior onto his parents.

Unlike other TA therapists, we believe that the patient will have reached an important point in his treatment when he is able to recognize that his parents were real people who suffered their own hurts and disappointments. For then he will begin to forgive them, not in a maudlin way, but as a result of his deep gut recognition that his parents weren't witches or monsters; they were just two people trying to get along, hurting, and passing on some of the hurts—what Fanita English calls the Hot Potato.

The contract. As is well known, the contract, as that term is used in Transactional Analysis, refers to the agreement the therapist makes with the patient to work on the patient's goals. In practice, the contract, as formulated by the patient provides us with data which are crucial to the success of our therapeutic efforts. Thus we ask the patient what he wants to achieve now, or today, or this week, or in the next eight weeks. Then we look for the Injunction, the script or first act, the early decision, the games, and the rackets—in short, we look for all the ways in which the patient denies his autonomy.

We listen to the patient's words—try, can't, want, should, ought to, why-because—all ways he has of saying won't, of copping out. And now we ask him to get in touch with the real power of the won't: If he's been saying *"I want to quit smoking,"* for example, we ask him to say *"I* won't *quit smoking"* instead. And then we ask him to fantasize where he will be in five years, or ten years, or fifteen years, if he continues to smoke, and let him realize the full implications of his life pattern. We let him feel enough organismic shame or disgust, to use Simkin's term, so that at that moment he will make a Redecision, feel the change in his guts, feel the flood of relief of having made a real decision to grow, or play, or live.*

What we try to do, then, is to work quickly to put the patient in touch with himself, to make him aware of himself, of the lack of congruence between what he thinks and what he feels, the lack of congruence between what he says and his behavior; we try to make him see how he maintains the same kinds of feelings, regardless of the situation, how he sets things up so that he can stay in the bad feelings that support the injunction and the script he's in, and how he thus robs himself of his own autonomy. We don't allow him to talk about his past relationship with his mother or father; we ask him to sit in a chair facing one or the other parent, and talk to them now. We ask him to take both parts, and frequently in this way he is able to get to the roots of the basic core position in life which he has held on to for many years.

> A forty-year-old woman was able to find all sorts of things to feel guilty about, until she had collected enough guilt to seriously consider knocking herself off. We asked her to be thirty-five ("What do you feel guilty about now?") ; then thirty, then twenty-five, then twenty years old, etc. At forty, she felt guilty about driving her husband away; at thirty-five she was guilty about how she was raising her children; at thirty she felt guilty because she didn't have orgasms; at twenty-five she felt guilty about having become pregnant at twenty before she was married; at twenty, she felt guilty about being pregnant; at fifteen she felt guilty about not getting her household chores and homework done; at ten she felt guilty about masturbating; at five she felt guilty every time she made too much noise, or did something her parents didn't like.
>
> Finally, we asked her to be a newborn baby: What did she feel guilty about now? She didn't know, so we asked her to put herself in her mother's skin and tell Carol (the patient) what was wrong with her. As her mother (Edna), she told herself that all her (Edna's) troubles started when she became pregnant with Carol, that her whole lousy life was Carol's fault, that it was Carol's fault that she had been conceived. When Carol made Edna say this, she stopped playing the part of her mother, and started to laugh. "*That's silly,*" she said, moved back into her own chair, "*You're blaming me for my own conception. You're nuts, and I'll be damned if I'm going to feel guilty about being alive anymore.*" At that point, then, she had more than Adult cognition of the reason she continued in her rackets. Deep down, she felt that she was really OK.

This is a far cry from the method of one TA therapist who shouts "You're OK" at his patients, thinking that this will change them, or

---

* Incidentally, both Mary and I quit smoking after writing this.

of other classical TA people who look carefully for the right words to give patients. In this case, the patient gave herself the words which put her in touch with the incongruity of her position. Once she recognized this incongruity, she could begin to break loose from her old life pattern by checking herself whenever she did something, or felt something, or behaved in some way that fit that pattern. No one I know has worked through an impasse and then changed forever, but the enthusiasm and excitement the patient feels at the moment of breakthrough, and shares with the group, are unique. Moreover, these feelings give the patient a new frame of reference for his every-day activities. His feelings and behavior are no longer predetermined by his overwhelming sense of guilt. Then, having acquired a new sense of his own worth, the patient can get out of his old script.

For instance, Carol was really in a Cinderella script: She had been scrubbing the hearth, waiting for her fairy godmother to come and release her, and feeling guilty and depressed while she waited. From time to time she had entered treatment, and had briefly given up her mother's Injunction to drop dead, and the script, but only to go into the Counter-Injunction, "work hard, scrub the hearth": thus, if she was a good girl, and worked hard in therapy, then the therapist would magically reward her with a coach and four, and she could give up her script. The trouble with fairy tales is that the writers were crooks: They took a real life situation and tacked a phony ending on to it; little girls who read fairy tales and wait for the magic prince to come and get them out of the set are doomed to disappointment.

The real success in therapy comes when the patient is able to work through an impasse, to get on the other side by both redeciding and feeling the redecision. Making what Simkin calls an "intention" to change is not the same as changing. The patient who makes a redecision to enjoy life, or to live, or to be close makes it at the moment that he feels it in his bones and guts, at the moment he feels the real joy of being free. Only then can he really let go of his injunctions and counter-injunctions, his games, his rackets, his script.

The function of the group. When Carol stopped feeling guilty, and was able to make a Redecision to live and to take positive steps to implement that Redecision, she got strokes from the rest of the group for her work. Thus, she became aware of the fact that the rewards she could expect for living surpassed the rewards she had been getting for being depressed. She then proceeded to establish a different life style for herself.

The function of the group, then, is not to help members work through their transference problems while the therapist sits passively by, waiting to give his weekly interpretation. The group is used to provide an encounter experience for the working patient. We no longer sit by and wait for someone to say something; we take a strong lead. We do a great deal of one-to-one work in the group, ask other patients to intervene when they have something to say, and analyze their games when they intervene. We do not use encounter tricks, but use the group to reinforce the patient's Redecision. For example, it will be recalled that we asked a young patient to tell each member of the group that she was no longer a baby. In contrast to the patient's parent, the group gives the patient strokes for change; thus it can be and often is a force for change.

SUMMARY

The detailed account of a weekend group marathon session appended to this article (Appendix A) will help to further clarify the therapeutic concepts and innovations described herein. To summarize our philosophy: We believe that change must occur on an emotional level, but that it is often facilitated by cognition. We use ourselves to facilitate change, but not as new parents. If the patient chooses to cast us in the role of parents, we need to make sure that he will not set up his old games with new referents. Thus autonomy, complete and free, is our goal, and we believe that the techniques used in TA therapy to foster cognition, combined with the guts work of Gestalt therapy, is the best way to implement that goal.

Appendix A

ANNOTATED TRANSCRIPT OF A GROUP
THERAPY WEEKEND MARATHON

The annotated transcript of a group therapy marathon which follows demonstrates, in greater detail, the clinical application of the theoretical concepts discussed above.

As mentioned earlier, we often deal with patients in the group on a one-to-one basis. During the particular weekend marathon which was taped for inclusion in this article, the following quotes focus on Tim, a twenty-one-year-old patient who was seriously ill, and suicidal. Tim had been hospitalized previously for treatment of a drug (LSD)-induced psychosis, manifested by delusions, hallucinations, irrational and bizarre behavior, looseness of associations, flight of ideas, etc. He had been out of the hospital for about five weeks when he attended his first group session.

Initially, Tim's behavior was rather provocative, and the other members of the group cooperated in his attempt to maintain his bad feelings about himself. However, once we diagrammed the moves of the *Kick Me* game he was playing, Tim agreed to stop (and, if he slipped, not to accept the payoff). Instead, he would get closer to the other members of the group. At the next two sessions, he did well in that he didn't play any serious games and participated, to some extent, in the work the others were doing. He wasn't working for himself, however. And at this point we invited him to take part in a marathon. Tim accepted our invitation, but after the marathon started, he sat around silently for a while and then proceeded to express some doubts about its value.

Tim: Bob and Mary,* I'd like to . . . I came here to get something done. And it's not been getting done too much, and I'm not enjoying myself too much. (By saying "It's not been getting done too much," rather than "I'm not doing it," he's relinquished all responsibility for what happens to him.)

Mary: What is it you still want to get done?

Tim: Um . . . I still want to decide to live for sure, and I don't really know how to ask you to help me do that. But I do want to do it. (This is the first move toward a Redecision.)

Mary: So you want to decide to live. And that you will go on living no matter what?

Tim: Yeah (*questioning note in his voice*). Well, not that I'm going to go on living, but that I'll be committed to life, to making things come out right. (This is encouraging. Now he's saying he's committed to "making things come out right, rather than "It's not been getting done. He's beginning to sound as if he's taking charge of things.)

Mary: What does that mean to you—making things come out right?

Tim: Uh—making things happy—uh—doing things for my own—uh —for my own happiness. Then I'd have 60 happy years. (This is another step toward a Redecision.)

Bob: You said for my own happiness, and shook your head *no*— what's the other side of it? (Apparently, part of him is not in agree-

---

* The marathon was led by cotherapists, Bob (Robert Goulding) and Mary (Mary Edwards Goulding). In general, we encourage patients to call us by our first names to counteract any tendency on their part to cast us in the role of "good" parents, who would tell them what to do, make decisions for them, etc.

ment. I want him to be in touch with that side too, to completely resolve this conflict.)

Tim: The other side is, I'll live and then I'll die.

Mary: So if you decide to live you'll have 60 happy years.

Tim: Yeah—that doesn't sound so bad now, but uh I have a way of interpreting things very strongly. I listen—just listen—take sounds as if they were coming out of the tape recorder, take all sights as if they were on a movie screen, and all smells as if God was blowing smells in my nose, and mixing them all together and coming out with uh a . . . (*looks at Bob*) You're not interested in hearing God, are you? (*Bob shakes head.*)

Mary: I'm not particularly, because I'm still back with the thing you said before that—about the 60 happy years—and I don't want to be construed as promising anybody full happiness. What I'm interested in is a decision that you're going to live, period. Do you see what I mean? You can get hung up if every day has to be happy.

Tim: Yeah, well I think I can make them pretty darn happy. I think I can—at the conclusion of each day—say I'm glad this day happened— no, that I made this day happen.

Mary: Yeah, it's important that you separate these too—that your life doesn't depend upon each day's evaluation—but that you decide to live no matter what.

Tim: Yeah.

Bob: I like what you just did, Tim, when you went back and said "No, I made this day happen." You heard yourself use the "this day happened," and you turned it around.

Tim: Yeah, but I don't know that I cured it—by just doing it. I'm aware of that, I'm aware of a lot of things that uh blow my mind, there are a lot of things I'm not aware of. I haven't laughed in a long time. I'm, I'm getting anaesthetized. I'm bored—nothing seems funny anymore. I don't say anything that's funny.

(Another participant, A, says—"Remember that laugh you had when you first came?")

Tim: I don't like that laugh, that's like blowing off steam. That laugh is all right, I'd rather laugh that laugh than no laugh, but I would much rather just laugh and I don't know what's holding me back (*painfully*). I don't know what's making me feel sad, making my face sad (*here he made a sad face*). (*pause*)

Mary: Will you go on? Put some words to that sadness you're feeling.

Tim: Well, I seem to feel sadder when I start talking about all the things I've lost.

Mary: All the things you've lost? What have you lost?

Tim: I've lost my laugh, my ability to laugh and uh and I've lost a relationship with a girl that started that was quite promising. I . . . well I felt like I was in control of that—the whole thing—and then I lost control. It went overboard, or else I controlled it to go overboard— either way I lost—that I've lost spontaneity.

Mary: So some of your goals for the future are to laugh more, to allow yourself to be more spontaneous, and to have a relationship with a girl or girls—(*Tim nods*)—and I hear basically this, that the decision that's needed is that you're going to live—not if you're happy, or if you're spontaneous, or if you have a girlfriend, but that you are going to live.

Tim: Yeah, that's about it. I don't understand why I'm here—who made me, why this world is here, how I got here, I don't understand. I feel that there is uh a loving spirit around me, but that spirit is calling me to be with it, through death—through deciding to die—and I won't do it.

Mary: It sounds right now as if at a point where you decide to act, to live, all of a sudden you trip back into some philosophizing—almost as if to take away your current action, ability to move—because you don't know how come the world is here, or how come a couple of cells join together and add up to a human being. Neither do I—but you're going off into that at a point where you're talking about committing yourself to living.

Tim: Yeah—the thing is I want to believe that I have a pipeline to God, and I want to believe that all of you people in this room have a . . . (Here he went into a long diatribe about God, most of which was psychotic.)

Mary: See how you get yourself off your stated desire that you decide to live? By going off a back street of depression—I don't understand that.

Tim: I want to live—that's my computer—thinking from one part of me. (*Long, long silence, and then he frowned.*)

Bob: What's the frown?

Tim: I'm nowhere again—anything I say from here on will have no meaning. It's just something I'm saying, something in my head.

Bob: Well, you said "I want to live," and you had some feelings about that, and then you frowned, and then you said that doesn't mean anything—and then you're back to what Mary was saying. At any given moment you can quickly run to something to feel bad about. Like how did I get here, or what's the world all about, or everybody is killing everybody, or something else. This ties in considerably with what we said the very first day—how I saw you doing things that ended up in your feeling badly. So that you can do something with someone else and end up feeling badly, or if that's not available, you can say "Oh, I can feel badly about . . ."—and then pick out something to feel badly about.

Tim: Yeah (*smiling*) I can always find something to feel badly about.

Bob: And then you can add up enough bad things to feel badly about. If you search hard enough, they're not too hard to find, and then you can say "Yeah, I can kill myself—to heck with it—it's not worth it"— and what Mary was suggesting was that you stay at this moment in feeling good about a decision you have made, rather than running off to something to feel badly about. So what I heard you say was, "I want to decide to live"—and right at this moment, what is keeping you from saying *"I am going to live."*

(*Long pause.*)

Tim: I don't feel capable of receiving love (*long pause*). It's from a human being that's not worthy of a soul—

Mary: I've got a hunch that you're supposed to feel badly about deciding to live. (This is a theoretical position that Mary took—the Injunction says "If you die I'll love you," so, of course, if he decides to live, his little Child will not get any love, and therefore he can't feel good, an impossible position if he stays in the Injunction.)

Tim: Yeah.

Mary: How come? Will you get with that? (We ask "will you," not "can you".)

Tim: I can tell you my head trip on that—I'm backing away from certainty to death—I'm scared of killing myself—that's why—I'm guilty of being afraid.

But I don't know if that's the right reason—I sure hope— (*voice drops*) it isn't.

Mary: If you were really feeling healthy right now—really feeling good, and wow, you're going to live out the rest of your life, and know where you're going, and all that stuff. All of a sudden you dropped the depression, dropped the philosophical side trips, and said "Hey, wow, I'm really here. I've really made it." Will you go there in your imagination right now?

Tim: Yeah.

Mary: In your imagination you say "Wow, I've really made it—I know where I am, I'm going to live out my life." What's scarey about that?

Tim: I'd have a hell of an inflated ego to believe I'm a super power, that I could control people.

Mary: And who would you want to control—can you name somebody?

Tim: Well, my mother, my family, my girlfriend.

Mary: Will you see your mother in front of you now, and you say "Wow, I'm really there. . . ."

Tim: Yeah.

Mary: OK, will you tell her how you are going to control her—from your really there position?

Tim: Well (*moves in his chair*)—it's not so much I want to control you, as I just won't buy crap from you—won't buy any crap from you—and not only that, I can see through the crap you are handing me and I can give you what you want, what you need, and what I want to give you which is my love. . . . (*The next few words were said in a very low voice.*)

Mary: From your really there position—can you visualize yourself walking out the front door, and saying "Goodbye, I'm really there, and I'm living a life for me now? And I'll see you at Christmas and Easter and when I'm in town."

Tim: Goodbye—that's a hard one to envision, that's the hardest one. Well, I'll be on my way—on my happy merry way—I'm leaving you to carry our load. (*Mumbled*)—You may have a mess, but I'm through with you now all right.

Bob: OK, so then you leave, saying "Goodbye, I'll see you at Christmas, and Easter, and times like that"—and what do you fantasize yourself doing between now and five years from now. I run into you in 1975, when you stop by on your motorcycle and say hello. OK—and what have you been doing, Tim, in 1975?

Tim: I could be up to 80—my story. . . .

Bob: Will you make up a story?

Tim: I would have found my way into a way of life. (He starts out very sadly, and I can see that the chances are very good he's about to go off on another sorry, philosophical, irrational, word salad—and at this point I want to hear from his creative and genius side, from the happy, spontaneous side, I know he has, and for him to get in touch with that—he has been in this depressed jazz long enough—and the idea of this exercise is to let him taste the other side—so):

Bob: Tim, will you go on a Time machine with me? I've got a big machine here (*I drag up two chairs*)—invisible walls, and it's a time machine. Will you get inside the Time Machine? (*Tim looks in.*) And we go Bzzzzzzzz, and it's 1975—OK—and here's the chair inside the machine. (*He gets in.*) We go Bzzzzzzz. It's now July 7, 1975 and I say "Wow, hi Tim how are you?"

(Tim and I went on a fantasy, in which he imagined being successful in 1975, with great enthusiasm, and again in 1980, with great enthusiasm. We went on a ride in his newly invented steam car, for instance, and his level of excitement got higher as he fantasized events. Without the fantasy trip, I don't believe that he would have gotten in touch with his own power at this time, and would not have reached the decision he ultimately reached.

At the end of the fantasy trip, we came back to the present. I asked him if he felt good about the things he had invented. He said yes, and then we had the following dialogue.)

Bob: So the way you got to do all these things was to look for ways to feel good?

Tim: Yeah.

Bob: OK, let's go back to 1970. Will you decide to live so that you can start doing those things? (This was a mistake, and slowed down the process. He was in this bind because of his father's demands that he succeed, among other things, and at this point I made what I thought was a reasonable request in view of the fantasy, but which he felt was a parental demand.)

Tim: (*After a long pause, sadly:*) Yes, I decide to live, I decide not to kill myself. I decide not to go to sleep forever.

Bob: You mean that?

Tim: Not all the way. I think I would be crying if I did. It's like if I decide that, I won't be able to receive love.

Bob: I can hear what you say, and I don't believe that you won't be able to receive love.

Tim: You don't believe it?

Bob: I believe that at this moment you believe it, but I don't.

Tim: Yeah, I think you're right.

Bob: Will you allow yourself to open up to receive love—from me?

Tim: Yes (*pause*) —I like the idea very much.

Bob: So if I love you as another human being that's OK with you? (I deliberately said, that I could love him as a human being, [not because he was an achiever] to get out of the bind I set up by the work demand I made previously.)

Tim: Yes, but it makes me feel like someone is clutching my heart.

Bob: I have no expectations for you—and what you do with the fact that I love you as another human being. . . .

Tim: I just can't believe that—I just look for evidence and it's not good enough.

Bob: Do you hear me? I have no expectations for what you do—I love you as a human being.

Tim: Yeah, I can see what you're saying more clearly. I think I have felt that too—I know I have.

Bob: So, how about the decision?

(He starts to cry. I wait a while and then say:)

Bob: I think I know—and you and I can find out—a lot of the reasons why you've felt the way you've felt in the past. I'm not sure it's that important to find out why, but I think we can if we look for them. I think we can find them a lot easier, if they're important, or maybe even drop the question if it's not important, if you first decide, "By God no matter what happens, I am going to live." I'm not going to kill myself, accidentally or on purpose—ever.

Tim: By God, I'm not going to kill myself, no matter if things get pretty tough. (*There is a two- or three-minute pause here, while he cries, Mary and I cry, and 30 other people in the room cry.*)

Mary: I'm so very fond of you, Tim without expectations, and with a great deal of willingness for you to say goodbye as soon as you're ready.

Tim: I just don't know when to be sure. What are the conditions for being sure? I know I felt sure about some things. I know I can do some things, because I can feel myself behind them. . . . I know I can get something done when I start it— (*mumble*).

Bob: That's the key. You don't know right now how you're going to make the decision come true, and that's not as important as making the decision. You—like I, and other people have—will find the way.

Tim: It seems like my voice is going to betray me, if I promise. . . .

Bob: I'm not asking you for a promise. This is a decision for you, not a promise to me. I'm here asking you to look at it, and decide it, for you. Not for mother, not for father, not for anybody else—not for Mary, not for Virginia, but for Tim, for you.

Tim: Yeah.

Bob: Then you can say goodbye to mother, goodbye to father, goodbye to Mary, goodbye to me, in all kinds of ways, then get on your motorcycle and ride over the mountains. The decision about living is for you.

Tim: Sometimes life isn't really worth it.

Bob: I know.

Tim: This last week has not been.

Bob: I know that sometimes life looks like it isn't worth it.

Tim: Then why live, if it's not worth it, even for one day?

Bob: Why die if it is?

Tim: I know the last week hasn't been worth it.

Bob: Are you blocking out the next ten thousand days? Because of your experience in the last week?

Tim: Yeah.

Bob: I think that you've been living under the early Decision (you made), a long time ago, not to live. You've been struggling with it a long time. And as long as you're in that struggle, whether to or not to, then you'll always find black clouds.

Tim: Yeah, that's true.

Bob: Yeah, I know, I've heard you.

Tim: (*With a warm chuckle*) I can always find white clouds too.

Bob: That's right, and I've heard that too. I don't think you know what it feels like to say "Hey, I'm going to live, I'm going to live. That's a decision I can make." I don't think you know what it feels like to make that decision. And you're never going to find out what it's like, until you make it.

Tim: (*Crying*) It's for me, the decision is for me!!!! It's really for me. It's for me, it's for me. Not for you, not for (*this is said very softly*) anyone. It's for me, to commit myself to life, to commit myself to something that's going to end in 70 years.

Bob: Or 80, or 90 or 100. I plan to live to be 150!!! At least.

Tim: Mmmmm.

Bob: I don't know whether I'll make it or not, but I'm planning on it.

Tim: Yeah (*long sigh, sniffle*) —uh—I suppose it doesn't matter how long you, and everyone else in this room, waits for me. (*Pause*) I'm not going to kill myself.

His Father (who was there): You really mean that?

Mary: At this moment will you be your mother, and say what you want to hear? Will you sit in this chair, and tell Tim, mother.

Tim (*as mother*): Gee, that's too bad. I'd rather have you for my own than have you free.

Mary: Will you be Tim and answer that.

Tim: That's too bad. (There was a resolution of the old oedipal situation at this point, and he laughed, then grinned happily.)

Bob: You did a good job on that.

Tim: Yeah, I'm not going to kill myself. That's the way it is. I'm not going to kill myself.

Mary: Will you tell your father?

Tim: All I see of him is a shell.

Mary: Will you tell him anyway?

Tim: Tell a shell?

Mary: Yeah.

Tim: Dad, I'm not going to kill myself. It's ridiculous. I'm not going to kill myself.

Tim (as Dad): You aren't? (*In an entirely different voice.*) Well, I'd rather have you kill yourself than live a life like Uncle Tom.

(Apparently, Uncle Tom was the family ne'er-do-well—and so now we see what the Injunctions were: Mother said "Don't grow up, stay my little boy." And father said from his Parent "Succeed," and from his Child "Kill yourself"—better be dead than no good.)

Mary: Will you respond to that?

Tim (as self): *That's Tough.* (*Firmly.*) I'm not going to kill myself. I'm sorry. (Then his face lit up with a great smile.) I'm *not sorry*, Dad. (Everyone in the room laughed with relief, enjoying this crucial last remark. And it really was crucial—the first automatic "I'm sorry" was a cop out, which he immediately heard, and retracted.)

(Tim then started to sob, and after a minute or two I said:)

Bob: Like you said, when you mean it you'll cry. I want to stop now. (Everyone then talked to Tim, and hugged him, stroking him for an important change in his life, instead of hugging and stroking him for the old rackets.)

Follow-up. Tim then went east for several months, and got a job on the East Coast. Some time later, his sister visited him and offered to supply him with grass, LSD, or any other drug he might want. Tim's response to her offer was, *"I've decided not to kill myself—and that's a way to kill myself—I'm not buying!"*

10

TELEVISION IMAGE CONFRONTATION IN GROUP THERAPY

Ian Alger, M.D.

Training Psychoanalyst, New York Medical College

INTRODUCTION

In recent years an increasing number of workers have used videotape playback in psychotherapy and several have written about its particular advantages in the setting of group therapy (5, 6, 14). Although the experience of being able to review an event in therapy immediately following its occurrence has unique advantages, and although the self-confrontation involved in such a procedure has a direct impact of its own, it is universally agreed that the use of video playback finds its special advantage, not as a unique therapeutic method, but rather as an important adjunct within a larger psychotherapeutic context.

The author has written on this overall theme as well as describing several clinical uses of videotape playback involving such entities as "image impact," and "second chance phenomenon," as well as the usefulness of videotape playback in communication problems involving messages at various levels of abstraction, sent over multiple channels (1, 2, 3).

In the present chapter very little attempt will be made to cover this comprehensive area, but rather the intent will be to focus attention on the application in group therapy of certain special uses of closed circuit television and video playback. Methods similar to several of those to be described have been used in other therapeutic frameworks, such as psychodrama (11), role play (8), gestalt (12), and transactional (7).

Many of the methods, because they focus attention on processes within the person (intrapersonal), find reference points in various theoretical systems in which hypothetical representations of various intrapersonal processes are designated; for example, the Freudian ego: super-ego: id; the Missildine formulations of inner child of the past: approving parent: disapproving parent (19); and the transactional model of parent: child: and adult. These various hypothetical representations and personifications can be understood as metaphorical ways of conveying personal experience of the self which in actual living seem familiar to all of us, and yet which, without some such system, tend to be extremely difficult to convey to another person.

In individual therapy much attention has been placed on the identification of these "feelings of self," and indeed much of the attempt to integrate theory during the past decade has revolved around an understanding of the concepts and feeling of self (identity, and self-systems), and in particular how they develop and operate within the contexts of interpersonal relationships, and larger systems and groups including society.

When such methods of investigating the self, originally developed in individual therapy, have been used in groups, many observers have noted that the results seem more like, "individual therapy in groups," rather than "group therapy," the latter implying greater attention being paid to group dynamic processes rather than to reactions of individuals (intrapersonal dynamics).

The aim of this chapter is to present ways in which video has been useful in creating a means whereby the methods now so often used with individuals in a group setting, can be adapted through the use of television, so that a more effective and dynamic group involvement develops.

The chapter will be divided into three main sections: first, a short technical description of equipment; second, a clinical description of several ways of using video in which special effects can be created to explore not only aspects of one's self-image, but also to explore the concept of one's self in relationship to one's interaction with others; third, a discussion of the ways in which some of the clinical methods described have been integrated into a more dynamic group involvement.

TECHNICAL METHODS AND EQUIPMENT

Only a brief outline of equipment and technical methods will be given here, primarily because each clinical setting requires a special survey by a trained television technician or engineer, in order that the most appropriate and the most economical system can be installed; and secondly, because technical developments in this field are moving so rapidly that any specific recommendations made here will soon be outmoded.

Nevertheless, certain basic pieces of equipment will be mentioned and the fundamentals of their use described. For the techniques under discussion, a minimum of two television cameras is necessary, each equipped with a zoom lens. A T.V. monitor of fair size (at least 23″ diagonal) is necessary as well as a videotape recorder. The final essential component is a special effects generator which permits the synchronization and mixing of signals from two different cameras so that superimposition of one image on another is possible, as well as the effect of splitting the screen so that the image from one camera is shown on the left side of the T.V. monitor, while the image from the other camera appears on the right side.

Opinion is varied among writers about the merit of having equipment hidden or freely visible to the group. In most of the techniques to be described, the monitor, of course, is visible and because of the intricacy and importance of the positioning of the cameras, both these in the author's experience, are more useful when no attempt at concealment is made. The other components can be better enclosed in an equipment room, particularly if the videorecorder is equipped with remote control features.

Finally, the importance of even and adequate lighting should be stressed, particularly when the double-profile method (described later) is tried. Also, too much emphasis cannot be placed on the importance of good sound recording when using T.V. In many instances a lavolier (neck-suspended) microphone gives the best results, and can be used in many of the special methods outlined.

SPECIAL EFFECTS ACHIEVED BY THE USE OF TELEVISION

As with other scientific instruments and mechanical tools, television and videoplayback represent a means of expanding, altering, and controlling human capacities, in this case particularly the human capacity for perception. Wilmer (16), has noted that the zoom lens adds to man's capacity the ability to focus increasingly closely on an image, a faculty that is not normally possible. In addition, television can provide electronic alteration of image size, simultaneous views from different perspectives, novel juxtapositions, and superimpositions of images. The capabilities of videotape playback allow for repetition of scenes, with or without sound, and for slow motion playback, or stopping of motion entirely, or for reverse playback. All these additional capabilities can be used in an endless series of innovations to sharpen, highlight, and reveal otherwise hidden or obscure aspects of human behavior, and can also provide a unique stimulus to encourage awareness of an individual's inner processes, his own thoughts and feelings which might otherwise go unnoticed, or ignored.

(a) Face-to-Face Self-Confrontation

This method was originally described by Tausig and Shaeffer (15), and later by Kubie (9), and also by the present author (4). The patient is seated before a television monitor, behind which is placed a television camera with a zoom lens. The subject then is face-to-face with his own image, being presented to him full-face, life-size (by means of adjusting the zoom lens). The effect differs from observing one's image in a mirror in two ways. First, the subject sees his image exactly as another person does, and not reversed, as one does in a mirror. Second, the subject cannot look directly into his own eyes because the camera is placed behind and slightly above the top of the television monitor. (The possibility of the subject looking into his own eyes could technically be achieved by having the television image projected onto a larger one-way mirror from a small television tube, in the same way as some of the early television home-sets operated. The camera could then be positioned directly behind the one-way mirror.)

The patient in one variation of the method is then instructed to free associate while he observes his own image. Kubie describes a fascinating series of reactions experienced by one analyst who agreed to act as an experimental subject. In that instance, the individual was able to make many important historical connections as he recognized expressions and mannerisms which were familiar to him from members of his early family. In another variation, the patient is instructed to look at the image on the screen as if it were another person, and then to speak to that person and tell him what the patient sees about him, and also to report what feelings the patient is experiencing as he watches. Later, the patient is asked to allow a reversal to occur, and to have the image speak to him from the screen, and to tell him what he thinks and feels about the patient. Following this, the patient is asked to attach identifying names to himself and to his image, and the two are then invited to hold a continuing dialogue. One can recognize the derivation of this adapted method from those methods in psychodrama and gestalt therapy using a change of chairs to alter roles, or age, while speaking to "another self" as one imagines that other self to be sitting in the chair opposite.

(b) Profile Self-Confrontation

In this method, the patient is seated directly in front of a television monitor. Two cameras equipped with zoom lenses are arranged one on either side of the patient, so that the one is televising the right profile while the other camera is televising the left profile. Signals from both cameras are processed through a special effects generator, which allows the screen of the monitor to be split, so that the emerging total picture is of the two profiles facing each other.

It is known that the human face is never symmetrical, and this has been simply demonstrated since the turn of the century by using photographic methods. Two entirely new photographs can be obtained by taking a full-face picture of anyone, then cutting the negative through the center line of the face, and then printing two new photographs, using in one the left-side negative used correctly to depict one side of the face, and printed reversed to represent the opposite side. The same procedure is followed with the right side negative. The two new photos (left-left, and right-right) are then easily seen to be entirely different from each other, and also different from the true representation of the subject. Theories have been formulated which suggests that one side of the face (the left in right-dominant subjects) portrays characteristics which represent private reactions; while the other side of the face represents more the attitudes shown to the world. Regardless of the merit of such a theory, it is usually remarkable to see the variation in expression of the two profiles. Of course among movie stars, and commonly among the rest of us also, the concern with having the "good side" taken is well-known.

When the double-profile is displayed on the T.V. screen, the patient is asked to comment on his observations and reactions to both sides. He is then invited to converse with one or both, and the profile-images are asked to respond. Soon a conversation develops among the three in the cast. At times the two profiles are directed to talk to each other, and attitudes and reactions which may surprise the patient suddenly emerge. As in the previous example, the patient is asked to identify each image with a name or some other designation so confusion as to which character is talking can be avoided.

(c) Juxtaposition of Images

Distance between participants in therapy as well as in all social behavior is known to be significant (13). Each culture has developed rules which determine the distancing in various contexts, and when variation of these accepted boundaries occur new significance is indicated, and this communication alters the whole transaction. Again by the use of two cameras, and the special effects generator and split-screen technique, two participants in a group can be placed side-by-side on the screen, even though in actuality they may be sitting on opposite sides of the group. If they are directly interacting, comparison can be more easily made as to the intricate series of behaviors they are serially displaying. Slow motion can be used on playback to examine minutely the start of any sequence. In one instance, for example, a man and a woman both seemed to move their right arms together, then both shifted together in their chairs, and then both together seemed to alter the position of their left arms, in a downward sweeping motion. On slow motion it became instantly clear that the woman in all three motions was moving first, although only by a fraction of a second, and that the man was tracking her movements. This information helped to uncover in the group discussion that followed his covert desire to placate her, and beyond that his fear of displeasing her, and this general realization was in direct contrast to the apparent commanding overt attitude he had been displaying towards her in previous group encounters.

Not only can two participants be placed side-by-side in this manner, but as in the method described under (b) above, the profiles of two participants can be placed facing each other on the split screen, and dialogue can ensue with this close face-to-face confrontation literally taking place not more than half an inch apart. This method has been extremely useful with married couples, many of whom have been encouraged to confront each other more directly in subsequent meetings after such a videotape playback exchange.

(d) Alteration of Image Size

The usefulness of videotape playback in presenting objective data for review has often been described, but the possibility of television being used to distort objective reality, and thereby create in that illusion a more accurate portrayal of the perceptive distortions of patients has received less attention. Again by using two cameras and a split screen method, two participants of a group are shown together. The two patients are chosen for this experience because of some indication that a difference in their experience of size towards one another has some discrepancy to reality. This discrepancy often is based on an age-awareness, in which one patient feels like the child of another, and therefore distorts his own and the other's images. It may also have a sex related factor, in which some patient may see certain women as much larger than they appear to be to others. When this type of situation exists, the patient who feels smaller is asked to advise the camera operators to vary the size of the two images until the difference feels "right" to him. In this mode a continuing interaction between the two is invited, and videotaped. The sizes are then reversed, and further interaction is encouraged, and finally both segments are replayed for reaction. Following this, a final segment is recorded with both images the same size, and a final replay and reaction time devoted to this.

(e) Transposition of Body Parts

This method also uses the capability of the two camera arrangement with a special effects generator, with the T.V. screen split horizontally, so the head of one person can be projected to appear on the body of another. In this way, a startling effect can be demonstrated which shows the non-verbal reaction of one group member to the verbalizations of another. An additional outcome of this has been at times the development in the speaker of greater empathy for his listeners.

(f) Superimposition of Image

This is another method favored by Wilmer (16), in which a closeup of one member is superimposed over a wide-angle shot of the entire group. This effect is also achieved with two cameras, and with a special effects generator allowing one picture to fade into the other, known as "ghosting." The advantage of this method over putting a closeup in one corner of an overall picture is that the size of the face in the superimposed way can be much larger, and no portion of the overall shot is missed. The large face can be switched from one group member to another, so the reactions shown by the member in focus can constantly be related on replay to the general group interaction and activity.

APPLICATION OF THESE SPECIAL EFFECTS IN GROUP THERAPY

Some of the methods outlined can be used in therapy with individuals, and these, of course, can be used in group therapy, where the group essentially plays the part of an audience. While some have called this "therapy in a group," as distinguished from "group therapy," it is frequently utilized in many Gestalt groups. Descriptions of the use of the video in this way will be followed by examples which demonstrate some of the unique values of T.V. and video playback in encouraging active involvement of the group. Special discussion then will be devoted to the use of negotiation between images, with emphasis on the facilitation provided by mediation.

(a) Image Confrontation—Group as Audience

A volunteer from the group is asked to seat himself in relationship to cameras and monitor in an appropriate position, depending on whether full-face, or double-profile is to be used. The therapist acts as director, giving instructions and asking questions of either the patient or the image (s) in order to encourage the development of the process. Throughout the procedure the rest of the group remains silent. One can speculate that, aside from the learning involved in the observation, group members could develop increased suggestibility to the process, and also could react competitively so that their performances when their "turn" comes, would be strongly affected by these factors. In addition, the position of authority of the therapist is almost certainly enhanced by this procedure, and in turn, tendencies for some patients to relate in a dependent way with either more compliance, or more rebelliousness may be encouraged. Because of these factors the author in his own practice tries to avoid techniques which tend to evoke an authoritarian approach. On the other hand, there is the undisputable fact that personal (inner) experiences are occurring constantly, and that at times it is most important that some exchange or communication about these experiences be encouraged in the group if the human possibilities of the group are to be more fully realized. It is precisely in this crucial angle, between the importance of the communication of personal reactions, and the importance of maintaining a group dynamic of active involvement, that the utilization of special video methods has a valuable contribution to make. A few of the following examples will illustrate how a patient can be helped to use some of the techniques.

The first two examples are of patients reacting with their own full-face images. Peter, a divorced man of 37, who had been in individual therapy for three years, but only recently had begun group therapy, participated regularly in group sessions by maintaining a silence presided over by a somewhat supercilious expression, rarely spoke except to make cynical or humorous self-deprecatory comments. His wit and cleverness usually served to keep most people at a distance because his barbs were pointed. He agreed to experiment with talking to his own image, and although he spoke disparagingly of the procedure, he mentioned as he sat in front of the T.V. monitor that he felt anxious. He was encouraged to speak directly to the image in the first person, just as if he were addressing another person, and was told to tell that other person what he observed about him, and what his feeling reactions were. He began by saying, "You really don't look very happy. And you're fatter than I thought you'd be. . . . (pause) . . . You really look very worried, and very unhappy. I feel sorry for you. You seem so lonely. Like you can't tell anybody how badly you feel." After several pauses, and continuing in the same vein, he said, "You really look so sad, it's as if you wanted to cry. You look so sad!" At this point tears were visible in his eyes, and he began to cry, and was encouraged to allow himself to experience this feeling, and to respond to it on the screen. During his crying he said, "I just never saw you like this. You really feel so badly!" At that point the therapist asked him to reverse, and to have the image speak for himself from the screen, to the patient. The image then said, "I never expected to be able to cry. I haven't cried for years. I just didn't realize I felt this way. I feel foolish, and cynical, and wonder what use this all is. But I feel amazed too. I never knew I felt this badly."

This experience was singularly important for this man, and he used it as a key reference during the ensuing months. It often served as a self-reminder, and in later sessions he would interrupt his own cynicism to recall the sadness he had experienced, and would say, "There I go with that putting-down routine . . . but it's true that I just hide my sadness . . . I remember my tears." At other times other members of the group would use the episode as a reference point, and tell Peter that they too remembered his tears, and refused to take his cynicism, and frequently he would be able to respond differently, with less distance and removal.

Another man, Morris, had been in combined group and individual therapy for three years. A common theme in group over this time had been his youthful appearance, and on several occasions he had become very angry when women in the group had reacted to him in a mothering way, or when one woman reacted angrily because he would not be more of a man with her. On the occasion of his facing himself on the T.V. screen, he began by talking to his image, and then a conversation between his image and himself ensued. "I just don't like the way you look. You just look like a young boy who doesn't know what it's all about! God, I just can't stand to look at you. Why the hell don't you do something! Grow up, God damn it!" A little later, with encouragement from the therapist, the image answered, "Well, I don't know. I just feel like I haven't anything worth saying. I don't know. I do feel mad at you for the way you talk to me." The patient replied, "Well, damn it, do something about it!" The image responded, and this time there was a detectable deepening of the tone of voice, "Well, what do you want me to do! You're always at me, and always criticizing me. Why don't you just shut up and leave me alone!" It was evident that the expression on his face was changing as the conversation proceeded. The boyish quality was vanishing, and a more certain expression with some sense of command was taking its place. The patient commented, "I like the way you're looking now. Why aren't you like that all the time?" And the image immediately came back, "Why don't you just stop making critical remarks about me and let me be! I'm tired of this little boy stuff too, but I don't need your constant criticism. I must say I really feel better now, and I'm tired of all the criticism." The patient came back by saying, "I feel better too. I just don't feel angry now, and I really feel just like you look there." At that point he smiled, and turned to the rest of the group and said, "I really do feel better, and I really am tired of that little boy stuff." In this instance also, the patient and the group were able to use this experience as a reference point, and that session marked a definite change in the patient's manner of relating to the others. When evidence of his little boy approach would occur, often he or the group would remember the exchange described, and the recall would result in a shift in the manner of the patient, and usually some awareness of the dynamics in the group which were involved in the reappearance of the old mode of relating.

The next example is of a woman, Mary, about thirty years of age, divorced, who had been in group therapy for nearly one year. The technique used was the split screen in which her two profiles were projected on the screen facing each other. At first she commented on the two images. "Oh, I can't believe how different they are. I look about ten years younger on my right side. And my left side is so sad, and looks so hurt, and angry too. I can't believe it. They hardly look like the same person." When asked to describe her feelings towards the two images, she continued, "The right side looks younger, and more pleasant, and yet I really don't like her. I feel I can't know her. She seems very closed off, or superficial, or something. Like I can't really expect that she will give me any real idea of how she's feeling. She just looks pleasant all the time, sort of frozen into a kind of smile. I see how her mouth turns up. But the left side. Very sad. I feel for her. I feel I could know her. I like her, but I feel a little frightened too. She looks angry, and her mouth turns down. Look at all the lines around her eyes. She has suffered a lot."

Mary was now encouraged to have the two images speak to one another, and to say what they felt about each other. Left started, "I really don't like the way you smile. It makes me feel sick." Right replied, "You frighten me. Please don't be angry." Left answered, "I'm not angry really. I just wish you'd stop all that smiling. I feel you're in the way." Right said, "I really do feel frightened of you. I feel scared of what would happen if people saw you." The therapist asked, "What would happen?" And right responded, "I just don't think anyone would like me, and I'd be left alone." Following this, the therapist suggested that other members of the group involve themselves, and this example will be continued in the next section of the chapter.

(b) Active Group Involvement

After some member of the group has participated in using the equipment as illustrated in the previous section, other members can be encouraged by the therapist to take an active part. After this more involved participation has been initiated, the members of the group will be able on their own to utilize these methods and often will suggest that an image confrontation method be tried, and will frequently not need any cue from the therapist, but will take active roles throughout.

In a continuation of the last example in the previous section, the therapist asked other members of the group to freely speak to either image of Mary on the screen. (The two images were by agreement designated Mary-left, and Mary-right.) In response to Mary-right's saying, I just don't think anyone would like me, and I'd be left alone,"· a man in the group said, "It's funny, but I feel I can respond so much more to you when I don't have to see that constant smile. That really puts me off, because it seems to be telling me that I mustn't do anything that would upset you. Like that would be just too much anxiety or something." Another man continued the discussion, saying, "That's true for me too. When I look at Mary-left I really feel interested. I feel for you, and I wish I could get to know more about you. It really feels like I can talk to you." Mary-left replied, "It feels so good to be able to hear that. I feel let free, as if I hardly ever have this chance to talk so freely." Mary-right said, "I feel so scared. I don't know what's going to happen. I just want to smile, and move away." The first man said, "Well, don't do it. Try and stay. I don't want to be put off!"

The dialogue continued, and finally was closed by the therapist suggesting that the members talk not any longer to the images, but to Mary herself. Mary said, "It is really a strange feeling now. I feel I am aware of so much I never realized before, and I know that that serious and sad side of me is something I sense in myself often, but I really rarely ever have felt that I could let anyone else know about it." One of the men said, "I'm looking at you now, and I don't know if you've changed or not, but I'm less stuck with your pleasant expression, and it seems I can see a whole other part to you I never noticed before. I really feel so much closer to you." He then reached over and embraced Mary for the first time, and she then said that she felt anxious by the physical closeness, but also that she had longed for that closeness so much of her life, and now began to feel that the smile put a kind of shield between herself and others. This experience was also referred to later in group sessions, and again a new kind of group reference point was established.

Active group involvement was especially helpful in one woman's experience while confronting her own image full-face. Janet was a married woman in her late fifties, a professional person who had worked well and hard, and who had raised a family, while at the same time she had taken care of her mother. Further, she had often sacrificed in order to provide care and attention for her husband, who frequently was overly dependent and demanding. In the ordinary course of group interaction, she seemed quite cheerful most of the time, and reflected an air of buoyancy and self-sufficiency. It was, then, a shock to her when she reacted to her own image by recognizing how worn and tired she appeared. "I can't believe how tired you look," she said to the image of herself on the screen. Tired beyond your years!!!" A woman group member questioned, "Why do you do so much for everybody, and sacrifice yourself?" And the image replied, "I really don't mind. I really enjoy being able to make things work out."

"That sounds like bullshit to me, and I think you just don't want to face what you see!!", interjected a man in the group. Another woman continued, "You really can't be that out of touch with how tired and resentful you feel."

The therapist asked the image to respond to the group with her own reactions, and suggested she speak directly to them. (It is interesting to note that when the image on the screen is asked to communicate directly to either the patient, or to other members of the group, the illusion is complete, in that the lips of the image then are not only perfectly synchronized with the spoken words, but the words themselves are experienced as appropriately coming from the image; whereas when the patient is asked to speak *to* the image, the lips in the picture are moving in synchrony, but the illusion is somewhat broken, because these words are the words of the patient, and to fulfill the illusion the image's lips should at that point be still.) The image responded, "I felt hurt by what you said to me, but that isn't all. I really feel that it is true. I have been feeling tired, and really somewhat hopeless and I haven't wanted to deal with it. I know now that I have to deal more firmly with my daughter, and stop being so available." The first woman in the group spoke again, "I really believe what you are saying. There is a determined look I didn't see before." And the patient herself joined in saying, "You bet there is!! I see it too. And I like it!!'

One of the men who had spoken now commented that he had been aware of the depressed attitude earlier in the group, but had not felt he could say anything to Janet about it because he thought it would be denied behind the cheeriness. He continued to say that only when the hopelessness and the tiredness had been so apparent on the screen had he felt able to speak directly to that image of the patient. Many of the group members then reacted by describing feelings of relief that the cheeriness was no longer so oppressively present, but had been displaced by the definiteness which had emerged with Janet's new resolve.

The other special effects described above, including juxtaposition of images, image superimposition, alteration of image size, and transportation of body parts all lend themselves well to group exchange in which the members can become actively engaged; however, inclusion of clinical examples in respect to their use would not add to any further understanding of the methods.

(c) Negotiation Between Images—Usefulness of Mediation

A final clinical example will be given to demonstrate the effectiveness of negotiation. The actual negotiation can occur between patient and image, between one image and another image, between image and another group member, or of course, between two actual members of the group. The place of mediation will also be demonstrated, and although the therapist was the mediator in the present example, other group members have taken this role in other instances.

Sarah, another woman in her fifties, divorced, and quite depressed and lonesome, agreed after much reluctance to look at, and to talk to her own image on the screen. She immediately hated what she saw, and began to express intense feelings of disgust. Sarah began by exclaiming, "Uhhhhhh . . . it's worse than I thought. You are hateful! Ugly! Ugly! I can't stand to look at you. I don't wonder no one wants anything to do with you. This is horrible. I can't stand you. Disgusting!! Disgusting!!"

The therapist asked the image to speak. There was no hesitation on the part of the image. She began vigorously, "You never were worth anything! How dare you even speak to me! I'll make you suffer! You are so worthless, and useless. No one could ever want to have anything to do with you. No one ever wanted you, and you are just afraid to admit it. You are so low, I can't even begin to describe you. You are just a nothing! A failure! A complete failure!!"

The dialogue continued in much the same vein for a few more minutes, and then the therapist interrupted by saying, "You know, I want to speak to both of you (patient, and the image). It seems evident that you can't bear each other, and yet the obvious dilemma is that you really have no choice but to live together. I want to make a suggestion. Perhaps since you have to be together, it may be possible for each of you to consider for a moment the likelihood that each of you has very hurt feelings, and that each of you might consider how you could make a move that would create a little more bearable life for the other. Sarah-on-T.V., tell me, is there any way you can suggest that you might make some move, or concession, which would make life a little easier for Sarah-in-the-chair?"

The image responded, "Well, I guess I could lay off some of this putting her down, if she'll promise to not be so disgusted with me."

The therapist then continued, "Sarah-in-the-chair, do you think you could agree?" Could you, say for one week, try to get in touch with some feeling of compassion for image-Sarah, in order to mellow a little bit your feelings of disgust?'"

Sarah said, "I guess I could try that for a week anyway." And the image said, "I'll try for a week too. I have just felt that if you won't accept me then I'll make you feel miserable so you won't be able to enjoy yourself anywhere."

During the development of this exchange, several group members noted a softening of expression on the patient's face. Of course, one can question whether there is any kind of carryover from this kind of experience. The impression at the time was that the exchange and the negotiation resulted in an integration of separate attitudes towards the self, and that the therapist's mediation was a useful intervention. The special value of the television was apparent in more clearly defining, and actually more tangibly personifying, dissonant and conflicting self-attitudes in the patient, and in providing in this way a new possibility for conciliation and integration.

COMMENTS

The use of television and videotape playback has the specific value of providing a new source of objective data in psychotherapy. The videotape capacity of bringing events to the screen for immediate review has enabled patients and therapists to look at their behavior together over and over again, and from this pursuit, old theories both personal and general have been challenged, and new theories have been developed.

As emphasized earlier, the use of videotape is understood by the author to be a most useful adjunct in therapy and, although there are effects which are unique, the videotape playback is not considered a method of therapy in itself.

In general the use of videotape has demonstrated its importance in capturing, and providing clarification of dynamics in interpersonal and group contexts. This chapter, however, had dealt primarily with another area of great clinical interest; namely, the intrapersonal, or intrapsychic processes. By providing novel techniques which permit a more concrete personification of various self-concepts, the T.V. and videotape methods can be most useful in helping a person identify, and integrate various self-systems. Further value of these methods can be achieved by their use in a manner which encourages a dynamic group process to develop in the utilization of therapeutic techniques which, because they emphasize inner personal experience, often have been used in group therapy with the group members participating primarily as audience.

In addition to the uses of the video equipment in investigating intrapersonal dynamics, the effectiveness of other special techniques derived from the unique possibilities of special television effects can be applied in groups, and can also provide incentive for a more intense group dynamic process.

In the clinical discussions little description was given of the use of videotape playback. This omission was deliberate in order not to further complicate the exposition of the various methods. Videotape playback was, however, used in most instances. It is an extremely important therapeutic adjunct; however, its valuable aspects are basically not related to the special effects under consideration here, but rather apply in general to all clinical uses of television recordings. By reviewing playback segments of group therapy for example, not only is there development of greater awareness of personal reactions, and interactions, but the task of working together on such a review enhances the mutual and cooperative endeavor of the group, and provides this additional therapeutic vector.

Finally, since the therapist is often included in the picture, and the recordings, the playback allows him to see himself, and to be seen by others as he actually behaves. One effect of this is to decrease the authoritarian structure, and to further encourage mutuality in the pursuit of greater awareness.

REFERENCES

1. ALGER, I. & HOGAN, P.: The Use of Videotape Recordings in Conjoint Marital Therapy. *Amer. J. Psychiat.*, 123:1425-1430, 1967.
2. ALGER, I.: Therapeutic Use of Videotape Playback. *J. Nerv. Ment. Dis.*, 148:430-436, 1969.
3. ALGER, I.: *Audio-Visual Feedback and Therapeutic Change.* Prof. School Psychol. Vol. III: 302-317, Grune and Stratton, N. Y., 1969.
4. ALGER, I.: Insight and Involvement in Individual Therapy through Videotape Confrontation. *Sc. and Psychoanal.* Vol. XVIII: 20-35, Grune and Stratton, N. Y., 1971.
5. ALGER, I. & HOGAN, P.: The Impact of Videotape Recording on Involvement in Group Therapy. *J. Psychoanal. Groups*, 2:50-56, 1967.
6. BERGER, M. M.: Self-confrontation through Video. *Amer. J. Psychoanal.*, 31:48-58, 1971.
7. BERNE, E.: *Transactional Analysis.* Grove Press, N. Y., 1961.
8. CORSINI, R. J.: *Role Playing in Psychotherapy*, Aldine Press, Chicago, 1967.
9. KUBIE, L. S.: Some Aspects of the Significance to Psychoanalysis of the Exposure of a Patient to the Televised Audiovisual Reproduction of His Activities. *J. Nerv. Ment. Dis.*, 148:301-309, 1969.
10. MISSILDINE, W. H.: *Your Inner Child of the Past.* Simon and Schuster, N. Y., 1963.
11. MORENO, J. L.: *Psychodrama, Action Therapy and Principles of Practice*, Vol. 3, Beacon Press, N. Y., 1969.
12. PERLS, F. S.: *Gestalt Therapy Verbatim.* Real People Press, Lafayette, Calif., 1969.
13. SCHEFLEN, A. E.: *Stream and Structure in Communication; Context Analysis of a Psychotherapy Session.* East. Pa. Psychiat. Inst. Press, Philadelphia, 1965.
14. STOLLER, F. H.: Videotape Feedback in the Group Setting. *J. Nerv. Ment. Dis.*, 148:457-466, 1969.
15. TAUSIG, T. N. & SCHAEFFER, S.: *Self-image Experience by Immediate Television Feedback: A Preliminary Report.* Unpublished paper.
16. WILMER, H. A.: Television as Participant Recorder. *Amer. J. Psychiat.*, 124:1157-1163, 1968.

11

ON THE RATIONALE OF TOUCH
IN PSYCHOTHERAPY

Elizabeth E. Mintz, Ph.D.

Faculty, National Psychological Association for Psychoanalysis

It is a source of recurrent amazement to this writer that the dimension of physical contact between therapist and patient has been almost ignored in literature in psychotherapy. Most contributors, even when discussing the patient-therapist relationship in detail, appear completely unaware of the possibility of touch as part of this relationship, or, like Menninger (1958, p. 40) regard any physical contact as "incompetence or criminal ruthlessness" on the part of the analyst.

Among contemporary experiential writers, physical contact is not anathematized, but it is usually regarded as a way of expressing the concern or the emotional availability of the therapist (Gendlin, 1964, p. 145). What is typically absent is any extended consideration of the occasions on which physical contact may be therapeutically valuable, and when it may be counter-indicated.[1]

Elsewhere (Mintz, 1969) this writer has discussed physical contact between analyst and patient and the historical background against which it became a taboo. I maintained there that physical contact involving either the promise or the actuality of direct genital fulfillment is invari-

---

Reprinted from Psychotherapy: Theory, Research and Practice, Volume 6, No. 4, Fall, 1969, pp. 232-234.
[1] An exception, striking because found in the work of so traditional an analyst as Edward Glover (1955, pp. 24-5), is a discussion of whether to shake hands or not, in which the point is made that this decision cannot be made as a general policy but only in terms of the patient's specific needs. He adds, "When in doubt behave naturally."

ably inappropriate, primarily because the essential nature of a helping relationship seems incompatible with the full mutuality of a healthy sexual relationship. Physical contact can be appropriate in certain specific situations: a) as symbolic mothering at times when a patient cannot communicate verbally; b) to convey the therapist's acceptance at times when the patient is overwhelmed by self-loathing; and c) to strengthen or restore the patient's contact with the external world when it is threatened by anxiety. These situations are not confined to overt or borderline psychotics, but can occur in deep analysis with patients who may possess considerable ego-strength.

In this contribution I further explore certain therapeutic aspects of touch.

1. *Touch as a natural part of a warm, ongoing relationship.* In our society many people, though not all, find it natural to express warmth through occasional physical contact—a particularly friendly handshake, a touch on the shoulder when another person is depressed, an embrace of congratulations on being told of some success or happiness. Although many psychoanalysts are willing to admit confidentially that they do allow themselves such demonstrations with patients, they are considered inappropriate because they may contaminate the transference and block the development of its negative aspects altogether.

This writer has conducted many analyses which, after the negative transference was worked through, were marked by deep feelings of mutual warmth, but in which there was never any overt physical contact except for an occasional handshake after a vacation.

When contact seems natural, however, may its absence not contaminate the transference more than would its presence? The traditional viewpoint is that any bodily contact would serve as an artificial stimulant for fantasies that the Oedipal or the dependent infantile wishes might actually be gratified; that it would hinder the pure development of transference based on early object-relationships and introjects; and that it might block the development and expression of hostile feelings. However, might a strict avoidance of physical contact not repeat a physical rejection by the parents? Could such avoidance not reinforce the denial of the physical aspect of human existence especially with obsessional and schizoid personalities? Might such avoidance not increase the likelihood that patients, especially the two latter groups, might depersonalize the psychoanalytic relationship as a defense against experiencing feeling? The traditional taboo against touch may be serving the resistance.

2.) *Touch as gratification of the patient's infantile needs.* If physical contact implies a danger of gratifying the patient to the point of interfering with his motivation toward growth and independence, then the maintenance of touch as a taboo would indeed be approprite. However, as has been pointed out even within the framework of the classical psychoanalytic structure (Roland, 1967), there are many patients, particularly those with severe neurotic character disturbances, who require a "real reparative object relationship" with the analyst, in addition to an opportunity to re-project and analyze harmful internalized objects.

Thus far, in private practice with neurotics and well-compensated schizophrenics, the writer has only a few times offered patients the experience of being held in an individual session, and only if a clearly experienced intuition of its rightness could be backed up by a sense of clearly understanding the patient's dynamics.

However, in groups, particularly time-extended marathon groups,[2] a participant has often been offered a close, sustained embrace, perhaps for fifteen minutes' duration, usually by me as a mother-symbol, but sometimes by another woman who can represent the mother, and sometimes by a male colleague or male participant as father-figure. In approximately 100 such episodes, this experience has never yet resulted in clinging, infantile dependency or in the precipitation of Oedipal passions.

3.) *Touch as gratification of the patient's manipulative needs.* The distinction between this meaning of touch, and the meaning discussed above, is sometimes difficult to make in practice, but is theoretically clear. There is a sharp distinction between the patient who reaches out for a temporary dependent and affectionate relationship which he was denied in childhood and the patient who seeks to use contact as a way to control the therapist and avoid self-confrontation.

A young man, a charmer of women who had always used his personal attractiveness to avoid responsibility, entered treatment in the depths of a depression, having worked with the writer some years previously in a different professional setting. At the end of a session in which he appeared genuinely despairing, he said, "You are my only hope," and turned at the door to embrace the writer, who accepted his embrace with a maternal feeling. No sexualization of the transference resulted, but it was the writer's belated impression that the subsequent course of treatment, which on the whole was unsatisfactory, was adversely affected by her failure to recognize and analyze his gesture as an attempt to cajole her into ignoring the dependency and rage behind his depression.

---

[2] The two-day intensive "marathon" groups focus on the individual needs of a limited number of participants, in contrast to larger "encounter groups" which have a different purpose and other values. In my opinion (Mintz, 1967) the former type of group may legitimately be regarded as an extension of psychoanalytically oriented psychotherapy.

A young married woman, suffering from vague anxieties and a poorly-developed sense of identity originating in a childhood during which she had been treated as a pretty toy without feelings or needs of her own, said wistfully to the writer, "If only you would hold me—my mother never held me." Subsequently she had a dream which apparently was about a homosexual relationship with the analyst. She was offered no gesture of affection, nor was the dream analyzed as genuinely homosexual, but instead we discussed her effort to induce the analyst to treat her as a toy object, repeating her childhood experiences. Results of analysis were gratifying; the marital relationship became more mature and the patient developed a strong, sustained interest in socially worthwhile activity.

These two cases fit into the writer's tentative conjecture that when a patient is able to ask assertively for physical contact with the therapist, he is probably strong enough to be able to find it in non-symbolic relationships outside therapy, and may indeed be attempting to cajole or seduce the therapist. The patient who is genuinely in need of reparative physical contact is likely to be unable to express his need clearly.

4.) *Touch as a means of eliciting feelings around aggression.* It is the writer's opinion that physical expression of hostility purely as a catharsis in the therapeutic situation is of slight value in itself. However, such expression is often valuable as an aid in developing insight and in furthering the breakthrough of repressed feelings.

Here, as in the procedure of holding a patient, the writer usually confines physical expression of hostility to marathon groups. When a participant is struggling with hostile feelings toward the mother, the therapist may offer herself as a target or opponent. When hostility or competitiveness is experienced toward a father, or toward a peer, an appropriate male participant almost always volunteers to play the part of father-surrogate. For these purposes, a variety of techniques can be used, including armwrestling, which permit a satisfying expenditure of physical energy without damage to either participant or to the surroundings.[3]

In a marathon group composed of colleagues, a competent, mature and well-defended man was telling his lifelong difficulty about expressing hostility toward his mother. The writer asked him to close his eyes, pretend that she was his mother, and grip her forearm as hard as possible (a procedure which can be easily sustained with very slight discomfort). With this physical expression of feeling to assist him, the participant was able to fantasy that he was actually speaking to his mother, and to express his bitterness and sense of deprivation, followed by a feeling of great relief. The participant

---

[3] The writer is indebted to Dr. William Schutz for introducing her to most of these techniques.

subsequently spoke of this experience as an important breakthrough, and no awkwardness followed in his professional or social relationship with me.

5.) *Touch as an expression of the therapists' feelings.* The therapist's expression of feeling is not necessarily therapeutic just because it is genuine. However, the converse does appear to be true: that, especially because many patients have been traumatized by constant uncertainty regarding the real feelings of their parents, any false gesture of acceptance or affection from the therapist could be destructive, repeating earlier trauma and diminishing the patient's confidence in his reality-testing.

Use of physical contact, then, seems to require not only an understanding of the patient's psychodynamics and an awareness of the probable effects of touch at that moment, but also a readiness for touch on the part of the therapist. This may at first seem to place and unrealistic burden on the therapist, and certainly any therapist to whom this type of communication seems alien or improper should confine himself to verbal communication. However, these criteria for the use of touch are not really very different from the criteria for other types of therapeutic intervention, which also require understanding of the patient, a reasonably-confident anticipation of the effect of the therapist's activity, and a reasonable degree of personal ease and comfort in the therapist.

The anxiety is sometimes expressed that any kind of physical contact may lead to inappropriate and destructive sexual acting-out. To the writer this argument seems specious: a therapist who could be swept away by touching a patient's hand or embracing a regressed patient could probably not withstand the sustained intimacy of the therapeutic relationship in any case.

The term "taboo"[4] implies a prohibition which is maintained on the basis of tradition rather than rationality; to the extent to which physical contact in therapy is a taboo, there can be no place for it in what is hopefully a growing science.

---

[4] This term was first suggested in regard to therapeutic touch by Ruth C. Cohn.

REFERENCES

GENDLIN, E. T. A Theory of Personality Change. In *Personality Change,* ed. P. Worchel & D. Byrne. John Wiley & Sons, New York, 1964.

GLOVER, E. *The Technique of Psychoanalysis.* Int. U. Press, New York, 1955.

MENNINGER, K. *Theory of Psychoanalytic Technique.* Basic Books, New York, 1958.

MINTZ, E. Touch and the Psychoanalytic Tradition. *The Psychoanalytic Review.* In press.

ROLAND, A. The Reality of the Psycho-analytic Relationship and Situation in the Handling of Transference-Resistance. *Int. J. Psychoanal.,* 48, Part 4, 1967.

12

BEHAVIOR THERAPY: ASSERTIVE
TRAINING IN GROUPS

Herbert Fensterheim, Ph.D.

Assistant Professor of Psychiatry
New York Medical College
Co-Director; Behavior Therapy Program, New York Medical College,
Metropolitan Hospital Center

Introduction

As is well known, during its brief history behavior therapy has challenged many of the basic assumptions of the traditional individual psychotherapies. Most recently, a growing number of clinicians have come to recognize that the various procedures subsumed under behavior therapy can be applied to the treatment of groups, as well as individuals. Careful research on the part of these workers has resulted in the systematic clinical development of behavioral groups which promise to provide useful and effective alternatives to the more established modes of group psychotherapy.

Behavior therapy in groups cannot be described as a specific treatment technique. Although all behavioral groups share certain elements in common, they utilize a wide range of treatment techniques which derive from different theoretical positions. At present, these different techniques are in various stages of development. Some have been well investigated, relatively speaking, and have been described in some detail in the literature; others have not yet been formally described. Assertive training would be included in this latter category. Indeed, although it is considered to constitute a major technique of behavior therapy, clinical and experimental reports on assertive training in groups is particularly sparse. An attempt has been made in this article to remedy this situation in part by providing clinical descriptions of two different types of assertive training groups.

It is logical to assume that these clinical descriptions will be better understood if they are preceded by a discussion of the principles and techniques of assertive training. In addition, as an appropriate preamble to the elucidation of the theory and practice of assertive training in groups, this article will include a concise statement of the characteristics of behavior therapy in general, and a brief description of the use of specific behavior therapy techniques in groups.

GENERAL CHARACTERISTICS OF BEHAVIOR THERAPY

Within the framework of behavior therapy, psychiatric syndromes are conceived of as collections of faulty habits which can best be modified if they become the direct focus of treatment. Thus the first task of the behavior therapist is to identify the patient's presenting problem in terms of his overt, objectively observable behavior. Once the specific behavior pattern (or patterns) which requires modification has been determined, the behavior therapist seeks to establish the conditions under which it occurs and the factors responsible for its persistence. After these data have been accumulated, the most suitable, i.e., potentially the most efficient, method (or methods, for several may be used) for changing the patient's maladaptive behaviors is selected from a growing array of such techniques, and systematically applied.

In contrast to psychoanalysis and the traditional psychotherapies which focus on subjective behavior, i.e., thoughts and feelings, in order to effect changes indirectly in the patient's overt behavior, behavior therapy focuses directly on the patient's overt behavior. No attempt is made to investigate either the genesis or dynamics of a particular behavior. Concomitantly, the behavior therapist finds no need to make the unconscious conscious, to delve into childhood memories or current dreams, or to elevate the therapist-patient relationship to the core of the treatment process. Reorganization of the patient's personality is not a major objective of behavior therapy. Instead the major emphasis is on correct identification of the disordered aspects of the patient's behavior and systematic attempts to modify these specific behaviors, preferably through methods which have been developed and validated in the experimental laboratory. When it is successful, this approach effects major changes within a short period of time.

THE USE OF SPECIFIC BEHAVIOR THERAPY TECHNIQUES IN GROUPS

The Operant Methods

The operant methods (i.e., the regulation of reinforcement contingencies), where the therapist systematically attempts to increase or decrease the frequency with which specific behaviors occur have been employed in a wide variety of group settings. Reports have appeared in the literature of its successful use on psychiatric wards (2), in training institutions for mental retardates (9), classrooms (13), and in a group program for the parents of schizophrenic patients (4). Yates (19) has provided a good general discussion of much of this work; specific illustrations of the application of these modification techniques are included in the volume of case studies published by Ullman and Krasner (16).

Liberman (11) has demonstrated the effectiveness of the operant methods in traditional group psychotherapy settings. The therapist in such a group systematically reinforced expressions of "cohesiveness' by the patients, and did not reinforce expressions of other aspects of group interaction. His efforts were successful. This group did manifest greater cohesion in the content of its productions and in its social structure than did a psychoanalytically-oriented control group. In fact, it has been suggested that this method be used to control and manipulate behaviors within the group (cohesiveness, anger toward the therapist, etc.), so that the effects of these behaviors on treatment outcome may be evaluated.

Relaxation Training

Relaxation training is used frequently in individual behavior therapy. Often, the patient's presenting complaint is a direct consequence of tension; it follows, then, that if his tension can be alleviated through deliberate relaxation, his problem can be brought under control. Relaxation training is also considered to constitute a potentially effective form of group treatment.

Baker, Kahn, and Weiss (3) have reported on group training in relaxation for the treatment of insomnia. The author's selection of this technique had been based on the dual premise that insomnia is often due to tension, and that tension can be treated directly through relaxation training. Ergo, insomnia can be treated through relaxation. Accordingly, they recruited a number of students who complained of long-term difficulty in falling asleep and trained them in relaxation in four thirty-minute group sessions, conducted over a two-week period. (The subjects also practiced relaxation outside of the group sessions.) Post-treatment evaluations showed that almost every subject had improved insofar as his ability to fall asleep; and a year after treatment had been terminated, follow-up revealed that all but one had maintained, or further improved this ability.

Relaxation training has proven effective on certain types of behavioral disturbances, and is considered an important ancillary treatment procedure for others. Obviously, group training in relaxation is more economical than individual training, it may offer another advantage as well: Clinical experience suggests that many people are able to relax more quickly and more deeply in a group than in an individual treatment setting. This author questioned about twenty-five patients who had received relaxation training in both settings, and two reasons were advanced to explain the fact that better results were achieved in a group setting. Some stated that in a group they were less conscious of being the center of attention, hence they were under less pressure to relax, hence they found it easier to relax. Others explained that they "did not want to hold the group back"; therefore, they worked harder at relaxing. Although their explanations differed, these patients were in agreement on one point: They found it easier to relax in a group.

Systematic Desensitization

Systematic desensitization is the most dramatic, and certainly one of the most studied, of the behavior therapy techniques, and it has been used frequently in groups. Typically, the members of the group are trained in relaxation, work together to construct a hierarchy concerning a common phobia, picture the stimulus scenes, and relax upon the therapist's instructions. The entire group is relaxed when the first patient signals tension while picturing the stimulus scene; hence the group proceeds at the pace of the slowest (most anxious) patient. There have been a number of variations of this basic model, such as the use of preformed hierarchies, or the use of a different hierarchy by each group member as he works on his individual phobia. Paul (14) has published a critical review of the studies in this area.

What needs to be emphasized is the fact that almost all the systematic desensitization groups reported on to date have been part of an experimental project where some variable of the desensitization process, rather than the group process, has been the object of study. Groups had been used simply for reasons of economy or efficiency. Under such conditions there is little interaction in the group; for the most part, communication is initiated by the therapist and directed to individual group members. Indeed, in the review cited above (14) Paul suggests that it may be more correct to say that the treatment was *in* groups rather than *by* groups." However, group processes would be expected to play a more significant role in the actual clinical use of desensitization. Presumably, group members would discuss the behavioral "problem," report positive changes in behavior, and examine difficulties in the achievement of change. Reports by individual members of their progress would receive positive reinforcement in the group, and the progress reported by others would encourage and serve as a model for those patients who find it more difficult to achieve change. Thus the fact that the group serves *in loco maternis* facilitates implementation of the therapeutic objective. Group processes such as universalization and social facilitation may be operative as well.

A description of the clinical use of systematic desensitization in groups has been provided by Lazarus (10). One of the groups described was organized for the purpose of treating four women with severe and long-term sexual frigidity. All the patients had received training in relaxation prior to the first group session; thereafter, the group met once a week for an hour. Each group session was divided into four relatively distinct treatment strategies: discussion of maladaptive attitudes towards sex, didactic lectures about sex, relaxation, and desensitization. The hierarchy used for desensitization consisted of the following scenes, embracing: kissing, being fondled, undressing, foreplay in the nude, awareness of husband's erection, intromission, and changing position during coitus. One patient could not respond to this treatment and was removed from the group at the end of the third session. Treatment was discontinued for the other three women at the end of the fourteenth session when the least improved reported orgastic satisfaction at least 50% of the time. The results of a six month follow-up were somewhat obscured by the amusing fact that each woman was at least three months pregnant.

From this very brief glimpse of different types of behavior therapy groups some common characteristics may be noted. These groups are organized on the basis that a common modification technique is applicable to all members. The groups are highly structured and goal oriented with their primary aim being to modify specific target behaviors (overt and covert) which in turn will ameliorate the problem situation. Attention is focused on behaviors in life situations rather than on interactions within the group. The role of the therapist is one of teacher-expert and he maintains fairly close control of what is done in each group session.

Assertive training groups also tend to possess many of these characteristics. However, before these groups are described some word need be said about the general principles of assertive training itself.

ASSERTIVE TRAINING IN GROUPS

Principles of Assertive Training

This author (6) has noted that problems in assertion often underlie mood disturbances, certain phobic conditions, such as hypochondria, low self-esteem, and complaints by the patient that he is being pushed around, regardless of whether the complaints are valid. Conversely, the individual's ability to assert himself, when appropriate, is associated with an active orientation, feelings of mastery, and the ability to communicate satisfactorily with others.

Assertion has been defined as "The action of declaring oneself; of stating, This is who I am, what I think and feel; [it] characterizes an active rather than a passive approach to life" (5). Assertive behavior is most evident in social and personal communication which is (a) open and direct, (b) honest, and (c) appropriate. Salter (15), who first formulated this concept within the Pavlovian model of excitation, notes that the frank and spontaneous expression of feelings of tenderness, as well as feelings of anger and aggression, leads to better interpersonal relations and to subjective feelings of well being. Thus the capacity for assertive behavior plays a crucial role in psychological functioning. Where it is lacking, the individual can be trained in this behavior in a deliberate and systematic manner.

There may be many reasons for the individual's apparent inability to act assertively. For example, the fear of rejection may be sufficiently strong to inhibit assertive behavior. When that fear is removed, assertive behavior will appear spontaneously. Most frequently, however, the individual's consistent failure to assert himself can be attributed to the fact that, for some reason, he never learned how to behave assertively. It is for such people that assertive training is indicated.

Techniques

Assertive training techniques are not as standardized as many of the other behavior therapy techniques; nor have they been as carefully investigated. There are two exceptions, however: Friedman's (8) excellent study of role-playing, and the study by McFall and Marston (12) of behavior rehearsal may indicate the direction of future research. Descriptions of the clinical methods used have been provided by Salter (15), Wolpe and Lazarus (17), Wolpe (18), and Fensterheim (7).

At present, clinical programs in assertive training are designed for the individual; as a rule, the techniques used in that setting fall into one of five general categories:

1. *Didactic.* The therapist teaches the concept of assertion and the principles involved in various types of personal interactions. In short, he teaches the patient the rules for handling a confrontation.

2. *Review of life situations.* The therapist helps the patient to formulate assertive responses which would have been appropriate in situations in which the patient has actually been involved.

3. *Behavior rehearsal.* The patient practices assertive behavior in simulated life situations. This rehearsal serves both to shape assertive behavior and to reduce the anxiety it evokes.

4. *Specific exercises.* The patient practices specific assertive acts, such as making eye contact, using the pronoun *I,* or using "feeling-talk" (e.g., "I like what you said") both in and outside the treatment situation.

5. *Assignments.* At each treatment session the patient is given talks, specifically designed to implement his assertive training goals, which must be performed by the next treatment session. Needless to say, the patient must be considered potentially capable of completing the assignment within the prescribed time limit.

The social nature of assertive training suggests that it would be particularly effective in the treatment of groups. More specifically, Alberti and Emmons (1) have noted several advantages to the use of assertive training in a group setting: A group provides a "laboratory" of other people with whom to work. Because the group is typically understanding and supportive, the patient is able, and encouraged to experiment with new behaviors. There is a broader base for social modeling and greater feedback in group than in individual assertive training. This author has also used groups to facilitate the application of what has been learned in individual treatment to life. To illustrate, extremely unassertive patients receive individual assertive training first, then practice this behavior in a group setting, and finally are able to apply this learning to actual life situations.

Clinical Descriptions

Although the advantages of assertive training in groups seem to be self-evident, and although a number of authors do refer to such groups in the literature, as noted above, clinical descriptions of the use of assertive training techniques in group settings are extremely sparse. To the best of this author's knowledge, only Lazarus (10) has published a detailed clinical description of such a group. It would seem appropriate, therefore, to present an account of a typical assertive group session, as conducted by this author, as a means of illustrating the general characteristics of such groups. This will be followed by a clinical description of a less orthodox type of assertive training group—the minigroup.

A TYPICAL ASSERTIVE TRAINING GROUP SESSION

The group discussed herein consists of nine or ten people, with an approximately equal number of men and women. The patients are roughly homogeneous with regard to socio-economic status, education, achievement, marital status, and age. They are also roughly homogeneous in terms of the severity of their behavioral disturbance, i.e., the degree to which their ability to function in life situations has been adversely affected. Group homogeneity in these respects is important in assertive training, for there is a correlation between these variables and the types of assertive problems encountered most frequently and the criteria for appropriate behavior. Moreover, by virtue of the fact that they share the same assertive problems, perspectives, and experiences, group members can learn from each other and so facilitate the development of the desired behaviors.

The group meets for two and one-quarter hours once a week. Sessions are held in home-like surroundings, and the group atmosphere is informal. Group members are seated in easy chairs or on a sofa. The furniture is placed to form a horseshoe; the opening at one end serves as a "stage" for role-playing and behavior rehearsal.

The group session is far from standardized or inflexible. Yet most sessions tend to follow a pattern:

Assignment reports. During the previous session each patient had formulated an assignment. This session begins with a go-round, where each member of the group reports on his success (or failure) in completing his assignment. Few details are given at this point, for one aim of this procedure is to set the pace and the working atmosphere for the session. At the end of the go-round, however, various group members may want to, or may be asked to, elaborate on their experiences. Successful task completion evokes compliments and expressions of approval from the therapist and from the other group members. Failures or questionable results are discussed by the group. In such cases, behavior may be shaped and rehearsed, so that the assignment can be completed for the next session. Often, particularly when the patient did not even attempt to tackle the assignment, the task is considered to have been too difficult or too demanding, and is reformulated for completion the next week. In fact, however, assignments are usually successfully completed, and these reports give the group the feeling of forward movement from the very beginning of the session.

Special problems. One or more members of the group may be facing a special situation in life. These special situations are presented to the group in a straightforward manner. The group discusses each such problem in turn, under the guidance of the therapist, and makes suggestions for its solution, with particular emphasis on what the individual involved can *do* (i.e., how he can act) about the situation. Modeling and the sharing of similar experiences are often part of the discussion. The group is usually friendly and supportive, and this is particularly true when one of the members brings in a distressing problem. Obviously, solutions to these problems are not always available, but the concern expressed by the group is reassuring and it's often helpful.

Assertive experiences. Group members had been instructed previously to keep a record of the assertive incidents they were involvd in between sessions, and these are now discussed. The emphasis is on the trivial, for it is these relatively uncomplicated situations that the principles of assertion are most easily mastered. When they are presented in the treatment situation, these incidents may provide the therapist with didactic opportunities. An opportunity may arise to teach the principles of initiating or sustaining a conversation, for example. The group then uses incidents to shape assertive behavior in the context of the principles they have just been taught or the principles they were taught previously. In any event, individuality of style is stressed. These new behaviors are also rehearsed.

Special exercises. These are laboratory exercises, designed to foster the mastery of specific assertive behaviors by an individual member of the group, or by the group as a whole. They may include such acts as talking in a loud voice, behaving in an unpleasant manner, telling an interesting story, or directly expressing a tender feeling toward another group member. Group members model these behaviors for each other, give each other constructive criticism, and provide a great deal of positive reinforcement as the performance improves.

The hierarchical nature of these exercises may be illustrated by describing those designed for a group member who was severely inhibited in the expression of his angry feelings. In fact, this patient could not express the mildest annoyance or irritation in a highly structured role-playing situation. Furthermore, he claimed that he had never even experienced such feelings in the past twenty years, since early adolescence.

The exercises included: (a) Portraying an angry role, reading dialogue from a script. (b) Portraying the same role, but improvising the dialogue, instead of reading the script. (c) Improvising an angry role from a scene briefly described to him. (d) Role-playing angry scenes from incidents that other group members had been involved in, incidents which were most dissimilar to his own experiences. (e) Role-playing the incidents reported by other members which were similar to his own life experience. (f) Role-playing scenes from his own current life as though he had felt annoyed or angry in those situations.

Each exercise was continued until the patient reported at least a minimal level of comfort during its performance, and until he achieved a minimal adequacy of emotional expression (as judged by the group). Other group members participated in these exercises as they were needed.

The patient spent from five to ten minutes of each group session on these exercises over a four-month period, and also rehearsed the exercises at home with his wife. Toward the end of that time he began to report subjective feelings of anger, as well as the overt expression of anger in specific situations.

Group desensitization. When systematic group desensitization is used as part of assertive training, it is usually introduced at this point in the session. Ten to fifteen minutes may be used to present up to three scenes from a common hierarchy previously prepared by the group. Fear of authority is one hierarchy which is used often.

Assignment for the week. At the close of each session each group member formulates an assignment to be completed by the next group session. If the patient has difficulty in thinking of an assignment, other group members or the therapist suggest one. The group as a whole evaluates each assignment in terms of its meaningfulness *vis-à-vis* the patient's therapeutic goals, and the realistic possibility of his completing it within the week.

Discussion. This description of a typical group session illustrates certain characteristics of assertive training groups in general. Such groups are task- rather than person-oriented. The emphasis is on the acquisition of specific behavioral skills to be employed in life situations, and on the reports of individual attempts to use these skills. Although irritation, criticism, and anger are expressed in the group, they are usually expressed in an appropriate manner and lead to a constructive interchange. The general atmosphere of the group is a friendly, supportive one; the members want to learn and to help each other to learn. The therapist acts as a teacher-expert and directs the course of each session. The attitude of the group members toward the therapist is one of liking and respect, but he is not considered to be infallible or beyond challenge. Perhaps the paradigm of the assertive training group is a noncompetitive advanced seminar with each student involved in his own project, yet learning from the experiences of his classmates, under the guidance of an experienced professor.

Minigroup Assertive Training

Three years ago, in an attempt to make assertive training in groups more efficient, this author developed a more intense and concentrated training program, designed to achieve limited assertion goals. Because these training groups are limited to a small number of persons (a maximum of four), and to a preset limited number of sessions (usually four or six), they are called "minigroups."

In this form of training, each group member attempts to achieve a specific assertive goal within the limited number of training sessions. The sessions themselves are devoted to exercises and rehearsal of the behaviors critical to the achievement of this goal. Great emphasis is also placed on assignments. Each session lasts an hour, is highly structured, and is busy and workman-like. Group members are aware of each other's goals, and often attempt to help each other, but there is relatively little spontaneous interaction among the members. The group has a definite classroom atmosphere.

A minigroup, consisting of three members, and limited to four sessions, is described in detail below.

The Patients: The group consisted of three bachelors, ranging in age from 35 to 41. All shared the common problem of social isolation. Their social relations were minimal, transitory, and dependent on chance encounters. None had really experienced a long-term, deeply emotional relationship with a woman. Indeed, they had trouble getting dates, often spent solitary weekends, rarely were invited out and never invited people to their homes, and had no close male friends. They had all been in individual behavior therapy before they entered the group assertive training program.

The program. It was understood that the group would meet in the therapist's office one hour a week for four weeks. The patients were assigned specific goals, and were told that they were expected to make definite progress toward the achievement of these goals during that period.

The therapeutic goals. The common goal of all the members of the group was to establish a set of behaviors that would lead to more social contacts and, eventually, to their becoming part of a social group. Each patient had an individual goal as well: Allen, whose speech was pedantic and evasive, was to achieve direct communication. Bruce was secretive, in constant fear of "being found out"; his goal was to achieve open communication. Carl tended to avoid social contacts because after talking to someone briefly, he wouldn't know what to say and would become extremely anxious. His goal was to learn how to sustain a conversation.

These goals were formulated in individual sessions prior to the first group meeting.

The initial group session. Each member had been told previously that he would be asked to talk about himself for two minutes, and would have an additional minute to describe his main assertive problems and his specific training goals. The imposition of the time limit forced each patient to organize his thoughts, and to come to grips with the problem of communication. Following these presentations, each group member was given an exercise designed to implement his assertive goal. Allen, who wanted to achieve direct communication, had to limit himself to simple feeling-talk statements and to reject impulses to qualify or elaborate on these statements. With help and with obvious discomfort, he finally managed. Bruce, whose aim was open communication, was instructed to tell Allen and Carl how he felt about them, and also to tell the group something he had never told anyone about himself. Carl, who found it difficult to sustain a conversation, was to tell each person a story about a personal experience he had had and make the story interesting enough to hold the attention of the other person. He proved to be quite good at this; he had just never thought of doing it in social situations.

The greater part of the initial session was spent explaining the nature of the assignments for each week. The group was shown a model list first, and then worked together to prepare a five-item list of tasks for each patient. In the process they learned details of each other's current life, discussed common problems, and shared the experience of working together on a personal subject. At the end of the session, each patient had his list of assignments to be completed by the next session. In addition, group members had been instructed to keep a record of those situations in which they had behaved assertively, and to prepare a list of ten tasks which would constitute their assignment for the following week.

The middle sessions. Both the second and third sessions began with a brief discussion of the assignments. Several of the items on Bruce's list serve to illustrate how the completion of these tasks may lead to increased social contacts.

1. *Task*: Lunch with people twice during the week. Bruce had no social contacts with the people with whom he worked, and lunch hours were particularly lonely for him. He was able to make dates for lunch without difficulty, and the task was given to him each week so that it would become a routine habit.

2. *Task*: Phone two people, one man and one woman, just to chat. Actually, Bruce had gotten to know a number of people superficially

just in the course of living. However, if they were not part of his immediate environment, he made no effort to contact them. He needed some behavior rehearsal in the group before he made the first call, but then he made more than the two calls his assignment specified. During the four weeks the group was in existence, these calls resulted in a dinner invitation, a lunch date, and an invitation to a party.

3. *Task* (third session) : Visit the art museum and speak to two young women. This was to help him to meet women who shared his interests in art and music. The week before, his assignment was to talk to any two people at the museum. The week after, he had to get into a real conversation with a woman and ask her out for coffee. Behavior rehearsal, and the fact that another group member had the same assignment, helped him to complete this task, and even before treatment was terminated, he had been able to make a date with a woman he had met in this manner.

Bruce had other assertive tasks as well, and the other group members had assignments adapted to their own special needs. Some of the tasks were similar, some were quite different. The first part of each session was spent in reviewing, and perhaps modifying, the assignments the patients had prepared for themselves for the next week. The middle part of each session was used to discuss incidents in which group members had behaved assertively, and to provide exercises in directness for Allen, in openness for Bruce, and in sustaining a conversation for Carl.

The final session. After discussing the assignments, the patients were instructed in the use of lists after the program was terminated. Although each member of the group had made considerable progress, none could be said to have completed treatment. They were all moving in the right direction, however, and needed time to consolidate their gains and expand the new habits they had learned. It was decided that Allen and Bruce would take a vacation from treatment, and would maintain telephone contact with the therapist. During the group sessions it had become clear that Carl also had great difficulty in expressing tender feelings. Therefore, it was decided that he would join another minigroup for training in this area while continuing to improve his social life.

This minigroup focused on expanding the social network of its group members. Other minigroups may have different aims. However, they all share certain basic characteristics in common: They attempt to achieve specific, limited goals in a very short period of time. Whereas the typical assertive training group was compared to an advanced seminar, the minigroup might be said to resemble a small laboratory class, engaged in simple experimentation. Because its goals are so limited, the minigroup is not an independent modality; it is used, when indicated, as an ancillary treatment procedure.

REFERENCES

1. ALBERTI, R. E., & EMMONS, M. L., *Your Perfect Right: A Guide to Assertive Behavior,* San Luis Obispo, Cal.: Impact, 1970.
2. AYLLON, T., & AZRIN, N., *The Token Economy,* New York: Appleton-Century-Crofts, 1968.
3. BAKER, B. L., KAHN, M., & WEISS, J. M., Treatment of Insomnia by Relaxation, *J. Abnorm. Psychol.,* 1968, 73.
4. CHEEK, F. E., LAUCIUS, J., MAHNCKE, M., & BECK, R., A Behavior Modification Training Program for Parents of Convalescent Schizophrenics. In R. D. Rubin, H. Fensterheim, A. A. Lazarus, and C. M. Franks (eds.), *Advances in Behavior Therapy 1969,* New York: Academic Press, 1971.
5. FENSTERHEIM, H. *Help Without Psychoanalysis,* New York: Stein & Day, 1971.
6. FENSTERHEIM, H. The Initial Interview in the Office Practice of Behavior Therapy. In A. A. Lazarus (Ed.), *Clinical Behavior Therapy,* New York: Brunner/Mazel, 1972.
7. FENSTERHEIM, H. Assertive Methods and Marital Problems. In R. D. Rubin, H. Fensterheim, and J. D. Henderson (Eds.), *Advances in Behavior Therapy 1970,* New York: Academic Press, in press.
8. FRIEDMAN, P. H., The Effects of Modeling and Role-Playing on Assertive Behavior. In R. D. Rubin, H. Fensterheim, A. A. Lazarus, and C. M. Franks (eds.), *Advances in Behavior Therapy 1969,* New York: Academic Press, 1971.
9. GARDNER, J. M., Behavior Modification in Mental Retardation: A Review of Research and Analysis of Trends. In R. D. Rubin, H. Fensterheim, A. A. Lazarus and C. M. Franks (eds.), *Advances in Behavior Therapy 1969,* New York: Academic Press, 1971.
10. LAZARUS, A. A., Behavior Therapy in Groups. In G. M. Gazda (ed.), *Basic Approaches to Group Psychotherapy and Group Counseling,* Springfield, Illinois: Charles C. Thomas, 1968.
11. LIBERMAN, R., A Behavioral Approach to Group Dynamics. I. Reinforcing and Prompting of Cohesiveness in Group Therapy, *Behavior Therapy,* 1:141-175, 1970.
12. McFALL, R. M., & MARSTON, A. R., An Experimental Investigation of Behavior Rehearsal in Assertive Training, *J. Abnorm. Psychol.,* 76:295-303, 1970.
13. MEACHAM, M. L., & WIESEN, A. E., *Changing Classroom Behavior: A Manual for Precision Teaching,* Scranton, Pa.: International Textbook Co., 1969.
14. PAUL, G. L., Outcome of Systematic Desensitization. In C. M. Franks (ed.), *Behavior Therapy: Appraisal and Status,* New York: McGraw-Hill, 1969.
15. SALTER, A., *Conditioned Reflex Therapy,* New York: Farrar, Strauss & Giroux, 1949; Capricorn, 1961.
16. ULLMAN, L. P., & KRASNER, L., *Case Studies in Behavior Modification,* New York: Holt, Rinehart, Winston, 1965.
17. WOLPE, J. & LAZARUS, A. A., *Behavior Therapy Techniques,* Oxford: Pergamon Press, 1966.
18. WOLPE, J., *The Practice of Behavior Therapy,* Oxford: Pergamon Press, 1969.
19. YATES, A. J., *Behavior Therapy,* New York: Wiley, 1970.

Area I—Section D

SMALL GROUP PHENOMENA

The purpose of the final section in this area is to confront the group therapist with the incredibly prolific small group movement in which group methods are employed primarily for non-therapeutic ends. An increasing number of persons have become involved in encounter groups, T-groups, sensitivity groups, consciousness-raising groups, marathon groups, etc. Perhaps the enthusiasm this movement has engendered can be attributed to the fact that participation in such groups, which in addition to treating pathology also address themselves to enhancing the joyful, creative aspects of human experience, often evokes intense emotional responses. Thus, it may be speculated that, in this respect at least, the small group experience and the use of various psychedelic, narcotic and stimulating drugs serve similar purposes: their magnetic attraction lies in the fact that both are capable of causing intense emotional and "mind-expanding" or consciousness-altering experiences, and both hold out the promise of enhancing human potential.

The fact that many of these new methods foster intense emotional experiences and the rapid disruption of defenses has engaged the interest of group therapists. It has been suggested that these powerful techniques could be exploited in the service of therapy, in that the emotional and open states they promote might accelerate the patient's achievement of insight into the distortions in his modes of relating and life style, and also facilitate his acquisition of new, more adaptive behavior.

THE PAPERS

In this section Parloff presents an excellent and comprehensive review of the small group field and of its relevance for group therapy proper. This paper is followed by a description of the widely used marathon method by Stoller, a pioneer of this technique.

In the final paper in this section Yalom and Lieberman discuss their fascinating and valuable assessment of encounter group casualties, which is part of a larger study designed to investigate both the process and outcome of encounter groups. The authors found that almost 10 per cent (16 out of 170) of the college students who comprised their research population manifested adverse reactions after attending encounter groups, evidence of the power and perils of this approach. In addition, they identified the three crucial variables responsible for these adverse reactions. The study findings indicate the casualties resulted from the interaction of a specific leadership style with the participant's pre-existing pathology and with his set or expectations.

Even more valuable than these specific findings, however, is the research methodology developed by Yalom and Lieberman for the investigation of outcome and process in the field of group therapy. Mention has already been made of the lack of good evaluative studies in the group and family field. Unfortunately, procedures now persist and flourish primarily because they "feel good" to patients and therapists, and because they engage and keep patients in treatment, not because their effectiveness has been systematically demonstrated. Future progress in group therapy can be assured only if we know with some certainty that group therapy is effective in the treatment of mental illness. Other basic questions need to be answered as well: If group therapy is an effective treatment modality, what are the crucial change agents? Are they specific or non-specific? And what is the comparative effectiveness of different group methods?

Yalom and Lieberman have provided a welcome example of the type of imaginative study that is urgently needed to fill this vacuum. We await with interest their reports that are still forthcoming of study findings pertaining to the positive effects of encounter groups.

SUGGESTED CROSS-REFERENCES

In Area V, further applications of small group methods are discussed by Vivian Gornick in her article on women's consciousness-raising groups; by Sager, who made extensive use of T-groups and other group methods in developing the staff for a community partial hospitalization program; and by Lubin and Eddy, who present a comprehensive description of the National Training Laboratory, where T-group methods used to enhance the skills, sensitivity, and self-awareness of group leaders and executives were developed. Bard also discusses his use of role playing and T-groups in his fascinating paper on training police officers to intervene in family crisis, also in this Area.

The therapeutic implications of some of the encounter and sensitivity methods described herein are discussed in the preceding section on New Approaches in group therapy, specifically in the four articles on experiential therapy. And Goulding, in his article in that section, describes the use of TA methods with the format of the marathon.

H.S.K.
C.J.S.

13

GROUP THERAPY AND THE SMALL-GROUP FIELD: AN ENCOUNTER

Morris B. Parloff, Ph.D.

Chief, Section on Personality, Laboratory of Psychology
National Institute of Mental Health

The small-group field appears to be confronted with a phenomenon that aspires to the rarely used accolade of "breakthrough." An ill-defined set of techniques has been broadly applied to groups of "normals," patients, and parapatients by leaders who are "normals," professionals, and paraprofessionals. The claims made concerning the consequences of such procedures are extravagantly immodest on the part of both proponents and adversaries.

The advocates describe these groups as a much needed antidote to current social ills and as a prophylactic agent against the further inroads of our sick culture on man's sacred humanness. Opponents see these groups as representing a force which subverts the basic tenets of our culture, undermines Christian morality, and debases the field of group psychotherapy.

While there is little agreement regarding the definition or characteristics of groups variously labeled as personal growth, human relations, sensory awareness, sensitivity training, self-awareness, leadership training, love-ins, psychological karate, etc., it is generally agreed that they represent a potent force for great benefit or great mischief.

Reprinted from THE INTERNATIONAL JOURNAL OF GROUP PSYCHOTHERAPY, Volume XX, July 1970, No. 3, pp. 267-304.

The author is deeply grateful to Donald S. Boomer, Allen T. Dittmann, Sara E. Greenwald, Leon Lurie, and Irvin Yalom for their assistance in the preparation of this paper.

Rogers has characterized the intensive encounter group as ". . . perhaps the most significant social invention of this century. . . ." (1968, p. 268), and Burton has said, ". . . all of us who do encountering work believe that something unique, transporting, and unifying has been found which is unmatched thus far by classical psychotherapy" (1969, p. 2).

It has not, however, escaped notice that, as with any powerful force, these groups have the potential for harm as well as good. One of the more grandiose characterizations was aired on the floor of the U. S. House of Representatives. A Congressman, on the basis of information made available to him, concluded that the impact of such group experiences resulted in ". . . confusion, frustration, and wholesale disorientation among our unsuspecting people." He also believes that such groups are being employed as ". . . a tool to indoctrinate the masses for a 'planned change' in the United States . . ." (Rarick, 1969, p. 4666).

Clearly these groups have powerful credentials for a claim on our attention. Not only are they described as potent but they appear to produce their powerful impact in a relatively short period of time and they emphasize procedures not classically employed by the professional psychotherapist. The psychotherapist, usually apathetic in response to novel theoretical formulations, is excited by the development of new and apparently powerful procedures and techniques. It is not always necessary that their claims be substantiated before he is willing to adopt them.

My purpose here is to review the available evidence in order to assess whether these dramatic innovations represent a valid breakthrough in psychotherapy's body of theory and practice, or simply another hernia.

Specifically, I propose to consider (1) the nature of the current small-group phenomenon, (2) the cultural context in which these groups have developed and flourished, (3) the evidence concerning effects and effectiveness, (4) the contribution, actual and potential, of the encounter groups to group psychotherapy practice, (5) the role and responsibility of professional group psychotherapists, and (6) some conclusions.

NATURE OF THE SMALL-GROUP PHENOMENON

Small-group theory is no more uniform and monolithic than conventional group psychotherapy theory. One approach to the problem of differentiating among the new varieties of small groups is to identify them in terms of the relative emphasis they place on the study of dynamics of *groups* as contrasted to the study of the dynamics of *individuals* in the group.

The Process-Centered Group

Initially the T-groups of the National Training Laboratories (NTL) and the Group Relations Conferences of the Tavistock Institute both placed primary emphasis on the study of small-group processes and only incidentally on the dynamics of individual members. The residential conferences of each follow a similar format of major "exercises": small group (T-group or study group), large group, intergroup, and theory. The small-group aspect of the program was developed as an educational device and emphasized the experiential basis of learning. These types of groups became increasingly popular and provided the basis for the present plethora of personal growth and development groups. While the focus of NTL has shifted somewhat toward the individual dynamics, the Tavistock program and its American counterpart, the Group Relations Center of the Washington School of Psychiatry (WSP), have maintained their focus on the group per se. Both of these centers have in fact gravitated toward the study of even larger interactional processes: between groups, between group and institution, among groups within an institution, and among institutions. The attention of the members of the "study group" is directed to such group-based issues as leadership, authority, and the role of group members *vis-à-vis* the group's primary task. Efforts by members to introduce personal material in such groups is interpreted by the consultant only in terms of the role which such behavior plays for the group.

The group-centered emphasis is also found in varying degrees in groups which have as their specific aim the improved functioning of institutions. Organizations such as NTL, Western Training Laboratories, Boston University's Human Relations Center, and UCLA's Institute of Industrial Relations all conduct groups as a management training procedure. These institutional growth groups usually include lectures and group problem-solving exercises as well as sensitivity training. These groups may be used in training community leaders, securing labor-management harmony, promoting better understanding between police and community, etc. Such groups usually stress group process in order to assist institutions and organizations to fulfill their primary missions. The group experts assist the participants to identify problems in formal structure and in the relationships among staff members.

The process-centered groups tend to be conducted by highly professional organizations which undertake to exercise close control over the training and selection of their group leaders.

The Individual-Centered Group

The classification "individual-centered group" is intended to include all groups which are primarily concerned with the behavior, feelings, fantasies, and motivations of the individual. Most such groups that are not specifically psychotherapy groups limit themselves to the goal of education and do not wittingly undertake the treatment of patients. These individual-centered groups encompass personal growth, human potential, self-awareness, encounter, confrontation, Gestalt, sensory awareness, and human relations, and have also borne such labels as truth labs, marathons, and T-groups. Perhaps the best known of these groups is the T-group, a term that is widely used to refer to all members of this proliferating class. The term "encounter group," however, recently introduced by Rogers, is more descriptive, and will, therefore, be used here interchangeably with the term "individual-centered group" to denote all members of the class.

The proponents of encounter groups do not appear to be interested in the amelioration of suffering and the overcoming of disability—the classical concerns of the psychotherapist—but aim, instead, at assisting the individual to attain new, increased, and sustained experiences of joy and self-fulfillment. Clearly the group leaders are less concerned with "head shrinking" than with "mind expanding" (Parloff, 1970). The attractive goals of such groups as described in their brochures include assisting the individual to achieve self-realization, fulfillment, peak experiences, body integration, peace, unity, joy, authenticity, love, openness, and honesty.

The general format is that of a small, unstructured, face-to-face group averaging about ten to fifteen members. Such groups meet for a relatively brief span of days during which the group meetings are massed rather than spaced. The techniques employed are aimed at stimulating intense, candid, highly personal interactions and confrontations. The leader may act as a model for the participants in that he expresses his own feelings "openly and honestly," and except in such groups as Synanon and the psychological karate types of groups, he is warm, accepting, and strongly supportive. He thus illustrates the role of ideal group member and encourages the direct expression of feelings. While many of these groups place heavy emphasis on the experience of warmth, love, and total acceptance in the group, others emphasize direct expressions of hostility and physical displays of aggression. It appears, then, that while some group leaders prefer to train their group members to turn to each other for help, others find it equally useful to train the members to turn on each other for help.

The techniques employed include the familiar verbal interactions but also stress nonverbal execises and games that have been devised to assist participants to overcome their usual resistances and social inhibitions. Such techniques include mediating, introspecting, exercising, fantasizing, touching, tapping, holding, hugging, dancing, wading, stripping, and the like.

A time-extended version of the encounter group has been given a special designation, "the marathon group," in recognition of its prolonged and sustained duration and stress. The time span of a marathon group may range from an afternoon to thirty-six or even forty-eight continuous hours (Casriel and Deitch, 1968; Stoller, 1968; Bach, 1966, 1967a, 1967b, 1967c; Mintz, 1967, 1969). The special value of this practice lies in the claim that by developing a high level of intensity and fatigue, group members will achieve a corresponding weakening or dissolution of their usual defensive patterns.

In contrast to the group-centered, the individual-centered groups may or may not have institutional sponsorship. With a few notable exceptions, persons who decide to lead individual-centered groups are self-selected rather than appointed by an organization on the basis of formal training, supervision, and demonstrated competence. As a consequence the quality of leadership of encounter groups is highly variable. Leaders range from the highly trained mental health professional to the "compleat" novice.

As these groups proliferate, it becomes clear that they attract participants who would ordinarily seek psychotherapy. The clients of the groups appear to be drawn primarily from young and middle-aged members of the middle class. The groups are especially attractive to students and professionals—particularly mental health practitioners themselves. These groups have been very aptly described as group therapy for normals (Weschler et al., 1962); however, the definition of normal is becoming increasingly ambiguous.

The issue of whether these groups are primarily educational or therapeutic in intent seems to many encounter group practitioners a meaningless and unnecessary distinction. While the initial goals of the T-group were clearly limited to the study of group processes, the current trend toward use of the group for personal growth, self-knowledge, and peak experiences has confounded the issue.

The NTL has attempted to reestablish this important distinction in its recent policy statement: "Insofar as it is possible to distinguish between education and psychotherapy, NTL Institute programs are applied for educational, not psychotherapeutic, purposes. The Institute does not design or conduct programs to cure or alleviate pathological, mental or emotional conditions" (NTL, 1959, p. 7). However, review of the brochures of many encounter group leaders suggests that, as with zealots of any new truth, their major aim is to spread enlightenment. They offer their truths promiscuously to all comers. There is little evidence that unaffiliated encounter group leaders attempt to screen out patients from nonpatients. This is a difficult enough task for the professional and a frankly impossible one for the layman. Neither the popularity of the concept of the "cultural neurosis" nor the encounter movement's failure to recognize the qualifications for patienthood make the problem any easier.

THE CULTURAL CONTEXT

Although the group movement did not spring Minerva-like from the Jovian brow of the NTL, I shall not undertake here to trace the vagaries of its growth. Excellent summaries of this history have already been written (Yalom, 1970; Gottschalk and Pattison, 1969). Let us rather consider the cultural epoch which generated the movement and continues to sustain it. It is important to recognize that the popularity of these groups has been nurtured by the same powerful social forces that have produced other significant changes within our culture and in current psychotherapy practice.

The social changes that are reflected in these groups may be characterized as belonging to a "counterculture" in terms of implicit and explicit values. The encounter groups emphasize direct action, freedom, growth, and direct expression of feelings.

Every age attempts to define man as he should be and presumably could be if he were given the opportunity. Today the humanist-existentialist view of man has taken root in the credibility crevices which seam our political and social structure. The culture is blamed for thwarting man's desire for self-actualization, love, and intimacy. Middle-class man, having satisfied his primary physical needs for shelter and food, *pace* Maslow, has looked about for residual deprivation and has become keenly aware of his alienation. He experiences a sense of meaninglessness in the mere attainment of what had earlier been touted as the good life.[1] Man's attention has shifted from his belly to his belly button and, now, to that of his neighbor.

---

[1] This is wittily illustrated by a pampered dog who is the heroine of a children's book by Maurice Sendak (1967). She had pillows, round and square, her own comb and brush, two different bottles of pills, eyedrops, eardrops, a thermometer, a red wool sweater, two windows to look out of, two bowls to eat from and a master who loved her. Yet, she decided to leave home, explaining, "I am discontented. I want something I do not have. There must be more to life than having everything!"

The exacerbation of the "adolescent" conflict between dependence and independence, passivity and dominance, alienation and intimacy, reserve and openness is seen as an important contribution and problem of our culture. The term "cultural neurosis" has been devised to describe a pervasive malaise.

The wish to change an unfortunate external state is frequently seen as occasion for changing one's internal state. Groups have classically played an important role in the achievement of this goal. It has now been rediscovered that small groups may provide reassuring, enlightening, and edifying sets of experiences of varying durability—from permanent conversion to transitory titillation. The encounter groups are now being advertised as the treatment of choice for the cultural neurosis.

Rogers, in the role of spokesman for the new social movement, states that he is offering participants a set of clearly counterposed values: ". . . becoming more spontaneous, flexible, closely related to their feelings, open to their experience, and closer and more expressively intimate in their interpersonal relationships" (1967a, p. 275).

Since encounter groups appear to be counterculture manifestations, they have been vigorously attacked by conservative individuals and groups who are not pleased to learn that their values have suddenly gone out of style. Troubled people, they believe, should be encouraged to bear their burdens privately, not to bare them publicly.

One aspect of the counterculture rebellion is its distrust of the overly rational. Thoughts, fumblingly expressed in words, fall notoriously short of the ideal of clarity and absolute honesty. Verbal communications require interpretation and may therefore obscure meanings as often as they clarify them. Only feelings and personal experience can be trusted. These have a compelling sense of immediacy and conviction that far exceed that of rational thought. The more intense the feeling, the more intense the associated conviction. This trend is also reflected in the extraordinary increase in the use of psychedelic drugs as well as the current popularity of audience participation in the theater.

According to the existentialist the most pervasive problems experienced by members of this society are boredom, fear of intimacy, fear of self-disclosure, and lack of commitment. While it may be argued that these problems do not fall uniquely in the area of competence of the psychotherapist, he is appropriately concerned when encounter group leaders undertake to treat individuals who either could be more usefully treated by psychotherapy or are so precariously balanced that the intensity of the group experience may precipitate serious decompensation.

The untrained encounter group leader can evade this sobering responsibility by pointing to the growing debate within the psychiatric community regarding the meaning of the term mental illness. The fact that this concept is largely a metaphor encourages the erroneous interpretation that the problem of differentiating between the psychiatric patient and nonpatient is purely one of semantics without identifiable referents or significant consequences.

The controversy over the encounter group as an inadvertent therapeutic arena is aggravated by a growing antiprofessional bias, clearly reflected in increased skepticism regarding the value of graduate training for the psychotherapist. "Often, he [the student] becomes so burdened with theoretical and diagnostic baggage that he becomes *less* able to understand the inner world of another person as it seems to that person. Also, as his professional training continues, it all too often occurs that his initial warm liking for other persons is submerged in a sea of psychiatric and psychological evaluation, and hidden under an all-enveloping professional role" (Rogers, 1965, p. 106). The concern regarding the negative effect of training is echoed by Carkhuff (1967).

Such questions, coupled with the real scarcity of trained individuals equipped to deal with the pressures of the community psychiatry programs, may contribute to the entrance of nonprofessionals into the group field. To the professional, however, this is an explanation, not an excuse. He views with jaundice the burgeoning number of paraprofessionals who treat parapatients in encounter groups. One of the reasons may be that these parapatients tend to be young, well-to-do, intelligent, highly motivated, verbal, successful, and only moderately disturbed. In short, they would make ideal psychotherapy patients.

THE EFFECTS OF THE NEW GROUPS

The kinship between group therapists and "new group" practitioners is perhaps most clearly illustrated in their unanimous avoidance of systematic and rigorous assessment of the effects of their efforts. The new group leaders, while eloquent and rhapsodic in describing the functions and goals of their groups, are quite inarticulate in presenting evidence of consequences. Outcome research here, as in group therapy, is sporadic, ill-designed, and inconclusive.

In part, the reluctance of the encounter group practitioner to subject his work to objective scrutiny stems from the bias which scorns the "uptight" investigator who demands objective evidence. The practitioner appears to share the view expressed in *Man of La Mancha*: "Facts are the enemy of truth."

The undeniable fact, however, is that the small-group movement is still growing and large numbers of people are attending these groups. This would appear to be a powerful testimonial to their effectiveness, but the question remains: Effectiveness for what? What kinds of changes occur, with what kinds of individuals, and under what kinds of conditions? As in the field of psychiatry this sort of research has yet to be done. It is with these reservations in mind that I shall undertake to scan the reports in the literature. Two basic questions are addressed here: (1) Are the stated goals achieved? (2) What are the dangers and negative effects?

Achievement of Goals

The major aims of small groups can be grouped into three categories: (1) enhancing organizational efficiency, (2) enhancing interpersonal skills, and (3) enhancing the sense of well being.

1. *Enhanced organizational efficiency.* Process-centered groups have as one of their aims training participants to experience and to recognize group forces and their own contribution to them. The test of such training is its practical application in expediting the work of task-oriented groups in the "back-home" situation.

One of the most sophisticated reviews of this sizable literature has recently been completed by Campbell and Dunnette (1968). I shall therefore cite their conclusions, with which I am in agreement. They bring in a Scotch verdict: ". . . the assumption that T-group training has positive utility for organizatons must necessarily rest on shaky ground. It has been neither confirmed nor disconfirmed."

2. *Enhanced interpersonal skills.* There are a number of reports which purport to show that experience in T-groups and encounter groups produces increased skills in communication, independence, flexibility, increased self-awareness, and sensitivity to others' feelings. These changes are not only observed in the group but are apparently maintained in the "back-home" setting. Comparisons of individuals who have completed a group experience and those who have not suggest that the experimental subjects show two to three times as many "changes" as do the control subjects. According to Bunker (1965), for example, approximately one-third of group subjects (N = 229) tended to show increases in openness, receptivity, tolerance of differences, and operational skills in interpersonal relationships, and improved understanding of self and others; only 15 to 20 per cent of the control group (N = 125) showed such changes.

An even higher percentage of favorable change in group participants (64%) was reported by Boyd and Elliss (1962).

While there is evidence in support of positive effects of T-group training, a number of problems exist in these studies. One of the difficulties is that the amount of change reported appears to vary with the source of the judgments. The trainee's opinion of the effectiveness of his behavioral change tends to be far more optimistic than that of observers. For example, Miles (1965) reported that of 34 high school principals who had participated in NTL programs, 82 per cent indicated improved functioning subsequent to their training. Ratings by their "back-home" colleagues, however, indicated that only 30 per cent had undergone changes. The fact that the participant's own responses are more enthusiastic than those of his associates was also found by Taylor (1967).

Campbell and Dunnette (1968) summarize the evidence for change: "In absolute terms about 30 per cent of 40 per cent of the trained individuals were reported as exhibiting some sort of perceptible change" (p. 84). These findings must be interpreted with caution, since there are two obvious methodological problems.

The interpretation of data submitted by judges is difficult in that peers tend to assign less change to colleagues who completed a group training experience than do either their superiors or subordinates (Valiquet, 1964). Compounding the serious problem of judge bias is the fact that these studies are based solely on opinions obtained at the conclusion of the training period. In the absence of a pretraining baseline the results are of questionable value.

3. *Enhanced sense of well-being.* A number of encounter group leaders view the major function of the group as simply providing an intense emotional experience. This shifts the criterion for assessing success to the internal subjective state of the participant. If one assumes that reactions to the encounter groups are to be treated as private events, such as aesthetic appreciation or recreational enjoyment, then such reports may be assumed to have face validity. The individual may take that which he chooses, or is capable of choosing, from the opportunity provided.

That most participants retrospectively report global satisfaction with their group experience is indicated by the survey findings of three investigators. Perhaps the most careful study was that conducted by Rogers (1967a), who was able to obtain responses to his questionnaire from 82 per cent (481) of clients who had participated in groups which he had led. Three-fourths reported that it had been a helpful, positive experience: 30 per cent stated that the experience had been "constructive," and 45 per cent described it as a "deeply meaningful, positive experience." An additional 19 per cent checked that it had been "more helpful than unhelpful" (1967a, p. 273).

Approximately the same degree of participant satisfaction, 78 per cent, is implied by Bach (1968), who states that his analysis of the self-reports of 612 participants is supportive of the clinical impressions reported by his colleague Stoller. Stoller is quoted as stating that only 20 per cent of participants do not get the kind of gain they seek and about one or two per cent undergo actual harm (cited in Bach, 1968, p. 246). An earlier report by Bach is even more sanguine, for he reports of 400 group members: "Ninety per cent of these Marathon Group participants . . . have evaluated their 24- to 40-hour group encounters as 'one of the most significant and meaningful experiences' of their lives" (1967b, p. 1147).

Mintz (1969) also undertook to obtain follow-up reports from her group participants and found that of 93 subjects who evaluated their experiences immediately after the termination of the marathon group, 66 per cent reported that they had profited greatly and 30 per cent reported that they had profited moderately. In a sample of 80 who evaluated their marathon group experience after a minimum period of three months or longer, 46 per cent had profited greatly and 41 per cent had profited moderately. A further analysis of the data reported by Mintz reveals that the rate of decline in enthusiasm appears to be differentially related to whether the participant is himself a psychotherapist or not. While 70 per cent of the nontherapists report immediately upon group termination that they are greatly profited, only 34 per cent still report after three months or more that they were greatly profited. On the other hand, psychotherapists tend to maintain their enthusiasm—or possibly increase it: 62 per cent in the immediate response period report having profited greatly, while 67 per cent in the follow-up period report similarly.

These studies permit us to conclude that most of the clients who choose to respond to the inquiries of their former group leaders report that they "gained something" from the experience. Neither Bach nor Mintz provide information regarding the number of eligible respondents who failed to reply to these questionnaires, and they do not attempt to compare the characteristics of the responder and nonresponder samples. Besides the issue of response bias, there are three other methodological problems which further limit the value of these studies. (1) There are no control groups to aid in assessing the impact of techniques, leader personality, style, level of training, length of meeting time, and other such obvious variables. (2) Measures were not taken prior to the group experience but only after the group had disbanded. This acts to increase the opportunity for rater bias. (3) The measures used are global rather than specific. It is not possible to determine the specific nature of the changes experienced—e.g., interpersonal sensitivity, empathy, warmth, objectivity, and other such presumed goals of the encounter groups.

When investigators have attempted to identify specific rather than general changes induced by encounter-type groups, e.g., changes in self-concept, changes in inner- or outer-directedness, and changes in attitude and personality, the findings are less positive. Stock (1964) found that the individuals who reported the greatest degree of change in their self-percepts were also those who had become much less sure of what kinds of people they were. Kassarjian (1965) attempted to determine whether sensitivity training influenced participants to become more "other-directed," as is claimed by some, or more "inner-directed," as claimed by others. He failed to find any reliable directional shifts in ten groups of subjects compared on measures taken before and after training. Kassarjian concluded that social character may not be one of the variables affected by such training. Students who were exposed to a program of sensitivity training were reported by Massarik and Carlson as showing no significant change in such standard personality measures as the CPI (cited in Dunnette, 1962), the MMPI, F-scale (Kernan, 1964), and the Cattell 16 Personality Factor Questionnaire (Cadden et al., 1969).

The paucity of standardized scales employed makes it difficult to assess the nature of attitude and personality changes that may be fostered in encounter groups. Of the attitude scales employed, only the FIRO-B appeared to give positive results (Smith, 1964; Schutz and Allen, 1966).

In summary, participants in encounter groups report favorable reactions and are frequently described by others as showing improved interpersonal skills. The evidence is meager that such participants undergo significant attitude change or personality change, and evidence that group training improves organizational efficiency is not compelling. What is clearest is that these groups provide an intensive affective experience for many participants. In this sense, the groups may be described as potent. As is the case with all potent agents, they may be helpful when properly administered, inert in "subclinical" dosages, and noxious when excessive or inappropriate.

B. Dangers

It is apparent from the public press and from an increasing number of articles appearing in professional journals that the enthusiasm for encounter groups is not universal. The public fear is that the very popularity of these groups may ultimately endanger society by encouraging the spread of values inimical to the standards and morality of our culture. The professional fear is that encounter group participation may produce psychonoxious effects in the individual during and/or after his group participation.

The evidence of the impact of encounter groups on our cultural values is unclear and even more inferential than are the inadequate data on its effect on the individual participant. Those who insist on ascribing a major role to such groups in either undermining or saving our society may be doing the encounter group much too much honor. I propose, therefore, to finesse the first issue and to limit this discussion to the area of primary professional concern to the group psychotherapist, namely, the assessment of the evidence of psychological and emotional damage to group participants.

Clinicians are becoming increasingly concerned about the sheer number of "new" patients who report that their earlier participation in one or another of the encounter groups precipitated serious emotional disturbances. While it is entirely appropriate to recognize that the clinician may be exposed to a highly selected sample—that is, those individuals who have had "bad trips" rather than those who have had favorable experiences—these observations cannot be lightly dismissed. Lazarus (1970), who is himself no stranger to experimentation with new techniques, has recently written that the number of patients who are "victims" of encounter groups is becoming so large as to constitute a new 'clinical entity.' "

I shall review three major areas of negative effects: (1) psychosis and other serious emotional reactions; (2) mild to moderate emotional disturbances; and (3) "re-entry" problems.

1. *Psychosis and other serious emotional reactions.* A number of case reports have cited compelling instances of psychotic and near psychotic reactions to encounter group exposure (for example, Odiorne, 1963; Marmor, quoted in Hoover, 1967; Jaffe and Scherl, 1969). A cursory review of these findings may give the impression that the association between encounter group attendance and serious pathological reactions is quite high. This may reflect only an increased incidence of negative reports rather than an increase of untoward reactions. However, both trends may be true.

The clinician who becomes aware that someone has suffered a serious breakdown subsequent to a group experience is understandably concerned; he is eager to inform his colleagues of the negative effects of the seemingly promiscuous and amateurish application of encounter groups to a wide spectrum of clients. He may not be much comforted by evidence that the occurrence of such gross reactions may be relatively rare with respect to the total number of persons who participate in groups. He is concerned only that pathological reactions occur at all. If a group experience is capable of precipitating severe psychological reactions, then the clinician will wish to take action to minimize this risk.

Granting the seriousness of even a single instance in which an individual is so stressed by a group experience as to become grossly disturbed, let us consider the evidence regarding the incidence of such events.

Rogers (1967a), who has achieved a considerable reputation as both a therapist and researcher, particularly in the field of assessing the effects of psychotherapy, reported that of a total sample of 587[2] subjects whom he treated in some forty groups, only two participants showed a psychotic reaction during or immediately following the intensive group experience. A further statement by Rogers suggests that he is including in this analysis only those cases in which psychoses were not transitory, for he states, "On the other side of the picture is the fact that individuals have also lived through what were clearly psychotic episodes, and lived through them very constructively, in the context of a basic encounter group" (1967a, p. 273). These data suggest that in his groups enduring psychotic reactions occurred in only 0.3 per cent of the reporting participants. It is not clear, however, what proportion suffered transitory psychotic episodes during the life of the group.

It is noted that in Bach's discussion of a study of 400 marathon group participants, he does not report a single instance of a seriously pathological reaction. He states ". . . but no one, so far, has ever complained of any real emotional or social damage to himself" (1967b, p. 1147). A subsequent report by Bach based on the cumulative sample of 612 "research subjects," although less optimistic, supports his earlier findings: ". . . we do not know of any instance of permanent deterioration due to marathon-group shock" (1968, p. 246). Similarly, Mintz's (1969) follow-up study, based on a sample of 173 respondents and the observation of a minimum of 279 participants, fails to mention the occurrence of any psychotic reactions.

The reports of these three encounter group practitioners, based on a sample of approximately 1500 group participants, suggests that the inci-

---

2 Sample size was computed on the basis of Rogers's report that the follow-up data from 481 Ss represented an 82 per cent return.

dence of psychoticlike reactions is quite small. There are, however, conflicting reports from other participants, observers, and researchers.

An unusually high incidence of psychopathological reactions was reported by Gottschalk (1966), and subsequently by Gottschalk and Pattison (1969). Gottschalk participated in one group and observed two others in the course of a two-week Human Relations Labortory. I shall consider here only his observations of psychotic and severe reactions. In a group of 11 in which he was a member, Gottschalk diagnosed "one borderline acute psychotic withdrawal reaction" and "two severe emotional breakdowns with acute anxiety." In another group of ten participants, he found "one frank psychotic reaction" and "two severe depressive reactions with anxiety." In a third group of 11 he found no severe emotional reactions (1966, p. 475; Gottschalk and Pattison, 1969, p. 833) Thus, of 32 participants, two (6.5%) showed psychotic reactions and 4 (12.5%) showed severe disruptions in performance. In total, the reports suggest that 19 per cent of the participants were seriously disturbed by their group experience.

A preliminary report of a research study conducted at Stanford University (Lieberman et al., in preparation) on the effects of encounter group experiences is based on a sample of 209 university students. As of the time of this writing, one student had suffered a manic state and another student had become "severely anxiously depressed." This suggests that approximately one per cent of the participants were seriously disturbed by the group experience. A third student committed suicide but the role of the encounter group seems minimally implicated.*

Another case report, this one originating at the Menninger School of Psychiatry (Lima and Lievano, 1968, personal communication), claims that two of 11 psychiatric residents who participated in the same T-group suffered "psychotic breakdowns" (18%), and one more became psychotic some seven months after (sic) the group had ended.

The difference between the low casualty rate reported by the encounter group practitioners (less than 1%) and the higher rates reported by other sources (1% to 19%) may be attributable to a number of factors other than the obvious interest of the practitioner in presenting his work in a favorable light.

Competence and skills of leaders. The encounter group leaders whose work is cited here are expert, and, therefore, members of their groups may suffer less risk than do participants in groups led by less expert

---

* Editor's Note: See Yalom and Lieberman's report on casualties of this study pp. 223-253 this volume.

group leaders. The hypothesis that untoward reactions are attributable to the inadequacies of the group leaders is an appealing and popular one. Bach (1968) notes that many instances of "flip-outs" have come to his attention but that these occurred in groups that were conducted by leaders who were incompetent in both the clinical and group-dynamics areas. Greatest leadership skill is required in both the control of the anxiety levels which are stimulated within the group—i.e., in the monitoring of "regressive levels" (Scheidlinger, 1968) —and in the therapeutic use of such experiences.

Differential significance assigned to transitory emotional disturbances. Encounter group practitioners and nonpractitioners place different weight on evidences of transitory psychotic manifestations. Practitioners, unlike observers, participants, and researchers, may tend not to report such episodes, for on the basis of their experience, they have become inured to the occurrence of brief, intensive reactions, even those of psychoticlike proportions. Observers and others who have less experience with such groups may not share the leaders' reassuring breadth of familiarity with such phenomena and will tend to report each instance as evidence of important untoward consequences. The occurrence of intense emotional stress in group members may be highly valued by leaders as evidence of the power of the "medicine." Powerful medicine promises powerful change. It is very reassuring to know that "something is happening."

For some encounter group leaders the mere fact that an individual may have a psychotic reaction is not taken as unequivocal evidence of an undesirable response. Concern is tempered by a rather optimistic view of the potential gains for the disturbed individual. It is argued that he will ultimately be benefited as his personality is reintegrated in a new and more constructive manner. The expectation that psychotic disruptions may permit more effective integrations of personality is not new in the field of psychiatry, but compelling demonstrations of the beneficial effects of psychotic reactions, particularly those which endure beyond the life of the group, have yet to be made. The group leader who encourages psychotic regressions must be prepared to provide a high level of professional service to his group members during and after the period of the group's existence. It cannot be assumed that a psychotic episode, without appropriate therapeutic interventions, will automatically lead to more effective personality integrations. Our back wards are filled with patients who even after many years have failed to attain maximum benefit from their psychoses.

c) Limitation of follow-up information. Since the leaders of brief intensive groups have contact with group members only for the duration of the groups, they usually remain unaware of the occurrence of negative consequences in members following termination of the groups. The clinician, on the other hand, sees only the casualties and not the successes.

2. *Mild to moderate emotional disturbances.* Each individual responds to the stress of group participation with homeostatic mechanisms. When he is unable to invoke his usual defenses or when the level of stress exceeds his capacity to compensate, symptoms of varying degrees of pathology may be evidenced. While the reports suggest that mild to moderate disturbances are not uncommon, it is usually difficult to determine whether and to what degree the reactions are transitory or enduring.

A psychiatrist who was acting as the psychiatrist-in-residence at a two-week group reported that the total incidence of emotional disturbances requiring his care was approximately 0.5 per cent (Sata, personal communication). Another psychiatrist who attended a lab sponsored by the same parent organization found that approximately 10 to 15 per cent of the participants consulted the lab psychiatrist for such complaints as anxiety, depression, agitation, and insomnia (Yalom et al., in press). An even higher rate of pathological reactions among participants in similar groups was reported by Gottshalk (1966). Of 32 members in three groups, not only did six subjects (19%), as previously noted, have serious pathological reactions, but an additional nine subjects (28%) showed milder but substantial psychological disturbances. Thus, the incidence of emotional disturbances in these three groups appears to be a phenomenal 47 per cent.

While Rogers (1967a) does not present direct evidence of the frequency with which negative experiences occurred among his group participants, he stated that a number (unspecified) found it necessary to seek psychotherapy to deal with the feelings that were stimulated but left unresolved in the "workshop groups." He added that in the absence of more specific information about each individual case, it is not possible to determine whether this observation is to be interpreted as a negative or positive outcome. While the assessment of negative or pathological responses usually requires a professional judgment, one may properly infer negative reactions from the self-reports of the participants. I am not here concerned with whether the participant was merely disappointed with his experience but whether he experienced it as damaging.

The follow-up study by Rogers (1967a) indicates that of the 481 subjects who assessed their group experiences after a period of two to twelve months, only two individuals described it as "mostly damaging"; another six cases described it as "more unhelpful than helpful" and 21 classified it as "mostly frustrating, annoying, or confusing." Thus, of those reporting, only six per cent reported negative reactions. It is not known, of course, how the 106 nonresponders would have described their reactions to the group experience.

Based on a survey of 612 marathon group participants, Bach reported that only four (0.6%) could be classed as having been damaged by the experience, that is, clients ". . . who get 'hurt' and stay hurt . . ." (1968, p. 246). Mintz's study revealed that only two respondents (2.5%) of a sample of 80 subjects, reporting after a minimum of three months following their group experience, indicated an increase in symptoms: ". . . increase in anxiety and depression lasting for several weeks" (1969, p. 94).*

In brief, the reports of mild to moderate emotional disturbances that occur *during* the group experience range from 0.5 per cent to 28 per cent; negative reactions that endure *subsequent* to the group experience range from 0.6 per cent to about 6 per cent.

Critics of encounter groups have suggested that participants may sustain significant injury in ways not ordinarily reported in the usual survey studies. They refer not simply to increasing instances of physical injury—contusions, strains, sprains, and broken limbs—as a consequence of relatively uninhibited expressions of feelings, but to the intensive group and individual assaults on a member's sensibilities. Too often, when a group member finds some group practices, particularly those involving physical intimacy or invasion of privacy, personally offensive, his reaction is explained simply as an instance of hypersensitivity or an indulgence in overly "precious" thinking. Some humanists, however, have begun to voice objection to group activities which, in the name of reverence for everyone's essential humanness, subject the individual to dehumanizing and humiliating experiences (Koch, 1969).

The clinician, researcher, and potential client will be more benefited by the identification of factors that contribute importantly to psychological accidents than by the derivation of reliable "morbidity" tables estimating the probabilities of serious emotional breakdowns among encounter group participants. The reports currently available provide little evidence concerning the influences of such variables as client, leader, group composition, techniques, duration, and setting. There is little to guide the clinician other than the commonsense advice to select participants with good ego-strength and ability to cope with stress (Jaffe and Scherl, 1969). The prospective group member, in turn, is urged to select a group leader who has been "well trained" and is "skillful." The

---

* Editor's Note: See Mintz's article pp. 151-155 this volume.

meaning of these terms is obscure, not only to the prospective client but apparently to many aspiring group leaders as well.

3. *"Re-entry problems.* There is evidence that some participants experience problems on returning to their homes and to the work-a-day world. Rogers (1967a), for example, has noted that an individual who attends an encounter group may be moved to recognize and confront marital tensions that he had previously sought to ignore. This experience, coupled with his greater openness and honesty, may lead to encounters at home of such candidness that the marriage may ultimately be endangered. The danger is enhanced if the spouse has not also been exposed to group participation. Rogers further observes that the sexual component of the warm and loving feelings which may develop between group members can constitute "a profound threat to their spouses if these feelings are not worked through satisfactorily in the workshops" (1967a, p. 274).

A nondiscriminating, single-minded adherence to the rediscovered ideal of directness and openness in one's interpersonal relationships may be greeted by one's employer and co-workers with more restrained joy than was evinced by the encounter group leader and one's fellow participants. Some encounter group graduates appear to have overlooked the point that skills in communication are not limited to directness but include the accurate assessment of the recipient's receptivity to the communication.

What appears to be seized upon by some participants is the attractiveness of an absolute and infallible standard: all behavior should be uniformly truthful, honest, direct, open, and unhesitatingly spontaneous. Compromise with these high standards is unerringly recognized as a falling-away from grace and as evidence of hypocrisy. This approach dismisses as misguided the socialization process which attempts to convey the complexities of Murray's (1938, pp. 136-137) tpmo formulas—the relation of the nature and intensity of one's behavior to the time, place, mode, and object.

There are reports that individuals are deeply moved by their experiences and appear to undergo rapid and radical changes akin to a conversion experience. One of the most common expressions of this type of dramatic change is the conversion of laymen, after a single workshop, lab, or T-group into encounter group leaders. So widespread is this extraordinary parthenogenetic transmutation that the authors of the NTL *Standards for the Use of Laboratory Method* twice allude to the phenomenon. They emphasize, "No capabilities as a T-Group trainer or consultant should be assumed as a result of participation in one or more basic laboratories or other short-term experiences" (1969, p. 11).

The change in self-concept may affect other areas of participants' lives. Some individuals are so impressed by their new self that they attempt to undo earlier life decisions regarding marriage, jobs, etc., that were made by the old self. This can be tragic when the new self melts.

For some group participants the reality of the encounter group is more attractive than the seemingly bland, cold, hypocritical, and compromising world. As a consequence, a new breed of escapists is developing—the group addicts. Once hooked, these people move from group to group in their attempt to regain the elusive "peak experience" and "meaningful" interchange with others.

In brief, there is evidence that emotional disturbances—serious and mild, transitory and enduring—may be precipitated by encounter group experiences. This finding is not challenged even by the encounter group's warmest and most enthusiastic supporters. The reports do little, however, to advance knowledge regarding the relevant variables responsible for negative effects. It is difficult to interpret meaningfully materials based on a wide variety of groups of varying purposes, techniques, leadership skills, composition, and duration.

The reported incidence of pathological reactions, however, does appear to be somewhat more ominous in the writings of participants, observers, and psychotherapists than in the publications of encounter group leaders. The issue of assessing the extent of iatrogenic reactions to encounter groups is analogous to the problem of interpreting military reports of casualties. Much depends on the size of the sample that is selected as the reference population from which a rate is computed. To the leader of a ten-man squad, three casualties represent "heavy" losses; to the commander of a company of 200 men of which the squad is a part, these three casualties are "light." Similarly, those associated with a single encounter group in which one or two serious emotional reactions are observed will be impressed by the high casualty rate. The group leader who has conducted 40 or 50 groups and uses some 400 to 600 participants as his baseline experience will be less disquieted by the occurrence of a relatively few pathological reactions. While all agree that every effort must be made to reduce or eliminate such reactions, encounter group leaders also appear to be sustained by one or more assumptions which act to minimize the potential threat posed by clients who suffer psychotic or other serious reactions to encounter group experiences. Encounter group leaders seem to believe that: (1) such responses are merely transitory; (2) they are potentially beneficial as they may make the individual accessible to personality reorganization; and (3) the potential benefits outweigh the risks.

Let us consider the last assumption, as it is basic to the problem of making recommendations to prospective participants. Clearly, there is a degree of risk involved in encounter group participation, but the studies fail to shed much light on the critical problems of risk of what, risk for whom, and risk under what conditions. Clinicians are left, then, to make their day-to-day decisions on the basis of clinical experience and professional biases regarding the selection of appropriate subjects and the prerequisite training for group leaders. That the individual may experience stress as a result of "treatment" may not in itself be a sufficient basis for rejecting the treatment form. In some instances the possibility of increasing a patient's discomfort may be viewed as an acceptable risk in the light of the potential gain. Surgery presents the classical example of this phenomenon, for it always produces some new symptoms. Frequently, useful medicines have side effects. Whether the risk of iatrogenic effects of interventions are tolerable depends on the seriousness of the condition being treated, the probability that the treatment will achieve a more desirable state, and the intensity and duration of the discomfort concomitant to such treatment.

The individuals who present themselves for encounter groups are presumably not seriously disturbed. If they are, then all responsible practitioners are agreed that they do not belong in encounter groups. Participation in encounter groups may be classed as an elective cosmetic operation rather than as an urgent life-saving procedure. If the analogy is apt, how much risk should one be willing to take? This is a highly individual choice, and ideally it should be made by each candidate on the basis of unambiguous information and expert opinion regarding his suitability. Unfortunately, neither of these conditions can be adequately fulfilled. The degree of risk an individual might be willing to endure in order to "grow," "self-actualize," and experience himself more deeply is a highly personal matter. The acceptable risk level might be somewhat less for the same individual if the goal is to learn more about group processes and to improve organizational efficiency.

Having only the evidence currently available in the public press and professional journals, the circumspect clinician who wishes to advise prospective group participants regarding possible dangers can, with confidence, offer only the following kind of advice: participation in most encounter groups is likely to be more dangerous than attending an office Christmas party and somewhat less dangerous than skiing.

THE CONTRIBUTION OF THE ENCOUNTER GROUP TO GROUP PSYCHOTHERAPY

Encounter group practices are of interest to psychotherapists, and particularly to group psychotherapists, because of their claimed advantages in (a) accelerating the development of conditions prerequisite for the treatment process, (b) attaining goals overlapping with those of psychotherapy despite use of techniques different from those emphasized by therapists, and (c) expediting the training of mental health practitioners.

Development of Prerequisite Treatment Conditions

Most psychotherapists believe that the process of therapy involves three conditions: (1) stimulating or re-creating in the treatment setting the patient's emotional conflicts, (2) increasing his accessibility to new experience (via support, permissiveness, confidence in the potency of the treatment, etc.), and (3) introducing those procedures which the therapist assumes will bring about therapeutic change. The first two steps are common to all forms of therapy while the third is determined by the theoretical assumptions favored by the therapist. The encounter group approaches may have a special contribution to make in establishing the first two conditions.

In addition to the usual group therapy procedures, the encounter group adds an expanding repertoire of verbal and nonverbal exercises. Direct interchange, including varying degrees of physical contact and intimacy, is encouraged. The techniques include a wide spectrum: sensory awareness, role-playing, meditating, fatiguing, wrestling, rocking, restraining, dancing, fantasizing, "spread-eagling," "crotch-eyeballing," etc. The nature and range of the techniques suggested seem to be limited only by the ingenuity and *chutzpah* of the leader. There appears to be an escalation in the race among technique-innovators to invent procedures which are stimulating, exciting, and, above all, different. As a consequence the unique advantages of varying degrees of nudity in groups are undergoing a thorough scrutiny at such research centers as Esalen. It has been reported that some groups have discovered the distinctive benefits of nonsexual manipulation of nude participants (Lawrence, 1969). I am confident that by the time this paper is published, the advantages of frankly sexual manipulation will also have been discovered.

The capacity of some of these groups quickly to establish an atmosphere of warmth, mutual acceptance, and love is by now well documented. Their techniques are effective both with groups of complete strangers and with groups of individuals who have pregroup relationships, some of which are expected to continue after the group terminates.

Overlapping Goals—Different Techniques

Both encounter groups and therapy groups appear to share such aims as aiding group members to become increasingly sensitive to their impact on others and to their own misperceptions and distortions, and helping them to learn more effective ways of relating. In the encounter group, such goals are the end points of the training program, while in the therapy group, increased awareness and the acquisition of new social skills are only intermediate goals. The ultimate goals in psychotherapy are relieving the patient's discomfort and assisting him to function more effectively, not only in the group but in his life situations. Further, the group therapist is concerned not only with "teaching" new patterns of behavior but with helping the patient to unlearn old ones, and with increasing the patient's capacity to discriminate between present life situations and earlier ones.

The group therapist, particularly the analytic rather than "existential" or "supportive" therapist, deals with the member's group behavior principally as it provides clues to the patient's underlying motives. The central concern is with covert processes, and only secondarily with overt behavior. In the encounter group, the interest in group behavior is in highlighting group-shared motivations and conflicts.

The group therapist is interested in the techniques employed by encounter group leaders not only because both groups share some of the same goals but also because the encounter group leader claims to be able to achieve the shared goals relatively quickly. More importantly, the encounter group leader claims to reach these goals by the use of techniques and approaches not usually employed by psychotherapists.

One of the major contributions of encounter group practice for the analytic group therapist may be the development of procedures which facilitate rapid group formation and group cohesion. The heightened psychological stimulation achieved appears to increase suggestibility and emotional contagion, thus producing a climate characterized as group formative regression. The analytic therapist, unlike the encounter group leader, does not regard this level of group functioning as an end point but attempts to utilize it in the development of "therapeutic regression" —temporal and topographical. It may be possible for the psychoanalytically oriented therapist to adopt some of the group formative procedures of the encounter group in order to accelerate the process of analyzing resistances, defenses, transferences, distortions, free associations, dreams, and fantasies.

An objection frequently raised by classical therapists is that the encounter groups emphasize the "affective" and "here and now" at the expense of insight into the underlying, unresolved emotional conflicts of the past. These psychotherapists believe that an interpretation may produce useful insight if it is well-timed and/or correct. Such an interpretation is accompanied by an affective response. It may be debated whether the useful insight and affective response occur because the interpretation is "correct" and, therefore, convincing, or whether the compelling nature of the insight is due less to its accuracy than to the degree of associated emotional experience.

In my view, the encounter group procedures which enhance the affective experience of the participants may be useful to the insight-oriented psychotherapist even if they do not arise as a result of conventional interpretation. If the patient can be assisted to experience an intense affective state, then he will be accessible to a plausible and congenial interpretation which appears to explain that emotional state. It seems to be in the nature of man to seek to understand the meaning of any powerful experience.

> Tiger got to hunt,
> Bird got to fly;
> Man got to sit and wonder,
>   "Why, why, why?"
>
> Tiger got to sleep,
> Bird got to land;
> Man got to tell himself
>   he understand.
>
> (*Vonnegut,* 1968, p. 124)

The view that "interpretations" offered after affective arousal have useful impact is supported by a study conducted by Hoehn-Saric et al. (1968).

Analytically oriented group psychotherapists, such as Mintz (1967), have found it very useful to employ arm wrestling, rocking, restraining, holding, etc., in order to assist individual members to "get in touch with their feelings" and to stimulate recall of repressed and suppressed material. These and other encounter group procedures may assist the analytically oriented group therapist to accomplish the mediating goal of re-creating emotional conflicts of the past in the present group situation.

The encounter group has been used by psychotherapists to supplement treatment programs for their patients. Group therapists are now undertaking marathon groups with their patients in order to deal with group resistances, to stimulate strong affective experiences for patients, and to provide them with a further opportunity to intensively explore their interpersonal relationships.

Therapists recognize that a strong emotional experience is not necessarily therapeutic per se; however, patients who are gifted intellectualizers and well practiced in the art of obsessing may find the affect-arousing stimulation of the encounter group particularly useful. It may provide an important step in the total treatment process. The therapist and patient can then collaborate to utilize this new experience in the subsequent "working through" process.

Training of Mental Health Practitioners

Many training programs for professional therapists are being expanded to include trainee participation in one or more sensitivity training groups. The Annual Institutes sponsored by the AGPA have increasingly veered from didactic workshop training to an almost exclusive concentration on training via the experiential "process group" and encounter group. These personal growth groups play an important training role in a variety of psychotherapist training programs, including the Group Psychotherapy Training Program of the Washington School of Psychiatry and that of the New York State Psychiatric Institute (Berger, 1969). Many universities have made attendance at T-groups part of the required training for psychologists, psychiatrists, public health workers, etc.

While the encounter group may be a particularly useful procedure for dramatically demonstrating certain group phenomena to the trainee, in my view, it is not a substitute for participation as a patient in a psychotherapy group.

THE ROLE AND RESPONSIBILITY OF THE PROFESSIONAL GROUP THERAPIST

If the preceding discussion is a fair representation of the nature, bases, effects, and usefulness of encounter groups, what stance should the professional group psychotherapist adopt *vis-à-vis* such groups?

Typically the public pronouncements and recommendations emanating from professional organizations and their spokesmen are represented as being motivated exclusively by a wholesome and selfless interest in furthering the welfare of the society. That what is seen as furthering the welfare of the public happens to be highly correlated with what enhances the welfare of the profession is dismissed as a coincidence. In this case I believe I do not need to invoke a disclaimer regarding conflict of interests.

The welfare of the group psychotherapist does not seem particularly threatened by the new group movement. The inherent dangers of the current trends are far more ominous for the established T-groups and group process organizations than for the professional group therapy societies. Group dynamics organizations are being threatened with extinction by the influx of self-appointed—and self-annointed—encounter group leaders from two sides: the professional group therapist and the overzealous and undertrained layman. Gresham's law—bad money drives out the good—may have an analogous application for these groups. Its corollary certainly holds: Good money brings in bad leaders. This possibility has not been overlooked by those most concerned. Recently the NTL has published the first of what promises to be a series of statements specifying standards of ethical practice, training of leaders, and a guide to the selection of suitable clients. Such efforts are to be applauded and vigorously supported. We must, however, resist the temptation to identify as the sole problem the fact that the leadership of the small-group field has been infiltrated by psychodynamic illiterates. While it may be an exhilarating exercise to hurl polemic missiles at this group, at this point we have neither the authority to enforce acceptance of our recommended standards nor the power to impose sanctions on those who violate them.

It is highly probable that ultimately some formal organizations will be identified as authorized to offer appropriate training, and perhaps still other practitioner-organized societies will arise to monitor the ethical practices of the encounter group leaders. In any event, I do not see the AGPA as a likely candidate to take on these responsibilities.

The fact that no professional society of encounter group practitioners has yet been constituted leaves the field without minimal standards for assessing qualifications of potential leaders and without a formal set of ethical standards. While such practitioners are not usually liable to malpractice suits, since they do not "hold themselves out" as offering treatment, they still are legally responsible under tort law for any injury —physical or emotional—which their clients sustain. Clients who believe that they have been injured may sue for damages "in order to be made whole again." That the pursuit of such legal recourse has not become a more common practice suggests that it may not provide adequate protection, is not widely recognized, or is not justified.

The professional group therapist frequently becomes preoccupied with the question of whether or not the nonclinically trained encounter group leader is perpetrating psychotherapy on his witting or unwitting clients. A related question, but not identical, is whether psychiatric patients are being "treated" in encounter groups. Both questions are an embarrassment and are better tabled. Psychotherapy cannot be defined either by evidence of its unique effects or by its professionally specialized and restricted techniques. Psychotherapy is defined simply by intent. The nonclinically trained encounter group leader does not publicly undertake to offer psychotherapy. He is, therefore, not performing psychotherapy. It would be difficult to prove that someone is performing psychotherapy accidentally or against his will.

The second question revolves about the definition of the state of being a patient. While the professional psychotherapist appears to be able to discriminate individuals into two classes—psychiatric patients and non-patients—this is admittedly a difficult task. Many challenges have been made of the concept of the "psychiatric" patient and of the entire concept of mental illness. The problem has not been clarified by the psychotherapist's reluctance clearly to define the limits of patienthood. The waters are further muddied by the fact that the term has recently been extended by therapists to include the nonpatient class of "cultural neuroses." If the trained professional extends the limits of the class designation, "patient," he must expect that at any given time one or more patients will be found frolicking on the encounter group floor. The therapist, presumably, is not objecting because such patients are being effectively treated but because they are not being helped or are, indeed, being injured in some way. This concern invites the clinician to choose among a number of alternative courses of action. He could, for example, attempt to prevent the nonclinically trained from leading such groups, or he could encourage such leaders to seek further training, supervision, consultation, etc., or he might, himself, offer to provide such services to leaders, or he might choose to deliver service directly to the group members.

These alternatives are painfully familiar to the medical psychotherapist, who over the years has somewhat reluctantly been forced into the position of training the nonmedical practitioner. The psychiatrists' efforts to enforce the exclusion of the "layman" from the field of psychotherapy have proved to be impracticable. I predict no greater success with regard to encounter group leaders.

While I am sensitive to the fact that untrained encounter group leaders —particularly those not exposed to clinical practice or to professional societies which can enforce ethical practice—constitute a serious problem, I am also aware that exhortation and finger-wagging are tiresome and unprofitable exercises. It is my intention, therefore, primarily to address professional group therapists—among them those who may have already undertaken to lead encounter groups and those who aspire to roles of leader, supervisor, consultant, and advisor.

The group therapist who elects to offer his services to the encounter group leader must be modest about the areas of his competence. By virtue of the clinician's training and experience he can be of greatest help to the nonclinician group leader in aiding him to recognize the limitations of the participant's capacities to withstand stress and to recognize those clients who require psychiatric referral. Given the opportunity, the group therapist might also be useful in the selection of members and the composition of groups.

The group therapist must recognize, however, that his clinical training does not automatically equip him to conduct such groups. The effective leadership of encounter groups requires an intimate knowledge of group processes, a facility with a wide range of techniques, and a knowledge of when to employ them consistent with the level of group development. The clinician who wishes to lead encounter groups for his patients or for nonpatients must supplement his training. A plausible description of minimal training requirements is given in a recent NTL brochure: *Standards for the Use of Laboratory Methods in NTL Programs* (1969).

While I have chosen to emphasize the potential value of encounter group techniques for the clinician, I do not imply that the group therapist is to be encouraged to use these techniques for the treatment of acute and chronically disturbed patients.

It is appropriate that the therapist be familiar with the approach and procedures of the encounter groups in order to determine whether they have anything to offer him in increasing his usefulness in the treatment of his patients. The group therapist is primarily concerned with providing his patients with the opportunity to recognize their needs and conflicts in order that they be better prepared to find gratification outside of the group. The encounter group, however, emphasizes the direct gratification, albeit in attenuated form, of needs and wishes for closeness, affection, love, sex, and even pain. It is not appropriate that the group psychotherapist impulsively adopt procedures simply because they exist or that he shift his practice from leading therapy groups for the emotionally disturbed to conducting "sheltered workshops" for the alienated, disenchanted, and unloved.

The group therapist may be called upon to assess the suitability of patients and other clients for membership in an encounter group. If the recommendation is to be made independent of knowledge of the qualifications of the prospective group leader or of the particular nature of the group procedures to be employed, then the decision must be made solely on the strengths and weaknesses of the individual in question. A permissive group atmosphere may not be particularly useful to those who require more, rather than less, ego controls, such as the characteristically hostile, the chronically asocial, the psychotic, and the flagrantly hysteric.

Ethical Standards

Professional group therapists are guided by the ethical standards developed and enforced by their own professions and professional societies. These standards will, of course, be applied by the professional in the conduct of encounter groups. While it may be unnecessary, therefore, to spell out in detail all relevant ethical considerations, I believe it is appropriate to emphasize three principles which are basic to sound clinical practice: (1) informed consent, (2) freedom of choice, and (3) establishment of safeguards.

1. *Informed consent.* Prior to entrance into the encounter group the patient/client should be provided with as full information as possible to permit him to make a decision as to whether the purposes, leaderships, techniques, duration, costs, etc., are acceptable to him. The ideal of providing adequate information is, like all ideals, a goal to be striven for but not likely to be attained in any absolute sense. The prospective participant has, in fact, little opportunity to assess in advance the skills and intentions of the leaders, the nature of the specific exercises in which he will be expected to take part, and the likely consequences of his group participation.

If it were possible to present the candidate with complete information sufficient for him to make an intelligent choice, then it would be possible to invoke the principle of "consenting adults." The idea that mutually consenting adults may engage in private acts which are not injurious to others is gaining acceptance. As human beings we may have reservations about the morality of some acts, and we may as professionals offer some opinions about possible negative psychological consequences; however, once the prospective participant has been apprised of these possibilities the right of decision remains with him. Unfortunately, the responsible group leader cannot invoke the principle of consenting adults, for it will usually be impossible to provide a group candidate with all information prerequisite for meaningful "informed consent." The leader must, therefore, retain responsibility for selection and for the consequences of an individual's group experiences.

The problem of meeting the conditions for informed consent is complicated because leaders may wish the subjects to remain in ignorance about the nature and purposes of certain procedures. This decision is presumably justified by the rationale that the effects of certain procedures will be enhanced if they are presented "spontaneously" and in a context conducive to their usefulness. These considerations may be valid, but they require that the leader undertake to further protect the individual by guaranteeing the right of free choice and by providing the necessary safeguards.

One of the dangers of withholding information is that the leader may not be able to anticipate which of the practices may be offensive to the participant. Many leaders will assume this risk in the hope that in the course of the group a climate will be established in which the participant will find certain activities inoffensive which he might otherwise have found objectionable.

The implementation of the principle of informed consent is particularly difficult because the validity of the information provided may be highly debatable. The client organization—church, school, industry—employs the services of group trainers and consultants in the hope that a specified goal or set of goals may be achieved. Responsible group relations organizations will undertake to tailor the group experience to the particular client needs specified (Schein and Bennis, 1965); however, some group leaders assume that no modification of procedure is required. They appear to believe that the indiscriminate and stereotyped attempts at breaking down defenses, the induction of regressions, and the "Zen Master" scrutiny of group process are invariably useful in the service of any and all goals. At best, such an approach may be irrelevant, and, at worst, a damaging breach of contract.

2. *Freedom of choice.* Since the prerequisite conditions of informed consent are difficult to achieve, it is necessary that scrupulous attention be paid to preserving the client's right of free choice. This includes the client's right to withdraw from any given activity or from the group itself without being exposed to pressures from the group members or leadership. The principle of free choice is not to be violated even when the practitioner is confident that his own motivation is simply that of doing good unto the client. Ethical standards require that proper respect be shown for the convictions, sensibilities, and values of the clients. It is unethical to attempt to impose any morality on the subject that is contrary to his own.

The group leader must be prepared to protect the individual member from the subtle and overt pressures exerted by the group to force the "deviant" member to conform to the group norms. The mere announcement that participants are free to decline participation is no assurance that the rights of the nonconformist will be protected. The group leader must actively protect the participants' freedom of decision. Free choice can only be exercised when the individual is not threatened by humiliation, reprisal, rejection, or ridicule.

A special problem is presented by the practice of some industries and universities of requiring employees and students to participate in encounter-type groups. Ethical considerations require that such potential group members be excused from the group if they prefer not to participate. It is necessary that the sponsoring agency be familiarized with and respect the principle of free choice. No adverse action should be taken against those who decline to enter such groups.

3. *Establishment of safeguards.* It is the leader's responsibility to provide adequate facilities and resources to protect the subject against the possibility of psychological or physical injury. The most relevant safeguards are, of course, the leader's sensitivity to the psychological states of the participants and his skillful regulation of stress levels in order not to exceed the coping abilities of the individuals involved.

The skilled therapist is careful to permit an optimal level of regression, namely, a level which does not overwhelm the patients' capacity to utilize primary-process materials constructively. The skills required in the stimulation of regression and, more importantly, in the promotion of the effective use of such material by the observing, synthesizing, and controlling ego cannot be assumed to be present in the casually trained or untrained encounter group leader. The leader must also assume responsibility for dealing with crisis situations should they arise and for making use of appropriate referrals as indicated. The leader must be willing to remove from the group any individual who may harm others or himself by his continued participation in the group.

CONCLUSIONS

The burgeoning growth of the encounter groups, which may now be nearing its asymptote, cannot be dismissed as a fad. Such groups will survive after the more bizarre aspects fade, just as the basic tenets of psychoanalysis survived the period of "wild analysis."

There is evidence that the majority of participants report satisfaction with their encounter group experience and indicate that it helped them to feel more related to themselves and to others. There is but little evidence that such subjective changes are enduring or that these changes are followed by behavioral, personality, or performance improvements. As with any intensive and emotionally stimulating experiences, they result in transitory emotional disturbances in some participants and enduring pathological changes in a few.

While leadership training and the adherence to sound ethical practices cannot guarantee elimination of negative effects, they can do much to minimize their occurrence. The dangers of indiscriminate application of these procedures by undisciplined leaders to the psychologically unstable are apparent.

Some of the principles and techniques of the encounter group may be usefully explored by the analytic group psychotherapist in order to expedite the treatment of patients. However, a number of group therapists appear to be moving in the direction of leading encounter groups of nonpatients. The therapist's primary responsibility remains with patients—psychotic, schizoid, depressed, obsessive, compulsive, phobic, anxious, and sociopathic. He has no special responsibility or unique competence in dealing with others who have as their primary goals the seeking of a new purpose and new meaning in life.

Man's ultimate motivation appears to be that of finding and maintaining a state of happiness. It is not surprising, therefore, that over the centuries various proposals have been put forth for the achievement of this goal. What is surprising is how few proposals have emerged and how recurrent these few are. The encounter group movement appears to proffer only one of the classical views. Necessarily, it conflicts with other classical prescriptions. I will not presume to enter into the philosophical debate over which is the true *summum bonum*. I suggest only that concepts such as the reification of openness and honesty, the celebration of the body, and regard for one's inner experiences deserve no less respect than the set which urges the benefits of self-denial, self-discipline, and self-mastery as prerequisites to the joys of competence, intellectual achievement, and productivity. Both views are due the reverence accorded to age and survival. Neither has led to a Golden Age. However, the individual who has access to alternative views and alternative routes to happiness may be less despairing when he finds himself at a road block.

Admittedly the fields of "small groups" and of group psychotherapy, like society itself, are in flux. The basic challenge is the familiar one summarized by Whitehead: "The art of progress is to preserve order amid change and to assure change amid order."

REFERENCES

BACH, G. R. (1966), The Marathon Group: Intensive Practice of Intimate Interaction. *Psychol. Reports*, 18:995-1002.

—— (1967a), Marathon Group Dynamics: I. Some Functions of the Professional Group Facilitator. *Psychol. Reports,* 20:995-999.

—— (1967b), Marathon Group Dynamics: II. Dimensions of Helpfulness: Therapeutic Aggression. *Psychol. Reports,* 20:1147-1158.

—— (1967c), Marathon Group Dynamics: III. Disjunctive Contacts. *Psychol. Reports,* 20:1163-1172.

—— (1968), Discussion. *This Journal,* 18:244-249.

BERGER, M. M. (1969), Experimental and Didactic Aspects of Training and Therapeutic Group Approaches. *Amer. J. Psychiat.,* 126:845-850.

BOYD, J. B. & ELLISS, J. D. (1962), *Findings of Research into Senior Management Seminars.* Toronto: Hydro-Electric Power Commission of Ontario.

BUNKER, D. R. (1965), Individual Application of Laboratory Training. *J. Applied Behav. Sci.,* 1:131-148.

BURTON, A. (1969), *Encounter.* San Francisco: Jossey-Bass, Inc.

CADDEN, J. J., FLACH, F. F., BLAKESLEE, S., & CHARLTON, R., JR. (1969), Growth in Medical Students through Group Process. *Amer. J. Psychiat.,* 126:862-867.

CAMPBELL. J. P., & DUNNETTE, M. D. (1968), Effectiveness of T-Group Experiences on Managerial Training and Development. *Psychol. Bull.,* 70:73-104.

CARKHUFF, R. R. (1967), Requiem or Reveille. In: *Sources of Gain in Counseling and Psychotherapy* ed. B. G. Berenson and R. R. Carkhuff, pp. 8-20.

CASRIEL, D. H., & DEITCH, D. (1968), The Marathon: Time-Extended Group Therapy. In: *Current Psychiatric Therapies,* ed. J. H. Masserman. New York: Grune & Stratton, pp. 163-168.

DUNNETTE, M. D. (1962), Personnel Management. *Annual Rev. Psychol.* 13:285-314.

GOTTSCHALK, L. A. (1966), Psychoanalytic Notes on T-Groups at the Human Relations Laboratory, Bethel, Maine. *Comprehensive Psychiat.,* 7:472-487.

——, & PATTISON, E. M. (1969), Psychiatric Perspectives on T-Groups and the Laboratory Movement: An Overview. *Amer. J. Psychiat.,* 126:823-840.

HOEHN-SARIC, R., FRANK, J. D., & GURLAND, B. J. (1968), Focussed Attitude Change in Neurotic Patients. *J. Nerv. Ment. Dis.,* 147:124-133.

HOOVER, E. (1967), The Great Group Binge. *West Magazine, Los Angeles Times,* Jan. 8, pp. 8-13.

JAFFE, S. L., & SCHERL, D. J. (1969), Acute Psychosis Precipitated by the T-Group Experiences. *Arch. Gen. Psychiat.,* 21:443-448.

KASSARJIAN, H. H. (1965), Social Character and Sensitivity Training. *J. Applied Behav. Sci.,* 1:433-440.

KERNAN, J. P. (1964), Laboratory Human Relations Training: Its Effects on the "Personality" of Supervisory Engineers. *Dissert. Abs.,* 25:665-666.

KOCH, S. (1969), Psychology Cannot Be a Coherent Science. *Psychology Today,* 3:14-20.

KUEHN, J. L., & CRINELLA, F. M. (1969), Sensitivity Training: Interpersonal Overkill and Other Problems. *Amer. J. Psychiat.,* 126:841-846.

LAWRENCE, S. B. (1969), Psychology in Action. Video Tape and Other Therapeutic Procedures with Nude Marathon Groups. *Amer. Psychologist,* 24:476-479.

LAZARUS, A. A. (1970), *Behavior Therapy and Beyond.* New York: McGraw-Hill.

LIEBERMAN, M. A., MILES, M., YALOM, I. D., & GOLDE, P. (in preparation), Encounter Groups: Process and Outcome—A Controlled Study.

LIMA, F. P., & LIEVANO, J. E. (1968), Personal communication.

MILES, M. B. (1965), Changes During and Following Laboratory Training: A Clinical-Experimental Study. *J. Applied Behav. Sci.,* 1:215-242.

MINTZ, E. E. (1967), Time-Extended Marathon Groups. *Psychotherapy: Theory, Research, and Practice,* 4:65-70.

—— (1969), Marathon Groups: A Preliminary Evaluation. *J. Contemp. Psychother.,* 1:91-94.

MURRAY, H., et al. (1938), *Explorations in Personality.* New York: Oxford.

National Training Laboratory (1969), *Standards for the Use of Laboratory Method in NTL Institute Programs.* Washington, D. C.: NTL Institute. (Monograph)

ODIORNE, G. S. (1963), The Trouble with Sensitivity Training. *Training Directors Journal,* October 1963, pp. 9-20.

PARLOFF, M. B. (1970), Assessing the Effects of Headshrinking and Mind-Expanding. *This Journal,* 20:14-24.

RARICK, J. R. (1969), Sensitivity Training. *Congressional Record—House of Representatives,* June 10, 1969, H4666-4679.

ROGERS, C. R. (1965), The Therapeutic Relationship: Recent Theory and Research. *Australian J. Psychol.,* 17:95-108.

—— (1967a), The Process of the Basic Encounter Group. In: *Challenges of Humanistic Psychology,* ed. J. F. G. Bugental. New York: McGraw-Hill.

—— (1967b), A Conversation with the Father of Rogerian Therapy. *Psychology Today,* 1:20.

—— (1968), Interpersonal Relationships: Year 2000. *J. Applied Behav. Sci.,* 4:265-280.

SATA, L. (1967), Personal communication.

SCHEIDLINGER, S. (1968), The Concept of Regression in Group Psychotherapy. *This Journal,* 18:3-20.

SCHEIN, E. H., & BENNIS, W. G. (eds.) (1965), *Personal and Organizational Change through Group Methods: The Laboratory Approach.* New York: Wiley.

SCHUTZ, W. C., & ALLEN, V. L. (1966), The Effects of a T-Group Laboratory on Interpersonal Behavior. *J. Applied Behav. Sci.,* 2:265-286.

SENDAK, M. (1967), *Higglety Pigglety Pop! or There Must Be More to Life.* New York: Harper & Row.

SMITH, P. B. (1964), Attitude Changes Associated with Training in Human Relations. *Brit. J. Soc. & Clin. Psychol.,* 3:104-113.

STOCK, D. A. (1964), Survey of Research on T-Groups. In: *T-Group Theory and Laboratory Method,* ed. L. P. Bradford, J. R. Gibb and K. D. Benne. New York: Wiley.

STOLLER, F. H. (1968), Accelerated Interaction: A Time-Limited Approach Based on the Brief, Intensive Group. *This Journal,* 18:220-235.

TAYLOR, F. C. (1967), Effects of Laboratory Training upon Persons and Their Work Groups. In: Research on the Impact of Using Different Laboratory Methods for Interpersonal and Organizational Change, (Chairman) S. S. Zalkind. Symposium presented at the Meeting of the American Psychological Association, Washington, D. C., September, 1967.

VALIQUET, I. M. (1964), Contribution to the Evaluation of a Management Development Program. Unpublished Master's Thesis, M.I.T.

VONNEGUT, K. (1968), *Cat's Cradle.* New York: Dell.

WESCHLER, I. R., MASSIRIK, F., & TANNENBAUM, R. (1962), The Self in Process: A Sensitivity Training Emphasis. In: *Issues in Training,* ed. I. R. Weschler, and E. H. Schein. National Education Association: National Training Laboratories, pp. 33-46.

YALOM, I. D. (1970), *The Theory and Practice of Group Psychotherapy.* New York: Basic Books.

YALOM, I. D., FIDLER, J. W., FRANK, J., MANN, J., PARLOFF, M. B., & SATA, L. American Psychiatric Association Task Force Report on Recent Developments in the Use of Small Groups. *Amer. J. Psychiat.* (in press).

14

ACCELERATED INTERACTION: A TIME-LIMITED APPROACH BASED ON THE BRIEF, INTENSIVE GROUP

Frederick H. Stoller, Ph.D.

Formerly, Senior Psychologist, Camarillo State Hospital (California)

"Accelerated interaction" is a recent development in the use of groups for the purpose of personal change which utilizes continuous group interaction over several days as its major source of impetus.[1] Other important ingredients of this new approach are time-limited contact, negation of the illness model, and the promotion of plans for the future.

Succinctly, accelerated interaction proposes that people can sit down together for several days and engage in an intense, meaningful, and memorable experience leading to important and enduring changes. Of prime importance is the experience of being deeply involved with others, honestly focusing on the here and now. The total gestalt of what impinges upon a participant may be of more importance than the specific techniques that are introduced.

In a certain sense, the development of the group therapy movement has been an extension of individual psychotherapy. The length of sessions

Reprinted from THE INTERNATIONAL JOURNAL OF GROUP PSYCHOTHERAPY, Volume XVIII, April 1968, No. 2, pp. 220-235.

[1] Preliminary work emerged out of the collaboration of the author and George Lokie, Andrew Morrison, Ronald Waller, and Roger Wickland, the early history of which is available (Stoller, 1964). This paper represents the author's current practice and views and he takes full responsibility for differences that may have developed. Appreciation should also be extended to George Bach for the stimulation and encouragement he offered.

and duration of treatment have paralleled the older movement, and group practice has not developed its own rhythms. Most of the important concepts have been borrowed from the dyadic situation. The group experience offers unique opportunities and is potentially a process which has a power in its own right. Accelerated interaction places great emphasis upon enhancing the resources which are inherent in the group.

Several concepts are central to accelerated interaction: (1) an ahistorical focus, (2) avoidance of the mental illness model, (3) emphasis upon the responsibility of the individual for his own fate, (4) concentration upon the future and upon the potential of people rather than upon their difficulties. These are trends which are found in the views of the following influential figures: Maslow (1962), Rogers (1961), Jourard (1964), Berne (1961), and Bach (1954).[2] It also partially reflects the sensitivity training movement (Bradford et al. 1964). The particular combination of developments is unique, however, as is the attempt to put them to immediate use.

Accelerated interaction has been adapted to a number of different settings. For clarity the most general model will be described: a group of individuals who come together on a weekend for an intensive group experience. The motives and purposes of these individuals, usually strangers to one another, resemble those of most private-practice clients.

THE TERMS OF THE CONTRACT

Service relationships always involve agreements over fees, type of service to be rendered, and the scope of the responsibility carried by both parties. The contractual terms in the typical therapeutic relationship are usually quite explicit about the fee as well as the time and length of the individual appointments. The duration of the service is kept indefinite with the understanding that the relationship will terminate when both parties feel sufficient benefit has been obtained. Expectations of patients and therapists as to length of time involved in therapy often differ markedly (Garfield and Wolpin, 1963).

It is highly questionable whether most therapeutic alliances end in a rational manner; a large proportion terminate for many reasons other than therapeutic considerations. Indeterminate therapeutic relationships raise problems which are not often considered. The effect of not having a limited time in which to work undermines the sense of urgency of both parties. Apparently, a patient can even become accustomed to paying high fees without necessarily developing a high motivation for termina-

---

2 It is clear that developments such as accelerated interaction represent a climate of thought current within the helping professions.

tion. Put in its most exaggerated form, it is as if both parties are saying, "If we don't get to it this year, we'll get to it next year." Evidence is accumulating that effective change is not necessarily a function of long-term therapy (Wolberg, 1965; Schlien, 1957).

Within the framework of accelerated interaction, the contract is always time-limited. In the weekend program the group meets at 8 P.M. on Friday and runs until midnight or later. Members reconvene at 10 A.M. Saturday morning and again meet until at least midnight or beyond. On Sunday the group meets between 10 A.M. and 6 P.M. Meals are eaten together. Except for an evening follow-up meeting about six weeks later, this constitutes the limit of the time commitment of all the participants.

At the beginning of each group, the leader states, as explicitly as he can, what is going to occur. He outlines the hours of the meeting, the goals of the group as he anticipates them, the general content of the interaction as he sees it, and the role he intends to play in the group. It is felt that this sets the tone of the experience from the very beginning: honest, direct, and open communication.

When there is only a limited time available, a built-in urgency is likely. In a sense, everyone, including the group leader, realizes that unless an individual comes to terms with himself and his world during the weekend, a unique opportunity will have passed. The motivation of everyone concerned heightens, and the participants exert a degree of effort they are unlikely to make in other situations. It can be said that a crisis situation has been provided. Given an urgent situation, marked involvement, and a sense of special opportunity, the possibility of breakthrough is maximized.

One of the difficulties of a prolonged psychotherapeutic relationship is its inherent dependency. Therapeutic contracts of unlimited duration enhance the dependency which is already a prominent quality of many seeking help. This type of difficulty is almost totally circumvented in accelerated interaction. Not only does the multiple group identification dilute dependency upon a single individual, as is common to groups, but the time-limited contract creates expectancies leading to independence from the group leader. It has been my experience that long-term dependency situations do not occur. When given the expectation that they will be able to take care of themselves, people do a remarkable job of doing just that.

THE STRUGGLE WITHIN THE ARENA

In any therapeutic situation the therapist sets most of the rules of the encounter: what will be talked about, the nature of interventions, and the emotional tone to be sought. The nature of these rules are largely determined by the therapist's personal qualities, his image of man, and his concept of how change is brought about. Above all, the therapist's expectancies, as communicated to participants, color the proceedings and the results.

At the opening of an accelerated interaction session, the group leader states the goals that are being sought and, to some extent, the manner in which they will be pursued. He may make a statement such as this: "We are going to be together continuously for a good period of time and we will get to know each other pretty well. I am going to ask you to do something here that is very difficult. We are going to try to talk to each other as directly and as honestly as possible. As we get to know one another, we are going to try to spell out the kinds of reactions aroused in us: how the others make us feel and how they make us behave toward them. In a very real sense the world is going to shrink down to this group. Your behavior in the group will represent a fair sample of your way of being in the world, and you will have ample opportunity to change aspects of yourself which you find are both unrewarding and unnecessary. We will be much more interested in what goes on between us than in going into history. If I, or anyone, feels you are going too far afield from what we think is important or relevant, we will let you know. It is our hope that you will come away from this weekend having dropped a number of your masks and that you will find that, without them, you are freer and more sure of what you want and of what you are capable."

Once the stage is set, participants seem willing to give up the search for historical explanation. They recognize everyone's tendency to say, in effect, "Let me explain to you why I have to be the way I am," and when alternate routes are provided, they have a way of ridiculing any attempt to invest heavily in explanation or speculaton. This is not to say that personal history has no place in the arena; it can contribute to how much a person lets himself be known. Some individuals remain a mere outline, and after a weekend together, others may not know whether this person has any brothers or sisters, whether he is rich or poor, whether he has had an easy life or a hard one. Rather than the content, it is the quality with which facts about one's self are shared that is important. Thus, a relatively minor incident or seemingly unimportant relationship shared with the group in such a way that they are moved and touched is more valuable than a momentous event told in a detailed but mechanical fashion.

The way people talk and the manner in which they permit themselves to experience one another constitutes the principle struggle within the group arena. Most people are rarely able to sustain direct, honest, adult-to-adult communication over any appreciable portion of time. Ordinarily the goal is to have an interesting or amusing but, above all, comfortable time together. When serious goals are involved, maneuver becomes the prime ingredient of social intercourse.

Where the manifest purpose is to solve personal difficulties, such as in group psychotherapy, interaction style undergoes still another change. Basically, it can be categorized as: "Don't touch me!" In a purposeful search with others, people tend to explain themselves away, justify their particular stance, bemoan their burdens, or paint monochromatic self-portraits. The very style of talking is often distinctive: the shrillness of self-justification, the studied reasonableness of explanation, and the quickened rush to accumulate grievances.

Talking about "problems" is a subtle way of building barriers rather than bridges. Ostensibly the purpose is to present difficulties the person encounters in his life. Most characteristically, it involves framing the words in such a way that the individual discusses the "problem" as if it were something outside himself. Because there is an apparent attempt to deal with what is relevant to the therapeutic goal, the avoidant nature of the maneuver can be very elusive. Nevertheless, the object is actually to talk about "something" rather than focus on one's way of moving through the world. In the continuous group, people can see that a person's impact upon the world is of more urgency than problem-solving.

To show oneself to others in a face-to-face encounter is to be vulnerable and exposed. To be open reveals our weaknesses, inadequacies, inconsistencies, guilts, and inner wishes. It is the enormous energy which goes into remaining hidden which constitutes much of the difficulties and limitations with which we struggle. Without our disguises, we have a potential for greater use of our resources of intellect and organization, a greater depth of feeling as well as a greater strength and resilience for recovering from disappointment and injury. An important key to personal change lies in permitting oneself to drop some masks, staying with the consequences of this exposure, and learning that the masks are not so necessary. The accelerated group gives time and opportunity for this to happen.

Because the nature of the interaction constitutes the major struggle, the rules of the arena are of prime importance. An individual's current stance and his accumulated impact as reflected by his group participation become the main interest. Anything that tends to move too far afield from this is minimized. Anything that would tend to dilute genuine contact is discouraged. The group experience becomes the prime mechanism of change.

THE GROUP LEADER AS A PARTICIPANT

If the group experience is the major vehicle of change, the group leader's major responsibility is in setting up experiences which provide such opportunities. The demands placed on him are less in the direction of applying techniques and categorization and more in setting the tone and atmosphere of the group, actively rather than passively. He acts as a model for the group style from his opening statement.

If it is the aim of an accelerated interaction group to attain a sustained experience in direct, adult-to-adult interaction, the leader must set the pace. He is the member of the group who is less fearful of direct encounter, who has the most feeling for the group direction. He is more skillful at providing feedback and is particularly adept at presenting it in a helpful way, that is, in providing the individual with alternatives to his customary behavior.

Not only should the group leader be open and honest but he should refrain from establishing himself in a superior or inferior relationship to anyone else in the group. The conventional role of psychotherapist militates against this because the therapist sees people within the context of a theoretical framework, is bound to a set of techniques, and is provided with a special kind of knowledge about the individual. Ultimately the group leader must learn to read his own inner responses to people and it is to these that he must direct his attention. Constant contact with a person provides an accumulation of responses which has a special relevance; a sense of what living with the person is like is a particular advantage of the intensive group. It is an inevitable phenomenon that an individual's behavior in the group, over a period of time, is a direct reflection of his way of moving through the world.

By leaning heavily upon his own personal reactions, a group leader runs the risk of perceiving a person through his own set of distortions rather than as that person actually rubs up against the world. Group settings become especially valuable under these circumstances; the group leader is only one voice in a consensus and it is the consensus with which the individual must ultimately deal. If a leader's response is not echoed by the rest of the group, the leader should accept this as a special distortion of his own rather than an accurate reflection of the person's impact. In this fashion, the group gives the leader the freedom to be a truly reactive person.

Being confronted by a group consensus, rather than an individual reaction, has powerful consequences. It is particularly compelling when the involvement with the other group participants is intense. The individual's regard for the others and his concern for their feelings about him is often a highly potent force for change. However, it should not be assumed that group reaction is a sufficient condition for inducing change in behavior and attitudes. A member must often be helped to relate to the group differently.

If the group leader wishes the experience to be characterized by openness and sharing, he can do no less than lead the way. Rather than remaining a distant figure who lives and breathes only as a therapist, he must be a very real person. Only to the degree that he presents himself as a variegated human being filled with the juices of human frailties and assets, does he get the same behavior from others. To this end the group leader may share specific details about himself; in particular, aspects of his own difficulties and struggles which seem to parallel those of other participants. Often this results in the group leader's entering into a mutual exploration with others. At times the group leader is able to make a personal breakthrough for himself, unburdening some unnecessary and troublesome manner of functioning. Not every group presents such an opportunity but the leader should conduct himself so as to be open to such a self-therapeutic possibility.

Holding oneself to a very restricted role, attempting to keep others at a distance, guarding one's responses and ordering them so as to create a particular effect in someone else are exhausting ways of conducting oneself. It takes an inordinate amount of energy to maintain roles and stances; the more intensive the situation, the more burdensome they can be. Free of the necessity to constrict himself, a group leader can enter a very grueling and demanding endeavor without excess strain. In fact, following twenty-four to thirty hours of almost continuous psychotherapy, a group leader may emerge feeling exhilarated and renewed. Fatigue is temporary, while the positive features have a way of lingering. A well-conducted and well-functioning accelerated interaction group will renew and fulfill the group leader almost as much as it does the other participants.

In order for this to be so, the leader must not be chained to theory, and particularly, not to systems which tend to categorize people. There is a tremendous temptation to lean on diagnostic frameworks and on various ways of ordering behavior. Clinical caution often engenders fear and inhibition on the part of the therapist. However, such structure gets between the one who relies on it and the direct experience of the other person. In the same fashion, leaning upon case history material gives a biased and generally derogatory picture of the person. The only way to meet someone in the intensive group is as they appear in direct interaction.

The mental illness-mental health model is particularly inappropriate in the arena of intensive encounter. Such a framework forces one person to function as the authority who passes judgment on another's health. It is quite apparent that the very act of judging highlights certain features, and an appreciation of the individual's potential is invariably missed. When judgment as to the mental health (or illness) of the person is inconsequential to the purpose at hand, new aspects of the individual emerge. It can be argued that viewing people within the mental illness framework does not, of necessity, force a downgrading approach, that it is possible to develop the freedom to appreciate the person for what he could be within the more conventional clinical approach. But, as currently practiced, conventional therapy does not foster this appreciation. A group leader in an accelerated group experience functions much more effectively the more he relegates his clinical training to the background.

THE NATURE OF THE INTENSIVE GROUP

A number of phenomena emerge when the group experience is concentrated in time which are rarely found in other group therapy situations. These new phenomena represent important ingredients for the growth experience which have not been appreciated until now and which require considerable investigation before they are fully understood or their dimensions clearly seen.

At the present stage of development, it is appropriate to point only to some observable characteristics of such groups. More objective examination is possible and will be the object of further study. As a preliminary, the following observations should be noted:

1. The higher the level of involvement with others, the higher the level of tension and concentration. In the conventional group meeting periodically, tension rises within each session and breaks at the end. In each new session the group tension must begin building once more, though it may start at a slightly higher level. Over many sessions there is a gradually rising curve of tension and involvement consisting of a series of peaks and valleys.

In the weekend session, the curve of tension and involvement is not broken but shows a continuous, sharp rise. As a consequence, levels of tension and involvement are reached which are rarely encountered in the conventional therapeutic setting. This is evidenced by tremendous interest in and concern for fellow group members. Under these circumstances, groups are generally able to get beyond the usual poses and stances inherent in most social contacts, even that very special social situation called "group psychotherapy." Participants become less concerned with "looking good" and more concerned with closely experiencing the others. Above all, people grow together and are genuinely moved by one another's struggles. The way in which people talk to one another alters in a marked manner, and communication is designed to foster closeness and openness rather than distance and camouflage.

2. The participants' sense of time and place undergoes profound alterations. In view of the crowded series of events and interactions as well as the physical restriction, such changes are understandable. There seems to be some value in experiencing social interaction under other than customary hit-and-run circumstances. New views of conventional social practices are provided to the participants against the background of this new experience.

Within the experience itself, the sense of prolonged time has two specific advantages. A feeling of having lived with other individuals yields a new dimension for appreciating the consequences of intimate involvement with him. This is very different than experiencing another in short bursts, particularly when he is only talking about his life situation rather than living through it. It is equally true for married couples: their prolonged intimacy is inevitably excluded from observation and comment by others and involves such a history of maneuvering that helpful intervention is rare.

The unusual social arrangement of time and place sets the occasion aside as something special and out of the ordinary. Expectations for such special events are different, as is the investment of effort. Placing a change-inducing experience in a setting that stands out from routine life has consequences that are not entirely appreciated and that need investigation.

3. Within the confines of the brief intensive group, mask-wearing and role-playing become extremely fatiguing; their usual cost in terms of energy is rarely appreciated because such behavior is so ubiquitous in everyday life. Within the intensive group, the effort that it takes to maintain a particular mask becomes evident. With the mounting strain of holding a usual distancing and alienating pose, the likelihood of change is increased. There is likely to emerge genuine concern and regard for others, an uncharacteristic strength and humanity, a lessening in self-justification, a reaching into the self for sharing with others, and a determination and dedication to seek out goals congruent with actual desires.

Avoiding and distancing postures can be maintained relatively easily over the conventional time span of most therapy sessions. Being together for many months, as happens in long-term therapy, does not necessarily facilitate mask dropping: people may simply accommodate to each other's disguises and collude so that no one is ever put in a position of really being touched by anyone else. Being together continuously, however, in the context of honest and direct encounter, highlights the considerable effort that goes into maintaining the pose. When people talk together without the necessity for sustaining their usual front, the difference in the tone and the quality of their self-presentation is startlingly different. Conventional psychotherapeutic modalities rarely attain this.

4. Behavioral breakthroughs occur within the accelerated group. It invariably happens that various participants will begin to show different facets of themselves. With change, different feedback is received. When people begin to talk to one another with an unmistakable quality of honesty and directness, the regard and appreciation they receive is highly reinforcing; such regard is earned in the crucible of the group struggle.

Considerable doubt may be entertained as to whether a sudden breakthrough is effective, whether it can feasibly replace the long-term growth, learning, and insight which are the goals of conventional therapy. For the most part, in conventional therapy, people work on only one aspect of themselves at a time, and behavioral change rarely takes place in highly charged, emotional circumstances. The electric quality of the intensive group experience appears to provide a different type of learning situation. There is good reason to believe that significant portions of new behavior remain as parts of the individual's behavioral repertoire. The actual incidence of such outcomes, as well as their extensiveness, will have to be studied in the years to come. However, it is premature to assume that substantial and lasting changes in life styles and attitudes cannot occur in a brief, intensive experience.

5. Intense elation and excitement is a consistent and unique element in this type of group. Exactly why it occurs (and why it occasionally does not occur) is not entirely clear and should be studied carefully. It would be of some use to speculate as to what might be involved.

The excitement and elation occur in the later phases of the group experience and often extend for a week or two beyond. However, they are transitory effects and fade away. Group excitement seems to occur only after successful struggle. It seems to be a feeling which says in effect: "I have placed myself on the line before others, and they have seen something of me without my usual protection. Not only have I come through this relatively unscathed, but people feel better about me than I dared hope."

Part of the feeling of courage, triumph, and enhanced self-regard is the sense of there being alternatives. The participant can now see many new possibilities for himself. Even the fact that he is only growing toward a new stance rather than having attained it has exciting possibilities.

The feeling of self-regard which increases in the closing phases of the group is accompanied by an emerging appreciation for the other group members. Continuously growing involvement is accompanied by a rich mixture of feelings: concern, identification, directness, honesty, helpfulness, the joy of participating in someone else's growth, as well as the friendship that is synonymous with mutuality. All these contribute, in immeasurable fashion, to the inner and outer excitement which is so unique to the brief, intensive group experience.

It is likely that elation is not central to the important changes that can occur in accelerated interaction. Experience has shown that extremely important breakthroughs can occur without the excitement and should not be confused with more important, but less spectacular, processes which are operating. Nevertheless, it does represent a phenomenon as yet little understood and whose potential for impelling movement and providing reinforcement is only beginning to be appreciated. Most exciting of all, it may provide participants with a feeling of what is possible when one conducts one's lfe with openness and honesty. Should this be the case, the final phase of the intensive group may be an instance in which true adult growth is possible, in contrast to the reparative or "band-aid" aspect of most psychotherapy.

It should be apparent from the impressionistic observations that have been presented that the intensive group involves characteristics and processes that differ appreciably from those of the more conventional group. These qualities have an interest and importance which are compelling to anyone who has experienced them. It is highly likely that they represent extremely potent forces for movement which have been only dimly suspected in the past. In any event, they deserve more study, and some of the preliminary work for these studies is now being initiated.

THE AFTERMATH OF THE STRUGGLE

Accelerated interaction has a very specific goal: appreciable change on the part of the participants. Success implies significantly different conduct. It may involve embarking on a new course, dealing differently with people, or making a series of decisions which have heretofore been impossible. Less explicitly, but perhaps of more importance, it may enable an individual to approach new crises in a more creative and growth-inducing manner than has been thought possible.

Self-understanding, in the sense that it enables a person to talk more about himself, to explain himself away, is irrelevant. Words, insofar as they are brought in as ammunition for self-justification, are considered to be the antithesis of meaningful change. When people really change, when they drop an aspect of themselves, there is a tendency to move on to new things. What has been left behind is something they no longer care about; there is little need to explain it, understand it, or rationalize it. With real change there is a tendency to react more quickly and spontaneously, to feel right about a particular response without having to question oneself or to speculate about what others will think or how they will react.

Accelerated interaction is a rich experience in which a great variety of reactions, stimuli, ideations, identifications, and responses impinge upon an individual within a relatively brief period of time. Such a wealth of stimulation creates a state which can only be characterized as "stirred up." It is as if a person comes to a group experience with an internal organization. The experience stirs him up and causes the internal organization to undergo a state of excitation and movement. When he begins to settle down, his internal structure settles back into a state of greater stability. But it now represents a new organization which is not quite the same.

The degree of change differs among individuals. There are those who undergo a marked and startling change that is noticeable to anyone who has any enduring contact with them. There are others who seem to behave as before but meet crises in a different fashion and can recognize that they now arrive at solutions which are more purposeful and less self-defeating. Some feel differently about themselves and others; their emotional framework becomes much more pleasing to themselves. Still others find a renewed faith in themselves; it is as if they had undergone a self-validating experience. For many there is a realization of strengths and resources within themselves of which they had been only dimly aware. But, of course, there are those who show little or no change and for whom the experience can be said to have been a failure.

The gains and breakthroughs which follow a group experience take some time to jell. Follow-up sessions are held approximately six weeks following the original group experience. It would appear to take approximately that long for the original elation to fade and for the new aspects of the individual to have emerged and stabilized. At this interval, some estimate of the permanence of the gains can be made. If the gains are temporary, they will have faded within six weeks; judged too early, the person may be in a state of flux which will give a misleading picture of the final result. It is still premature to evaluate how long gains made in this very brief situation will last, but informal inquiries have revealed breakthroughs that have been maintained for at least a year.

Another type of growth has been found in persons who have gone through a number of marathon group experiences. Their entire initial experience may have revolved around whether or not they could permit themselves to be touched by others. Upon entering a second group experience, the person may involve himself in a very different manner than he did in the first group; his struggle will be of a different order and, as a consequence, will permit him to deal with different aspects of himself. There is reason to believe that people can engage in step-by-step growth with successive group experiences providing they are not permitted to grow "group-wise," to learn how to get by in a group of this sort by playing the game.

On the basis of purely subjective observation, approximately twenty per cent of the participants do not get the kind of gain from accelerated interaction that is sought. About one or two per cent undergo actual harm in that they seem worse after the experience than before. How to determine who will not benefit and, in particular, who will be harmed is not easy. While it is clear that motivation is as important here as it is in any approach, many who are ambivalent become mobilized by the momentum of the group. Diagnostic or psychopathological considerations are not as central for determining who might be harmed as might be assumed. Many whose involvement with mental illness would seem to rule them out have made enormous gains. In contrast, some who have had the most difficulty in the group have had no history of disturbance. The need to maintain a rigid role may be the most important feature for anticipating difficulties. But this is strictly speculative and cannot now be used as a basis for screening.

On the assumption that the risks are actually quite small in contrast to the probable gains, participants are now taken into groups as they apply. Sometimes the feelings of the group leader toward a prospective participant, whether he finds he wants to spend a long period of time with him, are the best indicator.

VARIATIONS AND APPLICATIONS

The primary technical consideration for accelerated interaction is that a group meet continuously over several days and that it be time-limited. Two or three days would seem to be optimal as judged by experience. More time does not necessarily mean more will be accomplished by the participants. Parkinson's law is applicable to psychotherapy: people will take the time allotted to them to achieve the goals they seek.

Settings for marathon groups vary with the demands of the situation. However, my preference is for home settings; many of the groups are held in my own home with my wife participating. It should be noted, however, that the attitude of the participants, particularly the group leader, is far more important than the setting. One of my most effective groups was held in an abandoned dormitory of a prison, as sterile a setting as can be imagined.

Many clinicians assume that the intensive group experience is too powerful for people who have undergone hospitalization or profound disorganization, but it is my experience that such people are not bruised by the experience and often achieve considerable gains. The primary limitation would seem to be for persons whose resources are too limited or who are too bogged down in immediate reality difficulties. If there is no room in which to apply new behavior or patterns, such people quickly become overwhelmed by the demands of their lives.

This can be clearly seen in an institutional setting. Accelerated interaction has been applied in mental hospitals and prisons for drug addicts, and the structure of institutional life is such that it is very difficult to sustain the gains that are frequently achieved. Because of this, it has become advantageous to think of this approach as faciltating the individual's utilization of the institutional program. In this sense, accelerated interaction may be utilized to promote a greater degree of meaningful participation on the part of inmates rather than as a primary tool to change life styles.

It should be re-emphasized that precise time goals are important. Attempts to prolong the therapeutic relationship for purposes of support undermine the growth potential of this experience. If necessary, it is preferable to have the individual undergo another accelerated experience; the growth under this situation is often much more meaningful than if the initial experience is prolonged.

SUMMARY

Accelerated interaction is a new approach mainly characterized by continuous group interaction over several days with a very definite time limit to the therapeutic contact. It utilizes the urgency and independence-fostering qualities of the time-limited contact while taking advantage of the impact of intimate group life. Elements of the group process emerge under continuous interaction which are scarcely realized under most conventional circumstances and which have profound implications for promoting social change in people. By stressing involvement, honesty, directness, and mutuality, the accelerated group promotes an intense experience in living with people which opens many possibilities for personal growth. The role of the group leader shifts from that of commentator and technician to that of participant who reacts in an immediate fashion. Holding such groups in homes rather than the usual office or clinic setting places the emphasis on personal growth and new possibilities for living instead of on correcting defective functioning. In addition, accelerated interaction has advantageous applications for institutional programs.

REFERENCES

BACH, G. R. (1954), *Intensive Group Psychotherapy*. New York: Ronald Press.
BERNE, E. (1961), *Transactional Analysis in Psychotherapy*. New York: Grove Press.
BRADFORD, L. P., GIBB, J. R., & BENNE, K. D., Eds. (1964), *T-Group Theory and Laboratory Method*. New York: Wiley.
GARFIELD, S. L., & WOLPIN, M. (1963), Expectations Regarding Psychotherapy. *J. Nerv. Ment. Dis.*, 137:353-362.
JOURARD, S. M. (1964), *The Transparent Self*. Princeton, N. J.: Van Nostrand.
MASLOW, A. H. (1962), *Toward a Psychology of Being*. Princeton, N. J.: Van Nostrand.
ROGERS, C. R. (1961), *On Becoming a Person*. Boston: Houghton-Mifflin.
SCHLEIN, J. M. (1957), Time-limited Psychotherapy: An Experimental Investigation of Practical Values and Theoretical Implications. *J. Counsel. Psychol.*, 4:318-322.
STOLLER, F. H. (1964), Accelerated Interaction: A Collective Presentation by Members of "Swing," A Professional Cooperative of Group Psychotherapists. Mimeographed paper.
WOLBERG, L. R. (1965), Introduction. In: Wolberg, L. R. (Ed.), *Short-Term Psychotherapy*. New York: Grune & Stratton.

15

A STUDY OF ENCOUNTER GROUP CASUALTIES

Irvin D. Yalom, M.D.

*Associate Professor of Psychiatry, Stanford Medical School,
Stanford, California*

and

Morton A. Lieberman, Ph.D.

*Associate Professor of Psychology, Committee on Human
Development, University of Chicago*

SYNOPSIS

Two hundred and nine university undergraduates entered 18 encounter groups which, over a ten-week period, met for a total of 30 hours. Thirty-nine subjects dropped out of the groups, while 170 completed the group experience. Of these, 16 subjects were considered "casualties" —defined as an enduring, significant, negative outcome which, according to our judgment, was caused by their participation in the group. The most reliable method of identifying casualties was to solicit the opinions

Reprinted from ARCHIVES OF GENERAL PSYCHIATRY, Vol. 25, No. 1, July 1971. Copyright 1971, American Medical Association.

Acknowledgments: The authors wish to express their gratitude for the significant contributions of Matthew Miles, Stephen Miller and E. Kitch in this study.

This study was supported by grants from the following: 1. Ford Foundation Grant 68-742; 2. Ford Foundation Fund for Innovations in Education; 3. Mary Reynolds Babcock Foundation; 4. Stanford Medical School Student Research Assistantship Grant; 5. NIMH Grant #MH 19212-01; 6. Carnegie Foundation; 7. Stanford University General Research Support Grant.

of the other group members; the leader was not a valuable judge of casualty states. The frequency, severity and mode of psychological injury varied considerably amongst the 18 groups. The highest risk leadership style was characterized by high stimulus input, aggressivity, charisma, support, intrusiveness, individual (as opposed to interpersonal or group) focus. The most vulnerable individuals were those with low self-concept and unrealistically high expectations and anticipations of change.

How psychologically dangerous are encounter groups? For several years mental health professionals have been in the uncomfortable position of having to answer this question without the necessary information. Despite, however, the lack of systematic information, there has been no dearth of polemics.

On the one hand, many, alarmed by case reports of severe psychological decompensation following an encounter group experience (so-called "encounter group casualties") have branded the whole encounter group field as dangerous. Some medical societies have proposed that state governments legislate regulations for encounter group practice. Clinicians' views towards encounter groups are based on heavily skewed information: they often see casualties or read about them in their professional journals, but they rarely have contact with encounter group members who have had satisfying experiences. Some psychiatric associations have attempted to garner relevant evidence by polling members for a list of all the casualties they have seen. Such an approach can demonstrate the existence but not the frequency of danger. Knowing the number of casualties without knowing the total number of participants from which the casualties issue offers useful but severely limited information. Anecdotal case reporting has another intrinsic flaw: multiple reporting may spuriously inflate casualty rates. An untoward outcome in a group member is generally a striking event not easily forgotten by the other group members; if the other 20 members (or, in a residential laboratory, 100 members) all describe this event to colleagues or friends, the single casualty soon assumes alarming proportions.

Encounter group leaders, enthusiastic members, and administrative staff of growth centers often take an opposite position. They report few casualties and generally do not view the encounter group as a hazardous venture—a not unexpected viewpoint. Most encounter group leaders and growth centers are limited in their source of information. Their groups are generally brief; once ended, the members scatter and the leaders have little opportunity, even were they so inclined, to gather follow-up data. A psychological decompensation occurring after the end of the group would be unlikely to come to their attention.

There are, in addition to actual limitations of information, ideological sources of bias. Many encounter group leaders reject psychiatric definitions of "adverse effect"; they feel that extreme psychological discomfort, even to the degree that professional aid is required, may be not a failure but an accomplishment of the group. They view psychological decompensation, like the legendary "night journey" as a stage, even a desideratum, of personal growth. Other leaders express a lack of interest in adverse effects since their ideological base stresses the necessity and ability of each individual to assume responsibility for himself. They believe that the leader who takes responsibility for the welfare of others thus infantilizes them and impedes their growth.

The American Psychiatric Association was sufficiently concerned with these issues to commission in 1969 a task force (chaired by one of the present authors, I. Y.) to survey the current state of knowledge. The Task Force Report (1) reviewed the literature and noted that there was "distressingly little data": the available evidence consisted entirely of anecdotal reports or loosely designed studies which lacked a post-group follow-up.

With this background in mind, the current authors when designing a systematic research project on encounter groups attempted to pay careful attention to the negative as well as to the positive outcomes of encounter groups.

METHODOLOGY

In the spring of 1969 we* conducted an intensive study of a large number of encounter groups led by leaders from different ideological schools. The group members, all Stanford University undergraduates, were studied in a variety of ways. They completed a large battery of self-report questionnaires before beginning the groups, after each meeting, at the end of the group experience and again, for a final follow-up, six months later. The groups each met for a total of 30 hours: some had spaced (10 three-hour) meetings, others a massed format in which the groups met for only a few time-extended "marathon" meetings. The encounter group participants received three academic credits; no preparation paper or examination was required, the only requirements (though unenforced) were attendance and cooperation in the research endeavor. The groups, with a few exceptions, met on or near the Stanford campus; each meeting was tape recorded and rated by two trained observers.

---

* The principal investigators in the entire project were Morton A. Lieberman, Irvin D. Yalom, and Matthew Miles, with the collaboration of Peggy Golde and Herbert Wong.

Eighteen groups were conducted. We deliberately selected leaders from a wide variety of ideological schools. Our eighteen groups thus had these labels:*

1. N.T.L. Sensitivity groups (T-groups)	2 groups
2. Gestalt therapy (Esalen—Fritz Perls derivative)	2 groups
3. Psychodrama orientation	2 groups
4. Psychoanalytic	1 group
5. Transactional analysis	2 groups
6. Sensory awareness focus (Esalen derivative)	1 group
7. Marathon (a. Rogerian; b. eclectic personal growth)	2 groups
8. Synanon	2 groups
9. N.T.L. West—"personal growth," black-white encounter focus	2 groups
10. Tape groups (leaderless; Bell & Howell Peer Program) (3)	2 groups

Once we selected the "types" of groups, we then attempted to identify the most competent, senior leaders of each ideological school in Northern California. The leaders were well paid ($750 for the 30-hour groups, plus two to three hours of research interviews and questionnaires). We were fortunate enough to recruit highly experienced, well recommended leaders. Indeed several of the leaders have national reputations. The instructions to the leader were minimal: they were asked to lead the encounter groups in their usual manner—to "do their thing."

When students registered for the course they were randomly assigned (stratified by sex, race and previous encounter group experience) to one of the 18 groups. Two hundred and nine students began the groups, 39 dropped out (i.e. missed at least the last two meetings) and 170 completed the group. Seventy-five control subjects were studied: approximately half of these came from the ranks of students who registered for the encounter group course and then (generally because of time-scheduling conflicts) did not attend the group, the other half were gathered by asking the experimental subjects for a list of friends who probably would have wanted to take the course but who could not because of scheduling conflicts. We drew a random sample from this list.

The goals of the project were ambitious. We attempted a thorough study of the process and outcome of experiential groups; in short "everything you ever wanted to know about groups." This article describes only that part of the project pertaining to negative outcome. The reader

---

* Our results indicate that the labels or derivative schools of the leaders convey relatively little information about their actual group behavior. On the basis of observer ratings of leader behavior and member descriptions, we evolved a different typology of leader behavior which we shall use in describing outcomes. The leader style typology is described in detail elsewhere (2).

is referred elsewhere (2) for a complete description of the experimental methodology and the measurement of process and of positive outcome.

A study of the casualties of encounter groups posed some basic moral problems for the experimenters. We rapidly appreciated two conflicting sets of allegiances: those to our desire to conduct a well controlled, powerful experiment and those to our sense of ethical and moral responsibility to our subjects. On the one hand, we wished to execute an *in vivo* study—one which was not so far removed from life that it would have no generalizability. On the other hand, however, we felt uneasy about deliberately placing our subjects in high risk situations: this would violate our sense of responsibility both as researchers and as clinicians.

Our final design represented a compromise between these allegiances. Our desire for experimental power resulted in:

1. No pre-group screening of the subjects (since growth centers and encounter group leaders almost never screen).

2. Random assignment of subjects to groups.

3. No intervention by the research staff during the course of the groups. The research observers were trained never to give feedback to the leaders or to any members of the group.

4. Inclusion of some aggressive highly confrontive leaders. These styles of leadership were already very much in evidence on the Stanford campus. In fact, encounter groups of all types are so common that approximately 50% of the student population has been in at least one group. Attention to our conscience and ethical sense resulted in:

1. Our informing all subjects before entering the study that "participation in encounter groups sometimes results in considerable emotional upset." They were also given the names of University mental health facilities and the name of one of the principal investigators to consult should they require help. During the midst of the project one of the group members committed suicide. When this happened we informed all leaders and requested them to remind their members of the existence of the mental health facilities on campus. (This was the single intervention the research staff made during the course of the groups.) To insure that the students gave informed consent, we attempted to communicate what to expect in an encounter group by a pre-group microlab exercise.

2. Imposition of research conditions which introduced some moderation in the groups. Each meeting was observed by two researchers (a different pair for each meeting); each meeting was tape recorded; each meeting was followed by 15-30 minutes of questionnaire administration.

In our judgment the overall effects of the research conditions were to *reduce* risk. The leaders knew, of course, that they were being observed, evaluated and compared with other leaders. They knew that the results would eventually be published, and we surmised that such conditions could only serve to put them, as it were, on their best behavior.

IDENTIFICATION OF CASUALTIES

A casualty, by our definition, was an individual who, as a direct result of his experience in the encounter group, became more psychologically distressed and/or employed more maladaptive mechanisms of defence; furthermore this negative change was not a transient but an enduring one, as judged eight months after the group experience.

Since it was not possible to interview in depth all 209 subjects who began the groups, we used eight criteria to identify a potential high risk subsample who could then be studied more intensively.

1. *Request for Psychiatric Aid.* The most obvious mode of identifying a casualty, and the one used in most previous research, is the request for emergency aid during the course of the group.

2. *Dropouts from Groups.* We expected that those who dropped out of groups might have done so because of a noxious group experience.

3. *Peer Evaluation.* At the end of the group, all members were asked, "Did anyone get hurt in your group? Who? How?"

4. *Self-esteem Drop.* The Rosenberg Self-esteem measure (4) was used as one measure of outcome. We calculated the pre-post change in self-esteem and studied the lowest ten percentile (the 17 subjects who decreased the most in self-esteem) of the subjects.

5. *Subject Testimony.* At the end of the group the subjects were asked to rate their group on a number of seven-point differential scales (e.g. constructive-destructive, low learning-high learning, pleasant-unpleasant, turned off-turned on, etc.). Again, the lowest ten percent were included in our high risk sample.

6. *Psychotherapy.* At the six-month follow-up all subjects were asked whether they had started psychotherapy since the beginning of the group. All subjects answering positively were studied.

7. *Leaders' Ratings.* The leaders were asked at the end of the group to rate each student on the amount of progress he had made on a number of dimensions (e.g. self understanding, positive self image, happiness, openness, sensitivity, ability to collaborate with others, etc.) The subjects (lowest 10%) who had had the lowest leader ratings were included in the high risk population.

8. Several miscellaneous sources of information were available to us. For example, the observers occasionally reported concern about some member of a group which they observed, or subjects during an interview expressed concern about another member.

> *Example*: One casualty was in fact identified by a rather remarkable method. One researcher was interviewing the 30 subjects who, on the basis of self-report questionnaires, appeared to have had the most *positive* outcome. It was clear that one subject not only had *not* benefited from the group but in fact had had a very negative experience and had scored himself highly on questionnaires in a vain and self-deceptive attempt to turn a destructive experience into a constructive one. The fact that a casualty appeared on the high positive change list suggested to us that our methods of identification were not exhaustive and might have erred on the conservative side.

Once a list (n = 104) of casualty suspects was compiled, the next phase of the project began. Approximately eight months after the end of the group, one of the authors attempted to contact each suspect by phone. If in a 15 to 20-minute telephone interview there was any suspicion that the subject had had a psychologically destructive experience, he was invited in for an in-depth personal interview. If distance did not permit a face-to-face interview, it was conducted over the telephone. The interviewer informed the subject that the investigators, in their study of the effects of the encounter groups, were interviewing a large number of students to obtain their retrospective view of the group. Did they now view the group as an overall constructive, neutral or destructive experience? Was the group stressful to them? Had they been made uncomfortable by the group? For how long a period of time? In which ways? Specific inquiries were made about interpersonal functioning, academic effectiveness and self-concept. If the group had a negative effect, had they by now (eight months later) recovered back to the level of comfort or adaptation that was present before the group? Were there concurrent life circumstances that may have also been responsible for the subject's deterioration during the period of the study? Had they sought help from professional or informal sources? To enhance the flow of information we often mentioned our mode of identification (e.g. decreased self-esteem on their self-administered questionnaires, or co-members citing the subject as having been harmed by the group) and proceeded to investigate these areas. Some dropouts may have been in the group for only a couple of sessions; to refresh their memories, a tape recording of their last meeting was played for them. In general, however, no memory refreshing was necessary; we were struck by the vivid recall eight months later of almost all subjects—even those who described the group as dull and plodding.

Our definition of casualty was fairly stringent: not only must the student have undergone some psychological decompensation but it must have been persistent and there must have been evidence that the group experience was the responsible agent. We did not consider as casualties several subjects who were shaken up and severely distressed by the group but who, a few days later, had recovered their equilibrium. Nor did we include several subjects who during the group or in the six months following had had some psychological decompensation that was due not to the encounter group but to other circumstances in the life of the individual.

> *Example*: The case of D.A. is illustrative. D.A. was the major tragedy of the study. A few days after his second meeting he took sleeping pills and committed suicide. It would have been easy to impugn the group as being responsible. However, upon careful study, we learned that he had a long history of psychiatric disturbance and had, during the course of the group and over the preceding three years, sought help from a number of sources. (In fact, the main reason he had recently transferred to Stanford was because he heard that the student health psychiatric service was excellent.) In the months preceding the project he had been in a number of local encounter groups. Six months before his death, he had begun both individual and group therapy in two University health facilities (without, incidentally, informing either therapist of his work with the other). Not only was he in two forms of psychotherapy while he was in the project, but we learned from a friend that he was, concurrently, in another encounter group in a nearby growth institute. We reviewed the two meetings he attended and found that they were low affect meetings in which D.A. had participated in a constructive manner. The group leader reported that he had been helpful in moving the group along by participating in an open, non-defensive manner. The questionnaires he completed at the end of these sessions also suggested optimism about the group.
>
> It is impossible to conclude with certainty that the encounter group did not in some way contribute to his suicide. However, after considering all the evidence, we decided that his participation in the encounter group was more a manifestation than a cause of his despair and did not, therefore, consider him a "casualty."*

---

* The suicide note D.A. left is an angry one which appears to indict therapy and encounter group members, past and present:

"I felt great pain that I could not stop any other way. I would have been helpful if there had been anyone to understand and care about my pain, but there wasn't. People did not believe me when I told them about my problems or pain or else that it was just self pity; or if there had been someone to share my feelings with, but all they said was that I was hiding myself, not showing my true feelings,

RESULTS

A total of 104 casualty suspects were identified. Of these 79 were contacted by telephone and 25 could not be located. Sixteen casualties were identified: this represents 7.5% of the 209 subjects who began the groups, or 9.4% of the 170 subjects who completed the groups.

The severity and type of psychological injury varied considerably. Three students during or immediately following the group had a psychotic decomposition—one a manic psychosis, one an acute paranoid schizophrenic episode, and the third an acute undifferentiated schizophrenic-LSD episode. Several students had depressive and/or anxiety symptoms ranging from low grade tension or discouragement to severe crippling anxiety attacks to a major six-month depression with a 40-pound weight loss and suicidal ideaton. Others suffered some disruption of their self-system: they felt empty, self-negating, inadequate, shameful, unacceptable, more discouraged about ever growing or changing. Several subjects noted a deterioration of their interpersonal life; they withdrew or avoided others, experienced more distrust, were less willing to reach out or to take risks with others.

The comparative efficiency of the various modes of identifying casualties is illustrated in Table 1. Note that the most effective method is "Peer Evaluation." A total of 30 subjects were listed by their comembers as having been hurt by the group and of these 30, 12 were casualties. There were 11 subjects who were multiply chosen (i.e. more than one member of their group listed them); of these 11, eight were casualties (and a ninth was D.A.—the subject who committed suicide). There were four casualties with only a single nomination, but three of these four were self-selected. *Therefore, if a group member is cited by more than one member of his group, or cites himself as having been hurt by the experience, it is highly probable that he represents a casualty of the group.* (In our sample, the probability is 73%.) Furthermore, all of the more severe casualties were identified by this method.

Table 1 also indicates that the leaders' ratings were a highly inaccurate mode of identifying casualties. Of the 20 subjects with the lowest leader ratings, only three were casualties. Moreover some of the severe casualties were missed by this mode.

---

talking to myself. They kept saying this no matter how hard I tried to reach them. This is what I mean when I say they do not understand or care about my pain; they just discredited it or ignored it and I was left alone with it. I ask that anyone who asks about me see this; it is my only last request."

TABLE 1
MODES OF CASUALTY IDENTIFICATION

Casualties	Request Emergency Psychiatric Aid	Drop-out	Peer Evaluation	Self-Esteem Drop	Subject Testimony	Psychotherapy Began During Group	Psychotherapy Began 6 Mos. Following Group	Leaders' Ratings	Miscellaneous
1 S.C.		X	X						
2 N.I.			X						
3 B.V.									
4 L.L.			X		X				
5 E.L.			X	X			X	X	
6 C.L.	X	X	X			X			
7 D.R.			X	X	X	X			
8 H.I.									
9 T.G.							X*		X
10 O.O.			X	X	X				
11 M.A.					X				
12 E.D.	X	X	X				X		
13 S.C.			X	X	X	X			
14 M.M.		X	X			X			
15 D.H.		X	X			X		X	
16 H.P.			X		X		X	X	
Total (Casualties)	2	5	12	4	6	4	3	3	1
Total (Non-casualties)	0	28	18	15	11	10	0	17	0

* Did not begin therapy but stated that, as a result of the group, he had been strongly considering it.

TABLE 2

MODES OF IDENTIFICATION FOR CASUALTIES AND CASUALTY SUSPECTS

| | Total Number of Indices | | | | Total N |
	1	2	3	4	
Casualties	5	2	3	6	16
Casualty Suspects	65	20	3	0	88

The usual mode of counting casualties—noting the number who seek help—was an insensitive index. Only two casualties came to our attention in this manner: one was seen in the emergency room in an anxious depression, the other in a manic psychotic state.

Table 2 indicates that the casualties were likely to have been identified by more than one of our modes of identification. Sixty-two percent of the casualties were identified by three or four different modes compared to only three per cent of the casualty suspects (who in interview were not considered to be casualties). Unfortunately, two of the three suspects with three indices of suspicion could not be located for interview, thus raising again the possibility that our reported casualty rate is low.

Table 1 indicates, too, that of the 17 subjects beginning psychotherapy either during or within an eight-month period after the group, seven were casualties. Three subjects could not be located for a follow-up interview. However, a study of the 14 available subjects revealed some interesting interrelationships between encounter group participation and psychotherapy. Table 3 indicates that it is three times more likely that a subject who is in an encounter group will seek psychotherapy during the time he is in the group, or in the eight-month follow-up period, than a control subject.

Why does he enter psychotherapy? Information from interviews with the 14 subjects suggested several reasons:

1. Five sought psychotherapy for repair. They were all casualties and were so upset by the group experiences that they needed help in order to regain their equilibrium.

2. Six (including two casualties) entered psychotherapy for the same reasons they had entered the encounter group. Psychotherapy and the encounter group experiences were not causally related; both were manifestations of the individual's search for help.

3. Two had a very constructive encounter group experience and entered therapy to continue work started in the group. They credited the

TABLE 3

ENCOUNTER GROUP MEMBERS ENTERING PSYCHOTHERAPY

	Never	Yes—Prior to Group	Yes—During Group	Yes—Within 6 mos. After End of Group	Totals*
Experimentals (excluding casualties)	130	20	0	10	160
Casualties	4	5	4	3	16
Controls	50	9	1	1	61

* The totals are less than the original experimental and control N, since not all subjects were available for the six-month follow-up questionnaire study.

group with helping them to identify their problems and showing them that it was possible to obtain help by talking about them and working on them.

4. One entered therapy for reasons entirely unrelated to the encounter group, a crisis in his life arose months after the end of the group.

RELATIONSHIP BETWEEN THE TYPE OF ENCOUNTER GROUP AND THE CASUALTY RATE

Table 4 indicates that the casualties were not evenly distributed amongst the 18 groups. Six groups had no casualties, while three had two casualties and one group had three casualties. To understand this skewed distribution of casualties we attempted to cluster together leaders with similar style. As we have previously indicated, the ideological school of the leader and his actual behavior were largely unrelated so that, for example, the two transactional analysis leaders were no more likely to resemble one another than they were to resemble leaders of any of the other schools. A new taxonomy of leadership style was therefore required —a task of no little complexity.

The entire methodology of the derivation of this taxonomy is described elsewhere (2) but, in brief, leader behavior was examined through two lenses—participant questionnaires, designed to tap the symbolic value of the leader to each member, and observer schedules. Observers rated, exhaustively, the leaders' behavior, their global style and their primary focus in the group (group, individual, or interpersonal issues). Observers also recorded their personal reactions to the leaders. In all 48 scales of leader behavior were rated by observers and participants. By means of factor analyses, these 48 categories were reduced to four basic dimensions

TABLE 4

Incidence of Casualties in the Eighteen Groups

Leadership Style	Group No.	Casualties	No. of Subjects Beginning the Group	Dropouts*	Number of Groups	Percent of the 18 groups	Percent of Casualties
A "Aggressive Stimulation" Charisma	1	0	11	0	5/18	27.8	44
	2	3	13	1			
	3	2	13	0			
	4	2	23				
	5			10			
B "Love"	6	0	13	2	3/18	16.7	6.2
	7	0	9	0			
	8	1	15	1			
C "Social Engineer"	9	1	10	0	3/18	16.7	17.8
	10	1	11	2			
	11	1	12	0			
D "Laissez-Faire"	12	0	11	4	2/18	11.0	12.5
	13	2	14	5			
E "Cool, Aggressive Stimulation"	14	1	9	1	2/18	11.0	12.5
	15	1	10	4			
F "High Structure"	16	1	11	1	1/18	5.6	6.3
G "Encounter Tapes"	17	0	11	1	1/18	5.6	0
	18	0	13	3			

* Excluding the five casualties who dropped out.

of leader behavior—emotional stimulation, caring, meaning attribution, and executive functions. These four dimensions accounted for 70% of the variance of total leader behavior. By means of statistical clustering, all the leaders in the study could be subsumed under seven types of leaders.

Type A Leaders—"Aggressive Stimulators." These five leaders (the two Gestalt leaders, one psychodrama leader, and the two Synanon leaders) were characterized by their extremely high stimulus input. They were intrusive, confrontive, challenging, while at the same time demonstrating high positive caring; they revealed a great deal of themselves. They were the most charismatic of the leaders. They were authoritarian and often structured the events in the group. They focused upon the individual in the group rather than upon the group, and they often provided the individual with some cognitive framework with which to understand himself and the world. They asserted firm control and took over for the participants. They seemed ready, willing, and able to guide participants forward on the road to enlightenment.

Type B Leaders—"Love Leaders." These three leaders (NTL T-group leader, a marathon eclectic leader and a transactional analytic leader) were caring, individually focused leaders, who gave love as well as information and ideas about how to change. They exuded a quality of enlightened paternalism; they were "good daddies"; they had an established frame of reference about how individuals learn which they used in the group but which they do not press.

Type C Leaders—"Social Engineers." These three leaders (NTL, Rogerian and psychodrama) focused on steering the work of the group as a whole rather than on the individual or interpersonal relationships. They offered relatively low levels of stimulus input and rarely confronted or challenged individuals. They were perceived by participants as being low on authoritarianism and were not perceived as charismatic. The distance between them and the participants was psychologically felt to be small compared to, for example, the Type A leaders.

Type C Leaders—"Laissez-faire." These two leaders (psychoanalytic and transactional analytic) offered very little stimulation input; no challenging, no confrontation, and made very little use of themselves as an issue in the group; they offered little support and generally remained distant and cool; they were experienced by the participants as technicians and their major input to the group was the occasional communication of ideas about how people learn. They offered very little structure to the members.

Type E Leaders—"Cool, Aggressive Stimulators." These leaders (two personal growth leaders) were aggressive stimulators, but not to the extent of the Type A leaders. They offered little positive support and were nonauthoritarian in that they rarely structured the meeting; they tended to focus more on the group ("social engineering") than did most of the other leaders except, of course, the Type C leaders.

Type F Leaders—"High Structure." One leader (sensory awareness—Esalen) was so different from all others that he must be classified separately. He used a large number (an average of eight per meeting) of structured exercises—group "games." He was exceedingly controlling and authoritarian.

Type G Leaders—the Tape Leaders. These are two groups which had as their leader the Bell & Howell encounter tape (Peer Program). At the start of each meeting the members turned on a tape recorder which gave the group instructions for the conduct of that meeting. The tape programs focused upon learning how to give and receive feedback, how to make emotional contact with others, how to self disclose. They fostered a warm, supportive climate and deemphasized interpersonal conflict.

Table 4 presents the number of casualties in each group and each typology. The "A" (aggressive stimulators) style of leadership was the highest risk method and the five Type A leaders produced seven of the 16 casualties (44% of the total casualties). Not only were there more casualties in Type A groups, but they were the more severe casualties. The "B" (love) leaders produced only one casualty, whereas Type "G" (tape) leaders produced none at all.

The probable mode of injury also differed considerably amongst the 18 groups. Our interviews with the subjects uncovered several types of prototypical group events to which they attributed their negative outcome, (see Table 5):

1. Attack by leader or by the group
2. Rejection by leader or by the group
3. Failure to attain unrealistic goals
4. "Input overload"
5. "group pressure" effects

These are, of course, arbitrary *post hoc* categories and often several modes occur for one individual. At times boundaries between them blur. Attack usually implies lack of acceptance, whereas the reverse is not necessarily the case. Some experienced such a massive attack that the lack of acceptance was, oddly, not a crucial issue: the subject either

TABLE 5
MODE OF SUSTAINING INJURY

Leadership Style / Casualties	Attack Leader	Attack Group	Rejection Leader	Rejection Group	Failure to Attain unrealistic Goals	Input Overload	Group Pressure Effect
A "Aggressive-Stimulation" Charisma							
1 S.C.	X						X
2 N.I.	X		X				
3 B.V.	X		X				
4 L.L.	X	X				X	
5 E.L.	X	X					
6 C.L.	X	X					
7 D.R.	X	X				X	
B "Love"							
8 H.I.			X	X		X	
C "Social Engineer"							
9 T.G.					X		
10 O.O.		X		X	X		
11 M.A.			X				
D "Laissez-Faire"							
12 E.D.		X			X		
13 S.C.						X	
E "Cool, Aggressive Stimulation"							
14 M.M.		X	X	X			
15 D.M.						X	
F "High Structure"							
16 H.P.					X		X
G "Encounter Tapes"							
None							

dropped out of the group or was, in a figurative sense, too concerned about survival to afford himself the luxury of asking for love.

Table 5 indicates that *"Attack by leader"* is cited only in Type A groups, and is associated with some of the more severe casualties. We should note that the categories of injury mode were developed before and independently of the taxonomy of leader styles. A clinical example is illustrative:

> N.N., was unequivocal in her evaluation of her group as a destructive experience. Her group, following the model and suggestions of the leader, was an intensely aggressive one which undertook to help N.N., a passive, gentle individual, to "get in touch with" her anger. Although the group attacked her in many ways, including a physical assault by one of the female members, she most of all remembers the leader's attack on her. At one point he cryptically remarked that she "was on the verge of schizophrenia." He would not elaborate on this statement and it echoed ominously within her for many months. For several months she remained extremely uncomfortable. She withdrew markedly from her family and friends, was depressed and insomniac; she obsessed so much over her leader's remark about schizophrenia that she dreaded going to bed because she knew her mind would focus on this point of terror. Often she lapsed into daydreams in which she relived, with a more satisfying ending, some event in the group. The only benefit of the experience, she said, was to help her appreciate how lonely she was; however, her discomfort has been so great that she has been unable to make use of this knowledge. We consider N.N. a severe and long term casualty; at the interview eight months after the end of the group, she felt that she was gradually reintegrating herself but was not yet back to the point she was before the group began. Her negative experience was a function of aggressive, intrusive leadership style which attempted to change her according to the leader's own values by battering down her characterologic defenses.

The other five subjects whose negative outcome was related to attack by the leaders were similar to N.N. The Type A leaders were charismatic, highly revealing of their own feelings and values, challenging and intrusive. They were unpredictable in that they displayed both high levels of anger and of support. They focused on the individuals in the group and one by one each member was "worked on." The Type A leaders loomed very large for their group members. The casualties in their groups remembered with remarkable clarity months later the leader's remarks to them. There was an intensive focus on each member as he occupied the "hot seat." There was no place to hide and in a 20-hour marathon meeting in one group members were physically prevented from leaving the group. In the two Synanon groups, this aggressive approach resulted in an exceedingly high dropout rate (10 of the 23 members (43%) dropped out of the groups).

Attack by the group was a mode of injury that occurred either in the Type A groups, in conjunction with attack by the leader, or in groups led by leaders who were distant and modelled little or no positive supportive behavior. These occurred in groups led by a "laissez-faire" leader (D), by the least caring of the "social engineers" (C), and by one of the "impersonal" leaders (E). The following case was a subject in a group led by a laissez-faire leader:

E.D. answered the question "Was anyone hurt in your group?" In the following manner: "Me. The last meeting I didn't want to come to and came out of 'responsibility.' I was not in the mood for 'encountering' and was almost forced to. I don't trust anyone in the group and felt threatened by it. I came away feeling insecure and having many self doubts without being able to resolve them within the group. I overheard another member of the group describing my actions with his roommate, and he was reinforcing my own self doubts about myself. I didn't want to participate, was forced to participate unnaturally and then was emotionally upset by the experience for several days afterwards. Our group had no cohesion, no group feeling, no real understanding and I felt pressured to 'produce' and show myself at the last meeting. I shouldn't have gone to it. In fact, I should have dropped out several times before."

He depicts his group experience as a catastrophe. He was unable to trust the other members who were aggressive and dominant. The group lacked cohesiveness and a feeling of warmth and support. The leader, he felt, was "crummy" and lacked any idea of how to deal with people. The last meeting was particularly bitter for him since he was vigorously attacked for his passivity and uninvolvement. He recalls nervously picking at the carpet during the onslaught; he was criticized for that and when he stopped he was criticized for his passivity and suggestability. He was so shaken that he soon could not interpret comments to him and perceived all statements as criticism. The group planned a post-group beach party, but he did not attend because he felt so bitter about his experience. E.D. stated that were it not for the last meeting he might have escaped relatively unscathed since he had previously rationalized his failure in the group by refusing either to take the group seriously or to involve himself emotionally.

Following the group he felt deeply depressed for about a week. Following this he was left with a residue of deflation, helplessness, self-disgust and discouragement. Even months later he continued to feel anxious, depressed, and less trustful of others. His isolation increased and he made plans for transferring to another collage. He has avoided participation in any other group, but several months after the end of the group he sought individual psychiatric help.

We consider E.D. a moderately severe casualty of long duration. His negative outcome was multidetermined. He entered the group with relatively severe problems including strong homosexual conflicts. He had been lonely and isolated at college and entered the group, in part, to search for friends.

He soon experienced so little support or trust in the group that he was unable to disclose any personal feelings at all, much less his homosexual inclinations. The deviant role which he thus assumed generated even more anxiety and reinforced his alienation and negative self-concept. The group, a non-cohesive, low support group led by a laissez-faire leader, whoe major and almost sole mode of participation was to comment on the interpersonal process (in the language of transactional analysis), was not considered in the testimony of the members, a successful one. Towards the end it attempted to salvage itself by extra-group social events and by forcibly attempting to convert E.D.—one of the major deviants. The other members had little appreciation of his discomfort and first coaxed, then ignored and finally frontally assaulted E.D.

Rejection played a role for six casualties. For some the experience of rejection overlapped so heavily with the experience of attack that the distinction was but a semantic subtlety; others, however, explicitly emphasized being rejected by the leader and/or group. One subject, for example, stated: "I wanted some reassurance about my existence . . . to be found acceptable . . . to be told I was O.K. . . . to dig myself." He felt that he did not get that acceptance from the group and left feeling even worse about himself. Another subject, a Mexican-American, entered the group especially hoping for acceptance from the white members. He was so prepared for rejection that he perceived criticism of his circumlocution and his guardedness as total, blanket rejection. Another member, the only casualty in a Type B leader's group (and of minor severity), explicitly described his failure to be accepted into the group. It reminded him of rushing for a fraternity and not making it. To his eye, the leader established an in-group of individuals "who mouthed radical jargon and were in the drug culture." He felt he couldn't "swing" in the way the leader wished and grew increasingly uncomfortable and anxious about his peripheral membership.

Perhaps the starkest example of rejection was a white female in a group led by a Type E leader (impersonal, aggressive stimulator). She had, prior to the group, struggled with a deep sense of shame and yearned for validation from others. Having planned her agenda in advance she revealed very early in the group a great deal about herself, including such material as intimate details of her sexual liaisons with black men and her deeply held racist feelings. She was not sensitive to the state of receptivity of the group which had several black members and was at that time preoccupied with dealing with black-white tensions. The other members were not prepared for the degree of intimacy she demanded: self-disclosure by one group member places implicit demands on the others for reciprocal disclosure. They withdrew from her and regarded her as a problem, a "sex maniac" to whom they could not relate. This sequence of events was extremely noxious to her and for many months thereafter she felt great shame and self-contempt.

Failure to Achieve Unrealistic Goals: Four of the casualties entered the group with unrealistically high expectations given their existing defenses. Their needs were extreme and would have been an appropriate ticket of admission to any psychotherapy group. One of the casualties, for example, had transferred to Stanford simply because his only friend had recently done so. He had strong schizoid trends and felt emotionally restricted and unable to make emotional contact and empathize with others. He had previously sought psychotherapy for these very problems. The three others can be described in almost identical terms. They all entered the group with great expectations: to learn to relate, to break through their restrictive schizoid strait-jacket, to get in touch with their emotions. Each explicitly hoped to find friends in the encounter group. Despite their vigorous personal resolutions to do things differently (resolutions which were abetted by the current optimistic mystique surrounding encounter groups) they found, to their great dismay, that their behavior was more locked, rigid and repetitive than they had known. They soon recreated and reexperienced in their encounter group the same interpersonal environment from which they had fled in the outside world. They were flooded with discouragement and abandoned their abortive attempts to communicate and relate differently. All of them left the group more discouraged and more pessimistic about ever changing. In general encounter group leaders and members share the subject's unbounded initial optimism and press very hard for the ever-elusive will-of-the-wisp of the encounter group—the "breakthrough." One individual stated it explicitly: "I tried to overcome my defenses as best I could but couldn't do it. The leader kept pressuring me to express my feelings but I didn't know what I felt. When I said this I was attacked as a phoney. This reinforced my defenses so later in the sessions I just withdrew and watched."

Group Pressure Effects: Two casualties reported unusual reactions to the group. Both, unable to accommodate to the group pressure to experience and express feelings, ended the group with a sense of hollowness. They couldn't keep up with the others in a pell-mell charge to levels of deep intimacy. They grew alarmed at their failure and defined themselves as deficient or empty. If they acceded to the group pressure by feigning intimacy, they privately felt duplicit as well.

There is a well-known experimental analogue of this sequence of events. Asch (5) and Sherif (6) have demonstrated that it is difficult and anxiety-provoking to oppose group pressure. Individuals will misperceive or misrepresent their perceptions to align themselves with the remainder of the group. If, in a group which demands a vigorous display of emotions (like leadership styles A or F), there are experienced groupers who begin to express deep feelings in the opening minutes of the first meeting, then some real problems are posed for group beginners. This is especially stressful for individuals who are not labile, are already concerned about the texture of their feeling tone and, in addition, lack the opportunity or confidence to seek consensual validation.

Input Overload: Several casualties seemed to have suffered from "overstimulation"—a mode of injury as vague as it is inferential. Three of the five subjects involved had had psychotic episodes beginning, during or shortly after the end of the group. Six months later they were still too disturbed to cooperate in the research interview and our evidence for input overload derives from their therapists and the group leaders. For example, one member had a severe manic psychosis which erupted during the fourth week of his group. The leader (a psychiatrist, Type D, laissez-faire) felt strongly that the subject would have had a psychotic episode even were he not in a group, but that events in the group ("the intense stimulation, feedback, and pressure to open up") all hastened and perhaps intensified the course of his illness.

Another subject (in a Type E group) was briefly hospitalized for an acute paranoid schizophrenic psychosis approximately one month after the end of the group. Her psychiatrist notified us that, in his opinion, her encounter group experience contributed to her illness. He thought that the group overstimulated her and imposed values of freedom on her which she could ill manage. Rather, she needed at that time reinforcement of order, structure and suppression.

Another subject in a Type B group had a far less severe reaction, but he too was "stirred up" in a manner not constructive for him. His group, because of members with severe sexual problems, had dealt at great length with homosexuality. Although he denied homosexual concerns, he remained rather vaguely troubled by his memories of the meetings and less confident of himself in social and especially heterosexual situations. The interviewer concluded that some poorly understood sexual conflicts had been awakened but not resolved. Similarly his hierarchy of life values was strongly challenged as the leader and the group questioned his "success orientation." However, here too he remained only shaken as he did not have, or make, the opportunity to work through the issue in the group and lacked the resources to do so outside the group.

PREVENTION OF CASUALTIES

In studying the casualty suspects we interviewed many individuals who resembled the casualties in some manner (character structure, goals, type of group, experience in the group, etc.) but did not have a negative experience. What accounted for these different outcomes? Our interviews suggested several *post hoc* explanations which were, for the most part, untestable in the present study.

Many of the subjects interviewed appeared to have taken a more casual stance to the group than did the casualties. They had neither a pressing need nor great expectations for the group. Intellectual curiosity or the three easy academic credits loomed a bit larger; loneliness, depression or other psychological hang-ups were more rarely mentioned. "Uninvolvement" was often mentioned. They stayed out of the vortex of the group, they "did not take it seriously," the group was "artificial," "not meaningful," "boring," "plodding." One subject in Synanon stated, "It's unreal, you know, for a group of strangers to meet once a week and scream at one another. How can you really take it seriously?" They detoxified the group by maintaining their objectivity, by forming an alliance with an observing ego which kept before them the fact that the group was an artificial, time-limited aggregation in which deliberate magnification of emotions occurred. Others disengaged themselves physically and dropped out of the group. (Obviously such lack of involvement which reflects a safety or a survival orientation to the group experience also precluded the possibility of positive, constructive gain.) Others could rely upon their positive self-concept to evaluate with proper perspective a negative group reaction or critical feedback. Their center of gravity remained within themselves unlike several of the casualties who had low stores of self-esteem and whose sense of worth rocketed up and plummeted down with the appraisal of others. Others used an outside refernce group for validation. For example, one subject, an experienced grouper in a Type A group, handled attacks upon herself by referring to internalized phantoms of past groups or by actively working it out with members of the commune where she lived. Her commune functioned as a slightly attenuated but perpetual encounter group and emotionally dwarfed the impact of the time-limited group on her. Another well integrated girl responded very adaptively to the same Synanon attacks which devastated others. She stated that the group pointed out the "dark sides" of herself but she also realized the universality of these aspects. She maintained her ability to objectify: "Yes, they attacked me for being a virgin but I know that they have different cultural backgrounds and different attitudes toward sex. I didn't let it fluster me." The group turned out to be an "eye-opener" for her. She had led a heavily sheltered life and found the group to be an educational venture which, though smacking of a slumming experience, was a personally meaningful and integrative one.

There were several subjects who, in our view, might well have become casualties were it not for skillful management on the part of the leader. It appeared to us that some subjects started the group in highly vulnerable states, yet benefited considerably from their group experience. Several were not active central members of their groups but seemed to profit both from a sense of belongingness and vicariously from observing others work through problems. Some explicitly expressed gratitude towards their leaders who invited, encouraged, but did not demand participation and who always permitted them to select their own pace. One Type B leader who led a low-risk group, very explicitly asked each member repeatedly to make the choice of what he wanted to work on and how far he wished to proceed in a particular meeting. This is in marked contrast to Type A leaders who made that choice for their members and developed a hot-seat, no-escape-hatch format.

One subject early in the group aroused concern in the research staff. He was an encounter group buff, attempted to assume leadership, inappropriately urged the group onto deeper levels of forced intimacy and catharsis, had a grab bag of group gimmicks for every occasion, and would have been a thorn in the side of any leader. Furthermore, he was a vulnerable individual who joined the group for therapeutic purposes when in the midst of a severe identity crisis and at times veered close to a borderline state. We suspect that without firm leader intervention, he would have soon created an unviable role in the group and evoked a withering degree of group hostility upon himself. The leader very deliberately "kept the lid on." He gently suppressed the subject and guided him into a less vulnerable, albeit less colorful role in the group. He ended the experience somewhat disappointed and frustrated with his group but none the worse for it.

Another subject assumed a hazardous role in his group. He declined to participate verbally except for occasional enigmatic comments and from the outset took copious written notes during the meeting—a highly sophisticated method of committing suicide in a California encounter group! The group, as to be expected, focused heavily upon him, but the leader (Type B "love" leader) helped to establish tolerant, gentle, nondemanding norms and, even though the subject continued much of this behavior throughout the meetings, the other members were able to accept him as he was without experiencing a sense of failure because they hadn't broken through his defenses. In the follow-up interview, the subject expressed a positive attitude toward the group experience.

PREDICTING AND SCREENING OUT CASUALTIES

To what extent does the psychological functioning of the individual and his attitudes and anticipations toward encounter groups predict psychological risk? We have learned that to a considerable extent the type of group a person enters accounts for the amount of risk. The fact that casualties did not occur in some styles of groups and that the population in the various groups was randomized would indicate that the power of prediction of personality variables must be limited in this study. (If, for example, all the groups had been led by leaders with the same style, then the power of prediction of personality factors would be much greater.) However the practical implications of screening are so compelling that an attempt was made to determine in this study, *post facto*, what information could be garnered that might help subsequent encounter group leaders predict and screen out subjects likely to have a negative reaction to the group.

A wide variety of tests and questionnaire information was available on all our participants prior to the group experience. From the pre-group data, the following 11 scales or indices were selected to test out whether casualties could be predicted.

1. *Attitudes toward encounter groups* (three scales)

2. *Current status* on such dimensions as intimacy, spontaneity, etc. (seven self-rating scales)

3. *Environmental opportunities*—the amount of opportunities the individual's environment offered to fulfill such needs as intimacy, expressivity, etc. (eight scales)

4. The seven current status scales and the eight environmental opportunity scales were also used to measure level of anticipation—the *amount of change the individual anticipated* from his participation in the encounter group.

5. *Interpersonal values*—scales tailored toward the assumed emphases of encounter groups (five scales)

6. *Personal growth orientation*—an open-ended instrument (the life space questionnaire) was developed for life values and an index was derived from this instrument which assessed the individual's investment in personal growth or change.

7. *Wanted and expressed interpersonal needs* measured by the FIRO-B (four scales)

8. *Self-esteem* measured by the Rosenberg Self Esteem Scale (4)

9. *Self concept* and *self ideal discrepancy* measured by an adaptation of the Kelly Role Repertoire Test (2). Eight factor analytically derived self concept scales and three self-ideal discrepancy scores were developed.

10. *Coping styles.* An instrument was developed which assessed styles of coping with personal dilemmas (2). Twelve factor analytically derived scales were used (i.e. denial, flight, understanding, take action, etc.)

11. Lastly, sex and previous encounter group experience were entered into the pool of predictor variables.

Technical Note: The number of variables hypothesized to be potentially relevant to predicting casualty status were far too numerous to adequately test the predictors' hypothesis. Furthermore, a number of these indices were especially constructed for the research with only minimal test-development and hence the problem of measurement error loomed large for predictive statistics. A series of statistical procedures were designed (9) to reduce measurement error and to make possible an adequate statistical test of the prediction hypothesis. Principal component analyses were computed on those specially constructed instruments which contained multiple scales. Thus, a reduced number of dimensions (the first and second principal component on each instrument) were generated. Those new dimensions were then subjected to a linear discriminate analysis which estimated the maximum discrimination on all the variables between the non-casualty and casualty samples. The linear discriminate analysis is a stepwise multivariate analysis which maximizes selection of independent variables for further analysis. In other words, this procedure was used not to test the hypothesis, but rather to develop the most likely independent variables for hypothesis testing. On the basis of these procedures the 71 original separate scores were reduced to 20 dimensions which could be used to test the prediction hypothesis. The statistic chosen for testing the hypothesis was a multivariate analysis of variance.

TABLE 6

PREDICTION OF CASUALTY STATUS

Variables	Means		Step Down F	P level (2 tailed)
	Non Casualty, Non drop	Casualty		
1. Previous Encounter Group Experience	1.44	1.47	.15	.09
2. Expected Danger	26.2	27.3	1.06	.30
3. Expected Superficiality	27.5	29.1	1.37	.24
4. Acceptance of Influence	5.0	4.5	.83	.36
5. Desire to Control	3.8	2.9	1.50	.22
6. Self-Esteem	3.9	3.5	2.26	.13
7. Growth Orientation	26.5	42.7	4.85	.02
8. Self-Ideal Discrepancy on Enthusiasm	5.7	7.6	.01	.88
9. Anticipation of Change*	.05	00	.30	.58
10. Anticipation Opportunity	00	.86	1.84	.17
11. Positive Self-Concept	1.36	00	3.99	.04
12. Interpersonal Perspective	00	.01	.14	.70
13. Interpersonal Problem Solving	.35	00	5.76	.01
14. Use of Understanding	.35	00	.70	.40
15. Take Action	00	.07	.47	.49
16. Planned Alternatives	.29	00	1.12	.29
17. Flight-Substitutive Activity	.18	00	.63	.42
18. Escape-Leave Situation	.01	.11	2.38	.12
19. Expect Worst	.09	.07	.17	.67
20. Denial-Not Worry	.10	:02	.02	.88

Coping Styles — variables 12 through 20.

* Indices 9-20 are based on principal component analyses; means represent transformed scores.
overall p = .086

Table 6 shows the means for the non-casualty and casualty samples on these 20 variables as well as giving the step down F value and P levels. The p levels shown are for two-tailed test of the hypothesis, although the anticipation of directionality is clear in many of the dimensions and thus the reader may divide the p levels by 2.

Findings: The multivariate analysis of variance produces an overall probability level of .086, which indicates that at a moderate level of confidence indices can be measured prior to an individual's participation in the encounter group that are associated with casualty-non-casualty status. Six of the 20 dimensions were particularly sensitive in discriminating between the casualties and non-casualties. Those who became casualties showed, before beginning the group, significantly lower levels of self-esteem and a lower level of positive self-concept than did those who did not become casualties.

Furthermore the casualties had a higher growth orientation and a greater anticipation that the encounter group would provide opportunities for fulfillment of their needs. Perhaps they overinvested in the possibility, perhaps they were more needy individuals who saw in the encounter group the unrealistic possibility of personal salvation. Whatever the origin of the more intense need, or the more "unrealistic" expectation—those individuals who came believing in miracles were more likely to reap pain.

The last area of specific prediction was in the coping-ego defense scales, which indicate that individuals who are *less* likely to use direct interpersonal modes and *more* likely to use escape modes had a greater probability of becoming casualties.

A history of previous psychotherapy is worth noting, but adds relatively little predictive power. Five (31%) of the 16 casualties had seen a psychotherapist prior to the group as contrasted to 9% of the non-casualty experimental population, and 18% of the control population (see Table 2). Of these five, four had only brief encounters with a therapist while only one had had ongoing psychotherapy.

What are the implications of these findings? The instruments we have examined for testing the hypothesis that personality, attitudinal and anticipatory dimensions are related to development of casualties were in the large not designed for this purpose and, as indicated previously, becoming a casualty is in large part dependent on the particular group the participant found himself in. Nevertheless, our effort to demonstrate casualty predictability have yielded a model which has considerable psychological consistency. It is reasonable to assume that with closer and more deliberate study some of the individuals who are emotionally traumatized in the encounter groups could be guided out of attending such situations. It is more than likely that some questionnaires which particularly focus on the individual's expectations and anticipations about what it was he would gain from encounter groups would yield the best payoff for screening instruments; the measurement of mental health or its related concepts though complex and inconsistent can serve as a supplemental aid in screening.

DISCUSSION AND SUMMARY

Eighteen encounter groups led by leaders with diverse styles were offered as university undergraduate courses. The process and outcome of these groups were intensively researched. We developed several criteria to identify potential casualties of the groups. We defined a casualty as an individual who, as a result of his encounter group experience, suffered considerable and persistent psychological distress. The most effective method of identifying casualties was to ask the group members at the end of the group whether anyone had been harmed by the experience. One of the least effective methods was a rating of negative change by the leaders; indeed many of the leaders were completely unaware that there had been casualties in their groups. This finding has some obvious and significant implications. Group leaders who do not provide themselves with the opportunity for follow-up interviews with their group members simply do not have the necessary information to make a statement about the hazards of their groups. That the members themselves were more accurate in identifying casualties is not surprising. There are a number of studies which attest to the evaluative sensitivity of peers; for example, the Peace Corps candidates were able to predict which of their number would eventually fail in their duties more frequently than were the instructors (10).

Two hundred and nine subjects began the encounter groups. There were 16 casualties. This represents a very appreciable casualty rate. Although one aspect of our design—the random assignment of the subjects to one of the 18 groups—may have increased the risk, it was our impression that our casualties rate may, in fact, be a conservative estimate. The overall design of the project, in our opinion, decreased the risk of the groups. The research conditions imposed some restraints on the groups: all groups were observed, tape-recorded, and the leaders were cognizant that they were being evaluated. Furthermore we defined "casualty" in a rigorous manner and finally, some "high risk" suspects could not be located for study.

A major finding of the study is that the number and severity of casualties and the manner in which the casualties sustained injury are all highly dependent upon the particular type of encounter group. Some leadership styles result in a high risk group.

Particularly stressful is a leader style (Type A) which is characterized by intrusive, aggressive stimulation, by high charisma, by high challenging and confrontation of each of the members and by authoritarian control. We shall focus on the A style of leadership since groups led in this manner accounted for far more than their share of the total number of casualties: the five Type A leaders accounted for seven (44%) of the 16 casualties. It was our impression, too, that these groups generated more severe casualties and furthermore that they bore more responsibility for the casualty. (The casualty seemed truly *caused*, not merely hastened or facilitated, by the leader style, and is thereby preventable by a change in leader style.) The Type A leaders were forceful and impatient. If some significant sign of growth or change (crying, testimonial, breakdown or breakthrough) was not given to them in the group, they increased the pressure on the participants. The "A" leaders appeared to operate on an immediate gratification system; they paid little heed to the concept of "working through" and demanded that their members change and change "now."

Another important characteristic of the Type A leaders was their lack of differentiation of the individuals in their groups. It appeared as though these leaders felt that everyone in the group had the same needs and had to accomplish the same thing in the group. There is a curious paradox here. The Type A leaders appeared highly unorthodox and innovative; they displayed at the same time the widest and yet the narrowest range of techniques—narrow because of a lack of discernment of the scope of intra- and interpersonal problems. After all, not *everyone* needs to express himself more vigorously and spontaneously, to shuck his societal restrictions, to achieve a greater degree of freedom, to abandon all success-oriented goals. Some individuals may need quite the opposite: they already express themselves with far too much lability, they need more, not fewer controls, they need more, not less of an ego boundary, they need, perhaps, a more structured, more traditionally based hierarchy of values.

One other observation of interest concerning the Type A leaders was their religious aura. These charismatic leaders had their own internalized charismatic leader. Synanon is still guided by the hand of Dietrich, its founding father, and many of the Synanon activities have distinct ceremonial, ritualized overtones. The gestalt leaders, too, have a highly revered, idealized leader in the person of the late Fredrick "Fritz" Perls; in fact there is a published gestalt therapy prayer with which some leaders begin their meetings. The fifth Type A leader was heavily invested in a Far Eastern religious order, and at the time of this writing he had been persuaded by his religious Elder to abandon his career as a group leader. Perhaps the religious element helps us to understand these leaders' failure to discriminate between individuals since they may tend to imbue the individual with a system of beliefs and values (a single and final common pathway to salvation) rather than to encourage the individual to change according to his own needs and potential. (During the meetings, the Type A leaders all reveal, to a greater extent than other leaders, their own personal belief systems.)

Whereas four of the Type A groups had a total of seven casualties, one "A" group had no casualties, and although this leader resembled in many ways an "A" leader who had three casualties, he differed from him in a significant fashion. He stated that he realized immediately that there were several restricted, fragile individuals in his group and therefore he deviated from his usual style: "I pulled my punches, I didn't get into the heavy intrapersonal material I usually focus on, I did more interpersonal work, more classroom work, I gave them a type of tasting session so that they could see what groups could be like . . . I was constantly aware of keeping the lid on my group." The A leader whose group had three casualties, on the other hand, commented that it was a stubborn group, full of people "too infantile to take responsibility for themselves and to form an adult contract" with him. "I saw that most of the group didn't want to do anything so what I did was to just go ahead and have a good time for myself."

Occasionally a casualty from attack by the members, not leaders, occurred in groups led by laissez-faire or leaders who modeled little positive, caring behavior. (Laissez-faire leaders paid another type of penalty for their lack of involvement or low stimulus input—large numbers of their groups dropped out because they found the pace slow and plodding.)

Other mechanisms of injury included rejection by the leader or by the other members. That a member may have a truly destructive experience because of rejection is a function of several factors: the norms of the group which mediated the existence and degree of rejection, the consistency of self image of the subject, the presence of internalized anchor groups and the presence of other interpersonal resources to which the subject could turn for support.

Other casualties were caused (or perhaps, more accurately, hastened) by "input overload"; they were so challenged and overstimulated that rather than assimilate new perspectives on themselves and their world they were instead sucked into a maelstrom of confusion and uncertainty. The "unfreezing" process that occurs in almost any encounter group may produce this type of casualty. Clearly, we found that these subjects had some pre-existing significant pathology which met the process halfway.

A final mode of injury occurred in a curious manner. The subject observed other members quickly experiencing and expressing high intensity affect. Noting the apparent discrepancy between the others' productions and his own comparatively pallid affect, he judged himself as emotionally deficient and thenceforth identified himself as one of the hollow men.

The low risk groups were those led by Type B leaders and the two tape groups. The subjects in the tape groups had a positive, though not deeply intensive, experience. The Peer Program tapes promoted supportive, low-conflict groups. On the few occasions that negative interaction occurred, it was dealt with by flight: with no leader to help the group understand and resolve conflict, the members generally avoided unpleasant issues. The Type B leaders offered considerable positive support for members. They helped create an accepting, trusting climate in the group which permitted members to participate at their own pace.

Although this paper is concerned only with the hazards of encounter groups, we wish to remind the reader that the positive gains from the experience were far-reaching for many subjects. There was, as we describe elsewhere (2), even more variation amongst the 18 groups in positive outcome than there was in casualty rates.

Although there were pre-group differences apparent between those subjects who went on subsequently to have a destructive experience and those who did not, these differences are not likely to provide us with powerful predictors at the present state of development. Our best means of prediction remains the type of group the subject enters and our best means for prevention is *self-selection*. If responsible public education can teach prospective encounter group members about what they can, with reasonable accuracy, expect in terms of process, risks and profit, from a certain type of group then, and only then, can they make an informed decision about membership. Individuals who are psychologically vulnerable and who overinvest their hopes in the magic of salvation of encounter groups are particularly vulnerable when they interact with leaders who believe that they can offer deliverance. Such an interaction is a potent synergistic force for destructive outcome.

REFERENCES

1. "Encounter Groups and Psychiatry," Task Force Report #1, American Psychiatric Association, Washington, D. C., 1970.
2. LIEBERMAN, M. A., YALOM, I. D., & MILES, M.: Encounter Groups: First Facts, in preparation.
3. BERZON, B., & SOLOMON, L. N.: The Self-Directed Therapeutic Group: Three Studies, J. Cons. Psychol., Winter 1966.
4. ROSENBERG, MORRIS: Society and the Adolescent Self-Image, Princeton, New Jersey: Princeton University Press, 1965.
5. ASCH, S. E.: "Interpersonal Influence: Effects of Group Pressure upon the Modification and Distortion of Judgments," in Maccoby, E. E., Newcomb, T. M. and Hartley, E. L. (eds.): Readings in Social Psychology, New York: Holt, Rinehart and Winston Inc., 1958, pp. 174-183.
6. SHERIF, M.: "Group Influences upon the Formation of Norms and Attitudes," in ibid., pp. 219-232.
7. BLANK, LEONARD, GOTTSEGEN, GLORIA B., & GOTTSEGEN, MONROE G. (eds.): Encounter: Confrontations in Self and Interpersonal Awareness, New York: Macmillan Press, in press.

8. SCHULZ, WILLIAM: *FIRO, A Three Dimensional Theory of Interpersonal Behavior*, New York: Rinehart & Co., Inc., 1958.
9. KITCH, E.: *Prediction of Encounter Group Outcome as a Function of Selected Personality Variables*, unpublished Ph.D. dissertation, Committee on Human Development, University of Chicago, 1971.
10. BOULGER, J., & COLEMAN, J.: *Research Findings With Peer Ratings*, Research Note No. 8, Division of Research, Peace Corps, Washington, D. C.

Area II

FAMILY THERAPY

Family therapy has opened new vistas for psychotherapy and additional parameters for understanding human behavior. Concurrent with theoretical and technical advances, family therapy has gained the acceptance of a growing number of professionals who vary considerably in training and background. The number of family units in teaching and training institutions is increasing, as are efforts to reorder the delivery of mental health services to center around a family rather than an individual approach. The family approach is in the tradition of community psychiatry. As the basic social unit in the community, the family becomes the natural modal point for primary and secondary prevention, as well as for treatment.

The family is the social-biological unit which exerts the greatest influence on the development and perpetuation of the individual's behavior. Most family therapists agree that consideration of both the individual *and* his family is essential to the formation of a total clinical picture. The question of whether the individual or the family is to be considered the malfunctioning unit, and hence the focus of treatment, poses a misleading dichotomy. The family therapist does not focus his efforts on the family to the exclusion of the identified patient; nor, conversely, is the patient viewed as the basic unit of treatment. Rather the therapist's focus on each family member is complemented by his concomitant focus on the entire family's transactions.

Family therapists subscribe to the proposition that altering the family system, and hence the transactions between the persons (sub-systems) who are part of that larger system, results in changes in the individual. Therefore, change at *any* point in the system may well affect any or all of its components.

Strategies and Tactics

The family therapist views behavior and symptoms as products of family processes, which influence and are influenced by each family member's intrapsychic dynamics. Accordingly, processes and changes in the ecological systems, rather than insights alone, are seen as the major change-producing agents, although techniques for achieving such change vary greatly.

256

Within the matrix of this systems approach family therapists employ numerous strategies and tactics. Many of these are borrowed or adapted from other treatment modalities, e.g., group therapy, behavior therapy, gestalt therapy, psychoanalysis, transactional analysis, or derive from various theoretical models, e.g., games theory, communication and information theory, linguistics, kinesiology, etc. In fact it has been said that there are as many family therapy techniques as there are family therapists. The point is that any one of these diverse therapeutic styles may be effective under a particular set of circumstances. Thus, the availability of a wide spectrum of attractive and potentially valuable theories and techniques permits the family therapist to exercise considerable flexibility in the use of therapeutic alternatives.

The crucial questions as to the effectiveness of these techniques, or whether the use of family therapy improves the outcome of treatment of specific disorders cannot be established with certainty until more and better evaluative studies have been conducted. Perhaps the greatest value of family psychiatry lies in the significant contribution to our knowledge of the multiple determinants of "normal" and "abnormal" behavior, and to our understanding of the mechanisms by which the forces which underlie behavioral disturbances can be modified.

NEWER DEVELOPMENTS

In his paper, Ackerman refers to stages in the development of family therapy. Although these overlap in time, for schematic purposes they can be delineated as follows: during the first stage, family therapy took the form of counseling which focused on the realistic aspects of family life. The second stage was characterized by the application of psycho-analytically-oriented techniques within a family treatment setting. At the third and present stage in its development, family therapy utilizes general systems theory as its conceptual substrate.

Most recently the principles of the systems approach have been extended to apply to a super-system comprising the relatives and friends of the nuclear family. In this approach, which its innovator, Ross V. Speck, has termed network therapy, this "latent" system is mobilized in treatment to effect changes in the nuclear family system. Other workers have developed temporary super-systems, consisting, for example, of a number of families with similar problems. Thus, multiple family therapy refers to the use of this super-system to affect each of the family subsystems and their component parts.

The emergence of the ecological systems concept constitutes another logical extension of family systems theory. The eco-systems approach proceeds on the assumption that the determinants of behavior are not limited to the individual's interactions within his family system, but include his transactions with all systems with which he has an interface with the total environment. Accordingly, the therapist attempts to modify the individual's transactions with the most pertinent of these social systems and institutions as a means of changing his behavior.

THE PAPERS

Family therapy can be discussed from a variety of viewpoints: its underlying theory, recently advanced hypotheses, or the countless treatment techniques currently in use, etc. However, we have not attempted to order the material contained in this area on the basis of any such schema because to so categorize these papers would be to sacrifice their essential flavor, i.e., the simultaneous interpenetration of myriad ideas which makes each therapist's contribution a mosaic rather than a monolithic structure. Accordingly, we have attempted to organize the articles in this area in a sequence which will illustrate the flow of recent technical and theoretical advances.

In the first article Haley attempts to delineate the variables which distinguish the experienced family therapist and his function from novices in this field. The paper thereby calls attention to the fact that the practice of family therapy for the behavioral scientist who received his training in individual psychotherapy requires a rather drastic change in orientation, which extends well beyond the therapist's heightened awareness of the role of family factors as determinants of psychopathology.

A central thesis of family therapy states that the transactions within the family system are major determinants of individual behavior. Framo uses this concept as the foundation for a transactional theory of symptom formation. He then proceeds from consideration of the parameters of family therapy to the beginning of a highly interesting transactional theory of human behavior. Family therapy may ultimately make its most significant contribution to a multi-causal theory of behavior within this frame of reference.

The use of the ecological systems approach in family therapy extends the systems concept to include the effects of the wide spectrum of systems that impinge on the individual. Auerswald's paper defining the clinical ecological systems approach is currently considered a classic in the field. The usual clinical application of this approach involves enlisting the support of other systems on behalf of their client and teaching the individual (or his family) to negotiate those systems (welfare, unemployment, health facilities, etc.) more effectively. Auerswald, however, also attempts *to change that system* when it has noxious effects on the client. When the major therapeutic thrust is directed at the ecological systems, treatment may differ significantly from what are currently considered accepted forms of family therapy: the therapist may spend more time dealing with the representatives of those systems which affect the family's functioning than he does with the family itself.

Minuchin and Barcai combine the advantages of the ecological systems approach with crisis intervention and certain aspects of behavior therapy. They induce a family crisis which makes it possible to effect changes in the family system with a resultant alleviation of the destructive behavior of individual family members.

Several other articles in this area also attest to the rapidly escalating influence of behavior therapy and learning theory in family therapy: Liberman describes his use of behavior therapy techniques in family and couple therapy. Ferber and Ranz, in a detailed case presentation, illustrate the application of behavior therapy strategies in the context of a complex family system.

Having discovered they cannot study a family system without affecting and changing it, family therapists have learned to capitalize on this well-known phenomenon by consciously putting information into the family system as a means of producing a particular effect. Almost every contributor to this area has employed this strategy. Such euphemisms as "information in-put," "setting tasks and goals," "paradoxical instructions," or the more straightforward "side-taking," the term Zuk uses in his paper, do not conceal the growing popularity of manipulation, which is no longer a dirty word in family therapy. In developing his triadic approach to family therapy, Zuk places emphasis on the therapist's go-between role among family members, mediating and taking sides as necessity dictates. This article elaborates on the side-taking techniques.

Very little has appeared in the literature to date on the participation of the young child in family therapy. Whatever the reasons, the fact remains that all too frequently the younger child is overlooked as a significant part of the family system, a potential source of useful information, and another focus for intervention. In response to our request, Zilbach and her colleagues have prepared a superb discussion of the role of the young child in family therapy. Specifically, they deal directly with the problems involved, and suggest techniques designed to facilitate and enhance the child's participation which are of practical and theoretical import.

Different families may have similar or overlapping problems. Laquer contends that if several such families are brought together to form a new (transient) system they are helpful to one another. In an article written specifically for inclusion in this volume Laquer provides an excellent discussion of the application of General Systems Theory to family and multiple family therapy, as an integral part of his elaboration of his own theory and practice of multiple family therapy. Systems theory has also been extended in another direction; as noted earlier, Speck and Attneave broaden and enlarge the nuclear family system to create a family network or "tribe" of at least forty persons. In their article the authors provide a clear exposition of the clinical procedures involved, and also deal with the crucial issue of staff training for the administration of network therapy.

It is difficult to predict the future course of family therapy. The tasks of unifying theory and of distinguishing therapeutic fads from the truly meaningful innovations which have emerged in recent years pose major problems. Ackerman, in the last paper he completed before his death, demonstrated his concern with these and other issues which have relevance for the future progress of family therapy if we are to develop rational and effective treatment methods.

SUGGESTED CROSS-REFERENCES

Many of the articles included in other sections of this volume deal with various aspects of family psychiatry. Strictly speaking, Area III, on Marriage and Sex, would be considered to constitute a sub-section of this area on Family Therapy, as would Section IV-A, which focuses on the role of family in the etiology of schizophrenia. In addition, in his article in Section IV-B, Spotnitz describes a new and highly innovative approach to the treatment of adolescents in a family therapy setting. Spark and Brody in the same area discuss the highly significant role of the aged as family members.

In his paper on transactional analysis, included in Section I-C, on New Approaches in Group Therapy, Goulding discusses the implementation of therapeutic techniques that are related to Framo's transactional theory of behavior.

Further material on the use of behavioral approaches in group and family modalities is contained in Fensterheim's article on behavior therapy in groups in Section I-C, and Stuart's paper on operant conditioning in marital therapy in Area III.

Finally, Durkin's article in Section I-A on General Systems Theory and its relevance for group therapy supplements the theoretical section of Laquer's paper which deals with the application of general systems theory to family and multiple family therapy.

C.J.S.
H.S.K.

16

FAMILY THERAPY

Jay Haley

Director of Family Research, Philadelphia Child Guidance Clinic

The clinicians who began to do family therapy in the early days were largely people who had been trained in the ideology and practice of individual therapy. Whatever their professions, their focus had been upon how to change a person. As they began to discover the new problem of how to change a family, each of them developed a unique approach. Often their approaches were each different because the therapists were innovating on their own and did not know that other people were doing family therapy. As a result, a number of schools of family therapy had developed which have their students and their followers. New approaches continue to develop as clinicians take up family therapy in different parts of the country and develop unique ways of working. Comparing different family therapists is difficult because they differ markedly in their techniques of intervening into families. However, as family therapists have gained experience they seem to have developed a shared body of premises about human problems and the nature of change despite working with families in quite different ways. Some family therapists, particularly those embedded in academic psychiatry or the tight professional organizations of a large city, do not seem to change their views with experience. Yet most family therapists have gone through a similar transitional process and share a basic shift in their ideas which comes about from the experience of working with families. At least one can assume that the shift in ideas comes from exposure to families, since

Reprinted from INTERNATIONAL JOURNAL OF PSYCHIATRY, Volume 9, 1970-71, pp. 233-242.

often family therapists shift to a common view even though they have not been exposed to the work of other family therapists. At about the time a family therapist passes his 200th family, he usually changes his perspective markedly and finds himself in a different conceptual world from the one in which he was trained. One way to describe this shift in thinking about therapy is to describe where a family therapist begins and where he often ends. Contrasting the premises of a beginning family therapist with those of a person who has had many years of experience can help clarify what is new in the family therapy field.

METHOD VS. ORIENTATION

The beginning family therapist tends to see family therapy as a method of treatment—one more procedure in a therapist's armamentarium. As he gains experience, the therapist begins to view family therapy not as a method but as a new orientation to the arena of human problems. This conceptual difference has practical results. For example, when asked what are the indications and countraindications for family therapy, the beginning family therapist will attempt to answer the question. The more experienced family therapist will appear puzzled since he finds himself defining any kind of therapy as a way of intervening into a family. Having shifted his unit of diagnosis and treatment from the single person to the processes between people, he defines psychopathology as a relationship problem. He cannot say that this person should receive individual therapy and this person family therapy, because he views individual therapy as one way of intervening into a family. The therapist who treats a wife may be dealing with the woman's fantasies, fears, hopes, and so on, but by seeing the wife and not seeing the husband the therapist is intervening into a marriage in a particular way. The family therapist might also interview only the wife, but it would be with an assumption that her problem involves the context in which she lives and the treatment must change that context. Even if drugs are given to only one person, the family therapist does not see it as drug therapy in the usual sense; it is the introduction of a drug into a family system with consequent concern about who is being labelled as the patient or labelled as the one who is at fault by this act.

Whether family therapy is seen as an orientation or a method is similar to the contrasting approaches in psychiatry forty years ago when psychodynamic theory developed. It was not a question of deciding whether the neurological method of treatment or the psychodynamic method of treatment was indicated; the issue was the difference in conceptual framework between the two approaches, because each represented a different way of thinking about the psychiatric problem. Similarly, one cannot contrast individual and family therapy as two different methods: They are not comparable at that level.

COLOR THE PATIENT DARK

The beginning family therapist tends to emphasize the individual patient as the focus of treatment and the remainder of the family as a stress factor. He may even do a style of family treatment which is called interviewing the patient in the presence of his family. The more experienced family therapist gives family members more equal weight and struggles to find a better term than "patient" for the family member who is chosen to be it. Terms such as "the identified patient" or "the supposed patient" or the "person in pain" or the "person expressing the symptom" are used. While the beginner tends to see a particular individual as a container of psychopathology or a person with a low stress threshold, the more experienced therapist sees the family system as needing some individual to express the psychopathology of the system. For example, if a child is agitated and is quieted, the mother will become agitated, and if mother and child are quieted then father or a sibling will become agitated because the system is of such a nature that this is necessary. In a similar way, the beginner tends to see the family as a collection of persons who are describable with the past language about individuals. He sees relationships as a product, a projection, of intrapsychic life. For example, he will emphasize how a wife is being mistreated by a sadistic husband, the husband is expressing his aggression and the wife is satisfying her masochistic needs. The more experienced family therapist sees intrapsychic process as a product of the relationship situation. He will describe such a couple as involved in a game in which they must both contribute behavior which keeps the distressing sequence going. In a similar manner, the beginner often sees the child as a victim of the parents' strife or as a scapegoat, while the more experienced therapist will view the child as a contributor and an essential part of a continuing sequence of events among all the people involved. As a result of this difference, the beginning therapist tends to intervene to get a person to shift his ideas or behavior while the more experienced therapist intervenes to change a sequence of behavior involving several of the people. For example, in an interview the father will be interrogating the child and the child will weakly protest. At a certain point the mother will come to the support of the child and attack the father. The father will back down and apologize.

After awhile, the sequence will begin again and repeat itself. The more experienced family therapist will see the sequence occur, and when it starts again he will intervene at a certain point to change it. He might intervene while father is interrogating the child, just before mother comes in to attack father, or just before father backs down when mother attacks. His goal is to give the sequence a different outcome, and he may or may not point out to the family the nature of the sequence. The beginning family therapist will tend to see the behavior in smaller units, and he will usually intervene to interpret to father that he should not behave as he is doing, or to help him understand why. He will be thinking about the father's motivations and possibly his history with his own father rather than about the current sequence that is happening in the family.

WHERE IS HISTORY?

The beginner seems much more interested in history than the experienced family therapist. He tends to see the family as a collection of individuals who have introjected their pasts, and the therapeutic problem is lifting the weight of this "programming" out of their inner space. The more experienced family therapist learns to see the present situation as the major causal factor and the process which must be changed. He inquires about the past only when he cannot understand the present and thinks the family can discuss the present more easily if it is framed as something from the past. Assuming that what is happening now has been happening for a long time, the therapeutic problem is what is happening now. At times a therapist may emphasize the past when he is trying to define a time when the family members were enjoying each other more; this is both a way of labeling the current problem as a temporary upset and a way of clarifying a goal of the therapy. In general, the more experienced the family therapist, the more he assumes that a current problem must be currently reinforced if it is continuing to exist.

WHAT IS DIAGNOSIS?

The beginner tends to put more emphasis upon diagnosing and evaluating the family problem and prefers to gather information before intervening. He tends to use diagnostic ideas in an individual language, and he prefers to try to define the family dynamics in as much detail as possible. The more experienced family therapists tend to find themselves always working with minimal information. Since they view the opening session as important to the ultimate therapeutic outcome, particularly when it is a time of family crisis, they wish to intervene as rapidly as possible to take advantage of this opportunity to bring about change. Therefore, they are intervening as soon as they have some grasp of what is going on and do not like to delay therapy for diagnosis and evaluation. Many of them think careful diagnosis is for the anxiety of the therapist and not for the family's benefit. Such therapists in conversation spend much less time talking about differences in family dynamics and more time talking about ways they have intervened to bring about changes. Generally, they like to end the first therapy session with some therapeutic aim accomplished so that the family has gained something from the immediate encounter and knows what the therapeutic experience will be like. This more action-oriented point of view does not mean that family therapy is always brief therapy. Often it is long-term, but it is brief when it can be. Whether treatment is short or long-term, most experienced therapists share an awareness of how much can be accomplished with active intervention at a time a family is in crisis and unstable. Some experienced family therapists say that if adolescent schizophrenia is not resolved with family treatment, the case has been mishandled. However, they are referring to family treatment at the time of acute onset of the family crisis and not after the adolescent has been hospitalized and the family has stabilized. When hospitalization is involved, family treatment can become interminable because each improvement leads to renewed hospitalization.

The more experienced therapist looks upon long-term therapy as necessary to accomplish particular ends, rather than meritorious in itself. If the job can be done more quickly, it is. It is also typical of more experienced therapists to see change as occurring in discontinuous steps, and they "peg" a change when they get one so that the family continues to the next stage of development and does not slip back. Instead of the desultory movement one sees in the beginner's family treatment, the more experienced therapists tend toward a developmental improvment in the family.

IS THE THERAPIST PART OF THE DIAGNOSIS?

A major difference between the beginner and the more advanced family therapist is the way the beginner tends to leave himself out of the diagnosis. He describes the family as a set of problems independent of him, much as the individual therapist used to describe the patient's productions in therapy as if they were independent of the therapist. The more experienced therapist includes himself in the description of a family. For example, the beginner will say that the family members are hostile to each other; the more experienced therapist will say the family members *are showing me* how hostile they are to each other. This is not a minor distinction. As a consequence, the more experienced person does not think of the family as separate from the context of treatment, and he includes himself in that context. He will consider, for example, whether the particular difficulty he sees between a husband and wife is created by the way he is dealing with the couple. A vignette can illustrate this area. An experienced therapist was supervising a beginner by listening to a tape recording. After listening to five minutes of the first session, the supervisor said that several minutes had passed and the therapist had not yet made a therapeutic intervention. The beginner replied that it was an evaluation interview in which he was gathering information about the family problem. The experienced supervisor replied, "Evaluation of a family is how the family responds to your therapeutic interventions." This example illustrates how much more rapidly the experienced person prefers to work, and how he sees the family problem in terms of how the family responds to *him*. With such a view there are not different diagnostic categories of families, there are different families in different treatment contexts. An important aspect of this more contextual view is the realization of experienced therapists that they must take not only the family into account, including the extended kin who always influence a problem, but also the other helping professionals who might be involved. In some cases a family has been divided up with each fragmented part being treated by some professional, often without knowledge of each other. The record might be a family in California which had fourteen professional helpers. To deal with the family unit, the experienced therapist finds he must also deal with the wider treatment morass, or the total ecological system. Until he gains experience, the beginner tends to see the other helpers as irrelevant.

In relation to diagnosis, a sharp difference between the beginner and the experienced therapist is the concern with using a diagnosis which defines a solvable problem. Unless the diagnosis indicates a program for bringing about change, it is considered irrelevant by the more experienced therapist. The usual psychiatric categories are rarely used, not only because they apply only to individuals but because they have nothing to do with therapy. The beginner tends to think of diagnosis as something that he has not created but which exists independent of him: and he must live with it. For example, a beginning family therapist who worked in the conservative network of a large city posed a question to a more experienced family therapist from the provinces. The beginner said she was working with a family, and after three diagnostic sessions she had concluded with the family which was unresolvable. The beginner asked, "What would you do with this problem?" The experienced therapist replied that he would never let that be the problem, and she did not understand what he meant. She saw the problem not as one which she defined but one which was independent of her and that she must struggle with even though she had defined it as unsolvable. Given the same family, the experienced therapist might have concluded with the family that when the daughter began to move toward independence the mother became upset and that there was open conflict between the mother and father. This diagnosis indicates ways of bringing about change, and by the third session an experienced therapist would already have begun change and not be dwelling on diagnosis.

THE POSITIVE VIEW

The beginning family therapist tends to feel that it is helpful to the family to bring out their underlying feelings and attitudes no matter how destructive these might be. He interprets to family members how they are responding to each other and expressing their hostility, through body movement and so on. Often he feels this is a way of giving meaning to the family members.

The more experienced family therapist has less enthusiasm for the idea that interpreting feelings and attitudes brings about change. In particular, he does not feel it is helpful to confront family members with how much they hate one another. Instead, he tends to interpret destructive behavior in some positive way, for example as a protective act. His premise is that the problem is not to make explicit underlying hostility but to resolve the difficulties in the relationships which are causing the hostility. Therefore, the more experienced therapist is more sparse with his interpretations except when using them tactically to persuade family members to behave differently.

At times the beginner can seem to be torturing a family by forcing them to concede their unsavory feelings about each other. The more experienced therapist feels this is a waste of time and not therapeutic. For example, a beginning family therapist working with a family of a schizophrenic observed the mother pat her son on the behind. He could not overlook this opportunity to help her by interpreting this behavior as the product of an incestuous desire, with the result that mother and son avoided each other even more than previously. A more experienced family therapist would probably have congratulated the mother on being able to show some affection toward her son. Although more experienced family therapists do not emphasize negative aspects of family living, they are quite willing to bring out conflicts if they are necessary to break up a particular pattern.

THE PROBLEM IS THE METHOD

The beginning family therapist, like the beginner in any field, would like to have a method which fits everyone who comes in the door. Being uncertain, he would like to have a set of procedures to follow each time. The more experienced family therapist tends to feel that any set procedure is a handicap; each family is a special problem which might require any one of several different approaches. Instead of fitting the family to a method, he tries to devise a way of working which varies with the particular problem before him. In contrast, the beginning family therapist tends to set rules which include seeing the whole family for a set length of time at set regular intervals. Typically, a family therapist begins to work with families by always seeing the whole family group, but as he gains experience he finds this too restricting. With experience he shifts, sometimes seeing the whole group to get a total portrait of the situation, and sometimes interviewing a single person, or a marital pair, or the siblings, or any combination that might seem appropriate for the problem involved. The therapist might also see a family regularly or quite irregularly, and they might have a session of several hours at certain points to save months of more regularly spaced sessions. There is also a willingness to experiment when a particular approach is not working. As a result, some family therapists are now trying out multiple family therapy and network therapy where not only the famliy but friends and neighbors are brought into treatment sessions.

EQUAL PARTICIPATION

When the experienced family therapist interviews the whole family group together, he puts special emphasis on getting all the members to participate. If a family member is not speaking, the therapist becomes uncomfortable and tries to involve him. Often the experienced family therapist will turn the family upon each other so they talk together rather than to him, and when he does this he likes them all to talk. The beginner often focuses upon one person at a time and tends to have the family members talk largely to him rather than to each other.

THE FACTIONAL STRUGGLES

When a therapist intervenes into a family, whether he interviews one person or the whole family group, he is caught up in the struggle of family factions with each other. The beginner tends to side with some part of the family. Often he sides with the child patient against the victimizing parents, or if he is older he may side with the parents against the child. In marital struggles the beginner is likely to find himself joining one spouse against another. The more experienced family therapist appears to assume quite flatly that if the therapist sides with one part of a family against another, there will be a poor therapeutic outcome, this is particularly so if he joins one faction while denying he is doing so, which often happens if the therapist still responds to one person as the "patient" but is trying not to. When experienced therapists take sides, they state this explicitly and announce that they are doing so, usually defining it as temporary.

LIVE SUPERVISION

Since the vital part of bringing about change is the ways the therapist behaves in a session, the experienced person wants to know what is happening when he is supervising a trainee. The beginner tends to think in terms of traditional supervision where he makes notes about what happened and carries them to his supervisor for discussion. This kind of delayed, content-oriented conversation arouses little enthusiasm in the experienced family therapist. He prefers to watch the trainee in session through a one-way mirror or on a replay of a videotape, so that he can give instructions in the technique of interviewing, which is the essence of therapy. More commonly the experienced family therapist is doing live supervision by watching a session and calling in on the phone to suggest changes, calling the trainee out to discuss what is happening, or entering himself to guide the session. In this way a trainee learns to do what should be done at the moment something happens, not later when the opportunity to change his form of intervention is long passed.

EMPHASIS UPON OUTCOME

The beginning family therapist tends to emphasize what is going on in the family; the more experienced therapist emphasies what therapeutic results are happening in terms of quite specific goals. Some beginners become so fascinated with family history, family dynamics, and the complex interchanges in the family that they lose sight of the goals of treatment. Often the beginner will seem to define the goal as proper behavior by the family—if the family members are expressing their feelings and revealing their attitudes, and if the therapist is making sound interpretations, then therapy is successful.

The more experienced family therapist emphasizes whether the family is changing, and he shifts his approach if it is not. This does not mean that family therapists scientifically evaluate the outcome of their therapy, but it does mean that outcome is a constant focus as well as a subject of conversation among experienced family therapists. They talk about family dynamics largely in relation to family change. The willingness of therapists to shift their approach if it is not working is one of the factors that makes family therapy difficult to describe as a method. Not only will a particular therapist's approach vary from family to family, but his way of working evolves into new innovations from year to year as he attempts to produce better results.

What family therapists most have in common they also share with a number of behavioral scientists in the world today: There is an increasing awareness that psychiatric problems are social problems which involve the total ecological system. There is a concern with, and an attempt to change, what happens with the family and also the interlocking systems of the family and the social institutions in which the family is embedded. The fragmentation of the individual into parts, or the family into parts is being abandoned, and there is a growing consensus that a new ecological framework defines problems in new ways and calls for new ways in therapy.

17

SYMPTOMS FROM A FAMILY TRANSACTIONAL VIEWPOINT

James L. Framo, M.D.

Chief, Family Therapy and Training Unit, Department of Psychiatry, Jefferson Medical College

It is characteristic of all scientific breakthroughs to be followed by rethinking about the basic nature of a phenomenon as well as by widening of perspectives and stimulation of new discoveries. Family therapy, a revolutionary development, has evolved into a transactional theory of human behavior which goes well beyond the merits of a specific technique or form of therapeutic intervention with the family as a unit. From this viewpoint, aside from questions of psychopathology, whenever a group of people are closely related to each other, as in a family, they reciprocally carry part of each other's psychology and form a feedback system which in turn regulates and patterns their individual behaviors. Experience in family therapy has shown that disordered behavior or psychological symptoms, which are frequently etiologically and dynamically obscure from the standpoint of individual psychology, can often be decoded and made intelligible when viewed within the matrix of their intimate social systems. Family transactional findings suggest further the momentous prospect that the intrinsic nature of psychopathology, usually seen as solely the outcome of insoluble intrapsychic conflict, may have to be recast and broadened as a special form of relationship event which occurs between intimately related people.

Reprinted from *Family Therapy in Transition,* an issue of THE INTERNATIONAL PSYCHIATRY CLINICS, Vol. 7, No. 4, pp. 125-171, edited by N. Ackerman. © 1970 Little, Brown and Company, Boston.

The implications of the transactional perspective drastically modify all traditional concepts of etiology, diagnosis, and treatment. Etiology has a different meaning when one considers all behavior as "normal," in the sense that no matter how deviant it may appear, all behavior is adaptive in its context. Diagnosis in individual terms depends on the kinds of intrapsychic defenses which the ego chooses for its protection, but from a transactional point of view we may be labeling only subordinate, cursory parts of a whole complex when we classify individual pieces of behavior as, say, "obsessive-compulsive" or "paranoid." Treatment concepts are widened to include efforts to change contexts.

It is, surely, impossible at this stage of understanding to study simultaneously the total range of a transactional field. The family context is focused on here, not only because of its manageability, but because of the conviction that the family is the most vital, lasting, and influential force in the life of man. Such social contexts as the community, neighborhood, school, work, and friendship networks can never approach the unique and powerful effects of the family, due to the deep emotional and blood ties, the family's personality-forming influence, and the special rules (that is, distorted, organized beliefs known as family myths) which apply to family relationships. Friends and colleagues can be replaced; one pretty much *has* to be involved with one's family whether one wishes to or not, even if one does not see the family very often or at all.

Many problems present themselves in shifting to this new frame of reference, not the least of which is the lack of a language to express field or contextual concepts. For instance, the very term *symptom* comes from an individual, medical framework, and in a certain sense it is inappropriate to apply this word to pathological phenomena of a system complex such as the family. In order to conceptualize the psychopathology of the family it is necessary to have some standard or model of family health or "normality"—an immense undertaking which has hardly begun (26, 29). It certainly makes little sense to use for family diagnosis a classification system developed from individual psychology. As more knowledge is accumulated, a meaningful nosology for families may be developed, far beyond the present crude practice of using the symptoms of one family member to characterize a family, such as "schizophrenic family" or "delinquent family." Some preliminary efforts at classifying family types have already been undertaken (1, 3, 12, 14, 35, 36).

In this paper the term *symptom* is used in its broadest sense, encompassing not only subjective complaints of individuals, but the observations of others (family members, associates, professionals) that something is wrong with someone's feelings, thinking, or behavior. People present their difficulties in the only way they know how, running the full spectrum of emotional pain or dissatisfaction with oneself or others, whether in the area of physical, personal, or social disturbance. This admittedly loose use of the term *symptom* has the shortcoming of being individually oriented as well as lacking scientific specificity. Nonetheless, using *symptom* temporarily in this commodious way does reflect the way it is used operationally by both laymen and professionals, and it enables the writer to communicate while attempting to bridge the transition from individual theory to family transactional theory.

Departing from the conventional, simplistic view of symptoms as intrapsychic entities and as stemming from a central illness process, the purpose of this paper is to document, with theoretical and clinical family transactional situations, the postulate that symptoms are formed, selected, faked, exchanged, maintained, and reduced as a function of the relationship context in which they are naturally embedded. Finally, a concluding discussion will present the formulation that symptoms are concomitants of the universal conflict between individuating, autonomous strivings, and loyalty to the family relationship system.

SYMPTOM-PRODUCING FAMILY SITUATIONS

The following series of family relationship situations is intended· as suggestive rather than exhaustive, and no particular importance should be attached to the order or sequence, with the exception of the extended discussion of irrational role assignment, which is considered fundamental. Furthermore, the situations or constructs are not mutually exclusive.

While the phenomena to be described are probably universal and present to some extent in all families, they function more pervasively and can be most strikingly observed in families described by Bowen (8) as being at the lower end of a scale of "differentiation" or in a state of "ego fusion." Furthermore, though of course symptoms appear in anyone, most of the situations to be cited focus on the symptoms of the children —usually the immediate stimulus which propels the family to seek help —because these examples are more readily communicable.

Irrational Role Assignment or Projective Transference Distortion

Human needs operate most forcefully in the family setting, with struggles over love, hate, rejection, hurt, gratification, and jealousy being a continuous dynamic process from one generation to the next. The implicit or explicit irrational assignment of roles* in the family—role being defined as a pattern or type of behavior which a person builds up in terms of what significant others expect or demand of him—reflects unconscious attempts by the parents to master, reenact, or externalize their intrapsychic conflicts about these powerful human needs, derived from relationship experiences in the family of origin. Before discussing further this concept of *interpersonal resolution of inner conflict* it is necessary to take a brief sojourn into intrapsychic psychology.

Among the theories which can provide an explanation of the genesis of irrational family role assignment and intrafamilial transference distortion, there is one model which to the present writer best fits the clinical facts.

Object-relations theory. Fairbairn (13), elaborating on some of Freud's and Melanie Klein's concepts, has postulated that man's need for a satisfying object relationship constitutes the fundamental motive of life. His object-relationship approach is contrasted with Freud's theory of the pleasure principle and instinctual gratification as primary in man. For Fairbairn, instinct is a function of the ego, pleasure is incidental to the object-seeking, and aggression is a reaction to frustration when the sought-after object denies satisfaction.

When the parents' behavior is interpreted as rejection, desertion, or persecution, the child, unable to give up the external object or change it in outer reality, handles the frustration and disappointment by internalizing the loved-hated parent in order to master and control the object in the inner psychic world, where it is repressed and retained as an introject, a psychological representative. It is the emotional relationship between the self and some external figure which is internalized, not feelings as such; moreover, these internal objects are not just fantasies but become subidentities and part of the structure of the personality. The bad (unsatisfying, exciting-frustrating) internal object, according to Fairbairn, is split into the dependent, unrequited love need (libidinal ego) and the dangerous, rejecting object (antilibidinal ego). Good objects are retained as satisfying memories, and the ideal object, the nucleus of the original object divested of its exciting and frustrating elements, can be safely loved by the central ego as a desexualized and perfect object. The bad internal objects remain as "internal saboteurs" or warring forces in the inner world—furious, guilty, hungry, anxious, conflic-

---

* Conscious, formal, instrumental family roles, described by sociologists, are not under discussion here because they are not very pertinent to psychopathology; it is the discrepancy between the irrational, informal role assignment and the natural family role that creates the difficulties.

tual—consuming psychic energy which the central ego should have available for evaluation of reality and investment in external relationships.

The earlier in life splitting occurs and the more painful and frustrating the external object world, the more dependence on the inner object world and the more incomplete the personality, a state of affairs with grave consequences for the development of psychopathology and symptom formation. For instance, an individual with early personality splits, resulting, say, from early loss of a parent, is likely to develop the symbiotic relationship dilemma: yearning for merger and fusion with those he loves so that they are part of him, but feeling possessed, tied, trapped, and losing his personality, then having to break away from independence, resulting in his feeling lost, isolated, lonely, and depressed. During the course of development of the individual, external real figures may be assimilated in successive strata or by fusion into the existing bad object situations; other people are seen only in terms of the individual's own libidinal wishes toward them, or as carrying for him his own guilt-laden, denied, split-off traits. More important for the present subject, life situations in outer reality are not only unconsciously interpreted in the light of the inner object world, resulting in distorted expectations of other people, but *active, unconscious attempts are made to force and change close relationships into fitting the internal role models.*

This theoretical formulation, greatly oversimplified in this presentation, while it sounds abstract and easy to caricature as "objects bouncing around in the psyche like little men," is nonetheless supported by innumerable clinical observations in that it does decipher a variety of puzzling human predicaments. For example, it helps explain why the psychology of intimate relationships is different from the psychology of other social relationships, and it sheds light on why some people have to select object attachments that bring them so much distress. It helps understanding of why so many people can become vocationally successful or accomplished in social adjustment terms yet be unable to tolerate the intimacy of a close relationship or form a viable marriage.* The inner psychological splitting of which Fairbairn speaks can have its real, external counterparts; individuals will seek representatives of the libidinal and antilibidinal objects in their external relationships. For instance, some people are

---

* Aldous Huxley's novel, *Genius and the Goddess* [20], gives a fascinating account of an internationally famous scientist's infantile behavior in the home. Research in the behavioral sciences, which usually uses social adjustment criteria of maturity or mental health, should take into account how people function in their intimate family relationships as well as their capacity to function in the outside world. There are many renowned, gifted people in positions of great responsibility whose marriages or children are very disturbed.

able to maintain a love relationship with one person only if someone else is related to as the enemy—a woman fantasies a love relationship with her psychotherapist while her husband is seen as a monster. Or one child in the family may get all the concern and "love" while another is ignored or subject to unreasoning prejudice. (Children in both these positions lose this game—the favored child has to struggle with the guilt, and the rejected child may fight eternally to gain the favor impossible to obtain and feels murderous toward the sibling.)

Marital interaction. Henry Dicks (11) was one of the first to translate Fairbairnian concepts into an interactional framework, focusing specifically on the marriage relationship. He focuses on the unconscious, object-relational needs which flow between marriage partners, and discusses in the following words the dovetailing of two inner worlds in the collusive marriage:

> This stressed the need for unconscious *complementariness,* a kind of division of function by which each partner supplied part of a set of qualities, the sum of which created a complete dyadic unit. This joint personality or integrate enabled each half to rediscover lost aspects of their primary object relations, which they had split off or repressed, and which they were, in their involvement with the spouse, re-experiencing by projective identification. The sense of belonging can be understood on the hypothesis that at deeper levels there are perceptions of the partner and consequent attitudes towards him or her *as if* the other was part of oneself. The partner is then treated according to how this aspect of oneself was valued: spoilt and cherished, or denigrated and persecuted (11, p. 69).

The partners in the disturbed marriage mutually use scapegoating, projection, and representation by the opposite in their unconscious attempts to force the spouse to fit or repudiate the split-off internal objects, even when the partner's real personality drastically contradicts the projection. Idealization is postulated by Dicks as being the link among all of the defense mechanisms in the marital field, whereby spouses attribute to the partner those bad feelings they must not own themselves or else make the partner all good while themselves taking on the badness. Dicks believes that warring couples have a deep, unconscious commitment to each other and need to protect their investment in the spouse. He states:

> By protecting the image of the partner (for example as a "drunk" or as "sexually inadequate" or "slovenly," and so forth) they are in the other secretly cherishing the rejected, bad libidinal ego with its resentments and demands while *within* the dyadic system they can persecute it in an interpersonal framework (11, pp. 122-123).

Family projection process. In previous publications (15, 16) the present writer has attempted to widen Fairbairn's object-relations theory beyond marital interaction to include the several generations of the family. Without going into family *system* theory at this point, the present focus is on irrational role assignment involving the children, who are also dynamic agents in the field. This writer has stated:

> The various children in the family come to represent valued or feared expectations of the parents, based on parental introjects; sometimes the roles of the children are chosen for them even before they are born (e.g., the child who is conceived to "save the marriage"), , , , In every family of multiple siblings there is "the spoiled one," "the conscience of the family," and "the wild one"; the assigned roles are infinite (15, p. 192).

Boszormenyi-Nagi has also discussed the role assignment in the larger than dyadic system, and, speaking of the "captivity of object-role assignment," he stated that:

> The unconscious fantasy through which the parent assigns his own parents' role to his children may result in bizarre, inappropriate actions. The connection between acting-out patterns and their underlying needs—e.g., the one for the assignment of parental roles, may be completely unconscious. Such regressive fantasies of the parents may result in demands for premature responsibility on the part of the children, who may comply with the parents' wish through precocious development. Feelings of hatred and wish for revenge originally connected with a parental introject can be acted out toward the child in unconscious transference, as illustrated by the tragic cases of severe child beatings and murder (6, p. 95).

Altrough not explicitly within a Fairbairnian framework, the work of the family therapists Bowen (7) and Brodey (9) is congruent with this thinking. Bowen has graphically described the "family projection process" whereby the problems in the family are transmitted to one family member, usually a child, and then fixed there with the unwitting assistance of the professional who lends the stamp of official authenticity to the process. Brodey utilizes the mechanism of externalization (defined as a projection plus the selective use of reality for verification of the projection) to describe the narcissistic relationships (defined as a relationship with a projected part of the self as mirrored in the behavior of another) which obtain in the more undifferentiated family. He notes that:

> . . . The inner world is transferred to the outside with little modification, and the part of the outer world attended to is selected

only as it validates the projections, *other impinging realities being omitted* (9, p. 385).

Brodey further described the disturbed family in the following formulation:

> A network of narcissistic relationships, in which ego-dystonic aspects of the self are externalized by each family member and regrouped into allegorical roles, each epitomizing a part of the major conflict which was acted out in the original marriage. . . . The constellation of roles allows the internal conflict of each member to be acted out within the family, rather than within the self, and each family member attempts to deal with his own conflicts by changing the other (9, p. 392).

Speaking of the very young children in such a family Brodey states:

> The infant perhaps would learn that survival within this relationship depended on expressing his own needs in a way and at a time conforming with the mother's projected expectation. The long-term reinforcement of the needs which happened to match the mother's, and the frustration of the needs omitted by the mother, would then alter the child's behavior in the direction of validating the mother's projection (9, p. 385).

When the projection process operates in more extreme fashion, every aspect of the child—his appearance, the way he crawls, walks, talks, cries, laughs, burps—is interpreted within the framework of the assigned traits or role, as proof that the trait is indeed present.* Aspects of the child which refute the assignment are blocked out, denied, or rationalized away. Psychotherapists to whom parents have brought a child for treatment are often struck by the discrepancy between the parents' overalertness by one behavior of the child, such as his lying or stealing, and their indifference to another aspect of the child, such as his being withdrawn or friendless. In accordance with these views, Laing has stated:

> . . . We are denoting something other than the psychoanalytic term "projection." The one person does not wish merely to have the other as a hook on which to hang his projections. He strives

---

* I am indebted to Carl Whitaker for the following incident: A father came to a family therapy session with Dr. Whitaker with the conviction that his own son was a Mongolian idiot because he had read in the *Ladies' Home Journal* that such children have a wide space between the large toe and the next toe. Dr. Whitaker skillfully handled the situation by requesting that everyone in the room take off his shoes and socks, and after examining everyone's toes the group concluded that the psychiatric resident was the Mongolian idiot.

to find in the other, or to induce the other to become, the very *embodiment* of that other whose cooperation is required as "complement of the particular identity he feels impelled to sustain (21, p. 101).

One can ask the question, since the parent's projections are his and his alone, why not treat him on an individual basis? The answer is that these kinds of people, even though they have a great impact on their intimates, never seek treatment for themselves but bring others to therapy. Family therapy is probably the only way to involve them in a therapeutic setting.

A number of family therapists and theoreticians, then, have independently corroborated the phenomenon of irrational role assignment or projective transference distortion which occurs in families. Although the phenomenon had been hinted at in the individual framework, it was not until the advent of family therapy that it was observed in full force, and its implications realized. Prior to family therapy, it was not "seen" because psychotherapists, due to cultural and professional taboos, had never observed families interacting in a diagnostic or therapeutic setting.

One can ask what functions the projection process serves for the individual family members and the family system, aside from avoidance of inner anxiety and the maintenance of psychological equilibrium. Projective transferences, externalization, vindictive fantasies, vicarious participations, all serve the function of recapturing the symbolically retained old love objects who have their representation in current real family members, thus delaying the pain of loss and mourning. Object possession, perhaps the chief motive underlying irrational role assignment, helps prevent individuation which can result in the catastrophe of separation, the old dread of abandonment, and facing of the fact that one has irretrievably lost one's mother or father. In many of the families treated the parents have, in fact, lost one or both parents at an early age, and one can observe the desperate efforts to keep the childred tied to them, notwithstanding impassioned statements to the contrary or the family seemingly flying apart with hostility. In the more undifferentiated families there is no opportunity for the children to experiment with a wide range of flexible roles necessary for functioning outside the restrictive, limited family culture, and if one of the purposes of family life is to prepare the young for life outside the family, these families fail.

The present author believes that the phenomena being described occur in some measure in all families, as a basic fact of human existence. It shuld not be necessary tó emphasize that the projection processes resulting in role allocation, like any other family system phenomenon, are not the result of intent on the part of the family members. Even labeling the processes unconscious does not communicate how they have a life and rhythmatic, gyroscopic force of their own, outside the plan or control of anyone involved, as in any group process which takes over as a regulatory mechanism beyond what anyone desires or expects. The "family way" of seeing and doing things becomes automatic and unquestioned, like the air one breathes. It is very difficult for anyone, no matter how mature, to avoid the family role assignment when he is in the presence of his family. Whether his role is that of "the quiet one," "the smart one," "the slick one," "the troublemaker," "father's protector," or any one of countless assignments, he will find himself behaving accordingly despite himself. The family role can appear incomprehensible, strange, or even ludicrous when viewed by outsiders; the "fighter of the family" may be the smallest, weakest-looking member, or "the crazy one" may be the only family member who makes sense. Years of "training" went into the designation, considered as an absolute given in some families. The assignment is further reinforced by family myths and rules and is ritualized into the family structure. The most powerful family persuasion to bring someone into line who has strayed from his role is to impute disloyalty to the errant one, and in some families veiled threats of emotional or even legal disowning are used on those who resist the symmetrical role.

Still, everyone needs a family, and those who cut themselves off from their families pay a costly price, as the statistics on high rates of psychiatric disorder and suicide for isolates will testify. One risks a great deal in going against the projections. Those who renounce their family of origin and have nothing to do with their parents or siblings, tend to repeat with others the old conflicts; others spend a lifetime trying unsuccessfully to get back into the old system. Many people never really leave home when they marry, by living in the same neighborhood as the parents and marrying the kind of people who, perhaps because they need a family for themselves, will allow frequent contact with the family of origin. Still others deceive themselves into believing that individual psychotherapy or analysis will unstick them from the family emotional system. A universal dilemma consists of the question, how can one keep relating to his family and yet stay free of the irrational aspects of the emotional system and be a person in his own right?

What does all of this have to do with symptoms? It should be obvious that the entire range of symptomatology can come into play concomitant with being boxed in by a "transference fix." The present author has previously stated:

To be on the receiving end of a projection of someone else's internal image can be a particularly frustrating and perplexing experience if that someone else is a vitally needed person; you must be seen as malevolent, spoiled, prematurely grown-up, deceitful, or what have you, and nothing can be said or done to change this view (15, p. 153).

If a father, say, zeroes in on his son as the cause of his misery, one can empathize with the hurt, bewilderment, and futility of this child who cannot get his father to like him even if he sacrifices his life. Projections of those who do not matter can be easily brushed aside. We do not understand the complicated factors which determine whether a given child accepts the designated role, fights it, internalizes it, pretends to accept it, flees from it, or is in conflict about it.* In general, it would seem that some symptoms are developed as a function of efforts to escape the role assignment and others as reflections of the designation. Some symptoms are manifested only within the family culture, as bargaining positions or as stakes in the intrafamilial relationship struggles, while others come into play only outside the family. (Family members often say, "But when I'm not with my family I'm an entirely different person.")

Children whose family role is limited to the reciprocation of the projection and who, in order to maintain a shaky identity, *become* the role set for them, whole and undigested, are likely to have the family role as the foundation of their personality and consequently are high risks for psychosis. The psychotic outbreak may come when attempts to establish the role (for instance, "the baby of the family") are inappropriate outside the family culture; for this person, being outside the family is lke being a fish out of water. Because everyone has some autonomous strivings there may be periodic attempts to establish narcissistic relationships outside the family in the form of proxy family relationships, but these kinds of outside relationships are fraught with instability since the kinds of people who lend themselves to such an arrangement have their own irrational demands to make. When such outside relationships fail, the individual may renounce all extrafamilial relationships and settle for the family role, feeling that the family system, however crazy, is at least predictable and seems more real.

---

* Not under discussion in this paper are some identifiable factors which can affect how irrational role assignments are handled by the child, such as basic personality differences in children, whether one fixed role is assigned with the collusion of the whole family or whether various roles are ascribed, the effect of the sibling subsystem or extended family or diluting or reinforcing the process, fortuitous factors such as opportunities that the child has for extra-familial relationships, the capacity of the child to gain distance from the role or to select from, change, or integrate the projected roles.

Another reaction to wholesale incorporation of the role assignment is to break away violently from the family, to "cop out" and become a hippie, with life being based on a refutation of the parents. This kind of individual will often suffer from the kinds of symptoms described by the existentialists—alienation or lack of meaning or connectedness with life. Some of the rebellious ones unconsciously arrange their lives in a way which guarantees their being pulled back into the old system (for instance, forming a disastrous marriage from which the parents have to rescue them, or getting in trouble with the law, thus inviting parental intervention).

Just as there are symptoms which ensure one's staying in the family system, preventing true individuation, so there are symptoms which are designed to help one get out of the system. For example, a child finds the home situation so unbearable that he behaves in such extreme fashion that institutionalization is required. Being removed from the family in this way cannot be interpreted as really wanting to leave, which carries implications of being disloyal. One adolescent seen at the juvenile court had been setting a series of fires, and at one of the fires he left his wallet containing his name and address. This boy's father had deserted the family, and the mother began drinking heavily. He often had to undress his mother to put her to bed. Once, when she remonstrated with him about his getting in trouble, he said, "Mom, I'll make a deal with you. If you stop drinking I promise I'll behave."

Some children, in response to irrational projection, develop a negative identity and exaggerate, with a vengeance, what they are led to believe they are. Accordingly, they may act out at home, in school, or in the community with a variety of behavior problems, such as destructiveness, truancy, stealing, or unmanageableness. Still others may playact at the role while they are with their family, always feeling phony, as if they have a false self; this kind of child may be "good" at home and a holy terror at school, or vice versa. Such children often develop character disturbances of the "as if" variety, going through life as if it were a charade, and their neurotic symptoms feel ego-alien. They may state in treatment, "I don't know why I do or feel these things—it isn't me." These individuals do not really know who they are. Those children who struggle internally with their part-identities and their ambivalence about the role assignment and their parents, are more likely to develop the kind of intrapsychic conflict which leads to the classic neurotic symptoms of phobias, obsessions and compulsions, or depressions. Some children unconsciously accept the appellation and consciously assail it. Many adolescent suicides are aborted resolutions of these conflicts, resulting in punishing the parents from the grave. The victimization which occurs within lower-class Negro ghetto families, documented by Rainwater (30), Pavenstedt (27), and Minuchin and his colleagues (25), while framed within the white caste system, has devastating effects on the identity development of children. Intense feelings of rage are often heir to real and projective exploitation, and since the fury often cannot be vented in the family, it is frequently displaced outside in the form of crimes of violence, riots, and even assassination of public figures.

In the case illustration which follows, the irrational role projection or intrafamilial transference distortion process is obvious and massive. Usually, the process operates in much more subtle fashion.

> *Case example.* Mr. and Mrs. B., in their determination to prove that their son Joe, age 17, was "schizophrenic," would go to any length to find corroboration of this diagnosis by professionals, and to greater lengths to demonstrate that they were good parents, as witness the fact that they never argued with each other and that their other son, George, age 14, and their daughter, Grace, were so "normal." The parents said they "sensed something different" about Joe from the time he was born. The parents believed, moreover, that Joe was a reincarnation of Mr. B.'s mother, who had been in and out of mental hospitals as a schizophrenic most of her life. Mr. B. felt that Joe was not "all boy" and he decided to turn his upbringing over to his wife and mother-in-law, who lived in an adjoining house with an interconnecting passageway between the two homes. He had nothing to do with this first son, and when George was born he felt he got a second chance to have a "real boy," subsequently investing his aspirations in his second son.
>
> Joe, symbiotically close with mother and grandmother, was teased and beaten up at school for being a sissy, and in response to his father's withdrawal, the suffocation from his mother, and being without friends, he became desperately unhappy and occasionally had screaming temper tantrums. On one occasion, in order to control Joe's tantrums, the parents managed to sneak him into a psychiatric ward of a hospital and there they showed Joe the mental patients, warning him that if he didn't behave he would end up like these patients.
>
> The parents, convinced that the tantrums were symptomatic of schizophrenia, then went from one clinic and psychiatrist to another to get him hospitaliezd. The clinics, after doing thorough work-ups, and the private psychiatrists, after examining Joe and the situation, refused to hospitalize, saying that his condition did not warrant institutionalization. The parents, on one occasion, hid a tape recorder in Joe's bedroom, provoked a tantrum (they said they knew how to trigger one) and then proudly took the tape to a psychiatrist to show how Joe had fooled him. Fortunately, in this instance, the psychiatrist refused to listen to the tape. After

numerous work-ups and psychological testings the parents were finally able to find a psychiatrist who did, indeed, hospitalize Joe, but he was discharged in two days because hospital personnel could see no reason to keep him. Subsequently, the parents initiated a law suit against the hospital for releasing a mentally ill person. The parents on their own gave huge doses of Thorazine to Joe to "control him," often forcing the liquid down his throat.

At a family evaluation session Joe, on cue, presented one of his temper tantrums, and after he calmed down he dared go against the system by disagreeing with his parents that they never argued. Father and mother indicated that he must be crazy to say such a thing and they both turned to the 14-year-old son as the responsible parent of the family to render the final decision. George made his pronouncement that the parents never argued. After being excluded from the family, Joe spent the rest of the session trying to take back what he had said and attempting to get back into the family again.

The family chose not to undertake family therapy, and at last reports were continuing to search for some doctor or agency who would hospitalize Joe.

Blurring of Generational Boundaries

Considerable clinical evidence has accumulated from family therapy observations to demonstrate the symptomatic consequences of parentification of children, role reversals of husband and wife, and crossing of generational boundaries. Cultural factors are intertwined with psychodynamic ones in accounting for the frequency of violation of appropriate age and sex roles in the contemporary American family. Emotional overburdening of the modern urban family has increased as a function of loosening of extended kinship ties, increased mobility, child-oriented trends, all occurring in an age of cultural revolution and rapidly changing values. With all relational needs expected to be filled through each other, parents overinvolve children in matters which should only concern elders.

Schmideberg (33) predated the family therapy findings when she gave numerous clinical examples of how chronological adults are dependent on their children—a woman could not buy a dress without consulting with her 9-year-old daughter; a father was unable to discipline because of fear that his child would not love him or might retaliate in kind. Parentification of the child is one of the most enduring findings derived from family therapy; seen in vivo, these phenomena are often shocking. Parentification may be direct and obvious, as when one of the parents is explicitly allied with one of the children against the mate (making real the child's fantasies of dividing the parents and violating the incest barrier), or when the parents turn to the children to settle their arguments, setting the stage for intrapsychic conflict in the child over divided loyalties. The alliance between parent and child may be more disguised, as when mother secretly goes to her son to complain about her husband; the excluded father often becomes rivalrous with his son and family wars may result, sometimes ending in murder. (Murder, by the way, statistically occurs much more frequently between family members than between strangers.)

When the child is parentified the real parent loses his parental authority and limit-setting function, feeling he has no right to require compliance. Parental abdication is often rationalized as an attempt to establish togetherness or democracy in the family, where "the dignity and rights of the children are being respected." Parents who are unable to establish the kind of benevolent dictatorship required for effective family life and who are impotent with their children are frankly bewildered when the children respond with rage reactions and later with assaults against the establishment. The consequences of crossing of generations, of the inability of the parents to work as a team in exercising their parental role, and of the parents not fulfilling their sex role, are felt in all the psychiatric and other societal institutions which have to deal with the products of these disordered family lives.

> *Case example.* Mr. and Mrs. S. requested family therapy because they felt they had ruined their other children's lives and wanted to make sure they did not destroy the last remaining at home, 13-year-old Stanley. The other children refused to be involved in the family sessions, maintaining that the only way they could keep their sanity was to have nothing to do with their parents. One older son, contacted by telephone, told of having to intervene constantly in violent battles between his parents, fights which often threatened to result in someone's death; he also said that he had had to raise Stanley, for example, giving him his bottle feedings during the night. When family therapy started Stanley had been having numerous somatic problems for which there was no medical basis and, in addition, suffered from a mixture of anxiety and depression.
>
> In the family sessions Stanley's role as the mediator of his parents' marriage was immediately evident. Whenever his parents fought they each used him to express hostility to each other. Mr. S., feeling helpless in dealing with his wife, used Stanley as a front man, sometimes literally putting the boy in front of him while he fed Stanley the complaints to say for him. Stanley said he was not able to do his school lessons because when he went to his room one or both parents would pop in every few minutes. (The family telephone was in his bedroom.) The parents never went out together; on the one occasion that the therapist was able to get them to go

to a movie together without Stanley, the father had to leave in the middle of the show to telephone Stanley. The mother had frequent tumultuous emotional outbursts, described by Stanley as "being like a wild woman." Stanley was expected to control these episodes for her, a particularly embarrassing task when she would scream out on the street, in view of the neighbors. The most extraordinary overinvolvement of Stanley had to do with how he got pulled into their sexual life. Mrs. S. said her husband was "sexually obsessed" and that if she wanted to buy something she had to bribe her husband with sex. Further, whenever she took a bath her husband would come into the bathroom and make a pass at her, knowing Stanley was downstairs and would hear her protests against "this disgusting behavior." Mrs. S. found her husband's advances so unbearable that in order to get him to stop she made her husband sit down with Stanley and write out in detail everything he did to her sexually.

Changes in the Family Relationship System

Unusual events of family life, such as the death of one of the parents or a child, hospitalization or imprisonment of a parent, marital separation or divorce, accidents and physical handicaps, economic reverses, and so forth, can, of course, produce catastrophic strain and disruption in a family. An epigenetic view of the family, however, centers on the crises which arise as a function of developmental events which occur as a natural part of the family life cycle. Every family has to adjust to the changes and stresses which accompany each natural successive stage of family development, all the way from the transition from a state of singleness to marriage, parenthood, the children going to school and later leaving for college or getting married, sequential marital stages, retirement, advancing age, and death. Symptomatic eruptions may be precipitated by the unusual family events, but may also occur in one or other family members at developmental junctures, that is, whenever someone enters or leaves the family system. Grunebaum and Bryant (19) have described a program of family diagnostic interviews which are oriented around family developmental crises, and they stress the importance of the family's style of feelings which are aroused by the life crises.

Sometimes the outbreak of symptoms is more subtly associated with some change in the family system; the flare-up in the child may be timed to some breakdown in relationship between a parent and grandparent. In the more undifferentiated families biological maturation of the children is often perceived as a threat, with the children getting the feeling that by growing up they are rejecting their parents. Levenson, Stockhamer, and Feiner (22), in describing the family transactions in the etiology of college dropouts, found that the failure of the student played an important homeostatic role for the family in that successful individuation threatened the family integrity. They stated:

We have seen previously bland marriages explode and break up when the students go away. Parents often come shockingly into contact with the aridity and disappointment of their lives when the child leaves home. Students are often cued in by telephone calls and letters to come home (22, p. 144).

Case example. Mr. and Mrs. B., both of whom had lost their parents at an early age, married on the basis of an explicit contract that Mr. B. was to be his wife's "father." They did not have romantic feelings about each other, did not even kiss during the courtship, and Mr. B. told his wife openly that he had run around enough and wanted to settle down with his pipe, television, and a newspaper. This arrangement was initially acceptable to Mrs. B., who said she was so glad to at least have a father. But she became increasingly dissatisfied with the lack of affection and the fact that they never went anywhere together.

Despite this arrangement, two daughters were born, Louise and Jane, each of whom was fitted to provide for gaps in the "marriage." Mr. B., unable to discuss anything with his wife, turned to Louise for relationship; the week she married he had to be hospitalized for depression. Mrs. B., terrified of losing her children, started with Jane when she was a small child, always finding something wrong with every friend the child had and repeating to her that people were not to be trusted. Mrs. B. always suspected that her daughters were up to no good and would constantly accuse them of doing bad things which they had not done. Despite her appreciation that Jane would get in trouble, she left Jane in Louise's care for weeks at a time. After Louise got married, Jane began to act out by becoming truant, taking drugs, becoming a hippie, and geting an abortion for a pregnancy. She and Mrs. B. had violent daily arguments, in the midst of which they would telephone Louise to decide who was right.

In family therapy sessions Mrs. B. spoke tearfully of how she was dying from lack of affection, that she had lost Louise, and that Jane, who used to be so loving toward her, was now drifting away and, furthermore, was doing all the awful things she had always been afraid that Jane might do. Mrs. B. was especially frightened of being alone with her husband, whose only words to her when he was home was to ask what they were having for dinner. Now she was afraid that if Jane ever got married she would only have the family dog to love and kiss.

Dynamic Economy of a Relationship System

There are many intimate relationship systems where the symptoms of one member, although regarded on one level as noxious by all concerned, are a necessary ingredient for the maintenance and even survival of the relationship. It is not uncommon for a marriage, for example, to be structured on the basis of one partner being the functioning "independent" one, and the other partner being the "dependent" 'helpless one; the nonfunctioning person may be continually ill physically, always tired, have frequent, vague pains or frank psychiatric symptoms, be unable to hold down a job or take care of the house. The words "independent" and "dependent" are put in quotes because these roles can shift, so that when one partner is up the other is down. On the other hand, there are marital situations which are relatively stable in this respect, where the husband, say, an executive or a doctor, is married to an alcoholic, chronically ill, or childlike wife whom he has to take care of. The nurtured one ensures the continuity of the relationship and helps the parental one to conceal his own dependency by displaying it for him.

If the weak one changes, by psychotherapy or other ways, or if they separate, there can be a rapid reversal of roles, revealing the basic picture of mutual dependency. Scheflen (32) has described the "gruesome-two-somes"—regressive, infantile, one-to-one relationships (husband and wife, homosexual partners, parent and child) characterized by limitations of relatedness outside the dyad, decreasing gratification within the relationship, and maintenance of the attachment by mutual exploitation of the partner's anxieties. Abandonment is the ultimate danger and "symptoms" are used as gambits or blackmail to create guilt or anxiety in the partner; if one partner gets interested in a third party the other gets jealous, sulks, or develops a "headache" or "asthma attack" to pull back the offender. Since one partner gets hurt if the other gets involved in anything which takes away from the relationship, there are restrictions in job advancement, interests, and hobbies, often resulting in what the analysts call "inhibition symptoms."

In the psychoanalytic or individual therapy situation the mutual role that the symptoms play in the maintenance of needed relationships is often missed. One wonders in this connection how many unnecessary divorces there will be because husband and wife seeing two therapists separately never had an opportunity to examine the intermeshing of their dyadic pathology and the nature of their marital bond. Symptomatic functioning in one member of a relationship system usually has its reciprocal in the overfunctioning of another (the all-powerful mother and schizophrenic offspring, or the overadequate woman and nonfunctioning husband). Family therapy observations have revealed how the symptoms of one member often serve useful and necessary functions for the others, how the underlying system reciprocity is revealed by symptoms appearing in a previously asymptomatic member when the symptomatic one improves, and how a marriage may rupture when the symptoms which had been built into the relationship are no longer present. During the course of family therapy, as the role of the symptoms in the dynamic balance of the family is exposed, there can be dramatic spontaneous "cures" in the designated patient, but often someone else develops symptoms. Symptomatic behavior in one of several members may express a displaced family conflict in symbolic form. For example, a brother or sister who are always fighting with each other act as a representation for parents who never get openly angry with each other. In this situation it is easy to see how the children may stop their squabbling as the hidden resentments of the parents come forth.

The realization that symptoms can equilibrate family as well as intrapsychic forces has momentous theoretical and practical implications. Multiperson systems, whereby one person carries part of the motivations and behavior of another person, are only beginning to be understood; the close other can become a structural part of the self. *Whenever two or more persons are in close relationship they collusively carry psychic functions for each other.* The collusiveness can be in the benign form we see in all our relationships, such as when something frightening happens when we are with someone—if he is scared, he carries our fear for us and we can be brave; or if he is responsible we can be irresponsible; or if our wives take the soft line with the children we can take the hard line. The deal can be more unconscious—"I will be your slave or your bad self if you will never leave me." The referent point of a feeling or behavior is always an Other who will have some predictable reaction. One can always detect the interlocking of motivations when it is noticed that the individual will not take a personal stand on some issue and instead claims he is not free because of the other person. Such an individual will not take a clear position in the form of, "I want this," or, "I don't like that"; instead he or she will say, "You won't let me do this," or, "You should not do that because it's not nice." The relational environment is manipulated so that others are maneuvered into being chastizing parents, monitors or expressors of one's sexual or hostile impulses, faithful servants, oppressors, or what have you, in order that more primitive conflicts will not come to the surface.

People are constantly acting out old conflicts and they seek through marriage, children, friends, enemies, psychotherapists, the supporting responses which will enable the relationship with the internal role models to continue. This is to say, they avoid painful symptoms by interpersonal choice. The reciprocal roles are found with exquisite accuracy:

George and Martha of "Virginia Woolf" fame found in each other the desired lover-persecutor; Hansel and Gretel found their witch; the King Lears will find their Cordelias to reject; the hurt lover his unrequited love object; the flirtatious woman her jealous husband; and the Little Red Hen will find her selfish associates and triumph over them.

Character defenses—the habitual, ingrained styles of warding off anxiety—only fail when the reciprocating others will not or cannot cooperate. It is at this point that the more standard symptoms are likely to develop (such as the depression which follows divorce of a couple who fervently anticipated how well off they would be without each other). This phenomenon has its parallel in the way an agoraphobic will never have symptoms so long as he is living in a monastery. Psychopathology in one member of an intimate relationship system, then, can be very protective of the other members.

> *Case example.* Mrs. S. had seven episodes of depression and "paranoid" emotional outbursts, on each occasion being hospitalized briefly and given electroshock treatments. The psychiatrist who referred the patient and her husband for couple therapy finally noted a pattern in Mrs. S.'s "illnesses"—whenever the couple had an argument Mr. S. would take his wife to the hospital for EST and she would dutifully comply. When she was not on courses of EST Mrs. S. was kept heavily tranquilized.
>
> In the first marital therapy session, when the couple entered the office, Mr. S., a successful businessman, took his wife's coat, folded it carefully, took his coat, folded it carefully, went back to the coats three times to check if all the wrinkles were out of them, then sat down, picked lint off his suit, stopped and picked some lint off the rug, and then made his first statement: "Doctor Framo, our big problem is my wife's compulsiveness."
>
> In subsequent sessions, after Mrs. S. came out of her lethargy, due to medication being stopped, she became extremely bitter and hostile to her husband, who reacted, sequentially, with shock that his wife was angry at him, amusement, smiling, and finally ceremonious and overpolite behavior. Her chief complaint, that he responded like a mechanical robot, was not real, and wiped her out as a person by not acknowledging her feelings, added further to her fury. Following some therapeutic work, Mr. S. began recognizing her wrath and began getting angry himself, and there then ensued a phase of ritualistic aggression between the two of them of such intensity that the pictures on the wall were shaken; occasionally they had fist fights outside the sessions.
>
> During this phase it was learned that neither one had any friends, that they never had people at their house and never went out, that whenever one tried to buy something without the other being present or tried to make a friend or join an organization, the other

would react by hurt withdrawal and threats to separate, have an affair, or kill himself. The couple would conduct "experiments" with each other. Mr. S. once fell to the floor and feigned death to test whether his wife cared. She did: she became panicky and told him she loved him. Mrs. S. once made up a story that she had a job, predicting correctly that her husband wouldn't speak to her for a few days. Their symptoms played into each other in various ways. Mr. S. was afraid to walk on the streets alone, but he said he had to accompany his wife on the street because she had this "street phobia." After the ritualistic aggression was redirected, in line with Bach's (5) and Lorenz's (23) work on aggression, they began to deal with the real issues between them.

It was learned that Mr. S. had been raised by a psychotic mother who, when she was not in the hospital, was involutional and frequently could not respond to questions. Mr. S. had always been frightened of going crazy, so he married someone who, while "a nice, sweet girl, so I thought," had a "crazy look in her eyes which intrigued me." In effect, Mr. S. dealt with his own irrationality by obsessively handling it in his wife, which is why he was most solicitous about getting her into treatment, so his own illness would be well taken care of. Mrs. S., on the other hand, played the role of patient for years because she was guilt-ridden by strict religious training and her fantasies of promiscuity and, in addition, felt that her husband would love her and she would be doing her wifely duty by acceding to his wishes that she get shocked out of her strong emotions. As the sessions progressed various symptoms shifted back and forth between the marital partners until they were able to achieve some differentiation from each other.

SYMPTOM CHOICE

What determines the specific content of a symptom? There has been little investigation of this extremely important and complicated question. From the point of view of individual psychology, the kinds of symptomatic pathways selected can be understood on the basis of the idiosyncratic history of the individual. Prior to the family system approach, family influence on the choice of symptoms was considered in terms of such factors as the child identifying with the symptoms of a parent—the offspring of an alcoholic will usually have problems around drinking—or the effect of a neurotic parent's fixation—a mother who is preoccupied with anal functions may give her child numerous enemas, so it is no surprise when the child develops symptoms around elimination.

More sophisticated knowledge of family dynamics has increased understanding of differential responses of several children to the same deleterious situations. For instance, if the marriage of the parents is characterized by immutable turmoil, demeaning of each other, and noisy battles, although all the children may share common feelings of fear, shame, disgust, being torn apart, yet wanting to save their parents' marriage, each child may incorporate separate aspects of the marital relationship. One child may identify with the aggressive role, going through life victimizing others; another child may incorporate the victim role and always get in situations which provoke abuse; another child may incorporate both aspects as an intrapsychic conflict; and still another child may block it all out and become silent and withdrawn, inwardly feeling, "Things are bad enough; I cannot make demands because it might make matters worse." To be sure, there are many factors which will affect such outcomes: the extent to which the children are pulled into the marriage difficulties, which child is selected as the marriage counselor, the birth order, sex, and ages of the children, the stage of the marriage into which each child was born, how much support the siblings are able to give each other, and so forth.

In addition to intrapsychic and family dynamics, wider cultural influences, such as the ethos of various societies, historical changes, value conflicts within societies, and ethnic, religious, and, social class distinctions, certainly play a part in the manner in which symptoms are manifested. An outstanding example of the way cultural change affects fads in symptoms is that since the passing of Victorian repressiveness the conversion hysterics of Freud's day are almost never seen. Everyone recognizes that behavior which is regarded in one culture as pathological or anathema may not only not be so regarded in another culture but may be rewarded. Every society has its own defined ways of patterning human needs and giving approved expression to distress, and each culture has its own standards, criteria, and precepts regarding what is and is not deviance.

Family Interpretation of Psychopathology

The dimension of the family relationship system, unknown before the introduction of family therapy experience, has increased understanding of the process whereby a family member's behavior is interpreted as abnormal by the family intimates, as well as the process of choice of symptoms. Behavioral scientists have long been puzzled by the phenomenon that some behaviors which to outsiders, including professionals, are patently not abnormal are defined by family members as mental illness; and other behaviors which are clearly seen as disordered or perilous from a psychiatric or social adjustment point of view are denied, blocked out, minimized, or explained away by one or more family members. It seems that sickness, like love or beauty, is in the eyes of the beholder.

Different investigators have offered various explanatory concepts to account for the interpretation of "sick" behavior on the part of another family member: tolerance of deviance (18); the relationship between the definer and the symptomatic one (34); whether or not the referring family member was a target of the behavior (10); and the degree of satisfaction with the relationship (31). Psychodiagnosticians and therapists often get their data for diagnosis or treatment of a patient, particularly a child, by interviewing the relatives *about* the patient. Who else but parents should know their own child? Yet, in another sense, the last person in the world able to evaluate or interpret accurately the behavior or degree of pathology in another's behavior is a member of the family. The lack of congruence in systematic investigations of this problem can perhaps be made intelligible by an elusive variable which rests on knowledge of how family systems work.

The informant's psychology is intimately tied up with and even a constituent of the psychology of the "patient," and together they are part of a regulatory system which, quite out of awareness, has built-in biases and falsifications, sometimes of massive proportions, which stem from the vital relationship needs which are at stake. If a wife needs a husband for her psychic survival she may state about his severe delusions that, "Everybody gets peculiar ideas now and then." On the other hand, if the system requires that someone in the family have particular symptoms, no amount of outside evidence to the contrary is convincing. For example, two brothers had been stealing cars and were finally caught and sent to juvenile court. The parents insisted that one son be punished and detained because he was "bad clear through," and they dismissed the antisocial behavior of the other son, characterizing his actions as "childish pranks." Sometimes the family's overconcern with one symptom and ignoring of others can have disastrous consequences—for example, the parents of an adolescent boy focused on his reading disability by requiring constant tutoring, and they were oblivious to an obvious depression and frequent threats of the suicide which was eventually carried out.

In general, the recognition and specificity of the symptom depends on what the family system does or does not allow, and families usually seek help only when the system is hurting, that is, when someone in the family is expressing antisystem symptoms. In a system no one element is more important than another. When the nature of the "deviant" behavior threatens the integrity of the homeostatic balance of the family system, that is, when there is a true change in a role which demands modification of a reciprocating role, there can be intense family anxiety. No matter how bizarre or dangerous a symptom is, on the other hand, if it does not have a system function it is simply not acknowledged, although neighbors, school, or the police may force the family to do something.

SYMPTOM MAINTENANCE AND SYMPTOM REDUCTION

Whatever dynamic family process is involved in the formation and shaping of symptoms is also a part of what determines whether symptoms are short-lived, episodic, unnecessary, or chronic. Generally speaking, symptoms are maintained or reduced to the extent that they serve relationship system functions and are an integral component of and bonding force in the relationships. Symptoms which sustain relationships and are embedded in stagnant contexts are likely to be the ones most intractable to change, as some individual therapists ruefully recognize when they find that after lengthy psychotherapy many of the original symptoms in their patients are still present. According to psychoanalytic views of therapeutic change (24), when the ego gets stronger in its control and synthetic functions, it can better deal with the demands of the id, superego, and external reality, including the family pathology. There is, however, a relentless stickiness in the quality of a dyadic or triadic close relationship which has a force of its own, and individual treatment is likely to have a greater effect on the patient's nonintimate relationships than on those relationships which carry transference meaning and rely on repetitive, characteristic feedback. It is true, as Luborsky and Schimek say, that "favorable changes in patients (in analysis) do not always imply that all symptoms are gone. Symptoms may sometimes be present after treatment, even though the patient may have accomplished much change" (24, p. 88). One wonders, however, how many therapeutic failures are the result of lack of appreciation of the symptom in its context; it could well be that the only symptoms which change in individual therapy or analysis are those which do not have family system functions. Of course, changes occur in people and in symptoms in circumstances other than formal psychotherapy, most often when the context changes, that is, when the symptoms no longer have meaning in a given relationship system in time.

Experienced family therapists are no longer excited by the striking "spontaneous cures," even of long-standing symptoms, which can occur early in family therapy. They know the power of an approach which, by moving the system just a small notch, can unfurl a process of change which can spread to all the relationships in the family; small system changes, in other words, can make a great difference in total family functioning. Indeed, the very fact that some families come to a session at all and discuss important matters with each other for the first time can have lasting effects, even if the family never returns. Opening up of communication on real issues between the parents, for example, often leads to invigoration of the marriage, almost invariably followed by symptom reduction in the children. Or, when a family member is able to dispute an irrational role assignment, the process of change has begun. Visiting professionals observing family sessions for the first time have been very impressed with the early dramatic changes, not knowing how family systems work and not recognizing that removal of symptoms in designated patients represents a very limited goal of family therapy.

Among the countless ways that symptoms are maintained by the supporting surround, only a few examples will be mentioned.

Secondary Gain

When one person in the family has fixed neurotic, characterologic, or psychotic symptoms there are always consequences for the family system beyond what has been called secondary gain. To be sure, the symptomatic one unconsciously exploits his illness in a variety of ways. Families do indeed suffer when a hypochondriac extracts his worry dues, a compulsive housewife tyrannizes with her nagging, a depressed parent makes everyone feel guilty, a paranoid family member snipes behind the privileged sanctuary of psychosis, and a fire-setting child keeps everyone on edge. Secondary gain, however, can function only in a cooperative medium; when the system is resistant, that is, when the symptoms truly do not meet the needs of other family members, the symptomatic one must resort to other defenses, changing the character of the disorder. Usually one person in the family is permitted to have his symptom because this arrangement allows the trading bargain of an unwanted behavior, reward, or defensive protection for someone else—"My husband is so miserable to live with, I figure I have a right to play around." Some families require that one of its members be symptomatic, a fact which partially explains the revolving of symptoms around the various family members during the course of family therapy. Changes in the system which result in the family no longer needing a patient, while difficult to achieve, represents one major goal of family therapy.

Hospitalized Member

A common, tragic situation consists of the one in which the family's having a hospitalized, psychotic member has become fixed and integrated into the system as a way of life for the family. One can witness the melancholy ritual every Sunday in all the state hospitals across the country: family members visit the hospitalized one year after year, bringing food, asking the same questions of the patient and staff, and not really expecting any change. Some of these families, feeling the illness of the patient as the cross they have to bear, do get some surplus advantages from this arrangement; for some, the only social life they have is involved with hospital visits and activities, and such situations can become so calcified that attempts to get the patient out of the hospital will be sabotaged by the family.

PSEUDOSYMPTOMS

The modifier "pseudo" is used hesitantly to characterize those symptoms which are even less "genuine" than those mentioned thus far. Labeling them less genuine does not necessarily imply fakery or malingering or conscious intent to assume a symptom. Rather, under discussion here are those symptoms which come into being, either momentarily or over a long period of time, to meet the conditions of some family system contingency. Some of these symptoms disappear rapidly when the contingency context changes, but others may develop into "real" symptoms or character traits, sometimes on the basis of functional autonomy.

For instance, in the situation where a divorce is imminent between parents, it would be surprising if the children did not develop symptoms of some sort. The young children may wish to sleep with mother (further increasing the threat if followed through), may somatize, lose interest in things, become irritable and impatient, or may act out in order to forestall the dire threat. These symptoms, which began originally as conscious or unconscious attempts to force the parents together, may quickly vanish or may become fixed and internalized.

There are some situations which are so ominous that pretty much any symptom will do, so long as it diverts attention from the main threat. As a matter of fact, a large proportion of the symptoms which people initially present in psychotherapy, either on an individual or family basis, are diversionary pseudosymptoms. It is not infrequent, for example, for the parents in family therapy to start off talking about some problem in the child in the first session and then never to mention it again during ensuing months. This finding has led some family therapists to call the child's symptoms a passport for the parents to get treatment. Symptoms may be nonspecific attempts to introduce variability or excitement into a congealed, dead family, or they may be distress signals, dilatory tactics, games, manipulations, bribes, attempts to achieve closeness or distance, or any combination of innumerable strategic interpersonal gambits.

The purpose of some symptoms may be to block changes in the system in order to maintain the status quo. For example, a child can be given the power to divide the parents and turn them against each other, and his symptoms may add to the parental struggle. It is not uncommon in family therapy for the symptomatic child, who presumably has the most to gain from changes in the family, to be the one who is most obstructionistic, although careful examination sometimes reveals that the child is a spokesman for one or both parents.

There are several symptom phenomena which have important theoretical and practical implications for evaluation of psychopathology. A person shows different sides of his personality to different people in different situations, and certain behaviors are manifested only in the actual, physical presence of particular people. The presence of family members introduces the greatest effect on an individual's behavior; it is very difficult, for instance, for the most mature adult to avoid feeling like a child when he is with his mother or father. Some symptoms, therefore, will be exhibited only in proximity of either the family members or others who have family transference meaning for the person (the boy who whines or has a tic only when with his mother, or the girl who is always an angel when her father or therapist is around).

Self-consistency, then, is a myth, but so is object constancy. The current, actual real mother of an adult is not the same, transactionally, as the historical introject of mother; the relational meaning is different. Everyone at times behaves toward the present-day mother as if she were the mother of childhood (occasionally noticing with shock the grey hair), but the more undifferentiated the personality the more the individual responds not to mother as she is today, but to the early imago. The schizophrenic adult views his mother almost exclusively in terms of the introjected mother, an observation which can be confirmed by witnessing the interaction between the two. This writer has had the experience of treating patients in individual psychotherapy and suggesting that they bring in one or both parents; the patients' near-panic which followed this suggestion is probably due, at least in part, to the threat of confrontation of the discrepancy between the introjected and the current, real parent. Most often the patients said they felt that great harm would befall their parents if they came to the sessions, but this altruistic concern overlay protection of the fantasy introject. One patient, who had been describing how "impossible" her mother was, finally admitted she needed to see her mother as impossible and felt her actual presence in the sessions might destroy the coveted image.

There are also interactional behaviors which make their appearance only under specified relational conditions. For example, a couple may fight only when the children are around or play their sadomasochistic games only when there is an audience, such as at a party, and behave very differently when they are alone together or with their in-laws. Because particular combinations of people in a particular context exhibit some behaviors and not others, this crucial factor must be taken into account when the professional wants to generalize from the behavior he himself observes, whether he is evaluating dynamics, selecting who should attend family therapy sessions, or determining the composition and design of a family interaction experiment.

Another important related symptom phenomenon has to do with the observation that some people are able to be spontaneous, human, creative, real, questioning, only when they are nonrational or symptomatic. Warkentin and his colleagues (37) highlighted the value of certain kinds of episodes of disorganization, provided the people close to the person can accept the behavior. Some people are able to deal with the real issues with close others only when they are drunk, psychotic, under drug influence, or in other ways "not themselves." For example, a woman was hospitalized on many occasions over a period of 15 years, each time following a period of great upset during which she would despair over her husband's lack of affection and cruelty and declare her intention to get a divorce; each time she returned home from the mental hospital she would claim that she loved her husband and couldn't understand why she said those crazy things. There are occasions, then, when giving up symptoms means returning to a stultifying, restrictive conformity to the system patterns. Families and, too often, professionals are sometimes too quick to assess these occasional therapeutic symptoms as pathology.

SHARING AND EXCHANGE OF SYMPTOMS

Just as a phobia, in intrapsychic terms, is an attempt to localize anxiety within a single situation while saving the ego from recognizing the real problem, and just as an obsessional isolates his symptoms from the rest of his personality and does not feel them as his own, so will people isolate, localize, and place forbidden tendencies and anxieties onto their intimates, manipulating others into expressing and carrying their problems for them.

For example, a mother is having one of her "attacks"; she screams that she is going blind and is going to die. Her young son gets all upset, frantic, and worried, and starts crying. Once the shift has occurred, mother is no longer anxious, placates her son, and asks, "Why are you upset?" or she may even get angry at him for being worried. Later on, when the son learns to ignore the attacks and not get hooked or tied up in knots, he is accused of being uncaring. Irrational fears, thinking, and memory can be transmitted from one person to another through these double-binding means, often getting to the point where one's own senses, perceptions, recollections, and feelings are mistrusted.

As we have seen in previous sections, one person can express a symptom *for* some other close person; several family members can, overtly or covertly, jointly share symptoms; and family members can manifest interchangeable depressive, paranoid, or aggressive symptoms in their interaction with each other, yet be symptom-free in their extrafamilial relationships.

The following examples are some representative prototypes of the sharing and exchange of symptoms within family relationship systems.

Mutual Secondary Gain

Secondary gain is usually discussed in terms of an individual "patient," but that which is gain for the patient may also be gain for the significant other. Bilateral secondary gain in a marriage, for example, may be the critical ingredient which helps create, maintain, and determine the fate of symptoms in each or both partners. Mutual secondary gain represents an investment and safeguard in the relationship itself, and the motivational interlockings and misalignments can themselves be the very constituents and essence of the disorder. It is in this sense that family therapists speak of the marriage itself or the family as being the patient. One can speculate how often more observable symptoms in one person serve to conceal, protect, and mask symptoms in an intimate; indeed, symptoms in one person can bind and protect a whole family constellation.

At woman was in psychotherapy because she suffered unbearable anxiety about her husband's health, even going so far as to lie awake at night listening to him breathe and dreading the cessation of breath that signaled a heart attack. Her husband was usually tolerant of his wife's overconcern, sometimes amused, but occasionally annoyed because her concerns imposed restrictions on his freedom of movement; he had to stay near a telephone at work because if he did not answer the phone quickly she would become panicky. So long as she was carrying his fears he was unconcerned about his state of health. It was noted, however, that whenever her concern about his health abated, he would "develop" chest pains.

Monitoring

Symptoms never exist in a void, and even before family therapy it was recognized that symptomatic people usually need someone to monitor their symptoms, the monitoring one usually being considered by the therapist as a constant, however. Take, for example, a married couple where the wife is obese. She demonstrates that in order to indulge her wish for food she needs another who will forbid this activity. Her husband is disturbed by her need to gratify herself and her inability to exercise discipline, so he chastizes her. She assuages the hurt from the chastisement by eating more. Deeper exploration reveals that the husband cannot allow indulgence for himself, so he participates vicariously in her eating and in subtle ways encourages it, such as giving her a pie for her birthday.

Reciprocal gain is seen in the mates of alcoholics, gamblers, and other addicts where both members of a pair have a problem, and one manifests it while the other protests. There is the husband who handles his anxiety about being a male by taking care of the children and house because his wife is always "sick," or the wife who claims that because of her husband's fear of driving she has to drive him places, thereby not having to face her own phobia or what she gets from assuming the parental role with him.

Open Sharing

Some relationships are kept in dynamic balance by virtue of an openly shared symptom which can constitute the cementing "third party." This transactional situation is apparent in an alcoholic couple who are both married to the bottle, or a marriage maintained by mutual fantasies of the mate's infidelity with a rival.

Scapegoated Member

Systems are often maintained on the basis of containing a scapegoated member whose symptoms have sacrificial value for the others. For example, a child may be the continuing focal point of a marital dispute, with the father saying to his wife, "You always spoil that kid," and the mother countering with, "I wouldn't have to if you loved him enough." The parents argue incessantly about the child and threaten separation, at which point the boy starts underachieving at school, develops enuresis, or manifests any of many symptoms. Whether or not the child's "symptoms" continue depends largely on what happens to the marriage relationship; what happens in the marital relationship may depend on what happens with the child's symptoms. The child may be taken for treatment, and he may be willing to go if he feels he can escape being the battleground for the marriage or if he feels his going to a therapist will help his parents get along better. The professional to whom the child is referred will then usually evaluate the child and treat him as *the* patient, with the handling of the marital problem either being ignored or treated on an ancillary basis.

Vicarious Participation

Another common mechanism through which symptoms are shared is through vicarious participation and gratification. For example, Mrs. E. was in show business from the time she was a teenager, and although she was tempted to be as promiscuous as the other girls in the nightclub where she worked, she controlled her behavior and warded off advances of many men. One reason she did so, in addition to moral reasons, was that she had a sister who had been so promiscuous that she had had to be institutionalized in a home for wayward girls. Mrs. E. married a man who could not be demonstrative, and occasionally she went out on dates with other men with her husband's knowledge and approval. She insisted, however, "I never did anything wrong because I respect my husband too much." But she felt cheated out of something important, so she began living through her daughter, who cooperated by living a free sexual life. She fought with her daughter constantly about her behavior, yet would listen in on her daughter's telephone conversations about boys, would open her daughter's mail, and would follow her on dates. On one occasion she told her daughter she was going out and wouldn't be back until late, and she placed herself outside a window of the house to peek at her daughter making love. The next week Mrs. E. convinced her husband that the daughter needed treatment, so they took her to a child guidance clinic.

DISCUSSION

The first real bridge and juncture between the personal and the social exists in the development of family transactional theory whereby man is viewed not as a personality constellation with defined limits, but as being linked to, shaped by, and shaping the natural habitat within which he is involved, feels, and behaves. Family transactional theory and family therapy, in this writer's judgment, represents a major break-through which compels reexamination of the fundmental nature of psychopathology. The view that psychiatric illness, craziness, or odd disordered behavior is a socially intelligible response orchestrated to an odd, crazy, or disordered system has a significance as momentous as the Freudian revolution in psychiatry. On the basis of the material presented in this paper, one can question whether psychopathology can ever be contained within the boundaries of one individual, even if one grants the precondition of intrapsychic conflict for neurotic symptoms. It is this writer's view that although all symptoms are not interpersonally determined, they always have interpersonal and relationship consequences which will determine their nature, course, preservation, or removal. That is to say, the substance of psychological disorder can consist of the reciprocal interlocking of a multiperson motivational system, not only in terms of etiology, maintenance, and reduction of psychopathology in the individual members and *between* the members, but also characterizing the interacting unit itself. Symptoms, in other words, can be looked upon as disordered relationship events. Although intrapsychic psychology and inner experience have been minimized in this paper, it should be recognized that neither the intrapsychic nor transactional levels can be replaced by the other or reduced to the other, and that both are necessary for the whole picture, even though the enormous complexity of the relationship between the two levels has only begun to be explored.

Psychodynamic theorists and practitioners have known for a long time of the close relationship between family dynamics and symptoms, but it was not until actual treatment of the family together that the how and why of the kinship between the two were forcefully brought home by the transactions. Any complete theory of symptom formation could not be limited to the construct that a symptom is a compromise between instinctual gratification and the defense. This writer postulates the theory that the universal human conflict between autonomy and reality on the one hand and the need to be accepted by intimate others on the other hand would have to be included in any comprehensive explanation of the development of psychopathology. The power of life-sustaining family relationship ties is much greater than instinctual or autonomous strivings. Whereas life preservation for animals depends on instinctive regulation in unfolding sequence, the human being must depend much longer on parental care, and the feelings surrounding the early symbiosis persist as an aspiration throughout the life span. For the sake of approval by the parents, and because abandonment has such disastrous consequences, the child will sacrifice whatever ego integrity is called for in order to survive. If the price for acceptance is to absorb unrealities, accept an irrational identity or role assignment, be persecuted, be overindulged, be scapegoated, be parentified, or what have you, this price will have to be paid; to be alone or pushed out of the family either physically or psychologically is too unthinkable.*

Adults, too, require specific reciprocal identities in their intimate others in order to maintain their own identities. Family members are most content when everyone behaves according to the others' expectations. Family members are extremely emotionally involved, but not so much with each other as with their imprinted inner role formulas which require confirmation in the others' behaviors. The consequences of someone not cooperating with their assigned role can be calamitous. Bach, who studied intensely a sample of spouse murderers, found the following:

> Actually, all the spouse killings we investigated, including the few suicide displacement murders, can be conceptualized as punishing a partner for not fitting into a *role, image or situation* as defined and wished for by the other partner (4, p. 6).

It is suspected that instances of murder of children by their parents involve a similar dynamic. At any rate, in order to adapt to the system the child will deny, repress, distort, or project as much as he has to; the resulting symptoms, however, are by-products of the imperious, compelling importance of family dependence. The psychoanalytic investigator, Weigert, has expressed this idea in a similar vein:

> The child needs, before all, the constancy of being accepted. In his emotional conflicts, he often sacrifices the (for him) inferior value of pleasure gain or pain avoidance for the (for him) high value of object constancy and ego identity. . . . Man in his existential anxiety has to make conscious decisions between being and nothingness, between his responsbility for personal self-preservation and his loyalty to family and larger units of solidarity (38, pp. 226-236).

---

* The tone of this paper thus far might suggest that psychopathology is the inevitable fate of family process, and that the family is a closed system. Certainly, wider social factors influence family dynamics. Assuredly, too, the positive aspects of family living, although also not under discussion in this paper, are many indeed; families provide the safest emotional refuge from outside stress. Moreover, fortuitous life circumstances over the course of an individual's or family's life can have more salutary effects than the changes brought about by formal therapy.

One wonders whether any child can self-actualize without having to depend on parental figures for acceptance. Weigert addresses herself to that extremely rare instance when:

> The child loves himself not only when he feels loved by his family; in growing independence he loves himself in spite of rejection by others. But such firmness of self-esteem is hard to reach, because of the power of human interdependence and solidarity (38, p. 231).

Though most psychological symptoms are painful and matter much to the person who suffers from them or who has to deal with those who have them, in another sense symptoms are relatively superficial manifestations, by-products, and precipitates of complicated processes arising from the nature of relationship struggles among intimates. Indeed, in a literal sense the word *symptom* means a sign or token which stands for something else. It is difficult to see how those systems of psychotherapy which deal only and directly with symptoms can achieve results without getting involved in the processes which bring them about. Insofar as the *therapy* aspect of the family approach is concerned, symptoms themselves are generally bypassed and are translated into the deeper dynamic relationship occurrences which produced them. The family therapist uses symptoms transactionally, as components of the system, and the symptoms themselves provide the therapeutic leverage for producing change. Ackerman (2) sees the goals of psychotherapy in general as (1) symptom relief, (2) self-realization, and (3) integration of the individual into his group, and he suggests further that the health of the group will determine whether people will get well and stay well. In constructing a theory of treatment involving intrapsychic and family system factors he states:

> Conflict between the minds of family members and conflicts within the mind of any one member stand in reciprocal relation to one another. The two levels constitute a circular feedback system. Interpersonal conflict affects intrapsychic conflict, and vice versa. Generally speaking, interpersonal conflict in the family group precedes the establishment of fixed patterns of intrapsychic conflict. Psychopathic distortion and symptom formation are late products of the processes of internalization of persistent and pathogenic forms of family conflict. Potentially, these disturbances are reversible if the intrapsychic and symptom-producing conflict can once more be externalized, that is to say, can be reprojected into the field of family interaction where a new solution can be found (2, pp. 75-76).

Once one has had the experience of treating families and being part of the process of emotional face-to-face encounters and reciprocal influences on each other's experience and behavior, it is almost impossible to go back to the old way of describing psychopathology in such standard individual terms as "strong sadistic impulses," "oral-passive needs," "inappropriate affect," "unrealistic ideas," "poor judgment," "withdrawn," and so forth. These stereotyped statements, seen in every psychiatric or psychological report, have little meaning without knowledge of their place in the matrix in which they are displayed. It is necessary to specify when these characteristics are expressed, toward whom, under what conditions, and the part they play in a given relationship system.

The behavioral sciences, in research as well as in clinical practice, are caught up in a anachronism by operating from the assumption that people have fixed personality characteristics which endure over time regardless of the situation or the relationships involved. Of course, there *are* durable personality traits, and behavioral scientists *know* that situational contexts may drastically alter experience and behavior, but in research practice the major effort is aimed at eliminating and controlling for the variability of human response rather than an analysis of the contexts which give shape and meaning to the behavior. The trend toward fractionation is seen in the fact that entire professional organizations and journals are devoted to the study of single, particular symptoms. (One recent publication on learning disabilities lists 250 different kinds of learning disorders.) Without devaluing the contributions of dedicated scientists and practitioners who devote their professional lives to the study of particular symptoms, contextual analysis, nontheless, is likely to have many more scientific and therapeutic payoffs.

The isolating, individual point of view has consequences in fields outside the behavioral sciences. The law, for example, judges behavior only as a function of the properties and responsibility of the individual, even though this legal ethos is tempered by defense efforts to show the situational and extenuating circumstances under which a crime was committed. Despite the movement of the helping professions toward social factors, clinical practice is still overwhelmingly oriented toward the principle that there is an individual patient with a focal disorder. The alternative being offered here is that most people's problems stem from the difficulties arising from the familiar social systems in which they presently live, and that when there is family distress the symptoms may appear in any form, in any member, as a function of what is going on in that system. The symptoms of one or more family members may involve many community agencies and members of the helping professions, *each dealing with a limited sector of the family process, leaving the system untouched.* A marital difficulty, for instance, may spill over into the children, presenting problems in school or in the community, may involve the police or juvenile court, family social service agencies, psychiatric intervention, visiting nurses, Alcoholics Anonymous, religious organizations, institutions for the aged involving grandparents, medical hospitals, and so forth. Because of lack of awareness of the total family situation there is inefficient duplication of services, and sometimes the various agencies serving the family are working at cross-purposes. One family that came to our attention was simultaneously involved with 18 agencies. The psychiatrist who does a consultation, the clinical psychologist who administers tests, the social worker who sees a relative, none of them is in a position to understand the meaning of the presenting symptoms he is called upon to diagnose or treat.

It is for these reasons that it is recommended that intake family diagnostic interviews be done on a routine basis, no matter what the symptoms are of any member of the family. This is not to say that everyone should do family therapy or that there is no place for other forms of psychotherapy; indeed, not all families can make use of conjoint therapy, although most families can profit from short-term family therapy when they are in the midst of an acute crisis. (One practical consequence of great import is the promising finding of a crisis unit in Colorado (28) that family therapy can keep most patients out of mental hospitals.) Rather, it is believed that clinical practitioners, when they observe the family interacting with each other, can make superior diagnostic appraisals of what is really going on and will see symptoms in an entirely new perspective. These insights will be of great value even if the professional continues to evaluate or treat only on an individual basis.

The family approach lends itself, furthermore, as a central integrative process for the entire scope of clinical services of a community mental health center, with referrals being made to the various services on the basis of diagnostic family interviews. Because psychiatrists, clinical psychologists, and social workers have not had the kind of training which equips them to view psychopathology transactionally, one of the first undertakings should be modification of training programs along the lines espoused in this paper. The family approach offers a meaningful supplanter to the medical model which, while supported financially and emotionally as a vested interest, is proving increasingly inappropriate for these times of sweeping cultural change.

There is much resistance to the family approach and many professionals have developed scotomata when it comes to the family. Perhaps this state of affairs results from attitudes about the sanctity of the family which most cultures have; another factor is the charged, emotional aspects of family life, which family therapists themselves feel when their own past or present family life is moved by the treated family's transactions (17).

In conclusion, Dicks has said:

> It is my contention that the treatment of individuals "in vacuo" by whatever method of in-patient or out-patient handling, is an obsolescent concept. Unless we are dealing with an isolate, the meaningful unit of therapeutic action is the presenting individual's primary group: parents and siblings, spouse and children, sometimes also the work group. If this be granted, then the approach to diagnosis and therapy in large areas of psychiatry demands appropriate new techniques for analyzing such interpersonal networks which all attending psychiatrists and psychotherapists (including analysts) should possess. I will go so far as to assert that they do not know what opportunities for rapid insight and critically decisive help they are missing daily in their work by not having this conceptual and operational equipment (11, p. 325).

Acknowledgment—Appreciation is expressed to Dr. Ivan Boszormenyi-Nagy for reading the manuscript and offering suggestions. Most of the family therapy observations discussed in this paper evolved from work done at the Division of Family Psychiatry of the Eastern Pennsylvania Psychiatric Institute, directed by Dr. Boszormenyi-Nagy.

REFERENCES

1. ACKERMAN, N. W., & BEHRENS, M. L. A Study of Family Diagnosis. *Amer. J. Orthopsychiat.*, 26:66, 1956.
2. ACKERMAN, N. W. *Treating the Troubled Family*, New York: Basic Books, 1966.
3. ACKERMAN, N. W., BOSZORMENYI-NAGY, I., BRODEY, W. M., & GIOSCIA, V. J. The Classification of Family Types: A Panel Discussion. In N. W. Ackerman, F. L. Beatman, and S. N. Sherman (Eds.), *Expanding Theory and Practice in Family Therapy*. New York: Family Service Association of America, 1967.
4. BACH, G. R. *Intimate Violence, Understanding and Prevention.* Unpublished manuscript, 1967.
5. BACH, G. R., & WYDEN, P. *The Intimate Enemy*. New York: Morrow, 1969.
6. BOSZORMENYI-NAGY, I. A Theory of Relationships: Experience and Transaction. In I. Boszormenyi-Nagy and J. L. Framo (Eds.), *Intensive Family Therapy*. New York: Hoeber, 1965.
7. BOWEN, M. Family Psychotherapy with Schizophrenia in the Hospital and in Private Practice. In I. Boszormenyi-Nagy and J. L. Framo (Eds.), *Intensive Family Therapy*. New York: Hoeber, 1965.
8. BOWEN, M. The Use of Family Therapy in Clinical Practice. *Comp. Psychiat.*, 7:345, 1966.
9. BRODEY, W. M. Some Family Operations and Schizophrenia. *Arch. Gen. Psychiat.*, 1:379, 1959.
10. CLAUSEN, J. A. The Marital Relationship Antecedent to Hospitalization of a Spouse for Mental Illness. *World Congress of Sociology IV, Stresa*, 1959.

11. DICKS, H. V. *Marital Tensions*. New York: Basic Books, 1967.

12. EHRENWALD, J. Family Diagnosis and Mechanisms of Defense. *Family Process*, 2:121, 1963.

13. FAIRBAIRN, W. R. D. *An Object-Relations Theory of the Personality*. New York Basic Books, 1952.

14. FALLDING, H. The Family and the Idea of a Cardinal Role. In G. Handel (Ed.), *The Psychosocial Interior of the Family*. Chicago: Aldine, 1967.

15. FRAMO, J. L. Rationale and Techniques of Intensive Family Therapy. In I. Boszormenyi-Nagy and J. L. Framo (Eds.), *Intensive Family Therapy*. New York: Hoeber, 1965.

16. FRAMO, J. L. Conceptual Issues and Clinical Implications of Family Therapy. Discussions of a Theoretical Position for Family Group Therapy, by John Bell. In *Creative Developments in Psychotherapy*. Cleveland: Western Reserve Univ. Press. In press.

17. FRAMO, J. L. My Families, My Family. *Voices*, 4:18, 1968.

18. FREEMAN, H. E., & SIMMONS, O. G. *The Mental Patient Comes Home*. New York: Wiley, 1963.

19. GRUNEBAUM, H. V., & BRYANT, C. M. The Theory and Practice of the Family Diagnostic. *Psychiat. Research. Rep. Amer. Psychiat. Assn.*, 20:140, 1966.

20. HUXLEY, A. *Genius and the Goddess*. New York: Harper, 1955.

21. LAING, R. D. *The Self and Others*. Chicago: Quadrangle Books, 1962.

22. LEVENSON, E. A., STOCKHAMER, N., & FEINER, A. H. Family Transactions in the Etiology of Dropping Out of College. *Contemp. Psychoanal.*, 2:134, 1967.

23. LORENZ, K. *On Aggression*. New York: Harcourt, 1966.

24. LUBORSKY, L., & SCHIMEK, J. Psychoanalytic Theories of Therapeutic and Developmental Change: Implications for Assessment. In P. Worchel and D. Byrne (Eds.), *Personality Change*. New York: Wiley, 1964.

25. MINUCHIN, S., MONTALVO, B., GUERNEY, B. G., ROSMAN, B. L., & SCHUMER, F. *Families of the Slums*. New York: Basic Books, 1967.

26. OTTO, H. A., Criteria for Assessing Family Strength. *Family Process*, 2:329, 1963.

27. PAVENSTEDT, E. A Comparison of the Child-rearing Environment of Upper-Lower and Very Low Lower-class Families. *Amer. J. Orthopsychiat.*, 35:89, 1965.

28. PITTMAN, F. S., LANGLEY, D. G., KAPLAN, D. M., FLOMENHAFT, K., & DEYOUNG, C. Family Therapy as an Alternative to Psychiatric Hospitalization. *Psychiat. Res. Rep. Amer. Psychiat. Assn.*, 20:188, 1966.

29. POLLAK, O. Design of a Model of Healthy Family Relationships as a Basis for Evaluative Research. *Soc. Serv. Rev.*, 31:369, 1957.

30. RAINWATER, L. Crucible of Identity: The Negro Lower-Class Family. In G. Hendel (Ed.), *The Psychosocial Interior of the Family*. Chicago: Aldine, 1967.

31. SAFILIOS-ROTHSCHILD, C. Deviance and Mental Illness in the Greek Family. *Family Process*, 7:100, 1968.

32. SCHEFLEN, A. E. Regressive One-to-One Relationships. *Psychiat. Quart.* 34:692, 1960.

33. SCHMIDEBERG, M. Parents as Children. *Psychiat. Quart.*, 22 (Suppl.):207, 1948.

34. SCHWARTZ, C. G. Perspectives on Deviance—Wives' Definitions of Their Husbands' Mental Illness. *Psychiatry*, 20:275, 1957.

35. SINGER, M. T., & WYNNE, L. C. Thought Disorder and Family Relations of Schizophrenics. *Arch. Gen. Psychiat.*, 12:187, 1965.

36. VOILAND, A. L., & ASSOCIATES. *Family Casework Diagnosis*. New York: Columbia Univ. Press, 1962.

37. WARKENTIN, J., FELDER, R. E., MALONE, T. P., & WHITAKER, C. A. The Usefulness of Craziness. *Medical Times*, June, 1961.

38. WEIGERT, E. V. Narcissism: Benign and Malignant Forms. In R. W. Gibson (Ed.), *Crosscurrents in Psychiatry and Psychoanalysis*. Philadelphia: Lippincott, 1967.

18

INTERDISCIPLINARY VERSUS ECOLOGICAL APPROACH

Edgar H. Auerswald, M.D.

Director, Applied Behavioral Sciences, Jewish Family Service
(New York City)

The explosion of scientific knowledge and technology in the middle third of this century, and the effects of this explosion on the human condition, have posed a number of challenges for the behavioral sciences that most agree are yet to be met. The overriding challenge is, of course, the prevention of nuclear holocaust, but such problems as crime and delinquency, drug addiction, senseless violence, refractive learning problems, destructive prejudice, functional psychosis and the like follow close behind.

Practically all behavioral scientists agree that none of these problems can be solved within the framework of any single discipline. Most espouse a putting together of heads in the so-called "interdisciplinary approach." The notion is not new, of course. The "interdisciplinary team" has been around for some time. Some new notions have emanated from this head-banging, but there have been few startling revelations in the last decade or so.

However, a relatively small but growing group of behavioral scientists, most of whom have spent time in arenas in which the "interdisciplinary approach" is being used, have taken the seemingly radical position that the knowledge of the traditional disciplines as they now exist is rela-

Reprinted from FAMILY PROCESS, Vol. 7, No. 2, Sept. 1968, pp. 202-215.

tively useless in the effort to find answers for these particular problems. Most of this group advocate a realignment of current knowledge and re-examination of human behavior within a unifying holistic model, that of ecological phenomenology. The implications of this departure are great. Once the model of ecology becomes the lattice-work upon which such a realignment of knowledge is hung, it is no longer possible to limit oneself to the behavioral sciences alone. The physical sciences, the biological sciences, in fact, all of science, must be included. Since the people who have been most concerned with constructing a model for a unified science and with the ingredients of the human ecological field have been the general systems theorists, the approach used by behavioral scientists who follow this trend is rapidly acquiring the label of the "systems approach," although a more appropriate label might be the "ecological systems approach."

These terms are currently being used metaphorically to describe a way of thinking and an operational style. They do not describe a well formed theoretical framework as does the term "general systems theory." It is with the former, the way of thinking and the operational style, that I am concerned in this paper.

The two approaches described above differ greatly. Let us examine why the difference is so profound. The ongoing accumulation of knowledge and its application to practice follows a well known sequence. This might be broken down into steps as follows: the collection of information or data, the ordering of that data within a selected framework, analysis of the data, synthesis of the results of analysis into hypotheses, the formulation of strategies and techniques (methodologies) to test the hypotheses, the construction of a delivery plan for use of these strategies and techniques, the implementation of the plan, and the collection of data from the area of implimentation to test its impact, which, of course, repeats the first step, and so on.

The key step in this sequence is the second one, the ordering of data within a selected framework, because it is this step, and this step alone, that gives structure to the rest, all of which are operational. Not only does the nature and outcome of subsequent steps depend on this structuring framework, but so does the prior step, the collection of data. What data among the infinite variety of available natural data are considered important, and are, therefore, collected in any given arena, will depend on the conceptual framework used. It is here that the difference between the two approaches is to be found.

The "interdisciplinary" approach maintains the vantage point of each contributor within his own discipline. While it has expanded the boundaries of the theoretical framework of each discipline to include concepts borrowed from other disciplines, only those concepts which pose no serious challenge or language difficulties are welcomed. More importantly, I think, the interfaces between the conceptual frameworks of different disciplines are ignored, and, as a result, the interfaces between the various arenas of systematic life operations (e.g., biological, psychological, social or individual, family, community) represented by different disciplines are also ignored.

The structural aspects and the clarity of context of the data collected are lost as a result. The precise source, pathway, and integrating functions of messages passing between various operational life arenas in the ecological field cannot be clearly identified. Analysis of such data depends almost entirely on the *content* of these messages, and much distortion can and does take place.

The "systems" approach, on the other hand, changes the vantage point of the data collector. It focuses precisely on the interfaces and communication processes taking place there. It begins with an analysis of the *structure* of the field, using the common structural and operational properties of systems as criteria for identifying the systems and subsystems within it. And by tracing the communications within and between systems, it insists that the structure, sources, pathways, repository sights and integrative functions of messages become clear in addition to their content. In my opinion, this, plus the holistic non-exclusive nature of the approach, minimizes the dangers of excessive selectivity in the collection of data and allows for much more clarity in the contextual contributions to its analysis. And the steps which follow, including prescription and planning of strategies and techniques, gain in clarity and are more likely to be rooted in concrete realities.

There are some very practical advantages that accrue as a result of the above. At the level of *theory*, for example, the ecological systems model, by clarifying and emphasizing the interfaces between systems, allows for the use of a variety of theoretical models which have to do with interactional processes and information exchange. These models form bridges between the conceptual systems of single disciplines. Information theory, crisis theory, game theory, and general communications theory for example, represent some of the bodies of research and knowledge which become useable in an integrated way.

Knowledge that has been accumulating from the study of specific ecological systems, such as the family and small groups, the development of which lagged until recently because the systems did not fit neatly into the bailiwick of any one traditional discipline, can also be included without strain. And the developmental model of the life cycle of the individual man and of various larger human systems as they move through time in the ecological field of their environment assumes meaning in a larger context.

In addition, the use of this model in planning has demonstrated its many implications for the design and operational implementation of delivery systems, especially for community programs (e.g., "comprehensive community health" programs). The ecological systems approach insures that the entire process of planning for a community is rooted in the realities and needs of that community. The organized identification of the ecological systems making up a target community allows for the planned inclusion of information collection stations in each key system and at primary interfaces which provide feedback to the planning arena, thus setting up a servo-system which assures that planning will remain closely related to changing need. Over a period of time, as a picture of a target community emerges from such data, it will emerge as an idiosyncratic template of the structural and operational configurations of that community. It will not, as in the "interdisciplinary" approach, emerge as a predetermined template of the theoretical structure of the dominant discipline.

As a result, program designs constructed in this manner are deeply imbedded in the target community. They will develop as another ecological system among the many, thus greatly clarifying the context in which any program can be integrated into the life of the community as a whole. Furthermore, the delivery organization itself becomes viewed as a system with assigned tasks made up of sub-systems performing sub-tasks including intra-organizational tasks. This allows for more clarity in the selection of staffing patterns, in the definitions of staff role functions, in the construction of communication systems and data collection (record-keeping) systems, and of the assignment of tasks within the organizational structure to staff members best equipped to handle them. Of special import to community programs is the fact that with the clarification of specific tasks to be performed comes the increased possibility of identifying those tasks that can be carried out by staff members or volunteers who need relatively little training.

At the *operational* level the strategies of evolution and change can be more clearly designed. More important, perhaps, use of the ecological systems approach allows for the development of a whole new technology in the production of change. Many techniques have, as a matter of fact, already appeared on the scene, largely within organized movements aimed at integration in its broadest sense, such as the Civil Rights

Movement and the "War On Poverty." Some community organization and community development programs, techniques using economic and political pressure, and techniques which change the rules of the game such as the non-violence movement, all represent a new technology, and all have their relevance to the broadly-defined health needs of socially isolated individuals, families, and groups.

In service programs working with individual people and families this new technology is also emerging, more slowly perhaps. Many new ways of coping with familiar situations are being developed. Techniques of treating families as systems, for example, represent one advance. In particular, an emphasis which stresses the organization of events in time and traces the movement of the developing infant-child-adolescent-adult-aged individuals's degree of participation versus his isolation in relation to his family and to the flow of surrounding community life—such an emphasis makes it possible to determine with much more clarity in what life arenas the individual, the family, or a group of individuals needs assistance, and thus to more effectively combat the anomie and dehumanization characteristic of our age. The result is that the targets of therapeutic activity are much clearer and therapeutic work is more clearly focused on forces and situations that are truly etiological in a given problem situation. Techniques of producing therapeutic change can be brought to arenas much larger than the therapy room or even the home. I think that a single story will serve to illustrate more concretely what I mean.

In the story I wish to tell, two therapists, one a "systems" thinker, the other a member of an "interdisciplinary" team, became involved in the case of a runaway girl.

To give you some initial background, I should explain that I have been involved in designing and implementing a "Neighborhood Health Services System" for provision of comprehensive *biopsychosocial* care to a so-called "disadvantaged" community. The main aim in setting up this unit was to find ways to avoid the fragmentation of service delivery which occurs when a person's problem is defined as belonging primarily to himself, and he is sent to a specialist who is trained to deal primarily with that type of problem. The specialist naturally sees the problem not only as an individual matter, but defines it still further according to the professional sector he inhabits. He is not accustomed to looking at the total set of systems surrounding the individual with the symptom or to noticing the ways in which the symptom, the person, his family, and his community interlock, and he is often in the position of a man desperately trying to replace a fuse when it is the entire community power line that has broken down. Furthermore, the specialist's efforts to solve the problem are apt to be confined to arbitrarily chosen segments of time called "appointments." And finally, there is that unfortunate invention, the written referral, a process of buck-passing that sends many a person in trouble from agency to agency till he finally gives up or breaks down. As a beginning we decided that we would have to pilot some cases in order to gain some experience with the different approach we felt was needed.

At this point, a case providentially dramatizing the points we had in mind fell into our hands. (We have since found that almost every case that falls into our hands providentially dramaties these points.) One of our psychiatrists was wandering about the neighborhood one day in order to become better acquainted with it and to explore what sort of crises and problems our neighborhood program must be prepared to serve beyond those we already anticipated. I should say here that this psychiatrist,[1] by virtue of several years of pioneering work with families, including the experimental use of game theory and games in diagnosing and treating them, was particularly well qualified to handle the situation I will describe. His explorations that day had brought him to the local police station, and while he was talking to the desk sergeant, a Puerto Rican woman arrived to report that her twelve-year-old daughter, Maria, had run away from home. This was apparently not the first time. She described the child to the police, who alerted their patrols to look for her and assigned two men to investigate the neighborhood. Our psychiatrist, whom I will refer to from now on as our "explorer," was intrigued and decided to follow up the situation himself.

He first identified himself to the mother as she left the police station and asked if she would be willing to allow him to help her with her current difficulty. She agreed. He learned that she lived a few blocks away with her now absent daughter and another daughter, aged 14. Her own parents lived nearby, and she had a paramour who also lived in the neighborhood. The father of her two children had long since deserted his family, and she was uncertain as to his whereabouts. The exploring psychiatrist learned also that the runaway girl had been seeing a psychotherapist at the mental health clinic of a local settlement house. In addition, he ascertained the location of her school.

He then decided that his behavior might appear unethical to the child's therapist, so he proceeded to the mental health clinic, a clinic which prided itself on the use of the "interdisciplinary" team approach.

---

[1] Dr. Robert Ravich. I am indebted to Dr. Ravich for the case material reported.

The original therapist turned out to be a social worker of considerable accomplishment and experience, who agreed to cooperate with him in his investigation after he explained what he was up to and that he had the mother's permission. He read the child's case record and discussed the girl with the therapist at some length. He learned that at a recent team case conference, the diagnosis which was originally assigned to the girl, that of childhood schizophrenia, was confirmed. The team also decided that in the light of repeated episodes of running away from home, her behavior was creating sufficient danger to indicate that she be placed in a situation where that danger would be alleviated while her therapy continued. For a twelve-year-old Puerto Rican girl in New York City, especially one carrying a label of schizophrenia, this almost always means hospitalization in the children's ward of a state hospital. Accordingly, the arrangement for her admission to the state hospital covering the district had been made and was due to be implemented within a few days.

The next stop of our explorer was the school, where Maria's teacher described her as a slow but steady learner, detached from most other children in the class, vague and strange, but somehow likeable. The guidance counselor reported an incident in which she had been discovered masturbating an older boy under the school auditorium stairs. This behavior had led the school authorities to contemplate suspending her, but since they knew her to be in treatment they decided to hold off, temporarily, at least.

The exploring psychiatrist also learned at the school that Maria was involved in an after-school group program at the settlement house. He returned there and got from the group worker a much more positive impression of the girl than he had previously encountered. She participated with seeming enthusiasm in the projects of the group and got along very well with the other children. The group worker, by way of providing evidence that Maria had much potential, showed the therapist a lovely and poignant poem she had contributed to a newspaper put out by the group. It was never ascertained whether the girl had written or copied the poem. She had, nevertheless, produced it, and there was general agreement that its theme of isolation was one which was expressive of her.

Back at Maria's home, our explorer talked to Maria's sister, who at first grudgingly, but then with some relish, admitted that she knew where the girl had gone during her previous runaway episodes. She was the sometime mascot of a group of teenage boys with whom she occasionally traveled for two or three days at a time. The sister did not know where she went or what she did during the junkets, but she suspected that sex was somehow involved. She also volunteered the information that neither she nor her mother had ever found it easy to communicate with her sister, and that if the therapist really wanted to talk to someone who knew her, he should talk to her grandfather. So off to the grandparents' apartment he went.

The grandmother turned out to be a tight-lipped, highly religious Pentecostalist who was at first unwilling to say much at all about the girl.

The grandfather, however, was a different kettle of fish. Earthly, ebullient, jocular, bright, though uneducated, his love for Maria was immediately apparent. He spoke of her warmly, and bemoaned the lack of understanding that existed in her home. Remembering a passing reference in the case record at the mental health clinic to a suspicion that the grandfather may have engaged in seductive play with the girl, if not open sexual activity, our explorer raised the issue of the girl's emerging adolescent sexuality. This brought an outburst from the hitherto silent grandmother than confirmed the mutually seductive quality of the grandfather's relationship with the girl, followed by a return blast from the grandfather who revealed that his wife had refused to sleep with him for several years. He readily admitted his frustrated sexuality and the fact that he was at times aroused by his budding granddaughter.

I have presented only a sparse picture of the rich amount of information collected by our explorer up to this point. In a continuous five hour effort, without seeing the absent Maria, he was able to construct a picture of her as a child who had grown up in relative isolation in a home where she received little support and guidance. Communication between herself and her mother had become more and more sparse over the years, most likely because of efforts of her older sister to maintain her favored position in the home. She had turned to her grandfather, who, feeling frustrated and himself isolated in his own marriage, brought his sexually-tinged warmth willingly into a relationship of mutual affection with her. Furthermore, it seemed clear that with someone like the group worker who liked her and who, because the group was small, could spend time with her, Maria could respond with warmth and exhibit an intelligence that otherwise remained hidden. But, and this was, of course, speculative, the tools she perceived as useful in her search for a response from others would most likely be limited to infantile techniques of manipulation developed in early years prior to the need for verbal communication or, based on the relationship with the grandfather, some form of seduction where the currency of acceptance was sex. And, at the age of puberty, having been shut out of the female world of her mother and sister, she was using this currency full blast in the world of boys.

The next day our explorer talked again to the mother, who told him that the girl had been found by the police on the street and had been hospitalized at a large city hospital on the adolescent psychiatric ward. Before visiting her, he briefly questioned the mother about her paramour. It turned out that the subject of marriage had come up between the two of them, but because he earned a limited income, both he and the mother had decided against living together or getting married. Either action would result in loss of the support the mother was receiving from the Department of Welfare for herself and her two children.

All that had been predicted the day before was corroborated when our explorer visited the girl in the hospital. Her behavior with him, and, as it turned out with the resident physician on the ward, alternated between childish manipulation and seductive behavior of a degree which appeared bizarre in a 12-year-old. But she was, at the same time, a lithely attractive girl with a lively wit which blossomed once she felt understood. She was ambivalent about the alternatives of going home or of going to a state hospital, mildly resisting both.

Our exploring psychiatrist then returned to the mental health clinic to discuss what he had observed with the child's therapist and the consulting psychiatrist. He suggested a plan of action as an alternative to hospitalization. By targeting on key issues in various systems surrounding this child, it seemed theoretically plausible that the conditions which held her fixed in a pattern of behavior that had been labeled as sick and crazy might be changed, thus freeing her to accept new coping patterns which she could be helped to learn. An effort to re-establish communication between the child and her mother, who had shown with her other daughter that she could raise a child with relative success, would be one step. It might not be feasible to work with the grandparents' unsatisfactory marriage, but an explanation to the grandfather, who had already tentatively understood his contribution to the girl's dilemma, might be useful. If the Department of Welfare were willing, and if the boyfriend's income could be enhanced by at least a little supplementary public assistance, the mother and her boyfriend might be induced to marry. Teacher and guidance counselor could be helped to understand the girl's behavior more fully and might cooperate on a plan for helping the girl learn new ways of relating in school. The group worker's investment in the girl could be used to a good effect in this joint effort to help her grow. And the original therapist, instead of concerning herself with defense systems and repressed conflict could concentrate on helping the family provide the maximum of support and guidance possible, or, if she wished, could still work with the girl herself. With these suggestions, our exploring psychiatrist bowed out.

A month later, a follow-up visit to the mother revealed that the girl had been sent to state hospital on the recommendation of the resident on the adolescent ward who agreed with the diagnosis and felt that, since she was "a schizophrenic," she should be in a hospital. No one had made any counter-move and contact between all of the helping people except the state hospital doctor and the girl's family had been terminated. This outcome had occurred *despite the fact that the mother and her boyfriend had, after a conversation stimulated by our therapist-explorer, presented themselves at the mental health clinic and expressed their willingness to marry if it seemed wise, their wish to have Maria come home, and their hope that someone at the clinic would help them learn what they must now do for her as parents.*

I have, I realized, presented an unusual situation. Reasonable question could be raised, I suppose, as to how often this sequence could occur. And my own bias is obvious in the manner of my presentation. But I think the case illustrates the radical difference between the two approaches under discussion. The approach of the therapist from the interdisciplinary clinic and that of our exploring psychiatrist are not merely two points on a continuum of techniques. The "ecological systems" approach literally changed the name of the game. By focusing on the nature of the transactions taking place between Maria and the identifiable systems that influenced her growth, it was possible for the "systems" psychiatrist to ascertain what strengths, lacks, and distortions existed at each interface. Two things happened when this was done.

The first was that Maria's behavior began to make sense as a healthy adaptation to a set of circumstances that did not allow her to develop more socially acceptable or better differentiated means of seeking a response to her needs as a developing child. Thus, the aura of pathology was immediately left behind.

The second was that the identification of lacks and distortions in the transactional arena of each interface automatically suggested what needed to be added or changed. Thus the tasks of the helping person were automatically defined. Rigidity of technique in accomplishing these tasks could not, under those circumstances, survive. Flexibility, ingenuity, and innovation were demanded.

The implications of what can happen if this approach is used universally are obvious. If proper data is kept, it seems inevitable that new clusters of data will occur to add to our knowledge, and a new technology of prevention and change develop.

The case of Maria has a certain uniqueness that separates it from most similar cases across our country. The uniqueness is not to be found in the "interdisciplinary" approach used, but rather in the quantity of skilled people who were trying to help her. Despite their dedicated efforts, all they managed to accomplish was Maria's removal from the only system that could be considered generic in terms of her growth and socialization—her family—and her removal from the school and community which should provide the additional experience she needed if she were to become a participant in the life of her society. In addition, they succeeded in stamping a label on the official records of her existence, a label which is a battleground of controversy among diagnosticians, but which means simply to the lay public that she is a nut.

By chance, Maria wound up in a mental hygiene clinic where her behavior was labeled as sick. She might just as easily have joined the many girls showing similar behavior who wind up in court and are labeled delinquent. Either label puts her in a category over which various members of "interdisciplinary" teams are in continued conflict. The needs of the girl, which are not clearly apparent, in either arena, become hopelessly obscured. Decisions made by those charged with the task of helping her are likely to be made without cognizance of those needs, since they depend for their outcome too often on the institutionalized procedures and momentary exigencies in the caring organization or person.

As a final point, let me explore the nature of the communications breakdown that occurred between the two therapists.

In his explorations, our "systems" therapist collected a good deal of data that was not known to the "interdisciplinary" therapist and team in order to insure that he understood the operations that had been going on at each interface in which he was interested. This additional data only supplemented the data previously collected and agreed with it in content. Thus the two agreed substantially as long as they confined their communications to content and to inferred construction of the internal psychodynamics of the persons involved, Maria and the individual members of her family. And, as it happened, this was all they discussed until the exploring "systems" psychiatrist returned for a final chat. At that time, having ordered his data in such a way as to clarify the transactions which had been taking place at the interfaces between Maria and the various systems contributing to her growth, his suggestions flowed from a plan designed to affect those interfaces. The "interdisciplinary" team, including the original therapist, had not ordered the data in this way. Since the dominant disciplinary framework used in their arena was psychiatric, they had ordered the data around a nosological scheme for labeling illness. The outcome of their plan of action, therefore, was to apply a label signifying the nature of Maria's illness, and to decide, reasonably enough within this framework, that since treatment of her illness on an outpatient basis had not been successful, the next step was hospitalization, a decision backed by the assumption that her runaways were dangerous.

It was literally impossible, at the final meeting, for the suggestions of our "systems" therapist to have meaning to the "interdisciplinary" team. They fell on ears made deaf by a way of thinking which could not perceive them as meaningful. They came across as a dissonance which had to be screened out. Communication between the two approaches thus broke down completely.

This instance of breakdown is characteristic of efforts of communication between people from the two arenas. Conversations I have had with a variety of people who take the ecological systems view, backed by my own experience, seem to add up to the following:

There seems to be no serious problem of communication between the systems thinker who emphasizes structure and the experimental behavioral scientist who does basic research in his laboratory or even the researcher who is attempting to deal with a wide range of natural data. Such researchers have selected and defined the structure of the theoretical framework in which they wish to work and are the first to admit that the outcome of their research carries the label of validity within that framework alone.

The clinical scientist, whose emphasis is more on the content of his data, is for the most part a different animal. Most clinical theorists, planners, and practitioners, regardless of discipline, seem caught in the highly specialized sequence of their own training and intradisciplinary experience, upon which they seem to depend for the very definition of their personal identity. Generally speaking, a situation seems to exist in which the integration of the cognitive apparatus of the clinician is such as to exclude as a piece of relevant data the notion that his intradisciplinary "truths," which he carries to the interdisciplinary arena, are relative. He most often will hear and understand the notion when it is expressed. But, again speaking generally, he treats it as unimportant to his operations, as peripheral to the body of knowledge he invests with meaning. Why should this be?

I think it is because the clinician is a product of the specialized fragmentation of today's world of science. To him, admission of this fact would mean that he would have to rearrange his cognitive style, his professional way of life, and, all too often, his total life style as well, if he were to maintain a sense of his own integrity. Not only would he have to renounce his idols, but he would have to go through a turbulent period of disintegration and reintegration. He would have to be willing and able to tolerate the fragmentation of identity boundaries such a transition entails. He would have to leave the safety of seeming truths, truths he has used to maintain his sense of being in the right, his self-esteem, his sense of values, and his status in the vertical hierarchies of his society. He would have to give up the games he plays to maintain his hard-won position in his discipline, games such as those which consist of labeling persons from other schools of thought as bright but limited, misguided, or insufficiently analyzed. More often than not, he would rather fight than switch.

I imply, of course, that he should switch. Thus the question must reasonably be asked: Why should he? Why should he attempt such a fundamental change? After all, he can point with pride to the many accomplishments and successes of his discipline and his own work within it.

But to rest on his laurels, in my opinion, is to abdicate responsibility. It is like crowing over the 70% or so juvenile delinquents who become law-abiding citizens and, ignoring the 30% who do not. The major responsibility of today's behavioral scientist is to those who don't or won't make it, not those who do, to Maria, not to Little Hans, whom he already knows how to help.

The least he can do is examine his labels and how he uses them. In the life-space of Maria's world, there is a serious question as to which system deserves the prefix, *schizo*.

19

THERAPEUTICALLY INDUCED
FAMILY CRISIS

Salvador Minuchin, M.D.
Director, Philadelphia Child Guidance Clinic

and

Avner Barcai, M.D.

The Chinese character for "crisis" is said to combine the character symbolizing "danger" with that symbolizing "opportunity." The components of crisis are a dangerous situation and the opportunity of resolving it.

Crisis theory which, as conceptualized by Lindeman (1) and elaborated by Caplan (2) has become an integral part of many psychiatric interventions, seems to dovetail very neatly with the economic Chinese concept. Crisis is defined as a situation which presents elements so radically different from the ordinary (hence, danger) that the individual (or system) is forced to change in order to cope with the crisis situation. Therefore, inherent in crisis is the opportunity for change.

Crisis in this sense must be differentiated from emergency. An emergency may require the mobilization of resources to an unusual extent, but it does not require change. Unlike a crisis, an emergency can be coped with by the use of established methods and resources, though these may differ greatly in degree, according to the nature of the situation.

Because crisis requires change, at least temporarily, a period of crisis

Reprinted from SCIENCE AND PSYCHOANALYSIS, Volume XIV, 1969, J. Masserman, Editor. Reprinted by permission of Grune & Stratton, Inc.

may be an optimum time for establishing the foundation of permanent therapeutically indicated change.

We believe that therapeutic change cannot occur unless some pre-existing frames of reference are modified, flexibility introduced and new ways of functioning developed. Permanent change, however, cannot usually result from a radical departure from the old system. Successful permanent resolution of dilemmas depends on successful negotiation between the old patterns and news ways of responding. Only by mediation and the development of some continuity between the old and the new can permanent change be established.

We see the family as a system. In Grinker's description (3) "Each system maintains its organization or wholeness by regulatory devices which are homeostatic or equilibratory by goal-seeking, for example, drive-reducing activity. In addition, goal-changing activities such as exploratory behavior are actualizations in response to external conditions impinging on the system's potentialities and which result in novel reactions as in evolution and creativity" (p. 33).

As family therapists, we frequently induce and capitalize upon crisis induction (4). We are continually causing upheavals by intervening in ways that will produce unstable situations which require change and the restructuring of family organization.

The family therapist operating as a change-agent is not in the position of the "cool" professional, aiding a system from outside. By his intervention he forcibly enters a system, becoming a participant member, thus inducing change from within. Therefore, he must be prepared as a member of the system, to arbitrate the family's negotiation of permanent change. The system becomes unstable temporarily at least, as a result of his intervention, so it behooves him to remain available as an interim regulator, supporting the system from within while preparing it for a more autonomous existence.

The following is an example of an intensive use of crisis induction which indicates how much we usually depend on this method of triggering change in therapy. In this case change had to be radical and dramatic because one of the members of this family was responding to psychosomatic stress with potentially fatal bouts of diabetic acidosis. By transforming this medical emergency into an emotional crisis situation, we were able to create rapid therapeutic change.

Julie, aged 12, had been hospitalized seven times within the last 6 weeks with diabetic acidosis and impending coma. The hospital described her condition as labile, incorrigible diabetes, which could not be controlled medically.

Julie is a white, upper middle class child, living with her parents and her siblings, Carol, aged 16 and Tom, 14. Julie had been seen by a psychiatrist, who labeled her a very sensitive child, possessing no coping mechanisms. The rest of the famly was then described as well and healthy, the family's problem being Julie's poor adaptability to life.

Julie's repeated attacks of diabetes had caused a crisis for the medical staff, and this crisis sparked change in the pediatricians; they called in psychiatrists to help them with a medical situation they could not control by ordinary means. But for Julie's family, this was not yet crisis. For them, Julie's attacks were emergencies. Sometime in the morning or afternoon she would begin to get sick; sugar and acetone levels in the urine would increase. The family would call the pediatrician, who would recommend more insulin. The insulin would fail to work. A few hours later the symptoms of acidosis would be unmistakable. Julie would be seen to be dehydrated and hospitalization would be required. At this point, the issue before the family would be, who will drive Julie to the hospital? Whose daily routine will be interfered with? This practical problem would usually be taken care of mechanically. Whoever was around (usually father or mother) would deliver her into the trusted and capable care of the physicians. They would stay to see that she was started on intravenous fluids, politely ask the physicians when they should return for her, and disappear from the picture.

The psychiatrists were thus in a position of having to respond to the pediatricians' crisis by dealing with a family facing repeated emergencies. It became obvious even before we saw the family that the success or failure of therapy would depend upon their ability to make our intervention an experimental crisis for the family, not just another emergency connected with Julie's illness.

In the initial interview, the family was seen by two psychiatrists in a 3-hour session. The therapists began with an open reformulation of the problem. Julie's illness was not the problem, but only an indication that something was wrong with the family. It would be the task of these seven people to unravel whatever was wrong and find ways of changing it. Thus before gathering any detailed knowledge of the family or establishing a relationship with the family or any of its members, the therapists defined the goal of treatment as a restructuring of the family's organization. The path to induction of crisis was opened.

At this first interview, the family looked like a friendly and attractive unit. They seemed to be in good health, well dressed, pleasant, even jovial. The exception was Julie who was thin, awkward and glum.

We were strongly impressed by the bantering, jovial mood of the family. It seemed inappropriate in the light of the presenting problem, a potentially fatal illness, though we realized that the family's repeated success in saving Julie from impending coma had probably lessened their realization of the seriousness of the situation. But it soon became obvious that the bantering and enmeshment of the family's structure were defensive operations deflecting the need to deal with conflicts. The family was unable to focus on any issue or resolve any conflict. If a topic was broached by the mother, it would be echoed by father, Carol would pick it up, Tom would interfere, Julie would try to join, father would interrupt, noise, confusion and laughter would increase, and finally the topic would be lost sight of. An angry interchange might occur, but soon another topic would be brought up and the cycle repeated. Nobody could keep hold of an issue long enough for meaningful discussion to occur. It was impossible for two people to discuss an issue without being interrupted. Dyadic interaction or dialogue was almost nonexistent.

Constant in this process was the exclusion of Julie. If she tried to participate, someone would interrupt. She was cut off and detached from the rest of the family. During the session she became more and more gloomy and sulky. Later on, her sulkiness was used by the family as a device in order to shift from one issue to another.

Another family problem which became obvious in the first interview was the weakness of intergenerational boundaries. Carol and Tom acted as ancillary parents. The father and mother were seen to explain themselves to the children, and to follow their instructions. Any parental conflicts were picked up by Carol and Tom, who took over the discussion and excluded their parents until they felt it was safe to readmit them.

Because of the serious nature of Julie's illness the therapeutic team consisted of pediatricians* and psychiatrists. The psychotherapeutic team, when necessary, would meet with the pediatricians and family around Julie's hospital bed. The pediatricians and nurses would watch the psychotherapeutic sessions from behind the one-way mirror. The danger of Julie's situation and the likelihood that by producing turmoil in the family we would, for a while, be increasing the frequency of her diabetic decompensation, made it imperative for us to remain in close contact with the medical team. But, at the same time it was vital to force the family to redefine the nature of the problem facing them. The crux of the matter was the factors in the family which were causing Julie to decompensate. Therefore, in the psychotherapeutic sessions, we would deal only with the family's handling of interpersonal relationships.

To fight the diffusion of conflict and the weakness of intergenerational boundaries, the family was assigned two tasks. First, they were to make room for dyadic units within the family. If two people were involved in a conflict situation, the others were not to butt in. Secondly, the parents were given the responsibility of not letting the children interfere in their arguments.

As a result, of the family's attempt to comply with their tasks, the subgroupings of the family emerged more sharply. The mother and the two older children formed a contained central unit. The

* The pediatric team was composed of Drs. Lester Baker and Robert Kaye.

father and Julie were outsiders, Julie because of her illness, the father because he was assigned the role of family disciplinarian. When Julie tried to enter the central system, she was ignored; when the father tried, the others made a pretense of listening to him, but refused to allow him to participate meaningfully.

As a result of the assigned task, areas of conflict, particularly the father's peripherality, which had been diffused for years by these mutually regulatory maneuvers, came sharply into focus. A circular feedback between the wife's control and the husband's dependency had continued for years. The wife's fear of being alone or of being abandoned led her to maneuvers which were strongly controlling of her husband. She insisted that he call her often during the day and, because she was afraid he would drink heavily, that he be home by 6:15 every evening. Her husband dutifully called home twice a day and arrived home at 6:15, but he would make a point of telling her that he had taken two cocktails before getting there. This would start a typical family escalation. The parents would argue, Carol and Tom would join in, alternately blaming the mother and the father, until finally the situation would dissolve into another issue without resolution.

In a family session, this relationship was redefined. In the presence of the family, the husband was assigned the task of coming home later than his wife expected. He chose to do so one Friday, when the spouse had planned a weekend trip. This caused a quarrel which reached such proportions that the normally quiet, gentle wife attacked her husband with a pair of scissors. At 8:30 that evening a terrified Julie called one of the therapists, crying that her parents were killing each other. Shortly thereafter, the therapists and the family met in the home of one of the therapists.

At this interview, which lasted until one o'clock Saturday morning, parental conflicts which for years had been detoured by the intervention of the children were opened and debated without interference. The possibility of real negotiation became available to the spouses. At 1 A.M., they left for their weekend trip without the children. The next morning Julie had to be hospitalized.

Now, this particular attack of acidosis was Julie's reaction to the events of the session. The parents had reached the possibility of negotiating their own conflicts without the children's intervention. This was such a radical change from the family's accustomed ways of operating that the children were at a loss. Julie's requiring hospitalization was an attempt to restore the old patterns, bringing the family together.

But these patterns, because of the crisis-inducing intervention of the therapists in the family system, were changing; so were Julie's patterns of hospitalization. During the next 6 or 7 weeks, Julie regularly suffered attacks of acidosis which required hospitalization within 12 hours before or after a family session.

While family sessions continued, one of the therapists started seeing Julie in individual sessions, to explore her place in her ecological systems. These sessions dealt with the problems of her individuation in her family, organized as it was into coalitions she could not join, explorations of her coping, her effectiveness and the ways she could take a different part in the family interactions.

Meanwhile, the second therapist worked with the parents. He prescribed a new task. The parents were to deal with Julie only in positives for a specific period of time. This was extremely difficult for them to do, but they tried and their attempts unbalanced the old family system completely, intensifying crisis.

The tendency in a system is to preserve accustomed patterns, and now Carol and Tom attempted to restore the former homeostasis. Julie's old role, peripheral weak member, was assumed by Carol. She became depressed and unable to cope with school and social affairs. Consequently, family sessions focused for a while on Carol's involvement with and protection of the family. Individual sessions were scheduled with her to explore intrafamilial areas. When Carol began to experiment with age-appropriate adolescent separation from the family, Tom took on the role of weak member. He took the family car and drove it all over without a license, and one night at home he got drunk and vomited all over the furniture.

Although the treatment of this family is still in progress, we feel that there has been great change in all the members of the family in a very short time.

If we take Julie, however, as the indicator of family change, we note that she is now attending school (previously, she had to be tutored at home) and leading a much more normal life. In the last 5 months she has had to be hospitalized for acidosis only twice.

CONCLUSION

We would like to point up some of the interesting aspects of the early intervention with this case. The therapists began work by redefining the problem and delineating therapeutic goals. The family had understood the problem to be Julie's illness. The therapist declared that the problem was the family's interactional patterns; the goal of treatment was to change these patterns.

The therapists deliberately intervened in ways which increased stress and conflict within the family, then directed the family to resolve these conflicts. The family was given homework assignments designed to narrow the transactional field, eliminate static from family communication and increase awareness of conflict areas outside of the sessions. By assigning these tasks the therapists insured the continuity of the treatment process outside of the session.

Great flexibility in the planning of sessions was maintained. Since we conceptualize the family as an ecosystem composed of significant subunits, we often facilitated the exploration of systems of alliances and coalitions and accelerated the process of change by manipulating the format of the sessions.

Sessions were held with the total family, with individuals, with mother and daughters while father and son observed through a oneway mirror, with the spouses, and with other significant subsystems as the need appeared.

The length of the sessions was kept very flexible and we tried to follow the general practitioner model, making ourselves available according to the family's needs. During the first week of contact, for instance, the family was seen three times, in sessions of 3-4 hours. Most dramatic, of course, was the 4½-hour Friday evening session. But, having deliberately caused a crisis by our intervention into the system as ancillary family members and our assignment of tasks which weakened the old methods of intrafamilial regulation, we had to be on hand as interim regulators.

Recently, in the measure that the family has shown increased ability to handle their crises and conflicts by themselves, the length of the sessions has shortened and the interval between them has lengthened. We believe this flexibility in scheduling also facilitated change.

SUMMARY

In this case a family problem which had been seen as the response to emergencies created by the physical illness of one of its members was redefined as pathology in the workings of the family, to which its weakest member was responding. This redefinition and the tasks assigned to change the situation, induced a crisis situation, to which the family members had to respond by changing.

ACKNOWLEDGMENT

The authors acknowledge the assistance of Drs. Lester Baker and Robert Kaye and Mrs. F. Hitchcock in the preparation of this manuscript.

REFERENCES

1. LINDEMANN, E.: Symptomatology and Management of Acute Grief. *Amer. J. Psychiat.*, 101:141-148, 1944.
2. CAPLAN, G.: *Prevention of Emotional Disorders in Children.* New York, Basic Books, 1961.
3. GRINKER, R. R., SR.: Conceptual Progress in Psychoanalysis. In Marmor, J. (Ed.): *Modern Psychoanalysis.* New York, Basic Books, 1968.
4. MINUCHIN, S. ET AL.: *Families of the Slums.* New York, Basic Books, 1967.

20

BEHAVIORAL APPROACHES TO FAMILY AND COUPLE THERAPY

Robert Paul Liberman, M.D.

Assistant Clinical Professor of Psychiatry
School of Medicine, University of California at Los Angeles
Research Psychiatrist and Director, Clinical Research Unit
Camarillo State Hospital and California Department of Mental Hygiene

The current splurge of couple and family therapies is not simply an accident or passing fad. These increasingly used modes of treatment for psychiatric problems are anchored in a sound foundation and are not likely to blow away. The foundation of these newer therapies lies in the opportunity they offer to induce significant behavioral change in the participants by a major restructuring of their interpersonal environments.

Couple and family therapy can be particularly potent means of behavior modification because the interpersonal milieu that undergoes change is that of the day-to-day, face-to-face encounter an individual experiences with the most important people in his life—his spouse or member of his immediate family. When these therapies are successful it is because the therapist is able to guide the members of the couple or family into changing their modes of dealing with each other. In behavioral or learning terms, we can translate "ways of dealing with each other" into consequences of behavior or *contingencies of reinforcement*. Instead of rewarding maladaptive behavior with attention and concern,

Reprinted from AMERICAN JOURNAL OF ORTHOPSYCHIATRY, January 1970, Volume 40, Number 1, pp. 106-118. Copyright 1970 by the American Orthopsychiatric Association, Inc. Reprinted by permission.

the family members can learn to give each other recognition and approval for desired behavior.

Since the family is a system of interlocking, reciprocal behaviors (including affective behavior), family therapy proceeds best when each of the members learns how to change his or her responsiveness to the others. Family therapy should be a learning experience for all the members involved. For simplification, however, this paper will analyze family pathology and therapy from the point of view of the family responding to a single member.

Typically, families that come for treatment have coped with the maladaptive or deviant behavior of one member by responding to it over the years with anger, nagging, babying, conciliation, irritation, or sympathy. These responses, however punishing they might seem on the surface, have the effect of reinforcing the deviance, that is, increasing the frequency or intensity of the deviant behavior in the future. Reinforcement occurs because the attention offered is viewed and felt by the deviant member as positive concern and interest. In many families with a deviant member, there is little social interaction and the individuals tend to lead lives relatively isolated from each other. Because of this overall lack of interaction, when interaction does occur in response to a member's "abnormal" behavior, such behavior is powerfully reinforced (14).

Verbal and nonverbal means of giving attention and recognition can be termed *social reinforcement* (as contrasted with food or sex, which are termed *primary reinforcement*). Social reinforcement represents the most important source of motivation for human behavior (6, 19). Often massive amounts of such "concern" or social reinforcement are communicated to the deviant member, focused and contingent upon the member's maladaptive behavior. The deviant member gets the message: "So long as you continue to produce this undesirable behavior (symptoms), we will be interested and concerned in you." Learning the lesson of such messages leads to the development of maintenance of symptomatic or deviant behavior and to characterological patterns of activity and identity. Sometimes, the message of concern and interest is within the awareness of the "sick" member. Individuals with a conscious awareness of these contingencies are frequently termed "manipulative" by mental health professionals since they are adept at generating social reinforcement for their maladaptive behavior. But learning can occur without an individual's awareness or insight, in which case we view the maladaptive behavior as being unconsciously motivated.

Massive amounts of contingent social reinforcement are not necessary to maintain deviant behavior. Especially after the behavior has developed, occasional or *intermittant reinforcement* will promote very durable continuation of the behavior. Laboratory studies have shown that intermittant reinforcement produces behavior that is most resistant to extinction (6).

Many family therapists (7, 8, 21) have demonstrated that the interest and concern family members show in the deviance of one member can be in the service of their own psychological economy. Maintaining a "sick" person in the family can be gratifying (reinforcing) to others, albeit at some cost in comfort and equanimity. Patterson (15) describes how this reciprocal reinforcement can maintain deviant behavior by using the example of a child who demands an ice cream cone while shopping with his mother in a supermarket. The reinforcer for this "demand behavior" is compliance by the mother, but if she ignores the demand, the effect is to increase the rate or loudness of the demand. Loud demands or shrieks by a child in a supermarket are aversive to the mother; that is, her noncompliance is punished. When the mother finally buys the ice cream cone, the aversive tantrum ends. The reinforcer for the child's tantrum is the ice cream cone. The reinforcing contingency for the mother was the termination of the "scene" in the supermarket. In this reciprocal fashion, the tantrum behavior is maintained. I shall return to this important aspect of family psychopathology—the mutually reinforcing or symbiotic nature of deviance—in the case studies below. Indeed, the balance between the aversive and gratifying consequences of maladaptive behavior in a member on the other family members is the crucial determinant of motivation for and response to treatment.

Changing the contingencies by which the patient gets acknowledgment and concern from other members of his family is the basic principle of learning that underlies the potency of family or couple therapy. Social reinforcement is made contingent on desired, adaptive behavior instead of maladaptive and symptomatic behavior. It is the task of the therapist in collaboration with the family or couple to (1) specify the maladaptive behavior, (2) choose reasonable goals which are alternative, adaptive behaviors, (3) direct and guide the family to change the contingencies of their social reinforcement patterns from maladaptive to adaptive target behaviors.

Another principle of learning involved in the process of successful family therapy is modeling, also called imitation or identification. The model, sometimes the therapist but also other members of the family, exhibits desired, adaptive behavior which then is imitated by the patient.

Imitation or identification occurs when the model is an esteemed person (therapist, admired family member) and when the model receives positive reinforcement (approval) for his behavior from others (3). The amount of observational learning will be governed by the degree to which a family member pays attention to the modeling cues, has the capacity to process and rehearse the cues, and possesses the necessary components in his behavioral experience which can be combined to reproduce the more complex, currently modeled behavior.

Imitative learning enables an individual to short-circuit the tedious and lengthy process of trial-and-error (or reward) learning while incorporating complex chains of behavior into his repertoire. Much of the behaviors which reflect the enduring part of our culture are to a large extent transmitted by repeated observation of behavior displayed by social models, particularly familial models. If performed frequently enough and rewarded in turn with approval by others, the imitated behavior will become incorporated into the patient's behavioral repertoire. The principles of imitative learning have been exploited with clinical success by researchers working with autistic children (12), phobic youngsters (4), and mute, chronic psychotics (18). How modeling can be used in family therapy will be illustrated in the cases cited below.

I will limit the scope of the case examples to couples and families; however, the same principles of learning apply to group therapy (11, 17) and with some modification to individual psychotherapy (9). Although learning theory has been associated in clinical psychiatry with its systematic and explicit application in the new behavior therapies, it should be emphasized that learning theory offers a generic and unitary explanation of the processes mediating change in all psychotherapies, including psychoanalytic ones (1, 13).

TECHNIQUE

Before getting to the case material, I would like to outline the main features of an application of behavior theory to family therapy. The three major areas of technical concern for the therapist are: (1) *creating and maintaining a positive therapeutic alliance;* (2) *making a behavioral analysis of the problem(s);* and (3) *implementing the behavioral principles of reinforcement and modeling in the context of ongoing interpersonal interactions.*

Without the positive therapeutic alliance between the therapist and those he is helping, there can be little or no successful intervention. The working alliance is the lever which stimulates change. In learning terms, the positive relationship between therapist and patient(s) permits the therapist to serve as a social reinforcer and model; in other words, to build up adaptive behaviors and allow maladaptive behaviors to extinguish. The therapist is an effective reinforcer and model for the patients to the extent that the patients value him and hold him in high regard and warm esteem.

Clinicians have described the ingredients that go into this positive therapist-patient relationship in many different ways. Terminology varies with the "school" of psychotherapy to which the clinician adheres. Psychoanalysts have contributed notions such as "positive transference" and an alliance between the therapist and the patient's "observing ego." Reality therapists call for a trusting involvement with the patient. Some clinicians have termed it a "supportive relationship" implying sympathy, respect, and concern on the part of the therapist. Recent research has labeled the critical aspects of the therapist-client relationship: nonpossessive warmth, accurate empathy, and genuine concern (20). Truax and his colleagues (20) have been able to successfully operationalize these concepts and to teach them to selected individuals. They have further shown that therapists high on these attributes are more successful in psychotherapy than those who are not. Whatever the labels, a necessary if not sufficient condition for therapeutic change in patients is a doctor-patient relationship that is infused with mutual respect, warmth, trust, and affection.

In my experience, these qualities of the therapeutic alliance can be developed through a period of initial evaluation of the patient or family. The early therapist-family contacts, proceeding during the first few interviews, offer an opportunity to the therapist to show unconditional warmth, acceptance, and concern for the clients and their problems.

Also during the first few sessions, while the therapeutic relationship is being established, the therapist must do his "diagnostic." In a learning approach to family therapy, the diagnostic consists of a *behavioral or functional analysis* of the problems. In making his behavioral analysis, the therapist, in collaboration with the family, asks two major questions:

1. What behavior is maladaptive or problematic—what behavior in the designated patient should be increased or decreased? Each person, in turn, is asked, (1) what changes would you like to see in others in the family, and (2) how would you like to be different from the way you are now? Answering these questions forces the therapist to choose carefully *specific behavioral goals.*

2. What environmental and interpersonal contingencies currently support the problematic behavior—that is, what is maintaining unde-

sirable behavior or reducing the likelihood of more adaptive responses? This is called a "functional analysis of behavior," and also can include an analysis of the development of symptomatic or maladaptive behavior, the "conditioning history" of the patient. The mutual patterns of social reinforcement in the family deserve special scrutiny in this analysis since their deciphering and clarification become central to an understanding of the case and to the formulation of therapeutic strategy.

It should be noted that the behavioral analysis of the problem doesn't end after the initial sessions, but by necessity continues throughout the course of therapy. As the problem behaviors change during treatment, so must the analysis of what maintains these behaviors. New sources of reinforcement for the patient and family members must be assessed. In this sense, the behavioral approach to family therapy is dynamic.

The third aspect of behavioral technique is the actual choice and implementation of therapeutic strategy and tactics. Which interpersonal transactions between the therapist and family members and among the family members can serve to alter the problem behavior in a more adaptive direction? The therapist acts as an educator, using his value as a social reinforcer to instruct the family or couple in changing their ways of dealing with each other. Some of the possible tactics are described in the case studies below.

A helpful way to conceptualize these tactics is to view them as "behavioral change experiments" where the therapist and family together re-program the contingencies of reinforcement operating in the family system. The behavioral change experiments consist of family members responding to each other in various ways, with the responses contingent on more desired reciprocal ways of relating. Ballentine (2) views the behavioral change experiments, starting with small but well-defined successes, as leading to (1) a shift toward more optimistic and hopeful expectations; (2) an emphasis on doing things differently while giving the responsibility for change to each family member; (3) "encouragement of an observational outlook which forces family members to look closely at themselves and their relationships with one another, rather than looking 'inside' themselves with incessant whys and wherefores"; and (4) "the generation of empirical data which can be instrumental to further change, since they often expose sequences of family action and reaction in particularly graphic and unambiguous fashion."

The therapist also uses his importance as a model to illustrate desired modes of responding differentially to behavior that at times is maladaptive and at other times approaches more desirable form. The operant conditioning principle of "shaping" is used, whereby gradual approxi-

TABLE 1

A BEHAVIORAL MODEL FOR LEARNING
(adapted from E. P. Reese (16))

1. Specify the final performance (therapeutic goals):
   - Identify the behavior.
   - Determine how it is to be measured.
2. Determine the current baseline rate of the desired behavior.
3. Structure a favorable situation for eliciting the desired behavior by providing cues for the appropriate behavior and removing cues for incompatible, inappropriate behavior.
4. Establish motivation by locating reinforcers, depriving the individual of reinforcers (if necessary), and withholding reinforcers for inappropriate behavior.
5. Enable the individual to become comfortable in the therapeutic setting and to become familiar with the reinforcers.
6. Shape the desired behavior:
   - Reinforce successive approximations of the therapeutic goals.
   - Raise the criterion for reinforcement gradually.
   - Present reinforcement immediately, contingent upon the behavior.
7. Fade out the specific cues in the therapeutic setting to promote generalization of acquired behavior.
8. Reinforce intermittently to facilitate durability of gains.
9. Keep continuous, objective records.

mations to the desired end behavior are reinforced with approval and spontaneous and genuine interest by the therapist. Through his instructions and example, the therapist teaches shaping to the members of the couple or family. Role playing or behavioral rehearsal are among the useful tactics employed in generating improved patterns of interaction among the family members.

The therapist using a behavioral model does not act like a teaching machine, devoid of emotional expression. Just as therapists using other theoretical schemas, he is most effective in his role as an educator when he expresses himself with affect in a comfortable, human style developed during his clinical training and in his life as a whole. Since intermittant reinforcement produces more durable behavior, the therapist may employ trial terminations, tapering off the frequency of sessions prior to termination and "booster" sessions (1). The strategy and tactics of this behavioral approach to couples and families will be more clearly delineated in the case studies that follow. A more systematic and detailed outline of the behavior modification approach is presented in Table 1. The specification and implications of the items in this outline can be found in the manual by Reese (16).

Case #1. Mrs. D. is a 35-year-old housewife and mother of three children who had a 15-year history of severe, migranous headaches. She had had frequent medical hospitalizations for her headaches (without any organic problems being found), and also a 1½-year period of intensive, psychodynamically oriented, individual psychotherapy. She found relief from her headaches only after retreating to her bed for periods of days to a week with the use of narcotics.

After a brief period of evaluation by me, she again developed intractable headaches and was hospitalized. A full neurological workup revealed no neuropathology. At this time I recommended that I continue with the patient and her husband in couple therapy. It had previously become clear to me that the patient's headaches were serving an important purpose in the economy of her marital relationship: headaches and the resultant debilitation were the sure way the patient could elicit and maintain her husband's concern and interest in her. On his part, her husband was an active, action-oriented man who found it difficult to sit down and engage in conversation. He came home from work, read the newspaper, tinkered with his car, made repairs on the house, or watched TV. Mrs. D. got her husband's clear-cut attention only when she developed headaches, stopped functioning as mother and wife, and took her to bed. At these times Mr. D. was very solicitous and caring. He gave her medication, stayed home to take care of the children, and called the doctor.

My analysis of the situation led me to the strategy of redirecting Mr. D's attention to the adaptive strivings and the maternal and wifely behavior of his wife. During ten 45-minute sessions, I shared my analysis of the problem with Mr. and Mrs. D and encouraged them to reciprocally restructure their marital relationship. Once involved in a trusting and confident relationship with me, Dr. D worked hard to give his wife attention and approval for her day-to-day efforts as a mother and housewife. When he came home from work, instead of burying himself in the newspaper he inquired about the day at home and discussed with his wife problems concerning the children. He occasionally rewarded his wife's homemaking efforts by taking her out to a movie or to dinner (something they had not done for years). While watching TV he had his wife sit close to him or on his lap. In return, Mrs. D was taught to reward her husband's new efforts at intimacy with affection and appreciation. She let him know how much she liked to talk with him about the day's events. She prepared special dishes for him and kissed him warmly when he took initiative in expressing affection toward her. On the other hand, Mr. D was instructed to pay minimal attention to his wife's headaches. He was reassured that in so doing, he would be helping her decrease their frequency and severity. He was no longer to give her medication, cater to her when she was ill, or call the doctor for her. If she got a headache, she was to help herself and he was to carry on with his regular routine insofar as possible. I emphasized that *he should not, overall, decrease his attentiveness to his wife, but rather change the timing and direction of his attentiveness.* Thus the behavioral contingencies of Mr. D's attention changed from headaches to housework, from invalidism to active coping and functioning as mother and wife.

Within ten sessions, both were seriously immersed in this new approach toward each other. Their marriage was different and more satisfying to both. Their sex life improved. Their children were better behaved, as they quickly learned to apply the same reinforcement principles in reacting to the children and to reach a consensus in responding to their children's limit-testing. Mrs. D got a job as a department store clerk (a job she enjoyed and which provided her with further reinforcement—money and attention from people for "healthy behavior). She was given recognition by her husband for her efforts to collaborate in improving the family's financial condition. She still had headaches, but they were mild and short-lived and she took care of them herself. Everyone was happier including Mrs. D's internist who no longer was receiving emergency calls from her husband.

A followup call to Mr. and Mrs. D one year later found them maintaining their progress. She has occasional headaches but has not had to retreat to bed or enter a hospital.

Case #2. Mrs. S is a 34-year-old mother of five who herself came from a family of ten siblings. She wanted very badly to equal her mother's output of children and also wanted to prove to her husband that he was potent and fertile. He had a congenital hypospadius and had been told by a physician prior to their marriage that he probably could not have children. Unfortunately Mrs. S was Rh negative and her husband Rh positive. After their fifth child she had a series of spontaneous abortions because of the Rh incompatibility. Each was followed by a severe depression. Soon the depressions ran into each other and she was given a course of 150 EST's. The EST's had the effect of making her confused and unable to function at home while not significantly lifting the depressions. She had some successful short-term supportive psychotherapy but again plunged into a depression after a hysterectomy.

Her husband, like Mr. D in the previous case, found it hard to tolerate his wife's conversation, especially since it was taken up mostly by complaints and tearfulness. He escaped from the unhappy home situation by plunging himself into his work, holding two jobs simultaneously. When he was home, he was too tired for any conversation or meaningful interaction with his wife. Their sexual interaction was nil. Although Mrs. S tried hard to maintain her household and raise her children and even hold a part-time job, she received little acknowledgment for her efforts from her husband who became more distant and peripheral as the years went by.

My behavioral analysis pointed to a lack of reinforcement from Mrs. S's husband for her adaptive strivings. Consequently her depressions, with their large hypochondriacal components, represented her desperate attempt to elicit her husband's attention and concern. Although her somatic complaints and self-depreciating accusations were aversive for her husband, the only way he knew how to "turn them off" was to offer sympathy, reassure her of his devotion to her, and occasionally stay home from work. Naturally, his nurturing her in this manner had the effect of reinforcing the very behavior he was trying to terminate.

During five half-hour couple sessions I focused primarily on Mr. S, who was the mediating agent of reinforcement for his wife and hence the person who could potentially modify her behavior. I actively redirected his attention from his wife "the unhappy, depressed woman" to his wife "the coping woman." I forthrightly recommended to him that he drop his extra job, at least for the time being, in order to be at home in the evening to converse with his wife about the day's events, especially her approximations at successful homemaking. I showed by my own example (modeling) how to support his wife in her efforts to assert herself reasonably with her intrusive mother-in-law and an obnoxious neighbor.

A turning point came after the second session, when I received a desperate phone call from Mr. S one evening. He told me that his wife had called from her job and tearfully complained that she could not go on and that he must come and bring her home. He asked me what he should do. I indicated that this was a crucial moment, that he should call her back and briefly acknowledge her distress but at the same time emphasize the importance of her finishing the evening's work. I further suggested that he meet her as usual after work and take her out for an ice cream soda. This would get across to her his abiding interest and recognition for her positive efforts in a genuine and spontaneous way. With this support from me, he followed my suggestions and within two weeks Mrs. S's depression had completely lifted.

She was shortly thereafter given a job promotion, which served as an extrinsic reinforcement for her improved work performance and was the occasion for additional reinforcement from me and her husband during the next therapy session. We terminated after the fifth session, a time limit we had initially agreed on.

Eight months later at followup they reported being "happier together than ever before."

Case #3. Edward is a 23-year-old young man who had received much psychotherapy, special schooling, and occupational counseling and training during the past 17 years. He was diagnosed at different times as a childhood schizophrenic and as mentally subnormal. At age 6 he was evaluated by a child psychiatry cilnic and given three years of psychodynamic therapy by a psychoanalyst. He had started many remedial programs and finished almost none of them. He, in fact, was a chronic failure—in schools as well as in jobs. His parents viewed him as slightly retarded despite his low normal intelligence on IQ tests. He was infantilized by his mother and largely ignored or criticized by his father. He was used by his mother, who was domineering and aggressive, as an ally against the weak and passive father. When I began seeing them in a family evaluation, Edward was in the process of failing in the most recent rehabilitation effort—an evening, adult high school.

The initial goals of the family treatment, then, were (1) to disengage Edward from the clasp of his protective mother, (2) to get his father to offer himself as a model and as a source of encouragement (reinforcement) for Edward's desires and efforts towards independence, (3) to structure Edward's life with occupational and social opportunities that he could not initiate on his own. Fortunately the Jewish Vocational Service in Boston offers an excellent rehabilitation program based on the same basic principles of learning that have been elucidated in this article. I referred Edward to it and at the same time introduced him to a social club for ex-mental patients which has a constant whirl of activities daily and on weekends.

During our weekly family sessions, I used modeling and role-playing to help Edward's parents positively reinforce his beginning efforts at the J.V.S. and the social club. After three months at the J.V.S., Edward secured a job and now after seven months has a job tenure and membership in the union. He has been an active member of the social club and has gone on weekend trips with groups there—something he had never done before. He is now "graduating" to another social club, a singles' group in a church, and has started action on getting his driver's license.

The family sessions were not easy or without occasional storms, usually generated by Edward's mother as she from time to time felt "left out." She needed my support and interest (reinforcement) in her problems as a hard-working and unappreciated mother at these times. Because of the positive therapeutic relationship cemented over a period of nine months, Edward's parents slowly began to be able to substitute positive reinforcement for his gradually improving efforts at work and play instead of the previous blanket criticism (also, paradoxically, a kind of social reinforcement) he had received from them for his failures. I encouraged the father to share openly with Edward his own experiences as a young man reaching for independence, thereby serving as a model for his son.

The parents needed constant reinforcement (approval) from me for trying out new ways of responding to Edward's behavior; for example, to eliminate the usual nagging of him to do his chores around the house (which only served to increase the lethargic slothful behavior which accrues from the attention) and to indicate instead pleasure when he mows the lawn even if he forgets to rake the grass and trim the hedge. They learn to give Edward approval when he takes the garbage out even if he doesn't do it "their" way. And they learned how to spend time listening to Edward pour out his enthusiasm for his job even if they feel he is a bit too exuberant.

Our family sessions were tapered to twice monthly and then to once a month. Termination went smoothly after one year of treatment.

Case #4. Mr. and Mrs. F have a long history of marital strife. There was a year-long separation early in their marriage and several attempts at marriage counseling lasting three years. Mr. F has paranoid trends which are reflected in his extreme sensitivity to any lack of affection or commitment toward him by his wife. He is very jealous of her close-knit relationship with her parents. Mrs. F is a disheveled and unorganized woman who has been unable to meet her husband's expectations for an orderly and accomplished home maker or competent manager of their five children. Their marriage has been marked by frequent mutual accusations and depreciation, angry withdrawal and sullenness.

My strategy with this couple, whom I saw for 15 sessions, was to teach them to stop reinforcing each other with attention and emotionality for undesired behavior and to begin eliciting desired behavior in each other using the principle of *shaping.* Tactically, I structured the therapy sessions with an important "ground-rule": No criticism or harping were allowed and they were to spend the time telling each other what the other had done during the past week that approached the desired behaviors. As they gave positive feedback to each other for approximations to the behavior each valued in the other, I served as an auxiliary source of positive acknowledgment, reinforcing the reinforcer.

We began by clearly delineating what specific behaviors were desired by each of them in the other and by my giving them homework assignments in making gradual efforts to approximate the the behavioral goals. For instance, Mr. F incessantly complained about his wife's lack of care in handling the evening meal—the disarray of the table setting, lack of tablecloth, disorderly clearing of the dishes. Mrs. F grudgingly agreed that there was room for improvement and I instructed her to make a start by using a tablecloth nightly. Mr. F in turn was told the importance of his giving her positive and consistent attention for her effort, since this was important to him. After one week they reported that they had been able to fulfill the assignment and that the evening meal was more enjoyable. Mrs. F had increased her performance to the complete satisfaction of her husband, who meanwhile had continued to give her positive support for her progress.

A similar process occurred in another problem area. Mr. F felt that his wife should do more sewing (mending clothes, putting on missing buttons) and should iron his shirts (which he had always done himself). Mrs. F was fed up with the home they lived in, which was much too small for their expanded family. Mr. F resolutely refused to consider moving to larger quarters because he felt it would not affect the quality of his wife's homemaking performance. I instructed Mrs. F to begin to do more sewing and ironing and Mr.

F to reinforce this by starting to consider moving to a new home. He was to concretize this by spending part of each Sunday reviewing the real estate section of the newspaper with his wife and to make visits to homes that were advertised for sale. He was to make clear to her that his interest in a new home was *contingent* upon her improvements as a homemaker.

Between the third and sixth sessions, Mrs. F's father—who was ill with terminal lung cancer—was admitted to the hospital and died. During this period, we emphasized the importance of Mr. F giving his wife solace and support. I positively reinforced Mr. F's efforts in this direction. He was able to help his wife over her period of sadness and mourning despite his long-standing antagonism toward her father. Mrs. F in turn, with my encouragement, responded to her husband's sympathetic behavior with affection and appreciation. Although far from having an idyllic marriage, Mr. and Mrs. F have made tangible gains in moving closer toward each other.

DISCUSSION

There is too much confusion in the rationales and techniques underlying current practices in family therapy. Although attempts to convey the method of family therapy always suffer when done through the written word, I do not share the belief that "the vital communications in all forms of psychotherapy are intuitive, felt, unspoken, and unconscious" (7). Although this article is not meant as a "how to do it" treatise for family therapists, I do intend it as a preliminary attempt to apply a few of the basic principles of imitative learning and operant conditioning to couple and family therapy.

Although the rationalized conceptualization of family therapy practiced by psychoanalytically oriented therapists differs from the learning and behavioral approach described here, closer examination of the actual techniques used reveals marked similarity. For example Framo (7), in explaining the theory behind his family therapy, writes: "The overriding goal of the intensive middle phases consists in understanding and working through, often through transference to each other and to the therapists, the introjects of the parents so that the parents can see and experience how those difficulties manifested in the present family system have emerged from their unconscious attempts to perpetrate or master old conflicts arising from their families of origin. . . . The essence of the true work of family therapy is in the tracing of the vicissitudes of early object-relationships, and . . . the exceedingly intricate transformations which occur as a function of the intrapsychic and transactional blending of the old and new family systems of the parents. . . ."

Despite the use of psychoanalytic constructs, Framo describes the actual process of family therapy in ways that are very compatible within a learning framework. He writes: "Those techniques which prompt family interaction are the most productive in the long run. . . . It is especially useful to concentrate on here-and-now feelings; this method usually penetrated much deeper when dealing with feelings described in retrospect. . . . As we gained experience in working with families we become less hesitant about taking more forceful, active positions in order to help the family become unshackled from their rigid patterns."

Framo goes on to give illustrations of his work with families in which differential reinforcement for behavior considered more desirable and appropriate is given by the therapists. In dealing with angry and aggressive mothers, "we learned to avoid noticing what they did (e.g. emotional in-fighting) and pay attention to what they missed in life." Trying to activate passive fathers, "the therapists make every conscious effort to build him up during the sessions. . . . A number of techniques have been tried: forcing more interaction between the husband and wife; assigning tasks; having a female therapist give encouragement in a flattering way; occasional individual sessions with the father." Zuk (23) describes his technique of family therapy in ways that fit into a reinforcement framework. He views the cornerstone of the technique the exploration and attempt "to shift the balance of pathogenic relating among family members so that new forms of relating become possible." Zuk further delineates the therapist's tactics as a "go-between" in which he uses his leverage to "constantly structure and direct the treatment situation."

It should be emphasized that the behavioral approach does not simplistically reduce the family system and family interaction to individualistic or dyadic mechanisms of reinforcement. The richness and complexity of family therapist working within a behavioral framework. For instance, Ballentine (2) states: ". . . behavior within a system cannot be so easily modified by focusing on the behavioral contingencies existing within any two-person subsystem, since one person's behavior in relation to a second's is often determined by behaviors of others within the system . . . the behavioral contingencies within a family system are manifold and constitute a matrix of multiple behavioral contingencies."

The complexity of family contingencies is exemplified by a transient problem which arose in Case #3. As Edward developed more independence from his parents and spent less and less time at home, his parents began to argue more angrily. Edward had served as a buffer between them—taking sides, being used as a scapegoat for their hostility, and serving as a "problem child" who required joint parental action and solidarity. With their buffer gone, the husband-wife relationship intensified and friction developed. Since the therapeutic goals were limited to Edward's emancipation from his parents and since it seemed that the parents were sufficiently symbiotic to contain a temporary eruption of hostility, the therapist's major efforts at this point were aimed at protecting Edward from backsliding in response to guilt or family pressure. The strategy worked, and within a few weeks the parents had reached a new modus vivendi with each other while Edward continued to consolidate and extend his gains.

A behavioral and learning approach to family therapy differs from a more psychoanalytic one. The therapist defines his role as an educator in collaboration with the family; therefore, the assigning of "sickness" labels to members, with its potential for moral blame, does not occur as it does under the medical model embodied in the psychoanalytic concept of underlying conflict or disease. There is no need for family members to acknowledge publicly their "weaknesses" or irrationality since insight per se is not considered vital.

The behavioral approach, with its more systematic and specific guidelines, makes it less likely that a therapist will adventitiously reinforce or model contradictory behavior patterns. The behavioral approach, consistently applied, is potentially more effective and faster. When patients do not respond to behavioral techniques, the therapist can use his more empirical attitude to ask why and perhaps to try another technique. The orientation is more experimental and "the patient is always right," with the burden on the therapist to devise effective interventions. In the psychoanalytic approach, the tendency has been for the therapist to decide that their failures are caused by patients who were inappropriate for the technique rather than viewing the technique as needing modification for the particular patient.

The work of behaviorally oriented family therapists is not restricted to the here-and-now of the therapy sessions. As the cases described reveal, much of the effort involved collaboration and involvement with adjunctive agencies such as schools, rehabilitation services, medication, and work settings. Family therapists are moving toward this total systems approach.

The advantages of behavioral approaches to family therapy sketched in this paper remain to be proven by systematic research. Such research is now proceeding (5, 10, 15, 22). Much work will go into demonstrating that family processes are "essentially behavioral sequences which can be sorted out, specified and measured with a fair degree of accuracy and precision" (2). Hopefully, further clinical and research progress made by behaviorally oriented therapists will challenge all family therapists, regardless of theoretical leanings, to specify more clearly their interventions, their goals, and their empirical results. If these challenges are accepted seriously, the field of family therapy will likely improve and gain stature as a scientifically grounded modality.

REFERENCES

1. ALEXANDER, F. 1965. The Dynamics of Psychotherapy in the Light of Learning Theory. *Internat. J. Psychiat.*, 1:189-207.
2. BALLENTINE, R. 1968. The Family Therapist as a Behavioral Systems Engineer . . . and a Responsible One. Paper read at Georgetown Univ. Symp. on Fam. Psychother., Washington.
3. BANDURA, A., & WALTERS, R. 1963. *Social Learning and Personality Development.* Holt, Rinehart and Winston, New York.
4. BANDURA, A., GRUSEC, J., & MENLOVE, F. 1967. Vicarious Extinction of Avoidance Behavior. *Personality and So. Psychol.*, 5:16-23.
5. DUNHAM, R. 1966. Ex Post Facto Reconstruction of Conditioning Schedules in Family Interaction. In *Family Structure, Dynamics and Therapy*, Irvin M. Cohen, ed.: 107-114. Psychiatric Research No. 20, Amer. Psychiat. Assn., Washington.
6. FERSTER, C. 1963. Essentials of a Science of Behavior. In *An Introduction to the Science of Human Behavior*, J. I. Nurnberger, C. B. Ferster, and J. P. Brady, eds. Appleton-Century-Crofts, New York.
7. FRAMO, J. 1965. Rationale and Techniques of Intensive Family Therapy. In *Intensive Family Therapy*, I. Boszormenyi-Nagy, and J. L. Framo, eds. Hoeber Medical Division, New York.
8. HANDEL, G. (ed.). 1967. *The Psychosocial Interior of the Family.* Aldine, Chicago.
9. KRASNER, L. 1962. The Therapist as a Social Reinforcement Machine. In *Research in Psychotherapy*, H. Strupp, and L. Luborsky, eds. Amer. Psychol. Assn., Washington.
10. LEWINSOHN, P., WEINSTEIN, M., & SHAW, D. 1969. Depression: a Clinical Research Approach. In *Proceedings*, 1968 Conference, Assn. Advan. Behav. Ther., San Francisco. In press.
11. LIBERMAN, R. 1970. A Behavioral Approach to Group Dynamics. *Behav. Ther.* In press.
12. LOVAAS, O., ET AL. 1966. Acquisition of Imitative Speech by Schizophrenic Children. *Science*, 151:705-707.
13. MARMOR, J. 1966. Theories of Learning and Psychotherapeutic Process. *Brit. J. Psychiat.*, 112:363-366.
14. PATTERSON, G., ET AL. 1967. Reprogramming the Social Environment. *Child Psychol. and Psychiat.*, 8:181-195.
15. PATTERSON, G., & REID, J. 1967. Reciprocity and Coercion: Two Facets of Social Systems. Paper read at 9th Ann. Inst. for Res. in Clin. Psychol. Univ. of Kansas.
16. REESE, E. 1966. *The Analysis of Human Operant Behavior.* Wm. C. Brown, Dubuque, Iowa.
17. SHAPIRO, D., & BIRK, L. 1967. Group Therapy in Experimental Pesrpectives. *Internat. J. Group Psychother.*, 17:211-224.
18. SHERMAN, J. 1965. Use of Reinforcement and Imitation to Reinstate Verbal Behavior in Mute Psychotics. *J. Abnorm. Psychol.*, 70:155-164.
19. SKINNER, B. 1953. *Science and Human Behavior.* Macmillan, New York.

20. TRAUX, C., & CARKHUFF, R. 1967. *Toward Effective Counseling and Psychotherapy: Training and Practice.* Aldine, Chicago.
21. VOGEL, E., & BELL, N. 1960. The Emotionally Disturbed Child as the Family Scapegoat. In *A Modern Introduction to the Family,* N. W. Bell and E. F. Vogel, eds. Free Press, New York.
22. ZEILBERGER, J., SAMPEN, S., & SLOANE, H. 1968. Modification of a Child's Problem Behaviors in the Home with the Mother as Therapist. *J. Appl. Behav. Anal.,* 1:47-53.
23. ZUK, G. 1967. Family Therapy. *Arch. Gen. Psychiat.,* 16:71-79.

21

HOW TO SUCCEED IN FAMILY THERAPY: SET REACHABLE GOALS —GIVE WORKABLE TASKS

Andrew Ferber, M.D.

Director, Family Studies Section, Bronx State Hospital
Department of Psychiatry, Albert Einstein College of Medicine

and

Jules Ranz, M.D.

Clinical Director, Tremont Crisis Center of Bronx State Hospital
Department of Psychiatry, Albert Einstein College of Medicine

THE THERAPY IS DESCRIBED

Hello

The Farrells reached our doorstep by a somewhat circuitous route. Their nine-year-old daughter, Mary, had been suffering from a chronic debilitating illness almost since birth, requiring frequent medical check-ups at a nearby hospital. During one visit Mrs. Farrell described her home situation to Mary's social worker. She and her husband had recently undertaken to raise three nephews (aged 11, 10, and 6) who had

Reprinted from *The Book of Family Therapy*, edited by Andrew Ferber, New York, Science House, 1972.

We especially acknowledge the helpful additions suggested by Barbara Lewis, M.S.W., Rodman Hill, Ph.D., and Albert Scheflen, M.D.

Our special thanks to Adele Gottlieb, Myrna Rubin, Elmeta Phillips, and Irene Pisacano who did the dirty work.

346

been orphaned four months before by the death of their father. Their mother died a year previous to the father's death. Three other children of this marriage went to live with the mother's sister on Long Island. The Farrells, who had raised three extremely well-behaved children, were unprepared for the sudden onslaught of three active young boys. The oldest boy, Kevin Boyle, was a constant troublemaker, and the Farrells were having little success controlling him.

The social worker sensed that the Farrells would be receptive to family therapy as it might help them cope more effectively with their difficult situation. The financial hurdle, however, appeared to be insurmountable. Mr. Farrell was a hardworking small businessman, but there were eight people living in his household, and he also partially supported a son going to a nearby private college. Because of its large size, the family was eligible for Medicaid, and Mrs. Farrell was told to look into whether their insurance would cover family therapy. She did, and it did, and the first major hurdle was surmounted.

Mrs. Farrell called Dr. Ferber in November, 1969. She asked if he would see them to help them cope with Kevin. He asked if they had any other children. "Yes," there were Kevin's two younger brothers, Timmy and Joseph, and the Farrells own daughter, Mary. They would bring the boys, but preferred to leave Mary at home. "Why?" Her brother Henry had died just six months ago, a victim of cystic fibrosis at age 15. Mary, also suffering from cystic fibrosis, had been extremely close to Henry. She was very sensitive and they did not want to upset her unnecessarily. Besides, she was a very well behaved young girl, and presented no problems at home. Dr. Ferber explained that he liked to see everyone at home at least once and that Mary, in particular, needed to be there if he was to get a clear picture of the family. Mrs. Farrell agreed reluctantly. She asked if he wanted to see her mother and aunt, both widowed, since the two women also lived with the family. "Yes, indeed, bring them along." Dr. Ferber also told Mrs. Farrell that he would arrange for a colleague, Dr. Ranz, to join him in the sessions. "Why?" Dr. Ferber said he generally worked with a co-therapist, and with a family of eight, covering three generations, he needed all the help he could get.

It's Good to See You

When we walked into the conference room to meet the family for the first time, we shook hands with each person in turn, and noted the rather graphic seating arrangement.

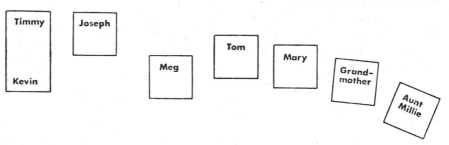

There was a tight semicircle made by the adults, with Mary firmly enmeshed within. We saw the two older boys forming their own group, with Joseph trying, rather ineffectually, to bridge the gap. We asked the parents to open out their circle to include the boys. This was attempted half-heartedly, and a distinct gap still remained. The boys refused to move even halfway, and preferred to stay on the couch when invited to move closer to the rest of the group.

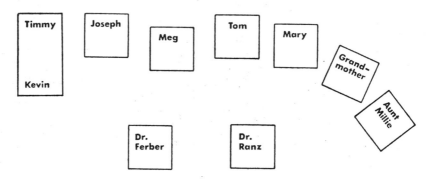

How Are You?

We acquainted ourselves with the complex makeup of the family and charted the family tree on the blackboard. Mr. and Mrs. Farrell were about 50, Irish Catholic, living in Newtown which was a small suburban community in Westchester County. The maternal grandmother had been briefly hospitalized in a state mental hospital during the past year because of senility. She and her sister currently occupied their own section of the Farrell's medium sized house. The two widows generally ate with the family and often cared for the children when both parents were out.

The Farrells had had three natural born children. Only one was still alive. Their first born, Ann, died at three of cystic fibrosis. Terrance, aged 21, was healthy and attending a Catholic college within a 20 minute drive of his parents' home. He visited frequently on weekends, and attended about half of our family sessions. The third child, Henry, had died recently. Mary was an adopted child, although this fact was never acknowledged in her presence during the sessions.

Each Person Makes a List

As soon as we had finished gathering this information, the parents made a concerted effort to thrust Kevin at us as their "problem" and as their sole reason for being there. They told us he repeatedly disobeyed them, and often started fights at home and at school. Kevin sat, disgruntled, on the edge of the couch as far from the others as he could be, and intermittently engaged in distracting laughter and whispered with Timmy.

At the end of the first session we gave everyone the following "homework": Each family member was to compose a list detailing what he liked about the family, and also what he would like to have changed; no person was to consult with anyone else about the lists until they came in the following week.

Standard Operating Procedures

Some of the rules we set forth in that first session are part of our standard operating procedures. We asked that all persons living at home be brought into contact with the therapeutic process, at least peripherally. We directly required that people talk to (not at or about) each other, emphasizing that adults should talk *to* children. To facilitate re-examination of sessions and to allow sick or otherwise absent members to keep up, we tape-recorded all sessions. Finally, we made it clear that while we would take responsibility for controlling the structure of the meetings, the family had the responsibility for initiating what was to be discussed.

Problems and Situations

When the family returned with their lists for the second session, we quickly learned that most members of the family wished to see less strife and do more things together. There was a striking absence of references to sickness and death which suggested considerable denial in a family that had very recently experienced three deaths, and had a chronically ill child. We agreed with the family that strife was a *problem* stemming from the stresses inherent in trying to bring together two families with such different life styles. We said we would work with them on this problem, if they so wished. We redefined Kevin's behavior, not as a problem in itself, but as a part of a larger problem . . . the family's apparent need for a scapegoat. Specifically, then, we could help them deal with Kevin's behavior, *only* if they agreed to work on it as part of the struggle to help change a pattern that required a scapegoat. The family skeptically accepted our quaint description of their "bad-boy" problem. We suggested to them that the absence of references to sickness and death pointed to incompleted mourning. The feelings and thoughts each person had about the deaths he had recently experienced, and Mary's ongoing illness, were not being shared. The family was treating this as a situation to be endured. They did not label the incompleted mourning as a problem. Finally, we agreed with the family that Joseph's being temporarily in crutches (he was suffering from Legg-Perthes disease, a chronic but not progressive bone disease of childhood), was a situation that did not need to be treated as a problem in family therapy.

By the end of that second session we had outlined a working plan acceptable to both therapists and family. We had set out three major goals, each stemming from an identified problem:

1. controlling strife by better uniting the two families
2. freeing the mourning process from its stuck track
3. unscapegoating Kevin.

Ghosts

At our third meeting we began to work on the mourning process. We encouraged each member of the family to bring forth personal memories of Henry and of the boys' parents, asking the listeners in turn to empathize and comment.* The boys' idealized their former home in Connecticut. They made numerous comments about how much they disliked Newtown, the school, their friends, etc., and how much better Connecticut had been. Indeed, the boys had been asking to return to Connecticut for a visit (they had not done so since their father's death), and although the Farrells had agreed to do this, no definite plans had been made. We encouraged the family to make the excursion as soon as possible, and to report back to us what the experience was like.

During the following week the trip was made. This made a tremendous impact on everyone. Kevin and Timmy enjoyed themselves immensely, collecting souvenirs which they displayed to us. Joseph was not

---

* We are following Operational Mourning models described by Eric Lindemann and Norman Paul (10) (12).

so comfortable there; he remembered few people and felt that Newtown was his real home. Joseph had been living with the Farrells about six months longer than his two older brothers. Kevin and Timmy reacted to Joseph's statements by calling him a "traitor" and not talking to him for the rest of the session. Mary, quite upset, said she felt things had been better before the boys came to live with them and she wished they weren't there. Mrs. Farrell recalled with some bitterness that her dead brother, the boys' father, had been such a well-behaved youngster, and that she felt his later drinking problem must have been caused by troubles with his wife. Mr. Boyle died of a bleeding ulcer, aggravated by heavy drinking in the years prior to his death.

In the fourth session there was some talk about Henry, the dead son.

> Meg: (talking about caring for Henry in the few months prior to his death) "He was so good, he never complained of all the suffering. . . ." (stops, becomes tearful)
> Dr. Ranz: "Go on. . . ."
> Meg: "I can't, I can't talk about this with all these people here."
> Tom: (gets up and whispers in Dr. Ranz's ear) "Mary—it's fatal. . . ." (Few moments of awkward silence)
> Timmy: (makes funny face at Joseph, who giggles)
> Kevin: (runs toward microphone to tap on it)
> Tom: "Get away from there!"
> Dr. Ranz: (to Mary, who is silent and very pale) "Would you tell us your last memories of Henry?"
> Mary: (very tearful—throws arms around Terrence, sobs)
> Meg: "She always gets. . . ."
> Dr. Ranz: (motions for Meg to stop) . . . (to Mary) "Do you want to talk?"
> Mary: (nods head yes—then begins slowly) "We used to play chess together. He would let me beat him (pause). . . . When I saw him in the casket I thought his lips moved. I wish he were still alive, I want him back."

After these few sessions, we felt that the mourning for the boys' parents had progressed well, particularly aided by the planned trip to Connecticut. Mourning for Henry, however, did not proceed quite so well. Following the above discussion, the family resisted further discussion of this topic. Looking back at this, we feel we colluded with the family's resistance to break open their particular pandora's box—Mary's precarious medical condition. Any attempts to further the group's mourning for Henry resulted in the inevitable comparisons between Mary and Henry. A successful resolution of this problem was not achieved during our sessions with the family.

Black Sheep, Scapegoats, and Little Lambs

During the fifth session, an attempt was made to scapegoat Kevin. Kevin got very annoyed at Timmy for interrupting a story he was telling and complained that Timmy always did that to start fights and to get Kevin in trouble. Mrs. Farrell acknowledged that that used to happen when the boys lived with their parents, but believed that Kevin was no longer being blamed for every fight. Still, she said, he never stops complaining. We remarked that Kevin complained so much because he was carrying the burden of all the children. Meg admitted she felt that Timmy was a nervous and fearful child who never revealed his fears to them. We pointed out that Timmy could not complain because it would be out of character. He had a role to play as problematic as Kevin's role of a scapegoat. He played the part of the ever-cheerful, mealy-mouthed milk-toast, expressing what he believed adults wanted to hear. For Timmy to do otherwise, would have been too frightening. It would have been courting parental disapproval, and a possible loss of love. We commented that each member of the family played a role. Mary was always the shy well-behaved child, inhibited and clingy. Joseph was regressed and constantly seeking physical comfort. Meg was the traffic cop, frantically harrassing everyone to "be good," while ignoring the issue raised, and Tom the disapprover who would withdraw and glower menacingly from a corner. The Farrells recognized that these roles were, at best, "parodies" of good behavior and began to see that the others were nearly as troubled as Kevin though less outspoken. The Farrells asked how they could help the children express what was on their minds. We said that direct questioning and encouragement (as we did with Mary) would help somewhat, but that it would be asking too much of the children to give up their distorted conceptions of "good" behavior just by talking about it. We suggested an experiment during sessions. The children would not have to worry about behaving well. They could speak up when they liked, and move about the room freely. They were invited to bring in material (such as toys, games, books) to play with during the session so that they might not get bored. We explained that children often express themselves more openly by their actions than by words.

As expected, the children proved to be quite eloquent in their activity. During the next (sixth) session, Joseph roamed about from one person to another, sitting on any available lap. Mary's movements were more patterned—she would go from Mother to Father to Terrance and always ended up sitting in the protection of one of the three. Kevin repeatedly set up walls about him—with chairs, blackboard, other people. Timmy chattered endlessly. The parents acted as if most of this activity simply wasn't happening, seemingly taking care not to attend to any child any more than the others. Indeed, the only consistent response that the parents gave, was to reprimand someone (more often Kevin than the others) for some behavior they felt they couldn't ignore. We suggested that much of the children's behavior appeared to be attention and attachment seeking in nature. Tom and Meg were advised to encourage the children to come to them for physical comforting. Meg responded positively with "That's the first concrete suggestion I've heard."

Kevin was skillful at subverting attempts to "unscapegoat" him. He quickly grasped that we wanted to break through the family's natural tendency to hide behind a facade of "polite" talk and behavior. He came prepared each week with provocative tidbits that always succeeded in arousing the rest of the family. He was following our direction yet remained the trouble maker. He was having his cake and allowing it to be smashed in his face. In the seventh session we asked the family to help Kevin by ignoring his provocative behavior when possible, and by attending to and encouraging his constructive behavior. This suggestion resulted in a warm and productive encounter at home in which Tom helped Kevin with his homework. Kevin's work improved and Tom reported pleasure in being able to deal with Kevin in a non-combative manner. We made a point to encourage continuation of this kind of encounter which was a good example of meaningfully changed behavior originated by the family. (Maxim: when you see something you like, applaud like mad!)

Ignore the Stress and Stone the Scapegoat

Meg was not at the eighth session because she wasn't feeling well. Tom and Terrance had a discussion about Terrance's social life and, much to their surprise, found they were able to have a mutually satisfying talk—something they did not do often. An unstated implication was that Meg was so puritanical that Terrance could not discuss his dates with her without feeling he was acting sinfully. Meg was still absent the following week. Tom explained that she was sick and in the hospital for tests. Further questioning during the session revealed little information and none of the children appeared particularly concerned or upset over her illness. After that session, Tom told us in private, that Meg had chronic gynecological difficulties and was in the hospital where hysterectomy had been contemplated, but then deferred.

Meg returned the following week. Though nobody would admit to being concerned about her health (just as nobody ever discussed sickness or death in this family), a smoldering feud between Timmy and Kevin flared up to crisis proportions and became the focus of the tenth session. Timmy complained that Kevin encouraged some of his friends to harass and "rough him up" after school. Kevin denied the accusation, saying he was trying to stop them from bothering Timmy. Tempers were such that even when separated by the length of the conference room, a word or a cross-eyed look between the two of them could precipitate a physical attack.

A Paradoxical Instruction

The boys were separated, not allowed to look at each other, and told not to interrupt each other until the other indicated he was finished talking. Kevin was able to follow this direction, but Timmy could not or would not. Several times he interrupted while Kevin was talking. After several such interruptions, Kevin stood up at his place, staring menacingly at Timmy. Tom yelled at Kevin to sit down, ignoring Timmy's provocative interruptions. During the eleventh session, Timmy and Kevin continued to provoke each other. We suggested a one week trial separation. The boys were not to talk to or deal with each other in any way at home or in school. When they returned the following week, both boys wanted the separation to end. They missed each other's company, support, and protection.

The Lid Comes Off

The change in the relationship between Timmy and Kevin seemed to "free" the other children and a torrent of troubled thoughts and forbidden activity was unleashed. In the thirteenth session Kevin and Mary were reprimanded for looking at pictures that Tom felt they shouldn't see. Kevin felt he received the brunt of the criticism and complained that Mary was favored by the parents over the other children. He further claimed that Mary played this advantage by provoking fights to elicit sympathy from her parents. Mary, tearful and angry, yelled that it wasn't true. Timmy told her to shut up, in a menacing manner. To this Tom erupted: "I won't have them talk that way to my child."

Tom's outburst struck a chord within Mary. She started crying and then surprised everyone by her next comment. She said she felt her parents fought too often and with too much vehemence, and that when they did so she was terrified one or the other might leave. Obviously shaken by Mary's feeling, the parents admitted they infrequently threatened each other in such a manner in the heat of their arguments, but both hastened to reassure Mary that she was in no danger of being abandoned by either. During the fourteenth session, Timmy reported a nightmare: He was in a swimming pool, surrounded by bodies of dead parents; the therapists were also swimming in the pool. The Farrells were standing around the edge of the pool, and Timmy was screaming for them to pull him out. Everyone talked about the dream, and the consensus was that it indicated movement toward the Farrells. At the very end of that session, Joseph spontaneously burst forth with his own complaint—he felt no one ever paid attention to him. He said he had gotten more attention when he was wearing his crutches, and now that he didn't need them nobody seemed to care for him anymore.

During this difficult period the Farrells listened without criticizing, gave reassurance when possible to Mary, held and hugged Joseph and Timmy when they looked upset. They were particularly bothered by Kevin's accusation that they played favorites with the children.

> Tom: "We treat all the children the same. They're all tied, we have no favorites."
> Dr. Ferber: "But the boys are tied for last."
> Tom: (*Furiously*) "I won't stand for that, you have no reason to speak that way to me."

This confrontation unnerved Meg. She pleaded for a quieter atmosphere.

> Meg: "We've tried to adjust to the boys but we just can't do it. We're too set in our ways. We can't bend. The boys will have to adjust to us."
> Kevin: "Well, I didn't want to live with you people. I want to go to Connecticut."

Tom, much calmer, told Kevin that he wasn't going to Connecticut. He revealed that the Farrells had taken the three Boyle boys since they were the most active of the six orphaned children. None of the other relatives felt they could handle the boys. The Farrells had known it would be rough, and they would not let trouble defeat them. In short, Tom's message was that they were now a family; he wasn't going to ship them off just because he was angry with them.

Graduation

During the next week Meg called to tell us they had been upset by recent meetings, and did not want to continue therapy. After some persuasion, she agreed to come to a session alone with Tom. At the meeting (sixteenth session), they told us "we feel you gang up on us . . . you make us feel guilty for everything, you never support us." We said we felt we were now ready to support them as they now were in a position to discipline the boys without the boys worrying that their behavior might precipitate abandonment.

They returned the following week with the whole family. We supported the parents' move to assert positive control of the family, only amending their demand "you should do this . . ." to "I want you to do this. . . ." Not surprisingly, the boys objected. Timmy wrote "strike" on their blackboard and then led the other children in a march around the room protesting "unfairness" by parents and therapists. The children were angry. They now directed their anger where it belonged—at the adults—while simultaneously maintaining a sense of humor that revealed the warm feelings and renewed confidence they felt towards their parents.

The following session, the eighteenth, opened with the announcement that the family had decided they didn't have to come anymore. We reexamined our goals as stated at the outset: 1) solidify the family, 2) help the mourning process, 3) unscapegoat Kevin, and decided that significant progress had been made towards all three goals. As Kevin was eager to point out, there was much left to be done, but he agreed with the others that the remainder could be worked on by the family alone. An extemporaneous graduation ceremony ended our last session with the Farrells.

SOME EXPLANATIONS ARE PUT FORTH

"Family" and "Therapy" Are Behavioral Systems

Carl Whitaker has said that the therapist is responsible for the therapy, and the family is responsible for their lives. We try to understand that epigram in this essay.

We put forth our views of how we were useful to the Farrells. Our discussion focuses on setting goals and giving tasks. We recognize that many other things happened during our sessions that we allude to only in passing, if at all. In our short professional lives families seem to have stayed pretty much the same, the treatment of their problems has changed a little, while explanations and justifications that therapists give have varied widely and wierdly. We have tried to be interesting and true to our experience in our explanations. The cost is a lack of theoretical closure and frequent inconsistencies.

BEHAVIORAL SYSTEMS ARE COMPOSED OF BEHAVIORS, NOT PERSONS

Families and family therapies may be viewed as behavioral systems. A behavioral system is composed of behaviors, not persons. Of course, the behaving is done by people. These people think, feel and remember, and although we cannot observe these phenomena directly, we know they are important in understanding people. Here, though, we have set ourselves the task of explaining what happened during our contact with the Farrells, and we believe we can do this without describing the subjective experience of each of the family members, nor by concerning ourselves with their total involvement outside the system under observation. To describe this system, we focus on behaviors, their patterns of occurrences and integrative relationships.

THE FAMILY SYSTEM IS CONTRASTED

The Farrells came, in effect, asking us to study their family system. This immediately created a new system, which we call the therapy system. These two systems are quite distinct. The family system's *duration* is continuous. After expected (e.g. birth of a child) and unexpected (e.g. early death of a spouse, divorce) crises and transitions, a gradual change into the next generation occurs. The therapy system lasts minimally for one brief meeting, modally 20 to 50 meetings in a year, and maximally several years of once a month to several times a week brief meetings.

The *membership* of American family systems are clusters of mother, father, and/or children with varying ties to lateral clusters of brothers and sisters and cousins, and lineal clusters of parents and uncles and aunts. The membership of a therapy system is the therapists and whatever members of the family they select to see. The behaviors of the family system occur in a very complicated site called the household as well as several other *locations*, often widely separated in space. The variety of *behaviors* is large and includes a ritual of daily activities from risings, greetings, feedings, and matings, to elaborate procurement and preparation of goods and services for one another, etc. The behaviors in the therapy system occur typically in a single cramped office and mostly consist of various sitting postures, movements, and a great deal of conversation.

The behaviors are integrated and organized by patterns at many levels. Researchers have described the most microscopic patterns of family behaviors as well as behaviors of families occurring over several generations. Mothers and infants move in rapid, rhythmic synchrony that can be demonstrated with slow motion film analyses (16). Three meals a day appear. Bills are paid monthly, Thanksgivings happen yearly. The clan appears once in each person's lifetime for his funeral. In the family therapy system, regular cycles of microbehaviors have been found by Condon (5) while repetitive and alternating patterns of postures, gestures, and topics, have been demonstrated by Scheflen (15), and Beels and Ferber (2).

The *plans* for the family system can be abstracted and are called child rearing, provisioning, maintaining a degree of closeness to each other, etc. Therapy system plans will be described later. The *leadership* of the family system is most commonly in the hands of the parents. The leadership of the therapy system, if it is to do its job, is in the hands of the therapist. The family system has a continuing set goal—the maintenance of a pattern of relationships. The therapy system has a finite set goal, the termination of relationships between therapist and family members. (See later for definitions of these terms.)

THE FAMILY SYSTEM IS INTEGRATED WITH THE THERAPY SYSTEM

There are some behaviors that appear both within the family therapy system and the family system. The family re-enacts its face-to-face systems of relationship and communication in therapy. These include the patterns of posture, voice, gesture, language, ways of representing information, developing plans, expressing feelings, scorning, supporting, etc. The therapists request that the family bring to the therapy session some of their plans for, and rules about, their actual behavior outside the therapy system. Therapists try to bring these plans into awareness, and make explicit the maps of certain parts of the family's life. The therapist's aim is to appraise and alter the face-to-face relationship systems of the family, and the plans and rules by which the family members conduct their lives.*

---

* We hope it is clear that with a different family, we would have had a different therapy system, hence a different therapy. (e.g. with families other than the Farrells, there may be more attention paid to the marriage, relations betwen adults and their parents, dreams and fantasies, sexual difficulties, etc.) Furthermore, therapy systems can endure for longer or shorter times than did ours with the Farrells. Longer therapies sometimes, but not always, become more complex. The communicative structure of the relationships amongst the family members are radically altered, and the attachment between the therapists and the family members becomes more personal and messy. These developments are called cultivating and analyzing a transfrence neurosis in psychoanalytic parlance. An example of such a case is "Changing Family Behavior Patterns" by Ferber and Beels (6).

FOUR MODELS FOR THE THERAPIST

We present four models of well known events to illustrate varying ways of looking at the relationship between the family system and the therapy system.

Mediator. A mediator's job in negotiating a new contract between management and labor resembles a therapist vis-a-vis a conflict of interest within a family system. The mediator attempts to create a situation where the two parties may resolve, under his auspices and supervision, previously unsolvable conflicts of interest. His only powers are his good offices, persuasion and the parties' wish to reach an amicable solution. It is often clear in such disputes that the mediator's function is to suggest compromises, then neither side need admit to a victory or a defeat, since the adversary did not initiate the new move.

Diplomat. A diplomatic model features family members as coming from different nations with different languages, customs, and rules of behavior. The therapist first must act as a translator, to be sure everyone understands one another. Furthermore, he must help each see the problems from the viewpoint of the others, so that meaningful discussion can take place. His most difficult task, perhaps, is to help develop areas of mutual trust, to allow the opposing parties to adjust to one another without resorting to warfare or bloodshed.

Director.. The therapy system is like a play wherein the therapist assumes the prerogatives of director and eventually co-author. The family appears and is asked to stage whatever aspects of their lives that they wish to seek some help with. The therapists must structure their meeting so that the family is able to reproduce the drama of their lives in the therapist's office.* As times goes on they gradually rewrite the script of the familiar dramas and, hopefully, leave when it has been adjusted to their satisfaction. This model highlights the family system as a stereotyped, painful trap which requires an outsider to lead it somewhere new.

Lone Ranger. As to the relative importance of the therapy system to the family system, an analogy and a quote from *War and Peace.*

We see the family as a ship on a long voyage. The therapists fly in by helicopter, somewhere in mid-voyage, conduct an inspection of some or much of the ship, peruse the charts of the waters ahead, the plans for the navigation, and the ship's log. They suggest some changes in the course of the voyage, perhaps fix some machinery gone awry, often clarify the relationships amongst the crew members, and attempt some

---

* The authors have been much influenced by Luigi Pirandello, Harold Pinter, T. S. Eliot and Peter Brook.

small changes in their relationships. Then they board their helicopter, usually leaving a wireless address, and fly off while the ship continues on its way. We recommend Tolstoy's General Kutuzov as a model to the family therapist.

> "He will not devise or undertake anything, but he will hear everything, remember everything and put everything in its place. He will not hinder anything useful nor allow anything harmful. He understands that there is something stronger and more important than his own will—the inevitable course of events, and he can see them and grasp their significance, and seeing their significance can refrain from meddling and renounce his personal wish directed to something else" (17).

Goals

THE GOALS OF THE THERAPY SYSTEM

Create and Maintain the Therapy System. The therapist's first job is to create and maintain a new system of relationships. We believe that all good therapists are in control of the process that unfolds during the therapy session (although of course such control may be exerted quite subtly) (1, 7, 18). While the culture encourages people to expect the therapist to direct the therapy and to be in charge of their meetings, a new set of ground rules must be established in each therapy contract and a dominance battle must be fought for the right to set the rules (see *Standard Operating Procedures*). Among the more common rules that therapists propose are those that state that both therapists and family members should appear at set times, remain in the room for the length of the meeting, and when there, talk to each other. During the meeting there should be no serious physical violence, no sexual intercourse, and the therapist and family should pay somewhat serious attention to the work at hand. Patients are expected to pay their fees or some equivalent thereof. Once the general rules are accepted and the therapist's control is acknowledged, at least for the moment, the therapist sets about prescribing a secondary set of rules that facilitate the development of the work of the therapy. These rules include: people are to say whatever is on their minds; one is to listen to what the other person is saying; children may be allowed to be on less than best behavior and to play with toys and crayons, etc.

In our favorite working posture we tell family members "You have become stuck in solving your problems, and that is why you are here. It is the *process* of problem solving rather than the particular solutions to problems that we can help you with. Please begin talking and working with each other on whatever point you have reached in the resolution of your difficulties. We shall then observe and when and if you get bogged down in your negotiations, we will try and help you proceed from there." We then face them toward each other, pointedly remove ourselves from the center of the communication position, and urge them to go at each other and attempt to resolve their difficulties. The adherence to these rules by the therapists and by the family member creates the new system of relationships.

Maintaining this new system is, unfortunately, more difficult than creating it. If the therapist runs interesting, lively, and friendly meetings, maintains a helpful context and helps solve some of the customer's problems, he has a good chance of maintaining the therapy system. A helpful context requires that the therapist refuse to allow fighting for the sake of fighting, and steadfastly maintain that everything done in the meeting be for the eventual betterment of the membership. This may require fancy footwork by the therapists, e.g. relabeling vicious attacks as misguided efforts at problem solving, as when Kevin's "complaining" was interpreted as a burden he carried. The therapists also continually feed warm smiles, approving headnods, benign interest, flirtatious gestures and postures, approving appraisals of the family's performance, etc., into the therapy system. This keeps a friendly and interested interpersonal climate in the room (14). It is also the therapist's obligation to ask interesting questions, lead and pace the discussions and presentations of material, and generally conduct the meeting as an interesting human event. If the patients try to make the meeting an unfriendly encounter or a drag, the therapists do what they can to counteract that, and as a last resort tell the patients that unless they stop doing that, they will all have to go home. The payoff is the solution of the customers' problems. *It is the production of new behavior by the family that is the raison d'etre of the family therapy system.*

Represent and Change Aspects of the Family System. The second major therapy goal is to represent and change aspects of the family system. We regard it as axiomatic that when a family enters family therapy they do so because at some level they perceive that something is wrong with the family's typical system of relatedness, and they are thus open to changing this system. The first step in this process is to present the family system, especially in its troublesome aspects. This is done in a rather straightforward way, by asking the family to "do their thing" in the presence of the therapists. Some of the tasks described in *Create and Maintain the Therapy System* do this. We expect family members to reenact their difficulties during the therapy session. The implicit understanding is that family members may relinquish some responsibility and be less guarded since the therapist is there to pick up the pieces.

While the family is performing, the therapists participate in the system so as to gain an appreciation of how it operates, and in particular, what needs to be changed.

THERAPISTS IN CONTROL OF THE THERAPY—FAMILY IN CONTROL OF THEIR LIVES

As a rule of thumb, we would recommend that therapists never fight a battle unless it is absolutely necessary, One way of doing this is to generally insist that you are in charge of the process within the office, and the family is in control of their lives.* Thus, anything that happens on the outside is not your responsibility and therefore you cannot be held accountable for it. However, there comes a time in some therapies when the therapists find they must announce that unless the family changes a specific type of behavior that is occurring outside the room, the therapy will have to stop.

When new behavior occurs, families will try to re-establish their accustomed ways. The nominal head of the household will often act as if the changes are a threat to his dominance and end up doing battle with the therapists for control of the therapy system. Thus Tom, seemingly following our suggestions that the family open each meeting with what was on their minds, would often tell the boys, "Tell the doctors what you did this week." Thus, he grabbed the chance to define what was to happen next and shifted the emphasis from "where were the people in the room at that moment" to "what did the bad boys do on the outside during the week." It is one of the therapists' most taxing tasks to watch for these attempts to restore the prior family equilibrium and to firmly continue to direct the therapy system to whatever new behavior evolves.

WHAT TO CHANGE: GOALS FOR THE FAMILY

Situations and Problems. Families come to therapists with a complicated pattern of lives which we may call their situations. They choose to label some aspects of their situations as problems. They generally believe that these problems create living situations that call for redress or change. A great deal of the therapy time is spent in negotiating labels.

---

* Clearly resembles the psychoanalytic caveats of (1) be abstinent (2) interpret the transference.

Some situations that the family has labelled problematic the therapists seek to unlabel. They would prefer that the family live with these rather than worry and fight about changing them. The therapists may seek to label other situations as problems and urge the family to try to alter these situations. We discussed the specific negotiations with the Farrells in the section titled *Problems and Situations*.

How Do Families Decide What They Wish to Change? We cannot discuss this exhaustively in this paper. What families label as problems and what they consider potentially remediable by family therapy are questions best answered by examining the value system of the culture from which the family comes. Therapists and families sharing class and culture may have similar assumptions about what are problems and what are their solutions. Therapists and families from different ethnic and social class backgrounds may have different expectations as to what are the problems and what can be done about them. It is a good idea to try to deal with the problems that the *family* labels as problems, or when this is impossible, to make it very clear how you get from their definition of the problem to your own definition of the problem.

How Do Therapists Decide What They Wish to Change? Not infrequently the changes therapists attempt to impose on families, derive not directly from what the family presents to us as a problem, but rather from certain (often unacknowledged) values therapists believe make for "the good family life." For example, we tend to believe that consistency is a value if it doesn't stultify creativeness, that overly rigid families would be better loosened up (and vice versa), that people should work hard, have fun and good sex, and obey most of the Ten Commandments. We recognize that some therapists may argue with one or another assumption. In fact, any and all of these mentioned values are subject to change when and if we see things by a different light.

Our ideals of family structure influenced the goals for the Farrells in many ways. We describe several below.

Attachment. There is an acceptable range of attachment between intimates. When this bonding becomes too close, it restricts the partners from taking different postures within the relationship. Mary's bond to her adoptive parents seemed too close to us and we worked at placing more distance between them. If the bonding is too distant, then no meaningful relatedness is possible. Kevin and Timmy seemed too distant from Tom and Meg. We worked to decrease this distance (4). It seemed that people must effectively mourn for lost family members for if they don't, they will not be free to relate fully to living family members. Our work towards completion of mourning embodied this concept.

Power and Responsibility. Parents do have more power and responsibility than children. Everyone should know and be able to discuss who has what power and who has which responsibility. The person with the responsibility for doing a job should usually have the power to decide if the performance is adequate, and to modify the performance if it is not. Tom and Meg had an arrangement for disciplining the children that was less than optimally effective, and put a hard strain on Meg. She was responsible for most of the discipline, yet Tom, in fact, had much of the power needed to implement Meg's decisions. The boys had long ago learned that they could depend on Tom to "soften" Meg's decisions (though not to change them). We urged Tom and Meg to clarify their power relationships, and, in particular, for Tom to assume more of the direct responsibility for disciplining the children.

Communication. We tried to enforce two rules about communication. The first is that anything that people do with one another may be accurately labelled and talked about. The second rule is that talk and communication about behavior should be consistent with behavior. This means we are against lying, hypocrisy, and "double-binding." A good example occurred when we supported the confrontation over the actual playing of favorites and the myth that "all children are treated equal" in the Farrell family.

Blaming. We believe that most family troubles are problems in the social system of that family and its transactions with other social systems. We take a strong stand against the blame game. The blame game is the cultural tradition which holds that when *something* is wrong, *someone* must be at fault.

We observed that the Farrell adults and Boyle boys were too distant from each other, and suggested that the adults begin to improve this by making the first move toward the children. The Farrells took this to mean we were blaming them for the problem. We said that no one was to blame. We had pressured them to make the first move simply because they were in a better position to do so.

It takes a good deal more work to counteract a family's tendency to repeatedly blame one member whenever stress occurs anywhere in the system. We helped the Farrells in this regard by labelling this problem "scapegoating" for them and then directing them to discover that other family members' concerns were being submerged in the general rush to "dump" on Kevin. But a "fixed" system of this kind is not so easily replaced: we have already seen how the family resorted repeatedly to scapegoating whenever the going got rough.

The question is *how* can the social system be changed, not *whose fault* is the problem. Finding a villain to blame and punish for the problem usually avoids any change in the social system that generates the problem.

This is only a partial and rather abstract list of ideals that we, the therapists, hold for the families we work with. We mentioned them because we think they are important for understanding the process of therapy. We think that negotiations involving therapists' ideals, therapists' actual behavior, families' ideals, and families' actual behaviors, eventually lead therapist and family into the courses of action that hopefully will alter the family situation.

Tasks

People Obey Instructions. Once goals have been set, and the proper moment arrives to intervene, what then? By task, we mean those behaviors that the therapists explicitly or implicitly, verbally or nonverbally, instruct family members to perform. The assumption is that through the performance of the behaviors which the therapist prescribes and proscribes, the family system will change.

For instance: when the Farrell family seated itself in two distinct "camps," an opportunity presented itself to use this seating arrangement as a problem to be worked on. We might comment on the seating arrangement, with minimal elaboration, and then drop back to see what, if anything, the family chooses to do with the comment. The comment is intended to help the family "see" the existence of a problem, and to give them further impetus to do something about it. This is a good tactic when the therapist feels it is inadvisable to move in too fast; the comment implies that something should be done about this without forcing anyone's hand. A similar, if less timid, tactic is to provide an interpretation: For example, the therapist might say, "I wonder if this seating arrangement suggests that everyone is afraid to make the first move towards the others?" This move goes further than a mere comment, it suggests a possible motivation lurking under the surface of the difficulty. Telling people why they do things is a time-honored practice in psychotherapy. It is often effective precisely because it works at several levels:

(a) A problem is brought to the family's attention.
(b) An unstated injunction is established by the therapist that tends to make the patient think twice about doing that again (at least in front of the therapist).

    (c) Hidden somewhere in the interpretation is a possible suggestion, as with our suggestion to the Farrells, "move toward each other."

    (d) People generally feel more in control of themselves when they think they understand why they are doing things.

Or, one may come out from behind the bushes and prescribe a task. The Farrell family was actually asked to move their chairs towards each other after the seating pattern was mentioned. The point of this task is quite straightforward: getting the family to physically move toward each other. This forces the family members to relate to each other in a new and unaccustomed manner which, under therapeutic guidance, will hopefully allow them to *experience* the better results of such new relatedness.*

People Change Themselves, People Imitate Leaders. Two other mechanisms lead the family toward new behavior. The situation itself demands change as the therapy situation is considered a place where people are expected to change their lives for the better. The other source of family change is its imitation of the therapists. In almost all primate groups a great deal of the behavior can be characterized as the membership imitating the leadership. We suspect that much of the change in family therapy systems stems from people imitating their therapists. In the rest of the paper we say no more of these two modes of change.

Plans of Tasks Reach Toward Goals. We will describe some of the tasks we have given the Farrell family to help move them toward the three goals we have featured in this paper. We design a plan which consists of several tasks that successively move the therapy system toward some new state. This is a developmental process. Each task is dependent upon the state of the system at that moment, and thus a second task can neither be designed nor proposed until the reaction of the system to the first task has been ascertained.

SET GOALS: FINITE AND CONTINUING

Set Goals Lead to the Deactivation of a Behavioral System. Many human activities are enactments in complicated goal directed and error

---

* Most readers of this paper will be familiar with the long raging battle as to whether behavioral changes produced by direct instructions are more superficial (or less longstanding) than changes induced by "insight" or some other indirect instruction. We would again like to emphasize the strength of the experiential approach which is often ignored: once a family has accomplished a change in relatedness, and assuming it is a healthy change for that family, the various members will begin to *experience* themselves and their relationships to other family members in a new light, and presumably will feel better about this new way of relatedness. We cannot imagine any better way to produce lasting change in any people or systems.

corrected plans. We continue to enact these goal directed activities until we achieve the set-goal, become temporarily exhausted or change the set goal.

We wish to distinguish between two categories of set goals: finite set goals, e.g., an orgasm, winning a game, the completion of an annual report; and the continuing set goals, e.g., proximity between a mother and a child; being within a territory (such as a house), maintenance of a superordinate-subordinate relationship in a social structure.

Completion of mourning is a finite set goal. Changing the usual relational distance, bringing the Farrells and Boyle boys closer together, is our example of a continuing set goal. Finite and continuing set goals require different strategies from the therapist. If the goal in therapy is helping family members move toward unconsummated finite set goals, then the strategy is to move toward that goal with all deliberate speed. If the goal is changing continuing set goals, moving off dead center and playful exploration of alternate possibilities is the order of the day.

Complete Mourning (Goal I): Tasks Toward a Finite Set Goal. In our first meeting, people spoke of the deaths of the boys' mother and father, 16-year-old Henry, and the long dead daughter, Ann, in a fashion that suggested incompleted mourning. The family's tense, hushed, reverential and awkward discussion of their dead people made us feel that this situation was not a dead issue. The next task was to negotiate an agreement with the family that this was something to work on. After we agreed to the general task of continuing the mourning for these several deaths, many specific tasks remained. We encouraged detailed recollections of the dead. We steered conversations to the dead, and urged people to push their memories until they were not choked up with tears, but were crying unashamedly and openly. Tears and a warm sad resigned feeling satisfied us. If things remained tense, angry, withdrawn, and depressed, it signalled incompleted work and we would press on and urge the family to recollect and talk some more. The trip to Connecticut was a key task in this sequence. If mourning is the task, it is often good to urge people to return to the graves of dead relatives, to visit living persons who knew the deceased, talk extensively with them about the deceased, to reflect upon photograph albums, records and other mementos of the deceased, and in general to bring back and work through as many memories of the dead person as possible.

To move a family toward a finite set goal requires that the therapist have at least a rudimentary knowledge of: what that goal is and which behaviors are steps toward reaching it and, which behaviors are merely side tracks or runnings away from the goal. It is only with fairly sure knowledge that the therapist can urge family members to do things that are often painful, uncomfortable and feel "unnatural." When people complain that they are not being spontaneous or sincere, the therapist may tell them that if they could do these things spontaneously, they would not need his help.

Decrease the Relational Distance Between the Farrells and the Boyles (Goal II): A Continuing Set Goal. Changing a continuing set goal requires a different strategy than changing a finite set goal. The hope is that the new set goal will be more satisfactory to the family members than the prior one. However, under force of habit, or whatever one calls the conservative tendencies in social systems, there is a continual short run pressure to return to the prior state of the continuing set goal. It is not as simple as changing the setting of a thermostat (9).

In the very first session, we noted the large distance between the Farrells and the Boyles and we asked them to move closer. They half-heartedly complied. Yet they mentioned the desire for a closer social distance between the two families. There was not much problem in negotiating this as an area to work on. There was a constant instruction from us to them to talk to each other rather than about each other to us. This had to be repeated frequently, especially when a difficult situation arose and either the boys or the parents would try to complain to us about the other. We noticed that the boys, especially Timmy and then Kevin, sat on our laps a lot. When we first saw them with Terrance, it became clear to us that they preferred his lap to Tom's and Meg's, and snuggled up to him a great deal. Joseph occasionally went to Tom and Meg for physical contact. We urged both the boys and the parents that whenever either of them perceived the boys to be upset or lonely, either party should initiate a hugging, approaching kind of contact. Furthermore, we told the parents that instead of backing off and sitting in a rejecting posture when they wished to control the boys, they should move toward them and even physically hold them when attempting to discipline or instruct them. We told Tom and Meg not to reject the boys when the boys rejected them. We urged them to make an explicit commitment to the Boyle children, and instructed the Farrells to make it clear that the relationship was permanent. The boys had no place else to go and whether they liked it or not they were with the Farrells. They could not provoke complete rejection. We could then tell the boys that since this was a permanent rather than a transient relationship, they might as well make the best of it. We told the parents to be firm and guiltless in their discipline of the boys since they were committed to care for them. They certainly had the prerogative of running the family in the fashion they chose. They did not have to do everything for the boys' benefit. We taught a new style of negotiating. Since the parents had the final say, why not solicit the boy's opinion before making decisions?

When Meg attempted to terminate therapy over the phone at about the sixteenth session, we refused and insisted on getting together and talking about it. Tom and Meg said we were blaming them for the family's difficulties by saying it was all their fault; they felt guilty. We said we liked them and suggested that if their feelings were hurt by us, they should tell us. We would try to accommodate to their complaint. We said they, not we, were in charge of the family. If they did not like our suggestions, they could tell us and need not run away from us. We consider this situation parallel to the boys' running away in lieu of complaining to Tom and Meg. The successful renegotiation of the therapy contract between therapists and parents, with the clarification of responsibility, was followed by a similar process between parents and children within the family. The preceding episode is an example of what has been called induction of the therapist into a pattern of the family system (11). It resembles the development of transference in individual therapy, and is handled in a similar way: by making an interpretation to the patient that indicates you are not what he is expecting you to be.

Families in treatment are often caught in power problems: power is either abused, absent, abdicated or the object of endless struggle. Family members readily regard the family therapists as potentially ideal models for the appropriate use of power. It is extremely important, therefore, for family therapists to become and remain aware of themselves (in effect if not in intention) as very influential executive power figures in the family therapy arena.

Small moves by therapists can seem gargantuan to family members. Thus it is even more important for therapists to exercise obvious restraint when intervening in families, to solicit comments and criticisms from family members about the therapists and to remain open for the re-negotiation of any and all deals in which they become involved. There is always the danger that therapists may fall into patterns of interacting that replicate and intensify the family's dysfunctional interactions; this is especially the case in the handling of power.

The therapist must know which behaviors of the family members are enactments of the relationship system that maintain the old continuing set goals, and which behaviors indicate an enactment of the new continuing set goals. There is a continuous interweaving of noticing and then forbidding or not reinforcing the old set goal, pushing any or several of the members toward enactments of the new continuing set goal and then reinforcing with praise, approval, etc., any performance of the relationship system as it oscillates around its new continuing set goal. Major impetus should be towards doing something different. It is not necessary beforehand to know exactly what the new continuing set goal should be. Families usually can be trusted to pick a new goal that suits them once they stop seeking an old one that does not.

BEHAVIORAL PROGRAMS

In the performance of their daily activities and in the pursuit of the individual or family set goals, families use sequences of behaviors which are culturally patterned and clearly recognizable. These have been described in several places and most clearly conceptualized in Scheflen's "Behavioral Programs" (13) and Harris' "The Nature of Cultural Things" (8). In a prior paper, "Changing Family Behavioral Programs" (6) Ferber and Beels pointed out how some of these organizations of behaviors can become cyclical dead ends. The task may be to change an unsatisfactory behavioral program which is getting in the way of reaching either finite set goals, or maintaining satisfactory continuing set goals. The particular dysfunctional behavioral program we discuss in this paper is a scapegoat system.

Unscapegoat Kevin (Goal III): Tasks Toward Changing a Family Behavior Program. The changing of the scapegoat pattern that featured Kevin as the bad boy was a very complex goal. While the family presented him as the problem, they did not present the scapegoat alignment that included him as a problem. We requested homework lists which required everyone to both make complaints and assign praise to various sections of the family's functioning. This gave everyone a new role in the therapy system (evaluator of the family) in addition to the one they had in the scapegoat system. We next had to accurately label the remainder of the scapegoat system, and then convince the family that everyone's behavior was interdependent, automatic, and less than optimally useful. This involved making clear how Timmy's goodness was as strange as Kevin's badness. Mary's fearful clinginess, Josep's lap searching, Meg's frantic and overwhelmed disciplinary efforts and Tom's withdrawal were sequentially and simultaneously illuminated as parts of the same picture. By the time of Meg's illness, the members acknowledged that all these behaviors could be simultaneously produced by stressing the family system, and that no one member was necessarily the instigator of the pattern. We told Kevin to be helpful. This involved asking Kevin to do things that were clearly good and then rewarding these. We started this by praising his active and eager participation in the sessions, and then asked the parents to find things for Kevin to do at home. A more difficult task was persuading the family to reward his good behavior and ignore his bad behavior. This acknowledges that once a person (Kevin) is part of a dysfunctional system (scapegoating) he will always play his part even when the others stop playing theirs (persecutor, protector, etc.). It takes all members of the system some time to change the program. If only one person changes, the rest of the family will usually pull him back. If a person changes, it is important to shift the focus to those members of the system that haven't moved, all the while encouraging those who have changed already to hold their new place.

By the eleventh session the focus was off Kevin as the only bad boy but still was on Kevin and Timmy as the fighting duo. The paradoxical task that was prescribed was that Kevin and Timmy should not talk to each other for an entire week. This not only revealed their strong need to be with each other, but also led to smoking out both the favoritism of Mary vis-a-vis the boys, and Tom's secret role as enforcer. This allowed us to tell Tom that the boys were perhaps in part fighting each other because they dared not accuse him of favoritism because he was so fierce when accused. When Meg was sick and in the hospital, no one spoke of it and everybody fell back into the scapegoat system. We concentrated on having them talk about Meg and how they were managing without her, and passed off as a matter of expectable course that they might fall back on an old, albeit useless pattern at such a time.

The message here is—talk about the stress, not about the old pattern after it is clearly understood and labelled by all as dysfunctional. We took the position that the scapegoat system was no one's fault, but rather a pattern they were trapped in. We taught them a new pattern in which to negotiate grievances, and some new ways to share concerns. We faced Kevin and Tom towards each other and asked Tom to solicit Kevin's opinion, then discuss matters with him and finally make a binding decision. We urged the parents not to feel guilty in running the family in a fashion that pleased them even if the children grumbled. We coached people in practicing new patterns, and then dropped back when they seemed to be doing well.

Ranz Returns and the Paper Ends

One year later, Dr. Ranz paid a followup visit to the Farrell home:
I was greeted at the door warmly by everyone except Kevin. I found

him watching television; he was in a bad mood. Tom came in to say he had the idea Kevin thought that they had called me and were planning to bring him back to therapy. Kevin acknowledged he had that idea, and seemed to accept my assurance that I had initiated the contact.

We discussed the preceding year. Terrance was away in basic training, having joined the service following graduation from college. Everyone had had a relatively healthy year. Kevin and Timmy had gone to camp during the summer, had enjoyed it, and planned to return with Joseph the next summer. Tom's older brother, who had been quite ill for some time, had died during the fall, but not before paying a visit to his own parents' graves in Ireland. Tom spoke warmly of his departed brother.

All family members seemed to be more at ease with their memories of deceased relatives. They talked freely of Henry and of the boys' parents, were openly tearful, and showed me many pictures. They also brought out a lovely essay about Henry, written by his girlfriend and dedicated to the Farrells after his death. The boys were able to bring forth memories of their parents freely, and without too much bitterness. Clearly, the mourning process we had helped to start, had progressed well in our absence.

The relational distance between the boys and the adults had maintained the closeness achieved during our sessions. There were no longer behavioral signs of two "warring" camps, and I observed genuinely warmer interaction amongst family members.

The most difficult problem, the scapegoat system, was still very severe. The Farrells placed heavy emphasis on Kevin's continued disobedience, while Kevin obediently played his role by sullen behavior and by setting up walls (as before, but noticeably less pervasively). Meg acknowledged they were so disturbed by his misbehavior they had tried to send him to other relatives, but no one would take him. I suggested the following task: Kevin was to choose *one* aspect of his life which represented a present struggle with his parents, and suggest his own resolution. If they felt it was appropriate, they would agree to try his solution. Every month a new contract was to be negotiated. Kevin suggested he be allowed to supervise bedtime for the other children when the Farrells were out for an evening. They said he just wanted to have control over the others. He said, no, they would determine what time the children were to go to bed, he would only insure they actually went to bed at those times. Meg responded, "That seems like a reasonable job for a 12-year-old—let's try it."

I was impressed by the quickness with which both Kevin and the Farrels grasped the purpose of the task and their readiness to make the

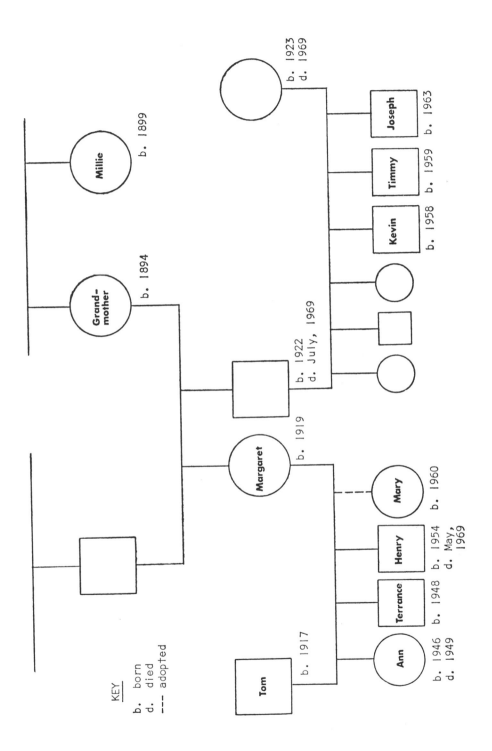

KEY

b. born
d. died
--- adopted

Millie b. 1899

Grand-
mother b. 1894

b. 1923
d. 1969

Joseph b. 1963

Timmy b. 1959

Kevin b. 1958

b. 1922
d. July, 1969

Margaret b. 1919

Mary b. 1960

Henry b. 1954
d. May, 1969

Terrance b. 1948

Ann b. 1946
d. 1949

Tom b. 1917

effort necessary to negotiate the new contract. The family had retained or could rapidly relearn some of what they had more slowly and painfully learned during their earlier contact with us.

Satisfied that the Farrell ship was headed once again on approximately the right course, I boarded my helicopter and departed.

AFTER THE FACT

Just before publication we learned that the Farrells had moved toward their own resolution of their scapegoat system—Kevin was sent to live at a private school for the duration of the school year. He had spent the previous summer at this school, and enjoyed himself immensely. Perhaps this plan was undertaken because Kevin wanted to go there, rather than because the Farrells wanted to get rid of him. At any rate, both the Farrells and Kevin report that they are happy with this arrangement.

REFERENCES

1. BEELS, C. C. & FERBER, A. Family Therapy: A View. *Family Process*, 1962, 8:280-332.
2. BEELS, C. C. & FERBER, J. Unpublished research on the semiotics of a family therapy interview.
3. BODIN, A. & FERBER, A. "The Presentation of Experience in Family Therapy and Family Therapy Training." To be published in *Becoming a Family Therapist*, New York: Science House, 1971.
4. BOWLBY, J. *Attachment and Loss.* Vol. I, New York: Basic Books, Inc., 1969.
5. CONDON, W. & OGSTON, W. D. A Segmentation of Behavior. *J. Psychiat. Res.*, 1967, 5:221-225.
6. FERBER, A. & BEELS, C. C. Changing Family Behavior Programs. *Interna. Psychiat. Clinics*, 1970, 7:27-54.
7. HALEY, J. *Strategies of Psychotherapy.* New York: Grune and Stratton, 1963.
8. HARRIS, M. *The Nature of Cultural Things.* New York: Random House, 1964.
9. HOFFMAN, L. "Deviation—Molifying Processes in Natural Groups." In Haley, J. (ed.), *Changing Families.* New York: Grune & Stratton, 1971.
10. LINDEMANN, E. Symptomatology and Management of Acute Grief. *Amer. J. Psychiat.*, 1944, 101:141-148.
11. MINUCHIN, S., MONTALVO, B., GUERNEY, B. G., ROSMAN, B. L., & SCHUMER, F. *Families of the Slums.* New York: Basic Books, 1967.
12. PAUL, N. & GROSSER, G. Operational Mourning—Its Role in Conjoint Family Therapy. *Community Mental Health Journal*, 1965, 1:339-345.
13. SCHEFLEN, A. "Behavioral Programs in Human Communication." In W. Gray, F. Duhl, and Rizzo (Eds) *General Systems Theory and Psychiatry.* New York: Little and Brown Co., Inc., 1969.
14. SCHEFLEN, A. Quasi-courtship Behavior in Psychotherapy. *Psychiatry: Journal for the Study of Interpersonal Processes*, 1965:28:245-257.

15. SCHEFLEN, A. Stream and Structure of Communicational Behavior. *Behavioral Science Monograph I*, Philadelphia: Eastern Philadelphia Psychiatric Institute Press, 1966.
16. STERN, D. A Microanalysis of Mother-Infant Interactional Behavior Regulating Social Contact between a Mother and Her 3½-Month-Old Twins. To be published in *J. Amer. Acad. Child Psychiat.*
17. TOLSTOY, L. *War and Peace*. New York: Heritage Press, 1938, Part 10, p. 198.
18. ZUK, G. The Go-between Process. *Family Process*, 1966, 5:162-178.

22

THE SIDE-TAKING FUNCTION IN FAMILY THERAPY

Gerald H. Zuk, Ph.D.

Family Psychiatry Division
Eastern Pennsylvania Psychiatric Institute (Philadelphia)

Evidence has been accumulating in the literature over the past dozen years for the hypothesis that certain triadic-based transactions, such as family coalitions and alliances or family efforts at arbitration and negotiations, may become pathogenic; that is, that they may tend to breed mental disturbance among the family members of the in-group and among the members against whom the coalitions are directed. While investigations have established a beachhead for a triadic-based psychopathology of family systems, little headway has been made in constructing a thoroughgoing system of family *therapy* based on a triadic model. Instead, family therapy has been heavily weighted with the blend of monadic and dyadic concepts that composes the psychoanalytical framework and other individual-centered psychological models.

In a series of recent papers (6-8) I have attempted to construct a triadic-based system of family therapy to correlate with the triadic-based psychopathology of family systems that has been under development. This system of family therapy is designated "go-between process," a special application to family therapy of the triadic concepts of mediation and side-taking. Even though in daily life one sees on all sides the immense influence of mediation and side-taking processes to bring about

Reprinted from the AMERICAN JOURNAL OF ORTHOPSYCHIATRY, Vol. 38, No. 3, April 1968, pp. 553-559. Copyright © 1968, the American Orthopsychiatric Association, Inc. Reprinted by permission.

major human change, for better or worse, psychotherapists have been reluctant to examine these processes as means to bring about beneficial change in psychotherapy. Particularly in American therapy, the therapist has been reluctant to view himself in the role of mediator and has often been adamant that side-taking is not part of his function. Yet it should be abundantly clear that the family therapist cannot avoid the role of mediator or side-taker, even though he may deny this to his patients and take steps to defend his position of complete neutrality. Such prominent spokesmen for family therapy as Haley (2) and Ackerman (1) have written recently in support of the view that mediation and side-taking are not only unavoidable in family therapy but are legitimate therapeutic functions that may promote beneficial change. In this paper I have three goals: (1) to identify the go-between process clearly as a triadic-based system of family therapy and to outline its relationship to a triadic-based formulation of psychopathology ("pathogenic relating") in family systems; (2) to describe the two types of change promoted by the therapist who conducts go-between process; and finally (3) to spell out in greater detail than in my previous papers the side-taking function in go-between process.

GO-BETWEEN PROCESS

The functions or terms of go-between process as conducted by the therapist vis-a-vis family members need defining. First, the therapist focuses on current issues on which family members are in conflict and attempts to get the members to express their conflicts with one another. Second, the therapist openly takes the role of go-between: he encourages family members to define and amend the areas and terms of disagreement among themselves; he sets limits or rules out certain behavior during the discussion of conflict; and he even suggests means by which the conflict may be resolved or at least attenuated. Third, the therapist engages judiciously in side-taking with respect to persons and issues, which means that he positions himself in favor of or against a family member, or pro or con an issue, in order to exert leverage against a coalition or alliance he has deemed to possess pathogenic properties.

PATHOGENIC RELATING

In a recent paper (8) I define family therapy as ". . . the technique that explores and attempts to shift the balance of pathogenic relating among family members so that new forms of relating become possible" (p. 71). By *technique* I refer to go-between process. By *pathogenic relat-*

ing I refer to certain kinds of coalitions, alliances, or cliques that tend to produce mental disturbance among members of the in-group or among those against whom these group processes are directed. Silencing strategies are examples of pathogenic relating; certain double-binds constitute pathogenic relating; the scapegoating process is another example (4, 5, 9). Threats of physical or psychological violence made by a coalition of family members against another member would constitute still another form of pathogenic relating. In my view the family therapist directs his efforts mainly toward breaking up these harmful associations, and I view go-between process as the means by which he can best accomplish this.

Additional forms of pathogenic relating have been observed in family therapy: (1) selective inattention to the presence of powerful affect, such as when one family member is depressed, mourning, or hostile and this appears to be ignored or not noticed by the others; (2) selective inattention to the presence of threat, such as when a husband has been physically violent to a wife or child but this information is studiously withheld by family members; (3) resort to unfair, incorrect, or scapegoating labels, such as when a child is unreasonably tagged "wild," "bad," "stubborn," or "stupid"; (4) myths or rituals that are of uncertain origin and cannot be clearly rationalized, such as when a member expresses the fear of a strain of insanity in his family but cannot state a clear basis for the fear, or when members attend celebrations that are disliked and which usually result in unpleasantness among family members; (5) family "noisemaking" activities, such as rapid-fire shouting by members or other forms of mutually approved distractibility that have the effect of discouraging the therapist from getting a word in edgewise.

In previous papers (see especially references 6 and 7) I may have left the impression that go-between process is aimed essentially at conflict resolution. This would be an erroneous impression, for go-between process is aimed primarily at undermining pathogenic relating in families and replacing it with more productive forms of relating. Evoking conflict is an especially useful means to expose pathogenic relating in families, although not the only means.

CHANGES IN FAMILY RELATIONSHIPS

The family therapist conducting go-between process promotes change in two ways: (1) through his presence as a "third party" he causes family members to redefine and restructure key elements of their relationships with each other; (2) through reputation as an expert in human relations and a figure of authority he causes the family to enter with him into a subtle contest to decide who—therapist or family—will control the type of change to occur, its rate of occurrence, and its magnitude and pervasiveness.

In connection with the first point, it seems clear that the mere presence of the family therapist (although, to be sure, he is never just merely present in the therapy situation) influences the family members to relate to each other in somewhat new ways, to use somewhat different terms to describe each other, to act toward each other somewhat differently, even to perceive each other in a somewhat different light. An example of this type of change promoted by the family therapist is the case of a husband and wife who agreed that the behavior of their nine-year-old son could only be called "silly." They agreed on very little else, for this was a disturbed marriage in which the son was being used as a pawn by both parents. He had entered (perhaps "been seduced" is the correct phrase here) into an especially close relationship with his mother from which his father was almost entirely excluded. The motives of the parents for labeling their child's behavior "silly" were not the same, but identical motives are not necessary for parents to act in collusion. Even the child agreed that his behavior could be called "silly," partly out of a desire to placate both parents. My aim as therapist conducting go-between process with this family was to get the parents to redefine the child's behavior and thereby, hopefully, to expose and break into a system of pathogenic relating in which the term "silly" played a key supportive role. Eventually the parents did decide that "silly" did not properly describe their child's behavior, indeed that his behavior was most meaningful and directly related to the disturbed family system. Such change in a labeling system employed by a family can have a powerful and pervasive effect on long-term relationships in a family; a beneficial therapeutic effect may also be almost immediately noticeable.

On the second point, a previous paper (8) described the "bargaining" transaction that occurs between therapist and family in which they subtly negotiate with each other the type of change to occur, its rate of occurrence, and its magnitude. In my view family therapy is an active confrontation between therapist and family in which both strive to control or delimit the efforts of the other: specifically, the therapist attempts to introduce his notion of beneficial change into the family; the family, on the other hand, attempts to undermine, contain, or neutralize the therapist's interventions in order to retain the safety and security of the status quo. Sometimes, families in treatment will effect a small change simply in order to forestall the therapist's demand for a much greater change. Of course, the therapist must carefully consider the timing and phrasing of a demand for change because there is always the risk that the family will break treatment. Still, it has been my experience that beneficial results can flow from an understanding and judicious application of the fact that family therapy is composed in part of a series of "bargaining" transactions in which therapists and family vie with each other for control of possible outcomes.

THE SIDE-TAKING FUNCTION

As therapists have become more "active"—and they have become so in all the psychotherapies in the past 20 or more years in American psychotherapy—they have inevitably engaged more extensively and unavoidably in side-taking. Even though "active" therapists have been typically reluctant to make such an admission, there have simply been too many clinical reports about the harmful influence on the patient of "dominating" mothers and "passive" fathers to accept without some skepticism the view that the therapists are not involved, directly or indirectly, at least to some extent, in side-taking. To be sure, therapists might offer the explanation that the so-called dominating mother or passive father *really* exists in many of their patients. (There are abundant studies which show that they *do* exist; others which show that they do *not*.) Or the therapists might accept the charge of side-taking but defend themselves against it by describing it as a function of their countertransference which they must "work through" in the course of their treatment.

Side-taking engaged in by the therapist is inherently neither good nor bad; it is simply inevitable and unavoidable, especially in family therapy. It is important to give close consideration to the side-taking function because it is a powerful device to either maintain or alter patterns of pathogenic relating seen in family therapy. As a rule of thumb, the family therapist should not be trapped into the position of siding *consistently* with one family member against others. Expert family therapists will jealously guard their prerogative to side with or against different family members at different times. Often they will defend this practice to the family by saying that the fact that they can change sides reveals how fair and unbiased they are.

The family therapist can side on behalf of issues or on behalf of persons, although in practice these two factors often overlap. He may take a point of view on an issue with the aim of weakening a group of family members who have formed a coalition in order to contest that particular issue with the therapist. The rightness or wrongness of the therapist's view in this case is not so critical as is the question of whether his action will bring about a disruption of the coalition that he views as pathogenic. The therapist may side with (or against) an individual in the family with the same goal in mind: to disrupt a harmful coalition of which that person may be either a member or the "object" against which it is directed.

The family therapist quickly discerns rather typical patterns of side-taking in the families he treats. In American families it is common to find mothers siding strongly with their sons (to a lesser extent, fathers will side with their daughters). A strong mother-son alliance can wreak havoc in a family, particularly when one of its goals is to undermine the man's role and sense of identity as a husband and father. In fact, a strong mother-son alliance is one of the stoutest defenses against the efforts of the family therapist to get beneficial change; he may have to find some way to weaken or circumvent the alliance before any beneficial change can occur.

Coalitions and alliances are complex processes that often include an element of subtle deception. That is, members of a strong alliance will develop means to disguise the existence of their alliance, means to arouse doubt as to its depth and extensiveness. The members of a strong alliance may even have developed means to hide the depth and extensiveness of their commitment *from each other*. Sometimes the family therapist can get a hopeful change in pathogenic relating simply by getting one member of a strong alliance to reveal an aspect of the depth and extensiveness of his commitment previously unknown to the others—or to reveal the absence of some aspect previously believed present by the others. Coalitions and alliances tend to break up when the degree of trust or confidence between the members is disrupted. Trust can be diminished when any information is introduced that reveals a special interest or desire for control in one of the members not previously known or agreeable to the others.

In the event of a strong mother-son alliance, it is predictable that the mother and son will make efforts to get the therapist to side with them against any "object" of the alliance, usually the father in the family. Sometimes a therapist will side with such a pathogenic relationship by default, as when a father *expects* the therapist to side with his wife and son because in his experience people have usually done so. In other words, a father may be so conditioned to losing out to a clever mother-son team aligned against him, he will assume that the therapist will also support that team. If the therapist does not inquire into this expectation and attempt to correct it, in effect he will be siding with the mother-son alliance against the father.

There are other ways in which the therapist can lose effectiveness by siding *with* a pathogenic relationship. This may occur simply as a result of the family's cleverly spotting some special feature about the therapist that can be manipulated—some aspect of the therapist's social class or of his educational, ethnic, or religious background; a distinguishing physical characteristic; and so on through an endless list. While Midelfort (3) sees a positive value in the family therapist being of the same ethnic and religious origins as his patients, such similarity may prove a two-edged sword, for the therapist may be so forced to defend the values of the ethnic or religious group to which he and the family belong that he loses important flexibility. The family therapist must be able to side, from time to time, *against* the family's expectation of how he will side in order to keep the family slightly off guard; that is, in order to maintain siding as a powerful device to disrupt pathogenic relating. He must, from time to time, be able to surprise the family with a position he takes. He must also be able to refuse to take a side, if by so doing he believes he is resisting or undermining a family maneuver to trap him into an impotent position.

In carrying out his side-taking function, the family therapist conducting go-between process is not seeking to impose his own set of moral or ethical values on the family, although to some extent no therapist can help doing this. The therapist mainly attempts to work within the moral and ethical value system of each family he has dealings with. He may vigorously side in favor of or against an ethical belief, but his aim in taking the position is primarily to shake up and thus hopefully minimize a pattern of pathogenic relating. The therapist may sometimes even be required to take a position on an ethical or moral issue with which he does not personally agree. (This should not strike the reader as especially Machiavellian, for I have known therapist-colleagues to express to their patients more liberal views on moral or ethical issues than they, personally believed or practiced in their private lives. I have also known a few to express more conservative views to patients than they personally held.) But ordinarily the therapist should not have to depart very far from his personal code of values in his conduct of go-between process in family therapy.

Side-taking by the therapist does not consist simply in his saying to one family member, "Now I am on your side and against the others." It is a far more subtle process involving nuances of both word and gesture, and it may be either active or passive. In active side-taking, the therapist takes a certain position because he has concluded that the position may interrupt pathogenic relating. In passive side-taking, he takes a position in order to turn aside an attempt of the family to get him to take another position less favorable to the promotion of beneficial change in the family. The family often carries out what might be called a counter go-between process vis-a-vis the therapist, undermining or minimizing the change desired by the therapist. The therapist must skillfully employ go-between process to isolate or circumvent these efforts of the family to limit beneficial change.

SUMMARY

Go-between process is a theory and technique of family therapy based strictly on triadic concepts. Features of the process are mediation and side-taking, both triadic concepts in that they require the presence of at least three persons, one of the three acting as a "third party." In conducting go-between process, the therapist functions as go-between and also takes sides in order to shake up the system of pathogenic relating he observes in the family; that is, he uses one function or the other as leverage to disrupt and minimize pathogenic relating, hopefully to replace it with more productive patterns of relating. Pathogenic relating refers to certain kinds of alliances, coalitions, or cliques that tend to produce mental disturbance among the family members of the in-group or among the family members against whom these group processes are directed. Scapegoating is an example of pathogenic relating, as are certain kinds of double-binds and silencing strategies.

Go-between process is directed primarily toward undermining pathogenic relating and replacing it with more productive forms of relating; it is only secondarily a means to promote conflict resolution in families. The family therapist conducting go-between process promotes beneficial change in two ways: (1) by enabling or compelling family members to redefine or restructure key aspects of their relationships with each other; and (2) by redefining or restructuring, in the course of treatment, key aspects of his own relationship with the family. The presence of the therapist as a "third party" brings pressure on the family members to deal differently with each other. The therapist and the family conduct subtle "bargaining" transactions with each other in which they negotiate as to what type, when, and how much change will occur in the family.

The side-taking feature of go-between process is a subject of special focus in this paper. In family therapy the therapist is unable not to take sides. Intelligently handled, side-taking can be a source of considerable therapeutic leverage; poorly handled, it can be a major obstruction in treatment.

REFERENCES

1. ACKERMAN, N. 1966. *Treating the Troubled Family*. Basic Books, New York.
2. HALEY, J. 1963. Marriage Therapy. *Arch. Gen. Psychiat.*, 8:213-234.
3. MIDELFORT, C. 1957. *The Family in Psychotherapy*. McGraw-Hill, New York.
4. ZUK, G. 1965. On the Pathology of Silencing Strategies. *Family Process*, 4:32-48.
5. ZUK, G. 1965. On Silence and Babbling in Family Psychotherapy with Schizophrenics. *Confin. Psychiat.*, 8:49-56.
6. ZUK, G. 1965. Preliminary Study of the Go-between Process in Family Therapy. In *Proceedings of the 73rd Annual Meeting*. Amer. Psychol. Assn., Wash., D. C.
7. ZUK, G. 1966. The Go-between Process in Family Therapy. *Family Process*, 5: 162-178.
8. ZUK, G. 1967. Family Therapy. *Arch. Gen. Psychiat.*, 16:71-79.
9. ZUK, G. 1967. The Victim and his Silencers: Some Pathogenic Strategies Against Being Silenced. In *Family Therapy and Disturbed Families*, G. Zuk and I. Nagy, eds. Science and Behavior Books, Palo Alto, Calif.

23

THE ROLE OF THE YOUNG CHILD
IN FAMILY THERAPY*

Joan J. Zilbach, M.D.

*Staff Psychiatrist and Director of the Family Therapy
Research Unit, Judge Baker Guidance Center*

Ernest Bergel, M.D.

Staff Psychiatrist, Judge Baker Guidance Center

and

Carol Gass, M.S.W.

Staff Social Worker, Judge Baker Guidance Center

INTRODUCTION

The concept of the "sick family," and the philosophy, goals, and methods of conjoint family therapy, have been widely discussed in both the popular and professional literature, and, presumably, are well understood. A closer look at the current clinical application of these theoretical and therapeutic concepts reveals a glaring inconsistency: some members of the family, notably, the younger children, are frequently excluded from treatment. Under such circumstances, the family, in fact, is not being treated.

Elsewhere in this volume Ackerman has commented on the fact that

---

* Investigation of the role of the young child in family therapy was conducted as part of a larger research project on family therapy currently in progress in the Family Therapy Research Unit of the Judge Baker Guidance Center, Boston, Mass.

although family therapy represents a relatively new addition to our therapeutic armamentarium, workers in this field have developed a wide variety of styles and formats—and, inevitably certain prejudices. One of the most common of these prejudices is directed against the inclusion of younger children in what is loosely referred to as family therapy. Thus we are faced with the contradiction that a fundamental principle of family therapy is being widely violated by its own adherents. As is well known, family therapy derives from the proposition that "The family is a unit," or, stated differently, that "The family must be treated as a whole." Apparently for many family therapists, the "unit" or "whole" encompasses only those family members who have reached certain prescribed stages in their mental and emotional development, so that they are able to express themselves adequately on a verbal level. Inasmuch as they cannot fulfill these criteria, most very young, non-verbal children, and those who have very limited verbal facility, are excluded from treatment. In the extreme case only the adolescent siblings are considered eligible for family therapy.

We believe that the future progress of family therapy depends in large measure on the elimination of these exclusionary practices. Accordingly an attempt has been made in this article to present those considerations which make treatment of the entire family desirable or essential; to describe methods specifically designed to facilitate the participation of the young child in the treatment process; and, finally, to explore the ways in which the participation of the young child may serve to implement the goals of family therapy.

Rationale for the Treatment of the Family as a Unit

Family therapy is neither the only, nor always the most desirable, mode of treatment. However, family therapy is based on the premise that a unit or social subsystem exists which represents in selected cases the preferred, and sometimes perhaps the only, locus of intervention in order to permit amelioration of certain discomforts, commonly called symptoms. These discomforts may present themselves as complaints by or about a single individual who is a member of that unit, but we nevertheless interpret them as signs that the whole unit is in difficulty.

What do we understand by this unit called "the family?" Wynne (1) who has pointed to the psychological boundaries that link members of a family together and separate them from others, has also pointed out the difficulty of making a decision *a priori* as to who is or is not a member of a specific family. All relativistic considerations notwithstanding, it must be clear that all minor and unmarried children living in the home must be considered an essential part of any family, even where the family itself would like to disown such children. There is no simple way to prove this and it may have rare exceptions, but from a common sense point of view it must be obvious that the care and education of young children is one of the prime functions of families in all societies where the children live primarily with their parents. Consequently, the whole family without all such children is a contradiction in terms, regardless of what other persons may need to be included or excluded from the family group to conform to its psychological boundaries as the family itself perceives them.

Furthermore a therapist cannot expect to fully understand a family's current situation, its past history as a family, or its future hopes and fears unless he knows all members of the family. To paraphrase Erikson, family development is epigenetic: the tasks of the family at each stage of its development are different and build upon each other (2, 3). The whole family participates in these tasks. Consequently, the way in which the younger, as well as the older, members of the family participate at specific stages of *family* development will greatly influence family life in its subsequent stages.

Finally, if the assumption that the whole family is in trouble is correct, the younger children must also need help in a troubled family. To leave them out of the unit in treatment is to run the risk that they may remain unhelped and be a source of future trouble for the family or themselves.

Thus the inclusion of the entire family including the younger children is essential to the therapist's understanding of the family's developmental history and current situation, to the family's sense of identity, and to make help available to all members of the family.

It would appear that both from a theoretical point of view and from practical necessity, the whole family should be included. Why then are younger children so often excluded from treatment?

The answer seems to lie in certain special characteristics of younger children that present difficulties to therapists and their ways of conducting therapy, and the special place younger children hold in many families. Therapists are accustomed to talk with their parents and through this medium to produce understanding, "insight," and improved "communications." Young children may be unable to talk or have a very limited vocabulary and understanding of abstract ideas. Children are restless and often literally unable to sit through the long sessions customarily used in family therapy. Even if the therapist is willing to put up with all this "inconvenience," he has to justify to himself that the children will not be hurt by being forced to witness unpleasant family confrontations and learn secrets from which they otherwise might have been safely insulated.

Parents, too, raise objections. While these often take a practical form, e.g., the children cannot miss school, or cub scouts, or would get home too late, the underlying theme is usually the parents' wish to believe their younger children as "normal." Bad enough that their older children have problems, they would at least like to believe that they have raised other "healthy" children. The thought that all their children may be affected by the family plight is frequently quite threatening to their self-esteem, since they feel that then they must be very poor parents.

The children themselves sometimes object (though less often than one might expect a priori). Family resistance to family therapy is as inevitable as individual resistance to individual therapy. Since family resistance frequently is expressed by some particular member of the family (who is then viewed as recalcitrant by the other family members and sometimes also by the therapists), it is not surprising that this spokesman is sometimes a young child. Indeed, the young child frequently still has a fairly direct and intuitive grasp of the parents' unvoiced feelings and is thus a good candidate to express their doubts and fears.

Last, but by no means least, even if a therapist is willing to make the technical modifications (see below) necessary to make it possible and emotionally safe for children to participate and is willing to work through the whole family's resistance to the inclusion of the younger children (from whatever part of the family it may come), he is still left with the burden of overcoming his own irrational resistances which are frequently experienced in rationalized form: the children are too young or too immature to understand or to participate. The truth is that it is by no means easy for adults to relate naturally to children. They tend to either ignore children or else to treat them with that condescending preciousness that implies that children are incapable of serious and well-thought out opinions of their own. While many children are very charming and well-behaved, others can be very trying. We can confess to having treated families with whom we were very glad to see the end of the hour. Finally, therapists have had to renounce the world of childhood with varying degrees of reluctance; the danger of having those feelings re-aroused is not to be discounted.

Given the many obstacles, internal and external, it is not surprising that many therapists have preferred to treat "the whole family" without the presence of younger children. We have ourselves made such accommodations, but in retrospect, always at the price of incomplete therapy.

In a family with two daughters, 18 and 14, and a 16-year-old retarded son who lived in a special school and only came home weekends, we elected to see the family without the son. Although the therapy showed some rather rapid success, later follow-up revealed a severe regression in the identified patient in response to the death of her paternal grandfather. A major factor in the regression was the depression of the father which the family had never permitted the therapists to approach. Since the father's depression was intimately tied up with his concern about having no normal male heir, we speculate that the question might have been more treatable in the presence of his retarded son, even though the latter was not directly involved in the daughter's problems, which seemed to improve dramatically. Our prejudices in regard to including a mentally retarded boy along with the four family members with normal intelligence no doubt contributed to our failure to explore more fully the possibility of his being included in the family sessions.

Facilitating the Participation of Young Children in Family Therapy

Given the need to include young children in family therapy and given the special needs of young children, how can family therapists conduct themselves so as to meet the needs of all members and their own. We have found a number of modifications useful. Many helpful suggestions are found in Satir's (4) chapter on "Including the Children in Family Therapy." We would particularly stress the following points:

The therapist must show consistent respect for two aspects of family life. He must respect each child as a *person* with a right to his own thoughts, feelings, and opinions and not merely as a *child*, which still carries with it the idea of being somehow inferior and of less importance and value than adults. On the other hand, he must also respect the parents' rights to be parents which includes the obligation to set and enforce standards of behavior for their children, even though those standards or means of enforcement may differ from those the therapist uses or would recommend. The lien is not as narrow as this account may make it appear, but is easily obscured by countertransference. We have found children observant and thoughtful about their families and frequently capable of making very valuable contributions. We solicit and value their opinions as we do those of older members.

Second, no one is ever required to answer any question, even if posed by one of the therapists. This is to some extent contrary to individual therapy and to the way some people conduct family therapy. However, it has the merit of protecting children from being "put on the spot." Many children have not yet learned how to shade the true or even to lie effectively. This would leave them defenseless against any intrusions into the privacy of their feelings unless they can have the right not to answer without having to give an excuse.

Third, we try to use simple language. However, being only human, we cannot watch or weigh each word. If we or others use difficult words, we or the person who used the word explains its meaning. Furthermore, the children are encouraged to ask if they do not understand something and they frequently make use of this freedom.

Finally, we make available and encourage the use of play materials of various sorts.

The Use of Play Activities to Facilitate the Child's Participation in Family Therapy

Play activity is the major factor that makes it possible to include young children in family therapy without treating them like miniature adults. Words are only one of many ways in which families communicate. Young children in particular, even when quite verbal, use more non-verbal modes of expression than adults. Play is a normal and important activity at home. Its inclusion permits the therapists to view an important aspect of family life. Furthermore, play serves the child not only for expression, but also as a defense against anxiety.

Convincing as is the case for letting children play during family therapy, we did not think of it spontaneously. We owe the idea to a 4-year-old girl in one of our first families who brought toys with her to her first session. From her example we learned that play can be a valuable addition to family therapy without interfering with the therapeutic work. Since then we have made available in the family therapy room the standard play materials used in child guidance clinics. These included drawing paper, crayons, water colors, finger paints, a blackboard and chalk, plasticine, building blocks, checkers, cards, soldiers, a toy pistol, and a furnished dollhouse with Flagg dolls. From the outset, the painting and drawing materials proved the most popular by far. But whatever their choice, we found that the use of these play materials made family therapy sessions more comfortable for younger family members. We refer, in particular, to children under ten. No matter how impressive their verbal skills, or their ability to listen to and comprehend what others are saying, children of this age group normally find it difficult to do nothing but "converse" for ninety minutes (5). The availability of play materials made it possible for these children to both express and defend themselves, thus putting them on a par with the family members who have more developed egos.

Play As a Mode of Expression

Through play, young children are often able to express fears which have gone unrecognized by their families. In so doing, they also clarify their own role in the family and the unique character of their relationship with crucial family members.

The 4½-year-old girl referred to above brought toys to the first session she attended. Her motives can only be surmised, but we suspect that both she and her family considered this the normal and appropriate thing to do for a little girl who was about to take a trip to a strange place. Small children quite frequently take some of their toys when going for a visit, especially if the visit is tinged with unpleasantness or anxiety. Perhaps her parents had also supported her bringing toys in order to encourage her to take a greater distance from the rest of the family in therapy, since at that time they saw her as "completely normal" and "too young" to participate in the therapy. They brought her only out of respect for our professional authority.

Although she was reluctant to come and her parents had their doubts, she was able to participate comfortably in our 90-minute sessions through the use of play. Since she was shy and at first reluctant to talk, she would have found sitting through the sessions without play difficult and it would have given her and her family additional rationalizations for not coming.

As we came to know the family better, it became clear that this girl had phobic symptoms that caused her great pain and her whole family very considerable inconvenience. Indeed she had more symptoms than the identified patient. There were multiple determinants for her parents' wish to exclude her. They wished to see her as normal and unharmed. Her symptoms were in an area to which the parents were not as sensitized as the identified patient's school difficulties. They no doubt hoped she would outgrow her difficulties. Most decisively, she was on good terms with both her parents and the peacemaker in the family, whereas her older brothers were each allied with one of the parents. The parent who was most active in initiating treatment selected as the identified patient the boy allied with the other parent, thus obliquely bringing some of the marital dissatisfaction into focus. By contrast, the girl represented the strengths and happy sides of the marriage and family life.

After two years of therapy, the now 6-year-old girl wanted to get some water from the bathroom to continue her painting. She asked her mother to go with her because she was afraid to go into a dark room alone. The mother agreed without hesitation although she was just in the middle of speaking. The therapists intervened and told the girl that it was important for mother to remain at the meeting. They suggested that she try to get the water by herself, and assured her that help would be available if she needed it. She was able to perform this task on her own and was visibly pleased.

This led directly and naturally to the subject of fears. When asked how she felt her parents could best help her to deal with her fears, the girl replied that she wanted them to help her get used to the fears. The discussion that followed brought out that the mother, too, suffered from multiple fears and was responding to her daughter's phobias as if there really were something of which to be afraid. The father then mentioned that maternal grandmother also reacted to minor difficulties with disproportionate anxiety approaching panic. Thus, not only did the mother learn how her attitudes perpetuated her daughter's fears, but a family pattern spanning at least three generations was revealed for further investigation. The play, which had begun as an expressive activity (painting) and had quickly turned into a defensive maneuver (being out of the room and trying to pull mother out), ended by giving the therapists an opportunity for role modeling and shed light on an intergenerational family problem and the manner in which it was passed from one generation to the next.

Play Activity As a Defense Against Anxiety

At times, particularly in early family therapy sessions, play activity may serve as a useful defense against anxiety. The availability of play materials gives children an opportunity to retreat into play when they feel too threatened, or when the therapists feel that the child's retreat into play in the face of overwhelming anxiety is preferable to the risk that his attempts to cope with his anxiety in the context of the therapeutic situation may disrupt the treatment process.

> The youngest of four children, an eight-year-old boy, was extremely uncomfortable during family diagnostic sessions, although the discussion centered around the difficulties his parents were encountering with their oldest child, a sixteen-year-old boy. Nor did this eight-year-old attempt to alleviate his discomfort by engaging in play activity. Instead, he dealt with his anxiety by frequently interrupting the family discussion with seemingly irrelevant material. It soon became apparent that he hoped that this material, which was supposed to cheer everyone up, would help to heal the breach in the family.
>
> It was too early in the treatment process for the therapists to deal with the boy's anxiety in depth without an inappropriate shift in focus from the diagnostic problem which was of immediate and rather urgent concern to the older members of the family. Conse-

quently, the only alternative was to strongly encourage him to use the play materials at his disposal. He then proceeded to try to comfort himself by painting pictures which conveyed the same rosy sentiments he had previously put into words. This respite gave the therapists time to proceed with the gathering of essential facts and dealing with the emergency created by the identified patient. The therapists could then apportion more of the treatment time to letting the youngest boy talk about his anxieties, which he was able to do without having to resort to the disruptive defensive behavior he had used earlier. He went on to make some valuable contributions to the family therapeutic work in his own right.

The fact that play may serve as a defense against anxiety makes it safer to include very young children in conjoint family therapy. Therapists can exert only limited control in the treatment setting over the issues raised and the manner in which they are discussed. Provided family members do not deal with each other destructively (and therapists do have considerable control over this), there seems little danger that anxiety will reach harmful levels for the adults in the family, regardless of what issues come up for discussion. However, this is not true for the child, especially the young child, who has not yet developed strong defenses against anxiety, and who has a greater propensity for misunderstanding or distorting what is said in terms of his own fantasies. The opportunity to retreat into play gives the child the freedom to defend himself against a threatening situation.

> While the parents engaged in sharp and bitter arguments, their two sons, one pre-adolescent and the other in late latency, seemed so deeply absorbed in their joint play that their parents doubted that the boys had been listening. In fact, if the boys were asked to participate in their parents' discussion at an appropriate point, it was obvious from their replies that they had listened carefully and were ready to make their own verbal contributions. However, if the argument grew more heated, and the material became too threatening, they would leave the room frequently to get water for painting, etc.

The therapists, in turn, are given the opportunity to adjust the dosage of the child's involvement in treatment to the extent they deem necessary. If the therapists feel that the child is not yet ready to deal with a particular issue, they can support his right to retreat into play. Telling a child that he does not have to answer a question asked by a parent, or even by the therapist, gives the child the freedom to maintain his defenses to the extent he feels necessary at that moment. If, later, when the therapists know the child's needs and ego strengths well, they deem his tendency to withdraw excessive, they may elect in various ways to help the child speak out in analogous ways to those used in individual therapy. The choice then lies between merely pointing out that the child is withdrawing, or that he seems to be withdrawing because the subject has aroused a great deal of feeling, or directly encouraging the child to tell how he feels. How vigorous the therapists are in encouraging the child depends on the stability of the family situation, the safety of the issue for the child, and the child's ego structure. In no case would we recommend pressuring a child or demanding that he speak. The final choice must be his. It has been our experience that children are usually eager to talk once they feel it is safe to do so—and that they are frequently more perceptive and honest than the adults in the family (6).

THE CHILD'S CONTRIBUTION TO FAMILY THERAPY

Granting that in one sense "family" therapy is unthinkable without the presence of all members, there remains the question of whether a young child has any specific personal contribution to make to the process of family therapy other than his physical presence. We believe that the answer is decidedly—"Yes." From our work with families which included very young children we can offer at least three specific ways in which their participation enhanced the process. First, the child through his behavior, play or words may act as spokesman for the underlying feeling of the family, and thus provide access to one of the family's problems. Second, his presence not only provides valuable clues toward understanding the quality of family interaction, but may also act as a modulator of the interaction of older family members. Third, as the child interacts with the therapists or elicits intervention from the therapists, the latter inevitably have an important, but natural opportunity to set the parents an example of how to handle their children.

Access to Family Problems

Children tend to be far more direct and honest than adolescents or adults. The younger the child, the more straightforward his communication is likely to be. We do not mean to imply that children are incapable of deception or of fierce loyalty in maintaining a family secret (they are); we are merely calling attention to the simpler ego structure of the child in the face of, at least relatively, more powerful instinctual drives. At other times children may use their partial immunity from retribution by adults to voice unpleasant truths that their parents are afraid to mention. At other times, they may express family problems through the use of play materials.

> All the children in a family, including one overtly psychotic child, were deprived of affection and warmth, and could only communicate their insatiable need for love through play and action. When the therapists responded by recognizing these underlying feelings and dealing with them appropriately, the children's attitude toward therapy became more positive.
>
> This freed the mother, who up until this time had been insisting that the children come, to show the negative side of her ambivalence without putting it into words. Because the therapists had been able to establish (in part through the instrument of play) a satisfactory relationship with the children, the latter felt safe enough to expose their mother's plan not to return for further sessions in time for us to initiate a discussion of the mother's feelings. Thus the abrupt and premature termination of treatment was averted.
>
> Later in treatment, as the parents continued to miss or cancel appointments, the children expressed their feelings by vying with one another for the privilege of writing the date and time of the next appointment on the blackboard.

As noted above, a child may catalyze the family's and therapist's understanding of some aspect of the family's problem. The fact that a child cannot speak does not preclude his functioning as a catalyst and consequently should not disqualify his inclusion in treatment. Such a child may play a crucial role in the family problem.

> A family with five children, who ranged in age from seventeen to two, was seen in consultation because of the learning difficulties of their 13-year-old third child. We decided to ask them to bring the youngest children, an eight-year-old girl and a two-year-old boy with them, although they allegedly had no problems. Certainly we might have been tempted to exclude at least the two-year-old, simply on the grounds that he had not yet learned to talk.
>
> Moreover, this family seemed to have ample problems without involving the youngest, healthiest members. The father had just lost his job; in addition, he had heart disease, and was not taking proper care of himself; the oldest child was in serious trouble with the school authorities who suspected her of selling drugs to other students; the 15-year-old boy was also having his difficulties in school; the third child, who was the identified patient, could not learn although she had an above average IQ; the mother was depressed and angry because her husband would not follow his doctor's orders.
>
> While there was considerable covert hostility among the five oldest members of the family, everyone seemed fond of the two youngest children, especially the baby. He was a very active little boy, who

wandered from person to person, including the two therapists in a friendly way. In fact, he demanded attention, and everyone catered to him in return.

Stimulated by his presence, the family began to talk about the changes that had taken place in their lives in the two years since his birth. The boy woke up at 4 o'clock every morning, and the mother felt that she had to get up when he did and feed him. Then she made breakfast for the rest of the family. Since she had no domestic help, she spent the day doing housework, when she was not taking care of the baby. Neither the mother nor the father could fall asleep until all the children had come in at night, which meant they frequently did not get to bed until 2 A.M. On the one hand, the parents resented their children's "lack of consideration" and the latter felt guilty about staying out late on dates or parties, because they knew that they were depriving their parents of their sleep. In fact, the mother was clearly exhausted by this schedule, which was frequently aggravated by the baby's habit of waking in the middle of the night. Indeed the children's school problems and a severe exacerbation of father's rheumatic heart disease seemed to date back approximately two years.

Thus, the diagnostic picture that emerged was very different both from the way the family saw itself (a family with a sick father, an overwhelmed mother, three difficult teenagers, and two problem-free innocent younger children) as well as from the constellation that the therapist might have anticipated (teen age children battling for independence from their parents with regression on both sides). Indeed, the self-destruction and mutual ambivalence among the five older members of the family was at least to an important extent a displacement of the hostility they all felt toward the defenseless and overindulged baby who was overtaxing the family's limited physical, financial, and possibly affectional resources.

Conversely, a youngest child can also be a source of unanimity and family cohesion. Some children will even use their privileged status to play the role of peacemaker. We have seen a number of youngest children of both sexes painting pictures with happy connotations, such as valentines, and asking for the appreciation of one or both parents at points where they sense great tension in the family.

Finally, a child's play activities may provide useful clues as to the underlying issue at a particular point in therapy.*

While his parents talked in a very critical way about the difficulties of the identified patient, the latter, a 12-year-old boy, painted a

---

* It should be noted, however, that the correct interpretation of the child's use of play material for this purpose usually requires prior training in play therapy techniques.

picture of a bleeding heart and colored the inside black. We took
this to represent both his wish to get close to his parents and his
depression about being unable to do so.

The Expression of Underlying Feelings

The feeling that one is not loved, or not loved enough, and the concomitant need for reassurance, are very basic issues that family members
—old and young alike—are often unable to put into words.

> The children in one family fought almost steadily throughout the
> first session over possession of the play materials in the room. They
> fought not only over single items, such as a particular doll, but also
> over items in plentiful supply, such as paper. This behavior, which
> was unchecked by their parents, provided us with clues to their
> unspoken need for love, a need which all the members of the family
> shared in common.

The Quality of Family Interaction

The availability of play materials provides the therapists with many
opportunities to observe the interaction among siblings, and between
the children and their parents. Thus the therapists are provided with a
sample of family interaction, centered around a commonplace daily
activity, which enhances their understanding of total family functioning.

> In one family, a great deal of fighting occurred between the two
> older children, while the youngest, who was not the identified pa-
> tient, usually played by herself. We soon learned that the older
> children actually had a close relationship that they could only
> express through fighting. They were excluding the youngest child,
> who made desperate efforts to buy the affection of both adults and
> children, in therapy and real life, with presents, often made from
> play materials during our sessions. In this family, we regarded as
> an improvement the youngest's increasing ability to join in the
> fighting and be less accommodating to parents and therapists.

Opportunities for Role-Modeling

Play activity also furnishes the therapist with built-in opportunities
to teach parents more effective ways of handling their children through
actual demonstration. These demonstrations come about inevitably as
the therapists are called upon to deal with the children's demands. In
general, the therapists should be quite permissive, placing few restrictions on the amount or type of play materials used and generous with
help and praise when a child needs reassurance. At the same time, how-

ever, the therapist must be prepared to set firm and consistent limits, with the proviso that the reasons for the limits are always explained.

In a family of five, the children's overt difficulties centered around sharing or taking turns with the play materials, playing games according to a prescribed set of rules, and the pathologically immature use of their parents as judges in disputes which arose in connection with their play activities. In fact, these particular aspects of their behavior served to express the intense need felt by each of these children to get more for himself than he could allow his siblings, since each doubted he would receive enough otherwise. Once the therapists recognized these underlying feelings, they were able to put their insights to practical use by offering the parents a model of how to deal with their children's fractious behavior without responding in a defensive or judgmental way. This demonstration, in itself, was enough to reduce the intense rivalry for supplies; later, the methods used were successfully emulated by the parents.

Inevitably, this family also provided the therapists with many opportunities to demonstrate how to set limits. On one occasion, when all three children were busily engaged in the mass production of finger paintings, they eventually ran out of places to put the paintings while they dried. The most disturbed child in the family then gave his father one of his paintings to hold. Somewhat reluctantly, the father agreed first to hold one and then a second. When the father clearly could hold no more, the boy turned to the male therapist with the same demand. The therapist refused in a decisive but friendly way, and explained that he felt that holding the paintings would distract him, and he would not be able to give his full attention to the discussion that was in progress. The father, following the therapist's example, was then able to say that he had similar feelings, at which point the boy was forced to face the fact that he had to stop painting temporarily.

Thus, in this instance, the father was made aware of one way of asserting his own needs without harming his son. The son, along with his whole family, learned that even insatiable desires have limits and that such limits need not have any catastrophic consequences.

SUMMARY AND CONCLUSION

Family therapy is still young. We wish to call attention to the desirability of changing some aspects of this treatment modality while it is still in a state of flux and before it becomes codified and rigid. In particular, one common phenomenon, violates the basic principles of family therapy: only a portion, instead of the whole, family is in treatment. Children, especially younger ones, are frequently excluded (7). Among the many reasons children are excluded, we assign particular importance to the fact that children express their thoughts and feelings more in play and action and less in words than adults. Many adults, including therapists, are not comfortable with these modes of expression. One way of facilitating the child's participation in family therapy is to make available play materials in the therapy room. This resource prevents the children from becoming restless and offers them a defense against excessively threatening material. The therapists have an opportunity to observe an added aspect of the family's life and a chance to model roles for the parents. The presence of the children, and sometimes their play itself, can provide valuable clues to the underlying feelings and issues in the family. Once they learn about family therapy, children are frequently more dedicated to the treatment process than their parents.

We have not seen any unfavorable responses by young children to family therapy and urge slight modifications of treatment in order to include the whole family.

REFERENCES

1. WYNNE, LYMAN: "Some Indications and Contraindications for Exploratory Family Therapy," in I. Boszormenyi-Nagy, and J. L. Framo (Eds.): *Intensive Family Therapy*. Harper & Row, Publishers, Inc.; New York, 1965, pp. 289-322.
2. ZILBACH, J. J.: Family Development. Chapter 14 in J. Marmor: *Modern Psychoanalysis*. Basic Books, Inc., New York, 1968, pp. 355-386.
3. ZILBACH, J. J., BERGEL, E. W., GASS, C.: The Family Life Cycle: Some Developmental Considerations. Proceedings of the IVth International Congress of Group Psychotherapy. Verlag der Wiener Medizinisches Akademie. Vienna, 1968, pp. 157-162.
4. SATIR, V. W.: *Conjoint Family Therapy*. Science and Behavior Books, Inc. Palo Alto, 1964, pp. 136-159.
5. BERGEL, E. W., GASS, C., & ZILBACH, J. J.: The Use of Play Materials in Conjoint Family Therapy. Proceedings of the IVth International Congress of Group Psychotherapy. Verlag der Wiener Medizinischen Akademie. Vienna, 1968. #IV-16.
6. GASS, C., BERGEL, E. W., & ZILBACH, J. J.: *Including Younger Children in Family Therapy*. Unpublished manuscript. (April 1968).
7. ACKERMAN, N. W.: Child Participation in Family Therapy. *Family Progress*, 9 (4): 403-410 (December 1970).

24

MECHANISMS OF CHANGE IN MULTIPLE FAMILY THERAPY

H. Peter Laqueur, M.D.

Director Family Study and Treatment Unit, Vermont State Hospital
Associate Professor of Clinical Psychiatry
University of Vermont Medical College

INTRODUCTION

The abstract character of general systems theory (GST), coupled with the fact that it has its roots in basic physics, make it seem remote from the practicalities of human suffering and psychotherapy. In fact, how-ewever, GST provides a conceptual framework which permits elucidation of the very complex systems the clinician must deal with in multiple family therapy (MFT), as well as the therapeutic techniques he employs to this end. An attempt has been made in this paper to explore this hypothesis in detail and, in so doing, to demonstrate the value of GST for the understanding and treatment of mental illness.

The Therapist As Systems Analyst

Within the framework of GST the individual is seen as a subsystem of a higher system—a dyad—and then again as part of the next higher system in the hierarchy: the family, the kinship system, the community. When the functioning of the individual or the family is threatened by maladaptation or pathological conditions, GST permits the therapist to identify the primary focus of disturbance, and to devise methods to improve the adaptation and integration of these disturbed individuals and families in the surrounding community.

Thus, with specific reference to family therapy, GST conceives of the family and its components as subsystems in a larger field of interrelated systems whose interface* problems can be studied and dealt with in much the same way a good mechanic understands and repairs the defective component parts of a complex machine. If the therapist subscribes to the view that family malfunction is caused by a specific malfunction of its component parts or of feedback mechanisms, he performs the functions of a systems analyst (analyzing feedback, perception, recognition, association, and planning for response). He can then propose to the family new and specific possibilities for repair and restitution that can lead to correction of the malfunction.

Basic Principles of Human Behavior: The Concepts of Program and Style in GST

The material structure and processes of a human being can be understood from the viewpoint of physiology, cybernetics, and technology, and can be demonstrated on a robot-model. But man is also capable of other mental processes, best described as spontaneous, or creative processes, which, although dependent on the material structure and function of the organism, are not identical with it. The selection of information, the spontaneity and originality of ideas, combinations of ideas, and the determination of a goal and purpose in life cannot be described in the same terms as the memory and pattern recognition area, the program, and the motor preparation area of a robot system.

It can be said, then, that each individual has a program which can be understood, at least in part, on the basis of statistical expectations and cybernetic models, and, in addition, a personal style that defies statistical predictions. The interaction of two or more persons is determined not only by their individual programs, that is, their statistically predictable structure and function, but also by their personal styles, that is, their personal selections, spontaneous associations, and creative goals and purposes in life.

In addition to its phylogenetic and ontogenetic particulars, the program includes unconscious, preconscious, and conscious mental elements, as well as much of what the individual has learned during his life span. In other words, the program represents the cybernetic struggle for survival.

In contrast, the handling of new and unexpected situations lies within

---

* *Interfaces* between systems are the areas where energy, matter, and information (i.e., knowledge, meaning, and affect) are interchangd.

the province of the individual's personal style. Confronted with problems of equal magnitude, one individual will deal with a stressful situation by imitating the problem-solving techniques of others; another will find new ways of coping creatively and intelligently with the situation. Whether an individual acts as a follower or a leader in a complex situation is determined by his personal style, not by the program that is built into all human organisms. Creativity in man transcends the cybernetic struggle for survival.

The concepts of program and style may appear to overlap in some areas. In the area of learning, for example, a distinction must be made between what is learned and how it is learned. What is learned (be it by a computer or a human being) is objectively and statistically measurable and is part of the program; how (by what method) it is learned is part of the original, creative, spontaneous approach to learning and characterizes the individual's personal style. A computer has a program but no personal style.

The program can develop normally or pathologically. When faulty ways of dealing with stresses, e.g., "bad habits," addictions, etc., insinuate their way into the program, they must be corrected through new experiences such as therapy or the introduction of another significant factor. The program becomes partially or completely disjointed in mental illness. The individual's personal style may or may not be affected by mental illness, but his program for adaptation to stress is always affected. This vulnerability can be explained by the fact that the program originates at the border of original mental and robot-like physiological structure; consequently, it encompasses primitive as well as more mature functions.

THE ORIGINS AND RATIONALE FOR MFT

The mental patient who bounces back and forth between home and hospital is a familiar problem. He is hospitalized when the family can no longer cope with him at home, improves under hospital care and returns home, only to be brought back to the hospital by the family after a shorter or longer interval. The development of family therapy can be attributed, in part, to the realization that the patient's home environment, i.e., the quality of his relationship with his family, was at least a contributing factor in his illness and relapses.

In contrast, MFT was born of necessity. When the state hospital with which this author was affiliated did not have the resources to provide enough therapists to conduct family therapy sessions, he and his colleagues began to treat four or five hospitalized patients and their families in a group. We soon discovered, however, that the presence of the second, third, fourth or fifth family was not only an expedient solution to the shortage of professional personnel, but that this approach had therapeutic advantages as well. For one, it seemed to us that MFT could induce changes in harmful patterns of interaction within a shorter period of time than could the treatment of individual families. As demonstrated below, when a group includes the members of several families, the therapist is able to use some of the participants in specific co-therapeutic roles to expedite the achievement of insight and the modification of pathological behavior.

*Problems in Individual Family Therapy and
Their Amelioration in MFT*

The difficulties inherent in the treatment of individual families which include a schizophrenic member have long been recognized. MFT provides a unique setting for the resolution of the core conflict which, in our opinion, plays a major etiological role in schizophrenia. More specifically, we see the schizophrenic patient's main problem as a conflict between his struggle to achieve differentiation, on the one hand, and his need to maintain his symbiotic attachment to primary family objects, on the other. The presence of other families and other hospitalized patients in the treatment setting seems to stimulate the patients to engage actively in the struggle toward increasing self-differentiation and independence. In MFT sessions patients and parents tend to recreate the primitive, long-standing family situations which gave rise to, and have served to perpetuate this conflict; thus, a patient or a relative may identify with a member of another family on a given occasion and learn by analogy with much less anxiety than is usually associated with such learning.

But apart from such considerations, the therapist is confronted by two major obstacles in his efforts to treat such families:

1. The code every family seems to develop for internal verbal and nonverbal communication among its members.
2. The resistance of the family to change.

The therapist must "break" the code if he is to understand the family, and be understood by the family in turn. To understand what goes on within the family, the therapist must learn to decode not only the normal intrafamilial language, but the semantically distorted language of the schizophrenic family member. To make his messages to the family understandable, the therapist must be able to translate his message into terms consonant with the internal family code. The help provided by other patients in facilitating this translation process is of great value. If four families are together, usually at least one can pick up the therapist's signal, and rephrase and amplify his message to make it comprehensible to the other three families. When problems of patient-family communication arise, very often schizophrenics can translate for each other, and do a better job than the therapist could.

The family's resistance to change is a second major impediment to treatment progress. In individual family sessions, the hospitalized patient finds himself in direct confrontation with his most intimate opponents, his family, and this is often perceived as a threat of such magnitude that strong defenses are mobilized in all the members of the family, tending to reinforce their normal resistance to change. The specific mechanisms available in MFT to overcome this resistance to change are discussed in detail below.

THE MFT SYSTEM

Phases in Multiple Family Therapy

For schematic purposes, the treatment process can be divided into three phases:

Phase I. Patients and families who are new to the group obtain some initial relief of anxiety, and some remission of symptoms.

Phase II. Their initial fears about exposing hurts and anxieties come to the fore, with a concomitant increase of resistance. An initial lowering of defenses is achieved by the therapist and those families who are older members of the group.

Phase III. Significant changes begin to take place. There is a growing realization on the part of patients and families of their deeper problems, and their ability to deal with them. Concomitantly, there is evidence of increased flexibility in their recognition of the alternative options open to them.

Mechanisms of Change in MFT

A description of some of the mechanisms which operate in the MFT will serve to illustrate the nature of the transactions performed by the MFT system. These include a) the use of families as co-therapists, b) competition, c) delineation of the field of interaction, d) learning by analogy, e) learning through identification, f) learning through the identification constellation, g) "tuning-in," h) learning through trial and error, i) the use of models, j) focus of excitation, and k) the amplification and modulation of signals.

a) *The use of families as co-therapists.*

As noted above, the therapist often uses less disturbed families as co-therapists in his efforts to reach the more disturbed families. This process is facilitated by the fact that all the families in the group have a common problem, i.e., a seriously disturbed member. Within this frame of reference, MFT gives patients and families the opportunity to improve communications, achieve better understanding, and exchange similar attitudes and experiences, on the assumption that this exchange will help to cope more effectively with frustrating realities. The use of families as co-therapists has relevance for other mechanisms as well, and will be described in further detail below.

b) *Competition.*

Competition among several families in the MFT system produces changes in their internal power distribution and behavior faster than occurs in the treatment of a single family. A threat to the status of a family or an individual member stimulates competition, which leads, in turn, to meaningful interaction of the family members at an earlier stage in treatment. At a later stage in the group process, competition among the families is replaced by cooperation.

c) *Delineation of the field of interaction.*

Following Lewin's approach, MFT studies the total field of interaction among subsystems (patient and family) and the suprasystem (the total social environment). The therapist tries to make the participants understand that the illness of the individual family member must be understood in the context of the total field of interaction: the behavior of one individual affects the actions, reactions, and general behavior of all the other people in his environment. The validity of this concept is clearly demonstrated in MFT. Thus, in therapeutic sessions, members of an MFT group have an opportunity to observe that people do not react to members of their own family, circle of friends, employers, and fellow-employees, but that each individual (subsystem), as well as the social environment (suprasystem), has a direct impact on the family and participates in the final result of treatment. The therapist uses this concept of the field of interacting forces to bring into the open the feelings, problems, and needs of participants that had previously been denied or covered up, and to explore new ways of handling them. Mutual recognition of problems and needs in a given field, in the presence of several fathers, mothers, children, and siblings, enables the therapist to choose a rational treatment program from a much wider range and variety of therapeutic approaches than would be available to him with single individuals or single families.

Clinical illustration

For the most part, Joan was uncommunicative at MFT sessions, and let her mother do all the talking. She also let her mother make her personal decisions. For example, she had responded to an insistent boy friend by simply handing her mother the telephone when he called.

Tom, who had been caught between the excessive demands of an overpowering father and the efforts of an overprotective mother to shield him from life, but who had begun to recognize this, pointed out Joan's extreme dependency on her mother. Joan's mother (Mrs. P) replied to Tom's statement by comparing Joan's attitude toward her to her attitude toward her own mother: She said she had never been able to "talk back" to her own mother, who she described as a very forceful personality with definite opinions on everything, and then added, "I still can't talk back to her." She then admitted that she was hurt by the fact that Joan seemed to function better without her. During a previous weekend, when she could not stay home with Joan, the girl had been very active: She had invited a girl friend to visit her, and had done some cooking in preparation for her company. But last weekend, when Mrs. P was home, Joan had slept twelve hours a day.

Tom tried to interpret Mrs. P's (and Joan's) behavior on the basis of his own experience: "Mrs. P, you can't talk back to your mother for fear of hurting her feelings, and Joan can't talk to you because she's afraid of hurting your feelings. I can't talk with my parents because I'm afraid of hurting them."

As a result of this interaction, Mrs. P realized that her attempts to control Joan, by convincing her that she "always knew best," stemmed from her resentment at being treated this way by her own mother. Tom's mother (Mrs. S) also gained some insight into her behavior. She said she understood Mrs. P's deference to her mother's wishes; she did the same thing with her husband "because he is so capable and can do everything so much better than I can." Only Mr. S, the most rigid member of the group, did not profit from this interaction. He brushed aside the pleas of his wife and son for better communication: "If I'm too forceful, I can't help it. That's the way I am."

d) *Learning by analogy.*

Members of an MFT group have many opportunities to observe analogous conflict situations. One family faced with a conflict it cannot resolve watches another family handle an analogous situation more successfully, and learns new ways of negotiating. Obviously, the knowledge that others "have been there" is an important incentive in learning, and this situation occurs with great frequency in the MFT group whose members present many diverse types of conflict.

Clinical illustration

Bob, who had just been taken off medication, was extremely tense: "When I started therapy I didn't think I had any feelings. For a long time I didn't feel anything. But now that I've stopped taking my medication I've begun to feel things for the first time. I get shaky, I get upset, I think I'm going to explode." The therapist then tried to find out what was upsetting Bob, at which point his mother interrupted to say that his excitement was due to the elimination of the medication.

Bob was clearly provoked by this gratuitous explanation: "I guess she wants me to go back on medication, so I can escape my feelings. I don't think you ever wanted to listen to me. And when I wanted to tell Dad something, he wouldn't listen either. Even when I banged my head on the wall, he wouldn't listed. He'd say, 'No, not now.' He just didn't want to take the time. You didn't want me to have any feelings."

It subsequently turned out that Bob's emotional distress had been precipitated by the fact that his mother, without his prior knowledge, had volunteered to provide some services on the ward, an intrusion he deeply resented: "My parents have always been involved in anything I've done. I've never been allowed to be independent." At this point, his mother said she would retract her offer to work as a volunteer on the ward, but Bob wasn't happy with this solution because he felt that her action would be dictated by her desire to overprotect him.

The therapist then attempted to involve the group in the discussion by asking them the question which seemed to be central to the difficulties between Bob and his parents: Should the feelings of individual family members always be attenuated at some point to keep "peace" in the family, or would it not be more productive in the long run to bring feelings out into the open, discuss them, and then try to resolve the disagreement?

The therapist's efforts to generalize from the situation between Bob and his mother stimulated the other members of the group to remember and relate conflict situations in their own families where the feelings of anger and resentment evoked by their relatives attempts to overprotect them had been covered up and left to smolder with unfortunate consequences.

e) *Learning through identification.*

MFT affords many opportunities for identification. Young people watch other young people deal with the older generation. Fathers learn from other fathers, mothers from other mothers, and married couples show better understanding for each other after observing other married couples. In other words, the fellowship of experience helps each member of the family to cope with existential and situational problems.

f) *Learning through the identification constellation.*

This is a more complex mechanism than simple identification, and one that probably is unique to MFT. Identical family configurations give rise to something that might be called an identification constellation. Thus, in a group containing four young female patients and their mothers (three of whom had been widowed for many years, and the fourth divorced since the patient was four years old), an extremely rapid identification of the four patients with each other and the four mothers with each other was observed.

g) *"Tuning-in."*

Not only the identification of one person or group of persons with another, but the identification of one situation with another frequently leads to important insights in MFT.

Clinical illustration

Despite the therapist's persistent attempts to make Jim's father understand that his excessive demands could have contributed to Jim's illness, the father vehemently denied having made such demands on Jim, and insisted that Jim's "drive" had made him overdo things. But Jim's mother recalled that her husband often tried to impress Jim with the importance of striving to excel by telling him how he himself had struggled to succeed—"I worked after school; I had to earn my own way," etc. At the same time, however, he showered Jim with all the material things he had never had as a young man. The therapist pointed out to the father that this put Jim in a very difficult position: "On the one hand, you wanted Jim to be a self-made man; on the other, you wanted to live vicariously so you gave him everything you had never had yourself. You can't have a silver spoon in your mouth and be a self-made man as well. You wanted Jim to be two different things at once."

At this point, the older brother of another patient suddenly saw things in a new light. "I think Melvin was in the same kind of situation with me. I started to work at a very early age, and I had had to do most of the earning; Melvin wasn't in a position to help. But I tried to do things for him, so he was in the same predicament as Jim in a way. When I want Melvin to relax a little, I bring up something that puts me at a disadvantage. Now I understand why that seems to give him a feeling of confidence."

h) *Learning through trial and error.*

The members of an MFT group have a unique opportunity to try out new modes of behavior and reinforce them if they meet with the approval of the group, or discard them if the group disapproves.

To illustrate, the MFT group is characterized by the simultaneous presence of many authority figures—the therapist, fathers, mothers, husbands, and so forth. In this setting the relationships between patients and various authority figures can be worked through fully and rapidly by means of the comparatively nonthreatening process of understanding through analogy and identification. The patient's positive transference feelings toward the therapist in the role of parent-surrogate may transiently diminish the parent's authoritarian status, thereby encouraging the patient to behave more independently, to be more "daring," in MFT.

The MFT situation also provides patients, as well as parents, with an opportunity to form new interpersonal relations. The patient experiences new relationships with parents other than his own which are less threatening to him. And his relatives may form similar relationships which are equally rewarding. Such gratifying experiences are much less likely to occur if the patient attempts to change the quality of his relationships within the context of his own family; when the individual family is treated as a separate unit, the patient meets with more intense and more frequent rejection by his family than he does in the MFT situation. Thus, the MFT paradigm, in which family relationships are pooled, provides broader and safer opportunities to try out adaptive behavior and new role relationships.

i) *The use of models.*

The therapist in MFT uses the healthier aspects of one family as a model and as a challenge to motivate other families to change their own behavior. The potential for this is enhanced by the fact that MFT groups are open-ended, so that each group includes families at different stages of treatment. This also increases the co-therapy potential of families to help one another. Usually, the persons with the most severe symptoms (i.e., the primary patients) are the first members of an MFT group to profit from this use of models. The attitudes of their relatives change later when the more mature behavior of the primary patients become manifest.

j) *Focus of excitation.*

The therapist who seeks to break through the resistance to change behavior typically manifested by the family with a schizophrenic member may find it helpful to ask himself how people integrate new experiences into their outlook on the world and their preparation for future behavior? Perhaps some clues can be derived from information theory, which postulates that those things have the highest information value that have the least probability of occurring, and yet do occur. In other words, a new pattern, i.e., a new sequence of signals producing an excitation focus in the nervous system, has significant information value.

Translated into MFT terms, a new, more realistic type of behavior manifested by one individual or family, as distinguished from their usual behavior, can act as a focus of excitation for the whole group, if it is used skillfully by the therapist.

Clinical illustrations

A patient whose speech habitually consisted of incoherent, neologistic sentences, especially when his parents were around, was suddenly interrupted by the therapist: "Look here, Irwin, we know that you're putting on this show to punish your parents. How about cutting out the nonsense?"

The patient didn't reply to this rather sarcastic statement, but continued to ramble about the helicopters his father, who, in fact, was a small shopkeeper, owned, and his great wealth. At this point the therapist began a rapid, rambling, loud, nonsensical discourse. Everyone watched him and Irwin. Suddenly, Irwin turned to his parents with an amazed expression. "What's the matter with him?" he asked, acting as if he had never been "out of it" himself.

The excitement flowing off from this "improbable event," namely, the "normal" talk of a schizophrenic patient, had a powerful effect on the other schizophrenic patients in the group. They, too, became less withdrawn and more to the point.

At another MFT session, the mood of the fairly dull "conversational" meeting changed instantly when John, a young patient who was usually subdued and quiet, said, "I've been in treatment so long, and nothing seems to change. I've lost all hope; I probably won't ever get well." His parents were shocked by these remarks which had been made in a quiet, sad voice.

John's atypical behavior touched off a great deal of inner turmoil in the other patients and families. The patients identified with John's fears, the parents with his parents' anxiety and guilt feelings. For the first time, John and his parents were able to come out of their shells a little. They were encouraged to do so by the intense concern expressed by the other members of the group, which had been mobilized by John's unexpected disclosure of his real feelings.

k) *The amplification and modulation of signals.*

A sensitive patient can pick up a signal from the therapist and amplify it, thereby sensitizing his family. This first family, in turn, will further amplify such signals for other families who, without this amplification, might not have responded to the therapist's signals.

Furthermore, the specific "I and Thou" relationship between the therapist and the first patient may, through reverberating communications and feelings, ultimately lead to similar feelings of empathy and identification among other families in the group, particularly those who feel that the first patient and his family "have been there," that they have experienced the difficulties they have not yet resolved. And these other families gain confidence from their observation that such difficulties can be resolved.

Clinical illustration

An overanxious father, Mr. A, and his rebellious daughter periodically quarreled violently at MFT sessions about the father's attempts to exert tight control over the daughter's movements.

After one such argument, the therapist, with a twinkle in his eye and a smile, turned to another patient in the group and said, "The same thing happened here several months ago between you and your mother, remember?" Mary B nodded, and immediately began to attack Mr. and Mrs. A: "You can't think that this will endear you to your daughter, or make her behave better. . . ."

Mary B's parents confirmed the fact that scolding and fighting had not gotten them anywhere with their daughter, but that a reasonable, open-minded approach and compromise seemed to have worked in their case. Other children in families C and D then pitched in to amplify the signal from the therapist to Mr. A and his daughter.

Moreover, the improved relationships in family B seemed to give the other families in the group an incentive to try new and different approaches to solve their own problems.

Program and Styles in MFT

The program of an MFT group is largely determined by the goals of the hospital or clinic in which it takes place. The goal of the MFT group is a given; it is designed to foster better mutual understanding between patients and their families in order to assure the patient's continued well-being after his discharge from the hospital. The way this goal is approached is determined by the personal style of the therapist. It goes without saying, of course, that the goals of the institution, the therapist, the identified patient, and those of his family must all come to approximate one another.

Threats of Systems Failure

All the qualities that form the personal style of the therapist, namely, originality in the handling of a new situation, the ability to adjust to cases of unusual malfunctioning, initiative in the choice of hitherto unused approaches in critical situations, and a sense of timing, are pre-requisites for clinical competence in every setting. However, these quali-ties are particularly important in the therapist of a MFT group, because such a group is quick to take on all the properties of a system that is threatened by failure when it is confronted by unexpected or unusual situations. Some examples of situations with which the therapist may have to cope in order to avoid such failures are described below.

Overload. Several families may begin to quarrel violently at the same time, and demand that the other participants arbitrate their conflicts, without paying any attention to the therapist's attempts to regulate "traffic" and assign priorities.

Breakdown of timing. This may include breakdown of the feedback in-put (delay in feedback loop). Private disagreements among members of a family, or among members of an identification constellation, when the therapist does not as yet understand their private code and does not know what is going on, lead to gaps in the therapist's knowledge and his consequent temporary inability to keep up with events.

Inflexibility. Instead of remaining flexible (more random), the thera-pist may see things according to a set of rules which are not appropriate for the group. His rigidity makes him "drive through warning signs," and instead of helping patients and families, he frightens and disturbs them.

Insufficiency of internal sensors. Lack of perception, sensitivity, and experience may cause the therapist to give academic psychodynamic in-terpretations which, although correct theoretically, will increase the patient's resistance.

Failure of external sensors. The therapist's failure to take into account changes in the administrative climate (in ward, hospital, or clinic) may bring members of the MFT group into conflict with the surrounding system and thus cause confusion detrimental to therapeutic progress.

Breakdown of components requiring bypass, overriding, or replace-ment. Co-therapists may make errors in interpretation which must be corrected promptly by changing the subject before greater damage is done. At other times, the behavior of a particular member of the group has such a disturbing effect that the therapist must arbitrarily change the subject of discussion, or even remove the patient who has evoked intense anxiety from the room. Only in rare instances, however, is it necessary to ask a whole family to withdraw from the group and replace it with another family.

It is understood, of course, that a great deal of tolerance is expected and required of all participants, since the primary purpose of the group is to promote freedom of expression in order to relieve existing tensions caused by insufficient communication among family members. However, the therapist often finds himself between the devil and the deep blue sea: On the one hand, he must "awaken sleeping dogs"; on the other hand, if too much anxiety-producing information is placed at the center of the stage too soon, some families may feel extremely threatened, in which event the possibility of systems failure must be considered.

FURTHER COMMENTS ON THE APPLICATION OF
GENERAL SYSTEMS THEORY TO MFT

As stated earlier in this paper, GST enables us to study MFT as a system, to analyze individual and family malfunction in order to identify the primary focus of disturbance, and to devise methods for better integration of the individual and family in their environment. Within this framework, we see the disruption and disturbance of communication in a family system as similar in many ways to the troubles that can develop in the functioning of a computer program. This concept merits discussion as a further illustration of the application of GST to our field.

To begin with, the basic elements of a computer program can be compared to those of its social counterpart, the family system: Every computer program must have a so-called "main procedure" which establishes the guidelines and the beginning elements of the program. The social counterpart of the main procedure would be the socio-economic environment in which the family finds itself, partly as a consequence of previous strategic decisions.

The second elements of the program are the sub-programs, or sub-routines as they are commonly called. A given program may include one or many sub-routines, each having a particular task. In some programs there is little or no interaction between sub-routines; in other programs, one routine is very dependent on another to the extent that the second routine makes it possible for the first to carry out its task. The social counterparts of the sub-routines would be the members of a family.

When a program is functioning normally, each main procedure has a starting point, and processing begins at this point and progresses one step at a time, in a straight line, so to speak. The sub-routines are brought into the processing as new conditions arise. And, once a sub-routine becomes active, the main procedure no longer continues in a straight line; processing then branches off into any number of directions, although it usually returns to given check points. If the program begins processing, and all the sub-routines perform within their parameters, and no malfunctions occur, the purpose of the program will be accomplished. There are many things that can go wrong, however.

One of the most common problems to arise among the sub-routines is the so-called "closed loop." In this situation one part of the program can progress no further, and returns to a point somewhere between its point of origin and the point of problem answer. It will then begin functioning until it reaches the problem area, repeating this process over and over until either the machine is turned off, or some other outside force intervenes to correct the problem or to modify the routine so that an escape from the closed loop is possible. Another type of problem is the "run-away equation." This is best explained by a division problem in which the resulting answer is an unending remainder ($\frac{1}{3} \times 100 = 33.333 \ldots$), and the sub-routine continues working but is accomplishing no useful results.

Since all sub-routines must work together if the program's goal, e.g., a successfully completed financial report or statistical chart, is to be realized, the outside intervention for a sub-routine with a problem such as the "closed loop" or the "run-away equation" must come either from another sub-routine—in our case another family member—or from the computer operator or programmer—in family therapy the therapist or the co-therapist, who, in *Multiple* Family Therapy, may be another family functioning as co-therapist.

The problems in a computer program's functioning, such as the "closed loop" and the "run-away equation" are reminiscent of the bizarre behavior patterns often manifested by disturbed families. The redundancies and the over- or under-reactions of family members are caused by the fact that people in given situations are not reacting only to the "here and now," but also to crucial figures in their past. Inevitably, other members of the family are surprised, puzzled, and hurt by such reactions, which actually were not meant for them. When such behavior patterns are repeated over and over, there is a gradual withdrawal of family members, a break-down in communication, and eventual disruption of the family.

Only by learning that there are other options for behavior, that behavior patterns can be changed, can the free flow of information be restored—or created. MFT brings about such changes through the intervention of the therapist and his co-workers, and especially through the rich opportunities it affords the participants of the group to learn from each other by analogy, by seeing themselves as in a mirror when other families recreate primitive, long-standing family situations and conflicts in therapy sessions. In MFT changes in behavior tend to precede insight.

THE CURRENT STATUS OF MFT

This author first reported on Multiple Family Therapy as a new treatment modality in 1964 (2, 3). In the years since, more than six hundred families have participated in MFT under my supervision. While there is no doubt that these families behaved differently after they had been exposed to MFT, there is an obvious need for more precise evaluative and follow-up studies; such studies are currently in progress. At present it can be said, however, that the introduction of MFT has reduced the frequency and length of hospitalization, enhanced the potential for preventing future crises, and facilitated the restructuring of intra-family relationships to permit greater mutual understanding and more realistic confrontation of family problems.

REFERENCES

1. BERTALANFFY, L. VON: General System Theory and Psychiatry. In: S. Arieti (Ed.): *American Handbook of Psychiatry*. New York, Basic Books, 1966.
2. LAQUEUR, H. P. ET AL.: Multiple Family Therapy: Further Developments. *Internat. J. Soc. Psychiat.*, Congress Issue, sect. K, 69-80, 1964.
2. LAQUEUR, H. P. ET AL.: Multiple Family Therapy. In: J. H. Masserman (Ed.): *Current Psychiatric Therapies*, Vol. IV, New York, Grune & Stratton, 1964.
3. LAQUEUR, H. P. ET AL.: Multiple Family Therapy: Further Developments. *Internat. J. Soc. Psychiat.*, Congress Issue, sect. K., 69-80, 1964.
4. LAQUEUR, H. P. & SAFIRSTEIN, S. L.: *Comparison of Treatment in the Psychiatric Division of a General Hospital and in a State Hospital*. Excerpta Medica Internat. Congress Series No. 150. Proceed. IV World Congress of Psychiatry. Madrid, 1966.
5. LAQUEUR, H. P.: General Systems Theory and Multiple Family Therapy. In: J. H. Masserman (Ed.): *Current Psychiatric Therapies*, Vol. VIII, New York, Grune & Stratton, 1968.
6. LAQUEUR, H. P. ET AL.: *Multiple Family Therapy in a State Hospital and Community Psychiatry*, VTFT. (Pages 13-19) (January Issue).
7. LAQUEUR, H. P., ZUNITCH, M. L., SMITH, G. E., & WELLS, C. F.: *Multiple Family Therapy and the Decision Making Process*. 2nd Internat. Congress of Social Psychiatry. London, 1969.

25

SOCIAL NETWORK INTERVENTION

Ross V. Speck, M.D.

Fellow, Center for the Study of Social Change (New York City)

and

Carolyn L. Attneave, Ph.D.

Clinical Associate Professor, Department of Psychiatry
Tufts University School of Medicine

In social network intervention we assemble together all members of a kinship system, all friends and neighbors of the family, and, in fact, everyone who is of significance to the nuclear family that offers the presenting problem. In our experience, the typical middle-class urban family has the potential to assemble about forty persons for network meetings. These meetings are held in the home. Gathering the network group together in one place at one time provides great therapeutic potential. The assembly of the tribe in a crisis situation probably originated with prehistoric man. Tribal meetings for healing purposes are well known in many widely varying cultures. Social network intervention organizes this group force in a systematic way.

THE INTERVENTION TEAM

When a social network is assembled, they meet with a team of network intervenors. It is doubtful if this type of therapy should routinely be undertaken by one person working entirely alone. The first strategy,

Reprinted from CHANGING FAMILIES. Edited by Jay Haley. Copyright © 1971 by Grune & Stratton, New York, pp. 312-332.

then, is the selection of a team. Preferably the team should be made up of two or three people who know one another well enough to have considerable trust in one another and who are familiar with each other's styles of relating and of general behavior. Division of roles and skills is important, but not a prerequisite. A particularly happy combination occurs when one of the team is skilled in large group situations, easily able to command the flow of attention and energy of a network, and knows when and how to turn it loose on itself.

The role of the leader is somewhat like that of a good discussion leader or a good theatrical director (particularly if he or she knows the Stanislavsky techniques). A sense of timing, empathy with emotional highpoints, a sense of group moods and undercurrents, and some charismatic presence are all part of the equipment that is desirable. Along with the ability to dominate, the leader must have the confidence that comes with considerable experience in handling situations and knowing human beings under stress. Equally important is his ability to efface himself, to delegate and diffuse responsibility, emphatically and pointedly, rather than to collect it for himself. This last characteristic is essential and often overlooked. One neophyte team commented that in their networks they did all the talking. By comparison, networks organized by experienced teams deceptively appear to run themselves. In fact, in several instances the team has been known to leave at about 11 o'clock, only to be told the next day, "We didn't even notice you'd gone until after 12:00 —and we kept right on talking until about 1:30."

The other team members should also have some of the leader's characteristics, but may contribute special skills. If the network includes several generations, it is often helpful to have one youth and one grandparent type on the team so that mingling between team and network and participation by many of the network will be facilitated. Also, suppression of manic, overanxious, or inopportune comments is easier if the network member concerned is matched in style and status by a team member. Team members who blend easily with the total network can effectively help focus the smaller groups into which the network divides, such as committees, buzz sessions, or free-floating conversations.

It should be pointed out that if the team has three or more members, one member will often be selected as a scapegoat and be telephoned or vilified whenever the network or any part of it is angry at the leader or frustrated by its own impotence. The scapegoat role may as well be anticipated, even though one cannot always predict before the first meeting whom the network will choose for this sacrificial position.

An important skill that should be represented in the team is familiarity with nonverbal encounter techniques and their impact on groups and individuals. Emphasis on the scientific, cybernated aspect of the world has caused the importance of feelings and emotions to be overlooked to such an extent that most rituals are omitted or even ridiculed while the youth of the land cry out for meaning and for some way of learning how to "feel." Not only are the nonverbal reactions of the group extremely sensitive cues and clues for the intervention team, but when the team plays upon them to build a nonverbal network experience a ritual takes place. The tension released by jumping, shouting, or screaming, the calming effect of group swaying, the solidarity that comes from huddling and handclasping, all of these knot the network together in a way that merely meeting and talking cannot do. One often notes that, if a pattern of nonverbal openers has been utilized in the first meeting, the network members feel uneasy if it is omitted at the next meeting. That newcomers or latecomers are most easily melded into a social setting via informal nonverbal ritual is almost self-evident if one observes the number of rituals that form part of common courtesy, such as offering chairs, moving over, touching, exchanging meaningful looks, etc.

The experienced intervention team scattered in the crowd can respond to the leader's directions spontaneously and dramatically, catalyzing contagion and drawing everyone into participation. If a dignified "doctor" is willing to take off shoes and sit on the floor, or look at the ceiling and let out a rebel yell or war whoop, or close his eyes and sway while the whole group is looking, then it becomes safe for the housewives and husbands, the kids and the parents, the relatives and the neighbors to do so, too.

Also, quick verbal and nonverbal exchanges of information are easier for a team that is used to working together. The leader may need to have a piece of information, understand a relationship, see a development of insight or resistance in some subsection of the network. When space and organization permit, small conferences make information flow easy and help the leader utilize the team to verify impressions, check strategy, switch roles, or just let off steam. However, when conditions are too crowded or the session activities do not permit *sub voce* team conferences, postural and body communications are important and the ability to break in or to toss the ball quickly and deftly about the team becomes more important. Network sessions last three or four hours, and leadership is strenuous. For the team to keep optimally fresh, some spelling off, as well as change of pace, is desirable.

The teamwork exhibited by the professional intervenors is sometimes fundamental as a model for the network. The effect of the teamwork model is most quickly seen in the network's activists, but the more passive members also learn that it is safe to fumble, to stick one's neck out, and to trust one another.

In one first network session involving a teen-age drug user and his friends and family, the network youth group was most reluctant to discuss openly their use of and experience with various drugs, as well as their ideas about drug use, until the matched youth team member spoke up frankly about his own curiosity and experience. While challenging this peer, the network youth found that the network's older generation was both interested in and attentive to their views. Once stereotyped defenses were down, the older members of the network were amazed to find themselves feeling defensive about diet pills and tranquilizers. Discussion was facilitated when the older team member insisted that discussion was relevant and necessary. The leader then capitalized on the commonality demonstrated, instead of the confusion in role reversals, and shifted the pressure away from stereotypes about drug addictions and onto the more pertinent relationships involved. Team member support allowed the leader to capitalize on the mirror-imaging between the generations—a task which otherwise would have been much more difficult.

Goals of the Intervention Team

Naturally the personality, physique, and aura of each individual denote some of the limits of his or her role on the team. The common goal of the team is something else, and whatever the ingredients, the team must be committed to it, regardless of the division of labor.

The goals of all network intervention are to stimulate, to reflect, and to focus the potential within the network to solve one another's problems. By strengthening bonds, loosening binds, opening new channels, facilitating new perceptions, activating latent strengths, and helping to damp out, ventilate, or excise pathology the social network is enabled to become the life-sustaining community within the social matrix of each individual. This does not happen if the intervenors act like therapists toward patients, since implicit in the therapeutic contact is delegation to the therapist of responsibility for healing, even though eventually most therapies provide a terminal phase where responsibility for self is returned to the patient or family.

However, the intervention team must be on guard at every turn to deflect therapist attempts and keep the responsibility within the network itself. This means being able to live with one's own curiosity when the network activists gain enough confidence to take over. It means real, not pseudo, confidence in network members, who know the problems, the landmarks and terrain of the distressed person's life space. They must be free to do the thinking and acting that will evolve more practical and efficient solutions than the professional could. It means the willingness of team members to be available to consult without being drawn in, and it means considerable clinical experience and intuition to be able to make quick and decisive judgments. Above all, it implies a shared working philosophy of faith in human beings and satisfaction in seeing them rise to occasions rather than a faith in a professional mystique and a need to be central and depended upon.

If this goal and faith is part of the fiber of the team, it is communicated to the network in a positive and safe manner. Even suicidal and homicidal gestures can usually be controlled and handled by the network. The professional judgment that quickly evaluates both the gesture and the network strengths is important. It takes a good deal of acumen to know when it is safe to say "Leave him out in the rain—when he gets wet he will come in, and he ought to find you drinking coffee in the kitchen, not hanging out the window whining."

We have found that in every network there are members whom we call activists. These network activists perceive the need for someone to take over temporarily, and they require support from the team when filling the breech. It takes guts on the part of a network committee of activists to sit with parents around the clock while they let their boy learn what it is like to earn his own living. It takes compassion to invite a defensive embattled couple to dinner, a card party, or a style show and make them comfortable amongst guests and strangers. It takes reserves of patience to find job after job for an inept and unwilling depressed person, and to help him succeed almost in spite of himself so that he finds out that he can "be somebody." Moreover, it takes considerable courage for most professionals to turn these responsibilities over to someone else who has nothing but his or her humanity, concern, and horse sense to guide him through the traps professionals know so well.

The experienced team has often observed that, if they wanted to, they could shift any network over to individual and family therapy and be busy for the rest of their professional careers. For it is not just the index patient's distress that is dealt with, but that of many other families and individuals in the network. As they bring their distress to the surface, the network deals with it. The network team working through the activists enables the network to begin the important human task of solving one another's problems. The ambivalence of one set of parents is resolved when they find someone dealing with parallel problems down the block. One man's need for manual labor is matched by someone else's inside track to a hideaway that is available. This is the way that society has always functioned best—whether in extended families, small communities, clans, communes, or fraternal organizations. It is this potential within any group of forty or more people related by common concern for one another that can be unchained by the network effect. *There is no other single goal—not care, not treatment, but enabling people to cope and to share their strengths in coping and also in reaping enjoyments and pleasures that restore their potentials and set them up to handle the inevitable next crisis of living.*

When these goals are clear, skills needed by the team are relatively simple to define. The ability to relate to people, to sense group and subgroup moods and strengths, and to facilitate, focus, and reflect back confidence. The particular disciplines and techniques are raw materials, not prerequisites. The intervention team will blend them with experience and use any and all when appropriate.

Sequences and Patterns

With experience, too, comes the sense of an order to the events that transpire, and a pattern falls into shape. This makes it easier to work with the numbers of people involved and their subgroupings. It makes sense of the highs and lows, the ploys and counterploys, and the permutations behind the seemingly infinite changes each network rings on the organizational possibilities of human social relationships.

Not all these patterns have been identified and explored yet. It is part of the fascination of network study and intervention that there are unmapped vistas and old mountains to be climbed before new ones are glimpsed. The sequences and patterning sketched here may after some years seem like the early maps of the new world that showed California as an island and connected the Great Lakes to the western seas. Had the earlier explorers waited for the surveyors, and later perhaps the aerial photographers, before opening trade routes and establishing outposts, the wilderness would remain and the cities of Europe and the coastal plain of the United States would be even more crowded and explosive than they are now.

The assembly or prenetwork phase has already been well described. The opening session is usually considered one of a series, although on two occasions a single network meeting has been held and subsequent follow-up indicated that the network effect had productive effects persisting for well over a year. Theoretically the one session intervention might be the ideal, but it is doubtful that it will be very often approximated when a network has to be assembled and created around the distress of an individual and his family. The experience of many religious groups who rely on the network effect of a conversion experience, as in revival meetings, suggests that even though this is a potent force it has to be renewed periodically or the group falls back into fragmentation. Other groups provide for renewal at a lesser peak through family reunions, seasonal festivals, life cycle celebrations of birth and marriage, and passage from one stage of the life cycle to the next, including death. Network intervenors need to be cognizant of this and, if possible, direct the energy of the network toward some such self-recharging cycle of its own, within whatever context seems appropriate to the group.

The principal reasons for continuing meetings beyond the tossing of the first rock into the pool are the need for practice, learning and development of insight, since one trial learning is usually not very permanent or predictable. The reinforcement that comes with shared coping experiences tends to make the network a stabilized social unit that can continue to function without professional coaching. A series of six meetings seems to be satisfying to all concerned, and practical, although sometimes three or four are adequate. The first session is usually one that ends on a high pitch of excitement and discovery of one another within the group. The reality of the fact that the professionals are not going to take over at some point or another is not always clear to the network at this time, and in fact the illusion of professional protection and sanction may be very important at this point to free the members of the network to explore one another more spontaneously. Hope and communication are both characteristic of this phase.

The strategy for the first session is plotted by the team on the basis of acquaintance with the problem gathered in the prenetwork discussions with the family about its distress. The leader will count on quick feedback from team members of subgroupings and moods as the network gathers. Individual team members arriving early and watching the host family and others can quickly sort out the alignments and the feelings as well as the relationships from the kinesics, the voices, and the clusterings.

New team members often ask "What do I do?" The answer is simple: Set the example of friendly interest, open communication, and unobstructive returns of the ball whenever anyone moves to put the professional in charge. If asked, identify yourself by name and, if pressed, by occupation or professional role. If not asked, let people assume you are another member of the network, because for the next few weeks that is what you will become. Use whatever social skills seem appropriate, establishing human contact with as many people as possible, but also do a lot of listening and observing. Locate the refreshments, the bathrooms, the cloakrooms, the kitchen, the back door, the fans, the extra chairs, the ashtrays, the telephone and its extensions. Help move furniture if necessary. Get to know the people and the environment thoroughly as quickly as possible. Likewise, the children. Above all, don't get caught with the team standing grouped together staring at the people like zoological specimens. Never seem to be talking at length about any interest that cannot be shared with part of the network. It is not only rude; it is also destructive of morale.

Be prepared for many anxieties and much fear at the first session. Very few people will have any idea why they are there, and there will be many who are apprehensive about the distress of the family who invited them, about the risks they may be taking themselves, and about much that they have read and heard and misinterpreted about the whole profession of psychotherapy. In fact, those who have had experience with such marathons as group or individual therapy may be even more wary than the completely naive. This anxiety has its function, since, as the session relieves it, the relaxation and confidence is a potent reinforcement for continuing with the network intervention model. However, the clinical skill and ability to relieve false fears and to focus feelings realistically can be important at this stage.

Once the group has gathered, the leader takes charge. He needs to introduce himself with an outline of the problem and the network intervention methodology. This is a brief sales pitch and, like many similar openings, has impact beyond the cognitive level. Information may not be retained so much as a sense of purpose and direction.

Almost immediately after this introduction the leader introduces encounter-sensitivity techniques. This rapidly inducts the network into what we have called a group high where enthusiasm, activism, and polarization can break down ordinary social barriers and defenses which isolate each network member prior to the assembly. A fight for control is often noted here as the distressed person, his family, or a network member attempts to not participate. The team scattered through the group stimulates, initiates, and infectiously pulls the fringers into the group. During this prelude the leader often establishes control not merely of the network but, through it, of the dissidents and distressed persons in a highly significant fashion. These nonverbal periods need not be long: three, five, or ten minutes at most. But they do seem to be the first breakthrough that begins the realignment of network bonds and binds.

These nonverbal rituals should end with the group feeling solidified, in contact with one another, and quiet. At this point, the leader quickly forms a structure for dialogue and discussion.

In conducting a new session, the leader's sense of timing is crucial, including his ability to shift the tempo and adapt the rate of change, introduce themes, and provide the staccato and legato marks that build to crescendos of maximum impact.

In introducing dialogue, the leader shifts the members' positions to form an appropriate grouping. The physical arrangements depend on the setting, which are usually the living room and dining room of homes. Frequently, people are seated on the floor as well as chairs, sofas, and stairways. One format that is adaptable to many such settings is the use of concentric circles.

An inner circle of six to ten people is rapidly designated and asked to sit on the floor in the center. These are the more outgoing, often younger members whose talk will stir up ripples and begin to polarize the group. Sometimes an outer group is designated because the older, less immediately involved group have naturally seated themselves on the comfortable peripheral furniture. At times there is a middle group interposed by the apparent vagaries of seating and furniture arrangement. This middle group may serve as a buffer or mediator between the inner and outer groups, which will soon be polarized by the task assignments of the conductor.

The leader not only selects the most communicative group first, but also arranges to polarize issues by dividing along generational lines, or in some other way dramatizing the tensions and differences that exist. He sets a topic for discussion and controls the outside group to prevent interruptions. This keep the discussion focused, with everyone promised, and later given, their turn for similarly interruption-free expression.

Often a fairly neutral, but subtly loaded question is good for a kick off, like "What do you think of John?" or "How many of you have used drugs?" or "What do you think the basic problem in this family is?" No one is allowed to escape from commentary, but no one is embarrassed. Skill at giving the sanction for open expression is of paramount importance, and both leader and team need to be alert to protect individuals even while encouraging openness.

The purpose of the multiple circles is to produce more intense interaction in smaller subgroups of six to ten persons. The forty-plus group of the assembled network is too large a group for free group discussion.

Also, the advantage of multiple polarization (within each subgroup) allows the development and synthesis of various dialectics. It is important to elicit competitive polarities with diverse opinions and resolve some of these. The wide range of topics discussed helps the network begin to select and focus on the major issues to be dealt with in order to resolve the predicament in a nuclear family. Each subgroup is given its turn to interact, with the other subgroups instructed to not interrupt and to listen. Later each will have a chance to criticize what has been said by the other subgroups. An empty chair in the inner circle is an excellent device to use when there is pressure to be heard by peripheral members. If the group is large and active, two empty seats may be placed in the inner circle. Anyone not in the focal group may take the empty chair to signal a desire to speak. Having spoken, he is then obliged to return to the outer group and give way to someone else. Other devices of this nature within the repertoire of every group leader or skilled teacher who uses discussion techniques. The important thing is to get the group talking to one another rather than holding a socratic dialogue with the professionals or rehashing old arguments among themselves.

As the discussion gets several ideas going and some confrontations emerge, the focal group is shifted off the center stage and another group is brought forward before premature resolutions are frozen into the system. At first it appears that very little is being settled. This phase is a kind of brainstorming. The leader and team are setting the ground rules for widespread participation and much airing of opinions, suggestions, ideas. The objective is to get out in the open misinformation that the group can correct, as well as information that the group can validate.

An important rule is no polite secrets. Indeed, the professional network intervenor not only does not promise confidentiality but establishes the precedent that there will be none. The team helps see to it that this is carried out. At first, the reverse of the usual professional ethics seems to shock everyone. Soon the network members demonstrate their relief at being able to speak openly about things they have already observed but could not deal with. "We knew you and John disagreed, but you would never let us help you understand before. . . ." "I was embarrassed after that night you drank too much at my house because you never gave me a chance to say I felt the same way. . . ." "I was angry because you didn't let me know about Aunt Minnie's funeral for three months, so I didn't think you cared. . . ."

It is quite usual for people to think that their secret fears, foibles, and worries are hidden when they are patently obvious. It is also true that often people only know half-truths about one another, when the whole picture makes far better sense. But most heartening of all is not only the way people can take it when truths and secrets are shared, but also how within a social network the resources for supportive acceptance appear, along with a common sense, hardheaded approach to the things that need to be changed.

The sequence of polarizing, shifting, and refocusing, with everybody listening is timed to end again with a restatement of a specific problem. At the end of the session, buzz groups or a free-floating refreshment and visiting period is in order. Before breaking up, the leader designates the next time to meet and sets the assignment of a specific, task-oriented topic with this in mind. This is usually enough to get everyone talking, and as soon as that is assured the team exits with minimal attention to goodbyes, beyond the bare amenities, until the next meeting.

INITIATING THE NETWORK PROCESS

Consider a case in its initial phases, where decisions as to the strategy to be employed have not yet been made. A nuclear family consisting of a mother and father in their late 40's, a 25-year-old daughter, and an 18-year-old son (Jim) came to the clinic for help following Jim's acute psychotic episode, during which he thought his mind was being tape recorded and his thoughts played over the local radio stations. He also thought that the telephone system in the house was monitored by outside wires and enlisted the aid of his parents in tracing the wiring throughout the house in a frantic effort to learn that the sister worked at a local radio station taping spot announcements and advertisements, and that she resisted the initial efforts to involve her in any family conferences.

At the first session with the whole family, an attempt was made by the intervention team to find out just what kind of help the family was looking for. Among the possibilities were hospitalization for the son, psychotherapy for the whole family conjointly, and the assembly of their loosely knit social network with an attempt at network intervention by our team. A potential goal in the minds of the team was the mobilization of a peer-supporting network that might enable Jim to move out of the house and find employment and social relationships more appropriate for his age and status. The family was opposed to hospitalization, and at first resisted family therapy by using the sister's work as an excuse for all being unable to attend. They were intrigued by, but even more frightened of, the thought of network intervention, insisting that it would be impossible to assemble the forty persons which we gave as a minimum number necessary. Jim began to assert himself at this point and expressed reluctance to include his friends and peers in the same network as his parents' peers and kin.

What we are trying to communicate by this anecdote is that the resistance to any form of therapy or intervention rests on the lack of familiarity with it. People are unable to conceptualize the processes and change modalities about to be unleashed. Human beings universally resist change, and those in distress are usually most defensive in the face of a choice about whether to introduce a new element or not. If they have never heard of network intervention, the vast majority of people will want to proceed cautiously.

In fact, both the intervenors and the nuclear patient nexus prefer as simple an intervention as feasible. However, where the simple measures such as counseling, individual psychotherapy, group therapy, and family therapy have also been rejected, and where they seem inadequate to solve the family's predicaments, the potential network intervenor has to expand his own horizons and begin formulating strategies around a new theoretical base. This is essential to get himself into a network set. Once he is able to do this, it is not extraordinarily difficult to guide the family into thinking about themselves and their problems in network terms. We believe that this line of thinking does not involve any unusual problem, but we underline the seemingly obvious fact that, *unless one thinks in a new frame of reference,* the likelihood of the intervenor's being overwhelmed by the difficulties he perceives often prevents him from doing the obvious.

To round off the illustration, the family in question, even before actually completing their own network assembly, discussed the idea with many others. A new family called the clinic and startled the intake worker by saying, "We have a son with a problem just like Jim's, and the Jenkinses have told us about how you assemble networks to help solve it. Do you think you could do one for us?"

The Assembly Process: Advantages of Rapid Assembly

Once again it might be well to examine the predicament, the distress, and the forces suggesting the appropriateness of network intervention. In this case a 42-year-old mother had four children under school age. The oldest, a girl, was not presented as having any problems. The next, a 3-year-old boy, was dramatically frightening everyone, mother, siblings, baby-sitters, neighbors, and kin by grabbing knives and threatening to kill them. He appeared to be trying to avenge his father's murder, which all the children and the mother witnessed. The killing was the aftermath of a neighborhood quarrel, when an older son of a neighbor, under the influence of drugs, invaded their home and stabbed the father in the presence of his family, who were watching a TV program.

The third sibling was severely damaged from birth defects affecting his central nervous system and was quite hyperactive. The last sibling, born after the father's death, was mongoloid and was in need of corrective plastic surgery.

Although the mother was not overtly depressed, she was drained of energy from coping with the four small children. She had moved from her previous home because of the overwhelming associations of loss and terror. She had lost contact with many of her old friends and had no extended kin since she had grown up in foster homes. However, there were some foster sisters as potential network participants.

The usual rationale for intervention in a case of this sort involves the treatment of the mourning and loss problems of mother and child (ren) and the search for social agencies to relieve the mother of some of the more pressing and energy-draining responsibilities of caring for defective children. One might suggest relieving the mother of her burdens by simply assuming them or handing them on to other professionals, if one were to follow the sick-and-needy person model. However, a rapid assembly of interested and able friends, neighbors, relatives, and, if indicated, agency personnel, the foster families of the past, and perhaps the church-related persons of the present could provide a large enough group to stimulate considerable change. Presented with the predicaments and given the responsibility to jointly participate in their solution, both mother and network members, under the stimulus of the network effect, may generate some innovative and creative solutions, support the control needed for the abreacting boy, help the mother not only mourn but find and form new nexus and clustering relationships. All this could be accomplished in a much more efficient and self-perpetuating fashion than the conventional assumption of professional responsibility and patient dependence.

Slower Assembly: Advantages and Disadvantages

Most reports of the assembly and creation of networks for therapeutic intervention deal with cases in crisis where there is virtually no option but rapid decisive action. We recently had experience with the assembly and creation of a loosely knit social network around a nuclear family with a son who had had an acute psychotic episode and was on the verge people that they and their son knew for a meeting at a given time and place. Instead they made a series of visits. They spent a couple of hours with each of about ten such friends, telling them about the network idea and discussing their own problems. Only after several weeks of this did they get into gear and begin phoning and settling specifics of time and place.

This slow-paced use of five or six weeks to mobilize the network is unique in our experience in the assembly and creation of networks and raises the following hypothetical formulations and theoretical questions: of hospitalization because of delusional ideas, erratic behavior, and family turmoil. Unique features in the network preassembly phase included reluctance of the family to do anything about their predicament but call and talk to the social worker for hours. They refused to relinquish control over their own situation; yet they kept asking for help. After accepting (hesitantly) the idea of network assembly, they reasserted this control by disregarding the instructions merely to call and invite all the

1. Slow assembly, controlled by the rate of dissemination of information which feels most comfortable to the nuclear nexus, sets the network-effect phenomenon into operation before the large assembly. Much of the network interventive action has already occurred before the larger meeting. Assembly in this case could confirm and validate actions and perceptions already shared, and could focus energy displaced by the directions already set in motion. The first actual meeting of the network might somewhat resemble a second- or third-stage meeting of a more rapidly assembled network.

2. Some danger of stasis might occur because the family has already selected its own system out of the available social matrix. In our experience the rapid assembly and creation of the network in a chaotic crisis situation seems to have the advantage of multiple foci which could be relatively easily rocked or shaken loose by various strategies in order to introduce new structures and form new vincula. The rapid assembly of social networks, within ten days or two weeks of our being consulted about a crisis situation, makes up the largest number of our interventions. It is our clinical impression that more significant changes in occupation, in role performance, and in network relationships (vincula) occurred when crisis situations forced the rapid assembly of the network. However, we have not yet seen enough slow assembly cases to be sure of these speculations.

3. One related type of impasse is the polarization which may result if the nuclear nexus controls the slower process of assembly. If there is sufficient binding, knotting, and stacking of vincula, the assembly presents the intervenors with a dialectic so energized that the task of disalignment and realignment is staggering. One wonders what elements of good fortune would have to be added to technique to

implode the plexus and produce the network effect. The potential violence unleashed if the implosion is successful may spill over to involve police action or other disagreeable effects.

The risk is particularly probable if the polarization occurs around two or more clusters within the network. The intervenors are then set up for a large-scale reenactment of the classical situation where a well-meaning mediator attempts to reconcile a battling couple and gets clobbered by each of them.

4. On the positive side, however, the slow assembly process, if contact is maintained with the distressed nexus, allows the intervenors access to more information than is usually available when rapid assembly is utilized. In one particular case, the son with the schizophrenic label revealed that he and his friends had been using a variety of drugs, including marijuana, hashish, barbiturates, amphetamines, and possibly mescaline and LSD. Because of the experience of one of the authors with similar cases on the psychedelic drug scene, he had a strong clinical hunch that the psychotic process would not be as ingrained as in cases where drugs were used in the absence of peer relationships, or in cases where drugs use had not been part of the clinical picture.

When the intervention team has advance information, it is possible to set goals for the network assembly that involve other less loaded areas of concern, which may enable the polarized factions to find common elements around which to reform. These might include appropriate employment for the son, who had graduated from high school six months before and was not yet motivated either for work or further education, and possibly moving the youth out of his home into a semi-structured or somewhat loosely peer-supervised living arrangement—a pad in the center of the city, for instance.

At this point in time, there is simply not enough experience to provide the criteria for selecting appropriate cases for slow assembly versus rapid assembly of the network. Nor is there evidence to decisively rule either process in or out as a method of choice.

INVOCATION OF PREEXISTING NETWORKS

The invocation and utilization of a preexisting group which possesses the membership variety characteristic of a social network is not as common as creating a new social network via the assembly method. It seems applicable where minority group members depend upon tribal-style assemblies, or where the nuclear nexus in distress centers much of its life around some organization such as a church or temple, a cousin's club, a block organization, or the like. If this group provides the heterogeneity of most rapidly assembled networks, much the same processes can occur.

If, however, it has factions, some of the dangers of the slow assembly process, such as selectivity of polarized clusters and stasis, may apply. In any case, such a group can add impetus to the network effect if it can be properly amalgamated in the network and involved in the task of solving the predicament of the distressed nexus.

Technical differences often center on how to arrange to invoke the network. It is usually not enough for the intervenors and the nuclear family or distressed individual to agree on the network idea. Preferably, one or more members of the intervention team should already be known, by reputation if not personally, to a plexus or authority figure in the group around which the network can be invoked. If it is a rather formal group, at some point the priest, medicine man, club president, or other role-assigned figure will have to be consulted. Usually a clustering person who has vincula with the authorized role representative can effect the team's introduction to the power structure.

Once introduced, the intervention team should demonstrate that they have no desire to take over the group or to reform it, as well as show mild positive empathy for its avowed goals and activities. If the team conveys the idea that the nexus in distress is somehow caught in a bind which prevents full utilization of the supports offered by the group, some expression of need for revitalizing the whole group is called forth from its leaders. From this point on the intervenors are on familiar ground, using their discretion in communicating confidence in the network effect's multiple impact without promising miracles.

Some differences in intervention technique will probably be required because some of the rituals familiar to the group have potential affect-laden charges that can be utilized in place of innovative nonverbal techniques to loosen binds, form bonds, and to stimulate growth of new vincula. Nonuse of a ritual response when it is expected is also effective in developing new perceptions and awareness.

Peer Networks: Special Cases

Peer networks are powerful social agencies in contemporary culture. They seem to be age-graded stratification phenomena with varying limits; probably a maximum span of about fifteen years is typical for older people and a narrower span for youth.

One needs first of all to recognize that peer networks exist and are as potent a force as the multigenerational networks if they can be properly invoked to assemble. They have varying degrees of tightness from a loose network to highly structured groups. When the generally loose-knit associations are assembled, the process is much like that of the creation of a network for a family, but the actual creation of a network of peers from scratch has not seemed feasible. Rather it seems more effective to take advantage of natural groupings, which abound.

Two natural sources of peer networks are adolescents and work associations. An example of a hippie peer social network and its interventions was seen in the course of a long-term observation in a pad. A group of college students who had formerly been part of a fraternity formed the plexus of the network. A formal fraternity group had been broken up because of the group use of drugs, and this nucleus rented a large old Victorian home and set up a commune living arrangement. Although several members dropped out of college, most of them eventually graduated.

The intervenor gained access to the peer group through the development of a therapeutic relationship with one of its members when he panicked after prolonged use of LSD and other psychedelic drugs plus amphetamines. When he described his living arrangements, he was asked if we could meet with all the persons who customarily assembled in his pad, and the result was our seeing from six to twenty of his peers on typical weekly visits.

Over the course of a year we got acquainted with about a hundred youths at this pad, many of whom comprised peripheral members of the peer system of the original nexus. Some of these peripheral members were connecting links with drug-dealing networks. Others were pad crashers who were freaked out or were runaways looking for a place to hide. At different times the peer network provided for one or more young persons in acute "schizophrenic crisis," who were allowed the isolation and security they needed, a chance to talk about their panic, and generally secure subcultural approval for the "trip" they were on in their personal distress. Network intervention in this instance was a matter of operating largely as part of a validating cluster with those involved at any particular time, and of utilizing the natural setting as innovatively as the youth who had adopted the life style in the first place.

By contrast, intervention with work associates as a peer network seems stiff and formal. On one occasion, the authors, together with Mrs. Jean Barr, were invited by a professional group of about 150 persons to do a network intervention on the vincula and structure of their organization. This group seemed to have a number of problems, among them an affective tone of depression ascribed to uncertainties about the usefulness of the organization. There was also an unperceived exclusion of new members and a general fearfulness about the general political climate expressed in much small talk about the manipulations of city and county governments and the availability of funds.

The disruption of the usual seating structure, business agenda, and task orientation of the group's annual meeting loosened the habitual bonds rather quickly. Some nonverbal group process techniques furthered the evocation of more fundamental relationships stripped of formal role restrictions. Freely formed subgroups were used, who were then directed to develop a polarized dialogue, and the heightening and relaxing of tensions to prevent clear-cut crystallization was carried out by the team during the course of a whole day, during which not more than ten people dropped out or were replaced by latecomers. The network session itself ended on a good high note, and the intervenors left the group with a feeling that the goals of involving the newer and younger members and revitalizing the relationships at many levels had been well initiated.

As in the case of invoking existing networks, the invocation of professional associations, unions, service clubs, and other formal peer group networks needs to be done at the invitation of someone in executive authority. Interestingly enough, the organization itself, as well as an individual or plexus within the peer group, may be the social unit in distress and may request help with its own predicaments. An outside intervention team is probably best utilized for this type of "therapeutic" activity, since any member of the group who could set off the network effect would probably be quickly organized into the hierarchy of the group structure or ejected by counterpressures from the threatened establishment in its resistance to change.

THE NETWORK EFFECT

Early in our experiences with various kinds of networks, we became aware of a phenomenon that seems appropriately called the network effect. Originally it was noted that a new process had been set in motion which had little to do with the intentions of the network intervenor. It was a bonus that in some ways made network therapy seem more fun and more interesting, but it seemed tangential to the goal-directed tasks of therapy. Later reflection and discussion have raised some theoretical questions which strongly suggest that perhaps this network effect accounts for much of the impact of the various types of network intervention, and that it is an essential characteristic of social behavior in a basic and fundamental way.

The network effect eludes description because it is largely nonverbal and unconscious. It might be more easily recognized removed from the therapeutic setting and examined in social settings, where it occurs spontaneously. For instance, in Preservation Hall in New Orleans, old black men from the early Dixieland era improvise jazz nightly. The audience of habituées and tourists begins the evening relatively unrelated to one another, at separate tables, and in couples or small groups. Under the mystical, religious, tribal, hypnotic, musical spell they become closely knitted together. They sit tightly pressed. The small group boundaries dissolve. They clap, sway, beat out rhythms, and move their bodies in a united complex response. The group mood is a euphoric high, and the conventional binds dissolve. New relationships melt away the conventional barriers of status, generation, territory, and sex. Young white women, lower-class black men, older spinsters, and hippie youths recognize a mutuality and express it in gesture, contact, and verbal expression. This lasts until the musicians give out and the people leaving form some new bonds. They leave in groups they might not have ever contemplated before they came. For those brief hours they have become involved with one another and with humanity in general in new ways, with new feelings, new relationships, new bonds. However briefly, they have been a part of a social network and they have felt its effect.

Other examples are rampant in the contemporary and historical scene. Religious revival meetings, tribal healing ceremonies, and alumni association "big game" celebrations are time-tested institutionalized examples of this process at work. Newer phenomena such as the Woodstock festival, peace marches, civil rights activities, and revolutionary militant group meetings are contemporary examples. Although neither might like to admit it, some hope of expressing this process unites the Lions Club in its group-singing climax to its regular meeting and the Beatles with their tribal photos as a trademark on their record albums. The network effect is a turn-on phenomenon of group interaction. Once people have made this initial change, they can never step into the same river of human relationships again.

Sometimes they do try, and indulge in all the defensive countermaneuvers used to repress or neutralize any other strong affective experience. This produces its own resonance and can produce counterwaves of new network effects if many people are involved. Utilizing and harnessing the network effect and steering it as it begins to carom about a group is one of the essential strategies of network intervention technique. The evocation of the effect is probably one of the strategies common to the variety of interventions involving networks, and the different foci used may help evolve a typology or classification that will make discussion more meaningful.

Perhaps a metaphor will help at this point: If the water in a deep pool represents the binding and bonding between people, the widening ripples following the fall of a large rock into the pool are the visible network effects changing the apparently smooth surface and stirring the whole mass into new relationships. Counterripples collide as the waves reach boundaries or are drawn into eddies that preexisted, setting up apparently never-ending patterns. More complex patterns can be quickly achieved by skipping small rocks off the water surface, by sending a boat across, or by opening a new channel. But unless something persistently stimulates the water, either by changing the flow or organizing new splashes, the pattern eventually subsides again, leaving the surface calm but the original relationships realigned.

In our clinical experience we have discovered the equivalent of all these phenomena and are considering the varying desirability of permanent and transient changes that can be effected. For instance, in the case of one young schizophrenic girl who was symbiotically bound to her mother, activation of several network members broke through the usually reticent relationships enough for them to find her an apartment, physically move her into it, and support her through the initial phases of disorientation as the symbiotic bonds gave way to more personal ego boundaries. The ripple effects were observed as the ringleader of this network group, who had been unemployed for several months, spending his time writing poetry, began to look for a job. In a matter of weeks the associated efforts had transformed him from a sloppy-looking, bitter, depressed, and angry young man into a clean-cut business executive type with medium long hair (no value judgment intended). Another member who had participated in breaking the index girl's symbiotic binds temporarily separated from her husband, saying that she had finally found the strength to stand up to him and renegotiate the relationship. The example could be spun out to illustrate the reactions that affected employment, marital, personal, and interactional patterns in the lives of at least a dozen members of the social network over the next six or eight weeks.

It would seem that the network effect begins once members realize that they are now part of a special human cluster. Therapeutic intervention labels this as a network and works within the newly formed associative groupings—tightening vincula, stimulating nexi, and coalescing clusters. The use of this vocabulary illustrates that the professional is not immune to the strong drive observed in most groups to try to develop rules that regularize and give the new associative bonds some permanence in the network-effect experience.

While these definitions will prove of some use later in this discussion, at present the phenomena can be described as first an experience of a new feeling of freedom. There are fewer rules, at least fewer formalized rules, in the new context. The network intervenors try to keep this openness, this sense of new options, alive so that the network members can learn for themselves how to be innovative and creative. Learning is rapid as they discard regulations which do not work or which are limiting and begin to cherish a certain looseness of regulations which potentiates freedom. This sense of freedom, validated through shared intimate experience, is a high, a euphoric experience which energizes the group with confidence so that they can begin to tackle their everyday problems. Their success is partially due to the fact that their problems have been redefined by the new group culture, which strips off old labels, collapses old roles, and punctures old bags that are difficult get out of. This last allusion is particularly apt, since the contemporary rediscovery and reapplication of this network effect in a therapeutic context belongs as much to the hippies and young radicals of today as to the professionals. A never-ending parade of examples of reinvented social values and cultural forms, as well as new realities, confronts anyone who looks for it in the contemporary scene.

When we began to conceptualize in this way we began to get rid of the "sick" model for many patients, and this felt good. We also began to get rid of the "healer" model for the therapist, and this left us uneasy—particularly in figuring out how to collect fees for an as yet undefined service, to a new population, in intuitively defined ways. Tradition tells society what is acceptable to the majority of the group by defining what is sick. When called upon, therapists take the sick person and tell him he must become like the majority, for which the system will reward him. What hasn't always been realized in using this model is that this system needs a certain number of persons to scapegoat—to define as sick—in order to define itself. Thus if one person gets over his needs for being scapegoated he has to be replaced by someone else. An alternative left for a patient is to find that being sick is more fun and to remain chronically ill. In either case, therapists are apt to find themselves in the middle of a cybernated pegboard game in which, if you press down one peg, sometimes two or three more pop up. Most of the time, only one pops up—but only occasionally and apparently by chance do no pop-ups occur.

The network effect can scramble the cybernated pegboard, open new feedback connections, make everybody both an experimenter and a validater of new options. Suddenly the only acceptable and needed epithets are WOW! FANTASTIC! RIGHT ON! *and no one is sick.*

IN CONCLUSION: SOME THOUGHTS ABOUT HUMAN SOCIAL SYSTEMS

In our world today, some workers in the social sciences have to become organized in their thinking about behavior and the modification of behavior in large human groups. In the McLuhan world of instant tribalization, each of us is influenced by mass behaviors—from protests to festivals. We are involved positively or negatively in the characteristics of what Abbie Hoffman has called the Woodstock nation or what Roszak has called the counterculture. This has some implications of a polarization of mankind into youth and adults which may be due to a fragmentation of social networks which in the past held generations together with a sense of unity in time and space.

Youths fear the destructive potentials of the cybernated technocratic world, which they feel have led to the imminent destruction of both man and nature. Adults, on the other hand, feel that we have an affluent and manageable system which can be exploited further to bring health, happiness, and security to the "motivated." Like it or not, this is the predicament facing mankind today. Therapists need to be willing to begin to experiment and study these human group phenomena at levels which have during the past couple of centuries been thought of as political. Unless we do this, it is questionable how relevant therapy, or indeed the social sciences in general, is going to be. The culture is changing so rapidly that the old methods of intervention with individuals, families, and groups are not meeting the requirements of the situation.

Rapid social change creates identity confusion in both the adult generation and in youth. Prescribed models for behavior no longer function effectively, and results of actions cannot be anticipated with confidence. This is readily seen in the way youth have established radical changes in dress codes and opened up to public view many relationships that were cloaked in Victorian mystery. They have also shaken up the adults as they have demonstrated their social and political skills in large assemblies, and as they have openly challenged many institutions disliked by the over-thirty generation who felt change could only occur slowly. Granting that there are many variables contributing to effectiveness, and that youth are not always successful in avoiding violence or achieving change, there is still ample evidence that they have established some new forms and uses of social relationships.

Such social mutations create new tensions and precipitate distress which should not be interpreted as a new guise for old pathologies. Clinically, adolescents seen today are not the same as the youth of the past two or three generations. They appear depressed and hopeless, but they admit it rather than blame themselves. They see the world situation as hopeless, and they are hungry—but for dialogue, not therapy. They are suffering from real distress of the soul, and so are their parents, teachers, and peers. Intuitively they sense something more than they can express about this change.

If the psychotherapist is to maintain relationships with human beings in this predicament, if he is to be of any value in relieving distress, he has to innovate.

It seems to us that social network intervention has much promise as a constructive innovation. It provides a chance for the healing of torn bonds and the gentle freeing of binds. Network intervention may be able to evoke the potential capacity of people to creatively and cooperatively solve their own problems as an antidote to the aura of depersonalized loneliness characteristic of postindustrial society.

REFERENCES

1. MARUYAMA, M., "The Second Cybernetics: Deviation-Amplifying Mutual Causal Processes." In W. Buckley (Ed.), *Modern Systems Research for the Behavioral Scientist*, Chicago, Aldine, 1968, pp. 304-313.
2. WIENER, N. *The Human Use of Human Beings*, New York, Anchor, 1954, p. 25.
3. HARDIN G. "The Cybernetics of Competition: A Biologist's View of Society." In P. Shepard and D. McKinley (Eds.), *The Subversive Science: Essays Toward an Ecology of Man*, Boston, Houghton Mifflin, 1969, pp. 275-295.
4. *Ibid.*, pp. 286-287.
5. BATESON, G. *Naven*, London, England, Cambridge University Press, 1936.
6. JACKSON, D. D. "The Question of Family Homeostasis," *Psychiat. Quart. Suppl.*, 31: 79-90, 1957.
7. HALEY, J. *Strategies of Psychotherapy*, New York, Grune & Stratton, 1963, p. 189.
8. HALEY, J. & HOFFMAN, L. *Techniques of Family Therapy*, New York, Basic Books, 1968, p. 227.
9. HALEY, J. "Research on Family Patterns: An Instrument Measurement," *Family Process*, 3:41-65, 1964.
10. DURKHEIM, E. *The Division of Labor in Society*. G. Simpson (Tr.), New York, Free Press, 1960.
11. COHEN, A. K. *Deviance and Control*, Englewood Cliffs, N. J., Prentice-Hall, 1966, Chapter 7.
12. ERIKSON, K. T. "Notes on the Sociology of Deviance." In H. Becker (Ed.), *The Other Side*, New York, Free Press, 1964, p. 12.
13. *Ibid.*, p. 19.
14. ERIKSON, K. T. *The Wayward Puritans*, New York, Wiley, 1966, p. 19.
15. GOFFMAN, E. *Asylums*, New York, Anchor, 1961, pp. 127-168.
16. DURKHEIM, E. *Suicide*, New York, Free Press, 1951.
17. FRIEDSON, E. "*Disability as Social Deviance*." In E. Rubington and M. S. Weinberg (Eds.), *Deviance/The Interactionist Perspective*, New York, Macmillan, 1968, p. 119.

18. BECKER, H. *Outsiders: Studies in the Sociology of Deviance,* New York, Free Press, 1963.
19. MARUYAMA, *op. cit.,* p. 304.
20. MILLER, J. "Living Systems: Structure and Process," *Behav. Sci.,* 10:337-379, 1965.
21. BUCKLEY, W. "Society as a Complex Adaptive System." In W. Buckley (Ed.), *Modern Systems Research for the Behavioral Scientist,* Chicago, Aldine, 1968, p. 491.
22. *Ibid.,* p. 500.
23. MARUYAMA, *op. cit.,* p. 312.
24. BATESON, G. *Naven* (rev. ed.), Stanford, Calif., Stanford University Press, 1965.
25. *Ibid.,* pp. 288-289.
26. HARDIN, *op. cit.,* p. 287.
27. BATESON, *Naven* (rev. ed.), p. 197.
28. MARUYAMA, *op. cit.,* p. 312.
29. SIMON, H. "Comments on the Theory of Organization," *Amer. Polit. Sci. Rev.,* 46:1130-1139, 1952.
30. RUESCH, J. & BATESON, G. *Communication: The Social Matrix of Society.* New York, Norton, 1951, p. 287.
31. *Ibid.,* p. 289.
32. MERTON, R. K. *On Theoretical Sociology.* New York, Free Press, 1967, p. 115.
33. HALEY. *Strategies of Psychotherapy,* Chapter 1.
34. MERTON, R. K. *Social Theory and Social Structure.* New York, Free Press, 1968, pp. 475-490.
35. RUBINGTON, E. & WEINBERG, M. S. *Deviance/The Interactionist Perspective,* London, England, Macmillan, 1968.
36. WILKINS, L. T. "A Behavioral Theory of Drug Taking." In W. Buckley (Ed), *Modern Systems Research for the Behavioral Scientist.* Chicago, Aldine, 1968, pp. 421-427.
37. VOGEL, E. F. & BELL, N. W. "The Emotionally Disturbed Child as the Family Scapegoat." In N. W. Bell and E. F. Vogel (Eds.), *The Family.* New York, Free Press, 1960, pp. 382-397.
38. DENTLER, R. A. & ERIKSON, K. T. "The Functions of Deviance in Groups," *Soc. Probl.,* 7:98-107, 1959.
39. DANIELS, A. K. "Interaction Through Social Typing: The Development of the Scapegoat in Sensitivity Training Sessions." In T. Shibutani (Ed.), *Festschrift in Honor of Herbert Blumer,* 1969.
40. HALEY & HOFFMAN, *op. cit.,* p. 205.
41. MACKAY, C. *Extraordinary Popular Delusions and the Madness of Crowds,* New York, Noonday, 1962.
42. BATESON, G., JACKSON, D. D., HALEY, J., & WEAKLAND, J. H. "Toward a Theory of Schizophrenia," *Behav. Sci.,* 1:251-264, 1956.
43. JACKSON, D. D. & WEAKLAND, J. H. "Conjoint Family Therapy: Some Considerations on Theory, Technique and Results." In D. D. Jackson (Ed.), *Therapy, Communication and Change,* Palo Alto, Calif., Science and Behavior Books, 1968, p. 270.
44. HALEY, J. "Toward a Theory of Pathological Systems." In H. Zuk and I. Boszormenyi-Nagy (Eds.), *Family Therapy and Disturbed Families.* Palo Alto, Calif., Science and Behavior Books, 1969, pp. 11-27.
45. DANIELS, A. K. "The Social Function of the Career Fool," *Psychiatry,* 27:218-229, 1964.
46. *Ibid.,* p. 229.
47. BATESON, *Naven* (rev. ed., p. 175.
48. *Ibid.,* p. 289.
49. HARDIN, *op. cit.,* pp. 288-289.
50. BATESON, *Naven* (rev. ed.), pp. 187-197.
51. LEDERER, W. J. & JACKSON, D. D. *The Mirages of Marriage.* New York, Norton, 1968, pp. 161-173.

26

THE GROWING EDGE OF FAMILY THERAPY

Nathan W. Ackerman, M.D.

*Late Director, Family Institute of New York, and Clinical Professor
of Psychiatry, College of Physicians and Surgeons, Columbia University*

Family Therapy as a Dimension of Family Healing

In its strictest sense, the term family therapy refers to a systematic method of psychotherapeutic intervention, designed to alleviate the multiple, interlocking emotional disorders of a family group. Thus defined, family therapy is new. In contrast, family healing proceeds in accordance with the basic laws of human behavior and is probably as old as the human family itself. Nevertheless, family therapy and family healing share many essential features in common.

As a natural behavioral phenomenon, family healing might be conceived of as encompassing a broad range of self-healing processes which occur spontaneously in family life. More specifically, family healing connotes revitalization through an experience in human closeness: It is based on the premise that there is a significant restitutive, regenerative potential in such events as family gatherings, religious observances, feasts and festivals, weddings and births, death and the rituals of mourning. For within the context of family healing, these shared experiences come to symbolize the triumph of life over death, of pleasure over pain; in short, they are perceived as a reaffirmation of the joy of being alive.

This is the Director's address at the Tenth Anniversary Conference of the Family Institute, New York City, October 24, 1970. A slightly different version of this paper appeared in *Family Process*, July, 1971.

But this orientation is not unique to family healing. As a clinical procedure, family therapy is human drama; it is a search for basic human truths; above all, it seeks to heal the wounds and disablements of family living. A major responsibility of family therapy, therefore, is the enhancement of the family's sense of relatedness and unity, and the concomitant mobilization of its natural self-healing functions. Finally, family therapy can also be said to constitute an experiment in nature, in that it provides a path of entry into a true group, in contrast to the artificial, contrived relationships which characterize traditional treatment modalities.

THE CURRENT STATUS OF FAMILY THERAPY

It is not surprising, in light of these considerations, that family therapy has received increasing respect as a new dimension in the science of behavior and the philosophy of healing. Yet the current status of family-therapy is ambiguous, to the degree that even the task of interpreting existing conditions presents formidable difficllties. On the one hand, there is a growing conviction that the principles of family treatment are important, and that the method works. On the other hand, the field has not yet been precisely defined, and its borders are extremely fuzzy.

Inevitably, growing interest in this treatment modality has given rise to multiple studies which have spiraled out in many directions at once. Thus, when one examines the evidence at the growing edge of family therapy, the experience is comparable to trying to follow an amoeba under a microscope. One sees a young, primitive, free-floating organism bobbing about in lively fashion, but extremely vulnerable to its surroundings. Then, under one's very eyes it changes shape, and begins to sprout its protoplasmic buds every which way. The organism flits up, down, sideways; it is difficult to keep it in focus. One grows dizzy with the effort of following its erratic, unpredictable path, and the longer one watches, the more perplexed one becomes.

Defined in more prosaic terms, the ambiguity which currently characterizes this treatment approach lies in the fact that no one can be sure where family therapy begins and where it ends, or how it articulates with other forms of therapy. But, above all, there is a conspicuous lack of consensus with respect to the theoretical foundations of this form of intervention. At this stage in the development of family therapy, the possibility that an integrated theory of family behavior and family healing will be achieved in the near future appears remote.

The Diversity of Treatment Approaches

On scanning the field, one is overwhelmed by the bewildering array of forms of family treatment. One has the distinct impression that each therapist is "doing his own thing"; but then, even as one watches, he changes his "thing." The fact is that developments in this area are turbulent, and often contradictory. Yet, family therapy is surrounded by an aura of excitement and innovative discovery. The forays into uncharted territory are bold, exploratory, and exhibit a distinct imaginative flair. And, as such, they are a fertile source of fresh thinking and fragmentary hypotheses concerning family transactions, role complementarity, and individual adaptation. Unfortunately, however, we lack the criteria which would enable us to put these partial hypotheses to an adequate test.

In a sweeping survey, one might identify some ten forms of family therapy.

1. Marriage counselling.
2. Family counselling.
3. Therapy which focuses on one or two strategically important family members, in order to achieve "detriangulation" and family change.
4. Modification of communication patterns.
5. Therapy which focuses on the emotional interchange among family members.
6. Experiential therapy; encounter and marathon therapy.
7. The crisis approach to family treatment.
8. An authoritarian, manipulative approach to the power alignments in family relationships.
9. Therapy for multiple families.
10. The eco-psychiatric approach, and network therapy.

This diversity in the approach to family treatment raises a number of questions which, for schematic purposes, can be said to relate to three major issues: First, one is tempted to speculate as to whether there are, in fact, almost as many forms of family treatment as there are therapists. Do these multiple approaches represent distinct forms of family therapy, or are they primarily projections of individual style and individual belief systems? And, to carry this line of reasoning one step further, how prevalent is the tendency among family therapists to aggrandize one or two favorite therapeutic techniques, so that these become the basis for a whole philosophy of therapy? Secondly, we are concerned with the effect of therapeutic bias on the efficacy of treatment: To what extent do therapists force the family to accommodate to their own idiosyncratic therapeutic techniques? The third issue relates to the origins of therapeutic bias: Are some treatment procedures a product of insufficient training and stereotyped understanding, and others the result of restricted training and over-specialization? If the therapist's training is inadequate for one reason or the other, it is logical to assume that his repertoire of treatment techniques will then become rigid and narrow.

When they are considered in combination, it becomes apparent that two basic questions underlie these issues: Is family therapy problem-oriented or technique-oriented? To what extent is family therapy art, and to what extent is it science? An attempt has been made in this article to explore these questions of depth.*

The Origins and Implications of Therapeutic Bias

Clearly, the diversity of therapeutic forms looms large. In fact, so vivid and dramatic are these differences that they tend to submerge any levels of agreement or common ground that may exist among family therapists. Differences of interpretation extend to all aspects of family therapy—to the what, who, where, and by whom. And the single over-riding force which shapes these variations is change—change in social forms, in the concept of mental illness, and in the principles of therapy.

Thus, the heterogeneous, transitional therapy of theoretical developments in family therapy can be attributed to the influence of changes in socio-cultural concepts and in our general understanding of family process. Concomitantly, transitional developments in the practice of family therapy, per se, are a product of changing perspectives in the science of behavior and the philosophy of healing. As is well known, some behavioral scientists, and particularly those who are engaged in mental healing, are extraordinarily susceptible to changes in the theoretical and therapeutic climate, while others cling tenaciously to established concepts. We have witnessed the emergence in our time of a consensus regarding surgical theory and practice, but this can hardly be said of

---

* The implementation of this goal posed certain "technical" problems to which the reader should be alerted at the outset. Essentially, these problems stemmed from the fact that these questions are closely inter-related, and could not be considered as separate entities. Obviously, some repetition of key concepts was inevitable under the circumstances. But, more important, it was not always possible to discuss the tangential issues in a systematic, orderly fashion, or to preserve the unity and continuity of this presentation throughout. This author was aware of the possibility that these defects might detract from the impact of this article. On balance, however, it was decided that the task of providing a comprehensive discussion of the crucial issues which presently confront family therapy must take precedence over such editorial considerations.

psychiatry. If anything, in recent years there has been an increase in the number of schools of thought concerning the nature of social and mental disorders, and the ways of dealing with them.

The lack of a unified theory regarding the nature and origins of mental illness and methods for its amelioration has created a huge gap in family therapy. And, inevitably, in the absence of validated hypotheses, therapeutic bias has run rampant. Thus, in tune with the vagaries of such bias, a given therapist may lean toward one or another conception of human nature, of social change, of family process, of personality development in health and illness, and finally toward one or another theory of therapy and the role of the therapist as a change agent. Accordingly, treatment procedures differ in the degree to which they emphasize intrapsychic, interpersonal, or situational factors. They differ also in the extent to which they focus on conscious or unconscious forces, content or affect, the past or the present. They differ further in the degree to which social factors are implicated in the etiology of psychological illness, and in the extent to which psychopathological phenomena are related to divergent value systems. Finally, family therapists differ in the degree to which they rely on re-education, manipulation, or the treatment of emotional conflict in depth as a means of effecting change.

The determinants of therapeutic bias are multiple and complex. In general, however, it is the product of the following variables:

1. The therapist's personality, his special gifts and special handicaps, and the way these affect his use of self in the therapeutic role.
2. The relative mental and emotional health of the therapist; the values and attitudes he holds vis-à-vis the family as a social institution; and his socio-cultural stance in general.
3. The therapist's professional training and theoretical orientation.
4. The special "fit" of a given family and a given therapist.

Because they frequently overlap, it may be difficult at times to identify the major determinant of therapeutic bias in a given therapist. But, regardless of its genesis, there is no question that therapeutic bias presently constitutes a prepotent force in family therapy. It shapes a series of highly significant choices:

1. The therapist's definition of the unit of treatment, i.e., whether it should consist of two members of a family, a triad, a nuclear unit, an extended three-generation family, a multiple-family group, or a social network.

2. The choice of treatment setting, i.e., whether treatment should be conducted in a hospital, a clinic, the therapist's private office, or at the patient's home.
3. The criteria for diagnostic assessment.
4. The definition of therapeutic goals, i.e., whether these should be limited to the resolution of symptoms, or to effecting changes in family relationships (and in role complementarity), or whether treatment should extend to every aspect of the behavior and attitudes of each member of the family, with the final goal of creating a new way of life for the family as a whole.
5. The orientation to conflicting theories of behavior.
6. The therapist's general orientation to conflicting theories of therapeutic process.
7. The use of single or co-therapists; the preferred use of professionals, paraprofessionals, or lay persons; the preference for brief or long-term treatment.
8. The tendency to favor a particular set of personal, familial, societal, and political values.

The Effect of Therapeutic Bias on the Efficacy of Treatment

It is not surprising that, given these many choices, family therapists tend to polarize and specialize: They intervene on selected aspects of the family phenomenon. And, as might be expected, in the final analysis each does what he likes to do and what he does best. This may account for the fact that, regardless of their approach, family therapists claim results. Nor can their claim that they induce change be disputed. However, a note of caution must be injected at this point: Obviously, the criteria for change used by a given therapist will reflect his individual therapeutic bias. Indeed, depending on his particular orientation, there is a danger that the family therapist may fail to distinguish between the effects of exposure to the therapeutic process and genuine change. Exposure to treatment may produce dramatic changes in the patient's behavior, but these changes may only be transient; and, even more important, they may not be therapeutic, in the true sense of the word. Depending on its nature, a minor change in the behavior system may be more therapeutic than a dramatic symptomatic improvement which involves the substitution of one symptom for another.

The fact is that despite the positive results claimed by family therapists in general, the lack of a unified theory in family therapy, and the consequent preoccupation with experimentation in therapeutic techniques, have had an adverse effect with respect to the efficiency of this treatment approach. Some of the family therapy procedures which are currently in vogue appear to be off balance. That is, they are over-weighted on the side of technique, and are not sufficiently oriented to the objective assessment of the problems of a given family. Obviously, technique is important, but the special fit or lack of fit of family and therapist is a crucial determinant of the outcome of treatment. A given family may accommodate collusively to a given therapist's style, or the family may simply balk and rupture the treatment. Clearly, creative experimentation in family treatment is of great potential value. But it is equally apparent that family therapy may suffer from the indiscriminate use of experimental methods. In short, we need to devise procedures which will enable us to test the theoretical validity and therapeutic efficacy of these new treatment approaches. Unfortunately, we are prevented from doing so at present by our insufficient knowledge of family dynamics, family diagnosis, and the criteria for change.

The Relationship between Practice and Theory

As noted above, the existence of so many diverse forms of treatment constitutes a major issue in family therapy. Thus we are concerned, first and foremost, with the uniqueness of these multiple approaches: Are the differences between them real, or are they more apparent than real? Are there some basic similarities which have become obscured behind the almost garish quality of their differences? Which of the current versions of family treatment are progressive, and which are regressive? Which are based on incorrect premises, and are likely to fade away? Which forms are truly viable and growing?

A close scrutiny of contemporary trends in family therapy leads to the impression that the multiple approaches which characterize this field do not, in fact, represent pure or distinct forms of treatment. They are "hybrids"; they overlap significantly, to the degree that one is tempted to characterize them as "non-types." In short, they reflect the therapist's individual style, rather than his distinctive approach to treatment.

If these areas of overlap are taken into account, the ten versions of family therapy listed earlier can be consolidated into five approaches:

1. Family counselling, consisting primarily of guidance and re-education, which is designed to influence the conscious organization of family relationships.
2. A therapy which focuses on the emotional interchange and complementarity patterns among family members.
3. A therapy which seeks to modify communication patterns, with specific emphasis on systems theory, on observable behavior, and on patterns of action.

4. Therapy for multiple families; families treating families under the guidance of a therapist.
5. The eco-psychiatric approach, and network therapy.

Within this framework, our attention is directed to a second core problem in family therapy, i.e., the relationship between practice and theory, incomplete as it is. The five levels of clinical intervention listed above have been deliberately listed in a certain order. The progression from Level 1 to Level 5 is meaningful, for, in a broad sense, this sequence parallels the chronological emergence, stage by stage, of particular perspectives on the dynamics of change. Thus the series begins with an emphasis on the re-education of conscious patterns of behavior; it then moves on to psychodynamic intervention, to the modification of patterns of communication, to the interaction of multiple families, and finally to the induction of change in the social system. However, perspectives on the dynamics of change are inextricably linked to a theory of behavior, a theory of family dynamics, a conception of health and illness, and a point of view concerning the essence of therapeutic progress.

The root experience of the therapeutic process is the case study and the insights derived therefrom. Insights into the sources of behavior arise from the clinical hunch, which must be tested, step by step, in the interactional hopper of clinical involvement. By definition, clinical study is distinct from the model of the controlled experiment. Clinical understanding grows out of the accumulation of experience which has been tested against real life; it does not derive from data acquired through the replication of experimental conditions.

Clinical intervention is a professional art, an intensely personal performance. But the approach to knowledge is a paradoxical one. It is through the subjective nature of clinical involvement that one reaches out for a more objective understanding of the problems of behavior. The therapeutic encounter is the royal road to diagnostic discernment. Yet the diagnostic process itself requires a theoretical orientation. It is through the subjective essence of clinical interaction that we trace the therapist's allegiance to one or another scientific framework.

Family therapists respond variously to the responsibility of relating practice to theoretical orientation. Some subscribe to Kurt Lewin's view that "There is nothing so practical as a good theory." Others agree with Donald Hebb's contention that "Theory is like skating on thin ice— keep moving or drown. . . . When theory becomes static, it becomes dogma." There is truth in both points of view, yet neither is entirely acceptable. Therapists cannot work without a theoretical orientation, but they cannot be rigid in this regard; rather they must remain flexible and open to change. Theory is not an end; it is a means to an end. It provides a conceptual framework for the design of studies which are crucial to the further progress of family therapy. Ideally, of course, we hope to arrive at a formulation that will give us the power of prediction. We are all engaged in a never-ending quest for the "elegant synthesis," but that goal continues to elude us. For the present we would do well to devote our efforts to the more pressing task of unravelling the knot of conflicting theoretical orientations which threatens to strangle family therapeutic process.

Family therapists are challenged to build a theoretical matrix that accommodates a special focus, the contributions of family experience to mental health. It is self-evident that a theoretical structure of this type differs from those models which view the family phenomenon from a biological, socio-economic, political, religious, or historic-anthropological perspective. The relevance of such constructs is indirect and tangential to our central concern with the family as the unit of health.

Basically, three theoretical models are involved at the five levels of family intervention cited above: a bio-psychoanalytic model, a psychosocial model, and a general systems model. No one of these theories is complete. Each lends itself to special uses; each reflects characteristic complexities and limitations. Perhaps the general systems model comes closest to constituting a unified theory. Yet adapting to this orientation may pose formidable problems for the clinician. He is not yet familiar with the new vocabulary of systems theory, and finds it difficult to apply systems concept to the solution of clinical problems.

GUIDELINES FOR THE FURTHER DEVELOPMENT OF FAMILY THERAPY

If it is to constitute an effective treatment modality, the ambiguity and confusion which presently characterize family therapy at every level must be resolved. A description of the program currently underway at the Family Institute, and its particular bias and posture with regard to the theory and practice of family therapy may provide some useful guidelines for this purpose.

The Evolution of a Family Therapist

In view of the major implications of therapeutic bias for family therapy, and in view of this author's role as founder and director of the Institute, it would seem appropriate to begin this discussion with a brief, personalized account of my professional development in order to shed some light on the origins of my own theoretical and therapeutic bias.

I am a psychiatric clinician first, committed primarily to the treatment of the family. My activities as an investigator of family dynamics and theorist are subordinate to my major preoccupation with clinical process.

Over a period of some thirty-five years, I have extended my orientation to the problems of behavior, step-by-step, from the inner life of the person, to the person within family, to the family within community, and, most recently, to the social community itself. Along the way, I have been influenced, in particular, by studies in family and child psychiatry, and by my special interest in the relationship of poverty, delinquency, and prejudice to mental health.

I received my early training in the theory and practice of psychoanalysis including personal analysis. However, the nature of my professional pursuits subsequently sensitized me to Sullivan's views on interpersonal relations and to the contributions of social science. The fact is that, essentially, I consider myself to be self-trained. Out of my background in psychoanalysis, psychosomatic medicine, family psychiatry and social studies, I assimilated selectively what I could document as valid on the basis of my own experience. Thus, gradually, I evolved a flexible, open-ended theoretical framework, which was appropriate to my clinical orientation in general, but which reflected on my primary interest in the psychiatry of the whole family. I began with a psychodynamic orientation, expanded this to include a psychosocial perspective, and then proceeded to a broader bio-psychosocial theoretical foundation. My approach to the relationship of family experience to mental health is humanistic rather than mechanistic.

For the greater part of my professional career, I had been stamped by my colleagues as a maverick. Now the younger innovators in family therapy accuse me of being too conservative. And, in fact, there is a germ of truth in this damning indictment. I have derived some comfort, however, from a statement made by Robert Oppenheimer to the effect that new knowledge does not displace old knowledge; it transcends it. I am also reassured by my strong resolution to keep pace with the young. I am with youth and for change. But this does not mean that I am willing to abdicate my interest in the three crucial tasks which face family therapy: constructing a theory of family dynamics, evolving a specific method of family psychotherapy, and building a system of family diagnosis. As long as there is some agreement with respect to these goals, there need be no generation gap.

Toward the Construction of a Theory of Family Dynamics

At the Family Institute my colleagues and I are reaching out for ways of describing families, of comparing and contrasting them, and of conceptualizing individual growth and development within the broader framework of family growth and development. We seek explicit answers to the following questions:

1. What are the functions and activities of family life, i.e., the "work" of the family group?
2. How is the work carried out? What is the organizational pattern? How does the family operate and to what ends?
3. How are the family's multiple functions integrated and balanced?
4. How do we conceptualize the complementarity of family role relationships?
5. How do we view the circular relationship of the internal and external aspects of family adaptation, the relationship of the nuclear family to the extended family, the relationship between the generations?

In essence, our goal is to design a theory which will include the physiology of the family, its homeodynamic equilibrium, its ability to maintain and restore balance under stress, and its capacity to protect potentials of learning and growth. Our approach to the relationship between clinical practice and theory is a pragmatic one: What we are seeking is the contribution of psychotherapy to a theory of family behavior and change.

At first glance, general systems theory would seem best suited to our purposes: It aspires to universality; it seeks to encompass the totality of relationships. But it is a pure and abstract theory. Those theories which most closely approximate mathematical models are also the most difficult to apply to concrete human situations. To quote Einstein, "Insofar as the laws of mathematics refer to reality, they are not certain; insofar as they are certain, they do not refer to reality." Therapeutic experience has demonstrated that a theory of behavior which aspires to universality must be reduced to a lower order of generalization before we can make practical use of it in the analysis of a clinical problem. One might speculate, therefore, that a middle range theory might provide a closer connection with the time- and space-bound vicissitudes of human conflict.

General systems theory lends itself to two interpretations: a mechanistic model of transactional relationships, and an organismic model which embraces the role and force of values. The mechanistic model of transactional relationships offers a powerful lure: In its preoccupation with the properties of systems, there is an unfortunate tendency to wipe out the person. This is in keeping with the new allegiance to the ecological orientation, which advocates an all-or-none approach to the family group. More specifically, what counts is the family system; the individual member, the person qua person all but fades out of the picture. But how can one choose between the family system and the person? The person is a sub-system within the family, just as the family is a sub-system within the community and culture. The problem is one of systems within systems. The interface between them becomes the arena of struggle with value differences.

Another defect of the mechanistic model of systems theory lies in its tendency to evade the value problem; it runs the risk thereby of dehumanizing the therapeutic responsibility. In contrast, the organismic model respects the importance of the person and the issue of values.

The theoretical posture which erases the person can best be illustrated anecdotally: Years ago at a research conference, The Elizabeth McCormick Conference on the Family, attended by twenty-five social scientists and a lone psychiatrist, myself, I listened to the repeated assertion that in family research the "intervening variable" was superfluous. The meaning of this assertion was not clear at first. Only after further discussion, did it dawn on me that the "intervening variable" was none other than the person. But I still fail to understand how one can study and treat problems of human behavior and ignore the person. An avid, exclusive enthusiasm for the mechanistic aspect of systems theory leads to an unwarranted reductionism. It rubs out the biological core of the human being. The person has a border, his skin. This makes him a separate organismic entity. The family, in turn, is what James Plant has called the "skin outside the skin"; it provides a "protective envelope" for the person. Thus, the family, in effect, becomes an extension of the biological border of the person. The struggle with values converges at the skin of the person and at the skin of the family.

Toward the Evolution of a Method of Family Psychotherapy

At present, new and fertile ideas have first priority. But the crucial problems of the relations of family experience and health do not yet lend themselves to precise measurement. Statistical studies provide facts, not truths. Considered from this viewpoint, clinical and experimental approaches are not so utterly different; in both cases the observer's final interpretation of his findings is shaped by his relation to his subjects.

In the study and treatment of two or three generations of a family unit we focus on the emotional interchange and complementarity patterns among the family members. But our perspective is by no means fixed or static. As we learn, we change our approach.

In general, however, we believe that emotion is bodily process; it is social; it is contagious and circular in its effects. The negative emotions, anxiety and rage, are infectious; so too are the welfare emotions of affection, intimacy, and mutual caring. In our view, deviant behavior and mental breakdown are largely a consequence of the contagion of disturbed emotion within the nexus of family relationships. From this vantage point, the concept of mental disorder is expanded to include a constellation of multiple vulnerabilities, now afflicting one family member, now another. These disturbances are interdependent and interpenetrating. The overt signs of breakdown in one or another member emerge in series across the life cycle of the family unit. To save any one member, we must mobilize the healing powers of the whole family.

In our conceptualization of family treatment, we move both from inside-outward and from outside-inward. Each perspective acts as a check on the other. We are concerned with articulating the dynamics of the inner and outer faces of the family, and the inner and outer faces of its individual members. We are interested not only in what the environment does to the family, but also in what the family does to the environment. There are two sides to the question: How does the family adapt to society? How does society accommodate to the nature of man and the family of man. In short, we are faced with a special challenge: We need to discover the essential distinctions between healthy and pathogenic social values, as these affect issues of mental health. In terms of the relationship between the family and society, the premise that everything is relative, that anything goes is no longer acceptable. No longer is the human family charged solely with the responsibility of blindly adapting to society. When a society fails to accommodate to the needs of the family, the family must change that society.

Toward a System of Family Diagnosis

Finally, workers at the Family Institute regard the problem of building a system of family diagnosis as crucial to the further advance of family therapy. Concomitantly, they recognize the need to establish normative standards of family health, and to delineate the relationship of family health to value orientation.

The problem of family diagnosis confronts us with some curious contradictions. To all appearances, we are making swift progress in the development of family therapy, and yet we are experiencing a critical lag in the building of family diagnosis. Actually, this contradiction is a result of changes in the orientation of behavioral scientists in general. Therefore, although this lack of interest in diagnosis is particularly conspicuous in family therapy, it is not unique to family therapy. More specifically, a widespread bias presently exists among mental health professionals against "labeling" people and families. Many regard the formal diagnosis of behavior as "passé," a waste of time; a few believe that it is actually harmful. With specific reference to family therapy, a number of workers maintain that within the limits of present-day knowledge a typology of families is simply not "do-able."

Do-able or not, the fact is that therapists inevitably formulate judgments regarding the families they treat. They compare and contrast them; they draw meaningful clinical distinctions between them. They cannot help but do so. The function of interpretation is inherent in the therapeutic process. Often, however, such formulations are designated as evaluations by family therapists, not as diagnoses. Presumably, they hope thereby to unshackle the interpretative function from the hobbling effects of the medical model of illness, to counteract scapegoating through psychiatric "labeling," and to avoid laying claim to a degree of accuracy we do not possess. Let us be very clear, however; there is no way to sidestep the responsibility of conceptualizing and categorizing family types. The need for diagnosis is not an issue. Rather, we must arrive at a consensus regarding what criteria shall be used for this purpose, toward what end, and with what measure of reliability.

There is another pertinent consideration: treating people is fun; diagnosing them is work. But, however arduous, the task of designing a clinically-oriented classification of families is a must. Without it, we are hampered in our efforts to evolve a science of the human family; without it, progress in family therapy may grind down to a slow halt. The danger, which has become increasingly apparent, is that family therapy may come to represent the expression of the idiosyncratic talent of individual therapists. Surely this is not enough. Although family therapy is an art, it requires a scientific foundation if it is to develop as a unique and distinct form of healing.

For the past twenty-five years, staff members of the Child Development Center, the Family Mental Health Clinic of the Jewish Family Service, and, most recently, the Family Institute, have worked to develop a system of family diagnosis. Admittedly, we have frequently felt discouraged and defeated. We have had to amend our outline for family diagnosis again and again in an effort to make it simpler, more practical, more authentic, and yet render a live image of the character of the family. We do not seek a still picture, but a picture of the family in action. Despite the fact that our efforts to date have not been entirely successful, we recognize that this work must continue.

The responsibility of designing a normative standard, a theoretical model of family health, epitomizes all the complexities of the concept of family diagnosis. The model of health is peculiarly elusive. The fiercer the chase, the more tenuous does our hold on it become. Nevertheless, a model of health is an essential component of a system of diagnosis. Both are needed for the measurement of deviations, for the formulation of treatment goals, and for the assessment of change. As long as we lack a concept of a well family, we may easily deceive ourselves about what really constitutes a sick family. The one perspective carries meaning only in relation to the other.

There are numerous paths for searching out the basis of a normative standard of family well-being. At the Institute we have attempted to conceptualize such a standard in terms of four parameters:

1. The species-specific characteristics of the human family, i.e., those uniform and immutable properties which are present regardless of any and all differences. This connotes the biological and transcultural core of the family phenomenon, the sine qua non of survival.

2. The common denominators of family life in the human and near human species.

3. a) The family's adaptation to society and to social change: the distinction between those forms of adaptation which are on the side of life and growth, and those forms of compliance and "adjustment" which lead to family disorganization and decay.

    b) Society's adaptation to the family: the distinction between those societal processes that offer essential supports for the viability of the family, and those that damage the viability of the family.

4. The role of values in the preservation of the family; the distinction between healthy and pathogenic values as these mold the destiny of the family.

Through this multi-level approach we hope to fathom the mystery of the concept of family health. We are searching here for a universal—but flexible—design for family organization, a framework which will provide for sub-types patterned by a range of environments. The principle of cultural relativity has its limits, however. The diversity of family shapes and forms is possible only when a basic denominator for human survival and growth has been established. As our world becomes smaller, more crowded, and more violent, it becomes equally apparent that nothing less than a universal design for family living will do. It is now widely recognized that families cease to breed and thus fate themselves to die under conditions of intolerable environmental stress. The hour is late. The sky turns dark, not only with physical pollution of the atmosphere, but also with a poisoning of the moral and social atmosphere. Szent-Gyorgy, the Nobel prize-winning biologist, contends that as a society we are death oriented not life oriented, and in his book, *The Crazy Ape,* he has provided ample evidence to support this contention. There are signs too, everywhere around us, that the family is dying. But we have not yet grasped the true significance of this aspect of the social revolution. Two thousand years of persecution have taught the Jews that the survival of one Jew is the survival of all Jews. Conversely, the world must learn that the death of one family is the death of all families, that the death of the family is the death of civilization itself.

In the final analysis, the real test of a healthy family embedded in a healthy community rests on its commitment to a sound set of human values. Our technological society has become isolated from these essential values. Instead, it has involved us in warfare, racial conflict, and violence; it has invaded personal freedom, distorted humanistic and spiritual values, and induced a loss of human connectedness. Technological society has created a "mass man," whose personal gods are power, manipulation, competition, and acquisition. It de-humanizes and brutalizes man so that he is rendered numb to the suffering of others. In short, society seems to be suffering a loss of soul. The big question is how to move away from the dedication to power and acquisition, and the master/slave pattern of exploitation, to get a set of values that are pro-life, not anti-life; for peace, not death and destruction; for respecting the dignity and worth of all persons, regardless of race, color, or creed; for sharing and cooperation, not destructive competition; for openness, honesty and intimacy in human relationships, not isolation and alienation; for recognizing the creative value of differences, not fostering prejudice and violence; for a meaningful place and function in society for youth and for senior citizens; for a relevant educational program that will help to implement the goals and values of a civilized society.

The family institute brings a new and eloquent voice to these critical problems. The creation of the first family institute in New York City ten years ago set a precedent for a nation-wide trend. In the years since, family institutes have been established in Philadelphia, Boston, Washington, Chicago, Los Angeles, and San Francisco. Their original focus on the mental health of the family has been expanded to include a concern with broad social issues. Thus the proliferation of family institutes has taken on the quality of a grass roots movement to cultivate and rehumanize family life within the changing community. But the evolution of this movement has other implications as well: It clearly demonstrates that while the edge of family therapy may be ragged, it is vital, vigorous, and vastly open to new discovery.

Area III

TREATMENT OF MARITAL AND SEXUAL PROBLEMS

The marital relationship and its vicissitudes exert a crucial influence on the quality of life. Most people seem more comfortable, secure and productive when they are involved in a lasting, mutually gratifying emotional relationship with a member of the opposite sex, than when they are alone. However, such love relationships are highly vulnerable to various disruptive influences, and as such are often the source of great unhappiness. Similarly, sexual difficulties, apart from depriving the person of erotic pleasures, may also cause serious emotional difficulties. Fortunately, in the last decade significant advances have been made in the treatment of marital and sexual problems.

MODERN MARITAL TREATMENT

In the recent past, when treatment was still monopolized by the analytic model, therapy focused exclusively on the individual and it was considered taboo for the analyst to have any contact with a patient's spouse, let alone to see them both concomitantly. In the early thirties, the psychoanalyst Dr. Bela Mittleman, impressed with the reciprocal effect of each partner's pathology upon the other, began to see spouses consecutively, i.e., after one had completed treatment, and later concurrently, but in separate sessions. Almost two decades later Henry V. Dicks experimented with seeing mates together. Since the sixties, it has become legitimate to consider the marital unit as the "patient" and marital treatment has developed into a distinct discipline.

Reflecting the pluralism that has recently enveloped the entire field of psychiatry, modern marital therapy utilizes a variety of innovative techniques that derive from three major theoretical sources: 1) the concept of marriage as a *transactional system*, which extends the focus of intervention beyond the individual spouse to include the marital relationship; 2) *psychodynamic* concepts, which continue to contribute valuable tools for dealing with the intrapsychic difficulties of each partner; and 3) *learning theory*, which identifies the mechanism by which pathological transactions are maintained and reinforced by the partners, and also provides, apart from insight, an additional modality for modifying behavior. While therapists may place emphasis on one of these approaches, in fact they usually employ an amalgam of all three concomitantly in clinical practice.

The *transactional approach* has greatly influenced the field by drawing attention to the interactional determinants of marital discord, which had previously been neglected. Accordingly, analyzing an individual spouse when there is marital dissonance is like treating a child for pin-worms when the whole family is infected; such intervention fails to alter the crucial sources of the problem. Clinicians have in the past tended to regard disturbances in the marriage relationship as symptoms of one partner's emotional illness. Thus it was assumed that once the patient's over-all functioning began to improve, there would be an automatic concomitant improvement in the marriage. However, the effects of a spouse's improvement, as a result of individual therapy, on the marriage is unpredictable, and indeed may have a negative impact. A mate's inhibitions and symptoms often serve the partner's own neurotic needs and thus, as one improves the other may covertly punish him or become disturbed herself. Clarification and resolution of such reciprocal dynamics constitute an essential aspect of the treatment of marital discord. Masters and Johnson in their paper on the rapid treatment of sexual problems explicitly endorse this transactional viewpoint. They hold that the primary sources of sexual dysfunction lie in the faulty interactions between the partners. Consequently they focus their highly effective therapeutic intervention on the sexual transactions of the "marital unit," which they view as the "patient."

Psychodynamics. The modern approaches to marital treatment employ a variety of therapeutic strategies and tactics, and no longer rely exclusively on psychoanalytic formulations. However, these have not been abandoned, as they have much of value to contribute to the understanding and treatment of marital discord. Thus, for example, the pathological interactions which beset troubled marriages are often the expression of inner conflicts that are best understood from a psychodynamic frame of reference, and marital interactions improve when these are resolved. In other words, transactional sources of marital distress have intrapsychic components. Therefore, the therapist intervenes both on a transactional and intrapsychic level. The paper by Sager *et al.* on the marriage contract describes the complemental use of both intrapsychic and transactional strategies in the treatment of marital discord. The interplay between intrapsychic and interpersonal factors is also illustrated in the paper by Markowitz and Kadis on the analytic treatment of couples in groups. According to these authors marital difficulties grow out of unresolved infantile needs which each partner hopes to gratify in the marriage. Resolution of these neurotic conflicts is the primary aim of treatment which is conducted in a group setting with both partners actively engaged in the therapeutic process.

Learning. The third theoretical contribution underlying developments in this field derives from learning theory and its technical offshoot, behavior therapy. The intimacies of marriage provide rich opportunities for spouses to reinforce and shape the relationship into destructive patterns, and also afford equal opportunities for effective therapeutic intervention. Although seldom explicit, learning factors are operative to some extent in all forms of therapy. However, reinforcement and extinction are generally utilized as an adjunct to insight or cognitive restructuring, which are usually considered to be the primary change agents. Recently, however, learning principles have begun to be employed as a major therapeutic tool. Thus Stuart's article on operant conditioning treatment for marital discord describes a technique wherein the therapist clarifies the subtle and unrecognized reinforcement contingencies that have resulted in the couple's problems. He modifies the relationship by having the spouses reinforce each other's more constructive behavior.

THE TREATMENT OF SEXUAL PROBLEMS

One of the most startling advances of the last decade is the development of rapid and effective techniques for the treatment of such vexing symptoms as premature ejaculation, impotence, retarded ejaculation, frigidity and problems related to sexual incompatibility. Hitherto such symptoms had been regarded as reflecting serious pathology and were considered to be amenable only to lengthy and costly treatment.

The basic treatment strategy of the new approach is essentially simple: the therapist attempts to identify and diminish the factors that inhibit the patient's sexuality and at the same time tries to augment the experience of sensuous and erotic feelings. Intervention is based on an appreciation of the multicausality of human sexuality. Accordingly, sexual symptoms result from deficiencies in various vulnerable determinants that operate on biological, intrapsychic, learned and ecological levels. Thus, for example, the effects of contraceptive medication or drug abuse, or her partner's ignorance of sexual techniques, or sexual inhibitions that derive from the past, or a pregnancy phobia, or poor communication with her lover, or the unrealistic expectation of reaching mutual orgasm with regularity, can all interfere with a woman's ability to achieve orgasm. Many of the underlying causes of sexual dysfunctions are amenable to the wide array of techniques employed in sexual therapy. However, to transcend the status of a technician who dispenses his remedies mechanically, the therapist who undertakes to treat sexual disorders also needs to understand the characteristics of sexual determinants as well as their vulnerabilities. For this reason we have included Money's article which reviews recently identified genetic, hormonal, fetal, experiential, sensory and social determinants of sexual behavior and of gender identity.

DUAL SEX TEAMS

The use of mixed gender co-therapist teams is enjoying increasing popularity in the practice of marital and sexual therapy. Interestingly, authors advance contrasting reasons for this preference. Thus, Masters and Johnson advocate mixed sex teams for the purpose of facilitating communication by providing each partner with a "friend in court," i.e., a therapist who understands and can identify that person's gender specific concerns. They also contend that the team approach minimizes transference phenomena which they feel are *undesirable*. On the other hand, Markowitz and Kadis favor the mixed sex team specifically *because* it elicits parental transferences, which they feel facilitates resolution of neurotic material.

The interesting hypothesis has been suggested that the use of male and female co-therapists fosters "in-vivo" desensitization of patients' fears of the opposite sex. At any rate, the ultimate validation of the co-therapist approach rests on studies, that are still forthcoming, comparing the outcome of treatment conducted by one as opposed to a team of therapists.

MARRIAGE

Some papers in this area were selected to reflect current interest in reevaluating our society's traditional concepts of marriage, and of gender specific roles. Stereotyped attitudes regarding these issues on the part of the professional who is asked to help in a troubled marriage may result in interventions which are based more on the therapist's defensive needs to preserve his personal prejudices concerning woman and marriage, than on the therapeutic needs of the patient. The danger that interventions influenced by defensive stereotypes may not be in the best interest of the patient is explored in the paper on psychiatric help when divorce impends by Whittaker and Miller. Pittman and Flomenhaft reinforce this notion by alerting us to the perils of intervening in relationships which serve as defenses against the eruption of severe pathology in one spouse. They describe the "doll's house" marriage which, although it runs counter to conventional models, often should not be tampered with by the therapist.

Alternatives to the conventional monogamous marriage model are being tried by many young people, and some of these seem to be viable. The therapist engaged in marital treatment widens his perspective and enhances his therapeutic potency by understanding such phenomena in depth. For this reason we have included Constantine and Constantine's paper on comarital and multilateral relationships, which describes various alternative arrangements. Their observations are derived from the Multilateral Relations Study Project, which aims to investigate the growing phenomenon of group marriages in the United States.

SUGGESTED CROSS-REFERENCES

For a theoretical discussion of the systems approach which is germane to the treatment of couples, see Durkin's paper in Section I-A. The numerous clinical papers in this volume that also emphasize ecological factors in treatment include Laqueur's paper describing multiple family treatment, the article on the network approach by Speck and Attneave, and the paper on ecological versus multidisciplinary approach in family therapy by Auerswald, all in Area II on *Family Therapy*.

In contrast, many papers in this book illustrate the value of psychoanalytic concepts to the group modalities. A collection of these are contained in Section I-B—*Analytic Approaches to Group Therapy*. In addition, Lidz's paper in Section IV-A employs concepts derived from a psychoanalytic frame of reference in the family-oriented treatment of schizophrenia in Section IV-B.

For further material on learning theory and behavior therapy see Fensterheim's article on behavior therapy in groups in Area I, as well as Ferber and Ranz's paper on how to succeed in family therapy by setting reachable goals, and Lieberman's discussion of behavioral approaches to family and couples therapy, both in Area II—*Family Therapy*.

The changing role of women is discussed from a different perspective in Vivian Gornick's article on women's consciousness-raising groups in Area V—*Applications and Extensions*.

Birk *et al.*, in their fascinating paper on combined group and behavior therapy of homosexual men, which is presented in Section IV-B, also employ male and female co-therapists.

H.S.K.
C.J.S.

27

SHORT-TERM ANALYTIC TREATMENT OF MARRIED COUPLES IN A GROUP BY A THERAPIST COUPLE

Max Markowitz, M.D.
Director, Adjunct Therapy Clinic, Postgraduate Center for Mental Health

and

Asya L. Kadis
Past Director, Group and Family Therapy Department Postgraduate Center for Mental Health

Our methodology in the therapy of couples is based on an appreciation of the effects in the here and now of the spouses' residual characterological problems originating in early familial experience. In most instances, compulsive strife between the spouses can be broken if either can be made aware of the similarity between his perception of relationship to, and expectations of the other and their perception of a significant parental figure. It can then be brought to awareness that these old problems are being replayed in the marital situation.

Once this situation is clarified, much marital distress can be alleviated when the other spouse realizes that the friction, fault-finding, or whatever, does not actually pertain as much to him personally as it does to intrapsychic difficulties connected with the past in his partner. This kind

Reprinted from NEW DIRECTIONS IN MENTAL HEALTH, B. F. Riess, Editor, Vol. I, pp. 50-68, 1968. Reprinted by permission of Grune & Stratton, Inc.

of effect and reaction is reciprocal. Further exploration of intrapsychic mechanisms in the group context, using the male and female co-therapists as a screen on which to project them, can be most useful in eliciting the nuclear situation and in initiating change.

Our approach to treating couples is based on the observation that almost all our patients perceive, in their family structures, one strong parental figure, usually the mother. Most patients state that mother was the stronger member of the family, that mother wore the pants, or that father was weak or absent. In other words, there is usually an indication of a residual distortion of the functional relationship between the parents.

We do not believe these perceptions to be necessarily based on the reality of the parental relationship. We feel, on the contrary, that they are usually strongly grounded in the patient's need to perpetuate his dependence on one or the other parent as a residue of the "unweaned state." He resists the process of growth which requires that he become a person, separate from the parental object, and dependent primarily on his own resources. The emotional state of such an individual is thus geared toward a struggle to maintain his primary dependency relationship.

The patient's perception and description of his parents' interactions become meaningful in this context. Underlying the failure to mature is a lack of constructive "weaning" experiences which may result from faulty parental interaction.

The child initially may perceive the mother-father relationship as an unwanted obstacle to his pleasure drives. As an expression of his narcissism, he reacts to the frustration with hostility. Learning to live constructively with this reality is, however, imperative. A mutually loving and respectful mother-father relationship is also imperative so that it may function as a psychological teething-ring for the child's personality development. The child needs parents whose own maturity is sufficient to enable them to handle his displeasure with understanding and without undue anxiety.

Undue parental anxiety and guilt are related to overidentification with and the need to placate the infantile omnipotent expectations of the child and represent a reflection of similar expectations residual in the personality of the parent. Dynamically, behavior between parent and parent, and between either parent and child, may be motivated by this child-centeredness and become destructive to all concerned. It is in such an atmosphere that the child perceives the "mothering" influence equalling unlimited gratification as pervasive and dominating in the family structure, whereas the "fathering" influence, as representative of the reality principle or limitation of gratification, is weak or absent.

Problems between the parents—difficulties in communication between them, as well as diadic alliance formations in the family structure—seem to have their origin in resistance to emotional growth determined by the dominance of the pleasure principle. This leaves a corresponding imprint on the child. As a result, in the present marriage interaction, each "imprinted" spouse tends to project upon the other a demand to play a role appropriate to his unconscious omnipotent, or unlimited, fantasy expectations. Failure to do so is reacted to with anxiety since the inherent threat is that of separation, distorted into permanent love-object loss. Separateness in itself—the capacity of each spouse to behave in a fashion allowing for independence in the other—is in most cases conspicuously absent.

Each spouse beats upon the other in the anxiety to obtain the emotional gratification that the other, realistically, cannot afford to provide. Thus, the intial problem for the therapist is to relieve the intolerable tensions arising from the mutual beating-upon-the-other behavior. A long step forward can be made through the re-creation, in the couples' group, of the early familial structure—thereby shifting the burden of expectation from the spouse to the group itself. By this process of displacement, the original separation problems can be elicited, understood and worked through, while simultaneously relieving the existing marital tensions.

SHORT-TERM THERAPEUTIC INTERVENTION

During the therapeutic process, the patient's underlying fantasy life may be seen as dominated by a denial of limitations with particularly unlimited expectations of the spouse in accordance with the pleasure principle. These individuals often behave as if individuation and its attendant limitations simply did not exist.

Such fantasy appears to fully control the behavior and emotional life of the patient, and to this extent we appreciate in him an inherent ego defect. It is as if the ego's capacity to discriminate and cope realistically was submerged and overridden by such fantasies of expectation.

Ironically, the nucleus of neurotic superego formation also arises in this kind of fantasy expectation, so that the individual bestows his all-demanding expectations not only on others but on himself as well, without regard for realistic limitations. Failure to live up to the magical expectations of the neurotic superego creates severely painful perceptions of the self as worthless.

In consequence, transference resistance can be understood as a compulsive striving on the part of the patient to maintain the status quo of his fantasy expectations. That these expectations not only cannot but *need not* be met is denied (the intent of the fathering influence and role). One spouse then thrusts upon the other the full force of these unlimited expectations; the other, victimized by his own unconscious agreement, or failure to identify with the fathering influence, feels trapped and can therefore only react with fight or flight.

For example, if the wife expects limitless gratification from her husband, he may unconsciously agree with the expectation and strive to make it possible. If he cannot, he feels guilty and inadequate. It is as if his ego, his capacity to assert his own realistic limitations, is overwhelmed by the neurotic superego expectation of himself. In this connection, the role of the male therapist is to provide himself as an identification by introducing appropriate fathering behavior.

We are impressed with how different the situation would be if the spouse could find the strength to separate himself from the demands made upon him. Then he could recognize his limitations as ego-syntonic rather than ego-alien and thus not feel obliged to comply with unrealistic demands. This would allow the vicious cycle of threat and counterthreat inherent in the fight or flight reactions to be broken. Consequently, the individual can now be experienced differently by his spouse. While, on the one hand, he does not comply, on the other, he can still remain in close contact, free to offer what support he is realistically able to offer.

In the contentious marriage, one spouse, overridden by his own neurotic superego invested as it is with pathological narcissism, reacts with neurotic guilt. This reaction, in itself, tends to justify the other spouse's expectations. Further, it feeds into the corresponding need to feel the victimized "good one." The tension resulting from this mutual neurotic seduction, or "sucking-in" between the spouses can be reduced as the therapeutic relationship becomes established.

The mechanism of displacement plays an important role in this connection. The focus of unrealistic expectations is transferred to the therapist pair whose function it is to recognize the process, assist in its recognition by the others and provide the necessary experiences to stimulate the ego's capacity to integrate the existence of separateness and its unpleasurable limitations as not only a necessary but also an equitable and justifiable state of affairs. Recognition and respect for separateness become the new bases for the relationship, replacing the former pattern of transferential expectation on the pathological symbiotic level.

In open-ended individual and group therapy, we have become increasingly aware that the therapeutic relationship seems to provide a gratifying experience of unlimited duration to the patient. Such perception, if not corrected by the therapist, reinforces the transference resistance and is contrary to the therapeutic objective: the learning of limitations, acceptance of their existence as necessary and equitable and rerouting of energy from the path of total dependency on the love object to a more realistic dependence on one's self and others.

The result of such experiences is that dependency is now perceived on a quite different basis. Behavior becomes essentially self-motivated, with the self-responsible individual developing possible relationships to independent others. A spouse has become aware that the other is acting in basic self-interest. He is not only not threatened by it, he find it egosyntonic, enjoying it in the other as in himself; thus he has been freed to relate to the other's behavior with optimal flexibility.

The rationale for a short-term approach to couples' therapy, therefore, relates to the question of limitations and the introduction of the reality principle.

By limiting at the outset the number of group meetings, we direct ourselves to a major manifestation of the analytic resistance, namely, that, in the fantasy lives of these individuals, there is a lack of awareness of time as the structure or as a limiting factor. It is our psychoanalytic understanding that this lack of awareness of limitations relates to primary process thinking and its persistence into adult life. Fantasies of omnipotence, particularly with regard to the expectations of the oral or infantile period, have never been constructively learned about and integrated into a more adult personality. To repeat, inadequacy of constructive weaning experiences frequently underlies the failure of maturation.

We conclude, therefore, that a definitely limited therapeutic experience can constitute an emotional weaning situation which will elicit the attendant anxiety and pertinent defenses relating to the "unweaned state" of the individual. These may then be subjected to a constructively corrective experience.

In summary, we postulate that the chief value of a short-term treatment aproach lies in the stimulating impact of the time limitation on the therapeutic process. The time limitation imposed as a nonalterable factor catalyzes the emergence of primary separation anxiety and bypasses compulsive repetitious defenses. In addition, therapeutic interaction by the co-therapists, as parental prototypes, provides opportunity for perceptual change and movement toward maturation.

THE GROUP COMPOSITION

One short-term analytic group recently concluded by the authors will be described. It consisted of five couples, who met together with the co-therapists for ten working and one summary session.

Jack and Florence. This couple originally consulted with A.K.; neither had had any previous therapy. They had been officially separated for six months. On the advice of a friend, Flo initiated the first contact. After two interviews with the couple, A.K. thought that a group experience might help them to get a better idea of what underlay their difficulties and arranged for a joint session with M.M.

Jack presented a façade of disinterest and disbelief that therapy could help. Flo seemed more motivated to try. At one point Jack mentioned that it was "cold living in New York." M.M. immediately perceived this as a sign of underlying loneliness and need for his wife and children; Jack affirmed this. Both therapists saw positive potential in the couple and felt that putting them into a couples' group might be rewarding.

Joe and Eloise. Joe and his wife were referred to M.M. by Joe's therapist, who felt that a marital focus was necessary. Progress in therapy had been at a standstill as Joe avoided self-confrontation, repetitiously over a period of four years finding fault with his wife. Eloise had had only a cursory therapeutic experience many years ago, from which she had not greatly benefitted. M.M. saw them individually and as a couple for a number of sessions.

Joe had deep feelings of inadequacy and insecurity. Unable to be masculinely assertive, he was a poor businessman like his father. He was contemptuous of aggressive businessmen as exploiters, meanwhile allowing himself to be exploited. He found security in civil service employment where he was underpaid in relation to his actual capabilities—a reflection of self-undervaluation. He rationalized his passivity with ideals of liberalism and altruism. His character armor was rigidly compulsive, with considerable detachment from real feelings.

Having perceived his mother's complaints as derogatory of his father, he unduly resented his wife for her complaints. He could relate only to her criticism, not to her underlying needs. He saw her as consistently degrading him in the eyes of the children. Identifying with them, he would also intervene protectively when she was critical of his sons. In this way, he was competitively overprotective and seductively "mothering" to his sons. As a result, one of them was already in therapy. Joe overtly expressed resentment of his wife's working and her relationship with her mother as undermining of him. Covertly, he was dependently passive of their contributions.

Eloise, on the other hand, was the daughter of a "dominant mother and passive father." Unable to find security in the male, she remained passively adapted to the mother figure, reactively contemptuous of and superior to the male. In the sessions with M.M., both transferred the passive-dependent relationship to him as the "mother" figure and competed bitterly to gain him as an ally to prove the other at fault.

M.M., unable to break through this pattern and feeling that to continue offered a poor prognosis, thought it might be helpful in altering the transference pattern to place the couple in a short-term group.

Sam and Doris. This marriage was Sam's second and Doris' first. He married out of his faith the first time, and after only a short time, his wife left for another man, hurting Sam deeply. In his remarriage, Sam felt uncommitted and trapped by Doris. In their marriage of 17 years, Sam felt unhappy and cheated, seeing himself as a good father and provider, staying married for the children's sake. He was always critical of Doris as unfeminine, neglectful of the home, the children and himself. He was subject to depressive reactions and phobic manifestations, particularly a fear of flying and travel.

Sam described early family relations as unhappy. His parents did not get along. His mother was hard-working and dedicated, but not warm to his father. The latter was seen as psychotically angry when mother took Sam into the bath with her. The oedipal implications are clear. Sam was an early winner.

Sam had been very successful financially, enabling him to retire at a relatively young age. He had been in therapy for many years with a male analyst who, in the past three years, had also taken on Doris. As the latter became more attached to the therapist, Sam perceived the analyst to be abandoning him in favor of Doris. Feeling rejected and angry, he left the therapist to seek treatment with A.K. who placed him in a group. He also entered individual treatment with another female therapist.

Doris, too, had had an insecure childhood. She saw her mother as dominant in the family, her father as weak. In contrast to her sister who was a "good girl" and pleased her mother, Doris became tomboyish and developed an unusually close relationship with her father, as if to negate and punish her mother. Doris repeated this pattern with Sam, to whom she transferred as a mother figure who was always displeased and rejecting of her. Remaining dependent on him, she acted out by defying his wishes and by having interests other than his. It was probable that she made a mother transference to Sam and a father transference to the therapist, becoming his favorite and displacing Sam from him.

Since Sam was making little progress in therapy and the marriage was increasingly threatened, A.K. felt that both could benefit from group experience as a couple with a therapeutic couple. After a joint session, M.M. concurred.

Frank and Jane. This couple came to A.K. on the verge of divorce. Two highly intelligent people, they were in constant strife in their ten-year marriage. Both had had considerable analysis and the wife was still with her female therapist. An immediate interview to include M.M. was arranged. As a result, both therapists concurred, in spite of the difficulties, in seeing considerable strength in the marriage. Since Frank particularly seemed to exchange productively with M.M. (to Jane's evident satisfaction), it was decided that they work with him as a couple pending group placement.

Frank's overt defense was a seeming superciliousness and distance. He was obsessed underneath by fear of castration by his wife. Any failure on her part to conform to his wishes was a threat to masculinity; he was unaware of her independent needs as a person and projected a tyrannical image upon her. Among other things, he demanded that she have children despite her lack of readiness, and that she go to work as well. He never raised a finger to help with household chores. Exploration into his early familial relationships indicated attachment to a strong and protective mother, defiance and antagonism toward his father for whom he had contempt as castrated.

Jane, on the other hand, far from being "strong," was anxious and insecure; this stemmed from her having felt abandoned when her mother died in the patient's youth. Shifting dependency to her father, she was traumatized by his remarriage. Losing trust in him, she made alliance with her stepmother, fearing and clinging to her. Feeling abandoned by Frank's insensitivity to her and his reaction to her security manipulations, she found her stepmother again in her analyst. In the latter, she found support in her neurotic denials of Frank, ostensibly as manifestations of her growing independence. She failed to recognize how this was driving a wedge deeper between them.

Murray and Olga. This long-standing marriage was strongly based yet consistently unhappy. Both spouses had sought help in analytic treatment in which they had been involved over too many years. Murray was with a male analyst in both individual and group therapy, and Olga similarly was in treatment with A.K. However, their inability to communicate persisted as their neurotic depressive responses to each other continued. It was observed that if the wife felt better and freer, the husband felt threatened and anxious, arousing a hostile response. In turn, this would set back the wife who became depressed. A.K. had felt for some time that an interruption of the pattern might best be accomplished by bringing the pair together in therapy. Finally, resistance to this overcome, she saw them as a couple for several months. Feeling the presence of M.M. necessary as a transference object, A.K. recommended the short-term group experience. This was concurred in by M.M. after a joint session.

As a child, Olga had felt abandoned by her mother who was greatly involved in caring for "the sick and depressed father." She felt displaced by her father as the center of mother's attention. Her hostility expressed to her mother was not understood and was countered with resentment. Feeling rejected, Olga would characteristically withdraw.

Murray, on the other hand, was the son of a depressed and withdrawing mother. Learning early that self-assertion would earn him her withdrawal, such self-assertion became taboo as an oedipal period defense. This ego-alienating response could be seen in its projection on his father and brother, whose self assertion he condemned as exhibitionistic. Murray needed to feel that he always pleased, and he expected the same from objects. Thus, when his wife was depressed, he reacted with unrealistic guilt and avoidance mechanisms which displeased her. When she became more self-assertive, he would become disapproving and critical as with his father. Much of this was perceived in the first interview by M.M. who felt that judicious and insightful use of his own self-assertiveness might be helpful in stimulating change as a model.

GROUP DYNAMICS

Flo and Jane lost their mothers early; Eloise maintained a ubiquitous relationship with hers. The women all present problems of sexual identification—being feminine, in a sexual sense, versus being a mother. And the ideal of motherhood supersedes all others. This is grounded in the fantasy of the omnipotence of the mother; consequently motherhood all but obliterates wifehood.

Olga, Eloise and Jane fall into the passive-dependent category. This can be seen in their relationships to their mothers and to other women. They relate in passive-dependent fashion to the fantasy mother and make corresponding expectations of the male figure, looking to him for the same mothering.

Doris and Flo, on the other hand, make aggressive identification with the mother figure to whom they react in an essentially paranoid fashion, suspicious and revengeful: Doris by acting out with papa; Flo, because she feels rejected by her mother in her dependency aspiration, is reactively aggressive. (Flo is married to one of the aggressive men, Jack; and Doris is married to the more passive Sam.)

All the women are placing a transferential expectation on their husbands to be all-good and all-feeding mothers to them—with money, words, admiration and catering. The men, in turn, need "feeding" from their women and demanded to be fed themselves, to be appreciated, given rewards, told how well they have done. Thus, there is a collision between mothering and mother-expectancy, with both spouses asking each other to be the good and feeding mother without complaints, an obvious impossibility.

Jack, Frank and Joe were definitely trying to protect their masculinity, and they saw women as trying to deprive them of it. The other two men, Sam and Murray, seemed to represent the other side of the coin, passivity rather than aggressiveness, with a concern for being accepted and cared for. Joe stands somewhere in the middle, showing both the aggressive and passive components. He is aggressive about his masculinity but is also extremely passive about his expectations of his wife.

Sam and Jack have in common a successful adaptation to the business world. The basic difference in their character structure is expressed in their reactions to frustration at home. In Sam's case, dissatisfied with his wife as mother in the the home, he finds it ego-syntonic to take over this function for himself. Sam expresses, in this manner, a strong, latent homosexual orientation. Taking on the role of mother is an aggressive act toward the woman. On the other hand, Jack could not take over in such a manner, because playing a feminine role was much too ego-alien. In this connection it is interesting to note that Joe overtly manifests both these attitudes, so that it is clear that a strong, latent homosexual component exists in him as well.

Joe is an excellent example of the passive and aggressive components, overtly and simultaneously present. On the one hand, he strongly defends his masculine position in the family but, at the same time, he plays a maternal role with his own children (much as Sam does, in direct competition with his wife). In effect, and unwittingly, he models for them a man who aggrandizes the power of the woman and by so doing undermines his own.

The structure of the group enables each male to find, in another group member, a mirror reflecting his own "dark side." It is, of course, important for each patient to learn about the totality of himself so he can integrate opposite components and thereby function more adequately. In the group, the man concerned with his masculinity can also learn to see his own underlying passivity, his need to be pleasing and to be cared for as reflected in his counterpart in the group.

Eloise says, "You have created a group in which we all see mirror images in each other. We're learning about ourselves through each other, how we react, how we hurt, all our feelings in fact."

Mirroring takes place as the participants compare notes on each other's lives. First, one person recognizes an aspect of himself in another and mirrors this back to the other: "You are like me." Next, another group member who also sees something of himself in both of them, but who also has seen *more* of himself than they have, now reflects back to them what he knows about himself. As others become involved, there is a growth of the perceptual image in multidirectional fashion. In addition, apparently nonparticipant members are also involved by their own identification with the mirroring process and can make excellent capital of the opportunities inherent in the situation. This amplification of ego functioning based on the process of identification is perhaps the most important contribution made by *group* therapy.

When Sam perceived Joe acting in a passively expectant rather than masculine way, he can really see himself. Through this kind of mirroring perception, it comes to the patients' awareness that objects are composed of more elements than had habitually been recognized. The powerful mother in the fantasy life of the individual, for example, comes to be appreciated for the human being she really is, powerful, to be sure, but with real needs as well. Where a parent's expectation of the child was perceived by the child to be authoritarian imposition on him by the powerful person, it can now be seen that this may represent not just an authoritarian imposition, but also a direct expression by the parent of his own needs as they relate to the child.

Seeing the shadow in another is the first step in seeing the shadow in the parent figure and in seeing in reality the latter's vulnerability and lack of omnipotence.

Illustrative of the core situation as it arose in the group is the following: The male therapist had occasion to assert the time limitation, insisting on the terms of the contract—so many sessions and no more. This was perceived as an authoritarian imposition at the time, as the male therapist's way of manifesting his power. Patients may, therefore, resent the therapist's being reality-oriented and not fulfilling of their omnipotent fantasy of continuous availability to nurture their needs. What is not immediately perceived, but what must finally become clear, is that the therapist's action represents his own need to carry out his prescribed function *plus* his need for cooperation from the patients.

It is necessary to learn to integrate the fantasy and the reality parts of the love object. The patient can no longer get away with his accustomed defensive meneuver of splitting the good and bad parts in order to maintain the fantasy (good) object. By the same token, through identification he may be enabled to integrate those "good" and "bad" parts of himself. In other words, one comes to terms with the part of oneself which is vulnerable, finite and therefore human, accepting oneself with one's limitations.

THE CLINICAL EXPERIENCE

While we do not have space here to outline completely the eleven sessions or to trace the progress of each patient, we will note some of the major themes and insights which occurred.

In the very first session, the latent content of the problem between the spouses begins to emerge as an underlying struggle for power and domination. The roots of this struggle are a residue of imprinted early familial experience affecting the marriage in the present.

Jack begins to construct the overall gestalt problem by talking of his mother as "the General." M.M. picks up this theme by allying himself with the feeling that no man wants to live with a woman who needs to dominate him. "With such a wife I would have a problem, too." In supporting the male position, M.M. is perceived as allying himself against the women and thereby arouses an anxiety reaction in them. This is crystallized by Doris who becomes their spokesman. She accuses M.M. of being destructive of A.K. "by grizzing her" (needling her). In effect, there was some reality to her perception. M.M. was indeed starting out to demolish the universal perception of the mother as all-powerful, but certainly not to degrade the reality mother image in the father-mother constellation.

Both therapists, by their interaction, had actively set up the emergence of the residual distortions of early life perception of the father-mother relationship. Alliances among the men and among the women thus are encouraged to emerge.

The idea of "having to be the good one" emerges and the "good one" is identified with the "victim." "Good" and "bad" are polarized, and the good one is felt to be the omnipotently giving mother. But it is agreed among the women that to *be* the good one doesn't *feel* good; they feel cheated and deprived by their "sacrifices." They blame their husbands for the way they feel, instead of attributing it to their own neurotic demands to suppress self-assertion.

Also, controlled by the equation, good one equals good mother, the men feel that assertiveness, doing things for yourself to fulfill your own needs, must be bad. Based on this value system, psychosexual confusion results. It becomes clear that the good mother orientation is everybody's problem, "We must always be good and give."

The danger lies in the maintenance of a one-sided view that it is blessed to give with the assumption that it is evil to take. There is ignorance of the fact that the act of taking for oneself in a love relationship can be immensely giving of gratification to the other. Love relationship here is meant as sexuality in its widest sense. Without such correction this kind of distorted overidealization can only result in a masochistic life style. Therefore, such ignorance must be eradicated.

Through the fifth session, the masochism of having to be the good one is engaged. At one point while Murray is talking, M.M. gets up to get himself an ashtray. He is immediately attacked for "not paying attention." In reply, M.M. exploits this situation by asking if the relationship of therapist to patient makes the former a slave. The problem of living up to expectations is considered, with the theme: "Am I a slave because I'm married?"

The necessity for each spouse to act assertively in his own self-interest and to recognize the same need in his partner begins to be clarified. Each begins to learn to do for the other person, not because it is expected, but because of identification with his needs.

During the eighth session A.K. is absent. A multitude of hostile feelings about her, which would not come out in her presence, emerge: negative feelings in reaction to frustrated expectations about the therapists, resentments about money, anxiety about the group continuing and their dependence on it, etc. Held-in grievances of one kind or another, which were evidently restrained previously out of transferential fear toward the bad mother fantasy figure prototype are brought to the fore.

The wish to extend the duration of the group is positively refused by M.M. Since mother, the General, the feared one, was absent, the group thought that father, the easy mark, could be prevailed upon or manipulated to take her place competitively. Upon M.M.'s refusal, Murray immediately reacts, stating: "If that's the way it is, let's get busy, folks."

Jane observes with regard to the neurotic superego, "If your standards are impossible, you have to suffer; there is nothing but trouble. With more realistic goals you can fulfill them." Jack, too, observes about his father, "I guess I should respect him for what he is, and not judge him for what he should be." Murray says, "I just can't give my wife as much as she wants," and turning to her he says, "Respect me for what I *can* do." Thus the theme of acceptance of limitations emerges as central to the eighth session—limitations in spouse, parents and self are recognized in this session and become ego-syntonic.

In the ninth session, Jack and Florence announced that they would skip the next session to take a vacation together. The enthusiasm of the therapists for this "reconciliation" let us to acquiescence to it instead of intervening, a countertransference manifestation. It has since been impressed upon us that a couple's wish to miss a session apart from absences declared by necessity needs to be actively dealt with at all times as a transference resistance.

In the last session, perceptions of the actual gestalt of the relationships between parents and spouses as well are clarified and corrected: father being pushed around by the all-powerful mother is fantasy and not reality. Jane as the spokesman for the group, in playful provocation asks again of M.M., in the presence of mama, whether there is a chance of continuing the group. The underlying meaning is clear: "Does father have the strength to hold his own in mother's presence? And, in turn, will mother support the position taken by father?" M.M. replies with an easy laugh, "Why don't you ask the real boss?" This is a direct interpretation of the latent meaning of her question, "Who *is* the real boss?"

A.K. raises her own and the group's anxiety that "the children might feel they are being abandoned, left up in the air." Her question is: does the group really feel that she is "bad" because she is abandoning the children? Frank replies in as easy a voice as M.M.'s, "Don't flatter yourself, mama, we won't be left up in the air at all. Our feet are on the ground now and we can survive without you." He is, in fact, a spokesman for the group at this point, confronting mother directly and indicating their capability and readiness to give up their symbiotic relationship with her.

OTHER GROUP PHENOMENA

Louis Coser has said: "One need not concern himself with the uniqueness of these events (in our case, the uniqueness of each couple's life patterns), but rather with their underlying uniformities. In formal analysis certain features of concrete phenomena, which are not readily observable unless such a perspective is applied to them, are extracted from reality. Once this has been successfully accomplished it becomes possible to compare phenomena which may be radically different in concrete content, yet essentially similar in structural arrangement."

This applies to our experience with the apparent diversity manifested by the individual couples, for we are struck by the similarity of the structure of the problems in each case, regardless of level of education or social stratum. Some of these recurring phenomena, which we have seen repeatedly in our couples' groups, are enumerated below.

Behavior toward the spouse shows a repetitious, rigidified, and distorted perception-response pattern, indicating transference. We can often immediately find the basis for this transference attitude in an unconscious identification of the spouse with a resented parent. Some examples from the group under discussion are included here: (1) Criticism of husband for laziness or inadequacy equals father was felt to be improvident and uncaring. Also unconscious is an identification with the attitude of mother toward the father, indicating an alliance against him. (2) Criticism of husband as insensitive and abandoning equals father was insensitive, uncaring, and abandoning in remarrying after the death of mother in early childhood. Unconscious feelings include resentment toward mother for dying and abandoning child. (3) Criticism of wife when she shows unhappiness or dissatisfaction, which is felt to be castrating and is responded to with anger, and/or impotence equals husband thinks his own father was castrated by his mother, whose favorite he sought to be. Unconscious is a homosexual anxiety related to a passive and seductive father who displaced his love onto his son. The son feels closeness with the father as a threat to his masculine identity. (4) Criticism of wife as being controlling equals felt his mother was controlling and his father weak. (5) Criticism of wife as sexually unresponsive equals had indulgent and ubiquitous mother and saw father as undermined and superseded by himself.

Evidence of pathological narcissism is universally present. Self-centeredness is the characteristic attitude, with expectations of total gratification. For example, (1) A male patient explodes angry at the male therapist when the latter gets up to get himself an ashtray while the patient is talking. (2) A female patient is orgastically impotent unless clitorally manipulated. (3) A male patient is devastated if his wife so much as looks unhappy. (4) A male patient takes over the mother's role in family because wife is not thoroughly catering. (5) A female patient takes hours to dress and cannot understand her husband's resentment.

There seems to be a universal failure to perceive object relationships, except in a rigidly stratified peer versus parental-object context. We conclude that all these patients have, in common, an immature self-concept. They see themselves as children of parents. Peers are also children of parents. They do not see themselves as parents in their own rights; hence, they feel no responsibility in this connection.

The unreality here lies in the fact that when peers marry, the consciousness of the peer status of the other is lost as the erstwhile peers become the object of all the expectations the child has of its parents. Even before marriage, one of the key features of courtship is that it seduces, with one partner promising the other the kind of special treatment one might expect a mother to give to her child. During the infatuation of the courtship, the illusion of rediscovering the lost omnipotent parent must be a primary motivating factor in the development of the relationship. Conflicting needs in the courtship period may be studiously avoided or rationalized and, when they emerge after marriage, the shock of disillusionment results. We repeatedly hear the statement, "You weren't that way before we were married."

Transference to the therapists is dichotomized. One therapist is seen to be good or powerful; the other is bad or weak. In our experience as a heterosexual couple, the female therapist is most often designated the good and powerful, although the male therapist occasionally finds himself cast in this role. However, the "dark side" of the transference attitude to the predominant figure is fear and anxiety connected with the threat of abandonment.

Transferences, when examined superficially, appear multitudinous and diverse. However, closer observation reveals the following: The therapist couple is split; one is the strong and *deeply feared* parent, while the other is the weak, ignored, undesired, or competed-with parent.

Transference reflects fixations of psychosexual development stemming from the nuclear family and projected onto the therapist pair.

As we can see, distortion of parental perception is influenced by two major factors: pathological symbiosis in relation to the strong and deeply feared parent, and pathological narcissism. This narcissism distorts perception. It overvalues the symbiotic object and devalues the co-parent into a competitor for the object. It also gives rise to subjective, nondiscriminating, magically colored judgments reflecting primary process thinking and a belief in omnipotence.

The roots of transference development lie in a perception of early narcissistic injury or threat from the strong object, and involve pregenital dynamics. Primary narcissism, which Freud described as "normally egotistic" as an expression of the instinct of self-preservation, becomes a source of anxiety if it arouses hostile reactions in the object. To be oneself is too dangerous, and so such tendencies go underground or into repression. Pathological clinging to the object ensues as an adaptive reaction.

To perceive the mother in both her "good" and "bad" parts may be too overwhelming to the young ego. Therefore, major defenses come into play: (1) denial—chiefly around separation and its attendant anxiety; (2) displacement—the split-of "bad" object is conveniently displaced onto another individual; the other parent, usually the father, and eventually the siblings, become the scapegoat for this displacement; (3) projection—the child's own feelings and attitudes, his anxiety to possess his object, to be its favorite and protected one, projected and felt to be present in the scapegoated object: "Father wants to kill me so he can have Mother to himself. . . ."

It might be useful at this point to speak of countertransference. Whatever has been said about the parents is significantly applicable to the therapist. His own blind spots reflecting residues of his own child-centeredness can induce feelings and attitudes parallel to those of the pathogenic parent. Common countertransferential attitudes are: (1) Overidentifying with the patient as a victim of his parents and covert support of destructive behavior toward them. "They deserve the way you feel about them." (2) Competing with the parents to be a better parent than they were. "I alone will make you happy." (3) Identifying with the patient as a hated younger sibling, plus reaction formation. "You poor fellow, you are so small and weak. I must not hurt you. If I take good care of you, I will be mother's favorite son . . . or my supervisor's favorite supervisee." (4) Seducing the patient to act out against the commonly hated authority figure in the co-therapy setting. (5) Needing to be liked and favored by the patients and competing with the co-therapist, either overtly deprecating or covertly undermining. (6) Persistently missing opportunities to intercede actively in support of the co-therapist when under attack by patients. (7) Being persistently impelled to help, rather than to let the patients help themselves; that is, seductively offering omnipotence and encouraging attachment rather than a separation experience. (8) Detaching oneself and failing to perceive what is going on.

In couples' therapy, the other group members are particularly useful since defensiveness in relation to self-image is mitigated through seeing oneself mirrored by a peer. "Instead of having to cope with the direct pain of seeing oneself in actuality, I am better able to see it as objectified in the individual who is doing what I am doing. I am better able to take in the image of myself, to identify by proxy and see what is going on on my dark side because I, myself, am seeing it and it is not being pushed at me. I am more available because I do not have to feel attacked as I would if the therapist were to push the confrontation directly at me." The value of the group context then lies primarily in the area of ego liberation as seen, in mirroring and identification, as the tyranny of the neurotic superego is overthrown.

Since maturation is a therapeutic aim, the couples' group is set up to include a "parental" therapist couple. This serves as a medium for: first, relieving intraspouse conflict by displacing transference expectations to a therapist; and second, ferreting out behavior ghosts–from imprinted nuclear family exiences, replaying them on the therapist pair, and subjecting them to group interaction and corrective experience. In addition, the therapist pair lend their understanding and reality testing to the patients' struggle to find self-esteem and personal freedom. And the group contributes to self- and other-awareness by providing the experience of universalization and mirroring.

The relationship of the therapist pair is of the essence in effecting a corrective experience. They must have the capacity to relate positively to each other, to accept differences between themselves, and be free to assert themselves individualistically in accordance with their sexuality and role distinctions. By and large Mama therapist tends to give sweeter milk than Papa therapist, but she can also be effectively sour at times; and, on occasion, he can "break down" and give some sweetness, too. But, in the face of inordinate expectations, both must be firmly secure in the knowledge that they not only cannot, but *need not*, live up to them. Their primary concern is to serve as models of *realistic* behavior.

CONCLUSIONS

We are convinced that a short-term group analytic experience can be of considerable value in the treatment of married couples. The most important feature appears to be the growth-stimulating effect of firm adherence to predetermined limitations. To our surprise and gratification, development of a capacity for alloplastic behavior was seen to emerge much more quickly in this short experience than in our usual therapy groups with their unlimited, open-ended structures.

We feel we have received affirmation that a group structure which includes both a male and female representative of the "parents" is highly productive in eliciting and altering fixed transferential patterns. With male and female co-therapists present, sex-syntonic identifications are more easily evoked; this confirms Flescher's notion that "direct evidence that the therapist is free of anxiety in contact with a member of the opposite sex is the greatest spur for sex-syntonic identification."

We also agree with Flescher that "the triadic setting is an oedipal setting, and thus an antidote for preoedipal and pregenital regressions which are defenses against more mature strivings."

Our impression that the therapeutic process can be speeded up in the type of group we have described appears to be confirmed by the fact that all the patients became involved in the transference production. In other words, analytically inexperienced people can be constructively introduced into such a group. However, therapists must keep in mind the fact that much can be stirred up in such patients which requires special consideration and handling during and after the experience.

Transference in a couples' group can be responded to and confronted directly. The therapists will not be tempted to assume, as a patient thrust into the role of co-therapist might in another group, the role of sexual savior. Whereas in a regular group therapy setting, there will usually be some patient who will be glad (out of his own distortions and transferential needs) to respond to such a call, in a couples' group the therapist will not accept at face value any transferential acting out. Rather, he will intervene with appropriate affect, response, or interpretation. In a couples' group, the identification and mirroring phenomenon is less transferentially distorted, since there are constantly "parents" and "children" simultaneously present.

In a regular group context, with a single therapist, one couple may become the "parental" targets. This is often very hard to take. That couple becomes the group's scapegoat, paying for the sins of all other parents. It then becomes much more difficult for the couple to deal with their own problems in the presence of their "children." Under such circumstances, it is often extraordinarily difficult, even for a skilled therapist, to recognize defensive transferences to manage heterosexual attraction, and to work through transference and counter-transference elements at the same time.

A distinct advantage of the couples' group is in the diminishment of destructive acting-out behavior, for the therapists' own behavior can set an example for the other couples. In an acting-out situation, the therapists communicate in one way or another that "this is not a solution to the problem." Since transference distortions in a couples' group are usually directed toward the co-therapists, they can react to the fantasy with a confrontation of the neurotic aim to split the parents into good and bad parts.

In our personal experience, AK has felt her male co-therapist to be of extraordinary value, not only for male identification as a father prototype, but also as a spouse interaction model: one who can survive storms and disagreement, and who can be mother-father oriented and at the same time male and female oriented. On working with a female co-therapist, MM has found greater opportunity to use himself more concentratedly as a challenger of the ubiquitous fantasy model. In contrast to situations in which he is the sole therapist, in the couples' group there is greater freedom to be that which elicits the "bad mother" transference—that is, to be challenging, to be frustrating, to be the representative of reality and limitations. The female therapist, because of her own natural inclination to be giving and concerned, is an ideal foil to complement this challenge to the ubiquitous mother fantasy. The authors have found the resulting transferences to be very sharply delineated, and therefore more amenable to ultimate correction, as their interaction becomes the prototype of constructive parental interaction in which the maternal vector and the paternal vector find complementarity and balance.

28

THE MARRIAGE CONTRACT

Clifford J. Sager, M.D.

Clinical Professor of Psychiatry, Mt. Sinai School of Medicine

Helen Singer Kaplan, M.D., Ph.D.

Clinical Associate Professor of Psychiatry
Cornell University Medical College

Ralph H. Gundlach, Ph.D.

Chief Psychologist, Department of Psychiatry
New York Medical College—Metropolitan Center

Malvina Kremer, M.D.

Associate Clinical Professor of Psychiatry
New York University School of Medicine

Rosa Lenz, M.D.

Assistant Professor of Psychiatry
New York Medical College—Metropolitan Center

and

Jack R. Royce, M.D.

Clinical Assistant Professor of Psychiatry
New York University School of Medicine

This article is intended to serve as an introduction to the concept of the marriage contract, which has proved to be a useful clinical tool for clarification and treatment of troubled marriages. Transactional as well as intrapsychic factors

From the Marriage Research Committee of the Society of Medical Psychoanalysts. Reprinted from *Family Process*, Vol. 10, No. 3, September 1971, pp. 311-326.

are important aspects of marital dynamics. The contract concept employs both these behavioral parameters and facilitates therapeutic intervention at both levels.

THE "MARRIAGE CONTRACT" AS A CONCEPTUAL MODEL

In our work with marital couples and families the concept of the "Marriage Contract" has proven extremely useful as a model for the elucidation of interactions between marital partners. Specifically, we seek to understand these interactions in terms of the congruence or conflict of the partners' reciprocal expectations and obligations. In our experience these "contractual dynamics" are powerful determinants of the individual's behavior, as well as the quality of the marital relationship. Thus it is logical to assume that analysis of marital transactions according to this model may clarify otherwise inexplicable behavior and events within the marriage and also provide a focus around which to organize effective therapeutic intervention when an individual, marriage, or family is in trouble.

We use the term marriage contract to refer to the individual's expressed and unexpressed, conscious and unconscious, concepts of his obligations within the marital relationship and to the benefits he expects to derive from marriage in general, and his spouse in particular. But what must be emphasized, above all, is the reciprocal aspect of the contract: what each partner expects to give and what he expects to receive from his spouse in exchange are crucial to this concept. Contracts deal with every conceivable aspect of family life: relationships with friends, achievements, power, sex, leisure time, money, children, etc. The degree to which a marriage can satisfy each partner's contractual expectations in these areas is an important determinant of the quality of that marriage.

THE TERMS OF THE MARRIAGE CONTRACT

The terms of the contract are determined by deep needs and wishes that the individual expects the marital relationship to fulfill. It goes without saying that these will include healthy and realistic as well as neurotic and conflictual needs. What is important in this context is the fact that while each spouse may be aware of his own needs and wishes, to varying degrees, he does not usually realize that his attempts to fulfill his partner's needs are based on the covert assumption that his own wishes will be fulfilled thereby. Furthermore, while each spouse is usually at least partially aware of the terms of his contract, and the needs from which these terms are derived, he may be only remotely aware, if at all, of the implicit expectations of his spouse. Indeed, a partner may assume there is mutual agreement regarding his own contract, when in fact there is not. Nevertheless, the individual then behaves as if an actual contract existed, and he and his spouse were obliged to fulfill its terms. In that event, when significant aspects of the contract cannot be fulfilled, as is inevitable, and especially when these lie beyond his awareness, the disappointed partner may react with rage and depression and provoke marital discord just as though a real agreement had been broken. This response is particularly likely to occur when one partner feels that he has fulfilled his obligations, but that his spouse has not.

THE SOURCES OF CONTRACTUAL DIFFICULTIES

The sources of contractual difficulties vary. The marital partners may be operating under two very different—and incongruent—contracts. A common source of such incongruence is the culturally derived difference in the role expectations of men and of women. Again, if one partner is conflicted on an intrapsychic level as to his needs and wishes, the terms of the contract he is trying to implement on another level of integration will reflect these conflicts and contradictions. Obviously, the "deal" can't work under those circumstances, and disappointment is inevitable. Frequently, one partner frustrates the expectations of the other in a specific area because some aspect of the transaction arouses a great deal of anxiety. But there are other relationships in which a sadistic partner enjoys the sense of power he derives from frustrating the other. Contracts fail in some marriages because they are based on unrealistic expectations; although one spouse fulfills his obligations, his own needs remain unfulfilled because his partner simply does not have the capacity to gratify them. This may happen, for example, when one partner is significantly less intelligent than the other or when one suffers from serious psychopathology. Finally, some expectations are doomed to disappointment because they are based on fantasies that no relationship can fulfill in reality.

SCHEMATIC MODEL OF THE MARRIAGE CONTRACT

For clinical purposes we have found it useful to consider the content of the marriage contract on three levels:

I. *Conscious, verbalized*: This would include what each partner tells his mate about his expectations in clearly understandable language. As noted earlier, however, the reciprocal aspects of these expectations are not usually verbalized or recognized.

II. *Conscious, but not verbalized*: We refer here to each partner's expectations, plans, beliefs, fantasies, etc., which may differ from the content at level I only in that they are not verbalized to the mate, usually because of the fear or shame connected with their disclosure.

III. *Beyond awareness*: Level III comprises those desires or needs, often contradictory and unrealistic, of which the partner has no awareness. These may be similar to or in conflict with the needs and expectations which are operative at levels I and II, depending on how well integrated the individual is.

Contracts on any or all levels are dynamic and may change at any point in the marital relationship. As might be expected, such changes frequently take place when there is a significant modification of needs, expectations, or role demands of one or both partners, or when a new force enters the marital system. Thus there are several points in time at which one might find the nature of the marriage contract of particular interest: during courtship, at the end of the first year of marriage, after the birth of children, during and after a dislocating experience, when children leave home, etc. For purposes of therapy, the nature of the contract at the time of the clinical examination would, of course, be considered most important.

It has been our experience that congruence of contracts on the first level may well lead the couple to the altar; disparity on the second level leads to difficulty early in the marital relationship, usually by the end of the first year; and incongruence on the third level, when non-ambivalent complementarity does not exist to a reasonable degree, contributes significantly to neurotic object choice and lies at the root of the problems one encounters most frequently after the first few years of marriage. The problems having their origin in contractual incongruence at level III are often expressed in seemingly petty differences on the conscious level that often do not reveal the true dynamics at play within the dyad. Thus the therapist's function is to bring these underlying issues to light, to clarify them, and to facilitate the resolution of the disparity between the partners' expectations on this third level.

As a general rule, we are able to elicit information regarding levels I and II, i.e., the conscious, verbalized aspects of the contract, and those which are conscious but not verbalized, directly from the partners themselves. However, for the contractual content which lies beyond awareness (level III) we depend on the therapist's interpretation of material that he selects from his patients' productions. The conclusions the therapist arrives at with respect to the contractual dynamics at level III will, of course, reflect his particular theoretical bias and must be regarded in this light.

The following clinical example will serve to illustrate the application of the marriage contract model to a marital relationship, as a means of elucidating the dynamics of that relationship. The major difficulty of the couple described below related to conflicts over power and control, and not surprisingly, these conflicts were expressed most dramatically in their sexual relationship. For purposes of clarity, we have focused on these aspects of their agreements and omitted contractual data relevant to a full clinical description of this couple. It can be stated, however, that the terms of their agreements, on all levels, clearly reflected problems related to the male and female roles in our middle-class culture.

The husband was a good-looking, well-dressed man of thirty-two and his wife an attractive woman of twenty-four, who appeared much younger despite the fact that she wore a conservative tailored suit with a slightly mannish cut. The husband was an English professor at a prestigious university; the wife was a graduate student in English at the same institution. They had been married for three years.

The Presenting Complaints

After the first few months, the marriage had been a stormy one. The couple's complaints centered on their frequent arguments, and the lack of pleasure in their lives. More specifically, the wife complained that she was anxious, irritable, subject to brief depressions, and felt chronically angry and dissatisfied. Further exploration revealed that she had been sexually experienced when she met her husband, while he had had little sexual experience. She had "taught him about sex" and continued to control their sexual activities. Although the wife protested that she wanted her husband to be more assertive sexually, in fact she rejected him when he took the initiative. Typically, he reacted by feeling hurt, going into a rage, or masturbating. Moreover, he was frequently impotent. At other times, when she did not reach orgasm during intercourse, which often happened, she would tell him to "go ahead and finish." His inability to gratify her at such times drove him to distraction; in contrast, she took it in stride and calmly told him not to be so silly. Finally, she was openly competitive with her husband in all areas, while he denied any competitiveness.

It was also apparent at the initial interview that this couple shared many values and ideas in common. Both were intelligent, valued intellectual pursuits highly, and both believed, on an intellectual level, in the full equality of men and women and tried to live in accordance with this principle. In fact, they were genuinely puzzled about the causes of their unhappiness. The husband, in particular, felt helpless and hopeless about the situation. He felt guilty and responsible somehow for his wife's moods and insecurity, and for their sexual problems as well. The wife realized that her complaints and feelings of dissatisfaction could not be explained entirely on a rational basis but had no insight into their underlying causes.

I. Conscious, Verbalized

Wife	*Husband*
1. Men and women are equal. Therefore I am willing to assume equal obligations and take care of you when appropriate and will not ask to be taken care of like a helpless individual. However, I expect to have the same rights and privileges as you do.	1. Men and women are equal. Therefore I will afford you the same rights and privileges I expect for myself. But I expect you to assume equal obligations and not ask to be taken care of like a helpless individual and to take care of me when appropriate.
2. You have the power to help me professionally since you are a professor and a gifted writer. I am just a beginner and insecure. I expect you to help and guide me to the best of your ability, and then I, too, will develop professionally with your help.	2. I have the means and I will be glad to help you develop professionally, and I will not be competitive with you in this area.
3. I am often depressed and emotionally labile. I expect you not to reject me at these times.	3. You are often depressed and emotionally labile. I will not reject you but will try to be helpful and understand.
(in exchange for the above)	(in exchange for the above)
1. I have the ability to help you sexually and will be glad to do so, and will not humiliate you in this respect.	1. You will improve in your moods.
	2. You are free and experienced sexually and have the power to help me. I am sexually inadequate and inexperienced and vulnerable. I expect you to help me and to teach me, and I expect to become sexually competent with your help.

Both spouses were aware, of course, of these consciously experienced wishes and had verbalized them. But they did *not* recognize the reciprocal or "in exchange" aspects of their contracts.

The verbalized terms of the contracts seem wholly compatible, and the couple's initially harmonious married life reflected this compatibility. He was supportive when she felt depressed and irritable, and actually helped her professionally. Indeed, initially, he derived considerable satisfaction from helping her because of the covert assumption that his sexual problems would be solved thereby. He did not exploit her in a chauvinistic manner but tried to respect her as an equal, and, in fact, this couple shared many household chores and made many joint decisions. In return, he expected her to be strong and supportive to him, to assume equal obligations and responsibility, and, most important, to respect his vulnerability about sex and to facilitate his sexual functioning.

Initially, she was glad to help him to overcome his sexual difficulty. She was sensitive and imaginative in her lovemaking and patiently reassuring whenever he showed signs of inhibition. She initiated him in the use of fantasy to enhance his sexuality. And he responded well and was satisfied with the marriage as long as she fulfilled the terms of her contract. However, within a few months she had become covertly rejecting during their lovemaking, which had an adverse effect on his sexual functioning. Their lovemaking deteriorated, they began to bicker about trivial matters, and she became irritable and depressed.

The question of why this couple's apparently compatible expectations and values did not continue to lead to satisfaction and growth in their marriage can be understood in terms of their contract. Without conscious awareness she had made a "deal" to exchange sex for professional advancement, but while she had fulfilled her part of the bargain, he had not done his part. Actually, he had tried in every way to help her, and to live up to his "obligations" under the "contract." He obtained an academic appointment for her, helped her to select courses, etc. His efforts were not truly effective, however, because she was inhibited and blocked in her work, and on some level of awareness she felt cheated and blamed him for her own inadequacies. Neither partner realized that there was a relation between her anxiety about professional success and their sexual difficulties.

The non-verbalized terms of their contracts effect these dynamics in greater depth.

As mentioned earlier, spouses do not communicate freely in all contractual areas because they fear rejection or anger, or feel guilty about their wishes. At the second level of this couple's contracts, uncertainties,

II. Conscious, Not Verbalized

Wife

1. I am anxious and afraid that I can never make it alone professionally. I can't compete. I am helpless and I am jealous of your professional status. I want your help so I can be as good as you and as good as other people, so I can feel acceptable.

2. I am afraid you will leave me because I am depressed and irritable, and you are really too good for me. I am not very good, so you must not leave me. I want you to remain insecure about sex because this is my hold over you.

(in exchange for the above)

1. You expect me to help you with sex. I want to and I will. I will make you appear to be an adequate sexual male before others.

Husband

1. I am willing to help you professionally, and I will not compete with you. However, I will try to get you to go into an area different from mine, because your competitiveness makes me uneasy.

2. I am willing to reassure you, but it really gets tedious. I hope you mature soon and become strong like ·my sister, who is really my ideal.

(in exchange for the above)

1. I want many women but they will not want me unless I improve sexually. You are my only chance at sexual freedom. I expect you to give me this for everything I do for you.

incipient conflicts, and disappointments emerged, which were consciously expressed to the therapist, but not to one another. Once again, neither partner had any insight into the fact that the broken "deal" aspects of their contracts were the true basis for their complaints.

Contract content at level II reveals some of the deeper roots from which the terms of the contract derive and also demonstrates the way in which marital transactions can function as attempted solutions to intrapsychic conflict. The wife's deep feelings of inadequacy, which stemmed from her profound "fear of success" and attendant work inhibitions, caused her to attempt to trade her sexual knowledge and sensitivity for the use of her husband's intellectual ability and professional status. This maneuver was doomed to failure, and her self-esteem was further injured when she compared his conflict-free and excellent functioning in the area of work with her own paralysis. The husband felt guilty and puzzled because his realistic attempts to help her and his frequent capitulation to her demands to control him did not alleviate her depression or put an end to their bickering.

Finally, the contractual elements beyond the couple's conscious awareness (level III) helped to further clarify the dynamics of their relationship, inasmuch as each partner's more intense and pathological conflicts were clearly discernible at this level.

III. BEYOND AWARENESS

Wife

1. I am nothing, but I want to be supreme. Only through you can I achieve this. You will be strong and powerful for me so that I can use your power to control, dominate, and compete. I will submit to you in exchange for the male power that I lack.

2. Females are passive—males are active. I want to destroy you for being a strong, active male. This makes me feel inadequate in comparison. I will not abandon you, if you let me destroy you.

3. I am excited by the thought of your having sex with other women. I will make you free, if you have other women for me.

4. I am afraid you will abandon me, if you compare me to other women. You must not have other women; in exchange I will make you sexually free.

5. We must be close and intimate.

6. We must remain distant and separate.

7. You must acquiesce to *all* these terms. In exchange, I will not leave you.

Husband

1. I am afraid to be sexually free. I want other men to envy me, but I am afraid of them. I can only be sexually free if I have your permission and protection. I expect you to make me free if I have your permission and women. I will make you powerful in return. I will let you dominate me in return.

2. Women are inferior. I want to dominate you. If you dominate me, I shall be angry at you and I shall despise myself for being so dependent. I will not hurt or abandon you if you let me dominate you and put you in an inferior position.

The aspects of the marriage contracts that are not accessible to conscious awareness may be regarded for clinical purposes as working hypotheses inferred from the behavior, fantasies, and other productions of each spouse. Marriage contracts on this level may have the irrational, contradictory, and primitive characteristics that are attributed to "the unconscious" according to the psychoanalytic model. As a rule, these terms of the contract cannot be fulfilled because of their mutually contradictory and unrealistic aspects. Marital discord arises from the failure of one or the other spouse to fulfill these unconscious contractual expectations, because such disappointments tend to evoke intense emotional reactions, which even the partner who experiences these reactions often finds puzzling.

In the case under discussion, the terms of the husband's contract at the third level contains such a contradiction: "I will let you dominate me—I want to dominate you." This contradiction reflects an unresolved conflict about women that derived from his neurotic relation with his sister. In his marriage he had tried to recreate and resolve that neurotic relationship. Specifically, he saw his sister as a powerful woman who would protect him from the injury he seemed to fear as retribution for his sexual feelings and impulses. In exchange, he would submit to her control. However, on an unconscious level, he resented this dependence and the price he had to pay for her protection; in fact, he felt very angry and competitive toward his sister, and the wish to dominate her had been extended to apply to all women, including his wife. Nevertheless, it may be speculated that this attempt to resolve his conflicts by means of his marital transactions might have provided a viable solution, were it not for the contractual disappointments that his wife experienced.

The wife's third level contract reflected deeper pathology than did her husband's and a number of noteworthy contradictions: "have sex with other women—don't have sex with other women; be strong and potent—don't be strong and potent; compete with me—don't compete with me," etc. Clearly, her conflicts surrounding assertion, power, femininity, and intimacy were profound, and her attempts to resolve these by means of her marital transactions were doomed to failure because of the multiple contradictions in her marriage contract. As noted above, she had no conscious awareness of their contractual dynamics. However, her profound rage and chronic irritability can be attributed to the contractual frustrations she experienced on an unconscious level: Although she had fulfilled her obligations to her husband (at least in part), her own wishes had not been met. Now we are better able to understand why, instead of the deep pleasure that is usually felt when a marital partner fulfills his obligations in a mutually satisfying contract, this woman experienced rage and despair, and then, to her husband's bewilderment, attacked him when her efforts had succeeded in making him happy.

Thus, when they are viewed within the conceptual framework of the marriage contract, it becomes apparent that this couple's marital problems derived, in large measure, from contractual disappointments of which they had no awareness.

Treatment

The couple were treated for five months by one of the authors (C.J.S.), who saw each partner separately once a week and also conducted a weekly joint session. The dual aim of therapeutic intervention was to help the spouses resolve their individual intrapsychic problems, as well as to improve their marital relationship.

In the treatment of married couples many therapeutic techniques are employed, and this was true of the couple described here. For purposes of clarity, however, this discussion will focus on the use of the marriage contract concept. More specifically, the therapist who subscribes to this approach assumes that contractual disappointments are a major source of marital discord. Accordingly, he attempts to clarify the significant terms of the contracts, and if these are being violated, to help the couple renegotiate more realistic ones. This may require prior resolution, by one or both partners, of basic intrapsychic conflicts, for, as we have seen, contractual transactions often represent attempted solutions of intrapsychic difficulties. Thus, the clarification of contractual transactions in therapy sheds light on intrapsychic factors, and vice versa, and the therapist's efforts are guided by his knowledge of both variables.

It is useful to introduce the contract concept early in treatment and to emphasize the mutually satisfying elements of a couple's contracts at the outset. In the case under discussion the contract concept was introduced in the first session, and the fact that the partners helped each other compete with and relate to others was cited as an example of the mutually satisfying elements of their contracts; e.g. "his position as professor gives you prestige in school; your attractiveness makes him appear to your friends to be sexually adequate." The emphasis early in treatment on positive contractual elements makes the couple aware of the valuable features of their marriage and helps to motivate them for the difficult therapeutic task that lies ahead. Later, as destructive contractual elements become clear, they are brought to the attention of each spouse singly or together, as indicated.

The interpretation of unconscious contractual material can evoke intense reactions that are potentially highly constructive but may also be destructive to a marriage. A patient usually experiences relief when he attains insight into the reasons for his smoldering rage and irritability, which may have been puzzling and disturbing. On the other hand, confronting a spouse with the deep disappointments he has suffered in marriage can be destructive initially, and the therapist must be sensitive to the potentially disruptive effects of his interpretations upon the relationship. The ultimate aim of treatment is open communication between the spouses on all levels, and each spouse is encouraged to verbalize to the other the unspoken aspects of their contracts. Nevertheless, at the outset, contractual material, especially when it reflects unconscious dynamics on the third level, is often discussed first with one spouse in individual session and may be brought up by the spouse himself in joint session only after he has been able to achieve some resolution of his conflicts. To illustrate, in the case described here, the wife's intense competition with her husband might have been threatening to their relationship and mobilized her resistance to treatment, if it had been exposed initially during the joint sessions. Accordingly, the wife's destructive feelings toward her husband were discussed with her individually first. At the time, she was reassured that her resentment of male domination was justified, but the neurotic aspects of her conflicts regarding power and female sexuality were also explored. Moreover, in subsequent joint discussions, the wife revealed that a good deal of her anger at her husband stemmed from her disappointment that the help she had given him sexually had not fostered her own self-esteem and assuaged her competitive feelings. Thus, the wife's realization that her anger revolved around her husband's getting a "better deal" was highly constructive to the marital relationship and also contributed to the resolution of her own problems.

The Outcome of Treatment

Clinically, both partners improved, as did their relationship. The couple became increasingly aware of the terms of their contracts and of the destructive effects upon their marriage of their intensely negative reactions to contractual disappointment. In addition, they were able to view themselves and their motives more objectively and could deal with their problems more effectively. There was less bickering and fewer crises. The husband continued to advance professionally; the wife, although still blocked in this area, began to deal with the problem constructively in therapy. Finally, their sexual relationship became more satisfying. However, grave marital and personal problems remained unresolved.

The husband achieved partial resolution of his conflicts surrounding power and sexuality. He gained insight into the unrealistic nature of his contractual expectations that his wife would free him from his sexual inhibitions in exchange for his support and compliance. And, as a result, he felt less submissive and also less angry with her. At the same time, he realized, with considerable relief, that her problems were not caused by his own failure to live up to his "obligations," and he was able to view her needs more objectively and to be more helpful to her, although he was also less tolerant of her erratic behavior. Insight into his contractual dynamics facilitated resolution of his intrapsychic conflicts. Thus, although he was still somewhat fearful of competing sexually with men, on the whole he was far less anxious about his sexual functioning and no longer felt as dependent on his wife for help in this area. In addition, he became more openly competitive with women and now wanted to play a more dominant and assertive role in the marital relationship.

The new contract he wanted to negotiate reflected these changes. He now wanted a marriage contract that would obligate his wife to assume a more independent, i.e., mature, and feminine role in the marriage. He wanted a child, and he wanted her to prepare some meals. In exchange he was still willing to be supportive and comforting when she felt angry and depressed and to help her in her career and share household tasks. Thus it would appear that some of the contradictory elements of his contract that had been beyond awareness prior to therapy had been resolved, at least to the degree that he was now able to construct a more realistic contract.

The therapeutic gains made by the wife were less noteworthy. Like her husband, she gained insight into the terms of her contract and some relief of her depression and tension. However, she lacked the resources to resolve her intense intrapsychic conflicts or modify as rapidly her pathological transactions with others. She was left with deep and pervasive feelings of inadequacy, which were intensified by her conflicts about female sexuality and power.

Instead of resolving these conflicts and working out a viable and more constructive contract, she formulated different, but equally unrealistic terms, which led to further marital difficulties. Once again, her new contract reflected an attempt to enhance her self-esteem by dominating a man in a sexual relationship. Since her relationship with her husband had been a disappointment in this respect, she wanted a "deal" that would enable her to find another more satisfactory partner and to punish her husband at the same time. Thus, she now wanted a contract allowing them both to engage in extramarital sexual relationships.

She became less defensive about assuming a share of so-called feminine role activities. However, her unresolved conflict in this area found expression in her contractual demand that her husband shower her with praise in exchange for every tender act on her part.

She remained conflicted about her husband's adequacy. On the one hand, she wanted to gain power by identifying with a strong mate; on the other, she could not tolerate his superiority. She was enraged by the thought of being submissive to a strong man but was afraid of being abandoned by a weak one. Thus, she was angry when her husband was adequate and felt threatened when he was not. At present these conflicts do not permit her to enter into a mature relationship with her husband.

Her problems contaminate all her transactions; because the primary purpose of her "deals" is to gratify her insatiable need for acclaim and power, they are doomed to disappointment. In short, her current contract works toward dissolution of the marriage.

DISCUSSION

When a marriage is viable, the clarification of marriage contracts usually leads to dramatic improvement in the couple's relationship and in the growth and development of the individual spouses. At some point in therapy each partner is confronted with realities that had previously been beyond his awareness: e.g., "I can't get A in this relationship, but I do get B and C," or "My wishes are unrealistic, and no one can give me what I want." Such insights tend to lead to increasing commitment to the marriage and to the decision to accept its realistic limitations, which, in turn, facilitates the resolution of presenting problems.

Occasionally, however, exposure of the terms of the marriage contracts results in the discovery of serious disappointments and incompatibilities, which may precipitate the dissolution of a marriage: e.g., "I can't get what I want from this marriage no matter what I give," or "I can only satisfy him if I am destructive to myself." A couple's decision to dissolve their marriage on the basis of realistic and comprehensive insights is not a treatment failure. On the contrary, under such circumstances, dissolution of a hopeless marriage can be a constructive experience for both. Moreover, we have found that the prolonged, agonizing, and destructive experiences that often accompany divorce can be minimized with this approach.

The outcome of the marriage described here is still in question. The ultimate resolution of their marital difficulties will be determined, to some degree, by the husband's further resolution of his hostility toward women, but to a much greater degree it will depend on the wife's progress in therapy. It is safe to assume that only if she can achieve further resolution of her problems and realistic acceptance of herself as a woman, so that she ceases to use the marital relationship as a vehicle for acting out her inner conflicts, will she be able to relate to her husband on the basis of a viable marriage contract.

Summary

The concept of the marriage contract is a useful clinical tool for the elucidation and modification of marital relationships. We have found it helpful to familiarize marital partners with their own and each other's contracts and to point out their troublesome aspects; couples are usually highly receptive to this way of structuring their problems. This technique is particularly valuable in conjoint sessions. Communication is facilitated, and spouses are able to understand themselves, each other, and their relationship much better when the terms of their contracts are revealed. The reasons for their unhappiness, apparently irrational behavior, and bickering or bitterness then become clear. Once they gain some understanding of the contractual disappointments each has suffered, marital partners often feel less helpless and are able to seek more realistic and effective solutions to their problems.

The couple's reciprocal expectations are powerful behavioral determinants. The therapist intervenes in the troubled marriage by manipulating and trying to alter crucial aspects of these interactional processes with the aim of improving the marital relationship and the quality of each spouse's life.

Intrapsychic as well as transactional factors are important aspects of marital and family dynamics. The contract concept integrates both these behavioral parameters. It clarifies interactional processes by referring to their intrapsychic determinants. Specifically, contractual dynamics derive from needs and conflicts that can best be understood in intrapsychic terms. Indeed, contractual dynamics can often be understood as adaptive attempts to resolve conflicts by means of specific interactions. However, the consequent interactional process, the contract itself, then becomes a crucial determinant of the quality of the marriage.

This article is intended to serve as an introduction to the concept of the marriage contract. As such, the many further applications and implications of this concept were considered to lie beyond the scope of this discussion. However, the promise of the marriage contract as a conceptual model and its therapeutic value clearly merit its further elaboration in future communications.

29

OPERANT-INTERPERSONAL TREATMENT FOR MARITAL DISCORD

Richard B. Stuart, D.S.W.

Professor, School of Social Work
Fellow, Center for the Study of Human Growth and
Development, University of Michigan

The operant-interpersonal approach to marital treatment rests on three assumptions concerning the character of marital interaction. First, it is assumed that the exact pattern of interaction which takes place between spouses at any point in time is the most rewarding of all of the available alternatives. This implies that the interaction between spouses is never accidental; it represents the best balance which each can achieve between individual and mutual rewards and costs (Tribaut & Kelley, 1959, p. 12). Thus when a husband consistently fails to leave his friends in order to spend time with his wife, it may be concluded that his friends offer greater relative rewards than his wife.

The second assumption is that while the specifics may vary for each couple, most married adults expect to enjoy reciprocal relations with their partners. Reciprocity has the general sociological connotation that "each party has rights and duties [Gouldner, 1960, p. 169]" and the specific behavioral connotation that each party to an interaction should dispense social reinforcement at an equitable rate (Patterson & Reid, 1967, p. 1). In effect, a quid pro quo or "something for something" arrangement underlies successful marriage (Jackson, 1965, p. 591). The exchange of rewards in marriage may be viewed as a quasi-legal contract affording

Reprinted from the Journal of Consulting and Clinical Psychology, 1969, Vol. 33, No. 6, pp. 675-682.

distinct safeguards to each partner. Whenever one partner to a reciprocal interaction unilaterally rewards the other, he does so with the confidence that he will be compensated in kind in the future. For example, if the husband agrees to entertain his wife's parents for a weekend, he does so with the expectation that his wife will accompany him on a weekend fishing trip at some time in the future.

Reciprocity develops as a consequence of a history of positive reinforcement. There is extensive empirical support for the proposition that ego will be more attracted to alter and will reinforce alter more if he has been positively reinforced by alter (Bachrach, Candland, & Gibson, 1961; Brewer & Brewer, 1968; Byrne, 1961, 1962; Byrne & Nelson, 1965; Homans, 1961; Komorita, Sheposh, & Braver, 1968; Newcomb, 1955; Pruitt, 1968).[1] When disordered marriages are evaluated in light of this reinforcement-attraction hypothesis, it is seen that each partner reinforces the other at a low rate and each is therefore relatively unattractive to and unreinforced by the other.

The third assumption is that in order to modify an unsuccessful marital interaction, it is essential to develop the power of each partner to mediate rewards for the other. In support of this assumption, it can be shown that individuals will be more positively attracted to each other when each has been successful in influencing the other to comply with his wishes (Thibaut & Kelley, 1959, p. 124; Thibaut & Riecken, 1955). Conversely, it can be shown that when one party to an interaction fails in his influence attempts, he becomes "socially bankrupt" (Longabaugh, Eldred, Bell, & Sherman, 1966, p. 87) as he lacks the resources needed to control the other's behavior; failing to gain control through positive strategies, he resorts to negative means of control.

In successful marriage, both partners work to maximize mutual reward while minimizing individual costs. A reciprocal exchange of potent social reinforcement is established in which each partner controls sufficient rewards to compensate the other for the rewards which are expected or received from him. In an unsuccessful marriage, both partners appear to work to minimize individual costs with little apparent expectations of mutual reward. In an effort to trim costs, few positive rewards are dispensed; positive reinforcement, as a strategy of behavioral control, is

---

[1] Byrne and Rhamey (1965) have postulated a law of attraction magnitude which takes the following form:

$$A_x = m \left(\frac{\Sigma (PR_x \times M)}{\Sigma (PR_x \times M) + \Sigma (NR_x \times M)} \right) + k,$$

. . . [where] X is a positive linear function of the sum of the weighted positive reinforcements (Number $\times$ Magnitude) received from X divided by the total number of weighted positive and negative reinforcements received from X [p. 887].

replaced by negative reinforcement (removal of an aversive event follow-ing the expected response).

Either or both of two broad patterns of behavioral control, coercion and withdrawal, are likely to emerge in unsuccessful marriages. In coer-cion, one member seeks to gain positive reinforcement from the other in exchange for negative reinforcement (Patterson & Reid, 1967). As an example, a husband might wish his wife to express greater affection; following the failure of his amorous advances, he might become abusive, accusing his wife of anything from indifference to frigidity, abating his criticism when he receives the desired affection. The three flaws in this approach are: first, to the extent that he makes himself unpleasant, he is less likely to receive affection; second, to the extent that he is abusive or accusing, he debases his wife's affection and simultaneously reduces its reinforcing properties for himself; and third, to the extent that her affection is offered in compliance to his demand, it will appear to be appeasement rather than a gesture of genuine affection (Haley, 1963, 1967).

The withdrawal which is likely to occur in unsuccessful marriages is analogous to one of several strategies available in a prisoner's dilemma game:

> If the structure of the situation is such that (a) the reward is small, (b) terminating the interaction is made difficult, and (c) the retali-atory response must take a form which is identical to the disliked other's harmful behavior, then cognitive consistency principles would lead one to expect an increase in ill will, but no retaliatory behavior [Swingle, 1966, p. 270].

Retaliatory behavior might require the husband to match his wife's actions; but to the extent that he devalues his wife for so behaving, consistency would demand that he behave otherwise. Withdrawal has the advantage of denying satisfaction to his wife while at the same time creating a situation requiring her to continue to behave assertively. Thus it is a low-risk tactic of control. The reinforcement for approach behavior on the wife's part would be termination of the husband's withdrawal. At the same time that the husband is withdrawn from his wife, however, he may also find other social and nonsocial reinforcers in his cronies, mis-tress, or can of beer.

Based on this formulation, the operant-interpersonal approach seeks to construct a situation in which the frequency and intensity of mutual positive reinforcement is increased. The effect of positive reinforcement in inducing positively "biased scanning" [Janis & Gilmore, 1965], or searching for assets rather than liabilities in the spouse, has been well demonstrated, particularly when the positive reinforcement is large and is offered under positive sponsorship (Elms & Janis, 1965, p. 53). It is anticipated that this positive scanning will replace negatively biased attitudes, making positive responding more likely. Positive responses, in turn, are intended to augment the range and importance of social reinforcement mediated by each spouse for the other, leading to reestablishment of successful interaction patterns.

TREATMENT CONSIDERATIONS

Operant-interpersonal treatment occurs in four orderly steps. The first step requires training the couple in the logic of the approach, consisting of two self-evident premises. The first premise is that the impressions which each spouse forms of the other is based on the behavior of the other. Accordingly, when one changes his behavior, there are corresponding changes in the other's impressions and expectations of him. Spouses who lose sight of this typically attribute marital difficulty to the personality of the other. For example, the wife who believes that her husband "is passive" implicitly suggests that her husband's personality must change before the marital disturbance can be overcome. Conversely, the wife who believes that her husband "behaves passively" need only find ways to modify her behavior (as she is in control of his actions) in order to modify his problematic responses.

This leads to the second premise, which asserts that in order to change interaction in a marriage, each partner must assume initiative in changing his own behavior before changes can be expected in his spouse. The typical couple is "locked into" problematic patterns of interaction as long as each requires a change in the other prior to changing his own behavior. If coercion and withdrawal are in fact basic problematic processes in discordant marriages, then spontaneous behavior change is highly unlikely to occur, as the response cost is too great and the potential reward too small.

Clients benefit from an explanation of the logic of the approach for at least two reasons. First, such explanations may help to free each spouse from his inaccurate and negatively biasing prejudices. Second, when each spouse is fully aware of the logic of the treatment, he can participate more fully in effective therapeutic planning and execution (Stuart, 1967).

The second step in treatment consists of asking each spouse to list the three behaviors which he would most like to accelerate in the other. This task is often subject to four difficulties. First, couples tend to begin by listing requests for decelerating negative behaviors, which may be expected in view of the fact that much of their interaction prior to seeking treatment has been negative. The difficulty with attempting to decelerate behavior is that its attainment would require the use of aversive stimuli or extinction paradigms, and the typical unhappy couple is already disproportionately committed to these negative strategies. Second, each spouse is likely to phrase his "three wishes" in molar rather than molecular units, and many of these are likely to be formulated in preverbal terms. For example, a husband is likely to list the request that his wife "act more feminine." "Feminine" is a modifier which is subject to varied interpretation and which may modify a wide range of behaviors. These molar requests must be reduced to specifics which include description of the desired behavior, its rate, and the context in which it is expected to occur. Third, each spouse is likely to proclaim that the other should "know what I want—if I have to tell him, then he is not as sensitive to me as he should be." Many unhappily married couples share the naïve expectation that their spouse should be clairvoyant, and it is therefore often necessary to stress the need that each must communicate his wishes to the other in order to increase the probability that they will be gratified. The fourth obstacle in this apparently simple listing of behavior change objectives is concerned with the punctuation of the behavioral chains. It has been observed that each spouse is likely to describe each unit of his own behavior as sandwiched between two negative actions on the part of his spouse (Watzlawick, Beavin, & Jackson, 1967, pp. 54-59). These three element chains (other-negative, self-positive, other-negative) obscure the true interaction, as the speaker omits reference to his stimulation of the other's initial negative actions.

The third step in the treatment calls for transcription of the three wishes of each as headings on a Behavior Checklist which is posted at some convenient point in the house. Each spouse is asked to record the frequency with which the other performs the act which he desires. While monitoring undoubtedly influences the rate of occurrence of each set of responses, this exercise does provide a crude base line against which to evaluate change.

The fourth step consists of working out a series of exchanges of desired behaviors. The typical couple complains of a "lack of communication," which is a euphemism for a failure to reinforce each other. On closer analysis, this complaint is frequently seen as a reference to low-rate conversational and sexual behavior. This communication gap is overcome in the fourth step by arranging for each partner to compensate the other for the behaviors which he identified as socially reinforcing to him.

In marriages which have not dissolved reciprocity into coercion or withdrawal, a simple exchange of behaviors is effective. Couples are asked to accelerate desired behaviors on an equal basis. For example, one husband complained that his wife failed to greet him at the door, that she did not straighten the family room in anticipation of his return home from work, and that meals were rarely ready on time. His wife complained that he failed to spend sufficient time with the children (it was agreed that 30 minutes before bed was sufficient), failed to take her out for an occasional movie, and failed to pay attention to meals when they were well prepared. Accordingly, each of these behaviors was restated as a positive (e.g., greet husband at door) and was listed on the Behavior Monitoring Form. Each person recorded the frequency with which the other completed the desired behavior. When these behaviors were accelerated at a sufficient rate, other goals were added.

In marriages in which reciprocity appears to be essentially absent, a token economy has proven useful. Where reciprocity fails, couples tend not to trust each other. It is therefore important to arrange for some immediate form of reinforcement. Tokens are an ideal media for such reinforcement because (a) they are given immediately (b) they can be redeemed for the specific consequences which the recipient deems desirable at that point in time, (c) they are concrete and unambiguous, (d) the giving and receiving of tokens is customarily associated with positive social interchange, and (e) they permit an exchange of behaviors which are not contiguous. Token systems have been used effectively in a wide range of settings (e.g., mental hospitals—Atthowe & Krasner, 1968; classrooms—Clark, Lachowicz, & Wolf, 1968; and institutions for delinquents—Tyler & Brown, 1967), and extension of this technique to marital treatment appears warranted.

ILLUSTRATION AND RESULTS

Four couples have used the token system to modify each other's behavior. Individuals ranged in age from 24 to 52 and in education from high school diploma to doctorate. The couples were married from 3 to 23 years and had a maximum of two children. Each of the couples sought treatment as a last-ditch effort prior to obtaining a divorce. In each instance, the wife listed as her first wish that the husband converse with her more fully, or at least that he not "close me out of his life even when he is at home." Considerable discussion was often necessary to identify what intensity level of conversation was positively reinforcing to the wife, and this was made clear and rehearsed during the treatment

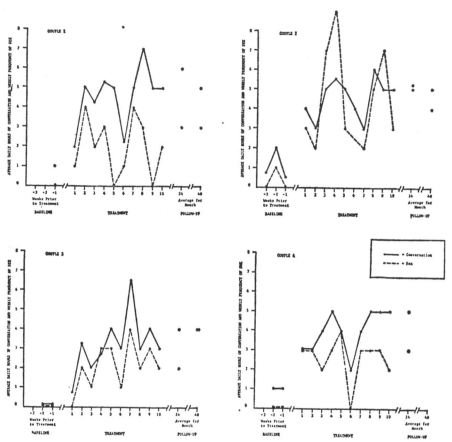

Fig. 1. Average daily hours of conversation and weekly rate of sex of four couples—
before, during, and after operant marital therapy.

sessions. The wife was then instructed to purchase a kitchen timer which
she could carry with her about the house. She was instructed to set the
timer as soon as her husband entered and to give him one token when
the bell rang after each hour in which he conversed at the criterion level.
If he failed to behave at the criterion level by the end of the first 30
minutes of each hour, she had to notify him of this and offer constructive suggestions, cueing him as to how his performance could be improved
upon. If she failed to do this, he had to be given a token even if he
failed to perform adequately. If he so requested, at the half-hour cue
time, the timer could be reset so that he could earn a token during the

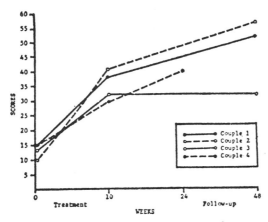

FIG. 2. Marital satisfaction assessment inventory scores of four couples—before, at last session, and at follow-up of operant marital treatment.

next hour (so that he waited 60 rather than 90 minutes before being rewarded).

The criterion level for conversation is naturally a negotiable factor. No one could be expected to talk to his wife constantly; if for no other reason, his children would not allow it. Therefore, conversational tokens can be earned for a wider range of responses ranging from intense conversation at one extreme to the wife's feeling free to interrupt her husband with a question at agreed intervals at the other extreme.

While tokens may have some intrinsic reinforcing properties in their own right (in addition to being associated with positive social responses when they are offered), they become more powerful when they function as contingencies for some other event. With the four couples cited, tokens were redeemable at the husband's request from a menu stressing physical affection. A different menu was constructed for each couple which took into account the base-line level of sexual activity, the desired level of sexual activity, and the number of hours available for nonsexual (in this instance conversational) interchange. Each of these couples had sex less than once per week (ranging from once in the year prior to treatment to once in the week prior to treatment), each desired sex an average of three times per week, and each had approximately 5 hours together on weeknights and 14 hours on weekends, making a total of approximately 52-54 hours per week. Accordingly, husbands were charged three tokens for kissing and "lightly petting" with their wives, five tokens for "heavy petting," and 15 tokens for intercourse. (These behaviors were not rehearsed during treatment sessions.)

Tokens earned and spent were recorded on the Behavior Checklist, which also provided data for continued graphing of interactional behavior. The performance of each of these couples is represented in Figure 1; where it will be seen that the rates of conversation and sex increased sharply after the start of treatment and continued through 24- and 48-week follow-up periods.

At the start of treatment, at the conclusion of regularly scheduled interviews, and at the time of follow-up, each spouse was asked to complete a brief inventory measuring the extent of his own and his perception of his spouse's satisfaction in and commitment to the marriage. This inventory was adapted from the work of Farber (1957). The results are depicted in Figure 2 where it can be seen that the rate of reported satisfaction increased in association with the reported behavioral changes. These changes enabled the couples to become more similar to nonclinic families on this dimension (Levinger & Breedlove, 1966, p. 369).

With each of these couples, all therapeutic sessions were held jointly. Sessions were held during the first four, the sixth, eighth, and tenth weeks, for a total of seven sessions. When it is considered that these couples were each on the brink of filing for divorce, this could be considered relatively inexpensive treatment. Follow-up contacts were held by phone or by mail, and all data, including that collected during sessions, were based on self-report.

DISCUSSION

The therapeutic recommendations of alternative courses of behavior are consistent with Goldiamond's (1966, p. 118) recommendation to his patients that: "If he wished his wife to behave differently to him, then he should provide other stimuli than the ones which produced the behaviors he did not like." Each spouse was directed in specific modifications on his own behavior in an effort to modify the behavioral environment in which his partner's behavior occurred. The antecedents for changed behavior were probably twofold: therapeutic recommendations exercised some discriminant stimulus control as did the expectation of changes in the behavior of the spouse. The therapist suggested that each party engage in behaviors which had doubtless been requested, cajoled, and demanded by each party countless times before. As therapeutic directives, these new requests were differentiated from the old in two important respects. First, they were clarified. Second, they were removed from the context of coercive demands in which granting the request would have been tantamount to reinforcing dysfunctional patterns of negative reinforcement. In addition, the treatment was characterized to each couple as a "game" in which each would be able to modify the general rules of the relationship so that positive rather than negative strategies would pay off.

It is impossible to isolate which aspects of this complex treatment approach carry the weight of the observed change. Behavioral rehearsal and the manipulation of social reinforcers were the objectively identified variables but other observers would undoubtedly stress other factors as well. One technical point of particular importance is the fact that at no time was an attempt made to "fade" (or slowly remove) the behavior modification system, replacing it with more natural processes of behavioral control (Krasner, 1965, 1966). Indeed, continued reliance on the therapeutic techniques as a means of programming and evaluating each other's behavior could result in considerable gain with low cost. In fact, one characteristic of an ideal therapeutic technique might be that it is transferable to the natural environment without change.

This pattern of treatment is likely to be challenged on two counts. Some critics will charge that the therapeutic strategies of this approach are "trivial" because they are based on "superficial" changes in behavior. Two counterarguments should be stressed. First, the only data which are available to the therapist as a scientist are observable behaviors, and it is at the level of behavior that changes must be sought (Skinner, 1953). Second, it must be stressed that these were the changes sought by the clients and were therefore in accord with the therapeutic contract. To have sought other goals would have meant ignoring the presenting complaints.

In response to the triviality argument, it is also relevant to cite the data concerning the level of marital satisfaction. However, these must be considered to be "soft data" as they are based on global self-ratings such as "How committed are you to stay in this marriage?" and "What proportion of time spent with your spouse would you consider to be fully satisfying?" It is impossible to determine exactly what degree of meaningfulness can be attributed to answers to such questions and they should, at best, be interpreted as indications of trend.

REFERENCES

ATTHOWE, J. M., JR. & KRASNER, L. Preliminary Report on the Application of Contingent Reinforcement Procedures (Token Economy) on a "Chronic" Psychiatric Ward. *J. Abnorm. Psychol.*, 1968, 73:37-43.

BACHRACH, A. J., CANDLAND, D. K., & GIBSON, J. T. Group Reinforcement of Individual Response Experiments in Verbal Behavior. In I. A. Berg and B. M. Bass (Eds.), *Conformity and Deviation*. New York: Harper, 1961.

BREWER, R. E. & BREWER, M. B. Attraction and Accuracy of Perception in Dyads. *J. Personality and Soc. Psychol.*, 1968, 8:188-193.

BYRNE, D. Interpersonal Attraction and Attitude Similarity. *J. Abnorm. and Soc. Psychol.*, 1961, 62:713-715.

BYRNE, D. Response to Attitude Similarity-Dissimilarity as a Function of Affiliation Need. *J. Personality*, 1962, 30:164-177.

BYRNE, D. & NELSON, D. Attraction as a Linear Function of Proportion of Positive Reinforcements. *J. Personality and Soc. Psychol.*, 1965, 1:659-663.

BYRNE, D. & RHAMEY, R. Magnitude of Positive and Negative Reinforcements as a Determinant of Attraction. *J. Personality and Soc. Psychol.*, 1965, 2:884-889.

CLARK, M., LACHOWICZ, J., & WOLF, M. A Pilot Basic Education Program for School Dropouts Incorporating a Token Reinforcement System. *Behav. Res. and Ther.*, 1968, 6:183.

ELMS, A. C. & JANIS, I. L. Counter-norm Attitudes Induced by Consonant versus Dissonant Conditions of Role-playing. *J. Experi. Res. in Personality*, 1965, 1:50-60.

FARBER, B. An Index on Marital Integration. *Sociometry*, 1957, 20:117-134.

GOLDIAMOND, I. Self-control Procedures in Personal Behavior Problems. In R. Ulrich, T. Stachnik, and J. Mabry (Eds.), *Control of Human Behavior*. Chicago: Scott, Foresman, 1966.

GOULDNER, A. W. The Norm of Reciprocity: A Preliminary Statement. *Amer. Sociol. Rev.*, 1960, 25:161-178.

HALEY, J. *Strategies of Psychotherapy*. New York: Grune & Stratton, 1963.

HALEY, J. Marriage Therapy. In H. Greenwald (Ed.), *Active Psychotherapy*. New York: Atherton Press, 1967.

HOMANS, G. C. *Social Behavior: Its Elementary Forms*. New York: Harcourt, Brace & World, 1961.

JACKSON, D. D. Family Rules. *Arch. Gen. Psychiat.*, 1965, 12:589-594.

JANIS, I. & GILMORE, J. The Influence of Incentive Conditions on the Success of Role Playing in Modifying Attitudes. *J. Personality and Soc. Psychol.*, 1965, 1:17-27.

KOMORITA, S. S., SHEPOSH, J. P., & BRAVER, S. L. Power, the Use of Power, and Cooperative Choice in a Two-Person Game. *J. Personality and Soc. Psychol.*, 1968, 8:134-142.

KRASNER, L. Operant Conditioning Techniques with Adults from the Laboratory to "Real Life" Behavior Modification. aper presented at the meeting of the American Psychological Association, Chicago, September 1965.

KRASNER, L. The Translation of Operant Conditioning Procedures from the Experimental Laboratory to the Psychotherapeutic Interaction. Paper presented at the meeting of the American Psychological Association, New York, September 1966.

LEVINGER, G. & BREEDLOVE, J. Interpersonal Attraction and Agreement: A Study of Marriage Partners. *J. Personality and Soc. Psychol.*, 1966, 3, 367-372.

LONGABAUGH, R., ELDRED, S. H., BELL, N. W., & SHERMAN, L. J. The Interactional World of the Chronic Schizophrenic Patient. *Psychiatry*, 1966, 29:78-99.

NEWCOMB, T. M. *Social Psychology*. New York: Holt, Rinehart & Winston, 1955.

30

TREATING THE DOLL'S HOUSE MARRIAGE

Frank S. Pittman, III, M.D.

Director of Psychiatric Services, Grady Memorial Hospital (Atlanta)
Assistant Professor of Psychiatry, Emory University School of Medicine

and

Kalman Flomenhaft, D.S.W.

Director, Institute for Teachers of Family Therapy
Philadelphia Child Guidance Clinic

The Doll's House, a common pitfall for family therapists, is an extremely unequal relationship in which one spouse's incompetence is required or encouraged by the other. This pattern of marriage is common in a sick population and is chosen by people with clear individual pathology. It may be stable and satisfying, but it is crisis prone. Doll's Houses are likely to be disrupted by the arrival of children, financial reverses, and, most important, the intrusion of another person upon whom the Doll is dependent and who sets out to equalize the marital relationship. A well-intentioned therapist with an intolerance for pathology can destroy the marriage. Therapy seems more successful when the therapist respects the basically unequal framework the couple has chosen and works toward greater understanding and respect for unique individual needs within that framework.

Reprinted from FAMILY PROCESS, Vol. 9, No. 2, June 1970.

This work was supported in part by NIMH grant #1577. The authors wish to express appreciation to their colleagues in the Family Treatment Unit, from which this paper emerged. These included Dr. Donald G. Langsley, Dr. David Kaplan, Dr. Pavel Machotka, and Miss Carol DeYoung. Dr. Alfred A. Messer, Emory University, Atlanta, also provided many helpful suggestions.

The zealous therapist eager to stamp out disease, can destroy a family. The same pathology which limits a family's healthy flexibility makes it crisis prone, and even brings it into therapy, may be cherished by the family, even may be the raison d'être for the family. There are times when one should leave bad enough alone.

A common pattern of marital pathology has been graphically described by Ibsen. His play, *A Doll's House,* has been cited many times before for its example of a marriage which fails. In the play, Torvald Helmer adores his child-wife, Nora, his "little squirrel." Nora is charming, flighty, helpless. She fits the dictionary definition of a doll—"a plaything; a pretty but empty-headed person." She seems retarded mentally and immature emotionally, completely dependent on Helmer, as she was on her father. In her words, she is a plaything in a doll's house. Unknown to Helmer, Nora, years previously, acted independently in his interest. As the secret nears revelation, a crisis occurs. Nora's friend, a self-reliant widow, makes well-intentioned, but uninvited efforts to use the crisis to equalize the marriage. When Helmer is forced to recognize Nora's capacity for independent action, he condemns it as incompetence. Nora's response is to end the marriage.

A Doll's House is, simply, a marriage in which one spouse cannot tolerate acknowledgment of his partner's competence. A marriage of this sort is not unusual. The authors, on the staff of the Family Treatment Unit of the University of Colorado Medical Center (1, 2, 3), have provided crisis therapy for families containing an acutely psychotic member. In 150 families in which one member was brought for psychiatric hospitalization, 30 of the marriages were of the Doll's House variety.[1] The essential features are much as Ibsen describes, extremely unequal relationships in which one spouse's incompetence is required or encouraged, or had been for long periods in the past. The Doll, usually the wife, is subservient, does not make independent decisions, and is seen by her Master as helpless, dependent, and perhaps defective mentally or emotionally. The Master is uncomfortable with any indication of competence on the part of the Doll. Nonetheless, the relationship may be accepted and enjoyed by both people for long periods of time—a stable, pathological equilibrium.

THE DOLL AND THE MASTER

The underlying pathology is overt and fairly straightforward. The Doll does not function as a competent adult. Usually she is truly incom-

---

[1] One of these 30 families is described in detail by Dr. Pavel Machotka, in Chapter VII of the Family Treatment Unit's recent book, *Treatment of Families in Crisis* (2).

petent, often actually retarded, more often schizophrenic. About half the Doll wives were schizophrenic. Whatever the cause of schizophrenia, it may result in some degree of incompetence, undependability, dependency, isolation, or inflexibility. It might be assumed that the husbands of these women were realistically assessing their capabilities and loving them despite their limitations. Such is often the case, but in these marriages, the opposite was true. The women were cherished *because* of their limitations; the helpless withdrawal of schizophrenia was encouraged as health, while independence, expressiveness, and attempts at competent functioning were seen as sickness. More than one Master decided to marry a Doll while she was overtly psychotic—even catatonic. The schizophrenic Dolls thus have the potential disability of schizophrenia enforced through Dolldem.

Sometimes the Doll is potentially capable, but, like Nora, has spent a lifetime feeling and being thought of as incompetent. Many of the younger women are poorly educated, socially awkward, unsure, and anxious when facing new experiences. Some of these were from rural or under-privileged families. An occasional Doll has struggled for years to survive independently or to support weak men, and collapses, angry and exhausted, when she finally finds a man who will let her do so. She may maintain her position through a sequence of disabling physical or emotional symptoms. It may even happen that a Doll's House marriage may develop from a more conventional marriage, as a woman becomes menopausal or invalided. In such situations, a temporary shift occurs and is so satisfying it is maintained.

Doll's House Masters are more constant in their psychopathology. Each of these men secretly feels helpless or incapable, castrated perhaps, an infirmity which must be hidden or denied. He considers himself incapable of winning or holding a real woman. He tends to be fearful of women, but may be comfortable in his dealings with men. He may be overtly paranoid, but more often is just rigid and suspicious. He is rarely alcoholic, but may be a reformed alcoholic with a second wife. (If he were overtly symptomatic, the Doll's House would crumble quickly; it is important that he maintain his wife's respect and confidence —if her dependency were rooted in fear, it would be quite a different relationship.) He usually had a dominant and demanding mother, whom he could never satisfy, but his fear of strong women may have come later after a first marriage to such a woman.

THE USUAL PATTERNS

The Doll's House is an unequal relationship, hardly a partnership, but as with Nora and Helmer, it may provide many years of satisfaction and happiness. A couple enters into such a relationship voluntarily and knowingly, though often the marriage was arranged by relatives. The Master is loving, may be successful and generous, and is usually faithful and attentive. He is rarely abusive or even inconsiderate. The Doll feels secure, loved, and wanted. She may feel far more attractive than she is. Sexual adjustment is rarely a problem for the Master, and, if the Doll is frigid, which certainly is not always the case, this may be well tolerated by both. Perhaps six of the dominant husbands were alcoholic, promiscuous, or brutal, but this represented episodic interruptions of more usual protective patterns.

In typical operation, the Master makes a steady living and provides a comfortable home. The Doll keeps house, usually well. The Master may do the shopping and menu planning, and the Doll may not even handle money or drive a car. The Doll's pleasures may be entirely domestic, and she is not likely to spend her day having coffee with neighbors. The Master may disapprove of her contacts with her relatives, or even his. The couple may have few friends and rarely go out socially, though they may have activities they enjoy together at home. Both may be disdainful of more equal marital relationships, and this may further restrict their circle of available friends.

There are variations in a Doll's House relationship. Milder degrees of inequality also exist, along the usual continuum. There may also be temporary marital inequalities, arising from a variety of circumstances such as an illness. Unequal "marriages" also occur among homosexuals.

A relationship not unlike a Doll's House may be sanctioned and supported by the surrounding culture. Southern "belles," Indian squaws, and Mediterranean or Japanese wives may, in external appearances at least, be only a few degrees away from Dolldom. In Colorado, many families of rural Spanish speaking origin, perhaps in this respect similar to the Puerto Rican arrivals to Eastern cities, prefer marriages in which wives are subordinate, even subservient. Good wives of this sort may pride themselves on their imagination and finesse in achieving the appropriate aura of male dominance, while retaining influence and even control over the family.

A Doll's House may also include a female Master and a male Doll. Such female Masters may be chronic martyrs, or they may have severe doubts about their attractiveness to more competent men and have masculine strivings. Five such Doll men were interesting. One had been a violent alcoholic for many years prior to his recent incapacity with amyotrophic lateral sclerosis. Now a helpless invalid, he was adored by a long-suffering wife who formerly loathed him. The four other men were incompetent, unemployed, chronic schizophrenics whose strong wives supported and cherished them and saw themselves as the envy of their friends. Interestingly enough these men seemed to be pursued by other women.

The early years of a Doll's House marriage are not so sublimely rigid. Either spouse may resist the other's expectations, and the battle may become intense. An alcoholic physician married a catatonic woman he had met while both were hospitalized. After he nursed her back to health, she expressed a desire to work. He tried to convince her she should remain an invalid, and he seemed determined to drive her crazy again. In a more common situation, a lovely young wife refused to care for her child, and, instead, wanted her husband to treat her as a child and ignore the baby. In still another marriage, a competent widow married a young man who had never held a job. She expected him to stay home caring for the children and became overtly psychotic when he insisted on working. In each of these three situations, the marriage could have dissolved, could have developed into a true Doll's House, or could have become more or less a partnership. As one partner struggles to establish a Doll's House, the other partner may cooperate, may acquiesce, or may rebel. (Therapy in these cases could be influential in determining the outcome because the patterns of the marriage are not yet rigidified.)

CRISES IN THE DOLL'S HOUSE

In Ibsen's description, the Doll's House relationship had succeeded for a time, but some crisis came. Few Doll's Houses seem to collapse under their own weight. It must be understood that we are speaking only of relationships which have been successful for a time; undoubtedly, many individuals attempt to establish such a marriage but are rebuffed by a prospective partner who wants something quite different from the marriage. There seem to be three major kinds of crises which disrupt previously successful Doll's Houses: a new baby, a change in the family finances, or the intrusion of another adult.

One major source of crisis in such an exclusive twosome may be the birth of a child. Only a few—the most pronounced—remained voluntarily childless. It may be that a child works to soften the Doll's House by giving the wife (or forcing her into) a more adult role and giving the husband a real child, but the wife may not want the new responsibility, and the husband may fear the experience will make his wife too adequate. In the few childless cases, it was more often the husband who chose not to introduce a third person into the relationship.

Either spouse might be temporarily resentful of a new child. One husband, who had left a former wife when she had children, was attempting to have his present wife declared an unfit mother (which she wasn't) by having her found insane (which she wasn't) in an effort to have the baby placed for adoption, even though he got enormous pleasure from the child, as did his wife. On the other hand, at least six of the Dolls had given away children previously, though five of these occurred in previous marriages which were not of the Doll's House variety. In the one Doll's House marriage in which a wife was determined to give away a child to her mother, the husband chose to keep the child and return the wife to the mother instead.

Once the children arrived and were accepted, they seemed to do reasonably well. None of the younger children of these families was overtly symptomatic. Considering the degree of pathology in the families, quite aside from the Doll's House marriage (it will be recalled that each family contained a member, usually the mother, who was overtly psychotic or otherwise considered hospitalizable), the children were happy and well cared for.

Older children were somewhat too mature and responsible for their age, especially when the Master included them in an alliance to reinforce the Doll's House relationship. Among the nine marriages with older children still at home, two adolescents were probably schizophrenic but functioning comfortably. In four of these older marriages, each marked by severe tension between the parents (these included the few marriages in which the husbands were openly unfaithful or alcoholic), there were adolescents with neurotic or behavior problems, with two of the boys dropping out of school as their fathers had, one girl being openly promiscuous, and one very bright boy desirous of a therapist for himself to help him with his feeling of disrespect for all women. The overall impression has been that children can be raised adequately in these families, after the initial shock of their births, and that the only specific problem these children face is a possible confusion about marital role differentiation.

Doll's House marriages are badly prepared for absorbing financial crises. In part, this is because Doll's House Masters are unwilling to admit any failures in this realm, so when they need to tighten their belts, they may continue a show of financial success. Obvious solutions, such as admitting a need to curb spending or letting the Doll spouse go to work, are usually closed to them. The Doll is more likely to be capable of working than the Master is to permit it. The result may be that the Master will withdraw from the Doll, become abusive, or even leave rather than let her help him. After twenty years of marriage, one husband found his business failing. He refused to admit the failure, even after losing the family home and savings. The Doll wife became depressed and anxious at his withdrawal from her, but with therapy, was able to go to work and help the family to be fed and clothed. Her husband became violently abusive, moved far from the bus line, and gave her car away to force her to quit working.

By far the most common problem for these marriages comes when other adults, in-laws, therapists, or adolescent children become horrified at the inequality of the relationship and determine to change it. A Doll's House wife, if she is more competent than her husband would like to acknowledge, may require, as Nora did, a companionate relationship with someone who can treat her as an equal. These women are rarely either subtle or bright, and, above all, they are dependent, so the Doll's House wife is likely to have few secrets from her confidantes. They may have professional confidantes, too, and may be particularly appealing to the rescue fantasies of these therapists.

The confidantes—people who would involve themselves with such inept and clinging creatures—are likely to be rather bossy and interfering, as a profession or as a hobby. The confidantes may be well intentioned when they encourage the Doll to feel guilty for liking the marriage's inequalities, to question her husband's love for her, or to rebel. The good intentions of the confidante may be based not on what would be best for the Doll, but what would be an acceptable marital relationship for the confidante. This is exactly what Ibsen described. In our series, the most likely disrupting confidantes were therapists and mothers-in-law. Friends or other relatives, including grown or adolescent children, occasionally performed this role.

THERAPY

Therapy with these families is problematic. Individual therapy of the Doll is particularly hazardous. The enthusiastic therapist is likely to side strongly with the aspect of the Doll's ambivalence which yearns for independence. The dependent Doll, ever striving to please, may obediently rebel against her husband—now identified as the villain. The result may be precipitous disruption of the family, desperate counter moves from the Master, or bizarre efforts at emancipation, calculated to fail, which leave the Doll even more convinced of her helplessness and guilty for having disappointed the therapist. The very existence of the therapeutic relationship may be so threatening that the Master will disrupt therapy and return the Doll oven more firmly to her Doll's House.

Family therapy is less hazardous, but presents its own problems. The structure of couples' therapy is based on a concept of marriage in which there are two equal partners with equal voice in decisions and with potential for compromise and "quid pro quo." The therapist takes the adult role to the two equal "children." Understandably, this structure is anathema to a Doll Master.

The authors, observing the crises and the results of different forms of therapy with Doll's House marriages, and making most of the expectable mistakes, have felt that therapy succeeds best when it respects the basic inequality of the marriage. It should not be too difficult for the therapist to appreciate that these two people have sought out one another and satisfied one another for some time prior to the crisis that has led to the request for treatment. Also, it should become apparent that the Master is not really a villain, although the Doll may gain much approval from her mother, her therapist, or her girlfriend by picturing him that way. The Doll's independence must be supported cautiously, slowly, and with careful consideration of her realistic capabilities and her husband's ability to tolerate it. In the authors' experience, if the Master is respected and if the basic inequality is not challenged, some compromise can be reached between what the Doll feels she wants and what the Master feels he can tolerate. The result may be far from a partnership and once the Doll has a little more freedom, she may anxiously give it up, if the therapist will let her. It must not be forgotten that there are other people involved too—friends and relatives who have some sort of investment in assisting the Doll's rebellion. Much of this quandry was described in Sampson, Messenger and Towne's book, *Schizophrenic Women* (4), though it seems applicable to non-schizophrenic Dolls as well. It may be necessary to answer the question posed by one Doll-wife, "Mother doesn't love me unless I'm fighting with my husband, but when I don't talk to her for a few days, I realize I like my marriage just the way it is. Do I have to want what she wants for her to love me?" This therapist must also ask if he is producing this quandary.

The following rather extreme case history will demonstrate many of the points about the phenomenon of a Doll's House marriage and about a possible approach to therapy.

CASE A

Mrs. A was thirty-five and childless after ten years of marriage. She has been raised in a rural, impoverished, German-speaking family and felt isolated and odd in school. She became a shyly awkward, overweight young woman who dropped out of school, kept house for the family, worked briefly and married. Her husband was an energetic and illiterate little man. Neither had had serious romantic involvements previously. Mr. A did maintenance work and provided a steady and adequate income. Mr. A did not want children, and Mrs. A acceded. The couple built a house in the mountains with no neighbors. The bedroom contained a double bed, the living room had two comfortable chairs before a television set, and the third room, the kitchen, contained a small table and two chairs. A large dog kept away intruders. The immaculate Doll's House was clearly built for two. A large guest room had been built onto a garage almost one hundred yards from the little house. It was here that Mr. A's mother stayed when she made her annual visit. The mother, after her most recent divorce, was increasingly dissatisfied with the couple's failure to have children. First she tried to change her son, but failed. Then she began working on Mrs. A. Her visits were increasingly stressful as she encouraged Mrs. A to defy her husband in various ways. Mrs. A was more malleable than her husband had been, and a series of psychiatric hospitalizations resulted. Each time, Mrs. A failed in her efforts, blamed her husband, threatened to leave, and developed symptoms of acute schizophrenia. In the hospital, she was made asymptomatic with phenothiazines, encouraged to rebel further, and sent home with plans to go to work, plans which invariably dissolved. This pattern was repeated through three hospitalizations in three years. The fourth year, during the mother-in-law's visit, Mrs. A again began to feel dissatisfied and inadequate. Her first act of independence was to discontinue her medication. A few days later she fought with her husband over the recurrent question of children, packed her bags, and dramatically left home. She was found sitting beside the road a few hundred yards away, hallucinating.

Mrs. A was brought in for what would have been her fourth hospitalization in four years. She was not hospitalized, but treated at home with her family. On medication, her symptoms cleared as before. She was not pushed toward independence, instead she was encouraged to see the benefits of her position, while her husband realized he would run less risk of losing her by giving her a little more freedom. He voiced some of his fears that he didn't deserve such a marvelous woman. Perhaps the most important aspect of the treatment was the focus on the mother-in-law and other relatives in the area. They were encouraged to see that the A's marriage was as the A's wanted it and was best left alone. This was accomplished in a few visits. Three and a half years later, Mrs. A remained free of major symptoms on a small dose of phenothiazine. She was still childless, still unemployed, still in her Doll's House, and still "happily" married. The only change was a more active social life and freer contacts with her relatives. The mother-in-law still visited but respected the peculiar but satisfying relationship of the A's.

CASE B

The reversal of the sexes produces little real change in the nature of the relationship, or the problems of therapy, as evidenced by the B Family.

Mrs. B married her husband because he was so different from other men. When she met him, he was sitting immobile with his head in his hands. He remained there all evening. She was immediately attracted to him and quickly married him. She became a nurses' aide, moved the family to an old mountain cabin belonging to her mother, and produced several children. At first, Mr. B worked when he was not in a psychiatric hospital for his chronic paranoid schizophrenia. As household duties became more bothersome for Mrs. B, she left her husband at home to care for the children and the house. During the warmer months, he made a few dollars by repairing cars for friends. He wintered in a Veterans' Hospital. Winters were hard for him at home because it was too cold to work on cars in his unheated garage. Each winter, as he had no cars to work on, he began to accuse his wife of putting saltpeter in his coffee and otherwise plotting to rob him of his masculinity. After Mrs. B had herself declared head of the household and was sent to practical nursing school, Mr. B's symptoms increased and he was brought for his sixth psychiatric hospitalization. Instead, he was medicated and referred to Vocational Rehabilitation. His wife begged him to stay at home, instead, and he did, staying in bed for days at a time. He talked of opening a real automobile repair shop at home. His wife okayed it, but the therapists discouraged it and pushed for full outside employment. A year later, he became less affectionate to his wife and more attentive to another woman. He refused to take medication and became more paranoid. Again, he was refused hospitalization and referred to Vocational Rehabilitation. This time he went, and performed admirably. Mrs. B made a suicide attempt, began staying home from work, and encouraged Mr. B to stay with her. Separation was urged by the therapists. The couple separated, Mr. B dropped out of his program, took a job on a farm, worked two weeks, was contacted by his wife, and returned home, not working but keeping house, instead, and refusing further contact with the therapists.

RESULTS

The authors have followed 30 families for up to five years. Most remained together. Two of the couples have been separated by death—in each case a chronically invalid Doll dying of a chronic neurologic disease. Only two couples chose to separate for any period of time. One woman left her philandering husband of twenty years on the ·advice of all. her relatives and friends. The husband took a young mistress even more helpless than his wife had been. The wife, clinging and intermittently employed, after exhausting the patience of her relatives and scaring off prospective suitors with her dependency, found herself isolated, alcoholic, illegitimately pregnant and suicidal.

The second couple fared little better in separation. The wife had left her only child for her mother to raise. When the boy was eight, his grandmother felt he should be with his parents, though they didn't want him and he preferred his grandmother. The mother again felt unable to raise him. The husband, forced to choose between his wife and his son, chose the son and returned the non-psychotic wife to her mother, who had her hospitalized at the state hospital where the mother worked. Two and a half years later, the hospital noted that the young woman seemed to have found a home there and had little motivation to prepare herself for life outside. The author's impression from this experience has been that disruption of the marriage is not a solution to be taken lightly.

DISCUSSION

Doll's House marriages are pathological and, because one spouse must remain incompetent, limited in their repertoire of responses to crises. There will be crises which may require professional help. At such times of imminent change, the therapists may be tempted to push for more change than is necessary for crisis resolution. When the basic inequality and attitudes of the Doll's House are respected, many small changes can be made in the workings of the relationship, and the repertoire can be expanded. Mr. A can take his wife square dancing, can let her visit relatives, can even let her learn to drive and do the shopping alone, though he cannot let her have a child. Mrs. B can let her husband supplement the family income by repairing cars, though she must remain officially head of the household. But these important little changes can't be made if the therapists threaten to make the marriage "healthy" and thereby frighten the couple out of therapy.

There are few people who want to change, however strongly they may want relief of pain. In a Doll's House, the desire to remain the same may seem even stronger than the desire for comfort. This may become apparent if the therapist takes seriously the patient's complaints and, willingly or not, encourages the Doll's rebellion. In his concern with making every family member "grow," he may destroy the family. The patient may be forced to choose between her husband and her therapist, an unhappy alternative either way.

Grandiose goals for families or individuals may sound impressive, especially in the absence of data to evaluate results. More important, the setting of grandiose and global goals may prevent realistic change from being recognized or even attempted. An appropriate goal of family therapy is to help people to live together (or apart) without driving one another crazy. This usually can be accomplished within a family framework not too different from that chosen by the family. Families with a variety of configurations have been successful. It rarely is necessary or appropriate to push the family toward some norm or ideal chosen by the therapist.

It is the impression of the authors that there is wide variation in patterns of successful marriage and that the therapist who respects uniqueness, and thereby encourages others to do so, is most likely to be helpful.

REFERENCES

1. HALEY, J. & HOFFMAN, L. Techniques of Family Therapy, "Cleaning House: An Interview with Frank Pittman, III, Kalman Flomenhaft, and Carol DeYoung," 1, New York, Basic Books, 1967, pp. 361-471.
2. LANGSLEY, D. G., KAPLAN, D. M., PITTMAN, F. S., MACHOTKA, P., FLOMENHAFT, K., & DEYOUNG, C. D. The Treatment of Families in Crisis, 1, New York, Grune and Stratton, 1968.
3. PITTMAN, F. S., DEYOUNG, C. D., FLOMENHAFT, K., KAPLAN, D. M., & LANGSLEY, D. G. "Techniques of Crisis Family Therapy." In J. Masserman (ed.), Current Psychiatric Therapies, 6, New York, Grune and Stratton, 1966, pp. 187-196.
4. SAMPSON, H., MESSENGER, S. L., & TOWNE, R. D. Schizophrenic Women: Studies in Marital Crisis, 1, New York, Atherton Press, 1964.

31

A RE-EVALUATION OF "PSYCHIATRIC HELP" WHEN DIVORCE IMPENDS

Carl A. Whitaker, M.D.

Professor and Chairman, Department of Psychiatry, University of Wisconsin Medical School

and

Milton H. Miller, M.D.

Professor, Department of Psychiatry, University of Wisconsin Medical School

It was Hippocrates who said, "Physician, at least do no harm!" In attempting to provide aid to those couples who are experiencing marital discord, the members of the family, the would-be friend, and the psychiatric clinician alike may well take heed. Marriage is a complex matter and divorce no less so. Each marital unit represents a system all its own—no two are alike. When trouble occurs, no simple formula gained from past success will necessarily apply.

Before consulting a psychiatrist, most couples in difficulty have struggled together for long periods and have talked individually with their friends, possibly with their minister, occasionally with the lawyer. Then, one or both turn for assistance to the psychiatrist. We suggest that in a circumstance where divorce impends the ordinary and customary styles of reacting to an appeal for help characteristic of general psychiatric

Reprinted from AMERICAN JOURNAL OF PSYCHIATRY, 126: 5, November 1969, pp. 611-616. © Copyright 1969 American Psychiatric Association.

Read at the 125th anniversary meeting of the American Psychiatric Association, Miami Beach, Fla., May 5-9, 1969.

practice may be inappropriate, ineffectual, or, at worst, substantially detrimental.

Although the courts have held that "a high degree of intelligence is not essential to understand the nature of the marriage contract," the significance of that contract and the factors that go into its maintenance or its dissolution are by no means well understood. Many "well-adjusted marriages" dissolve, whereas other marriages, characterized by storm, travail, highs and lows, episodic fisticuffs, jealousy, recrimination, and occasional trips to the lawyer appear to sustain and satisfy.

Key words in understanding a marriage appear to be "engagement," "involvement," "locked in together." It is ordinarily a lessening of "engagement" in a marriage that leads to a provocative act by one partner or the other. Thus, in a cool marriage with a marital temperature dropping slowly toward the freezing level, there may occur an incident that on the one hand seems to provoke divorce but that may, conversely, represent an impetus for "reengagement," "reinvolvement," "getting locked in together." The provocation for divorce may constitute simultaneously a possibility for a heightening of engagement in a marriage that had grown stagnant. Clearly a turning point. Enter the psychiatrist.

PROVOCATION LEADING TO ENGAGEMENT NOT WITH
THE MATE BUT WITH THE THERAPIST

Case 1. Mrs. B, desperately agitated, thinking of suicide, tearful, was referred to a psychiatrist by her girl friend. Mrs. B had been separated from her husband for three weeks as a result of his great anger when she confessed an act of infidelity one week before. Her husband of seven years—rather critical and cold, a frequently unfaithful man—was powerfully hurt by what his wife told him and after a week of passionate rejection and reconciliation, he struck her and she left.

She was in great turmoil, as was her husband, who was quite certain that she had left him to return to her lover. Her lover was, however, in Mrs. B's eyes, something of "an innocent bystander." During the first few interviews with the therapist she was terribly depressed and anxious, alternately defensive, ashamed, and filled with proclamations of love for her husband. followed by statements of indignation at his treatment of her and determined announcements of her intention to seek redress.

Mrs. B was a sensible, proud woman, 30 years old, the product of a somewhat distant home with considerably older parents. In her marriage she and her husband appeared to take turns in periods of anger, hurt, and withdrawal. They had difficulty coming together in a loving way. They alternated in turning down the heat on their marriage burner. She was more outwardly loving, though masochistic; he was more domineering, perhaps less secure. Together they developed something of an indifferent marriage. Indeed, they were unaware of how involved they could be with each other until the interval after Mrs. B's infidelity.

Because of the level of the patient's despair, the therapist saw her two or three times each week in a supportive manner during a period of four or five weeks after she first consulted him. He attempted to play a non-decision-making role, reflected her feelings, expressed confidence in her ability to make an ultimately sound decision, questioned her about the coldness in the marital relationship, but at the same time reassured his patient that the problem in the marriage was not hers alone.

Four weeks after Mrs. B was first seen, there was a joint interview with the husband. However, the husband was greatly threatened by what he experienced as a coalition against him. He responded with a belligerent assault on his wife, calling her "a cold whore" and warning the therapist not to be deceived by the wife as he had been, etc. The husband was incapacitated when he faced his wife's newest allegiance and he put on a very bad performance. He felt outnumbered, outgunned, in danger of assault or humiliation.

The impact of this interview was perhaps decisive in leading to the divorce that followed. The therapist concluded privately, "He's worse than she told me." In the succeeding weeks both the husband and wife were involved in casual sexual contacts outside the marriage. Approximately three months after the initial separation, both the husband and wife had discovered that there was little steam left within the marriage. The glue had dried with the partners separate. The engagement, weakened before, had become a disengagement.

For Mrs. B, however, her hours with the therapist assumed the central position in her life. She was grateful to her therapist for his support to her during the most trying period in her life. Her husband, from whom she became divorced three months later, continued to resent the therapist very much and referred to him as "her $30 lover." She appreciated the fact that her doctor had not tried to influence her decision. From our vantage point, he was more influential than she knew.

THE IMPACT OF A DIAGNOSIS—A SICK MATE OR A MARITAL PROBLEM

Case 2. Professor R, a 36-year-old language instructor, called to request an appointment with a psychotherapist. When questioned over the telephone, he explained that he was very concerned about his inability to consummate his marriage of three and one-half months. When he was asked to come with his new wife for the first appointment, he protested that the problem was strictly his, that he had had psychotherapy off and on for a number of years, and that there were matters he did not want to discuss in the presence of his bride. The therapist was insistent, however, and after some protest the two appeared together for the first appointment.

The husband proved to be a most eccentric man. He was deeply entangled with his widowed mother, a woman given to spiritualism and a belief in the living occult and who, over the years, had demonstrated a determination to protect her son against sinfulness. The mother had opposed the marriage. She appeared to take poorly to strangers.

The husband had experienced transient homosexual contacts through most of his life but he had never experienced sexual intercourse. Although he had informed his wife about past periods of homosexuality, she had not been discouraged about marrying him. She had been a graduate student in her husband's department and had "loved him from afar" for many years. She was, however, very upset about his inability to consummate the marriage. She proclaimed her love for her husband, as he did for her. She was alternately self-castigating and very angry with him. She was 33 years old, had never been married, but had had a few prior sexual experiences.

Psychiatric examination revealed a very eccentric and narcissistic man, creative but extremely conflicted in the sexual area. He carried to that first interview a Rorschach protocol, one product of a psychiatric examination he had undergone a few years earlier. The protocol hinted broadly, and perhaps not incorrectly, at a psychotic diagnosis. His manifest problems were considerable; the latent problems overwhelming.

The patient's wife appeared to be a much more stable person. She was very attractive, shy, extremely proper, and very female. It is easy to become overidentified with the sexually deprived mate in a psychotherapeutic circumstance and she was that kind of person. Despite the obvious problems of the husband and the apparent stability of the wife, this couple was viewed as sharing in a 50-50 way a need for help to resolve the heterosexual difficulties of the marriage. Despite efforts, first by one, then by the other, to gain an individual appointment, they were always seen together.

After a period of approximately six weeks of reassurance, support, and relatively gentle interpretation, the husband and wife together had successfully consummated their union. They were lovingly proud of having worked through a very difficult problem together, an achievement undiluted by major involvement of a third person. The couple was seen at intervals over the next six months, always together. They were first seen some seven years ago and since that time Christmas cards with the growing family pictured and an occasional letter from both speak of the successful union.

The therapist saw himself as a catalyst to the love and desire for success that was present in this union. Had one person been labeled in the marriage as "the sick one" (albeit with some basis), a less desirable outcome might well have resulted. And importantly, there was time later to go toward a more elaborate therapeutic endeavor if necessary. The demonstration of psychopathology, the search for a basis for the husband's anxiety, analysis of his homosexual conflicts, or the explication of the wife's reason for picking a sexually reticent mate were not precluded later if this simple, more direct intervention in the marriage was not successful.

In this instance the husband was not without reason for seeking psychotherapy. He qualified by most standards as warranting psychiatric therapy. The therapist's choice, however, was to take no step to take the action out from the marriage and to take as few steps as possible that put him, the therapist, into the marriage. The therapist viewed his task as one of getting the mother-in-law out of the bedroom, replacing a former student with a wife, assuring the husband that it was okay to enter the bedroom, and keeping himself, the therapist, out of that bedroom. Perhaps most important, the therapist elected to assign heavy weight to the fact of the marriage, recognizing its fragility but affording it particular reverence nonetheless.

RETURNING THE UNWANTED MATE TO A PARENT OR A PSYCHIATRIST

It is always good to know that one's mate of 25 years will not be badly hurt by being divorced and/or that one could divorce one's mate and at the same time, in absentia, take care of her (or him). One way is to provide a rich divorce settlement. Another is to find a lover for the abandoned mate. A third system is to return the mate to his or her parents; a fourth is to find a psychiatrist who will take over.

> *Case 3.* Mr. D, a 44-year-old lawyer, confronted his wife with the news that although he loved her he loved his partner's wife even more, and he wanted a divorce. Their marriage of 22 years had been quite civilized and in some ways rather productive and fruitful.
>
> He had become a very successful man in his profession. Apparently he had been somewhat threatened by the departure of the older of their two girls for college and on that occasion, two years earlier, he had his first extramarital encounter. Puzzlingly, this first affair, although supposedly unknown to the wife, seemed to warm up the marriage slightly and moved it from its rather habitual and civilized form into a period of brief excitement. This did not last too long, however.
>
> Mrs. D, a socially active club woman, was devoted to her family but somewhat on the distant side. She was extremely upset following her husband's announcement, and her husband immediately referred her to a psychiatrist in order to help her through the difficult period. The psychiatrist saw Mrs. D several times, then insisted that the husband should come for an appointment. At that time, Mr. D explained his deep affection for his wife and his expectation that they would always be, in one way or another, friends, voiced great

concern about her suicidal threat, and with great feeling repeated his hope that the doctor would take good care of this woman. That evening, as if to underscore her husband's words, Mrs. D made a suicidal attempt, ingesting ten sleeping capsules.

The psychiatrist found himself catapulted into caring for this woman in the hospital and, despite his ambivalence, accepted her as a psychotherapy outpatient. He worked with Mrs. D through the enormous ordeal of her impending divorce, saw her through the anger, despair, animosity, and humiliation of the divorce itself, and worked with her for another year afterwards. The loss of her husband was, she felt, endurable only because of the assistance that he had provided.

Two years later the husband, who had ultimately failed in his attempt to marry his partner's wife because of the latter's reconciliation with her husband, committed suicide.

USE OF THE TELEPHONE DURING ENFORCED SEPARATION

Case 4. Mr. R, a handsome, likeable, 28-year-old married, unemployed, thrice hospitalized only son of a prominent Milwaukee family, returned to his parents' home unexpectedly in the middle of the night from the Texas university community in which he and his wife had been living. His wife remained in Texas. He seemed mildly dazed, had been drinking heavily, and spoke in vague terms about his inability to find meaning, etc. Diagnostically, he seemed to be on a seriously troubled continuum with severe character problems and poor controls, strong sexual conflict, alcoholism, and, more ominously, a strong paranoid predilection. Attempts to arrange therapy at the time of earlier hospitalization had, as with so many of this man's plans, washed away.

He had been married for three years to a college classmate. His wife was teaching in a Texas high school. He had drifted out of college five years earlier, and his work record in the succeeding years had been very spotty. He was somewhat vague about the status of the marriage but had been living with his wife prior to coming to his parents' home. He had left the evening before without much discussion with her.

In considering this young man's situation, the psychiatrist felt that one of his solid therapeutic assets, and he had few, was a three-year-old marriage to an apparently more stable and loyal wife. The therapist asked the patient to be in touch with his wife the first day by telephone. The second day, therapist, patient, and wife, by three-way phone, held a ten-minute discussion of treatment plans, reviewed the possibility of continuing therapy "there or here," reviewed the wife's ideas as to reasons for current trouble and her explanation as to why previous recommendations for therapy had been overlooked, etc.

Mr. R had a long history of ineffectual moves in the face of stress. Drifting from the marriage toward his home appeared to be the newest in that series. He needed help. It developed that there were psychiatrists in Texas as well as Wisconsin.

DISCUSSION

The psychiatrist confronts a number of complex professional questions when he is called upon for assistance by a person who is one of a marital pair. He walks a fine line between wishing not to intrude into the intimacy of a marriage and, at the same time, honoring his own credo, which holds that any person who needs professional help should find an answer to his appeal. As a result of these often conflicting pressures clinicians have explored various therapeutic deployments and assignments to make it possible to work with a married person without disturbing the marital relationship. A number of patterns have been tried, but as yet no predictably satisfactory system of intervention has been developed.

Intervening therapeutically on one side or another in a marriage remains a risky business. A number of unsatisfactory results develop. It may be well to list a few examples of what we mean. There are a great many instances of prolonged individual therapy for one or both mates followed by divorce; therapists have worked in prolonged psychotherapy with one partner who does very well in psychotherapy, matures, and grows, while the mate is unable to keep pace; there are those particularly uncomfortable occasions in which a patient sustains a dreadfully barren marriage by embarking on a prolonged "therapeutic marriage" with a doctor that becomes intractable because the termination of therapy threatens the termination of "both marriages."

Of course, the technique of deployment of one or more therapists is perhaps less important than the attitudes of the therapist, his sense of his own therapeutic role, and his unconscious fantasies about the patient (or patients) and the possibility of the patient's divorce. When the therapist is asked to mediate in an impending divorce situation and he agrees to work with one or both of the pair, his own feelings about himself, his own marriage, and his patient's marriage will inevitably play an important role in determining what happens next. The most natural course is to go where his own life is going: i.e., if he himself has never been divorced, he can watch the marital pair progress toward divorce or reunion and extrapolate from his observations answers to questions of what could happen in his own marriage.

The third option, perhaps the ordinary stance, is for the therapist to move toward a state of apparent neutrality, asserting, "I am neutral. I will not take sides. The matter of a divorce is for them to decide. I want for them what they want." The patient or patients, however, particularly in the kind of stressful situation represented by marital discord, may utilize the therapist's "neutrality" to project onto him a sense of support for their private decision making, thereby moving on toward their own fantasied objective.

The patient or the couple may pick a side for the therapist, put him on that side, and act as if he said "okay" even though he does not know what side they have put him on. They may make it clear to each other that the therapist wants them to get divorced and thinks that they should become divorced because he frowns at the end of the second hour, or they may decide that the therapist obviously wishes them to stay together since he smiled when they talked about the good old days.

The stance of neutrality is comfortable for the therapist. In theory, when he assumes no responsibility, he may be in a position of such strategic weakness as to contribute negatively to the outcome of the therapy. That weakness may be understood in this way: The gradual, manageable psychotherapeutic transference that often occurs in one-to-one relationships is not easily available in therapy with a couple. The couple are ordinarily substantially "transferred" to each other. Unless the therapist moves in such a way as to displace the mate, he becomes a kind of bystander and he is either a catalyst in their relationship or he is nothing. When the therapist elects to talk seriously with the couple about their impending decisions, which after all may be the result of ten or twenty years of struggle and ambivalence, he faces an almost insurmountable problem. He ordinarily lacks the power needed to move such an entrenched team.

Even when the marital tie is a very powerful one and where divorce is not an imminent question, treating a married person and hoping that the result will generalize into the marriage usually does not work. Where the marital tie is weak and divorce threatens, intervention with one of the pair seems routinely to be disruptive. We are impressed that moving unilaterally into a marriage relationship, taking one of the two as the patient and referring or ignoring the mate, is very often a tactical blunder.

What is the alternative? A psychiatrist ordinarily moves toward a person who calls for help and offers to listen to him and to see him again. What should he do when there is a marriage in question? The therapist ordinarily feels that in almost any situation something useful can come from honest and open discussion. What should he do if one member of a marital pair wishes to talk unbeknown to the mate? What should the therapist do when there is a suggestion that one member of a marital pair is emotionally disturbed and needs some kind of assistance?

CONCLUSIONS

We believe that psychiatric intervention when divorce impends cannot be regarded as a routine matter. The therapist should view his entrance into the situation as calling for his broadest perspective. He must see what is going on between him and his patient, already a difficult task. Even more than that, he must see what is implied by the fact that he and his patient are sitting down together without the mate. Any move by the therapist that discounts the significance of the marriage may be unexpectedly influential. Thus, the ordinary medical system of replying affirmatively to a request for help by one person in a marriage, excluding the other, may in effect be an intervention favoring divorce.

In working with a married individual, or with a couple who contemplate divorce, the therapist confronts a system under stress. He could do well, ordinarily, to respect the marriage as a continuing fact·until the legal divorce is complete. No matter what the degree of complexity, no matter how seemingly collapsed the patient's marriage is, the therapist should not presume to discount its ongoing power, its possibility of resurrection, its beating heart. If there is to be a death certificate, the trial judge of a divorce court of record is the one to sign the document.

Accepting in therapy one member of a troubled couple should be viewed by the therapist as very possibly a step toward preventing a reconciliation. For many couples on the verge of divorce, the therapist becomes an alternate mate no matter how scrupulous his efforts to avoid it. In the history of many, many ongoing marriages, one finds episodes of apparent cruelty, of separation periods, of affairs, of litigation, along with an episodic move toward divorce followed by reconciliation. Therefore, the therapist should be aware that he may be intervening and changing a process that, when nature takes its course, will heal. In a general way, we feel that the burden of proof is on the therapist who elects to work with a couple in such a way as to take the action out of a marriage, either in the first or during subsequent interviews.

Divorce inevitably has many ramifications for children and families of origin. These others, significant others, should be considered for inclusion in the psychotherapy. Our own experience suggests that involving the children and parents of a couple in the midst of marital discord is often a powerfully helpful device. The majority of our patients who were asked to bring family members in for interviews have agreed and in no case did we regret their presence. That the technique is often a useful one we feel quite sure. We are less certain why. Whether the inclusion of other family members offers an opportunity for correcting basic discord or whether its usefulness rests upon a symbolic proof of the seriousness with which the therapist views the possibility of dissolution of the marriage, we are unable to decide. Bringing the other family members in, however, coincides with our general philosophy that it may be better to err on the side of too much respect for the fact of the marriage, particularly in the early interviews.

We often find it necessary to remind ourselves that as therapists we are in no position to offer a real substitute relationship for the mate who will be disappearing; not at the time, not in one month, six months, nor in a year, and certainly not four years hence. This may be especially relevant if the therapist himself is comfortably married and enjoys a marriage where there is parity, affection, and reliability. A comfortably married person is rarely able to anticipate or appreciate the loneliness, despair, and tedium in the life of a divorced person. Even statistical studies that appear to demonstrate rather conclusively that divorce is hardly a road to happiness (1) tend to be forgotten when one is working with an aggrieved, or apparently aggrieved, member of a marital pair.

An observation passed down through the generations advises that almost any couple during a lifetime of marriage could find ample opportunity to break up, depending upon who is around when divorce impends. We hope that it will not be one of us.

REFERENCES

1. SROLE, L., LANGNER, T. S., MICHAEL, S. T., OPLER, M. K., & RENNIE, T. A. C. *Mental Health in the Metropolis: The Midtown Manhattan Study*. New York: McGraw-Hill, 1962.

32

THE MARRIAGE/DIVORCE PARADOX

Robert A. Ravich, M.D.

Assistant Attending Psychiatrist, Gouveneur Hospital (New York)
Assistant Clinical Professor of Psychiatry, Cornell
University Medical College

In the course of studying many thousands of marital and premarital dyads with tne aid of the Ravich Interpersonal Game Test (1, 2) (RIG/T), an unusual pattern of interaction has been encountered in about one per cent of the couples. Clinical experience with approximately thirty couples that demonstrated this pattern led to the realization that for every case in which it appeared, divorce was the inevitable outcome. I have termed this the marriage/divorce paradox (M/DP). The present article will describe and discuss various aspects of this phenomenon and comment upon its possible significance.

Method

The marriage/divorce paradox has been recognized by means of the RIG/T. This is an instrument that presents the structural situation illustrated in Figure 1 to two individuals. Over a series of trips, each person must maneuver a vehicle from separate starting points located at opposite ends of a small table. A panel divides the two sides of the table so that each person can see his own vehicle and the track system along which it can travel, but cannot see the other person's vehicle or track system.

On successive trips, each person must decide whether to move his vehicle to its destination by way of the short Direct route or the long Alternate route. Collisions may occur along a section common to both

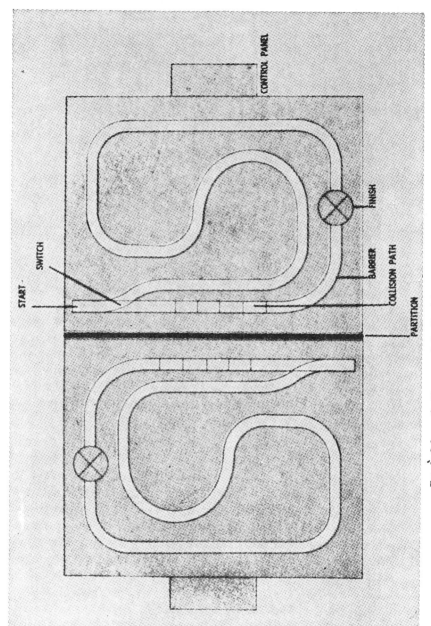

FIG. 1: Schematic diagram of the Ravich Interpersonal Game/Test.

Direct routes. In addition, each person controls a barrier that can be closed to stop the other person's vehicle if it is on the Direct route. If the longer Alternate route is taken by one or both individuals no collisions can occur. Also, a vehicle on the Alternate route cannot be stopped by closing the barrier. Scoring on each trip is determined by the time required for the vehicles which travel at fixed velocity to reach the destination against a standard time (0). A vehicle that travels unimpeded on the Direct route can reach the destination in $T = + 1$, while a vehicle on the Alternate route can do so in $T = - 1$.

The Pattern of Interaction of M/DP Couples

A wide range of options on any single trip exists and the series of twenty or more trips that constitute a test allows an almost infinite array of possibilities. We are concerned here with a small group of couples (about one per cent) that select one particular option and adhere to it with near or total absolute consistency.

The pattern is quite simple. On any single trip, one individual takes the Direct route and the other individual takes the Alternate route. On each successive trip the two switch routes.

This can readily be expressed as follows:

S_1	D	A	D	A	
S_2	A	D	A	D	
Trip	1	2	3	4	20

where D is the Direct and A is the Alternate route. A further condition is that neither individual closes the barrier.

The scoring on any one trip for $S_1 + S_2 = +1 - 1 = 0$. At the end of each trip the score achieved by each individual is announced, so that both are aware throughout the test exactly what their payoffs are.

It is important to recognize that this pattern of interactional behavior, while quite simple, nevertheless requires a high degree of agreement and coordination of decision and actual behavior. To accomplish it, both individuals must agree never to be on the same route at the same time as the other person, to change routes on successive trip, and to accept a payoff of $+1$ and -1 on each successive trip, so that the overall payoff for each person and for the dyad is 0.

The amount of verbal interaction required to develop this pattern ranges from none at all to a great deal. Couples who do not talk to each other at all before establishing this pattern or while carrying it out have said that they "know" where the other is going to be, and what the other will do, and act in such a way as to always avoid them. At the other extreme are couples who discuss the pattern that they set up extensively, choose this pattern out of various alternatives that they recognize and then rigidly adhere to it, even while they continue to talk about the zero individual and combined payoff and its attendant frustrations.

Whatever the amount of verbal interaction, perfect coordination in terms of non-verbal interaction is required. It is understandable in view of this requirement that the same pattern has not been observed in couples that have not had an on-going relationship.

On the other hand, the same pattern·has been observed in several brother-sister sibling relationships characterized by marked mutual dependency and considerable anxiety.

It is not unusual to observe the occurrence of the pattern that has been defined over a few trips. When the pattern appears during the early phase of the test, e.g., trips 1 through 6, and then is replaced by other patterns and does not reappear, it does not indicate imminent divorce. However, when it appears in the early phase, is replaced by some other interactional behavior, and then returns again in the later phases of the test, it does appear to connote that significant periods of separation have or will occur.

Another variation on the marriage/divorce paradox is one in which barriers are used by one or both individuals. When both use the barriers, or when the person who is on the Alternate route closes the barrier on the other's Direct route, this indicates that a real hostility exists within the relationship which serves as a bond. Such bonds of hostility may be sufficient to forestall separation and divorce for a considerable period, but the probability of this as the ultimate outcome is quite high.

Significance of the Marriage/Divorce Paradox

The highly structured pattern of interaction that has been described has in every instance in which it was observed led to divorce. This has occurred even in situations where at the time of testing no significant marital discord was known to exist. For example, it has been observed among couples that were considered to be "normal controls." Subsequently we learned that divorce had eventuated.

In some cases, one is not surprised to find this pattern emerge, since it accords with clinical observations of the relationship. However in others its occurrence is unexpected.

Couples may display very obvious emotional distance and elaborate distancing behavior which is expressed in the course of the RIG/T by the M/DP. More often, however the dyads that display this pattern of inter-action describe themselves as having many sporadic "fights." Upon closer investigation it becomes evident that these fights are not the cause of the pattern, but are instead an attempt to overcome the nearly total alienation and the consequent absence of contact in the rela-tionship.

This clinical observation of the "pseudo-fights" in the M/DP serves to focus attention upon a central feature of the interaction within the test situation. These dyads agree upon the necessity to avoid any possi-bility of a collision. In game theory terminology, these couples make a non-zero-sum game into a zero-sum game. The same purpose may be expressed in the course of the RIG/T by other couples, but they do not manifest it to the extreme degree of the M/DP. The behavior of these other avoiders may be directed toward avoiding collisions, but a certain risk of collision is nevertheless present. The M/DP dyads take no such risk. In effect, they establish a set of rules that insures no contact and precludes even the possibility of contact.

Therapeutic Implications

Our experience in treating such couples is limited because of the rela-tive rarity with which they are seen—about one in a hundred. Whether or not this proportion is representative of the general population is un-known. Studies regarding the M/DP seem clearly indicated in two situa-tions. Couples who seek legal dissolution of their marriage should be investigated by the RIG/T in order to ascertain the incidence of the pattern in this population. It would also be very useful in establishing predictive data to know how many couples enter marriage with the M/DP already established. This could be done at the time that marriage licenses are obtained, or in the course of pre-marital counseling that is offered by various religious groups and agencies.

The theoretical importance of the M/DP is great, for it constitutes an absolute interactional value which closely approximates to zero. The recognition of absolute zero is highly significant in the physical, chemical and biological sciences, and is of similar import in the behavioral sciences.

Clinically, couples that demonstrate this pattern may need therapeu-tic help in resolving the paradox of being divorced behaviorally, but married socially and legally. These couples will not, in our experience, remain married and this is so even when they seem to be motivated in seeking marital therapy. Repeatedly we have been forced to recognize that therapeutic intervention can do no more than help these couples to terminate legally and socially a relationship that has reached absolute zero in terms of interactional behavior. Such assistance may be of considerable value to these individuals and their families, since it ends the marriage "myth."

It should be pointed out that many couples seen together, or many individuals seen individually, may describe their relationship as having the characteristics of the M/DP. However, the RIG/T findings in these cases may be quite different.

Of course, couples displaying M/DP are not the only ones that end in divorce. Rather the M/DP couples are the only ones that (in my range of experience) *always* end in divorce.

REFERENCES

1. RAVICH, R. A. The Use of an Interpersonal Game-Test in Conjoint Marital Psychotherapy. *Am. J. Psychiat.*, 23:217-229, 1969.
2. RAVICH, R. A. A System of Notation of Dyadic Interaction. *Family Process*, 9:292-300, 1970.

33

COUNSELING IMPLICATIONS OF COMARITAL AND MULTILATERAL RELATIONS

Larry and Joan Constantine

Senior Research Associates
Multilateral Relations Study Project

Couples involved in altered forms of marriage present a unique challenge and opportunity for the counselor. The trend toward broadening the scope and form of marriage is clear (Constantine and Constantine, 1970a; Orleans and Wolfson, 1970; Otto, 1970). The counselor can expect to encounter an increasing number of novel marital situations involving not only the traditional dyad but other intimates as well.

While it is not now known what portion of marriages significantly depart from the traditional monogynous model, indications are that non-conventional structures represent a sizable minority. The Breedloves statistically estimated that some six to nine million individuals have regularly exchanged partners with the knowledge and consent of their spouses (Breedlove and Breedlove, 1964). Kafka and Ryder found that about three percent of the National Institute of Mental Health panel of young marrieds espoused—at marriage—an ethos which explicitly valued comarital involvement (Kafka, *et al.,* 1969). (These marriages were termed "open ended" by Ron Mazur in the opening address at the 1970 National Council on Family Relations meeting.) Twenty-five percent of respondents to a *Psychology Today* poll indicated some interest in group marriage (Athenasian, 1970).

537

The implications and conclusions drawn here are based on research conducted since May 1969 in the Multilateral Relations Study Project (Constantine, 1970b). The specific thrust of this project is an empirical investigation of contemporary group marriages in the United States. The discussion here will include mate swapping (swinging) only as a secondary phenomenon. There is reason to believe that social mate swappers are comparatively unlikely to seek counseling (Denfield and Gordon, 1970). The reader interested in research on social mate swapping should also consult Symonds (1966, 1967), Smith and Smith (1970), Bartell (1970), O'Neill (1970) and Breedlove (1964).

Comarital Relations. A comarital relation is an intimate involvement, probably including sexual intimacy, which is an adjunct to an established dyadic marriage. Comarital relations are distinguished from extramarital relations in being open rather than covert and based on prior mutual agreement. This is no mere relabeling of proscribed behavior in order to avoid pejorative connotations. Comarital and extramarital relations are operationally and psychodynamically distinct phenomena. Specifically, comarital relations are a part of the marriage and constitute potentially constructive rather than divisive factors.

A couple might be involved in separate comarital relations or jointly with the same individual or couple. The relationships, as with all interpersonal relations, may be isolated or a part of a common pattern; involvements may be short or long term, intense or passive, rewarding or unsatisfactory. From the standpoint of the dyadic marriage on which the counselor's attention is focused, the effects may be positive or negative.

Of special interest is the intimate network first described by Stoller (1970). Such a network consists of several separately domiciled families joined by intimate comarital bonds, committed to openness and mutual supportiveness. The intimate network offers even fairly conventional families numerous advantages, especially an alternative to nuclearization with concomitant strength and stability but including, additionally, a high growth potential and, if desired, sexual variety in a stable, supportive community of intimates. We see such networks as a growing trend (Constantine and Constantine, 1970a).

Multilateral Marriage. Comarital relations can become so integral and intimate as to constitute "marital" relations. We define a multilateral marriage as a voluntary family group of three or more persons, each of whom is committed to and maintains a relationship with more than one other person in a manner regarded (by the participant) as essentially "married." This form of marriage, more popularly called group marriage, is actually being pacticed on a small scale today. At this writing, a body of substantive non-fiction of this and related structures is just beginning to accumulate (Constantine and Constantine, 1970b).

We will not here discuss the potential advantages of a multilateral family structure, which at any rate are as yet unproven. What the counselor must realize is that his clients very often do believe in these advantages and desire to make the multilateral rather than the conventional dyadic relationship work. Perhaps here is one dimension in which we are dealing with a new phenomenon, for *both* husbands and wives (and their cohusbands and cowives) may genuinely want the expanded intimacy instead of one or more seeing such involvement as undesirable, even immoral.

We feel this is essential, that comarital and multilateral relationships be seen as unique, possibly new, potentially very productive family models and not be seen only from a conventional pejorative perspective.

THE COUNSELOR'S ROLE

The counselor could be confronted with any of these forms of alternate family structures, or even with permutations as unique as the individuals participating in them. Our own experience, the correspondence reaching one popular author,* and the opinion of others (cf. Orleans and Wolfson, 1970) coincides in indicating that simple triads are likely to be the most common in the future. While one man-two women triads *may* predominate, it is not at all certain at this point, especially considering the greater portion of women at ease with ambisexual involvement (see below). In the current study both the average and the mode is for tetrads of two men and two women, not necessarily two previously married couples.

The counselor should, of course, strive simply to see every marital situation in its full uniqueness, no more than we expect of a good counselor faced with a conventional dyadic marriage. The point is that sometimes this may involve strengthening rather than truncating a supposedly "extramarital" situation.

The criterion the counselor must give priority to is what is best for his client and his client's family, necessarily from his client's perspective rather than his own. It must be emphasized that the client's family in a multilateral marriage includes not only his legal spouse and their children but the rest of the "expanded family." If it is legitimate for the

---

* Robert Rimmer, author of *Harrad Experiment* and *Proposition 31*, both dealing with multilateral family structures, has received thousands of letters from readers.

counselor to face conventional dyadic counseling giving emphasis to the preservation of the marriage and the family, the same must be true for at least some multilateral situations. The counselor, at least, must be capable of some level of veridical perception of the situation and to refrain from attempting simply to superimpose his own moral and ethical framework on the client's. This does not necessarily mean that the counselor's personal morality must be as liberal as that of participants in multilateral relations. The issue is more one of his acceptance of pluralism of moral perspectives and concomitant marriage and family structures. In our own experience, we have found some quite personally conservative professionals capable of non-evaluative confrontation with multilateral relations.

Approach. Although it is largely speculative at this point, we feel that conjoint therapy techniques (cf. Satir, 1967) are the most promising, for obvious reasons. This includes dealing with comarital relations in which the secondary relationship or relationships are not shared by both spouses. The resulting confrontation and mutual attempt at communication and problem solving could be most revealing and suggestive of novel methods of resolution not even evident from dealing with the primary dyad jointly but isolated from the other parties.

One counselor working with a group marriage in our study has found that conjoint family therapy along with concurrent (individual with same therapist) to be a worthwhile combination. Some guidance in approach might be carried over from the dyadic experience, and the reader is referred to Grunebaum, *et al.,* 1969.

The opportunity for small group techniques being used among the partners of a single group marriage is almost without precedent. Otto's various "positive" experiential techniques (Otto, 1969) are especially indicated. We have several cases of group marriages conducting resident basic encounter groups as an on-going process for building the marriage and dealing with complex interpersonal difficulties. One of these employed an outside professional facilitator with favorable results, although in the long run the group underwent a partial dissolution and subsequent "reorganization."

Counseling Aids. An essential criterion for the methodology of the Multilateral Relations Study Project is that the insights gained be shared with the participants in responding groups (Constantine, 1970b). We have found the Edwards Personal Preference Schedule (EPPS) to be of major value not only in understanding the structure and functional basis of a multilateral involvement, but in providing insights and productive stimuli for the group itself. The EPPS is a paper-and-pencil instrument measuring the relative magnitude of fifteen normal personality needs. It has long been used in individual counseling; the immediate precedent for our use is in premarital counseling of dyads (Kilgo, 1969). Drewery (1969) developed a framework based on perception and metaperspective of needs to study the structure of dyadic marriages. Our usé is essentially an adaptation of Drewery's and appears to be one of considerable clinical value.

Respondents in the study complete the EPPS in the usual manner. They then rate what they perceive to be the level of their own needs on each of the fifteen scales. They do the same for each of the other members of the group. Finally, they record how they think each of the others will rate them. Special forms which include a discussion of needs and need-satisfaction and brief descriptions of each need are used for this purpose.* What is revealed is a very rich picture of perceptions and misperceptions, self-insight and its absence, misunderstanding that is recognized and misunderstanding that is unseen. All results, including the actual EPPS profiles, are returned to the group as the basis for open discussion. In almost every case, major insights into the underlying perceptual basis for various aspects of group functioning and dysfunctioning have been generated in the discussion. It was one of the groups which devised a worthwhile adjunct in which each possible dyad meets separately in open encounter using the Edwards/Drewery profiles as a departure point for understanding some of the essentials of their relationship.

We have found certain prior conditions to be essential to the success of this experiment for groups and believe these concepts would apply to the use of most psychometric techniques in counseling multilateral relations. The relationship between examinees and the administrator must be fairly well established. Presumably this would be the case with counselees. (Jourard and Resnick (1967) have shown that examiner self-disclosure significantly affects results using the EPPS.) It is also important that the test is seen as an opportunity to learn, not as psychological rape. A respondent completing a schedule for his own edification responds significantly differently than when the testing is exclusively for the enlightenment of others.

Finally, we have found that what amounts to a belief in the validity and reasonableness of the testing methodology is important. There is, especially among younger people, a widespread distrust of and dislike for psychometric methods. It is generally believed that the methods are invalid and can always be easily and completely faked. Indeed, it is

---

* Copies of this form are available from the authors.

probably at least true of most of the college population that a testing situation is viewed as a game, the basis of which is to "figure out" the test, the goal to beat the system by successfully creating a false picture. Faking and validity checks are just not entirely sufficient to counter the psychological sophistication of the contemporary young person who in many cases knows or can figure out exactly what checks have been built in. We finally found it valuable to share the entire basis of the experiment with respondents, including explaining the rationale of the EPPS and our reasons for feeling that it does a fair job of measuring what it purports to measure. We do not exclude our reservations or its known shortcomings. The respondents generally enter the experiment with a realistic attitude toward what the instrument can accomplish and an awareness that their own willingness to be candid and realistic in their responses will in large part determine the value of the resulting information. Although this can be done with a straightforward instrument like the EPPS, it may not be possible with others. It is also important to present the schedule in a non-threatening manner, stressing that it does not deal with how sick a person is.

Naturally, the counselor's own preferences and prejudices on the use of standard instruments must be the final criterion. Some place a heavy reliance on them, others consider them totally inadequate. We feel that the chief value of such tests is as a departure point, an original stimulus for further insights. The EPPS/Drewery scheme has a particular advantage in relation to multilateral situations in that it reveals a detailed picture of the group structure at reasonable cost to investigator and respondent alike. The structure of a six-person marriage can be so complex that even the most elementary understanding must otherwise be extracted from protracted discussions with the group and with each individual. While the EPPS/Drewery scheme deals with only one set of dimensions of group structure, this is an especially important and revealing one. An analysis of the relationship of need-perception structure and group functioning will be reported in a later paper.

Communication. It is not surprising that multilateral, like dyadic relationships are most frequently troubled by communication problems. To the counselor's advantage, most participants have a strong growth orientation (Constantine, 1970a) and already strive for openness and authentic self-disclosure; introducing the concept of directness and honesty and convincing the clients of its value is unlikely to be a problem.

The multilateral aspects are both advantageous and potentially productive of dysfunctional behavior. We find that groups can take advantage of the alternate paths of communication between any pair in a multilateral situation. If one path becomes blocked, another is still open. On the other hand, this can be abused and communication through third parties becomes a substitute for direct communication.

Fostering direct, candid communication may be the counselor's most important function, as this enables the group to resolve its own current and future problems.

One group marriage has developed a concept and specific method of possible value to professionals. They became aware that many of their communication difficulties, especially in decision-making situations and in sensitive areas, such as sleeping arrangements, arose from conscious or unconscious attempts to give what they termed "processed data." A processed statement is one which includes the speaker's attempt to take into account the perceived feelings and opinions of others rather than simply to express the isolated, spontaneous, individual feeling of the speaker. When most responses are processed, the group may never be able to assess or discern the real or "raw data" feelings and thus arrive at consensus, resolution, or understanding.

Undoubtedly most dyadic marriages at times experience the resultant difficulties. However, there the structure is simpler and the dynamics of both the processing incorporated into communications and the task of unearthing the raw data are not nearly as complex as in the multilateral situation.

This particular group gained practice in giving raw data in all their decision making activities. They found it essential to make it absolutely clear that raw data answers would not "be held against anyone." When polling, all were reminded that they could later offer a processed statement, even if contradicting their raw data, which would be accepted as their vote, opinion, or preference. Not being committed to raw data statements makes them easier to supply.

When communication breaks down in a multilateral marriage it is impossible to ignore. We have seen the unusual form of coping in several cases of very poor communication—participants began *writing* messages. We now consider any volume of written communication on substantive matters among intimates who are in daily face-to-face contact as symptomatic of extreme failure in communication. On the other hand, it is sometimes better than no information transfer at all. Each situation will have to be individually analyzed; in some cases, written pronouncements have had bomblike effects on the family.

SPECIAL COUNSELING AREAS

Some problems, like communication, are common to conventional dyadic counseling situations as well as multilateral ones, although there may be new factors which must be taken into account in the counseling approach. There are, however, problems unique to the multilateral situation or which in monogynous marriages do not emerge as such significant issues.

Possessiveness and Jealousy. Acceptance of, if not enthusiastic affirmation of, intimate relationships by a spouse with others is the *sine qua non* of comarital and multilateral involvement. For the kind of meaningful relationships we are concerned with, this means more than "gymnastic non-jealousy." Acceptance of true concurrent intimacy includes acceptance of genital sexual expression, while willingness to share a spouse sexually in itself may even carry a proscription on meaningful interpersonal relationships, as often appears to be the case among recreational mate swappers.

We have come to view jealousy as a behavioral manifestation of diverse underlying intrapsychic experiences. Jealousy may emerge as the result of a desire to own, possess, or control; it may result from the need or desire for assurance or for a special or unique relationship; it may show fear of loss, and the threat may be either real or imagined, though it is always real to the experiencer. In general, jealous behavior must not simply be denied or ignored or suppressed. It constitutes an important signal about the group experiences or those of some individual. If, for example, it results from the fear of loss of an intimate to another, this must be ascertained. Unjustified fear can then be corrected. If the fear turns out to be justified, serious confrontation on the basis of the multilateral involvement is in order.

Possessive jealousy is fundamentally antagonistic to multilateral relations. We find that individuals can and do outgrow their culturally implanted possessiveness, although this may take years of multilateral involvement. It is perhaps a counselor's central responsibility to facilitate growth in truly nonpossessive intimacy. Indeed, regardless of the outcome of the specific comarital involvement, the central dyad will function more smoothly and be more conducive to consolidation of other personal growth if the partners can be helped to relate nonpossessively.

We do not as yet understand *how* this particular dimension of growth can be facilitated. A strong prior intellectual conviction—that capacity for sharing is better than possessiveness—is probably good so long as the intellectual conviction is not taken for gut-level arrival. The nature of any early multilateral involvement may be a critical factor. If each spouse is simultaneously enthusiastically involved in a positive relationship, prognosis is good. A sense of *inclusion,* of being a part of and sharing in the alternate involvement seems to be facilitory. Early situations carefully designed to be warm, positive, and non-threatening, as well as a *gradual* deepening of involvement, also appear to be good.

The existential reality of sharing a beloved can be profoundly different from the intellectual acceptance. Perhaps it is most important that participants be brought to confront each other, the situation, and their deep feelings on sharing and possession. More than once, suppression of jealousy on moral grounds (the new morality) has eventually resulted in violent explosions with more than minor aftermaths.

Problem Solving Behavior and Need Satisfaction. Beltz (1969) has proposed a model of behavior among couples with altered marital contracts which should be understood by counselors and counselees alike. The concept is based on learning theory and probably represents a fundamental relationship that will obtain unless specific counteractions are taken. As married partners admit additional intimate relationships and find them satisfying, they learn that some needs they would otherwise have to satisfy through their spouse may be more easily satisfied in comarital relations. As this is learned, it is less likely that any particular level of effort will be expended with the spouse to satisfy needs not directly satisfied by the spouse. The basis of this is that a person will satisfy his needs in the easiest way open to him. The end result could be a couple less likely to attempt to solve a problem in their own relationship and more likely to turn to other sources of satisfactions without, in turn, ever attempting to *solve* interpersonal problems.

Our own extension of this model is that each dyad must have elements or mechanisms which assure that effort will be expended to solve problems and build the relationship. An arbitrary barrier to expansion of the circle of intimates serves such a purpose. Marital fidelity may be applied to multilateral as well as monogamous marriages, and indeed is an element of most of the fiction on group marriage (Heinlein, 1966; Rimmer, 1968). It is probably more effective if each pair simply have a sufficient mutual commitment to a growing relationship, a willingness to work at mutual need satisfaction and problem resolution*

In this regard, it is the counselor's responsibility to make the clients aware of the potential for not trying sufficiently hard to reach resolution within any given dyadic relationship, not only endangering the rela-

---

* Most, but not all, of the respondents in the Multilateral Relations Study Project appear to have chosen commitment rather than a fidelity ethic. It is interesting to contrast the social mate swappers (swingers) who deal with this problem by compartmentalizing interpersonal relations, isolating physical sex as the sole modality for multilateral involvement (Denfield and Gordon, 1970).

tionship but not helping the participant to learn more about how to solve such problems.

The group marriage, with its multiplicity of easily accessible alternate relations *within* the marriage, may have a different problem, for Beltz's model would predict that each individual dyadic relationship would deteriorate. On the other hand, the *group* process works to strengthen dyadic relations, indeed the group cannot survive without a sufficient number of sufficiently successful dyads within it.

We have noted some tendency for prior dyadic marriages to deteriorate in the multilateral situation. In general we find groups devote an insufficient effort to continued integration or reintegration of the previously married couples, with negative effects on the whole group functioning. It would seem appropriate to provide specific times for each dyad to be together alone over an extended period, especially the previously married ones.

Dealing with Guilt. Some individuals experience guilt over their multilateral involvement. It is more likely to be those involved comaritally than in an actual group marriage, perhaps because of the closer similarity to extramarital involvement and some residue of more conventional morality. That a client feels guilty over a departure from conventional marital patterns should not be *a priori* reason for the counselor to restore the conventional involvement over which the guilt is experienced, and whether the guilt is tied to a genuine decline in the primary relationship or to a loss of satisfaction with the multilateral involvement for one or all parties.

Most important, the counselor's responsibility is to help the client deal with his guilt, preferably overcome it altogether, in order to reach a more rational, hopefully more beneficial, decision about continued involvement. The person burdened with guilt is hardly in a position to make an optimal choice.*

Sexuality, Homosexuality, and Ambisexuality. As with dyadic marriages, sex is an important element of the relationship in comarital and multilateral involvement. Indeed, the opportunity for sexual variety in a supportive atmosphere of on-going, genuine interpersonal intimacy is an important argument for group marriage. Counselors must not confuse the need or desire for a variety of sexual partners with variety in sexual experiences with the same partner. The overwhelming preponderance of experience indicates that a desire for a number of sxual partners

---

* This view of guilt in comarital involvement was brought to our attention by Ronald Mazur of Sex Education and Counseling Associates.

is normal and all but universal for men and women alike (cf. Johnson, 1970).

The orthodox psychoanalytic view that all multilateral sexual involvement is an expression of repressed homosexual interest is, with absolute certainty, too monolithic. Our own experience indicates that almost the full range of attitudes and personal orientations toward homosexual involvement is evident among those participating in multilateral relationships. There are those who acknowledge strong aversion to, even fear of, multiperson sex or homosexual relations, and perhaps these individuals possess a subconscious attraction. On the other hand, there are individuals who appear to be free of "hang-ups" over homosexuality and experience ambisexual situations as positive. Some, who seem to be equally free of "hang-ups," do not engage in either ambisexual or homosexual encounters, however. Among groups we have located there is but one individual who is significantly homosexual in orientation.

Ambisexuality, the capacity to relate sexually with members of both sexes, as appropriate to the situation and the relationship, is probably the healthiest orientation. The *exclusive* heterosexual, like the *exclusive* homosexual, may be regarded as somewhat crippled in his interpersonal relationships, lacking capacity for arbitrarily deep and physically expressive intimacy with his own sex. The individual who can give and receive physical expressions of affection with both sexes obviously has greater freedom in interpersonal behavior.*

Of course, the counselor should be prepared to assist where homosexual expressions or their absence are causing problems for a couple or group and, if necessary, refer for psychiatric or other individual therapy those who could benefit from it.

One trend is now evident, that more women than men have resolved their ambisexual component, and more easily. We find this to be most directly an effect of stronger cultural counter-conditioning to overt homosexual expression among men. This applies even (or especially) to simple warm physical contact beyond an occasional handshake. We feel that, at the very least, participants in group marriages should be helped to become comfortable with affectionate touching by the same sex, as this

---

* This area is, of course, highly controversial and in no way resolved. What we are expressing is an opinion, but one held by a widening circle, that ambisexuality, even if not specifically healthy, is at least not intrinsically pathological. That man is by birthright polymorphous perverse is, of course, orthodoxy. As Ellis notes (Ellis, 1965) seeking satisfaction with both sexes should not then, be regarded as unusual. He also notes (Ellis, 1956) prognosis is better for bisexuals than homosexuals undergoing psychotherapy. Healthy individuals also deal with bisexual involvement with alacrity (Stoller, 1968). Matther's commentary is particularly relevant.

is an important modality for communication and method for enhancing group integration.

The complex, often very difficult and painful process of forming a multilateral relationship holds the greatest potential for the counselor to play a truly productive role. Unfortunately, not many groups or individuals are likely to seek counseling during the early phases of a relationship. In a couple of cases we know of groups contacting professionals by reputation, but even where assistance is desired, it may not be sought for fear of a pejorative response.

We have found certain rather specific problems to be consistently encountered by those forming group marriages. Most of these have been previously discussed from a different perspective in Constantine and Constantine (1970c).

Alone Time and Territory. Time for isolation or solitude is frequently neglected. The participants are so intensely involved in the group process and in the new dyads that no time is left for each to be alone. Individuals, of course, differ in the need for "alone time," but the group may have to make a deliberate effort to see that time is available, in generous quantities, for this purpose.

Man's territoriality is a topic in vogue. We do find that groups who do not provide for individual property and "turf," an area that is the exclusive or primary domain of the individual, eventually experience difficulties over this. All the older groups have eventually provided for such areas. This can be a serious practical problem when four to six adults and another four to six children share the same household. Rather ingenious solutions have been worked out in some cases.

Prior Dyads. In the very early stages, one pattern has been characteristic. Participants become intensely involved with the new heterosexual dyads, both interpersonally and sexually, often to the exclusion of the legal spouse. Novelty may sustain such a "reversed" marital situation for some time, but eventually one individual will begin to desire renewed intimacy with his spouse. He is often perceived by the others as manifesting jealousy and possessiveness. It is important that the group be aware of the importance of periodic if not continuous reestablishment of the basis of the prior dyads. Spouses will need regular checks on how they feel about each other, what they are experiencing, how they are changing, etc. We have not found the *group* situation to satisfy this requirement. Separate dyadic encounters are probably needed for exchange of this sort of intelligence.

Growth in Relationships. There may be considerable pressure, open or implicit, for the various relationships to develop at the same pace or in the same way. It may take conscious effort or overt action on the part of the group to allow each relationship to develop in its own unique way and at its own pace. Pressure of this sort is most likely to be experienced in terms of sexual involvement, one dyad being pressured into intercourse before they feel ready for it by virtue of the other dyad having consummated their relationship.

Fun. It may seem a small thing, but groups frequently become so deeply involved in the integration process, in on-going encounter, and in dealing with personal and interpersonal difficulties, that little or no allowance is made for simple fun. We find that recreational or non-purposive activities with outside friends may be the most important. These activities not only provide pleasant relief from the "marathon encounter" of the group process, but provide an essential break in the tendency for the group to turn excessively inward and form a microcosm.

Personal Growth and the Pressure to Grow. It is in the area of significant personal growth toward self-actualization that multilateral marriages and expanded family situations offer the most potential. The basis for this and the orientation of participants has been covered in Constantine (1970b). There it was noted that the individual perceived by the group as being the "slowest grower" may be the object of considerable dysfunctional pressure. In essence the group says, "We've been through it, now it's your turn. Grow, damn it, grow!" This not only is not conducive to growth but may exacerbate problems holding back the one so exhorted.

OTHER IMPLICATIONS FOR THE CONVENTIONAL DYAD

The Multilateral Relations Study Project brings us in contact with a large number of couples and individuals interested in, considering, seeking, recovering from, or trying to get out of comarital and multilateral relations. Except for this, the couples are in traditional monogynous dyads.

The Reluctant Spouse. We are frequently approached by a husband (less frequently by a wife) who wants to know how to convince the spouse to try comarital or multilateral relations. Often there is an implication that there is something wrong with the spouse, that somehow she is less mature, less sophisticated, less self-actualizing, and the proof is her refusal to accept comarital relations. A great deal of resentment may be expressed by the husband.

Such a request may well indicate that professional counseling of the dyad is in order. It is not that the interest in comarital relations is pathological or symptomatic of problems, nor is, necessarily, the one-sidedness such an indication. What is significant is the attitude of the husband and a strong tendency to project all the blame for present marital difficulties on the wife. Under these circumstances, comarital involvement is most likely to lead to the couple bypassing resolution of existing problems in their dyadic relationship.

This type of situation is the one exception to the rule that interest and leadership in multilateral involvement is roughly equally distributed between men and women. As often as not, wives are the enthusiastic leaders.

Marital Problems in the Dyad. There is some tendency to view all forms of comarital relations as making up for deficiencies in conventional monogamy and even as offering solution to problems in the dyadic marriage. While there may be specific areas in which multilateral marriage has greater potential, we definitely do not believe it to be a solution to actual marital difficulties. In many ways, the multilateral situation will either exacerbate or at least make painfully obvious the problems already present. It must be stressed that the multilateral marriage is intrinsically many times more difficult and complicated than a dyadic one.

Resolution of the Triangle. Traditionally, the eternal triangle was resolved either by breaking up the extramarital involvement or by divorce and remarriage. Both alternatives can be especially painful to all parties under some circumstances. An affair with the spouse's best friend is not, in any sense, resolved by either alternative.

If the parties can be brought to accept the concept of a triadic marriage as a legitimate and viable alternative, they have opened the possibility of a true resolution. The very fact of involvement with a close *mutual* friend enhances the likelihood of a successful multilateral marriage. Moreover, we have found that triads are quite stable and substantially easier to form in the first place than larger marriages.

LEGAL QUESTIONS

There is some concern on the part of counselors with whom we have talked about the legality of multilateral marriage. Although statutes specifically directed against it are comparatively rare, in most states multilateral marriage participants would be violating more than one law. For the most part these are archaic statutes fallen into disuse (and misuse). The danger is from discriminatory application, and in essence, should anyone desire legal retribution on participants it would be readily achieved (Solis, 1970).

Clients, of course, should be made aware of this potential as a remote but possible consequence. We do not feel that the responsible counselor can in any way allow this to bias his own role in facilitating positive comarital and multilateral situations. Illegality is not used as an excuse to avoid suggesting oral-genital sex as an enjoyable adjunct to coital sex; it should not be in this context either. In the long run, we are convinced that the law will give recognition to a pluralistic view of marriage, just as other relationships among consenting adults are gradually being withdrawn from the legal arena.

CONCLUSION

In many respects counseling marriages which include a multilateral element is merely an extension of dyadic counseling. A very small number of characteristics may be regarded as intrinsically dissimilar. On the other hand, the relative importance of various aspects of the relationship are shifted. Moreover, the counselor too may find his job confounded by the very complexity that compounds the problems faced by those within the relationship.

Perhaps the end goal is to turn complexity from problem into strength. Thus the counselor can facilitate alternate paths of communication, promote use of the supportive potential of a many-person family, and encourage productive use of group process to facilitate growth and handle difficult decision-making functions. And there are many new options in terms of restructuring the multilateral situation for specific ends.

The real promise of this era is that the creative counselor has an opportunity at last to help to tailor the family structure to the people rather than to continue to try to mold individuals to fit one structure. This is not to say that conventional monogyny is a poor structure, but simply to realize that it may not be best for everyone. Neither should we hail group marriage as a new panacea as some segments have. It is but one form of marriage that some individuals, perhaps a small minority, will find particularly fulfilling. Both the challenge and the opportunity of genuine pluralism in marital forms are immense.

REFERENCES

ATHENASIAN, ROBERT, ET AL. "Sex." *Psychology Today*, Vol. 4, No. 2, July 1970, pp. 39-52.

BARTELL, GILBERT D. "Group Sex Among the Mid-Americans." *J. Sex Res.*, Vol. 3, May 1970, pp. 113-130.

BELTZ, STEPHEN E. "Five Year Effects of Altered Marital Contracts." In Gerhard Neubeck (ed.), *Extramarital Relations*. Prentice-Hall, Englewood Cliffs, 1969.

CONSTANTINE, LARRY L. "Personal Growth in Multilateral Marriages." *Radical Therapist* (in press).

CONSTANTINE, LARRY L. & CONSTANTINE, JOAN M. "Where Is Marriage Going?" *The Futurist*, Vol. 4, No. 2, April 1970, pp. 44-46.

——. "Group Marriage and Related Topics: An Annotated Bibliography of Non-Fiction." *Family Process* (in press).

——. "Pragmatics of Group Marriage: Year One." *The Modern Utopian*, Vol. 4, Nos. 3 & 4, Summer-Fall 1970, pp. 33-37.

DENFIELD, DUANE & GORDON, MICHAEL. "The Sociology of Mate Swapping: Or the Family that Swings Together Clings Together." *J. Sex Res.*, Vol. 6, May 1970, pp. 85-100.

DREWERY, JAMES. "An Interpersonal Perception Technique." *Brit. J. Med. Psychol.*, Vol. 42, 1969, pp. 171-181.

ELLIS, ALBERT. *Homosexuality: Its Causes and Cure*. Lyle Stuart, Inc., New York, 1965.

——. "The Effectiveness of Psychotherapy with Individuals Who Have Severe Homosexual Problems." *J. Consult. Psychol.*, Vol. 20, No. 3, 1956.

GRUNEBAUM, HENRY, ET AL. "Diagnosis and Treatment Planning for Couples." *International J. Group Psychother.*, Vol. 19, April 1969, pp. 185-202.

HEINLEIN, ROBERT A. *The Moon is a Harsh Mistress*. G. P. Putnam's Sons, New York, 1966.

JOHNSON, RALPH E. "Some Correlates of Extramarital Coitus." *J. Mar. and Family*, Vol. 32, No. 3, August 1970, pp. 449-456.

JOURARD, SYDNEY M. & RESNICK, JAQUELYN L. "Some Effects of Self-Disclosure Among College Women." *J. Humanistic Psychol.*, Vol. 10, No. 1, Spring 1970, pp. 84-93.

KAFKA, JOHN S., ET AL. A Nonconventional Pattern Within the Conventional Marriage Framework. Unpublished research report, NIMH, 1969.

KILGO, REESE D. The Use of the Edwards Personal Preference Schedule in Premarital and Marriage Counseling. Paper, National Council on Family Relations Annual Meeting, Washington, D. C., 1969.

MATTHEWS, JOAN. "Bisexuality in the Male." *J. Sex Res.*, Vol. 5, No. 2, May 1969, pp. 126-129.

O'NEILL, GEORGE C. & O'NEILL, NENA. "Patterns in Group Sexual Activity." *J. Sex Res.*, Vol. 6, May 1970, pp. 101-112.

ORLEANS, MYRON & WOLFSON, FLORENCE. "The Future of the Family." *The Futurist*, Vol. 4, No. 2, April 1970, pp. 48-49.

OTTO, HERBERT A. *Group Methods to Actualize Human Potential*. The Holistic Press, Beverly Hills, 1970.

RIMMER, ROBERT H. *Proposition 31*. The New American Library, Inc., New York, 1968.

SATIR, VIRGINIA. *Conjoint Family Therapy*. Science and Behavior Books, Inc., Palo Alto, revised edition, 1967.

SMITH, JAMES R. & SMITH, LYNN G. "Co-Marital Sex and the Sexual Freedom Movement." *J. Sex Res.*, Vol. 6, May 1970, pp. 131-142.

SOLIS, GARY. *Group Marriage and California Law*. Paper for class in Family Law, University of California, Davis.

STOLLER, FREDERICK H. "The Intimate Network of Families." In Herbert A. Otto (ed.), *The Family in Search of a Future*, Appleton-Century-Croft, New York, 1970.

STOLLER, ROBERT J. *Sex and Gender*. Science House, New York, 1968.

SYMONDS, CAROLYN. *Pilot Study of the Peripheral Behavior of Sexual Mate Swappers*. Unpublished Master's Thesis, University of California at Riverside, 1968.

——. *The Utopian Aspect of Sexual Mate Swaping: In Theory and Practice*. Paper, Annual Meeting of the Society for the Psychological Study of Social Problems, Washington, D. C., 1970.

34

THE RAPID TREATMENT OF HUMAN SEXUAL DYSFUNCTIONS

William H. Masters, M.D.

*Director, The Reproductive Biology
Research Foundation (St. Louis)*

and

Virginia E. Johnson

*Assistant Director, The Reproductive Biology
Research Foundation (St. Louis)*

An investigation of human sexual function was initiated in 1954 under the auspices of Washington University School of Medicine. This program has continued since 1964 as an important segment of the total research supported by the Reproductive Biology Research Foundation. Three major aspects of human sexual response have been foci of investigation. In chronologic order these research ventures have included various aspects of sexual physiology, variants in the treatment of sexual dysfunction and a combined laboratory and clinical evaluation of homosexual response patterns. Established Foundation policy requires that at least a decade be devoted to each area of human sexual functioning under investigation before reporting work in progress to the scientific community.

In the early years, the work in sexual physiology was handicapped by problems of funding and concerns for protecting the anonymity of the

From a paper titled "Current Status of the Research Programs," presented to the American Psychopathological Association Meeting, New York, N. Y., February 5, 1971.

study-subject population. Work was slowed frequently and even interrupted occasionally as funds ran out and/or as security techniques required revision. The primary objective, requiring the greatest amount
of time and consideration, was to eliminate, insofar as possible, influence
of the artificiality of laboratory environment upon the study-subject's
levels of sexual responsivity. A perpetual administrative problem was
created by continuous attempts of the blatantly curious to penetrate the
protective security established by those men and women who cooperated
to provide laboratory-oriented evidence of the basic physiological principles of human sexual function. Protection of study-subject anonymity
always has been and always will be a total commitment of the Foundation's professional staff. At least two, perhaps three years of research
time could have been salvaged had the work been conducted with any
semblance of adequate financial support and any significant evidence of
maturity in either public or professional curiosity.

In January 1959 the second aspect of the Foundation's research program related to human sexual response was initiated. This clinical component of the research design was designated "the rapid treatment of
human sexual dysfunction." Based upon preliminary experimentation, a
controlled clinical study was initiated which sought to integrate physiologic fact and psychosocial structure. This concept requires that therapists regard the interrelation of the psychologic and biologic systems as
an operational necessity. The fundamental tenets of this clinical research
were formulated in 1958 prior to establishing an eleven year period of
statistical control. Since objective evaluation of treatment techniques
depends upon appreciation of the precepts involved, they will be presented in some detail.

First: Each partner in a marriage handicapped by some form of sexual
inadequacy is considered to be responsibly (accountably) involved both
in the physical functioning and the psychosocial aspects of the marital
relationship. Therefore, both members of the distressed marital unit
must be seen in therapy, and, equally important, must voluntarily participate in the educative process that is the basis of the Foundation's
treatment of sexual dysfunction. The marital relationship always is the
primary target of therapeutic attention. Individual requirements, preferences and goals are given consideration within the context of this
relationship.

Second: It is believed that there are specific advantages inherent in the
use of dual-sex teams in treatment of marital units contending with
symptoms of sexual dysfunction. Although team members' responsibilities are too numerous to detail here, the primary purpose for the use

of a male-female team is to provide full and fair clinical representation for both members of a marital unit undergoing treatment. It is the female therapist's clinical obligation to help the wife define and express herself, to give support as she evaluates her position in the ongoing therapy process, and to interpret material of female orientation. It follows that the male therapist has similar responsibility for the husband.

Third: The process of education within the course of therapy is dependent upon daily review of the patients' participation in a learning opportunity, which has been provided when the marital pair "tries on" ideas and modes of interaction conceptualized for and with them during discussion sessions. The daily review is derived from the patients' account of their own attitudes and activities developing from the previous day's discussion. In this manner the marital pair explores the appropriateness and reliability of combinations of verbal and nonverbal, sexual and nonsexual communication in producing mutually desired feelings and attitudes. They subsequently may accept or reject any particular experience (and its means of attainment) as it does or does not support their mutual values and goals.

Content of any daily session may include an account of patient experience, discussion of related feelings and attitudes, as well as cotherapists' presentation of new information, correction of misinformation, and suggestions for altering patterns of behavior which have been defined as unsatisfactory by husband and/or wife. Repetition is employed frequently to achieve understanding and familiarity with effective patterns of interaction. Both exploration and experimentation are carried out by the marital partners under protective rules of conduct and, if necessary, intervention of the cotherapists. The team imposes three rules of conduct upon the involved husband and wife to help achieve this protective environment.

> a. Communication between the marital pair shall be an exchange based on self-interpretation and must never be allowed to impute feeling, meaning or intent by one partner to the other.
> b. Anger or frustration devoloping from breakdown in communication between the marital partners shall be held in abeyance, to be described and dealt with in the next day's therapy session.
> c. Those actions and ideas elected as appropriate and effective by either partner shall be introduced for the enhancement of both, but never at the expense of valued requirements of the other.

Fourth: This mode of psychotherapy presumes that human sexual functioning, like that of other animals, must be considered a natural process. It is not only unnecessary, it is impossible to "teach" the human male to achieve erection, the female to lubricate, the male to ejaculate or the female to experience orgasm. The basic principle that must be accepted by patient and cotherapist alike is that physical expression of sexual tension is a natural function. From this platform of general agreement, therapeutic techniques can be activated which are designed to contribute to progressive removal of psychosocial blocks inhibiting sexual responsivity. Possibly the key to professional and public acceptance of the concept of sexual response as a natural physical expression lies in appreciation of the fact that sexual function has a unique facility when compared to other physiologic responses of the human body. Sexual function so responds to psychosocial control that activity can be delayed indefinitely or even denied for a lifetime. No other basic physiologic process of the human body permits such a degree of inhibition without predictable impairment of body function.

Fifth: It is virtually impossible to establish treatment success with consistency when statistically evaluating a psychotherapeutic procedure. Particularly is this true when the process requires the element of self-evaluation. Treatment failure is considered far easier to ascertain, although measurement of contributing factors may not be conclusive. Therefore, treatment statistics have been and will continue to be reported relative to goal failure, rather than goal attainment.

Sixth: Regardless of the severity of the presenting clinical distress, symptom reversal during an acute phase of therapy is relatively unimportant, unless the newly-created, supporting patterns of communication and interaction are sufficiently appreciated and maintained by the marital pair to sustain symptom reversal after termination of treatment. If a therapeutic procedure is not to be judged a failure, the patient must evidence a trend of continued or progressive improvement after termination of therapy, regardless of the techniques employed and/or the duration of the acute phase of therapeutic support. Therefore, the concept of routine five-year follow-up of patients is applied to those marital units not identified as therapeutic failures during treatment for sexual dysfunction. Although the results would be of extreme investigative importance, rapid treatment failures are not followed in order to encourage every husband and wife whose problems have not been resolved by Foundation personnel, to approach other means of psychotherapeutic support.

The Foundation's second report, again reflecting eleven years of research commitment, was published in 1970. Hopefully, this report will give value to precepts involved in the use of dual-sex teams in the treatment of sexual dysfunction. The results obtained must be generally supported by similarly constituted dual-sex teams working in different geographic areas before scientific security in concept and procedure can be established. Of theoretical import is the intriguing possibility of using dual-sex team techniques in the treatment of yet other forms of psychopathology. The technique's inherent facility as an educative format only underscores the possibility of other applications of the method, since practically all forms of psychotherapy are, in large measure, educative processes.

Concomitant with first attempts at expansion of the professional staff during the last three years, the efficacy of this program of psychotherapy has been lowered significantly. There has been a significant reduction in effectiveness of the treatment of impotence and a major increase in failure to resolve problems of nonorgasmic return. These decreases in treatment efficacy have resulted in an indepth evaluation of the general therapeutic approach and of specific inadequacies in concept and technique of selection, training, and modes of evaluation of professional interaction for members of the professional staff. As a result of this self-evaluation conducted by the entire staff, some basic distractions to or inadeqaucies of staff function and of the psychodynamics of dual-sex team therapy have been demonstrated.

Four extraneous influences have contributed in large measure to the increased treatment failure rate. Hopefully, these factors have been resolved through reduction or elimination of their dominance in staff-time commitment. Excessive staff-time consumption has developed from:

(1) Problems inherent in the selection and training of additions to the Foundation's professional staff. In view of clinical demand for treatment, staff expansion was long overdue before that level of financial security necessary for such expansion became available. In addition, the severely overloaded permanent staff was constantly distracted by extraneous demands. Training requirements also further diluted staff commitment to patient care. Specific training techniques had to be developed and were, at best, far from adequate in those first years. All of these factors contributed to reduction in therapeutic efficacy. Successful expansion of the permanent staff has gone a long way toward resolving these problems.

(2) Major efforts to provide definitive sex information for public and professional consumption. The Foundation will have essentially withdrawn from this field by the end of 1971. Maturity achieved by such organizations as The Sex Information and Education Council of the United States (SIECUS) and the Center for the Study of Sex Education

in Medicine has obviated responsibility in this area. In the future, staff-time committed to the dissemination of information will be strictly controlled. It is the Foundation's fundamental responsibility to provide definitive sex information through effective research. Widespread dissemination of this information must be assigned to other organizations specifically designed for this purpose.

(3) Massive demand for treatment which overwhelmed somewhat frantic attempts of Foundation personnel to achieve selective balance and led to serious overscheduling at patient intake. Corrective measures have been taken and staff reaction has been entirely in a positive vein.

(4) In brief, the Foundation's professional staff has been spread entirely too thin during the rapid-growth period. Such overcommitment of time and effort will not recur. The professional staff has achieved approximately 75 per cent of its projected size. In the future, anticipated growth will occur at a slower, relatively nondemanding pace.

But there is no desire to overemphasize the negative in this discussion. There have been many positive returns in the past two years. Two of the three dual-sex teams trained to date are members of the Foundation's professional staff. The multiplicity of talents and disciplines these professionals possess argue well for improved therapeutic results in the future.

In January of 1971 the Foundation's long-anticipated postgraduate training program became a reality. Difficulties and inadequacies that were evident in prior training experience have underscored a number of principles vital to the new educative program: (1) Dual-sex trainee units must be closely integrated with the professional staff of the Foundation. The training period has been designated as one month but this time commitment may be altered as experience accrues. (2) Postgraduate training opportunity currently is being restricted to men and women with significant clinical experience. (3) One member of each trainee team must be a physician. Behavioral science orientation is highly desired as a credential for the other team member. (4) During the first year, postgraduate training will proceed at a deliberately slowed pace. This pace will enable the professional staff to analyze and revise these procedures as indicated.

A number of functional and psychosocial problems inherent in the practice of dual-sex team therapy have emerged over the past decade. At this point in time it seems appropriate to pinpoint some of these problems in professional adjustment for those who currently are or in the future, anticipate employing this manner of therapeutic approach.

(1), Experience suggests that the most consistently recurring problem is the arbitrary tendency of the male professional to assume control of therapy at any given time, or for the female therapy partner to engender such male dominance by failing to accept her share of responsibility in the course of therapy. This observation has remained constant for each of the four teams trained to date. Every male-female team must be continuously careful to negate those cultural influences that tend to engender imposition of male dominance as a prerogative in either personal and professional interaction. If the male therapist exercises dominance as a privilege he may commit the professional *faux pas* of attempting to describe or interpret for the wife of the sexually dysfunctional couple those details of sexual reaction that are particularly female in orientation. Examples of this type of therapeutic misfortune are provided by instances of a male therapist's attempt to verbalize the wife's subjective appreciation of sexual stimulation, the psychologic components of her approach to sexual interchange, or her objective or subjective appreciation of an orgasmic experience.

Obviously it is equally lethal for the female therapist to attempt any similar interpretive takeover of the husband's subjective or objective appreciation of sexual response.

(2) Another potential area of misadventure can be encountered when the female therapist attempts to interpret feminine accounts of sexual responsivity and psychosocial interaction from a masculine-oriented psyche. While this pattern of interaction remains somewhat enigmatic, many women who involve themselves in formal training in the interest of professional status and regard may undergo some degree of psychic reorientation. They respond with an essentially masculine input as a means to overcome the unfair competitive detours placed upon them in our culture. Psychosocial trauma during professional adolescence may show through the maturity of professional experience during professional attempts to interpret or react to a sexually distressed woman. Needless to say, a masculine clinical approach displayed by a female therapist is disconcerting or even traumatic to the female patient. The wife might fear that she does not have a female interpreter or true representation. As euphemistically described by Foundation personnel, she comes to the conclusion that she does not have a "friend in court." Such a conclusion, of course, is totally contrary to that intended by the dual-sex team concept.

(3) A problem possibly unique to the Foundation's professional staff is the necessity of developing a common language for clinical interchange. This stimulating problem of professional interaction probably has emerged from inadequate exposure to or appreciation of those profes-

sional disciplines in which a staff member has not received training. As currently constituted, each member of the full-time, clinical staff represents in fact or in part at least two different professional disciplines. Yet, no single discipline has more than one representative. It is apparent that there are tremendous advantages in having a variety of professional disciplines available to any treatment program. Each staff member must assume the responsibility of achieving some degree of familiarity with those multiple alternative disciplines to which he has not had sufficient prior exposure, before a common language can be established to describe finite nuances of patient reaction. For example, the significance of psychotherapeutic terminology might not be appreciated in totality by a professional trained as a pediatrician or an obstetrician. Similarly, the full portent of the multiple physiologic facets of human sexual response is hard to absorb by those trained in the behavioral disciplines.

Experience has made it apparent that the language of personnel communication must be that of the clinically trained psychotherapist. It must be used in combination with an in-depth appreciation of the physiology of sexual responsivity which, in turn, must become familiar not only to those with non-medical professional orientation, but to many of those formally trained in medical fields as well.

(4) Yet another problem area to emerge in the last few years has been the obvious failure of referring authority (usually medical) to associate superficial complaints of physical sexual dysfunction with a depth of underlying psychosocial trauma. In contradistinction, and equally delimiting in concept, is the categorical assignment of underlying psychopathology to all individuals complaining of sexual dysfunction. In many instances, clinical complaints of sexual dysfunction do represent the underlying existence of major degrees of psychopathology, but probably an equal or greater number of patients experience severe sexual inadequacy without evidencing symptoms of accompanying severe psychopathology.

(5) As stated previously, it is vital that psychotherapists dealing directly with clinical symptoms of sexual distress react from a sense of confidence ond comfort in their own sexuality and sexual functioning. There is a tendency for a sexually insecure therapist to lose objectivity when dealing with a sexually distressed patient, particularly one of the opposite sex. Any failure to maintain perspective has grave potential for undermining the effectiveness of the professional's therapeutic approach to the patient's complaint of sexual inadequacy.

(6) Problems of transference or a tendency toward countertransference have been observed despite the protective screen inherent in the tech-

nique of dual-sex representation in therapeutic counsel. When sexual dysfunction is the presenting complaint, there is a tendency for both male and female patients to attempt identification with the authority of the opposite sex. Although professionals are presumed sensitized to this tendency, there have been times when patient transference was encouraged, or at least not discouraged, by a member of the Foundation's professional staff. An occasional inclination toward countertransference has been identified during the daily case evaluation sessions which are conducted by Foundation personnel. In no sense is the Foundation impugning the effectiveness of controlled transference as a psychotherapeutic technique, yet it must be emphasized that such technique has no place in the rapid treatment of sexual dysfunction.

(7) When warring strangers (usually identified by such terms as husband and wife) are referred to the Foundation for treatment of sexual dysfunction, every effort is made to reconstitute their interpersonal relationships by catalyzing constructive communication. Identifiable, shared goals and common denominators of motivation provide the initial material for catalytic affect. Again and again the positive aspects of the unit's personal interactions must be emphasized if security in communication is to be established or restored. In the brief period of two weeks, both the husband's or wife's conscious or unconscious attempts at identification, each with the other, must be catalyzed successfully if there is to be a positive therapeutic return.

(8) The basic value systems of both the husband and the wife must be defined in depth sufficient to implement therapeutic effort successfully. A superficial scanning of the husband's or wife's set of personal values including their sexual value systems can indeed destroy therapeutic effectiveness. Superficiality of interrogation inevitably results in inadequate professional representation of the same-sex patient. The same-sex therapist must come to appreciate the patient's attitudinal approach to the psychosexual influences of our culture. Problems arise when a professional does not develop a history which adequately reflects patient values or life style, and, under pressure to meet demands of the therapy, imposes an interpretation based upon his or her own limited personal experience. With sufficient authoritative identification of the patient's individual value systems and of the context in which they function, it is far easier to keep the Foundation's educative program focused on those things truly desired by the individual rather than those possibly imposed by the therapist's own value system.

(9) There may be a tendency toward professional rigidity in assignment of highly structured roles to sexually dysfunctional husbands and

wives. Therapists must remain constantly aware that they are dealing with two different personalities, two sets of values and two individual expectations which have not been fully negotiated. Certainly they must anticipate the possibility of divergent concepts of life style developed from different experiential backgrounds. It must be kept in mind that a wide range of information is required to define common denominators from which to establish a secure foundation for patient interaction.

(10) Patient screening has been and remains a serious problem. There is no place for the acute psychotic or the borderline psychoneurotic in the Foundation's treatment program, unless the patient is referred with spouse after adequate preparation and returned immediately to post-treatment control by a competent psychotherapist. Foundation screening techniques must be improved to eliminate the referral of such seriously involved patients without such protection. For that matter, the screening techniques must be improved in other aspects as well. Currently this problem is being studied extensively by Foundation personnel.

Finally, a brief look to the future is in order. The decade of the seventies will find the Foundation's research commitments continuing to expand in both clinical and preclinical areas.

From a clinical point of view, there is yet another step to anticipate in the Foundation's approach to the concerns of sexual function and dysfunction. When approaching an essentially unexplored clinical problem, researchers usually follow the well-ordered patterns of moving first to the laboratory. Here every effort is made to provide, through basic science determinants, material pertinent to resolution of the clinical problem. As a second step, therapeutic suggestions and factual material developed in the laboratory are then applied to resolve the clinical concern. In the essentially unexplored area of human sexual function these first two steps have been taken in the last sixteen years. In normal progression, the inevitable third step, that of preventing distress, looms invitingly large. As a clinical research commitment, the next decade will be devoted to devising ways and means of prevention of sexual dysfunction. Obviously, every professional discipline available to the Foundation will be employed in this clinical venture.

The goal of the basic science program is to establish a neurophysiology laboratory comparable in quality to the Foundation's biochemical research area. There is little need to support here the necessity for such a facility. In brief, we know a great deal of the neurophysiology of cardiorespiratory function, so the quality of medical care in this area increases each year. We are reasonably well informed in the neurophysiology of bowel and bladder function, and, as a result, the quality of related patient protection continues demonstrably upward. Obviously, we know little of the neurophysiology of human sexual function, particularly at the extracranial level, and the quality of our patient care in this area reflects this ignorance. In no sense will devotion to this research concentration carry the implication that all of the answers to human sexual dysfunction will be found in a neurophysiology laboratory. What is implied is the belief that approaches to treatment of sexual inadequacy will be positively influenced by productive research in this area. Inevitably, clinical approaches based on a firm, basic science foundation reflect this security in progressively elevated levels of patient protection.

There is so much to learn of the multiple facets of human sexual behavior. In the last few years legitimate investigation in this area has not only been acknowledged as professionally challenging, but as socially acceptable. A massive, multidisciplined effort to interpret this last, essentially unexplored frontier of human function is long overdue.

35

DETERMINANTS OF HUMAN SEXUAL IDENTITY AND BEHAVIOR

John Money, Ph.D.

*Department of Psychiatry and Behavioral Sciences and
Department of Pediatrics, The Johns Hopkins
University and Hospital, Baltimore, Md.*

PRINCIPLE OF DIFFERENTIATION AND DEVELOPMENT

Sexual behavior in man, like the sexual anatomy itself, is by reason of man's place in the phyletic scale, dimorphic. That is to say, its growth from its inception onward is simultaneously a process of differentiation as well as of development. This fact tends to have been overlooked historically in psychiatry which has spoken mainly of psychosexual development. Sexual theory has been impoverished thereby.

Reduced to its barest essentials, traditional sexual theory in psychiatry is built on two constructs: libido and identification. Libido, the instinctual sexual force, has not been conceived of as sexually dimorphic, per se, though possibly as bisexual. Manifest difference in behavior between the sexes has been regarded conceptually as secondary to libido and mainly as the developmental product of identification: to somewhat oversimplify, little girls identify with their mothers, little boys with their fathers. It is possible, though by no means justified, to account for identification exclusively in terms of stimulus-response and reward-reinforcement theory. Thus, there has been grown up a strong current tradition

Supported in research by Grant #5-KO3-HD18635 and Grant #5-RD1-HD00325, U.S.P.H.S.

of explaining differences in behavior between the sexes—or deviations therefrom—as social-environmental or cultural in origin.

A theory in which the totality of dimorphism in sexual behavior is attributed exclusively to postnatal social and cultural determinants, is, *a priori*, open to the charge of being too narrow and simple. Moreover, notwithstanding the cogent evidence of the power of postnatal events in shaping gender identity and gender role in human beings, one would be hard-pressed to defend an exclusively cultural theory against the newly accumulating evidence of animal sexology on the fetal influence of hormones on the governance of sexual behavior by way of the central nervous system.

PRINCIPLE OF SEQUENTIAL DIFFERENTIATION

The antecedents of sexual dimorphism of behavior in human development are typically sequential, beginning with the genetic dimorphism of the sex chromosomes, XY for the male and XX for the female. Then follows the differentiation of the gonads and their differentiated fetal hormonal functioning, differentiation of the internal reproductive anatomy, differentiation of the external genital morphology, differential sex assignment at birth, differential rearing as a boy or girl, differentiation of a gender role and identity, differentiation of hormonal puberty, and differential response to falling in love, courtship, mating and parenthood.

CRITICAL-PERIOD PRINCIPLE

Differentiation of the embryonic gonads is normally governed by the sex chromosomes, but only if the genetic code written into the chromosomes is permitted to express itself normally (the genetic norm of reaction) without interference or disruption at a critical period from an environment liable to produce distortions. The most dramatic distortion of the genetic code of the sex chromosomes is one in which their role as sex determinants is completely reversed. Yamamoto (1962) was able to bring about such a complete reversal in the killifish, orizeas latipes, by exposing larvae to sex hormone. Exposed to estrogen, the female sex hormone, an XY larva destined to have differentiated into a male, thereupon differentiated into a female. Amazingly enough, this XY female was able to breed with a normal XY male and produce young. Twenty-five percent of the second generation larvae were then chromosomally XX (female), fifty percent XY (male) and twenty-five percent YY, which, if left untreated, would differentiate as males, but if treated with estrogen, would become YY females. In the succeeding generation, it was then possible to breed YY females with YY males, the resultant progeny all being YY and differentiating as males, if left unexposed to hormone experimental treatment. Yamamoto was also able to produce XX males by treating XX eggs with male sex hormone which exhibited the strong and competitively masculine mating behavior of YY males that has been studied by Hamilton, Walter, Daniel and Mestler (1969).

Yamamoto's experiment is not the first in which the germ cells have been reversed to produce ova instead of sperms, or vice versa, while still retaining their reproductive fertility. Many years ago, Witschi demonstrated that overripe toad eggs all devoloped as morphologic males. Not only the genetic males, but also the genetic females had the appearance of males and produced sperms, but without the male sex chromosome present in them (Witschi, 1956, 1965). Witschi and his coworkers (Chang and Witschi, 1955, 1956; Mikamo and Witschi, 1963) also succeeded in producing a similar reversal of genetic sex in toads by implanting sex hormones into the developing larvae. In 1964, Turner and Asakawa made a first step toward achieving the same result in a mammal by transplanting the gonads of fetal mice into a host animal, so that the fetal testis turned the fetal ovary into an ovotestis in which spermatogenesis progressed to the point of secondary spermatocytes. Burns (1961) had in 1956 used estradiol in the fetal opossum to convert a would-be testis into an ovotestis producing ovocytes.

It has not yet been reported experimentally possible to reverse the sex differentiation completely from that of the genetic sex of the fertilized egg in mammals. Nonetheless the fish and amphibian experiments demonstrate how profound can be the reversal of everything pertaining to genetic sex: morphology, behavior and fertility. These experiments require that one keep an open mind with regard to possible partial reversals of the expression of genetic sex in human beings, perhaps of direct relevance to sexual psychopathology, from causes as yet unknown.

The fish and amphibian experiments also point out a profoundly important principle in the theory of heredity versus environment (perhaps more appropriately designated as genetics versus environmentics). It is a principle that transcends the old dichotomy between nature and nurture by introducing the concept of the critical period. There is only a limited period during which a fertilized egg may be tampered with and forced to reverse the program for which it is genetically coded. After this limited, or critical period, the die is cast and the program cannot be changed or, having been changed, cannot revert.

The die is cast regarding the differentiation of the gonads in the human species at around the sixth week after conception. In the XY embryo, the core of the undifferentiated gonad proliferates to form into a testis, and the rind becomes vestigial; whereas in the XX embryo, the rind proliferates, while the core becomes vestigial, to form an ovary.

PRINCIPLES OF DIFFERENTIATION: VESTIGIATION VS. HOMOLOGUES

The principle of *commencing with the anlagen for both sexes, then allowing one to proliferate while the other vestigiates,* is one which nature extends from the differentiation of the gonads to the differentiation of the internal reproductive structures from the mullerian and wolffian ducts, both of which are initially laid down in parallel. Here another principle first becomes evident, namely this: *for the differentiation of a male, something extra must occur—something must be added.* In the total absence of gonads, whether by experimental castration of the fetus in utero, or by reason of a cytogenetic defect as in Turner's syndrome (typically $44 + XO = 45$ chromosomes), the fetus will develop as a female. There is no doubt about it that nature's first disposition is to make a female. Morphologically, for a female to be differentiated, it is not necessary to have fetal gonads able to release hormonal substances; whereas, for the differentiation of a male, it is absolutely necessary to have them and they must be testes. These fetal testes must release the so-called mullerian-inhibiting substance which causes the homolateral mullerian duct to regress, thus preventing the formation of the uterus and fallopian tube on that side. The fetal testes must also release an androgenic or male-hormonal substance which prevents regression of the wolffian ducts, thus ensuring the differentiation of the male internal sexual structures. When the mullerian-inhibiting substance fails, it is possible to have a male born with fully differentiated uterus and tubes. So far as is known, this rather extraordinary anomaly does not have any subsequent primary influence on sexual behavior. In the case of unilateral failure of the mullerian-inhibiting substance, only a half uterus and one tube is formed; subsequent external sexual development is liable to be hermaphroditic, with attendant risks of anomalously affecting sexual behavior.

Differentiation of the external sexual organs comes after that of the internal organs and proceeds on the basis of an entirely different principal—the *principal of homologues.* Here nature begins with the same anlagen and uses them for sexually different purposes: the genital tubercle becomes either the clitoris or the penis; the genital folds become either the hood of the clitoris and the labia minora or the foreskin and the wrap-around of the penis which forms the penile urethra; and the genital swellings become either the labia majora or the scrotal sac, joined by the same median raphe that fuses the penile urethra. It is between the second and third month of fetal life in the human species that external-organ differentiation takes place.

MASCULINE DIFFERENTIATION: ADDITIVE PRINCIPLE

The differentiating principle at this stage of embryonic development is once again: *add something to obtain a male*. The something added is *androgen*. In the absence of androgen, a fetus will differentiate externally as a female, regardless of chromosomal sex; and in the partial absence of androgen, differentiation will be as an unfinished male, that is with incomplete fusion of the penile and scrotal skin, the penis being diminished in size and the testes possibly being undescended. Conversely, in the presence of a sufficient quantity of androgen even an XX fetus will differentiate externally as a male.

Brain Differentiation

At around the same time as the external genitalia differentiate, (6 weeks after conception) fetal androgens exert an influence also on the developing central nervous system. In the lower, estrous species, androgen administered to the fetus at the appropriate critical development period counteracts its primary disposition to develop, subsequently, the cyclic estrous function of the female. The findings of different investigators using different techniques (reviewed by Harris, 1964; Money, 1965) converge on the hypothalamus as the responsible area of the brain. Nuclei in the hypothalamus govern, by way of their neural releaser-hormones, the pituitary gland's activity. The pituitary, in turn, by cyclically or noncyclically releasing its gonad-stimulating hormones, the gonadotropins, regulates the production of sex hormones from the ovaries or testicles.

The overall principle emerging from the foregoing neurohormonal (or neurohumoral) research is once again the familiar one: add something, androgen, to obtain a male. Whether the differentiation regulated by androgen follows the homologous pattern of the external genitals, or the vestigiation pattern of the gonads and internal organs, remains to be ascertained. One piece of evidence in favor of the vestigiation hypothesis is that of Fisher (1956, 1966) who was able to elicit simultaneous female (maternal) and male (mating) behavior in a male rat by injecting minute amounts of testosterone directly into the preoptic area of the hypothalamus. The schema of female behavior is dormant, of course, or vestigial in the male, under ordinary circumstances.

Masculinized Female Monkeys

The experiments that have so far been performed on primates, as contrasted with subprimates, have not shown a direct effect on hormonal cycling as manifested in the menstrual cycle. There is some evidence, however, to indicate a fetal effect on the central nervous system that will eventually influence sexual behavior. For example, investigators at the Regional Primate Research Center, Beaverton, Oregon (Young, Goy and Phoenix, 1965; Phoenix, 1966) have produced genetic female rhesus monkeys so effectively virilized in utero by androgen injections of the mother that they were born with a normal male-appearing penis and empty scrotum instead of a clitoris and vaginal orifice. In the juvenile years, these animals gained behavior scores for initiating play, engaging in rough-and-tumble play, making threatening gestures, and adopting the position in sexual play that were closer to the scores of normal control males with normal control females. As they approached puberty and adolescence, these anatomically masculinized females tended to lose the masculine trend in their behavioral scores, but the complete story has not yet been ascertained, and the complete repertory of appropriate tests remains to be performed.

Masculinized Human Females

In human beings, there are two clinical syndromes that are the counterpart of fetal monkey androgenization. One is the syndrome of progestin-induced hermaphroditism in females. The other is the female andrenogenital syndrome of hermaphroditism, specifically in cases where masculinization is restricted to fetal life, its continuance after birth being prevented by treatment with cortisone. It is superfluous to the needs of this chapter to digress into a full clinical description of these two syndromes and their differential etiology, prognosis and therapy; see instead Wilkins (1965) and Money (1968). It is sufficient for present purposes to note that, regardless of etiology, one has here examples of females subjected to masculinization in fetal life sufficient to enlarge the clitoris and partially fuse the labia, so as to create the appearance of hypospadias in the male. This anatomical abnormality is surgically corrected soon after birth, so that the appearance looks correctly female, in agreement with the rearing. Hormonal function, either spontaneously or by regulation, is female, and puberty is normal in onset. What then of behavior?

The evidence to date (Ehrhardt and Money, 1967; Ehrhardt, Epstein and Money, 1968) is that fetal androgenization in the above two syndromes does indeed influence the subsequent development of behavior, though only to a limited extent. It does not induce a complete reversal of gender role and gender identity in the sense that a girl feels she ought to be a boy or would like to change her sex. Nor does it automatically steer her in the direction of lesbianism. But it does tend to make her a tomboy, as judged by self-declaration and confirmed by parents and friends. Her tomboyism is defined, perhaps above all else, by vigorous, muscular energy expenditure and an intense interest in athletic sports and outdoor activities in competition with boys. It is not especially associated with aggression and fighting. It is accompanied by scorn for fussy and frilly feminine clothes and hairdos in favor of utility styles. It is incompatible with a strong interest in maternalism as revealed in the rehearsals of childhood doll play or in future ambitions for the care of tiny babies. It does not exclude the anticipation of romance, marriage and pregnancy, but these are regarded in a somewhat perfunctory way as secondary to a career. Career ambitions are consistent with high academic achievement and with the high IQ, which tends to be a characteristic of girls with fetal androgenization.

Antiandrogenism: Rats

The experimental opposite of fetal androgenization of the female is nonandrogenization or antiandrogenization of the male. The former can be achieved by means of fetal castration, a technically difficult operation even in a species like the rat in which the young are delivered fetally immature. Neonatal castration of the rat does indeed preserve cyclic functioning of the pituitary, as in the female (Harris, 1964). The use of antiandrogen is even more dramatic in its effect. When such a hormone is injected, with the proper timing, into the pregnant mother, then the fetal testes of the genetic males become dormant and fail to supply androgen to the anlagen of the external genitalia. In consequence, the animal, to be specific a rat (Neumann and Elger, 1965), is born with completely normal-appearing female genitals. By castrating the animal to eliminate all further influence of its own testes and giving replacement doses of female hormones at puberty, it is possible to obtain normal female mating behavior from these genetic males (Neumann and Elger, 1966). The stud males of the colony do not distinguish them from normal females. The sex-behavior reversal is complete.

Androgen Insensitivity: *Human*

In human beings, two clinical syndromes are close counterparts of experimental antiandrogenism in animals, namely Turner's syndrome and the testicular-feminizing or androgen-insensitivity syndrome (Wilkins, 1965; Money, 1968). In both instances, fetal androgenization of the external genitals fails so that the baby is born with normal-appearing female external genitals. In Turner's syndrome, there are neither ovaries nor testes as a result of the chromosomal error responsible for the syndrome, so that fetal androgenization is an impossibility. In the androgen-insensitivity syndrome, the testes are present and the chromosomal sex is $44 + XY =$ male. The testes produce male sex hormone in an amount normal for a male; and at puberty, they produce also female sex hormone in an amount normal for a male. It is not the testes that are at fault in this condition, but all the cells of the body which manifest a genetic inability to respond to male sex hormone. The body therefore responds to the testes output of female hormone; it develops a normal female appearance, including breasts at puberty. There is no uterus, however, since the testes produced their mullerian-inhibiting substance early in embryonic life, thus causing its vestigiation.

The behavior of girls and women with either Turner's syndrome (Money and Mittenthal, 1969) or the androgen-insensitivity syndrome (Money, Ehrhardt and Masica, 1968; Masica, Money, Ehrhardt and Lewis, 1969) is indisputably feminine. They are not tomboys. In childhood their interest is in traditionally feminine play and activities. They show strong maternalistic interests in doll play from an early age, generally like to take care of children as they grow through childhood, and rehearse fantasies of romance, marriage and motherhood as their primary ambition for the future. They are bitterly disappointed when their case is diagnosed and they learn the prognosis of sterility and motherhood by adoption. When eventually they do adopt children, they make good mothers. Their sex-lives in marriage are the same as for anatomically normal wives selected at random and subject to the same vicissitudes—except for the probability of needing long-term hormonal therapy and, in some cases of androgen insensitivity, surgical lengthening of the vagina for ease in sexual intercourse.

CORE GENDER IDENTITY: PRINCIPLE OF DISSOCIATION

Babies who will in future be diagnosed as having the androgen-insensitivity syndrome are almost never diagnosed at birth or in early childhood, for the obvious reason that they look normally female. The same is true for Turner's syndrome, except that various of the possible congenital defects of this syndrome may bring the child to earlier medical attention. It therefore happens that the differentiation of gender identity in these female-appearing people cannot be studied except under the reinforcement of a rearing that is female, like their appearance. The real test of the influence of sex of assignment and rearing on psychosexual differentiation is better studied in cases of sexual anomaly where the visible appearance is hermaphroditically ambiguous so that people of the same diagnosis can be found, differing only in that some have been assigned, reared, and surgically and hormonally treated as boys, the others as girls.

This condition, though rare, is met often enough to demonstrate the extraordinary power of postnatal events on the differentiation of gender role and identity. The typical finding is that gender role and identity differentiate in conformity with the sex of assignment and rearing. This conformity can withstand various partial contradictions which include: 1) even the extreme contradictory hormonal puberty such that a person raised as a girl virilizes like a boy or, being raised as a boy begins to grow breasts and pass menstrual blood through the urethra; 2) tomboyism of energy expenditure in a person raised as a girl; 3) imperfect pubertal virilization with a nonerectile stub of a penis in a person raised as a boy; and 4) a masculine type of threshold, in a person living as a woman, for erotic arousal in response to visual and narrative material as contrasted with the more feminine dependence on tactile stimulation.

There are exceptions, nonetheless, when gender identity does not differentiate in conformity with sex assignment. Disparity between the two is most likely to arise when the assignment itself is ambivalent. The parents may be given no medical conviction about their infant's sexual diagnosis, or even may be told to half expect that a sex change might be necessary later. Parental ambivalence can be further reinforced if the genitalia are left surgically uncorrected during childhood so that they not only are a reproach to the child, when he or she looks at them, but also may be the source of teasing by siblings, cousins or friends. Under such circumstances the child, sensing and then knowing full well that something is wrong, does not tolerate the cognitive dissonance of his ambiguity. It is very rarely that an hermaphrodite settled for an ambiguous or hermaphroditic gender identity. A resolution of ambiguity is achieved instead by the simple expedient of repudiating the attributed status, so obviously wrong and unsatisfactory, in favor of its opposite, which at least has the virtue of not having yet been proved wrong and unsatisfactory.

This process of reassignment, when it occurs, usually takes place early during an hermaphrodite's childhood; for the resolution of an ambiguous gender identity cannot feasibly be postponed. To achieve formal recognition of the change then becomes something of a cause célèbre and a real driving force in life.

The question of whether or not the influence of fetal hormones on sex differentiation of nuclei of the hypothalamus may have any bearing on an hermaphrodite's conviction of the need for sex reassignment cannot at present be answered. One can simply note (Money, 1969) that the decision seems to be arrived at more frequently by male than female hermaphrodites, and is more likely to require a female-to-male change of status than vice versa—which may have more to do with ambiguity of anatomy and of diagnosis of hermaphroditism than with assigned sexual status, *per se.*

The fact that some few hermaphrodites do not consolidate their gender identity from infancy onward, but reach a point of self-reassignment, contrasts strongly with those who do, and for whom a sex reassignment by edict would be a disaster. In the sex assignment of hermaphrodites, it is still relatively common for an on-the-spot decision to be made at the time of birth and then to have to be changed later, after completion of a full diagnostic work-up. As a result, a reannouncement of the baby's sex has to be made. Provided the parents are correctly guided through this dilemma, it need have no adverse effect, then or subsequently, on the differentiation of the child's gender identity.

It is somewhere between the ages of twelve and eighteen months, dependent on a baby's facility in the understanding and use of language, that a sex reannouncement becomes more than an adjustment problem for the parents alone, and one for the child as well. By the time he has command of names, nouns and pronouns differentiating the sexes, a boy has a clear concept of himself as a boy, and a girl of herself as a girl. There is now no such simple thing as a sex reannouncement: it will be a sex reassignment involving the child as a person. Psychologically, it is very serious business, for the child already has a self-identity as boy or girl; the core gender identity, to use a term increasingly in vogue, is already on the way to being firmly established. This is an aspect of psychosexual differentiation not accounted for in the traditional Freudian scheme of the oral, anal and genital stages of psychosexual development.

The differentiation of a core gender identity probably follows the same principle as the differentiation of the gonads and the internal reproductive organs. In other words, two systems are present to begin with, only one of which becomes finally functional. In the case of gender identity, however, the nonfunctional system does not become vestigial, in the true sense, but is dissociated—coded as negative and nonusable. Thus, a boy grows up to know how to do all the boy things, because he also knows how not to do all the girl things, or vice versa for a girl. It must be much the same type of coding as happens in the brain in bilingualism. Under special circumstances in the boy, the negatively coded girl pattern may be brought to the fore—as when, for example, a child reaches a decision of sex reassignment. The same may occur under circumstances of severe personality disorganization associated with adolescent psychosis. A behavioral sex change may emerge still later in life, in certain rare cases of temporal lobe epilepsy, or as a consequence of senile brain deterioration, and may be manifest in the form of personality changes, among others, toward transvestism or homosexuality.

PRINCIPLE OF MASCULINE VULNERABILITY

Except for impotence and frigidity, it is widely acknowledged that the incidence of psychosexual disorders is higher in males than females. The variety of psychosexual disorders is also greater in males than females; some of the more bizarre and exotic anomalies simply are not recorded in the female. It is quite likely that one has here a by-product of yet one more manifestation of the principle of sexual differentiation, namely that something must be added to differentiate a male. The something added that makes the difference between female and male in psychosexual erotic functioning might well, once again, be androgen. Its site of action, or absence thereof, would undoubtedly be the brain. Its mechanism of action would most likely pertain to threshold sensitivity for erotic arousal from a visual stimulus or, perhaps, its evocation in imagery from a narrative stimulus. After puberty, it is males who are girl watchers, not females who are boy watchers. Teenaged boys use nude pictures as masturbation stimuli, but girls do not. At puberty, the boy is self-presented with realistic erotic images in dreams accompanied by orgasm; the girl is not. The very sexual performance of the boy is categorically different from that of the girl, in that his penis must be aroused to erection before he can begin; and it must ejaculate in orgasm if reproduction is to be effected. In the girl, by contrast, it is possible for conception to occur without either arousal or orgasm. It is possible for the male to be erotically aroused by touch alone, a fact to which many long-married husbands can attest. But it is typically the visual image that lends an element of excitement and, above all, incites the male to be the one who takes erotic initiative. This principle of male initiative is widespread in the animal kingdom, and in many species is dependent on visual stimulation, the closest competitor being smell.

If nature seems always to need to add something to make a male, then she seems also more likely to fail in her effort. The birth ratio, 106:100, in favor of males, allows for the more rapid wastage of the male, and the conception ratio, estimated at as high as 140:100 shows even more dramatically how easy it is for a male to fail. There are no definite figures available, but the vulnerability of the male is again demonstrated at puberty, when, in the clinic, partial or complete failure of hormonal puberty is more common than in the female (excluding the postpubertal problems of ovulatory and menstrual irregularity). In the matter of psychosexual arousal, nature's difficulty in differentiating a male again manifests itself in the greater number of males than females who are "turned on" by a wrong stimulus, that is, one that has positive arousal value when it should be either neutral, negative or partial. All the anomalies in a textbook of sexual psychopathology can be interpreted in terms of being aroused by the wrong stimulus. Sometimes it is almost possible to glimpse how the wrong connections between behavioral components can be established by reason of their proximity of representation in the nervous system, as MacLean (1965) has pointed out with respect to oral-anal representations in the limbic system.

Vulnerability to errors of psychosexual functioning has no single source of origin. In some few cases gentics can definitely be implicated, as in the case of the XXY (Klinefelter's) syndrome or the XYY syndrome. Men with either of these cytogenetic anomalies are likely to have some or other peculiarity of sexual behavior. XXY men are also very weak in libido, as well as sterile.

Whether events in intrauterine life may predispose human beings to psychosexual errors later in life is uncertain. In animal experiments it has been found that androgenization of the female fetus can be blocked by barbiturates (Gorski, 1968). One wonders what effect, if any, sleeping pills taken by a pregnant mother may have on the unborn fetus.

The bulk of today's evidence points unquestionably to events in early post-natal life and infancy as of prime importance in relation to eventual psychosexual normalcy. Harlow's (1965) work with rhesus monkeys raised on dummy mothers and in isolation from playmates is too well known to need retelling here. It points to the hitherto unsuspected importance of clinging and the sense of touch in primate development. It points also to the need to be able to play at the appripriate critical period—sexual play included—if normal reproductive behavior and parenthood is subsequently to be achieved. Very recently, a new report from the chimpanzee colony in New Mexico (Kollar, Beckwith and Edgerton, 1968) shows that, like the rhesus monkey, these primates also are very vulnerable to errors of psychosexual function when captured from their normal jungle troop and imprisoned in captivity. In fact, their sex-behavior problems are uncannily human.

As for human beings themselves, there is no highly systematic body of knowledge concerning the contingencies between rearing and subsequent sexual behavior, though there is a store of clinical knowledge and hypothesis, too vast to be reviewed here. It is perhaps a safe generalization to say that almost any major disruption of a child's developmental experience, regardless of its origin or type, is a potential source of disturbance in subsequent psychosexual development—the more so the younger the child. The vulnerability of the psychosexual system to disturbance may simply reflect the fact that its differentiation is actively in progress during early childhood. It may also be a reflection of the fact that, in many societies, our own included, psychosexual development is subject to an excess of taboos, such as the taboo on sexual play in childhood. If one judges from the evidence of the other primates, then childhood sexual play is a necessary and normal rehearsal, in preparation for adolescence and adulthood. Perhaps we would do well to reexamine our policies on childhood sexual play as a determinant of adult sexual behavior.

PRINCIPLE OF LOVE AS AN IMPRINT

After the advent of hormonal puberty, a new milestone in psychosexual development is reached, namely the capacity to experience falling in love. Children in kindergarten have play romances, and children in the so-called latency period (not so very latent, either!) may play at copulation games, but they do not fall in love, unless precocious falling in love may itself be a specific sign of psychosexual maldevelopment. The capacity to be aroused and possessed by the stimulus of the love object is not simultaneous with puberty. It does not occur, for instance, in children with precocious puberty of infantile onset until they become older—twelve is probably about the youngest. By contrast, in children, most notably boys, with long-delayed puberty, it is possible though not routine to observe the experience of falling in love sometime from middle to late teenage, even when complete hormonal infantilism still persists (Money and Alexander, 1967). One suspects, therefore, that whereas one neurohumoral mechanism (or biological clock) in the hypothalamus turns on puberty by way of activating the pituitary, another mechanism, site unknown, activates the capacity to fall in love.

Falling in love resembles imprinting, in that a releaser mechanism from within must encounter a stimulus from without before the event happens. Then that event has remarkable longevity, sometimes for a lifetime. The kind of stimulus that, whether it be acceptable or pathological, will be the effective one for a given individual will have been written into his psychosexual program, so to speak, in the years prior to puberty and dating back to infancy. Especially in the case of psychopathology, a boy or girl may be shocked and guilty to be "turned on" by an abnormal stimulus, while at the same time secretly fascinated and obsessed with it because of the sexual feeling it releases. The effective erotic stimulus may not initially be revealed in full, so that there is some element of discovery and expansion to erotic experience with the passage of time. By and large, however, human beings stay remarkably stable in their erotic preferences. Thus, it is not possible to teach a man or even a teenager to be, say, a masochist or a peeping-Tom; and a few teenaged exposures to homosexuality do not create an appetite for more. The appetite has to be there in the first place. Earlier in childhood, the power of exposure and experience is probably far more impressive and lasting. However, a great deal more work needs to be done on the after-effects of childhood sexual experiences. There seem to be distinct personality types so far as falling in love is concerned, and they may correspond to the augmenters and diminishers of sensation as described by Petrie (1967). At one extreme are people of psychopathic or sociopathic personality disposition, the Don Juan and nymphomaniac types who are the experts at one night stands. These are perhaps diminisher-people whose experiences fade quickly and stand in need of constant repetition and novelty.

By contrast, at the other extreme are the augmenter-people who cannot let an experience go. It reverberates and enlarges in their memories, and haunts them. The love affairs of many schizoid and schizophrenic people have this quality. They may have an anguished love affair without ever declaring themselves to the partner; or even possibly conduct the whole love affair with an imaginary partner by way of a photograph.

The majority of mankind, of course, falls somewhere between these two extremes. Each tends to judge the other from within the solipsism of his own "egg shell" as being like himself. But the fact is that we are quite differently determined so far as sexual behavior goes.

ANDROGEN-LIBIDO PRINCIPLE

When a teenager who has a syndrome of sexual infantilism nonetheless has a falling in love experience, it is not as intense and full-bodied as it will be once he is given effective hormone replacement therapy. The sex hormones do not in any way govern the cognitional content of eroticism—they do not cause homosexuality, for example—but they do affect the intensity and frequency of its expression, though without exercising total responsibility in this respect. Androgen is probably the libido hormone for both sexes (Money, 1961; Herbert, 1966; Trimble and Herbert, 1968) though some women, notably those with androgen insensitivity, seem to be able to function adequately without it. Normal women tend to report a more receptive attitude of wanting to be possessed at around the time of ovulation, which is when the estrogenic phase of the menstrual cycle is in the ascendant. Estrogen tends to be an inhibitor of androgen. At the menstrual phase, when progesterone levels are higher, and androgen may be less inhibited, women are more likely to take an initiating role of inducing the male. The birth control pill may change this cycle, but in a way that seems to depend on the formulae of the different brands (Grant and Pryse-Davies, 1968). According to newly accumulating evidence from Hamburg and from Johns Hopkins (Money, 1968), antiandrogens may prove to be very beneficial in enabling certain sex criminals to gain a measure of control over their otherwise ungovernable sexual behavior. The effect is reversible when the medication is stopped, without adverse side effects. The same medication promises also to be helpful in the regulation of violent temper outbursts in some temporal lobe epileptics (D. Blumer, personal communication).

The hormonal changes of pregnancy have no routinely systematic effect on woman's sex life. The mechanics of carrying a baby affect different women differently, as does the psychologic effect of the meaning of pregnancy and parenthood. Being a parent affects husband and wife equally and may have a profound effect, it goes without saying, on their opportunities for sexual behavior.

As with the hormonal changes of pregnancy, those of the menopause have no systematic effect on woman's sex life, except insofar as the vaginal mucosa may become atrophic and too dry, with an adverse effect on sexual intercourse. This effect can be be reversed by the judicious prescription of estrogen (which also will serve as a protection against osteoporosis). The direct effect of the hormonal changes of the menopause on mood and temperament varies widely, as does the effect of the psychologic meaning of having reached the end of childbearing; consequently, both of these effects themselves bear no systematic relationship to postmenopausal sexual behavior. It is important for many couples to know that the menopause does not mark the end of woman's sexual desire and ability. Her sexual life may continue, and even be improved, far into old age.

The male's sex life also may continue far into old age, unmarked by any such dramatic hormonal event as the menopause of the female. The refractory interval between erections and between orgasms lengthens as age increases, but with great individual variation. Failing potency can generally be improved in older men whose own androgen levels have declined by the judicious prescription of testosterone. Impotence not associated with a falling-off in androgen production is not improved by treatment with hormones, and the same holds true for frigidity in women.

Apart from the aging effect, deficit or impairment of sexual behavior and its frequency has many different etiologies, requiring considerable astuteness to establish a diagnosis. It is necessary to consider that the symptom of deficient or impaired sexual activity may be a sequel to: a genetic defect; an error of metabolism; an endocrine error; a mechanical, neurological or circulatory defect; a traumatic injury; an adverse psychologic reaction to illness (for example, after a heart attack) ; a primary psychiatric disorder (especially depression) ; a disturbance of personality and the interpersonal relationship of sex; or a lack of sufficient timing, variety or novelty of stimulation.

An excess of sexual activity is more often regarded boastfully as an asset rather than as a symptom. Yet it may be a symptom, especially when it represents a change from a former lesser level, together with a change in the type of behavior. The most likely diagnostic considerations then are: an endocrine error; a neurological error (particularly a trauma, tumor, or senile atrophy of the brain) ; a primary psychiatric disorder (especially mania or hypomania) ; or a disturbance of personality and the interpersonal relationship of sex.

PRINCIPLE OF GENITOPELVIC SENSATION

It all but belabors the obvious to say that one of the determinants of sexual behavior is the integrity of the sexual organs with which coitus is performed. Yet the fact of the matter is that large amounts of sexual tissue can be removed without destroying the capacity for erotic response (Money, 1961) . Following amputation of the penis, whether by accident or because of malignancy, orgasm is retained. Sexual desire remains as before, sometimes creating a serious problem of morale in being unable to satisfy the partner.

A more complete loss of penile tissue is entailed in sex-reassignment surgery for male transexualism, for the corpora are extirpated and only the skin retained as a lining for the new vagina (Jones, Schirmer and Hoopes, 1968). Postoperatively and living as females, transexuals claim they experience erotic satisfaction in the female sexual role, and some report a climactic feeling of orgasm which, if different than they formerly experienced as males, satisfies them more because they are able to be in the female role.

Penile tissue is not lost but the corpora are, in many cases, functionally destroyed as a sequel to priapism. Erection is impossible, Here again orgasm and desire for intercourse are retained, while the morale may be seriously injured.

The morale problem is, by contrast, quite different in cases of paraplegia (Money, 1960) where the loss is not of genital tissue, but of all spinal chord connection with the brain. The genitalia are able to respond reflexly to local tactile stimulation, but the patient has no feeling and awareness of what has happened. A paraplegic male has no erection in response to erotic thoughts and imagery. The nearest he gets to an orgasm is by dreaming one, and even sexual dreams disappear as the years pass after the paraplegic injury occurred. The paraplegic knows that he has lost his sex life and would elect, if he could, to have it returned, but there is none of the quality of urgency and frustration found in men whose genitals can perform only a part of their sexual function without completing it. Signals from the genitals are obviously a principal component or determinant of sexual behavior.

In women as in men, ablation of genital tissue is compatible with the retention of erotic sensation and orgasm. The evidence comes from women who undergo radical resection of the vulva for epidermoid cancer, and from hermaphroditic females whose hypertrophied clitoris is resected or extirpated. According to the evidence of genital ablation, an orgasm is an orgasm regardless of the stimulation that triggers it—which is precisely the verdict of the Masters and Johnson (1966) research into the human sexual response. These authors effectively put to rest the ghost of the old controversy of the clitoral versus the vaginal orgasm as a determinant of mature sexual behavior in the female.

PRINCIPLE OF DIMORPHIC SIGNALS

Over and beyond the specifics of genitopelvic sexual behavior, there is a vast amount of human behavior that is sexual in the sense that it is dimorphic in relation to gender: what men do one way, women do another. This kind of gender-related behavior ranges from fashions of dress to conventions of work and earning a living, from rules of etiquette and ceremony to labor-sharing in the home. Though these various stereotypes of what is masculine and what is feminine may ultimately derive from such fundamental sex differences as urinary posture, menstruation, childbearing, lactation, stature, weight, and muscular power, the conventions themselves are defined by custom and may be arbitrary and subject to sudden changes of fashion or slow changes in the cultural pattern. It does not matter that they change. It is the fact that they exist in any given time and place that counts, for we human beings are sensitively dependent on our cognition of the signals and cues emanating from others—they are determinants of our own sexual behavior, just as are plumage differences in birds. We differ from birds in being able to adapt and change the signals historically, but we cannot obliterate them altogether. There is no more convincing evidence in support of this principle than the fact that the average man or woman tends to accept the impersonation put forth by a transvestite or a transexual—provided of course, that it is a perfect or near-perfect impersonation. It is then possible to accept the impersonation, even after the truth is known, as being more genuine than the sex of the sex organs. It is even possible for a psychosexually normal person to fall in love with a transexual impersonator. Resolution of the incongruity between impersonation and the sex organs is then achieved by responding to the impersonator as someone beset by misfortune who is deserving or needing medical or surgical help. There is no more cogent illustration of how compelling is the influence of the senses over that of judgment in determining human sexual behavior!

PRINCIPLE OF CULTURAL DETERMINANTS

Cultural tradition determines not only the criteria of sexually dimorphic behavior, but also various criteria of sexual interaction. The variety of possibilities is extensive but not limitless, although the limits have not yet been catalogued. Variability can be classified as pertaining to the following characteristics of partnerships:

* age: same or disparate
* physique: juvenile, adolescent or adult
* sex: same or opposite
* kinship: related or not related by blood, clan or race
* caste or class: same or different
* number: unity or plurality of partnerships
* time: sequential or contemporaneous partnerships, or one partnership only
* span: transient or constant partnerships

* privacy: public or concealed
* accessories: plain or modified by material artifacts, e.g., personal ornament, contraceptive device, etc.

To illustrate: the people of the lake region of northern Sumatra live in a cultural tradition that permits an age difference in a sexual partnership, ranging over the entire spectrum of physique, but only in homosexual and not heterosexual partnerships. In late childhood, it is not decent for children to stay sleeping in their parents' single-roomed house. A girl takes her sleeping mat to the home of a widow or old woman who accommodates about half a dozen girls who range in age from prepuberty to late adolescence. A boy joins a group of a dozen to fifteen males, his own age or older, who sleep in a boys' house specially constructed for them. There he learns from the adolescents and young men how to participate in paired homosexual play with them or older boys:[1] primarily mutual masturbation of penis held against penis, maybe anal coitus, but never fellatio. All members of the group may become one member's partner, in rotation. Relationships are not necessarily unobserved, but they are always in pairs, not in larger groups. Partnerships among group members do not involve falling in love, but they are constant up to the point where a young man opts to leave the group by marrying. No man is permitted to remain a bachelor.

When he is ready to marry, a young man asks his close friends to join him in a prescribed etiquette of approaching the chosen girl and his own family, to see if they have the wealth to pay the bride price and put on a wedding festival.

The young man in search of a wife narrates the procedure of his courtship to his companions in the boys' house. Once married, he discloses details about sexual intercourse. In this way information is transmitted down the generations, and a young adolescent is prepared to anticipate his graduation from the era of homosexual experience to heterosexual falling-in-love and marriage.

The homosexual era in adolescence, by sequestering the sexes, ensures that young women will be virgins until married. The sanctions against premarital sex are stringent, so that a girl who is discovered in transgression probably commits suicide. Once a marriage is effected, the parties discontinue homosexuality, though men away on working parties in the jungle may temporarily resume them.

---

[1] Information about homosexuality among females is conjectural among males, as talk about sexual activities, except between husband and wife, is taboo between the sexes.

By contrast with the allowable age disparities in homosexual partnerships, the heterosexual partnership is formed between people of like age in young adulthood, or else the girl may be younger, in her teens, than the' man, in his twenties. The relationship between the pair may be as close as cousins, but there is no special kinship obligation in the choice of a partner. There is a preference for partnerships within the racial-linguistic group. Marriage is the first and only heterosexual partnerships, except for remarriage after the early death of one of the spouses. A marriage cannot otherwise be broken. Being married is, of course, publicly announced. The coital relationship of marriage is, by convention private and unobserved, except that young children may awaken when the parents are copulating. They then must not disclose their observation, but ignore it. According to the formalities of the culture, they learn about sex not at home, but from their adolescent and young adult friends.

Changing Sexual Traditions in Our Society

The cultural traditions of a lakeside village in Sumatra have been able to survive intact for an unspecified number of generations, but now, under the impact of cultural contact through education and broadcasting, these traditions are yielding to change. Change is a hallmark of the cultural traditions of our own society in the present age of instantaneous broadcast communication, nuclear-space technology and, in matters sexual, effective contraception. Whereas to some, the change in sexual traditions is anathema, to others it is utopia, but to none is it very clear, what, exactly, is happening. In terms of the seven schematic categories above-listed, one may suggest the following. There has been no change of tradition with respect to a preference for pairing couples of similar age, with continuing toleration of a few exceptions of disparity within the adult years. There is still a rigid rule against juvenile sexual play, though the age of "sex education" is subject to radical downward revision, amidst sometimes acrimonious social controversy. There is no issue more heated than that of the rights of adolescents and young adults to have sexual and love affairs premaritally, with or without intention to marry and/or have children. The trend is toward greater freedom. Sanctions against homosexuality are being examined and eased, though ambivalently, in favor of consensual agreements between adults. Problems of kinship in mating continue to be singularly unimportant, so long as the incest taboo is respected. The issue of miscegenation is so explosive that it can scarcely be mentioned in public and political discussion, perhaps because it is a foregone conclusion that black-white intermarriage will become routine. Class and caste preferences and distinctions in sexual pairing remain otherwise about the same as ever.

The leading pressure point of change in our society's sexual traditions would seem to be toward a greater plurality of sexual relationships, for females as well as males, on a basis of mutual reciprocity. This change is registered in sequential more often than contemporaneous plurality of relationships, before or after marriage. Even contemporaneous relationships are constant, over a period of time, rather than transient. Availability of effective contraception is undoubtedly the material artifact that underlies this cultural change, though in the case of serial marriage and divorce, with children to be supported, the economic and legal emancipation of women is also a major factor. Despite the plurality of partnerships, the preference is still for episodic monogamy or fidelity, rather than running more than one affair contemporaneously. However, a new institution, its future still uncertain, is the "swinging scene" of partner exchanging and group sex, coexistent and compatible with contractual marriage and long-term loyalty and emotional allegiance to one partner.

Participation in any sexual relationship outside of marriage is still subject to at least a partial need for concealment, though increasing freedom is accorded to young adults to be frank and open about their non-marital sexual liaisons and living together. Coitus itself is still subject to the rule of privacy, though some group sex participants are indifferent to being observed or to engaging in activities with more than one partner simultaneously.

Whether or not these changes in sexual tradition constitute a sexual revolution or are simply variations of basic primate behavior has become a subject for rhetoric and politics as well as for science and medicine. The reader must formulate his own conclusions.

REFERENCES

BURNS, R. K. Role of hormones in the differentiation of sex. In *Sex and Internal Secretions*, W. C. Young, editor. Williams and Wilkins, Baltimore, 1961.

CHANG, C. Y. & WITSCHI, E. Breeding of Sex-reversed Males of Xenopus Laevis Daudin. Proceedings of the Society for Experimental Biology and Medicine, 89:150-152, 1955.

CHANG, C. Y. & WITSCHI, E. Genic Control and Hormonal reversal of sex differentiation in Xenopus. Proceedings of the Society for Experimental Biology and Medicine, 93:140-144, 1956.

EHRHARDT, A. A. & MONEY, J. Progestin-induced Hermaphroditism: IQ and Psychosexual Identity in a Study of Ten Girls. *J. Sex Res.*, 3:83-100, 1967.

EHRHARDT, A. A., EPSTEIN, R., & MONEY, J. Fetal Androgens and Female Gender Identity in the Early-treated Adrenogenital Syndrome. *The Johns Hopkins Medical Journal*, 122:165-167, 1968.

FISHER, A. E. Maternal and Sexual Behavior Induced by Intracranial Chemical Stimulation. *Science*, 124:228-229, 1956.

FISHER, A. E. Chemical and Electrical Stimulation of the Brain in the Male Rat. In *The Brain and Gonodal Function*, Vol. III of *Brain and Behavior*, P. A. Gorski and R. E. Whalen, editors. University of California Press, Berkeley, 1966.

GORSKI, R. Sexual Differentiation of the Hypothalamus. Paper delivered at a Symposium on *The Neuroendocrinology of Human Reproduction*, Wayne State University, Detroit, Michigan, 1968.

GRANT, E. C. G. & PRYSE-DAVIES, J. Effect of Oral Contraceptives on Depressive Mood Changes and on Endometrical Monoamine Oxidase and Phosphatases. *Brit. Med. J.*, 3:777-780, 1968.

HAMILTON, J. B., WALTER, R. O., DANIEL, R. M., & MESTLER, G. E. Supermales (YY Sex Chromosomes) and Ordinary Males (XY): Competition for Mating with Females. *Animal Behavior*, in press.

HARLOW, H. F. & HARLOW, M. K. The Effect of Rearing Conditions on Behavior. In *Sex Research, New Developments*, J. Money, editor. Holt, Rinehart and Winston, New York, 1965.

HARRIS, G. W. Sex Hormones, Brain Development and Brain Function. *Endocrinology*, 75:627-648, 1964.

HERBERT, J. The Social Modification of Sexual Behavior in the Rhesus Monkey. *Progress in Primatology*, First Congress of the International Primatological Society, pp. 222-246, 1966.

JONES, H. W., SCHIRMER, H. K. A., & HOOPES, J. E. A Sex Conversion Operation for Males with Transsexualism. *Amer. J. Obstet. and Gynecol.*, 100:101-109, 1968.

KOLLAR, E. J., BECKWITH, W. C., & EDGERTON, R. B. Sexual Behavior of the ARL Colony Chimpanzees. *J. Nerv. Ment. Dis.*, 147:444-459, 1968.

MACLEAN, P. D. New Findings Relevant to the Evolution of Psychosexual Functions of the Brain. In *Sex Research, New Developments*, J. Money, Editor. Holt, Rinehart and Winston, New York, 1965.

MASICA, D. N., MONEY, J., EHRHARDT, A. A., & LEWIS, V. G. IQ, Fetal Sex Hormones and Cognitive Patterns: Studies in the Testicular Feminizing Syndrome of Androgen Insensitivity. *The Johns Hopkins Medical Journal*, 124::34-43, 1969.

MASTERS, W. H. & JOHNSON, V. E. *Human Sexual Response*. Little, Brown, Boston, 1966.

MIKAMO, K. & WITSCHI, E. Functional Sex-reversal in Genetic Females of Xenopus Laevis, Induced by Implanted Testes. *Genetics*, 48:1411-1421, 1963.

MONEY, J. Phantom Orgasm in the Dreams of Paraplegic Men and Women. *Arch. Gen. Psychiat.*, 3:373-382, 1960.

MONEY, J. Components of Eroticism in Man. I: The Hormones in Relation to Sexual Morphology and Sexual Desire. *J. Nerv. Ment. Dis.*, 132:239-248, 1961.

MONEY, J. Components of Eroticism in Man. II: The Orgasm and Genital Somesthesia. *J. Nerv. Ment. Dis.*, 132:289-297, 1961.

MONEY, J. Influence of Hormones on Sexual Behavior. In *Annual Review of Medicine*, Vol. 16, A. C. Degraff, editor. Annual Reviews, Inc., Palo Alto, pp. 67-82, 1965.

MONEY, J. Hermaphroditism and Pseudohermaphroditism. In *Textbook of Gynecologic Endocrinology*, J. J. Gold, editor. Harper and Row, New York, 1968.

MONEY, J. Discussion: Clinical Effects of Agents Affecting Fertility. (Antiandrogen to Control Behaviour.) In *Endocrinology and Human Behaviour*, R. P. Michael, editor. Oxford University Press, London, 1968.

MONEY, J. Sex Reassignment as Related to Hermaphroditism and Transsexualism. In *Transsexualism and Sex Reassignment*, R. Green and J. Money, editors. Johns Hopkins Press, Baltimore, 1969.

MONEY, J. & ALEXANDER, D. Eroticism and Sexual Function in Developmental Anorchia and Hyporchia with Pubertal Failure. *J. Sex Res.*, 3:31-47, 1967.

MONEY, J., EHRHARDT, A. A., & MASICA, D. M. Fetal Feminization Induced by Androgen Insensitivity in the Testicular Feminizing Syndrome: Effect on Marriage and Maternalism. *The Johns Hopkins Medical Journal*, 123:105-114, 1968.

MONEY, J. & MITTENTHAL, S. *Personality Development in Relation to Cytogenetics and Physique: Turner's Syndrome.* In press.

NEUMANN, F. & ELGER, W. Proof of the Activity of Androgenic Agents on the Differentiation of the External Genitalia, the Mammary Gland and the Hypothalamic-Pituitary System in Rats. *Excerpta Medica*, International Congress Series No. 101: *Androgens in Normal and Pathological Conditions*, pp. 169-185, 1965.

NEUMANN, F. & ELGER, W. Permanent Changes in Gonadal Function and Sexual Behavior as a Result of Early Feminization of Male Rats by Treatment with an Antiandrogenic Steroid. *Endokrinologie*, 50:209-225, 1966.

PETRIE, A. *Individuality in Pain and Suffering.* University of Chicago Press, Chicago, 1967.

PHOENIX, C. Psychosexual Organization in Nonhuman Primates. Paper delivered at the Conference on Endocrine and Neural Control of Sex and Related Behavior. Puerto Rico, Dorado Beach, 1966.

TRIMBLE, M. R. & HERBERT, J. The Effect of Testosterone or Oestradiol upon the Sexual and Associated Behavior of the Adult Female Rhesus Monkey. *J. Endocrinology*, 42:171-185, 1968.

WILKINS, L. *The Diagnosis and Treatment of Endocrine Disorders in Childhood and Adolescence*, Third Edition. Charles C. Thomas, Springfield, Ill., 1965.

WITSCHE, E. Etiology of Gonadal Agenesis and Sex Reversal. In *Gestation, Transactions of the Third Conference*, C. A. Villee, editor. Princeton, 1956.

WITSCHI, E. Hormones and Embryonic Induction. *Archives D'anatomie Microscopique et de Morphologie Experimentale*, 54:601-611, 1965.

YAMAMOTO, T. Harmonic Factors Affecting Gonadal Differentiation in Fish. *General and Comparative Endocrinology*, Suppl. 1, 311-345, 1962.

YOUNG, W. C., GOY, R. W., & PHOENIX, C. H. Hormones and Sexual Behavior. In *Sex Research, New Developments*, J. Money, editor. Holt, Rinehart and Winston, New York, 1965.

Area IV

SPECIAL PATIENT POPULATIONS

To the extent that treatment is empirical, in contrast to rational, i.e. based on intuition rather than on a clear understanding of etiology, its effects are essentially accidental. It is not surprising, therefore, that treatment results with the many prevalent disorders whose causes remain obscure are still disappointing. With respect to the most urgent of these, schizophrenia, family studies have made invaluable contributions to the quest for rational treatment by identifying the family components of schizophrenia, and also by translating this data into clinically useful therapeutic tactics.

However, outcome of treatment may be poor even when causes are apparent. Here too the group modalities offer hope in part by drawing attention to the environmental factors that tended to be underemphasized by older treatment methods. Therefore, the promising group and family modalities are being explored and applied to many problem syndromes with the hope of improving their prognosis. These experiments are encouraging, but their final impact on specific disorders remains to be evaluated.

THE SECTIONS

The greatest payoff of these efforts has come from family studies of schizophrenia which have yielded promising novel treatment strategies and, more significantly, immensely important theoretical contributions as well. The following Section IV-A contains four papers that reflect both clinical and conceptual issues of current interest on this important subject.

The second section in this area, IV-B, contains papers that describe encouraging experimental group approaches with a variety of problem patients: homosexuals, the aged and adolescents.

H.S.K.
C.J.S.

Area IV—Section A
SCHIZOPHRENIA

Although schizophrenia remains in many respects a mystery, current treatment is much improved and the enigma is beginning to unravel. Family psychiatry has made substantial contributions to these advances. The papers in this section deal with accomplishments in separate aspects of this complex field. Therefore, in order to place them into perspective, a brief synopsis relevant to family therapy is presented.

HISTORICAL PERSPECTIVES

Originally considered to be either a toxic psychosis or an irreversible state of profound psychic regression, schizophrenia was regarded as hopelessly incurable. Later Fromm-Reichmann and others demonstrated that psychotherapeutic contact with schizophrenic patients could be made providing the therapist transcends conventional psychoanalytic concepts, and schizophrenia was readmitted to the ranks of the treatable disorders. Although the early psychotherapeutic efforts increased our understanding of schizophrenic psychodynamics, the outcome of treatment remained unpredictable and often disappointing.

In the early fifties the introduction of antipsychotic medication dramatically improved the treatment and prognosis of schizophrenia. These drugs rapidly eliminate, or at least substantially improve acute psychotic symptoms in the majority of patients. However, the drugs do not cure all. Their therapeutic effects appear to be limited to calming the frightened patient and to diminishing the acute disturbances of thought and perceptual processes. Unfortunately the basic vulnerability as well as the learned components of schizophrenia do not seem materially improved by medication, and so a large share of the burden of treatment must still be borne by psychological methods.

Nevertheless, the benefits of drug treatment are enormous in shortening the psychotic episode, and preventing deterioration, and facilitating psychotherapeutic contact. Thus the impact of phenothiazines shifted the treatment of schizophrenia primarily to an ambulatory basis.

Treating schizophrenics while they are living at home with their families soon revealed that family transactions play a crucial role in the vicissitudes of the disorder, while comparable observations implicating pathogenic influences of family relationships were made by clinicians working with schizophrenic children.

For these compelling reasons, investigators became interested in studying the families of schizophrenic patients. The investigations sought to clarify the influence of the ongoing family transactions on the current illness and also to identify possible early causal variables. It was found that the majority of schizophrenic patients come from clearly disturbed families having strange relationships, peculiar patterns of communications and other pathological features. An extensive literature describes specific peculiarities that are highly prevalent in families that produce schizophrenic offspring.

The hypothesis emerged that pathological family transactions, communications and relationships are primary causes of schizophrenia. Accordingly, it was said that the schizophrenic patient could best be understood as an integral part of the pathological family system. Indeed, schizophrenia was viewed by some as an expression, not of intrapsychic difficulties, but of the pathological family.

However, a comprehensive concept of schizophrenia must also account for compelling data which indicate that there are significant genetic contributions to schizophrenia, apart from the experiential factors that have been identified by family and psychodynamic studies. The genetic hypothesis has received strong support from an array of modern twin studies and also from several recent investigations of the offspring of schizophrenics who were reared from infancy by non-relatives. These studies all consistently show an appreciably higher incidence of schizophrenia or "schizophrenic-spectrum" disorders among biological relatives of schizophrenic patients.

A popular current genetic hypothesis recently reviewed by Rosenthal holds that the inherited components of schizophrenia have a polygenic basis, and that their expression is variously affected by experiential factors. According to this view, individuals harboring a "high dose" of "schizophrenic genes" have a high risk of manifesting the clinical illness, even if they are reared in relatively normal circumstances. "Low dose"

● Rosenthal, D., "Genetic Research in the Schizophrenic Syndrome," in *The Schizophrenic Reactions*, R. Cancro, Ed. Brunner/Mazel, N. Y., 1970.

individuals, on the other hand, have a lower risk and become clinically ill only under pathogenic conditions. The characteristics of the family environment which either facilitates or conversely protects against the symptomatic expression of schiophrenia in vulnerable individuals are not clearly understood and are currently the subject of intensive study in family psychiatry.

CURRENT CONCEPT

A model of schizophrenia, as a multicausal disorder that has a wide spectrum of clinical manifestations accommodates current data from the diverse genetic, biochemical, family and clinical studies on the subject. In clinical terms this model suggests that it may be useful for clinicians treating schizophrenics to regard the condition as a "psychosomatic" disease of the brain, or at any rate of brain functioning. Accordingly, thought processes that are reflected in such crucial functions as reasoning, discrimination of fantasy from reality and handling of sensory input, as well as emotional stability, are highly vulnerable in the schizophrenic and may disorganize under stress. Thus, as with other psychosomatic disorders, the therapist intervenes in a dual manner. In the acute phase he stabilizes the vulnerable "end organ," i.e., the brain, with antipsychotic medication, and also at the same time intervenes in various ways to reduce the immediate psychic and environmental pressures on the patient. After the acute phase is under control, the aim of treatment is to identify the specific intrapsychic and environmental stresses that have made the patient ill and help him master these and so prevent recurrence of acute psychosis. Unfortunately, present treatment methods cannot reverse the basic vulnerability. However, schizophrenia has proved to be highly amenable to interventions that modify psychosocial sources of stress.

ROLE OF FAMILY TREATMENT IN SCHIZOPHRENIA

According to current concepts, pathogenic family factors are prominent among the sources of stress that may precipitate and perpetuate schizophrenic illness. These operate both on an environmental and on an intrapsychic level, and the therapist intervenes in both.

Thus, if the patient is currently living with his family, the probability is high that his current relationships with his parents and siblings are ambivalent and emotionally stressful and so are impeding his recovery. If such is the case, conjoint family therapy which aims to resolve and modify the family pressures may be indicated.

In addition, early pathogenic transactions with family members may lead to crippling conflicts and also to pathological ways of relating to others which also add to the schizophrenic's problem. Modification of such intrapsychic and interpersonal determinants is the ultimate aim of psychotherapy with these patients. Understanding the typical "schizophrenogenic" family transactions thus aids the therapist in formulating a rational psychotherapeutic approach, as illustrated in Lidz's paper on this subject in this section.

Unresolved Issues

In summary, recent data deriving from family studies suggest that schizophrenia has a variable genetic component, that interacts in some manner with as yet unidentified experiential factors to produce clinical illness. If this model is confirmed, compelling questions are raised: What is inherited? Is it a faulty biochemical response to stress? A deficiency in information processing? Certain maladaptive reaction patterns? A perceptual style? What are the characteristics of the experiential family factors that precipitate and conversely protect against the development of schizophrenia? What is the role of the pathological family factors that have been identified as prevalent in families that produce schizophrenic off-spring? Do they cause a youngster to develop schizophrenia or is the schizophrenic member simply more sensitive to, and therefore unable to cope with, difficulties in communications that a normal youngster could handle without damage? Perhaps a non-schizophrenic youngster can handle double-bind messages without difficulties, while his brother who harbors "schizo-genes" is unable to make the appropriate discriminations? Is a schizophrenic produced by a peculiar family or does the presence of a schizophrenic member produce a peculiar family? Or both?

And finally—how may such information be applied to the treatment and the prevention of schizophrenia?

THE PAPERS

We have selected four outstanding papers which address themselves to some of these issues.

The first and final papers of this section are by Lyman Wynne whose views have had a powerful and well-deserved impact on the field. Wynne has been working towards a synthesis and comprehensive understanding of the genetic and experiential components of schizophrenia. He feels that certain behavioral reaction tendencies are genetically determined, while evidence suggests that specific aberrant family communication patterns predispose vulnerable persons to clinical schizophrenia. In the first of Wynne's papers he describes his finding that the communications of schizophrenics are ineffective for establishing normal relatedness with others. Wynne feels that this communication failure reveals fundamental deficits in the schizophrenic's basic "attentional-response disposition."

In the final paper in this section, Wynne expands the thesis that both the constitutional and experiential determinants of schizophrenia need to be more precisely identified and described in order to develop rational treatment and prevention methods. In this paper he discusses strategies for investigating this problem by means of longitudinal studies of families who are likely to produce schizophrenic offspring.

The second paper is by Lidz, who has studied the families of schizophrenic patients intensively for many years and in this paper exquisitely translates his vast knowledge into a therapeutic approach. He has identified what appear to be crucial determinants of schizophrenic pathology that stem from the patient's pathological interactions with his relatives. The aim of treatment is to reverse the psychic effects of these family interactions. Lidz's identification of prevalent pathogenic family relationships provides a highly rational scheme for individual as well as family therapy with the schizophrenic patient.

The third paper describes the fascinating observations and experiences of trained observers who "lived in" with families containing a schizophrenic parent. Anthony's findings that the patient may exert very powerful and pathological emotionally "contagious" effects upon the non-schizophrenic members of the family are of great interest to the clinician and to the investigator interested in preventive psychiatry.

SUGGESTED CROSS-REFERENCES

Family therapy exclusively or in combination with other therapeutic modalities is considered by many authorities to be the treatment of choice for schizophrenia. Thus, although not explicitly stated, all the papers in Area II, are in fact relevant to the treatment of schizophrenia. Specifically, Framo conceptualizes various schizophrenic symptoms as deriving from pathological family interactions. Speck and Attneave employ their "Network Therapy" techniques to manipulate pathological environmental influences, and cite a case of a schizophrenic patient treated by this method. Auerswald illustrates his ecological approach, which similarly is based on the concept of helping the patient by changing his environment, with a report of the impact of this method on a schizophrenic girl. Laquer in his article on multiple family therapy based his report on studies done with families that have had a member hospitalized because of schizophrenia.

Two papers, one by Pittman and Flomenhaft treating the "Doll's House" marriage and the other by Whittaker and Miller, on psychiatric intervention in impending divorce, both in Area III, discuss the clinical implications and dangers of treating couples who have created in their marriage a system that enables the schizophrenic spouse to function without decompensating.

Finally, in Section I—*Group Therapy*, Drs. Yalom and Lieberman, in their fascinating paper that evaluates the casualties of encounter groups, describe the patients who tend to react adversely to certain types of encounter group experiences as having "pre-existing pathology, poor ego-coping methods, low self-esteem and unrealistic expectations" as compared to low risk patients. It may be speculated that the authors are actually describing some of the schizophrenic and borderline patients who are highly represented among the casualties of intense group encounters.

H.S.K.
C.J.S.

36

COMMUNICATION DISORDERS AND THE QUEST FOR RELATEDNESS IN FAMILIES OF SCHIZOPHRENICS

Lyman C. Wynne, M.D., Ph.D.

Professor and Chairman, Department of Psychiatry
University of Rochester School of Medicine and Dentistry
Psychiatrist-in-Chief, Strong Memorial Hospital (Rochester)

We have much to learn from schizophrenics and their families—even more from them than about them—and, in so doing, about all of us. These families, as I seem them, starkly reveal pitfalls in dealing with a pervasive human problem—how to establish and maintain meaningful relatedness with one's fellows. The typical ways in which these families try to solve this problem are shared with many who are never officially designated as schizophrenic; and many others spend their lives in busy preoccupation with this same issue, or in careful avoidance and denial of its meaning.

My approach to this complex subject can be introduced by noting a striking contrast between two views of interpersonal relationships— between relatedness experienced primarily as a goal in its own right, and relatedness experienced more as a means for the fulfillment of some other task or objective.

In the first view of relatedness, which I shall call *expressive,* meaning- ful feelings, including experiences of warmth, affection, and in the broad-

This paper was presented before the Association for the Advancement of Psycho- analysis, March 25, 1970, at the Academy of Medicine, New York City as the Eight- eenth Annual Karen Horney Lecture. Reprinted by permission of the Editor of THE AMERICAN JOURNAL OF PSYCHOANALYSIS, 1970, Volume 30, No. 2, pp. 100-114.

est sense, human contact, are sought directly and immediately, without preliminaries, often in a rush of what is called "spontaneity." The content and the external task, if any, in the interaction are given secondary importance. Perhaps the fantasy about, and sometimes the experience in, the relatedness of mother and infant is both an example and a source of this form of relatedness. Romantic love is ordinarily regarded as taking this mode. And, in encounter and sensitivity training groups, directness in the immediate relation of the here-and-now is usually regarded as a primary, and ultimate, goal.

In the second, *instrumental* view of relatedness, greater value is given by the interacting persons to tasks and foci of attention external to themselves. The interpersonal relation is sometimes experienced as necessary or useful in pursuit or execution of a task, but is not valued in itself apart from its instrumental utility. The relationship of salesman and customer, of doctor and patient, are examples of this form of relatedness when the primary emphasis is on getting a job done.

To be sure, I have diagrammed extremes. What has started as a task-oriented relationship may become something much more personal and enduring. And what has begun in an affectionate glow may become a bond serving other purposes. Those relationships which seem most stable and reliably open to renewal and rejuvenation include both forms of experience. They are built up out of countless shared specific communicative interchanges—sustained participation together in specific tasks and in focused attention on the same events, comments and expressions of feelings. Such interchange defines and gives structure to the relationship, sometimes by explicit metacommunication but always including at least an implicit comment about the nature of the relationship (1, 2).

This formulation implies that communicative skills, both in understanding and carrying out goal-directed tasks and in the use of language and paralanguage, are a prerequisite for enduring relatedness. Actually, even in the seemingly spontaneous and incipient relatedness of mother and infant, considerable communicative skill is needed by both. Not only does the mother respond to signals of hunger, distress and contentment produced by the infant, but the infant must have the inborn capacity to produce these signals strongly enough so the mother can detect them, but modulated enough so she is not thrown into panic or agitation by them. The warmest initial attachment of mother and infant will have trouble flourishing and unfolding if an appropriate communicative "fit" through multiple specific interchanges is not achieved.

NOTES OF A GENERALIZED CONCEPT OF COMMUNICATION

My comments thus far imply a particular concept of communication processes. In this formulation, which can be outlined only very schematically here, there are three major levels: 1) the specific *message* or focal content to which shared attention is given in communication; 2) the *task* in which the communicating persons are engaged; and 3) the more or less enduring interpersonal *relationship,* which both provides a context for the task and the message and also is an intrinsic ingredient in the communication process as a whole.*

Let me exemplify what I mean by the levels or components of communication with a sequence from a tape-recorded Rorschach protocol of the communication between a psychologist and a 17-year-old girl, whom I shall call Amy. She was clinically diagnosed as a hebephrenic, "process" schizophrenic. In this paper, communications by this girl and her family will be used repeatedly for illustrative purposes.

The examiner introduced herself by name and as a psychologist. Assuming that Amy would fit into a conventional, unstated *relationship* context of examiner-subject, she proceeded to spell out the standard instructions for the Rorschach *task* in which the subject is asked to describe what she thinks the inkblots resemble. The psychologist completed the instructions and handed the card to Amy who threw it up in the air and then tapped it on the edge of the table. Despite these non-verbal messages suggesting a lack of readiness to join in the tester's task, she then responded:

"This looks like the back of your body." [By giving this *focal content,* Amy seemed to be communicating in accord with the task defined by the tester, but the "your body" suggests something more personal]

Tester: "O.K."

Amy: "That's all."

Tester: "Will you hold it a minute longer and see if something else comes to your mind?"

Amy: "O.K. What is your name?" [Tester had previously introduced herself.]

Tester: "Mrs. Thompson."

Amy: "Mrs. Who?"

Tester: "Mrs. Thompson."

---

* In the formulation of Watzlawick, Beavin and Jackson (2), content and relationship levels of communication are distinguished. However, these authors do not clearly delineate the here-and-now *task* in communication; perhaps they would subsume "task" under "relationship." Most "tasks" include numerous messages, but within a given relationship, extending over time, multiple, diverse tasks may be carried out.

Amy: "Mrs. Who?"

Tester: "Thompson."

Amy: "My name is Amy."

Tester: "Yes, Amy."

Amy: "Can we be friends?" [Amy wanted to clarify and define the relationship in her own terms.]

Tester: "Yep. Right." [Tester probably wanted to pass over Amy's redefinition of the relationship and to continue with the task.]

Amy: "I don't want to do this." [It sounds as if Amy felt that this task should not be part of a relationship between friends.]

Tester: "Well, look, you try to hold it a minute longer and see if anything else comes to your mind." [Task-orientation.]

Amy: "It looks like ah-ah—It looks like a [sigh]—it-it looks like a bat." [A popular response on this card.]

In this interchange the *content* of the particular percepts was not especially remarkable, and Amy appeared to understand the *task* which the psychologist had described. However, a serious communicational problem at the *relationship* level was apparent: Amy's understanding and preference about the relationship obviously differed from Mrs. Thompson's. Going on in this protocol, on the next Rorschach card, Amy asked:

Amy: "You going to help me here?"

Tester: "Mmmhnn. Certainly." [Speaking crisply, conveying in her tone of voice that she would prefer *not* to help.]

Amy: "I think this looks like the part of your front. Your stomach." (Tester: "Mmmhmm.") "A hole in the sto—not your stomach, but a hole in it. I like to touch people's navels."

And later, in the inquiry about this response:

Tester: "What made you think of a stomach?"

Amy: "Because it has a hole in your stomach."

COMMUNICATION DISORDER AND SCHIZOPHRENIC "THINKING DISORDERS"

In most situations Amy showed marked evidence of what is traditionally called "thinking disorder." In the above sequence such a disorder was not apparent initially but could be inferred from her tangential, "loose association" about people's navels and from the odd sentence structure and strange reasoning in the last response quoted here. One should keep in mind that the "thinking disorder" of schizophrenics, still regarded as the most crucial diagnostic feature is an *inference* by psychiatrists derived by looking at the language behavior or message level of communication. Typically, the psychiatrist defines in his own terms what he believes the context should be for the relationship and task levels of the communication in which the language behavior is embedded. Although patients may not share the same task-orientation or, as with Amy, be more preoccupied with the relationship level, psychiatrists are especially alert to messages or language which are at odds with the task which they have defined. For example, Eugen Bleuler described schizophrenic associations as "subordinated to some sort of general idea, but they are not related and directed by any unifying concept of purpose of goal" (3).

In terms of the concept of communication I am proposing here, one can restate Bleuler's formulation, in its application to the quoted Rorschach interchange, as follows: The patient is preoccupied with a personal, direct bodily relationship with the psychologist, who, in contrast, is more concerned with attending to the task and content levels of communication. When this patient's communications are viewed at the task and content levels, both in this excerpt and in many other clinical contacts, she seems to become more and more "disordered" in her "thinking" at the same time that there is, in fact, more and more reason for her to feel puzzled, uncomfortable or annoyed about the relationship in which she finds herself. This view of schizophrenic language and thought disorder is in accord with that of Sullivan: "The schizophrenic's speech shows characteristic peculiarities because of recurrent severe disturbances in his relationships with other people and the result is a confusion of the critical faculties concerning the structure of spoken and written language" (4).

Schizophrenics seem to have a profound distrust of the conventional meaning of language. They doubt that they can use language to improve their interpersonal relationships, or they are suspicious that language may be used malevolently to impair still further their relationships. Furthermore, although at an earlier time in their lives many of them believed that successful task-orientation would bring better relationships, this trust has not been confirmed by later experience; sharing language and tasks with others comes to be regarded as empty, meaningless and sometimes dangerous. Nevertheless, the remarkable fact is that despite a long and painful history of communicative perplexity and disaster, most schizophrenics remain enduringly responsive to the *potentiality* of relatedness. Searles (5) has vividly described the incredible personal loyalty of schizophrenics to their mothers, despite multitudinous events that would seem to undermine and discourage such feelings. However, schizophrenics are both fearful and unskilled in building up relationships through sharing in tasks and specific messages. Instead, when they renew their quest of relatedness, they attempt to do so directly and immediately—sometimes with a measure of success, temporarily, but all too often with a failure of reciprocity. When a degree of reciprocity is achieved, as in some long-term psychotherapeutic relationships, this unfortunately may have little carry-over for tasks and language usage in the context of other relationships.

SOCIOPATHIC COMMUNICATION

Despite the grave risk of overgeneralizing, I wish to note, at least schematically, a sharp contrast in the way in which relatedness fits into the communication patterns of so-called sociopaths and delinquents, compared to that found with the schizophrenics I have been describing. My thoughts on this subject have been stimulated by discussions with my colleague, Dr. Helm Stierlin. Sociopaths are typically very skillful at the levels of task-orientation and focal attention, often quite "slick" in their skill in achieving success in goal-directed tasks. However, relatedness is not sought in its own right, but is disparaged and used instrumentally as a means for achieving particular goals. The "con man" thus exploits relationships, uses people, and then drops them; they are no longer needed. The sociopath tends to regard interpersonal failures as bad luck or bad tactics, and continues in his exploitative way undaunted by interpersonal rebuffs in his pursuit of prestige, money, or other similar goals. He does not grasp why he is ultimately rejected or avoided when the quality of his participation in relationships is understood for what it is.

RELATEDNESS IN THE FAMILIES OF SCHIZOPHRENICS

A number of years ago my colleagues and I at the National Institute of Mental Health became impressed, on the basis of intensive psychotherapeutic work with the non-diagnosed members of families of schizophrenics, that the *whole family,* not just the identified patient, was typically caught up in an overriding preoccupation with the issue of establishing a *sense* of relatedness, even at the expense of the self-differentiation of the persons in the relationship and also at the expense of goal-directedness and language usage that has general acceptance in the broader community (6). We described three forms of relatedness: mutuality, non-mutuality and pseudo-mutuality.

"In pseudo-mutuality emotional investment is directed more toward maintaining the *sense* of reciprocal fulfillment of expectations than toward accurately perceiving changing expectations. Thus, the new expectations are left unexplored, and the old expectations and roles, even though outgrown, and inappropriate in one sense, continue to serve as the structure for the relation. . . .

"With growth and situational changes, altered expectations inevitably come into any relation. Then, at least transient nonfulfillment of expectations—that is, noncomplementarity—necessarily occurs. In pseudo-mutuality, the subjective tension aroused by divergence or independence of expectations, including the open affirmation of a sense of personal identity, is experienced as not merely disrupting that particular transaction but as possibly demolishing the entire relation.

"The alternative outcome is overlooked or cannot be awaited: that the recognition and exploration of difference may lead to an expanded or deepened, although altered, basis for the relation. Genuine mutuality, unlike pseudo-mutuality, not only tolerates divergence of self-interests, but thrives upon the recognition of such natural and inevitable divergence. In terms of role theory, a relation of mutuality is experienced as having a larger context than a particular role so that particular items of role noncomplementarity can occur as a stimulus rather than as a disruption to the relation as a whole" (6).

Later, I pointed out that pseudo-hostile relationships, in which the preoccupation is to maintain contact through enduringly unresolved bickering and turmoil, are dynamically very similar to pseudo-mutuality. Despite the difference in content, both pseudo-mutuality and pseudo-hostility help maintain vulnerable relationships in which it is feared that underlying wishes and impulses, opposite to those overtly expressed, would destroy the relationship (7). For example, tenderness and affection are experienced in pseudo-hostile relations as dangerous and destructive, sometimes as engulfing, sometimes an incestuous; embroiled bickering, no matter how unpleasant, is safer for the relationship (8).

FAMILY RESEARCH OBSERVATIONS

After working with ideas such as these on a clinical basis, particularly in conjoint family therapy, my colleagues and I about a decade ago began to add to our program other methods by which we could systematically evaluate family communication. The data that we have accumulated are too extensive to summarize here, but I would like to select certain findings which are especially relevant to the viewpoint being presented here.

1) *Individual Rorschach Evaluations*: Dr. Margaret Thaler Singer

and I have conducted a series of studies in which we have used the Rorschach technique in an unorthodox way (9, 10). We have regarded transcripts of verbatim, tape-recorded Rorschach transactions between a psychologist and a subject, not primarily as a means of studying percepts and projective fantasies, but rather as a relatively standardized starting point for sampling communication. We have been especially interested in evaluating what happens to the relationship between tester and subject and how the interpretive task is handled. In evaluating protocols blindly from all family members, the parents and well siblings, as well as the index patients, without identifying information about these individuals or about the index member, we found that both qualitative characteristics and quantitative severity of illness of an index offspring could be correctly predicted from the form of the communication samples of the other family members. Also, Dr. Singer successfully matched the index family members with the rest of the family on the basis of the test protocols alone (11).

The same principles were also used with other samples of communication, including the Object Scoring Test (12) and proverbs interpretation (13).

More recently, we have systematized our Rorschach evaluation procedures by developing a forty-one-category system for identifying communication deviances which our previous research had suggested would be especially frequent in the Rorschachs of the parents of schizophrenics (10). In selecting these scoring categories, we emphasized the importance of establishing and maintaining shared task sets and foci of attention in the transaction, in this study, between subject and examiner. We were not attempting to evaluate "thought disorder" in the parents themselves, but rather the impact that hypothetically important forms of communication would have upon the listener, and especially upon a growing child.

This scoring system has now been applied with a high degree of interrater reliability to two samples of families: first, fifty-nine pairs of parents of schizophrenic, neurotic, and normal young adult offspring tested in Houston by Dr. Seymour Fisher (14, 15). The second sample consisted of 116 families tested at NIMH. The adolescent and young adult index offspring were in five diagnostic groups: non-remitting ("process") schizophrenia; "reactive" and remitting psychoses; the so-called borderline syndrome; severe neurotic and personality disorders, including delinquency; and no clinically apparent psychiatric disorder. The patients, parents, and siblings of these indexes were all tested and their protocols scored.

The results showed that the parents, as pairs, of the schizophrenic patients consistently had a frequency of communication deviances above the total group median and the parents of the neurotics and normals all had scores below the group median. There was practically no overlap between these groups of parents. Most strikingly, in twenty-four families in which there was a schizophrenic offspring but neither parent showed any diagnosable psychopathology beyond ordinary neurotic levels, all twenty-four pairs of the parents showed high communication deviance scores. However, in the families of borderline patients, some of the parental pairs had a high frequency and some a low frequency of communication deviances (16).

In addition, it turns out that the parents of disturbed patients actually have higher deviance scores than their offspring, even though symptomatically the index offspring are all more clinically disturbed than their parents. Clinical disturbances such as thinking disorders are not common in the parents of schizophrenics, but disturbances at the relational and task levels of communication occur consistently (16, 17).

2) *Conjoint Family Procedures*: Another approach is to evaluate the communication of family members directly with one another. This has been done both with tape-recorded excerpts from conjoint family therapy (18) and a variety of experimental procedures in which the task level of communication is emphasized—for example, in reaching a shared consensus about Rorschach ink-blots (19, 20), in conflict-resolution (21, 22) and in solving a variety of experimental problems in which sharing of information would be useful (23, 24, 25).

Reiss, in our program at NIMH, has recently demonstrated that the families of schizophrenics frequently use a problem-solving set of strategies which he has called "consensus sensitive." These families, when together, "interact in ways that simplify and stylize their interpretation of the environment and maximize their sense of safety and integrity as a family by rigidly maintaining a fixed, agreed-upon view of the environment no matter how simple or distorted." They seek information from one another not to facilitate precise or comprehensive task solution, but to find out about one another's attitudes, that is, about the state of the relationship. They strive for "an *agreed-upon* rather than a *correct* interpretation of the environment" (25).

The experimentally-derived concept of consensus-sensitivity clearly has much in common with the clinical formulation of pseudo-mutuality. The communicative "coordination," as Reiss puts it, is good within these families in support of their quest for intrafamilial relatedness, at the same time that their communication about external tasks and problem-solving may be quite ineffective. In contrast to these consensus-sensitive families, other families, especially those with a delinquent offspring, make very little use of information from the other family members and go about problem-solving in their own way using other cues. The normal families are slower than the families of schizophrenics in reaching consensus but take time to use cues both from sources inside and outside of the family (24, 25).

Here I would like to turn to a more detailed description of a particular family in which the variations within the family were clinically initially puzzling. In this family, whom I shall call the Flemings, the index offspring was Amy, the 17-year-old process schizophrenic girl whose Rorschach was excerpted earlier. Using the communication deviance manual described above, the mother in this family had the lowest quantitative score of the parents of forty-four frankly schizophrenic adolescent and young patients. By looking more closely at the qualitative aspects of her communication, as well as that of her husband, perhaps we can see more fully how these parents function with each other and with their children.

Often when we retrospectively assemble a psychiatric history, we are vulnerable to our own criticism and that of others that the material is selectively supportive of a particular formulation or hypothesis. Both to give you a picture of the immediate communication data in this family and to convey something of the way that we work when we deal with communication data blindly, I shall therefore describe some of the test material which was obtained from this family and which was in fact evaluated blindly.

Mother's Rorschach: First, let us consider the individual Rorschach of the mother. I have noted already that she had a low frequency of communication deviances when compared with the scores of parents of other schizophrenics. Looking at her communication during the initial viewing of the Rorschach cards, we see that she volunteered very little, using a total of only ninety words on the ten first responses in the initial viewing. In contrast, 116 diverse mothers whose records we have studied spoke an average of 357 words in their first responses. The content of her responses was bland and she had only two minor deviance scores on the ten cards during the initial viewing. She gave the same impression which we obtained early in family therapy—of a taciturn but clear, well-organized lady.

Card I, response 1, initial viewing: "Looks like a bat."

However, in the inquiry portion of the Rorschach when the task shifted and she was asked to say more about *how* she saw the inkblots, she not only spoke more voluminously but also began to produce a quite large number of communication deviances of a particular variety: she consistently disqualified, forgot, expressed doubt about, and in general, failed to reach closure about her previously rather straightforward though mundane and abbreviated responses.

Card I, response 1, inquiry: "Well, of course, depends. I haven't seen a bat real close, but with the spread of the wings here, and looks like the wings here and the small head. And then what I thought was more of an eagle."

Both in therapy and in a variety of research communication samples, it became apparent that she was unable or unwilling to make a selection among alternatives, even when the suggested alternatives were her own and not in conflict with views of others. The quality of her contribution to a given relationship and task was superficially cooperative until it became necessary for her to participate actively and to clarify her own percepts. She did not sustain attention on particular, focal content to the point necessary for a shared understanding. From her test records we deduced that this woman would not appear actively malevolent to her children but would provide minimal or cryptic guidance and orientation to them, especially defaulting when questions or difficulties arose. In therapy one would expect that some of her specific remarks, by themselves, would hint at a capacity for an active relationship, but this would not be fulfilled in a shared task orientation. Certainly this turned out to be our therapeutic experience with her. Further, we deduced from her tests that she probably would be limited in her ability to correct or clarify confusion or craziness in her spouse if this occurred. On the other hand, if she had the good fortune of being married to a man who was unusually clear and perhaps was willing to offer ideas of his own, she might have a relatively favorable relationship with him and her children.

Father's Rorschach: Now let us look at a communication sample from her husband. In his individual Rorschach protocol he actively tried to define the relationship with the tester but always in terms that led to a breakdown of the specific task which the psychologist intended. Even when the psychologist was just starting to speak, before Mr. Fleming had heard what she was proposing as a task, he indicated his primary concern was to establish a relationship by repeatedly interrupting with an agreeable-sounding, "Yassuh." He then redefined the task by saying, "You mean say whatever it brings to my mind?" Rather than describing what he thought the inkblots resembled, Mr. Fleming's concept of the task involved giving a personalized, rambling set of associations to his work and past experience, only loosely related to the inkblots, with an emphasis on trying to establish actively a special but unshared relationship with the tester.

> For example, on card X, he stated: "I've seen this color in the water in the Pacific, especially in the sunset. It was very beautiful. You can see eight or ten different colors in the water. You want to really take a vacation sometimes—go to Honolulu and just watch the sunset going down behind the volcano. And then the harbor, it's great—the place where you enter—the water's the deepest blue you've ever seen—and you know, when the wind's blowing a little, winds cause the fronds and the palm tree to just blow in front of the lights and it makes it look like there's a million diamonds in the water. It's really worth seeing. I went through there four or five times during the war. And then they have the soft music, you know."

What I would like to emphasize here is that this father was restructuring both the task and the relationship with the examiner and almost leading one to forget the focal content of what he sees in the inkblots. I also would like to call attention to the fact that, in this example, his reference to many colors on card X is not particularly unusual. It is the *other* material *surrounding* this percept, in the communicative process as a whole, in which one finds a high number of communication deviances. Clinically, this father established relationships which were highly charged affectively. He proposed many contradictory ideas, and when faced with complex situations, his interpretation of them became distinctly paranoid.

Spouse Rorschach: Now let me go on to give a few brief examples from the consensus or "relation" Rorschach of the father and mother together. In this procedure, devised by Dr. Nathene Loveland (19, 20), the family members work on the task of reaching consensus about Rorschach responses without a tester present. Their performance is analyzed from a tape-recording. In the instructions, they are asked: "What we want you to do is see what agreements you can come to about the things you think this inkblot looks like. See how many resemblances you can find in it and on which you can both agree."

In this procedure, the failure of this parental pair to deal with the designated task in the here-and-now was especially prominent, with many references to what they or others may have seen on some other occasion, but rarely stating what they saw in the immediate situation. Here also it became apparent that the mother characteristically waited for her husband to make the first move, communicating with a style known in boxing as counterpunching; she readily expressed her views *after* her husband had expressed some other view. For example, on Card I of the Rorschach, he had spoken previously of having seen a bat; it was unclear whether he was seeing it now. His wife responded by saying, "I can see more definitely a figure in there now." When he asked what she meant, she went back to *his* percept: "No, this one looks like a bat I guess."

Father: "Yah."

Mother: "Does it look like a bat now?" [This question threw doubt on the agreement she had just expressed.]

Father: "I think it was the other card, wasn't it?"

Mother: "Well, when I first saw it I said it looked like a vertebrae but I don't think it does now."

Father: "Well, the bat one does."

Mother: "That's right. This one I thought looked like an eagle."

Father: "It looks like a figure of a woman with her hands raised. Is that what you had in mind?"

Mother: "Yah, and the backbone. I mean, does it look like a vertebrae at all?" [Note that the mother had previously suggested that it looked like a vertebrae and the father that it looked like a backbone, but now she is doubting her own response and taking on that of her husband's.]

Father: "Yah, it does—sure. At the lower part of the hips."

Mother: "Yes."

Later the parents marked independently on a location sheet what they each thought they had agreed upon. Here it became apparent that the father thought they had agreed that the "vertebrae" was a pelvic-like structure in the lower part of the inkblot, whereas the mother used this term to refer to a line down the middle of the blot, quite different in location. Thus, even when they thought they had agreed, they had not checked with each other sufficiently on the level of focal attention to achieve more than a "pseudo-mutual" consensus (6).

I can attest from considerable subsequent experience with this family in conjoint family therapy, with Dr. Harold Searles and I as cotherapists, that this kind of exchange was not atypical. However, in therapy, the mother was usually more cryptic and withholding and often contented that she did not need to explain what she had in mind because her husband or the therapists could read her mind anyway and thus save her the trouble of expressing herself. Alone, this woman appeared to be taciturnly normal, but when viewed in communication with her family she made a significant contribution to what Singer and I have called "transactional thought disorder" (26). This concept refers to "thinking" difficulties which are not fully apparent until one looks at communicational sequences between two or more persons.

Family Triad Rorschach: Thus far I have deliberately not introduced material from the presenting patient interacting with her parents. She thus can hardly be charged with having directly introduced and produced the communication problems of these parents either with the psychologist or with one another.

Now, however, I wish to give examples from a family triad Rorschach in which the index offspring joined with her parents in the same consensus task. Here a somewhat more complex pattern became apparent in which the parents expected their daughter to be an arbiter and negotiator between them.

For example, presented with Rorschach card VII, the father began by saying that it looked like a fur pelt. While the father was giving an elaborate explanation of a cut-up and patched fur that he had once seen, the mother interrupted to ask Amy what she thought it looked like. She said: "Two dancing people," quite an acceptable response for this card.

Mother: [to the father] "Well, I said two dancing lambs and you said a pelt."

Amy: "It does look like two dancing lambs" [modifying her response to agree with mother].

Father: [in loud angry tone of voice] "Well explain to Daddy and Mommie how-makes—"

Amy: "I'm scared (sic)."

Father: [in loud angry voice] "Why do you think it looks like two dancing—"

Mother: "Why are you scared?"

Father: "I'm not going to hurt you, sweetheart."

Amy: [softly] "I want to come home."

Mother: "I couldn't figure out these floppy things unless they look like—I said this looked like a pile of cotton."

Later, there was renewed argument between the parents about dancing animals and the fur pelt, a response to which Amy agreed. The father and Amy also agreed that part of the blot looked like a buttocks.

Mother: "I said it looked like cotton."

Father: "Well, it could look like cotton. That's right. Do we all agree that it looks like buttocks?"

Mother: "No, I don't agree with that because it's too fluffy."

Father: "Do we agree that it looks like a fur pelt?"

Mother: "Well, I think it can. I don't know whether Amy does."

Amy: "You don't think it looks like a buttocks?"

Father: "Yah I do."

Amy: "Looks like a buttocks."

Father: "What, Amy?"

Amy: "A *fur* buttocks."

Mother: "A fur buttocks! She's so mixed up now."

Thereupon Amy returned to talk about the dancing ladies and father asked, "Where did you see the dancing animals?"

Mother: "Yeh, that's the way I did, I thought I saw them that way exactly."

Amy: "Do you like me, Mommie?"

Mother: "What?"

Amy: "Yes or no."

Mother: "You're supposed to be concentrating on this."

Father: "You're supposed to be concentrating on this."

Amy: "Say yes or no."

Mother: "Supposed to be concentrating."

Father: "You're supposed to be concentrating on this."

Amy: "Can't you say yes?"

Family Rorschach including Index and Sib: Let us go on to still another consensus Rorschach procedure, here including both parents, Amy, and her sister, two years older. A very similar series of unresolved disagreements emerged. Each of the four contented in favor of percepts with which no one or only one other person at a time would agree. When one family member conceded to another, then the person who had originated the percept would abandon it and either disagree or ask the other what he or she meant.

Finally, in the midst of a chaotic sequence when all the members of the family had been talking simultaneously, Amy spoke up in a momentary pause, perhaps expressing the feelings of the whole family but sounding "crazy" to the others:

Amy: "I didn't throw things on the ceiling, did I?"

Father: "You just keep your big mouth shut."

Amy: "You're not mad at me, are you?"

Father: "Yes, I'm mad at you because you're not doing what we asked you."

Mother: "You're excluding the whole picture." [She was talking to the older sister and ignoring what was going on between father and Amy.]

The response which Amy had originally made was a "bee," but this was not acknowledged at the time by any of the other family members. However, now, much later, the mother said: "That looks like a bumble bee, spread out, dissected."

This in turn was ignored by the father, who said: "Well, we all agree on the jack-o-lantern?"

Older sister: "Well, what do you know, we got an agreement. Oh happy day!"

Father: "But we *don't* agree?"

This perhaps may suffice to give something of the flavor of the interaction in a family of the kind which I have characterized as "pseudo-hostile" (7), with a great deal of intense relating, mostly with negative affect. In these families, turmoil and crisis are a way of life, seemingly protecting them both from a sense of deadness and a loss of relatedness. Such relationships are not built upon communicative acts or tasks in which there has been a shared focusing of attention upon particular messages. Amy's "contaminated" response about the "fur buttocks" and her comment about throwing things on the ceiling seem to be very much an expression of the transactional disorder in the family, which goes on in her absence as well as in her presence. When "crazy" content is expressed by her, it temporarily helps to focus attention on her as the scapegoated troublemaker who is, supposedly, uniquely neglecting the family task. In these examples, and in many clinical situations, Amy was more concerned than the others in verbally defining relationships in positive terms. Her verbal insistence upon friendly and positive relationships with her parents (and in her individual Rorschach, with the tester) was at odds with the family subculture of chronic bickering. Actually, however, her insistent questions about whether others liked her were irritating to them and thus was experienced as part of the pattern of bickering.

These examples of communication in a family could be elaborated in much more detail from the psychotherapeutic data. On another occasion, Dr. Harold Searles and I plan to report this material and its implications for understanding family dynamics and some of the processes of family therapy.

DISCUSSION

Family versus Individual Classifications: Although the kind of communication exemplified by the Fleming family is not unusual in my observations of schizophrenics and their families, I must caution against the possible assumption that these particular communicational patterns are found in *all* families of all patients labelled as schizophrenic or that they are found *only* in families with an individual member so diagnosed. Descriptions and classifications of families which make use of relational and communicational concepts differ from the more usual classification of families based upon the psychiatric diagnosis of an individual family member. For example, "pseudo-mutuality" and "consensus-sensitivity" (6, 25) are concepts that are concerned primarily with the relationship level of communication, whereas traditional psychiatric diagnosis, especially as it pertains to "thinking disorders," is more concerned with the task and content levels.

Because the three levels of communication are partially linked with one another, one should expect a degree of correlation between difficulties described from these two vantage points. Communication problems at the relationship level reverberate sooner or later, as with Amy, at the task and content levels. And an exclusive preoccupation with content or task, with a neglect of the relationship context, will lead sooner or later to communicational confusion.

However, disorder at one communicational level does not seem to have any fixed or invariant consequences for a particular form of disorder at other levels. This issue deserves more detailed and extensive empirical study. In such investigations, the different levels of communication need to be distinguished as well as the extent to which persons communicating with one another have a shared understanding at all three levels. These distinctions are needed, I believe, to clarify a number of important problems in behavioral and communicational theory, including certain difficulties with double-bind theory (2, 28, 29).

Etiology and Pathogenesis: Although I am greatly interested in the problem of etiology and pathogenesis of schizophrenia, in this paper I have been more concerned with the *immediate* characteristics of the communication process in families in which a schizophrenic member has already been identified. However, methods and concepts developed in order to evaluate communication patterns in the here-and-now can and should, I believe, be incorporated into research more specifically concerned with etiology and pathogenesis. This includes research with special samples, such as those of twins and adoptees and families at high risk studied longitudinally. The communicational features studied are not the same, I wish to stress, as those described traditionally as psychiatric symptoms. However, these communicational and transactional processes may contribute to the emergence of symptomatology which at some point is given a psychiatric diagnosis in an individual family member.

However, for a comprehensive understanding of pathogenesis and etiology we must attend to other considerations as well. As I have explained in more detail elsewhere (16, 17, 27), communicational patterns can be regarded as building upon attentional-response dispositions which probably have an innate, genetically-determined component. I have hypothesized that the response dispositions, which are experimentally defined aspects of "temperament," constitute the genetic contribution to schizophrenia. There appears to be no compelling need to postulate a distinctive or special schizophrenic genotype. Rather, the evidence, as I see it, is more compatible with a developmental formulation of polygenetically inherited response dispositions which, in turn, contribute to the likelihood of a distorted maladaptive "fit" between the growing child and his family environment. Both our studies of family communication and the recent twin and adoption studies support a broad, rather than a narrow, concept of schizophrenia (27).

Without discussing the response-disposition concept in detail here, it can be briefly noted that laboratory tests of the members of the Fleming family indicated that they all had a tendency to "augment" their responsiveness (in the averaged evoked responses on the electroencephalogram) to light stimuli of increasing intensity. However, along other response dimensions, such as field dependence-independence and scanning control, they differed from one another. Amy, who was both markedly field dependent and a minimal scanner, in addition to having a low I.Q., seemed poorly equipped, in comparison with her sister, to organize and select focal stimuli. Thus, within this family in which some features were shared, there also were individual differences which can be plausibly connected to individual vulnerability to symptomatic breakdown.

Concluding Comments: The turning away from conventional task-orientations which is so common in the history of schizophrenics tragically undermines their potential capacity to establish and renew the very relatedness which they seek so despairingly. The universal need for relatedness takes on a special urgency in certain individuals and families. In a culture which is commonly experienced as mechanized and dehumanized, the quest for relatedness for its own sake is quite understandably heightened. The current appeal of encounter groups and encounter experiences probably arises from such sources.

Unfortunately, the expectation of instant relatedness may involve a premature repeated dismissal and neglect of the more grubby aspects of task-orientation and attention to specific content in communication. The consequences of an unsupported, inept quest for relatedness can be seen with special intensity and poignancy in schizophrenics and their families. We all, schizophrenic and otherwise, must deal with an ultimately unavoidable developmental and psychological dilemma: relatedness *cannot* be long sustained without reference to specific focal content and actual tasks; on the other hand, an *exclusive* preoccupation with specific messages and tasks, without building a relationship context is empty indeed, worthy of a computer, but not of a human being.

Martin Buber described this dilemma most beautifully in his concept of man's two-fold need for *both* I-Thou and I-It relationships. I-It relationships can, in my present terminology, be regarded as those in which task and focal content are in ascendancy. Let me conclude with a memorable passage from Buber that has enduringly influenced my thinking as expressed in partial form in this paper:

> "The world of *It,*" says Buber (30) , "is set in the context of space and time.
> "The world of *Thou* is not set in the context of either of these.
> "The particular *Thou,* after the relational event has run its course, is *bound* to become an *It.*
> "The particular *It,* by entering the relational event, *may* become a *Thou.*
> "These are the two basic privileges of the world of *It.* They move man to look on the world of *It* as the world in which he has to live, and in which it is comfortable to live, as the world, indeed, which offers him all manner of incitements and excitements, activity and knowledge. In this chronicle of solid benefits the moments of the *Thou* appear as strange lyric and dramatic episodes, seductive and magical, but tearing us away to dangerous extremes, loosening the well-tried context, leaving more questions than satisfaction behind them, shattering security—in short, uncanny moments we can well dispense with. For since we are bound to leave them and go back into the 'world,' why not remain in it? . . .
> "It is not possible to live in the bare present. Life would be quite consumed if precautions were not taken to subdue the present speedily and thoroughly. But it is possible to live in the bare past, indeed only in it may a life be organized. We only need to fill each moment with experiencing and using, and it ceases to burn.
> "And in all the seriousness of truth, hear this: without *It* man cannot live. But he who lives with *It* alone is not a man."

REFERENCES

1. RUESCH, J. & BATESON, G.: *Communication: The Social Matrix of Psychiatry.* New York: W. W. Norton, 1951.
2. WATZLAWICK, P., BEAVIN, J. & JACKSON, D. D.: *Pragmatics of Human Communication.* New York: W. W. Norton, 1967.
3. BLEULER, E.: *Dementia Praecox or the Group of Schizophrenias* (trans. by Joseph Zinker). New York: Int'l Univ. Press, 1950.

4. SULLIVAN, H. S.: The Language of Schizophrenia. In J. S. Kasanin: *Language and Thought in Schizophrenia.* New York: W. W. Norton, 1944.

5. SEARLES, H.: Positive Feelings in the Relationship Between the Schizophrenic and His Mother. *Int'l. J. Psychoanal.,* 39:569-586, 1958.

6. WYNNE, L. C., RYCKOFF, I., DAY, J., & HIRSCH, S.: Pseudo-mutuality in the Family Relations of Schizophrenics. *Psychiatry,* 21:205-220, 1958.

7. WYNNE, L. C.: The Study of Intrafamilial Alignments and Splits in Exploratory Family Therapy. In Ackerman, Beatman and Sherman's *Exploring the Base for Family Therapy.* New York: Family Service Assn. of America, 1961, pp. 95-115.

8. HOOVER, C. F.: The Embroiled Family: A Blueprint for Schizophrenia. *Family Process,* 4:291-310, 1965.

9. SINGER, M. T. & WYNNE, L. C.: Thought Disorder and Family Relations of Schizophrenics: III. Methodology Using Projective Techniques. *Arch. Gen. Psychiat.,* 12:187-220, 1965a.

10. SINGER, M. T. & WYNNE, L. C.: Principles of Scoring Communication Defects and Deviances in Parents of Schizophrenics: Rorschach and TAT Scoring Manuals. *Psychiatry,* 29:260-268, 1966.

11. SINGER, M. T. & WYNNE, L. C.: Thought Disorder and Family Relations of Schizophrenics: IV. Results and Implications. *Arch. Gen. Psychiat.,* 12:201-212, 1965b.

12. WILD, C., SINGER, M. T., ROSMAN, B., RICCI, J., & LIDZ, T.: Measuring Disordered Styles of Thinking. *Arch. Gen. Psychiat.,* 13:471-476, 1965.

13. SINGER, M. T., WYNNE, L. C., LEVI, L. D., & SOJIT, C.: *Proverbs Interpretation Reconsidered: A Transactional Approach to Schizophrenics and Their Families.* Presented at Symposium on Language and Thought in Schizophrenia, 1968, Newport Beach, California, Nov. 23, 1968. (To be published.)

14. SINGER, M. T.: Family Transactions and Schizophrenia: I. Recent Research Findings. J. Romano (Ed.), *Excerpta Medica International Congress Series,* No. 151, 1967, 147-164.

15. WYNNE, L. C.: Family Transactions and Schizophrenia: II. Conceptual Considerations for a Research Strategy. J. Romano (Ed.), *Excerpta Medica International, Congress Series* No. 151, 1967, 165-178,

16. WYNNE, L. C. & SINGER, M. T.: Schizophrenics and Their Families: III. Recent Rorschach Findings. (In press, *Brit. J. Psychiat.,* 1971.)

17. WYNNE, L. C.: Methodologic and Conceptual Issues in the Study of Schizophrenics and Their Families. *J. Psychiat. Res.,* 6, Suppl. 1, 1968, 185-199.

18. MORRIS, G. O. & WYNNE, L. C.: Schizophrenic Offspring and Styles of Parental Communication: A Predictive Study using Family Therapy Excerpts. *Psychiatry,* 28:19-44, 1965.

19. LOVELAND, N. T., WYNNE, L. C., & SINGER, M. T.: The Family Rorschach: A New Method for Studying Family Interaction. *Family Process,* 2:187-215, 1963.

20. LOVELAND, N. T.: The Relation Rorschach: A Technique for Studying Interaction. *J. Nerv. Ment. Dis.,* 145:93-105, 1967.

21. MISHLER, E. G. & WAXLER, N. E.: *Interaction in Families.* New York: John Wiley and Sons, 1968.

22. RAVICH, R. A., DEUTSCH, M., & BROWN, B.: An Experimental Study of Mental Discord and Decision-Making. I. M. Cohen (Ed.), *Psychiatric Research Report* No. 20, Amer. Psych. Assn., 91-94, 1966.

23. REISS, D.: Individual Thinking and Family Interaction: III. An Experimental Study of Categorization Performance in Families of Normals, Those with Character Disorders and Schizophrenics. *J. Nerv. Ment. Dis.,* 146:384-403, 1968.

24. REISS, D.: Varieties of Consensual Experience. III. Contrast between Families of Normals, Delinquents and Schizophrenics. *J. Nerv. Ment. Dis.,* 1970 (in press).

25. REISS, D. & SHERIFF, W. H., JR.: A Computer-automated Procedure for Testing Some Experiences of Family Membership. *Behavioral Sci.,* 1970 (in press).
26. WYNNE, L. C. & SINGER, M. T.: Thought Disorder and Family Relations of Schizophrenics: I. A Research Strategy. *Arch. Gen. Psychiat.,* 9:191-198, 1963.
27. WYNNE, L. C.: Schizophrenics and Their Families: I. Research Re-directions. (In press, *Brit. J. Psychiat.,* Jan. 1971.)
28. BATESON, G., JACKSON, D. D., HALEY, J., & WEAKLAND, J.: Toward a Theory of Schizophrenia. *Behav. Sci.,* 1:251-264, 1956.
29. WYNNE, L. C.: On the Anguish and Creative Passions of Not Escaping Double Binds: A Reformation. Presented in a Symposium on the Double Bind, Annual Meeting of the Amer. Psychol. Assn., Washington, D. C., Sept. 2, 1969.
30. BUBER, M.: *I and Thou.* Edinburgh: T. and T. Clark, 1937.

37

THE INFLUENCE OF FAMILY STUDIES ON THE TREATMENT OF SCHIZOPHRENIA

Theodore Lidz, M.D.

*Professor and Chairman, Department
of Psychiatry, Yale University*

*The honor of being invited to present this lecture has
particular meaning for me through again linking me to the
memory of Dr. Fromm-Reichmann, who was a friend and
mentor as well as a teacher. Some persons are revered most
by those who knew them only through their writings and
reputation: not so with Frieda Fromm-Reichmann, who was
not only respected and admired, but loved by those close to
her. She played an important part in my life, and she remains very much with me as a guiding idea. I give at least
fleeting thought to her each evening as I enter our study and
see the painting of the hills of Jerusalem by her friend Ger-
trud Jacob that for many years hung in Frieda's study, and
when I enter my office, where the sole certificate is that of
the first Frieda Fromm-Reichmann award for research in
schizophrenia.*

*Dr. Fromm-Reichmann's life as a psychiatrist was primar-
ily devoted to analytically oriented psychotherapy with
schizophrenic patients and to demonstrating that such persons, even when their condition had become chronic, were
not beyond the reach of the persistent and devoted ther-*

The Twelfth Annual Frieda Fromm-Reichmann Memorial Lecture, given on November 15, 1968, at the Department of Interior, Washington, D. C., under the auspices
of the Washington School of Psychiatry. Reprinted from PSYCHIATRY, Vol. 32, No. 3,
Aug., 1969, pp. 237-251.

apist. With the extraordinary determination and persistence that permeated her kindly small body she proceeded to demonstrate this potentiality to her colleagues and to the world. The treatment of schizophrenic patients has altered markedly since her death and I wish she could have lived to see the change. I cannot match the inspiring testament of her lifework given in Hannah Green's I Never Promised You a Rose Garden, *but I shall attempt tonight to link her work with the therapeutic advances that have resulted from the studies of the family environments in which schizophrenic patients grow up and that together with the tranquilizing drugs and the new concepts of milieu therapy have vastly altered the future lives of schizophrenic patients.*

Nowhere in medicine has it been so apparent that the hypotheses held concerning the nature and etiology of a condition influence treatment as in the case of schizophrenia. Belief in demonic possession led to exorcisms and burnings. The conviction that these patients suffered from a somatic disorder was, in large measure, responsible for the relegation of generations of patients to neglect in custodial institutions. The hypothesis, accepted as fact, that the brain or its metabolism was at fault provoked the damaging of countless brains by insulin, metrazol, electricity, and lobotomy. Jung's and Bleuler's beliefs that the psychological disturbances they described were secondary to a toxic disorder, and Freud's idea that the schizophrenic patient's narcissistic fixation and regression made a transference relationship impossible convinced psychoanalysts that these patients were beyond their approach. Indeed, when Sullivan, Fromm-Reichmann, and Hill demonstrated that transference relationships could be established, many other analysts were skeptical and even derogatory because the fact ran counter to accepted tenets. The theory that schizophrenic reactions, as the most profound regressions, are due to fixations during the oral phase, led to the focus on maternal rejection during infancy—a period beyond conscious recollection; this orientation has led some therapists to believe that supplying the nurture and love the patient lacked during infancy forms the cornerstone of treatment.

It is essential to have hypotheses to guide therapy, but science progresses when hypotheses are based upon ascertained data rather than primarily upon theoretic assumptions. For many years, I have, together with various colleagues, been engaged in an intensive scrutiny of the family settings in which schizophrenic patients have grown up (Lidz *et al.*, 1965). We started from the clinical observation that schizophrenic patients seemed always to have emerged from seriously disturbed families; and from the hypothesis that because the foundations of language and thought are laid down within the family, the thought disorder that forms the distinctive feature of schizophrenia might well be related to these disturbed family environments. We hoped to find something specific within the radius of the family circle that was related to the etiology of schizophrenia; but the global nature of the family pathology created difficulties. Something was seriously amiss with each aspect of the family and its transactions that we examined. Whereas some of the mothers had been unable properly to invest the patient as an infant, others had serious difficulties in establishing boundaries between themselves and the children who became schizophrenic. Most but not all of the mothers were strange if not seriously disturbed, but the fathers just as frequently displayed severe psychopathology. Many of the families were rent by serious schisms between the parents, but others were distorted by a skewed parental relationship in which an apparent harmony or pseudomutuality was maintained because the aberrant ideas and ways of child-rearing of one parent were not countered by the passive spouse. The failures of parents to maintain boundaries between generations and to adhere to their gender-linked roles led to incestuous problems, gender identity confusions, and homosexual tendencies in both parents and offsprings. The peculiarities of communication and the distortions of reality within the family fostered a proclivity toward irrationality in the children. The extrafamilial socialization of the child had been impeded by a variety of asocial influences in these families. I cannot review the nature of these difficulties but wish to emphasize that the serious problems found in virtually all areas in all of these families had started prior to the birth of the patient and were continuing when the patient became overtly psychotic in adolescence or early adult life. We described our findings as objectively as we could; and many others have published similar findings and amplified them. When the protocols of family studies carried out in Bethesda,[1] in Paris,[2] in Finland,[3] or in Palo Alto[4] are reviewed, they reveal essentially the same difficulties, even though sometimes differing in emphasis concerning what is considered most salient. It has become apparent by now that whatever else may enter into the

---

[1] See Bowen, 1957, 1960; Bowen, Dysinger, and Basamania; Wynne et al., 1957; Wynne et al., 1958.

[2] See Delay et al., 1957, 1960, 1962.

[3] See Alanen, 1958, 1960a, 1960b.

[4] See Bateson et al.; Jackson; Jackson and Weakland.

genesis of schizophrenia, the family problems have major pertinence (Lidz, 1967a).

Focusing upon the etiology and understanding of schizophrenic reactions, I have written relatively little about their treatment in recent years. However, our explorations of the families were carried out in a therapeutic setting and included analytically oriented therapy of the patients. In looking back over the past twenty years I realize that my own treatment of schizophrenic patients, and that of some of my colleagues as well, has been profoundly influenced by the data and the conceptualizations derived from these studies. I shall discuss some of these influences and effects.

The first consequence that I wish to note may seem almost trivial but I believe it has had great therapeutic moment. It is the assurance the therapist can have that he will find ample and tangible material for psychotherapeutic work. He can set aside concerns that he is confronted by some mysterious ailment of metabolic origin and that he is struggling with useless epiphenomena, doubts fostered by the weight of tradition and bolstered by the constant flow of articles announcing the discovery of some new metabolic defect, none of which is subsequently varified— doubts to which the therapist may be vulnerable because of the discouraging turns that are an inevitable part of the work with schizophrenic patients. He can also feel assured that the problems are not beyond the reach of a psychotherapeutic approach, or that they may also become accessible after prolonged analysis. Assurance is essential because the therapist must arouse glimmers of hope in a person who has abandoned hope of coping with the world and those who people it; and the schizophrenic patient is unusually sensitive to pretense of conviction.

Further, the therapist can feel assured that the material he needs to establish a meaningful relationship is not cryptic, for some guides are usually fairly obvious to one who can but observe and hear them.

Let us consider a 17-year-old high school student whom I saw on the day I wrote these paragraphs. He had been flown to the hospital from a preparatory school where he had started behaving strangely, expressing delusions and talking almost incoherently. When I asked what brought him to the hospital he responded "My mother." "Your mother?" I asked. "My mother is a witch!—A seductive witch—No, she's a wonderful person—She won't let me do anything I want—No one is good enough for me—She controls me and my father is a weak man who does what she wants—He's a strong man—He was a West Pointer—He beat the hell out of me when I was little." He slipped back and forth, talking of the preparatory school and the nursery school he had once attended, but through it ran themes of ambivalence to his two unhappy parents and their conflicts, and his inability to be free from his mother's needs and demands. Yet, not so many years ago much of what he said about his witch mother, who seduced and controlled, would have been disregarded as but a reflection of his schizophrenic illness.

Even when the patient is out of contact, highly pertinent directives may be inadvertently provided by the parents.

For example, a college girl was admitted to the hospital after having been removed from a train bewildered and acutely delusional. I interviewed her parents when they arrived. In terms of the history alone, the girl's desperate condition sounded much like a bolt out of the blue. She had been a fine student who was interested in writing, somewhat shy but sociable and well liked by her friends and roommates. However, the session itself was replete with material familiar to those who work with parents of schizophrenic patients. The mother did all of the talking, while the father, a wealthy art dealer, remained silent. When I directed remarks at him, I gained a response from his wife. Even when I turned my back on the mother and pointedly placed a question to the father, she intruded before he completed a sentence. It was difficult to learn much about the patient for the mother told about herself, her Pilgrim ancestry, and her ambitions as a writer. When I finally interrupted and asked about the daughter's college career and her interests, I learned that the girl's whole life revolved about becoming a novelist; she had a passion for Virginia Woolf. The mother became enthusiastic; she prayed that her daughter would become another Virginia Woolf. I hesitated, and then commented, "But Virginia Woolf had psychotic episodes and committed suicide." The mother did not hesitate when she replied, "It would be worth it."

I could form a working hypothesis that in this family the parents' marriage was skewed, with the mother dominating the family transactions, preempting roles usually filled by the husband and unable properly to fill the maternal expressive-affectional role, at least toward this daughter. The father, no matter how competent in his career, did not occupy much of the masculine, instrumental role in the family. The mother's interest in the patient was egocentric, seeking to raise a daughter who would carry out her own frustrated ambitions, and she was likely to be intrusive but impervious to the girl's own desires and needs. The girl probably felt accepted only insofar as she could salvage her mother's own frustrated ambitions.

While making rounds some weeks later I noted several novels by Virginia Woolf in the patient's room and asked about them. She replied in a flat voice, "Mother sent them—she has a thing about Virginia Woolf." Over the next months the patient talked of her despair over her inadequacies as a writer, her desires for a marriage in which she could help a husband assert himself, and her resentments over her obligation to live out her mother's aspirations for her. I had some difficulty in believing that she was complying to the extent of becoming psychotic like Virginia Woolf, which proved a serious, a fatal error. When the patient emerged from her psychosis, her mother insisted she continue her treatment on the west coast where they lived. At home, caught up in her mother's control, she relapsed, and then followed the fate foisted upon her by committing suicide.

The therapist can not only feel secure that meaningful material for psychotherapy will be available, but he can anticipate the nature of the problems upon which the therapeutic transactions will usually focus. As I have noted, difficulties exist in virtually all aspects of the family transactions throughout the patient's life, and we have set down our findings elsewhere. I would now like to extrapolate from this abundant material those difficulties that I currently believe are essentially schizophrenogenic.

When we began our studies, we considered that the patient's dependency and symbiotic needs followed upon the mother's inability to establish boundaries between herself and her child (Lidz and Lidz, 1951). Needing the patient to complete her own life, often to live out the life that was closed to her because she was a woman, she failed to differentiate her own needs and feelings from those of her offspring, who then could not develop as a separate individual. His energies and attention went primarily into giving meaning to his mother's life and supporting her tenuous emotional equilibrium, rather than into his own development. The child could not clearly distinguish his needs, feelings, and wishes from those of his mother. I believe that these observations, which had also been made by Reichard and Tillman and which were elaborated by Hill, were on the right track. However, it is not always the mother's inability to differentiate from the child that leads to the patient's failure properly to establish boundaries between himself and others and attain a distinct identity. The father may be the prime source of such difficulties, particularly with daughters, or with sons when the father has strong homosexual tendencies (Fleck et al., 1958; Raybin). Then, too, when the parents' marriage is markedly schismatic, the child may be caught in the conflict so thas his major investment lies in seeking to bridge the gap between the parents, perhaps even by serving as a scapegoat upon whom the burden of parental difficulties can be placed. The result is much the same in that his own emergence as a person is thwarted and sacrificed to preserve one or both parents. He is prematurely burdened by a task that stifles his development. Study reveals that one parent—or both—is profoundly egocentric; that is to say, the parent is seriously handicapped in being able to understand others in terms of his own life. Not only is the child understood merely as an extension of the parent's existence, but the spouse is also treated egocentrically; and events are perceived only in terms of the parent's life and needs, and are often distorted to fit into an extremely egocentric view of the world. Now, whereas the parent is limited, at least he or she has an egocentric orientation and strives to preserve his integration. The patient, however, is not as fortunate, for his orientation is mother-centered or parent-centered; he views the world according to the parent's feelings, needs, and defenses, and lives to protect the persons from whom he has not properly differentiated (Lidz, 1967).

Fortunately, this statement of the situation is something of an exaggeration. Most patients who become schizophrenic in late adolescence or adult life have been able to try to differentiate and live their own lives, but because they are poorly prepared to understand others and to relate to them, they become enmeshed in difficulties and give up. Successful regression is impossible, for it leads back to dependency upon the engulfing parent, who arouses homicidal impulses or provokes incestuous fears. The question of how the patient solves this dilemma and where he seeks refuge leads us to consider thought disorder that forms the essence of schizophrenia.

As various investigators have pointed out, the patient's foundations in the meaning system and logic of his culture had been faulty. My colleagues and I described the transmission of irrationality within the family because of the parents' proclivities to distort reality in order to maintain their own precarious emotional equilibria. Commonly patients had been placed in a "double bind" (Bateson et al.) in seeking to fill a parent's mutually exclusive demands in order to feel loved or accepted; or had become perplexed about the utility of verbal communication because of the discrepancies between what parents said and what they conveyed by their behavior, or because of "the mystification" (Laing), in their contradictory communications. As Wynne and Singer (1963a, 1963b; Singer and Wynne, 1965a, 1965b), have amply demonstrated, there is a strange amorphous or fragmented quality in the parents' communications. The patient who is parent-centered tends to perceive in terms of a parent's needs rather than in terms of how perception and communication help him master his environment and how others in his community perceive and understand. Those patients who had been caught between irreconcilable parents try to maintain irreconcilable versions of the world that can only be brought together and resolved paralogically.

There is another aspect of the problem of the schizophrenic thought disorder that is difficult to explain succinctly. In order to perceive, think, or communicate, one must divide the ceaseless flow of experience into categories. By and large the vocabulary of a language is a catalogue of the categories a culture uses in dividing experience. In learning the language the child learns what his society considers essential or useful in understanding the world, and also what can be neglected and what must be ignored. This division of experience into categories requires the separation of what is actually a continuity. Experience is continuous— categories are discreet. Each culture teaches its members to ignore what would blur boundaries between essential categories. A fundamental step in establishing categories that must occur in each child's life concerns the differentiation of the self from the non-self. Every culture places a taboo on things that had been self and become non-self, such as secretions and excretions (Leach) ; and upon fusions of the self and the mother, as in nursing and the oedipal ties; and also upon other blurrings of essential divisions, such as the attributes of the two sexes. In persons who become schizophrenic, such boundaries have never been clearly established—between the self and the mother, between what is masculine and feminine—and these failures affect subsequent category formation and conceptualization. It is in the hiatus, in the nebulous region that lies between categories that the schizophrenic finds refuge. Often he returns to fantasies of a vague union with the mother in which boundaries are obliterated, a union that is now sexualized in a polymorphous perverse manner; and to a state where he is neither clearly male nor female, and where the burdens of being an individual self have vanished (Lidz, 1968) . Others, perhaps less able to regress in this fashion, but still with poor boundaries between the self and others, attribute their own impulses to others in what we term projection, or seek to control forbidden impulses by extrojecting poorly internalized parental prohibitions as hallucinations and delusions.

I believe that this explication of what I currently consider to be the crux of the schizophrenic situation provides the therapist with guidelines through the maze of data and the perplexing contradictions of the patient's communication and behavior; it permits the therapist to gain and retain perspective despite the booby traps that the patient can so adroitly set for him, and despite the inevitable flights from reinvolvement with the world and the unreliable, egocentric individuals who people it.

The therapist can know that the basic therapeutic task lies in releasing the patient from the bondage of completing a parent's life or of bringing the divisiveness between his parents, and in enabling the patient to become a person in his own right, investing his energies in his own development rather than remaining tied to the problems of the preceding generation. The therapist persistently fosters the patient's latent desires for individuation that he has given up as hopeless, and counters his fears of rejection and abandonment if he asserts his own needs and desires and his terror that self-assertion and expression of his ambivalent hostilities will destroy his parents. The patient must become capable of perceiving his parents, their behavior, and the interpersonal environment differently from the way his parents need to see these matters and from the way his parents require him to see them, and he must learn to trust his own feelings and perceptions.

Now, such therapeutic tasks require an approach that differs in many ways from conventional psychoanalytically oriented therapy. Our emphasis is *not* on analysis of distortions of understanding arising from mechanisms of defense that are utilized to buttress the ego, but is rather on analysis of distortions that have been imposed by significant others to defend their egos. Rather than raise doubts in the patient concerning his perceptions and motives, we often seek to imbue him with trust in his own feelings and ideas, accepting them while questioning ideas and feelings that are essentially his parents' offered as his own. The patient constantly tests the therapist's ability to differentiate the two. We do not foster anxiety to achieve proper therapeutic movement, for anxiety is apt to disorganize further, but rather we convey respect and trust of the patient's ideas and feelings to foster the patient's expression of what he has long been taught to distrust. We do not evoke free association, for the patient needs to be guided into sharper conceptualization and common modes of communication. Thus, waiting and long silences have little use; the patient is weaned from his autistic world and idiosyncratic communication by the therapist's ability to hear what the patient seeks to express even as he seeks to conceal in terms of metaphor and cryptic associations. Our knowledge of the common dilemmas and life situations of schizophrenic patients, knowledge gained from direct family studies, has particular importance in permitting us to be alert to what the patient is saying in his strange ways. The schizophrenic must come to trust verbal communication, and he does so by learning that the therapist listens to what the patient says and means what he says, but is not im-

imposing his ideas upon the patient. Thus, the therapist does not interpret so much as seek clarification of nebulous material from the patient. Then, too, whereas a therapist commonly questions why a neurotic patient blames his parents, and interprets in terms of distortions created by oedipal conflicts, he encourages the schizophrenic patient to express feelings about parents even if those feelings contain projective elements —for only then can the patient begin to sort out his confusions about his parents and properly question their attitudes and demands.

The schizophrenic patient develops a transference relationship when he can trust, and he trusts when he feels understood and when he begins to dare believe that the therapist will not use him or abandon him because he is understood. But the therapeutic relationship is long a tenuous thread before it becomes a means of reliving and reevaluating childhood experiences. It is fraught with the actual dangers of the patient's childhood intrafamilial relationships. A therapist's interest, concern, care, and affection are apt to be equated with parents' intrusiveness and envelopment, and with their imperviousness to the patient's own needs and feelings. In brief, a major requirement for the therapist concerns the ability to care and refuse to give up while not needing the patient or his devotion. The therapist seeks to convey that even though he wants very much for the patient to improve and will go a long way and make personal sacrifices to foster such improvement, he pursues this goal neither for the parents' sake nor because of his own need for a therapeutic success.

Then, too, because the patient has learned to disregard what is said, the unspoken signals are of great importance. "I long ago learned to stop listening and note how mother was feeling," said one young woman. Much has been written about the schizophrenic patient's intuitive capacities. They have learned to base their interactions with parents on indications and to become skilled in responding to feelings. However, despite such abilities or because such abilities are based upon relationships with peculiar parents, schizophrenic patients often misinterpret. Similarly, it is often difficult to know what a remark will mean to the patient, who can plunge into inchoate blackness of despair because of an imagined rebuff. It is important to counter a patient's tendency to consider the therapist as omniscient, for errors and misunderstandings are bound to occur; and many schizophrenic patients have learned that they must accept the parent's views or be rebuffed. The relationship can also be threatened by the common practice of considering as projections the patient's concerns that the therapist will seduce, or that the therapist wishes to be rid of him. A woman who seems to believe firmly that her analysis will lead to an affair with her analyst may be projecting her wishes to some extent, but, basically, she is transferring to the therapist her hope and fear that if she shows affection, he will seduce her, even as her father had started masturbating her when she became pubescent.

As many schizophrenic patients were raised by parents who had vacillated between intrusive closeness and inattentive withdrawal into their own fantasies or problems, establishing a proper working distance in therapy presents difficulties. A patient's feelings that I was withdrawn in some sessions and oppressively intrusive in others depended upon inadvertent changes of two or three inches in the customary placement of her chair. In general, schizophrenic patients have been burned by having been seduced into involvement with their engulfing parents, and because of the pain have renounced forever hopes of any meaningful relationships. They are wary and must be wary. When they find their resistances to the therapist melting they are very likely to flee . . . flee the hospital, flee into panic, or flee into withdrawn states. The therapist who has properly been encouraged by the developing relationship can become profoundly discouraged and even give up. This is a critical moment in treatment that must be anticipated even though it does not always occur. Now the therapist is being tested and if he persists and surmounts the rebuff, therapeutic movement can gain momentum, for a less tentative relationship will follow.

I have, perhaps, dwelt too long on how certain core problems in establishing and maintaining a useful therapeutic relationship gain meaning in the light of the family studies. Knowledge of the types of settings from which schizophrenic patients emerge provides guidance in many other ways. I shall offer a few examples rather than endeavor to be comprehensive.

Let us consider the common preoccupations of schizophrenic patients with homosexuality and with fears of undergoing a change of gender. An appreciation of the parents' confused gender identities and failures to maintain the gender-linked roles provides a therapeutic approach that is more useful than ideas about innate bisexuality. A firm sexual identity forms a foundation of a stable ego identity. In these families a child does not have a suitable model for identification in the parent of the same sex, whose worth is further undercut by the parent of the opposite sex whose love the child seeks. Sometimes the parents have virtually reversed gender roles and in other cases a parent's homosexual tendencies are apparent. A schizophrenic youth with many effeminate traits and homosexual and masochistic preoccupations had an alcoholic father who had been an eminent football player. The father was contemptuous of his effete, artistic son, whereas the mother had fostered his esthetic development, conveying the idea that he must not become like his crass father. Eventually, the youth began to speak of his notions that his father had homosexual tendencies. They were not projections. His mother abreacted with a social worker the anguish she had experienced when her husband had admitted that his attraction to athletics involved his fascination with nude male bodies, and when his impotence and his intense attachment to a fellow athlete had marred the early years of their marriage. The homosexual concerns of the patient could be approached meaningfully in terms of his perceptions of his father, who represented the type of man attractive to his mother, and in terms of the unacceptability of masculinity when it meant the callousness he and his mother had experienced from his father—and later through attention to his unresolved identification with his mother.

Fears of incest, which create panic because the patient fears proximity to the parent he needs, are not simply regressions and projections but reflect both the parents' own incestuous tendencies and the pathological family structure. A young man who had brought a girl friend into the home to sleep with him after his father left his mother was incoherent when hospitalized, but his mother begged, "You must cure him—he is all of my life—when he started to become sick I slept with him just like man and wife." A young woman who had been hospitalized because of her confusion and public promiscuity had her genitalia examined by her physician father each time she returned home from a date to make certain she was still a virgin.

We learn, too, that not all of the poor habits and sloppiness of the patient are evidence of schizophrenic dilapidation; some are reflections of the failure of parents to inculcate basic social behavior and essential adaptive techniques. A young male patient befriended a schizophrenic young woman and took her out to dinner. He reported to his psychiatrist that he could not continue the friendship for he could scarcely eat because of his disgust with the girl's sloppiness. She not only spilled food all over herself but blew her nose in the napkin. When the matter was broached with the young woman, she wanted to know what was wrong—her father, an eminent professor, blew his nose in his napkin. Another young woman always appeared untidy, and the nurses observed that she did not know how to put her nylons on properly nor how to adjust her brassiere. At the age of 26 she would not go to buy a properly fitting bra; she did not know how, for her mother had always brought them home for her. Such lack of education concerning social amenities can, in turn, interfere with socialization with peers, from whom the adolescent must learn so much about interpersonal relationships. We have come to appreciate that many schizophrenic patients require guidance in techniques of living and need group experiences which promote interchange about personal behavior to supplement or offset the intrafamilial experiences.

Along similar lines, the patient's thought disorder requires specific attention. It is not simply a regression or an intrusion of autistic primary process material, but a complex resultant of the parents' amorphous or fragmented styles of communicating, of poor training in categorizing, of having been taught paranoid mistrust within the home, of the paralogical thinking that results from trying to elude the "double bind," of thinking irrationally to suit the parents' egocentric needs. The topic is too large to pursue here. However, a major function of the special high school for adolescents in the Yale Psychiatric Institute lies in providing a type of instruction that counters the schizophrenic patient's overinclusive thinking and enhances focal attention and clear conceptualization. The therapist can promote such changes by fostering clear boundaries between the patient and others, and by clarifying conflicting feelings and attitudes. Increasingly, however, I have focused specifically on freeing the patient from the need to distort his perceptions and meanings to fit into his parents' aberrant version of the world. It is a difficult passage, but when accomplished, the patient is out of the mire and on more solid ground. Conjoint family therapy when used as an adjunct to individual therapy can be particularly helpful. In the family sessions the patient may be unable to avoid realizing that one or both of his parents distort reality to their own needs, that they will reject the patient if he challenges their defenses, and that their remarks are untrustworthy. The patient may have become capable of assessing what his parents say through his experiences in therapeutic groups where participants challenge others and comment on defensive maneuvers. The patient finds it easier to cope with the actual parent with a therapist present than with the parent as a malignant introject. The woman who had not known how to purchase a brassiere had made little progress until conjoint family sessions were started. She had considered her mother as a perfect woman who had long sacrificed herself to keep the family solvent after the father had become depressed and ineffectual. In the family sessions, whenever the patient sought to discuss problems in the home that had troubled her childhood and adolescence, the mother consistently shifted to talking about the patient's difficulties as a child, intimating that no parent could have been successful with an inherently disturbed child. Yet, at other times, she would insist that the patient had been a normal but highly gifted child. With but slight help from the therapist, the inconsistencies came into focus. Then, in a crucial session, the patient saw her mother in a new light. The mother persistently asked to have the patient at home for a weekend, but in these meetings it became apparent that whenever the patient could make the trip, the mother found the occasion unsuitable. Eventually, the visit home could not be sidestepped. During the subsequent session the father criticized the patient for various trivial shortcomings during the weekend. The patient finally said that although it had been good to be home she would have enjoyed it more if her father had not nagged so much. The mother immediately snapped, "Your father never nags." The patient was silent, but later remarked, "You know, Mother, I am just realizing that I often feel ill at ease with you." To this the mother replied, "If you are, you are the only person I know who is." The bind had been placed, but it was too apparent. There was no argument, no blow-up, but the patient now began to express her own feelings and her own ideas.

The priority I have given to discussing how knowledge of the patient's family milieu can serve to guide psychotherapy does not indicate a disinterest in direct work with the family. Indeed, I believe that neglect of the family has been a major cause of therapeutic failure. Particularly with youthful patients efforts must be made to modify parental attitudes toward the patient as well as the patient's attitudes toward his parents. All too often when a patient is hospitalized a member of the staff elicits a history from the parents, notes that they are difficult or even troublesome, and lets them know that they have handed over their offspring to competent surrogates. Of course, it seems simpler if the staff can focus on the patient without the family's interference—but the family problems cannot be avoided through avoidance of the family. The opposite extreme—of hospitalizing the family with the patient, as carried out experimentally by Bowen and his colleagues (1957)—does not permit the patient the disengagement that is a major purpose of hospitalization.

If the parents were not difficult or peculiar, it is unlikely that the patient would be schizophrenic, but this does not mean that they are not intensely involved with their child, whose hospitalization is one of the unhappiest experiences in their lives. They require support lest one of them or the marriage collapse under the strain. They also need to face the family problems rather than believe that their child's illness is the major source of their unhappiness and difficulties. Commonly, therapists who know that months or years of intensive work will be required with a patient, somehow expect the parents to change simply because they are told to do so.

The premature removal of the youthful schizophrenic patient just as a good therapeutic relationship is being established is often a major frustration in hospital treatment (Fleck *et al.*, 1957). The parents are likely to remove their child for several reasons. The mother cannot believe that her son or daughter can survive without her, a concern that earlier had caused the school phobia from which many of these patients had suffered, and which had blocked their socialization with peers. Only a person who has worked with such mothers after their children have been hospitalized can appreciate the almost unbearable anxiety they suffer. The mother must control the treatment because no one can understand or really care for her unique child. The parent may also dread the patient's growing attachment to the therapist, experiencing it as total abandonment. Then, when as part of his improvement the patient displays hostility to the parents, they know that he has become sicker and find reasons to remove him from the hospital. If the staff members have been hostile to the parents or have neglected them, they can more readily believe that the hospital is turning the patient against them. Such crises must be anticipated and headed off. When someone on the staff understands the parents' problems, keeps them informed, and works with them to modify their concerns about the patient and their fears of losing their offspring, they are less likely to disrupt the therapy.

The removal of the patient from the family commonly creates an intrafamilial crisis. The difficulties with the patient had served to mask the incompatibilities of the parent; or the mother becomes anxious and depressed, deprived of the major focus of her life; or recriminations flare into the open, with each parent blaming the other for their child's illness; or another child now feels the brunt of the family difficulties. The hospital cannot fully shelter the patient from the aggravated family problems. Sometimes, the family established a new equilibrium without the patient, particularly when the parents have been excluded from the hospital. The family closes ranks, leaving no room for the patient, and despite protests to the contrary, will resist resuming any responsibility for him—a common cause of abandonment of patients in state hospitals.

Stanton and Schwartz made a major contribution to the understanding of the treatment process when they pointed out that flare-ups of disorganized behavior often occurred in response to disagreements among the staff members about the patient. The patient had become sensitized by being the focal point of the family schisms and sometimes had been a master at provoking them in his role as a scapegoat for parental conflicts. In the hospital he is apt to be sensitive to the expressed or covert disagreements about him between parents, or between parents and staff, and caught between his loyalties, he covers the situation by regressive behavior. It is worth a great deal of effort to try to unite the parents concerning the need for hospitalization and the plan of treatment, even if they cannot agree about anything else. Neglect of the parents, hostile exclusion of them, or condescension toward them often leads to aggravation of the patient's condition even though the psychiatrist may believe he is protecting the patient from their malignant influence.

Indeed, it has now become apparent—how had it been overlooked?—that the acute onset of many schizophrenic reactions, or the exacerbation that leads to hospitalization, follows upon the patient's being placed in an insoluble bind by his parents' impending separation. The patient is pulled in two directions by the competing parents—a condition reflected in the ideation of the catatonic excitement or stupor. A few days ago I listened to an interview with a graduate student who had suffered several catatonic episodes. She told of her delusions during the first episode, when she believed that everyone in the world loved her but she was responsible for their well being. At the time, her parents had finally decided to end their unhappy marriage. Both used the patient, their oldest child, as a confidant and sought her as an ally. Her mother told the patient that she feared that her father would seduce the patient's pubescent sister, with whom he frequently slept. The father confided that the mother was a Lesbian and a menace to the three daughters.

When one realizes that an acutely disturbed patient is responding to an approaching break-up of his parents' marriage in which he is torn between them or knows that he will be left irrevocably tied to the task of salvaging a parent's life, one can accomplish considerable therapeutic work even when the patient is inaccessible. A 16-year-old youth was admitted in an extreme state of excitation, believing that an atom bomb had destroyed the city, that he alone remained alive, and that no one else was real. During the several months during which he remained out of contact, it was possible to modify his parents' relationship so that they no longer planned to separate. At first, the mother, who claimed she had only remained with her highly eccentric husband for the children's sake, had become even more determined to leave him, blaming him for their son's psychosis. However, as discussions continued, she realized that they had both been at fault: Their marriage had never led to a proper family life because both were pathologically tied to their families of origin, each of which undercut the worth of the other. The patient, who had long sought to bridge this schism, had become terrified at the prospect of being the mother's major support in the absence of his grandiose father. Receiving emotional support from the hospital staff during the crisis, the parents stopped blaming one another and began to face their shortcomings as spouses and parents. They supported one another sufficiently to give up their stranglehold on their son and later to accept the advice to send their son to a preparatory school. Their difficulties were far from resolved—the father's severe pathology precluded any easy solution—but they managed to have their son remain away from home and from further involvement in their problems.

At present the current flows strongly in the direction of brief hospitalization for schizophrenic patients lest the hospital foster regression or increased withdrawal from socialization. A hospital that is a therapeutic community does not promote regression but provides a retreat from living situations that have overwhelmed the patient, and fosters the socializing experiences with peers he had lacked at home. The pathology of the family is extensive and can be changed only under fortunate circumstances and with prolonged and intensive therapeutic work with the family. It forms a pathogenic environment, particularly for the patient who has become sensitized to it. Even after a prolonged hospital stay, it is usually unwise for the patient to return to his family. It requires considerable work with the parents as well as the patient to make such separation possible, but it is often vital for any definitive and lasting change in the patient's life.

We would like to believe that we can alter the family transactions and modify the parents' attitudes sufficiently to permit the patient to return to more normal ways and resume his development. This is the goal of conjoint family therapy, which some psychiatrists now believe is the treatment of choice for schizophrenic patients. Undoing the influences that had been throttling or distorting the patient's development throughout his formative years is scarcely possible without intensive psychotherapeutic work with the patient. It is a very different matter from eliciting changes in the family when the child is still very young. Moreover, the parents are no longer youthful and their personalities and patterns of interaction are set. Still it is worth the effort for when inroads are made, changes in the family are followed by significant changes in the patient. Although conjoint family therapy has much to offer in clarifying family problems to the family members, and can open the way for profound changes in attitudes, my own experience leads me to doubt its effectiveness as the sole approach rather than as part of a more total program of treatment for both the patient and the family. Another highly useful form of family therapy is carried out in open-ended parents' groups. In these groups parents not only relate to others with similar problems and can together try to work out some solutions, but also may be able to see in others what they had been unable to see in themselves.

I have sought to present some of the influences upon the treatment of schizophrenic patients that have been emerging with the realization that these patients have grown up in seriously disturbed and distorting family environments, and with our increasing knowledge of what these families are like and just how they have failed to provide certain requisites for the patient's integrated development. I have considered some of the ways in which such knowledge provides directives for psychotherapy with the patient, and also for effecting changes in the family situation, in the parents' relationships with each other, and in their attitudes toward the patient. We cannot always change the situation and we cannot often change it profoundly. We can seek to make it possible for the patient to escape from it into a different way of living rather than into irrationality and delusion. Occasionally, the patient gains sufficient independence, rationality, and perspective to appreciate that his parents had been so derprived in their own childhoods, so caught up in a net created by their parents' difficulties, that they could not have been different than they were, and that he, the patient, cannot salvage their lives for them, but rather has all he can do to make something of his own and break the pathological chain that has extended from generation to generation. Then, the ambivalent animosities toward his parents and his fears of them can dissolve into compassion for them. It was such compassionate resolution that Tennessee Williams sought in writing *The Glass Menagerie* long after he had fled his home and that Eugene O'Neill strove to work out in the series of plays that culminated in *Long Day's Journey into Night*. The patient is unlikely to achieve such understanding if his therapist regards the parents as villains and feels hostile to them, rather than grasping the tragedy of the parents' lives even as he seeks to understand and empathize with the patient.

REFERENCES

ALANEN, YRJÖ O. "The Mothers of Schizophrenic Patients," *Acta Psychiatrica Neurologica Scand.* (1958) 33: Suppl. No. 124.

ALANEN, YRJÖ O. "Some Thoughts of Schizophrenia and Ego Development in the Light of Family Investigations," *Arch. Gen. Psychiatry* (1960) 3:650-656. (a)

ALANEN, YRJÖ O. Über die Familiensituation der Schizophrenie-Patienten," *Acta Psychotherapeutica et Psychosomatica* (Basel) (1960) 8:89-104. (b)

BATESON, GREGORY, ET AL. "Towards a Theory of Schizophrenia," *Behavioral Science* (1958) 1:251-264.

BLEULER, EUGEN. *Dementia Praecox or the Group of Schizophrenias* [1911]; Internat. Univ. Press, 1950.

BOWEN, MURRAY. "Family Participation in Schizophrenia," paper presented at meeting of American Psychiatric Assn., 1957.

BOWEN, MURRAY. "A Family Concept of Schizophrenia," in Don. D. Jackson (Ed.), *The Etiology of Schizophrenia;* Basic Books, 1960.

BOWEN, MURRAY, DYSINGER, ROBERT H., & BASAMANIA, BETTY. "The Role of the Father in Families with a Schizophrenic Patient," *Amer. J. Psychiat.,* 115:1017-1020, 1959.

BOWEN, MURRAY, ET AL. "Study and Treatment of Five Hospitalized Families Each with a Psychotic Member," paper presented at meeting of Amer. Orthopsychiatric Assn., 1957.

DELAY, J. DENIKER, P., & GREEN, A. "Le Milieu Familial des Schizophrènes: I. Proposition du Probleme," *Encephale* 46:189-232, 1957.

DELAY, J., DENIKER, P., & GREEN, A. "Le Milieu Familial des Schizophrènes: II. Méthodes d'Approche," *Encephale,* 49:1-21, 1960.

DELAY, J., DENIKER, P., & GREEN, A. "Le Milieu Familial des Schizophrènes: III. Résultats et Hypothèses," *Encephale,* 51:5-73, 1962.

FLECK, STEPHEN, ET AL. "The Intrafamilial Environment of the Schizophrenic Patient: II. Interaction Between Hospital Staff and Families" [1957], in Theodore Lidz, Stephen Fleck, and Alice R. Cornelison, *Schizophrenia and the Family;* Internat. Univ. Press, 1965.

FLECK, STEPHEN, ET AL. "The Intrafamilial Environment of the Schizophrenic Patient: Incestuous and Homosexual Problems" [1958], In Theodore Litz, Stephen Fleck, and Alice R. Cornelison, *Schizophrenia and the Family;* Internat. Univ. Press, 1965.

FROMM-REICHMANN, FRIEDA. "Transference Problems in Schizophrenia," *Psychoanal. Quart.,* 8:412-426, 1939.

GREEN, HANNAH, *I Never Promised You a Rose Garden;* Holt, Rinehart & Winston, 1964.

HILL, LEWIS. *Psychotherapeutic Intervention in Schizophrenia;* Univ. of Chicago Press, 1955.

JACKSON, DON D. "The Family and Sexuality," in Carl A. Whitaker (Ed.), *Psychotherapy of Chronic Schizophrenic Patients;* Little, Brown, 1958

JACKSON, DON D. & WEAKLAND, JOHN H. "Schizophrenic Symptoms and Family Interaction," *Arch. Gen. Psychiatry,* 1:618-621, 1959.

JUNG, CARL. *The Psychology of Dementia Praecox;* New York, J. Nervous and Mental Diseases Publ. Co., 1909.

LAING, RONALD D. *The Self and Others: Further Studies in Sanity and Madness;* London, Tavistock Publ., 1962.

LEACH, EDMUND. "Anthropological Aspects of Language: Animal Categories and Verbal Abuse," in Eric Lenneberg (Ed.), *New Directions in the Study of Language;* M.I.T. Press, 1966.

LIDZ, RUTH WILLMANN & LIDZ, THEODORE. "Therapeutic Considerations Arising from the Intense Symbiotic Needs of Schizophrenic Patients" [1951], in Eugene B. Brody and Frederick C. Redlich (Eds.), *Psychotherapy with Schizophrenics;* Internat. Univ. Press, 1952.

LIDZ, THEODORE. "The Family, Personality Development and Schizophrenia," in John Romano (Ed.), *The Origins of Schizophrenia;* The Hague, Excerpta Medica Foundation, 1967. (a)

LIDZ, THEODORE. Salmon Lectures, 1967, to be published. (b)

LIDZ, THEODORE. "Familie, Sprache und Schizophrenie," *Psyche,* 22:701-719, 1968.

LIDZ, THEODORE, FLECK, STEPHEN, & CORNELISON, ALICE. *Schizophrenia and the Family;* Internat. Univ. Press, 1965.

O'NEILL, EUGENE. *Long Day's Journey Into Night;* Yale Univ. Press, 1956.

RAYBIN, JAMES. "Homosexual Incest," *J. Nerv. Ment. Dis.* (1968) in press.

REICHARD, SUZANNE & TILLMAN, CARL. "Patterns of Parent-Child Relationships in Schizophrenia," *Psychiatry*, 13:247-257, 1950.

ROSENTHAL, DAVID (Ed.). *The Genain Quadruplets;* Basic Books, 1963.

SINGER, MARGARET T. & WYNNE, LYMAN C. "Thought Disorder and Family Relations of Schizophrenics: III. Methodology Using Projective Techniques," *Arch. Gen. Psychiatry*, 12:187-200, 1965. (a)

SINGER, MARGARET T. & WYNNE, LYMAN C. "Thought Disorder and Family Relations of Schizophrenics: IV. Results and Implications," *Arch. Gen. Psychiatry* 12:201-212, 1965. (b)

STANTON, ALFRED H. & SCHWARTZ, MORRIS S. *The Mental Hospital;* Basic Books, 1954.

SULLIVAN, HARRY STACK. "Conceptions of Modern Psychiatry: Therapeutic Conceptions," *Psychiatry*, 3:87-117, 1940.

WILLIAMS, TENNESSEE. *The Glass Menagerie;* New Directions, 1945.

WYNNE, LYMAN C., ET AL. "The Family Relations of a Set of Monozygotic Quadruplet Schizophrenics," in *Congress Report of the 2nd Internat. Congress of Psychiatry,* Zurich (1957) 2:43-49.

WYNNE, LYMAN C., ET AL. "Pseudo-Mutuality in the Family Relations of Schizophrenics," *Psychiatry*, 21:205-220, 1958.

WYNNE, LYMAN C. & SINGER, MARGARET T. "Thought Disorder and Family Relations of Schizophrenics: I. A Research Strategy," *Arch. Gen. Psychiatry*, 9:191-198, 1963. (a)

WYNNE, LYMAN C. & SINGER, MARGARET T. "Thought Disorder and Family Relations of Schizophrenics: II. A Classification of Forms of Thinking," *Arch. Gen. Psychiatry*, 9:199-206, 1963. (b)

38

THE CONTAGIOUS SUBCULTURE
OF PSYCHOSIS

E. James Anthony, M.D.

Blanche F. Ittleson Professor of Child Psychiatry
Washington University School of Medicine (St. Louis)
Training Analyst, Chicago Institute for Psychoanalysis

> *"Sometimes I ain't so sho who's got ere a right to say when a man is crazy and when he ain't. Sometimes I think it ain't none of us pure crazy and ain't none of us pure sane until the balance of us talks him that-a-way. It's like it ain't so much what a fellow does, but it's the way the majority of folks is looking at him when he does it."*
>
> (WILLIAM FAULKNER: "As I Lay Dying")

The Response to the Irrational and the Unrealistic

As investigators intermittently in contact with psychosis, we are becoming increasingly aware that our response to the irrational and the unrealistic is not quite the same as that of individuals living at home with a close psychotic relative. We seem to lack, or to possess in short measure, certain adaptive capacities that develop only with exposure to the vicissitudes of everyday psychotic functioning. However, when we intensify our contact over time by entering the family circle, a curious enculturation gradually takes place and early discomforts, stemming from mystification, gives way to a surprising acceptance of eccentric phenomena. The more participant and the less objectively observational that

Supported by U.S. P.H.S. Research Grants MH-12043-01 and RO1-MH-14052-01.

we are, the more striking is the change in this attitude of acceptance. Nevertheless, we never achieve, and never hope to achieve, full familial status within the disturbed milieu, and one of the main factors impeding total assimilation is the exaggerated rationality with which we tend defensively to counteract exposure to the irrational. Families within the subculture of psychosis do not, in general, take kindly to strangers, especially when they unconsciously flaunt their sanity like a professional badge of office. It is only after we begin to appreciate the elements of irrationality within ourselves, provoked into fuller awareness by the living-in experience, that the degree of acceptance by our ever-suspicious hosts is enhanced.

When we first enter the psychotic orbit, we carry with us some ingrained preconceptions and stereotypes about what constitutes rational attitudes and rational behavior. We tend to assume that the rational is synonymous with the healthy until we are brought face to face with a logical apologia for some ugly example of human destructiveness. The rational and irrational are, therefore, polarized in popular thinking and have come to imply antithetical concepts. This "agglutination of values," to use Hartmann's term, is an illustration of the universal human proclivity to segregate good things from bad ones and keep them relatively isolated from each other (3).

The discontinuous viewpoint, so powerfully supported by the cross-sectional interview in the clinic, becomes untenable when the psychotic is lived with at home under conditions of his own making. When the threat of evaluation is removed, the grosser facets of psychosis frequently subside and a normalization of interaction ensues. Dystonic manifestations will frequently make their appearance at the interface separating home from not-home, but within the domestic setting a wider range of syntonic behavior is more apparent. Lapses into more primitive, more emotional, more unreasonable and less predictable activities seem to occur with greater frequency in the psychotic milieu and following such lapses, sensibility and equanimity may take longer to reestablish than in the less disturbed family situation.

So intrinsic is the concept of discontinuity to the general culture (allowing for some variation within different cultures) that it took us a surprising amount of time to correct in our research approach. In mutual discussion we gradually realized that our initial proposition had collectively assumed that entering the world of psychosis was tantamount to walking through a Carrolian looking glass and discovering a bizarrely antipodal set of circumstances. Our crucial experiences in living-in taught us that between the rational and the irrational there lay a complete series of transitional behaviors along a continuum and that watertight compartments of rationality and reality were not compatible with the actuality of human life.

A similar continuum prevailed with regard to reality and unreality along which we also slide in both directions during the course of everyday life. At many moments in the day, under conditions of average stress, we make little compromises with reality refusing to acknowledge its existence at times when it fails to serve our more urgent needs.

Reality is not built in a day but has a long developmental history. Nor is it completed once and for all. Its construction comes about gradually through a demarcation of the self from the non-self and the parents play an essential role both in furthering the sense of reality as well as distorting it. The child takes in the reality of his parents as he takes in their food, their language, their attitudes and their behavior. He takes in reality as they perceive it and as they want him to perceive it. His testing of reality follows their rules and the eventual differentiation of inside from outside, object from object and thought from thing is part of the basic grammar of reality deriving from the parents. He is therefore very easily caught up in any temptation on their part to tamper with reality, and there are as many emotional rewards for those children conforming to the distorted reality that the parents present to them as for those who strive to meet the demands of realistic parents. An unrealistic parent can seduce a child into living in a never-never land as much as a realistic parent can help him to make the vital discriminations between fantasy and reality. However, the sense of reality and the capacity to test it both in terms of internal as well as external experience are gradually acquired and variable functions even within the non-psychotic setting in every individual's life, an internal system of irrational and unrealistic thoughts is maintained and, from time to time, outer reality is manipulated to fit in with this inner scheme of things. The coherence of the world depends on the ego's capacity to organize the internal and external realities in a way that ensures a more or less comfortable equilibrium, but in dealing with children, one has constantly to bear in mind that before the ego becomes the sole representative of reality, it is the parents who undertake this major task and it is they who subsequently inculcate a viable sense of reality in the child. In the case of the psychotic parent, the sense of reality tends to remain more vulnerable to the many pressures brought to bear on it.

Irrationality and Unreality Within the Family

It has long been recognized that the irrational character of an individual's behavior in a group may contrast sharply with his rational behavior outside the group. An apparent cleavage occurs within him so that he is able to accept, for example, cruel, destructive and primitive ideas as a member of the group and reject them with abhorrence as a private individual. A similar type of splitting may take place in the sense of reality. In families where delusional ideas exist, for instance, the children may learn to live according to a double standard of reality so that they admit a delusional notion within the family but discard it when away from the family. The deluded parent may make acceptance of her delusion a prerequisite to the love relationship leaving the children with no choice but to accept her irrational or unrealistic ideas. This means that the systems of rationality and reality within a given family are intimately bound up to the system of object relationships and may therefore vary with the operations of love and hate.

If this is true, and our experience leads us to believe that it is, it follows that conglomerated descriptions of family functioning or anecdotes abstracted from their total context conduce to the falsification of actuality. For example, to depict family life globally in terms of irrationality, paralogical thinking, mystifications, falsifications of reality, double-bind communications, pseudomutuality, unpredictable switches in feeling, symbiotic identifications, ritualistic obsessiveness, inappropriate behavior, oscillations between withdrawal and closeness, lack of organization and direction, "as if" tendencies in all the members and systematic "brain-washing" by the parents depreciates the "humanness," the helpfulness, the good humor and the coping skills that also operate from time to time in the most psychologically-dominated families. The mechanisms that have been isolated have the advantage of clarifying the psychopathology and abnormal interactions that undoubtedly exist, but the disadvantage of mechanizing dynamic developments and at the same time masking the fluctuating and more authentic portrayal of the family.

An anecdote, reported to the clinician and embalmed in the case record, may have a similar deleterious effect on the constructed picture of life as actually lived by a family. For example, Lidz tells of a schizophrenic woman whose twin boys for many years were under the impression that the term constipation meant "disagreeing with mother" because whenever one of them would argue with her, she would insist that they were constipated and in need of an enema. Both boys were then placed prone on the bathroom floor while the mother, in her undergarments, inserted the nozzle of the enema into the anus of each boy, at the same time fostering a contest to see which of them could hold out longer before succumbing to the pressure for evacuation. It was the loser's penalty to have to dash down to the basement lavatory (5). An illustration, as striking as this one, has the effect of fixating one's image of the family so that subsequent reports serve only to confirm and consolidate the clinical impression of bizarre life.

Involving and Noninvolving Psychosis in the Family

Although our experience, in general, argues against the existence of transactional constancy within the family, we have to add that certain categories of psychosis can fundamentally influence the general functioning of the family. In this respect, psychotic disorders in parents can be classified, as far as the children are concerned, into involving and noninvolving types. In the former, the psychosis invades every aspect of family living so that the children are caught up in the parent's delusional and hallucinatory systems, exposed unpredictably to his incongruous affects, overwhelmed by his murderous or incestuous impulses and sucked into a vortex of interchanges that perplex and frighten them. In the noninvolving psychoses, the effect on the children is altogether less direct and less dramatic. The parent is lost to the children through autistic withdrawal and they must learn to live without him as in the case of death or physical separation although the presence of a lost psychotic parent tends to raise more complex problems of adjustment for the family as a whole. The psychotic parent can be isolated from the general life of the family that can be structured without him rendering him essentially a non-person.

With the involving syndromes, the organizational climate of the family undergoes marked dedifferentiation and, as a result, the group becomes primitively reactive, impulse-ridden, hyperemotional, inconsistent, unreasonable, irresponsible and unreliable, prone to violent excesses, deficient in reality sense and highly suggestible. This is the picture of the group given by Freud when organization, leadership and controls are deficient and the group regresses to a lower level of functioning, dominated by the pleasure principle, raw instinctual behavior and wishful thinking (2).

In the noninvolving psychoses, the family may at times be overorganized so that daily life is structured and rigidified and there is little evidence of free and spontaneous interaction. Life is carried on in a low key and the impact of psychosis on the family can only be indirectly observed.

The differences, therefore, in family climate are mainly evident in the amount of tempestuous interaction in which the members are engaged and the degree to which such interactions are governed by the psychotic influence at work.

Another difference is in the facility with which attitudes, feelings and behavior are transmitted to the family orbit as if by contagion. When one lives with the family in daily contact over time, one begins to appreciate that miniature epidemics of irrationality and unrealism pervade the family from time to time and that in between such contagious happenings even the most psychotically-dominated families do many of the things that ordinary families do, such as shopping in supermarkets, attending church, taking a drive or spending an evening at a movie or restaurant. Family life is by no means grossly disordered at the time and we have found that these families run the whole gamut of traditional observance and are just as custom-governed as ordinary families. This observation is very much in keeping with Dewey's dictum that the part played by custom and tradition in shaping the individual's life far outweighs the effect of idiosyncrasies or eccentricities. As far as the individual is concerned, it is a useful index of ego strength and invulnerability to ascertain to what extent he is affected or unaffected by the contagious phenomena that episodically beset the family.

The Phenomenon of Mental Contagion Within the Family

The phenomenon of mental contagion has been recognized by clinicians for over 300 years and critical opinion has fluctuated in regarding it at various times as a myth, a mystique, a metaphor and a psychological mechanism. It has been mainly investigated in terms of *folie à deux* with the two partners, interviewed separately, demonstrating a concordance in their psychotic symptomatology. The mysteriousness of the transmission was over-estimated because the process of transmission was never actually under scrutiny. In our research on the influence of parental psychosis on the children in the family, we came across several variations of "parapsychosis" in which delusional ideas or depressive affects had been, in different degrees, imposed on one or more of the family members. A typical example of what appeared to us to be contagious communication presented itself in the very earliest phase of our study and stimulated us to explore the phenomenon more thoroughly.

A few sentences from the interview with the mother, hospitalized several times for paranoid schizophrenia, gives some impression of the intense pressure of persecution afflicting the patient.

"Every day the children and I pull all the blinds down in the living room so that no one can look in and then we watch right through the day in case these people come by the road. The children want to go out to play but I warned them that if they do they will be caught and killed by these people. We have our lunch around the window so that we can watch. Sometimes we take turns at watching but the children are not such good watchers and I have seen them turn away from the window to do something else. I try to make them understand how important it is never to stop watching. We would never be safe."

Here now is an interview with one of the children in this family, an eight-year-old girl long exposed to this kind of affect and verbalization.

"What struck me first about her was her hyperalerted behavior. She seemed to be scanning every fraction of the environment with a high degree of intensity. Said she after a while: 'You've only got two bulbs in that lamp and there is supposed to be three.' I smiled at her and said: 'I would be willing to get another lamp if you think it would throw light on any problem you might have.' She frowned at this and said: 'What do you mean?' I shook my head. 'Never mind. I was only making a little joke so as to get us talking.' To this she replied: 'I don't like jokes. I don't like people who make jokes. I think jokes try to make you look small and stupid.' I said immediately: 'I'm sorry you feel like that about jokes. I know they are sometimes meant to tease, but this time I was really trying to be helpful.' She gave no reaction to my apology, but after a while she said: 'You have only one door to this room. What would happen if a fire broke out and you had no way of escaping? You would be trapped here and you would burn to death.' I said that we were reasonably careful about such things and that there had been no fire during the fifty years that this particular building had been standing and that, therefore, I was not unduly concerned about it. However, I added that I understood quite well that someone who worried a great deal about bad things happening to her might expect it to happen anywhere at anytime. She said: 'You can never be sure of being safe. No one is safe in this world. Earthquakes can happen, tornadoes can happen, fires can happen. You can't be safe anywhere in the world.' I said: 'You know, you must be saying something about yourself. If a kid can't feel safe at home with her mom and dad, there is nowhere that she is going to feel safe. We have to try and make you feel safer at home first.' She turned her eyes down and said quietly: 'My mom doesn't feel safe at home.' "

It was evident that something had passed between mother and daughter for this little girl clearly lived in an unexpectable world that was far from average and that her only safeguard against catastrophe was to live within a wide margin of safety. Unless everything was "just so" and orderly, her anxious apprehensiveness developed rapidly. A joke was outside the realm of carefully controlled behavior and was therefore not to be tolerated. It was also viewed negatively as damaging and deflating to the ego and this was in keeping with the general expectation of attack.

This pilot case raised a number of additional problems regarding contagious phenomena. What were the special characteristics of the donor or of the recipient that facilitated transmission? What were the special characteristics of the family that permitted the growth of delusional ideas to go uncorrected by rational and realistic confrontations? Why were some children immune and others vulnerable? And finally, were nonfamilial individuals as susceptible to the contagious process as the family members themselves?

To answer these various questions in a way that would illuminate the process involved, it seemed to us to demand direct observation of the family as a whole over a sufficient period of time to allow for the emergence of contagion.

The original study by Lasegue and Falret in 1877 (4) pointed out that "naturally apprehensive children, confined in a limited environment," are especially disposed to become "the echoes of a delusion with which they are associated" if, in addition, they are physically undernourished and undersized, of relatively poor intelligence, and markedly submissive and closely related to the deluded person. Suggestibility would seem to play a critical role in such contagions.

Among the transmittable affects, suspiciousness, fearfulness and anxiety are all regarded as highly "infectious" followed by depression and elation and angriness and moodiness. Most clinicians seem to agree that the paranoid forms of psychosis occur most frequently in the "psychoses of association" and that the depressive forms are seen less often.

The phenomenon can occur at various levels; at the most primitive, archaic motor mannerisms and expressions such as scratchings, yawnings, stretchings, throbbings, rockings and other repetitive rhythms are all very contagious and it is difficult for even normal people to avoid being "infected." At this level, the egos have little to say to one another and the effect is mostly brought about by the operation of empathy. The responses take place largely outside consciousness provoking a deep inner resonance that culminates in a shared regressive fantasy. The preconditions demand a maximum of free-floating anxiety at the intensity of panic coupled with a transient or permanent dedifferentiation of the self and non-self. Children suffering from clinical degrees of undifferentiation are particularly liable to such contagiousness.

At the next level, the affects are especially prone to transmission with suspiciousness, apprehensiveness and depression among the most easily "caught." This level of contagion operates with the help of a more advanced ego system, the feelings being embedded in a powerful flow of verbalizations used more in the service of expression than communication. At a mature level, the ideas, attitudes and values are rapidly assimilated mainly through the mechanisms of imitation and identification. Meerloo formulated two laws of contagion, the first being that the more archaically communicative a human expression was, the more contagiously did it function; and the second, that the more archaic the expression was, the more unobtrusively did the message get across (6).

Our expectation, based on these considerations, was that the involving or reactive psychoses would manifest the more overt forms of contagion as expressed in the transmission of affects, ideas and values whereas with the noninvolving process psychoses, the contagious phenomena would involve archaic motoric behavior. Furthermore, we postulated that the former contagions would require a crescendo development as the affects increased in vehemence whereas with the latter contagions, it was felt that the transmission might take place at any time on a plateau of ordinary interchange. Finally, it seemed logical to suppose that the presence of an involving parent was essential to the development of the type of contagion generated by them but that the presence or absence of the noninvolving parent was not critical to the development of archaic contagions.

The Living-In Experience

To live with one's patients, particularly psychiatric ones, would seem to be out of line with the Hippocratic tradition; at one end of the scale of proper professional conduct, it suggests the acme of indiscretion and at the other, an active masochism for which treatment should be urgently prescribed. However, in the sphere of clinical investigation, the matter is a little different. Research offers many diplomatic immunities to the investigator under the aegis of science and there are sometimes good reasons for taking advantage of the additional freedom and flexibility provided. Moreover, the precedents for living-in are quite impressive. The great Johann Weyer who demolished the case for witchcraft and witch-hunting in the 16th century occasionally took patients home to stay with him so as better to understand and treat them and, in our own times, the phenomenological psychiatrist, Minkowski, lived with his patients for as long as two months at a time in order to further his firsthand and inward experience of their illness. More recently, Winnicott, the British psychoanalyst, took a disturbed boy into his wartime household and subsequently described what happened in a well-known paper whose title speaks for itself: *Hate and the Countertransference!*

By all accounts, it is not an easy thing to spend more than the standard fifty minutes, especially if he is psychotic, and when it comes to six hours plus, the field is gratefully relinquished to the paraprofessional.

Psychiatrists, for many good reasons involving the technical usefulness of their objectivity, their neutrality or their free-floating attention, as a rule, tend to restrict the time and space arrangements with their patients to an extent that is manageable and workable: not too long and not too short; not too far and not too close. It is not altogether clear whether the benefits from these restrictions are entirely for the patient.

Whenever the subject of living-in with a family is brought up, a number of questions invariably get asked, particularly when there is a schizophrenic patient in the household: How does one set about it? How do the families put up with it? How does one stand it? And does one learn anything different from doing it?

The family-sitter is under the joint supervision of an anthropologist and psychiatrist. Before embarking on her duties, she is given a short training on the recording process which is done on tape at the end of each day. So far, the family-sitters have been young, theoretically unsophisticated women undergraduates selected on the basis of their unobtrusiveness, their equanimity under stress, their objectivity and their reporting skills. Since they were mostly at home during the day with the mothers and younger children, it seemed more logical to use women, and our experience has been that they do blend more easily than men into everyday family life. During the day, the family-sitter helps with the household chores, the supervision of the children and the shopping, and in the evening and on weekends, she participates in the recreational activities of the family as a whole. The role assumed is that of a visiting relative or close friend and tends to be passive and compliant, but helpful. The multiple functions entailed in this role ensure multiple contacts at many different levels. At one end, she may be treated as a dependable baby-sitter and, at the other, may be regarded as an omniscient observer with the capacity for powerful psychological insights. She tries to be, in fact, what the family wants her to be and, in theory, never "psychologizes," never assumes a therapeutic role and is only active in the case of some emergency such as an accident to a child.

On various occasions during the day, she takes off time to make notes on what has been happening. In her recordings, she is asked to be as unselective and as undiscriminating as possible and is cautioned against categorization and against causally connecting up events or interpreting them in any way. She is asked to remember that she is a very special sort of camera sensitively reflecting what is taking place in front of her. When her stint is over, we go over the total record with her and capture some of her own "unbracketed" feelings and fantasies about the experience. In this way, we try to have the best of both observational worlds, the objective and the subjective.

The families are told that the living-in arrangement serves the purpose of validating the clinical and experimental findings of the research center and that by enlarging our understanding, it enables us to help those with a similar problem. We point out that only in this way can we determine what is "natural" for a particular family and what is an artificial response to the testing situations.

Our experience so far has been that a fairly strong bond is rapidly created between the family-sitter and the family, and the relationship may even persist after the period of residence is over. This acceptance of the stranger came as a surprise. When seen from the outside, the psychotic enclave seems encapsulated, entrenched, isolated and insulated with the indwellers apprehensive of novelty and mistrustful of strangers. We therefore anticipated some paranoid explosiveness. There was hardly any and, contrary to our expectations, the family-sitter was generally treated with a graciousness that seemed strangely out of keeping with the crazy feelings and attitudes that sometimes dominated the family.

The fact that she was introduced into the situation with a minimum identifying data—an enigma wrapped in a mystery—made her an ideal object for projection. She was variously endowed with capacities to clarify the mystifications of psychosis, to soothe the wildest psychotic turbulences and to restore to equilibrium the many imbalances disturbing family life. The affect-hungry children may constantly solicit her feelings and the parents may invite her to arbitrate in their often amorphous arguments. She is a captive audience for a wide range of exhibitionism, a target for sadistic and masochistic impulses, a standard for reality-testing and a model for normal, rational behavior. It is a hard load to carry for relatively inexperienced young people but we have found that with coaching and supervision, the individuals selected for the job demonstrate a surprising resilience to the many discomforts involved in the situation. With this method, we probably see a wider range of activity than is usual for the family since the visitor appears to catalyze any latent emotional elements and to thus bring out both the best and the worst in the family.

Habituation to her presence has been fairly quick and the families themselves have reported that they do not seem so aware of her presence after the first few days. This is especially so when small children are present since they have a way of falling back into their habitual patterns of behavior and carrying the rest of the family along with them in this direction.

The family-sitters consistently report that the families do not seem as crazy by the end of the visit, and there is no doubt that a curious dynamic adjustment begins to take place with the result that the earlier discomforts, stemming from the chaos and confusion that at times pervade the home, give place to a rising tolerance or eccentric and incongruous phenomena.

In time, she may develop symptoms of her own in reaction to her milieu or borrow symptoms from the family. Toward the end of her week, she may find herself responding divergently like a member of the family and may become alarmed by this.

> On a particular evening, the family-sitter had been listening to the mother's enranged account of the provocations that she endured from her two children. A little later, one of the children began fiddling with the visitor's cigarette lighter and she asked him repeatedly to put it down and as repeatedly he ignored her and continued to work with it. All of a sudden she reached out and smacked him and immediately felt catastrophically guilty and ashamed wondering how she could possibly report this to the supervisor. The mother's reaction was typical. She remarked with enormous satisfaction: "Now you know exactly how I sometimes feel."

At its height, the contagion is widespread and inescapable. The visitors have complained of vague feelings of victimization, confused thinking, oppressiveness, depression, malaise and a wide range of psychosomatic symptoms. One of them said at the end of the first day, "I really feel terribly confused and it's giving me a headache. At times I am not sure whether I am crazy or whether the family is crazy. Things simply don't make sense and I don't know whether I can stand it." Another had a distinct feeling that the family, in unison, was testing her sanity to see just how much she could stand. "I suppose that they won't really accept me unless I really become one of them." She pointed out that in order to fit in, she found herself passively imitating the family's responses and experiencing less and less dissonance in so doing. Following her assignment, another of the girls suffered for a while from unpleasant dreams amounting to nightmares. In one of these, she was reduced to helpless panic when, having cleaned and tidied up the house with great satisfaction, the schizophrenic father in a frenzy reduced all her careful work to utter chaos. (We explicitly instruct the family-sitters not to engage in heroic efforts, to organize or restructure a dilapidating household.)

Within a week after the living-in experience, these minor contagious manifestations had completely subsided.

Does one learn anything new from this method? The answer to this is "yes" since there is no other way in which one can obtain a living picture of the phenomenology of family life in continuity. Not only do we learn how a family lives, interacts, organizes itself and plans for its immediate or remote future but we also become intimately acquainted with its strategies for coping with disturbing affects and behavior as a group. We can follow the ebb and flow of irrationality and realism as they undergo profound vicissitudes in the course of daily living. We can examine at firsthand the collective mythologies and pseudo-histories by means of which families construct and reconstruct their own specific "psychic reality." Most pertinently, all this can be done within the context of familiar surroundings and the bread-and-butter existence. Before deciding how crazy a family is or how limited its coping skills, it would seem better by far to observe it in context than out of it. The living-in experience provides us with the range of family variability without which both diagnosis and prognosis can be no better than intelligent guesses. To do better, both diagnostically and prognostically, one needs to know something of the normal behavior of the abnormal family, its capacities for coping and its propensity for defeat, its readiness for change and its contentment with stagnation.

Most of all, the living-in experience gives some indication of how involving a psychosis is and how pervasively it enters into every facet of the development of the children. However, it tells us how contagious the illness is and, therefore, to what extent we can anticipate a steady growth in abnormal reactions in the different family members. The vulnerabilities and invulnerabilities, the needs and fears, the move to closeness and the flight from closeness are best assessed at the time of their development at firsthand and in a setting not contaminated by institutional procedures and pressures.

For all these reasons and purposes, the most strategic place to be, both physically and empathically, and for diagnosis, prognosis and treatment is within the family circle.

Illustrations of the Living-In Experience

THE CASE OF AN INVOLVING PSYCHOSIS
WITH THE SICK PARENT AT HOME

In this first extract, the family-sitter is living-in with a family in which the mother has suffered from repeated attacks of severe schizo-affective disorder of a highly-involving type. Her husband tries to do his best in this predicament but is constantly drawn into the whirlpool of her emotions. There are three children: Paul, age eleven, Frankie, age three and a half, and Carol, a baby eighteen months old.

The family was going on an outing. I went into the kitchen and asked where we were going but no one seemed to know. Mr. Mann just drove and drove and drove until finally we got out at a little roadhouse and he ordered hamburgers for everybody. The fight started between Mr. and Mrs. Mann because she had set the baby on the table and he protested that the baby might fall off. At this she got up and said: "Let me out. I am not going to take any of this. I am going out to sit in the car. You can have her." With this she dumped the baby on the seat and went off. Her husband kept saying: "Now ain't that something," but the children said nothing. We then drove on to look at the river and there was a fight about that. Mrs. Mann said: "Just go on and do anything you want. You think everybody is going to do what you want them to do." The boys seemed to be getting increasingly anxious and wanting to get out and Mr. Mann said to me: "Why don't you get out with the boys and go look at the river." We were hardly out when Mrs. Mann called us back. Her husband said: "Get in so that your mother won't have to be watching you all the time." He then announced that we were going home and at this the boys protested and started to cry, and the bickering between the parents got steadily worse until the screaming and yelling reached a pandemonium. At one point, Mrs. Mann said she was going to beat Frankie to death if he didn't stop misbehaving and later she threatened to throw him out of the car. Amidst all this, Paul turned to me and asked: "Are you happy?" And I countered with "Are *you* happy?" at which he looked down at the floor. However, for the rest of the trip he kept saying: "Isn't this a wonderful day!" and "Aren't we all having a grand time!" and other similar comments.

When we reached home, the baby was crying very, very hard and Mr. Mann kept saying that she was doing it on purpose. Paul tried repeatedly to comfort her saying: "Please, Carol, don't cry," but his father ordered him to stop it. Paul persisted saying: "She's my sister and you don't have to pester her," finally stomping off into his room. At the table, Mrs. Mann held the baby over her head and tickled her. This seemed to bother her husband who said: "Don't, you'll drop her." As she started to feed her, the baby had a look of dismay on her face which grew as the mother kept feeding her faster and faster. Eventually the baby began to spit out and the mother yelled that there was no reason for doing that. When the baby finally choked, Mrs. Mann said: "I bet you think Mother is trying to strangle you" and laughed. Then the baby threw up all over the tray and the mother became very upset and angry. In getting her out of the high chair, she jammed the baby's foot and the baby screamed. The mother then began lifting the baby to her face and saying: "Oh, I am sorry, baby, I am sorry" at which the baby stopped crying. Then she abruptly sat her back on her lap and told her that she was bad and the baby started to cry again. The mother started to laugh, lifted the baby again to her face and said: "I'm sorry, baby, I'm sorry," and once again the baby stopped crying. Mrs. Mann said: "The funny thing is that you're not even crying" and added "Bad," and the baby started to cry again. She repeated this cycle several times. Each time the baby cried, Frankie began to scream hysterically and Paul would hide his face in his hands saying: "Don't pester her; she'll die." Mother eventually put down the baby and turned on Frankie who shouted that she was going to kill him and fled upstairs. Paul was sitting stiffly in his chair staring ahead of him and his father asked him: "What's the matter with you? Didn't you have a great day?" Without looking up and in muffled tones, Paul said: "Everybody hates me in this house. Everyone's picking on me. It's no good. I just want to die."

When the children had gone to bed, Mrs. Mann began to look through a magazine and saw some pictures of women with fancy hairdos and asked if I ever thought of getting a wig and I said I had. She said that her husband had thought about getting her one but decided against it. He flatly denied this and she insisted. "What you really need," he said, "is a mask," and they both laughed. Now a gradual change came over Mrs. Mann. She lost most of her irritability, her nervousness, her extreme sensitivity, her chaotic, disorganized approach to everything and began to joke with her husband and enjoy his sarcastic banter. She giggled and seemed to become younger. At one point, her chin was resting on the table and she acted girlishly saying: "You once said you were going to get another girl, and he replied: "Maybe I will." They began to argue about who would take the children and he said that he would and she said that she was the one who bore them. He asked how she would ever be able to take care of them and she answered: "Oh, you would be surprised!" She insisted that she wanted the baby. The night was filled with this sort of banter but after a while it lost its playfulness and neither of them seemed amused anymore. Her comments became wilder and more far-out and he seemed to be leading her again into another disturbance. The bickering took over and they were soon at each other's throats. Mr. Mann said he wanted to go to see his mother and Mrs. Mann refused to do so: "Not when she send spies to spy on me at school. I don't need those spies. I don't want anything to do with anybody like that." A couple of times she declared that she was going to bed but stayed around. She started to talk about the fact that her husband said she was "nuts" all the time. "I don't have to take that from him."

Paul came out of his room and said: "I wonder how Mom is feeling?" And his father answered saying: "I guess she is feeling alright." Then Paul remarked that everyone in the family except his mother had brown eyes and hers were blue.

One can observe in this vignette the gradual culmination of intense effect after a low-key beginning. The feelings first disrupt the mother's functioning and then overflow onto the rest of the family in a way that causes them to become alternately angry, frightened, depressed and despairing. The baby has little recourse open to her except to scream and choke on her food and this she does almost interminably. With the children out of the way, the mother regains something of her composure, but very soon her feelings once again reach a disruptive level under the provocation of her husband. The oscillation of affect and behavior, as demonstrated in the feeding situation with the baby, appears to be a compelling pattern for the mother from which she derives almost sadistic pleasure. At this stage, her psychosis is starting to relapse and most of her interactions are ending up negatively and wildly.

THE INVOLVING PSYCHOSIS WITH THE SICK PARENT ABSENT

Mrs. Mann has been hospitalized. I am impressed by the difference in the children. Paul seems much quieter and more shy. He doesn't smile very much and withdraws from the family into his own room. He looks most like his mother—the same sad face and peculiar way of saying things. He seems to be playing "dumb" and is becoming increasingly backward at school. He asks me twice if his father has taken me out and suggests that I should take Frankie for a walk because Frankie would like that. He has a rather secretive suspicious air about him and his attitude towards Frankie seems to be almost too kind and too concerned.

Frankie used to be the most active person in this family but now seems greatly altered. He has lost most of his tan and has little circles under his eyes. He stays very close to his father and says of his mother sadly: "I want she to come back." Even when we go out into the backyard, Frankie doesn't seem as independent as he was before. He seems to be very conscious of the family now, saying things like: "I'm going to sit by my dad" and "I'm going to ride on my brother's shoulders." His outside contacts seem to have slimmed down considerably. He dawdles a great deal of his food.

The baby, Carol, is allowed to crawl around on the kitchen floor and this is entirely different than when her mother was here.

I get the same feeling as I got on my previous stay. This family cannot stand to be together and yet they stay together.

After I had settled in, Frankie and I and Mr. Mann sat together in the living room. Then Mr. Mann said he was going to start making lunch. He set the table, got out some lettuce and cleaned it up. He made me a club sandwich and told me to go ahead and eat it because he was going to feed Carol. He also made Frankie a sandwich and Frankie started playing up. His father did get a little bit annoyed but it wasn't anywhere near as high-pitched as it was last time I was in this house. The strife seemed much less. Mr. Mann fed Carol rapidly and she ate all her food without spitting it out. Mr. Mann then told Frankie that it was time for his nap and although Frankie protested, he did go into his room and was very quiet. I was surprised. Mr. Mann then put Carol on her potty. The baby did not smile very much and did not seem too lively or happy. However, when her father asked her to give him a big hug, she seemed very delighted to do so. The father began pressing Frankie to eat his sandwich and the boy kept saying: "Leave me alone; just leave me alone." He told his father that he was "bothering him." His father said: "I'm not bothering you," and Frankie said: "Well, you're looking at me." He put his hands up to his eyes when his father talked to him.

This return visit to the Mann family shows how much Mr. Mann has taken over the role of mothering the children. In place of the turbulence, there is a subdued, almost unreal, quality about the home. The shadow of the mother hangs over the family life. She is the ghost in the situation and they still respond to her but not as powerfully as when she is actually there. There is no focus of disturbance and no wave of contagion tripping across the family. The family-sitter is much more aware of the children as different people leading their own lives in their own way but the mother's influence is still very much apparent. In the quietness of the home without the mother, the observer was very much reminded of a period of commotion during her previous stay when Mrs. Mann kept yelling at all the children all the time and Paul turned toward the visitor and remarked: "I'm sure glad this world is in one piece."

THE CASE OF NONINVOLVING PSYCHOSIS
WITH THE SICK PARENT PRESENT

Ernestine, the psychotic mother, is home. She is fat and very much like the grandmother, Mrs. A, who is looking after the two children, Sidney, age nine, and Sonia, age eight. Sonia is sitting on my left and talking away. She points to my skirt and blouse and says: "I knew you were going to wear this today." She touches my skirt and says that it feels like corduroy and I tell her it is made of blue jean material. Mrs. A tells Ernestine to sit up: "Ernestine, we got company; sit up." Sonia leans over and takes my hand. She remarks that I am now wearing my hair down as compared with previously. I tell her that this is right. Ernestine is scribbling on a small piece of paper. She is very absorbed in this and holds it close to her face occasionally raising her eyebrows. She tilts her head to the left and takes a long look at the paper. She scratches her head and puts her hand to her mouth. She has not said a word. I notice Sonia scratching herself. Sonia remarks that when I don't smile I look kind of sad. Mrs. A tells Sonia not to bother me. Ernestine has taken another piece of paper and is scribbling. Sonia is picking at her fingernails. Ernestine is still sitting forward and scribbling on her piece of paper. Sidney comes over and sits close to me and Sonia begins to ·cry. Mrs. A tells her that she is crying because she cannot get to sit next to me. Sidney is smiling as he sits next to me. Mrs. A says to him: "You make the time good because that was her chair." Sonia is very angry because she can't sit next to me. Ernestine is still scribbling and hasn't said a word. Ernestine wants to know when her mother is going to get her some cigarettes. I give her a cigarette. She drops some ashes and Sonia remarks on this. (The children call their mother Tina and their grandmother "Mom.") Sonia insists that I sleep with her at night and Sidney remarks that Tina uses up a lot of room on the bed. Sonia asks if I spank children when their mothers leave them and I say "No." She asks me if I nag at them and again I say "No." She looks at Ernestine. Then she asks me what I would do if children kissed all over me. She offers me some crackers and kisses me on the cheek. Ernestine is still scribbling. Sonia sits by me and plays with my hair. She wants to know how many cigarettes I have smoked and I say that I don't know. Sidney suggests that I count the butts in the ashtray. Ernestine is now scribbling on a new scrap of paper and staring very intently at it. Sonia says she remembers when she had a friend who.hurt her finger and they put a tape around the finger. Ernestine is scribbling on her paper. The children watch T.V. An hour later Ernestine is still scribbling. She puts her hand up to her neck, sticks her neck out and rubs her head with her hands up and down about three times. Sonia tries to rock me to sleep. Then she begins to suck her thumb. Ernestine makes a fist and rubs the other hand over it and then she changes her hand smiling in a very childlike way. Suddenly she remarks that she had a sandwich when she got home and then two sandwiches before dinner and then dinner. Sonia asks me whether she would get fat if she ate all the food in the house. I say that I do not think she would be able to eat it all and Mrs. A says that she would get sick. Mrs. A adds that Sonia does not want to get fat. A little later, as we are having a meal, Ernestine comes in and stands by Sonia's chair. It seems that she cannot get through but she does not make any move to let anyone know this. Finally, Mrs. A tells Sonia to get up and let her mother through and she does. Mrs. A asks Sidney to get her some water so she can take her pills but he sticks out his lip. Mrs.A says: "I knew a man at the hospital who used to keep his lip out like that and I believe he was crazy." At this Sonia starts to laugh hysterically and Sidney gets a very sad look on his face, almost as if he could cry but doesn't. Mrs. A starts talking about animal instinct; the closer you get to it, the uglier it seems and the more afraid you become. She connects this with the look on Sidney's face. The children are now fighting and talking about killing each other and hating each other. Sonia comes over to me and says: "You haven't ever seen a fight before, have you?" and I say: "Yes," but she says: "Not like this," and I say: "No, I guess not." Sidney has his lower lip out again and is not looking very happy, and Mrs. A tells him that he is going to become a crazy old man setting Sonia off on another fit of hysterical laughter. Sonia is now leaning up against me with her head on my lap. She takes my arm and puts it around her. A little later she says: "Remember when you were sitting on the couch and I knelt down and looked at you and you didn't smile." Then she tells me about a woman who was so happy that she fell down.

NONINVOLVING PSYCHOSIS—MOTHER ABSENT

Sonia came over to me and smiled. Then Sidney came and sat on the couch. He and Sonia started going through a bantering routine and he would pretend to be angry at her. Then he turned to me and said that I had never seen him when he was really mad. Then he could beat the pulp out of Sonia. He looked at me out of the corner of his eye and said: "I was just kidding about beating the pulp out of Sonia." He said he was very strong and could bend a steel bar with his bare hands. Sonia came over to me with a book and wanted to read me a story. A little later both children stood up and started wrestling and play fighting but not hurting each other. Sonia wanted to try on my glasses. Then Sidney tried them on. Sonia wanted to touch my hair. She said it was soft and Sidney asked if I used any oil on it. Both children seemed very curious about me in general. The television was turned on and Sonia put her chair very close to mine and smiled. She asked me if I smiled all the time and Mrs. A remarked that it was nice to have somebody like that around. Sonia leaned against my knee and smiled. It was a very sleepy atmosphere and sort of contagious and I felt myself getting drowsy. Mrs. A suggested that the children go outside and play. She said that she knew they were acting normal but that sometimes they made her feel nervous. She thought that she herself was overly concerned with unchastity. She told me about a television program she had seen the night before about a woman who thought her husband was crazy and it turned out that she was the one who was crazy. She thought maybe that that was what was wrong with her. A little later Sonia began to draw a house which she made into a tall house because I am tall. She told me a long story about a mother who sent her child to the store to get food. When he came back, he sneaked some of it for himself and when his mother found this out, she chopped his head off and threw it down the basement stairs. Then the father came home and saw what the mother had done and he chopped her head off and threw it down the stairs. She eventually put me into the picture as well as a little baby and the two of us were the only ones who came out of the story alive. Both Sonia and Sidney were competing for my attention. They would say: "Look at me, Peggy; watch this." Sonia asked whether I would laugh if she tipped over in her chair. I said: "No" because she would hurt herself. Next she started climbing on the fence and I saw some loose prongs sticking out so I asked her to be careful with her bare feet because she might cut her foot. This led to a discussion as to whether or not I would laugh if she cut her foot. A little later Sonia started reading a story to me about a fish that asked the fisherman to let it go back into the sea in exchange for three wishes. Sonia asked me if I thought fishes could talk. I said: "No." She then asked Mrs. A who said that stories like that were made up to amuse people. They were not really true. Sonia then came over and attached herself to me leaning against my shoulder, sitting on my lap and putting her arms around me. She said that I was to sleep with her because she had a double bed. She wanted to know if I pushed people out of bed. A little later she asked me to lift her up and Mrs. A protested saying: "Sonia, you aren't a baby anymore." Sonia said: "Peggy should have been here when I was a baby so she could have lifted me up."

The mother, in this case, is suffering from a severe process schizophrenia and is almost completely out of touch with the world around her. On the level of verbal communication, contact and control, there is very little difference in the protocols with Ernestine present or absent. However, on a more primitive, nonverbal level, it was observed that a good deal of the mother's motoric behavior, especially in its more archaic aspects, seemed to be picked up by the children so that facial expressions, uncontrolled laughter, picking at fingers, scratching, yawning and touching passed from mother to children even when they seemed to be least conscious of her presence. There are many latent anxieties present—the fear of becoming fat (like mother), of becoming crazy, of becoming affectless. Both Sidney and Sonia behave like affect-hungry children and Sonia especially has a heightened sensitivity to the facial play of emotions. She is especially aware when Peggy is looking sad. Neither of them accept the mother as a mother and neither of them makes any concession to her presence, but both of them are more on the verge of breaking down emotionally when she is around.

DISCUSSION

The susceptibility to contagion varies considerably with different members of the family and the relationship that they have with the major pathogenic member. The more suggestible, the more submissive and the more undifferentiated rapidly respond to the rising tide of affect and irrationality and takes hold of the family from time to time. In the case of the involving psychoses, the spreading of affect, whether paranoid or depressive, is fairly manifest and easy to observe. With the noninvolving psychoses, the general atmosphere is characteristically low key and archaic, somatic elements are much more in evidence. At high levels of intensity, the contagious circuits appear to crystallize around some single member who may consequently feel rejected and victimized. When the family enters into states of panic with persecutory anxiety dominating the entire setting, there is a marked decrease in the level of rational and realistic interchange and the boundaries between participants appear almost nonexistent. Delusional ideas make their round and even halluicnations, for short periods, may become common property. For the family-sitter, these episodes of panic are especially threatening and she may find excuses at these times to leave the field and dictate her report.

Among the younger children in the family, one can sometimes observe the dispersion of paranoid play characterized by intense preoccupation, a high degree of magical control, a lack of organization and an absence of beginning and end to the content. In its more blatant forms, this kind of paranoid play also has its crescendo effect.

> One of the girls in the family sought me out in my room. "There is something about my mother I want to tell you." She began to whisper and I could not hear her but it seemed as if she were telling me that her mother was picking on her. She looked at the door: Are you sure no one can hear from the corridor? There could be somebody standing out there." She tiptoed to the door and peered out. "There is nobody there. Perhaps she is at the window. No, nobody there. What about under the table?" She bent down and peered all around. All the while she was getting more and more excited. "She might be under the carpet or in that crack in the wall or in that pencil there or anywhere, anywhere!"

There was nothing psychotic at all about this girl but her mother suffered from paranoid schizophrenia and was extremely difficult to interview because of her considerable suspiciousness. The reactions of the children in such households are like common colds, uncomfortable, disagreeable, transient but ready to be picked up by the next susceptible person in contact. The major clinical problem lies in separating the evanescent from the permanent and the living-in experience offers the best opportunity to gauge the possibility of eventual psychotic developments. The vicissitudes of identification and relationship govern the ebb and flow of contagious material between family members and at their acme may set up delusional love and hate affairs. The more encapsulated, entrenched and isolated the family is from corrective reality experiences, the more swiftly do the epidemics of irrationality traverse their ranks and inundate them all with psychotic experience. In the nuclear families of today, there are no available extensions through which to dilute some of the intensity of the emotional load. The family seems imprisoned within the domestic orbit and, like the Sartrian perception of hell, the exit is there but cannot be used. Within the psychotic enclave, the visitor is struck by the abrasiveness of all relationships. Almost every contact, however well intentioned, can set off a negative cycle of response ending in someone's pain. The arguments are, for the most part, around apparent trivialities and there is no expectation of a better outcome. Part of the problem lies in the low capacity for mutual satisfaction and part in the family's general incompetence in reconciling differences. Eventually, the situation becomes irreversible and matters can no longer be mended after destructive episodes. As reparation fails, the family assumes a trigger existence when the slightest provocation brings about a landslide of disturbance in its wake. Most of this tragic business is conducted indirectly so that it remains mystifying as to what forces are responsible for any particular contagious developments. What Winnicott refers to as "organized chaos" seems often to be set up in order to conceal a more serious underlying disintegration of the family.

The preconditions for contagion, therefore, include a disaffiliated social existence, relative insulation from the world outside, a high tolerance for intramural eccentricity, overcrowding within limited space and a corresponding lack of privacy, an absence of reality-oriented individuals, a chaotic, disorganized amorphous setting in which the individuals are out of touch with others but excessively in touch with one another either on an affective level (involving psychosis) or on a motoric level (noninvolving psychosis), a culture that is essentially simple-minded, undifferentiated and based on suggestion and submission, and finally, the presence of catalyzing agents who may initially challenge the preconceptions of the family group but may later find themselves reacting like members of the family as the defenses of hyperrationality and hyperrealism are discarded in the service of professional inquiry. The relative immunity of members of the family to the psychotic contagion has something of this professional quality about it.

Our living-in experience would therefore lend support to Ehrenwald's clinic-based distinction between psychological contagion with similar (homonymic) and dissimilar (heteronymic) clinical symptomatology (1). We would go further in suggesting that the penetrant nature of the former is a function of the marked emotional charge generated by paranoid, phobic and compulsive attitudes, whereas the contagiousness of the latter gains expression in disguised, chiefly somatic, forms as a result of archaic communication through organ or action language. We would agree that susceptibility is directly proportional to the duration of exposure and inversely proportional to the age at which exposure takes place, to existing tendencies to conformity and compliance prevailing in the family at the time, to the presence of certain predisposing traits (gene-determined?) in family members, to the vicissitudes of regression and ego strength within the group and to the counteracting forces of support and cooperation dynamically at work in the interactional sphere.

Our final agreement with Ehrenwald is with his statement that "the question of resistance—or immunity—to contagion is of paramount importance to the psychiatrist concerned with matters of prevention." His study was more with vertical contagion, whereas ours has focused on horizontal contagion, but preventive intervention along both axes would seem to hold the best promise for the production and preservation of good mental health.

REFERENCES

1. EHRENWALD, J. (1960) Neurosis in the Family. *Arch. Gen. Psychiat.*, 3:1, 232-242.
2. FREUD, S. (1955) *Group Psychology and the Analysis of the Ego.* Standard Edition, vol. 18. London: Hogarth Press.
3. HARTMANN, H. (1964) On Rational and Irrational Action. *Essays on Ego Psychology.* New York: International Universities Press, pp. 37-68.
4. LASEGUE, C. & FALRET, J. (1964) La folie a deux. *Amer. J. Psychiat.*, Suppl. 121, 4:1-23.
5. LIDZ, T., FLECK, S., & CORNELISON, A. (1965) The Transmission of Irrationality. In *Schizophrenia and the Family.* New York: International Universities Press, pp. 171-187.
6. MEERLOO, J. A. M. (1959) Mental Contagion, *Amer. J. Psychother.*, 12:66.

39

FAMILY RESEARCH ON THE PATHO-GENESIS OF SCHIZOPHRENIA:

Intermediate Variables in the Study of Families at High Risk

Lyman C. Wynne, M.D., Ph.D.

Professor and Chairman, Department of Psychiatry
University of Rochester School of Medicine and Dentistry
Psychiatrist-in-Chief, Strong Memorial Hospital (Rochester)

Present explanations of schizophrenia leave wide gaps between the presumed genetic endowment and the eventual psychotic breakdown in adolescence and adulthood. Concepts, methods, and data are needed to fill in convincing evidence about the developmental processes leading to the overt illness. Although recent studies of the genetics of schizophrenia have confirmed the usual assumption that *something* is in fact transmitted genetically in at least some persons diagnosed schizophrenic, the strength of the genetic factor seems to be weaker than was formerly claimed. For example, well-controlled recent twin studies find concordance rates of 25% to 38% in monozygotic twins (Kringlen, 1967), in contrast to the traditionally quoted figure of Kallmann (1946) of 86% concordance.

In addition, a closer, more qualitative look at symptomatic resemblances between twins and between schizophrenic adoptees and their biologic relatives suggests that genetic factors are not direct determinants

Presented at the International Symposium on Psychosis, Institut Albert-Prévost, Montreal, 5 November, 1969, and published in P. Doucet & C. Laurin (eds.): *Problems of Psychosis Vol. II*, pp. 401-412. Amsterdam: Excerpta Medica.

of a circumscribed disease entity. Kety, Rosenthal, Wender, and Schulsinger (1968) found that among the 150 biologic relatives of 33 schizophrenic adoptees, there was only one typical chronic schizophrenic, but 12 other relatives fell in a "schizophrenia spectrum," a broader concept which includes typical acute and chronic schizophrenia as well as borderline schizophrenia and inadequate personality. Among 156 biologic relatives of 33 control adoptees, there was also one typical schizophrenic but only two other relatives in the schizophrenia spectrum. Thus, a higher frequency of the *spectrum* disorders was found among the biologic relatives of the schizophrenic adoptees, but this result would not have been apparent if only cases of "core" schizophrenia had been counted in the relatives. Similarly, Rosenthal, Wender, Kety, Schulsinger, Welner, and Ostergaard (1968) found that the offspring of schizophrenics reared in adoptive homes showed an increase in schizophrenia *spectrum* disorders, compared to controls, but again the data do not point to the simple inheritance of a specific schizophrenic disease entity. As Rosenthal has concluded, "The genes that are implicated produce an effect whose nature we have not yet been able to fathom. It is clear that not everybody who harbors the gene develops schizophrenia" (Rosenthal, 1968).

These and other studies suggest that a *predisposition* to developing any one of a diversity of mental disorders, and perhaps a diversity of nonpsychiatric deviances, including greater creativity (Heston, 1966), is probably inherited, at least in a portion of cases. If this conclusion is correct, it is inappropriate to be content with diagnostic or symptomatic concordance in genetic studies; this traditional approach will have difficulties establishing more than the non-controversial point that an undefined genetic contributing factor is present, or that these disorders are polygenic, without clarifying the nature of the genetic components and without being able to say anything about how genetic factors interweave with other factors in pathogenesis and development.

Two Classes of Intermediate Variables

What appears to be needed are measurable indices of genetic endowment and reliable means of evaluating later contributions to the development of schizophrenia. I have suggested investigation of two main classes of *intermediate* variables between genes and symptoms (Wynne, 1967, 1968a, 1968b): 1) individual *response dispositions,* especially cognitive control principles, which are aspects of "temperament" that can now be measured with psychophysiologic, neurophysiologic, and perceptual methods (see, for example, Gardner, Holzman, Klein, Linton, and Spence, 1959; Silverman, 1967; Witkin, Dyk, Faterson, Goodenough, and Karp, 1962); and 2) *"transactional" processes, particularly intra-familial communication patterns,* which also can be now evaluated empirically (Singer and Wynne, 1966; Loveland, 1967; Singer, 1967).

Response dispositions appear to be significantly determined by genetic factors, while communication patterns probably are more strongly influenced by experiential factors. However, both classes of variables lend themselves to the study of somatic, psychologic, and social determinants without prejudgments as to their relative importance. Research in which these variables are explicitly examined can facilitate a more detailed scrutiny of the polygenic theory of the inherited aspects of schizophrenic disorders (Gottesman and Shields, 1967), and also will permit intensified study of the developmental interplay of genetic and environmental factors when applied to special samples (e.g., adoptive families). By turning to the investigation of intermediate classes of variables, such as those proposed here, a more orderly and stepwise picture of the development of schizophrenia may be obtained. Certainly, we cannot remain content with the etiologic truism that both heredity and environment are important and interact with one another.

Response dispositions, the first group of proposed intermediate variables, are an operational conceptualization of a series of dimensions characterizing how an individual receives, regulates, and modifies environmental and internal stimuli in standardized laboratory situations. These dimensions were labeled "cognitive control principles" by Gardner *et al.* (1959) and fall into patterns or profiles called "cognitive styles." The response dispositions to which we have been giving special attention in research at the National Institute of Mental Health are: field dependence-independence (Witkin *et al.*, 1962), stimulus sensitivity and stimulus intensity control, including the tendency to augment (amplify) sensory stimulation or to reduce (attenuate) stimulation (Petrie, 1967; Buchsbaum and Silverman, 1967, Silverman, 1968); and scanning control (Gardner and Long, 1962). Other important cognitive dimensions are: leveling-sharpening (Holzman and Gardner, 1959); constricted-flexible control (Gardner *et al.*, 1959; and conceptual differentiation (Gardner and Moriarty, 1968). Propensity to psychophysiologic arousal should also be considered with this broad class of variables (Venables, 1964; Mednick and Schulsinger, 1968), as well as sociability or social responsiveness, which Scarr (1965) has shown seems to have an inherited component.

On the basis of theoretical considerations and preliminary research findings, I have hypothesized (Wynne, 1968b) that *potential schizo-phrenics are drawn from the substantial portion of the population who have extreme patterns of response disposition.* I have suggested that some, but not all, of these dispositions, in their attentional, perceptual, neurophysiologic, and psychophysiologic aspects, are strongly genetically determined and *indirectly* constitute the "genetic component" in schizo-phrenia (Wynne, 1968b). However, extreme response dispositions, I have further hypothesized, lead to a vulnerability not just to schizo-phrenia but to a spectrum of other "deviant" outcomes, psychiatric and probably creative (Cf. Heston, 1966). Using these formulations we have now turned to a new, indirect kind of genetic study of schizophrenia: the genetics of response dispositions, instead of the genetics of the sympto-matic disorder. With this research strategy, usable data potentially can be obtained about *all* relatives of schizophrenics, not just about the minority who themselves are overtly disturbed. In addition, this method provides a reasonable basis for selecting persons and families at high risk for schizophrenia in the typical situation in which none of the immediate relatives are diagnosed as schizophrenics. However, such genetic studies clearly need to be combined with the investigation of other variables which are manifest *later* in the development sequences leading to overt breakdowns.

Intrafamilial communication patterns, the second class of intermedi-ate variables which I shall consider here, are not independent of atten-tional and cognitive styles and other aspects of response dispositions, but rather build upon these dispositions in the course of development. I have noted that how a person goes about sustainedly focusing attention is a key factor in how he selects language, organizes his thinking and com-munications, and copes with affects (Schachtel, 1954; Wynne, 1961). In addition, Dr. Margaret Singer and I have also used the concept of *sharing* foci of attention, a fundamental aspect of the communication process which involves how two or more persons engage one another in a rela-tionship system (Wynne and Singer, 1966). Out of such sharing, the family evolves as a small social system with patterned, more or less enduring characteristics of its own which are not *simply* an aggregate of the characteristics of the individuals and which constitute a new con-stellation of phenomena (Wynne, 1967). Our working assumption, sup-ported by recent experimental laboratory studies of families (Mishler and Waxler, 1968; Reiss, 1967) is that certain aspects of family inter-action are functions of the rules and roles of the family, not of particular personalities of the members. In these respects the family system, and more indirectly, broader aspects of social structure and culture, pre-

TABLE 1

DIFFERENTIATION OF PARENTAL PAIRS (N = 116 PAIRS)
41-Category Rorschach Scoring

		Parents (as Pairs) of:					
		"Typical" Schiz.	Schizo-Affective	Border-line	Neurotic	Normal	Total
Frequency of Communication Deviances	Above Median	42	5	10	0	1	58
	Below Median	0	1	10	28	19	58
	Total	42	6	20	28	20	116

sumably combine with innate predispositions to shape the actual resultant behavior of individuals, deviant and otherwise.

Empirically, Dr. Singer and I have found that measures of communication deviances *in parents* consistently differentiate families with schizophrenic offspring from those with neurotic and normal offspring, as well as families with different subtypes of schizophrenic offspring from one another. While there appears to be almost no overlap between the parents of schizophrenics and parents of neurotics and normals, we have found that the parents of borderline patients do overlap with the parents of schizophrenics on the one hand and the parents of neurotics on the other. Dr. Singer and I have discussed the methods and the initial findings of this research elsewhere (Singer, 1967; Singer and Wynne, 1965, 1966; Wynne, 1967, 1968a, 1968b). In addition, a book-length report is in preparation. Here let me illustrate our findings with summary data from a recent sample of 116 American families.

Using a 41-category scoring manual (Singer and Wynne, 1966), communication deviances were scored on typescripts of tape-recorded Rorschachs from the 132 parents in these families. The raters had no information whatsoever about the subjects; the protocols were identified only with coded numbers and were individually scored in an unselected order mixed in with similar protocols of normal and disturbed offspring. Here I shall report only the sheer quantitative frequency of deviances on the first responses of the ten Rorschach cards. A score obtained by taking the number of deviances per response for each parent was added together with the score independently obtained for his or her spouse. These sum scores for each parental pair were analyzed statistically. Table 1 shows the distribution of scores above and below the median for the total sample.

The results replicate an earlied finding on another sample (Singer, 1967; Wynne, 1967) : None of the parental pairs of the schizophrenics had low scores, and very few of the parental pairs of neurotics and normals had high scores.

Other aspects of our use of communication deviances in family research have been discussed elsewhere (Singer and Wynne, 1966; Singer, 1967; Wynne, 1967, 1968a, 1968b). Here I simply want to make two points: (1) *Parental* communication deviances, far more than parental symptoms, appear to be a subtle but consistent indicator of schizophrenia symptomatology in an offspring. (2) If these parental deviances predate the offspring's symptomatology, they should constitute a good device for identifying the families of preschizophrenics before the diagnosis of schizophrenia has been made.

What is the likelihood that parental communication deviances in fact predate the symptomatology of their offspring? Dr. Singer and I have planned our work from the beginning so as to maximize this possibility, though we cannot be sure about this until we move from cross-sectional longitudinal studies, as we now are doing with the help of colleagues, especially Dr. Helm Stierlin. As we have discussed at some length in earlier papers (Wynne and Singer, 1963; Singer and Wynne, 1965), we have tried to anticipate the need for longitudinal studies by emphasizing in our cross-sectional research stylistic or formal aspects of attention and communication rather than more transitory content, because of evidence that these relate to relatively enduring personality features and are likely to have existed in years past as well as the present (e.g., Witkin *et al.*, 1962). Second, along with this emphasis on formal aspects of thinking and communicating, we have deliberately *not* made use of interview or attitudinal data about feelings of overprotection or guilt between family members, which could be secondary consequences of the illness itself.

Third, because of our concern about the possible secondary effects of illness and hospitalization of a family member on the other family members, we have compared families of schizophrenics with families which have had a similar experience with the recent hospitalization of an offspring for a serious but nonschizophrenic psychiatric disturbance. Although more recently we also have added "normal" comparison groups, we have continued to hold the view that "an essential feature of comparison studies of families is the constant factor of a sick offspring, disturbed and disturbing. Families with normal offspring may be differentially motivated to take part in a program of testing and clinical interviewing. Also such families have not had to develop means of coping somehow or other with the presence of a sick offspring. Thus, we have not merely compared disturbed and non-disturbed families but families with different *varieties* of disturbance" (Wynne and Singer, 1963). Thus, we have some confidence that these methods will prove useful in longitudinal research; substantive evidence, however, must await the outcome of longitudinal studies for which the cross-sectional work was preparatory.

In order to evaluate and spell out more fully these formulations about intermediate variables within a developmental context, longitudinal research clearly seems necessary. Retrospective data, including even the best records of child guidance clinics and schools, will clearly not be appropriate for obtaining the kinds of experimental and behavioral data called for by the above formulations.

However, longitudinal studies of the developmental process present their own brand of difficulties. With an expectancy rate for schizophrenia of less than 1% in the general population, predictive longitudinal studies must, to justify the expenditure of time and resources, be selective both in the variables and the persons studied. This means that reasonable hypotheses have to be available both about variables that are likely to "pay off" predictively and about those groups of persons who are at high risk for the later development of a schizophrenic disorder.

Thus far in this paper I have sketched out hypotheses about two broad classes of intermediate variables which I believe have merit for longitudinal studies. An additional part of the "pay-off" in studying these intermediate variables is that we are likely to learn about how parents and children resemble each other, or differ, along specified, central dimensions which need study *in themselves,* apart from the special problem of schizophrenia.

VARIETIES OF HIGH RISK FAMILIES

In the remainder of this paper I shall consider alternative ways of selecting families who are at high risk for having a member develop schizophrenia. With each method of sample selection, the repeated direct study of intermediate variables over time is necessary in order to clarify many aspects of the developmental process. This discussion will be concerned with *prospective,* predictive research on families containing *candidates for schizophrenia,* that is, persons at high risk for being diagnosed as schizophrenic at a future date. The design of research with families at high risk should include comparable study of low-risk families, that is, families in which it is thought unlikely that anyone will develop schizophrenia. Also such investigations may advantageously include predictions about nonschizophrenic alternative outcomes both for low-risk families and for those members of high-risk families who, it is predicted, will not become schizophrenic. These other possibilities include not only psychiatric difficulties such as impulse disorders, neuroses, and personality eccentricities, but also positive "deviances," especially creativity. The study of these alternatives should help clarify the nature of those continua, or dimensions, which apply to schizophrenics and nonschizophrenics alike.

At present, I believe that five main strategies for selection of high-risk families deserve consideration: (1) families in which a person who is already schizophrenic and a "candidate" for schizophrenia have *both a biologic and a psychologic relationship* (e.g., families in which children are reared with a schizophrenic who is also their biologic parent); (2) families in which a schizophrenic and the candidate for schizophrenia have *a biologic but not a psychologic relationship* (e.g., the biologic families of schizophrenic parents whose children are reared in adoptive homes; ideally, for research purposes, neither adoptee nor the adoptive parents should know anything about the biologic parents); (3) families in which a schizophrenic and the candidate for schizophrenia have a *psychologic but not a biologic relationship* (e.g., families in which an adoptive parent or a stepparent is schizophrenic); (4) families in which one or more of the children have *incipient difficulties,* of adjustment problems, which are regarded as "pre-morbid" for schizophrenia (e.g., early adolescents with passive forms of school underachievement); (5) families selected on the basis of *extreme scores* by the parents *on tests* of communication deviances and response dispositions and then followed longitudinally, preferably beginning with the marital relationship before the birth of children. Clearly, some of these methods can be combined, such as the use of parental test scores, with any of the other selection procedures.

A detailed comparison of each of these sampling strategies is beyond the scope of this paper, but I wish to comment at least briefly on some of the merits and limitations of each approach. I shall not touch here upon the important ethical and scientific question of whether predictive longitudinal research should be combined with preventive or treatment programs. Rather, I would like to consider the extent to which each approach can help fill in what I have described as the wide gap between vaguely specified genetic endowment and far-removed symptomatic schizophrenia.

(1) *Families in which a biologic and psychologic relationship is combined*. Three such relationships will be considered—the children, sibs, and second degree relatives of schizophrenics.

(a) *Children reared by schizophrenic parents*: Because it has been assumed that it would be excessively difficult and uneconomical to sample non-sick populations, it has been quite naturally proposed, especially by Mednick and McNeil (1968), that the children of schizophrenics be selected as a high-risk group. This procedure deliberately combines genetic and environmental influences, with the assumption (perhaps unwarranted) that this is the best way to maximize risk in other family members. At any rate, this method permits the longitudinal observation of developmental processes in families in which there is quite a high likelihood that someone else, beside the original patient, will become symptomatically ill. This approach, then, is suited for the study of pathogenesis and development, but not for the differentiation of genetic versus environmental etiologic factors.

The great interest and value of these studies is apparent in the work of Mednick and Schulsinger (1968) but, as with each of the other research strategies, this method has certain limitations. First, because about 88% of schizophrenics do *not* have a schizophrenic parent (Slater, 1968), we are dealing with an atypical sample when a parent is or has been overtly schizophrenic. Sample skewing is, furthermore, likely with respect to particular subtypes of schizophrenia which are most likely not distributed in the same way in these families as in "ordinary" families of schizophrenics. Those schizophrenics who become parents are likely to be better organized and may well have different kinds of response dispositions and communication patterns from those who do not marry or have children.

Second, if a parent has been identified as schizophrenic while the child is growing up, there usually will be disruptions of the parental functions due to hospitalization of the parent or at least curtailment of parental functions due to the effects of the illness or the effects of drugs taken to treat it. Also, it is likely that if a parent has actually been identified as mentally ill, other relatives or persons from the community are apt to take a role in the rearing of the child which would again make for an atypical situation. In some cases, teachers are probably aware of the disturbance in the parent and may change their behavior toward the child either positively or negatively as a result (as well as being influenced in their contributions to research evaluations of the children.)

Third, a special way in which these families may be atypical is that when a parent is overtly disturbed and recognized as such by the community and the rest of the family, the child has a different task of coping with the parent than if the parent is more subtly peculiar in his or her communication and behavior. Manfred Bleuler (1968) and others have pointed out that even small children are able to realize what is grossly psychotic and what is not and can discount and cope with psychotic parents, sometimes helping to look after them. It is our clinical and research observation that parents have a more consistently disturbing impact upon their children's ability to communicate and think when the parents claim reasonableness and are tolerated as reasonable by the spouse and others but actually convey and teach peculiar and mystifying modes of language usage and thinking to their children (Wynne, 1968a). In addition, it should be noted that if the parent is *quietly* non-functioning in his or her parental role and no surrogate steps in, this may lead to deficiencies in the child's learning, with an amorphous, poor premorbid development of skills, as in "simple," process schizophrenics. In contrast, a more actively intrusive paranoid parent may be more difficult for a child to cope with and provoke more florid reactive defenses, including delusions and hallucinations. Another variant, pointed out by Grunebaum (1967), is that some schizophrenic mothers are able to be remarkably nurturant and capable while the baby is still small, but become less successful when the child is older.

Fourth, when the mother is schizophrenic, especially when she is actively psychotic during pregnancy, the likelihood of disordered fetal physiology and birth complications probably increases. Thus, a non-genetic biologic environmental variable, perhaps of importance, further complicates the evaluation of genetic and experiential factors. It may be preferable not to try to study so many major variables in the same sample. If the schizophrenic parent is the father, then the genetic component is retained but the factor of the mother's uterine physiology is eliminated from consideration.

Thus, parental schizophrenia itself may either exaggerate or attenuate various possible determinants of schizophrenia in an offspring, compared to the way these factors operate in the more usual families in which the children develop schizophrenia but neither parent is schizophrenic. At any rate, the developmental process becomes very complex indeed in these families with parental schizophrenics; generalizations to families in which neither parent is schizophrenic are difficult and hazardous. I am sure that current work with these groups will further clarify many of these issues. However, we cannot assume that we are obtaining a representative sample of schizophrenics or their families with this methodology.

(b) *Siblings of schizophrenics*: A second kind of family in which bio-logic and psychological influences combine arises when one offspring in a family develops schizophrenia; siblings, especially younger ones, can then be regarded as at high risk and their developmental course followed over the ensuing years in which a schizophrenic breakdown is likely. This strategy is mostly applicable to short-term predictive studies, rather than long-term investigations begun before disturbance was apparent in a family. However, predictions as to which of the siblings are going to be disturbed, and in what ways, may be very fruitful if dimensionalized measures are used. For example, predictions can be based upon the degree to which response disposition scores as extreme for one sibling compared to another. Also, predictions can be based upon the evaluation of the pathogenicity of the family environment for males compared to females (Fleck, Lidz, and Cornelison, 1963). Slater (1968) concludes that the expectation of schizophrenia for sibs of clearcut schizophrenics is only 8.7%. However, by evaluating all of the sibs with measures of intermediate variables, data about the factors differentiating those who break down from those who do not can be obtained.

Pollin (1969) has recently proposed an ingenious variant of the above procedure for studying sibs of schizophrenics prospectively. He has pointed out that an especially high risk for developing schizophrenia can be found in monozygotic twins during the first five years after one of the twins has developed schizophrenia; the co-twin is then at a very high risk during the ensuing five years for developing the same disorder. There are obvious practical problems in locating such a sample. How-ever, large twin registers, such as that set up in the past by the National Academy of Science can make such research efficient and feasible.

(c) *Second-degree relatives of schizophrenics*: As I have noted when discussing research on children reared by schizophrenic parents, there are many secondary psychological complications caused by the fact of parental psychosis, such as increased parental absences and the likelihood of parental surrogates entering the picture. An alternative research strat-egy is to sample families in which the "candidates for schizophrenia" are nieces, nephews, or grandchildren of index schizophrenics. This approach would reduce the gross family disruptions likely when a parent is ac-tively psychotic but would retain an increased genetic loading, compared to random populations. Such families are relatively common, compared to families in which schizophrenic parents rear their own children, so that better sampling for age, sex, and social-demographic variables can be obtained. Also, because both response dispositions and communica-tion patterns are apt to be widely divergent and often quite extreme in such families, the use of these intermediate variables should facilitate making an interesting array of distinctions within and between such families.

Thus, from a number of standpoints, this sampling procedure has practical and theoretical advantages over other methods. A partial disadvantage is that parents often compare their children with another family member and may have anxieties and expectations which could lead them to push a child toward, or away from, a more thoroughgoing resemblance to a schizophrenic relative. The child, conversely, may fear becoming like the schizophrenic relative, even (or especially) if he has no extensive personal contact with this relative. Nevertheless, these psychological influences may not be greatly different from those found in other families in which there are no close relatives at all who are schizophrenic. The dynamics and structure of the nuclear family potentially can be studied comprehensively, while other, less predictable influences have to be noted carefully about the course of development in any event.

(2) *Families in which the "candidates for schizophrenia" have a biologic but not a psychologic relationship to an index schizophrenic.*

(a) *Adoptive versus biologic families*: The adoption studies of Heston and Denney (1968) and of Rosenthal, Wender, Kety, Schulsinger, Welner, and Ostergaard (1968) have been of great importance in establishing that a genetic factor contributes to the breakdown of a portion of schizophrenics. Heston followed up 47 persons born to schizophrenic mothers in a state hospital and discharged within 3 days of birth to a foundling home or to relatives, typically the father or paternal relatives. Five of these experimental subjects were later diagnosed as schizophernic, while none of the 50 control subjects reared in foundling or foster homes became schizophrenic. However, a clearcut genetic interpretation of these findings is blurred by the fact that the experimental subjects may have had nongenetic fetal or birth complications associated with the fact that their mothers were hospitalized psychotics during pregnancy. Also, the relatives who reared 22 of the 47 experimental subjects presumably knew that the mother was a disturbed psychiatric patient, a psychologically important circumstance which could well have altered their expectations of these children; it is not clear what the foundling-home caretakers for the other 25 subjects may have known about the mother's illness.

In the Rosenthal *et al.* (1968) study in Denmark better control was achieved over these contaminating factors. I have already commented upon the theoretical implications of their findings concerning an increased incidence of schizophrenia spectrum disorders in the offspring of schizophrenics reared in adoptive homes. This method of selecting a high-risk sample *after* the illness has emerged as suited for etiologic research in which the goal is to separate overall but unspecified genetic and experiential factors. However, detailed and direct behavioral comparisons of both the adoptive and the biologic parents have not yet been carried out. Gross diagnostic and symptomatic reports on which prime reliance is placed clearly need underpinning with other research methods. Especially because of the *spectrum* of behaviors reported in the adopted biologic offspring of schizophrenics, it will be of critical importance to study this range of behaviors in both the biologic and adoptive parents with additional methods, such as those I have mentioned in this paper, with which data can be obtained from *all* of the subjects, not just those who have found their way into a psychiatric register. If one is interested in the more explicit identification of the genetic and environmental factors involved, and a clarification of how and when they interact during the course of development, then adoption studies must also be carried out prospectively and longitudinally.

Another difficulty, not overwhelming but worthy of attention, is that better normative studies are needed with adoptive families. Our knowledge of the psychology and sociology of adoption is appallingly meager; we need to know much more about the characteristics of adoptive samples in relation to the general population and in comparison with ordinary non-adopted persons who becomes schizophrenic. It is my impression that adoptive families have a special psychologic problem in achieving a workable "fit" between the characteristics of the parents and the adoptees. Some adoptive parents realistically expect their children will differ substantially from themselves and take a positive approach to the development of these individual differences. However, another subgroup of parents are disappointed and intolerant when such differences appear —differences which are more likely, on genetic grounds, to occur in adoptive families than in non-adoptive families. Direct research data on response dispositions will help clarify how psychological problems of family members may fit together and unfold in the course of family development. These views also suggest that many basic questions about genetic-environmental interaction cannot be adequately understood with only *outcome* studies, even in the very valuable special samples of adoptees. Rather, prospective longitudinal studies will also be necessary with adoptive families.

(b) *Twins and siblings reared apart:* It has long been recognized that monozygotic twins reared apart are an especially strategic research sample. Their obvious scarcity is a serious problem however. Even when twins are geographically separated, the problem of *psychologically* important relationships, fed by fantasies of the well twin based upon partial knowledge of the sick twin, constitute an important difficulty about which information should carefully be obtained.

Siblings reared apart are a more commonly available sample, but there are likely to be difficulties in obtaining tests and other data directly from the two rearing families.

(3) *Families in which the "candidates for schizophrenia" have a psychologic but not a biologic relationship to an index schizophrenic.*

In addition to the detailed study of adoptive families, another possibility seemingly has not been considered for schizophrenia research. With current high frequencies of divorce and remarriage, consideration should be given to the study of families in which there is a step-parent. Perhaps it would be especially interesting to focus on the not rare situation in which the spouse of a schizophrenic has remarried; such a parent may have children both by a schizophrenic and by a nonschizophrenic spouse. The timing of the remarriage would be an important variable in such samples.

Step-parents are partially similar to adoptive parents and some of the same questions can be asked of both samples, especially if detailed dimensionalized data are obtained, rather than simply diagnostic labels.

(4) *Families with Adolescents and Children Showing Incipient Psychiatric Difficulties*:

A high-risk method which is being used in the Adult Psychiatry Branch of NIMH in a program under Dr. Helm Stierlin uses the strategy of studying the families of adolescents beginning at age 15 and continuing for at least 5 years. Adolescents in these families have been referred by the public school system as "under-achievers," namely, students with low academic records in relation to their relatively high test intelligence. Dr. Stierlin has assumed that the current and future psychiatric status of these students will vary considerably, including relatively successful normalcy, delinquency, various personality difficulties, and schizophrenia. During an intensive 3-month period of research evaluation and family therapy, detailed clinical predictions are made about the future of the family and the adolescent and a series of tests are conducted which can be independently used for predictive purposes. The tests being used at present include the response disposition battery of perceptual, cognitive and neurophysiologic tests mentioned above, as well as studies of communication problems of the individuals and the family members together in such procedures as the consensus Rorschach. In addition, the families are tested together in experimental problem-solving situations by Dr. David Reiss. Standardized psychiatric assessments are conducted by Dr. John Strauss in accord with interview procedures developed in WHO research on schizophrenia.

This sampling strategy, which is being used with different procedures by Dr. Michael Goldstein in Los Angeles, has the advantage that the period of maximal risk for schizophrenia will typically fall in a relatively brief time span 5 to 8 years after the subjects are first studied, thus lending itself to the accelerated longitudinal approach recommended by Dr. Richard O. Bell (1954). Another advantage of this approach is that the index offspring may not have an official or formal psychiatric diagnosis and is not clearly launched on a psychiatric career at the time of study, but is, rather, ordinarily seen as having some not uncommon school problems. The NIMH study, which has now been under way for about two years, is at too early a stage for a report of predictive findings, but the pattern of "fit" among family members with respect to their response dispositions and test communication scores, "make sense" in terms of independent clinical observations.

A disadvantage of this approach is that it can be argued that precursor features of schizophrenia may have already been present at the time of the baseline evaluation and have influenced to some extent the relationships and communication patterns of the index and other family members. However, this strategy does provide an opportunity to study the details of the important developmental phase which occurs before and during the "resolution" of adolescent separation from the family. This approach also lends itself to studying and predicting a variety of other important outcomes in addition to schizophrenia, such as delinquency and adaptive success.

(5) *Populations sampled on the basis of tests of (a) parental communication and (b) response dispositions of family members*: A more rigorous and ultimately satisfactory approach than any of the above procedures, in my opinion, is to select stratified samples of the population, taking into account social, cultural, and demographic variables, as well as such factors as intactness versus brokenness of the family. As in ongoing longitudinal studies of ordinary family and child development by the Child Research Branch at NIMH, couples can be screened early in their marriage prior to birth of the first child. Several types of communication samples, such as those from abbreviated individual Rorschachs, consensus Rorschachs, individual and conjoint proverbs, and other procedures can be quite quickly administered and can serve as a broad initial screening for the selection of high versus low risk groups. After screening a large number of couples (about 2,000 are needed) with a brief series

of procedures, preliminary identification of high risk and low risk groups can be made, to be followed by a more extensive test battery of response dispositions and other variables administered to these smaller groups. By making predictions prior to the birth of a child, the complications brought about by the impact of the newly born infant on the parents can be overcome and the total developmental process studied.

Obviously, the problems of feasibility are considerable with this approach, but it is my view that the time will soon come when this approach is sensible. I believe the findings in our cross-sectional family studies are encouraging in this respect and raise the possibility that on-target predictions are more possible than I have assumed in the past. My present feeling is that a continuation of the study of twin samples, adoptive samples, and samples in which there are incipient difficulties, such as the under-achiever adolescent group, will provide within a very few years enough further data to justify more comprehensive programs of prospective longitudinal research with respect to the issue of prediction of schizophrenia and the study of its developmental context, together with comparisons of low-risk families. The study of families in which an uncle, aunt, or grandparent is schizophrenic perhaps can be combined with sample selection which is purely on the basis of test scores.

In conclusion, it seems that a number of alternative sampling strategies are emerging as both feasible and promising in the task of expanding our understanding of the pathogenesis and development of schizophrenia and related disorders. At the same time that such research proceeds, I hope that we can look more comprehensively at the broader range of behaviors of which the schizophrenias are but a portion.

REFERENCES

BELL, R. Q. (1953): Convergence: an accelerated longitudinal approach. *Child Development*, 24, 145.

BLEULER, M. (1968): Comments quoted by Rosenthal, D. in Rosenthal, D. and Kety, S. S. (eds.): *The Transmission of Schizophrenia*. Pergamon Press, New York.

BUCHSBAUM, M., SILVERMAN, J. (1968): Stimulus intensity control and the cortical evoked responses. *Psychosomatic Medicine*, 30, 12.

FLECK, S., LIDZ, T. & CORNELISON, A. R. (1963): Comparison of parent-child relationships of male and female schizophrenic patients. *Archives of General Psychiatry*, 8, 1.

GARDNER, R. W., HOLZMAN, P. S., KLEIN, G. S., LINTON, H. & SPENCE, D. P. (1959): Cognitive Control: *A study of individual consistencies in cognitive behavior*. Psychological Issues, Monograph 4. International Universities Press, New York.

GARDNER, R. W. & LONG, R. I. (1962): Control, defense and centration effect: A study of scanning behavior. *British Journal of Psychology*, 53, 129.

GARDNER, R. W. & MORIARTY, A. (1968): *Personality Development at Preadolescence.* University of Washington Press, Seattle.

GOTTESMAN, I. & SHIELDS, J. (1967): A polygenic theory of schizophrenia. *Proceedings of the National Academy of Sciences,* 58, 199.

GRUNEBAUM, H. (1967): Personal communication.

HESTON, L. L. (1966): Psychiatric disorders in foster home reared children of schizophrenic mothers. *British Journal of Psychiatry,* 112, 819.

HESTON, L. L. & DENNEY, D. (1968): Interactions between early life experience and biological factors in schizophrenia. *Journal of Psychiatric Research* 6 (Suppl. 1), 363.

HOLZMAN, P. V. & GARDNER, R. W. (1959): Leveling and repression. *Journal of Abnormal and Social Psychology,* 59, 151.

KALLMANN, F. (1946): The genetic theory of schizophrenia: an analysis of 691 schizophrenic twin index families. *American Journal of Psychiatry,* 103, 309.

KETY, S., ROSENTHAL, D., WENDER, P. & SCHULSINGER, F. (1968): The types and prevalence of mental illness in the biological and adoptive families of adopted schizophrenics. *Journal of Psychiatric Research,* 6 (Suppl. 1), 345.

KRINGLEN, E. (1967): *Heredity and Environment in the Functional Psychoses. An Epidemiological-Clinical Twin Study.* University Press, Oslo and London.

LOVELAND, N. (1967): The relation Rorschach: A technique for studying interaction. *Journal of Nervous and Mental Disease,* 145, 93.

MEDNICK, S. A. & McNEIL, T. F. (1968): Current methodology in research on the etiology of schizophrenia. Serious difficulties which suggest the use of the high-risk group method. *Psychological Bulletin,* 70, 681.

MEDNICK, S. A. & SCHULSINGER, F. (1968): Some premorbid characteristics related to breakdown in children with schizophrenic mothers. *Journal of Psychiatric Research,* 6 (Suppl. 1), 267.

MISHLER, E. G. & WAXLER, N. E. (1968): *Interaction in Families.* John Wiley and Sons, New York.

PETRIE, A. (1967): *Individuality in Pain and Suffering.* University of Chicago Press.

POLLIN, W. (1969): Methodological issues in research with groups at high risk for the development of schizophrenia: The use of twins as a potential high-risk sample. Position paper for Conference on High-risk Research, NIMH, Bethesda, Maryland, June 9, 1969.

REISS, D. (1967): Individual thinking and family interaction—II. A study of pattern recognition and hypothesis testing in families of normals, character disorders, and schizophrenics. *Journal of Psychiatric Research,* 5, 193.

ROSENTHAL, D. (1968): The heredity-environment issue in schizophrenia: Summary of the conference and present status of our knowledge. *Journal of Psychiatric Research,* 6 (Suppl. 1), 413.

ROSENTHAL, D., WENDER, P., KETY, S., SCHULSINGER, F., WELNER, J. & OSTERGAARD, L. (1968): Schizophrenics' offspring reared in adoptive homes. *Journal of Psychiatric Research,* 6 (Suppl. 1), 377.

SCARR, S. (1965): The inheritance of sociability. *American Psychologist,* 20, 5.

SCHACHTEL, E. G. (1954): The development of focal attention and the emergence of reality. *Psychiatry,* 17, 309.

SILVERMAN, J. (1967): Variations in cognitive control and psychophysiological defense in the schizophrenias. *Psychosomatic Medicine,* 29, 225.

SILVERMAN, J. (1968): A paradigm for the study of altered states of consciousness. *British Journal of Psychology,* 1114, 1201.

SINGER, M. T. (1967): Family transactions and schizophrenia: I. Recent research findings, in Romano, J. (ed.) *The Origins of Schizophrenia, Excerpta Medica International Congress Series,* No. 151, 147.

SINGER, M. T. & WYNNE, L. C. (1965): Thought disorder and family relations of schizophrenics. IV. Results and implications. *Archives of General Psychiatry*, 12, 201.

SINGER, M. T. & WYNNE, L. C. (1966): Principles for scoring communication defects and deviances in parents of schizophrenics. Rorschach and TAT scoring manuals. *Psychiatry*, 29, 260.

SLATER, E. (1968): A review of earlier evidence on genetic factors in schizophrenia. *Journal of Psychiatric Research*, 6 (Suppl. 1), 15.

VENABLES, P. (1964): Input dysfunction in schizophrenia. In Maher, B. A. (ed.): *Progress in Experimental Personality Research*, 1, 1. Academic Press, New York.

WENDER, P. (1968): Vicious and virtuous circles: The role of deviation amplifying feedback in the origin and perpetuation of behavior. *Psychiatry*, 31, 309.

WITKIN, H. A., DYK, R. B., FATERSON, H. F., GOODENOUGH, D. R., & KARP, S. A. (1962): *Psychological Differentiation*. John Wiley and Sons, Inc., New York.

WYNNE, L. C. (1961): Principles for the study and differentiation of the families of schizophrenics, presented at NIMH, Bethesda, Maryland and the Second World Congress of Psychiatry, Montreal, June 1961.

WYNNE, L. C. (1967): Family transactions and schizophrenia: II. Conceptual considerations for a research strategy. *Excepta Medica International Congress Series*, No. 151, 165.

WYNNE, L. C. (1968a): Methodologic and conceptual issues in the study of schizophrenics and their families. *Journal of Psychiatric Research*, 6 (Suppl. 1), 185.

WYNNE, L. C. (1968b): Schizophrenics and their families: Recent research findings and their etiologic implications, Mental Health Research Fund Lecture, London.

WYNNE, L. C. & SINGER, M. T. (1963): Thought disorder and family relations of schizophrenics: I. A research strategy. *Archives of General Psychiatry*, 9, 191.

WYNNE, L. C. & SINGER, M. T. (1966): Schizophrenic impairments of shared focal attention. Roberts Memorial Lecture, Yale University.

Area IV—Section B

GROUP AND FAMILY APPROACHES TO OTHER SPECIAL PATIENT POPULATIONS

This section describes group and family approaches to three kinds of difficult patients: homosexuals, the aged and adolescents.

HOMOSEXUALS

In the past, homosexuality has been regarded as resistant to treatment. Recently, however, therapists using psychoanalytic techniques, behavior therapy and group therapy have all reported some successes. Birk and his colleagues have developed a fascinating method, that, while emphasizing group procedures, combines these three approaches. The first paper in this section describes the experiences of the male-female cotherapists who conducted the group phase of the project. The authors are carefully evaluating the outcome of treatment, and preliminary results seem highly promising. However, the emphasis on evaluation of outcome did not preclude consideration of process and the authors have tried to identify the crucial change-producing factors. Specifically, the effects of learning, interactional process, as well as psychodynamic features were studied.

SUGGESTED CROSS-REFERENCES

The use of mixed sex teams in the treatment of marital and sexual problems is discussed from different perspectives in two papers; one by Masters and Johnson and also in the article by Markowitz and Kadis. For a contrasting approach to the treatment of sexual problems, which deals more directly with symptoms rather than dynamics, the reader is referred to Masters and Johnson's article on the "Rapid Treatment of Sexual Dysfunctions" in Area III.

THE AGED

The next two papers address themselves to the long neglected aged. It may be speculated that a major obstacle to interest and involvement with our psycho-geriatric population has not been based on technical difficulties—because the aged are often pleasant, grateful patients—nor on poor prognosis, because if goals are realistic, results of treatment can often be highly gratifying. Perhaps our professional neglect is more often due to intensely negative emotional feelings related to death, loss, helplessness and hostility towards our elders, that may be evoked by intimate contact with aged persons. Hence, we have erected perceptual defenses and avoid seeing the need, the opportunities and the potent and reciprocal impacts that the aged members of our families, our profession and our society have upon us.

In the paper, "The Aged Are Family Members," Spark and Brody suggest that, contrary to our defensive non-perceptions, the aged often play a significant role in family pathology. They cite cases illustrating the complex effects of unresolved parental relationships with elderly parents on family dynamics, and on its members. Aged family members are included in conjoint family sessions for the purpose of helping younger members clarify and resolve crucial pathological perceptions and relationships. In addition, and surprisingly, the aged have retained capacities for psychic growth and change and thus can also benefit from therapy.

This view of the aged as capable of change is also reflected in the paper by the Bergers in which they describe a multi-dimensional, group oriented day care program for the aged. The Bergers' approach reflects optimism that derives from the feedback of the responsive aged patients to their rational and humane treatment approach.

ADOLESCENTS

The essential issues of the adolescent's crises seem to involve conflicts produced by his need, on the one hand, to establish an adult identity and to act autonomously, free of the need for parental approval; and his continuing feelings of dependency and insecurity about his own abilities, on the other. Successful transition from the dependent child to autonomous adult seems to depend, at least in part, on the establishment of a more equal relationship with his parents. To make this transition without severe emotional and interpersonal distress is difficult for many youngsters and for their families as well.

It may be speculated that the same forces that generate adolescent problems also contribute to their resistances to therapy. Specifically, the conventional intense relationship with a parental figure that is required in most diadic therapy is often experienced by the adolescent as "counter-revolutionary," that is, in conflict with his healthy strivings to individuate and liberate himself from dependence on his parents. The therapist (often with some cause) may be seen as the parent's or society's agent, paid "to psyche" him into accepting the role and behavior assigned him by parents or other adult authorities. Hence, it is not surprising that adolescents may be resistant to treatment.

Spotnitz in his paper, "Constructive Emotional Interchange in Adolescence," suggests a novel approach designed to overcome such resistances. He enlists the young patient as a "helper" in the family therapy situation, and thereby fosters the development of the more realistic and equal parent-child relationship that is a prerequisite to healthy maturation and individuation. The method also helps young patients achieve a feeling of mastery and awareness of their own assets and strengths.

The second paper on adolescents by Didato describes a technique whereby peer groups are employed in treatment of that most formidable group of adolescents, delinquents. Didato's peer group approach avoids some of the resistances that may be engendered by interaction with adults alone. In addition, Didato speculates that aggressive youngsters may evoke the counter-transferential hostilities of the "parent within" of some therapists, and that such counter-transferential factors are anti-therapeutic. His own methods appear to owe their success in engaging such youngsters in treatment, at least in part, to the exorcising of such counter-transference.

SUGGESTED CROSS-REFERENCES

Various methods have been devised to reach the adolescent. In the preceding section Lidz describes the treatment of an adolescent schizophrenic patient, which is based on the author's intensive study of the families of schizophrenics. In contrast, in Area II, Ferber and Ranz discuss an interesting behavioral approach to treatment that is applicable to families that contain adolescents; while Minuchin and Barcai illustrate their method by producing a crisis to foster changes in the behavior of a family in which the symptomatic patient is an adolescent.

H.S.K.
C.J.S.

40

GROUP PSYCHOTHERAPY FOR HOMOSEXUAL MEN BY MALE-FEMALE COTHERAPISTS

Lee Birk, M.D.

*Assistant Professor of Psychiatry, Harvard Medical School
and Director, Behavioral Psychiatry Laboratory,
Massachusetts Mental Health Center
Research Phycsiatrist, Harvard University Health Services*

Elizabeth Miller

*Clinical and Research Associate, Behavioral Psychiatry Laboratory,
Massachusetts Mental Health Center*

and

Bertram Cohler, Ph.D.

*Lecturer on Clinical Psychology, Department of Social Relations,
Harvard University
Research Fellow in Psychology in the Department of Psychiatry,
Harvard Medical School*

This is a clinical paper based on the treatment of 25 homosexual men. This experience came as a part of our involvement in a clinical research study which will be briefly described. The outcome of this controlled study, statistically evaluated, will be the subject of a later paper. Of the 26 patients, 16 were subjects in the research study throughout the period they were in treatment; for these patients we have corroborative data

Reprinted from ACTA PSYCHIATRICA SCANDINAVICA, Supp. 218, 1970, pp. 7-37.

in especially rich detail, including pre-treatment and post-treatment evaluations by outside clinicians. The other 10 patients in the series were in private group therapy and were not a part of the formal research study.

BACKGROUND

Homosexuality as a clinical entity[1] has long been regarded with therapeutic pessimism, from Freud (1924) to Curran and Parr (1957). Within the last ten years, however, three modes of treatment—psychoanalysis, group therapy, and behavior therapy—all have been reported to be effective in the treatment of male homosexuality.

Bieber (1962) reported that 29 of the 106 male homosexuals (27%) became exclusively heterosexual after 150 to 350 hours or more of analysis. Mean treatment time was not specified but a majority of the patients who became exclusively heterosexual had "more than 350 hours" of treatment. Bieber's study made a real contribution by unequivocally documenting the treatability of this group of patients, and by delineating the dynamic structure of their families. Treatment of this kind, however, requires much time and money.

Hadden (1966a, 1966b) beginning about 1955, pioneered in the development of group therapy as a way of helping homosexuals. He works with open-ended groups of homosexual men meeting from one to one and a half hours per week over a period of several years, typically 2 to 4. Hadden reported that 12 of 32 patients (38%) have shown "exclusively heterosexual adjustment" as well as a general decrease in neurotic behavior. Five of his patients (16%) have married and have remained married, "apparently happily." Hadden was the first to point out a number of important specific advantages of group therapy for homosexual patients. Group therapy has the added advantage of being financially within the reach of most people.

Feldman and MacCulloch (1964, 1965), using a behavioral treatment method (an anticipatory-avoidance learning technique), have reported the following results: 18 of 25 patients (72%) have shown "a complete or near-complete absence of homosexual fantasy . . . (and) were either actively practicing heterosexuality or had strong heterosexual fantasies." (Follow-up 1-14 months; mean 6 months.) A treatment technique for homosexuality which requires at most about 20 hours of treatment and claims 72% results certainly promises much but bears close scrutiny.

---

[1] The best comprehensive view of homosexuality we found to be "Sexual Inversion," edited by Marmor (1965). This book examines homosexuality from genetic, biological and anthropological points of view as well as from a clinical psychoanalytic vantage point.

One of course must reserve final judgment when such a brief period of follow-up is reported, and when the criteria for "improvement"—markedly decreased homosexual interest and increased heterosexual interest —were so narrowly defined. Certainly "strong heterosexual fantasies" for example, even if present in 18 of 25 patients treated, cannot directly be compared to 5 of 32 "lasting apparently happy marriages." And, of course, even lasting marriage is not equivalent to satisfactory heterosexual adjustment and therefore in itself may not be an adequate criterion for recovery from a sexual deviation.

The authors' research goal has been to try to take the best from each of these treatment approaches, apply it clinically, and then to evaluate treatment results. The research study was undertaken with the goal of working out and testing a maximally efficient method of treatment. We hoped to develop and test a method addressing itself not just to "modifying homosexual behavior," but to the full range of problems of individual homosexual patients.

In the study our treatment approach is an amalgam of group therapy, conditioning, and brief individual therapy coinciding in time with the conditioning treatments.

A subsequent paper will deal statistically with the results of the intial trial of this combined treatment program, and in particular with the results of a controlled clinical trial of the behavioral conditioning method we have developed. The current paper discusses our developing ideas about group therapy, which has been the most important part of the treatment program for all patients in our series, whether or not they also received conditioning treatments. In the group work we use a male-female cotherapist team[2] and feel this has been especially valuable.

SETTING FOR CLINICAL OBSERVATIONS

The first two authors (L.B. and E.M.) worked together for two years as a male-female cotherapist team with three separate groups. In this way we saw in extended group treatment a total of 30 homosexual men. Of course, 26 were seen in sustained weekly therapy, most for a full two years. (One third of our patients had group psychotherapy only, one third had group therapy plus "placebo" conditioning treatments, and one third had "real" conditioning treatments.) In the group work the male and female therapists worked together directly. Both therapists attended and took an active part in each group meeting.

---

[2] Since we began using the male-female cotherapy team in 1966, Singer & Fischer (1967) reported one year of experience with the use of a male-female cotherapist team in treating a group of 8 homosexuals.

CHARACTERISTICS OF PATIENTS TREATED

All patients were voluntary outpatients, well enough motivated to pay modest fees ($3-$8 a week) for their treatment. The patients ranged in age from 19 to 36 with a mean age of 23. Their intelligence clustered in the bright-normal to superior range. Generally they were well-educated, with a mean of 14½ years of education. One-half of the patients (13 of 26) were college or graduate students, and 4 were educators. Two patients were medical technicians, 4 were semi-skilled, and 4 were essentially unskilled.

Patients were considered for treatment if they were non-psychotic and without history of psychosis, if there was unequivocal evidence of homosexual orientation together with a genuine interest in treatment, with or without a definite expressed goal of changing to heterosexuality. The treated patients in this series were selected from 60 people referred and evaluated. In practice, if candidates for treatment met the basic requirements listed above, we tried to select those who seemed most clearly motivated for treatment and most likely to remain in treatment for a full two years or more. Thus the authors make no claim to having selected a representative sample of homosexual men, or even of homosexual men who want treatment. Rather, we selected a group of non-psychotic homosexual patients who we thought would remain in treatment long enough to be available for re-evaluation in two years.

Degree of Distress. Three patients had made multiple suicidal attempts, and two were active and serious suicidal risks. Nearly all of the patients were deeply distressed about their lives; they were lonely and isolated people who wanted help. Six more were also judged to be substantially depressed, but habitually tried, mostly with little success, to hide this fact from themselves and others. Of these covertly depressed patients 5/6 were among the 11 who habitually frequented gay bars. Seven of the 26 patients in the series were rather noticeably effeminate in some aspect of their dress or grooming, but only two were ostentatiously so, posing and flirting during the early group meetings.

Amount of Work Inhibition. Fifteen of our 26 patients suffered from some substantial degree of work inhibition, three severely so and 12 moderately. Of those severely affected, one complained of a "writing block" and had to drop out of college in his senior year. Another was both a graduate school dropout and chronically unemployed. Of the 12 moderately work-inhibited patients, all were working or studying at a level considerably below their capacities; 2 had a history of marked instability in their job records, and 3 were near academic failure. Four of the 26 patients in the series were over-achieving graduate students who used work as a defense against involvement with people.

Sexual Orientation. Two patients were bisexual, and having heterosexual intercourse at the time therapy began, but without real physical satisfaction or positive object ties to their heterosexual partners. Four more had bisexual histories, having had transient heterosexual experiences several years earlier. The other 20 were exclusively homosexual. One was a pedophile and 2 were hebephiles.

All patients were people who sought therapy because they were unhappy. Twelve felt homosexuality was a central problem and stated they wanted to become heterosexual. Ten felt homosexuality was probably contributory and when asked whether they wanted to become heterosexual, gave skeptical qualified "yes" answers. Four were only grudgingly willing to concede that their lives might be better if they were able to shift to heterosexuality.

Characteristics on Psychological Testing. Subsequent papers will deal with pre- and post-treatment data on TAT, Rorschach, and Phillipson Object Relations Test responses, as well as with the details of the MMPI data, in the light of comparison data from a "normal" control group. The mean pre-treatment MMPI profile for the 16 intensively studied patients is reproduced in Figure 1.

This modal MMPI profile closely approximates the "8-4-2" profile described by Marks and Seeman (1963) and Gilberstadt and Duker (1965) in their manuals for the diagnostic study of psychiatric patients. Patients with this MMPI profile may be described as feeling alienated, distant, and aloof from others, and as afraid of emotional involvement with others. These persons are moody, irritable, and resentful of the demands which they feel others make of them. Typically, such patients handle their conflicts by blaming others for their own difficulties, rationalizing their own problems, and acting out these problems. Patients with this profile generally feel hopeless about the possibility of change and are difficult to involve in treatment. Finally, it should be noted that the high peak on Scale 5, the so-called Masculinity-Femininity scale, is consistent with the patients' presenting problem, that of homosexuality.

Socioeconomic Status. Of the patients who remained in treatment for more than one year, 25 of the 26 were Caucasian and one was Negro. (Another Negro was accepted for treatment but dropped out after a few months.) All but 4 were children of American-born parents. One was born in Ireland, one in Venezuela, and one in South Africa; the fourth was the son of Italian immigrants. Patients clustered in the upper middle class but ranged from working class (4 patients) to upper class (1 patient).

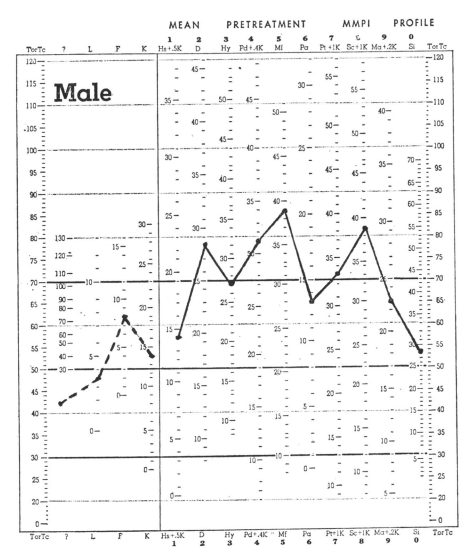

FIGURE 1

*Comparison of Patients Treated to Those Treated by Hadden
and by Bieber et al.*

Socioeconomically the patients in this series are comparable to those treated by Hadden. (Personal communication.) Only one of our patients, however, was a court referral. The patients in Bieber's series were able to afford the cost of analysis, whereas only one of our patients could have afforded this.

"HOMOSEXUALS" AS PEOPLE

The setting in which most of our observations have been made—group psychotherapy—has provided an opportunity to get to know well a sizeable number of homosexual patients as people, interacting with each other and with us. It has been particularly revealing to see the unfolding and changing of their attitudes toward the woman therapist, and to interact with them as they tried in various ways to master the triangular therapeutic situation. This human experience has forced the authors to confront their own initial largely unrecognized prejudices and cultural suspiciousness of "homosexuals." Although our initial biases about "homosexuals" were subtle and relatively sophisticated, they did require working through before we could make real progress in the group work.

The Problem of Differentness. In the beginning the authors and the many colleagues with whom we discussed our work seemed not to think but to feel that these patients were somehow basically different from us. This feeling of "differentness" seems to be a root problem from which many mistaken ideas grow. Even therapists of long general experience may discover that they have unworked through and/or unrecognized needs to feel "different" from their overt homosexual patients in a way that they would not feel, say, about patients with phobias. When this happens, it can interpose a crucial barrier to effective therapy.

Patients take pains to cultivate this illusion of "differentness." Initially many of our patients were clinging almost belligerently to the defensive chauvinism of the gay subculture. These patients found various ways to assault us with their differentness from us. They made ostentatious use of the words "queer" and "gay," and "fag," and they barraged us with talk about ribald times in the gay bars, and orgies in public rest rooms and Turkish baths. One of our patients is a highly intelligent and erudite man who knows personally a great many of the professional homosexual models across the country; he boasted that he had slept with "about 2,000" men over the past dozen years. At the outset of the very first group meeting he provocatively passed around a color slide of a "frontal nude," a commercially available picture of a nude homosexual model posed to display his penis prominently. As each group member in turn gawked at the picture, he observed airily, "Women I suppose aren't very interested in pictures like this because . . . they are different . . . and don't have really strong sexual drives like . . . we do. . . ." Prophetically this opening move was the first of many attempts by group members to drive wedges of "you're different, you're straight etc.," between themselves and their heterosexual therapists. To understand the patients' need to do this is to understand much about what it does for people to categorize themselves as "homosexuals" in the first place. The dynamics, in part, seem to be:

> "You, with your heterosexual interests and desires, are different from me. Unlike you, I have no heterosexual desires (or at least no strong preferential ones); because I am a homosexual, and homosexuals just aren't that way."

It is obvious what safety this position provides from the Oedipal anxiety stirred by conscious recognition of heterosexual feelings. Also this position seems to protect patients from experiencing directly their anger at both their parents—because it permits them to avoid again confronting the feeling of being attracted to a woman. For them this is an experience which has been historically linked not only to Oedipal fears of retaliation, but also to intensely frustrating feminine seductiveness, with rage at the mother for doing this, and at the father for permitting it. The psychodynamic details here are speculative of course, but what is wholly unspeculative is that for the most overt homosexual men, it is a keystone of their defensive structure to present themselves and think of themselves as different from others, "straight people," in terms of sexual matters.

Probably it is a by-product of the need and intensity with which homosexuals in our culture generally pursue these goals that most of us "straight" therapists[3] begin their experience working with homosexuals, almost inevitably having already in part accepted the party line of the gay subculture that homosexual people are different. (The official party line is, of course, that gay people can be good, moral, kind, trustworthy, talented, responsible, etc., though different, but the important psycho-

---

[3] Therapists may be ready to embrace the notion of homosexuals as "different" because of countertransference issues. Such a belief can operate to make male therapists feel safely different from their homosexual patients, and so to insulate them from confronting as bluntly their own unsettled concerns about passivity and masculine identification. Parallel but more complex countertransference factors also can make it tempting for female therapists to cling to the notion of differentness.

dynamic core of this complex statement, however, is simply that they are different.)

ADVANTAGES OF GROUP THERAPY

As Hadden has shown, group therapy has specific advantages for treatment of homosexual men. First is the fact that the "gay" defense—which in individual therapy can be very difficult to resolve—turns out to be a remarkably superficial matter in group treatment, even for patients who have been thoroughly assimilated into the gay life. This results because unwelcome interpretations come from homosexual peers who are seen as having no axe to grind. Also, homosexual love relationships—among our patients at least—are typically short-lived and phasic in character. Early in these relationships there is much idealized hope and expectation, but disappointment and disillusion soon follow. Thus there is nearly always one patient who from his own recent bitter experience is only too ready to "tell it like it is" when someone else is at an idealizing stage. Typically others are stimulated to recount their own past disappointments. Then when the group's assessment of the relationship is borne out by eventual sad events, this has a profound impact. It takes but a few cycles of this till there is a group consensus, or near-consensus, that homosexual liaisons tend to be illustory and not to "work" fulfillingly and lastingly.

A second important advantage of a group for homosexual patients is that it can provide these lonely people with objects, in a setting where relationships are not immediately sexualized. Among overt homosexual patients, especially those with some investment in the "gay" subculture, it would be hard to overestimate the importance of depression, loneliness and a feeling of interpersonal isolation. There is often a chronic state of deprivation of real and sustained personal intimacy. Against such a background of object hunger, group therapy can be immediately useful to the homosexual patient.

Group therapy then can quickly break down patients' rationalizations that they are not unhappy to be homosexual, and can reduce pressure toward homosexual activity by decreasing object hunger. There are additional advantages to support therapy. It can provide much-needed support during the phase of early heterosexual experimentation. It is also important that members get to see each other change and progress. Generally they come to reinforce each other for progress. A climate of useful pressure develops for members to work toward goals of self-understanding, responsibility, and "not acting out," and toward understanding and confronting fears of heterosexual expression. Group pressure eventually is brought to bear on certain members to relinquish their homosexual or "swishy" ways of dressing and acting. The commonality in the dynamics of individual members leads to insights and ventilative experiences, shared affectively by many members. This leads to early recognition by the group that their plight is experientially determined and therefore changeable. As the group begins to see some members actually changing in concrete ways, group confidence and motivation for real therapeutic work are greatly augmented.

GROUP THERAPY: PHENOMENA AND TECHNIQUE

In the group meeting the therapists tried to be open and non-judgmental, generally leaving the initiative as to what comes up in the meetings largely with the patients. The main ground rule was that all strong feelings be brought out and discussed, whether these related within the group, and whether the feelings were angry, fearful, specifically sexual, or tender and loving. Often the most persistingly difficult inhibitions for patients to overcome are in the realm of positive feelings for each other. It can also be hard for patients to speak of their sexual feelings, especially early in treatment, and especially when these involve each other or one of the therapists. At first, when homosexual episodes come up, they tended to be spoken of reticently, in a way which blurred who did what to whom, much less why. A flustered but stubborn vagueness is communicated by descriptions like "So I took him home, and we had sex. . . ." Often the presence of a woman is given as a reason for blurring but the impression is that it is difficult for patients to talk of these things at all. Both therapists tried to break through these inhibitions by setting an example of unembarrassed frankness, and by being calmly relentless in pursuing the nitty-gritty. We asked as many questions as necessary to pin down the facts as to who did exactly what to whom. Such an approach finally succeeded in establishing that "we had sex" really meant ". . . yes . . . I sucked his penis." Here the inquiry would be pressed further: "Why. . . ." "What did it do for you? . . ." "What did you really want? . . ." Questions like these can stop some patients cold, and induce the beginnings of a sober reflectiveness about what it all does mean. This can be an important therapeutic step particularly if the therapist is prepared to follow up by helping the patient with the answers to such questions by understanding well himself the various common dynamics of homosexuals acting out.

Although both therapists most of the time usually were rather inactive and careful to leave most of the initiative up to the group, there were many times when both therapists were active, directly participant and candid, even to the point of openly disagreeing with each other about certain issues. Also there were usually several times per month when the male therapist was not only active, but quite aggressive, when the situation seemed to call for it. This happened a couple of times, for example, when patients were challengingly disclaiming responsibility for paying bills. Another notable example was when a group member was on the verge of accepting a car as a wedding present from his mother. He and his fiancée wanted a Volvo, but his mother wanted to dictate the type of car they would have by making her gift conditional on her doing the choosing, thus obviously perpetuating her dominance over him and extending it to his new wife-to-be. The male therapist pointed this out in the most vigorous and persistent way, emphasizing the pattern being established and the distress it was causing his fiancée. Following the therapists' lead, the entire group took a very strong stand on this matter. The next week this patient returned gratefully with the paradoxical news: "Well, group cost me $5,700 last week!" At times, in other words, it seems important to intervene decisively; this can be useful we feel because these patients have lacked, need, and can utilize, a model of appropriate male assertiveness.

It is worth noting that early on many of the patients began calling the therapists by their first names. Such easy informality and implied camaraderie is not a usual therapeutic stance for the authors. Of literally dozens of previous individual and group patients, only one had ever before called one of us by his first name, and that one happened to be a married homosexual patient in individual therapy. These facts alone mean nothing, but it has been our impression that homosexual patients experience an unusually urgent need to establish an atmosphere of intimacy with their therapists. (On this point Dr. Irving Bieber in a personal communication provided the following consensual validation: "Dr. William V. Silverberg told me some years ago that when a male patient early called him by first name he suspected him to be homosexual or to have serious homosexual conflicts".) In group therapy with male-female cotherapists, it seems that there is additionally a certain tendency to regard the group as an extended close family and to idealize the therapists as wished-for parents who are permissive, who relate to each other cooperatively, and who allow them to relate to the man and the woman simultaneously. First naming no doubt also has to do with a felt need, probably in reaction to feeling weak, inferior and afraid of the man, to feel on equal footing with the therapists.

When patients one by one began to call us by our first names, we, of course, were assiduous in taking up what this meant to them, with widely varying feelings coming out. Always, however, this was done with the implied or explicit permission to call us anything they chose so long as the feelings about it were discussed. One man, the child of parents who had been maddening caricatures of liberal overpermissiveness, held out in calling the male therapist Dr. Birk, because, he explained, when he was little, he remembered being in bed calling for his father to bring him a glass of water. After many repeats of "Daddy, Daddy, Daddy," in a burst of omnipotent exasperation he finally shouted, "Bob!" whereupon his father promptly carried out his wishes. "I felt I had killed my father . . ." he said, "and I always called him by his first name after that." This patient continued to call the male therapist "Dr. Birk" for two full years, then abruptly switched to calling him "Lee." This change came just after the male therapist successfully dealt with a contrived gesture of defiance by the patient, distinguishing him in the patient's mind from his overpermissive father, whose manipulatibility made him feel dangerous and lethally omnipotent, yet at the same time weak because unable to respect his father.

Extra-group social contacts between patients were the rule in all three of the therapy groups. This has some obvious disadvantages; namely, clique formation, inhibition of the expression of hostile feelings toward each other, and occasional joint sexual and other acting out. However, we feel the advantages far outweighed the disadvantages. Socialization between members began naturally enough (as is common in group therapy) with a kind of "after-group group phenomenon." Patients would often still be thinking and talking about what had gone on in group after the meeting had ended, as they walked out of the building. Later contacts became more intimate and deliberately sought out. People would plan to share automobile rides with each other or would arrange to meet another member for the subway trip to the group meeting. Still later, people phoned each other and arranged to have lunch together, to go to the movies together, or to invite each other to parties. At the most intimate and difficult level (with some previously very isolated people), socialization included invited visits to each other's living quarters "just to talk." One touching and mutually and beneficial example of this occurred between Bill, a tremendously over-intellectual isolated graduate student who had been an only child and whose only acquaintances were overly intellectual people like himself, and Mike, a rough and ready cursing lower class Irish immigrant who had been a high school dropout and who despite his rather high native intelligence had labored under a tremendous feelings of intellectual and general inferiority.

For many patients these social contacts represented the first time in their adult lives that they fraternized easily with other males, without either immediately sexualizing or "narcissizing" the relationship, or retiring into an aloof, distant, basically fearful stance characteristic of the way "gay" men relate to "straight" men. Most patients formed one or more group friendships which were marked by unprecedented honesty, openness, and mutual understanding. Extra-group contacts seemed to deepen the meaningfulness of the object ties that these lonely people found in the group.

The only rule about extra-group contacts was that all important happenings, insights, feelings, events, mutual acting out, be brought up with the entire group. The resultant discussions often proved especially valuable.

> One pair of members in the early months of therapy became almost constant companions. They formed a relationship which though not overtly sexual was thoroughly neurotic and homosexual in interpersonal tone, and thoroughly typical for each of them. One member of this dyad became the dominant one, in a caricatured, autocratic way, while the other dutifully (but resentfully) took the role of his puppy-dog-loyal compliant friend. Eventually the loyal member of the pair became disenchanted and overtly resentful of his subservient role, and it was possible in the group for both members to analyze and partially modify this need in themselves to form such relationships.

More than a year later, other people in the group picked up subtle nuances of dominance-submission patterns harking back to this striking object lesson.

The problem of preventing dropouts is a current one of course in psychotherapy, espectially group psychotherapy, and homosexual patients in general are rather notorious for their wavering motivation and failure to persist in therapy. We feel, however, that if patients are well selected, and are people who have come to terms with wanting therapy, problems with dropouts tend to be minimal. Especially for patients with homosexual orientations, the timing of treatment is crucial. In our experience many still developing homosexuals must have an opportunity to see for themselves that they are not going to "grow out of it" and that the gay life is not so gay. The fantasy of growing out of it is common in teenage homosexuals; disillusionment with the gay life seems to occur when patients are in their twenties or later. Obviously these things are highly individual but it can be a positive injury to people to push them too early into treatment before things have crystallized and they have seen for themselves both that homosexuality *is* their life style, and that it is not a happy one for them.

With well selected patients, group therapy becomes an engrossing emotional experience and an important part of the week, essentially immediately. No doubt because of widespread cultural prejudice and the need to maintain either secrecy or a facade of "gay" exuberance, the open honest atmosphere of group produces striking involvement, commitment, and cohesion very early in treatment. The problem of minimizing and interpretively warding off dropouts then, assuming patient selection has been well done, is largely a problem of not fumbling, and of managing well certain crises that tend to develop.

Common pitfalls are in the management of overdue bills, of transference anger, and of a wish to quit therapy in order to maintain a highly cathected relationship with a lover, currently focused on as a hoped-for solution to all problems. Unpaid bills in therapy generally can lead to premature guilty termination, but it is particularly important, we feel, to be alert to the problem of mounting balances with this group of patients. Partly this is because so commonly many of them enter treatment with an unusual need to perpetuate a view of themselves as incompetent at coping. This fits in with and reinforces their need to think of themselves as safely homosexual and not threatening to potential feared rivals. Another pitfall, one which caused us to lose one patient, is the maintenance of an over-aloof stance, without enough early interpretation, and willingness to give a little, when patients get intensely involved in transference anger, particularly at not being given to by a man. As for the last problem—patients' need to follow lovers out of therapy—we feel at times the only workable solution is to interpret this as fully as possible and then to let them go, but with the door open to come back. More often than not interpretation of the situation, particularly by peers, succeeds in keeping the patient in treatment, but sometimes it seems that nothing anyone can say will deflect a patient from such a course. Such a situation can make the therapists feel they are dealing with a delusion, almost, and when this happens, nothing but testing it seems to suffice.

Acting out in the homosexual therapy group, we feel, is mainly a countertransference problem in terms of its being conceived of as a major threat to ongoing therapeutic work. Homosexual patients in a homosexual group, and in therapy, of course at times act out their feelings and, of course, this is at times homosexual. The point is that if the group is effectively handled, there is more than enough therapeutic momentum to make patients value it, and to keep sexual acting out from becoming epidemic and more valued than the goals of therapy. The acting out that does occur, especially that between members, often can be used to advantage therapeutically in the group. This is not to minimize the importance of labeling, examining, and reducing to a minimum sexual and other acting out. In fact, our approach has emphasized educating patients about acting out as a concept. To get the idea across requires examples and plain talk, but once they get the idea what acting out really means in their own lives, patients call each other on it quite effectively.

It becomes evident with experience then that dropouts and acting out are not big problems. One thing that does not come quite as naturally is the matter of getting to the deeper levels of the dynamics of homosexual behavior, especially paralytic unconscious fears of retaliation for sexual interest in women. One of the best avenues into this has been through the use of dreams. One man dreamed of frolicking on a bed with a beautiful young woman with long blonde hair. In the dream they were having a wonderful time, laughing and enjoying each other, when the woman left for a minute to go into the kitchen to get something. While she was gone, a dark hairy arm appeared, knife in hand, menacing, from under the bed. It is notable that for this patient male hairiness is in waking life an erotic stimulus. In the dream the hairiness appears uncamouflaged as a source of terror, obviously connected with heterosexual wishes and fears of retaliation. Discussion of this dream and others like it led into the issue of retaliation fears, with the eventual result that the whole group became aware of this dynamic.

Another patient associated to the dream just described by telling a repetitive nightmare of his own:

> I was on a train at night. . . . There was a murderer loose somewhere on the train. We had formed a kind of posse and were searching for the murderer. . . . Then . . . my father and I were alone together in the baggage car, closed in. . . . My father was standing at a grinding wheel sharpening a long knife. . . . I was kneeling right beside him turning the grindstone while he was sharpening the knife. Then he stopped and ran his finger along the edge of the knife. I looked up and when I looked into his eyes, I realized that he was the one. I knew he was the murderer . . . and . . . I knew he was going to kill me.

Another patient dreamed of a lifeless male body lying face down on a railway track, run over by a train: "He was face down. I didn't know whether it was me or my father. . . ."

Another man dreamed of exploring a "dark, slimy, cavernous vagina" with his whole arm: ". . . when I tried to pull out my arm, it came off inside—when I pulled it out, it was cut off at the elbow. . . ." Even more plainly another patient dreamed of having intercourse with a woman, and ". . . when I tried to come out after sleeping with her, my penis came off inside of her. . . ."

In the first two dreams the dread of retaliation from a man is unusually clear. In the very first, both the crime (heterosexual pleasure) and the punishment (the attacking hairy arm with the knife) are present. In the second, the retaliating lethally dangerous person is clearly the father. In the third, the outcome is definitely fatal for someone, and either a father or a son is killed. The fourth and fifth dreams are obviously about castration, plainly enough, and castration occurring during sexual intimacy with a woman, but in these dreams the element of danger is displaced onto the female organs. In a group, patients get to hear each other present dreams like these, each one of which presents one or another element more or less undisguised. Often they resonate to each other's dream with feeling, and one senses that the experience may help them to put together into a meaningful whole the various elements that in separate dreams appear undisguised.

We are not saying that all our patients' dreams expressed aspects only of male retaliation fears, nor do we wish to minimize the importance of other unconscious dynamics of various kinds in individual patients. For example, one patient dreamed aggressively of having intercourse with a woman; in the dream, he said, "I stuck it right through her; I split her right in two." Another man dreamed, again of a train killing someone violently, but for him the person killed was his mother, and he left the scene quickly feeling profoundly guilty.

MALE-FEMALE COTHERAPY

Our primary rationale for having a female cotherapist in the group was that we felt these patients would stand to gain from experiencing a relationship with a woman different from the frightening seductive-exploitative one they had experienced with their mothers. The advantages of this have been reported by Toby Bieber (1967). We realized that in the aversive conditioning procedure we might have an effective technique for blocking homosexual feeling and behavior, but that unless we could succeed in helping these patients to be able to obtain gratification heterosexually, these effects would be transient and not conductive to a happy life. We hoped that having a woman in the group therapy could help to reduce fears about women, and over time that a kind of *in vivo* desensitization might result. We also felt to recreate in the treatment the triangular situation would enrich the content of the therapy sessions.

Two years' experience have shown us that these advantages are even more significant and important than anticipated. We found that generally patients were not much inhibited, even in the beginning, by the presence of a woman. Of the 26 patients, only 2 had more than a little difficulty in overcoming these inhibitions, but eventually did so. We were also a little surprised that overt hostility toward the female therapist was not more blatant, and surprised by the relative easy availability of heterosexual feeling, in abundance, within the protective setting of the treatment situation. Indeed the most improved patient in this series tended to be the same ones in whom we could document especially clearly this phenomenon of the elicitation of heterosexual feelings in the treatment situation, repetitively experienced, without the dreaded retaliatory male reprisals, and then generalized to other available females. Nearly all of our patients however—all but 2 of the 26—acknowledged directly or indirectly a definite sexual interest in the female therapist, many quite directly and early in treatment. (These were *not* the same 2 who expressed inhibition initially at talking in the presence of a woman.) Many patients commented directly in the group meetings about their attraction to her. Such remarks typically are made nervously, often with perceptible monitoring of the reactions of the male therapist. Watching this, fantasies of male retaliation seem not very inferential. In the group meetings and out, different patients at different times have expressed feelings toward the female therapist by behaviors ranging from coy but unmistakable flirtatiousness, to direct but usually backhanded compliments about her hair, dress, legs, figure, "bod," (body) personality, to open statements about actual desire towards her.

An interesting sidelight of the cotherapy experience was that the female therapist could frequently sense when patients came to group fresh from some homosexual episode. At such times, before this came up explicitly as group content, she noticed a certain atypical defiant flirtatiousness toward her, along with a faint aura of bravado toward the other men in the group.

In the fourth month of treatment one Kinsey 6 patient who had never been out with a girl in his life cornered the female therapist just after a group meeting, and whispering to her, asked her for a date. This patient did later begin to date and now considers himself unofficially engaged. In a different group, another Kinsey 6 patient, also in about his fourth month of treatment, a man who had dated before but only to

maintain appearances, was speaking in the group of a brand new heterosexual relationship with a woman, Dinah. He was speaking of the growth
of his attraction for Dinah when he slipped and said: "Things have
been much different since the beginning of my relationship *with Elizabeth* . . ." (the female cotherapist). In subsequent meetings he made
almost identical slips two more times, meaning to say Dinah and saying
Elizabeth. He is now happily married to Dinah and they are expecting
a baby.

It seems to be advantageous for patients to work with both a man
and a woman in their therapy and to have the experience of seeing them
work together without dominance or exploitation on either side. As is
later elaborated, the dynamics of the families in which these patients
developed their problems apparently always involve a defective family
setting in which the relationship with mother, the relationship with
father, and the relationship between mother and father all were grossly
aberrant. They need a man to identify with and to help them feel safe
about their heterosexual feelings, a man who does not punish or retaliate
against them. Instead he subtly encourages them toward heterosexual
ventures and permits them to feel safe, for example, in expressing interest
in the woman. One patient in an evaluation interview described his
feelings about a petting experience as follows:

> Patient: ". . . I started wanting to escape . . . I started to get those
> feelings about wanting to get out. I would start thinking about
> Lee, and I would say "if I ever needed you, I need you now!·. . . uh
> and uh so that uh things went pretty well!"
> Interviewer: "*You think of Lee while you were making love to the
> girl?*"
> Patient: "Yeah."
> Interviewed: "*And how would that help you?*"
> Patient: "I would just figure if he can do it, so can I!" (laughter.)

As for the specific value of a woman—another patient in an evaluation
interview explained his early reactions to the female therapist as follows:

> "I didn't realize the first time I met her, I just—I didn't realize
> what my reaction was, but when . . . I saw her, I sort of jumped
> and I wouldn't look at her. . . . Well the reason she frightened me so
> much was that her hair was all down and it wasn't done. When my
> mother had her hair down and not done, she was you know—just
> impossible to get along with . . . really dangerous. . . ."

He went on to explain that his mother was given to "strikingly different
moods . . ." alternating between being sweetly seductive and violently
angry.

The moods, he explained, were paralleled by the way she dressed and the way she wore her hair. When she was dressed up she would wear her hair up and carefully done, and at such times "she would put on a kind of pseudo-sticky-sweet-behavior—it was seductive type behavior. . . ." He went on to explain that this phase could never last long—"maybe a half day or maybe an hour . . . before she was going to get very angry . . . and come at me with something or throw something at me. . . ." At times, he said, his mother always had her hair down and not "done." On one such occasion she hurled a ceramic pot full of boiling hot coffee at his head, and when it missed him and crashed against the wall, she screamed at him "Now look what you have done!" This man has now terminated and for nine months has been happily married to a woman whose personality attributes he considers similar to those of his former therapist.

Many patients have made similar though less dramatic statements about the importance to them of getting to know a woman in the group. It has been a repetitive theme explored by all three groups that the female therapist ". . . is somehow . . . a different kind of woman." When the meaning of this phrase was pursued with one patient, he stumbled and hesitated as he tried to formulate it, then said reflectively that he thought that the most different thing about her was that she didn't seem to want or need anything from him; she wasn't interested in coaxing him into involvement with her out of her own needs. Finally he blurted out "I don't know—she's just different—well, what I mean is she's different from my mother!"

DYNAMICS OF HOMOSEXUAL BEHAVIOR AND FEELINGS

Oedipal Factors and Defective Masculine Identification. In the modern clinical literature on the psychodynamics of homosexuality, strong emphasis has been given to the central role of Oedipal factors. The patient, denied during his developmental years an adequate opportunity to identify with a capable male, and heavily exposed during those same years to female seductiveness of extraordinary intensity, develops especially intense and severe Oedipal fears of retaliation. Thus he comes to deal with his normally pressing sexual appetites by safely renouncing interest in heterosexual objects, and by rechanneling his libidinous drives toward male objects. This affords him a greater feeling of safety while allowing him release of sexual tensions, and it also tends to fit in with and further reinforce various degrees of "feminine identification," a process which began much earlier, during the earliest years of paternal unavailability and maternal pressure not to be like father.

We fully concur with the centrality and root-problem-importance of these factors, but we are here suggesting that many other identifiable dynamic patterns also exist, and that these can be very profitably focused on in therapy. These "other" dynamic factors usually are much more nearly conscious, and they vary among individuals and even quite strikingly from homosexual act to act. They may frequently be simply the top layer of the dynamics; however, tactically in group therapy we have found it useful to work first with these nearer-the-surface patterns, while concomitantly laying the foundations for deeper interpretations as to the root dynamics outlined above. In this way, early on in treatment, patients can get a feeling of accomplishment and of some control-through-understanding of part of their behavior. This helps to shape patients toward being usefully analytical about their sexual impulses and helps to create a positive and appropriately hopeful attitude toward therapy. We believe that these other nearer-the-surface dynamics are not as much emphasized in the literature as their importance and in particular their usefulness would warrant.

Other Dynamic Factors. We have seen many instances of particular homosexual episodes arising from feelings on unbearable loneliness, from depression and specific disappointments, from anger triggered by identifiable life events, and from feelings of yearning for the father. At other times it seems clearly a matter of a deep conviction of masculine inferiority, physically felt, with irrational fantasies of somehow gaining parity as a man by a particular homosexual act with a particular man felt to be especially virile, competent and masculine. In other cases, patients have recognized and acknowledged that they actively sought out homosexual encounters because of inner cues arising from unusual success either with a woman or with other competitive masculine endeavors. In such cases, patients often say clearly "I guess I just couldn't stand things going so well; somehow I had to screw it up, and make myself feel small and . . . no good. . . ." Here it seems that the success phase both provokes anxiety about retaliation from males, and produces guilt about the possibility of successful competition. The acting out phase then apparently serves both as a self-punishment to expiate the guilt and to terminate anxiety by concretely reconfirming the patient's identity as "just a homosexual," therefore safe from the reprisals of jealous men.

Finally, many times patients use homosexual activity, the more demeaning the better, to act out anger at their parents, their therapists, or others. Sometimes there are strong wishes, which may or may not be acted out, to inform the parents about these things, "so they know just how much they have screwed me up. . . ."

Clinical Examples of "Other Dynamic Factors"

Unbearable Loneliness: The patient is a superficially happy and friendly man of 36, an immigrant from Ireland who lives alone and has no real friends, and no family in this country. On the surface he is glibly jovial, but with people he keeps communication at a very shallow level. Describing picking up someone for a sexual episode, he has often said things like "I just wanted to be with someone . . . and be happy, and not feel so terribly lonely and depressed. . . ." As this patient has learned from repetitively hearing himself describing such loneliness-sex sequences, and as he has learned in the group to relate to people more directly and satisfyingly, he has become much happier and less driven, though his sexual orientation is "still as queer as ever." Recently he described meeting a homosexual acquaintance in the subway station. He said "I could see he was sad and wanted to cheer him up." However, when a sexual exchange was proposed, the patient responded, "No, a quick blow job in the men's room is not my cup of tea . . . but I'd like to talk to you. . . ."

Depression: The patient is a 30-year-old hairdresser who generally lives alone, though several times he has had transient roommate-lovers. Even during his first months in treatment, he could freely acknowledge that he knew such liaisons were "no good" and that they never last. This man leads a chronically isolated, emotionally impoverished life. Generally his loneliness is unbroken except for the "friends" he meets in the gay bars, and except for his contacts with his mother, who is exploitative and grossly feminizing toward him. He sees her usually only once a week when he returns home to have dinner with her and "do her hair," as well as the hair of several of her matronly friends. His friends from the gay bars are people he meets when the need to be acknowledged as attractive becomes urgent. Then he dresses flamboyantly, preens himself, carefully styles his own hair, and goes to the bar with a facade of artificial gaiety, determined to be looked at and admired, but not touched. His pleasure comes from rebuffing the attentions he has so painstakingly courted. This man has repeatedly said things like "I was just feeling so depressed, I couldn't stand it so . . . I went to the bar, and I picked somebody up . . . I took him home, and we had sex . . . I knew nothing would come of it, but . . . I just had to do something; I couldn't stand feeling so depressed. . . ."

Anger Triggered by Identifiable Life Events: The patient is a 25-year-old law student with a history of being pushed very hard by his mother always to be at the top of his class, which he always was throughout his precollege and college years. He is chronically embittered toward and disappointed in his father. This is partly because of his father's real deficiencies and subservience to patient's mother, and partly because of lifelong exposure to a constant barrage of histrionic undermining propaganda directed at his father by his mother. When this patient entered graduate school, he felt he was competing in a world of men, not boys, and felt an acute need of affective moral and financial support from his father. In a mutually tearful (and rare) man-to-man talk, his father promised support. Then over the course of the following year, he received a series of letters from him essentially reneging on this promise. He was enraged. More than once receiving one of these letters from his father, the patient would angrily seek out a demeaning homosexual contact. Once he said "so I read the letter . . . and felt furious . . . enraged . . . so I just put the letter down and went out . . . the next thing I know I ended up in a public john . . . ; I just stayed there until finally I got someone to blow me. . . ."

Profound Yearning for the Father: The patient is a 33-year-old unemployed professor of English literature from the old South. This man's father was a harsh, hard-drinking, millionaire businessman who was almost a caricature of masculine success. He was ". . . terribly practical and mechanical . . . ; he ran a construction business which was highly successful . . . ; he was aggressive and hard-driving and . . . (explosively opinionated) . . . ; for relaxation he owned an airplane which he flew himself." Until the patient was 17, his father was drunk much of the time he was home, and when drunk he alternated between tenderness and frightening brutality toward the patient. The latter was triggered repeatedly by the way the mother had taken over the boy and lavished her love on him, excluding the father.

After age 17, his father reformed and became a teetotaler and "was accepted again into my mother's bed" . . . "but" . . . he said "it was too late. . . . For those first 17 years she so completely shielded me from him and so constantly told me 'your father is a *mess*, you don't want to be like him,' that when the time came for me to accept him and be like him, I just couldn't be, and that was that."

That was *not* that, however; this patient has never gotten over his profound yearning for his father. He struggles with it daily, still, though he is now in his mid 30's. This patient's feeling of yearning for his father qualitatively is typical of what many in our series experience, but for him the yearning seemed both extremely intense and blended with guilt and need for punishment. The atypical intensity, and his guilt and need for punishment are not surprising in view of his history—when his father died of a heart attack 10 years ago, the patient was openly blamed. His father's death had been sudden and had occurred at the height of an ongoing vicious verbal battle between the patient and his father. The battle had begun because his father had just learned that "that fancy Eastern school" had ruined his son by turning him both "pink" (liberal) and "queer." His last conversation with his father was by telephone; his father had screamed at him "I'll fix you so you can never get a degree from there!" After his father's death, the patient fixed himself—shortly before he was to receive his Ph.D. he brazenly stole a pair of socks from the University operated department store. This was but the last of a long series of provocative deeds with the University administration, and he was expelled "not to be readmitted under any circumstances."

This patient kept in his living room a huge, full length larger-than-life sized photograph of his father "dressed in his leather pilot's outfit, standing beside his airplane, looking young and strong and handsome. . . ." The patient himself has related his brooding, lonely, often all-night pursuits of a sexual partner to yearning for his father. Once, after a sexual episode, he reported that he had actually experienced a vivid visual image of his much longer-for-father, just at the time of orgasm.

Masculine Inferiority: The patient is a 24-year-old college senior majoring in psychology, a Negro brought up in a city in the deep South, "in a matriarchal society." His mother and his two aunts are college educated, well-respected teachers who hold advanced degrees; his father carries out groceries in a supermarket and has a grade school education. The patient always regarded him as "stupid" and "crude" and "brutal" and was determined not to be like him.

Now, however, he feels (quite nonrationally) that he is too fat and soft and that his hips and buttocks are too thick and wide and feminine. This feeling of lacking masculine attributes and power extends also to a host of ordinary problems of coping with life. Repeatedly in group he spoke of "becoming aroused by some guy with a great body. . . . He reported experiencing conscious wishes to be like the man and said that he thought he knew it was irrational, he felt that by sucking the man's penis, he could "somehow get what he has—the masculine 'bod,' the aggressiveness . . . the ability to make it. . . ." In this case, the patient was generally aware of much of this before therapy began. However, his explicit repeated acknowledgment of this sequence of "always looking for the archetypal male stud" led finally in the group to his being unable to slide easily into this magical search for manhood and so to evade the reality and responsibility of his own real power to cope as a man. As in fact he coped more and more responsibly with his therapy bill, his school work, his career plans, his dating life, and finally his draft status, he became less driven to look for masculine competence in his magical way.

Unusual Success and Retreat from Masculine Heterosexual Competence: One of the best examples here is from the work with Melvin, the same patient cited as an example of anger; this illustrates our earlier statement that patients may indulge in homosexual behaviors at different times out of quite different psychological needs.

Patient was enjoying himself at a party. While there he met Donald, a fellow patient from the group, with his newly acquired girl friend-lover, Sandy. Sandy made a point of being especially friendly with Melvin, and told him he was a "very attractive man." She further implied that her attractive former roommate, Ellen, now the patient's apartment neighbor, liked him and would be quite capable of being interested in him as a man. He had very much enjoyed himself at the party for the previous 4 hours or so, but inside another hour he had gotten himself thoroughly drunk, and shortly thereafter left the party to seek out a homosexual episode. Afterwards he said, "I felt so good . . . when Sandy told me all those things . . . I guess I just couldn't take letting myself feel so good. . . ."

On another occasion, this same patient was praised by his law school professor in class, in front of his peers. Hours later he found himself in the subway men's room getting blown.

We do not wish to contend that psychological mechanisms like these underlying particular homosexual behavior sequences are unique to homosexuality. Very similar sequences of course often underlie impulsive heterosexual behavior, especially where loneliness or depression is a mainspring force. In homosexual syndromes one is struck, however, by the centrality of anger-sex sequences, by the importance of feelings about or deriving from the father, and by the frequency and clarity of masculine success-phobia as a mechanism. The important point is that these dynamics are readily accessible and workable right from the very first day of therapy.

SOME THOUGHTS ABOUT "HOMOSEXUALS" FROM THE GROUP EXPERIENCE

The tendency to regard homosexual patients as rather alien creatures leads to vague fears and to emotional reactions basically not unlike say midwestern farm attitudes about "city folks," "Easterners," or "foreigners." This promotes the growth of many false stereotypes.

One of these is the idea that practicing overt homosexuals tend to be people who are wildly gratifying their impulses. There is a temptation to accept at face value accounts of orgiastic sprees; some patients can make it sound as if they are spending their lives in a perpetual round of near-unimpeded gratification, with very little inhibition and almost no holds barred. This is sadly untrue. Of the patients in our sample, the ones who initially talked the biggest and wildest were typically the very ones who turned out to be the most pathetically and consistently inhibited. They want and pursue not just sexual release, but love and a feeling of enduring closeness and contentment: "I just wanted to make him happy . . . I wanted to feel loved and special . . . and like the whole thing really meant something. . . ." Our patients generally found this impossible, certainly in any long range way. Also they often were too inhibited to obtain even sexual release.

For our patients, romantic homosexual liaisons have been either quite transient, with lengths usually measurable in days or even hours, and/or for both partners mixed with so much unfulfilled yearning, covert anger, spite and frustrated vindictiveness, that in retrospect the affairs seem quite a fiasco to them. Rather than being perpetually gratified by their sexual activity, our patients were perpetually frustrated and disappointed by it. They seemed to be people continuously searching to find partners with whom they could experience deepening rapport and lasting personal ties. Some search and hope but fail to find even a shadow of what they yearn for. Others, often quite repetitively, find mirage-like romantic relationships which soon become bitter and mutually destructive. One man over several months' time wrote 109 unanswered or rebuffed love letters to his intended, without ever having any sex at all during this time. Later, this same patient "fell in love with" another man. For several months he agonized verbally about his new love in the group; during this time it remained love from afar. Finally he got the opportunity to sleep with the man, but he found himself impotent and embarrassed. When he finally reported "success" in sleeping with this man, he spoke in a flat, depressed, nihilistic tone and said simply "well . . . I finally did it. I screwed him . . .; but . . . it wasn't very good. . . ." Another patient after months of parading his "gay" ways eventually complained explicitly about his severe sexual inhibitions, even homosexually:

> *Patient*: "You see, I have a certain problem. I can—I can't climax with anybody blowing me. And there's a mental block there. . . . So the first time I tried to see just what it was like in a men's room . . . I was sitting in a stall, and I didn't know who the heck was in the next stall. . . . And he told me like slip myself up underneath you know, so that he could get at me and blow me. . . ."

Interviewer: "*Under the stall?*"

Patient: "Right; partition."

Interviewer: "*You got down on the floor you mean?*"

Patient: "Right. So I—so I did and he started blowing me and I was amazed because I got sexual pleasure from it and I never even get any sexual pleasure from anybody blowing me. In fact, I didn't like it. It bothered me. It irritated me. And I got sexual pleasure from it. And I climaxed within a few seconds. I tried this again, and it still worked. . . ."

Interviewer: "*But you never saw the guy?*"

Patient: "No. That's the difference. . . . That's the difference. I never saw the guy. And then I tried . . . I tried it different other ways. I tried, in other words, seeing one person go in the stall and seeing that he was cute and trying it. Well occasionally I got sexual pleasure from it but I had great difficulties. It took me longer to climax than before. And then to say, go into the same stall with the same person and be facing the person—I—I had trouble doing that. Uh—if I sort of blocked out the person and said: "I don't care about you, just—just get it over with, I could climax. But if I looked at the person, and if I had the . . . slightest bit of interest in the person I couldn't climax . . . it's almost like being impotent. It makes me feel bad and I wish I could take on that fault and get rid of it, so that I could have sexual satisfaction like any other person."

Another misconception, we feel, is the idea that specific types of sexual activity necessarily are correlated with discrete characterological types of homosexuals ("active," "anal," "passive," "oral," etc.). Indeed, there are homosexual men who strongly prefer a particular kind of sexual activity and who in general eschew other kinds, and others who invariably are dominant and aggressive and active in seeking out and relating to their partners, and still others who play a compliant, acceding passive role with their partners. However, we feel it is misleading rigidly to categorize homosexuals into types and subtypes with each grouping (like "active anal" for example) being felt to possess distinctive characteristics. The patients we have seen engage in a great variety of activities with different partners or the same partners at different times. Very often patients are willing to do sexually whatever their partner wishes, often with an intense desire to please him, even though he might be a total stranger. The wish to please certainly more often dictates the type of sexual activity engaged in than some bookish classification. Such intense wishes to please are common, apparently with narcissistic dynamics: They want to give what they desperately yearn to get, in the only way open to them. And like the rest of us, what they want to get is a sense—however false or transient—of being loved. From our experience, what homosexuals do sexually is typically highly variable, and depends heavily on what is the composition of the underlying feelings of the moment. Even more centrally, especially when a felt need for human love and closeness is the dominant feeling of the moment (versus anger for example), what they actually do sexually is pathetically dependent on what they hope will please their partners.

FAMILY DYNAMICS

The case histories of our patients of course differ from each other in important ways, which require thoughtful individualization in terms of treatment, but there are common patterns, and what we have learned here has corroborated the work of Bieber (1967). It was striking that every one of our patients grew up notably lacking in rapport with his father. In each case there has been evidence of a profound unsatisfied yearning for a good close relationship with a strong, competent and approachable father. In a small minority of cases (3/26) the father was seen as effective, even highly competent, but inaccessible (3/26) and/or "probably homosexual himself," (2/26). In these cases also, however (when the father was seen as an effective male), the quality of the father-son relationship was poor. It is not simplistically a matter of patients lacking an effective father with whom to identify, however. Rather, and again corroborating Bieber's findings, all our patients seemed to have relationships with their mothers which also were defective, and defective in the context of a disordered family setting in which mother and father did not take appropriate roles toward each other as husband and wife. Often even in very transparent ways, these sons served as husband-substitutes and/or confidants for their mothers. It is interesting that of our 26 patients, no one came from a "broken home." This is consistent with the apparent importance of the intact but disordered family setting, with its conflict between mother and father, and its pressures on sons not to be like their fathers, and its demands on the sons to serve sexual and other neurotic needs for their mothers.

Most of the mothers were "close-binding-intimate," seductive and exploitative. Most patients presented their mothers as clearly bent on opposing and retarding their development into being a masculine person. These mothers typically discouraged athletics, Cub Scouts, and other masculine peer activities, as well as contact and closeness with fathers. Many said openly: "Your father is a failure, and you are going to be different." Subtly or quite baldly, these mothers undermined developing adolescent heterosexual interests and relationships.

One mother said about a potential girl friend, "You know, I think her father owns a whore house." Another mother of a patient who is so sexually inhibited he cannot even be successfully homosexual, sternly warned him repeatedly, "Remember—one moment of pleasure can ruin your whole life!" Another mother, still at it though her son is in his late 30's, said about a girl friend—"Virginia is such a nice girl. Do you suppose she has false teeth?"

A common denominator among families in our samples seems to have been great pressure on sons not to identify with their fathers. Pressure not to be masculine came always from mothers, and usually was over the issue of mothers wanting their sons to be unlike their fathers. The family dynamics are by no means entirely stereotyped, however. In one of our cases, a whole extended family cooperated in feminizing a male child. This patient, Joe, was born "the baby" of a large Italian family of boys. He is a large baby-faced man who from the neck down looks like an overweight football lineman. He was to have been born not "Giussepe" (Joe) but "Giussepina" (Josephine), his mother's dreamed of little girl. In this family the father and all the siblings cooperated in the signing over for this unfortunate male child to his mother. He was not allowed to play with his brothers. While they played football, his lot in life was to peel potatoes, wash dishes, help his mother, and keep her company.

At least 5 of our sample of 26 patients had mothers who were quite overtly bizarrely feminizing: One mother, for example, dressed her son as a girl until he was 4; another nicknamed and derisively called her son "Mary Jane"; another continued to encourage and praise her son when he paraded around in her high heeled shoes, even when he was an adolescent, old enough to know better. Even after this patient was 21, she was giving him her cast-off jewelry.

RESULTS AFTER TWO YEARS OF THERAPY

A detailed consideration of therapeutic results will be presented in the later paper which is to deal with results with and without the behavioral conditioning treatment technique, by comparing patients receiving group therapy plus "real" conditioning treatments versus those receiving group therapy plus placebo conditioning treatments. Here we merely want to outline in a general way what our overall results have been after the first two years of therapy. Most patients remain in treatment, and most we feel are still changing and improving. Figure 3 for example, which gives both two-year results and three-year results, illustrates the apparent trend toward continued gains.

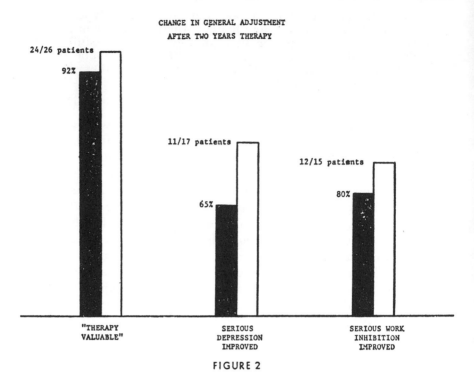

FIGURE 2

Of patients who remained in group long enough to be considered in therapy—three months or more—only 4/30 dropped out. Of those who did persevere in treatment for two years or more, all but 2 considered their therapy valuable. (See Figure 2). Of the patients who were most seriously chronically depressed at the time they began (including two serious suicidal risks), 9/11 improved substantially. Of the persevering patients with substantial work-inhibition as a symptom, 12/15 have definitely improved, 3 quite dramatically so.

In terms of sexual changes (Figure 3), in the first two years of therapy, 9/26 patients shifted to or toward heterosexuality, and 8/26 experienced heterosexual intercourse for the first time. (One patient had experienced heterosexual intercourse before, but many years before and only with prostitutes, while in the Army.) Three patients married during the first two years of treatment and three more became engaged. Of those who married, two have remained married happily. One married impulsively very early in treatment and is unhappily married. Of those who became

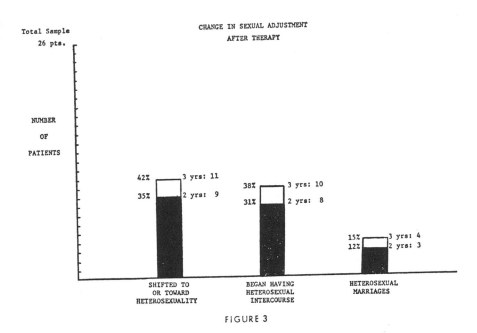

FIGURE 3

engaged, one is now married, one lost his fiancée by death and one has set a wedding date.

CONCLUSIONS AND SUMMARY

The author's experience during the first two years in treating 26 overt homosexual men primarily by group therapy, and using a male-female cotherapist team, has proved rewarding, with nearly all patients considering their therapy valuable and showing substantial improvement in their lives in general, and with about a third (9/26) shifting to or toward heterosexuality. The question of whether and to what degree the addition of an aversive conditioning technique to the treatment regimen of 8 of the patients in our series has contributed to our results will be considered separately in a later paper. Briefly, however, we can say that while we have evidence to present that the conditioning technique was useful, several of our most improved patients came from each of the three categories—group therapy only, group therapy plus placebo conditioning treatments and group therapy plus "real" conditioning treatments.

From a public health point of view it is important that these results have been obtained quite economically in terms of professional time and treatment cost. The patients in this series—even the most improved ones —were all treated in a total of 79 to 140 hours, nearly all of which was in group therapy. Many patients, of course, continue in therapy and it seems many continue to improve. Our still continuing experience with group therapy has convinced us, with Hadden, that it is an effective treatment technique, low in cost, which deserves to come into wider use. We also feel that the use of a male-female cotherapy team has been valuable and hopefully will be tried by other investigators.

ACKNOWLEDGMENT

The authors wish to express their indebtedness to the psychiatric staff of the Harvard University Health Services, who have cooperated with our work throughout. We are especially grateful to Dr. Paul Walters; without his encouragement and help the study would not have been possible.

We also want to thank Dr. Alfred O. Ludwig, and Dr. Stanley Kanter, of the Massachusetts Mental Health Center, who were of great value as clinical consultants. Drs. Irving and Toby Bieber, Dr. James Mann, Dr. Lenore Boling and Dr. Sheldon Roth served as independent clinicians assessing the outcome of the treatment program. We are grateful to Drs. Irving and Toby Bieber, and to Dr. Samuel Hadden for their valuable suggestions about the manuscript.

Finally, we want to thank Dr. Jack R. Ewalt, Bullard Professor of Psychiatry, Harvard Medical School, whose encouragement and support made this research possible.

This research was supported in part by a grant from the National Institute of Mental Health, MH 14455.

REFERENCES

BIEBER, I., et al. (1962): Homosexuality. A Psychoanalytic Study of Male Homosexuals. Basic Books, New York.

BIEBER, I. (1967): On Treating Male Homosexuals. *Arch. Gen. Psychiat.* 16, 60-63.

CURRAN, D., & PARR, D. (1957): Homosexuality: An Analysis of 100 Male Cases Seen in Private Practice. *Brit. Med. J.* 1, 361-367.

FELDMAN, M. P., & MacCULLOCH, M. J. (1964): A Systematic Approach to the Treatment of Homosexuality by Conditioned Aversion; Preliminary Report. *Amer. J. Psychiat.* 121, 167-172.

FELDMAN, M. P., & MacCULLOCH, M. J. (1965): The Application of Anticipatory Avoidance Learning to the Treatment of Homosexuality—I. Theory, Technique and Preliminary Results. *Behav. Res. Ther.* 2, 165-183.

FREUD, S. (1924): Psychogenesis of Homosexuality in a Woman. *Collected Papers,* Vol. 2 (p. 207) Hogarth Press, London.

GILBERSTADT, H., & DUKER, J. (1965): Handbook for clinical and actuarial MMPI interpretation. W. B. Saunders, Philadelphia.

HADDEN, S. B. (1966): Group Psychotherapy of Male Homosexuals. *Current Psychiatric Therapies,* Vol. 6. Ed.: Masserman, J. New York: Grune and Stratton.

HADDEN, S. B. (1966): Treatment of Male Homosexuals in Groups. *Int. J. Gr. Psychother.* 16, 13-22.

MARKS, P., & SEEMAN, W. (1963): Actuarial Description of Abnormal Personality. Williams and Wilkins, Baltimore.

MARMOR, J., et al. (1965): Sexual Inversion, The Multiple Roots of Homosexuality. Basic Books, New York.

SINGER, M., & FISCHER, R. (1967): Group Psychotherapy of Male Homosexuals by a Male and Female Co-therapy Team. *Int. J. Gr. Psychother.* 17, 44-52.

POSTSCRIPT

Six more patients have now been treated for a total of two years or more in group psychotherapy. Five of six of these have shifted to or toward heterosexuality. Two of six have begun having heterosexual intercourse for the first time and one more who previously had no conscious sexual interest in women whatsoever now goes to bed regularly with women, pets heavily and seems at the point of actualizing a consummation with his present sexual partner. One of six has already made a happy marriage.

If we pool all these figures for the new six patients who have now had two years of therapy with those who have remained in treatment on followup, the following adjustments would have to be made:

In Figure 3 on page 35 of the reprint:

1. Ordinate line—32 patients have now been treated (instead of 26).
2. First bar graph—17 patients or ex-patients have shifted to or toward heterosexuality (vs. 11 in the original graph).
3. Second bar graph—12 patients or ex-patients began having heterosexual intercourse for the first time (vs. 10 in the original graph).

There were also 4 more patients who experienced heterosexual intercourse, making a total of 16, but these patients have yet to be able to sustain a non-sporadic heterosexual pattern.

4. Third bar graph—6 patients or ex-patients have now been successfully married (vs. 4 patients in the original bar graph). Five of these 6 are happily married and 2 have become fathers.

41

THE AGED ARE FAMILY MEMBERS

Geraldine M. Spark

*Associate Director, Division of Family Psychiatry, Eastern
Pennsylvania Psychiatric Institute (Philadelphia)*

and

Elaine M. Brody

*Director, Department of Social Work
Philadelphia Geriatric Center*

MULTIGENERATIONAL RELATIONS

Gerontology and family-oriented therapy have common bonds. Both experienced their major growth during the past two decades and both struggled counter to the main currents of thought. Family treatment was hampered by the predominant orientation of approaches which focused on the individual, while gerontology strove for a place in the scientific sun alongside the more fashionable younger phases of life. The purpose of this paper is to stimulate a dialogue in order to integrate the new knowledge of these disciplines in the practical interests of the clients being served.

The first section will offer some information about the aged and their intergenerational relationships and some observations of family dynamics when an elderly family member becomes the focus of a family

Reprinted from FAMILY PROCESS, Vol. 9, No. 2, June 1970, pp. 195-210.

This is a revised version of a paper presented at the Conference on *Family Therapy and the Family Life Cycle* sponsored by the Family Institute of Philadelphia, Benjamin Franklin Hotel, Pennsylvania, May 23, 1969.

problem. The second suggests that the elderly are a crucial ingredient in family practice.

The family approach shifted the therapeutic focus from the individual to the family as a whole. Till now, concentration has been primarily on the family in its relatively early phases, reflecting the same preoccupation on the part of theoreticians, researchers, and practitioners in the psychological and social sciences. An additional shift in perspective is suggested so that the conceptual framework includes all generations, even those legitimate family members, the aged. Otherwise, the process of scapegoating by exclusion will simply be moved up a generation: the "bad" parents of the first half of the century will become the "bad" grandparents of the second half. Equally important, such exclusion will continue to disadvantage the younger generations as well as the aged themselves.

How did it come about that the later life phases of the individual and of the family have been so neglected?

Psychologically, aging is a painful subject with its connotation of death and disease. As individuals and as professionals, the tendency is to avoid it if possible. The family situations confronting us are unique to our time if only because a large aging population simply did not exist at any previous time in history. At the turn of the century only one of 25 Americans was 65 or over. Now the aged represent one of every ten in the total population—20 million strong—and are increasing both numerically and proportionately. More families include more older people all the time. Thus, when psycho-dynamic formulations of human behavior began, the aged were not much in evidence and emphasis was placed on the young nuclear family. Phases of development were conceptualized as far as "genital maturity" where they were presumed to end. Aging, when considered at all, was viewed as a gradual decline till death—as a disease process rather than a natural process (17).

Simultaneously, social theorists, impressed with the impact of industrialization, mobility and urbanization, postulated the isolated nuclear family as being the modal, functionally optimal type in modern industrial society. The "last stages in the development of the family were systematically disregarded" and "only pessimistic predictions of the dissolution of family relationships" were made (31).

Consequently the central theme underlying investigation and controversy in gerontology had at its core the issue of *segregation versus integration* (9). Some expressions of the issue were: Do the aged wish to remain part of society or to "disengage?" Should they live in segregated living arrangements or interspersed among young people? Are they isolated from their families, or are they integrated via continuity of family ties?

The last question is the primary concern of this paper. Fortunately, a good deal of information has been assembled which debunks prevalent myths and fantasies.[1]

In the past 50 years, more marriages, earlier marriages, earlier child-births, and fewer large families have reduced the span in years between generations. Currently, 82% of those over 65 have at least one surviving child and most have 3 or more children; of those with children, 93% have grandchildren and 40% have great-grandchildren. Thus, the vast majority of old people belong to 3 generation families, and *"the four generation family is now a common phenomenon!"*[2] (31, p. 171).

What does this mean for family practitioners? If they subscribe to the myth of separation of the aged, they may say: So what? Multigenerational families may in fact exist, but old people have been abandoned by the younger generations; are sick, "senile," and dependent; to a great extent have been institutionalized; live apart from their children, and therefore are not physically or psychologically part of "the family"; are rigid and incapable of psychological growth and change; and are . . . well, old people.

To accept such propositions is to deal in fiction and fantasy, rather than fact. Old people are not a homogeneous group. They vary widely in health, personality, behavior and socio-economic background. The processes of aging vary from one individual to another, within each individual's organs, parts, and body systems, and progress at different rates. The span of years of the aging phase of life can be longer than that of any other phase. The aged now include several generational strata: there are significant numbers of adult "children" who are themselves in the aging phase of life (5).

Unfortunately, senescence, which simply means aging or growing old, is often incorrectly equated with "senility." Physical and mental illness are not inevitable concomitants of old age. While chronic and mental impairments do become more prevalent with advancing age, the vast majority of old people get along with no difficulty whatsoever.[3]

---

[1] Major texts which summarize and analyze this information and report research findings are listed as references (25) and (26).

[2] A word of statistical caution: These figures denote the number of over 65's who belong to multi-generational families, not the number of other individuals who do so. Since the average age at which one becomes a grandparent is 54 for women and 57 for men, the figures under-represent the number of people who comprise the oldest or second generations in multi-generational families.

[3] About 7% of older people suffer severe chronic brain syndrome (i.e. "senility")

The stereotypes of families "dumping" their aged is a myth. Of all old people, only 4% are in institutions of any kind. When families place their older members they are often elderly and ill themselves, have exhausted all other alternatives and have endured enormous social, psychological and economic stress in the process. The notion of abandonment has been researched so thoroughly, so competently, in so many different geographical areas and in relation to so many different kinds of institutions that it has ceased to be an issue of any kind of gerontology.

No doubt there are instances of abandonment of the aged. However, human psychopathology can exist at any age level and there are also young parents who abuse, neglect or abandon their young children. Popular belief to the contrary, a long inventory of research studies has documented that, ties between old people and their families continue to be viable (29, 22, 23), that families in general behave responsibly in helping their aged (20, 30), and that when they are unable to do so a constellation of personal, social and economic forces may be at work (18, 10). These facts are not to be construed as meaning that old people in general live in multi-generational households, since less than 25% actually share a dwelling with an adult child.[4] Though separate living arrangements are the rule, continuing contacts and exchange of mutual services have been well documented (23, 24, 25, 22).

The sociological theory of the isolated nuclear family has been thoroughly destroyed (21, 29). In Rosow's words, "Seldom has social science had the opportunity to settle disputes through a concise body of definitive research on which a discipline can clearly agree" (21). However, he points out that granting the continuation of responsible intergenerational *behavior,* we must turn to the study of the emotional quality and meaning of intergenerational relations. This is a prime concern of practi-

---

and another 7 or 8% mild to moderate damage (11). With regard to physical functional capacities, of every 100 persons over 65, 82 get along with no difficulty whatsoever, 7 do not need help but have some trouble getting around freely, 5 need a special aid of some kind, 2 need the help of another person and 4 are confined to their homes (7).

[4] Three-fourths of old people live within 30 minutes of at least one child, and in a recent major survey, more than four-fifths had actually seen an adult child in the previous week (25). Of the 96% of the aged who live in the community, the vast majority (90% of the 8 million men and 80% of the 11 million women) live in their own households either as heads or wives of heads of the household. Of those, many (15% of the men and 35% of the women) head households in which they live alone or have taken in nonrelatives). About 20% of the older women and 10% of the men live in someone else's household, usually that of a member of their family (8). Households consisting of an aged married couple or a widowed (or divorced or separated) parent and married or unmarried children constitute about 16-34% of the living arrangements of persons 65 and over (27).

tioners, since those engaged in family treatment can, if they wish, have the direct opportunity to experience and observe them in depth.

There is little information about how the addition of a third- and sometimes fourth-generation has affected the delicate shifting balance of family relationships, nor about the effect on the younger generations and on the family personality. Without question, the generational composition has profound significance. In exploring what that may be, it must be remembered that the "good old days" do not offer a model against which to measure change[5] (13). There are no guidelines for "normative" behavior.

Much confused thinking about intergenerational relations centers about the concept of dependence-independence. Parenting has often been misunderstood to mean helping the child from the total dependence of infancy through childhood and adolescence with the goal being total independence and separation. Pathological dependence at any phase of family life should be distinguished from normal, healthy interdependence. In psychic terms, there is no total separation or total independence at any phase of life. When normal family relationship phases of growth and change have not been resolved, extremes of overt behavior in either direction may occur.

The healthy family is characterized by flexibility, and the capacity to meet changing needs of family members. In the later phases of life the changing capacities of older people may compel additional shifts in the family homeostasis. The family experiences another "Period of Adjustment" in the continuing process which never really ceases. This time, however, the goal cannot be as it is with children, to help the dependent members move out of the nest. The dependency of the old foreshadows not less dependence, but continuing or increasing dependence.[6]

Observations of increased dependency needs of older people have led to incorrect formulations of "role reversal" and "second childhood." There can be no true role reversal and no second childhood. The specific instrumental help given by an adult child to his older parent cannot

---

[5] For example, as Donald Kent phrased it, "the three-generation family pictured as a farm idyl is common, yet all evidence indicates that at no time in any society was a three-generation family ever the common mode, and even less evidence that it was "idyllic" (13).

[6] The ambivalence of gerontologists has been reflected in the polarization of attitudes about whether the aged should be urged towards "independence" or whether all-out efforts should be made to "meet their dependency neds." As Lawton phrased it, the "Bleeding Heart Gerontologists, hell-bent on squeezing tears from us as they describe the poor, frail, helpless older person and his need to have services given to him, contrast with the 'marine sergeants,' who outragedly berate the manner in which the tough independent person . . . is infantilized by the Bleeding Hearts" (14).

be equated with psychological relationship. In feeling, though the adult child may be old himself, he remains in the relationship of child to parent. He does not become parent to his parent. The behavior of a brain-damaged regressed old person may appear child-like but he is not a child. Half a century or more of adulthood cannot be wiped out.

In conceptualizing developmental phases beyond genital maturity Blenkner has postulated the phase of "filial maturity." She defines this as the mature adult's capacity to be *depended on* by the parent, and as marking a healthy transition from genital maturity to old age. Thus it is not "role-reversal," but fulfillment of the filial role rather than parental role to one's own parent and implies resolution of earlier transitional phases (3). This model, must, of course, be modified by consideration of the adult child's own situation:—physical, emotional and social. When, for example, the adult child is himself in the beginning phases of the aging process, requiring major adaptation on all levels of functioning, the expectation that he meet the parents dependency needs implies a capacity which may not be present, achievable, or realistic (5). Performance of the filial task is qualified also by the aged person's capacity to be dependent—i.e. to permit the adult child to become filially mature.

Thus, filial maturity requires the adult child's capacity to accept and resolve what he can *not* do, as well as mature acceptance of the can-and-should do in the filial role. Those in the helping professions walk a thin line in making the clinical judgment to either "relieve guilt" on the one hand, or to help the adult child "behave responsibly" on the other.

The aged person rarely, if ever, is referred for family treatment as the "designated" client, but is invariably the designated client at institutions for the elderly. At the Philadelphia Geriatric Center, thousands of families have been seen at the point when institutional care is requested for an elderly family member. Experience and practical necessity confirm that the family is the client rather than its aged member alone, since each family member feels the impact of the crisis of aging whether or not he plays an overt role in its resolution (6). The family behavior at such a time is part of the natural continuity of past relationships from which it flows, not a sudden idiosyncratic departure from previous relationship patterns.

The prospect of institutional placement may constitute a crucible in which family patterns are revealed in full strength. The behavior of the families seen represents the entire spectrum from "health" to pathology. When severe relationship problems have historical roots in the younger family, pathology may be evidenced by the manner in which the family deals with the prospect of placement.

Some re-current themes occur of which the following are examples:

1. Family One. An adult daughter agreed with her 82 year old mother that the latter should enter the Home for the Aged. The son, who had not spoken to his sister for many years, opposed the plan and for a time sabotaged it successfully by refusing to participate in financial planning. Both siblings were extremely well-off economically. Each attempted to obtain recruits for his side of the battle, approaching social workers, physicians, nurses, and administrative personnel of the institution. They induced influential community figures to exert pressure—the daughter to force admission and the son to prevent it. Spouses of the adult children and the grandchildren participated fully in the furious accusations. The manifest problem of financial support finally culminated in a bitter court battle. For hours, the principals and their three attorneys attacked and counter-attacked. The judge openly stated that he feared hearing this vituperative case had caused his ulcers to flare up.

2. Family Two. Widowed in her 30's, an 85 year old applicant had been separated from her 61 year old adult son only for the year of his unsuccessful marriage, which was followed by divorce. Finally, the aged woman's increasing incapacity became more than the son could manage physically. In describing their difficulties in contemplating placement, they used the language of the marital pair: "Our home has been a happy one, we have been happy together, we always got along well together."

3. Family Three. An adult son alone among several siblings, took physical and economic care of his mother. After her admission to the institution he visited so frequently that he rarely was able to have dinner with his own wife and children. Another son, who did "nothing" remained the "favorite." The "burden bearer" (6) continued for years his futile, doomed-to-failure attempt to gain his old mother's affection. Finally, keeping a long death-vigil at her bedside, he was rewarded with her last words: his brother's name.

4. Family Four. An adult daughter was locked in a symbiotic relationship with her mother, the latter completely disoriented, incontinent, needing constant supervision to prevent her from wandering away or setting fires. The two women shared the marital bed while the son-in-law shared his 15 year old son's room. The grandson could not bring his friends home and had difficulty finding a place to study. The daughter was unable to place her mother despite the husband's ineffectual threats of divorce.

One can only speculate retrospectively as to the family relationships of such families in earlier phases of their family life cycles. It can be hypothesized that the pathology, in its impact on the younger family members will be perpetuated in succeeding generations. Just as the child is said to be father to the man, the young family is precursor to the older family and to succeeding generations of families as well.

Gerontologists have begun to look in some depth at intergenerational relations. It has become evident that the goal of helping the aged, individually or collectively, cannot be achieved except in the context of the needs of the younger generations.

For those engaged in family treatment, older families and intergenerational family relationships are in the main a clinical frontier. The concepts of family treatment have applicability to the understanding of the dynamics of older families. In the older phases of family life, as in the younger phases, there are scapegoats, parentified or rejected children (though they may be 70 years old), dyadic alliances, "absent" family members, and symbiotic relationships. Those concepts have much to contribute to the understanding of family relationships in the later phases of the life cycle. Inclusion of appropriate older people in the treatment of younger families can be a preventive measure to forestall cyclical repetition of pathological patterns. Indeed, if the younger generations are to be served well, we cannot afford a tunnel vision focus on the younger generations, excluding the aged who psychologically and in reality are family members. But they must be accorded full acceptance and equal status—i.e., not viewed solely as "acting on" the younger generations, but as "acted upon" reciprocally.

In short, leadership must be exercised in integrating further the view of the "whole family" of which the philosophical concept of the whole man was the harbinger. Neither an individual nor a generation should be accepted as the "designated" client.

IMPLICATIONS FOR PRACTICE

In turning to consideration of the potential value of including older family members in family treatment, it is reiterated that the main purpose of this paper is to heighten awareness of both reality factors and myths concerning intergenerational relations.

Research and clinical experience with older families have demonstrated that the links between generations continue to be strong. Observations of family therapists working with younger families also have noted the viability of such ties. For example, Meissner has emphasized that the nuclear family is influenced by emotional currents in the extended family. "Emotionally significant events and sequences of events occurring in the respective families of origin and in their collateral branches exercise an ongoing contemporary influence which is often of major significance." (16)

In studying families with a schizophrenic member, Lidz reported that in 5 of 8 marriages studied, "the focus of the partners' loyalty remained in their parental homes, preventing the formation of a nuclear family in which the center of gravity rests in the home. The grandparents or the parental siblings often carried out much of the expressive and instrumental roles rather than the marital partners" (15).

A further review of the literature reveals that there have been many studies of the extended family. Most have been done from a sociological point of view, from psychological tests administered to older family members, and from histories taken in individual sessions. Experience which actually included the aged in conjoint family sessions has been minimal. In the main, authors were not describing the "inner world" of relationships which exist between nuclear families and their families of origin. Parenthetically, in the very few interviews described in which the aged person was included, he was never the designated patient.

Some authors emphasized the constructive influence of grandparents, while others emphasized the significant negative influences. For example, Ackerman described one family in which the maternal grandmother lived in the home with the nuclear family (1). His goals were,

1. "to break the regressive symbiotic alliance of mother and grandmother."
2. "to counteract grandmother's role as omnipotent destroyer; to puncture her hypocritical pretense of always being right, and of loving the granddaughter better than the parents did."
3. "to wean the mother from grandmother, eliminating the need for complicity with her, and to encourage the mother to accept the male monster, and for the first time, to join the husband in marriage, to counteract the image of sex as violence."

Rappaport also felt "there can be a detrimental influence," his thesis being that "the presence of grandparents infantilizes the parents and creates feelings of omnipotence in the grandchild if the grandparent is also weak. In addition, grotesque and bizarre character traits are apt to develop because of grandparental identification" (19).

Bell has a different point of view. He wrote that, "as for the relatives, seeing them legitimizes their interest in the nuclear family, bringing this interest under some control" (2). In his experience he found that "the therapists were able to neutralize their involvement in the nuclear families and get for themselves a broader perspective of the nuclear family."

Sussman stated that, "family continuity is increased when a pattern of mutual aid exists, in moderation, between two sets of families" (28). Hader also wrote in this constructive vein that "regarding grandparents, it is obvious that the grandparent can serve as a modulating function of significance in view of both their presence and concern and real position of objectivity and experience. They can fulfill and be fulfilled. The goal of thoughtful involvement containing an appropriate degree of emotion by oldsters with their younger relatives should be studied and encouraged" (12).

Thus, grandparents have been seen as stimulators of conflicts and competing objects or as positive sources of support and indulgence. To put it another way, the first, second, or third generation may be the objects of constructive or destructive attitudes and behavior. However, the above viewpoints do not necessarily describe the mutuality of involvement that exists between the generations.

Whether the nuclear family or the family of origin are constructive or negative influences on each other, the reality is that intergenerational continuity does exist. If practitioners ignore the existence and involvements between the generations, it is tantamount to thinking of and treating the nuclear family as a closed system. If families are expected to move to higher levels of maturation, not only the nuclear family, but other close kin must be considered and selectively included in treatment.

Hopefully, a body of experience and knowledge will in the future be accumulated regarding criteria for involvement of the older family members. At present, it is possible to cite a few instances in which such involvement appears to be indicated:

1. A mother-in-law lives in the home, takes care of the household chores and the children. Her son works at night and her daughter-in-law works during the day. The wife spends five days a week working with her mother in a factory. On Saturdays, the young wife and her own mother spend the day shopping together.
2. The grandmother lives separately from her daughter, son-in-law and grandchildren. However, a minimum of one and a half hours daily are spent on the phone, as the grandmother is consulted and supervises her daughter's current family.
3. A young mother is severely depressed and is having marital difficulties. The adopted children are uncontrolled and experiencing academic and behavior problems in school. Until recently, the grandmother had been spending three or four afternoons in the home. Recently the grandmother went to work in her son's business and her daughter feels emotionally abandoned.

These cases clearly demonstrate pathologically prolonged intense emotional attachments. It is essential to consider the effects on the nuclear family (marital partners and children) of such continuing over-involvement with the families of origin. Such interlocked bonds and ties should be explored if the growth process is to be stimulated via family treatment.

Basically, family practioners attempt to intervene to help those families which sustain distortions or myths that are reprojected by family members from one generation to the next. Symbiotic, binding relationships result which deter individuation, healthy separation and maturation, and intensify suffering. Such conflict-ridden, ambivalent families are committed unconsciously and collusively to family systems which do not permit gratifying relationships or mature functioning either within the family or with persons outside the family system.

In the author's experience, when families and grandparents have willingly and mutually decided to participate in ongoing therapy sessions, it has proved to be constructive for family members and offered valuable learning for the therapists. A stimulus was provided for the growth processes of all the generations. This is particularly applicable when families had been at a stagnant, fixated level of relating which supported and continued destructive, circular, scapegoating mechanisms.

The following observations are made with the caveat that conjoint treatment of families with aged members is largely unexplored, and are based on some limited experience with the inclusion of a grandparent as a regular participant in ongoing family therapy sessions. It is suggested tentatively that there may be potential for therapeutic gain along the following lines, and that the suppositions must be checked out by experience.

1. The grandparents or children may be relieved of the roles of being objects blamed as the source of all the anger and disappointments. Relationships between the generations may be improved when each family member can be experienced as an available and mutual resource. Instead of divisiveness and fragmentation, each family member may thus become an active source of help or support in coping with the emotional and physical stresses which confront all family members in all phases of life.

2. Confrontation between all three generations may help past and still existing distortions or myths to be clarified and mutually corrected in the light of the current reality.

3. Generational and sexual roles and the family member's respective

physical and emotional needs may become more clearly defined and gratified.

4. The grandparent has an equal opportunity to discuss and describe his own life difficulties; to be regarded as a human being who like the younger family members has conflicts, weaknesses and strengths. His past and current reality, helps pierce the internalized and projected myths in which he had previously been considered the all-giving, or non-giving, rejecting omnipotent figure. Such vital and active participation provides an opportunity for all family members to mourn over unfulfilled wishes, which in reality may never have been possible. When the grandparent is perceived as a real person, the fantasy that any human being could be the total source of infinite gratifications may be given up. He becomes a family member whose needs were also unmet and who still struggles for change and improved family relationships despite the existence of generational differences.

5. Internalized and reality images are discussed in the immediate context. The validity of feelings is reviewed in terms of current reality needs of all family members and may be contrasted with the time when any of them were helpless and dependent children. Past hurt and angry feelings and behavior can be understood and now experienced as the result of inexperience, misunderstandings, unawareness, and internal-external pressures, rather than as intentional behavior to hurt, anger, humilitate, or be deliberately destructive.

According to Nagy, the ideal goal "of family (and individual) health is a relational situation which is characterized by rich interaction and well-differentiated and responsibly acting members" (4). Family treatment aims at helping families to develop more reliable methods of coping with conflicts to create a more constructive equilibrium between the sexes and the generations. Such balance is, of course, an ideal. In disturbed families, walls are unconsciously erected between nuclear and extended family members, between all generations, resulting in loneliness, despair, isolation and psychic death. Such emotional barriers, maintained from generation to generation, permit avoidance of feelings of loss and deprivation which are too painful to be faced. These feelings of hurt and anger, hidden and unexpressed, prevent the open display of intimacy and genuine affection. Complete expression of hurt and anger may lead to murderous feelings and overtly destructive actions: at the other extreme, repression may result in silencing or in emotional or geographic distancing.

In conclusion, it is hypothesized that through the inclusion of grandparents in selected cases, intergenerational relationships could be modified so that each family member would gain strength, support, understanding, and gratification from the others. It is in no way implied that the inevitable conflicts existing in all close relationships would be eliminated, since they are the fundamental stimulants of the growth process in all phases of family life. It is hoped that blaming or scapegoating grandparents, parents, or children would be minimized during and after treatment. Thus, each generation would be considered in the context of survival for all. The cost of change and growth for one generation should not be the destruction of another.

REFERENCES

1. ACKERMAN, N. W. & FRANKLIN, P. F., "Family Dynamics and the Reversibility of Delusion Formation: A Case Study in Family Therapy," in Boszormenyi-Nagy, I. and Framo, J. L. (Eds.), *Intensive Family Therapy,* New York, Hoeber Medical Division, Harper and Row, 1965, p. 286.
2. BELL, N. W., "Extended Family Relations of Disturbed and Well Families," *Fam. Proc.,* 1:175-193, 1962.
3. BLENKNER, M., "Social Work and Family Relationships in Later Life with Some Thoughts on Filial Maturity," chap. 3 in Shanas & Streib, op. cit., 1965.
4. BOSZORMENYI-NAGY, I., "From Family Therapy to a Psychology of Relationships: Fictions of the Individual and Fictions of the Family," *Compr. Psychiat.,* 7:408-423, 1966.
5. BRODY, E. M., "The Aging Family," *The Gerontologist,* 6:201-206, 1966.
6. BRODY, E. M. & SPARK, G., "Institutionalization of the Aged: A Family Crisis," *Fam. Proc.,* 5:76-90, 1966.
7. BROTMAN, H. B., "Every Tenth American," paper presented at State Conference, Iowa Commission on the Aging, Des Moines, Iowa, October 2, 1968, mimeo.
8. BROTMAN, H. B., "A Profile of the Older American," *Useful Facts #31,* Administration on Aging, U.S. Dept. of HE&W, Washington, D.C., November 20, 1967, mimeo.
9. FRIIS, H., TOWNSEND, P. & SHANAS, E., "Old People in Three Industrial Societies; an Introduction," chap. 1 in Shanas and Associates, *Old People in Three Industrial Societies,* New York, Atherton Press, 1968.
10. GOLDFARB, A. I., "The Senile Older Person," in *Selected Papers, Fifth Annual National Conference of State Executives on Aging,* U.S. Dept. of HE&W, Office of Aging, #123, August 1965, p. 43.
12. HADER, M., "The Importance of Grandparents in Family Life," *Fam. Proc.,* 4:228-240, 1965.
13. KENT, D., "Aging—Fact and Fancy," *The Gerontologist,* 5:51, 1965.
14. LAWTON, M. P., "The Psychological Status of the Elderly," paper presented at 21st Annual Conference on Aging, Univ. of Michigan, Ann Arbor, Michigan, August 1968, mimeo.
15. LIDZ, T., CORNELISON, A. R., FLECK, S. & TERRY, D., "The Intrafamilial Environment of Schizophrenic Patients. II Marital Schism and Marital Skew," *Am. J. Psychiat.,* 114:241-248, 1957.
16. MEISSNER, W. W., "Thinking About the Family-Psychiatric Aspects," *Fam. Proc.,* 3:1-40, 1964.
17. PINCUS, A., "Toward a Developmental View of Aging for Social Work," *Soc. Work,* 12:33-41, 1967.

18. *Psychiatry and the Aged: An Introductory Approach,* Report #59 of the Groups for the Advancement of Psychiatry, New York, 1965.
19. RAPPAPORT, E. A., "The Grandparent Syndrome," *Psychoanal. Quart.,* 27:518-538, 1958.
20. REID, O. M., "Aging Americans, A Review of Cooperative Research Projects" in *Welfare in Review,* U.S. Dept. of HE&W, 4:1-12, 1966.
21. ROSOW, I., "Intergenerational Relationships: Problems and Proposals," chapt. 15 in Shanas & Streib, eds., op. cit.
22. SHANAS, E., "Family Responsibility and the Health of Older People," *J. Gerontology,* XV:408-411, 1960.
23. SHANAS, E., *Family Relationships of Older People,* Health Information Foundation Research Series 20, October, 1961.
24. SHANAS, E., *The Health of Older People: A Social Survey,* Cambridge, Harvard University Press, 1962.
25. SHANAS, E. & ASSOCIATES, *Old People in Three Industrial Societies,* New York, Atherton Press, 1968.
26. SHANAS, E. & STREIB, G. F., Eds., *Social Structure and the Family: Generational Relations,* Englewood Cliffs, N. J., Prentice-Hall, Inc., 1965.
27. STEHOWER, J., "The Household and Family Relations of Old People" in Shanas and Associates, op. cit. p. 218.
28. SUSSMAN, M. B., "Family Continuity: Selective Factors which Affect Relationships between Families at Generational Levels," *Marriage Fam. Liv.,* XVI:112-120, 1954.
29. SUSSMAN, M. B., "Relationships of Adult Children with their Parents in the United States," chap. 4 in Shanas & Streib, eds. op. cit.
30. TOWNSEND, P., "The Effects of Family Structure on the Likelihood of Admission to an Institution in Old Age: The Application of a General Theory," in Shanas, E. and Streib, G. F. (Eds.), *Social Structure and the Family,* Englewood Cliffs, N. J., Prentice-Hall, Inc., 1965.
31. TOWNSEND, P., "The Household and Family Relations of Old People," chapt. 7 in Shanas and Associates, *Old People in Three Industrial Societies,* New York, Atherton Press, 1968, p. 178.

42

PSYCHOGERIATRIC GROUP APPROACHES

Milton M. Berger, M.D., F.A.G.P.A.

Assistant Clinical Professor of Psychiatry
College of Physicians and Surgeons, Columbia University

and

Lynne F. Berger, A.T.R.

Executive Director, Center for Adults Plus

Selective Review of the Literature

In 1951 Zeman (1), a long-time friend of the aging and the aged stated, "Too many physicians, nurses and social workers have in the past allowed their sense of frustration at not being able to understand the aged to be projected as resentment against old people. Those of us who have worked with the aged know how challenging and stimulating this work can be, what wonderful patients old people are, how appreciative they are of small attentions and what marvelous results modern medicine and surgery, as well as psychiatry, can achieve even in the highest age bracket."

The authors of the publications discussed below share these views. Thus they have reported on their efforts to improve psychiatric care for the aging and aged by investigating and modifying staff attitudes, by fostering better understanding of the aging process, and, finally, by developing more effective group treatment techniques. No attempt has been made to organize these publications according to subject matter. Rather, they are discussed in chronological order. We hoped, thereby, to provide an overview of the evolution of psychogeriatric group treatment during the past twenty years. We have, in addition, attempted to bring this account up to date, so to speak, by presenting a detailed description of a group psychotherapy program for the aging and aged which is currently in progress.

Group therapeutic efforts with psychogeriatric inpatients have been reported as far back as 1950, when Silver (2) published a milestone paper on "Group Psychotherapy With Senile Psychotic Patients." His group consisted of seventeen senile psychotic inpatients who had been hospitalized from one to thirteen years. The patients met twice weekly for their group psychotherapy sessions which were interrupted about twenty minutes after they began so that tea could be served. The tea renewed their flagging interest in being together and talking. Silver found that specific obstacles to successful therapy were the short attention span of these patients, their amnesia, and the persistence of ideas. However, improvement was noted in their morale, personal cleanliness, and general behavior, and a significant added dividend was found in the greater cooperation manifested by the patients' relatives.

In 1954, Linden (3) concluded that certain facts concerning pathologic senescence merited restatement: "For simplification the entire psychogeriatric group will be referred to here as the senile or chronologically senile. The person in this category is the sum of interrelationships among three processes: (1) Biologic and pathologic functions of the organism inherent in this period of the human life cycle; (2) lifelong personality traits, the functions of an unconscious mainstream of psychologic mechanisms; and (3) socially directed attitudes in reaction to cultural values. These are woven together so intimately in the senile individual as almost to defy analysis. There is, however, some reason for optimism on this score. Paradoxically, it is the very interrelatedness of these primary factors that makes it possible to estimate the requirements of the senile person. The decremental physiologic alterations of senility constitute a real threat to the effectiveness of psychologic defense mechanisms, so that the most dominant defenses emerge as strongpoints, become overdetermined, exaggerated, and employed to extremes. Proceeding from this realization is the conclusion that the senile is a caricature of himself."

In 1955 Meerloo (4) made a similar effort to elucidate the nature of pathologic senescence: "The onset of involution and decline differs widely in many persons. We may suppose that much of it depends not only on the somatic body instrument and the decline of homeostatic capacities, but also on underlying compulsions and lifelong frustrations. In some people the process of what might be called psychosclerosis may start early in life. Others are able to develop new capacities in very old age."

In 1965 and 1967 Liederman and Green (5, 6) reported on a group therapy project with geriatric outpatients, designed to prevent or postpone their confinement to nursing homes or hospitals and, when possible, to improve the patient's patterns of living. The authors were concerned about the negative implications of the term "crock," and the frequency with which it was used by the providers of health services to describe patients over sixty-five with multiple vague somatic complaints, interrelated organic and functional illness, poor attention span and recall, verbal ramblings—and inadequate financial resources.

The authors had concluded that the treatment of choice for patients whose symptoms are functionally determined is a nonsymptomatic approach within the group setting. Specifically, the therapists' function was to encourage the group members to confront reality; only rarely did the therapists make such confrontations themselves. Routinely, the sessions ended with a summarization by one of the co-therapists of the reality components of the problems discussed. All the members of the group showed some improvement, and their increased level of social functioning, which is the primary goal in the treatment of psychogeriatric patients did, in fact, serve to prevent institutionalization.

In his capacity as psychiatric consultant to the Section on Aging of the National Institute of Mental Health, Baruch (7) has found that the use of the experiential group approach with staff could best assure a successful group psychotherapy program for geriatric patients. At a modern home for the aged, staff group meetings not only allowed for partial resolution of disturbing administrative problems, but also led staff members to appreciate the value of the open give and take of a group experience. When the staff began to participate in psychotherapy groups with the residents of the home, there was a decrease not only in patient irascibility, discontent, and depression, but also in episodes of incontinence, congestive heart failure, and social breakdown.

Hall (8) has also reported on the effect of staff attitudes on geriatric group programs. When recreation groups include both the older and the younger patients in an inpatient community mental health service setting, she found that recreation workers, who are often young and physically able themselves, enjoy recreational games, particularly those involving physical activities, more with younger than older patients. As a result, the older patients tend to sit around with their essential need for recreation and exercise ignored as recreation workers focus on and experience personal satisfaction or gratification with younger patients. Older patients lend themselves to "copping out" by saying, "We're too old for that" or "I'm afraid" or "We can't" or "Oh! Let the younger ones play." Her conclusion is that passive, detached, introspective, shy and non-gregarious older patients tend to get lost "on the sidelines" in an inpatient setting as far as their recreational needs are concerned, unless staff members identify with, understand, and attempt to fulfill their specific needs for recreation and activities which will keep them in touch with their bodies, with enjoyment of such activities as a way of letting-go as well as having fun, without which there can be no mental health for patients of any age. Hall's observation that music and movement together are interesting and attractive to older patients confirms our own findings.

Hinkle and Chisman (9) found that the youthfulness of mental health trainees like themselves stirs up many counter-transference problems when they work with psychogeriatric patients. They agree with Kubler-Ross (10) that the therapist must be able to face his own feelings about loss, physical and social limitations, incapacitating illness and death. If he does not face these feelings, his own need to deny them will make it impossible for him to help his patients come to grips with these central issues. Young co-therapists working with such aging and aged patients also have to work through their counter-transference feelings toward their own parents and grandparents who are contemporaries of the group members. This may account in large measure for the fact that it is difficult to generate professional workers.

THE CENTER FOR ADULTS PLUS

The major goal at the Center for Adults Plus (11), like those of Linden, Liederman, and many other workers in gerontologic group psychotherapy, is the resocialization of the individual patient. The Center offers aging and aged psychogeriatric patients the following services: *continuity of after-care services,* if they have been hospitalized previously; *a program to prevent hospitalization* in psychiatric facilities, nursing homes, or general hospitals; and *an out-reach program* to seek them out in their homes in order to motivate them toward the use of resources which can help them to give up their isolation, despair and sense of futility and to enjoy their remaining years helping themselves and others.

Our goals for group participation with the aging and aged vary from person to person and may consist concurrently or alternately of: Resocialization and reduction of isolation through increasing interpersonal verbal and nonverbal communication in the here-and-now; rebuilding a sense of self-esteem and self-worth even though the patient may be retired and not working gainfully at a regular job. In addition, we seek to foster reality testing and reality contact in order to catalyze or maintain intellectual functioning and restore memory and socially appropriate behavioral patterns; to reduce the patient's preoccupation with anxiety, fears, guilt, self-hate, and feelings of uselessness; to provide opportunities for the discharge of pent-up tension, anxiety, anger, and affection; to provide an opportunity to improve motor coordination, discharge aggression, and feel bodily aliveness through movement, exercise, or dance; to increase or restore attention span, concentration power, and the capacity for abstract thought; to stimulate independent thought and behavior, creative self-expression and the development of interest in new activities or people. Finally, we encourage sibling support, assurance, and acceptance.

We agree with Goldfarb's (12) recent assessment of psychogeriatric group therapy: "Through the group experience we find that behavior, particularly disruptive behavior, can be changed even though the basic personality remains unchanged. Sometimes work or sexual performance can be improved although the basic personality remains the same. Behaviorally speaking our old people are highly malleable."

Criteria for Participation in Group Therapy

The eligibility of outpatients in our day center to participate in our therapy group, which encompasses discussions, movement, dance, art, crafts, and other activities, is based on the following criteria:

1. The patient has the ability to walk, be wheeled, or escorted to the center;
2. he is functioning in the "here-and-now";
3. he is not unmanageable to the degree that he cannot sit still because of undirected restlessness;
4. he does not suffer from unremitting bowel and bladder incontinence or advanced deafness;
5. he is willing to participate voluntarily;
6. he is able to recognize and acknowledge that he needs emotional or psychological help;
7. he is able to understand the language used in the group (English, Spanish, Yiddish).

Given their eligibility to fulfill these basic criteria, it is our opinion that, of all patient categories (those patients who are over 55 are the ones who have to be most carefully selected, prepared for, and fitted into a group with specific goals for them. It is all too easy to assume that patient A, in his seventies or eighties, who suffers only from an acute situational depression, will fit appropriately into a group of patients who are approximately the same age, but whose lives have been spent in marginal depression, emotional and intellectual impoverishment, and quiet desperation. In fact, there is a strong possibility that patient A will become a group dropout early, for he obviously does not fit into such a group and will find it difficult to be with people who stopped living—and growing—emotionally, sexually, and intellectually too early.

THP GROUP APPROACH

The Composition of the Group

We will now describe our approach with a group of psychogeriatric patients over 67, heterogeneous with respect to sex, age, physical and psychiatric diagnosis. All had difficulties, to varying degrees, with memory loss, psychosomatic symptoms, depression, disorientation, and anxiety. However, they were able to function in the here-and-now, to interact and be aware of their impact on each other. The group described consisted of three men and five women:

1. Mr. N., who is a 67 year old, is an agitated, unmarried, blind man who was a shoe salesman until he lost his vision from glaucoma at the age of 50. His father died when he was 9, and he remained quite dependent on his over-protective mother who died ten years ago. He then became depressed and suicidal, but was not hospitalized. Mr. N., who was referred to the Center by an agency social worker is the most vital and verbal member of the group and has suffered the least memory loss.

2. Mr. R. is a 72-year-old anxious and very agitated, married restauranteur, whose depression is related to his being unable to carry on his business. Emotionally, Mr. R. decompensated rapidly after surgery for a hypertrophic prostate because he found himself completely impotent sexually, and he has not returned to work since. He also suffers from a profound loss of memory due to cerebral arteriosclerosis.

3. Mr. J. is a 71-year-old music teacher who got married for the first time at 51 to a brilliant woman lawyer of 35. Their child is now 15. At 69, he began to show signs of senile dementia, and his condition grew worse after a hernia operation 6 months ago. Since then he has talked in a rambling, disoriented fashion; most of the time he lives in a fantasy world in which he is preoccupied with designing fashions and getting his piano repaired.

4. Mrs. S., a 74-year-old divorcee, suffered a cerebral stroke two years ago, and has a long history of intermittent short depressions which she recovered from without hospitalization. She has a complete loss of memory most of the time, but when she is free of anxiety she has return of memory traces from her middle years and is better able to remain in contact with what transpires in here-and-now interactions.

5. Mrs. C., a 76-year-old widow with generalized arteriosclerosis, suffers from major memory loss. She lives with her 77-year-old sister who treats her like an object.

6. Mrs. K., who is 80 years old, is married to an 85-year-old orthopedist, who is still in practice. She is disoriented and disruptive in her demands for attention. She has some present here-and-now memory, but little or no memory for the past including the fact that she has a married daughter and three grandchildren. She is symbolically involved with her husband who is her "great man," and is very much in awe of him. Dr. K, brings his wife to the Center, but she is able to return home alone by bus.

7. Mrs. L. is a 68 year old married housewife who has a lifelong pattern of psychotic breaks when confronted with family stress. She is depressed at present, and complains of a tight band around her head. Her husband is a manic, expansive person with poor reality testing.

8. Miss H., 67 years old and unmarried, has never had to work for a living, having inherited enough money from her parents to give her a marginal income. She has been hospitalized many times for serious depressions. Correctly, Miss H. is living with a 40-year-old lover who she is supporting. She has agreat deal of self-hate, and talks about the fact that she gets no satisfaction, sexual or otherwise, from her relationships with others.

The Group Process

The group meets for three hours, from 1 to 4 p.m., three afternoons each week. As each member arrives at the Center, and again as he enters the group meeting room, he is given a warm but normal last name greeting, i.e., "Hello Mrs. Duncan. It's good to see you again," or "glad you could come again."* At the beginning of each meeting, the group members sit in a circle with no table or other impediments in front of them. In addition to the eight patients described above, group meetings are attended by a senior psychotherapist, an occupational therapist, and a social work student.

---

* Although it is our practice to refer to patients in adolescent and adult groups by their first name, we believe it is of value to address patients in our psychogeriatric groups as Mr., Mrs., or Miss, as a way of indicating respect for their age.

Music. Each group meeting begins with ten minutes of listening to recorded *music* chosen by one or two of the eight members of the group or by a staff member. There is often some unstructured, informal conversation between group members while they listen to the music and wait for late-comers to arrive. These moments of commonly-shared experience serve to bring the group together so that they then move along cohesively as well as interactionally. When group members recognize each other as they enter the treatment room, even if they cannot remember each other's names, there is a sense of familiarity, pleasure, anticipation, and family reunion. At this point, the patients frequently shower the staff members with compliments in a manner reminiscent of school children bringing an apple to the teacher.

During this initial phase of the group meeting, and intermittently in the course of the meeting as well, it is necessary to assure and reassure patients with memory deficiencies that "It's o.k.!" They are told that if they are not so anxious about their loss of memory, they will probably be able to remember more. There are very strong feelings about brief or persistent loss of memory. It evokes not only a sense of confusion and disconnectedness between the past and the existential here-and-now, but also a pervasive sense of inadequacy and impotence. These feelings are often accompanied by depression and paranoid thinking. The reassurance required must be extended on many levels, and it must come from the patient's peers in the group as well as staff members. In essence, its message is "We accept you even though you are no longer as adequate as you once were."

Breathing exercises. Following the initial phase, which might be described as group "re-entry," the music is stopped and members engage in *breathing exercises* under the direction of a staff member. Patients are not encouraged to hold their breath for long periods; nor do we emphasize deep breathing; obviously, these activities could have disastrous consequences. Rather group members are encouraged to breathe in as deeply as they can without distress, in order to enjoy the satisfaction of letting go as they breathe out.

The pleasurable effects of letting go are enhanced by expression of the sound of umm! umm! Patients breathe in from one to five times at most, and are cautiously observed by staff members during this period in order to spot incipient signs of distress. After the exercises the group relaxes and talks about how it feels to let go or not to let go and about other feelings.

Movement therapy. The next phase of each meeting is devoted to *movement therapy.* Group members emulate staff as they reach upward with their arms outstretched, fingers groping in the air. A staff member will ask the group, "What are we reaching for?" Typical answers are, "We're reaching for the sky"; "We're reaching in order to feel better, and it does feel good to stretch." Following another period of relaxation and talk about reaching toward and reaching for, we move toward some self-involving and self-loving movements. Group members are directed to lightly tap and feel their own faces and to caress themselves lightly and slowly, and then to move their fingers through their hair and massage their scalp for a few moments. Everyone is encouraged to hug himself while stating, "I am worth loving."

As a group we may now begin the relaxing movements involved in letting go with hands, arms, and legs, while sitting in our chairs.

To improve blood circulation and skeleto-muscular mobility, group members, following the lead of a staff member, then spend a few minutes gently rotating their wrists, fingers, shoulders, and feet. Saying "No" with their feet as if they were stamping or kicking may lead to the question, "No to what?" One group member answers, "No! I don't want to be sick!" Another says, "No! I don't want to have pain in my shoulder!" A third says, "No! I don't want to have memory problems!" We then talk about the feelings which go with such statements, and the need to learn to accept what needs to be accepted so we don't remain angry because we are helpless to change what cannot be changed.

Then we stop to talk again about how it feels to be so much more in touch with our bodies and to find how much they can respond and move when we make the effort to pay attention to them, when we make ourselves move instead of spending our time sitting on a park bench or in front of a television screen.

Mrs. C. comments, "Oh! I didn't even feel my head!" Mr. N. says, "I feel more alive."

Word game. After the movement therapy we play a "word game." One patient says a word, and the next one picks it up and says another word which he believes is connected to the previous word or phrase. For example, the first patient starts with "like," another follows with "love," "only me," "I want to get better," "I feel," "No I don't feel," "hate," "love," etc. Sometimes words are repeated. The leader picks up from phrases like these and encourages the group member to elaborate. For example, what does he mean by "only me?" "Well I am all alone, and I feel like no one wants me or needs me." Another person in the group may then say, "But we want you." The patient says, "Yes, but when I leave the group I feel bad."

As the group meeting progresses, various subjects, thoughts, fears, etc., are stirred up or brought forth by the spontaneous interaction, or the stimulation of music, movement, or free associations in the word game. Problem areas are then discussed by the group members and staff in an educative supportive session which will help to alleviate the group member's anxiety, self-hate, or depression. No attempt is made to do deep reconstructive character analysis. Counseling or advice is given when appropriate.

In 1959 Ross (13) stated that "progress in clinical psychiatry and geriatrics has mitigated the therapeutic nihilism which heretofore vitiated the attack upon the emotional ills of the elderly," that "any aura of therapeutic nihilism in regard to this increasing patient population is unjustified." We share this view. Ross also discussed the therapist's relationship with the older patient: The good son-daughter therapist "should not feel guilty for being younger." An almost paternal attitude may be developed, if necessary; but above all the therapist must be secure enough to deal with the older patient's hostility and with his efforts to make the younger man feel guilty and defensive for being younger. Ideally, the therapist who has resolved his unconscious feelings of guilt and ambivalence toward his own parents will not be overbearing, patronizing, idealizing, or avenging, but will be able, in Grotjahn's (14) words, to "offer himself quietly and calmly in order to repeat and analyze the reversed Oedipus situation as a therapeutic experience."

We believe that *Activity* is the basis for "joie de vivre" at any age. Passivity breeds paralysis and pessimism. This is further compounded by isolation and depression. Exercising one's capacity to learn and to be active appears to delay the onset of any loss of ability to learn and to be active.

Group psychotherapeutic approaches to the aging and the aged in outpatient as well as inpatient settings can provide that degree of interpersonal activity and involvement with others which can diminish isolation, regressive behavior, and despair. At the same time, self-eteem and self-respect can be revived through discussion and emotional and physical touching, even as psychogeriatric patients are helped to accept their limitations and the fact that their lives have not been lived in vain.

REFERENCES

1. ZEMAN, F. D.: "Constructive Programs for the Mental Health of the Elderly," *Mental Hygiene,* 35:221-234, 1951.
2. SILVER, A.: "Group Psychotherapy with Senile Psychotic Patients," *Geriatrics,* 5:147-150, 1950.

3. LINDEN, M. E.: "The Significance of Dual Leadership in Gerontologic Group Psychotherapy: Studies in Gerontologic Human Relations III," *International Journal of Group Psychotherapy*, 4:262-273, 1954.
4. MEERLOO, J. A.: "Psychotherapy With Elderly People," *Geriatrics*, 10:583-587, 1955.
5. LIEDERMAN, P. C. & GREEN, R.: "Geriatric Outpatient Group Therapy," *Comprehensive Psychiatry*, 6:51-60, 1965.
6. LIEDERMAN, P. C. et al.: "Outpatient Group Therapy with Geriatric Patient," *Geriatrics*, 22:148-153, 1967.
7. BARUCH, J.: Personal Communication.
8. HALL, C. G.: Personal Communication.
9. HINKLE, S. & CHRISMAN, K.: "Some Observations on Group Treatment of Geriatric Patients in a Psychiatric Hospital." Unpublished paper.
10. KUBLER-ROSS, E.: *On Death and Dying*, London, 1969, p. 28.
11. BERGER, M. M. & BERGER, L. F.: "An Innovative Program for a Private Psychogeriatric Day Center," *Journal of the American Geriatrics Society*, 19:332-336, 1971.
12. GOLDFARB, A. I.: "Group Approaches With the Elderly." Address given at the Center for Adults Plus One, New York City, January 16, 1971.
13. ROSS, M.: "A Review of Some Recent Group Psychotherapy Methods for Elderly Psychiatric Patients," chap. 39 in Group Psychotherapy and Group Function, co-ed., Rosenbaum, M. and Berger, M. M., Basic Books, New York, 1963.
14. GROTJAHN, M.: "Analytic Psychotherapy with the Elderly," *Psychoanalytic Review*, 42:419-427, 1955.

43

CONSTRUCTIVE EMOTIONAL INTERCHANGE IN ADOLESCENCE

Hyman Spotnitz, M.D., Med.Sc.D.

THE PSYCHODYNAMICS OF ADOLESCENCE

Whereas the dominant problem of the adult relates in some way to his adaptation to the external environment, that of the adolescent relates to the need to control his internal impulses. More specifically, the decisive psychological issues in adolescence relate to the biological maturation of the genital and reproductive drive systems, and the concurrent resurgence of pregenital sexual impulses, combined with the development of genital potential. Thus the major tasks of adolescence include the resolution of old issues, and the achievement of a new status; concomitantly, a different kind of relationship with the parents is called for. These tasks are pursued over a period of years, which accounts for the fact that adolescence is normally marked by turmoil and upset. Indeed, as is well known, these upheavals are generally regarded by workers in the field as external indications that internal adjustments are in progress. Thus Anthony (1) has referred to the inherent problems and difficulties of this developmental stage as the "normal depression of adolescence." And Anna Freud (2) considers tranquility during adolescence an indication for treatment.

It is not surprising, in light of these considerations, that the disturbed adolescent presents a paradoxical clinical picture. On the one hand, according to Anna Freud (2), "adolescent manifestations come close to

This article is a revised version of a paper presented at a meeting of the American Society for Adolescent Psychiatry (Conference on the Adolescent in Family and Group Psychotherapy), New Orleans, January 1971.

symptom formation of the neurotic, the psychotic or dissocial order and verge almost imperceptibly into borderline states and initial, frustrated, or fully fledged forms of almost all mental illnesses." On the other hand, fluctuations in mood and behavior that would be stamped as pathological at other stages of life are generally considered to be part and parcel of the transition from puberty to maturity. Moreover, since adolescence is a rite of passage from the late winter of childhood to the early spring of adulthood, it is often difficult to differentiate between the normal use of adolescent defenses and their pathological manifestations.

In fact, the difference between normal and pathological adolescence are primarily quantitative: The pervasiveness and persistence of a particular symptom picture are the only reliable criteria for differentiation in diagnosis. For example, transitory states of ego fragmentation do not belie the essential health of the ego; conversely, despondency, seclusiveness, and a preoccupation with sex are highly suspect when these behavior patterns are prolonged and exaggerated. Another problem in diagnosis stems from the fact that it is difficult to understand the adolescent's symptoms in terms of his current life experience. Careful scrutiny of the patient's past history for evidence of previous disturbances in his personality development and in his relationship with his parents and other family members may help to resolve such diagnostic uncertainties.

Treatment of the Adolescent: General Considerations

Psychotherapy during this critical developmental phase is equally complex, for, as noted above, during adolescence the patient is part child, part adult. To treat him as a child is to insult the adult components of his personality; to treat him as an adult necessarily entails some degree of failure to meet the maturational needs of the child.

Psychotherapeutic techniques used with adults are generally applicable to this patient population as well. But despite certain basic similarities in symptomatology, it is the opinion of this author, based on extensive clinical experience, that each adolescent presents a special problem and must be understood as an individual. For schematic purposes, patients in this age group can be divided into two categories: The first category would comprise those patients who are particularly vulnerable to the development of high tension states and who, therefore, require minimum intervention on the part of the therapist. In contrast, the second category would consist of emotionally hungry patients who manifest strong tendencies to regress to the dependent relationships of childhood and who, therefore, require a treatment setting which is structured to provide them with the emotional supplies they require.

The fact that these variables have not received sufficient attention may help to explain the contradictory opinions expressed by clinicians with respect to the response of adolescents to analytic psychotherapy. When the therapeutic techniques utilized are evaluated in terms of the specific needs of the individual adolescent patient, the reasons for the treatment failures reported in the literature become apparent.

With respect to the first category of emotionally overcharged adolescents, treatment was unsuccessful when undue pressure was placed on the patient to make progress. In contrast, these patients responded favorably to treatment when their vulnerability to the development of high tension states was borne in mind by the therapist, and they were permitted to proceed at their own pace. Thus it is safe to assume that the most effective treatment techniques for this segment of the adolescent patient population are, by and large, less stimulating than those employed with children.

More specifically, the emotionally overcharged adolescent responds to a calm treatment climate; he needs to discharge his tensions with a minimum of stimulation. An obvious prerequisite for the maintenance of such a climate is the therapist's ability to time and formulate his communications in terms of the patient's contact functioning, that is, the patient's conscious and unconscious attempts to elicit a response. In such a climate, intervention is indicated only when the patient demonstrates a desire for information, or when a communication from the therapist is clearly required to preserve the treatment relationship. To illustrate, this approach was very effective in the treatment of an obese adolescent who had developed a pattern of overeating to relieve his anxieties. When he was able to talk without interruption in a permissive, but "cool" setting, he became less anxious and, consequently, had less need to overeat.

As noted above, however, this approach would not be considered suitable for all patients. Typically, the emotionally hungry, narcissistic adolescent who has strong tendencies toward regression cannot tolerate a situation in which there is little communication from the therapist. Presumably, such a patient would be more responsive to a familial situation that is structured to provide him with the type of emotional nurturing he requires. Constructive Emotional Interchange, as a specific form of treatment which involves the participation of the family, constitutes an attempt to meet the needs of this particular patient category.

Rationale for Participation of the Family in Treatment

It may be helpful to precede the detailed discussion of Constructive Emotional Interchange which follows by a review of those factors which argue in favor of participation of the family in the treatment of adolescents.

Granted the fact that the ego defenses used in adolescence constitute potentially useful ways of implementing the tasks intrinsic to this stage of development, the manifestations of these defenses may be extremely distressing to others, and to the adolescent's parents in particular. On the other hand, his parents' response to his behavior may have an adverse effect on the adolescent's further development and maturation.

Perhaps what needs to be re-emphasized in this connection is the fact that adolescence marks a period of transition from puberty to maturity, rather than an abrupt break with childhood. And, of course, this is especially true of those adolescents who manifest strong tendencies to retreat to the dependent relationships of childhood. In such cases, recognition and support not only by the community but by his parents are particularly crucial to the adolescent's efforts to achieve a new status, i.e., to develop a new identity and new standards of behavior, for these responses enable him to develop his capacity for work, expand his social relationships, and progress toward adulthood. Conversely, the adolescent's difficulties are compounded when the people around him bombard him with feelings that he cannot assimilate because they are in direct opposition to his essential goals. Moreover, the persistent expression of hostility, aggression, etc., by his parents and other family members may add impetus to the adolescent's tendency to attempt to resolve his problems by engaging in deviant forms of behavior.

Children are generally believed to be more vulnerable than adolescents to the feelings of their parents. But the adolescent is much more capable than the child of responding to negative feelings in personally and socially damaging ways. Infants and toddlers lack the physical strength and mobility to do much harm, and children in latency do not experience the tension states which precipitate such responses. The adolescent's feelings are more intense, and he commands the physical power and intellectual resources to destroy himself and others. One need look no further than *Romeo and Juliet* for evidence of the capacity of adolescents to commit murder and suicide under the sway of passion.

Today the adolescent's tendency to give vent to his feelings is exacerbated by his increased awareness of the multiple threats of human survival, the new sexual freedom, lurid presentations by the mass media of acts of violence, and, of course, the greater availability of drugs, guns, etc.

CONSTRUCTIVE EMOTIONAL INTERCHANGE

Definition

Constructive Emotional Interchange can be defined concisely as an indirect approach to the treatment of adolescents whose pathological behavior can be attributed, in large measure, to disturbances in the parent-adolescent relationship. The use of this approach is predicated on two observations: First, for the emotionally hungry patient, a constructive relationship with his parents (and other family members) is crucial to the successful implementation of the tasks of adolescence. The second observation relates to the fact that these adolescents, like children, have strong urges to meet the emotional needs of their parents. For example, a child's provocative behavior in the home may be motivated by a desire to help his mother blow up. Sometimes such behavior improves the family climate; sometimes it is destructive to the child. If the child goes into treatment and is helped by it, typically, he wants his parents to be helped too. Similarly, I have been greatly impressed by the need expressed by adolescents who are recovering from serious emotional disturbances to help their parents, to influence them, re-educate them, and change them.

In order to improve the quality of the parent-adolescent relationship, the therapist exploits the adolescent's need to help his parents by casting him in the role of the therapist's assistant. In other words, the customary policy of enlisting the cooperation of parents on behalf of their child or adolescent is *reversed*. The family interviews are so managed as to make it possible for the patient to help his parents verbalize their feelings with awareness and regard for his capacity to assimilate these feelings. In essence, this is the formula for constructive emotional interchange.

Eligibility for Treatment

Once again I would stress the fact that the emotionally overcharged adolescent, who, according to the clinical evidence, responds more favorably to a less stimulating therapeutic climate, would not be expected to improve in this or any other type of group setting. Rather, this method is tailored for the emotionally hungry adolescent with narcissistic problems. The greater his desire to help his parents, the more responsive he will be to this approach.

The parents who qualify are those who, basically, have appropriate feelings for the patient, but must be educated to control their expression. In the past, they have expressed feelings of love and concern, or of disapproval and hostility, at the wrong time or in the wrong dosage; or they may have lacked the verbal facility to communicate their feelings effectively. Finally, the participants, who may include the patient's siblings as well as his parents, must be willing to cooperate with the therapist; moreover, they must be able to work together.

The Advantages of Constructive Emotional Interchange

What needs to be emphasized at the outset is that the use of the adolescent as a target for the release of parental feelings would *not* be regarded as Constructive Emotional Interchange. As noted above, the untimely or overly strong expressions of parental feelings can overwhelm the adolescent to the degree that they may stimulate suicidal impulses, as well as rebellious behavior which is destructive to others. Nor does this approach center on the use of the parents as a target for the expression of adolescent feelings of hostility and aggression.

Treatment is structured to provide a mutually beneficial experience. In the process of being trained to provide the patient with the type of psychological food he requires, at the tempo he can digest it, the parents are helped to deal with the negative feelings his behavior has aroused in them. The patient himself benefits in two ways: For one, functioning in the role of the therapist's helper bolsters his ego. Secondly, the feelings he helps his parents to verbalize appropriately serve to meet his maturational needs, and facilitate his transition to adulthood. The description which follows of the use of Constructive Emotional Interchange in the treatment of an adolescent who had not benefitted from individual psychotherapy or hospitalization may serve to further elucidate the advantages of this approach.

Clinical Illustration

A somewhat moody boy, Paul had been a model student and appeared to be developing normally until the age of twelve. The emergence of his emotional problems coincided with the departure of his older sister, his only sibling, for college in another part of the country. Once his sister left home, he became the focus of his parents' attention: At times, he received more attention than he wanted; at other times, he was neglected because of their active social life.

Both individually and as a team, his parents handled him inconsistently.

Paul's mother, an attractive and energetic woman, was inclined to act on impulse. When her impetuous behavior got her into trouble, she would become frightened and try to reverse herself. Paul reacted to her occasional attempts to discipline him by locking himself in his room or storming out of the house. Paul's father, a successful manufacturer, was given to fits of anger. He oscillated between entrusting his wife with full responsibility for Paul's upbringing and suddenly stripping her of that responsibility when she was unable to control the boy. Although Paul's parents were happy together for the most part, their son's behavior had become a source of increasing friction between them.

Paul began individual psychotherapy at twelve, when it became apparent that he had emotional problems. He continued to deteriorate, however. Although he had expressed his willingness to cooperate during the initial interview, once he was on the couch he manifested strong resistances and withheld important information from the therapist. Individual treatment was terminated when the boy attempted suicide—a panic reaction to threats of exposure from boys with whom he was taking drugs. He was fourteen years old at the time.

Paul was hospitalized after his suicide attempt, which, in fact, culminated a series of failures at school and increasing strife at home. He had been truanting from school to go on drug trips with cronies his parents regarded as undesirable companions, and taking money from his father's wallet to pay for pot and pep pills. When reprimanded for his failing grades, he threatened to drop out of school. Moreover, although he liked music and was a talented violinist, he dropped his music studies.

Paul did no better in the hospital than he had as an outpatient. Within a year he was moved from one institution to another, and he was discharged from the second institution after several months as an incurable schizophrenic. Greatly alarmed, his parents again consulted the psychiatrist, and at this juncture a series of family interviews was suggested.

The problem was presented to the family in the following terms: The parents needed help in dealing with the feelings their son's behavior aroused in them. Paul would work in the interviews to help them modify these reactions, and give him the feelings he needed. Helping them in this way, the family was told, would help Paul too.

Paul made no secret of the fact that he had no confidence that he would be helped. He immediately expressed the opinion that the "crazy" psychiatrist had dreamed up this scheme "in desperation," because nothing else had worked for him. But, despite his reservations, he was willing to cooperate if the interviews would help his parents.

Rules of conduct that were agreeable to Paul, his parents, and the therapist were enunciated as needed. Each deviation from the rules was studied, and, when the reason it had occurred was understood, attempts were made to correct it. The parents agreed, for example, to restrain their expressions of anger at Paul. When his father exploded in rage, Paul told him to "cool it," and together they explored the reasons for such behavior. Over a period of months, Paul discovered that his father's anger had its roots in fears which were evoked by his son's delinquent behavior, or his wife's anxieties. At other times, the father's anger had its source in his unconscious feelings about himself *vis-à-vis* Paul as a growing adolescent. Another rule, that the mother would not talk until Paul gave her permission to do so, was implemented only occasionally. Nevertheless, his feeling of being stifled by her gradually diminished, and he developed a sense of power and control in their relationship.

One of the major sources of disturbance in the family stemmed from the fact that each member consistently misinterpreted the behavior of the other members. For instance, when his mother nagged him to stop smoking pot, Paul interpreted this as an attempt to control his life and deprive him of freedom of action, whereas, in fact, she nagged him because of her intense fear that he was damaging himself. Similarly, Paul interpreted his father's anger as an attempt to dominate him, and characteristically reacted by avoiding contact with his father.

Initially, the youth insisted that if his parents had the right to drink Scotch, he was entitled to take drugs. But even if they gave up liquor, he would not give up drugs. To his parents this was a deliberate defiance of their wishes. Paul contended that in the face of their strong pressure for compliance he was obliged to make some effort to assert himself. Besides he had a right to do anything that helped to make life more tolerable for him. In view of his manifest difficulties, their highly emotional reactions were irritating and inappropriate.

Yet, even as he was contemptuous of his parents' behavior, Paul demonstrated a growing interest in helping his mother to resolve her tendency to behave impulsively. He became increasingly aware of the relationship between his own behavior and her acute anxiety; and, in time, he came to realize that she nagged him because she was anxious. He obviously sympathized with her, and expressed these feelings. But, more important, he was willing to take positive action to help her. After the family interviews had been conducted for several months, he announced that he would give up drugs.

Needless to say, this dramatic change in his attitude gave his mother new hope; indeed, the emotional climate of the home was suddenly transformed. Other changes in Paul's behavior were equally notable. His performance at school improved rapidly. And he proved the sincerity of his avowed intention to give up drugs by studiously avoiding his former pot-smoking cronies, and by being more discriminating in his choice of new friends.

Discussion

As mentioned earlier, Paul did not expect to benefit from the family interviews. He did not believe that in the process of becoming aware of his parents' feelings, and helping them to deal with their intense anxieties over his repeated failures—at home, in school, and in treatment—he would also be dealing indirectly with his own emotional problems. Although it was clear to the others that his behavior was influenced by their anxieties, Paul himself did not perceive this. Since he failed to see that his parents' feelings could affect him, except to make him angry, he was not motivated in terms of his own interests to participate in the family interviews. He perceived only that his parents were suffering, and he wanted to help them. It was his strong desire to ease their stress that helped him to alter the pathological aspects of his behavior.

The interchanges with his mother and father in the treatment sessions enabled Paul to recognize that the reactions he had experienced as verbal attacks were the involuntary responses of concerned parents who loved him. He became aware of the manifold anxieties which motivated their attempts to help him extricate himself from the dangerous situations he had gotten into and to protect him from a repetition of these experiences. In short, they really loved him, and had trouble dealing with the fears that had been stirred up by his previous escapades.

Paul's ability to influence his parents to control the expression of their feelings and his efforts to reduce their anxieties by improving his own behavior made them more amenable to his wishes. As a result, he began to acquire a greater sense of freedom from parental controls, and his rebellious defiance gave way to self-assertiveness. On the other hand, his parents, by meeting his maturational needs for expressions of warm, positive feelings—love, admiration, and respect—made him more amenable to their wishes.

Thus, at the end of the first year of the family interviews, Paul was attending school regularly and doing well in his classes. He had also resumed his music studies, and was contemplating a career as a violinist. In fact, Paul is now willing to concede that the family interviews have helped, but he still finds it difficult to believe that mutual helpfulness and understanding can produce such dramatic improvements.

Conclusion

In Constructive Emotional Interchange the therapist operates on the assumption that helping parents to understand the psychodynamics of adolescence, facilitating their recognition of the types of emotional interchanges within the family that the adolescent experiences as disagreeable, and helping them to make constructive changes in these interchanges will make it possible for the young patient to alter his pathological behavior. In conducting the interviews, the therapist intervenes primarily to influence the timing and dosage of the parent's expression of feelings, so that the emotional ingredients that the patient wants and needs are verbalized in ways that make him feel more secure.

The fundamental prerequisite for this approach is the adolescent's willingness to help his parents. When the parents have a reciprocal need to help the patient and cooperate with him in his efforts to *help them,* Constructive Emotional Interchange is a powerful tool for improving the adolescent's functioning, not only in his family milieu but also in a broader social context.

REFERENCES

1. ANTHONY, E. JAMES. Two contrasting types of adolescent depressions and their treatment. *Journal of the American Psychoanalytic Association,* 18:841-859, 1970.
2. FREUD, ANNA. Adolescence. In *Psychoanalytic Study of the Child,* Vol. 13. New York: International Universities Press, 1958, p. 275.

44

DELINQUENTS IN GROUP THERAPY: SOME NEW TECHNIQUES

Salvatore V. Didato, Ph.D.

Supervising Psychologist and Assistant Director of Research
The Morton Prince Clinic for Hypnotherapy

A number of specialized techniques were utilized with 28 juvenile delinquents over a period of 13 months in a short-term group therapy program. The groups were structured along the line of the democratic model used by Lewin, et al (1939).

Psychodynamic profile of the groups showed personality characteristics generally associated with the so-called psychopathic personality. Latent homosexual themes with attendant anxiety emerged from time to time, and behavioral compensations for feelings of male sex role inadequacy were frequently noted. The results obtained were generally consistent with those of Lewin, et al and also in line with work by Sherif (1948). Both these studies used normal boys.

Four major therapeutic goals evolved as the group developed:

1. To increase capacity to experience powerful affects (positive or negative) without acting them out.
2. To increase capacity for empathy.
3. To strengthen identification with the therapist.
4. To encourage new behavioral patterns in helping the group resolve intergroup conflict through nonphysical, verbal means.

Reprinted from ADOLESCENCE, Vol. V, No. 18, Summer, 1970, pp. 207-222.
This work was done while the author was a staff psychologist at the Catholic Charities Guidance Institute, N.Y.C.

Various techniques are discussed in achieving these goals.

The special role of the therapist is discussed in terms of his necessity to abandon his traditional perception and role expectation of himself as therapist and utilize maximum flexibility of therapeutic technique. Personality characteristics of therapists as significant variables in the outcome of the therapy are discussed in relation to work with specialized groups such as schizophrenics, drug addicts, etc.

This is a report of a short-term group psychotherapy program for delinquents with a specific focus. The goal was to help the boys make the transition from school, where they were having difficulty, to jobs in the community. This therapeutic focus has been attempted elsewhere with success (15).

The boys ranged in age from 11 to 17 years and were referred by the juvenile court for a variety of offenses, including petty stealing, gang fights, illegal entry, phoned bomb threats to school, personal assaults, school truancy, and sexual molestation of children. The groups formed were of mixed racial background. They were taken randomly from court referral lists, with no regard for psychodiagnostic status, and were age-divided into 11-14 and 15-17 year old groups. Twenty-eight boys were accepted into the program with no attempt to screen out those who had acting-out problems, as advocated by some researchers (6).

Dividing delinquents into therapy groups according to the nature of their basic problems has been attempted with success (3, 9, 18), and although it may require keen and discriminating diagnostic judgments, it should be encouraged as an innovation for future research.

Individual sessions were held with each boy at intervals ranging from weekly to monthly, averaging three per month for each boy. If the therapist thought it to be therapeutically profitable, boys were seen in twos and threes in addition to the group meetings. Both group and individual attendance was irregular at first, but improved in time.

PSYCHODYNAMIC PROFILE OF THE GROUP

The delinquent possesses personality characteristics generally associated with the character disorders. In addition, he attends reluctantly, with great suspicion, hostility and defiance. Repeated assurances that the therapist is not an agent of the courts, schools, police, or church in the community seem to be insufficient to offset his perception of the therapist as an authority who will either censure or punish him. As if by reaction formation, patients rarely discussed family activities. Their main preoccupation seemed to be with their own exploits. One is struck by the flagrant braggadocio with which one is assailed in the group session. This is done either openly or subtly, but it often may be recognized as an attempt to gain peer status and prestige in the group.

Delinquents spend a great deal of time thinking about attacking and being attacked. Many sessions were spent in which various techniques of self-defense were enumerated and illustrated by the boys. Many of the boys studied books on judo, karate, jiu-jitsu, etc. One boy boasted that he had broken several knuckles by repeatedly slamming his fist against a wall. By doing this, he eventually shattered nerves in his hand which made it insensitive to the repeated blows which he could give others. With great pride, some boys boasted of their knowledge of karate and enumerated various critical points in the human body which, when struck, would disable or kill a man. The entire preoccupation with fighting and self-defense becomes a kind of cult in the subculture of the delinquent. Body building, weight lifting, fighting and boxing, skills with the use of knives and other weapons, all play into the delinquent's enhanced prestige and status among his peers.

PSYCHOSEXUAL DEVELOPMENT

In general, the boys were sexually precocious. However, much guilt and anxiety was observed when sexual topics arose. It was also observed that much anxiety emerged when latent homosexual themes were brought forth. Bragging and exaggerated tales of heterosexual exploits were frequently in evidence as obvious compensations for feelings of sex role inadequacy.[1] There was exhibitionism, boasting, emphasis on creating a physically mature appearance (and to be stylish, "in" and "camp"), defiance of authority often bordering on protean orneriness, boasting of sexual or antisocial exploits, glorification of the body, etc.

Considerable intragroup punitiveness occurred. Each member had his turn in attacking some other member, in peck order fashion. These aggressive outbursts often took the form of a verbal attack with sexual terms used for emphasis. Instances of incest anxiety were frequently displayed as members attacked each other by making aggressive comments about the sexual behavior of the mother of the boy attacked. The entire area of sexual discussion, in terms of jokes, books, pictures, personal experiences, profane language, etc., was readily used as an arena for the expression of hostility toward each other.

---

[1] For an interesting theory explaining the delinquent's conflict in terms of a struggle with feelings of social difference with other cultural groups around him, see Turk (23).

FAMILY LIFE

One might expect a similar pattern in the family life of each of these boys. It was generally characterized by the usual pathognomic pattern typical of these cases (6, 24). There were weak parental controls, little parental interest and involvement, poor relationships with siblings, weak father figures, and mothers who were unable to discipline their children. Most of the mothers seemed to be victimized by their social anomie.[2] In general, they were overtaxed by family responsibilities. They were intellectually and culturally impoverished, and seemed to offer no enthusiasm for living to their children. It might be mentioned that the boys seemed to be lacking in inspiration to aspire to higher levels of performance. Of all the patients in this study, only two came from intact homes. All the others had experienced some disruption in the family unity, such as the death of a parent, a desertion, a separation, a remarriage of a parent, or outright abandonment of the child to a relative or friend. Some of the boys were out-of-wedlock children.

RATIONALE FOR TECHNIQUES USED

The theoretical framework which provided us with a guide in the selection of our therapeutic techniques may be deduced from the following comments. The delinquent may be seen as a product of the group experience, not as a causative determinant in its formation. He undergoes an acculturation in his group through adoption of its value systems, social attitudes, general life philosophy and style of response. The group becomes the social matrix in which he develops an antisocial frame of reference which alienates him from society. Since the delinquent shows greater responsiveness and sensitivity to group processes, it is hypothesized by many that he may best be treated in a group setting.

We were influenced by the work of Lewin, *et al* (13) in trying to structure the groups in terms of a democratic experience. Throughout the program a quasi-group centered approach was utilized in trying to foster within the group its own norms for the guidance of subsequent behavior. Presently there emerged in this "sub-culture" what might be described as a scaffolding of a social system with its norms and values, which has been described by Sherif in detail in his group work with adolescent boys (20).

After some time the boys demanded more and more structure, how-

_____

[2] Prior to the formation of the groups, interviews were held individually with the mother or legal guardian of the boy wherever possible.

ever. They did not look to the therapist for this, but began to question themselves as to how this could be achieved. They hit upon the idea of electing a president, which they did. They believed that some system of rewards and punishments had to be devised to control the group's actions. Out of their own invention they first developed a discipline system based on demerits. However, they later decided that members should be rewarded with merits if they did something constructive for the group.

Various "problems" arose from time to time, which were common to all group members, such as setting the exact time of the session, seating arrangements, punishment for lateness and absence, responsibility for buying and distributing candy and milk, bringing games from home (checkers, cards, chess, Monopoly, etc.). All decisions regarding these tasks were arrived at through a group vote. Whenever possible, patients were encouraged to assume increasing amounts of responsibility in achieving the various aims of the group. Glasser explains his technique of "reality therapy" in these terms, and focuses upon increasing the delinquent's capacity for greater and greater amounts of responsibility (8).

At this juncture, a word is in order which may further clarify our technique rationale. Both Eissler (7) and Aichhorn (1) describe the easily lost motivation of the delinquent in the therapy situation. They recommend keeping him involved by constantly stimulating interest in the relationship. Eissler advises against saying anything or doing anything the delinquent already may expect, but, rather, maintaining heightened interest by surprise moves. Aichhorn, over a decade earlier, suggested that this could be achieved "by arousing surprise without causing fear, exhibiting strength without threatening, pretending to attract without promising anything." With these concepts as a backdrop, several techniques were employed with a conscious effort to maximize interest and involvement.

Four major therapeutic goals evolved as the group developed:

1. To increase capacity to experience powerful affects (either positive or negative) without acting them out and then to encourage the boy, within the group setting, to express them in more successful ways than before.
2. To increase capacity for empathy.
3. To strengthen identification with the therapist.
4. To encourage new behavioral patterns in helping the group resolve its own intra-group conflict through non-physical verbal means.

COPING WITH POWERFUL AFFECTS

Therapy may be seen as a kind of training for the development of new reactions through corrective emotional experience which brings new meanings for the patient; as a novel permissive situation in which to develop and try out new behavioral adaptations to rising, powerful inner affects. The emotional responses of the delinquent which get him into trouble (his "symptoms") are essentially negative, i.e., aggressive, sadistic, assaulting, etc. The therapy, then, necessarily becomes a situation charged and bristling with these very contents. In a sense the therapy becomes a situation for "fight training" similar to that advocated by Bach (2), in which the patient must learn new ways of effectively dealing with hostile (anti-social) feelings. More will be said later about the therapist's personal characteristics and his own capacity to deal with these powerful, hostile emotions.

Because of his limited capacity to cope with powerful affects, the delinquent's style of handling a strong anxiety is to discharge the emotion by acting it out symbolically. The therapy situation was structured in such a way that the therapist maximized every opportunity for the fullest and strongest buildup of affect and held it at this high level as long as he judged that the tolerance of the group would permit it. In this highly charged emotional context, an attempt was made to structure and guide the outcome into a new and fresh style of managing the emotions and the attendant anxiety. Strong positive affects (caring, affection, etc.) may be just as threatening to a patient as strong negative affects. An effort was made to elicit any covert positive feeling as well as unexpressed negative feeling which members bore for each other in any ongoing interchange, and to deal with it in new terms, i.e., to allow the fullest appropriate emotional catharsis through verbalization.

Whenever possible, fantasy and imagery techniques were used in expressing and then resolving aggressive feelings in order to lessen the possibility of acting out (16). Frequently, members verbalized fantasy situations in which they were the aggressors toward particular persons they disliked. One particular session, for example, involved the repressed sexual sadism and incest anxiety of the group. At a certain point in the discussion the boys, one at a time, began to fantasy what they would do to a sexual aggressor who attacked their mothers. Needless to say, this session elicited a great amount of verbally-expressed hostile feeling.

EMPATHY

In working with delinquents, one is struck with the empathy deficit. They may discuss personal episodes which might involve brutality, violence and daring with little sign of upset. More normally adjusted children do not show this deficit and act differently; it has been shown experimentally, for example, that they react to facial expressions of others and respond to these cues with appropriate affect. Delinquents, however, show deficit in this regard (25). This empathy deficit is possibly associated with affect blunting and may possibly be utilized as a defense against, anxiety, which (defense) actually enables the delinquent to commit his flagrant antisocial acts. Every opportunity was utilized to focus on feeling and emotion as it occurred, in order to strengthen the impoverished empathic ability of the boys. Situations which normally would elicit emotional reactions of a more positive nature—such as a mother's hospitalization, a boy's accident, the retelling of the death of a loved one, a father's loss of job, etc.—were focused upon in an effort to elicit feelings in the group. It was found that, initially, the tolerance for this more positive empathy experience was marginal, and anxiety defenses against it were massive.

Attention was strongly focused upon bodily processes in eliciting the self-awareness of feeling. The therapist frequently shot questions around the group, asking the boys what they were feeling, where they were feeling it, and how it was being felt. It was observed repeatedly that when the anxiety level became too high for the boys, their first defense against it was withdrawal and denial. The boys frequently changed the subject or minimized the affective aspects of the topic under discussion. Occasionally, they used a second line of defensive reaction by "acting in." The boys might leave their chairs, pace about the room, pick up objects and toss them to each other, look out the window, laugh and joke, go for drinks of water, etc. It was expected, and later confirmed, that the anxiety tolerance level was highest when the boys themselves brought up the charged topics, rather than when the therapist initiated discussion of them.

IDENTIFICATION WITH THE THERAPIST AND RESOLUTION OF CONFLICT

As sessions progressed, the greater the identification with the therapist and the stronger the positive transference, the more the group began to adopt, as might be expected, the implicit and unexpressed social values and superego of society through the person of the therapist. For example, the boys consistently questioned, criticized and disciplined each other when they were late or absent or out of order in the group. As another example of these emergent superego attitudes, the boys chose to set up a mock trial—complete with jury, judge, defense and prosecuting attorneys—after one member of the group openly stated he was suspected by the therapist of stealing something from the offices on the lower floor in the building. The boys asked logical, rational questions about the whole affair. The therapist spoke quite freely and openly concerning his opinions on the matter, and the "defendant" did likewise in his own defense. After a secret vote of the jury, the verdict of guilty was announced. The accused was noticeably upset and angry. He sulked and, for a time, continued to maintain his innocence. Emotional tension was at an extremely high level. The group pressure upon the boy was very great. Finally, he admitted he had stolen the item. He was noticeably guilt-ridden and as the group dispersed he tried to make up to the other boys by joking with them and generally trying to get back into their good graces. The boys seemed superficially tolerant, but there was a marked disdain for him and what he had done. This example illustrates powerful possibilities for utilizing inherent strong conscious structures in delinquents. As is commonly known, these patients severely discipline each other in their own group settings when group taboos are violated. The notion that the juvenile delinquent possesses little or no conscience structure (superego) has always been controversial. It might be recalled that the 19th-century taxonomists took an extreme position on this and referred to them as "moral imbeciles," with even so great a scholar as G. S. Mall labelling the adolescent offender as "morally insane" (11). The example above again points to the emergent wishes for self-government and autonomy in groups of this kind, and is in line with work by Sherif (20).

THE THERAPIST'S SPECIAL ROLE AND PERSONALITY CHARACTERISTICS

It is generally accepted that the therapist's anxiety tolerance level must be high to work with this provocative type of patient who unconsciously endeavors to destroy positive elements in his relationships with authorities. The successful therapist resists such efforts on the patient's part to draw him into such stratagems. A common mistake is for the therapist to be provoked into forcing discussion of the delinquent's "offense." Perhaps the greatest initial problem facing the therapist in an outpatient setting is the high rate of absenteeism. During the first month of the program, approximately one out of three appointments was broken. There is a striking lack of regularity, order and systematization in the life of the delinquent. Unlike normal children, they lack a consistent behavioral habit pattern. Driven by a fitful unrest, they seek excitement in an aimless fashion, moving from one situation to another as fate would command them. This short-run hedonism is always in flux. There are few anchorages in the social structure, and to motivate these patients to attend group meetings regularly, in itself a herculean task.

The therapist abandoned his role and perception of himself as therapist in the traditional sense, and a wide flexible variety of approaches were utilized. All attempts were made to reach the boys and strengthen a positive transference, disregarding the usual rules of standard analytic therapy. For example, the boys were encouraged to use phone calls, letters, notes, drop-in visits and any other form of communication whenever they wished to contact the therapist.

An added task for the therapist is that he must exercise the utmost effort to establish his identification in his own right—apart from his authoritative affiliations elsewhere—as an interested, objective point within the life of the delinquent.

From time to time, therapist identification with various members will occur. He may recall adolescent anxieties and fears associated with violence which were once part of his own life. The therapist's fears and hostilities are very much in the forefront in this type of work. They must constantly be analyzed either as induced countertransferences or true countertransferences, historically derived. A therapist may find himself making interpretations in a retaliatory manner and subtly expressing his hostility toward some group member, *albeit* that the heightened suspiciousness of the delinquent already disposes him to construe most *any* interpretation as an attack on him. The therapist may overly protect a weaker group member when the latter is being attacked. He may try to overcome his personal anxiety by taking an authoritative stand on moral or ethical issues. He may feel impelled to defend himself rigidly when provoked by verbal attack.

It is only within the last decade or so that the attitudes of the therapist have come to be recognized as highly significant variables in the achievement of the goals he sets for his patients. Many therapists believe delinquents to be untreatable. Some believe that patients who reject their therapy initially may not or cannot be helped. It may be stated that in every case in our study, all boys initially rejected the concept of therapy totally. Research does indicate strongly that patients initially displaying negative attitudes toward therapy are helped more than is realized (14, 17, 19). The success of the therapy in these cases is very likely a function of the therapist's motivation (4, 7, 21). Studies also suggest that therapists achieve the best results with patients for whom their expectations for progress are high, and with patients having similar socioeconomic backgrounds as their own (21, 22)

Work with delinquents, who have traditionally been considered poor prognostic bets, elicits powerful countertransferences which must be dissolved before progress in therapy can occur. It cannot be emphasized too strongly that no therapy should be attempted with highly resistant, suspicious, hostile and negativistic patients until the therapist resolves his conditioned aversion to such patients.

A careful exploration of countertransferential reactions may yield valuable data concerning the therapeutic failure of certain "unpopular" patient groupings such as homosexuals, schizophrenics, and those with character disorders, which includes criminals, drug addicts, and delinquents. Perhaps more assessment in depth of the therapist's attitudes toward his patients—as advocated by some writers (10, 12, 22)—should be attempted before they are assigned to him. This, indeed, would be an innovation in the usual procedure of patient-therapist assignments and, hopefully, would increase overall therapeutic efficiency in work with delinquents.

REFERENCES

1. AICHHORN, A. *Wayward Youth.* New York: Viking Press, 1935.
2. BACH, G. "A Theory of Intimate Aggression." *Psychol. Rep.,* 1963, 12, 449-450.
3. DeSOUSA, C. "Fundamentals of the Natural Classification of Delinquents." *Revista de Psicologica Normal Patologica,* 1926, 8, 21-38.
4. DIDATO, S. "Note on Therapy Failures: Pride and/or Prejudice of the Therapist?" (In preparation)
5. DIDATO, S. "Juvenile Delinquency: Some Recent Trends." *Mental Hygiene,* October, 1969.
6. DOUGLAS, E. D., FIKE, D., & WIERZBINSKI, E. "Effects of Group Counseling." *Crime and Delinquency,* 1965, 2, 360-365.
7. EISSLER, K. *Searchlights on Delinquency.* New York: International Universities Press, Inc., 1949.
8. GLASSER, W. "Reality Therapy." *Crime and Delinquency,* 1964, 10, 135-144.
9. GOLDSMITH, J. & BERMAN, I. "Middle Class Jewish Delinquency." *Journal of Jewish Communal Service,* 1962, 39, 192-196.
10. HAASE, W. "The Role of Socioeconomic Class in Examiner Bias." *Mental Health for the Poor.* New York: Free Press of Glencoe, 1964, pp. 241-247.
11. HALL, G. S. *Adolescence: Its Psychology and Its Relation to Psychology, Anthropology, Sociology, Sex, Crime, Religion, and Education.* New York: Appleton-Century, 1904, p. 330.
12. HARARI, C. & CHWAST, J. "Class Bias in Psychodiagnosis of Delinquents." *Crime and Delinquency,* 1963, 2, p. 145-151.
13. LEWIN, K., LIPPITT, R., & WHITE, R. "Patterns of Aggressive Behavior in Experimentally Created Social Climates." *Journal of Social Psychology,* 1939, 10, 271-299.
14. LYTLE, M. "The Unpromising Client." *Crime and Delinquency,* 1964, 10, 130-134.
15. MASSIMO, J. & SHORE, M. "The Effectiveness of a Comprehensive Vocationally-oriented Psychotherapeutic Program for Adolescent Delinquent Boys." *American Journal of Orthopsychiatry,* 1963, 33, 634-642.

16. PERL, W. "Use of Fantasy for a Breakthrough in Psychotherapy Groups of Hard-to-reach Delinquent Boys." *International Journal of Group Psychotherapy*, 1963, 13, 27-33.

17. ROGERS, C. *Counseling and Psychotherapy*. New York: Houghton-Mifflin, 1942, p. 159.

18. SADOVNIKOV, V., BENSON, R., & PACKARD, G. "Problems Encountered in Establishing , an Institution-to-community Group Therapy Program for Delinquents." *International Journal of Group Psychotherapy*, 1963, 13, 156-166.

19. SCHMIDEBERGE, M. "Treating the Unwilling Patient." *British Journal Delinq.*, 1958, 9, 117-121.

20. SHERIF, M. & SHERIF, C. *An Outline of Social Psychology*. New York: Harper Brothers, 1948.

21. STRUPP, H . (Ed.) *Research in Psychotherapy*. Baltimore: French-Bray Printing Co., 1962.

22. STRUPP, H. & WALLACE, M. "A Further Study of Psychiatrist's Responses in Quasi-therapy Situations." *Behavioral Science*, 1965, 10, 113-134.

23. TURK, A. T. "Toward a Theory of Juvenile Delinquency." *Journal of Crime, Criminology and Police Science*, 1964, 55, 215-229.

24. "Hearings, 83rd Congress, 2nd Session," U.S. Senate Subcommittee to Investigate Juvenile Delinquency, Washington, D.C., 1954-55, United States Printing Office.

25. WASHBURN, W. C. "Interaction Cues Involved in Perception of Authority Figures by Delinquents and Nondelinquents." *American Journal of Orthopsychiatry*, 1953, 23, 13-21.

Area V

APPLICATIONS AND EXTENSIONS

The methods used by the group and family modalities have applications which extend beyond their primary therapeutic aims. Group processes are potent forces for changing and controlling human behavior in a variety of contexts, and as such have wide applications both within and outside the field of mental health.

Group procedures have been used extensively to improve the delivery of psychiatric services in community mental health centers, and in the training of mental health professionals and paraprofessionals who staff such programs. Community mental health centers were established to provide psychiatric services to previously neglected populations. Initially, group procedures were employed at these centers primarily for reasons of expediency, i.e., so that more patients could be seen by scarce mental health professionals. It became apparent early on, however, that the problems typically encountered in community mental health centers are highly amenable to group procedures. Environmental and social forces play a visibly important role in the mental disorders of impoverished minority-group patients. Hence, a core principle of the community mental health movement stipulates that, concurrent with psychological treatment, the patient's ecology be changed and that the cooperation of his community be enlisted to this end. Accordingly, group procedures have been developed to reach the persons who live with, work with, teach and employ the identified patient, and also to teach patients the skills he requires to negotiate his social system.

In her article in this area Christmas describes the adaptation of group processes to the unique needs of a community mental health center that serves the people of Harlem. Specifically, her polymorphous therapeutic approach is designed to intervene at levels which are crucial to the patient who lives in a black ghetto, but is often overlooked by other therapeutic approaches.

Similarly, Sager describes a partial hospitalization program which is based primarily on a number of group and family therapeutic procedures specially adapted to the needs of disadvantaged chronic psychiatric pa-

760

tients. The successful implementation of such a program requires that the mental health professional relinquish his traditional role behavior because it subtly impedes the therapeutic process. Unfortunately, however, such roles and attitudes are as tenacious as they are ubiquitous. Thus, Sager's article describes various group procedures which did, in fact, include crucial additional changes among the staff of the partial hospitalization program he developed, and thereby enhanced its effectiveness.

SOCIAL APPLICATIONS

Power seeking individuals and institutions appreciate the awesome potential of group procedures in molding and influencing the human mind. Group process has been used in various ways to control the thoughts and sentiments of human beings by governments, industry and labor, in religion, the military and in political movements of various persuasions. Obviously, the moral and ethical application of group procedures is not inherent in the process. Like atomic energy, group processes can be used for good or evil.

The Destructive Use of Group Forces

The Nazis are a prime example of the use of group processes for evil: they relied on group forces to unite their supporters, to foster compliance to their program and to crush resistance to the movement. More horrifying, however, was the Nazi's effective use of group forces to cause millions of persons to submit to, and even participate in their own destruction.

The military use of group procedures to affect morale and purpose in the armed forces may, under certain circumstances, be similarly classified as "evil." This practice is as old and as universal as are armies themselves, hence, the fact that Charlie Company participated in a "morale building" session the evening before the My Lai massacre was not, in itself, unusual. In his article Rabkin advances the hypothesis that this session inspired the violence at My Lai. Rabkin develops a thesis concerning the transference of suffering which has broad implications for family and social psychology, and raises moral questions that deeply concern all of us.

Constructive Uses of Group Forces

Although some readers may disagree with the editors' value judgment, we have included as an example of the constructive use of group forces

Vivian Gornick's article on women's consciousness-raising groups which are currently gaining increasing popularity. Women's liberation is one of many recent social movements which has made extensive use of groups to enlist, inspire, control and motivate prospective adherents.

Training

In the course of the educational process, the student learns a body of necessary information. In addition, however, education involves the acquisition of new and different attitudes and behavior. In this phase of training which, although subtle, is perhaps the most essential in fields that rest upon the interactions between individuals, group methods are extremely useful. Hence, the use of group methods is in ascendancy in training programs in many service fields, such as education, business, politics, law, medicine and social welfare.

In this volume the application of group processes to training is illustrated by three articles:

In the first paper, Lubin and Eddy describe the model developed at the National Training Laboratory which has served as the prototype for the use of group processes to enhance the skills and sensitivities of such non-patient populations as business executives, administrators, army officers, etc.

The second deals with the "Theme-Centered Interactional Workshop," a powerful method for the rapid acquisition of skills and attitudes which has become increasingly popular. Ruth Cohn, its innovator, uses her abilities as a poet, psychoanalyst and group therapist to weave a dialogue with the reader which serves, at the same time as an exposition of her method.

The third example of the use of group methods for training purposes is provided by Bard, who describes his highly creative and important project which involved training police officers to intervene in family crises while maintaining their role as police officers.

The final paper in this volume consists of a review of the best of the currently available training films in group and family therapy. We asked Dr. Gladfelter to prepare this article because films are assuming an increasingly important role as teaching instruments. This excellent review should be invaluable to those involved in training in group and family therapy.

SUGGESTED CROSS-REFERENCES

Further material on the non-therapeutic applications of group processes is contained in Section I-D, in "Small Group Phenomena," which consists of papers that explore the potentials and perils of the proliferating encounter and marathon groups.

Durkin's paper on general systems theory in Section I-A and Auerswald's on the ecological approach in treatment, in Area II, elucidates the conceptual foundations for the broad-based mental health programs which are described in the papers by Christmas and by Sager.

The changing role of women, which is the subject of Vivian Gornick's paper in this area, is considered from a different vantage point by Larry and Joan Constantine in their article on comarital and multilateral relations in Area III. Pittman and Flomenhaft are concerned with the question from a therapeutic perspective in their article on the "doll's house" marriage, also in Area III.

Ruth Cohn's theme-centered workshop relies heavily on gestalt methods which are discussed in further detail by Simkin in Section I-C, on the newer therapeutic approaches in group therapy.

Finally two of the films reviewed by Gladfelter were created by authors whose work appears in this volume: two films on family therapy of schizophrenia by Nathan Ackerman, and also "The Scream Inside" on group techniques by Milton Berger. In addition, the films reviewed illustrate some of the newer therapeutic approaches described herein, e.g., the use of behavior therapy in groups, the group marathon process, the therapeutic use of video tape and various other aspects of family therapy.

C.J.S.
H.S.K.

45

GROUP REHABILITATIVE APPROACHES IN SOCIALLY AND ECONOMICALLY DISADVANTAGED COMMUNITIES

June Jackson Christmas, M.D.

Chief, Division of Rehabilitation Services, Department of Psychiatry, Harlem Hospital Center, and Research Associate, Columbia University College of Physicians and Surgeons

Overview

In recent years the efficacy of group rehabilitative approaches, in general, has been clearly demonstrated. It has also become apparent, however, that group rehabilitation programs, as they are presently structured, are not equally appropriate for all patient populations. More precisely, it has become apparent that the forces which impinge upon those individuals who are not only physically or mentally disabled, but socially and economically disadvantaged as well, are interwoven, intricate, and complex, and cannot be altered by a single-faceted approach to rehabilitation. For these patient populations there is an obvious need for a broader, more comprehensive socio-psychiatric approach to rehabilitation. Yet, few attempts have been made to date to develop innovative group programs which would provide effective rehabilitation techniques and, at the same time, forge a link between the recovering individual and his social environment.

One such program, which has been initiated in the low-income community of central Harlem, in New York City (3,4), has addressed itself to this need, and, as such, served as the proving ground for the theoretical and therapeutic concepts discussed herein. Briefly stated, this program seeks to implement the traditional goals of psychiatric rehabilitation, i.e., improved psycho-social functioning, educational advancement, and the development of vocational skills and potential. But it is also concerned with the psychological, physical, social, and economic factors which can enhance or deter the rehabilitative process. Underlying these aims are certain assumptions, shaped by a social systems orientation, regarding the person-situation configuration and the transactional nature of man and society.

The Dynamics of Socio-Psychiatric Rehabilitation

Socio-psychiatric rehabilitation is characterized by the use of multiple, comprehensive, coordinated interdisciplinary interventions, all of which are designed to help the individual to achieve productive social, psychological, physical, educational, and vocational roles, within the limits of his capacities and potentialities. The range of interventions used for these purposes includes, but is not limited to, various forms of psychotherapy, actional approaches, counseling and guidance, and supportive therapy. Intervention may also include educational and training programs; it may take the form of self-development and self-help programs; or it may involve the initiation of programs which seek to foster individual and group social action.

The referrents of socio-psychiatric rehabilitation are intrapsychic, interpersonal, and social (in the broad context of education, work and leisure, and relationships between individuals, groups, and social institutions). In keeping with this orientation, all socio-psychiatric rehabilitation programs are concerned with the implementation of social, therapeutic, educational, vocational, and environmental goals, albeit to varying degrees. Each of these goals has social components, however, inasmuch as successful human relationships are essential to its implementation.

Since, as noted above, all socio-psychiatric rehabilitation groups include these elements, they can best be classified according to their specific "vehicles of change." For example, in therapeutic groups, psychological treatment is the specific vehicle used to effect change. In socialization groups, the vehicle is social relationships. The learning process produces change in educational groups. In actional approaches (socio-therapies, work and training groups, and environmental groups), activities and interactions with animate and inanimate objects are the vehicles of change. In the group setting, the group leader and the patients act as agents of change in various social systems. More specifically, within the framework of group dynamics, goals, sanctions, leadership, norms, identification, and support are used to mobilize the potential for change in each individual member/client.

Evolution

It is an unfortunate paradox that economically-disadvantaged central cities, which have the highest admission rates to public psychiatric hospitals, suffer from deficits in mental health services in general, and, in particular, from a lack of adequate rehabilitation services. Few facilities are available to meet the multiple needs of the individual who has been discharged from a psychiatric hospital, and re-enters the community without funds, without a job, undereducated and without vocational skills, often without adequate housing to which he can return.

When they were first instituted, group rehabilitation programs (and advances in psychopharmacology) seemed to offer a solution to the urgent need for increased services. However, these expectations that the implementation of approaches would require less staff time have not been sustained (2). Instead, the complex issues arising within groups, the plethora of information elicited, and the deeper awareness on the part of the staff of the social and economic problems which typically complicate the recovery of these former psychiatric patients frequently lead to increased demands for staff time and the provision of supportive services beyond those provided within the formal group program.

Program Planning: General Guidelines

Residents of the disadvantaged inner cities share certain crucial characteristics in common: Their income is generally substandard, and, to varying degrees, they bear the psychological, emotional, and social scars which are the inevitable concomitants of extreme poverty. Nevertheless, within this framework, they are heterogeneous in many respects: Urban central city communities are comprised of people who range in age, and come from different social classes; some were born and spent their early years in rural communities, others have lived in the city all their lives. They differ with respect to their work roles as well. Thus one finds among them the unemployed man or woman who is "on the street," and the skillful hustler who lives on the edge of the law; the aged woman who is on welfare, and the woman who must struggle alone to raise her children on the meager earnings of a domestic servant; the stable middle-class white-collar employee and the marginally, but regularly, employed blue-collar worker.

Obviously, program planners must take these and significant psychological and social variables into account. For only then can they develop specific groups whose goals and modes of intervention are consonant with the needs of patients, clients (i.e., ex-patients), or family members. For example, interventions can be directed at various targets: Thus, the target of change may be the individual member of the group, sub-groups of the entire group, the marital unit, the family group, the small or large rehabilitation group, or the program itself. Efforts to effect change, as part of rehabilitation, can also be directed at the "establishment," i.e., at community agencies or groups, or social institutions.

Rationale for the Use of Group Treatment Methods in Socially and Economically Disadvantaged Communities

Group therapy has been described in the literature as the treatment of choice for individuals whose apparent inability to cope with the vicissitudes of life can be attributed to their limited knowledge and narrow perspectives, but who are nonetheless overwhelmed by feelings of helplessness and inadequacy. It is considered suitable for those persons whose functioning is impaired by the stereotyped values they share with members of the community with whom they identify. Other authors have stressed the value of group treatment for patients whose problems stem primarily from disturbances in the socialization process. In addition, it is generally conceded that group therapy counteracts poor motivation and resistance to treatment may be due to their characteristic hostility toward and suspicion of authority, as epitomized by the therapist.

Obviously, these characteristics are not limited to specific patients populations. However, they are particularly prominent among members of disadvantaged communities. As such, they constitute indications for group treatment, and merit further elaboration within this frame of reference.

It has been postulated that the socially and economically disadvantaged individual is exposed to special conditions which gives his personality a distinctive configuration. Obviously, a detailed discussion of this hypothesis lies beyond the scope of this article. It is logical to assume, however, that social and economic discrimination would be expected to produce tendencies toward low self-esteem, frustration, rage and aggression, or feelings of apathy, depression, and hopelessness. In any event, there is ample evidence that in poor communities there are distinct

advantages to easily accessible and readily available mental health services. The administrators of mental health programs can meet the need
for immediate service by initiating various group approaches, i.e., evening
and weekend groups, walk-in or vestibule groups, waiting-list groups, and
open-end intake groups.

The advantages of group intervention become apparent with the initiation of service. The initial treatment session provides an opportunity
for early contact with others who seek help, not only with the middle-
class psychiatrist or social worker, who may be perceived as a threatening
figure. Thus group interaction relieves the stress of the screening situation. Obviously, the therapist's interest will be reassuring, but for the
disadvantaged patient an encounter with others with similar problems
will be infinitely more reassuring. Feelings of resistance about entering
treatment, misconceptions regarding the nature of its therapy and goals
can be dealt with in the intake sessions. Finally, intake group screening
can serve to initiate the ex-patient into a new social role, that of rehabi-
litant: Within the group setting, his identity as member or client rather
than patient is established. The immediate contact with others with similar problems, the universalization which is a unique feature of group
treatment, works against dropouts early in therapy. This phenomenon
permits those whose frame of reference does not include the concept of
psychological determinism to acquire some understanding of the psychodynamics of their behavior by identifying with others with similar problems or life histories. The cooperative and democratic aspects of groups,
as exemplified in the therapeutic community, encourage the person who
is the designated recipient of help to begin to help himself and others;
moreover, regardless of whether his efforts are valued or criticized, he is
the focus of attention and concern—usually for the first time in his life.
Thus, as group members relate to one another, they may move from the
alienation and anomie which they experience, to develop a sense of
being and belonging.

Not surprisingly, the typical poor patient who has frequently had disturbing experiences with hostile authority has strong resistance to the one-
to-one relationship with a therapist from another social class and/or
race. Apart from his conviction that the therapist cannot possibly act in
his interests or really understand his problems, he may fear that he will
be malevolently controlled or abused. For, in fact, this has been his experience in past encounters with authority. Universalization and the commonality of certain aspects of life can lead to the gradual development of
trust in the change agent, who is often perceived initially to the point
where he is able to use his specific therapeutic skills. Other elements work

toward this end as well: The fact that groups foster a cooperative and democratic rather than an authoritarian approach, can also contribute to the gradual development of trust. It goes without saying, of course, that members of a group will react differently in this regard. Some will begin to accept the rational help and talents of the designated group leader while continuing to test their perceptions of malevolent or disinterested authority. Others will accept his help unquestioningly and passively, and demand omnipotence, control, and manipulation of the group leader.

CLASSIFICATION OF GROUP REHABILITATIVE APPROACHES

An attempt has been made below to classify socio-psychiatric group rehabilitative approaches in terms of their goals and levels of intervention. It should be noted, however, that the goals of any given group may be altered in time by expressed group interest or by the inherent group process. In guidance groups based on common problems or need, for example, the emphasis may move from the solution of the particular problem to coping mechanisms in general, and from the present and the past to the future. Rehabilitative groups can combine several approaches, social, actional and verbal, and thus, be modified to meet the needs of group members at a particular time in the life of the group or on the basis of its composition. This flexibility is dependent, however, in part, upon the skills of the therapist, and, more particularly, on his ability to remain "in touch" with group dynamics, individual psychodynamics, and the changing social environment.

Group Psychotherapeutic Approaches

Low socio-economic communities have a high incidence of persons with chronic, severe mental illness, generally diagnosed as schizophrenia. These patients may be less threatened by group approaches modified to meet their psychosocial needs than by more intensive therapeutic approaches which foster the development of strong individual identifications, transferences, and strong emotional reactions.

Those who are triply damaged by poverty, mental disability, and racism, and who, therefore, experience the full weight of social discrimination, may prove suitable candidates for constructive group psychotherapy. Within this therapeutic framework, group interaction compels individuals to examine their own behavior patterns, while the use of conscious material helps them to cope with current reality problems. Thus, the patients' patterns of behavior, personality difficulties and strengths, social functioning, and their relation to the "real world" are dealt with as the focus of concentration.

This is in contrast to more intensive reconstructive analytically-oriented group therapy, where analysis of transference, counter-transference, resistance, fantasies, and dreams is the instrumentation of change. This is not to say that analytic insights and knowledge of intrapsychic mechanisms are not useful in group therapy with socially and economically disadvantaged people. Obviously, the therapist's knowledge is crucial to his understanding of motivation and of individual behavior, and his ability to judge the capacity of a member/client to tolerate the stresses of rehabilitation. Unfortunately, however, the use of reconstructive group therapy in disadvantaged communities is necessarily limited by the amount of time and effort which it requires.

Apart from the variables discussed above, the choice of the appropriate depth of psychotherapy also depends on the kind of commitment the individual is willing to make to the group. A lower socio-economic class individual, considering rehabilitation, may not accept the commitment implicit in analytically-oriented groups, that is, the commitment to personality change. Initially, he may only be able to accept relief from the disturbing symptoms of loneliness, to improve his social functioning, through a successful orientation to work, or, at best, to learn to modify his behavior, at least to some degree. In time, however, he may be ready to re-examine and renegotiate his "contract," and this must be a collaborative effort by patient member/client and staff.

Actional Approaches

The need of lower-class patients for concrete answers, direction, and guidelines can be satisfied through the use of groups which operate on an educational, counseling, or guidance level. The patients' need to understand his repetitious and self-destructive behavior can be met through groups which focus on social learning and problem-solving. Skill development can be built into groups which operate on a socio-therapeutic, educational, or pre-vocationally oriented actional level.

Socio-therapy groups offer certain advantages to poor persons who are also poorly educated in that they are actional rather than solely verbal. Moreover, they can be conducted in a language which the participants understand. This is particularly true when adequately trained local community residents are recruited to serve as group leaders or as co-leaders with professionals who have some knowledge of the local culture.

An understanding of processes transpiring within the here-and-now in the group, and over the life span of the group, can enhance the patient's self-understanding. The opportunity to deal with the concept of causality in a group can heighten one's sense of personal and interpersonal responsibility, and lead to intrapsychic change as well. For poor men and women, who have learned the futility of future orientation, the understanding derived from group approaches may enable a crucial change in life style—from living-for-the-moment to more effective modes of adaptation.

Once the patient member/client becomes aware of the effects of his feelings and behaviors on others, and realizes that change within himself can elicit altered responses in others, his feelings of helplessness or powerlessness become less acute. This kind of social learning can be equally beneficial when it is applied in a staff group setting and in the staff-patient sub-group. Moreover, ultimately, it has significance for individual and group action.

Particularly in the days when inner cities cry out for evidences of black or brown power, ethnically homogeneous groups may fill the need for a sense of brotherhood, comradeship, and humanity. Skillful leadership can help bridge the gap between group social problems, individual self-understanding, and increased life options. On the other hand, communications among group members in the language of the deprived community can broaden the knowledge of the therapist (who often comes from a different class and/or race), both in regard to the culture in which he works and with respect to the psychodynamics of individual group members. Groups which include persons from several races may provide an arena for dealing with interracial attitudes and relationships, feelings of inferiority or superiority, self-concepts, and love and hate. They can also lead to the resolution of identity crises, to conflict resolution, and to group problem-solving.

Those groups which, following the socio-psychiatric model, utilize the paraprofessional or professional services of community residents who themselves have experienced the stresses of living in a deprived community, exemplify the self-help principle. The change agent is himself rehabilitated, while serving as a role model and, in many instances, entering upon a new career as a rehabilitative and therapeutic agent (1). The introduction of significant numbers of these new careerists into health services can also have a positive effect on the quality of these services. There is a tendency of these professionals and paraprofessionals, once they have assumed their new roles to unite in an effort to improve existing services and foster institutional change.

The primary goal of groups which operate on a social level is to mobilize individuals to move from isolation and constriction to action (7). Transactions among socialization groups and social activities with non-patient groups in the community are used to gain improved social functioning, to assist in relearning long-lost social skills, or to provide a habilitative experience.

One of the goals of rehabilitation in disadvantaged communities is the enhancement of the potential for autonomy. Self-help groups may be particularly appropriate to the achievement of this goal. Thus, the socio-psychiatric orientation has led to the development of groups which focus on economic development, self-education, and sheltered workshop activities (5).

On another level, the use of group approaches patterned after the socio-psychiatric model in deprived communities can lead from unproductive social isolation to opportunities for more productive social action. Community organization and social action groups, whether successful or not in the accomplishment of their short-term goals, can be truly educational in that they can provide an experience in group planning and action, an opportunity for reality testing, and a social learning experience undertaken with other who do not bear the label of patient or ex-patient. Failure of group social action is not always viewed as negatively as is individual failure. Rather, it can be a stimulus for the development of social network strategies and activities designed to affect the causes of deprivation. Planfully conceived and implemented, socio-psychiatric group rehabilitation efforts can be directed not only toward individual growth and change, but also toward institutional and social change (4).

SUMMARY

Ideally, rehabilitative groups should lead to a decrease in psychopathology, improved interpersonal relationships, the development of social and vocational skills, and a concomitant sense of satisfaction and self-worth. Yet, few coordinated social and vocational rehabilitative group services are projected in long-range community mental health program planning (6). And even fewer reach the inner city which is in dire need of such mental health services.

An understanding of group processes and of the needs of economically deprived populations can be applied productively to programs concerned with rehabilitation of the chronically mentally ill, who comprise a large proportion of those seeking psychiatric services in the inner city. However, this requires a meaningful involvement with the local culture, the community, and its informal social networks. Once these prerequisites have been fulfilled it is possible to implement a coordinated, interdisciplinary, socio-psychiatric approach which can make a major contribution to the rehabilitation process.

REFERENCES

1. BROOKS, M. H. What's happening to new careers? Paper presented at the Annual Meeting of American Orthopsychiatric Association, Washington, D.C., March, 1971.
2. CHRISTMAS, J. J. "Group Therapy with the Disadvantaged." *Current Psychiatric Therapies: 1966,* edited by Jules H. Masserman. Grune & Stratton: New York, 1966.
3. CHRISTMAS, J. J. "Group Methods in Training and Practice: Nonprofessional Mental Health Personnel in a Deprived Community." *Psychiatric Agents: New Roles for Nonprofessionals, Parents and Teachers,* edited by Bernard G. Guerney, Jr. Holt & Winston, Inc.: New York, 1969.
4. CHRISTMAS, J. J. "Psychiatric Rehabilitation in the Inner City." *Training Manual,* edited by Leonard V. Wendland. University of Pittsburgh: Pittsburgh, 1971.
5. FAIRWEATHER, G. W. *Social Psychology in Treating Mental Illness.* John Wiley & Sons: New York, 1964.
6. PATTISON, E. M. Group psychotherapy and group methods in community mental health programs. *Int. J. of Grp. Psychother.* 20:516-539.
7. RICHARDS, H. "The Relationship between Group Approaches and Social Action in Community Mental Health Settings." *Current Concepts in Clinical Nursing,* edited by B. Bergensen *et al.* C. V. Mosby Co.: St. Louis, 1969.

46

STAFF DEVELOPMENT FOR A THERAPEUTIC COMMUNITY

Clifford J. Sager, M.D.

Clinical Professor of Psychiatry, Mt. Sinai School of Medicine of the City University of New York

INTRODUCTION

In essence, the therapeutic community is designed to provide the day hospital and hospitalized psychiatric patient with a series of "corrective emotional experiences" which may serve to counteract the psychological damage he sustained as a result of the vicissitudes of his past and current relationships with crucial figures and systems that compose his environment. The logic of this approach is self-evident. It is equally apparent, however, that the implimentation of such a program may pose a major challenge for the staff of a service. If he is to be offered the kind of relationships which are so crucial to his recovery, staff members at every level must be willing to modify their traditional roles and attitudes toward the patient. Similarly, if the patient is to be offered an opportunity to participate in new experiences which will heighten his sense of autonomy, enhance his self-image, and increase his capacity to cope with stress, the staff must be prepared to institute radical changes in the organization and structure of the service.

In light of the acknowledged validity of the theoretical concepts on which it is based, it is safe to assume that it is the magnitude of the task of staff reorientation which accounts for the reluctance of workers to put this approach into operation. Hopefully, this detailed account of our experience in this regard may help to foster the implementation of these therapeutic principles.

The relationships established between patients and staff are, of course, partly the result of patient expectations. But to a much greater extent they are the result of traditional concepts of "proper" organization and structure of psychiatric services. That is, they are based on the covert, but commonly held, assumption that the psychiatric patient is ill, disturbed, helpless, etc., and therefore in need of the services of a staff which is omniscient, powerful, firm and "detached." Professional roles and attitudes which are based on these assumptions can be expected to foster sick and dependent attitudes in patients, and may also act as a barrier to the intense involvement between patients and staff which facilitates the treatment process. In short, the roles and attitudes of the staff and the organization and structure of a psychiatric service form a system which can in itself constitute an anti-therapeutic factor. It follows, then, that if one subscribes to the premise, stated above, that the relationships offered the psychiatric patient are a major determinant of the success of treatment, one must also concede the need to modify traditional professional roles and attitudes. There is an equally apparent need to modify the traditional organization and structure of psychiatric services which reinforce these roles and attitudes, and which further contribute to the desocialization and regression of the patient.

The treatment program outlined below grew out of our desire to put this hypothesis into the operation, organization, and structure of our psychiatric unit in order that we might modify the relationships which are traditionally offered the psychiatric patient, and thereby enhance his prospects for recovery. Within this conceptual framework, the overriding objective of the program was to exploit the therapeutic potential of all transactions—those between patients, between patients and staff, between staff members, and finally among the patients and their community and the staff.

We felt that this objective could best be served through the application of a total group and family approach, not only with respect to treatment techniques per se, but also with respect to the orientation, organization and structure of the unit. Thus, as an alternative to traditional roles, we structured a system analogous to a positive family-like ecology which would facilitate the acquisition of adaptive, constructive behavior. More specifically, the staff was conceived of as the patient's "alter-family," and was considered to constitute the major agent of therapeutic change. The methods we employed to train the staff and to equip them with the theoretical knowledge, techniques, and attitudes which would enable them to function effectively in that capacity are the focus of this report, and will be discussed in some detail. However, if the training program is to be viewed in proper perspective, this discussion must be preceded by a brief description of the treatment unit, the characteristics of the patient population served, and, finally a more precise delineation of our therapeutic orientation.

THE TREATMENT PROGRAM

We felt that a partial hospitalization program which, by definition, is designed to promote the emotional, social, cognitive, and vocational rehabilitation of the psychiatric patient offered an ideal vehicle for the implementation of our therapeutic approach. The Partial Hospitalization Program which was put into effect to this end provided for the operation of a day center, an evening center, and a weekend family center.*

The Patient Population

The district served by the Program includes one of the most poverty-stricken areas of New York City—a section known as East Harlem, which has a large black and Spanish-speaking population. However, it also includes pockets of white middle and working-class neighborhoods, and, although we did not count them among our patients, a section which houses some of the city's wealthiest residents—fashionable Park and Fifth Avenues.

The great majority of the patients selected for admission to the program had been diagnosed as chronic schizophrenics. Typically, such patients are apathetic, defeated, hopeless—and helpless; and their prognosis is considered to be extremely poor. Concomitantly, patients assigned to this diagnostic category are generally regarded by clinicians as the most difficult and least rewarding to treat.

The Therapeutic Orientation

We conceived of our program as an antidote to the roles and relationships these patients had assumed over the years, partly as a result of

---

* The Partial Hospitalization Program is part of the Community Mental Health Center, which is operated by the Department of Psychiatry of the New York Medical College and Metropolitan Hospital. The Program was conceived and instituted by the Family Treatment and Study Unit of the Department of Psychiatry, at the request of the Chairman of the Department, Dr. Alfred M. Freedman, and with his cooperation; it was funded by the National Institute of Mental Health and the Community Mental Health Board of New York City.

their exposure to more traditional treatment approaches. Thus, in order to counteract the noxious effects of these roles and relationships, which were characterized earlier as powerless, regressed, etc., patients are given an opportunity to learn that they can control their own destiny. More specifically, we organized the unit so that patients might participate with the staff in making decisions regarding the operation of the Program in general, as well as their own treatment plans. For example, patients attend staff meetings at which their progress is evaluated. Moreover, no decisions are made regarding the patient without his knowledge, that is, unless he participated in the decision-making process.

A major aspect of our basic therapeutic philosophy has been described by Auerswald (1). as the ecological systems approach. We are aware of the possible peril of exposing seriously ill psychiatric patients to excessive external or internal stress, but we also appreciate the peril of attempting to protect them from all stress. Accordingly, we intervene in any area of life that generates distress or conflict which the patient cannot cope with adequately. Foci of intervention may include the patient himself, or his relationship with relatives, friends, school authorities, the welfare system, the courts, police, etc. Our major emphasis, however, is on helping the patient to find more effective ways of coping, of negotiating the complex systems that impinge on him. Concurrently, we communicate our expectation that the patient behave rationally. Irrational behavior is understood and treated, of course, but it is regarded as alien to the patient and his interests. On the other hand, it has been our experience that behavior which appears to be irrational at first glance may, at times, turn out to be adaptive when it is considered in relation to the total ecological field within which the patient must operate (5).

As noted above, the family-like group structure, in which the staff is perceived by the patient as an "alter-family" is considered to constitute the core agent of therapeutic change. Hence, group (and family) therapy, which may take many forms, are utilized as the major treatment modalities: group treatment methods include daily community meetings which are attended by all staff members and patients; group therapy sessions (6-10 patients per group, with two co-therapists); therapy for married couples; activity therapy (which includes the utilization of arts and crafts, as well as play and recreational activities); family therapy; family life education seminars for patients and staff; psychodrama; use of television confrontation techniques and vocational guidance sessions. In general, group sessions are based on the principle of group dynamics, rather than the principles of insight or analytic therapy.

In addition to the procedures listed above, we also encourage less formal group activities, e.g., meetings of the patients' organization, informal discussion in the living room of the Center, and the practice of having patients and staff eat together. Finally appreciating the appropriate medication is an essential aspect of the treatment of schizophrenia, all patients were carefully evaluated and medicated when indicated. Indeed, medication was a frequent subject of group discussion.

STAFF DEVELOPMENT

From the outset we realized that training the 35 professionals and paraprofessionals who staffed the Program to treat these "difficult" patients in a highly unconventional manner would require a great deal of work, the inculcation of a specific orientation—and boundless optimism. In light of these considerations, a brief description of staff recruitment and orientation procedures, and the general characteristics of the staff, may serve as an appropriate preamble to a more detailed discussion of the procedures employed to facilitate the modification of traditional staff roles and attitudes.

Staff Recruitment

We had three months, prior to the date patients were officially admitted to the Program, in which to hire the nucleus of our staff, to set up basic procedures, and to begin to work together to implement these procedures. The key staff members were hired by the Program Director, and they then participated with him in hiring other personnel. Subsequently, a hiring committee was set up to interview all applicants and make recommendations to the Director regarding their possible participation in the Program. Only one restriction was rigidly imposed with respect to eligibility for employment: At least one-half of the staff must be black or Spanish-speaking. Consequently, a professional (or nonprofessional) white person, no matter how well qualified, would not be hired if this meant that we would have to reduce our quota.

At this early stage in the development of the Program the administration firmly resisted establishing limiting job descriptions. Obviously, each professional was expected to carry out the particular functions for which he had been trained: the psychologist was to administer psychological tests, the vocational counselor was to provide vocational and avocational guidance and training, etc. But beyond those basic considerations, the role of each staff member vis-a-vis the patients was not specifically defined. We felt that these were "grey areas," which could be clarified only on the basis of experience. In fact, this is precisely what happened; eventually staff members wrote up their own job descriptions which were then confirmed—or further clarified—by their colleagues.

Staff Composition

Initially, the staff was widely disparate in almost every way: the professionals represented different theoretical biases and disciplines (psychiatry, social work, psychology, nursing, occupational therapy, etc.); similarly, the non-professionals had formerly been engaged in a wide variety of occupations (they included housewives, industrial workers, welfare department aides, poverty program workers, etc.). The staff came from middle and working class backgrounds, and several had been welfare department clients previously. With respect to their educational background, some members of the staff were high school drop outs; and others had completed post-doctoral training in their specialty. Finally, as noted above, the staff included representatives of different ethnic groups. Yet, despite their diversity, the members of our staff— professionals and non-professionals alike—shared two crucial features in common: a desire to help their fellow man, and an expressed readiness to work in a setting with disturbed patients. Commitment to the Program had special implications for the professional staffs and for the psychiatrists in particular. Whereas formerly they had remained sequestered in their offices for the most part, and had seen patients "on schedule," they now agreed to spend their work day in almost constant contact with their patients and to share responsibility for their treatment.

Preliminary Indoctrination

The staff was hired with the understanding that they were in agreement with the over-all philosophy which governed the operation of the Program, and would comply with the basic procedures which would be employed to implement that philosophy. Nevertheless, we realized that we must expect dissension to arise from time to time, once these highly unconventional procedures were put into practice. Staff members were encouraged to express their objections and reservations openly at meetings, without fear of reprisal by the administration.

Apart from their participation in these formal procedures, the staff was expected to comply with certain ground rules laid down by the administration as a condition of their affiliation with the program. In general, the staff was encouraged to develop attitudes based on their understanding of the psychiatric patient's need to assume new roles and form more meaningful relationships in the treatment setting. To facilitate this process, staff members were expected to interact with patients in a variety of ways. For example, patients were to be included in staff activities, and patients and staff were encouraged to socialize on the premises of the Center, and on trips sponsored by the Program. On the other hand, extramural socialization was discouraged, and when it did occur, such contacts were to be entered on the patient's chart. We hoped thereby to avoid the dangers of cliquism, favoritism and exploitation of either patient or staff member. Finally, staff members were encouraged to explore the therapeutic potential of all activities, which, as noted earlier, were to be conducted within the framework of a family-like ecology. From the outset, the staff demonstrated its understanding of the importance of their role as the patient's "alter-family." Thus, shortly after he had joined the Program, one staff member suggested that patients who were isolated socially be invited to celebrate national holidays at the Center. Equally significant is the fact that other members of the staff agreed to join him and remain "on duty" during holidays. In short, the staff manifested an *esprit de corps* which can be attributed, in turn, to their shared enthusiasm for our orientation.

On the other hand, our expectation that dissension would arise once our program had been put into effect proved justified. In the following paragraphs the Program's operational system is discussed in further detail from another, more relevant vantage point, i.e., in terms of the problems we encountered in the course of our efforts to implement these concepts and procedures and their ultimate resolution.

Basic Concepts

The modification of traditional professional roles. Reference was made earlier to the fact that the function of each staff member *vis-a-vis* the patients was not specifically defined at the outset; we hoped thereby to reduce the tendency, common among workers, to work in rigid roles and to foster the exploration of new functions and ways of collaborating with others. We encountered some resistance to this after the Program had been in existence for only three months, at which point we had our first staff casualty. An extremely well-trained professional who had been most helpful in conceptualizing various procedures on paper, found that the "lack of organization" was distressing, and that she could not work effectively when roles were not sharply defined. This first resignation and the few others which followed subsequently can be understood in terms of the need of these professionals to operate within well-defined roles in a setting where their authority was recognized and honored. Interestingly, although we expected the casualty rate to be highest among the psychiatrists on this account, only two resigned. (However, several psychiatrists who had expressed an initial interest in joining the Program withdrew their applications when they realized that although they might command a higher salary because they held a degree, only the quality of their work and of their relationships with patients and other staff members would earn the respect of their colleagues.) Although psychiatrists were ultimately responsible for diagnosis and for prescribing medication, they had no more authority regarding treatment than did any other member of the team. Decisions in this regard were made by the team and the patient—within the theoretical and therapeutic framework of the Program.

The therapeutic orientation. For reasons noted above, it was clearly understood from the outset that group and family therapy would be utilized as the major treatment modalities. On the other hand, it is generally recognized that the superiority, in terms of outcome, of any one psychotherapeutic modality has yet to be established. Moreover, we recognized that a therapist's enthusiasms for, and confidence in his own style is an important determinant of the efficacy of treatment. Accordingly, staff members were encouraged to use the therapeutic techniques with which they were most comfortable. Theoretical differences were acceptable as well; for example, a group therapist was free to use analytic technique if he wished to. Yet, despite this flexibility, one professional left the Program because he felt that individual therapy was the only effective treatment modality, and he could not, in good conscience, participate in a program that emphasized group methods which he considered only ancillary approaches and of little value.

The modification of traditional patient roles. Our efforts to modify traditional patient roles gave rise to problems as well. Initially, many staff members were ambivalent and confused about patient participation in decision-making conferences. And, not surprisingly, they balked at the demand subsequently presented by the patients' organization that they be represented on the staff hiring and firing committee. Nevertheless, since patients served on all other committees, they had ample opportunity to express their complaints against individual staff members, and it is interesting to note in this connection that no patient has tried to date to get a staff member fired, although they know their complaints are given careful consideration. Most important, it was apparent from the outset that giving the patients the right to be critical of the staff had important therapeutic value. Obviously, it heightened the patients' sense of autonomy. But of particular relevance in this context is the fact that the staff frequently learned a great deal from the patient's reactions to their efforts, and usually responded well to such criticism—not by lip service, but by modifying their attitudes and actions.

Training Procedures

The didactic training program. Another objection to the modification of traditional professional roles was expressed by psychiatrists and psychologists who strongly resisted the idea of sharing some of their psychotherapeutic functions with non-professionals, on the grounds that non-professionals were not qualified to discharge these functions adequately. Our task was to create a new role and job, not to make the paraprofessional a junior psychiatrist. We attempted to supply the necessary training and experience as expeditiously as possible. Required reading lists were distributed to all non-professionals on the staff. Seminars were held on theory and clinical practice. And we arranged to have non-professionals attend the course in basic psychiatry given at the New York Medical College for second-year medical students. A supervisory system was established.

At first, the staff participated in these activities with great enthusiasm; they seemed to feel that they were part of an exciting adventure. But after the first flush of their enthusiasm for academia had faded, those staff members with the least training, and the mental health workers in particular, no longer wanted to be burdened with seminars, courses, or reading assignments. Several participants regarded the didactic training program as an unnecessary diversion, for they were firmly convinced that they were qualified to engage in clinical activities. In fact, some were even resentful of supervision. This led to a decline of the formal aspects of in-service training, and the development of a peculiar competitiveness between those staff members with more experience and training and those with less. By the end of the year, however, this anti-intellectualism had begun to dissipate. By this time staff members at both ends of the spectrum realized that they had much to learn from one another. Accordingly, new seminars were set up by staff committees which were better suited to the needs of non-professionals, and to the needs of the Program. For example, at one such seminar an expert from another division of the Department of Psychiatry of the New York Medical College was invited to talk with the entire staff about the use of medication as a therapeutic agent, a concept which many staff members (on the professional as well as the non-professional level) had previously regarded as an anathema.

The sponsor system merits special consideration because it served to foster the integration of treatment services, and underscores the contribution of the non-professional staff members to the Program. Briefly, each patient was assigned to a sponsor who saw to it that the patient was seen by the necessary members of other disciplines, and who scheduled planning and evaluative conferences at appropriate intervals. The sponsor was also available for individual treatment sessions and served thereby as a counterfoil to the various forms of group treatment in which the patient participated. At first, the more experienced professionals served as sponsors; later any professional who wished to could become a sponsor. Eventually, mental health workers served as co-sponsors. Thus the sponsor system was also considered to constitute a learning experience; moreover, the sharing of responsibility promoted staff unity. But apart from these considerations, the mental health workers contributed to the efficacy of this procedure. They were able to establish a rapport with patients from the outset, because they came from the same neighborhood and were similar ethnically and culturally.

On the other hand, we recognized early that the sponsor system also had its drawbacks: at times a sponsor developed a proprietary attitude toward a particular patient, and jealousy guarded his relationship with that patient. When that happened there was a strong possibility that the patient would be deprived of available services or therapy sessions with other staff members. Although some staff members were never able to fully resolve this problem, it was possible to reduce the intensity of their over-protective proprietary attitude. However, our intervention was selective: We did not interfere with the special and intense relationships which we felt had great therapeutic potential, but tried to correct only their constrictive components. In any event, these crises usually led to important insights. Once he was ready to concede that he had not been acting in the patient's best interests, the staff member was also forced to face the fact that his technique was not necessarily unique and superior and that from time to time he had to accept help from those who used other approaches. Concurrently, staff members were motivated to become more familiar with these other approaches.

Joint decision-making. The Director frequently brought perplexing administrative problems to the daily community meeting, not only for help in their resolution, or as a means of fostering staff and patient involvement in the Program, but because patients were given an opportunity to assume another role in this setting, and this, in turn, fostered the modification of traditional staff roles and attitudes. The following example may serve to underscore the therapeutic—and administrative—advantages of this procedure.

When it became apparent that we could not help patients who were addicted to heroin in our setting, the Director raised this issue at several community meetings, on the assumption that it concerned the entire community. Obviously, this problem was of special interest to the staff. But it affected the patients as well, inasmuch as those among them who suffered from drug addiction frequently exerted a disruptive influence on the Program. The decision ultimately arrived at reflected these considerations. Specifically, it was decided, in due course, that addicts who were off drugs at the time they applied for admission to the Program would be accepted for treatment, but those applicants who were still using drugs (with the exception of prescribed methadone) would not be eligible for treatment in this setting. Moreover, any patient who was currently using hard drugs was to be dismissed from the Program, but might reapply when he was clean. This policy proved to be a wise and effective one. Most important, since this decision had been made, after careful deliberation, by the patients as well as the staff, the patients helped to enforce it without rancor. And their efforts in this connection further enhanced staff-patient relationships.

The T-group. The procedures described above facilitated staff growth, but, most importantly, our honest evaluation of ourselves, of our performance, and of one another paved the way for our work with patients. A T-group, which was started within a few months after the Program had been established, was particularly crucial in fostering staff self-awareness and cooperation. The open expression of hurt feelings, doubts, and misapprehensions permitted relative freedom from the destructive aspects of competitiveness, and contributed thereby to the development of a highly effective therapeutic team. Essentially, the group, in which both the Director and Coordinator of the Program participated on an equal basis with other staff members, was oriented toward the enhancement of staff-patient interaction.

The T-group went through an interesting evolution, in terms of its organization and structure, which can be schematized as follows:

Phase 1. The effectiveness of the first T-group was limited because its leader, an expert who had been recruited from outside, was determined not to reveal himself or become involved, an approach which, of course, was incompatible with the basic philosophy of the unit. The staff decided, therefore, to look for another leader whose approach was more conducive to openness and growth. At the same time, however, they appreciated the fact that this first leader's unswerving stand on this issue had fostered their sense of unity and served to underscore the need for open involvement in their own relationships with patients.

Phase 2. A talented part-time member of the staff was then named leader of the T-group on popular demand. This worked out well for a while, but the members of the group gradually became increasingly competitive and began to actively resent their colleague's special status as group leader. Moreover, they were neither willing nor able to be sufficiently open about their feelings of competitiveness in the group; instead, they withdrew.

Phase 3. In the third stage, a leaderless group was established which remained in operation for approximately five months. At the end of that period the group realized they needed a leader, and they were ready to accept one.*

Phase 4. At this point, the staff formed two separate groups which were led by two T-group leaders, neither of whom was centrally involved in the program. The members of Group "A" described themselves as members of the "out-group." The self-appointed "in-group" (Group "B") comprised those staff members who had greater experience as therapists—and considered themselves superior on that account. Group "A" worked effectively, and its members developed; the members of the "elite" group (Group "B") competed with one another, as well as with the group leader, and did not accomplish their basic task of removing blocks to better team functioning. Additional difficulties arose when competitiveness between members of the two groups developed, and the staff was divided into two factions. However, we realized that this competition had certain positive aspects when it became apparent that Group "A" had proved itself to Group "B" by accomplishing the tasks of its T-group.

Phase 5. Membership in the T-group now became entirely voluntary, and there was only one group. We hoped thereby to avoid the divisiveness that had occurred in Phase 4. The fifth T-group, which was led by the "outside" professional who had successfully led Group "A" during that period, has continued to operate most effectively.

To summarize our experience with T-groups, in general, we found them invaluable as a means of promoting staff cohesiveness and sensitivity to patients. However, we also came to some specific conclusions with respect to the operation of such groups: We believe they should be task-oriented, that they should have a well-trained leader, and that the

---

* This decision coincided with the dissipation of the anti-intellectualism, referred to earlier, which had temporarily brought the more academic aspects of our in-service training program to a near standstill.

leader will be more effective if he is not a member of the staff. We also learned that, even under ideal conditions, T-groups are vulnerable to a variety of problems which may derive from one of several sources—the personality of the leader, competitiveness among group members and poorly defined goals. It is necessary to be alert to these problems so that they can be resolved before they reach crisis proportions.

Evaluation of Training Procedures

In summary, the various procedures and techniques described above enabled the relative resolution of earlier problems involving staff self-identification and role rigidity, the reluctance on the part of the non-professional staff to learn necessary treatment techniques, and the competitiveness and hostility among staff members which precluded their effective collaboration on behalf of the patient. In time, individual staff members learned to recognize their own limitations and abilities—and the limitations and abilities of others. The mental health worker who had been suspicious of the psychiatrist initially came to respect him instead. With the help of the mental health worker, the psychiatrist was able to acknowledge the irrational fears and assumptions he held with regard to the under-privileged and was able to refrain from judging them in terms of his own value system.

VICISSITUDES OF STAFF DEVELOPMENT

Regression in Staff-Patient Relationships

Inevitably, from time to time, staff members would regress to earlier ways of perceiving patients as children who had to be directed and disciplined; or they "took over" in the interests of expedience. In fact, such lapses occurred regularly; but, as a general rule, the openness of the system allowed for their discovery and correction.

There was one exception, however: The failure of the staff to encourage patients to become involved in community affairs constituted a problem which persisted until the late Spring of 1968. At that point, patients and staff elected to charter a bus and participate in the poverty march on Washington. And, shortly thereafter, patients began to bring representatives of their neighborhood organization, their welfare workers, ministers and other people with whom they were involved to the Program's community meetings. This shift marked a new stage in our efforts to cooperate with neighborhood agencies. The fact that this, as well as many other innovations, was initiated by patient action is of particular interest. But even more significant is the fact that we were able to provide a milieu which fostered the development of such initiative.

Intra-staff Dissension

Just when everything seemed to be going smoothly, we were confronted by a major staff crisis. It was at this point that blacks militantly began to implement their demands for power on the community level on a nation-wide scale—and a long-smoldering problem burst into flames. As part of this movement, several health services operated in black or Spanish-speaking neighborhoods were taken over by members of the community. For example, mental health workers seized control of one hospital in New York City and forced the director and other administrators to leave. Services at that hospital were disrupted, and the program had to be discontinued. And we appeared to be moving in the same direction: Blacks and Spanish-speaking members of our staff became polarized from each other and from the white staff members. However, we were able to deal with this potentially explosive situation effectively, within the structure of the total Program. Furthermore, our method of solution served to enhance the Program's therapeutic effectiveness.

From the outset, we had had many discussions at our community and staff meetings about prejudice, black power, discrimination in the Program, the role of the Spanish-speaking staff, how best to reach various minority groups, etc. In other words, this problem was not new to us, and it seemed for a while that the Director's efforts to work toward staff integration and patient integration would be successful (despite the fact that he was white, a psychiatrist, and had a middle-class background). Then, gradually, there was growing evidence of unrest: Two black staff members left the Program for more prestiginous positions, which paid higher salaries. Shortly thereafter, the mental health workers, who were lowest on the economic and prestige ladder, presented demands for a large pay increase, time off for study, and several other demands, all worthy of consideration. The Spanish-speaking staff then voiced their feeling that they were consistently "put down," that they were not respected by other staff members, and that they were assigned only Spanish-speaking patients. And as further evidence of the low esteem in which Spanish-speaking people were held, they pointed out that many patients in this ethnic group had withdrawn from the day center because they felt they were not fully understood or given adequate help. In contrast, those assigned to the weekend family center, where all the staff members spoke Spanish, were generally satisfied with the Program. In order to counteract the feeling that Spanish-speaking staff and patients were discriminated against, it was suggested that community meetings should be conducted bilingually.

Now staff discussions seemed to lead nowhere. There was a great deal of talk but no real resolution of problems; and there was no significant change in the behavior of staff members or the operation of the Program. Tempers grew short. Cliques continued to develop along ethnic lines. Individuals were criticized not for their behavior, but on ethnic grounds. White staff members were accused of white chauvinism, and they refused to even consider the possibility that such accusations might have some basis in fact. All our efforts to work toward a resolution of this crisis failed. And, inevitably, the patients began to manifest similar attitudes of disquiet and tension.

The call of the day in the arena of the "outside" world was for separatism, and our efforts to continue to operate as a racially integrated unit seemed to be doomed. At this point, the Director decided to call a staff meeting in a final attempt to save the Program. The proceedings were sufficiently interesting to justify our quoting from the minutes at some length:

> *Director (white)*: The Partial Hospitalization Program was originally conceived in terms of working toward a true integration of patients and staff along racial, professional, economic, and other lines. However, previous failures to find solutions have made it clear that integration can only take place among persons and groups who are recognized equals. It cannot occur until black, white and Spanish-speaking persons are accorded and feel respect within themselves. I suggest then, that we organize ourselves into caucuses divided along racial and ethnic lines—black, white and Spanish-speaking— each group to work independently, with the ultimate purpose of improving the treatment of patients most like themselves. I suggest that each caucus have the responsibility of determining what is needed for the care of patients of their own ethnic group, and of communicating this material to the other groups. Each group can decide how much of what went on in the meeting they wish to share with the rest of the staff. The point is that, at this time, integration cannot occur unless there is separation first, and then consolidation.
>
> My intent today is for us to meet first as a staff and then quickly to involve patients.
>
> (Each group was instructed to appoint a chairman and a recorder and to report back to the entire staff later that same day. The whites

greeted the announcement with dissension. The blacks and Spanish-speaking groups concurred in the suggestion; the blacks expressed agreement in a militant manner. Theirs would obviously be an organized caucus, meeting to press for certain demands which probably had already been formulated.)

Discussion:

R. (white) : What about the Jewish people?

O. (black and the 2nd administrator) : Jewish people are *white!*

R. (white) : What are you so angry about?

W. (black) : A double message is being given here. On the one hand, the hope is to open communication. But the other message is that it's all right to hold back communication.

Director: The caucus has to have the right to decide what will be brought back.

O. (black) : But you don't have to give the caucus this permission. *Question*: Isn't this furthering separatism?

V. (Spanish-speaking) : It is always the whites who don't want this. Perhaps, if it is the official result of a meeting, the others will listen. There are things that can only be discussed among one's own.

Director: Is there a role for an organization such as ours? Can we work out a way of working together as a group? I don't know the answers, but we have to work in a different way than we did before.

R. (white) : (With sarcasm) Our district goes down to 72nd Street. Maybe the white staff should see patients who live below 96th Street (a fashionable white neighborhood) and the black and Spanish staff treat those who live above it (the East Harlem ghetto area).

Director: Maybe we should. It's something for the caucuses to discuss. The white caucus can meet here. The black caucus can meet in my office. . . .

O. (black) : The black caucus will meet in *MY* office!
(Meeting adjourned with a great deal of ferment and buzzing, so that first caucus meetings could be held.)

The caucuses were organized that day. The black and Spanish-speaking staff members functioned effectively, in that they focused on their position *vis-à-vis* the staff and on ways to improve patient care. The whites spent a lot of time brooding and feeling sorry for themselves. Some among them could not understand why some of their colleagues considered them to be racists when they had the best of liberal intentions.

"Truce." Predictably and with some justification, the black and Spanish-speaking staff members felt that the white staff were more likely to empathize with the better educated white patients, and did not devote themselves assiduously to working with other ethnic groups. The caucus approach was most helpful in clarifying issues of this nature, and in illuminating the feelings of individual staff members within each caucus. In fact, within a month after the caucuses began to meet, many significant changes were instituted in the Program. Paradoxically, separatism led to a closeness among staff members on a deeper level than had existed before, and an improvement in patient care was an inevitable result of this closeness. The issues had also been taken to the patients by their representatives, and their involvement contributed to the further refinement and clarification of these issues and the remedies. Once again, staff and patients were able to view the Program in a favorable light, and they communicated their positive response to our efforts to their representative leaders in the community. By taking this action, they were able to halt a growing coalition that was threatening to "take over."

We realize, of course, that the problem of racial conflict and the strong feelings it engenders, will not be completely resolved in the unit until it is resolved in the larger social and political arenas. But what needs to be emphasized is that we were able to work together by recognizing our differences as well as our similarities, and using this understanding to restructure—and strengthen—staff relationships and, concomitantly, the relationships between staff and patients and with the community we serve. Thus, once again, staff openness and discussion provided a dividend for patients.

COMMENT

The fact that staff and patients lived together for seven hours a day in a helping, rational setting, coupled with the availability of a broad spectrum of therapeutic modalities undoubtedly contributed to the efficacy of the treatment program. But it is equally apparent that the most important factor in the effectiveness of the treatment program was the staff's involvement with the patients and the Program, their respect for the patients, their expectation of healthy behavior, and the models they were able to provide. Even the most frightened, withdrawn, and depressed patients found it difficult not to relate in this setting after two or three weeks.

Like infinity, the goal of perfect staff functioning is never achieved—but it can be approached. Our involvement in the Program served to heighten our awareness of the prerequisites for the fulfillment of this ideal: We found that constant self-examination by the staff, and their concomitant awareness of the patients' reactions to their behavior, were essential, and that this orientation could best be fostered by group process. Periodically, something would happen to make us aware of our deficiencies. When we realized that we had slipped in one or another area, we would try to find out why, make sure our original decision had been correct, and, if not, revise it and begin all over again.

But our assessment of the effectiveness of the Program (and of our performance) did not occur only in times of crisis. Each year patients and staff would retire to the Academy of Medicine to hold a retreat (which, with characteristic optimism, we called an "Advance"). The purpose of the Advance was to evaluate the Program in terms of its results, and to this end papers on various aspects of the Program were presented for general discussion by individuals and committees of patients and staff. These annual Advances constituted our most serious and effective evaluation procedure; invariably, they led to significant changes in staff functioning—and to concomitant improvements in the psychological functioning of our patients.

On reflection, we believe our experiment has been successful. Admittedly, the Program bears some semblance to a utopian community. In fact, however, great emphasis is placed on teaching the patient to cope with the real world; this is a basic goal of treatment—and it was successfully implemented within the framework of this "utopian community."

Without a dedicated staff with varied gifts and training, and the willingness to risk exposing themselves to change, the Program could not have evolved. Staff growth and development was facilitated by the use of group methods designed to enhance the staff's ability to form psychologically healthy relationships with patients, to transmit to patients their openness and faith in them. Finally, we would emphasize, above all, that it was the importance we attached to staff growth and development, in terms of their attitudes and real relationships with our patient population, that made it possible to put into effect methods of treatment which are often discussed (and extolled) but rarely practiced.

REFERENCES

1. AUERSWALD, E., "Interdisciplinary Versus Ecological Approaches," *Family Process,* 1968, Vol. VII, pp. 202-215.
2. JONES, M., *The Therapeutic Community,* Basic Books, New York, 1953.
3. JONES, M., *Beyond the Therapeutic Community,* Yale University Press, New Haven, 1968.
4. JONES, M., "From Hospital to Community Psychiatry," *Community Mental Health Journal,* 1970, Vol. 6, pp. 187-195.
5. SAGER, C. J., BRAYBOY, T. L., & WAXENBERG, B. R., *Black Ghetto Family in Therapy,* pp. 238-240, Grove Press, New York, 1970.

47

EVIL AS A SOCIAL PROCESS: THE MY LAI MASSACRE

Richard Rabkin, M.D.

*Director, Social Design Division, Community Research
Application (New York)*

Evil is a concept that is usually limited to theology. Because not many people currently participate in or observe theological debates, it is a concept that is seldom considered. It has value, however, and a relevance that extends beyond the scope of theology. I believe that the nature of evil can be meaningfully considered from the perspectives of the behavioral sciences. An attempt has been made in this article to illustrate this view: Using a well-publicized contemporary act as a point of departure, the concept of evil is examined within the conceptual framework of the behavioral sciences and shown to be comprehensible within a systems-oriented view of psychopathology.

The Events at My Lai

In the late 1960's, the general strategy followed by the United States in Viet Nam called for the physical removal of the South Vietnamese population from the countryside, in order to "flush out" and annihilate enemy guerrillas. As a first step, the inhabitants of the villages in a given area were warned to leave; then, regardless of whether or not it was defended, the region was subjected to intensive aerial bombardment and ground operations, i.e., "search and destroy" missions. As a result of this strategy, which was designed to conserve American lives, one-third of the entire South Vietnamese population has become refugees. By August

1967, the relocation centers in Quang Ngai Province to which South Vietnamese civilians were moved after they had been routed from their native villages were so overcrowded that American field units were requested not to "generate" any more refugees. The Army complied with this request to curtail the generation of refugees by eliminating their efforts to warn villagers of impending air strikes or ground operations; the "search and destroy" missions continued. In other words, the Armed Forces continued to carry out their missions in areas that must have included villages inhabited by the South Vietnamese; yet there was no appreciable increase in the population of relocation centers, for the inhabitants of these villages were no longer offered the option of becoming refugees and removing themselves to "pacification camps." This strategy set the stage for My Lai.

The events at My Lai are, of course, a matter of public knowledge. Apart from the newspaper reports, detailed accounts of the incident have been published (1, 2), and it has been discussed by behavioral scientists (3). The factual data provided in these various sources can be summarized briefly: On March 16, 1968, Charlie Company, which was stationed in Quang Ngai Province, entered on foot a hamlet which was listed on American maps as My Lai 4, part of the village of Son My, in the mistaken belief that they had entered another hamlet where the Viet Cong were known to be active. Unaware, of this error,* the men of Charlie Company herded together 400 non-combatants, who had not been forewarned of this raid (and thus given an opportunity to become refugees), and who, in any event, offered no resistance, and then shot them. At approximately the same time, Charlie Company's sister unit, Bravo Company, killed an additional 100 civilians (according to conservative estimates) at another sub-hamlet of Son My, which was located near My Lai.

Quantification of Evil

In most reports of the "My Lai Massacre," the incident is cited as an extraordinary act of evil, comparable to the most infamous deeds of history. What these representative evil events seem to have shared in common is number, the fact that they involved mass atrocities. That is, there seems to be a direct correlation between the number of victims of an evil act and the degree to which that act is condemned. Thus, an evil act, such as the murder of two people, is considered more reprehensible than the murder of one person. And, at first, this seems only rea-

---

* It has been suggested that the leaders of Charlie Company subsequently became aware of their error, but proceeded nonetheless to carry out their mission. However, this has not been established.

sonable. Clearly, then, from a quantitative point of view, the My Lai Massacre of 400 people is extremely evil. In fact, it has been so well-publicized and has aroused strong public indignation precisely because of its quantitative aspects, not because such events as the deliberate killing of prisoners and non-combatants were singularly unusual in the Viet Nam War.**

Nevertheless, quantity is not a good criterion of evil. If the killing of 400 Vietnamese by Charlie Company was labeled a massacre, does this mean that the killing of 100 civilians at approximately the same time by its sister unit, Bravo Company, was not a massacre—and, by implication, not as evil? Is not one such death as evil? I believe that one such death *must* be seen as equally evil because to quantify evil is to unwittingly sanction it, if only partially. Partial sanctions of evil may be based on other criteria as well: In some ancient regimes it was considered more evil to kill someone Sunday than on weekdays. Until quite recently, the State could execute a pregnant woman at a stage in pregnancy at which an abortion would be a crime. Partial sanctioning leads to a gradual and progressive callousness as there tends to be a drift to higher and higher thresholds of evil under repeated exposure to quantitative thinking. With respect to prevention, it is difficult, under such circumstances, to determine the level at which intervention is called for.

Another conceptual framework is required for the analysis of evil. Further examination of the cumulative experiences of Charlie Company may serve to demonstrate the application of a transactional point of view to an understanding of this phenomenon.

The Psychogenesis of Evil

Charlie Company had suffered considerable losses in the weeks prior to March 16, the day it entered My Lai, and was severely demoralized. Six members of the Company were killed and twelve were badly wounded by mine explosions on February 28. Just two days before the massacre a very popular and highly respected sergeant had been killed. On the eve of the massacre the captain delivered a "pep talk" and funeral oration, in the course of which he discussed the pain the men felt as a result of these deaths. He encouraged the men to deal with their feelings by giving vent to these emotions; they were urged to "let it out, let it go." Morale was to be heightened by seeking revenge, making others suffer in place of the company. Thus, members of Charlie Company who

----

** Such events are hardly unique to the Viet Nam War. Indiscriminate killing occurred in previous wars as well—e.g. the bombing of Dresden, London, Hiroshima.

were present at the funeral have testified that they were told that "nothing should be left walking, growing, or crawling" in the area which had been selected as their next target. This discussion will focus on two aspects of the experience of Charlie Company: First, the function of revenge. Secondly, I am interested in the alternatives which were open to Charlie Company, i.e., in the possibility that its losses may have been compensated for in other ways.

The Communication of Evil

Simon Weil, the French philosopher, believes that evil spreads and flourishes in the world because it is passed on from victim to victim in the form of suffering. It is Weil's contention that a victim of evil finds relief from his own suffering by causing suffering in others. A single evil act may thus travel, inasmuch as the effects of that act—its essence, so to speak—can be transmitted from person to person, in an endless chain much like the energy of a wave which travels great distances. For purposes of this presentation it is important to emphasize Weil's basic proposition that the infliction of suffering on another person by a victim frequently gives rise to feelings of relief rather than remorse.

Charlie Company's desire for revenge or, more precisely the attempt by these men to alleviate their own suffering by causing others to suffer, exemplifies Weil's hypothesis. Nor is this an isolated example of the transfer of suffering. At one time or another, practically everyone has had experiences with evil, although it is not usually perceived or labeled as such. To illustrate, I once had the misfortune to witness a suicide. I happened to be looking out of the window of a hospital room when a young girl jumped off the roof of the building directly across the street. Shortly afterward, I met a friend in the hospital corridor to whom I described in detail the event I had just witnessed. The friend's whole demeanor changed, and the expression on his face clearly reflected the horror and revulsion he felt; in contrast, I experienced a sudden and dramatic sense of relief. My friend staggered off, perhaps to pass the burden to another person, while I, without giving the matter another thought, ate a hearty lunch. In short, I had caused someone else to suffer and relieved my own suffering in the process. In Weil's opinion, I was guilty of an evil act. Although the incident at My Lai is extraordinary because of its quantitative aspects, it does not differ in other respects from the trivial experience described above.

The need to transfer suffering is not easily frustrated. Once again, an episode in which I participated serves to illustrate the point. Prior to a conference of family therapists, I was approached in the coffee room by one of the participants who was so depressed by the conditions at the State Hospital where we all were working, that he was barely able to muster the strength to go to the conference. When it became apparent that he was about to transfer his burden, I tried to stop the process. I explained that I wanted to guard against the transfer of suffering, and the other therapist agreed to change the subject. He then proceeded to talk about his experiences in the Air Force which were initially entertaining but unaccountably began to resemble events in all bureaucracies, including the State Hospital. And, before I knew it, I was feeling terrible, and shaking my head about the "waste and corruption and the hopelessness of it all." Despite precautions, the other therapist had successfully shifted to me his feelings of despair. When we entered the conference room, I was depressed and apathetic, barely able to muster the strength to attend "another one of those conferences," but my friend felt fine.

It is this process of transferring suffering, whether it results in 400 deaths or has the trivial consequences described above, which is suggested as the proper criterion of evil.

Clinical Examples of Transfer Phenomena

Transfer phenomena are crucial to an understanding of all psychopathology from a systems point of view. Ross V. Speck (4), who has discussed these phenomena within the framework of family therapy, reports that such transfers are almost daily events in the social units he refers to as "schizophrenic families." Speck has related his observations to Jackson's concept of homeostasis within the family. And he has commented on the relationship between the transfer phenomenon and the clinical syndrome of *folie a deux*. When it was first described in 1877, *folie a deux* was also called *folie communiquee,* suggesting the process of communicated evil described by Weil.

The psychoanalytic literature includes an excellent article by Wangh (5), in which he describes a woman with insomnia who repeatedly transferred this symptom to her husband by waking him up to tell him how worried she was about their teen-age son who stayed out too late. Once her worries had been shifted to her husband, and he was sufficiently distressed—and incensed—to wait up for the boy, the wife was able to sleep soundly. When the son finally did come home, his father would proceed to chastise him loudly. And the noise would wake the wife, who, since her own anixety and anger had been dissipated, would then calmly join her son for a midnight snack. This is a rather rare example of the transfer of a symptom (i.e., insomnia), which took the same form in both the perpetrator and her victim.

Although Wangh was able to notice the shift of insomnia because of his intimate psychoanalytic knowledge of the perpetrator, such transfers usually go unnoticed by therapists. When successful, the person who perpetrates the transfer feels fine and is not likely to seek psychiatric help. It is only when he fails that his maneuvers may come to the attention of the psychiatrist. For instance, in the case of the transfer of insomnia reported above, if the husband were to go for treatment of insomnia, his wife's behavior probably would go unnoticed. On the other hand, if the wife's maneuvers were unsuccessful, she would be seeking the psychiatrist's help, and there is a possibility that her efforts to transfer her symptoms might come to light in the course of treatment. What needs to be emphasized here is the fact that it is only in family therapy and in systems-oriented or ecological studies that transfer phenomena are fully elucidated.

What must be revised before the relationship between transfer phenomena and psychiatric entities can be further clarified are the mistaken notions that all psychiatric symptoms serve a useful purpose, and that they are effectively executed by all who display them. In fact, standards of competence can be applied to all disordered behavior including manifestations of symptoms. For example, many paranoid patients ineptly carry out their behavior and seem merely ludicrous to others. In contrast, a competent paranoid can actually create a hostile environment. And when the paranoid maneuver is superbly performed, those who are involved with the patient can be made to display foolish or even deranged behavior.

Regardless of the nature of his symptom, if the transfer maneuver is successful, the perpetrator is relieved of his burden. Recently, a student stood up during a medical school lecture and offered his unsolicited opinion that the lecture was abysmally poor. The lecturer was provoked (and enraged) by this comment; nevertheless, to be on the safe side, for some time he omitted any reference to the material the student had objected to in the examinations he prepared. Later, he scheduld an additional meeting of the class to discuss in depth the material his critic felt had not been covered adequately, thus eventually thwarting this student's attempt to shift the weight of his pre-exam anxiety to the lecturer.

One other aspect of the incident described above is of particular interest: The anxiety which the student felt, although similar, was not identical to the anger which the lecturer experienced once the transfer had been successfully executed. In fact, it doesn't seem to matter whether the symptom which is transferred takes the same form or not. Thus, a patient with a history of frequent psychotic episodes was worried about a thyroid operation, and was able to transfer this concern. As a result, she was given special attention during her hospital stay, and helped considerably by the ward personnel who were worried about the possibility that she would have another psychotic break. The patient remained calm throughout; but the ward personnel were under a considerable strain.

Finally, mention should be made of symptom substitution (e.g., the substitution of a phobia for, let us say, enuresis), which might be classified as a sub-category of the transfer phenomenon. In any event, it is an extremely incompetent solution, and requires a particularly inept individual. For one thing, symptom substitution does not execute a sufficiently distant transfer; it merely shifts systems within the same personality. Secondly, it does not achieve transfer of the burden to the point of relief, except insofar as an exchange of symptoms can be beneficial in certain instances.

The disadvantages of symptom substitution serve to point out that one of the prerequisites for a successful transfer is an interface between social systems—a gap in the communication process, a gulf between people. Needless to say, very little is achieved by the husband who transfers his burden to his wife who then transfers it back to him in ping pong fashion. However, if a relatively distant person is the victim of the transfer, he carries the burden outward, away from the social system in which it previously existed. When there is no interface between perpetrator and victim, the perpetrator feels remorse not relief following the transfer, contrary to Weil's understanding of the matter.

Absorption as an Alternative to Transfer

According to Weil, the chain of evil can be broken by one who is willing to sacrifice himself in Christ-like fashion, who is willing to eliminate some of the world's evil and suffering by absorbing it without yielding to the temptation to cause others to suffer. The reference to Christ is somewhat misleading, however. One might willingly absorb evil, but if the martyr is seriously hurt in the process, we are once again submitting to the temptation to quantify evil. Such a martyr may help to eliminate evil, but if he himself will be a victim, we will have scored only a minor victory over evil. This solution has other flaws as well. Although they have different connotation, the phenomena of martyrdom and scapegoating are closely related. It depends on whether one views the role from the standpoint of the system (scapegoating) or of the individual (martyrdom). Typically, one thinks of the scapegoat as a victim of the system, while in contrast, the role of martyr is self-selected. But in family therapy one is frequently called upon to rescue scapegoats who are self-selected.

There is an alternative, however. The resilience of any system depends on its ability to transfer external challenges or absorb them. In the case of evil, a system may choose to pass on the evil to which it has been exposed, to seek revenge, as Charlie Company did. Or it may absorb it— as a system. To use a non-human example, a tidal marsh can absorb the enormous force of a hurricane because it is a spongy mass which bends with the storm and yields to its pressure; but a rigid house in the same storm might be blown away. The fact that the marsh is spongy means that each of its elements is able to absorb some of the force of the storm and fall back on the next element, thereby diluting the pressure on the individual front-line element. In human social systems, mourning, when it involves the sharing of stress, is a very similar process. It is not the *transfer* of pain from person to person in an endless chain, or its transfer to a single martyr, or scapegoat, but a diffusion of the original pain. Grief, as the old saying goes, is itself a medicine, but not when the burden of pain must be borne alone. Mourning provides relief only if other people are available to "help to carry the cross," to use a more appropriate Christian metaphor. In short, studies of human social systems can help the victims of misfortune to recognize, and guard against their tendency to find a scapegoat, to "get even" by hurting others.

War As a Special Problem

Pacifists have challenged the notion that war can be waged honorably, yet most people still seem to believe it is possible. Shifting from ethical to pragmatic considerations, one can hypothesize that a pre-condition of an honorable war would be a social system sufficiently absorbent to cushion the enormous burden of pain and suffering which war imposes. Such a system would counteract the alternative tendency to handle such stresses by transferring the burden across an interface. For, in that event, the evil perpetrated might come home to roost. This was Gandhi's truth: Evil done to others in a crowded world of interconnected networks of people is very likely to damage the social system in which the perpetrator resides. This was demonstrated by the My Lai Massacre. Apart from the fact that Americans at home were demoralized by the disclosure of the events at My Lai, the international prestige of the United States declined. It was also possible that the evil of My Lai might be transferred to American prisoners of war, which might have led, in turn, to still another My Lai incident.

Behavioral scientists have observed that the sharing of suffering within a family group can counteract its possible pathological manifestations. This applies to other social groups as well, in war or peace. Thus, to begin with, an honorable war would have to allow time for mourning, or for the formal expression of sorrow. A proper and greatly expanded funeral for their sergeant was the alternative for Charlie Company. It might not have decreased the suffering that war causes, but it would have decreased the evil—that is, the desire to cause others to suffer simply as a means of assuaging one's own sorrow and pain.

REFERENCES

1. HAMMER, R. *One Morning in the War: The Tragedy at Son My.* New York: Coward-McCann, 1970.
2. HERSH, S. M. *My Lai 4: A Report on the Massacre and Its Aftermath.* New York: Random House, 1970.
3. SANFORD, N. & COMSTOCK, C. *Sanctions for Evil, Sources of Social Destructiveness.* San Francisco: Jossey-Bass, 1971.
4. SPECK, R. V., The transfer of illness phenomenon in schizophrenic families. In Nagy, ed., *Psychotherapy of the Whole Family.* New York: Springer, 1965.
5. WANGH, M., On the evocation of a proxy. In *Psychoanalytic Study of the Child*, Vol. 17. New York: International Universities Press, 1962.

48

CONSCIOUSNESS ♀

Vivian Gornick

In a lower Manhattan office a legal secretary returns from her lunch hour, sinks into her seat and says miserably to a secretary at the next desk: "I don't know what's happening to me. A perfectly nice construction worker whistled and said, 'My, isn't *that* nice,' as I passed him and suddenly I felt this terrific anger pushing up in me. . . . I swear I wanted to *hit* him!"

At the same time, a thoughtful 40-year-old mother in a Maryland suburb is saying to a visiting relative over early afternoon coffee: "You know, I've been thinking lately, I'm every bit as smart as Harry, and yet he got the Ph.D. and I raised the girls. Mind you, I *wanted* to stay home. And yet, the thought of my two girls growing up and doing the same thing doesn't sit well with me at all. Not at all."

And in Toledo, Ohio, a factory worker turns to the next woman on the inspection belt and confides: "Last night I told Jim: 'I been working in the same factory as you 10 years now. We go in at the same time, come out the same time. But I do all the shopping, get the dinner, wash the dishes and on Sunday break my back down on the kitchen floor. I'm real tired of doin' all that. I want some help from you.' Well, he just laughed at me, see? Like he done every time I mentioned this before. But last night I wouldn't let up. I mean, I really *meant* it this time. And you know? I thought he was gonna let me have it. Looked mighty like he was getting ready to belt me one. But you know? I just didn't care! I wasn't gonna back down come hell or high water. You'll just never believe it, he'd kill me if he knew I was tellin' you, he washed the dishes. First time in his entire life."

None of these women are feminists. None of them are members of the Women's Liberation Movement. None of them ever heard of consciousness-raising. And yet, each of them exhibits the symptomatic influence of this, the movement's most esoteric practice. Each of them, without specific awareness, is beginning to feel the effects of the consideration of woman's personal experience in a new light—a political light. Each of them is undergoing the mysterious behavioral twitches that indicate psychological alteration. Each of them is drawing on a linking network of feminist analysis and emotional upchucking that is beginning to suffuse the political-social air of American life today. Each of them, without ever having attended a consciousness-raising session, has had her consciousness raised.

Consciousness-raising is the name given to the feminist practice of examining one's personal experience in the light of sexism; i.e., that theory which explains woman's subordinate position in society as a result of a cultural decision to confer direct power on men and only indirect power on women. The term of description and the practice to which it alludes are derived from a number of sources—psychoanalysis, Marxist theory and American revivalism, mainly—and was born out of the earliest stages of feminist formulation begun about three years ago in such predictable liberationist nesting places as Cambridge, New York, Chicago and Berkeley. (The organization most prominently associated with the growth of consciousness-raising is the New York Redstockings.)

Perceiving that woman's position in our society does indeed constitute that of a political class, and, secondly, that woman's "natural" domain is her feelings, and, thirdly, that testifying in a friendly and supportive atmosphere enables people to see that their experiences are often duplicated (thereby reducing their sense of isolation and increasing the desire to theorize as well as to confess), the radical feminists sensed quickly that a group of women sitting in a circle discussing their emotional experiences as though they were material for cultural analysis was political dynamite. Hence, through personal testimony and emotional analysis could the class consciousness of *women* be raised. And thus the idea of the small "woman's group"—or consciousness-raising group—was delivered into a cruel but exciting world.

Consciousness-raising is, at one and the same time, both the most celebrated and accessible introduction to the woman's movement as well as the most powerful technique for feminist conversion known to the liberationists. Women are *drawn,* out of a variety of discontents, by the idea of talking about themselves, but under the spell of a wholly new interpretation of their experience, they *remain*.

Coming together, as they do, week after week for many months, the women who are "in a group" begin to exchange an extraordinary sense of multiple identification that is encouraged by the technique's instruction to look for explanations for each part of one's history in terms of the social or cultural dynamic created by sexism—rather than in terms of the personal dynamic, as one would do in a psychotherapist's group session. (Although there are many differences between consciousness-raising and group therapy—e.g., the former involves no professional leader, no exchange of money—the fundamental difference lies in this fact: in consciousness-raising one looks not to one's personal emotional history for an explanation of behavioral problems but rather to the cultural facts of the patriarchy.)

Thus looking at one's history and experience in consciousness-raising sessions is rather like shaking a kaleidoscope and watching all the same pieces rearrange themselves into an altogether *other* picture, one that suddenly makes the color and shape of each piece appear startlingly new and alive, and full of unexpected meaning. (This is mainly why feminists often say that women are the most interesting people around these days, because they are experiencing a psychic invigoration of rediscovery.)

What *does* take place in a consciousness-raising group? How *do* the women see themselves? What *is* the thrust of the conversation at a typical session? Is it simply the man-hating, spleen-venting that is caricatured by the unsympathetic press? Or the unfocused and wrong-headed abstracting insisted upon by the insulated intellectuals? Or yet again the self-indulgent contemplation of the navel that many tightlipped radical activists see it as?

"In this room," says Roberta H., a Long Island housewife speaking euphemistically of her group's meetings, "we do not generalize. We do not speak of any experience except that of the women here. We follow the rules for consciousness-raising as set out by the New York Radical Feminists and we do not apply them to 'woman's experience'—whatever on earth that is—we apply them to ourselves. But, oh God! The samenesses we have found, and the way in which these meetings have changed our lives!"

The rules that Roberta H. is referring to are to be found in a mimeographed pamphlet, an introduction to the New York Radical Feminists organization, which explains the purpose and procedures of consciousness-raising. The sessions consist mainly of women gathering once a week, sitting in a circle and speaking in turn, addressing themselves—almost entirely out of personal experience—to a topic that has been preselected. The pamphlet sets forth the natural limitations of a group (10 to 15 women), advises women to start a group from among their friends and on a word-of-mouth basis, and suggests a list of useful topics for discussion. These topics include Love, Marriage, Sex, Work, Femininity, How I Came to Women's Liberation, Motherhood, Aging and Competition with Other Women. Additional subjects are developed as a particular group's specific interests and circumstances begin to surface.

When a group's discussions start to revolve more and more about apparently very individual circumstances, they often lead to startling similarities. For instance, a Westchester County group composed solely of housewives, who felt that each marriage represented a unique meaning in each of their lives, used the question, "Why did you marry the man you married?" as the subject for discussion one night. "We went around the room," says Joan S., one of the women present, "and while some of us seemed unable to answer the question without going back practically to the cradle, do you know?, the word love was never mentioned *once.*"

On the Upper West Side of Manhattan, in the vicinity of Columbia University, a group of women between the ages of 35 and 45 have been meeting regularly for six months. Emily R., an attractive 40-year-old divorcée in this group, says: "When I walked into the first meeting, and saw the *types* there, I said to myself: 'None of these broads have been through what I've been through. They couldn't possibly feel the way I feel.' Well, I'll tell you. None of them *have* been through what I've been through if you look at our experience superficially. But when you look a little *deeper*—the way we've been doing at these meetings—you see they've *all* been through what I've been through, and they all feel pretty much the way I feel. God, when I saw *that!* When I saw that what I always felt was my own personal hangup was as true for every other woman in that room as it was for me! Well, that's when *my* consciousness was raised."

What Emily R. speaks of is the phenomenon most often referred to in the movement, the flash of insight most directly responsible for the feminist leap in faith being made by hundreds of women everywhere— i.e., the intensely felt realization that what had always been taken for symptoms of personal unhappiness or dissatisfaction or frustration was so powerfully and so consistently duplicated among women that perhaps these symptoms could just as well be ascribed to *cultural* causes as to psychological ones.

In the feminist movement this kind of "breakthrough" can occur no place else than in a consciousness-raising group. It is only here, during many months of meetings, that a woman is able finally—if ever—to bring to the surface those tangled feelings of anger, bafflement and frustrated justice that have drawn her to the movement in the first place. It is only here that the dynamic of sexism will finally strike home, finally make itself felt in the living detail of her own life.

Claire K., a feminist activist in Cambridge, says of women's groups: "I've been working with women's groups for over two years now. The average life of a group is a year to 18 months, and believe me, I've watched a lot of them fold before they ever got off the ground. But, when they *work!* There is a rhythm to some of them that's like life itself. You watch a group expand and contract, and each time it does one or the other it never comes back together quite the same as when the action started. Something happens to each woman, and to the group itself. . . . But each time, if they survive, they have *grown.* You can see it, almost smell it and taste it."

I am one of those feminists who are always mourning after the coherent and high-minded leadership of the 19th century. Often, when I observe the fragmented, intellectually uneven, politically separated components of the woman's movement I experience dismay, and I find myself enviously imagining Elizabeth Cady Stanton and Lucretia Mott and Susan B. Anthony sitting and holding hands for 40 years, sustaining and offering succor to one another in religious and literary accents that make of their feminism a heroic act, an act that gave interwoven shape to their lives and their cause. And I think in a panic: "Where would we all be without them? Where would we be? They thought it all out for us, and we've got not one inch beyond them." Lately, however, I have changed my mind about that. . . .

I was on my way to a meeting one night not too long ago, a meeting meant to fashion a coalition group out of the movement's many organizations. I knew exactly what was ahead of me. I knew that a woman from NOW would rise and speak about our "image"; that a Third Worlder would announce loudly she didn't give a good goddamn about anybody's orgasms, her women were starving, for chrissake; that a Radicalesbian would insist that the woman's movement must face the problem of sexism from within *right now;* and 10 women from the Socialist party would walk out in protest against middle-class "élitist" control in the movement. I knew there would be a great deal of emotional opinion delivered, a comparatively small amount of valuable observation made, and some action taken. Suddenly, as the bus I was on swung westward through Central Park, I realized that it didn't matter, that none of it mattered. I realized it was stupid and self-pitying to be wishing that the meeting was going to be chaired by Elizabeth Cady Stanton; what she had done and said had been profoundly in the idiom of her time, and in the idiom of *my* time no woman in the movement was her equal, but something else was: the consciousness-raising group.

I saw then that the small, anonymous consciousness-raising group was the heart and soul of the woman's movement, that it is not what happens at movement meetings in New York or Boston or Berkeley that counts, but the fact that hundreds of these groups are springing up daily—at universities in Kansas, in small towns in Oregon, in the suburbs of Detroit—out of a responsive need that has indeed been urged to the surface by modern radical feminism. It was here that the soul of a woman is genuinely searched and a new psychology of the self is forged. I saw then that the consciousness-raising group of today is the true Second Front of feminism; and as I thought all this I felt the ghost of Susan B. Anthony hovering over me, nodding vigorously, patting me on the shoulder and saying: "Well done, my dear, well done."

That ghost has accompanied me to every movement meeting I have attended since that night, but when I am at a consciousness-raising session that ghost disappears and I am on my own. Then, for better or worse, I am the full occupant of my feminist skin, engaged in the true business of modern feminism, reaching hard for self-possession.

And now let's go to a consciousness-raising session.*

Early in the evening, on a crisp autumn night, a young woman in an apartment in the Gramercy Park section of Manhattan signed a letter, put it in an envelope, turned out the light over her desk, got her coat out of the hall closet, ran down two flights of stairs, hailed a taxi and headed west directly across the city. At the same time, on the Upper West Side, another woman, slightly older than the first, bent over a sleeping child, kissed his forehead, said goodnight to the babysitter, rode down 12 flights in an elevator, walked up to Broadway and disappeared into the downtown subway. Across town, on the Upper East Side, another woman tossed back a head of stylishly fixed hair, pulled on a beautiful pair of suede boots and left her tiny apartment, also heading down and across town. On the Lower East Side, in a fourth-floor tenement apartment, a woman five or six years younger than all the others combed out a tangled mop of black hair, clomped down the stairs in her Swedish clogs and started trudging west on St. Marks Place. In a number of other places all over Manhattan other women were also leaving their

_____

* Editors' Note: The session described is not reported verbatim.

houses. When the last one finally walked into the Greenwich Village living room they were all headed for, there were 10 women in the room.

These women ranged in age from the late 20's to the middle 30's; in appearance, from attractive to very beautiful; in education, from bachelor's degrees to master's degrees; in marital status, from single, to married to divorced to imminently separated; two were mothers. Their names were Veronica, Lucie, Diana, Marie, Laura, Jen, Shiela, Dolores, Marilyn and Claire. Their occupations, respectively, were assistant television producer, graduate student, housewife, copywriter, journalist, unemployed actress, legal secretary, unemployed college dropout, school-teacher and computer programmer.

They were not movement women; neither were they committed feminists; nor were they marked by an especial sense of social development or by personal neurosis. They were simply a rather ordinary group of women who were drawn out of some unresolved, barely articulated need to form a "woman's group." They were in their third month of meetings; they were now at Marie's house (next week they would meet at Laura's, and after that at Jen's, and so on down the line) ; the subject for discussion tonight was "Work."

The room was large, softly lit, comfortably furnished. After 10 or 15 minutes of laughing, chatting, note and book exchanging, the women arranged themselves in a circle, some on chairs, some on the couch, others on the floor. In the center of the circle was a low coffee table covered with a coffeepot, cups, sugar, milk, plates of cheese and bread, cookies and fruit. Marie suggested they begin, and turning to the woman on her right, who happened to be Dolores, asked if she would be the first.

Dolores (*the unemployed college dropout*): I guess that's okay. . . . I'd just as soon be the first . . . mainly because I hate to be the last. When I'm last, all I think about is, soon it will be *my* turn. (*She looked up nervously.*) You've no idea how I *hate* talking in public. (*There was a long pause; silence in the circle.*) . . . Work! God, what can I say? The whole question has always been absolute hell for me. . . . A lot of you have said your fathers ignored you when you were growing up and paid attention only to your brothers. Well, in my house it was just the opposite. I have two sisters, and my father always told me I was the smartest of all, that I was smarter than he was, and that I could do anything I wanted to do . . . but somehow, I don't really know *why*, everything I turned to came to nothing. After six years in analysis I still don't know *why*. (*She looked off into space for a moment and her eyes seemed to lose the train of her thought. Then she shook herself and went on.*) I've always drifted . . . just drifted. My parents never forced me to work. I needn't work even now. I had every opportunity to find out what I really wanted to do. But . . . nothing I did satisfied me, and I would just stop. . . . Or turn away. . . . Or go on a trip. I worked for a big company for a while. . . . Then my parents went to Paris and I just went with them. . . . I came back . . . went to school . . . was a researcher at *Time-Life* . . . drifted . . . got married . . . divorced . . . drifted. (*Her voice grew more halting.*) I feel my life is such *waste*. I'd like to write, I really would; I feel I'd be a good writer, but I don't know. I just can't get going. . . . My father is so disappointed in me. He keeps hoping I'll really do something. *Soon.* (*She shrugged her shoulders but her face was very quiet and pale, and her pain expressive. She happened to be one of the most beautiful women in the room.*)

Diana (*the housewife*) : *What do you think you will* do?

Dolores (*in a defiant burst*) : Try to get married!

Jen (*the unemployed actress*) and Marie (*the copywriter*) : Oh, no!

Claire (*the computer programmer*) : After all that! Haven't you learned yet? What on earth is marriage going to do for you? Who on earth could you marry? *Feeling* about yourself as you do? Who could save you from yourself? Because that's what you *want*.

Marilyn (*the school teacher*) : That's right. It sounds like "It's just too much to think out so I might as well get married."

Lucie (*the graduate student*) : Getting married like that is *bound* to be a disaster.

Jen: And when you get married like that it's always to some creep you've convinced yourself is wonderful. So understanding. (*Dolores grew very red and very quiet through all this.*)

Sheila (*the legal secretary*) : Stop jumping on her like that! I know *just* how she feels. . . . I was *really* raised to be a wife and a mother, and yet my father wanted me to do something with my education after he sent me to one of the best girls' schools in the East. Well, I didn't get married when I got out of school like half the girls I graduated with, and now seven years later I'm *still* not married. (*She stopped talking abruptly and looked off into the space in the center of the circle, her attention wandering as though she'd suddenly lost her way.*) I don't know how to describe it exactly, but I know just how Dolores feels about drifting. I've always worked, and yet something was always sort of confused inside me. I never really kenw which way I wanted to go on a job: up, down, sideways. . . . I always thought it would be the most marvelous thing in the world to work for a really brilliant and important man. I never have. But I've worked for some good men and I've learned a lot from them. But (*her dark head came up two or three inches and she looked hesitantly around*) I don't know about the rest of you, but I've always wound up being propositioned by my bosses. It's a funny thing. As soon as I'd be doing really well, learning fast and taking on some genuine responsibility, like it would begin to excite them, and they'd make their move. When I refused, almost invariably they'd begin to *browbeat* me. I mean, they'd make my life miserable! And, of course, I'd retreat. . . . I'd get small and scared and take everything they were dishing out . . . and then I'd move on. I don't know, maybe something in my behavior was really asking for it, I honestly don't know any-more. . . .

Marie: There's a good chance you *were* asking for it. I work with a lot of men and I don't get propositioned every other day. I am so abso-lutely straight no one *dares*. . . . They all think I am a dike.

Sheila (*plaintively*): Why is it like that, though? Why are men like that? Is it something they have more of, this sexual need for ego gratifi-cation? Are they made differently from us?

Jen (*placing her coffee cup on the floor beside her*): No! You've just never learned to stand up for yourself! And goddammit, they *know* it, and they play on it. Look, you all know I've been an actress for years. Well, once, when I was pretty new in the business, I was playing opposite this guy. He used to feel me up on the stage. All the *time*. I was scared. I didn't know what to do. I'd say to the stage manager: That guy is feeling me up. The stage manager would look at me like I was crazy, and shrug his shoulders. Like: What can I do? Well, once I finally thought: I can't stand this. And I bit him. Yes, I bit the bastard, I bit his tongue while he was kissing me.

A Chorus of Voices: You *bit* him????

Jen (*with great dignity*): Yes, dammit, I bit him. And afterwards he said to me, "Why the hell did you do that?" And I said, "You know goddam well why I did that." And do you know? He respected me after that. (*She laughed.*) Didn't *like* me very much. But he respected me. (*She looked distracted for a moment.*) . . . I guess that is pretty funny. I mean, biting someone's tongue during a love scene.

Veronica (*the assistant TV producer*): Yeah. Very funny.

Laura (*the journalist*): Listen, I've been thinking about something Sheila said. That as soon as she began to get really good at her job her boss would make a pass—and that would pretty much signal the end, right? She'd refuse, he'd become an S.O.B., and she'd eventually leave. It's almost as if sex were being used to cut her down, or back, or in some way stop her from rising. An *instinct* he, the boss, has—to sleep with her when he feels her becoming really independent.

Lucie (*excitedly*): I'll buy that! Look, it's like Sampson and Delilah in reverse. *She* knew that sex would give her the opportunity to destroy his strength. Women are famous for wanting to sleep with men in order to enslave them, right? That's the great myth, right? He's all spirit and mind, she's all emotion and biological instinct. She uses this instinct with *cunning* to even out the score, to get some power, to bring him down —through sex. But, look at it another way. What are these guys always saying about women's liberation?—"All she needs is a good ——." They say that *hopefully*. *Prayerfully*. They know. We *all* know what all that "All she needs is a good ——" stuff is all about.

Claire: This is ridiculous. Use your heads. Isn't a guy kind of super if he wants to sleep with a woman who's becoming independent?

Marie: Yes, but not in business. There's something wrong every time, whenever sex is operating in business. It's always like a secret weapon, something you hit your opponent below the belt with.

Diana: God, you're all crazy! Sex is *fun*. Wherever it exists. It's warm and nice and it makes people feel good.

Dolores: That's a favorite pipe dream of yours, isn't it?

Sheila: It certainly doesn't seem like very much fun to me when I watch some secretary coming on to one of the lawyers when she wants a raise, then I see the expression on her face as she turns away.

Marie: God, that sounds like my mother when she wants something from my father!

Veronica (*feebly*): You people are beginning to make me feel *awful!* (*Everyone's head snapped in her direction.*)

Marie: Why?

Veronica: The way you're talking about using sex at work. As if it were so horrible. Well, I've *always* used a kind of sexy funniness to get what I want at work. What's wrong with that?

Lucie: What do you do?

Veronica: Well, if someone is being very stuffy and serious about business, I'll say something funny—I guess in a sexy way—to break up the atmosphere which sometimes gets so heavy. You know what I mean? Men can be so pretentious in business! And then, usually, I get what I want—while I'm being funny and cute, and they're laughing.

Diana (*heatedly*): Look, don't you see what you're *doing?*

Veronica (*testily*): No, I don't. What am I *doing?*

Diana (*her hands moving agitatedly through the air before her*): If there's some serious business going on you came in and say: Nothing to be afraid of folks. Just frivolous, feminine little me. I'll tell a joke, wink my eye, do a little dance, and we'll all pretend nothing's really happening here.

Veronica: My God, I never thought of it like that.

Laura: It's like those apes. They did a study of apes in which they discovered that apes chatter and laugh and smile a lot to ward off aggression.

Marilyn: Just like women! Christ, aren't they always saying to us: *Smile!* Who tells a man to smile? And how often do you smile for no damned reason, right? It's so *natural* to start smiling as soon as you start talking to a man, isn't it?

Lucie: That's right! You're right! You know—God, it's amazing!—I began to think about this just the other day. I was walking down Fifth Avenue and a man in the doorway of a store said to me, "Whatsamatta, honey? Things can't be *that* bad." And I was startled because I wasn't feeling depressed or anything, and I couldn't figure out why he was saying that. So I looked, real fast, in the glass to see what my face looked like. And it didn't look like anything. It was just a face at rest. I had just an ordinary, sort of thoughtful expression on my face. And he thought I was *depressed*. And, I couldn't help it, I said to myself: "Would he have said that to you if you were a man?" And I answered myself immediately: "No!"

Diana: That's it. That's really what they want. To keep us barefoot, pregnant, and *smiling*. Always sort of *begging*, you know? Just a little supplicating—at all times. And they get anxious if you stop smiling. Not because you're depressed! Because you're *thinking!*

Dolores: Oh, come on now. Surely, there are lots of men who have very similar kinds of manners? What about all the life-of-the-party types? All those clowns and regular guys?

Claire: Yes, what about them? You *never* take those guys seriously. You never think of the men of real power, the guys with serious intentions and real strength, acting that way, do you? And those are the ones with real responsibility. The others are the ones women laugh about in private, the ones who become our confidantes, not our lovers, the ones who *are just like ourselves*.

Sheila (*quietly*): You're right.

Lucie: And it's true, it really does undercut your seriousness, all that smiling.

Sheila (*looking suddenly sad and very intent*): And underscore your weakness.

Dolores: Yes, exactly. We smile because we feel at a loss, because we feel vulnerable. We don't quite know how to accomplish what we want to accomplish or how to navigate through life, so we act *feminine*. That's really what this is all about, isn't it? To be masculine is to take action, to be feminine is to smile. Be coy and cute and sexy—and maybe you'll become the big man's assistant. God, it's all so sad. . . .

Veronica (*looking a bit dazed*) : I never thought of any of it like this. But it's true, I guess, all of it. You know (*and now her words came in a rush and her voice grew stronger*), I've always been afraid of my job, I've always felt I was there by *accident*, and that any minute they were gonna find me out. Any minute, they'd know I was a fraud. I had the chance to become a producer recently, and I fudged it. I didn't realize for two weeks afterward that I'd done it deliberately, that I don't *want* to move up, that I'm afraid of the responsibility, that I'd rather stay where I am, making my little jokes and not drawing attention to myself . . . (*Veronica's voice fadad away, but her face seemed full of struggle, and for a long moment no one spoke.*)

Marilyn (*her legs pulled up under her on the couch, running her hand distractedly through her short blond hair*) : Lord, does *that* sound familiar. Do I know that feeling of being there by accident, any minute here comes the ax. I've never felt that anything I got—any honor, any prize, any decent job—was really legitimately mine. I always felt it was luck, that I happened to be in the right place at the right time and that I was able to put up a good front and people just didn't *know* . . . but if I stuck around long enough they would. . . . So, I guess I've drifted a lot, too. Being married, I took advantage of it. I remember when my husband was urging me to work, telling me I was a talented girl and that I shouldn't just be sitting around the house taking care of the baby. I wanted *so* to be persuaded by him, but I just couldn't do it. Every night I'd say: Tomorrow's the day and every morning I'd get up feeling like my head was full of molasses, so sluggish I couldn't *move*. By the time I'd finally get out of that damn bed it was too late to get a baby-sitter or too late to get to a job interview or too late to do anything, really. (*She turned toward Diana*). You're a housewife, Diana. You must know what I mean. (*Diana nodded ruefully*.) I began concentrating on my sex life with my husband, which had never been any too good, and was now getting really bad. It's hard to explain. We'd always been very affectionate with one another, and we still were. But I began to *crave* . . . passion. (*She smiled, almost apologetically*.) What else can I call it? There was no passion between us, practically no intercourse. I began to *demand* it. My husband reacted very badly, accused me of—oh God, the most awful things! Then I had an affair. The sex was great, the man was very tender with me for a long while. I felt *revived*. But then, a funny

thing happened. I became almost hypnotized by the sex. I couldn't get
enough, I couldn't stop thinking about it, it seemed to consume me; and
yet, I became as sluggish now with sexual desire as I had been when I
couldn't get up to look for a job. Sometimes, I felt so sluggish I could
hardly prepare myself to go meet my lover. And then . . . (*She stopped
talking and looked down at the floor. Her forehead creased, her brows
drew together, she seemed pierced suddenly by memory. Everyone remained quiet for a long moment.*)

Diana (*very gently*) : And then?

Marilyn (*almost shaking herself awake*) : And then the man told my
husband of our affair.

Jen: Oh, Christ!

Marilyn: My husband went wild . . . (*her voice trailed off and again
everyone remained silent, this time until she spoke again*). He left me.
We've been separated a year and a half now. So then I *had* to go to work.
And I have, I have. But it remains a difficult, difficult thing. I do the
most ordinary kind of work, afraid to strike out, afraid to try anything
that involves real risk. It's almost as if there's some *training* necessary for
taking risks, and I just don't have it . . . and my husband leaving me,
and forcing me out to work, somehow didn't magically give me whatever
it takes to get that training.

Laura (*harshly*) : Maybe it's too late.

Diana: Well, that's a helluva thought. (*She crossed her legs and stared
at the floor. Everyone looked toward her, but she said no more. Jen
stretched, Claire bit into a cookie, Lucie poured coffee and everyone
rearranged themselves in their seats.*)

Marie (*after a long pause*) : It's your turn, Diana.

Diana (*turning in her chair and running thin hands nervously through
her curly red hair*) : It's been hard for me to concentrate on the subject.
I went to see my mother in the hospital this afternoon, and I haven't been
able to stop thinking about her all day long.

Jen: Is she very sick?

Diana: Well, yes, I think so. She underwent a serious operation yesterday—three hours on the operating table. For a while there it was
touch and go. But today she seemed much better and I spoke to her. I
stood by her bed and she took my hand and she said to me: "You need
an enormous strength of will to live through this. Most people need
only one reason to do it. I have three: you, your father and your grandmother. And suddenly I felt furious. I felt *furious* with her. God, she's
always been so strong, the strongest person I know, and I loved her for it.
I felt like saying to her: "Why don't you live for yourself?" I felt like

saying: "I can't take this burden on me! What are you doing to me?" And now suddenly, I'm here, being asked to talk about work, and I have nothing to say. I haven't a goddamn thing to say! What do I do? After all, what do I *do*? Half my life is passed in a fantasy of desire that's focused on leaving my husband and finding some marvelous job. . . . At least, my mother worked *hard* all her life. She raised me when my real father walked out on her, she put me through school, she staked me to my first apartment, she never said no to me for anything. And when I got married she felt she'd accomplished *everything*. That was the end of the rainbow. . . .

Dolores (*timidly*) : What's so terrible, really, your mother saying she lived for all of you? God, that used to be considered a moral virtue. I'm sure lots of men feel the same way, that they live for their families. Most men *hate* their work. . . .

Marilyn: My husband used to say that all the time, that he lived only for me and the baby, that that was everything to him.

Lucie: How did you feel about that? What did you think of him when he said it?

Marilyn (*flushing*) : It used to make me feel peculiar. As thought something wasn't quite right with him.

Lucie (*to Diana*) : Did you think something wasn't *quite right,* when your mother said what she said?

Diana (*thinking back*) : No. It wasn't that something wasn't quite right. It seemed "right," if you know what I mean, for her to be saying that, but terribly wrong suddenly.

Lucie: That's odd, isn't it? When a man says he lives for his family it sounds positively unnatural to me. When a woman says it, it sounds so "right." So expected.

Laura: Exactly. What's pathology in a man seems normal in a woman.

Claire: It comes back, in a sense, to a woman always looking for her identity in her family and a man never, or rarely, really doing that.

Marie: God, this business of identity! Of wanting it from my work, and not looking for it in what my husband does. . . .

Jen: Tell me, do men ever look for their identities in their wives' work?

Veronica: Yes, and then we call them Mr. Streisand. (*Everybody breaks up, and suddenly cookies and fruit are being devoured. Everyone stretches and one or two women walk around the room. After 15 minutes. . . .*)

Marie (*peeling an orange, sitting yogi-fashion on the floor*) : I first went to work for a small publicity firm. They taught me to be a copywriter, and I loved it from the start. I never had any trouble with the people in that firm. It was like one big happy family there. We all worked well with each other and everyone knew a bit about everybody else's work. When the place folded and they let me go I was so depressed, and so *lost*. For the longest time I couldn't even go out looking for a job. I had no sense of how to go about it. I had no real sense of myself as having a transferable skill, somehow. I didn't seem to know how to deal with Madison Avenue. I realized then that I'd somehow never taken that job as a period of preparation for independence in the world. It was like a continuation of my family. As long as I was being taken care of I functioned, but when I was really on my own I folded up. I just didn't know how to operate. . . .And I still don't really. It's never been the same. I've never had a job in which I felt I was really operating responsibly since that time.

Sheila: Do you think maybe you're just waiting around to get married?

Marie: No. I don't. I know I really want to work, no matter what. I know that I want some sense of myself that's not related to a husband, or to anyone but myself, for that matter. . . . But I feel so lost, I just don't know where it's all at, really. (*Five or six heads nodded sympathetically*.)

Claire: I don't feel like *any* of you. Not a single one.

Dolores: What do you mean?

Claire: Let me tell you something. I have two sisters and a brother. My father was a passionately competitive man. He loved sports and he taught us all how to play, and he treated us all exactly as though we were his equals at it. I means, he competed with us exactly as though we were 25 when we were 8. Everything: sailing, checkers, baseball, there was nothing he wouldn't compete in. When I was a kid I saw him send a line drive ball right into my sister's stomach, for God's sake. Sounds terrible, right? We loved it. All of us. And we thrived on it. For me, work is like everything else. *Competitive*. I get in there, do the best I can, compete ferociously against man, woman or machine. And I use whatever I have in the way of equipment: sex, brains, endurance. You name it, I use it. And if I lose I lose, and if I win I win. It's just doing it as well as I can that counts. And if I come up against discrimination as a woman, I just reinforce my attack. But the name of the game is competition.

(*Everyone stared at her, openmouthed, and suddenly everyone was talking at once; over each other's voices; at each other; to themselves; laughing; interrupting; generally exploding*.)

Laura (*dryly*): The American dream. Right before our eyes.

Diana (*tearfully*): Good God, Claire, that sounds awful!

Lucie (*amazed*): That's the kind of thing that's killing our men. In a sense, it's really why we're here.

Sheila (*mad*): Oh, that love of competition!

Marie (*astonished*): The whole idea of just *being* is completely lost in all this.

Jen (*outraged*): And to act sexy in order to compete! You degrade every woman alive!

Veronica (*interested*): In other words, Claire, you imply that if they give you what you want they get *you?*

Diana (*wistfully*): That notion of competition is everything we hate most in men, isn't it? It's responsible for the most brutalizing version of masculinity. We're in here trying to be men, right? Do we want to be men at their worst?

Lucie (*angrily*): For God's sake! We're in here trying to be *ourselves*. Whatever that turns out to be.

Marilyn (*with sudden authority*): I think you're wrong, all of you. You don't understand what Claire's really saying. (*Everyone stopped talking and looked at Marilyn.*) What Claire is really telling you is that her father taught her not how to win but how to lose. He didn't teach her to ride roughshod over other people. He taught her how to get up and walk away intact when other people rode roughshod over *her*. And he so loved the idea of teaching *that* to his children that he ignored the fact that she and her sisters were girls, and he taught it to them, anyway. (*Everyone took a moment to digest this.*)

Laura: I think Marilyn has a very good point there. That's exactly what Claire has inside her. She's the strongest person in this room, and we've all known it for a long time. She has the most integrated and most *separate* sense of herself of anyone I know. And I can see now that that probably has developed from her competitiveness. It's almost as though it provided the *proper* relation to other people, rather than 'no relation.

Sheila: Well, if that's true then her father performed a minor miracle.

Jen: You're not kidding. Knowing where *you* stand in relation to other people, what you're supposed to be doing, not because of what other people want of you but because of what you want for yourself . . . *knowing* what you want for yourself . . . that's everything, isn't it?

Laura: *I* think so. When I think of work, that's really what I think of most. And when I think of *me* and work, I swear I feel like Ulysses after 10 years at sea. I, unlike the rest of you, do not feel I am where I am because of luck or accident or through the natural striving caused by a healthy competitiveness. I feel I am like a half-maddened bull who keeps turning and turning and turning, trying to get the hell out of this maze he finds himself in. . . . I spent 10 years not knowing what the hell I wanted to do with myself. So I kept getting married and having children. I've had three children and as many husbands. All nice men, all good to me, all meaningless to me. (*She stopped short, and seemed to be groping for words. . . .*) I wanted to *do* something. Something that was real, and serious, and would involve me in a struggle with myself. Every time I got married it was like applying Mercurochrome to a festering wound. I swear sometimes I think the thing I resent most is that women have always gotten married as a way out of the struggle. It's the thing we're encouraged to do, it's the thing we rush into with such *relief*, it's the thing we come absolutely to *hate*. Because marriage itself, for most women, is so full of self-hatred. A continual unconscious reminder of all our weakness, of the heavy price to be paid for taking the easy way out. Men talk about the power of a woman in the home. . . . That power has come to seem such a lopsided and malevolent thing to me. What kind of nonsense is that, anyway, to divide up the *influences* on children's lives in that bizarre way? The mother takes care of the *emotional* life of the child? The vital requirement for nourishment? Out of what special resources does *she* do that? What the hell principle of growth is operating in *her*? What gives a woman who never tests herself against structured work the wisdom or the self-discipline to oversee a child's emotional development? The whole thing is crazy. And it nearly drove me crazy. . . . What can I say? For 10 years I felt as though I were continually vomiting up my life. . . . And now I work. I work hard and I work with great relish. I want to have a family, *too*. Love. Home. Husband. Father for the children. Of course, I do. God, the loneliness! The longing for connection! But work first. And family second. (*Her voice split wide open in a big grin*). Just like a man.

Lucie: I guess I sort of feel like Laura. Only I'm not sure. I'm not sure of anything. I'm in school now. Or rather "again." Thirty years old and I'm a graduate student again, starting out almost from scratch. . . . The thing is I could never take what I was doing seriously. That is, not as seriously as my brother, or any of the boys I went to school with, did. Everything seemed too long, or too hard, or too something. Underneath it all, I felt sort of *embarrassed* to study seriously. It was as if I was really feeling: "That's something the *grownups* do. It's not something for *me* to do." I asked my brother about this feeling once, and he said most men felt the same way about themselves, only they fake it better than women do. I thought about that one a long time, and I kept trying to say myself: What the hell, it's the same for them as it is for us. But . . . (*she looked swiftly around the circle*) it's not! Dammit, it's *not*. After all, style is content, right? And ours are worlds away. . . .

Veronica: Literally.

Lucie: I don't know. . . . I still don't know. It's a problem that nags and nags and nags at me. So often I wish some guy would just come along and I'd disappear into marriage. It's like this secret wish that I can just withdraw from it all, and then from my safe position look on and comment and laugh and say yes and no and encourage and generally play at being the judging mother, the "wise" lady of the household. . . . But then I know within six months I'd be miserable! I'd be climbing the walls and feeling guilty. . . .

Marilyn: Guilty! Guilty, guilty. Will we *ever* have a session in which the word guilty is not mentioned once? (*Outside, the bells in a nearby church tower struck midnight.*)

Diana: Let's wrap it up, okay?

Veronica (*reaching for her bag*): Where shall we meet next week?

Marie: Wait a minute! Aren't we going to sum up? (*Everyone stopped in mid-leaving, and sank wearily back into her seat.*)

Lucie: Well, one thing became very clear to me. Every one of us in some way has struggled with the idea of getting married in order to be relieved of the battle of finding and staying with good work.

Diana: And every one of us who's done it has made a mess of it!

Jen: And everyone who *hasn't* has made a mess of it!

Veronica: But, look. The only one of us who's really worked well—with direction and purpose—is Claire. And we all jumped on her! (*Everyone was startled by this observation and no one spoke for a long moment.*)

Marilyn (*bitterly*): We can't do it, we can't admire anyone who *does* do it, and we can't let it alone. . . .

Jen (*softly*): That's not quite true. After all, we *were* able to see finally that there was virtue in Claire's position. And we *are* here, aren't we?

Marie: That's right. Don't be so down. We're not 102 years old, are we? We're caught in a mess, damned if we do and damned if we don't. All right. That's exactly why we're here. To break the bind. (*On this note everyone took heart, brightened up and trooped out into the darkened Manhattan streets. Proof enough of being ready to do battle.*)

49

THE LABORATORY TRAINING MODEL: RATIONALE, METHOD, AND SOME THOUGHTS FOR THE FUTURE

Bernard Lubin, Ph.D.

Professor and Director of Training in Psychology, Department of Psychiatry, University of Missouri School of Medicine at Kansas City

and

William B. Eddy, Ph.D.

Professor, School of Administration, University of Missouri at Kansas City

The laboratory training method, as Bunker notes, ". . . had its beginnings in the wedding of social action and scientific inquiry" (1965, p. 131). Since its inception in 1947, laboratory training has exerted an important influence on developments within a number of fields, including education, industry, religion, community development, and volunteer and professional agencies.

The definition of laboratory training as an educational method, which gathered momentum from its roots in the field of research and theory

Reprinted from THE INTERNATIONAL JOURNAL OF GROUP PSYCHOTHERAPY, Volume XX, July 1970, No. 3, pp. 305-339.

The authors wish to thank Leland P. Bradford, Jerry B. Harvey, Alice W. Lubin, Kurt Olmosk, David Peters, Oron South, Duane Thomas, and F. Lee Van Horn for their assistance.

in social psychology, can be traced from its inception (Benne, 1964; Bradford, 1967). Within the past few years, however, the definition has become less clear as a result of the tendency by the public and some professionals to use interchangeably such terms as laboratory training groups, sensitivity training groups, T-groups, encounter groups, therapy groups, etc. Part of the confusion arises from the development in recent years of a large number of experimental groups and part from recent developments in the laboratory training method itself.

The laboratory training model refers to a range of experience-based learning activities in which participants are centrally involved in goal setting, observing, feeding back, analyzing data, planning action or change steps, evaluating, etc. Data which are within the learning situation itself provide the material for learning. The format may take a number of forms; the best known form, the "laboratory," has the character of a conference. It is the form that will be discussed in this paper.

The laboratory consists of ". . . different groupings of participants with differing technologies of training in the service of various learning objectives. Staff members are in continuous communication in order to establish and maintain relationships among the parts of the laboatory experience. As the laboratory proceeds in time, participants are brought together in integrating sessions designed to help them relate the parts of their overall laboratory experience. Integration of learnings becomes a central concern for participants in work on problems of application of laboratory learnings in their home situations" (Benne, 1964, pp. 108-109).

"Laboratory" has been used on occasion as a synonym for T-group, and vice versa. The T-group is an important component of the laboratory and is crucial for certain types of learnings. It is one of the "groupings" referred to by Benne above, but using the term as a synonym for the overall laboratory contributes to the confusion of terms.

This paper attempts, where possible, to differentiate laboratory training from therapy groups and encounter groups. An historical overview, information on rationale and method, and some thoughts for the future are presented.

HISTORICAL OVERVIEW

The intellectual climate of the third and fourth decades of the twentieth century was optimistic, pragmatic, and oriented toward exploring the use of social-psychological knowledge and methods in the solution of social problems. This was the period when John Dewey made his contributions. Also, during this period, the social-emotional components of the educational process were recognized.

The workshop method of teaching and learning began in the summer of 1936 at Ohio State University (Diederich and Van Til, 1945) and was quickly recognized as an educational vehicle that accelerated the productivity of participants as they worked on solutions to practical problems. At about this same time (1938), Ronald Lippitt and Ralph White, under the direction of Kurt Lewin, conducted their well-known studies on autocratic, laissez-faire, and democratic leadership. Kurt Lewin, during this period, was experimenting with the potential of the small group for changing attitudes and behavior. He developed field theory and was engaged in various action-research projects. For several years during this period, Leland P. Bradford was exploring and developing improved methods for use in adult education. While in the same period, at Teachers College, Columbia University, Kenneth D. Benne had become convinced ". . . that the social-psychological processes of building a community out of conflicting orientations were a part of the basis for building informed and authoritative decisions leading to effective action" (Bradford, 1967, p. 129).

In the relationship that developed between these men over the next half a decade was the basis for collaboration in the summer of 1946. During the summer of 1946 the Connecticut Interracial Commission, the Connecticut Department of Education, and the Research Center for Group Dynamics (then at M.I.T.) jointly sponsored a training-research workshop at the State Teachers College in New Britain, Connecticut. The purpose of the workshop was to develop more effective local leaders to assure the success of the Fair Employment Practices Act. The Research Center for Group Dynamics was to conduct research on the effects of workshop experience and the later application of learnings.

Participants invited to the workshop were mainly from teaching and social work backgrounds. Kenneth D. Benne, then at Columbia University, Leland P. Bradford of the National Education Association, and Ronald Lippitt of the Research Center for Group Dynamics (R.C.G.D.) comprised the training staff; Kurt Lewin, R.C.G.D., Ronald Lippitt, and three graduate students in social psychology who served as research observers (Morton Deutsch, Murray Horwitz, and Melvin Seeman) were the research staff.

The design of the workshop initially consisted of three ten-member groups discussing back-home problems. Role-playing was used for diagnostic clarification and for practice of potential solutions. Using pretested schedules, a research observer in each group coded interactions and behavioral sequences for the purpose of reporting in the evening meeting to the training staff—*not* to the small groups.

A few participants who requested permission to attend the evening staff meeting were allowed to do so. Their obvious interest in, and involvement with, the observer's feedback of the interactional data attracted other participants. Soon all participants were attending the evening staff meetings and reporting that they were much more interested in the interactional data than in the substantive discussions around which the observations were made and that these observations were helping them to understand their own behavior and the development of their groups.

In 1947, with the direct sponsorship of the National Education Association and the Research Center for Group Dynamics of M.I.T., the above-named training staff organized a three-week summer session at Gould Academy in Bethel, Maine.[1] An isolated "cultural island" location was selected because of Lewin's conviction that change was more likely if the usual situational forces which acted to resist change could be left behind.

The Basic Skills Training Group (BST) was included in this three-week summer session. It contained an observer who fed back behavioral data for the group discussion. A staff member referred to as the training leader assisted the group to evaluate the observations made by the observer, as well as data supplied by the participants in the group.

Benne (1964) summarizes the expectations that the staff held for the BST groups:

> In the first place, one of its functions was to help members internalize some more or less systematic sets of concepts. One was a schema of deliberate or planned change and the skills required by the agent of such change. Another set had to do with indices and criteria of group development which in turn presupposed knowledge of and sensitivity to a rather complex set of group variables.
>
> A second expectation was that the group would provide practice in diagnostic action skills of the change agent and of the group member and leader. Skill practice, through role playing, thus played a fairly heavy part in the methodology of BST Groups in 1947 and 1948.
>
> A third expectation was that the behavioral content would run the gamut of "human organization" from the interpersonal level and the group level to the intergroup level (both in formal organizations and

---

[1] Bethel, Maine is synonymous with laboratory training for many people because it began there and for a number of years it was the only site where it took place. Over the past ten years, however, the number of sites at which laboratory training is conducted has continued to increase. The 1970-71 NTL Institute announcement lists laboratories of various kinds conducted in more than fifty locations throughout the United States, Canada, Mexico, Great Britain, and Europe.

in "communities"). There resulted a competition between discussing here-and-now happenings which of necessity focused on the personal, interpersonal, and group levels, and discussing outside case materials. This sometimes resulted in the rejection of any serious consideration of the observer's report of behavioral data. More often, it led eventually to rejection of outside problems as less involving and fascinating.

A fourth expectation was that the BST Group would help its members to plan the application of laboratory learnings to back-home situations and to plan for continuing growth for themselves and their associates. A fifth expectation was that members would gain a more objective and accurate view of themselves in their relations to other persons in the group and to the developing group as a whole.

A sixth expectation was that participants would develop a clearer understanding of democratic values. These values were to be operationalized in terms of principles of methodology for functioning as a leader or member of a group and as an initiator and facilitator of change.

A seventh expectation was that members of the BST Group would not only acquire skills and understandings to help them function more adequately as change agents and as group members but that they would also acquire trainer skills and understandings required for communicating these to others [pp. 85-87].

Although this set of expectations was soon seen as overly ambitious and unrealistic for accomplishment in one session, the experience was to generate more than twenty years of experimentation with objectives, groupings, technologies, and client systems.

The BST Group evolved into the T-group. "Two Periods in T-group Evolution" are delineated by Benne (1964):

> The first period, roughly from 1949 through 1955, is marked by a variety of experimental attempts to create training formats and technologies to serve learning objectives seen as extraneous to those peculiarly within the province of the T-group [training group]. This led at times to virtual segregation of T-group activities. Separate groupings were formed for skill practice, for application of laboratory learnings, and for the study of change, among other activities. Sometimes, separate staff units for handling T-group activities and nonT-group activities were recruited. This experimentation was greatly aided by two large grants from the Carnegie Corporation of New York for the development of NTL's program.
>
> The second period, roughly from 1956 to the present, is marked by efforts to reintegrate T-group experiences into the designs of laboratories. Experimentation with new designs and with new uses of T-groups continues [pp. 87-88].

Bradford's comments (1967) [2, 3] tie together the historical developments of laboratory training and the organizational development of the NTL Institute:

> [The first period (1949 through 1955)] . . . saw a variety of efforts to solve the problems of multiple learnings. Community case studies, skill clinics, large-meeting experimentation, conference planning, massive total-laboratory role playing for a week at a time of a complicated community problem were all experimentations in the more difficult task of training change agents to work in large and complicated social systems.
>
> In recent years, separate programs in community leadership, conflict management, and consultation skills have been directed toward this problem.
>
> During the 1950's three trends came into being. Regional Laboratories emerged autonomously: the Western Training Laboratory, the Pacific Northwest Laboratory, the Intermountain Laboratory for Group Development, and the Boston University Summer Laboratory. Some have now merged or collaborated with NTL as a national program has steadily grown.
>
> The second trend was the development of occupational laboratory sessions held during the year—most notably in the fields of industry and religion. . . .
>
> Another trend, beginning in the late 1950's, has been that NTL and Network members have been engaged increasingly as change agents in organizational growth and development. . . .
>
> The 1960's have seen the extension of NTL activities into many new social and occupational areas leading toward the establishment of the five Centers: (1) Center for Organization Studies; (2) Center for the Development of Educational Leadership; (3) Center for Community Affairs; (4) Center for the Development of Leadership in Government; and (5) Center for International Training.[4] All of these are part of the new NTL Institute for Applied Behavioral Science [pp. 141-142].

Regional development continues. The Midwest Group for Human Resources based in Kansas City, Missouri, is now the Midwest Division of the NTL Institute, and metropolitan offices have been opened in Chicago, Illinois, and Portland, Oregon, with movement toward develop-

---

[2] The history of laboratory training in the United States is predominantly the history of the NTL Institute for Applied Behavioral Science. We have drawn to a large extent from published material by the NTL Institute and its faculty who are based at various universities.

[3] Leland P. Bradford has been Executive Director of the NTL Institute for Applied Behavioral Science since its inception in 1947.

[4] During the past year, two new Centers have been opened, the Center for a Voluntary Society and the Black Affairs Center.

ment of regional centers in Northern California, San Diego, California, New York City, and Atlanta, Georgia.

Over the past fifteen years a number of people from Europe and Great Britain have participated in various NTL laboratories and trainer development programs and have developed laboratory training activities on their return home. NTL maintains a close relationship with the European Institute for Transnational Studies in Group and Organizational Behavior, many of whose members have served on the staff of NTL laboratories. For a number of years, staff members of the Tavistock Institute and other educational and training facilities throughout the world have served as staff members of NTL Institute programs, thereby facilitating considerable interchange of ideas and technologies.

Regional development has facilitated creativity in programming by providing opportunity for experimentation and field testing of new designs. The Midwest Group for Human Resources-NTL, in its Midwest Executive Development Laboratory, has developed a unique, experience-based learning situation for managers which devotes a substantial portion of the second week to the issue of human problems involved in merging organizations (Eddy et al., 1968).

The Western Training Laboratory has produced the philosophical underpinning for what is now called the "Laboratory with a Personal-Interpersonal Emphasis." The "Self in Process" model of training (Weschler et al., 1962) was developed by three members of the NTL Network on the faculty of the Graduate School of Business Administration, UCLA: Irving R. Weschler, Fred Massarik, and Robert Tannenbaum. The model was instrumental in branching some training activities away from the group process model.

Following are the authors' statements of rationale and desired learning outcomes for their method:

> The network of social relationships which vitally influences our lives is replete with contradictory demands and inconsistencies. These not only take their toll of the clinically recognized psychotic, but they also affect the lives of most of us who seem to be getting along tolerably well with the world and the people around us.
>
> While the obviously ill often are pushed with irrevocable force toward seeking a solution for their acute discomfort, the rest of us relatively healthy individuals find ourselves in a dilemma. In most respects we seem adjusted in our day-by-day activities. We appear to behave appropriately with regard to the demands made upon us by our families, friends, and jobs. Yet this appearance is deceptive. Internal doubts and schisms persist. As no convenient learning vehicle is typically available to the 'pseudo-healthy' person, tensions below the

surface debilitate realization of potential capacities, stunt creativity, infuse hostility into a vast range of human contact, and frequently generate hampering psychosomatic problems.

Our recent approach to sensitivity training represents one means for facilitating the personal growth of persons who, while 'normal' by most accepted cultural standards, may indeed be affected in subtle and complex ways by these very standards. For us (and, no doubt, for many others), sensitivity training is no longer primarily a technique for the improvement of group functioning, the development of interpersonal skills, the intellectual discussion of human relations problems, or the more surface discussion of neurotic manifestations. (It should be noted that in the early 1950's the predecessor to our present UCLA program was called "Skill Practice in Supervision.") Rather, sensitivity training is now pointed in the direction of total enhancement of the individual.

Our version of sensitivity training increasingly concerns itself with strengthening of the individual in his desires to experience people and events more fully, to know himself more intimately and accurately, to find a more significant meaning for his life, and to initiate or sustain a process of individual growth toward ever-increasing personal adequacy.

We are beginning to deal with life values which come to be deeply reflected in the total pattern of a person's attitudes and behavior. We are involved, for instance, with his tendency to control or be controlled by others, with his management of anger, with his ability to express and receive love or affection, with his feelings of loneliness, with his search for personal identity, with his testing of his own adequacy, and with other similar concerns. Any one of these themes is typically of somewhat greater personal significance to one person than to another, yet each is likely to have real meaning to all, as they go through a training experience together.

Consideration of these issues in training involves two concurrent processes—the group's activities may revolve around the exploration and personal experiencing of the meaning of these values, often without using the specific labels, while theory sessions may deal explicitly with these same issues. Thus, our present training methods touch on live values both in the language of feelings and behavior and by efforts to spell out underlying concepts in cognitive terms [pp. 34-35].

Although this approach de-emphasizes group-level learning, it is important to note that the authors, while championing the role of affect, retain an important status for the role of cognition and understanding.

During recent years NTL-Institute for Applied Behavioral Science has responded to the diversity of participant and staff interests, the broad range of emphases that seem to be technically feasible within the laboratory and T-group format, and the rich fund of skills, both within and

TABLE 1

BASIC LABORATORIES IN HUMAN INTERACTION

DESIGN FOCUS	INDIVIDUAL AND ORGANIZATIONAL RELEVANCE	EXPERIENCES
PERSONAL AND INTERPERSONAL	more openness and honesty in dealing with self and others/reduced defensiveness and game-type behavior/increased ability to learn from one's own behavior/expanded awareness to growth potential/increased awareness of racially conditioned feelings and attitudes	T-Groups Nonverbal Painting Improvisation and fantasy Body movement Interpersonal confrontation Racial confrontation
	improved communication with others/development of new ways of working with others/locating feelings that block satisfactory and effective relationships, and bringing these out for examination/working for creative resolution to conflict	

INTERGROUP	effects on your behavior when your group is working with another group/looking at you, loyalties in multigroup operations/diagnosing intragroup problems brought on by intergroup work/examining the effect of different racial mixtures	T-groups
		Competitive and
		  collaborative exercises
		Observation of groups
		Conflict models
		Multiple loyalty simulations
		Construction of
		  conceptual models

	examining intergroup consultation, cooperation, and competition (corresponds to interdepartmental relationships in a firm)/how changes can be made between groups/looking at payoffs for collaboration and competition/conceptualizing and confronting conflict, including that generated by racial differences	

GROUP	increasing ability to act in different ways in a group and to live with different types of group climate, including that in which race is a problem/getting feedback on your group style and work methods/using your own feelings to help understand group process/feeling freer in groups	T-groups
		Role analysis
		Cluster and large groups
		Team building
		Consultation
		Helping relationships
		Construction of
		  conceptual models
		Group problem-solving
		  exercises

	understanding stages of group life and development/leadership and membership in groups (such as departments, task forces, teams, classes)/learning why some problems get "solved" over and over, and why some decisions don't stick/constructive methods for dealing with problem members/experimenting with different methods for handling racially generated problems	

outside the NTL network of trainers. In their public laboratories (sometimes called "stranger laboratories"), which are residential conferences of from one to two weeks in length offered throughout the year at various locations, NTL now offers labs at different levels and with considerable variation within each level.

The most recent NTL announcement lists types of Basic Human Interaction Laboratories, their design focus, their individual and organizational relevance, and the type of experiences that are likely to be included (see Table 1).

A number of additional basic training experiences of a specialized nature are listed, as well as eight different advanced laboratories and six professional development programs.

The trend toward greater differentiation of laboratories acknowledges the wide diversity in client needs and permits the development of more organic and concentrated laboratory designs.

RATIONALE AND METHOD

Even a few years ago the practice of laboratory training outstripped the development of sound theory. Today the gap has widened considerably. The situation seems to us to be very much analogous to that of group psychotherapy. And similar to the situation in the field of group psychotherapy, there are a number of theories about the method of learning in laboratory training. Only bits and pieces of these theoretical structures, however, have received empirical test. (For statements of theory, the reader is referred to Bennis and Shepard [1956], Bradford et al. [1964], Schein and Bennis [1965], Mann [1967], Hampden-Turner [1966], and Argyris [1968].)

We have decided to present a few of the assumptions which guide the design and conduct of laboratories and some hypotheses about the process of attitudinal change. The assumptions are highly synoptic and contain within them meta-assumptions about the nature of the generalized client, his needs, and the potentiality of the laboratory situation to relate to these learning needs. They are intended to be illustrative, not necessarily representative.

1) Participants have been culturally conditioned to inhibit the expression of the emotional aspects of their communications, thus reducing interpersonal effectiveness.

The laboratory method legitimizes feelings and facilitates experiencing, expressing, and examining the emotional aspects of communication.

2) Participants, however well they may function interpersonally, have

developed resistances against attending to certain classes of cues about the effect of their behavior on others. Thus, their potential for learning newer, more functional behaviors is inhibited.

The laboratory provides an opportunity for each participant to receive information about how his behavior is seen and to learn about his impact on others.

3) Even though participants might have opportunities in everyday life situations to receive such information as mentioned above, it is extremely difficult for them to feel free enough to practice new behavior because of the real or imagined high risk involved.

The laboratory sanctions, encourages, and provides opportunities for the practice and analysis of new behavior.

4) Although participants function more or less well in leadership and membership roles in a variety of groups back home, the press of substantive factors in their groups and other considerations make it unlikely that they have opportunities to examine important dimensions of the group at work (decision making, communication, problem solving, etc.) and their own performance in relation to these group dimensions.

The laboratory, especially those with a group or organizational focus, can and does provide opportunities, both structured and unstructured, to learn about the many forces at work in groups and to study one's own performance in relation to these forces.

5) Participants may have considerable cognitive knowledge about the "principles" of leadership, communication, group dynamics, etc. However, they may not be able, for a variety of reasons, to translate the knowledge into action.

The experience-based laboratory approach may help them to operationalize their knowledge.

Schein and Bennis (1965) have addressed themselves to the manner in which attitudinal change takes place in laboratory training. The model would seem to be heuristically useful and consonant with several theories.

> Essentially, the model specifies that attitude change consists of three stages or phases which correspond closely to what Lewin identified as the stages of change: (1) unfreezing, (2) changing, and (3) refreezing. The first two of these stages are necessary conditions of change, the third is concerned with the stability of whatever change occurs. Under each of these stages, we can identify certain key mechanisms, as follows:
>
> *Stage 1.* Unfreezing
>   1. Lack of confirmation or disconfirmation.
>   2. Induction of guilt-anxiety.

    3. Creation of psychological safety by reduction of threat or removal of barriers to change.

Stage 2. Changing
    1. Scanning the interpersonal environment.
    2. Identifying with a model.

Stage 3. Refreezing
    1. Personal—integrating new responses into the rest of the personality and attitude system.
    2. Relational—integrating new responses into ongoing significant relationships.

    . . . attitude change begins with a dis-equilibrium, with some information about a person that leaves him uncomfortable because it is unexpected or violates his image of himself. Often such disconfirming information leaves him feeling anxious or guilty. In order for change to occur, however, some psychological safety must be present in the situation or else the person will simply become defensive and more rigid. Though this process sounds somewhat cognitive, we wish to emphasize the basically emotional features of becoming unfrozen.

    If the person comes to feel safe, he will begin to seek some new information about himself which will allow him cognitively to redefine some beliefs about himself or his relationships to others. Such new information will be obtained by one of two basic mechanisms: (1) scanning the available interpersonal environment for relevant cues, (2) identifying with some particular other person whose beliefs seem to be more viable.

    The changee, in other words, may begin to try to view himself from the perspective of another person or from the perspective of an array of others. As his perspective, his frame of reference, shifts, he develops new beliefs about himself which, in turn, lead to new feelings and behavioral responses.

    If these new feelings and responses fit well with the rest of the person's personality and attitudes and/or if they are confirmed or reinforced by others, a new cycle of unfreezing and changing is initiated until the person finds attitudes (feelings, beliefs, and responses) which do fit and which are reinforced [pp. 275-276].

A major short-coming of most theories is that they do not deal adequately with the phenomenology of the participant (Lieberman et al., 1969). Schein and Bennis (1965) touch on this area when they attempt to account for some of the factors producing participant discomfort at the beginning of the laboratory or in its early sessions:

    Tensions have different sources: (1) dilemmas created by the unfreezing forces—how to establish a viable identity in the group, how to control others, how to insure that the group goals will include his own needs, and how to keep the group discussion at an appropriate level of intimacy; (2) the heightened consciousness of self that brings with it the possibility of discovering something within himself that will prove to be unacceptable; (3) the actual possibility of getting honest reactions to himself from others, which have always been relatively unavailable and may prove to reveal unacceptable parts of himself, or worse, may prove himself to be entirely unacceptable; (4) defensive reactions to feedback already obtained, either because it was hostile and retaliatory or because it was too threatening; (5) the belief or assumption that he may not be able to change behavior which is unacceptable to others (therefore it may be better not to learn about it in the first place) ; (6) the belief or assumption that feedback is always evaluative and always deals with inadequacies or things that are wrong [p. 301].

The initial tension soon dissipates as participants have opportunities to test assumptions, apprehensions, and fantasies against the reality that they observe. Different sets of tensions replace some of the initial ones; the latter seem to be associated with intercurrent events in the group, stages of self-discovery, and the vicissitudes of various interpersonal relationships.

Some questions that are frequently raised:

How are T-Groups opened? The laboratory typically opens in a general session in which, among other things, the broad objectives are stated, staff are introduced, group rosters are distributed, etc. This may or may not be followed by some warm-up activity.

The first few minutes of the first T-group session requires some statement from the trainer regarding himself and the group. The statement is usually quite brief and is usually distorted by participants as a result of their state of tension. Opening trainer statements vary according to the values of the trainer, the nature of the laboratory (emphasis), and the sense of urgency that the trainer feels in helping to establish certain norms. A few examples follow:

> This group will meet for many hours and will serve as a kind of laboratory where each individual can increase his understanding of the forces which influence individual behavior and the performance of groups and organizations. The data for learning will be our own behavior, feelings, and reactions. We begin with no definite structure or organization, no agreed-upon procedures, and no specific agenda. It will be up to us to fill the vacuum created by the lack of these familiar elements and to study our group as we evolve. My role will be to help the group to learn from its own experience, but not to act as a traditional chairman nor to suggest how we should organize, what our procedure should be, or exactly what our agenda will in-

clude. With these few comments, I think we are ready to begin in whatever way you feel will be most helpful [NTL Institute News and Reports, 1969a].

This opening would seem appropriate for several types of laboratories (Basic Human Interaction Laboratories, Group Emphasis Laboratories, Organization Development Laboratories).

In labortories which emphasize personal-interpersonal learning, the following T-group opening might be appropriate:

> We will meet together in this group for a number of sessions in order to deepen our understanding of who each of us is and how we relate to each other. In order to accomplish this, we will need, as much as possible, to try to communicate openly with each other and share our reactions, feelings, and perceptions. I see my role as that of a facilitator rather than the usual leader. From time to time, I might suggest an activity that I think would be helpful, but it is important to remember that it is only a suggestion—as anyone else can make at any time in here. Now we need to find a way to begin.

If the laboratory has an emphasis such as "Laboratory in Conflict Resolution," and if the trainer is concerned that the T-group achieve an organic integrity with the rest of the laboratory, he might mention in his opening statement that the T-group, in addition to other possibilities, can provide opportunities for each person to learn directly from the T-group experience about conflict resolution. On the other hand, he might think that it would be wiser to omit the statement and, instead, give special attention to that class of phenomena as it occurs.

Trainers vary as to how much value they place on the initial floundering of the group after the opening statement. Most agree that it is important for the group to experience the fact that they have developed a great deal of dependence upon familiar structural properties of groups (designated leader, agenda, etc.). Some feel the need to assist the group in beginning to establish the experiential "here and now" norm. In this case, the trainer might say something along the line of:

> We can talk about anything we want to in here. But the more we keep our discussions within the group—our feelings, reactions, what's going on here, among us—the more will we be using this situation for our learning.

Regardless of the form that the opening takes, subsequent trainer interventions can be seen as influencing the development of group norms. Psathas and Hardert (1966) present some interesting data on trainer interventions and normative patterns in seven T-groups. They found that trainer interventions having to do with ". . . norms pertaining to the categories of Analyzing Group Interaction or Process, Feelings, Feedback, and Acceptance Concern . . . are the most frequent (in this order)" (pp. 165-166).

Later, they speculate:

> One norm-category may show a high frequency because establishing this behavior is a necessary prerequisite for later group development. Another norm-category may show its highest frequency only when conditions are so favorable that an intervention can have its greatest impact and the norm is most likely to develop. The occurrence of a critical incident in the group could also serve to crystallize an operating norm to which the trainer may later have to labor to direct the group's attention. His interventions can be concerned with directing the group to reexamine its procedures and revise its operating norm, particularly if these are not compatible or consistent with other norms he seeks to develop [p. 167].

How are participants selected? Selection is not a suitable concept for describing the process by which participants are admitted to laboratories. Descriptive materials about the laboratories are widely distributed and applications from individuals are accepted. For laboratories oriented toward specific occupations and levels within organizations, applicants must meet the stated criteria.

In NTL Institute programs, however, emphasis has recently increased in regard to being explicit with applicants about the purpose and nature of programs. Policy is defined in the manual on "Standards for the Use of Laboratory Method in NTL Institute Programs" (1969) in the following excerpts:

> . . . Institute programs should be directed to the specific purposes and needs of the client group as they are agreed upon by consultant and client. They should be designed to include only those processes and techniques appropriate to the agreed-upon purposes and needs [1969, p. 6].
>
> Insofar as it is possible to distinguish between education and psychotherapy, NTL Institute programs are applied for educational, not psychotherapeutic, purposes. The Institute does not design or conduct programs to cure or alleviate pathological, mental, or emotional conditions [1969, p. 7].
>
> 1. Programs using laboratory method are deemed appropriate for persons of any age, occupation, or educational level, provided they are designed and conducted in keeping with the standards presented in this paper.

2. A person undergoing psychotherapy or intensive counseling should consult his therapist before enrolling in a laboratory training program.

3. Persons in the following categories should not ordinarily participate in a laboratory training program:

Those whose participation is based primarily on the wishes or demands of another, e.g., an employer, rather than on any degree of personal motivation.

Those whose goal in participating would be to cure or alleviate a severe mental or emotional disturbance.

Those with a significant history of incapacitating response to interpersonal stress.

To the limited extent that personal difficulties are predictable and screening procedures make it possible, prospective participants should be screened for these conditions [1969, p. 9].

The policy is operationalized in printed materials announcing programs. The brochure announcing the 1970 NTL Institute programs points out, for example, that "NTL Institute Programs are not designed or intended as psychotherapy or as a substitute for psychotherapy. Nor are the training laboratories to be construed as professional preparation for conducting laboratory training." A typical brochure statement might say, "These programs are intended to assist successful, normally functioning persons to further increase their effectiveness in understanding and working with others."

As the considerable amount of research being conducted on laboratory training progresses, it may be possible to spell out more definitively some of the screening criteria. Argyris (1964) has discussed some issues to be taken into account when evaluating potential participants:

People who learn in T-groups seem to possess at least three attributes:

1. A relatively strong ego. . . .

2. Defenses which are sufficiently low to allow the individual to hear what others say to him (accurately and with minimal threat to himself), without the aid of a professional scanning and filtering system (that is, the therapist, the educator).

3. The ability to communicate thoughts and feelings with minimal distortion.

. . . [Those who profit from training laboratory are] . . . relatively healthy individuals capable of learning from others how to enhance their degree of effectiveness . . . [p. 67].

No one should be encouraged to attend a laboratory as an act of administrative discipline, e.g., "to get him straightened out." Organizations which have a program of routinely supporting laboratory attendance for people at certain levels should make every effort to insure that attendance is voluntary. One method might be to have several optional development programs available to the individual, including laboratory training.

Undoubtedly, the issue of who should or should not attend training laboratories needs additional consideration.

Trainer Development and Certification

In the early stages, those who took trainer roles in NTL programs transferred their skills from fields such as adult education, group dynamics, and clinical psychology. But as the popularity of the approach increased and additional resource persons were needed, it became necessary to conceptualize the trainer role more objectively and to develop training programs for trainers. Benne (Bradford et al., 1964, pp. 110-113) recalls that during the first ten years of its operation NTL depended primarily upon an apprenticeship system to train new trainers. The usual model was for persons holding doctorates in one of the social sciences to attend a laboratory as a participant and then to act as co-trainer in a number of programs before assuming full responsibility for a group. Later several "training of trainer" programs were held for laboratory alumni and other specialized groups.

The first formalized internship program was held in Bethel during the summer of 1960. It combined participation in a laboratory, co-training experience, and seminars on the various theoretical and methodological issues relevant to training. Subsequent intern programs have followed the same general format. Emphasis is placed upon competence in personal and interpersonal understanding and interaction, as well as mastery of cognitive material. Currently, NTL conducts internships in Applied Behavioral Science and in Group Leadership primarily for behavioral scientists interested in becoming professional trainers. In addition, there are a variety of programs in organization development, planned change, educational consultation, and community change intended for persons who plan to occupy training and consulting roles within their own organizational settings.

A number of university graduate programs have also provided training techniques and related skills, either as a part of doctoral programs in social science fields or as an elective minor focus. Some of the schools that have, at varying times, provided trained personnel to the laboratory training field include Boston University, M.I.T., University of Michigan,

UCLA, University of Cincinnati, Case Western Reserve University, and University of Kansas.

Throughout the history of laboratory training there has been continuing concern with the problem of standards for qualifications and conduct of trainers. NTL has never accredited trainers in a formal sense. Professionals elected as Associates or Fellows in the NTL Institute have usually completed one of the internship programs and thus have been screened at several stages. However, admission to associateship or fellowship status means that the individual has entered the resource pool from which staffs for NTL labs and other programs will be drawn, not that he has been certified. This condition, however, is often misunderstood, and membership in NTL is sought by many individuals who wish to enhance their professional legitimacy in the training field. There is, in this sense, "de facto" certification being carried on.

As one step toward clarification of the criteria for trainer qualification the NTL Institute has recently ratified by Board action and published a statement entitled "Standards for the Use of the Laboratory Method in NTL Institute Programs" (1969). One section deals with standards for trainers and consultants *who represent the NTL Institute and/or hold staff roles in NTL programs.*

Standards for Trainers and Consultants

1. NTL Institute endorses the *Ethical Standards of Psychologists* of the American Psychological Association and urges its members to guide their conduct accordingly.

2. In relationships with individual clients and client groups, persons representing NTL Institute are expected to discuss candidly and fully goals, risks, limitations, and anticipated outcomes of any program under consideration.

3. NTL Institute trainers and consultants are expected to endorse the purposes and values and adhere to the standards presented in this paper.

4. NTL Institute trainers and consultants are expected to have mastered the following skills:

Ability to conduct a small group and to provide individual consultation using the theory and techniques of laboratory method.

Ability to articulate theory and to direct a variety of learning experiences for small and large groups and for organizations.

Ability to recognize their own behavior styles and personal needs and to deal with them productively in the performance of their professional roles.

Ability to recognize symptoms of serious psychological stress and to make responsible decisions when such problems arise.

5. NTL Institute trainers and consultants are expected to have a strong theoretical foundation. This ordinarily implies graduate work in a behavioral science discipline or equivalent experience in the field.

6. NTL Institute trainers and consultants are expected to complete the following training experiences:

Participation in at least one NTL Institute basic Human Relations laboratory.

Supervised co-training with senior staff members.

Participation on laboratory staff with experienced trainers in programs for a variety of client groups.

Participation in an NTL Institute or university program specifically designed to train trainers.

[This sequence of activities usually requires a minimum of two years to complete].

7. NTL Institute trainers and consultants are expected to continually evaluate their own work, to seek individual growth experiences, and to contribute to the evaluation and development of the art and science of training and consultation.

NOTE: Basic human relations laboratories, executive development programs, and similar beginning-level programs are designed to help participants be more effective in personal and job roles, not to become trainers. No capabilities as a T-group trainer or consultant should be assumed as a result of participation in one or more basic laboratories or other short-term experiences [pp. 10-12].

Stress in Laboratory Training. Currently, there is a great deal of concern being raised by various persons concerning actual or potential psychological injury associated with laboratory training. Some of this concern seems to be genuinely motivated in terms of a wish to protect the public welfare, while the motivation in other instances, because of its "shotgun" approach, seems questionable.

One concern that has been mentioned is that laboratory training, in general, produces a pathologically high level of stress. What is the evidence? The only data on this subject as yet available comes from the study by Lubin and Zuckerman (1969). The most stressful level in four T-groups of an NTL Institute laboratory with a group emphasis was compared with the stress conditions in a six-hour, an eight-hour, and a twenty-four hour perceptual isolation experiment. The Multiple Affect Adjective Check List (Zuckerman and Lubin, 1965), a self-report instrument that measures anxiety, depression, and hostility, was used in the stress and nonstress conditions of the perceptual isolation studies; in the laboratory it was administered before the conference began and at the end of each T-group session. The most stressful session in the four T-groups was significantly lower on all three scales than the three perceptual isolation conditions.

When raw scores were converted to T scores according to the instrument's standardization sample, in the four T-groups no individual achieved a T score of 70 (psychometrically deviant), while each of the three perceptual isolation studies produced some T scores at that level (32%, 24%, and 31%).

Using this as a start, we are collecting data in other life situations said to be stressful for comparison purposes. Preliminary analysis seems to indicate, for example, that T-group stress (highest point of emotional arousal) is of the order of that experienced by college students just prior to an examination.

> NTL Institute records indicate that of 14,200 participants in its summer and industrial programs between 1947 and 1968, for 33 (.2%) the experience was stressful enough to require them to leave the program prior to its completion [NTL Institute News and Reports, 1969b].

The only other published figures are those from an intensive program of laboratory training in the YMCA:

> A systematic effort was made to track down each instance of allegedly severe negative experience in YMCA sensitivity training for professional staff. Out of the approximately 1,200 participants, four negative experience cases were finally identified [.3%]. Even for these four cases, however, the experience as a whole was not completely negative. Data gathered from careful interviews with the principals themselves, their work supervisors, their sensitivity group trainers, other group participants, and, where applicable, with clinicians working with the principals, indicate that for three out of four persons thus involved the disruptive experience actually turned out to be helpful and is now appraised by them as being a valuable learning experience which has enhanced their effectiveness as individuals and as YMCA Directors. In the fourth case, although the individual does not evaluate the experience as being a positive one for him, he has not been incapacitated by the experience and is continuing to do an effective job in his position as a YMCA Director [Batchelder and Hardy, 1968, pp. 83-84].

Jaffe and Scherl (1969) report on two cases of acute psychosis resulting from small-group activity. Although the title of the article contains the term T-group, the text refers in one case to a weekend experience which, by description, would seem to be more of an encounter group than a

T-group. The other situation, two weeks in length, was a leadership training experience "required by his company." Both situations are a bit unusual in the size of the reported T-groups (15 and 19).

Several branch societies of the American Psychiatric Association have requested their membership to report to a central register all casualties from the various kinds of small groups. We believe this to be a potentially useful activity, but unless data are collected systematically and in relevant detail, it is likely to produce more confusion than illumination. To tabulate the number of casualties from unspecified or improperly specified small groups would be similar to a statement about the number of people who had adverse reactions to "medications." We need to know about participant characteristics, the kind of small group, if possible the type of activity that seemed to precipitate the distress, the qualifications of the leader, etc. Such documentation would be important.[5]

Recognizing the fact that participants sometimes have medical needs while away from home, the NTL Institute over the past few years has been making available inresidence medical consultation in summer laboratories.

Laboratory Training in Comparison with Group Psychotherapy and Encounter Groups. In the opening section of this paper, a brief description of the components of a laboratory design was presented. Important for comparison purposes at this point is the fact that there is more than one T-group in the laboratory model, multiple groupings are used, multilevel learnings (personal, interpersonal, and, in some laboratories, group and organizational) are sought, prior staff planning attempts to match client learning needs with a range of group technologies, conceptualization of experience is encouraged, and opportunity for integration and discussion of transfer of learning to back-home situations is provided. Also, laboratory training is defined as an educational rather than a therapeutic procedure.

Laboratory Training Groups and Group Psychotherapy. Despite increasing variation in the practice of group psychotherapy (see Gottschalk and Pattison, 1969) the adult outpatient group seen in psychiatric clinics or community mental health centers still represents the mode and can be used as a point of comparison.

Scheidlinger (1967) described group psychotherapy as:

> . . . a psychosocial process wherein a trained practitioner (usually psychiatrist, psychologist, or social worker) utilizes the emotional

---

[5] The NTL Institute is currently conducting a national survey of training procedures and materials in order to evaluate their major values and limitations.

interaction produced in small, carefully planned groups to effect 'repair' of personality malformation in individuals specifically selected for this purpose.

Since group psychotherapy has, with very few exceptions, evolved from the general field of psychotherapy, its concepts and techniques naturally reflect this fact. There is, thus, first of all, a primary emphasis on curing individual mental ill health [p. 54].

It was this type of group that Frank (1964) had in mind when he made comparisons between it and the T-group with a group emphasis. Similarities that he found were: both emphasize the importance of accurate communication, both attempt to assist members to change attitude and behavior, responsible functioning of members is valued in both, early sessions in both are characterized by uncertainty about the group's purpose and lack of trust in the method used, early sessions in both reveal more than moderate tension in members, and "in both . . . the most useful meetings seem to be those in which there is an issue or 'focal conflict,' which is of interest to most or all of the members, and arouses their emotions. . . . Moreover, some of these issues are the same in both groups—such as conflict over dependence on versus rebellion against authority and between desire for and fear of closeness to peers" (p. 447).

Some of the differences between group psychotherapy and the group emphasis T-group as seen by Frank are: therapy group members are seen by themselves and others as having psychological problems and needing help, whereas T-group members are seen as relatively well-functioning individuals interested in improving old skills and learning new ones; attitudes which therapy attempts to modify are usually concerned with persons who are close to the patient and therefore more central and resistant to change, whereas the T-group attempts to modify more peripheral attitudes; the therapist is a much more central person than the trainer and dependency upon him continues to be strong throughout; and the T-group, focusing less upon the individual, evokes more moderate emotional responses.

To this list of differences can be added the fact that the group emphasis T-group deals almost exclusively with the "here and now" of group development and transactions among members, to the exclusion of genetic material. The therapy group, on the other hand, frequently searches for the factors associated with conflicts and perceptual distortions in the patient's past life experiences. Dreams, fantasy and discussion for the work of the therapy group. The patient in group therapy is not interested in and does not attend in order to learn about "groups." For of patients' relationships with people not in the group are very legitimate him the therapy group mainly exists as the medium through which the amelioration of his suffering or help with personal problems takes place. Conversely, the group emphasis T-group member has a high investment in learning about groups and improving his leadership and membership skills.

In the T-group which has a personal-interpersonal emphasis, one again finds members defined as relatively well-functioning people. They are primarily concerned with learning about themselves in interaction with others, and less concerned with group level learning. By definition, this type of T-group will deal with attitudes that are more central to members, e.g., life style and values. The personal-interpersonal T-group may include encountering methods, other nonverbal techniques, role play, the use of fantasy, etc., in addition to verbal discussion. The position of the trainer seems to be more central in the personal-interpersonal T-group than in the group emphasis T-group.

Laboratory Training Groups and Encounter Groups. Published accounts of encounter groups are largely anecdotal and/or autobiographical and do not contain a clear statement of theory or method. Encounter groups differ very much among themselves, partly because of the very central role of the leader. The uniqueness of his personal style and his inventiveness are highly prized and very influential. Otto and Mann (1968) have put together a series of articles, all within the domain of the encounter group movement. The title of the book, *Ways of Growth: Approaches to Expanding Awareness,* appropriately indicates the individualistic, currently nongeneralizable nature of the field. As Burton (1969) observes, "Encounter groups have been so busy being expressive that they have had little time to look to their theories" (p. ix).

Despite the many differences in approach of the various encounter groups, most of them have emerged from the existentialist and humanistic tradition and some of them have been heavily influenced by Eastern philosophy. Martin Buber, Viktor Frankl, Wilhelm Reich, and Fritz Perls are some of the progenitors frequently mentioned as sources of ideas and methods.

Encounter[6] group practitioners believe that man functions at a small fraction of his potential and that methods which remove blockages and release this potential enable him to integrate at substantially higher levels of functioning. The encounter has been defined as ". . . a sudden,

---

[6] For purposes of this paper, we consider the marathon group as an extended encounter group, for several of its features (therapeutic change goals, intensity, centrality of the leader, methods that circumvent the defenses, etc.) are similar to those of the encounter group.

spontaneous, intuitive meeting with another person in which there is an immediate sense of relatedness . . ." (Moustakas, 1967, p. 45). Perls et al. (1951) use this notion in a broader sense to include clear communication and contact between parts of the self. Such strategies as increasing sensory awareness, relaxation methods, fantasy and dream study, nonverbal games, physical contact, meditation, etc., are utilized to circumvent the restrictions maintained by the censoring ego, to enable participants to get in contact with early "feeling memories," to experience feelings at deeper levels, and to make the unconscious conscious. Encounter groups vary from those which emphasize somatopsychologic methods (Schutz, 1967) to those that are mainly verbal (Rogers, 1967). The group exists as the environment in which these activities take place. The group, however, is *not* the object of study.

The centrality of the encounter group leader and his prerogative to structure the experience of participants are accepted by participants. In contrast, participants in laboratory training are encouraged to examine their feelings about and their perceptions of the various roles that the trainer takes during the laboratory as part of the learning process.

The nature and timing of the feedback model utilized in the different types of groups seems to be another important factor. The study by Psathas and Hardert (1966) found that in the group emphasis T-group, trainer interventions regarding feedback were third in frequency among the norm categories throughout the lab and second in frequency during the middle of the lab. This confirms our impression that personal feedback is reinforced relatively later in the group emphasis T-group. Personal feedback is legitimized and reinforced early in the personal-interpersonal T-group.

In the encounter group, since the role of the leader is so central to what takes place in the group, the occurrence of feedback from peers is variable and depends upon the leader's style. In the gestalt encounter group, for example, the leader may work in a one-to-one manner with an individual for an extended period of time. It might be quite awhile before other group members have the opportunity to share impressions and feelings with the protagonist.

To recapitulate, laboratory training (including both the T-group with a group emphasis and the T-group with a personal-interpersonal emphasis) retains a strong tie to its origin as an educational method, is concerned with cognitive as well as affective learning, and values the ability of the participant to transfer learnings to the back-home situation. It differs from group psychotherapy (the form practiced in many adult outpatient clinics) in that lab participants are seen as relatively well-functioning individuals, repair and restoration of function are not among its objectives, the leader is less central to the process, and the perspective is upon current group developments and interpersonal transactions.

The T-group with a personal-interpersonal emphasis resembles some encounter groups in some of the methods that are used, but it deals less with personal-historical material and has more of an educational focus. Psychotherapists sometimes refer patients to encounter groups as a means of breaking through impasses and inhibitions, but the NTL Institute does not encourage attendance by this group of clients in its programs.

Encounter groups resemble therapy groups in the depth of participant change that is sought and in the centrality of the leader to the process.

The forthcoming report of the Task Force on Recent Developments in the Use of Small Groups of the American Psychiatric Association (*Encounter Groups and Psychiatry,* in press) notes an important point of contrast among T-groups, therapy groups, and encounter groups: "T-groups, springing from the field of social psychology, have behind them a long tradition of research in group dynamics. No comparable body of knowledge has been generated by group therapy, a field notoriously deficient in any systematic research. Thus, what is presently known of the basic science of group psychotherapy stems almost entirely from social-psychological research with task groups and T-groups; psychotherapy owes to the T-group much of its systematic understanding of such factors as group development, group pressure, group cohesiveness, leadership, and group norms and values. Furthermore, T-group research has elaborated a wealth of sophisticated research techniques and tools of which the group therapy field is now slowly availing itself . . . the variegated new forms of the encounter group are, of course, even less research-oriented than the group psychotherapy field" (p. 23).

Unlike NTL Institute laboratory training programs and group psychotherapy conducted by members of the American Group Psychotherapy Association, encounter group practitioners do not have a national organization which defines standards of practice and concerns itself with accreditation or certification. Many encounter group leaders are doctoral level professional people who conduct their activities in a manner that would be acceptable to various professional societies. On the other hand, the fact that there are no national standards is a matter of concern, for it permits anyone to conduct encounter groups. Moreover, encountering techniques, similar to hypnotic induction techniques, are powerful instruments and are simple to learn. There is no indication that leaders of encounter groups caution group members about potential hazards in the use of these techniques nor are distinctions made between client experience and experience designed for the development of encounter group leaders.

The call for a comparative analysis of the full range of groups concerned with "promoting personal growth, behavior modification, or development" issued by Lieberman, Lakin, and Whitaker (1969) is one with which we very much concur. This seems to be the most promising possibility for increasing our knowledge of process and outcome and of freeing practitioners of various persuasions from the bondage of their own rhetoric.

SOME THOUGHTS FOR THE FUTURE

Some of the readers of this *Journal* are probably interested in the more clinical aspects of laboratory training. Increasingly, the method is being used, for example, in training programs for group psychotherapists in order to provide trainees with information about how their behavior is perceived by others and to enable them to experience the effects of various group phenomena. However, the future of laboratory training will be concerned with broader issues. Predictable developments can be seen in the areas of system change, organizational development, temporary systems, social issues, and the new university.

System Change

Society's institutions are growing increasingly complex, more impersonal, and sometimes less relevant to human needs. Behavioral scientists are focusing upon complex systems and have begun to develop conceptual schemes and technologies intended to bring about constructive change. The late psychologist, Douglas McGregor, wrote a management classic entitled *The Human Side of Enterprise* (1960) in which he related Maslow's theory of human motivation (1954) to the relationship between the employee and his organization. Since that time there has been a progression of experiments in applying laboratory training and its allied technologies to the changing of systems. Increasing interest is developing in these conceptualizations and technologies.

One major approach has involved using laboratory training for managers of organizations. The assumption has been that managers who are more sensitive to the needs and feelings of peers and subordinates, more aware of their own styles, and more perceptive about the workings of social systems can build organizations which are both more humane and more productive.

The focus of change and development has begun to shift more directly from the individual to the social system within which he functions. There is growing consensus that re-education and behavior change are unlikely to endure unless the back-home environment supports and reinforces the new behavior and encourages continuing development. Thus, approaches that deal with changing the operations and norms of systems are being explored. It has become clearer in recent years, for example, that laboratory training must be conducted at top management levels where the organizational influence is greatest. There is every reason to believe that NTL Institute programs for presidents, key executives, and high-level managers of organizations are likely to expand.

At the level of community, the orientation is toward establishing community problem-solving and decision-making processes which will facilitate the development of a "more mentally healthy society."

There is evidence that a large proportion of the responses elicited from citizens to their "problems in living" involve indigenous resources outside the professional mental health ranks. The total community can usefully be viewed as a system of resources for dealing with a variety of human problems, including, but not limited to, those defined as "mental health" problems (Eddy et al., 1970).

Klein (1968) asserts that, "The community cannot remain only the setting in which mental health agencies operate; instead, it must become the essential source of mental health itself." He advocates the use of community development approaches, techniques of education (including laboratory methods), and strategies of social intervention as tools of change. He describes a variety of concepts and methods for instituting community development and change processes. These deal with such issues as building interorganizational collaboration, managing conflict, increasing citizen participation, and developing more viable approaches to understanding and solving problems.

Programs for individuals who can act as "change agents" in a variety of settings are increasing, and are likely to continue to do so. In addition to general programs in planned change, the NTL Institute and its affiliated organizations offer professional development programs in such areas as educational, community, and industrial change. A vocational role as "professional change facilitator" is emerging, and a clearer definition of this role will be available.

Organizational Development

Paralleling the focus upon system change, the emphasis upon organization development (OD) during the next decade undoubtedly will greatly expand. OD combines the theory and technology of laboratory training with the methodologies of organizational change and management education. Objectives of an OD project are:

1. To create an open, problem-solving climate throughout the organization.
2. To supplement the authority associated with role or status with the authority of knowledge and competence.
3. To locate decision-making and problem-solving responsibilities as close to the information sources as possible.
4. To build trust among individuals and groups throughout the organization.
5. To make competition more relevant to work goals and to maximize collaborative efforts.
6. To develop a reward system which recognizes both the achievement of the organization's mission (profits or service) and organization development (growth of people).
7. To increase the sense of "ownership" of organization objectives throughout the work force.
8. To help managers to manage according to relevant objectives rather than according to "past practices" or according to objectives which do not make sense for one's area of responsibility.
9. To increase self-control and self-direction for people within the organization [NTL Institute News and Reports, 1968, p. 1].

In the next decade, laboratory training methods will be applied with increasing sophistication (Davis, 1967) toward the basic aim of helping organizations more effectively use their own resources for organization renewal and problem solving.

Temporary Systems

Work and social relations are increasingly being carried out within the framework of temporary structures: committees, project teams, task forces, conferences, consulting relationships, etc. (Miles, 1964; Bennis and Slater, 1968). These temporary systems in communities and organizations frequently bring together persons with differing skills, roles, and backgrounds to pool their resources for more effective problem solving. If the attitudes, goals, and styles of the members happen to mesh in the right way, the group may be productive. If not, much potential is lost and disappointment in group work occurs. Often the problem is too important to justify leaving the development of teamwork to chance.

There are a variety of implications of temporary systems for organizations, but an issue directly related to laboratory training is that the skills of effective membership are frequently lacking. Individuals need to know how to move quickly into team relationships in which mutual trust, collaboration, and communication support satisfying and productive operations. The laboratory is, itself, a temporary system, and the analysis of the development of the laboratory and its small groups provides the participant the opportunity to learn more about the functioning of temporary systems. It allows him to examine his own behavior and feelings in such situations and the impact of these upon the functioning of the group. Organizations which are finding temporary systems an increasingly important aspect of their operation are relying on laboratory training or its variants (such as managerial grid training [Blake and Mouton, 1964]) to help their members develop skills and perspectives to operate effectively in team situations.

Social Issues

In addition to a general focus on system change, many behavioral scientists are committed to working on specific social problems through their research and action skills. Recent issues of the *Journal of Applied Behavioral Science,* a publication of the NTL Institute, have carried articles on such topics as helping teachers improve classroom group processes (Schmuck, 1968); consultation with a civil rights organization on its internal problems (Nadler, 1968); cross-cultural training for the Peace Corps (Harrison and Hopkins, 1967); planning behavior change in juvenile offenders (Lenrow, 1966); reinforcement of police neutrality in civil rights confrontations (Shellow, 1965); the reduction of prejudice (Rubin, 1967). Another important social application of the laboratory method is in the training of administrators and professional staff of comprehensive community mental health centers (Dupre and Lubin, 1970).

The variety and number of social problems to which laboratory training will be applied will continue to expand.

The New University for the Applied Behavioral Sciences

These challenges and the many more that will arise during the coming decade have led logically to the creation of a degree-granting educational institution which will train applied behavioral scientists to add to the more than 500 members of the NTL Institute network.

The formation of The New University for the Applied Behavioral Sciences, which will be located in the Washington, D.C., area, has been announced by the NTL Institute. Major organizational units of the university are: The NTL Institute, the College of Applied Behavioral Science, and the Institute for a Voluntary Society.

According to Leland P. Bradford, Executive Director, the purposes of the university will be: (1) To train postdoctoral scientists in the theory, processes, and skills of the application of behavioral science knowledge and method to practical problems, (2) to train paraprofessionals who are leaders on many levels and in many areas of the social scene as change agents, competent at their level to encourage and maintain necessary adjustments in their organizations, (3) to expand the theory, research, and model development of processes of change, (4) to develop collaborative "think tanks" consisting of scholars, researchers, and leading practitioners in order to facilitate the linkage necessary for change to take place, and (5) to continue to provide programs which will encourage social and organizational growth and development.

Applied behavioral scientists must come out of their university laboratories and use their knowledge to help society bring about the changes that must come if the many pressing problems are to be resolved. The new university seeks to develop scientists who are not only willing to come out of the laboratory but who know how to use their knowledge and skills to deal effectively with real social and organizational problems (Bradford, 1970).

Addendum

Since the publication of "The Laboratory Training Model: Rationale, Method and Some Thoughts for the Future," the following changes have occurred:

I. Dr. Vladimir A. Dupre has been appointed President of the NTL Institute for Applied Behavioral Science.

II. Early in 1971, the International Association of Applied Social Sciences (IASS) was incorporated as an organization independent of the NTL Institute. Purposes and objectives of the new Association are to encourage and improve the quality of professional practice in two areas of applied social science: (1) Education through the use of laboratory methods; and (2) Social system change through the use of laboratory methods.

Some of the activities in which IASS will engage are:

(1) Defining the discipline for each form of professional practice;
(2) Setting standards of competence and standards of ethical performance;
(3) Developing and applying procedures for admission of persons to membership in the Association on the basis of these standards;

(4) Developing and applying procedures for disciplining members;
(5) Protecting the public's interest in these two forms of social practice; and
(6) Protecting the profession and its members in the exercise of their professional responsibility.

III. The Midwest Group for Human Resources has completed its merger with the NTL Institute.

In the interest of greater efficiency, the management of midwest training and consulting activities of the NTL Institute has been moved to Chicago from Kansas City, Missouri.

IV. NTL Institute is programmatically moving in new directions emphasizing (1) professional and career development, (2) substantive research and development, (3) organization and system approaches to supplement individual change strategies, and (4) educational materials production through the establishment of an independent NTL-Learning Resources Corporation.

REFERENCES

ARGYRIS, C. (1964), T-Groups for Organizational Effectiveness. *Harvard Bus. Rev.*, 42: 60-74.
—— (1968), Conditions for Competence Acquisition and Therapy, *J. Appl. Beh. Sci.*, 4:147-177.
BATCHELDER, R. L., & HARDY, J. M. (1968), *Using Sensitivity Training and the Laboratory Method: An Organizational Case Study in the Development of Human Resources*. New York: Association Press.
BENNE, K. D. (1964), History of the T-Group in the Laboratory Setting, In: *T-Group Theory and Laboratory Method*, ed. L. P. Bradford, J. R. Gibb, and K. D. Benne. New York: John Wiley & Sons, pp. 80-135.
BENNIS, W. G., & SHEPARD. H. A. (1956), A Theory of Group Development, *Hum. Relat.*, 9:415-437.
——, & SLATER, P. E. (1968), *The Temporary Society*. New York: Harper & Row.
BLAKE, R. R., & MOUTON, J. S. (1964), *The Managerial Grid*. Houston: Gulf Publishing Co.
BRADFORD, L. P. (1967), Biography of an Institution. *J. Appl. Beh. Sci.*, 3:127-143.
—— (1970), Personal communication.
—— et al. (eds.) (1954), *T-Group Theory and Laboratory Methods: Innovation in Re-Education*. New York: John Wiley & Sons.
BUNKER, D. R. (1965), Individual Applications of Laboratory Training. *J. Appl. Beh. Sci.*, 1:131-148.
BURTON. A. (ed.) (1969), *Encounter: The Theory and Practice of Encounter Groups*. San Francisco: Jossey-Bass.
DAVIS, S. A. (1967), An Organic Problem-Solving Method of Organizational Change. *J. Appl. Beh. Sci.*, 3:3-21.
DIEDERICH, P. B., & VAN TIL, W. (1945), *The Workshop: A Summary of Principles and Practices of the Workshop Movement*. New York: Hinds, Hayden & Eldridge.
DUPRE, V. A., & LUBIN, A. W. (1970), *A Community Mental Health Workshop-Laboratory: A Report on the Experiential Sequences*. Washington, D.C.: NTL Institute.

EDDY, W. B., GLAD, D. D., & DUPRE, V. A. (1968), The Midwestern Laboratory for Executive Development. *Hum. Rel. Train. News,* 12, No. 3:3-5.

——, PAAP, S. M., & GLAD, D. D. (1970), Solving Problems in Living: The Citizen's Viewpoint, *Ment. Hyg.,* 4:64-72.

FRANK, J. D. (1964), Training and Therapy. In: *T-Group Theory and Laboratory Method,* ed. L. P. Bradford, J. R. Gibb, and K. D. Benne. New York: John Wiley & Sons, pp. 442-451.

GOTTSCHALK, L. A., & PATTISON, M. (1969), Psychiatric Perspectives on T-Groups and the Laboratory Movement: An Overview. *Amer. J. Psychiat.,* 126:823-839.

HAMPDEN-TURNER, C. M. (1966), An Existential "Learning Theory" and the Integration of T-Group Research. *J. Appl. Beh. Sci.,* 2:367-386.

HARRISON, R. L., & HOPKINS, R. L. (1967), The Design of Cross-Cultural Training: An Alternative to the University Model. *J. Appl. Beh. Sci.,* 3:431-460.

JAFFE, S. L., & SCHERL, D. J. (1969), Acute Psychosis Precipitated by T-Group Experiences. *Arch. Gen. Psychiat.,* 21:443-448.

KLEIN, D. C. (1968), *Community Dynamics and Mental Health.* New York: John Wiley & Sons.

LENROW, P. B. (1966), A Framework for Planning Behavior Change in Juvenile Offenders. *J. Appl. Beh. Sci.,* 3:237-303.

LIEBERMAN, M. A., LAKIN, M., & WHITAKER, D. S. (1969), Problems and Potential of Psychoanalytic and Group-Dynamic Theories for Group Psychotherapy. *This Journal,* 19:131-141.

LUBIN, B., & ZUCKERMAN, M. (1969), Level of Emotional Arousal in Laboratory Training. *J. Appl. Beh. Sci.,* 5:483-490.

MANN, R. D. (1967), *Interpersonal Styles and Group Development.* New York: John Wiley & Sons.

MASLOW, A. H. (1954), *Motivation and Personality.* New York: Harper & Bros.

MCGREGOR, D. (1960), *The Human Side of Enterprise.* New York: McGraw-Hill.

MILES, M. B. (1964), On Temporary Systems. In: *Innovation in Education,* ed. M. B. Miles. New York: Teachers College, Columbia University.

MOUSTAKAS, C. (1967), *Creativity and Conformity.* Princeton, N. J.: Van Nostrand.

NTL Institute News and Reports (1968), 2, No. 3:1-2. (Developed by Jack Fordyce and W. Warner Burke).

—— (1969a), 2, No. 2:1-2. (Taken from a paper written by Charles Seashore for the Mid-Career Education Project, Wayne State University, Department of Political Science, April, 1969.)

—— (1969b), 3, No. 4:1.

NADLER, E. B. (1968), Social Therapy of a Civil Rights Organization. *J. Appl. Beh. Sci.,* 4:281-298.

OTTO, H. A., & MANN, J. (eds.) (1968), *Ways of Growth: Approaches to Expanding Awareness.* New York: Grossman Publishers.

PERLS, F., HEFFERLINE, R., & GOODMAN, P. (1951), *Gestalt Therapy.* New York: Julian Press.

PSATHAS, G., & HARDERT, R. (1966), Trainer Interventions and Normative Patterns in the T-Group. *J. Appl. Beh. Sci.,* 2:149-169.

ROGERS, C. R. (1967), The Process of the Basic Encounter Group. In: *Challenges of Humanistic Psychology,* ed. J. F. T. Bugental. New York: McGraw-Hill.

RUBIN, I. (1967), The Reduction of Prejudice Through Laboratory Training. *J. Appl. Beh. Sci.,* 3:29-50.

SCHEIDLINGER, S. (1967), Current Conceptual and Methodological Issues in Group Psychotherapy Research: Introduction to Panel-Part I. *This Journal,* 17:53-56.

SCHEIN, E. H., & BENNIS, W. G. (1965), *Personal and Organizational Change Through Group Methods: The Laboratory Approach.* New York: John Wiley & Sons.

SCHMUCK, R. A. (1968), Helping Teachers Improve Classroom Group Processes. *J. Appl. Beh. Sci.*, 4:401-435.

SCHUTZ, W. C. (1967), *Joy: Expanding Human Awareness.* New York: Grove Press.

SHELLOW, R. (1965), Reinforcing Police Neutrality in Civil Rights Confrontations. *J. Appl. Beh. Sci.*, 3:243-254.

Standards for the Use of the Laboratory Method in NTL Institute Programs (1969), Washington, D. C.: NTL Institute.

WESCHLER, I. R., MASSARIK, F., & TANNENBAUM, R. (1962), The Self in Process: A Sensitivity Training Emphasis. In: *Issues in Human Relations Training,* Vol. 5 of National Training Laboratories Selected Reading Series ed. I. R. Weschler. Washington, D. C.: National Education Association, pp. 33-46.

ZUCKERMAN, M., & LUBIN, B. (1965), *Multiple Affect Adjective Check List: Manual.* San Diego, California: Educational and Industrial Testing Service.

50

STYLE AND SPIRIT OF THE THEME-CENTERED INTERACTIONAL METHOD

Ruth C. Cohn

Director, Workshop Institute for Living-Learning (New York City)

INTRODUCTORY NOTES

The theme-centered interactional group method is based on a conceptual framework of axioms, theories, hypotheses, principles and techniques. The liveliness and impact of the method is, however, significantly determined by a specific style which emphasizes fluidity, surprises, and interruptions. I will attempt to convey theory and techniques of the theme-centered interactional model as I conceived and conceptualized it in a writing style which reflects the spirit of a theme-centered interactional group. The writing style attempts to demonstrate the fluctuating movements toward and away from the theme as they appear in such a workshop.

The structure of the theme-centered interactional model emphasizes the importance of balancing three factors within a fourth:

1) the theme under discussion
2) the group
3) the individual
4) the environment and auspices under which the workshop takes place

The group leader guards the equilibrium of the dynamic process between these factors and uses his influence to shift balances in the interest of the progressing work. Group and leader, students and teachers are learning and teaching a theme while promoting awareness of their personal and interpersonal engagement and growth. Academic settings and organizational meetings concentrate on studying and communicating subject matter. However, learning does not proceed in a vacuum in the absence of a learner; neither does teaching. When students and teacher are fully concentrated—that is physically, emotionally and intellectually at one with themselves—studying proceeds without interference. If, however, people's divergent emotions, perceptions, thoughts and sensations are neglected or negated, interferences handicap the learning and communication process. The theme-centered interactional method gives precedence to the dissolving of distractions and disturbances in the learning process. I deduced this technique directly from psychoanalytic theory and practice which has established that work on resistances against the therapeutic process takes precedence over search and communication of any other factors. Dealing with resistance against the theme, the group, the leader and other personal disturbances help communication, learning and integration to proceed faster and more meaningfully. The totality of a person, the group and the circumstances are recognized and respected and intrapsychic and interpersonal disturbances are optimally prevented from undermining secretly the constructive work on hand.

In this article I will attempt to induce in the reader a feeling for the process of the theme-centered interactional group by giving precedence in time to personal and situational interferences during the writing process. However, this symbolic interaction is a present reality, while in writing, the audience, as the interactional partner, is invisible. The contact with the reader, therefore, is exclusively one of imagination.

You, the readers, are encouraged to get involved in this presentation, being aware of the content of reading as well as of your own incoming ideas and thought-splinters, physical sensations, emotions, and preoccupations. I believe that if you read this article as suggested, you will become acquainted with the theme-centered interactional method in an experiential way. This will facilitate studying the structure, concepts and techniques and will, so I hope, be an enjoyable experience by itself.

I want to write to you in the style of the theme-centered interactional group so as to reflect the fluidity of work processes and distractions, personal experience and theme-centered involvement. I would like you, in reading, to enter an experiment in reading as I enter an experiment in writing.

Learning and teaching occur in the here-and-now, never in the past and in the future. The past and the future can be brought into the here-and-now by thought and images. But the here-and-now is where I live and the vantage point from which I think back or look ahead.

Here and now I sit in a comfortable chair in a little attic room in a friend's house. I am warm. Outdoors it is cold. The little windows carry some ice-paintings, and tree branches wave in the sunny morning light. The wind bristles around the attic tower. I hear my friend's voices from downstairs.

I feel excited and a bit anxious. I know a lot about the theme-centered interactional method: its history, its philosophy, theory and applications. I spent many months in a cottage on top of a mountain trying to conceptualize that which I had done for years in order to teach it. But I do not know you, the invisible readers, for whom I write.

In writing to you, I must use my imagination as to who you may be: you are not here to tell me and a group what you expect, need, feel, sense, think, wish for. If you were in an interactional workshop with me and a group of maybe eight to twenty counselors or counselors to be and if I were the leader of this group, I might ask you to relax and to be silent for a few minutes. I might tell you to use a few minutes of this silence to think about the concept of counseling as you have learned or thought about and worked with . . . what you expect of yourself in the counseling profession and what you expect of this workshop series which I have set to be five two-hour sessions.

I would like to ask you, having read to here, to put down this book for five minutes and to *think* about what you know and have experienced in your work; and what you want to achieve in reading this particular article on the theme-centered interactional method. Take your time: think and reflect in the here-and-now on your experiences, knowledge, skills, thoughts about counseling, and your expectations for learning about the theme-centered interactional method.

I assume you tried to follow my directions. I meanwhile used my five minutes, in which I stopped writing, to imagine you, my group of readers. Maybe you followed my suggestion and put the book down. Maybe you were also able and willing to follow the instructions. Maybe you thought about other things. You may have wanted to concentrate on the task and succeeded; or you may not have wanted to try. One thing I am sure of, that you not only thought something or other but also had feelings about my suggestion which may be anticipation, joy, rage, indolence, impotence, excitement, boredom, etc. I also know that your physical being, your body, was involved in this venture—you were sitting, walking, lying down or standing up, feeling good or fatigued or pained.

Each muscle, limb, organ has been part of your five minutes of silence, some of it in awareness, some less so, some not at all.

If you were in a workshop with me, I might now say: "Please remain silent and switch your attention to something else: how does it *feel* to be in this group with colleagues whom you don't know (or do know, as the case may be) and to be asked to think about the theme you came for. How do you *feel* having been challenged to be silent and to think about counseling experiences and counseling theories in this group here and now?"

In a workshop group, I, too, would follow my own instructions. How do I feel in this group, thinking about the subject? I may feel comfortable and excited or anxious about how this group will react. I might look at each face and intuit or project into it my perception of what each person is feeling about my request. I might feel my stomach to be tense or my breathing heavy in fear of failure, or I might feel light and happy, expecting success and the fun of giving what I know and getting something new in return.

I would now like you to stop reading for another few minutes. I would like you to observe yourself the same way: how do you feel reading this article as you have? I am in my little sunny attic room. The house is quiet now. And you? I would like to know whether you are comfortable reading this, whether you are or are not following my suggestions, whether you are active, questioning, puzzled, furious . . . whether you shake your head, laugh at me, feel superior, or, maybe you feel the excitement of something new and promising. How do you feel in this relationship with me and the imaginary group over time and space? I fantasize a group of counselors and students reading this together, this sentence, "Please put the book down and feel whatever you feel about this book and the group you really are in, or the fantasy group of your own."

I have followed my own instructions to be aware of my feelings as I write about this method in its own style. As I fantasize you, I don't see a group in a circle, but figures in the fog of my mind—faces of men and women, perhaps twenty to forty years old. I see your clothes and positions—on chairs, on beds, in dormitories, in libraries, in subways, some in twos or threes, mostly alone. I feel like running out to you, to these foggy figures, asking you to please continue reading and try to follow this ebb-and-flow writing because I do not know of any other way to convey to you the essence of the theme-centered interactional group process.

I often start a workshop group with this "triple silence" technique. I ask the participants in a first period of silence to think about the theme they came for. After a few minutes I ask them to be aware of their feelings in this group and the challenge I have provided. In a third period of the same silence I bring a task to the group which connects the given theme to the present situation. This third suggestion is always carefully prepared in advance by fantasizing what kind of people the group is likely to consist of and what is my own purpose for this group?

For a group of counselors I would find some task to bring the idea of counseling into the immediacy of our gathering. So I imagine now that you are a workshop of counselors who do not know each other. My third suggestion in the silent period is: "Please remain silent and choose one of the participants to be your personal counselor. Tell him why you came to visit him and what you want to gain from this visit. Then reverse the situation. Choose another group member whom you would like to counsel. And imagine any reason why this counselee has come to you."

In this enforced long triple silence, as one of the techniques to open up a workshop series, I ask the group to perform three tasks:

1) to think about the theme they came for;
2) to experience and feel how it is to be in this group;
3) to connect a theme-oriented task with the present group.

After this third period of silence, I would say something like: "Let us now communicate about whatever we want to—the theme, my suggestions to you, your experiences, thoughts, feelings, whatever you want to communicate about. Please be your own chairman and try to get whatever you want to get from the group and to give to the group whatever you want to give. I will do the same being my own chairman, and the chairman of the group. Do interrupt when you are bored, distracted, angry or anything else which prevents you from full participation."

The group then might slowly or quickly communicate about their pent-up thoughts and feelings. They would relate to the various suggestions, preoccupations, concerns within the frame of reference of the theme and their personal and interpersonal involvements. The leader would recognize and accept everything that is being said, leaving room for a large variety of communications and relating them to the immediate situation, the theme or both.

At first sight, the multiplicity of intrapsychic and interpersonal processes as they weave in and out of the theme are confusing. Yet such a situation reflects all living processes. Nothing alive grows in simple sequence and abstract rational fashion.

Right now, I feel somewhat flat and discouraged. I miss a response. I do not know where to go from here. Nothing comes to my mind. My stomach feels empty—there is just a muted pain inside. Thoughts flash in and out of my mind. Suddenly I know what is needed. This experience right now illustrates something I wanted to talk to you about:

In the theme-centered interactional workshop, disturbances to the theme take precedence. If my stomach hurts or my mind goes blank because I resent the group leader or something that has been said, I cannot be fully involved in the study processes. I am not at one with myself; my body feelings, thinking, spirit, drives are compartmentalized. If any group member absents himself in anger, withdrawal, preoccupation, the whole group interaction loses something—some content, some coherence. Therefore, disturbances have to be dealt with. If one person's feelings are out of touch with the theme under discussion, the group suffers a loss. To bring this person back into the group as a participant, therefore, takes precedence over dealing with the theme. The group members are informed of this rule: each person is responsible for his attentiveness and participation, and if he is hurt, bored, angry or uninvolved, it is essential that he communicate this to the group. The closer each participant accepts and works within this rule, the more he asserts his right and responsibility for his autonomous and authentic participation. He acts as his own chairman. The group gains cohesion by each individual taking responsibility for giving to and in getting from the group what he needs to achieve with regard to himself and the theme. This is the essence, the belief in living-learning in group interaction: content is dead print or dead words unless living people bring it to life.

Distractions are taken seriously and worked through to the extent that they don't interfere with the work, or they can be assimilated into the theme and the discussion. Sometimes deeper disturbances need to be acknowledged. The loss of a lover or parent can, of course, not be worked through in a theme-centered workshop session, but acceptance of mourning feelings and their respectful recognition lessens their distractive impact.

Why, I imagine you ask me, do you start with these "triple silences?" Do you always do this? No, I don't. I start in various ways. But all ways have some principles and hypotheses in common. They are the base of the theme-centered interactional approach.

1) Man is a somatopsychic unit. All learning, teaching and studying are at their best when both soma and psyche are respected. Man has physical, emotional, intellectual and spiritual experiences, drives and needs. They are not packed into separate drawers or boxes, but repre-

sent facets of the same integrating unit: man. If any one faculty is touched by another intraphychic or interpersonal event, the entire person responds to this change.

2) Man is part of a social unit, i.e., he is interdependent. He is always in the process of taking in and giving out. He is neither totally self-sufficient nor totally dependent. His autonomy lies in the choice of the pattern of give and take.

The structure of a theme-centered interactional workshop group promotes awareness and use of these principles. All of my introductory procedures are geared to direct the participants' attention on the pertinent theme, on feelings and physical sensations, on group interaction and how these may be used in the here-and-now.

The choice of the initial structure depends on the specific group, the leader, the given environment and the theme.

The "triple silence" beginning of a workshop session works well with a new group, especially with alert and curious people who are eager to learn and study. It is not wise to choose an initial silence in groups where a great deal of anxiety or resistance can be anticipated. Young adults, however, who come for counseling, react well to a three-step silence technique. Non-voluntary groups require a rather direct approach; this is true also for adolescents. I may start a high school group whose problems are stated as difficulties in learning with a startling question such as "Have you ever turned on with anything?" And if some surprised and giggling answers have been given, continue with the next question, "Can you imagine that you could turn on with things such as American History or Mathematics?" Such simple questions contain emotional and intellectual challenges. There is rarely any difficulty in getting older children and adolescents to communicate on simultaneously personal and objective levels.

I once started a workshop with a group of teachers who were told by their authorities to participate in a workshop series. The teachers were suspicious of being judged or of in some way being spied on. I was aware of this fact before my first visit. On my way to the school, I reflected about possibilities to reduce the teachers' anxiety and distrust. I felt that any question or explanation would not relieve the situation. So I started off this session with a detailed history of my interest in education prior to and during my work as a psychoanalyst and how and why I had been recommended to this school system. This relatively lengthy introduction did not, of course, dispel the group's fears, but it reduced them sufficiently to make an initial contact.

I mentioned in my introductory statements that I use the words, "Be your own chairman." To be my own chairman as a group member means to take responsibility for getting and giving, in learning and teaching. It is my responsibility when I choose to speak up or to be silent, when I want to communicate or to observe and let things fall into place. As a group leader, I give and get like all other participants but *I function mainly as the guardian of the method* which keeps the group interaction, the theme and individual needs in balance.

I am trying to put myself in the role of the reader. Would these written words convey to me what the theme-centered interactional method could mean for me as a counselor in schools, agencies or organizations? I think I would have gained an inkling of it, at least of the initial procedure.

Without exception, a new group tends to direct all statements to the leader, at least for ten or twenty minutes. This group looks for approval, directives, answers. One person might say, for instance, in our imaginary theme-centered interactional group, in counseling, "I thought of some of my college kids who can't concentrate on their studies. I can't send all of them into psychotherapy and I don't know how to help them." I might respond to this by acknowledging it as an important question. Or I might ask for some concrete examples, to enlarge the question or to make it more specific. I might use similar examples from my practice. I will promote communication by personal interest, recognition of the validity of the statement by specificity or generalization, by re-stating the problem or making open-ended suggestions toward interaction. Another person might say, "I was terribly anxious during all this silence . . . I felt my heart beat like crazy." I might reply with my own feelings ("Sometimes I feel that way too—today I have been relaxed—or anxious," whatever the truth may be) or I might show interest in other people's reactions during that same period of silence. Or you might say, "I didn't come here to be silent. I expect you to teach me something about counseling" and I might reply "Yes, I'm teaching about counseling the best way I know of." Or perhaps you might say, "When you gave the directive of choosing somebody in this group to learn something from, I choose you: how do you deal with kids who take drugs?" And I might state perhaps among this group there is somebody who has a lot more experience with kids and drugs than I—let's find out about that.

All my responses are geared to be direct, realistic and, in the opening phase, to emphasize the positive elements of whatever is being said. This attitude creates a free and constructive group atmosphere. When the participants have experienced the group spirit as benevolent, all feelings, including the most disturbing and hostile ones, can be assimilated. Negativism and hatred can be integrated by a group when emotions are accepted as people's inalienable right to be recognized. We may confront another person with positive or negative judgments, with appreciation or disapproval, but realistic encounters grant, rather than deny, each person's right to his feelings even though we may want to influence them and channel them into different directions.

In psychotherapy, where more time is available, the reverse procedure of getting at hostile feelings right at the onset has been followed by most analysts, including myself. Under the impact of workshop experiences, I have lately tried to experiment with similar initial procedures in group therapy—that is, to establish a positive and accepting atmosphere with similar techniques in the first sessions of a new group therapy group. It seems to me that if we start from the platform of general acceptance of all emotions, flaws and negative elements within patients are easier to see and to assimilate than when we start in the depths of self-defeat and hostility.

For the first 10-20 minutes, I accept and even promote the "star relationship" to the leader. Everybody seems to direct his statements to me. I respond to everything anybody says by drawing out the positive elements of what has been said. Thereafter, invariably some interaction between group members ensues—the one-way directedness to the leader is broken up and interactional group communication takes place.

The group leader remains the guardian of the method and uses the interactional process in the service of the theme. If, for instance, in your group, two members would repeatedly state their dislike for each other, I would lead this event back to our theme "Counseling and Group Interaction": what do these fighting counselors do to each other? What do they gain or lose? How did this process come to pass? How does this handling of feelings relate to counseling and to the ability to learn in both peer and in authority relationships? How do you X, and you, Y, experience this fight and what does each group member feel and think about it? Make the rounds and let each person state his experiences and thoughts. What do we learn from this point about each person? Somebody may get stifled by watching a fight because his parents' fights seemed deadly. Another person might enjoy watching this fight because he has experienced fighting as a relief in the emotional dearth of his childhood. Such fights can be used by each individual to gain greater awareness about feelings of anger, dislike, etc.

As a leader, I might say, "Stay deeply with your feelings. Don't try to change them and see what happens to you." Or, "I see your left hand in a fist—follow the motion of your fist into the air. What does this motion bring out in you?" Or, "What about X made you that angry?"

The leader of an interactional theme-centered group has to keep the delicate balance between letting the group interaction go deep enough to be an important experience and not to drown in group interaction around deeper pathology. Pathology in interactional groups is dealt with as far as necessary for the group interaction but not as a theme in itself. Only in group therapy proper can pathology be the main theme.

It is evening and I feel unable to continue writing although I am still excited. I feel the need to read my friend what I already have written.

It is two weeks later. I am alone in my own apartment. It is 11 P.M. I am tired. But I would like to try working on this article—even if only for an hour. My daily work has left me without writing time.

The group leader of a theme-centered interactional group invariably goes through periods of peace and periods of unrest. There is a disquietude in holding the responsibility for the balance between the concerns of people and the theme. When do I interrupt? When do I gently shift communications by expressing myself with my own feelings and thoughts? When do I ask questions? When and how do I intervene? When do I ask a specific group member whether he would like to join the theme discussion or whether he needed to continue discussing his feelings? When do I interrupt a theme-discussion to point out process to the group? The groups generally express relief about intermittent, strongly-guided directions within a free-floating interaction around the theme. I feel that I work best with a minimal amount of anxiety which is concerned with the question whether the group has gone too deeply into academic discussion and conceptualization, or too deeply into interaction. There is content and process. The leader must steer the boat between the scylla of too much content and the charybdis of too much process. The leader's ability to interrupt and to re-direct is crucial for the functioning of the theme-centered workshop. In general, the "process party" is stronger than the "content party." People are generally more concerned with themselves, their own experiences, and other people, than about any work theme.

As a leader, I experience both the agreeable feelings that come from being admired, and the fear and hurt which come from the experience of criticism. It is necessary to accept both as part of the job of group leading and to be aware of the various feelings which accompany the work. I do not throw off any admiring or critical communications as "transference"—I try to discern any possible grain of truth and enjoy, regret, and shift correspondingly. When I work as a group therapist, I pick up transference and countertransference as important aspects of the therapeutic relationship. In theme-centered interactional workshops, I usually deal only with the reality considerations of the relationships.

When I started to work with the theme-centered interactional method, sub-group delegates came to me requesting that I split up the group, so that learning could proceed without the other sub-group's "nonsense." I remember groping with these confusing aspects of "group dynamics"— the splitting-up into sub-groups, which I can now deal with much better. Yet even now, after many years of practice, every session brings periods of confusion and attentive awaiting for the enlightenment of the moment when I will know how to re-establish group cohesion and balance.

Often in the beginning of a workshop, the group complains about the "lack of structure." To be told to take responsibility to his giving and getting in terms of theme does not at first strike people as a stringent structure. Yet it is a firm structure which promotes autonomy in living and learning and in living-learning. I feel personally very happy when I lead groups this way. I feel good because I experience myself as fully employed.

I am very tired. It is midnight. I feel like going on with my writing to you, but I really can't. Mozart sings on my left side, my right shoulder hurts—it may be a long time again till I can continue with my writing.

It has been six weeks since I started writing this article. I am back in the little attic room. I feel sad and heavy. A child died of leukemia, a friend lost her husband, a friend accused me of something. I am tired from having worked too much, traveled too much and slept too little. I pick up a booklet. Max Siegel says: "To live creatively is to live truthfully as one himself sees the truth."

My truth is a feeling of being stuck. My truth is the thought of a deadline for this article. My truth is the faith that I can go beyond the stuckness by allowing myself to be stuck, to be uncreative, to ride out the wave of being hollow and unalive, by not fleeing from the task in leaving the room again and joining the family and happy child noises from the park. My truth now is to stick it out.

This is agony. I feel embarrassed to let you read this. Yet also proud and truthful if I do. This is the kind of anxiety stuckness and confusion that is part of being a member or a leader of interactional groups. The truth as I see it is that all creative growth is a process which involves the excitement of potency and achievement, the anxiety of being stuck and the silent happening of progress and resolution.

I feel a bit closer to you now. Now I get an image of being in a group with you and others who have sympathetic and understanding expressions as if I had said something that was of importance to them.—"It is all right to be yourself—you have given us something now—just by allowing yourself to be stuck—to ride it out—to be confused and to share it with us—and to go beyond."

I remember a young woman, a graduate student, in last week's weekend workshop in Atlanta on "Freeing Creativity." She felt that she gave her attention to what was going on only part of the time. Part of the time she felt being "on the fringe." I said to her: "Stay on the fringe and feel the feeling of being on on the fringe—just stay with it fully." Later on she said: "If nothing else had happened in the workshop but this suggestion to accept and to live the feeling of 'being on the fringe' and being allowed to be an in-group member with an out-of-it feeling, this would have been enough for me to take along and to integrate into my living." It is all right to have all kinds of feelings, using all of them, instead of accepting one and rejecting another.

"Being on the fringe"—I guess this example came to my mind on the track of multiple and symbolic meanings. I thought of my writing to counselors as dealing with a subject on the fringe of my profession, since my background has been psychotherapy in the clinical sense, and not counseling, as an educational vocation. And I think of you counselors as a group on the fringe of psychotherapy since most of you, I assume, have been trained and experienced in education rather than in clinical work.

And now it is easier to find my way from the fringe to the essence of what I wanted to say to you as "truthfully as I myself see the truth" about the connection of psychotherapy and education in some of my personal history and thinking that have gone into the formation of the theme-centered interactional method:

Thirteen years ago I created the first theme-centered interactional group. It was a training group for psychoanalysts. The theme was Countertransference. The method used free associations around the treatment situation between a patient and a therapist, interaction between all group members, and my own participant leadership. The format of this workshop was "a happening," rather than a design. I merely presented a case I had difficulties with in free associations to a student group. I hoped that my young colleagues would learn how to use self-analysis of countertransference problems by observing me. This I assumed would lessen their anxiety about being imperfect. I asked them to be silent during my case presentation as I free-associated around the case. In the long silence of listening, the group intuited much about me and the patient but also projected much onto the situation from their own feeling background. Similarly, I had realistic and transferred feelings and thoughts about my listening silent audience. This was discussed in the subsequent highly emotional interaction between all group members and myself. The success in detecting and dissolving the countertransference situation in my case and the subsequent case presentations of other group members led to the conceptualization of the "countertransference workshop method." The theme-centered interactional method has been its offspring.

The countertransference workshop became a continuous open-end group. After several years' experience, I came to the shocking realization that the therapeutic effect of these educational workshops was generally speedier and greater than that of conventional therapy groups.

I spent uncountable hours trying to figure out what was more curative in the countertransference workshop than in the group therapy session. How were they alike and how were they different?

Alike was the atmosphere. Alike were the promotion of "creative truthfulness," acceptance of emotions and promotion of open communication. Alike were free interaction and attentiveness to unconscious processes. Present and past experiences as well as projections into the future were attended to in both the countertransference workshop and the group therapy sessions.

There were also differences. In group therapy, free interaction and evolving and fluctuating themes were the essence of the method. In the countertransference workshop, the first part of the session was devoted to only one person and essentially one problem—a case presentation; the remainder of the session, although allowing for free interaction, still was focused on the initial theme. I was an analytically observant and interpreting therapist, keeping my personal experiences to myself—unless they were used as transference reactions, induced by the participants' projections. In the countertransference workshop, I became a participant group leader, sharing my experiences and feelings freely with the group. In this way, leadership changed from a hierarchically superior position of authority to an authority of function—guiding the process by attentiveness and giving the example of open communication on deeper levels.

The countertransference workshop which had been conceived of as an educational enterprise turned out to be of therapeutic value. Therapy and education now prepared to be a unified field with shadings of emphasis rather than two decisive entities. In the countertransference workshop, each person was a therapist and a patient, a teacher and a student. We helped each other by encounter, knowledge, and interpretation. The work theme belonged to a field to which each person contributed.

I saw the therapeutic effect of this workshop mainly deriving from the fact that we discussed individual countertransference problems. Each countertransference situation relates to the disturbed childhood and fixated part of the therapist. It seemed likely that the therapeutic effect of this workshop rested upon the working through of the analyst's neurotic problems with his patients. However, I became more and more fascinated by the question whether themes other than countertransference treatment could be productive for the personal development of individuals and the penetration of themes.

In 1962, seven years after the first countertransference workshop, I started to translate its techniques into a method for other purposes. Since then, I developed and conceptualized the interactional theme-centered method for education and community purposes, which include business, organizations, schools, churches, etc. Since 1966, the staff of the Workshop Institute for Living-Learning has joined me in this endeavor of research, practice and training of counselors and community leaders.

Some weeks have passed since I spoke to you. I have just now looked through the draft and am pleased that a functional sequence of sub-themes seems to have evolved from the simple initial attempt to write this article in a style which would reflect the method. The concentration on the theme has created a functional structure without a pre-conceived outline.* This is equally true for a workshop series. Animated growth—like trees—never proceeds in straight lines. Trees are not like the walls of a house—they adjust to the living conditions of wind, sun, soil and rain. Structure grows out of needs and circumstances in more complex and complicated ways than outlines provide for—but they seem to be more functional.

I imagine you to be sitting with me in a circle. I want to see your faces and learn to know about your personalities a bit more. I would like to pretend that we are in the middle phase of our workshop series, talking about our concerns in counseling.

---

* *Editors' Footnote.* As this article had to be shortened for practical reasons, some of the "free flowing structure" may have suffered a bit. However, we, the editors, have done our utmost to keep the content-process interrelationship intact.

I am where I really want to be with you now: at a friend's country place. I want to be here with you because it is an early forsythia spring day in softly green mountains and because this house has meant a lot to me. It was here that I spent my first several teaching week-ends with theme-centered interactional training groups.* The participants were colleagues and close friends who later on formed the Workshop Institute for Living-Learning with me.† In this house we found time, space, a congenial atmosphere and a cooperative community group of patients and staff to work with.

If you were really here with me I would probably not be distracted, as I am, by the mild breeze around my cheeks and hands, the droning-by airplanes or the beauty of pastel green and yellow around a bright-blue swimming pool in the distance. If you were really here I might not even hear the birds sing or the humming dishwasher from the nearby house.

I want you to sit in a circle with me on this lawn. You may spontaneously talk about your experiences since our initial encounter and your feelings, thoughts and questions. If this were the second of a 5-session workshop series, you would probably be bubbling all over with the excitement of your experiences. Your students talk to you in a way they never did before. You relate differently to your families—were more open, more interested and less anxious. You had innumerable new ideas of what to do in counseling sessions and with counseling groups and even talked more freely to your superior. If it were a third session, you'd likely be withdrawn, depressed or hostile. Things just snapped back into old tracks or were worse than ever. Established ways have good reasons for being established and the old structures could be better than the new one. If it were a fourth or fifth session, it would likely be constructive and optimistic without the ecstasy of the second session or the depression and feeling of futility of the third one. (This is the way it usually goes.)

I try to see your faces now. You seem to wait for me to say something and I want to encourage you to be your own chairman: "What would you like to get from or give to the group?"

> Bob: (*A sturdy, broad-shouldered man about 35 years old, with sparkling brown eyes.*) I put five of my high school seniors, all boys, into a group after the last session. I had seen them individually before. They all seemed to have one concern in common and I thought it might be good to have them discuss their concern in a group,

---

* The Workshop Institute for Living-Learning (W.I.L.L.) is a training institute for group leaders sponsoring the team-centered interactional approach.
† "The Country Place," Renée Nell's Half-Way House in Connecticut.

especially since I really don't know how to handle it with them individually. These five boys are against the war in Vietnam and want to avoid the draft by going to college or going to jail or to Canada. They even spoke of crippling themselves. I really don't know how to handle this. I thought of you all the time (to me), how would you handle this? (His question is directed to me.)

I feel the anti-war rage with the boys. I feel the anxiety of Bob, the counselor, to do the "right thing" and not knowing what this is. I don't know his set of values and convictions. He has not told us about them. He asks for technical advice: Shall he tell the boys what to do? What he feels about the issue? Tell them to re-think the matter?

The group seems to hesitate for a second with their responses as I do.

> Elaine: (*A maternal looking woman of about 40. She wears brown slacks with a gray print blouse.*) She turns to Bob with a warm smile: I know exactly how you feel. You sit there and think you know what is right and what is wrong but how will you ever make them see it. I have a girls' group in my high school. I put them together a few weeks ago. All they are concerned with is romance and sex—nothing else matters to them. They'd give up school for good for an adventure. They even stay away from home when they feel like it, overnight. Sometimes they don't. The parents feel help-less and so do I. If you involve the police, they may send them to a reform school and that would only make things worse. What they talk about are pre-marital relationships, birth control pills, the "ar-rangement." Telling them about dangers does not do anything—but what does? And what should we do?

A heated discussion ensues.

> Nick: (*45, slim, in a gray business suit with a plain navy blue tie.*) We have to understand them but guide them toward a proper sense of reality and reality values. If the guys don't want to go to war—we must understand their fears, but also help them associate the needs of this country and the ultimate threat to our freedom.
> And those girls—they are like two-year-olds running across the street where cars can kill them. We have to show them dangers and their irresponsibility in taking risks. Help them to become responsi-ble citizens—that is what I would do with these boys and girls.
> Henry: (*About 30, turtleneck short, a small beard and long hair.*) I wouldn't be drafted for anything today—I don't know whether I would be for any war—certainly not for this one. We condemned the Germans for not following their individual consciences during the Nazi regime. Shall we guide our boys to develop their own con-sciences or follow mass hysteria and bad rulers? Progress has always depended on men like Martin Luther King who are a cause célèbre

after they have been killed—not when they lived—and spoke up against unjust laws.

Mary: (*25, with a blond pony tail, light blue shirt-dress and a freshly plucked daisy in her hair.*) How can kids of 15 or 16 develop meaningful relationships if they sleep around at that age? I have nothing against having a boyfriend and not being married when you know what you are doing—but they really don't know yet and they are really asking for help when they tell you about it. They know they are wrong and scared and they want you to discipline them—or tell their teachers and parents to help them. When I brought my first boyfriend home at midnight, I was terrified that my parents had gone to bed but I wouldn't let them know and played sophisticated.

May: (*A Negro woman, dark complexion, about 30, in black slacks and a yellow cotton shirt.*) Why do you want young people to be sexually frustrated? That's the time to experiment and to get to know what people are like. We want to have them live through all kinds of educational experiences in other areas. Why do we exclude sex?

Nick: Law and tradition are wiser than each individual person can be. That's why we have laws: to preserve wisdom and to protect.

May: These laws are made by people whose interests they protect.

Elaine: Birth control pills are not proven to be safe—one of my friends got pains in her breasts and another one was in a hospital with thrombosis. I was depressed myself when I took them. But the girls don't want to hear that.

Nick: You are dead wrong about that. There is nothing dangerous about the pills. My wife has been taking them for years and is fine. Her doctor wouldn't give them to her if they weren't safe. That's the wrong track to take with the girls. They are right if they don't listen to you for that. The pills are ok, but the girls have no right to take them before they are mature enough to have adult relationships.

Henry: The kids are going to take pills and drugs whether you like it or not. They'll steal them from their mother's medicine chests or get their boyfriends to hassle. You won't cure the generation gap by being moralistic.

Nick: There is a real moral issue involved here. If kids just want to get pleasure out of whatever—sex, drugs, draft evasion—society will perish as it did in the Roman days and whenever people loaf in luxuries and perfumes.

May: If society will die, it is not because of draft evasion and sexual pleasure. It's because most people don't want the world to change—it's a comfortable lawful world for them—only that the laws protect only those who make them.

This discussion has led from two concrete questions of counseling to the larger general issues of our society. I have been deeply involved in the interaction without speaking up. I want the interaction to be free for some time without giving any direction from my side. The group must have enough time for the issues each person is involved in to come to the surface. Too early or too much questioning or even stating viewpoints by the leader often prevents group members from coming out with their own concerns and viewpoints. I intervened at this point by stating a general rule.

Group Leader: Please speak per I. Do not talk per we or it. I want each of us to take a personal stand rather than to speak for other people. I can never be so sure what you think or feel anyway.

Mary: I think this is becoming too involved for me. Next thing we will be discussing War and Peace, and Black and White. We forget all about the kids.

Group Leader: Mary, please speak for yourself. What do *you* want?

Mary: I want to discuss one point at a time and restrict it to counseling. Elaine and Bob want answers, don't you? I don't want to get off these questions. Why can't we finish one question at a time?

Henry: They do belong together.

Bob: If we look at these issues point by point, I want to know who is right and I want to know where each person stands and learn from them. Or we may take a vote at the end and trust the majority.

Mary: We will still have the issues to contend with whether a vote makes an issue right. May has a point. Laws and votes may only protect the majority.

Henry: I am furious. This is just a—forgive me—bullshit group like all others. Talk, talk, talk and nobody really spills his guts. I am disappointed with you, Ruth, letting this crap go on. How do you feel, people, *feel* about yourselves and me and whatever you are saying? You avoid getting down to whatever it is with you and me—and the group here.

Mary: But we are not a sensitivity group. I want to learn something here. I want to improve my counseling. I can talk about myself with my husband and friends. They can tell me things about me better than you could.

Henry: I want to learn more about myself and about you, here. Then I'll know something about the kids, too. They are just like us—people—ordinary, lousy, good people.

May: I'll tell you something about you, Henry. I like you very much. But I don't like it when I look at your face and you look like you are looking down on me and all of us. I noticed that the first time we met and Ruth asked us to be silent. You seemed to be furious right then.

Bob: I thought he was just shy and thoughtful. I never want to ask him questions when he is silent. In fact, when my kids are silent, I never want to ask them either—it's like breaking into their privacy.

Nick: I agree with you on silence. I think it is better to let it be. I want to know from you, Ruth, whether I am right about that. I have a college group, co-ed, and they have talked about girl-friends and boy-friends, all of them, but one girl—she didn't say anything. And then I thought that wasn't right. She should have a turn, too. And so I asked her about her dates. And she just said, "Yes, I date, too." And that was all she said. And I felt bad then, as if I had done something wrong in asking her.

I might have intervened with various responses, questions or self-revelations sooner if I had been an active leader of this group rather than a writer-leader. In writing, I became so eager to have a counselor group evolve that I may have been more silent than I would be in reality.

Now I became acutely aware that you, the real readers, you are not these figments of my imagination, but people who will read about them.

Please put your book down for a few minutes and think about the discussion you just read and whatever comes to your mind now. What have Bob's and Elaine's questions stirred up within you? What else has been of interest to you in whatever way? Please think awhile about this. Be aware of what you feel now and pick up the book again. Re-read this piece of interaction and see what happens to you and the fictional people in this process.

(I, too, put my writing down.)

I was surprised when I looked at my watch. It was time for lunch. I had been writing without conscious interruption for about 1½ hours. There had been many distractions, but they did not interfere with my concentration on the work.

Re-reading the discussion has given me a new perspective of the group interaction and the individual personalities. In writing, it was the *content* of the imaginary discussion which occupied my mind. In reading, the group process came into focus. I react the same way in the workshop sessions. Spoken words can easily drown out my visual perceptions. Or introspective and abstract processes. I then remember to step back from listening to words and let the sound of voices rather than word-content sink into me. All I concentrate on is watching facial expressions and bodily positions. Here in this imaginary interaction episode, my awareness of the content of discussion has overshadowed my watching the process. I picked up the process by revealing my own feelings about Elaine's brown eyes which look at me like those of a helpless child. I watch my intrapsychic response and feel put upon as expected to give answers which I do not have.

> Group Leader: Elaine, you look at me as if I had all the answers to your questions. I feel uncomfortable when you look at me this way.
> Elaine: But you are the expert here. You must know how to handle these girls.
> Group Leader: I am really less of an expert with high school girls than you. But I wonder whether words like "expert" and "handle" get in your way of being alert to your own convictions and feelings —and maybe the girls'?

At this moment, in picking up Elaine's quest for irrational authority, I have become aware of the session's subtheme: the search for functional vs. irrational authority. Bob presented his high school boys' questioning the government's authority for drafting them for a cause they reject; Elaine's girls question society's and their parents' authority to regulate their sex and love life. May opposes unjust rules and laws. Henry questions my skill as an authority; why do I keep silent? Nick too challenges me to talk. The analysis of content and of process leads to the central subtheme of this session as: testing and evaluating authority.

I turn back to Elaine. Her overt request for an answer to a practical question contains a request for personal attention. I use this request for attention to elucidate her own and the group's involvement with the authority problem.

> Group Leader (to Elaine) : I would like you to remember how it was to be 15 years old. Take your time to remember and now pretend you are 15 years old. Remember a situation where your father, mother, or a teacher told you what you ought to do.

Elaine gives a few important incidents. She points out that her mother was the one person she would go along with blindly: She felt contempt for her father's and teacher's demands. I now request: "Pretend you are 8 years old. Somebody asks you to do something." And after the same response, I go on: "And when you were 3 years old?" To Elaine's surprise, she feels that she would obey her teacher at 8 and her father at 3. Then she breaks into tears: she realizes how much she had loved her father when she was little. Later on, he seemed to be a worthless stranger while her mother seemed to be close and important. Henry comes through spontaneously, telling experiences of watching his parents fight and cheat one another, while they gave him much personal attention: he never trusted them. He stopped obeying them at an early age. Nick's father was the president of a large corporation and demanded respect for his authority from his son without developing personal intimacy. Nick learned to live by objective rules without questioning them much. May's father was educated, her mother was not. He expected everything from his daughter, nothing from his wife. May learned to balance between her wish to be her father's favorite and not lose her mother's closeness.

The participants talk and listen intently now. The atmosphere is closer than it was when the talk concerned counselees and general problems. Each story is different. But the ingredients are similar. The stories speak about being insecure, happy, rejected, victorious, dependent, trusting, suspicious. The group is closely knit. Intimacy in interaction is strengthened whenever the focus is on feelings and processes, rather than on thoughts and problems. This bond of understanding seems to grow beyond this circle out into the space to groups anywhere—classrooms, offices, society. People are alike in different ways. They need to be affirmed as individuals.

I push myself to make my thoughts overt statements. In a therapy group, awareness experience and interpretation of self and others are the essence of the work. In a theme-centered interactional workshop, all awarness is being re-channeled into the study of the theme.

I lead the discussion back from our experience to our theme. Knowing personal problems with authority does not alter the significance of personal and social questions. But it helps each person to elucidate and understand their role and to make decisions. If I am aware of deeper personal and emotional entanglements I can work toward their resolution. I am less likely to make rationalizing brain decisions, to be swept by public opinion, or to be irrationally opposed. Bob may help his boys, Elaine her girls, by investigating with them their feelings about authority. They may see their presenting problems differently and recognize them as dim rebellion or as genuine conviction of individual and social revolutionary meaning.

The question of functional versus dogmatic authority is a key theme for leaders and co-leaders of the theme-centered interactional group. The method involves promotion of awareness, personal feelings and thoughts, and their interpersonal communication. In my experience, the leader's functional authority is best established when he can convey his personal here-and-now experiences with courage and faith in the validity of truthfulness. Some feeling for timing and tactfulness in the way he expresses himself is, of course, often necessary. Invariably, if leaders have held back the expression of feelings or intuitive recognition of an event, the group process has been slowed down or disturbed. The leader may get stuck in a feeling of annoyance with a group member; if expressed, it would help this group member, and the leader could investigate their attitudes and proceed from there. Or he may suppress the communication of an intuitive recognition about the participant's dynamics which could be rejected or integrated as valid by this person and be of value to others. Unspoken words about feelings usually serve as hydraulic brakes in the group process.

The expression of opinions about issues is much less important and often undesirable—especially in new or immature groups. As long as a leader is seen as a parental figure, the group members respond to his opinions with their usual pattern of always accepting or always rejecting authority rather than to consider what is being said on its merit. When the leader expresses his feelings and inner experiences, his real personality is likely to break through the group members' transferential image of authority. His opinions are then seen for what they are: that is, only one person's convictions.

At some time I know it will be right for me to tell Elaine and Bob what I think about the problems they brought up. I see our adult task in promoting the spirit of openness to feelings, and creativeness in the younger generation by fulfilling our own creative destiny and by the kind of communication which keeps my own needs and those of the students in mind. I want to convey my feelings to Elaine that there are many ways of enjoyment and fulfillment. They include bodily warmth, sexual electricity, and the recognition of experiencing different feelings for different individual men. I see no virtue in withholding sexuality from pre-marital constructive relationships. The question whether relationships are constructive is the essential point of discussion. Counseling will consist in helping the young student to become more aware of himself and his partner and to evaluate the feeling and reality situation. I will tell Bob at some time that I am in union with opposers of this war, but that I may lack the courage or conviction for overstepping legal boundaries. I have faith that working with young people in the service of awareness and communication may help the young generation to grow up to find new roles which are theirs to be discovered.

If you were here with me, fighting off the coolness of the storming-in evening clouds, you would respond to me. I miss this badly now. I think I will quit for today.

It is the Saturday of Memorial Day Weekend. I want to finish this draft today. I want to write about the process and content of terminal sessions in a workshop series. I feel intent and purposeful. We have gone a long way together—it has been exciting—this writing—like being in a roomful of interesting people. I hope, so very much, that this excitement will carry over to you, the reading collaborators of this experiment in writing.

The frequent and long interruptions were at first hard to take. I experienced them as obstacles which I had to deal with. Then I included them into the process of writing and I experienced them as constructive stimuli—the opportunity to let thoughts develop and grow slowly.

Sometime in the middle of a series' last session I usually stop the group process and say something like this: "Please be silent for five minutes and imagine that you are on your way home. Something comes to your mind you wished you had asked for or told to somebody. Please let us be silent. Thereafter, let each one of us try to give the group what we may have wanted to and not gotten around to and to get what we still want to get."

I put my writing down. The one-sided interaction between us makes me feel rather impotent. What do I still want to give you now?

There have been many "leftovers" for me in writing this article. I have wanted to write about co-leading groups, about experiences and thoughts concerning young people's workshops, about various teaching and community workshops, about thoughts related to the imaginary experience I wrote last time, etc. I will choose only some important factors. I want to convey to you the image of a geometrical figure of the theme-centered interactional model. I am always conscious of it when I pre-design the beginning of a workshop series and keep dimly conscious during each session. This figure is an onionlike glass globe. It contains the interactional triangle. The triangle's points are 1) the individual in the group—"the I,"; 2) the individuals in the group, centering around the theme—"We"; 3) the theme of the group—their focus. The onionlike glass globes are the environmental time, space and human surroundings. The leader is inside the glass globe, shifting his weight to the point wherever such weight is needed to keep the triangle in balance.

The globe of environmental circumstances is the initial point of planning and remains a substantial point of concentration all along. It comprises the time and place where the workshop takes place, the sponsors of the series, their motivation for the program, the community which supports or opposes the event in its financial and factual meaning, voluntary and compulsory reasons for the enrollment, and the leader's own motivation.

I become aware of wanting to give you instructions and advice. I wonder whether this spontaneous shift in attitude and style has something to do with "the last session syndrome"—which in the psychologist's lingo is usually referred to as "separation anxiety."

Yes, I feel driven. I want to "fill you up" with practicable suggestions —like handing you little food baskets with sandwiches and apples before you go on your way. And this after all my cautioning statements about not giving advice! And I rationalize that by now, in our last session, you know me well enough to take my opinions as those of a functional rather than transferential authority. And there is a difference in advising people on personal or on technical issues.

These thoughts lead me to think about the three base points of the triangle: you, the individual; we the group-as-a-whole; and It, the theme.

In most successful workshop series, the participants feel strongly about their being "a group" and would like to prolong the series. There is sadness about the coming of separation and the desire to continue learning. In my experience, it is not wise to change a previously set-up structure—be it in time (prolongation) or by change of the theme. The time structure as well as the setting-up of the theme, are powerful ingredients of the group process. If they are altered, the group structure rarely adjusts smoothly. It is better to announce a similar workshop for some time later. It is useful to plan for such workshops as a new enterprise, allowing for some change in membership.

Separation anxiety is a deeply rooted characteristic in most, maybe all, people; ultimately, it seems to be related to the fear of being born and the fear of dying. I believe that the group's wish to stay together beyond the given structure contains a great deal of separation anxiety. It is hard to accept the reality of necessary separation. Each step of separating means a step toward independence, autonomy and the openness to new relationships and ventures. The best medicine against separation anxiety and an elixir for progressive living seem to be the full exploration of any here-and-now, the ability to be fully in each Hello, in each experience, and in each Good-bye. The leader's suggestion to the group to use this last ½ hour to the brim of give-and-take is a tool for making use of the "now" and thus strengthen the ability to leave. Sometimes, when a group member feels hopeless, fearful, and very afraid of leaving, I ask him to fantasize that he will die in 5 (10, or 15) minutes.

How would he use these last minutes? Pursuing the countdown, and being fully related to him, usually leads to this person's living successfully through intense anxiety and its resolution. This to me is one of the major validated experiences. Disturbing emotions leave people who dare to be deeply and fully aware of them and live with and through them. Half-hearted awareness and dim anxiety keep us emotionally disturbed.

Again I feel the need of giving you "the sandwich basket." I feel filled with the need to give—since I really cannot, in writing, get anything from you but imaginary responses. I would like to be "in touch with you," rather than alone here. I am sitting on a wooden, backless bench at a quiet pond in the forest, somewhere in New Jersey. I am alone with croaking frog sounds, some bird and bee noises and the soothing brook-like sound of water going down the drain pipe. The air is satiated with the odor of freshly cut grass. I feel a bit guilty about not helping my friends who own this lovely, lonely pond to weed away grasses around their blossoming iris and blackberries. I don't want to take time out from writing. I feel my rush to convey content to you much more so than I ever experienced in a last workshop session. It seems that the lack of real interaction promotes my need for giving more. I felt, months ago when I started to write to you, there was time to be quiet and to contemplate. Now I feel like the magician's apprentice—driven by the figments of my own imagination, driven to fulfill imaginary demands.

Maybe I should now take the medicine I just described and fully sense my driving need as a cure toward relaxation. I choose, however, to weed the grass around the purple and golden iris.

In pulling cat briar, nettles, plain grass and lots of leafy little things whose names I do not know, two major issues ("leftovers") came to my mind which I do want to write about. 1) The handling of pathology, or "deviant" in a theme-centered interactional group, and 2) an incident from the imaginary group session which I had not touched upon but observed—May's preoccupation with the racial issue.

We may call people "deviants" or those who are "out-of-it" people who are continually in variance from the rest of the group. They may, for instance, be always silent or always talking—monopolizers—or actively ill individuals. I would like you to look at these persons from the point of view of the theme-centered interactional model: 1) they are individuals, 2) they are group members, 3) they can relate to the theme, 4) they are in this group because of their own or their superior's wish, personal and social circumstances.

As a leader, I observe and experience the "out-of-it" group members' behavior as their personal expression of needs and attitudes. I accept their ways as what they must be at this moment. I see the group's reaction and my own as equally determined. As my job as a leader is to recognize and to skillfully communicate reality, I would perhaps in the presence of a silent member say: "Seven people speak, one person is silent," or, in the presence of a monopolizer: "One person talks and seven are silent." Such descriptions may either lead to an affirmation and continuation of the situation, or, more likely, change the group's behavior. This intervention does not condemn anybody's autonomous activity, but stimulates the group toward change. The description arouses curiosity and the group members' recognition of what they are doing at this moment. Silent group members, or those who join discussions only tangentially, need attention. I look for non-verbal cues. If people look comfortable in their silence, I usually do not question them but sustain some eye-contact. Occasionally, I might state that I feel comfortable with their silence, but want to make sure that they do, too. Yet there are also ominous silences—those which belong to a face with shifting (paranoid) eyes, empty stares, hostile expressions, or very tense body posture. I relate myself to such silences in various ways. I usually try to elicit some personal response; most likely such persons are deeply disturbed. In such instances, as well as with openly psychotic people, I feel it is important to resist attempts at individual psychotherapy in this situation. To treat a psychotic in a theme-centered interactional workshop is non-functional for the group's purpose and therefore to the structured goal. It is therefore important to learn and develop specific ways and techniques with which we can relate to deeply disturbed people in interactional group sessions. I usually direct my intense personal attention for several minutes on the disturbed person and give the group and myself some time to listen to the depressed, anxious or hostile expressions or inappropriate stories. I then distinctly do *not* explore intensity, veracity and further personal experiences of this group member, but try to elicit facts which give his experiences and communications value to himself and to other group members and especially to the theme under discussion. The leader is responsible for keeping the balance of the four points of the group interaction. In one group, a young girl seemed to want to listen to others only, but not to explore herself. I encountered the group's request for her talking with my statement that sometimes people need recognition for silence before they wish to talk; in this case, I put my arm around the girl's shoulder for a long time. She then felt free enough to cry and to provoke the group's recognition of her distress. Techniques to deal with such specially vulnerable people include: the sincere, intense and brief acceptance of their personal communication of internal stress or interpersonal needs followed by relating this episode to the theme; translation from communication about their disturbances in living and in intrapsychic conflicts to the events in this room; finding ways to make such communications useful for the group process and the content of the theme; support through interest in the disturbed person but not especially in his disturbance. Ego support is established by accepting the person's need for recognition and his usefulness in the group, rather than by exploring his pathology. Only in rare cases has exclusion from the series proved to be necessary. Summarizing: deeper disturbances of group members cannot be handled therapeutically in a workshop setting, even if the group leader is a qualified therapist. The balance of the interaction (group, individual, theme, and circumstance) must be respected, or the group invariably loses cohesion and develops antagonism against the deviant person or the group leader, which is likely to be destructive.

It is late, late night. The Saturday passed away hours ago. It is Sunday. Rain falls outside the dark moth-ridden windows. A little wood-burning stove keeps me flickering company. I hope I can stay awake and alert. I want to finish this draft tonight. I do not want to disrupt the flow of thoughts again.

I want to return to May in the imaginary group. May was Negro. She was soft and personable, warm and empathic. Yet she seemed to feel that none of us could be close to her before we white people would respect black society and black power as separate.

In writing this last paragraph I feel the release of having written what I wanted to say. I need not, as I wanted to, pick up May's unfinished interaction with the group. I feel I have conveyed to you in this last hour my concern as a private person, as a leader of interactional groups, as a group member of our national and world society. This happens in the flow of writing as it happens toward the end of a last session. The leader becomes less and less the guardian of the method and more and more a participant group member.

As I and you strive to have the courage of deepened emotional and intellectual awareness and clarity, and strive toward communication of whatever we happen to be, we seem to open up some workable pathways for ourselves and those we meet. This is my hope for our society.

It is 6 A.M. The night has passed. The rain is still falling: The black, moth-ridden night windows have been replaced by green leaves on dancing branches reaching into a light gray sky.

51

TRAINING POLICE AS SPECIALISTS IN FAMILY CRISIS INTERVENTION

Morton Bard, Ph.D.

*Professor of Psychology, Graduate Center, the City
University of New York*

BACKGROUNDS AND GOALS

INTRODUCTION: THE FUNCTION OF THE POLICE

In large urban centers, rapid social change, alienation, increasing population density, and ever more complex economic competition conspire to subject the family and the individual to exacting pressures. For the disadvantaged in urban society, the personal effects may be extreme. Resulting frustration, despair and hopelessness often make for a volatile, aggressive mixture kept inert only by the presence of the police . . . society's agents of control.

The police may be regarded simply as a domestic army which keeps civilian order, or they may be regarded as individuals involved in highly complex functions that often extend far beyond mere repression. Indeed, it has been estimated that almost ninety per cent of a policeman's function today is concerned with activities unrelated to crime control or to law enforcement (11). A recent study by Cumming *et al* (9) revealed that about one-half of calls for assistance received by an urban police department involved complaints of a personal and interpersonal nature.

This article is a condensed version of the monograph of the same title by Dr. Bard, PR-71, U.S. Department of Justice, Law Enforcement Assistance Administration, National Institute of Law Enforcement and Criminal Justice, May, 1970.

A. Family Crisis Intervention as a Specific Function of the Police

The problem centers, then, on isolating those non-crime functions of the police which realistically make greatest demands upon police officers and which traditional police training methods ignore. Preliminary investigation reveals that "family fights" or "family disturbances" constitute one such "non-crime" function. Accurate estimates of the scope of this police function are difficult to determine with any precision: usual police statistics reflect recognized crime categories and do *not* report incidents which do not involve a reportable crime. However, personal communication with experienced police officers attests to the frequency of the occurrence of "family disturbance" calls. As a matter of fact, such calls for police assistance are common not only in urban centers, but in rural communities as well.

B. The Need for Specific Training

Despite indications of need for police training in techniques for managing families in crisis, there is little evidence of such content in existing recruit or in-service training programs. As a consequence, the police officer called upon to intervene in a family fight is usually unable to render effective service and, indeed, may be needlessly exposed to personal danger because of deficits in knowledge about this kind of disordered behavior. A family crisis which has deteriorated to the point of threatening violence is in critically delicate balance and requires a high level of skill on the part of the intervening authority who is expected to mollify the situation. Regretfully, the police officer, if he is unprepared for this function and left to draw upon his own often biased notions of family dynamics and upon his skills as a law enforcer, may actually behave in ways to induce a tragic outcome.

C. Relationship of Family Crisis to Crime

There is no way of knowing at present how many crimes are a direct outcome of uncontrolled aggressive outbursts within families. There are indications, however, that their number may be considerable. If one considers only the category of homicide, the evidence is impressive. There are numerous studies which support Durkheim's observation (10) that "while family life has a moderating effect upon suicide, it rather stimulates murder." In 1965 there were 634 homicides in New York City, of which 35% involved family members or close friends (19). A study of homicide in Houston, Texas, by Bullock (7) concluded that most felonious assaults result from either petty quarrels, marital discords in which one spouse kills another, or love or sex disputes in which the deceased was slain by someone other than a spouse. Bensing and Schroeder (4) studied 622 homicides committed in Cleveland, Ohio, and said, "Homicides committed during robberies receive much publicity but do not represent as great a number of killings as do marital discord and quarrels between friends." In Wolfgang's study (24), sixty-five per cent of 500 homicide victims were relatives, close friends, paramours, or homosexual partners of the principal offender, while only twelve per cent were complete strangers.

THE NEED FOR PREVENTIVE MENTAL HEALTH APPROACHES

In addition to increasing social pressure on the police, there is similar pressure upon mental health professionals to develop novel service strategies in keeping with changing needs. Traditional methods of diagnosis and treatment appear to have lessening impact as the demand for psychological services quickly outdistances professional manpower resources. It is increasingly apparent that preventive mental health approaches hold the greatest promise for resolving the dilemma. The program in family crisis intervention, based upon an emerging body of theory and research, defines a method which joins preventive approaches in mental health with those of crime prevention. It rests on the convergence of at least three distinct tracks of theory and research: 1) the use of the paraprofessional mental health worker; 2) the role of family dynamics in determining disordered behavior; and 3) preventive crisis intervention.

A. The Use of the Paraprofessional Mental Health Worker

The Joint Commission on Mental Health and Illness (14) has recommended that relief of manpower shortages in mental health be undertaken through the effective utilization of paraprofessional personnel. In 1963, Rioch and her associates (22) reported on the results of a pilot experiment to test the hypothesis that carefully selected mature people can be trained to do limited psychotherapy.

More recently, Reiff and Reissman (21) have written extensively on the use of indigenous mental health aides as a community action strategy. In an effort to extend the social impact of the highly trained mental health professional, they call for the use of trained paraprofessionals. There appears to be little question that intelligent laymen can be trained to render effective mental health services under the consultative direction of the more highly trained professionals. In this approach, the highly trained consultant is involved in *little direct service* himself but instead influences the functioning of the paraprofessionals directly providing service, thus extending the social impact of his education and experience.

In the present project it was hypothesized that a similar approach could be employed in using the police as mental health paraprofessional personnel; and it was proposed that selected policemen, already engaged in quasi-mental health service roles (9) *but without training*, be trained to function in those roles more effectively.

B. Family Dynamics as a Determinant of Disordered Behavior

In recent years there has been a growing recognition of the extent to which the family shapes the personalities of its children and of the complexity by which the shaping occurs. The importance of the family environment in the genesis of behavior pathology is well documented by a number of studies (1, 3, 16). The results of these research investigations suggest that early identification of and intervention in families where the parents live in a perpetual state of hateful and sadistic involvement may have significant preventive mental health implications for their children.

At the moment, most disordered families are diagnosed and treated only *after breakdown has occurred* and only *after seeking help.* Families who seek help are generally well educated and sophisticated in mental health matters; they come from the middle classes and usually have the resources and awareness requisite to seeking help. Undoubtedly there are large numbers of families in difficulty whose class and educational limitations prevent their identification by usual mental health case-finding methods. It is the contention here that the identification of such families would be facilitated by the use of atypical "case-finders" . . . in the present instance, the police. Those families who lack knowledge and sophistication in matters pertaining to mental health resources are the very ones most likely to involve the police when family crisis approaches breakdown.

C. Preventive Crisis Intervention

Human adaptation to crisis has come to occupy a singularly important place in behavioral science. Reaction to disasters and natural catastrophes, as well as responses to personal dangers, are increasingly important in the understanding of normal personality development and of the origins of psychopathology. Successful resolution of life crises during development can contribute much to ego growth. By the same token, many emotional disorders appear to begin or to be aggravated by an important life crisis. Caplan (8) believes strongly that the prevention of ego damage in children often centers on openness and vulnerability during crisis—an event he maintains "involves both danger and opportunity." This notion conceives of a crisis situation as one in which typical personality defense patterns are breached in the face of threat (openness), thus presenting unusual opportunities (vulnerability) for modification of usual behavior by direct intervention. Alein and Lindemann (15) contend that effective intervention techniques will not only relieve the crisis but will often serve to bring about personality change as well. Other crisis researchers present convincing evidence to support these observations (3, 20).

Police constantly meet states of openness and vulnerability as they find themselves enmeshed in countless life crises. But most particularly for the police project, their skillful preventive intervention in a specific life crisis, the "family fight," holds special promise as an effective means of behavior modification.

SUMMARY

The police project sought to demonstrate the effective utilization of selected police officers in a program of crime prevention and preventive mental health. There is evidence that police are currently engaged in a variety of quasi-mental health roles with little or no training equal to them. There is evidence that their lack of training is often personally dangerous and is wasteful to society as an opportunity lost for preventing certain classes of crime and for relieving manpower shortages in mental health. The area for study involved a common police complaint —the "family fight" or "family disturbance." This project sought to demonstrate the viability of training police in techniques of intervention and to define methods for extending such specialized training in the preparation of police for existing functions.

THE DEMONSTRATION PROJECT PLAN

PRE-PROPOSAL ACTIVITY

The preparation of the proposal which eventuated in the Police Family Crisis Training Project involved a full year of intensive activity prior to funding by OLEA. The investment of that effort by The Psychological Center of The City College of New York demonstrates the obligation of a consultative facility—The Psychological Center—to familiarize itself in depth with the consultee institution.

A. 30th Precinct: Commanding and Executive Officers

In the spring of 1966, after preliminary expression of interest by Police Commissioner Howard Leary, the commanding officer of the 30th Precinct (Capt. Ferranti) was invited to the College in the first of a long series of visits between staff members of The Psychological Center and of the Precinct. The rationale of the proposal was renewed and explained, and the active assistance of the Captain (and his executive officer) was enlisted in resolving specific administration problems. Cooperation at this level was invaluable, since it insured a plan that made sense in the context of the realities of police administration. This plan was reviewed with Commissioner Leary in June of 1966 as the basis for a draft proposal. During the fall and early winter 1966-67, there were continuing consultations with the new commanding officer of the Precinct (Capt. Agoglia), his executive officer, and the training sergeant. In November the Divisional Inspector and his staff met at The Psychological Center for a thoroughgoing review of the entire project plan. These meetings were invaluable for obtaining the "middle-management" support essential for any enterprise. Suggestions coming from these meetings served to further strengthen the plan and make it the shared product of many minds.

B. Station House Interviews

By January a draft proposal was ready for dispatch to the Office of Law Enforcement Assistance. What had been intended as a preliminary draft proposal proved sufficient as the proposal upon which the grant award was finally made. February of 1967 was devoted to a month-long pilot study of family crises and a preliminary run of the data collection and debriefing procedures. Preliminary forms of the basic "Family Crisis Card" were distributed to the men of the 30th Precinct going out on patrol. The commanding officer and desk officers instructed out-going platoons in the use of the cards and introduced the Project Supervisor to answer questions. This was not only the first test of the data collection, but, in a sense, was the first test of the relationship between The Psychological Center and the 30th Precinct. The results were most gratifying and proved an augury for the rest of the project. The patrolmen not only completed a new and physically unfamiliar form, but also gave of their own time to discuss or debrief the material after their tours of duty.

These debriefing sessions in the station house muster room yielded a sampling of case material upon which much that followed could be realistically based.

C. Headquarters Conference

By March, 1967, the time had arrived to set the final details. The grant award had been made.

A central feature of the plan was that the Family Crisis Intervention Unit which was to be created would not become detached from the patrol strength of the precinct. They would continue to work all tours, around the clock, in uniform, and be responsible for all normal patrol duties in a sector assigned to their car when not engaged in responding to a family crisis call. Thus the new Unit would not deplete the precinct's roster. However, the plan did call for a month of intensive on-campus classroom training before the Unit went operative. This month presented problems. The Psychological Center needed time to prepare for it: select the men, hire the instructors, and buy the educational materials with the funds that had just become available. The Police Department had no time as the demands of summer rapidly approached. The month of June was a compromise which represented pressures and sacrifices on both sides.

Other sensitive issues were studied and resolved at this meeting by the Department's legal and administrative heads. Follow-up visits to measure the effectiveness of instruction were reluctantly prohibited as a possible infringement of the rights of privacy. Ethnic identification and national origin inquiries were eliminated from the demographic data to be collected. Hard decisions were made, risks assessed, and the "go" signal was given.

D. Comparison Precinct

There was concern about the control precinct (24th). Evaluation is often the weakest aspect of many projects and the lack of comparable control data is usually responsible. The choice of a comparison precinct was difficult to make; *even more difficult was the problem of insuring the motivation and interest of those who might feel their role of secondary importance.* Worse still, "comparison" seems somehow associated with "individuals." While the commanding officer of the 24th Precinct was involved and his executive officer actively participated, there was always some question about reaching the men of the precinct on whose cooperation so much depended. The same techniques which seemed so effective in reaching the men of the 30th Precinct did not seem equally effective in the 24th. Although the latter has a larger population and a larger complement of men, a comparable period in the 24th Precinct did not produce half the response of the trial run in the 30th. Obviously we could not conduct a double blind study without contaminating the findings. Therefore, although it is possible to point to a record of careful and detailed preliminary work, the techniques for reaching and motivating comparison areas are still to be refined and improved.

THE PLAN

The plan which emerged as a consequence of the year's planning contained elements faithful both to intended innovative objectives and to normal New York City Police Department organizational functioning. It was regarded as essential that the design demonstrate enhancement of usual police performance within the context of usual institutional structure. Any departure from usual procedure was designed to be minimally disruptive in order to demonstrate that the intended objectives could be achieved within the existing organizational framework of the Police Department.

In essence, the plan called for the selection and training of eighteen patrolmen in one Upper West Side Manhattan precinct. This group of officers (approximately 8-10% of the precinct's complement patrolling a lower class to lower-middle class, stabile, largely black, residential community of about 85,000) would be designated as the Family Crisis Intervention Unit (FCIU). The Unit was to be trained intensively for one month and then function operationally for the duration of the two-year project period, with weekly consultations provided by The City College Psychological Center. During its operation, the Unit was to be divided into three teams of six men each; each team to be available for duty under the normal three-platoon system. It was anticipated that, even with absences for illness, vacation, etc, at least two men of the team of six would be available to man the "family motor patrol" on each tour of duty. The car designated for this function was to patrol a regularly assigned sector, in keeping with usual practice, but would be dispatched to *any* sector of the precinct when a family disturbance occurred. If, by chance, the men in another sector inadvertently responded to a family disturbance, they were under instructions to summon the "family car."

The development of police "generalist-specialists" was an essential feature of the plan. That is, the FCIU patrolmen were to perform general patrol functions but, in addition, were to be available as a precinct task force—able to deliver a form of professional police service.

In addition to the service to be provided by the members of the FCIU, it was intended that they collect vital information on family disturbance as a police function. Little specific information on the event is available in police records anywhere or in behavioral science research. The operations of the FCIU offered an opportunity to determine some of the parameters of family conflict as an aspect of human behavior. The Unit officers therefore were to be trained also in observational techniques and data collection methods to enable the investigators to arrive at conclusions regarding domestic disturbance.

Two key issues were undercurrent in the design:

1. It was recognized that the skills required for effective intervention in highly volatile family crises would, in large measure, be dependent upon significant alteration of the interpersonal perceptual set of each participating police officer. To ensure *gradual change over time* in personal attitudes and values in order to develop necessary interpersonal objectivity, traditional classroom instructional methods had to be supplemented by innovative educational techniques. Drawing on recent developments in the behavioral sciences, a central feature of the design called for a period of intensive training along more traditional lines to be followed by an extended period of weekly individual consultations and group discussions.

2. Role identity confusion was a potential threat to the integrity of the project—not to speak of its potential as a personal threat to each of the men who would operationally staff the project. The essential task was to engender the attitudes and skills of a helping professional without in any way compromising the police officer's basic peace-keeping mission. Throughout the project's duration, the selected personnel would be reinforced in their general police role despite their specialized function in relation to family disturbances.

The project design, then, consisted of three stages: a Preparatory Phase, for selection and intensive training of the Unit personnel; an Operational Phase, in which the Family Crisis Intervention Unit would function with consultative support; and an Evaluative Phase, for analysis of data.

Project evaluation was restricted to the effectiveness of the program in relation to crime control and police personnel safety in both the demonstration precinct (30th) and the comparison precinct (24th). The data in the comparison precinct were to be collected by the normal patrol force. While otherwise desirable, it was outside the scope of the present effort to attempt a large-scale assessment of the project's effort upon the community. The following evaluative comparisons were planned:

1. Changes in the total number of family disturbance complaints in the demonstration precinct and as compared with the comparison precinct.

2. Recurrence of complaints by the same families in the demonstration precinct and as compared with recurrence of complaint rate in the comparison precinct.

3. Changes in total number of homicides in the demonstration precinct and as compared with changes in the comparison precinct.

4. Changes in the number of homicides among relatives in the demonstration precinct and differences in comparison with similar data in the comparison precinct.

5. Changes in total number of assaults in the demonstration precinct and as compared with similar data in the comparison precinct.

6. Changes in the number of assaults among family members in the demonstration precinct and as contrasted with the comparison precinct.

7. Changes in the number of injuries sustained by patrolmen responding to family disturbance complaints, both within the demonstration precinct and as compared with the comparison precinct.

8. Follow-up visits to determine outcome in families served by the FCIU as compared with families served by the comparison precinct. (As noted before, follow-up visits were precluded by the New York City Police Department's concern for the civil and individual rights of the families visited by the police.)

THE PREPARATORY PHASE

During this phase of the project (May 1, 1967-June 30, 1967) four activities were predominant: A. selection of the 30th Precinct Family Crisis Intervention Unit; B. recruitment and preparation of professional project personnel; C. design and preparation of data collection and operational forms and procedures; D. intensive on-campus training of the FCIU.

SELECTION OF THE FCIU

An early decision was made to staff the experimental program with volunteers. The nature of the experiment indicated the advisability of selecting men with at least three years, but no more than ten years, of service. The minimum assured participation by experienced officers; the maximum would eliminate those men whose seniority might contribute to an inflexible quality. To ensure a satisfactory number from which to select eighteen officers, announcement was made by commanders in each of four precincts comprising the Police Department's Fifth Division, the administrative command of the Upper West Side of Manhattan. Each precinct commander made the initial selection of applicants after giving each man some indication of the nature of the project. The applicants were given to understand that they would be frozen in their FCIU assignment for the duration of the project and that the only tangible reward would be the education they would receive during the course of the project, as well as three college credits from the John Jay College of Criminal Justice of The City University of New York. In addition, advanced students enrolled in the College could receive three additional credits in an advanced social science research seminar.

Final selection was made by Dr. Morton Bard, Project Director, and Dr. Bernard Berkowitz, Project Supervisor. The selection procedure was kept as simple as possible and involved only a brief clinical assessment interview. Psychological tests were not used for two reasons—one, there was considerable doubt that they could reliably discriminate the factors considered important; and, two, their dubious value was far outweighed by their negative effects in possibly convincing the officers that the real intent of the college-based project was to permit psychologists to "psych cops" or otherwise to use them as "guinea pigs."

In view of the ethnic composition of the 30th Precinct area, it was decided to effect an ethnic balance in the Unit and, hence, nine black and nine white officers were selected. It was intended that the men be paired bi-racially in order to enable the investigators to gain some insight into the possible effect of ethnicity on successful family crisis intervention in a largely black inner city community.

SELECTION OF PROJECT STAFF

A. Group Leaders

The project design focused upon the importance of the group discussion leaders in the weekly consultations during the operational phase. Three highly skilled psychologists were recruited: Drs. Selwyn Lederman, Wilson Meaders, and Henry Sindos. Each had considerable formal post-graduate training as individual and group psychotherapists. However, each had extensive experience in non-therapeutic group leadership as well. This combination of therapeutic as well as non-therapeutic group leadership was regarded as ideal for the achievement of project goals. Therapeutic experience ensured a depth of perception and sensitivity to deeper-lying issues; non-therapeutic leadership experience ensured the flexibility necessary to adapt experience to the specific needs of the project.

B. Summer Psychological Advisors and Research Assistants

Since the FCIU was to begin its operational phase on July 1, 1967, when classes were not in session at the College, graduate student consultants were required to function until the beginning of these classes in September. With the onset of the fall semester, the most advanced class of doctoral students in clinical psychology were to be available to provide individual consultations. However, during the summer months' operation, the FCIU would require consultative support, and four graduate students were retained (A. Blum, N. Papouchis, C. Silverstein, and E. Welker), as was a research assistant (L. Goldsmith). All five were provided with an orientation and preparation along with the group leaders. (An unusual feature of the project design called for the group leaders to supervise the individual consultants who were providing consultations to Unit patrolment in each leader's group. This afforded a unique opportunity for educational feed-back and will be discussed more fully later in this report.)

C. Social Worker

While not exclusively assigned to the project, The Psychological Center's social worker (Mrs. E. Bain) devoted herself almost exclusively to the needs of the project during the preparatory phase. In addition to her own orientation and preparation, she was primarily charged with responsibility for establishing community resource contacts, developing a community resource file for use by the Family Crisis Unit and arranging field trips to health and welfare agencies which were planned for the final week of the intensive training month (June).

DATA COLLECTION: FORMS AND PROCEDURES

A. Family Disturbance Report

The report to be completed by Unit patrolmen was to be the basic data source of the entire experiment. It was necessary that its design be such that essential information could be readily recorded with clarity and that the form itself should be easy to manage in the field. In addition to the collection of the usual demographic and descriptive data, the form was designed to encourage the patrolmen to report impressions and judgments based upon their professional training.

B. Family Car File

In addition to its usefulness as a basic research data source, the Family Disturbance Report was intended to serve an important operational purpose. A card file was permanently installed in the family car to enable Unit patrolmen to have readily available to them reports of all interventions conducted by members of the Unit. The file was designed so that reports were filed according to street address and apartment number. This permitted the patrolmen to determine on being dispatched if there had been a previous intervention in that family, what the circumstances had been, whether or not weapons had been involved, and what action had been taken by the previous intervention team. This procedure had obvious advantages for personnel safety but, in addition, it assured a kind of continuity of service which would otherwise be unavailable to those seeking police aid.

C. Community Resource File

A continuously up-dated and cross-indexed family resource file was instituted as a permanent feature of the family car. Actually in the form of a samll loose-leaf binder, it contained references to community agencies with specific agency staff liaison personnel and telephone numbers which would permit specific consultative guidance to the men at the time of the actual intervention if necessary. This feature proved so successful that, at the suggestion of the Unit patrolmen, a personal file has been developed in a form which permits its insertion in each patrolman's memo or log book.

D. Referral Form

To facilitate referrals, a special form was developed. Designed to be similar to a physician's prescription pad, it was also intended to serve as a "flag" for agencies to which referrals were made. It was hoped that a person applying for service could be quickly identified on intake as having been referred by the FCIU, thus enabling more rapid identification of these cases for statistical follow-up purposes.

E. Agency Follow-up Form

This form was intended to facilitate the acquisition of information regarding individuals referred to other agencies. It was designed to be simple and to make minimal demands on overburdened social agencies. The primary goal was to learn whether or not family members were actually making efforts to act upon the officers' suggestions.

F. Consultation De-briefing Form

This form had a dual purpose: 1) to ensure uniform data collection *in depth,* beyond the limitations imposed by the brief Family Disturbance Report, and 2) to add an element of structure to the individual consultation process. Since there were educational advantages to the students serving as consultants, the de-briefing form served to focus the otherwise free-ranging aspects of the consultation. For both the consultant and the consultee, the form was intended to introduce an element of structure and discipline which had educational significance in the supervisory process.

DATA PROCESSING

At the outset of the project, a decision was made to develop a system for rapid information and data retrieval in order to allow for continuous monitoring of the project. Unfortunately, the system selected (Keydex Information and Data Retrieval System) did not prove useful for this purpose and also proved to be far more complicated and time consuming than had originally been anticipated.

INTENSIVE TRAINING PROGRAM

As indicated earlier in this report, a basic assumption in this demonstration was that training police as family crisis intervention specialists required two levels of approach: 1) learning selected and highly specific behavioral science content relevant to functions to be performed and 2) gradual modification of personal values and attitudes and a generalized increase in self-understanding to facilitate the sensitive nature of interpersonal intervention to be attempted.

The intensive training period entailed full-time attendance for four weeks by the entire Unit of eighteen selected officers. The first week was designed largely as an orientation and familiarization period with gradual introduction to the significance of psychological factors underlying observable behavior. Most of the first week's content was intended to be easily related to the world of the policeman and was presented in a lecture context during the mornings. Afternoons were devoted largely to group discussions or workshops. During the afternoon sessions, the officers had their first opportunity to begin working with the group leaders who would be their group consultants through the entire course of the project.

During the second week, the mornings were devoted to content specifically related to "The Family." Again, the afternoons were largely group oriented and quite naturally evidences of openness and group cohesiveness began to be apparent. During the last afternoon of the week, the men were requested to complete sociograms to provide a basis for establishing bi-racial teams. It was intended that assigned pairs would work together as partners for the duration of the project. Also, pairing was accomplished at the end of the second week to enable each pair to practice intervention in the feature of the third week designated as Laboratory Demonstrations. Dr. Bard and Dr. Berkowitz used their own observations of the men, as well as their sociograms, to pair the Unit officers. Of nine pairings made on this basis, there was one refusal. The strong objections of both officers were respected and two different pairings were arranged with no further difficulty.

The third week of intensive training was intended to deal with conflict resolution and specific techniques of intervention. Again, the morning lecture format was used, with continuing opportunity each morning for a "feed-back" session to discuss the material and events of the previous day.

For three afternoons during the third week, all that had been learned up to that point was afforded opportunity for expression in the Family Crisis Laboratory Demonstrations.* These demonstrations proved to be a highlight in the intensive training period. On each of three successive afternoons, specially written family disturbances of about eight minutes' duration each were enacted by professional actors in their entirety three times. Six members of the Unit in uniform were kept in another room as the remaining twelve members of the Unit observed each run-through of the play. At the conclusion of each run-through, two patrolmen who had been paired as partners entered upon the scene as they would in reality and practiced intervention techniques, data collection and referral, if indicated. There were no scripted conclusions to the plays; the

---

* Plays for Living, a division of Family Service Association of America, 44 E. 23rd St., N. Y., N. Y.

actors were instructed to improvise in relation to the behavior of the patrolmen.

The repeated performances permitted the patrolmen in the audience to gain added insight into causative and precipitating factors in the dispute. But, most important, they permitted the officers to witness how *the same set of events (by script) could eventuate in entirely different outcomes, depending upon the behavior of the intervening officers.* After each intervention, the officers involved retired to a room to confer. After the third run-through had been completed, the first pair of officers was summoned to present to the audience their evaluation of events as they found them on arrival at the scene and to provide a rationale for the approach they took. The actors, in turn, frankly stated their reasons for having improvised as they had—giving all the officers an opportunity to see how often well-intended behavior can have an entirely opposite effect. After the three pairs of officers had made their presentations and had their confrontations with the actors on each day, the actors were dismissed and the entire group of officers, audience and participants, engaged in a general discussion and critique led by a project staff member. In the course of the three afternoons devoted to Laboratory Demonstrations, all nine pairs of patrolmen had an opportunity to "learn by doing" in actual practice interventions with professional actors.

The final week of intensive training was largely concerned with referrals. In order that social agencies be more than an abstraction, field visits were arranged, with the men reporting back to the group as a whole the nature of each field visit. During the final week, there were continued group discussions in the afternoon and an effort at evaluation of the experience.

It was the staff's impression that the officers found most of the training useful, but, as in all educational settings, the impact of the material was often related to the skill of the teacher. It was, therefore, difficult to evaluate the relative importance of different content areas. There was further evidence in support of an old collegiate axiom—"You take the teacher, not the course." In any case, the officers felt that the intensive training had significance for them.

At the conclusion of the project, almost two years later, the consensus among the FCIU officers was similar to the impression of the project staff. There was general agreement that four weeks of intensive training was overly long, that two weeks of training would have served as well. This view is probably a valid one, although it should be noted that the eighteen officers had an attendance record of 100% during the four-week intensive tarining period, despite a number of minor illnesses during that time.

On the final day of intensive training, a graduation ceremony was held, during which each patrolman was presented with a Certificate of Completion. This document was also intended to be used as evidence of completion for those men who would later seek credit for the course at the John Jay College of Criminal Justice of The City University of New York.

On the evening of the last day of intensive training and after certificates had been awarded, there was a graduation party and, in effect, this was the last time all eighteen would be together. On the following day, July 1, 1967, the Unit became operational and, hence, according to the specially devised duty chart, each group of six men would be working a different tour. The specially created chart also provided for each group of six to be on campus for consultation on a different day of the week.

THE OPERATIONAL PHASE

THE FAMILY CRISIS RADIO MOTOR PATROL

The radio car was the central structural feature of the project's operational phase (July 1, 1967-May 30, 1969). In a departure from usual New York City Police Department practice, one 30th Precinct radio car was assigned to the FCIU for use in processing all family disturbances in the precinct. Typically, family disturbances are processed by the cars assigned to the sectors in which they occur. The FCIU car was usually assigned to a specific sector, but was authorized to leave the sector when dispatched on a family disturbance anywhere in the precinct, regardless of the sector in which it occurred.

While this feature of the plan ensured FCIU access to all family difficulties in the study area, it had other objectives as well. For one thing, it aided in the reinforcement of professional identity. That is, *the Unit officers were generalists performing all police functions and not specialists devoted to one function alone.* When not engaged in a family intervention, Unit patrolmen provided the same patrol services as other members of the command. This style of specialization avoids the problem common to all fields—professional rejection of those performing exclusively specialized functions. For example, general physicians often regard psychiatrists as not being "real" doctors, just as policemen often regard the Youth patrolman or community relations officer as not being "real" policemen. Because they were charged with general functions, it appeared that Unit officers were accepted by other members of their command and were aided as well in not becoming confused about the fact that they were, first and foremost, police officers.

It was difficult to devise a duty chart which would enable the FCIU car to be manned by Unit members 24 hours a day. With six of the eighteen men assigned to each tour, theoretically it should have been possible always to have two men in the car. Actually, the specially created chart had to make provision for vacations, days off and on-campus training time. The New York City Police Department, after considerable difficulty, did construct a suitable chart which served quite effectively.

INDIVIDUAL CONSULTATION

After the summer of 1967, when summer staff performed individual consultative functions, consultations were conducted by advanced doctoral students (3rd year) in the clinical psychology program at The City College. There were nine students in the third-year class during this project's first year, each student serving as consultant for a pair of patrolmen. The consultations, however, were conducted individually, thus affording an opportunity to identify individual differences in perceptions by each patrolman when they occurred. During the second year of the program (beginning September 1968), when the third-year class had twelve students, six students from two other educational institutions were afforded the opportunity for training in providing consultation to police officers.

The individual consultations were successful from an educational standpoint. Both officers and student-consultants reported distinct advantages in the experience. The students learned how to translate highly complex abstractions about human behavior into practically-oriented terms which could be useful to people called upon to take specific action. The officers, on the other hand, learned how to "think through" and conceptualize about human behavior, thus being enabled to take more effective action.

Our impression that mental health professionals must receive specific consultative training experience early in their careers was confirmed in this project. For the clinical psychology students, it forced self-confrontation on deeply held prejudices and opened to them a world of the psychological "front lines" which would have remained an abstraction at best. For the policemen, it caused some reexamination of attitudes about "intellectuals" and students; it demonstrated, too, the value of thought as well as action.

SUPERVISORY SESSIONS: STUDENT CONSULTANTS

Because the project began between academic years, from June through September 1967 three salaried assistants, students between their second and third years of doctoral training, served as consultants. Since these assistants had also participated in the initial month of on-campus training along with the officers, their orientation to police and police work was unusually facilitated. They benefited from the presentation of material on the role of police in society; particularly telling was their observation of the dramatized family conflict interventions. Their reaction was similar to that of most civilians when they have an opportunity to observe police at work. Not only did they have the response, "I had no idea how difficult the policeman's job is"; they also could appreciate more than most laymen what the police function entailed in clinical terms. "A clinician," one of them exclaimed after a dramatization, "would take days of tests and interviews to make the kind of judgment that these guys have to make under pressure, often at the risk of their own skin." This kind of enthusiastic appreciation greatly simplified the supervisory burden with the first three consultants. Supervisory sessions afforded a weekly opportunity for the consultants to review the working relationships they were building, as they negotiated the middle-ground between "know-it-all" and "what-do-you-know?"

For the first full academic year of the project (September 1967-June 1968), the three who had served during the summer were joined as consultants by six more third-year students, each of whom met individually with a pair of officers. Supervision was in groups of three consultants meeting with the group leader of the same six men who were their consultees. The feeling of newness was worn off for the leaders as well as for the three students who had served as consultants during the previous summer. The latter were assigned, as a kind of leavening, to each of the three supervisory groups. However, the six new consultants were handicapped in not having shared the classroom experience and the shakedown period of the project. They were also handicapped in that theirs was an assigned experience in community consultation, whereas the first three consultants had been voluntarily adding to their income and training by summer employment on the project. Concentrated orientation in the fall of 1967 could not quite serve to bring the six new people to the level of the initial three. The fall of 1967 was also the time of the beginning of serious campus disturbances at Berkeley, California, marked by violent encounters between police and students. The consultants, all graduate students, were all vocationally oriented and not militant undergraduates. But the six new consultants had not had sufficient time to overcome their stereotyped and predictable attitudes toward police. Fortunately, the leaders in the supervisory sessions, with the help of the "experienced" consultants, were able to deal with the feelings the news stories evoked in the students. The leaders' task was facilitated in some instances by the officers themselves, who discussed the students' reactions in their group sessions and talked things out with their respective consultants. The patrolmen were afforded an unexpected community relations opportunity and the students received an added educational dividend. Although disturbances continued to sweep campuses in this country and abroad, in some cases coming close to the College, by spring, 1968, close bonds of understanding and respect existed between student-consultants and police-consultees. This relationship was severely tested during the disturbances on the Columbia University campus. Some of the FCIU were assigned as part of the police detail, and they identified completely with the police point of view. Most of the student-consultants, on the other hand, shared prevailing campus abhorrence of police tactics and behavior, although they did not completely endorse what the Columbia students had done. For a while, some of the consultants could not face their consultees, and it appeared the project would be seriously threatened. An intensive round of meetings with the students, and the supervisory sessions, served to resolve the difficulty. Although some of the students had personally witnessed incidents of overreaction, they could be helped to discriminate and individualize, rather than to lump all police in stereotyped fashion. They could appreciate, after their initial emotionally charged reactions, that the police response had been deliberately provoked in order to radicalize student sentiment. The entire experience on the Columbia University campus provoked a vivid and sobering example of the unenviable difficulties of dealing with a studied intent to provoke violence. Consultations and good working relationships were resumed.

The fall of 1968 presented new problems for supervision which might be summarized as "too many, too late." The third-year doctoral candidates for 1968-69 numbered twelve. This number was supplemented by three graduate students from Teachers College and the post-doctoral Fellows from Columbia University College of Physicians and Surgeons. The supervisory task was to deal with the feelings of the consultants that were not making a sufficient contribution, beyond seeing to the systematic collection of data. Their restiveness was a tribute to the degree of training the officers had achieved. But the challenge of the first year was missing.

The arrival of student disturbances at The City College helped make it clear that the consultants were not disaffected with the project or with the police. When The City College SDS chapter turned on the project in search of an issue, in the spring of 1969, many of the student-consultants were indignant. Despite bitter denunciation in the student press, leaflets and picket-lines chanting about "Pigs Off Campus," the militants could not use the project to strike the kind of spark that would inflame any substantial number of undergraduates. In part, this was due to the respect the officers and the project employed on campus. In part, it was due to the spontaneous efforts on the part of the graduate student-consultants. They defended the project and the officers in spirited exchanges and quiet conversations with militants, pickets and those on the fence. Their efforts culminated in a meeting at which the consultants convincingly allayed the fears of those who could be reached in rational discourse. This event marked the end of the attempt to use the project as an issue, despite later events which paralyzed the College and shut it down. That this group of liberal-intellectual graduate students (the psychiatric Fellows were no longer serving as consultants in the spring semester of 1969) should so actively and effectively defend a police enterprise was due to their first-hand contact with the police officers and to the supervisory group discussions of their relationship with their consultee-teachers.

It is clear that this dual-purpose training program—police and graduate students—benefited significantly from the arrangement and placed group leader and supervisor functions with the same set of persons.

GROUP LEADERS' MEETINGS

The group leaders each brought impressive credentials to their task and had the benefit of two months' preparation to orient them to the specifics of the project before it became operational. But the small discussion group has its own "entrance requirements." Particularly in a police setting, the "outsider," no matter how qualified, must patiently earn the right to be counted as "insider." Each of the leaders, though experienced and qualified, was facing new challenges of a sometimes very personal nature. The monthly leaders' meetings, chaired informally by the project Supervisor, and usually attended by the project Director, provided the forum for airing experiences and observations, and for drawing conclusions. The meetings provided an opportunity to take the pulse of the project and keep it on course. The issues and crises of the preceding sections of this chapter were all brought into the leaders' meetings for discussion and clarification. Not all crises and issues could keep for scheduled meetings, but the unpressured periods provided time for reflection on the meaning of the project and its impact and demands on the leaders. The leaders had to face their own hesitations. While their training and experience was in understanding human behavior and finding the underlying causes and meanings, they did not know much about dealing with violence or how police were accustomed to dealing with it. They, therefore, had to admit to themselves and to their groups that they were on unfamiliar ground.

In the group leaders' meetings, the leaders shared their experiences. As Meaders puts it in referring to his work with the group in this project, "As a leader in this type of training group, I tended to talk rather freely about my own feelings, about my professional work, and about personal issues that affect my perception of other people." In this manner, the leader could provide a role model of personal openness. This was one of the ways to decrease the apprehension of the members of the group that they were subjects of analysis, rather than co-workers who were trying to understand themselves in relation to other people. The leaders had to avoid anything resembling either analytic objectivity or a highly structured student-teacher relationship. By being an active participant who shared his own feelings and experiences with the group, as well as providing information about his own particular area of expertise and knowledge, the leader could hope to encourage an identification with his own curiosity about how the officers could do their work better.

The leaders' meetings discussed the various ways of viewing the leaders' role. If the officers were to be seen as full partners and professionals in their own right, then a highly structured format set out by the leader would be impossible. Otherwise the professions of partnership would be just empty language that would breed distrust. On the other hand, the leader could not be led by the group and abdicate his own professional responsibility. Passivity on the leader's part only served to increase anxiety in the group. Each of the leaders had his own personal style as he carefully found his way between the extreme. The discussions in the leaders' meetings helped clarify these issues.

In addition to demonstrating that they could honestly talk about their own feelings, "show their cards," the group leaders were subjected to varying amounts of "cop talk" that at first was not easy to understand or to accept. Gradually it became clear that some kind of hazing or testing process was taking place. Police are exposed to the seamier aspects of life; the vividness of some descriptions, however, seemed related to their shock value. In the warm weather, the usually unseen pistols became intrusively apparent—and an uncomfortably new experience for the leaders. At times, it seems that the casual display of weaponry and the descriptions of violent encounters (not related to family crises) were intended to impress the leader, test his courage, and perhaps allude obliquely to the dangers experienced by the police. Some of these behaviors, new and somewhat unsettling to the leaders, are not uncommon in locker-room sessions, and were to be regarded as much as signs of acceptance as of testing. The different leaders reacted in terms of their own personalities, as well as in terms of their theoretical orientation. A variety of styles was evolved, including variations in degrees of structuring and different points on the activity-passivity continuum.

Many meetings were devoted to consideration of the "counter-transference" problem, or how to promote understanding by the officers of attitudes and reactions which facilitate or impair their functioning—without invading their personal preserves. The concept of "the public vs. the private counter-transference" proved useful in guiding the discussions (2). Simply put, the leaders have not attempted to analyze the officers or to explore their personal lives or their histories. Instead, they have attempted to help the officers to understand what they feel, to use the feelings induced in them by others as a source of information about the family and the other person, and to avoid letting their feelings interfere with their understanding and effectiveness (18).

In summary, the group leaders' discussions helped to identify and clarify their own experiences and professional postures; helped define what was occurring in the officers' and the supervisory groups; and provided a forum for considering strategies to deal with emerging situations. Matters of theoretical interest and professional contributions were also considered in this setting.

GROUP SESSIONS

Learning to think psychologically, to read the language of behavior was, perhaps, the major task of the group sessions. The concept of self-esteem is easily grasped as an abstraction, but to see its operation as a precipitator of violent emotions requires repeated reviews of specific manifestations. As one group leader reports:

> These were all men raised and educated in an ethic in which behavior is viewed as either good or bad, and is to be responded to accordingly. In the first month of training, the men were confronted by actors letting them know how they experienced these moralistic attitudes. This was the first time many of them realized the effect of a "right or wrong" attitude on a disputant.

I saw my first objective as training the men to see behavior as being purposive, having a cause or motivation and a comprehensible objective. I attempted to teach the men that emotions have a language of their own where neither right or wrong, or even logic, prevails. . . .

Officer G, at the beginning of the project, felt strong urges to retaliate when cursed. Near the end of the project, he saw that when a father called him a m-f, that was a sign of that man's frustration and feeling of impotence. To retaliate out of the officer's own injured feelings would only serve to make the man feel smaller. Mature, reasonable behavior couldn't be expected from someone who sees himself as so little. Pointing out to the man in a few simple words that the officer could see he was up against a tough situation helped rebuild self-esteem and eventually helped the man to look good before his family. In my opinion, this kind of outcome won the kind of good will for the police that no amount of public relations gimmicks could ever achieve. All of this was achieved through frequent discussions of case material in which the focus was on the meaning of words and behavior, rather than on the goodness or rightness.*

The small group proved to be an ideal setting for such learning for it provided the "binocular" vision of the professional psychologist and the professional police officer. The officers reporting on an intervention were helped over their blind spots by peer judgments and reactions to a greater extent than by the leader alone. Listening to another officer's report and helping him to deepen his understanding constantly interchanged teaching and learning roles. Interactions between members of the group could sometimes illustrate the material with incomparable vividness and immediacy.

A. The Effects of Psychological Understanding

Police training places great emphasis on respecting the public to be served. The project has helped put this respect on a more knowledgeable basis:

A major goal of the group process has been to increase the police officers' understanding of their own feelings in dealing with a variety of other people. They have come to recognize that people who seem very different at first are similar to themselves in having similar feelings, needs and concerns to deal with in their lives. . . .

Usually, police officers understandably hate to be called in on family fights because the situations are upsetting emotionally, and because they do not have concepts for understanding what is going

---

* Henry Sindos, M.S. Group Leader, Concluding Report, May, 1969.

on with the family or for coping with their own feelings and responses. Through open discussion in the groups, the officers have learned to know what they are feeling, and to accept it. They have become more comfortable dealing with "upsetting topics," such as sexuality, money, parent-child conflicts, alcoholism and feelings of fear and depression (18).

Until and unless it is experienced, it is difficult to illustrate the subtle interplay between self-knowledge and the ability to understand others. One of the officers found that he "turned off" and let his partner take over whenever they had to deal with a man who had been drinking. Even if the man was not drunk, he couldn't interest himself in trying to communicate or relate, except in the most perfunctory ways. The effect was one of indifference or contempt, so that the partner's task was made more difficult. During one of the sessions, the other members of the group observed that the officer in question always took the side of the woman in such instances. As he talked about his feelings of irritation with men who had drinking problems, he connected his reaction to a family experience with alcoholism. The experience was not pursued in depth, but it served to illustrate how his personal prejudice had interfered with his effectiveness in family crisis intervention. While he had subscribed to the principle of "impartiality," he could not have attained the ability to refrain from taking sides without such group sessions.

The experience of another officer illustrates the technique of using his own responses to help him understand a family situation and help the disputants. An eminently respectable, middle-class father who had succeeded in his own efforts in rising from humble beginnings evoked the antipathy of the officers toward his rebellious teenage daughter. The girl refused to study or go to college, to the dismay of her ambitious, industrious father. She had the ability, and her refusal to apply herself puzzled the officers. As one of the officers was talking to the father, he experienced a feeling of irritation in himself. The father could not seem to relate to what the officer was saying but kept repeating a catalogue of all he had sacrificed for his daughter. The officer exclaimed that he could understand what the girl might be feeling. Perhaps she, too, wanted to be listened to, to be regarded as a separate person, and not just an extension of the father's ambitious hopes. It was apparently an eye-opening experience for both father and daughter.

B. Preventing Assaults on Police

One of the aims of the project was to reduce injuries to police responding to family disputes. It had been assumed at the outset of training that the patrolman's self-esteem was an important element in his ability to avoid the kind of interchange which leads to violence. The training program, and particularly the group sessions, enhanced the officer's sense of adequacy.

The group session restructured the value system of the officers. It has been possible to deal with the "masculine mystique" which has helped make police so malleable at the hands of those who have been interested in provoking violence. Group pressures and sanctions have served to afford recognition to the skillful and effective officer who can "cool" a situation to the point where the disputants can begin to communicate with each other. The men were encouraged to develop their own style for restructuring the initial perceptions of the disputants toward police. The response repertoire of the officers has been expanded, and their sense of mastery enhanced (5).

Everyone connected with the project kept uppermost in mind the awareness that the officers of the Unit were policemen first and foremost, and they were not to be confused as to their role-identity. In one instance which came to the attention of the project staff, a pair of officers were in an apartment interviewing a family. Someone reported that the teenage friend of one of the family was in the hall with a shotgun. The report proved to be erroneous, but the men went into action with holsters loose.

The men of the Unit appreciated the need to communicate quickly to enraged disputants that they were people as well as policemen and that they regarded the combatants as people. They reported back to the group sessions the ways they used to accomplish these ends. One officer, an inveterate cigar smoker, would at times ask for permission to smoke. Others, depending on the season, would ask for a glass of water or a cup of coffee. Another, noticing a fishing rod in a corner, stunned an enraged husband out of his temper by speaking of his own interest in fishing and asking for advice on likely places and lures.

The group discussions of the language of behavior focused on the visible signs of tension. The men learned to observe posture and muscular tension, throbbing blood vessels, clenched teeth and hands, breathing and pupilary contraction and dilation. One officer described a man seated like a coiled spring, nostrils flaring, eyes darting suspiciously, obviously ready to attack or defend. Very elaborately, the officer also sat down. He put his night stick on the floor, took off his hat, slowly unbuttoned the top of his shirt and loosened his tie. He sighed, shook his head, and without a word gave every sign of being hot and tired. As the suspiciously watching man slowly relaxed, the officer smiled and started to talk in a measured way about the heat and the long flights of steps leading to the apartment. It was an effective demonstration of non-verbal suggestion. The description of the scene in the group session was obviously relished. In the underlying competitive group situation, others contributed accounts of keen observation and effective countermeasures against tension.

C. Interlocking Patterns of Conflict and Intervention

The following excerpt from the concluding report of one of the group leaders shows how the group discussions helped the men to understand more deeply what was meant by "seeing both sides":

> My goal in training the officers was to teach them that fights between people, couples, parents and children, had mutual causes, that their patterns were interlocking, and that in a crisis perhaps they would be even more highlighted. The team of officers coming in could have strong reactions to what was going on but they were not to get personally involved. By personally involved I mean they were to learn how the disputes came about, what each person's part was, how the parts meshed to make the problems worse, and to share this information with the family. On the basis of this information the next step was for the officers to see if the couple could respond to the comments made by the officers about what they had observed. If there was discussion and agreement and the couple came to some understanding of what each was doing, the officers could make suggestions about how the problems could be resolved by the disputants or to get the couple to accept a referral to a social agency. Towards the end of the project, my approach changed to having the officers help the disputants understand the problems and then to get the couples to try to come up with their own solutions rather than the officers' suggesting them to the couple. . . .
>
> By focusing on case material and pointing out that, while each officer might have a different impression of what was going on, each could nevertheless be valid and even complementary and that there was a connection between . . . what they felt and what the families they worked with felt . . . it wasn't a question of good or bad but . . . of different points of view which had to be reconciled. Getting the officers as much as possible away from the concept of "good" and "bad" . . . was the most challenging part of the work. . . .

A list of the steps in most effective interventions would probably read as follows:

1. Prevent violence by separating the disputants.
2. Allow only one person to talk at a time.

3. Take the disputants into separate rooms.
4. Switch officers so that the stories can be checked out.
5. In listening to the stories, try to find out in each case what each individual contributed to the conflict.
6. If one of the disputants holds himself to blame, find out in what ways the other shares the blame.
7. Ask questions so as to get the details as clear as possible.
8. Find out if there has been a previous history of this kind of behavior.
9. See if the history goes back to before the marriage to other relationships or similar relationships in the present.
10. Give each person the opportunity to speak in detail.
11. Bring the couple together to tell their stories to each other. Again, make sure only one person speaks at a time.
12. Point out similarities and discrepancies in the stories.
13. Point out the part that each is playing.
14. Get a reaction from both about what the officers say they see is going on.
15. Ask what the couple plan to do in response to what has transpired and to the officers' reactions. If they seem to understand and say they want to try to work it out, accept.
16. If you disagree with their response, suggest that they seek other help. If necessary, make a referral.
17. Tell them that if there is another dispute and they see that they are coming close to violence or to repeating the same pattern they should go again for counseling or contact the FCIU.
18. While noting that there will be further difficulties, assure them that if they sit down and talk at least they can come out in the open and try to resolve it.
19. If not in the beginning, then before you leave, make sure that they know your name.*

AGENCY LIAISON

What appeared at the outset to be one of the most promising features of the project proved to be one of its most consistent frustrations. The officers were delighted to learn of the variety of social resources available in New York City, and they started out making many referrals. The agencies, for their part, seemed to welcome the creation of the FCIU and offered their help. But, despite their unquestioned interest and intentions, the realities of the organization resulted in disappointment and frustration. The agencies are geared to serve the middle-class client who will travel to the office, go through an application process, accept and keep appointments, sometimes after long waiting periods. Their work loads and clerical problems were such that it was impossible to learn

---

* Selwyn Lederman, Ph.D. Group Leader. Concluding Report, May, 1969.

with any degree of accuracy how many referrals resulted in visits to the agencies, how many of these received agency services, and what the outcomes were.

In an attempt to find some solution to the frustrating impasse with the agencies, three kinds of liaison efforts were made. After the initial field trips by the officers during the first month of training, the Psychological Center staff social worker (Mrs. Bain) undertook to maintain contact with the agencies. Since the response was not satisfactory, it was thought that a more personalized liaison than the social worker's time would allow might be more fruitful. As a part of their training experience, the student-consultants were each assigned an agency. Finally, the officers themselves were urged to see if their personal requests for information and service would improve agency responsiveness. With minor exceptions, the agencies could not adapt their policies and practices to the demands made on them by the FCIU.

SPOKEN SPANISH INTRODUCTION

Another way in which the Center responded to the suggestion of the officers was to organize Spanish language classes. The officers felt they would be somewhat less completely at the mercy of interpreters in dealing with Spanish-speaking residents of the precinct if they had some instruction in the colloquial idiom. In cooperation with the Romance Language Department of The City College (Prof. Taffel), a faculty member (Dr. Ramirez) recruited a corps of undergraduate language majors native to Latin America. These students and their faculty advisor developed a specialized vocabulary of highly idiomatic words and phrases and were able to bring most of the officers to a point of proficiency. The officers were all able to indicate some familiarity with the language as a means of establishing contact. Some reported that they had reached the point where they could elicit all the information needed for the data collection purposes of the project.

EVALUATION

STATISTICAL FINDINGS

The findings to be presented are, in each instance, those specifically described as evaluative criteria in the original plan.

Changes in the total number of family disturbance complaints in the demonstration precinct as compared with the comparison precinct.

The 30th Precinct FCIU   intervened on 1,388* occasions with 962 families during the project's operational phase. The 24th Precinct (comparison) recorded 492 interventions with 484 families. The total number of family disturbances reported by the FCIU of the 30th Precinct is about three times that reported by the regular patrol force of the 24th Precinct. This finding is not consistent with expected incidence. While the population of the 24th Precinct is larger and while regularly reported crime statistics are proportionally similar in both precincts, it is unlikely that the real numbers of family disturbances would be so disparate. Ethnic differences in the two precincts (30th, largely Negro; 24th, largely Puerto Rican) would not appear to explain the lower incidence in the 24th Precinct.

The demonstration precinct (30th) engaged in a significantly greater number of family crisis interventions than did the comparison precinct (24th) during the project ($p = <.001$). This was reflected in each quarter ($p = <.001$) and during each month except March, 1969, when the difference approached a significance of .05 by the Chi-Square Test.

Comparing the two precincts in terms of the cumulative total of interventions over time reflects the dramatic difference in both total number of interventions and the rate at which such interventions occurred.

One possible explanation of the difference in totals could be the motivation to record incidents as they occurred. The FCIU obviously had high motivation to record each incident despite the abundance of "paper work" ordinarily required of patrolmen. It may be that the demands of "paper work" on the patrol force of the 24th Precinct resulted in the expedient of not completing a family disturbance report where, in the judgment of the officers, the incident was not sufficiently serious to so require. Although explicit instructions to the regular patrol force of the 24th Precinct required their completion of a report on each family incident, it would appear that the comparison precinct patrolmen established their own "expedience priority system." It is interesting to note that, during a three-month pilot experience in the 30th Precinct, before the onset of the present project, there were 91 family incidents reported. This attests to the common tendency in all police departments to underreport this particular event.

> Repeated interventions in the demonstration precinct as compared with the recurrence rate in the comparison precinct.

---

* This figure includes interventions made on 57 occasions by non-FCIU patrolmen but which were recorded and maintained in the FCIU data bank as well as in the family car file.

The 30th Precinct FCIU clearly demonstrated consistency in recording repeated interventions with the same families. The FCIU recorded a significantly greater number of repeat cases (p = <.001) than did the 24th Precinct during each quarter and throughout the project. While 30.7% of all FCIU interventions (1,388) were repeats, only 13.8% of all 24th Precinct interventions (492) were repeats. The difference in percentages between the two is significant at the .05 level of confidence.

The significantly greater percentage of repeat interventions by the 30th Precinct FCIU probably reflects the greater attention to family disturbance as a police function which was inherent in the project. However, the more rigorous data collection in the 30th Precinct undoubtedly reveals a more nearly accurate estimate of family disturbance as it affects police manpower utilization than has been available through traditional recording practices.

On the other hand, the availability of a more effective police service in this connection may have resulted in greater and more effective community utilization of the FCIU. While the 30th Precinct showed a smaller percentage of "once-only" calls (30th, 75.7%; 24th, 89.4%), the difference was not statistically significant. However, the *tendency* for the 30th Precinct to have a smaller percentage of "once-only" interventions may be mute testimony to the unreliability of comparison precinct data. That is, if initial cases went unreported and the same families were later visited, they would erroneously be reported as initial cases rather than repeats. By the same token, the FCIU percentage of repeat interventions would have to be greater as a result of greater accuracy of recording. However, it should be noted that a significantly greater percentage of 30th Precinct repeat interventions could indicate that chronically disordered families may have become better able to utilize the police as an acceptable alternative to violent acting out.

> *Changes in the total number of homicides in the demonstration precinct as compared with changes in the comparison precinct.*

In order to establish some base-line statistics on homicides and assaults, the number of such crimes for the two-year period preceding the demonstration was computed. Total homicides increased considerably (three and one half-times) in the demonstration precinct, while their was a one-third reduction in homicides in the comparison precinct.

Clearly, the operation of the FCIU failed to effect any change in overall homicide incidence in the demonstration area. Also, it is difficult to explain the reduction of homicides in the comparison precinct. It should be noted, however, that there has been a general homicide increase city-wide during the period covered by this study.

Changes in the number of homicides among family members in both the demonstration precinct and the comparison precinct.

The number of family homicides increased in the demonstration precinct and remained constant in the comparison precinct, when compared with the period preceding the operational phase of twenty-two months. However, in at least two instances of family homicide in the 30th Precinct, the victim and the perpetrator were not residents of the precinct but were transients at the time of the slaying. More important, too, it should be noted that *not one of the five families had previously been known to the FCIU.*

This finding has at least two possible implications. One, it may be that family homicides are a phenomenon which occurs with such suddenness as to preclude any warning that a fatal outcome is imminent. That is, families who solicit police intervention may, in fact, be less inclined to violent and homicidal acting out than those who do not ask for police intervention. On the other hand, it may be that there would have been an even greater number of family homicides in the 30th Precinct had the FCIU not been available as a resource. Skillful police intervention may have presented families in conflict with an option which served as an alternative to violence.

Changes in total number of assaults in the demonstration precinct as contrasted with assaults in the comparison precinct.

The total number of reported assaults in the demonstration precinct is less than that reported in the comparison precinct over the project period. However, as contrasted with the base-line data of the previous twenty-two months, the 30th Precinct shows a slight and non-significant increase in the total number of assaults. Changes in rate of reported assaults do not appear to have been affected by the operations of the FCIU.

Changes in family assaults in the demonstration precinct as contrasted with such assaults in the comparison precinct.

No base-line data are available for the twenty-four month period prior to the demonstration project's onset due to the fact that family assaults were not separately recorded during the 1965-67 period.

During the project's duration there were about one-third more family assaults in the comparison precinct than in the demonstration precinct. Family assaults in both precincts comprised about 19.5% of total assaults. Arrests for assault in family disturbances were 2.5% less in the demonstration precinct than in the comparison precinct. The significance of this difference is difficult to interpret, because there is no assurance of uniformity of the data from each precinct. However, there is the suggestion that the FCIU may have maintained a lower arrest rate in family disputes through the use of mediation and referral techniques. This, in turn, may have reduced the burden on the courts of cases wherein, as is commonly found, the complainant ultimately drops the charge. This finding would tend to support questions which have been raised concerning the appropriateness of existing judicial processes in dealing with family conflict.

Changes in the number of injuries to patrolmen responding to family disturbances within the demonstration precinct and in comparison with the comparison precinct.

During the entire period of the demonstration project, *no injuries were sustained by members of the FCIU*. Two members of the regular patrol force of the 30th Precinct and one member of the 24th Precinct patrol force sustained injuries while intervening in family disputes.

This finding is particularly striking in that the FCIU patrolmen had a much greater probability of being injured in view of their greater individual exposure to family disturbance. The absence of injury despite the greater likelihood of injury would have to be attributed to the skill acquired by Unit officers in moderating family disputes. The implications of this finding are profound. The injuries sustained by three *non-FCIU* patrolmen in the 30th and 24th Precincts can be projected for the New York City Police Department as a whole. Although exact numbers are not a matter of public record, there are approximately 30,000 members of the New York department. Estimating the *average* complement of officers in each of 77 precincts at about 200 men, it would appear appropriate to estimate that about 18,000 men might be involved in police duties which include family disputes. Given the validity of these estimates and based upon the experience of this project, a projection of 135 patrolmen injured city-wide in a similar twenty-two month period would not be unrealistic. The absence of injury to the eighteen men of the high-risk FCIU becomes even more significant in light of this projection.

*Follow-up visits to determine outcome in families served by
the FCIU as compared with families served by the comparison precinct.*

As previously noted, follow-up visits were precluded by the concern
of the New York City Police Department for the civil and individual
rights of the families visited by the FCIU.

SUMMARY OF STATISTICAL FINDINGS

The demonstration of Police Family Crisis Intervention was evaluated
primarily in relation to a police function as it affects certain categories
of crime. Over the life of the project, the demonstration precinct reported
a significantly greater number of interventions; there was an increase
in total homicides (significantly) and in total assaults (not significantly); there was an increase in family homicides but there were no
homicides in any of the 962 families previously seen by the FCIU; family
assaults decreased; and there were no injuries to any officer in the Family
Crisis Intervention Unit. In addition to the formal evaluative criteria,
there were a number of impressions and observations bearing upon the
demonstration project.

OBSERVATIONS AND IMPRESSIONS

A. Implications for the Community

Community acceptance of the FCIU can be inferred in a number of
ways. Unit members reported an increasing number of referrals of
families by other families previously served. In addition, there has been
an increase in the number of families entering the station house to ask
for specific Unit patrolmen. The Unit patrolmen reported community
acknowledgment of their status by such comments as, "Oh, you must be
those special cops."

After a time, it became apparent to the officers that the family radio
motor patrol was known in the community; residents apparently learned
the family car number. The officers commented on the noticeable absence
of "freezing" when the car rolled into a block. The men reported an
unusual absence of tension in most instances of interaction with the
citizenry. There were any number of personal expressions of interest and
support by community leaders and by ministers, educators, etc.

One of the most telling signs of a positive community response to the
FCIU was a negative one—that is, in the absence of a reaction. In these

times of community organization for action, a program like this one would have been a natural target for attack if the community felt it to be inimical to its interests. The fact that a law enforcement agency was involved makes this an even greater likelihood. However, in no instance did a community organization, regardless of its militancy, object to the service provided by the FCIU. In fact, it is particularly noteworthy that a personal attack on Dr. Bard and the project by The City College Students for a Democratic Society and Youth Against War and Fascism failed to rally any community support. There is every reason to believe that this form of tacit community acceptance speaks as loudly as would the most strident expression of opposition.

B. Implications for Law Enforcement

The initial reaction of most policemen to the experiment (including some Unit patrolmen themselves) was one of cynicism and skepticism. The regular patrol force of the 30th Precinct were initially overtly cool to the experiment largely because they saw the Unit as functioning in an exclusively specialized manner which would remove its members from "real" police duties. As the operational phase progressed and the other officers became aware of the generalized patrol functions of the FCIU, there was a noticeable change in attitude, particularly among the younger members of the command. FCIU patrolmen were approached by other officers and queried about what they did and how they did it. Apparently it was the younger officers who showed the greatest interest; more senior policemen tended to minimize the significance of the project throughout.

Police Department statistics give every indication that the basic professional identity of the Unit officers remained intact. One measure of this is to be found in the favorable disciplinary record of the Unit and in the fact that non-family enforcement activity of the FCIU was on a par with other members of the command (e.g., summons enforcement for parking, moving and other violations, arrests for burglaries and robberies, etc.).

Superior officers at the precinct level made repeated reference to the high morale of the Unit. It is our impression that increased professional responsibility increased job satisfaction. Mastery of technical skills and the challenge of decision-making responsibility are conducive to high morale in all occupations.

It is our impression also that policemen themselves feel more secure and less defensive generally when they have professional skills equal to the increasing complexities of their role. To lessen the gap between community and the police, law enforcement personnel can generate respect and trust by performing their complex order-maintenance functions in ways that are consistent with the citizens' hopes. It would appear that the FCIU members demonstrated to some extent the viability of such an outlook.

C. Implications for Mental Health

As a community mental health resource, the police are an agency without parallel. In the interlocking network of helping agencies, the police have stood in a unique position in the psychological front lines. By increasing the sensitivity and professional perceptiveness of policemen, an unusual early warning mechanism for identifying psychological and social pathology is made available to the community.

While the intent of this project was to deal with domestic disturbances, the FCIU became a resource for a range of human problems. Their trained ability to discriminate among the problems and their knowledge of the options open to them permitted the officers to move in helpful directions and yet to remain faithful to their basic peace-keeping mission.

In many instances, what appeared on the surface to be a domestic disturbance turned out to be a problem of a very different nature. For example, a husband and wife dispute might have been precipitated by the frustrations and desperation produced by three weeks of the husband's unemployment. Stereotypical management of the dispute might have prevented discerning the underlying cause of the friction in an otherwise good relationship With such knowledge, patrolmen can foster rational insights in the disputants and, if necessary, make an appropriate and helpful referral. In a sense the patrolmen becomes a "case-identifier," but, even more important, an initial screening or intake professional. And it must be emphasized that this level of performance in no way compromises police authority or responsibility.

An unexpected impression gained from the experience of the FCIU is the wide range of human difficulties which are masked by the designation "family dispute." Health problems, social difficulties, housing problems, and mental illness all came within the purview of the FCIU, yet in each instance the complaint was originally designated as a "family dispute." In a number of instances, for example, the domestic disturbance was a thin veneer for a helpless father's or mother's request that the police act as a father surrogate to regulate the behavior of an adolescent out of control. ("Officer, you talk to her! I can't do a thing with her!")

It became quite clear during the course of the project that police officers are in a unique position to identify emotional disorder at its earliest stage. Often summoned to deal with bizarre behavior, they are summoned just as frequently to deal with situations in which subtle behavior changes may connote an incipient or decompensating mental illness. For example, the ability to detect an agitated depression and deal with it appropriately has far-ranging potentials.

If primary prevention has any validity as a mental health concept, there is no helping agency in a better position to put it to the test than the police. However, it is important to emphasize that by so doing the police need not be identified as psychiatrists or social workers. Indeed, to confuse the professional identity of the policeman would in itself constitute a violation of the concept's validity. The aims of community mental health can be served within the framework of the peace-keeping mission of law enforcement.

Social Agencies as Resources. The role of community social and mental health agencies in supporting the efforts of the FCIU is particularly worthy of note. In the early months of the project, the Unit members referred a high percentage of cases to other agencies. Insecurity about their experimental role and unrealistic expectations regarding community agency potentials contributed to this early tendency to excessive referral. However, as the men gained a sense of mastery, they tended to rely on their own mediative skills and to make referrals only when the outside agency could be enlisted to provide a service outside the arbitrator's limited crisis role.

On the other hand, the officers experienced a growing disenchantment with social agencies. Much disappointment was expressed that agencies appeared to be overburdened and seemed unable or unwilling to provide flexible crisis services often required in support of a front-line operational group like the FCIU. On many occasions, the men expressed the wish for a social agency to be available 24 hours a day; one to which they might refer people at any time of the day or night.

The officers of the FCIU were encouraged to exercise their own judgment in the matter of referrals. The preferred outcome of course was one in which resolution of the conflict was brought about through the officers' intervention . . . the theory being that skillful intervention at the height of the crisis is more meaningful than even extensive treatment when the situation has cooled and defenses are again intact. It was impressive, however, that the Unit referred to a wide range of agencies indicating their learned ability to discriminate the special needs of each case. There was a total of 785 referrals to 719 families in the 30th Precinct by the FCIU. There was a total of 268 referrals to 263 families in the 24th Precinct.

Over the course of the project, one-quarter of all interventions were processed without referral. Of the 74.8% of all the families seen in the project who were referred, 34.8% were referred to Family Court. Indeed, Family Court referrals comprised almost one-half (48.7%) of all referrals. This rate of referral to Family Court may be because Family Court services are extensive (psychiatric, social and family counseling) and the Court's interest in the project ensured a continued and reliable referral resource. Another frequently utilized resource was the local Catholic Charities Family Counseling Unit (17.4% of referrals). It was a frequent choice for referral primarily because it is located centrally in the 30th Precinct.

Closer examination of the referral patterning in both precincts reveals additional significant findings. Family Court referrals by the 24th Precinct patrol force was 88.4% of all referrals made. The significantly greater percentage of such referrals by the 24th Precinct may signify less discrimination in the use of the Court. However, the 30th Precinct FCIU made a significantly greater number of referrals to hospitals for both physical and psychiatric reasons and a significantly greater number of referrals ($p = .05$ or better) to at least six other welfare or social agencies.

Given the difficulties mentioned earlier in this report regarding follow-up, it was particularly important to attempt to learn if individuals or families referred actually took action upon the referral. It is somewhat discouraging to note the large numbers for whom *no information* is available. Except in relatively rare instances, routine inquiries were made each month by form. Either the form was not returned or, if it was, it may have contained no entries. The cooperation of some agencies was clear, most agencies were either unwilling or unable to cooperate.

It is important to note that about 20% of all families referred (and about whom we have information) actually did apply for assistance at the agency recommended by the FCIU. It is interesting that these data indicate the greatest likelihood of acting upon the referral occurs when concrete or tangible services are expected of the agency (e.g., hospital or welfare agency) by the applicant. The more abstract or intangible the service offered, the less likely the person is to apply to the agency. This finding is consistent with previous experience in social service.

D. Implications for Education

In many ways the project constituted an experiment in education as well as one in law enforcement and mental health. On the one hand, it attempted to provide technical skills usually associated with the helping professions to a group of police officers whose personal safety has been traditionally thought to be associated with a very different kind of professional identity and personal performance. On the other hand, the project attempted to broaden the scope of professional training for clinical psychologists by exposing them to a world usually alien to them.

Police Education. The major educational departure in this project was the rejection of the traditional military training model. Most police instruction is devised to conform to a model in which disciplinary control is overriding and in which technical information is conveyed "by the numbers." Much of the instruction is provided by lecture (with or without audio-visual aids) in conjunction with instructional manuals. The approach is conductive to rote learning for automatized functions; it may well be inimical to functions which require analysis, discrimination, decision-making, and flexibility.

A major assumption in this project was that many of a policeman's functions are service-oriented, and hence learning them should be developed by "educational" means rather than by disciplined "training" methods. The distinction between education and training is nowhere as clear as when one carefully examines the objectives of the program or course involved.

In this project, we eschewed typical and traditional training to some extent. We added new techniques of individual and group interaction with an emphasis upon self-understanding, in order to increase the capacity for flexibility in selecting appropriately from among an increased repertoire of response options. We also assumed that education of this kind could not be accomplished immediately but, rather, that it required reinforcement over time.

The educational program for the FCIU contained elements of the traditional training model and the newer educational model. The intensive training period was essentially concerned with informational input in an accelerated form. But, even during the intensive training period, the officers were engaged in the early stages of enlarging their cognitive experience through interpersonal experiencing. Th subsequent weekly consultations were calculated to permit growth and change over time; to allow for the gradual absorption of knowledge not on an intellectual level alone, but on an inner-experience level as well.

We believe that our approach has been successful. The most telling finding in this connection is in the absence of injury to the officers of the FCIU. Traditional police training leaves the law-enforcement officer unprepared for the subtle complexities of human conflict. His limited response repertoire and his lack of personal insight lead to fear and a rigidity which often prompts inappropriate behavior leading to a tragic outcome. None of the FCIU was injured despite a high probability that they would be, by the very nature of the project. That they were not injured testifies, in some measure, to their successful educational experience and consequent personal and professional growth.

Psychological Education. The traditional process by which students of behavior are produced leaves much to be desired. Rooted in disciplined scholarship, much of the method of developing psychologists who specialize in *human* behavior is astonishing in its exclusiveness. A clinical psychologist, for example, may acquire his professional identity having been exposed almost exclusively to laboratories populated by experimental rats or experimental sophomores; or, if his experience has extended beyond the campus, to the sterile and highly disciplined hospital or clinic environment.

There is a growing realization in psychology and elsewhere that "life is with people." The psychological professions have come slowly to understand the importance of altering traditional training procedures to make them more appropriately educational. This approach requires immersion of the professional psychologist in the world of real people who live as real people live. This kind of education requires the enlargement of purely cognitive learning by procedures which enhance self-confrontation and the development of insight. It should ideally increase the range of adaptive alterantives to permit the psychologist to "know" human behavior on an emotional as well as a purely intellectual level.

This project has sought to achieve this kind of enlargement in the education of clinical psychologists. The project afforded an opportunity to learn techniques of consultation by providing consultations to an "atypical" professional colleague. It assured the confrontation with issues of authority often engendered by policemen. More than anything, perhaps, in exposing them to life as it really is, it may have helped our doctoral students to relinquish some of the omnipotence and grandiosity that is often a by-product of training in the helping professions.

It is our impression that the experience in this project provided our psychology doctoral students with a foundation which cannot help but serve them well in the future. In addition, many of them have altered their understanding of law enforcement, being enabled to perceive the myriad and complex professional responsibilities the officer has thrust upon him by society. And, finally, in the process of consulting and interacting, the students were exposed to rich case material for real life— the kind rarely seen in the restricted middle class and highly verbal world from which most students come and with which they are so comfortable. For the foregoing reasons, it was our impression that the project was successful as an educational experience for our doctoral students.

E. Implementation and Institutionalization

The primary problem of institutionalizing the demonstration in family crisis intervention relates to the enormous size of New York City, its complexity, and to the large numbers involved in its policing. The educational and logistical problems associated with extending the approach developed in this project are staggering. Indeed, these problems cannot be minimized when considering the implications inherent in the methods of the project.

Earlier in this report, reference was made to the fact that traditional methods of police training parallel those of the military. Much of this attitude is probably directly traceable to the repeated necessity for rapidly training large numbers for para-military functions. And, as with the military, the attitude prevails that the training function can be effectively discharged only by those who are themselves a part of the system. While understandable, this is an attitude which militates against effective extension of the methods and the approach embodied in this project.

If past experience is any guide, there will be a tendency to legitimatize family crisis intervention as a police function by curriculum insertions in present training programs (recruit and in service) and by developing a "how-to" instructional manual. Such an approach, while both predictable and understandable, represents a rejection of the basic contribution of the present demonstration. What is more, it implies the illusion of change where no change in fact occurs.

Extension of the approach to an aspect of law enforcement developed in this demonstration must be considered in the light of the setting in which the experiment was conducted. As a limited demonstration in a circumscribed area, it may have been regarded as manageable; as a limitless operation in the distant reaches of a vast institution, it may appear mind boggling in complexity. But, regardless of the awesome complications involved, the validity of the demonstration effort can be maintained only if its integrity is preserved.

The approach undertaken in this project demonstrated a viable method for accomplishing collaboration between professionals in law enforcement and in mental health. Usually operating in mutually exclusive isolation, these two groups have, in this project, demonstrated the capacity to collaborate successfully to their mutual advantage and to the advantage of the community as well. For each to retreat to traditional positions of isolation violates one of the most vital aspects of the demonstration. The measure of the demonstration's effectiveness will be reflected in the extent to which such collaboration continues. National and international interests in this project by both professional groups suggests efforts at "action-collaboration" will indeed be carried forward.

Any institution must move with caution in extending an innovative program. When the innovation involves collaboration with those outside the institutional system, past experiences with "outsiders" is a critical determinant in the process of implementation and institutionalization. The police have learned through bitter experience that most "intellectuals" and "do-gooders" fail to understand their problems, that such individuals tend to be critical and fault-finding, and that they frequently fail the most fundamental tests of trust. These reality experiences may stand as a primary barrier in the process of institutionalization.

Whether in relation to large urban centers or to small towns, however, the project has succeeded in highlighting what may well be a most significant but unheralded aspect of law enforcement. Traditional police training and the very organizational structure of most police departments fail to acknowledge or to reward the intricate web of interpersonal services performed by policemen. The necessity for developing organizational means for accomplishing human conflict resolution; the development of a system of incentives and rewards in relation to "order-maintenance" as well as to "enforcement"; the introduction of educational methods appropriate to functions to be performed; and the abandonment of a stance of exclusive isolation are the implicit requirements of institutionalizing the methods of this demonstration.

Finally, in encouraging and providing exceptional cooperation for this experiment, the New York City Police Department evidenced remarkable depth of understanding of the problems of modern law enforcement. The Department's commitment to the program is an expression of its sensitivity to the needs of a changing society. Its willingness to undertake the risks inherent in this project speaks well for its ability to meet the challenges of the future.

SUMMARY

Training police in family crisis intervention was intended to demonstrate innovative methods of crime prevention and preventive mental health. Processing family disturbances constitutes a major aspect of police work. Traditional police approaches to the problem do not reflect the realities of this aspect of the police experience. There is evidence that a significant proportion of injuries and fatalities suffered by police occur in the highly volatile family conflict situation. The present project attempted to modify family assaults and family homicides in a circumscribed area, as well as to reduce personal danger to police officers in such situations.

In addition, the project attempted the development of a new preventive mental health strategy. Assuming that family conflict may be an early sign of emotional disorder in one or all of the participants, the project attempted to utilize policemen as front-line "case-finders" in keeping with theories of primary prevention. It was proposed that selected policemen could be provided with interpersonal skills necessary to effect constructive outcomes in deteriorating situations which require police intervention.

Rejection of an exclusively specialized role for the police officers involved was a major emphasis. The program assiduously avoided the conversion of policemen into social workers or psychotherapists. The officers were expected to perform all generalized police patrol functions but were the individuals dispatched on all family disputes in a given geographical area of about 85,000 residents.

The project was organized in three stages:

1. Preparatory Phase. During the first month, 18 police volunteers were selected; all had had at least three years of service and gave evidence of motivation and aptitude for family crisis specialization.

The second month entailed an intensive, 160-hour, on-campus training course involving the entire Unit. In addition to lectures and field trips, there was active participation in "learning by doing" through Family Crisis Laboratory Demonstrations. These demonstrations involved specially written plays depicting family crisis situations enacted by professional actors and in which the patrolmen in the Unit actively intervened in pairs. Practice intervention were subjected to group critique and discussion. Finally, human relations workshops were conducted to sensitize the patrolmen to their own values, attitudes, and automatic responses.

2. Operational Phase. For the two-year duration of the project one radio patrol car was reserved for family crisis work in the experimental precinct. It was dispatched on all complaints or requests for assistance that could be predetermined as involving a "family disturbance." The car responded to calls anywhere in the precinct without regard to sector boundaries. The 18 men in the Unit were able to provide continuous

coverage, and at most times on each tour of duty four additional family crisis specialists were available to assist in processing calls during peak evening and weekend periods.

Discussion groups of six men each met with group leaders who were familiar with the work of policemen. Consideration of current crisis situations evoked assumptions, preconceptions, and misapprehensions about human behavior and family relationships that may have been implicit in the attitudes and performance of Family Crisis Unit members.

In addition to continuous group experience, each family specialist was assigned an individual consultant for at least one hour's weekly consultation. The individual consultants were advanced clinical psychology students who acquired in this way an unusual community consultation experience. The reciprocal effect of these encounters on the students and upon the policemen is self-evident.

3. Evaluation Phase. The evaluation phase encompassed the last four months of the project, although normal operations of the Family Crisis Intervention Unit continued during that time. Systematic data collection took place over the duration of the project, with an emphasis on simple tabulation in order to assess changes over time in a number of variables.

To facilitate evaluative procedures, a neighboring police precinct with a population composition somewhat similar to that of the demonstration precinct served as a basis of comparison. Comparisons were made based on changes in the total number of family disturbance complaints in the demonstration precinct as compared with the control precinct, differences in recurrence of complaints by the same families within the demonstration precinct and within the control precinct, and changes in the number of homicides and assaults involving both family members and policemen responding to family fight complaints.

The demonstration in Police Family Crisis Intervention was evaluated primarily in relation to a police function as it affects certain categories of crime. Over the life of the project, the demonstration precinct reported a significantly greater number of interventions; there was an increase in the total homicides (significantly) and in total assaults (not significantly); there was an increase in family homicides but there were no homicides in any of the 962 families previously seen by the FCIU; family assaults decreased; and there were no injuries to any officer in the Family Crisis Intervention Unit. In addition to the formal evaluative criteria, there were a number of impressions and observations bearing upon the demonstration project. These impressions and observations are discussed, along with implications of the project for law enforcement, mental health, and education.

CONCLUSIONS

It is our impression that the experimental project in police family crisis intervention demonstrated the following:

1. Sensitive and skillful police intervention in family disturbances may serve to reduce the occurrence of family assaults and family homicides.
2. The presence of trained police specialists in family crisis intervention may have a positive effect upon police-community relations.
3. Personal safety of police officers can be greatly increased through the use of psychologically sophisticated techniques in dealing with highly charged human conflict situations.
4. The professional identity of police officers can remain intact despite their acquisition of the skills and techniques usually associated with the helping professions.
5. Policemen are in an unusual position for early identification of human behavioral pathology and, if trained, can play a critical role in crime prevention and preventive mental health.
6. Police officers can function as generalists and, at the same time, and according to personal capability, can acquire highly specialized capacities within their law enforcement role.
7. Professionals in law enforcement and in psychology can successfully collaborate; each group can realize its primary mission and yet improve its service to the community.
8. Psychological education directed at specific police functions can enhance law enforcement in general and order-maintenance in particular.

It is recommended that:

1. Efforts be made in a variety of settings to replicate the program developed in this project.
2. Attention be given to the refinement of the generalist-specialist model as it applies to the range of interpersonal services policemen are expected to perform.
3. Universities be encouraged to collaborate with law enforcement agencies as a method for greater community involvement and as a means for extending knowledge of human behavior in the laboratory of the real world.
4. Law enforcement agencies acknowledge their communality of interest with both the learned and helping professions and thereby reduce their traditional isolation.

REFERENCES

1. ACKERMAN, N. W. *The Psychodynamics of Family Life.* New York: Basic Books, 1958.
2. BALINT, MICHAEL. Psycho-analysis and medical practice. *Int. J. Psychol.* 47, 1966, 54.
3. BARD, M. Implications of analytic psychotherapy with the physically ill. *Amer. J. of Psychotherapy* 13, 1959, 860-871.
4. BENSING, R. C. & SCHROEDER, O. *Homicide in an Urban Community.* Springfield, Ill.: Charles C. Thomas, 1960, p. 77.
5. BERKOWITZ, B. Alternatives to Violence. Symposium on Violence and Its Regulation. Amer. Orthopsychiatric Assn. N. Y. March 31, 1969.
6. BRADFORD, L. T., GIBB, J. R. & BENN, K. D. (eds.) *T-Group Therapy and Laboratory Method.* New York: Wiley, 1964.
7. BULLOCK, H. A. Urban homicide in theory and fact. *J. of Crim. Law, Criminology and Police Science* 46, 1955, p. 572.
8. CAPLAN, G. (ed.) *Prevention of Mental Disorders in Children: Initial Explorations.* New York: Basic Books, 1961.
9. CUMMING, ELAINE, CUMMING, IAN & EDELL, LAURA. Policeman as philosopher, guide and friend. *Soc. Prob.* 12, 1965, 276-286.
10. DURKHEIM, EMIL. *Suicide.* Glencoe, Ill.: Glencoe Press; 1951, p. 354.
11. EPSTEIN, CHARLOTTE. *Intergroup Relations for Police Officers.* Baltimore, Md.: Williams & Wilkins Company, 1962.
12. *FBI Law Enforcement Bulletin.* January 1963, p. 27.
13. JACOBSON, D. D. (ed.) The Etiology of Schizophrenia. New York: Basic Books, 1958.
14. Joint Commission on Mental Health and Illness. *Action for Mental Health.* New York: Basic Books, 1961.
15. KLEIN, D. C. & LINDEMANN, E. Preventive intervention in individual and family crisis situations. In: Caplan, *op. cit.,* pp. 283-306.
16. LIDZ, T., FLECK, S. & CORNELISON, A. R. *Schizophrenia and the Family.* New York: International Universities Press, 1965.
17. McCLOSKEY, C. C. JR. Executive Director, Division of Police Administration Services, Office for Local Government, State of New York, Albany, New York. Personal communication.
18. MEADERS, WILSON E. Group Techniques for Training Policemen to Deal with Violence and Aggression. Symposium, Council for Psychoanalytic Psychotherapy, February 9, 1969.
19. New York City Police Department. Press Release #30, March 31, 1966.
20. RAPOPORT, R. Normal crisis, family structure and mental health. *Family Process* 2, 1963, 68-80.
21. REIFF, ROBERT & RIESSMAN, FRANK. *The Indigenous Non-Professional: A Strategy of Change in Community Action and Community Mental Health Programs.* U.S. Dept. of Health, Education and Welfare, Report No. 3, November 1964.
22. RIOCH, M. *et al.* National Institute of Mental Health pilot study in training mental health counselors. *Amer. J. Orthopsychiatry* 33, 1963, 678-1969.
23. TOCH, HANS. *Violent Men.* Chicago: Aldine Press, 1969.
24. WOLFGANG, M. E. *Patterns in Criminal Homicide.* Philadelphia: Univ. of Penn. Press, 1958.

52

FILMS ON GROUP AND FAMILY PSYCHOTHERAPY

John Gladfelter, Ph.D.

Films for use in the teaching of psychotherapy became generally available in the 1950's. The first film on group psychotherapy to become available during this period was S. R. Slavson's "Activity Group Therapy."* This film, which is now considered a classic, represented a pioneer effort to communicate basic group therapy concepts, and undoubtedly had a positive influence on the growth of this treatment modality in the United States. Admittedly, the film is limited to the use of activity group techniques with adolescents; because of the clarity with which these techniques are presented, however, it is evident that this approach has validity for other age groups as well.

In the years since, a number of films, on a variety of therapeutic techniques, have been distributed. Thus, at present, there are sixty-two films available which would be classified under the general rubric of group and family therapy. This article will cover thirteen films which were made from 1968 to the present, and are representative of recent productions in the area of group and family therapy. Thus it should be noted, in this connection, that in selecting films for discussion this topic was given a liberal definition, so that variants of these therapies, e.g., sensitivity groups, marathon groups, etc., could be given consideration. More precisely, this article includes a brief description of the film creator's

---

* This film can be obtained from the New York University Film Library, 26 Washington Place, New York, New York 10003.

intent and the content of each of these thirteen films, as well as a critical evaluation of the film under discussion, with specific reference to its value as a teaching aid.

Some General Comments on the Use of Films

All too frequently the viewer of films of therapeutic operations hopes to see therapeutic techniques in action, so to speak; that is, he expects the film to show him "what is really going on." He is, of course, doomed to disappointment in this respect. Films cannot look inside patients or therapists and show change or growth. On the other hand, films can give the viewer an awareness of the processes by which therapists and patients communicate, and transmit something of the "feel" of their interactions.

All films share these basic characteristics in common. But, as is true of therapists in general, the film makers also vary greatly in their approach to psychotherapy; consequently, the appeal (and value) of any given film will range widely, depending on the audience to which it is shown. The descriptions presented herein of the content and purpose of current films on group and family therapy can provide a useful guide to the selection of films. However, they cannot serve as a substitute for the actual previewing of these films. Granted this is a time-consuming procedure, it is an absolute necessity for the instructor who wants to select the most appropriate film for his particular purpose.

Practical Considerations

For clarity of presentation, the name and address of one source for each of the current films discussed herein is listed in the Appendix to this article. No attempt has been made, however, to include rental or purchase prices. Although only one source has been listed, in fact, many of these films are available through several distributors. Consequently, prices vary considerably, and the reader is advised to contact the source of the film directly for such information. Parenthetically it should be noted that this is one reason film listings and catalogs rarely provide uniform data with respect to the number of films available for distribution, their rental and purchase prices, and the sources from which they can be obtained.

Certain films can only be shown to selected audiences, if wide distribution would violate the confidentiality of the "actors" involved. When a known limitation has been placed on audience viewing, this will be mentioned in the description of the film to which it applies and in the Appendix as well. As a general rule, it is well to observe restrictions which have been imposed on the distribution of films. Litigation in regard to film showings is a matter of record, and has caused the withdrawal of films from the market in the past.

Finally, the reader should be alerted to the fact that the more popular films must be reserved several months in advance; therefore, early inquiry is advisable. In an emergency, however, a copy of a sought after film may be obtained from local or state mental health agencies which maintain film libraries.

Films on Group Psychotherapy

1. *"Broad Spectrum Behavior Therapy in a Group,"* which was made by A. Lazarus, differs a bit from the other films in this listing because of the nature of behavior therapy and the use of the group for particular therapeutic purposes. The film presents segments of group behavior in which Lazarus is shown utilizing and directing the behavior of his subjects, all of whom are students, toward specific goal behaviors. Foci of attention in the group are behavior rehearsal, assertiveness, and desensitization using assumed norms of social behaviors as the referrents for behavior models. In view of the disparity between the basic concepts of group therapy and the conceptual roots from which this methodology grows, it is pleasantly surprising to find similarities in process and the applicability of behavior therapy to current group therapy practices.

Although the effectiveness of this approach is not at issue in this discussion, it should be noted that the film succinctly demonstrates the progress of individuals who participate in this kind of experience. Moreover, it presents new ideas which clearly merit examination: The effectiveness of suggestion as a therapeutic technique should be of particular interest to advanced group workers. However, the prospective user would be well advised to become acquainted with the literature on this approach before ordering the film.

2. *"Journey into Self,"* made by Carl Rogers, should prove something of a surprise to viewers who are familiar with Rogers' earlier films. The surprise is a pleasant one because this film, which differs markedly from his previous efforts, reflects Rogers' personal and professional growth and development over the years.

The film setting is a marathon (sixteen-hour) encounter group, and the processes presented are most interesting. Skillful professional filming and editing have permitted the encapsulation of the dynamic interactions of a group in an intensified form. Carl Rogers and Richard Farson are shown leading the group through the experience of searching for meaning in their lives in relation to other people and themselves. In general, this film is capable of evoking strong reactions in viewers. When the film was shown to participants in a workshop conducted by Carl Rogers it evoked intense feelings and stimulated interaction in small-group processes following the showing. But regardless of the professional qualifications of the audience, showings of this film should be accompanied by skillful interpretation. Audiences which are not familiar with marathon groups or lack sufficient knowledge of the basic concepts of group therapy would be expected to have difficulty in evaluating this type of group experience. Such issues as the utilization of marathons for purposes other than the clearly defined aims of psychotherapy are bound to arise, and will require clarifications on the part of the professional person showing the film. On the other hand, group therapists in training will find many valuable things in this film: It captures the transitory processes which produce intense emotional reactions, the resistances to feeling, the behaviors which typify locked-in role models or scripts, and the diverse ways of human experiencing as these emerge in the group setting. Indeed, this film will bear repeated showing to this audience, and minute-by-minute dissection, as a means of demonstrating the final points involved in the working through process.

Nevertheless, the film is not without its limitations: In its present form, it provides only limited opportunity to observe selected group members, and we see little of the actual group interaction. If the film had been edited less skillfully, it might have come to a standstill at times, but that would be a more authentic portrayel of the nature of groups. This edited version is misleading, in that the inexperienced therapist may get the mistaken impression that groups are always as intent in their work as they are in this film. Yet, this is a relatively minor complaint. The best films are those made with a clear purpose in mind, and the purpose of this film is clear from the outset—the exposure of the self in the marathon. Thus, on balance, this is a superb film, an Academy Award winner, and a worthy addition to any group therapy teaching program. If it is widely distributed, and it certainly will be, this film will have much to do with shaping group therapy practices and attitudes for some time to come.

3. "Group Therapy" is a film of a therapy session attended by the staff at Warrendale, a treatment center in Canada which specialized in the treatment of disturbed children. At Warrendale, group psychotherapy was a compulsory part of staff training, and the film presents the stress, anxiety, and emotion which evolve in any treatment group. In fact, the use of group therapy as part of a staff training program is a controversial

notion; howevef, the nature of the process presented by this film suggests that such a program has certain positive aspects.

Apart from the fact that it provoked some intial self-consciousness on the part of group members, apparently, the filming process was unobtrusive. Moreover, the film was produced by highly talented professional film-makers who were able to capture the group process and the continuity basic to therapy. Crises in professional and human relationships surface during the group session, and the group members engage in the working through process in a way that bears evidence of the fact that this is an on-going group, well along in treatment, under the leadership of a skilled therapist.

Experienced group therapists will feel at home with this content; others with less experience may have difficulty with the abrupt changes, the historic approach, and the affective undercurrents in the group.

On the whole, however, "Group Therapy" is an excellent film and would be particularly effective as a means of exposing students to the impact of feeling tone generated by group therapy sessions. It has other advantages as well: For one, since this is a film of a group of child care workers rather than patients, it would be expected to foster professional audience identification more readily than other films. Secondly, inasmuch as the film presents a group session in its entirety, with only minor editing, it permits the analysis of focal conflicts, as they emerge as a by-product of group interaction. Careful analysis of the on-going interaction is also warranted, with respect to both verbal and non-verbal communication. It is unfortunate that financial considerations and the time involved in such an effort preclude production of a series of similar films which could capture the historic sequence of the group, and thus enable the student to see the remarkable changes which flow from the therapeutic process.

4. "Group Therapy: The Dynamics of Change," made by Richard Abell, represents a departure from the traditional approach to the cinematic presentation of group therapy in that professional actors and contemporary television production techniques are used to convey the "message." The film was created to illustrate the application of basic psychoanalytic concepts in group psychotherapy: Richard Abell, using a transcript of an audio tape, wrote the script, in which a two and one-half hour psychoanalytically-oriented group therapy session is condensed into a thirty-one minute film. Particular focus is placed on the life experiences of one patient, the way in which they are translated into behavior, and her eventual insight into the nature of this relationship. In the

process, however, parallels between this patient's life and the lives of others in the group become apparent.

This is truly a film for the beginner; it captures just enough feeling tone to be interesting. Yet, he will gradually acquire increased understanding of the concepts underlying the group process.

The experienced therapist will enjoy watching this film because the sound, color, camera work, editing, and production are the work of professionals who know how to hold the attention of the audience. The use of actors as participants in the group session is a highly successful venture; the actors are talented and, through direction, are able to simulate life styles with a clarity that real patients often avoid. Despite his admiration for its technical aspects, the experienced group therapist may feel that the film lacks the lustre of spontaneity. But for the beginning therapist the clarity with which therapeutic concepts are presented might well provide the impetus for further interest and involvement in group therapy.

This approach to film-making could also be used to demonstrate the effectiveness of group psychotherapy over time. For example, a sequel to this film, which showed a therapy session of this group (portrayed by the same actors), a year or two later would present an exciting view of change in therapy.

5. *"The Scream Inside . . . Emergence Through Group Therapy,"* made by Milton Berger, represents still another approach to film-making —the use of videotape with an on-going therapy group. In this film, Berger, who regularly videotapes group sessions held in his private office, provides unusual taped sequences which illustrate the group process and the emergence of conflict areas in the lives of individual patients, and capture the spontaneous process of working through. The film also depicts unique experiences in the life of the individual and of the group which stimulate the resurgence of early conflicts with full emotional potency.

The film serves multiple purposes: It demonstrates the group process, the therapeutic use of videotape, the essential components of a therapy group, and the application of group therapy concepts to family therapy. As such, it would be suitable for both experienced and inexperienced group therapists. Because the film shows actual group interaction, it provides verification of the senior therapist's observations, and may serve to further stimulate his interest in this approach. The student may find it loose and confusing, but nonetheless provocative. The film should be previewed before it is shown, and the instructor should use the teaching guide which accompanies the film as a basis for discussion. The teaching guide is a synopsis of Milton Berger's approach to group therapy, and is of considerable value in itself as an aid to teaching group therapy. Indeed, it is hoped that in the not-too-distant future Berger will elaborate on and publish in book form the intriguing concepts which are only hinted at in the guide.

6. *"A Nude Marathon,"* made by Paul Bindrim, is bound to be popular if only because its title is likely to evoke the prurient interests of prospective professional audiences. As a rule, once he has seen the film, the viewer is both relieved and disappointed. He is disappointed because his prurient expectations have been frustrated, and relieved because major emphasis has been placed on the threapeutic process. This film enables the viewer to see the marathon and nudity demonstrated in a natural context, and the skillful use of these techniques by an experienced leader. The focus on verbalization rather than acting out places therapeutic endeavor in the forefront of what might otherwise be highly controversial and questionable experiences.

The format of the film is documentary; it was made for and televised by the Canadian Broadcasting Company. The participants are normal adults who are shown making the transition from physical isolatisn to nude body contact in a heated pool. Needless to say, this is a provocative film and could be of value in stimulating discussion in professional audiences who are concerned about such issues as nudity, marathons, sensitivity groups, and similar unorthodox approaches. Preview of the film by the instructor is essential if it is to be fully effective.

Films on Family Therapy

Films on family therapy differ from films on other forms of therapy in several respects. For one, they rely on cinema vérité techniques with real families, and restrictions are imposed with respect to the audience to which they can be shown. Secondly, they differ qualitatively from other films in that the complexity of family processes requires some sophistication on the part of the viewer in respect to therapy and particularly group therapy. Because it is a relatively new approach, only a limited number of films have been made on family therapy, and for the most part these are available from only two sources. In light of the growing interest in this area, one may speculate that within the next few years there will be an increase in the number of films made on family therapy, and some variation in film-making techniques. Indeed, this is essential, since problems of confidentiality and the disclosure of private information as it applies to children, in particular, have seriously hampered film production up to now.

7-11. Walter Kempler has made a number of films on family therapy. The five films selected for discussion here will be treated as a single entity, although they are rented individually, have individual titles, and have individual integrity, inasmuch as they depict the treatment of five different families. The titles of these films are: *"Patient Resistance—A Myth," "A Runaway Girl from a Runaway Family," "The Family Is the Patient," "Breaking Through,"* and *"The Facts Are Not Enough."* Each of these films presents an entire therapy session with a family, unedited, and with no comment or explanation other than that which evolves from the therapist-family dialogue.

In the brochure circulated by the Kempler Foundation their films are described as demonstrating "experiential psychotherapy, an historic approach which encourages the therapist's personal participation." Experienced therapists may feel that these films provide an exciting and stimulating challenge to work with families. Kempler comes through as a real person, helping families to do real work by way of extricating themselves from the unreal work of neurosis and psychosis. Sometimes he succeeds and sometimes he fails, but the work of therapy is apparent throughout, as is the encouragement and aid which the therapist provides. To the student, the film's content may seem disconnected and chaotic, and the therapist may appear to be autocratic and controlling. For this reason, these films can be used most effectively by an instructor who is experienced in family therapy, in a situation where ample time can be allocated to discussion. But apart from these considerations, since the personal participation of the therapist is a controversial issue in some quarters, the films should be previewed by the instructor lest he find that some of his own views on this issue are seriously challenged. The instructor must also be wary of the possibility that the inexperienced therapist may be so taken by Kempler's directness that he will attempt to parrot him rather than discover his own way.

The production quality of these films varies greatly; several of the films seem to be the work of professionals; others are definitely amateurish. This variation is particularly unfortunate in light of the uniform excellence of the therapy sessions. In fact, even those films with the worst sound and picture quality are worth the extra concentration and attention they require.

Two films on family therapy made by Nathan Ackerman are currently available: *"The Enemy in Myself,"* and *"In and Out of Psychosis: A Family Study."**

---

* These films antedate the other films listed in this article. It was decided to include them, nevertheless, in order to maintain the integrity of this discussion of films on family therapy.

12. *"The Enemy in Myself"* is a composite film of four family sessions, conducted over a period of a year and a half, showing the processes which evolved during that time span. The processes by which the parents and their nine-year-old twin sons work through the suicide attempt of one son is captured effectively. Ackerman is direct and open in his encounters with the family, and interacts with them in a guiding and involved way. A printed transcript of the dialogue accompanies the film to enhance discussion.

This is a good film to use to introduce beginning family therapists to the processes they will face, and to stimulate discussion of those aspects of family therapy which are frequent sources of conflict and concern. Typically, students are dismayed by the film initially; but, in time, this dismay usually gives way to involvement and enthusiasm. This film requires careful preliminary study if it is to be used effectively. For example, brief segments of the film can be shown to advantage as a means of demonstrating specific techniques of confrontation and interpretation.

The quality of the film production is only average, but this does not usually interfere with viewing. In any event, the quality of the content of the film more than makes up for its technical inadequacies.

13. *"In and Out of Psychosis: A Family Study,"* a more recent film by Ackerman, explores the psychotic process in the sixteen-year-old daughter in a family with great sensitivity and awareness. Actually, very few films on psychosis have been made in either group or individual therapy. And, with the exception of this film, no attempt has been made in those which are available to portray psychosis as a plausible human phenomenon, or to give the viewer some understanding of the dynamics of this process. In the context of family therapy, psychosis becomes a human experience with meaning and hope for resolution; indeed, the point of this film is hope. This is not a film for beginners, and should be used only after it has been previewed. It is a film which lends itself to in-depth study not only of family therapy and diagnosis but of the dynamics of severe psychopathology. The treatment process, as it unfolds in the film, permits the viewer to identify family processes, and also delineates the role of the therapist in this setting. Finally, this two-hour film is accompanied by a transcript of the dialogue to facilitate detailed discussion of these phenomena.

The Future for Films on Group and Family Psychotherapy

Those who are interested in making teaching films on group and family therapy should know that there is a small but eager market for their product. Moreover, although many good films are available, a number of important areas have not yet been explored:

Specialists in non-verbal communication urge therapists to be aware of the degree to which groups communicate on this level, and stress the importance of such material in group process. Obviously, a film in which the entire group is visible for the entire session would be extremely valuable in this regard, and the use of wide-angle and fish-eye lenses would make such productions feasible. Although current films allow some analysis of body language, the use of multiple cameras, split screens, and special angles is essential to underscore the importance of the total human body as a vehicle for communicating meaning to other individuals or the group as a whole. The study of kinetics is sufficiently advanced to make significant contributions to psychotherapy and particularly to group and family therapy.

Supervisors and teachers are aware of the need for a film series which will illustrate the sequential nature of the group process, and permit demonstration of the focal conflict model as a means of understanding group interaction. Group absences, silences, and acting out, among other things, require session-to-session comparisons for clarification of the dynamics of such phenomena.

The use of films would make available to beginning therapists very subjective but convincing evidence as to the effectiveness of psychotherapy as a method of changing human behavior. Research methodology and argument often blunt the meaning of change in behavior; films depict actual events, and the viewer can then make a judgment as to the precise nature of the changes which occur in patients on the basis of what he has seen.

Within the next five years, videotape equipment may completely obviate the use of films in teaching. Certainly the hardware and the technology currently in existence could make films obsolete, even if no further advances were made in this area. On the other hand, problems of distribution and the economic feasibility of using videotape have not yet been resolved. And, as is true of film production, confidentiality and invasion of privacy are issues of major importance which have precluded the wider use of such equipment to date. Indeed, it is apparent at this point that only the ethical and responsible handling of films and videotape by therapists can assure their increased use for teaching and training purposes in the future.

APPENDIX
CURRENT FILMS ON GROUP AND FAMILY PSYCHOTHERAPY (1968-1971)

Group Therapy

Film Title	Film Maker	Name and Address of Source
1. "Broad Spectrum Behavior Therapy in a Group"	A. Lazarus	Pennsylvania State University Audio-Visual Services, University Park, Pa. 16802
2. "Journey into Self"	Carl Rogers	Western Behavioral Sciences Institute, 1150 Silverado La Jolla, Calif. 92037
3. "Group Therapy"	Professionals (at the Warrendale Treatment Center)	Grove Press Film Library 53 East 11th Street New York, New York 10003
4. "Group Therapy: The Dynamics of Change"	Richard Abell	Association Films Inc.,* Roche Film Library 600 Grand Avenue Ridgefield, N. J. 07657
5. "The Screen Inside . . . Emergence Through Group Therapy"	Milton Berger	Sandoz Pharmaceuticals,* Medical Education Services Route 10 Hanover, N. J. 07936
6. "A Nude Marathon"	Paul Bindrim	Pennsylvania State University Audio-Visual Services, University Park, Pa. 16802

* Films made by the Roche and Sandoz pharmaceutical companies are often available through local company representatives.

*Family Therapy**

Film Title	Film Maker	Name and Address of Source
7. "Patient Resistance— A Myth"	Walter Kempler	Kempler Foundation 6233 Wilshire Boulevard Los Angeles, Calif. 90048
8. "A Runaway Girl From a Runaway Family"	"	"
9. "The Family Is the Patient"	"	"
10. "Breaking Through"	"	"
11. "The Facts Are Not Enough"	"	"
12. "The Enemy in Myself"	Nathan Ackerman	Family Institute 149 E. 78 Street New York, N. Y. 10021
13. "In and Out of Psychosis: A Family Study"	"	"

* Distribution of films on family therapy is restricted at present.